C0-DBT-661

DICTIONARY OF LITERARY CHARACTERS

DICTIONARY OF LITERARY CHARACTERS

VOLUME I

A–C

Michael D. Sollars

Facts On File
An imprint of Infobase Publishing

DICTIONARY OF LITERARY CHARACTERS

Facts On File, Inc.
An imprint of Infobase Publishing
132 West 31st Street
New York NY 10001

Library of Congress Cataloging-in-Publication Data

Sollars, Michael David.
  Dictionary of literary characters / Michael D. Sollars.
    p. cm.
  Includes bibliographical references and indexes.
  ISBN 978-0-8160-7379-5 (hc : alk. paper) 1. Characters and characteristics in literature—Dictionaries.
I. Title.
  PN56.4.S66 2010
  809'.92703—dc22   2009042853

Facts On File books are available at special discounts when purchased in bulk quantities for businesses, associations, institutions, or sales promotions. Please call our Special Sales Department in New York at (212) 967-8800 or (800) 322-8755.

You can find Facts On File on the World Wide Web at http://www.factsonfile.com

Text design adapted by Kerry Casey
Composition by Hermitage Publishing Services
Cover printed by Sheridan Books, Ann Arbor, Mich.
Book printed and bound by Sheridan Books, Ann Arbor, Mich.
Date printed: November 2010
Printed in the United States of America

10 9 8 7 6 5 4 3 2 1

This book is printed on acid-free paper.

CONTENTS

PREFACE

Welcome to the *Dictionary of Literary Characters,* an immense and unique collection of more than 40,000 literary figures found in novels, short stories, and plays from the United States, Great Britain, and all over the world. The literary works examined here range from ancient Greek classics such as Euripides' *Medea* and Sophocles' *Antigone* to 21st-century prizewinners such as Jeffrey Eugenides' *Middlesex.* No other reference covers so many characters in so many different works.

This set contains all the character entries published previously in Facts On File's *Dictionary of American Literary Characters* and the *Dictionary of British Literary Characters,* both of which focused exclusively on novels. To those thousands of characters have been added many thousands more, from British and American novels published in the last 20 years, from classics of world literature, and from short stories and plays of all periods and places of origin. The result is a truly comprehensive collection of characters from the world's greatest literature.

The body of this dictionary consists of literary characters listed alphabetically (letter by letter) according to the character's last name, if a last name is available. Mark Twain's Huckleberry Finn, for example, is listed under the Fs. Huck's companion Jim, however, whose last name is ambiguous, is listed under the Js. Foreign-language surnames beginning in a particle such as "de" are filed per the convention of the language in which the work the character figures in was originally published. Anonymous narrators are listed under the work they narrate. An extensive appendix lists all authors included in the dictionary in alphabetical order, in addition to the works included and the characters that have entries here. A briefer appendix lists all the works included in the set in alphabetical order. Readers who cannot recall the exact name of the character they wish to research can therefore easily find it by consulting these appendixes.

The development of this collection involved a commitment of many years by many scholars. Choosing which authors and works to include was the first challenge, and perhaps the greatest. We examined curriculum lists, reference works, and textbooks as well as lists of winners (and even short-lists of potential winners) of such major prizes as the Nobel and Pulitzer Prizes, National Book Award, PEN/Faulkner Award, Edgar Allan Poe Award, O. Henry Prize, and awards outside the United States such as the Prix Goncourt and George Büchner Prize. Some acclaimed best-selling works of popular and genre fiction were also marked for inclusion. Furthermore, suggestions from our contributors, editorial advisers, and other scholarly supporters were considered. Because a writer is included does not mean that characters from all of his or her fictional works are included. In some instances most of an author's works appear, while in other instances a writer's fiction is represented by a single major work.

A further goal was to include works from every continent and as many languages as possible. Classic works often neglected in American classrooms are included here, such as Murasaki Shikibu's medieval *The Tale of Genji;* Shudraka's Sanskrit play *The Little Clay Cart;* and the classical Chinese play *The Circle of Chalk,* which spotlights the intriguing young heroine Chang-hi-tang. Some important works that today are rarely anthologized, perhaps because of changes in literary fashion, have been resurrected here. An example is Conrad Aiken's "Silent Snow, Secret Snow."

The entries in the dictionary are brief but informative. They often include descriptions of the significance of those characters in the plots of the works. Characters that are also historical figures, such as Socrates, Abraham Lincoln, and Pancho Villa, are treated in the same manner as solely fictional characters.

This compendium of characters will aid the reader in many pursuits, whether academic or leisurely. We hope this reference will encourage readers to consider characters the primary subject of literary works, as opposed to plot. Exploring characters is often the best way to seek out the heart of any literary work, but too often we readers, no matter how experienced, focus instead simply on what happens. In Edgar Allan Poe's "The Tell-Tale Heart," for example, we should examine first the state of mind of the mad first-person narrator, whose inner life is so much more dramatic and thrilling even than the story's stunning plot. Furthermore, this collection will be of use to students and scholars in providing an overview of how an author treats characters over the span of his or her work, or how a number of related authors treat their characters. Finally, by providing a global perspective, this collection enables students to explore how different authors from different backgrounds create their characters—both the similarities and the differences can be striking. Most important of all, we hope this reference will encourage students and general readers to return to the great works in which these characters are featured.

Michael D. Sollars, Editor

A Daughter of Nimni and Ohiro-Moldona-Fivona in Herman Melville's *Mardi.*

"A" Moribund woman at age 92, invalided, and facing death's door; autocratic, proud, vain, and naturally mean-spirited nonagenarian; recalls to two other women named B and C at her bedside her past as once a poor young girl who married into money; life filled with expensive jewelry, riding horses, and love affairs; lost her husband to prostate cancer; her son seldom visits; attempts to put her will and papers in order in Edward Albee's play *Three Tall Women*

A . . . Narrator's young wife whose name is never given; suspected by her husband of having an affair with Franck, a neighboring plantation owner; her every gesture is minutely described in an accusatory manner, although no wrongdoing is ever confirmed; agitated by a centipede that Franck crushes to death in her and her husband's presence; travels with Franck to the port, where they remain together for a night, raising further suspicions in the mind of the intensely observing narrator in Alain Robbe-Grillet's *Jealousy.*

A—, Lady Louisa Aristocratic recipient of Mrs. Darnford's letters on education; she seeks to hire Mrs. Darnford as a governess for her daughters, who are to be educated at home in Clara Reeve's *Plans of Education.*

A—, Lord Aristocratic husband of Lady A—; he once proposed to Mrs. Darnford and occasionally comments on her letters in Clara Reeve's *Plans of Education.*

A—, M. French Academician, who dines with Mr. Home de Bassompierre in Charlotte Brontë's *Villette.*

A—, Marquis of Wily and successful statesman, who is a member of the Scottish Privy Council and a kinsman to Edgar Ravenswood; he aids Edgar in his struggle against Sir William Ashton in Sir Walter Scott's *The Bride of Lammermoor.*

Aardvaark, Captain (Aarfy) Fraternity man and navigator in Yossarian's squadron; rapes an Italian chambermaid and throws her out a window to her death to avoid a blot on his reputation in Joseph Heller's *Catch-22.*

Aaron Jewish moneychanger hired by the Prior of Saint Mary's to testify against Hugh Woodreeve in Ann Radcliffe's *Gaston de Blondeville.*

Aaron Moorish lover of Tamora and father of her son; orchestrates the plot to kill Bassianus and rape and mutilate Lavinia; kills his baby's nurse; gleefully confesses his crimes to Lucius in exchange for his son's life; buried up to his neck to starve by Lucius in William Shakespeare's play *Titus Andronicus.*

Aaron Hebrew son of Amram, brother of Miriam (and perhaps of Moses), and first high priest of the Israelites; killed and entombed by Moses on Mount Hor in Zora Neale Hurston's *Moses, Man of the Mountain.*

Aaron, Jimmy Young black man who is murdered when he returns to the plantation to organize and lead his people during the civil rights movement in Ernest J. Gaines's *The Autobiography of Miss Jane Pittman.*

Aaronow, George Past his prime in productivity as a salesman in the high-pressure Chicago real estate office where a group of hungry salesmen lie, cheat, bribe, and even steal to make sales; shows a lack of confidence and hope in front of the other men; investigated in the theft of the firm's sales leads and furniture in David Mamet's play *Glengarry Glen Ross.*

Aaronson, Michael Barbara Vaughan's Jewish cousin in Muriel Spark's *The Mandlebaum Gate.*

Aashild, Lady Aunt of Erlend Nikulaussön and a known witch-wife in Sigrid Undset's *Kristin Lavransdatter.*

Abagail, Mother See Freemantle, Abagail.

Abakumov, Victor Semyonovich Zek (prisoner) engineer serving his second term in the Marfino gulag prison camp located in the Moscow suburbs in Aleksandr Solzhenitsyn's *The First Circle.*

Abarak Failed seeker after the sword of Aklis; he assists Shibli Bagarag in finding the sword and afterward in George Meredith's *The Shaving of Shagpat.*

Abaschwili, Natella Birth mother of the child Michael; abandons the baby during her flight from the invaders of the palace, as she considers clothing and jewelry more important to her; does not search for her son afterward; later sues Grusha, the young woman who has cared for the child since its abandonment, in court and tries to prove herself the rightful mother in the famed Caucasian Chalk-Circle; harshly pulls her child from Grusha's hands and out of the circle, but loses the baby because the judge realizes that she, in willing to inflict pain on the child to possess him, does not love him as fully as Grusha in Bertolt Brecht's play *The Caucasian Chalk-Circle.*

Abate Abbot who refuses to help Vincentio di Vivaldi in releasing Ellena Rosalba from the clutches of the Abbess of the San Stefano convent in Ann Radcliffe's *The Italian.*

Abate Maniacal, politically ambitious abbot of the Saint Augustin monastery, who betrays Julia de Mazzini to her father the Marquis in Ann Radcliffe's *A Sicilian Romance.*

Abath (Vasidol) Mety Vasidol's daughter, who has an affair with Robayday Anganol and later falsely testifies against him in Brian W. Aldiss's *Helliconia Summer.*

Abbé of Perigord Unctuous, impudent, fawning, gossipy, this clergyman introduces Candide to a marquise of ill-repute and cheats him out of his money and jewels in Voltaire's *Candide.*

Abbess Elqidia's sister, who has a bad temper and is jealous of the relationship between her sister and Natura in Eliza Haywood's *Life's Progress Through the Passions: or, the Adventures of Natura.*

Abbess Religious figure in E. T. A. Hoffmann's *The Devil's Elixir.*

Abbess Sadistic abbess of the San Stefano convent, who gives Ellena Rosalba the ultimatum to become a nun, to marry the man of Marchesa di Vivaldi's choice, or to be locked in the dungeon in Ann Radcliffe's *The Italian.*

Abbess, Benedictine Norman aunt of Eveline Berenger; when Eveline refuses to take her advice to break the engagement to Hugo de Lacy, she withdraws her protection from Eveline in Sir Walter Scott's *The Betrothed.*

Abbess, Lady Head of the convent to which the Lady Lucy is taken after being attacked and abandoned by her husband; the Abbess later spreads the story of Lucy and Lewis Augustus Albertus so that all may be inspired by the example of virtue and religion in Penelope Aubin's *The Life and Adventures of the Lady Lucy.*

Abbess, Lady Isabella's aunt, who hopes to gain Isabella's estate for the nunnery if Isabella takes holy orders in Aphra Behn's *The History of the Nun.*

Abbess, The Mother Superior at Imber Abbey and spiritual adviser to Michael Meade in Iris Murdoch's *The Bell.*

Abbess of Ursuline Convent Prim and earnest recluse, who shelters Isabelle de Croye and is anxious to have her become a nun in Sir Walter Scott's *Quentin Durward.*

Abbeville, Horace Bigamist and debtor; commits suicide after settling accounts with Lee Chong the grocer by exchanging a fish-meal storage building for his debt in John Steinbeck's *Cannery Row.*

Abbie Concentration camp prisoner at Birkenau, a part of Auschwitz; jokes that he has figured out a new way to burn prisoners: Set fire to the children's hair in Tadeusz Borowski's *This Way for the Gas, Ladies and Gentlemen.*

Abbot, Martha Officious lady's maid at Mrs. Reed's residence, who has no kind words for Jane Eyre in Charlotte Brontë's *Jane Eyre.*

Abbot, Mrs. Widow after the suicide of her journalist husband; she takes in two children deserted by their father and ultimately remarries in George Gissing's *The Whirlpool.*

Abbot, Richard Down-to-earth romantic friend of Jane Weatherby; he takes up with Liz Jennings when Jane dismisses him for John Pomfret in Henry Green's *Nothing.*

Abbott Midshipman who fails at his duties during an attack on a fort in C. S. Forester's *Lieutenant Hornblower.*

Abbott, Caroline Conventional, agreeable, romantic young woman, who chaperones Lilia Herriton to Italy, where she too falls in love with Gino Carella in E. M. Forster's *Where Angels Fear to Tread.*

Abbott, Elizabeth (Liz, Gillespie Emerson) Woodcarver and clock winder who reconstitutes the Emerson family and salvages their neglected Baltimore home; as Gillespie, becomes the wife of Matthew Emerson and the mother of two children in Anne Tyler's *The Clock Winder.*

Abbott, Hannah Hufflepuff student in Harry Potter's term in school; "pink-faced" with blonde hair worn in pigtails; worries about O.W.L. exams; sports a "Support Cedric Diggory/Potter Stinks" badge during the Triwizard Tournament; Hufflepuff prefect; joins Dumbledore's army; marries Neville Longbottom and becomes the landlady of The Leaky Cauldron in J. K. Rowling's Harry Potter series.

Abbott, Horace Gentle husband of Sally Page Abbott; dies of a heart attack as a result of a Halloween prank in John Gardner's *October Light.*

Abbott, John Pastor of Faith Baptist Church in Ellington, North Carolina, and father of Elizabeth Abbott in Anne Tyler's *The Clock Winder.*

Abbott, Julia Wife of John Abbott and mother of Elizabeth Abbott in Anne Tyler's *The Clock Winder.*

Abbott, Sally Page Eighty-year-old liberal who in self-defense plans the injury or death of her brother, James Page, until she nearly kills her niece, Ginny Hicks; widow of Horace Abbott in John Gardner's *October Light.*

Abby See Freemantle, Abagail.

Abderames Emperor of the Moors; Julian the Apostate, as a Spanish king, forces him into war by refusing to pay the yearly tribute of one hundred virgins in Henry Fielding's *A Journey From This World to the Next.*

Abdul Musician with a taste for intoxicating "green honey" in Umberto Eco's *Baudolino.*

Abdul, General Turkish ambassador in Tunis and friend of Aunt Augusta Bertram; he helps her with shady investment deals in Graham Greene's *Travels with My Aunt.*

Abdulla Arab trader to whom Willems betrays the navigation of the River Pantai in Joseph Conrad's *An Outcast of the Islands.*

Abdullam Arab merchant in Luxor who sells Jane Mallory the head that looks like Jimmy Assad in John Fowles's *Daniel Martin.*

Abdul-Mickey Cook, waiter, and proprietor of O'Connell's Pool House, the misnamed greasy diner frequented daily by Archie Jones and Samad Iqbal; one of six brothers, all named Abdul by their Muslim father so that they would learn humility in Zadie Smith's *White Teeth.*

Abe Elderly government lawyer running away from corrupt politics and grief over the death of his wife and son; befriended by Anne and Phil Sorenson before plunging off a cliff to his death in Frederick Busch's *Manual Labor.*

Abe Son of Lucy; slave who is sent to sea, where he dies trying to assist distressed sailors in John Pendleton Kennedy's *Swallow Barn.*

Abednego, Moses Jewish clerk in the Independent West Diddlesex Fire and Life Insurance Co.; his father precipitates its collapse in William Makepeace Thackeray's *The History of Samuel Titmarsh and the Great Hoggarty Diamond.*

Abednego, Uncle Elderly black man from the almshouse who is the Birdsongs' gardener in Ellen Glasgow's *The Sheltered Life.*

Abel (Abelito) American Indian and World War II veteran who is imprisoned for murder in N. Scott Momaday's *House Made of Dawn.*

Abel, Francis (Frankie) Jill's older brother; son of Max, Pearl's second husband; twenty-seven-year-old gambler who spends time in jail in Marge Piercy's *Braided Lives.*

Abel, James Poor Farm inmate and witch digger in Jessamyn West's *The Witch Diggers.*

Abel, Leo Jill's oldest brother; son of Max, Pearl's second husband; thirty-year-old who lives with his mother and stepfather when escaping the law in Marge Piercy's *Braided Lives.*

Abel, Mary Poor Farm inmate and witch digger; sets the fire that kills Christian Fraser in Jessamyn West's *The Witch Diggers.*

Abel, Mr. (Abel Guevez de Argensola) Venezuelan adventurer in W. H. Hudson's *Green Mansions.*

Abellino See Rosalvo, Count.

Abelone Aunt of the protagonist Malte and with whom the protagonist has a love affair in Rainer Maria Rilke's *The Notebooks of Malte Laurids Brigge.*

Abenaide, Princess of Morocco Exquisite daughter of Sultan Abenamin of Morocco and Eloisa Clinton; her father smuggles her out of Morocco disguised as a male page; she marries young Harry Clinton in Henry Brooke's *The Fool of Quality.*

Abenamin, Emperor of Morocco Rescuer of Eloisa Clinton, whom he marries after his conversion to Christianity; the father of Abenaide, he flees to England to protect his daughter and to be among Christians in Henry Brooke's *The Fool of Quality.*

Abencerrage Rebellious son of Sultan Abenamin of Morocco and a concubine; his threat to the throne and his lust for his half sister Abenaide contribute to the sultan's reasons for fleeing to England in Henry Brooke's *The Fool of Quality.*

Aben-Ezra, Raphael Rich, educated Jew, actually Miriam's son; initially a troublemaker and enamored of Hypatia, he loses all faith in human nature, gives up his wealth, and becomes the student of his dog, Bran; he recovers some faith, is finally converted to Christianity by Augustine, marries Victoria, and tries to save Hypatia in Charles Kingsley's *Hypatia.*

Aberavon, Lord Rowland Deceased shipping magnate and art patron and the maternal grandfather of both Barbara Goring and Eleanor Walpole-Wilson in Anthony Powell's *A Buyer's Market.* Paintings from his collection—by Isbister, Deacon, and others—unvalued and dispersed at the time of his death, are sought by collectors in *Hearing Secret Harmonies.*

Aberdeen, Mrs. Rickie Elliott's servant at Cambridge in E. M. Forster's *The Longest Journey.*

Abernathy, Carol Wife of Hunt Abernathy and mistress of Ron Grant; head of Hunt Hills Little Theatre and occultist in James Jones's *Go to the Widow-Maker.*

Abernathy, Hunt Husband of Carol Abernathy and friend of Ron Grant; general manager of a brick-making and lumberyard establishment in Indianapolis in James Jones's *Go to the Widow-Maker.*

Abidaga Primary overseer in the construction of the Drina Bridge in Ivo Andrić's *The Bridge on the Drina.*

Abigail Servant in the household of Count Melvil; she is the victim of the scheme by Ferdinand and Teresa to cheat Mademoiselle de Melvil in Tobias Smollett's *The Adventures of Ferdinand Count Fathom.*

Abigail, Mrs. Any of several maidservants in Henry Fielding's *The History of Tom Jones.* Also see Honour Blackmore.

Abilene Pool shark, oil-well driller, and richest man (in cash) in Thalia, Texas, in Larry McMurtry's *The Last Picture Show.*

Ablewhite, Godfrey Suave lay preacher and cousin of Rachel Verinder, to whom he becomes engaged for a while in order to gain her fortune; he sees Franklin Blake remove a diamond from Rachel's room, and then he makes off with it himself; he is murdered by Hindu priests to recover the jewel sacred to their temple, where it originally lodged in Wilkie Collins's *The Moonstone. A Romance.*

Ablewhite, Mr. Apoplectic father of Godfrey; angered by Rachel Verinder's refusal to marry his son, he refuses to become her guardian as desired by the will of her late mother, Lady Julia Verinder, in Wilkie Collins's *The Moonstone. A Romance.*

Ablewhite, Mrs. Downtrodden mother of Godfrey and two daughters; she escorts Rachel Verinder to London, where she and her irascible husband intend to provide Rachel with shelter after her mother's death in Wilkie Collins's *The Moonstone. A Romance.*

Ablewhite, The Misses Godfrey Ablewhite's two giggling sisters, dubbed the Bouncers by Gabriel Betteredge; they are guests at Rachel Verinder's birthday celebration, where the yellow diamond is shown off and stolen in Wilkie Collins's *The Moonstone. A Romance.*

Abner Arthur Abner's son, a Jew whom Matey Weyburn protects as a schoolboy in George Meredith's *Lord Ormont and his Aminta.*

Abner Incompetent, disloyal shepherd employed by George Fielding on his ranch in Australia; he leaves and is followed and "killed" by Jacky but recovers to return and complain to George in Charles Reade's *It Is Never Too Late to Mend.*

Abner, Arthur Man who arranges for Lady Charlotte to hire Matey Weyburn as a tutor in George Meredith's *Lord Ormont and his Aminta.*

Aboan Friend of Oroonoko; he seduces the king's old wife, Onahal, so that Oroonoko may see Imoinda, who is under her guardianship, in Aphra Behn's *Oroonoko.*

Aboan Younger man with whom Onahal, the discarded mistress of the king, becomes enamored; politically savvy about the women in the king's harem; uses Onahal's interest in him to help Oroonoko secretly see Imoinda; goes to Onahal's bed, a strategy allowing Oroonoko and Imoinda to consummate their marriage in Aphra Behn's *Oroonoko.*

Abo of Fossanova Benedictine monk and abbot of an abbey in northern Italy; he asks William of Baskerville to investigate the mysterious murders taking place, in order to protect the good name of the abbey; dies as a victim of a murder himself in Umberto Eco's *The Name of the Rose.*

Abou Tired "aged negro with haunted sin-sick eyes" who helps deliver bouquets for Bachir from the Duchess of Varna's flower shop in Ronald Firbank's *The Flower Beneath the Foot.*

Abraham Biblical patriarch, who almost loses his wife to Totis, king of Egypt; he refuses gifts of Charoba, but when he discovers she slipped jewels into his supplies, he spends them on pious works in the appended romance "The History of Charoba, Queen of Egypt" in Clara Reeve's *The Progress of Romance.*

Abraham Faithful servant of Richard Annesly in Henry Mackenzie's *The Man of the World.*

Abraham Mandelbaum's nephew; he goes with the smugglers to Hungary to escape the Holocaust; however, he is forced by the Gestapo to send a fake letter to Vladek that says the smugglers can be trusted; Vladek meets him in Auschwitz, where Abraham tells him the truth; Abraham is presumed to have died in Art Spiegelman's *Maus.*

Abraham Pious Jew and keen businessman in Lodz; stern patriarch and father of two sons born minutes apart—Jacob and Simcha; later considers Simcha dead because of the young man's scheme to steal his father's position at the Huntze steam mill in Israel Joshua Singer's *The Brothers Ashkenazi.*

Abraham, Captain Master of the *Patricia,* sent to tow the crippled *Archimedes* to safety after the hurricane; he resolves an impasse over authority with Captain Edwardes by kneeling to make his assurances in Richard Hughes's *In Hazard.*

Abraham, Mr. Young Indian Christian man who serves as a guide for Being of the Fort St. Sebastian ruins in Madras; assiduously elegant and recently the recipient of a master's degree in commerce from the University of Madras; listens to test-match cricket from New Zealand on a transistor radio; his deportment has a protective haughtiness in Bharati Mukherjee's *The Holder of the World.*

Abramowitz, Mrs. Effusive button-shop proprietor in Joe's neighborhood with a knack for cheek-pinching unparalleled in Wolf Mankowitz's *A Kid for Two Farthings.*

Abrams, Eliot Raised by two gay men after parents' death; lover of Philip Benjamin; roommate of Jerene Parks; sophisticated and selfish; leaves Philip and goes to Europe in David Leavitt's *The Lost Language of Cranes.*

Abrams, Mike Lawyer; early romantic interest and later good friend of Salley Gardens in Susan Cheever's *Looking for Work.*

Abramson, Dr. Abe Physician; older cousin and surrogate father of Zeke Gurevich; patron of freethinkers in Greenwich Village in William Herrick's *The Itinerant.*

Abravanel, David Egyptian Jewish lawyer to Mrs. Khoury and father of Leah Strauss; he advises Mrs. Khoury to put her possessions in his name to avoid their confiscation by the Egyptian government; he dies in his sleep in P. H. Newby's *Something to Answer For.*

Abrazza Bachelor king of Bonovona in Herman Melville's *Mardi.*

Abreskov, Paul Young, elegant Russian turned Bolshevik; he is determined to capture Princess Saskia and her jewels and take her back to Russia; he drowns in a storm in John Buchan's *Huntingtower.*

***Absolute Beginners,* Narrator** Open-minded, intelligent teenager living and working in London in the 1950s as a freelance photographer; he is at odds with the establishment and a defender of the independence and lifestyles of teenagers and of his friends, who include prostitutes, hustlers, and homosexuals; disgusted by racism in the city, he aids endangered blacks during racial riots; he is in love with Suzette and devoted to his father in Colin MacInnes's *Absolute Beginners.*

Abstrog, Athenat Janol Angand's personal priest who advocates the union with Oldorando in Brian W. Aldiss's *Helliconia Summer.*

Abuelita Aging grandmother of the young female narrator; after her death, her granddaughter washes her body to purify it in Helena María Viramontes's "The Moths."

Abundio Traveler who leads a string of burros and shows Juan Preciado the way to Comala in Juan Rulfo's *Pedro Páramo.*

Abyssinia (Sister 'ssinia) Dressmaker who travels with Arista Prolo as a costume designer; confides the story of Arista's life and death to Black Will in Carlene Hatcher Polite's *Sister X and the Victims of Foul Play.*

Acaste Wealthy young marquis who has great influence at the king's court in Moliere's play *The Misanthrope.*

Accountant, The One of the five men on board the *Nellie* waiting for the tide to change on the Thames; listens as the protagonist, Marlow, recounts his strange tale of traveling up the Congo to find the mysterious Kurtz in Joseph Conrad's *Heart of Darkness.*

Ace, Josh Son of a team of Hollywood screenwriters from the 1930s and lover of Isadora Wing in Erica Jong's *How to Save Your Own Life.*

Achille See LAFITTE.

Achille, M. Fellow bachelor with whom Roquentin shares an awkward moment at Camille's bistro; is heartened by Dr. Rogé's overbearing self-importance; slavishly admires Dr. Rogé's extroversion and self-confidence; is the object of Roquentin's pity and contempt in Jean-Paul Sartre's *Nausea.*

Achilles Hero whose spirit the author encounters in Elysium in Henry Fielding's *A Journey From This World to the Next.*

Achilles Greek hero at Troy and lover of Helen; joins her in Egypt in H. D.'s *Helen in Egypt.*

Achon Emperor Seth's uncle who, although the legitimate heir to the throne, has been kept prisoner for many years in a remote monastery; when he is released by the combined military forces of General Connolly and the Earl of Ngumo and is crowned emperor, the strain becomes so great that he collapses and dies in Evelyn Waugh's *Black Mischief.*

Achorn, Charlie Cracker-barrel philosopher, temporary farmhand, and resident of Pretty Pass in Peter De Vries's *I Hear America Swinging.*

Achthar, Anophel Villainous fop, who unsuccessfully attempts to have his way with Anthelia Melincourt in Thomas Love Peacock's *Melincourt.*

Ackerman, Noah Lonely Jewish social worker whose marriage to Hope Plowman deeply enriches his life; drafted into the army during World War II, where he is subjected to anti-Semitic taunts and distinguishes himself as a hero, in Irwin Shaw's *The Young Lions.*

Ackley, Robert Ill-groomed student who lives next to Holden Caulfield at Pencey Prep in J. D. Salinger's *The Catcher in the Rye.*

Ackroyd, Flora Niece of Roger Ackroyd, whose will leaves her £20,000 in Agatha Christie's *The Murder of Roger Ackroyd.*

Ackroyd, Luke Intelligent working man in love with Thyrza Trent; he is rejected and temporarily falls into evil ways in George Gissing's *Thyrza.*

Ackroyd, Mrs. Cecil Roger Ackroyd's widowed sister-in-law; she and her daughter, Flora, live in financial dependence upon him at Fernly Park in Agatha Christie's *The Murder of Roger Ackroyd.*

Ackroyd, Roger Successful manufacturer turned country squire; he is murdered in his study at Fernly Park in Agatha Christie's *The Murder of Roger Ackroyd.*

Acky Mercenary unfrocked clergyman and owner of a "short-time" house who finds consolation for his betrayals through his grotesque wife's genuine affection for him in Graham Greene's *A Gun for Sale.*

Acoraci Guard at the exit from nester in Scott Spencer's *Last Night at the Brain Thieves' Ball.*

Acorn, Lawrence Horse thief and accomplice of John Burrows in the murder of Farmer Trumbull in Anthony Trollope's *The Vicar of Bullhampton.*

Acosta, Remedios Village gossip who relays information about Americans Richard and Sara Everton to inhabitants of Ibarra, Mexico, in Harriet Doerr's *Stones for Ibarra.*

Acte Christian and a former concubine of Nero; plans Lycia's escape from a probable death sentence from Nero in Henryk Sienkiewicz's *Quo Vadis.*

Acton, Elizabeth (Lizzie) Guileless sister of Robert Acton; marries Clifford Wentworth in Henry James's *The Europeans.*

Acton, Mrs. Invalid mother of Robert and Lizzie Acton in Henry James's *The Europeans.*

Acton, Robert Sophisticated, well-traveled cousin of William Wentworth; courts Eugenia Münster in Henry James's *The Europeans.*

Actor Traveler on the wagon who intercepts the Ale-Wife's bottle and who mimics everyone in Charles Johnstone's *Chrysal: or, The Adventures of a Guinea.*

Actor, The Alcoholic who hates the gambler and cheat Satine; one of the many poor boarders in the lodging owned by the ill-tempered landlord Kostilyoff in Maxim Gorky's play *The Lower Depths.*

Actress Traveler on the wagon who speaks in "heroicks" and turns up her nose at everything and everyone in Charles Johnstone's *Chrysal: or, The Adventures of a Guinea.*

Ada Manager of the seedy Golden Peach Club, where Arthur Blearney gives Charles Lumley a job as a bouncer when he is down on his luck in John Wain's *Hurry On Down.*

Ada Servant girl; having grown up in Hilda Lessways Clayhanger's service, she criticizes her demanding mistress and leaves with no notice, confirming Edwin Clayhanger's judgment of Hilda as an incompetent household manager in Arnold Bennett's *These Twain.*

Ada, Aunt Arthur Seaton's aunt, who tells him what to tell a woman to do to have a miscarriage in Alan Sillitoe's *Saturday Night and Sunday Morning.*

Adair, Ace Husband of Jewel Adair; killed by a train in William Goyen's *Come, The Restorer.*

Adair, Addis Adopted son of Ace and Jewel Adair; searches for his biological father and becomes a saintlike figure in the wilderness in William Goyen's *Come, The Restorer.*

Adair, Azalea Essay writer and dedicated wife from Nashville, Tennessee; abused and driven to poverty by her alcoholic husband, who wastes whatever money she makes; delicate southern woman of exquisite education who lives in a rundown house that still shows signs of its former grandeur with a black coachman and a maid called Imp in O. Henry's "A Municipal Report."

Adair, Jewel Wife of Ace Adair; seeks to fulfill her lustful desires in William Goyen's *Come, The Restorer.*

Adair, Mr. Pamphlet writer on the Irish question; he is conceded to be helpful to Mr. Gladstone, but is considered a bore by the debutantes in George Moore's *A Drama in Muslin.*

Adair, Walter (Wat, Watty) North Carolina Tory sympathizer who betrays Arthur Butler; captured following the battle of King's Mountain; dies of a bite from a rabid wolf in John Pendleton Kennedy's *Horse-Shoe Robinson.*

Adalantaland Queen Ruler who lives no better than her subjects; she tells Ambien II all that she knows of her people's history and their many laws—most of which were given them by the Canopians in Doris Lessing's *The Sirian Experiments.*

Adam Husband of Ruma and father of Akash; often travels for his work; supportive of Ruma and more relaxed than she about asking her lonely father to live with them; cannot fathom Ruma's anxiety in making such a simple decision in Jhumpa Lahiri's *Unaccustomed Earth.*

Adam Old, former servant of Sir Rowland de Boys; chastises Oliver for his treatment of Orlando, and warns Orlando of Oliver's plot against him; offers Orlando his meager life savings and accompanies him in exile; taken in and cared for in the forest of Arden by Duke Senior and his men in William Shakespeare's play *As You Like It.*

Adam Texas soldier who has an affair with Miranda; dies from influenza in Katherine Anne Porter's *Pale Horse, Pale Rider.*

Adam, Captain Jacob R. Adam Owner of the S.S. *Thespian,* home of Adam's Original and Unparalleled Floating Opera, and master of ceremonies of the minstrel show in John Barth's *The Floating Opera.*

Adam, Father Constant companion of Dean Jocelin, who refers to him as "Father Anonymous" in William Golding's *The Spire.*

Adam, Judge Magistrate in the court of Huisum, a village near Utrecht in the Netherlands; appears in court in a disheveled and disreputable state, including lacking his ceremonial wig and sporting obvious bruises to his face; fears the sudden inspection of his corrupt court by the visiting investigator Counsellor Walter in Heinrich von Kleist's *The Broken Jug.*

Adam, Miss Young lecturer in history at the women's college that Dolores Hutton attends in Ivy Compton-Burnett's *Dolores.*

Adam, Sir Rich Jew whom Lucy, Sebastian's mother, considers marrying in Vita Sackville-West's *The Edwardians.*

Adams Coroner's Clerk who investigates the death of Percy Higgins in David Lodge's *Ginger, You're Barmy.*

Adams Head boy at Dr. Strong's school in Charles Dickens's *The Personal History of David Copperfield.*

Adams, Abraham Learned country parson, whose virtue prompts him to support the innocent or afflicted and condemn the hypocritical despite the consequences; he accompanies Joseph Andrews and Fanny Goodwill to their home parish in Henry Fielding's *The History of the Adventures of Mr. Joseph Andrews and of His Friend Mr. Abraham Adams.* He is the editor's friend, who perused and evaluated the manuscript that is published as *A Journey From This World to the Next.*

Adams, Alice (Lady Alicia, Alys Tuttle) Daughter of Virgil Adams; has a summer-long romance with Arthur Russell, but gives up her dreams of a life in high society and enrolls in a business college in Booth Tarkington's *Alice Adams.*

Adams, Amos Philosophic and idealistic editor of the *Harvey Tribune;* husband of Mary Adams, father of Grant Adams, and grandfather of Kenyon Adams in William Allen White's *In the Heart of a Fool.*

Adams, Captain Willie Boat owner who warns Harry Morgan that Morgan's bootlegging has been discovered in Ernest Hemingway's *To Have and Have Not.*

Adams, Carter American acquaintance who introduces Charlie Stark to the beauty of the Hawaiian Islands in Peter Matthiessen's *Raditzer.*

Adams, Darryl Sells cocaine for Rodney Little at Ahab's, a fish restaurant; is cheating Rodney by selling only half of what he is supposed to; is shot and killed by Victor Dunham in Richard Price's *Clockers.*

Adams, Dick (Jack) Parson Adams's favorite child, who is reported drowned and prompts the parson's disproportionate grief; this behavior contradicts his admonition to Joseph Andrews to love in moderation in Henry Fielding's *The History of the Adventures of Mr. Joseph Andrews and of His Friend Mr. Abraham Adams.*

Adams, Dr. Country physician who drives the child Lucy Cane to take Hazel back from Nuthanger Farm to the Down in Richard Adams's *Watership Down.*

Adams, Elizabeth Daughter of wealthy businessman; meets Calvin Marshall while an exchange student at Fisk University; becomes his lover and executive assistant; tells Andrea Marshall Calvin's last words were to tell Andrea he loved her; marries Gregory Townley after Calvin Marshall's death in Julius Lester's *And All Our Wounds Forgiven.*

Adams, Geoffrey Cousin of Elizabeth Trelone; he is an East End preacher who befriends Sirius, broadens his experience with human nature, and allows him to sing in his church; Adams is later killed in the World War II bombing of London in Olaf Stapledon's *Sirius: A Fantasy of Love and Discord.*

Adams, George Handiman afflicted by advancing age and senility in Henry Green's *Concluding.*

Adams, Grandfather Grandfather of Pookie Adams; supplies Pookie with Casey Ruggles comic strips in John Nichols's *The Sterile Cuckoo.*

Adams, Grandfather Grandfather of Stephen Grendon; takes Grendon's side in arguments and teaches him that all love is just a fight against time in August Derleth's *Evening in Spring;* also appears in *The Shield of the Valiant.*

Adams, Grant Father of Kenyon Adams; carpenter, reformer, and labor organizer in love with Laura Nesbit Van Dorn and killed by an anti-union mob in William Allen White's *In the Heart of a Fool.*

Adams, Jake Streetwise eighteen-year-old who makes his living in the drug underworld of St. Louis; main character in Herbert Simmons's *Corner Boy.*

Adams, Jane Striking and talented actress who escapes an abusive marriage to find success on the hit television series *Manhattan* in Danielle Steel's *Secrets.*

Adams, John English sailor who escapes from Africa with Peter Wilkins in Robert Paltock's *The Life and Adventures of Peter Wilkins.*

Adams, John See Smith, Alexander.

Adams, John R. Major, veteran of the Philippine campaign, and commander of the First Marine battalion in France during World War I in Thomas Boyd's *Through the Wheat.*

Adams, Kay College girlfriend and later the second wife of Michael Corleone in Mario Puzo's *The Godfather.*

Adams, Kenyon Illegitimate son of Grant Adams and Margaret Müller; reared as the son of Amos and Mary Adams; musician and artist who marries Lila Van Dorn in William Allen White's *In the Heart of a Fool.*

Adams, Marian and Bob Aunt and uncle of Pookie Adams; their Los Angeles home is a haven for Pookie in John Nichols's *The Sterile Cuckoo.*

Adams, Mary Sands Wife of Amos Adams and mother of Grant Adams; with the help of James Nesbit, claims her grandson Kenyon Adams as her own son in William Allen White's *In the Heart of a Fool.*

Adams, Mildred See Gale, Mildred Adams.

Adams, Mrs. Long-suffering, self-interested wife of Parson Adams; she objects to his support of Fanny Goodwill and Joseph Andrews against Lady Booby, which threatens the welfare of Adams's own family in Henry Fielding's *The History of the Adventures of Mr. Joseph Andrews and of His Friend Mr. Abraham Adams.*

Adams, Mrs. Wife of Virgil Adams and mother of Alice and Walter Adams; nags her husband to start his own factory so she and their daughter can join high society in Booth Tarkington's *Alice Adams.*

Adams, Mrs. Charles Fine Elderly woman who brings to the narrator's library a book on growing flowers in hotel rooms by candlelight in Richard Brautigan's *The Abortion.*

Adams, Nick Veteran of World War I who bears both psychic and physical scars from his duty at the Italian front; returns to the northern Michigan woods where he grew up; hikes, camps, and fishes there; regains some of the spiritual vitality he lost overseas by practicing simple but proven rituals for living off the land in Ernest Hemingway's "Big Two-Hearted River." Also the young man who witnesses the preparations for the assassination of Ole Andresen and, when the victim has not shown up, goes to warn him in Ernest Hemingway's "The Killers."

Adams, Old Man Father of Jake Adams; factory worker close to retirement in Herbert Simmons's *Corner Boy.*

Adams, Phil Boyhood friend of Tom Bailey; teaches Bailey self-defense; becomes the consul at Shanghai in Thomas Bailey Aldrich's *The Story of a Bad Boy.*

Adams, Pookie (Pooks) Girlfriend of Jerry Payne; whimsical storyteller who falls in and out of love and finally commits suicide in John Nichols's *The Sterile Cuckoo.*

Adams, Robin Fiancé of Angela Crevy; he is jealous of and disgusted by Angela's wealthy new friends in Henry Green's *Party Going.*

Adams, Shirley Neddy's ex-lover whose house lies on his pool route as he attempts to swim across the country by going from one neighbor's pool to the next; less than pleased to see him arrive at her pool, tells him she will not give him any more money or any alcohol in John Cheever's "The Swimmer."

Adams, Virgil (Virg) Father of Alice and Walter Adams; longtime loyal employee of J. A. Lamb who starts his own glue factory but is eventually bought out by Lamb, in Booth Tarkington's *Alice Adams.*

Adams, Walter (Wallie) Son of Virgil Adams; despises the high society his mother and sister Alice aspire to; takes up with disreputable companions and becomes an embezzler in Booth Tarkington's *Alice Adams.*

Adamson, Gerard (Gerry) Chairman of the English department at Quirn College, philosopher-poet, and husband of Louise Adamson, who leaves him for Vadim Vadimovich in Vladimir Nabokov's *Look at the Harlequins!*

Adamson, Jack Unscrupulous partner of John Caldigate in a gold-mining venture in New South Wales; he conspires with Timothy Crinkett to blackmail Caldigate over his alleged bigamous marriage; he confesses to perjury in the case in Anthony Trollope's *John Caldigate.*

Adamson, Ken Attractive, well-mannered patient in Clive Ward who is popular with other patients and the nursing staff; in the hospital because of a car accident, he is concerned about his souring marriage to Maevis and his dubious involvement in the traffic accident that resulted in the death of a motorcyclist in John Berger's *The Foot of Clive.*

Adamson, Louise Young wife of Gerry Adamson, whom she leaves for a less than felicitous marriage to Vadim Vadimovich, whose third wife she becomes in Vladimir Nabokov's *Look at the Harlequins!*

Adamson, Maevis (Maeve) Beautiful model and wife of Ken Adamson; pampered, indolent, and self-centered, she visits Ken only once in the hospital in John Berger's *The Foot of Clive.*

Adam the First Old man from the town of Deceit; he tries to stop Faithful at the Hill of Difficulty in John Bunyan's *The Pilgrim's Progress from This World to That Which Is to Come.*

Adare, Adelaide Red-haired Polish woman who deserts her three children during the depression by flying off with stunt pilot The Great Omar; mother of Karl Adare, Mary Adare, and Jude Miller in Louise Erdrich's *The Beet Queen.*

Adare, Dot (Wallacette) Stocky, willful, aggressive part-Chippewa girl who at age 18 becomes the Beet Queen in Argus, North Dakota; daughter of Celestine James and Karl Adare in Louise Erdrich's *The Beet Queen.*

Adare, Karl German-Polish boy deserted by his mother, Adelaide Adare, at age fourteen; glib salesman whose life is marked by an absence of meaningful relationships; lover of Wallace Pfef and Celestine James; father of Dot Adare in Louise Erdrich's *The Beet Queen.*

Adare, Mary German-Polish girl deserted by her mother, Adelaide Adare, at age eleven; foster child of Pete and Fritzie Kozka, who takes over operation of the Kozkas' butcher shop in Louise Erdrich's *The Beet Queen.*

Adcock (Sparks) Radio operator who signs on with Captain Bennett to go on an unknown mission for good pay and is the only person who survives the experience; he is narrator of Alan Sillitoe's *The Lost Flying Boat.*

Addams, Frances (F. Jasmine, Frankie) Twelve-year-old protagonist infatuated with her brother and his bride; disrupts their wedding in an attempt to accompany them on their honeymoon in Carson McCullers's *The Member of the Wedding.*

Addams, Jarvis Older brother of Frankie Addams; bridegroom in Carson McCullers's *The Member of the Wedding.*

Addams, Royal Quincy Jewelry store owner, father of Frankie and Jarvis Addams, and employer of Berenice Sadie Brown in Carson McCullers's *The Member of the Wedding.*

Adderly, Jack Northerton's fellow ensign, who joins him in teasing and insulting the new volunteer, Tom Jones, in Henry Fielding's *The History of Tom Jones.*

Addie One of two very elderly women who share a room at the Old Ladies' Home; visited by the 14-year-old Marian, who has come to spend time with them as part of her Campfire Girls' obligation in Eudora Welty's "A Visit of Charity."

Addinsell, Charles Arthur Middleton's oldest friend; he becomes successively involved with Arthur's wife, Diana; Arthur's younger love interest, Annabel Paynton; and Annabel's close friend, Clair Belaine; in Henry Green's *Doting.*

Addison, Joseph Essayist whose soul the author encounters in Elysium in Henry Fielding's *A Journey From This World to the Next.* He appears as a critic and poet in William Makepeace Thackeray's *The History of Henry Esmond.*

Addison, Judah Investor in Frank Cowperwood's natural gas project in Theodore Dreiser's *The Titan.*

Adela Bernarda's youngest and most attractive daughter; dreaming of escape and freedom from the living hell of the house, she defies the domestic hierarchy of mother and sisters to initiate an illicit relationship with Angustias's fiancé that will lead to her death in Federico García Lorca's play *The House of Bernard Alba.*

Adela Emma Greatheart's maid who says that she never lays a finger on anything dead in Ivy Compton-Burnett's *Mother and Son.*

Adela Josephine Napier's maid in Ivy Compton-Burnett's *More Women Than Men.*

Adela Nurse for Sefton and Clemence Shelley; she is kind, trustworthy, and attached to the children in Ivy Compton-Burnett's *Two Worlds and Their Ways.*

Adelaide Mistress of Charles the Simple; she procures the downfall of Julian the Apostate, in his incarnation as court jester, after he makes fun of her appearance in Henry Fielding's *A Journey From This World to the Next.*

Adèle Beautiful young daughter of the Colonel and Mummy, although her biological father is the sinister Jacob

Hummel; a fragile spirit who spends most of her hours in the hyacinth garden; finds the world, when its stark truths are revealed, too bleak to live in and dies as a result in August Strindberg's play *The Ghost Sonata.*

Adele Daughter of Lillian Beye in Anaïs Nin's *Ladders to Fire* and *Seduction of the Minotaur.*

Adele Young woman and daughter of Roas Frumetl; her mother marries the rich patriarch Meshulam Moskat to ensure her dowry; modernized by European schools, she finds Warsaw too "Asiatic," and like her Jewish identity, the city is seen as foreign and unsettling; later marries Asa, although he still loves Hadassah; has a son, David, by him in Isaac Bashevis Singer's *The Moskat Family.*

Adelhu Heir and only son of King Oeros of Hypotosa and the lover and husband of Eovaai; after he is exiled through the evil machinations of Ochihatou, he disguises himself as Ihoya and acts as protector of Ijaveo in Eovaai's absence; he rescues her from Ochihatou and they are happily reunited in Eliza Haywood's *Adventures of Eovaai, Princess of Ijaveo.*

Adelina Mexican wife of Harrison; asphyxiated in Nicholas Delbanco's *News.*

Adeline Innocent young woman abandoned to thieves by her "father," Louis de St. Pierre (Jean d'Aunoy); she is rescued by the La Mott family and remains with them in an abandoned abbey until La Mott plans to relinquish her to the evil Phillippe, Marquis de Montalt; captured by Montalt, she escapes with her lover, Theodore Peyron, only to be recaptured by Montalt and returned to the abbey; she is released by La Mott to escape to Savoy, where she is sheltered by the clergyman Arnand La Luc; ultimately she testifies against Montalt, is discovered to be his niece and heir to the Montalt fortune, and marries Theodore in Ann Radcliffe's *The Romance of the Forest.*

Adelmo of Otranto Benedictine monk; he is a young illustrator of manuscripts; commits suicide due to his guilt for a homosexual affair with fellow monk Berengar in Umberto Eco's *The Name of the Rose.*

Adeppi Young orphaned street singer in the Italian village of Castiglione; befriends Nino and lives with Arsella and Pipistrello in John Hawkes's *The Goose on the Grave.*

Adept Alchemist who, while searching for the philosopher's stone, manages to free the spirit Chrysal from a small portion of pure gold and records the narration of the spirit in Charles Johnstone's *Chrysal: or, The Adventures of a Guinea.*

Aderyn the Bird Queen Llewellyn's apparent mother, a Welsh women famous for her trained bird act in a traveling circus; she is uneducated but shrewd and ambitious in Anthony Burgess's *MF.*

Adey, Max Fabulously wealthy young man, who plans and pays for the fog-delayed holiday of his friends; he is torn between loving Julia Wray and Amabel in Henry Green's *Party Going.*

Adimari, Euthanasia dei Beautiful, virtuous childhood friend and later the lover of Castruccio Castracani dei Antelminelli; she becomes Countess of Valperga and a benevolent ruler; she tries unsuccessfully to maintain neutrality in the Guelph-Ghibelline conflict of Florence and Lucca; an innocent idealist, she becomes disillusioned by the corrupt power tactics of her lover and finds her love for him changed to grief in Mary Shelley's *Valperga.*

Adimari, Lauretta dei Cousin of Euthanasia dei Adimari and wife of Leodino de Guinigi; she is consoled by Euthanasia at Valperga after her husband's execution by Castruccio dei Antelminelli in Mary Shelley's *Valperga.*

Adimari, Messer Antonio dei Chief of the Guelph party in Florence, father of Euthanasia, and a blind scholastic, who engrains love of peace and liberty in his daughter in Mary Shelley's *Valperga.*

Ad'jibid'ji Young daughter of the protagonist and strike leader Ibrahima Bakayoko; sneaks into a railway workers' union meeting in Bamako where the African workers vote to strike against the French owners of the Dakar-Niger line of the West African Company in Ousmane Sembène's *God's Bits of Wood.*

Adlan Supernormal being, an Egyptian who lives nearly four hundred years and, thirty-five years after his death, makes telepathic contact with John Wainwright, influencing the establishment of John's colony in Olaf Stapledon's *Odd John: A Story Between Jest and Earnest.*

Adler Member of Ward Bennett's crew seeking and failing to reach the North Pole; loyally remains with Bennett afterwards, encouraging him to make another voyage to the Arctic, in Frank Norris's *A Man's Woman.*

Adler, Dr. Vain physician and professor of internal medicine who lives in comfortable retirement in New York's Hotel Gloriana; uncaring father of Tommy Wilhelm in Saul Bellow's *The Victim.*

Adler, Irene Retired operatic figure who was previously engaged to the king of Bohemia; possesses a photograph of both Irene and the king; threatens the king by saying that she would send the photograph to the family of the king's prospective wife; now engaged to and later marries Godfrey Norton, a lawyer; understands that Sherlock Holmes is investigating to rescue the compromising photograph; leaves England for the Continent before Holmes arrives to seize the photo; leaves a letter for Sherlock Holmes and a different photograph of her for the king; always referred to by Holmes under the honourable title of 'the woman' in Sir Arthur Conan Doyle's "A Scandal in Bohemia."

Adler, Joe American looking for a good time and finding it with Laurie Gaynor in Jean Rhys's *Voyage in the Dark.*

Adler, Liza Marxist who corresponds with Paul Hobbes in John Clellon Holmes's *Go.*

Adler, Myron (Mike) Successful and even-tempered businessman who, out of friendship and concern, reveals Joseph's decline into bad temper in Saul Bellow's *Dangling Man.*

Admiral Achiever of rank through phlegmatic indolence and servility of soul; he sells contracts to pursers at a great profit and accepts bribes in Charles Johnstone's *Chrysal: or, The Adventures of a Guinea.*

Admiral's Clerk Employee who keeps track of the Admiral's accounts and enriches himself at the same time in Charles Johnstone's *Chrysal: or, The Adventures of a Guinea.*

Admiral's Executive Officer Active man who appeals to his sailors' sense of patriotism and greed before he leads them into battle; he gives Chrysal to the sailor who first spots land in Charles Johnstone's *Chrysal: or, The Adventures of a Guinea.*

Adolf Aging patriarch of a large Swedish family in the remote and isolated farm in Ulvaskog; refuses to modernize his farming methods and watches as his empire crumbles; all but one of his children, his favorite, Mari, leave for the city in hopes of a brighter future; ultimately murders Mari on the eve of her departure to Stockholm in Vilhelm Moberg's *Clenched Fists.*

Adolf New medical chief at Auschwitz who recently arrived from Dachau; possesses a pleasant nature; charged with training new medical orderlies such as the narrator, Tadek, and Staszek—two concentration camp prisoners; hopes that the new orderlies will improve the health of prisoners and morale of the camps to which they will return in Tadeusz Borowski's *This Way for the Gas, Ladies and Gentlemen.*

Adolf, Father Priest who is supposed to offer repentance and support to despairing members of the congregation, but instead instills fear of deceit in them; performs his best when conducting funerals; gets rid of the Hussites; has his failings as a priest, but is held in solemn respect; has supposedly met Satan face to face and defeated him; arrests Number 44, who is disguised as Balthasar, and escapes before being burned; eventually gives up trying to arrest the Duplicates as well; remains very superstitious and eager to assert his power as a church official in Samuel Langhorne Clemens's "The Mysterious Stranger."

Adolph Servant who accompanies Swithin Forsyte on a drive with Irene Forsyte to the site of Soames Forsyte's country house in John Galsworthy's *The Man of Property.*

Adolphe, Monsieur Perfectly attired, rosy-cheeked, cosmopolitan reception-manager in Arnold Bennett's *Imperial Palace.*

Adon-Ai Male spirit who is the friend and familiar of Zanoni in Edward Bulwer-Lytton's *Zanoni.*

Adonijah Old Jewish doctor who provides a haven for Alonzo de Monçada after Fernan di Nunez is interred; he makes a study of Melmoth the Wanderer and tells Alonzo de Monçada of Donna Isadora di Aliaga (Immalee), who was shipwrecked as an infant and grew up on an uninhabited island until she was visited by the Wanderer in Charles Maturin's *Melmoth the Wanderer.*

Adorno, Andy Weekend guest of Celia and Quentin Villiers and boyfriend of Diane Parry; he is rowdy, aggressive, and obsessed with his macho image; a number of perverse and violent acts, culminating in murder, are committed during a decadent weekend in the country, and Andy turns out to be the perpetrator in Martin Amis's *Dead Babies.*

Adraste Maid of Helen; becomes pregnant by Damastor in John Erskine's *The Private Life of Helen of Troy.*

Adrian Man involved in a brief relationship with Kate Fletcher Armstrong in Margaret Drabble's *The Middle Ground.*

Adrian Friend of Imogene King in Isabel Colegate's *Orlando at the Brazen Threshold.* Adrian becomes Imogene's lover in *Agatha.*

Adrian Poetic, sensitive second Earl of Windsor, son of the late King of England, and true friend of Lionel Verney; he vainly loves Evadne Zaimi, assumes the duty of Lord Protector, believes in republican government, and leads the last of mankind toward the safety of the Alps in Mary Shelley's *The Last Man.*

Adrian, Boris (B., King B.) Critically respected film director who directs a pornographic movie in Terry Southern's *Blue Movie.*

Adriana Small, thin, but stern and resolute woman who decides to convince her boyfriend, Mario, to accept the challenge to fight Jacob for the 500 pesos at stake, which would allow her to marry Mario in Juan Carlos Onetti's "Jacob and the Other."

Adriana, Doña One of two owners of a bar at the Naccos camp who are suspected by the investigator Lituma of hiding the secret about the disappearance of three men in Mario Vargas Llosa's *Death in the Andes.*

Adso of Melk Son of Baron of Melk and Benedictine novice; he is the scribe and apprentice of William of Baskerville; helps his mentor investigate the mysterious murders in the abbey; as an elder monk, he writes his memories on the events that have taken place in the monastery in Umberto Eco's *The Name of the Rose.*

Adverse, Anthony (Toni) Illegitimate son of Maria Bonnyfeather and heir of John Bonnyfeather; has many adventures in his travels as he makes his fortune in Hervey Allen's *Anthony Adverse.*

Adye, Colonel Port Burdock chief of police and friend of Dr. Kemp; he is shot by Griffin while trying to prevent Griffin's murder of Kemp in H. G. Wells's *The Invisible Man: A Grotesque Romance.*

A. E. See George Russell.

Aearchus Parasite who ingratiates himself with the duchess, Gigantilla, and has an affair with her but forsakes her in the end in Eliza Haywood's *The Perplex'd Dutchess; or, Treachery Rewarded.*

Aegistheus Lover of Clytemnestra; conspires with her to kill her husband and king Agamemnon; marries Clytemnestra and becomes the king of Argos; forces the citizens of Argos to repent for the crime and is in turn killed by Orestes and Electra, two children of Agamemnon and Clytemnestra, in Jean-Paul Sartre's *The Flies.*

Aegisthus Lover and husband of Clytemnestra; when his wife hears about Orestes' fake death, she joyfully sends for Aegisthus and thus unwittingly lures him to his death; back in the palace, he is slain by Orestes in Aeschylus's *The Libation Bearers.*

Aegisthus Clytemnestra's lover, Agamemnon's cousin, and the only surviving son of Thyestes, who was Atreus's brother and Agamemnon's uncle; Atreus had killed two of Thyestes' sons (Aegisthus's brothers) and served them to Thyestes for dinner; realizing the horror of having eaten his own children, Thyestes proclaims a curse on the House of Atreus, which Aegisthus has sworn to execute in Aeschylus's *Agamemnon.*

Aegisthus Ancient Greek figure; lover of Clytemnestra; conspires with her to murder Clytemnestra's husband, Agamemnon; killed by Orestes in John Erskine's *The Private Life of Helen of Troy.*

AEH Edwardian poet and professor of classics Alfred Edward Housman immediately after his death at age 77; best known for his collection *A Shropshire Lad,* inspired by his unrequited love for fellow Oxford student Moses John Jackson in Tom Stoppard's *The Invention of Love.*

Aehle, Miss Professional music teacher who tutors the narrator's older sister on the piano and Richard Miles on the violin; spinster who supports herself and her paralyzed father in Tennessee Williams's "The Resemblance Between a Violin and a Coffin."

Aelis, Dame Wife of Herbert le Gros Anisiau, a reprobate who nearly kills his wife before his son Haguenier steps in to defend her from his cruel father in Zoé Oldenbourg's *The Cornerstone.*

Aeore (Child-Star, Riri'an) Niaruna Indian warrior who becomes a jaguar-shaman and chief rival of Lewis Moon in Peter Matthiessen's *At Play in the Fields of the Lord.*

Afanasi, Vladimir Eskimo leader of Desolation, Alaska; builds successful community by integrating modern civilization and native practices in James Michener's *Alaska.*

Afanasyevitch, Ivan Statesman and a man of modern political and enlightened ideas; he takes Marmeladov back into the service on his own responsibility in Fyodor Dostoevsky's *Crime and Punishment.*

A Few Fleas Son of Roman Diosdado and barman at the Farolito in Malcolm Lowry's *Under the Volcano.*

Afflick, Jackie Good-humoredly vulgar owner of a coach-tour business in Agatha Christie's *Sleeping Murder.*

Afflock, Colonel the Right Honourable Sir Rupert, M.P., J.P., F.R.S. Eminently versatile Secretary of War; he is humiliated by Lord Raingo and schemes to bring about Raingo's defensive speech in the House of Lords which seriously taxes Raingo's heart in Arnold Bennett's *Lord Raingo.*

Afrany Head of Procurator's Secret Service; given orders in a very circumvent manner by Pilate to kill Judas in Mikhail Bulgakov's *Master and Margarita.*

Africana Somewhat physically disadvantaged kid goat passed off as a wish-granting, magical unicorn; it becomes the source of fantasy-play and the imaginary panacea to more mature adult wants and aspirations in young Joe's world in Wolf Mankowitz's *A Kid for Two Farthings.*

African Flower See Lavoisier, Angela Williams.

African Woman, The Described as wild and gorgeous, an African woman whose hair is done up to look like a helmet and who is adorned by large layers of jewelry; appears to have been Kurtz's mistress and mysteriously comes to the shore twice when Kurtz is forced to leave his African empire by Marlow on the steamer in Joseph Conrad's *Heart of Darkness.*

Afrosinya Drunken woman witnessed by Raskolnikov as she unsuccessfully tries to drown herself in a canal; she had formerly attempted to hang herself in Fyodor Dostoevsky's *Crime and Punishment.*

After Birth Tycoon See O'Leary, Salvador Hassan.

Agamemnon Ancient Greek warrior at Troy; brother of Menelaos and husband of Clytemnestra; killed by Clytemnestra and her lover Aegisthus in John Erskine's *The Private Life of Helen of Troy.*

Agamemnon King of Argos and Clytemnestra's husband; as the older brother of Menelaus, whose wife, Helen, was abducted by Paris, he commanded the Greek armies during the 10-year Trojan War; in order to obtain favorable winds for his ships, he sacrificed his daughter Iphigenia to the gods; upon victoriously returning home he is killed by his wife to punish him for sacrificing Iphigenia; first his wife has him blasphemously step on a crimson tapestry, then he is slaughtered like an ox in Aeschylus's *Agamemnon.*

Agar, Robert Specialist in keys and safecracking and an accomplice of Edward Pierce, whom Agar turns in to the police in Michael Crichton's *The Great Train Robbery.*

Agaric, Father Clergyman of Penguinia on the mythical island of Alca; seeks to restore the king of Alca to the throne in Anatole France's *Penguin Island.*

Agata Beggar woman who wanders during the winter to collect money for a funeral in Władysław Stanisław Reymont's *The Peasants.*

Agate Man who barks at the taxi drivers for their lack of backbone in striking; insults Fatt, one of the union leaders and a suspected mole for the company; incites the drivers by telling them that the rich are killing them off; says the "reds" have helped in the past and not to wait for Lefty, who may never appear; shouts "Workers of the world, unite!" in Clifford Odets's play *Waiting for Lefty.*

Agate, Sergeant Julian Flagrantly homosexual soldier in Sergeant Richard Ennis's unit; he becomes Ennis's friend and roommate but not lover; upbeat and irresponsible, Agate flaunts his homosexuality in Anthony Burgess's *A Vision of Battlements.*

Agatha Beatrice's maid and a practicing Christian who consistently reacts to guests based on their economic class in Chinua Achebe's *Anthills of the Savannah.*

Agatha Beloved of Redhead and wily waiting maid to the queen of Utterbol; she assists Ursula to escape the evil king of the Kingdom of the Tower in William Morris's *The Well at the World's End.*

Agatha Orphan girl whom Elisabeth brings home; her parents, drug addicts, committed suicide; invited into the secret room where Paul and Elisabeth carry out their imaginative games and lives; becomes enamored with Paul, raising Elisabeth's jealousy, which leads to the death of both Paul and Elisabeth in Jean Cocteau's *The Holy Terrors.*

Agatha Wealthy spinster who, though terminally ill, superstitiously refuses to make a will; she expects her great niece, Mary Whittaker, who lives with and cares for her, to inherit in Dorothy L. Sayers's *Unnatural Death.*

Agatha Beauty parlor assistant and girlfriend of Raymond; at Raymond's request, she visits the ailing Jake Brown in Claude McKay's *Home to Harlem.*

Agatha, Lady Lord Henry's aunt who works in the London slums and engages in other charitable work in Oscar Wilde's *The Picture of Dorian Gray.*

Agathe Sister of the Austrian protagonist, Ulrich, during the years leading up to World War I; engages in a mystical and incestuous journey with her brother in Robert Musil's *The Man Without Qualities.*

Agatson, Bill Former Harvard University student who drinks heavily and craves excess; killed in the New York subway in John Clellon Holmes's *Go.*

Agave Cadmus's daughter, sister of Smele, aunt of Dionysus, and mother of the Theban king Pentheus; joins the Dionysian rituals and becomes a Bacchant, a female follower of Dionysus possessed by his spirit; moved by Dionysus, she murders and dismembers Pentheus under the impression that he is a lion, only to realize her crime later in Euripides' *The Bacchants.*

Aged Gallant Aurora's titled and rich admirer, who lives a life of gallantry and cannot divert himself from the passion of love in Francis Coventry's *The History of Pompey the Little.*

Agelastes, Michael (Elephas, The Elephant) Philosopher and highly influential court wit; publicly an austere sage, in private he is a voluptuary; though seemingly attached to Emperor Alexius Comnenus, he secretly plots to ascend the throne himself but is killed before succeeding in Sir Walter Scott's *Count Robert of Paris.*

Agellius Callista's suitor, a farmer, who first tells her of the Christian faith; his uncle Jucundus and his brother try to dissuade him from it in John Henry Newman's *Callista.*

Agent Go-between who arranges Her Grace's patronage interviews for a gift of cash in Charles Johnstone's *Chrysal: or, The Adventures of a Guinea.*

Agha Turkish overlord of the remote village of Lycovissa in the mountains of Anatolia; obese glutton who drinks during the day and enjoys handsome boys at night; discusses with the other village elders the upcoming Passion Play; refuses to help the priest Fotis and his throng of beleaguered people who are searching for a new homeland in Nikos Kazantzakis's *The Greek Passion.*

Agha, Abdi Tyrannical feudal landlord in a village in Turkey; oppresses the poor; rages against Memed when he attempts to elope with Hatche and leave the village; finally defeated by Memed and loses his vast lands and fortune to the peasants in Yashar (Yaşar) Kemal's *Memed, My Hawk.*

Agilulf Emo Bertrandin of the Guildivern A model knight in Charlemagne's army who is an empty suit of white armour. His rigid devotion to rules and regulations allows him to maintain his existence; assigned Gurduloo as his squire. He earned his knighthood by saving Sophronia, the King of Scotland's virgin daughter, but his knighthood is contested by Sophronia's son Torrismund, who claims that his mother was not a virgin at the time of the deed; this accusation prompts Agilulf's quest. Before the truth about Sophronia is revealed, Agilulf believes that he does not deserve to be a knight, and leaves behind his armor for Raimbaut in Italo Calvino's *The Nonexistent Knight.*

Agliè Man who may or may not be the immortal Count Saint-Germain in Umberto Eco's *Foucault's Pendulum.*

Aglone Former slave who lives with the Pinseau family after the Civil War as their cook and housekeeper in Grace King's *The Pleasant Ways of St. Médard.*

Agnes Aged attendant of Maud, Lady Rookwood, in William Harrison Ainsworth's *Rookwood.*

Agnes Gilbert Imlay's lover; a childlike street minstrel; she laughs often and over very little in Frances Sherwood's *Vindication.*

Agnes Ill-disposed servant of Mme. Walravens; she lives off the generosity of M. Paul Emanuel in Charlotte Brontë's *Villette.*

Agnes Lorenzo's sister and Raymond's lover, who finds herself condemned to live a life she detests, inasmuch as she has been forced to become a nun; falls to sexual temptation and becomes pregnant; sentenced to death for this reason; clever and daring, she makes fun of religious superstitions and convincingly argues in her defense; attempts to escape from the convent but is imprisoned in the crypt, where her baby dies soon after birth; her final rescue comes as the only happy ending in the story in Matthew Gregory Lewis's *The Monk.*

Agnes The Heriots' under-housemaid who fell because of the broken back steps in Ivy Compton-Burnett's *The Last and the First.*

Agnes, Sister See Udolpho, Laurentini di.

Agnew Mortuary superintendent who helps Morgan perform the autopsy on the body of Lady Ashbrook in C. P. Snow's *A Coat of Varnish.*

Agni, Roland (Rollie) Talented rookie outfielder forced to play on the worst team in the Patriot League and bat eighth all year; reminds Angela Whittling Trust of her only true love, Luke Gofarmon, in Philip Roth's *The Great American Novel.*

Agni of the Daylings Warder of the Thingstead or holy place of the Markmen, where Thiodolf and Otter are chosen as war-dukes to lead the Gothic clans in their resistance against the Romans in William Morris's *A Tale of the House of the Wolfings.*

Agocho (Agocho Koh Tli-chu, Fig Tree John, John, Red Fire Bird) Apache Indian who seeks revenge on all whites for his wife's murder in Edwin Corle's *Fig Tree John.*

Agon Tall, aquiline-featured, white-bearded and vindictive high priest of the Zu-Vendi people; he fiercely hates Allan Quatermain and his English party; he joins General Nasta in rebellion against Queen Nyleptha and is killed by Umslopogaas in H. Rider Haggard's *Allan Quatermain.*

Agoropoulos, Mme. Woman kept from the social gatherings of the Cabala; honored when Alix d'Espoli accepts her invitation in Thornton Wilder's *The Cabala.*

Agravaine Brother of Gawaine in Thomas Berger's *Arthur Rex.*

Agrippa One of Octavius Caesar's officers; proposes that Antony marry Caesar's sister Octavia in order to strengthen the bond between the two men; at one point orders Caesar's troops to retreat from a resurgent Antony in William Shakespeare's *Antony and Cleopatra.*

Agrippa, Menenius Roman patrician, friend to Coriolanus and the hero's fatherlike figure, his relationship with Martius is quasi-paternal; seen as persuasive and wise; his apologetic speech on the parts of the body displays his rhetorical art, which he uses to avoid class conflict; unable to convince Coriolanus that he should not fight against the Romans in William Shakespeare's play *Coriolanus.*

Agrippine Ambitious widow of Emperor Claudius and omnipresent, possessive, and doting mother of Néron, the son of her former marriage to Domitius Ahenobarbus; possibly played a role in Claudius's death, which made Néron Caesar; fearing for her continued domination over Néron, especially after her adviser, Pallas, is banished, she plots to make Britannicus, Néron's stepbrother, emperor; after Britannicus's assassination, Agrippine knows that she will be Néron's next victim in Jean Racine's play *Britannicus.*

Agrippinilla Claudius's niece and mother of Nero; after marrying Claudius, she rules Rome in his stead, finally poisoning him to make way for Nero's accession in Robert Graves's *Claudius, the God and His Wife Messalina.*

Agronomist, The Friend of the Colonel; given custody of the Cartographer ostensibly because of his horticultural skills, he sets him free to spare the Colonel the difficulty of a trial at which the Cartographer was to be the principal witness in Nigel Dennis's *A House in Order.*

Agua, Dr. Pedro del Royal doctor ordered to mummify deceased husband with heart intact in Carlos Fuentes's *Terra Nostra.*

Aguecheek, Sir Andrew Cowardly fool who plots to regain his riches by marrying Lady Olivia; assisted in his matrimonial scheme by Sir Toby Belch, Olivia's uncle; decides to abort his plan but is pressured by Sir Toby to pursue the marriage plot in William Shakespeare's play *Twelfth Night.*

Agueda Old servant and only companion to the elderly Sophie; suddenly dies, leaving Sophie alone in the sprawling hillside home with her cat and the young male celestial angel in Dora Alonso's "Sophie and the Angel."

Aguerra, Monsignor Investigator sent by the church to study Leibowitz to determine the trajectory of his canonization; plays the role of God's Advocate in the process, which ultimately leads to Leibowitz's canonization in Walter M. Miller, Jr.'s *A Canticle for Leibowitz.*

Aguirre, Joe Foreman of a ranch where Jack Twist and Ennis del Mar work with sheep on Brokeback Mountain in Arizona; spots the two men in a homosexual embrace while they are guarding the sheep herd, but does not mention it to the two men at that point in Annie Proulx's "Brokeback Mountain."

Ahab Captain of the *Pequod* whose pursuit of Moby-Dick leads to the death of everyone aboard the ship except Ishmael in Herman Melville's *Moby-Dick.*

Ahab, Gil Night-shift worker whose truck is used to transport workers to the Past Bay Manufacturing Company factory during the strike; religious fanatic in Robert Cantwell's *The Land of Plenty.*

Ahearn, Mickey Unmarried mother of a child she calls Willy and sends via railroad freight to Will Brady in Wright Morris's *The Works of Love.*

Ah Fong Chinese baker on Manukura who dies in the hurricane before he can return to China in Charles Nordhoff and James Norman Hall's *The Hurricane.*

Ahineev, Serge Kapitonich School's writing master who gives a party for the wedding of his daughter; object of a joke, rumor, and slander, fostered by Vankin, an assistant usher at the ceremony, that he kissed the cook, Marfa, at the nuptial feast; becomes increasingly embarrassed as the tale spreads to the other wedding guests; the story grows, and the two are now rumored to be having a love affair; confronts Vankin, who denies that he has told anyone the rumor in Anton Chekhov's "A Slander."

Ahineev's Wife Wife of the school's writing master, who believes the rumors that her husband has started an affair with their cook, Marfa, and turns angry toward him in Anton Chekhov's "A Slander."

Ahmed Male name given to a baby girl born to hajji Suleyman, a tyrannical figure emblematic of the Moroccan male-dominated society; raised as a boy and then a man, even though female, for 20 years in Tahar Ben Jelloun's *The Sacred Night.*

Ahmed Turkish man working at the hotel in Istanbul where the Global Foods conference is going on; assigned to assist Kate Brown, he innately understands her role as "nanny" and its similarity to his own role in Doris Lessing's *The Summer Before the Dark.*

Ahmed Zahra's brother, favored as a child and given the choicest food; his family's ambitions for him remain unfulfilled in the context of war, and he joins a militia group and loots the homes of those he helps or kills in Hanan Al-Shaykh's *The Story of Zahra.*

Ahmed, K. Y. See O'Leary, Salvador Hassan.

Ahmose One of the protagonists and third of three pharaoh kings in a line of succession during the end of the 17th and start of the 18th dynasties in Egypt; one of three kings to lead his armies in a battle to regain Thebes and Egypt from the Hyskos king Apophis; only one of the three defending kings to survive the lost battle; years later returns to drive out the invaders in Naguib Mahfouz's *Thebes at War.*

Ah-Siu First wife and a barren woman of the wealthy tax collector; she becomes jealous that her husband's second wife, Chang-hi-tang, has borne him a son; plots to kill her husband, blames Chang-hi-tang for the murder, and claims the child as her own; later loses the child to its rightful mother in a test of true love for the infant in Li Hsing-tao's play *The Circle of Chalk.*

Ah Wing (Ah Sing) Chinese cook of the *Flying Scud,* wounded and buried alive at sea by the crew of the *Currency Lass;* his place is taken by Joseph Amalu in Robert Louis Stevenson's *The Wrecker.*

Aida Neighbor who helps Noumbe in Sembene Ousmane's "Her Three Days."

Aigredoux, Mme. Pauline Home's former schoolmistress, who did not like Mr. Home constantly in her school in Charlotte Brontë's *Villette.*

Aiken, Forney Alcoholic photographer who darkens his skin while researching his latest book on black life in the South in Walker Percy's *The Last Gentleman.*

Ailwyn, Godfrey Priest who notifies Lewis and Margaret (Hollis) Eliot that Maurice Hollis plans to marry in C. P. Snow's *Last Things.*

Aimata See Pomaree Vahinee I.

Aimee Daughter of Iris and Alex Thomas and Sabrina's mother; grows estranged from her mother and does not know her father's identity in Margaret Atwood's *The Blind Assassin.*

Aimor Rebellious Jamaican slave, who protects Matilda from his hostile compatriots in Sophia Lee's *The Recess.*

Ainger Sometimes facetious butler to the Middletons; he gossips and eavesdrops on the family in Ivy Compton-Burnett's *The Mighty and Their Fall.*

Ainger, Alfred Butler to the Clare family; he identifies with Cassius Clare, the master, and advises the family not to call for a doctor when Cassius seems to be making a second pseudo-suicide attempt in Ivy Compton-Burnett's *The Present and the Past.*

Ainley, Mary Ann Ugly, unselfish old maid, whose good works Caroline Helstone takes as a model but finds too difficult to follow in Charlotte Brontë's *Shirley.*

Ainnle Brother of Naisi and Ardank who defies the dictates of Conchubor, the high king of Ulster; murdered along with his brothers by Conchubor in John Millington Synge's play *Deirdre of the Sorrows.*

Ainslie, Earl of High-principled father of Lady Muriel Orme; he has an interest in science, particularly botany, in

Lewis Carroll's *Sylvie and Bruno.* He appears in *Sylvie and Bruno Concluded.*

Ainslie, Mollie Massachusetts teacher who becomes a major landowner in Kansas; marries Hesden Le Moyne in Albion W. Tourgee's *Bricks Without Straw.*

Ainslie, Oscar Brother of Mollie Ainslie; makes Mollie promise, as he is dying of consumption, that she will remain in a healthful Southern climate in Albion W. Tourgee's *Bricks Without Straw.*

Aiolfo Father of Medardo who gave up his title for his son; spends his time looking after the aviary; after Medardo's "bad half" rips a beloved bird in half when Aiolfo sends it up to see how his son is doing, the old man stays in his bed located in the aviary and dies in Italo Calvino's *The Cloven Viscount.*

Aire, John de Calais citizen who urges Eustace St. Pierre to sacrifice his kinsmen to English conquerors in a parable told by Charles Meekly in Henry Brooke's *The Fool of Quality.*

Airish, Miss Loose lady of the town in Eliza Haywood's *The History of Miss Betsy Thoughtless.*

Airman, Noel (Saul Ehrmann) Songwriter with a crooked arm who is the social director and head of the entertainment staff at South Wind, an adult camp; love of Marjorie Morningstar in Herman Wouk's *Marjorie Morningstar.*

Airport Check-In Agent Jamaican female worker who reiterates to Oliver that he must substitute his additional luggage with cardboard boxes due to airport codes that deny passengers onboard with overweight, multiple luggage, unless they pay in Oliver Samuel's play *Airport.*

Air Vice Marshall Structured, determined, controlling speaker; glimpses of humanity show through his intimidating exterior in Rex Warner's *The Aerodrome: A Love Story.*

Aisgill, Alice Handsome, passionate, affectionate, empty woman, whose husband no longer loves her but will not divorce her; she is lonely until she meets Joe Lampton; their breakup results in her suicidal death by auto "accident" in John Braine's *Room at the Top.* She is the subject of talk in *Life at the Top.*

Aisgill, George Controlling, conservative, sarcastic woolman; he does not like his wife Alice's friends and does not love her in John Braine's *Room at the Top.* He is an upstanding and strange man in the community in *Life at the Top.*

Aisha Member of a middle-class Muslim family in Cairo, headed by al-Sayyad and his wife, Amina; marries and nearly loses her entire family to typhoid in the 1920s in Cairo; becomes an old woman at 34 and has taken to smoking in Naguib Mahfouz's *The Cairo Trilogy.*

Aissa Malay mistress of Peter Willems; she murders him out of jealousy over his wife in Joseph Conrad's *An Outcast of the Islands.*

Aitken, Mr. Scots landing agent for a mining firm in Africa; he helps subdue the native uprising and finds the diamond pipe in John Buchan's *Prester John.*

Aitken, Robert Philadelphia printer who hires Thomas Paine to start the *Pennsylvania Magazine,* only to fire him when Paine starts writing too plainly about American independence, in Howard Fast's *Citizen Tom Paine.*

A. J. (Merchant of Sex) Financier of Islam Inc.; international playboy and practical joker in William S. Burroughs's *Naked Lunch;* sponsor of Homer Mandrill for president in *Exterminator!;* also appears in *The Soft Machine* and *The Wild Boys.*

Ajali Store clerk in Sergeant Gollup's General Store who likes and at the same time despises Johnson; he is a witness against Johnson in the murder of Gollup in Joyce Cary's *Mister Johnson.*

Ajax See Jacks, Albert.

Akakievich, Akakiy Poor government clerk and copyist in the Russian capital of St. Petersburg; dedicated employee who becomes the butt of office jokes because his overcoat is threadbare; starves himself to pay for a fine new coat, soon stolen by robbers; finds no help from the authorities; falls sick with fever and dies. His ghost goes on to haunt St. Petersburg in search of his overcoat in Nikolai Gogol's "The Overcoat."

Akash Three-year-old son of Ruma and Adam; a proper American child in language and habits; often resistive, presaging for his apprehensive mother the rift that will inevitably develop as he grows; learns to love his grandfather during his short stay and enjoys his time outside as his "Dadu" is busy gardening in Jhumpa Lahiri's *Unaccustomed Earth.*

Aked, Adeline Small, dark-haired, grey-eyed orphan; her solitary youth and her inheritance from an uncle give her an independence of mind which surprises Richard Larch when he fails her test of love in Arnold Bennett's *A Man From the North.*

Aked, Richard Elderly, thin, intense former solicitor's clerk and uncle of Adeline Aked; his erratic enthusiasms fire Richard Larch's literary ambitions until Larch recognizes that neither the old man nor he will ever achieve significant authorship in Arnold Bennett's *A Man From the North.*

Akerman, Mr. Keeper of Newgate Prison in Charles Dickens's *Barnaby Rudge.*

Akiba Religious fanatic who has a mania for constant religious purification, even declining to touch his wife, Gina, in Isaac Bashevis Singer's *The Moskat Family.*

Akiko Wife of Nobutoshi and daughter-in-law of Shigezō; cares for Shigezō after his wife's death; confronts the difficulties both the elderly and caregivers of the elderly face; grows to love Shigezō dearly and grieves for him after his death in Sawako Ariyoshi's *The Twilight Years.*

Akissi African woman with whom the protagonist Clarence is living in Camara Laye's *The Radiance of the King.*

Aksinia Married to Stepan, but the mistress of Eugene Listnitsky, a rich Cossack in the Ukraine district; finds herself tossed aside when her lover marries Olga in Mikhail Sholokhov's *The Don Flows Home from the Sea.*

Akuebue Best friend of Ezeulu, the chief priest, and a wise man who is always trying to push Ezeulu in the right direction in Chinua Achebe's *Arrow of God.*

Akukalia Emissary from the Nigeria region of Umuaro, who is sent to Okperi to announce the war in Chinua Achebe's *Arrow of God.*

Akulína Young woman waiting in the woods for her lover, Viktór Alexandrovitch; lacks education and social position; begs the man for an endearing word before he leaves for a lengthy trip abroad with his master; finds it unbearable that he will not offer a word of encouragement, not to mention marriage or love, in Ivan Turgenev's "The Tryst."

Akunna One of the respected elders of Umuofia; engaged in amicable discussions with Mr. Brown about their different religious beliefs in Chinua Achebe's *Things Fall Apart.*

Al One of the two mafia hitmen sent to kill Ole Andresen in Ernest Hemingway's "The Killers."

Alabaster, Professor Art critic who plans to write a biography of Gulley Jimson in Joyce Cary's *The Horse's Mouth.*

Alacran, Rosario "Baby" Homely, sickly daughter of the wealthy, well-connected Alacran family who is considered a burden by her parents; lonely, unloved, apolitical teenager who quits high school and elopes with Pepe Carreon in Jessica Hagedorn's *Dogeaters.*

Alacran, Severo Wealthy head of the leading business conglomerate in the Philippines; charismatic womanizer who frequently argues with his wife; neglectful husband and father; father of Baby Alacran in Jessica Hagedorn's *Dogeaters.*

Alamanack, Jack Former wealthy textile designer who chooses to become a street philosopher and is befriended by Michael Cullen in Alan Sillitoe's *A Start in Life.*

Alamo Lead steer of the Del Sol trail herd that travels from Texas to Abilene in Emerson Hough's *North of 36.*

Alan Honest hand on the *Hispaniola* who won't join the mutiny; he is killed by Long John Silver in Robert Louis Stevenson's *Treasure Island.*

Alan Husband of Sabina in Anaïs Nin's *A Spy in the House of Love.*

Alan, Catharine Elderly spinster who travels to Italy with her sister, Teresa, in E. M. Forster's *A Room with a View.*

Alan, Teresa Elderly spinster who travels to Italy with her sister, Catharine, in E. M. Forster's *A Room with a View.*

Alancon, Chevalier de Father of the young nobleman Katherine de Maintenon loves; he gives her and Belinda (Madam de Beaumont) shelter when they run away from their convent in Penelope Aubin's *The Life of Madam de Beaumont.*

Alancon, Colonel de Young nobleman loved by Katherine de Maintenon; she runs away from her convent to marry him in Penelope Aubin's *The Life of Madam de Beaumont.*

Alanno Chief of Hio-Hio who criticizes King Bello in Herman Melville's *Mardi.*

Alanthus (Formator) Hero who rescues Amoranda and falls in love with her immediately; he disguises himself as the elderly guardian Formator in Mary Davys's *The Reform'd Coquet.*

al-Araj, Ahmad Son of al-Shareef Saadi and Hasan's schoolmate in Fez; suffers from alienation because of his physical impairment; establishes a small army of fighters in the south of Morocco to attack the Portuguese; relies on Hasan in his negotiations with the sultan of Fez in Amin Maalouf's *Leon the African.*

Alarcon, Arthur Los Angeles Superior Court judge who replaces Alfred Peracca in the second trial of Gregory Powell and Jimmy Smith in Joseph Wambaugh's *The Onion Field.*

Alasco, Demetrius (Dr. Doboobie) Evil alchemist and astrologer, who poisons Thomas Ratcliffe, Earl of Sussex, tries to poison Amy Robsart Dudley, plays on the fears and ambitions of Robert Dudley, Earl of Leicester, with his astrological forecasts, and dies from inhaling his own concoction in Sir Walter Scott's *Kenilworth.*

Alastair ("Long Al") Charlie's alcoholic, chauvinistic lover, who physically and mentally abuses her and is mysteriously summoned back to England by an Israeli device so that Gadi Becker can entice Charlie away from her theatrical family in John le Carré's *The Little Drummer Girl.*

Alaster Rob Roy MacGregor's minstrel in Sir Walter Scott's *Rob Roy.*

Alba Narrator and granddaughter of Esteban Trueb; professes her progressive and radical social attitudes in modern Latin America, in contrast to her grandfather Esteban Trueb's traditional aristocratic views in Isabel Allende's *The House of the Spirits.*

Alba, Bernarda Odiously authoritarian domestic tyrant; twice widowed with five daughters whom she abuses verbally and physically; her power lies in rigid conformism and local gossip; unable to avenge herself on Pepe el Romano, and faced with Adela's suicide, she fatuously proclaims Adela's virginity and demands silence to maintain the family reputation in Federico García Lorca's play *The House of Bernarda Alba.*

Alban, Frank Jacqueline Armine's brother; he leaves his slum parish in Birkpool for a pulpit guaranteed to make him an "important figure in the Church" in John Buchan's *A Prince of the Captivity.*

Albany Husband of Goneril, compassionate and honorable; chides Goneril over her treatment of her father and is criticized by her for his "milky gentleness"; rebukes his wife as a fiend for turning Lear out and having Gloucester blinded; marshals his troops to defend from the French invasion, but is alerted by Edgar of his wife's courtship of Edmund; arrests Edmund and Goneril for treason in Shakespeare's play *King Lear.*

Albany Misanthrope born in Jamaica who haunts Cecilia Beverley to burden her conscience as a rich woman; he takes her to people who need her assistance and tells her his life story of disappointed love in Frances Burney's *Cecilia.*

Albany, Bert Former miner who works in Zar's saloon; courts and marries a prostitute, with whom he leaves Hard Times when Clay Turner returns to raze the town, in E. L. Doctorow's *Welcome to Hard Times.*

Albany, Duke of (Robert Stewart) Younger brother of King Robert III and uncle of the Duke of Rothsay; he conspires with John Ramorny in the murder of Rothsay in Sir Walter Scott's *The Fair Maid of Perth.*

Albemarle, Earl of Host of the masquerade at which young Harry Clinton displays his dancing skills and parries the flirtations of several women in Henry Brooke's *The Fool of Quality.*

Albemarle, Lord Elderly and paralytic noble gentleman in London in 1872; remains the only advocate who believes that Phileas Fogg can succeed in his circumnavigation of the world in 80 days; wagers £5,000 on Fogg in Jules Verne's *Around the World in Eighty Days.*

Alberic, Captain Estranged husband, a reported "wrong 'un," of Eustace Cherrington's old friend, Nancy Steptoe, from whom she is separated when Eustace meets her again in Venice in L. P. Hartley's *Eustace and Hilda.*

Alberic de Montemar Duke Richard of Normandy's young vassal, who becomes his trusted friend and advisor in Charlotte Yonge's *The Little Duke.*

Albert Older son of Lionel Verney and Idris in Mary Shelley's *The Last Man.*

Albert Friend of Cecil Braithwaite in John Edgar Wideman's *Hurry Home.*

Albert Husband of Celie; marries her to provide a housekeeper for his children when his wife dies; beats her; hides letters sent to her by Nettie; lover of Shug Avery; comes to understand himself and modifies his behavior as a result of Celie's growing independence in Alice Walker's *The Color Purple.*

Albert Government employee and husband of Lotte; his practical mindset and the rival for Lotte's love make him

Werther's main opponent in Johann Wolfgang von Goethe's *The Sorrows of Young Werther.*

Albert One of the circle of Hunt's people whom Kate Fletcher (Armstrong) found interesting when she was aged sixteen; he is "lank, silent, vain" in Margaret Drabble's *The Middle Ground.*

Albert Young son of Mercédès and Ferdinand Mandego; challenges the Count of Monte-Cristo, actually the disguised Edmond Dantès, to a duel to avenge his father's disgrace; saved from the mortal dispute by his mother's intervention in Alexander Dumas, pere's *The Count of Monte-Cristo.*

Albert, Dr. Stephen Lover and connoisseur of Chinese culture and literature; randomly picked out of the phone book by the spy Yu Tsun to be killed—as he has the same name as the town where a British artillery park is located—because this is the only way to signal the city that has to be bombed in Jorge Luis Borges's "The Garden of Forking Paths."

Alberta Maid with mixed blood who is the object of Gamaliel Bland Honeywell's early desires in Ellen Glasgow's *The Romantic Comedians.*

Alberta Young woman and the mistress of the married protagonist Troy Maxsom; dies in giving birth to Raynell, a baby raised by Troy's wife, Rose, in August Wilson's play *Fences.*

Alberto One of the young cadets at Leoncio Prado, a paramilitary academy in Lima, in the 1950s; meets Teresa, the girl that Slave loves, and starts to date her; unsuccessful in his attempt to buy the questions to an exam stolen by other cadets in a secret organization called the "Circle"; believes that his friend Slave has been murdered by Jaguar, another cadet, in retaliation for Slave's part in turning in Cava for cheating in Mario Vargas Llosa's *The Time of the Hero.*

Alberto Brother of Cristina Colamartini; seduced by Bianchina Girasole, bringing scandal to his family; enlisted by Paolo Spada into the revolutionary forces against the government; goes to Fossa with Bianchina in the revolutionary cause in Ignazio Silone's *Bread and Wine.*

Albertus, Henrietta Beautiful and virtuous daughter of Lady Lucy and Lewis Augustus Albertus; she marries a nobleman of great fortune from Heidelberg in Penelope Aubin's *The Life and Adventures of the Lady Lucy.*

Albertus, Lewis Augustus Handsome and gentlemanly but jealous German officer, who marries Lady Lucy; falsely believing she and Frederick are having an affair, he kills Frederick and stabs Lucy, leaving her to die in the woods; he leads a life of debauchery until wounded in battle, whereupon he begins to feel remorse and vows to live virtuously; he lives in a hut as a hermit, vindicates Arminda and reunites her with her husband, falls sick, and is nursed by Father Joseph, who discovers his identity and reunites him with Lady Lucy and his family in Penelope Aubin's *The Life and Adventures of the Lady Lucy.*

Albertus, Lewis Augustus (the younger) Son of Albertus and Lady Lucy; he lives in the convent with his mother until he is five; then he stays with Father Joseph in the abbey, where he meets his father, who is living as a hermit in Penelope Aubin's *The Life and Adventures of the Lady Lucy.*

Albertus, Lucy Beautiful and virtuous daughter of Lady Lucy and Lewis Augustus Albertus; she marries the noble son of Henrietta and Lord Lycidas in Penelope Aubin's *The Life and Adventures of the Lady Lucy.*

Albin, Herr Blond young man with a childish and theatrical fondness for guns and knives, with which he likes to scare the women in the hospital; his pneumonia does not keep him from smoking like a chimney; tempts the female patients with chocolate; at the end he provides the pistols for Naphta and Settembrini's duel in Thomas Mann's *The Magic Mountain.*

Albine Agrippine's confidante who flatters her mistress, provides background information, conveys the sentiments of the Roman people, and reports the massacre of Narcisse in Jean Racine's play *Britannicus.*

Albine, Salathiel (Little Turtle) Child captured and reared by Indians; eventually works his way from life in the forest to one in civilization in Philadelphia, in Hervey Allen's *The Forest and the Fort, Bedford Village,* and *Toward the Morning.*

Albini, Agnes D' (Ida) Lost daughter of Angelo D'Albini and Gabrielle Di Montmorency; she lived in Germany after her escape from Pierre Bouffuet and fell in love but gave up her lover to please her adoptive parents; she finally ends up locked in a convent by her father in Charlotte Dacre's *The Libertine.*

Albini, Angelo D' Libertine count, who refuses to marry the mother of his children, takes many mistresses, ruins his son by example, and locks his daughter in a convent after killing her lover in Charlotte Dacre's *The Libertine.*

Albini, Felix D' Aristocratic son of Angelo D'Albini and Gabrielle Di Montmorency; his self-love and rejection of his mother are encouraged by his nurse; he ends up a thief in Charlotte Dacre's *The Libertine.*

Albright, Dewitt Lawyer turned underworld handyman who hires private investigator Easy Rawlins to locate a missing woman, Daphne Monet; unpredictable, dangerous, and lacking morals or scruples, he attempts to ambush Rawlins, but is shot by Raymond "Mouse" Alexander in Walter Mosley's *Devil in a Blue Dress.*

Albright, Mavis Fugitive mother who abandons her family after the accidental death of her two youngest children; is one of the Convent women, a group of women with sullied pasts who now live together on the outskirts of Ruby, Oklahoma, an all-black town; is haunted by the ghosts of her two dead children in Toni Morrison's *Paradise.*

Albuquerque, Armênio Lawyer who typifies pedantic shallow intellectuality in Erico Verissimo's *Crossroads.*

Albury, Helen Sister of Robert Albury determined to prove her brother's innocence in Dashiell Hammett's *Red Harvest.*

Albury, Lady Rosaline Marchesa Baldoni's sister and Sir Harry Albury's wife; she is fond of her cousin Colonel Stubbs; she befriends Ayala Dormer, inviting her to visit and doing all she can to further a match between Ayala and her cousin in Anthony Trollope's *Ayala's Angel.*

Albury, Robert Assistant cashier of the First National Bank in Personville who is desperately in love with Dinah Brand, embezzles money to court her, and is charged with the murder of Donald Willsson in Dashiell Hammett's *Red Harvest.*

Albury, Sir Harry Jovial Master of Foxhounds who provides Ayala Dormer with a pony so that she can ride during her visit to his country place in Anthony Trollope's *Ayala's Angel.*

Albuzzi, Mrs. Loquacious lady of rank; she finds democratic principles loathsome in William Beckford's *Azemia.*

Alcacer (Mr. d'Alcacer) Embassy official who loved a young woman who died; he accompanies Mr. and Mrs. Travers on the *Hermit* to Batavia and secretly admires Edith Travers in Joseph Conrad's *The Rescue: A Romance of the Shallows.*

Alcasan, François French radiologist, executed for poisoning his wife; his head is recused by the N.I.C.E. (National Institute for Coordinated Experiments) and becomes the medium of communication between the Macrobes and the inner circle of the N.I.C.E. in C. S. Lewis's *That Hideous Strength.*

Alcázar, Don Luis Dashing young man from Madrid in 1765; rich in title but poor in his purse except for his rich uncle's benevolence; desires to marry Margarita Pareja, the daughter of the wealthy tax collector Don Raimundo Pareja; refused by Margarita's father because of his poverty; finally gains Margarita as his bride after she falls deathly ill from love loss sorrow in Ricardo Palma's "Margarita's Chemise."

Alcazar, Maria Katerina Lorca Guerrera (Kat) American lesbian of Cuban descent; hired by Angel Stone as companion, secretary, bodyguard, and detective; narrator of M. F. Beal's *Angel Dance.*

Alcée Arobin Seducer who has an affair with Edna Pontellier in Kate Chopin's *The Awakening.*

Alceste Highly principled, irritable, and despiser of all humanity for its hypocrisy; states that people should always honestly say what they think of others and not hide their true thoughts behind false compliments; creates many enemies for his brutal honesty, including Oronte, who has asked Alceste to offer honest and frank criticism of his new love poem; Alceste's unwavering demand for uncompromised virtue also destroys the love Célimène has for him in Moliere's play *The Misanthrope.*

Alchemist Arab who lives at the Al-Fayoum oasis and possesses exceptional powers; meeting with the alchemist in the desert helps the young man discover his inner strengths and brings the seeker closer to realizing his destiny in Paulo Coelho's *The Alchemist.*

Alcibiades, Don Man of limited means who brings the beautiful female protagonist from Obera to his Mendihondo country place to enjoy her curvaceous body; fails to reward her with gifts and treasures; returns unexpectedly from a trip to find the woman and his hired hand El Circo embracing in the hammock; shoots the young man and tortures the woman but is soon shot to death by the woman in Luisa Mercedes Levinson's "The Cove."

Alcidiana Miranda's younger sister, upon whose fortune Miranda and Tarquin rely; when Alcidiana threatens to marry against her wishes, Miranda plots her murder; Alcidiana survives two attempts made on her life and eventually obtains a pardon for Tarquin and her sister in Aphra Behn's *The Fair Jilt.*

Alcock, Mr. Bath innkeeper who, with the help of his Methodist scullery maid Deborah, guides Geoffry Wildgoose to the Methodist meeting place in Richard Graves's *The Spiritual Quixote.*

Alcot, Madeline Young society matron, Lady Kitty Ashe's social rival in Mrs. Humphry Ward's *The Marriage of William Ashe.*

Aldama, Margarita Mother of landowning Señor Pablo Aldama; older woman who seeks to dominate her daughter-in-law, the protagonist Señora Laurita, in Elena Garro's "Blame the Tlaxcaltecs."

Aldama, Señora Laurita Woman who seems to live two lives; married in one life to Señor Pablo Aldama, a wealthy landowner, and to her Cuitzeo Indian cousin, a native rebel, in another; finally leaves the Aldama household behind and disappears in Elena Garro's "Blame the Tlaxcaltecs."

Aldama, Señor Pablo Landowner and husband of Señora Laurita; hot-tempered man who resorts to punishing his wife for her infidelities with her Cuitzeo Indian cousin in Elena Garro's "Blame the Tlaxcaltecs."

Aldclyffe, Cytherea Bradleigh Wealthy unmarried woman who, as the girl Cytherea Bradleigh, fell in love with Ambrose Graye but mysteriously refused his offer of marriage; having inherited a fortune and taken the family name Aldclyffe, she hires Cytherea Graye as lady's maid and Aeneas Mansion as steward and resorts to deceit to promote their marriage; after Mansion's death she reveals to Cytherea Graye that he was her son by a cousin who deserted her and the reason for her refusal of Ambrose Graye's hand; she dies, leaving her property lo Cylherea Graye in Thomas Hardy's *Desperate Remedies.*

Alden, Harriet Bumstead Mother of Oliver Alden in George Santayana's *The Last Puritan.*

Alden, Nathaniel Boston landlord and half brother of Peter Alden in George Santayana's *The Last Puritan.*

Alden, Oliver Idealistic student of philosophy; the last Puritan in George Santayana's *The Last Puritan.*

Alden, Peter Alden Father of Oliver Alden in George Santayana's *The Last Puritan.*

Alden, Roberta (Mrs. Clifford Golden, Mrs. Carl Graham, Ruth Howard) Lover of Clyde Griffiths and pregnant by him; falls from a boat and drowns as Griffiths fails to rescue her in Theodore Dreiser's *An American Tragedy.*

Alden, Thomas (Tom, Tommy) Davenport author who sponsors Felix Fay at literary activities, even though Fay is a socialist, in Floyd Dell's *Moon-Calf.*

Alderigo Cousin to Castruccio dei Antelminelli; a rich London merchant, he persuades Edward II of England to exile his friend Piers Gavaston and advises Castruccio in affairs of the English court in Mary Shelley's *Valperga.*

Alderston, Sir John An owner of South Eastern Railway in Michael Crichton's *The Great Train Robbery.*

Aldi, Leonora Italian aristocrat; she marries an Englishman who is later killed in the Napoleonic wars; she marries Captain Brooks and then dies after the births of Owen and Beatrice Brooks in Caroline Norion's *Lost and Saved.*

Aldom Manservant of the Shelleys; he mimics family visitors for the children's amusement; he is the unacknowledged natural son of Sir Roderick Shelley in Ivy Compton-Burnett's *Two Worlds and Their Ways.*

Aldom, Mrs. Mother of the Shelleys' manservant by Sir Roderick Shelley; she is now willing to sell back the Shelleys' farm in order to be able to move to town in Ivy Compton-Burnett's *Two Worlds and Their Ways.*

Aldova, Don Gomez d' Physician who attends the feverish Amelia de Gonzales and instantly falls in love with her in William Beckford's *Modern Novel Writing; or, the Elegant Enthusiast.*

Aldrete, Toribio Accused in a lawsuit by Pedro Páramo of falsifying land boundaries; hangs himself in Juan Rulfo's *Pedro Páramo.*

Aldrich, Karen Susan Former mental patient who finally succeeds in committing suicide in Judith Guest's *Ordinary People.*

Aldridge, Aline See Grey, Aline Aldridge.

Aldridge, Grace Wrote the autobiography Jean is typing; has had many husbands and is engaged to Edward Quill when she dies from falling down stairs in Ann Beattie's *My Life, Starring Dara Falcon.*

Aldrovand, Father Norman priest, who serves as Eveline Berenger's father confessor, and who competes with Wilkin Flammock as her chief advisor in Sir Walter Scott's *The Betrothed.*

Aldwick, Rodney Friend of Neil Kingsblood; turns against his friend when Kingsblood's black ancestry is discovered in Sinclair Lewis's *Kingsblood Royal.*

Aldwinkle, Irene Lilian Aldwinkle's frank but naïve niece, to whom Lord Hovenden proposes in Aldous Huxley's *Those Barren Leaves.*

Aldwinkle, Lillian Aging, self-styled patron of the arts and hostess in her Italian villa to a myriad of guests; after rescuing the poet Francis Chelifer from a water accident, she makes preposterous advances to him which he skillfully avoids in Aldous Huxley's *Those Barren Leaves.*

Aldworth, Mr. Wealthy landowner and magistrate who, over the objections of his clerk Mr. Newland, assumes that Geoffry Wildgoose and Jeremiah Tugwell are innocent until proven guilty with regard to a stolen horse in Richard Graves's *The Spiritual Quixote.*

Aleema Priest from Amma who is killed by Taji in Herman Melville's *Mardi.*

Alehin Seemingly wealthy young man who owns the lavish country estate where Ivan Ivanovitch and Burkin take shelter in the rain; hardworking man who speaks of how busy he has been, barely having time to wash; receives the two men hospitably, however, and gives them a place to stay for the night; listens to Ivan Ivanovitch's story and then retires, since he gets up at three in the morning in Anton Chekhov's "Gooseberries."

Alehouse-Keeper's Daughter Purchaser of Pompey from the Maiden Aunt's footman; she takes him to live in a garret in Smithfield in Francis Coventry's *The History of Pompey the Little.*

Alejandra Young Mexican girl who lives on the La Purisima Ranch while not attending boarding school, and with whom John Grady Cole falls in love; she is forbidden to see him again after her grandaunt, Duena Alfonsa, pays Cole's ransom to secure his release from prison in Cormac McCarthy's *All the Pretty Horses.*

Alekseyev, Pavel Leonidovich (Pasha) Deputy commander of the Southwestern Theater for the Soviet Army who, with Marshal Rozhkov and Admiral Mazlov, plans Operation Polar Glory (invasion of Iceland) and seizure of Arabian oil fields; personally commands forward troops in action against NATO forces around Alfeld; engineers the coup that puts Sergetov in power and ends the nuclear threat; negotiates cease-fire with General Robinson (SACEUR) in Tom Clancy's *Red Storm Rising.*

Aleman, Fred Sober businessman to whom Joan Mitchell is engaged in Shirley Ann Grau's *The House on Coliseum Street.*

Alencon, Duke of Officer in the army of Francis I; he leads a small body of soldiers in an orderly retreat following the battle of Pavia in William Godwin's *St. Leon.*

Alehaw Yuli's father, who teaches Yuli to hunt and is killed by the phagors in Brian W. Aldiss's *Helliconia Spring.*

Ale-Wife Traveler on the wagon who drinks a great deal and offers a bottle of gin to the Disguised Gentleman in Charles Johns tone's *Chrysal: or, The Adventures of a Guinea.*

Alex Friend of Rosamund Stacey; he writes copy for an advertising agency in Margaret Drabble's *The Millstone.*

Alex Meddling man who attends a cocktail party hosted by Edward and Lavina in their London flat; enjoys telling stories about his many travels in T. S. Eliot's play *The Cocktail Party.*

Alex Waitress at the summer camp in Margaret Atwood's "True Trash."

Alex Working-class graduate of a Corrective School; ignorant and violent, yet surprisingly intelligent and sensitive to serious music, he is the leader of a gang of young delinquents specializing in crimes of violence; he speaks a futuristic, degraded English intermixed with slang and vulgarized foreign words; extremely antisocial, he is temporarily reformed by a psychological treatment while in prison in Anthony Burgess's *A Clockwork Orange.*

Alex (Uncle Alex) Alabama farmer, husband of Caroline, and employer and benefactor of Ollie in George Wylie Henderson's *Ollie Miss and Jule.*

Alexander, Alex One of the wealthy socialites trapped in a fog-bound London railway station; his rudeness and lack of tact frequently annoy Angela Crevy and his other friends in Henry Green's *Party Going.*

Alexander, Dr. Assistant lecturer in biodynamics and government agent; brings Adam Krug to a university meeting the night Krug's wife, Olga, dies; later exterminated for bungling in Vladimir Nabokov's *Bend Sinister.*

Alexander, F. Upper-class author of the fictional book *A Clockwork Orange* and a slightly demented intellectual fanatically opposed to the current government; he and his wife have been the victims of robbery and rape at the hands of a gang of delinquents, and he rightly suspects Alex of having been the gang's leader in Anthony Burgess's *A Clockwork Orange.*

Alexander, Mr. Lord Singer and songwriter from Trinidad; he successfully performs on the radio and in cabarets in Colin MacInnes's *City of Spades.*

Alexander, Raymond "Mouse" Friend and partner to private investigator Easy Rawlins; kills stepfather in inheritance dispute; violent and unpredictable, he values loyalty; saves Rawlins's life on several occasions in Walter Mosley's *Devil in a Blue Dress.*

Alexander, Roland Four-year-old boy who dies after accidentally swallowing rat poison left in his bedroom; as a result of this tragedy, his father almost beats his mother to death before being locked up by police in Alexis Deveaux's *Spirits in the Street.*

Alexander, Rose Militant feminist dedicated to the subversion and destruction of patriarchal society; takes part in a bank robbery, during which an elderly male guard is killed; goes into hiding; is eventually arrested after being tricked by Spenser, a private detective hired by Harvey Shepard in Robert B. Parker's *Promised Land.*

Alexander, Suicide Manager of the California baseball team that signs Henry Wiggen when Wiggen is released from the New York Mammoths in Mark Harris's *It Looked Like For Ever.*

Alexandra Daughter of Beatrice and Hallam and the niece of Rosamund Stacey in Margaret Drabble's *The Millstone.*

Alexandra, Sister Charismatic candidate in the election for Abbess who represents the old order even as she uses electronic devices to track her competitors in Muriel Spark's *The Abbess of Crewe.*

Alexandritch, Viktór Young pretentious and pompous man for whom the pretty but peasant girl Akulina waits in the woods for a rendezvous; exaggerates his importance despite being a valet of a wealthy gentleman; hopes to get on in society on the coat tails of his master; indifferent to Akulína's pleas for an endearing word of love or marriage before he leaves with his master for several years abroad in Ivan Turgenev's "The Tryst."

Alexis Servant at Bellfont who acts as one of Philander's go-betweens to Sylvia in Aphra Behn's *Love Letters Between a Nobleman and His Sister.*

Alexis Budding playwright and narrator who records the thwarted lives of young people living in her Harlem neighborhood in Alexis Deveaux's *Spirits in the Street.*

Alexis See Potts, James.

Alexis, Dr. Paul Official of the German Ministry of Interior and an Israeli sympathizer; he investigates the bombing at Bad Godesberg and is surprised when Marty Kurtz magically unravels the atrocity in John le Carré's *The Little Drummer Girl.*

Alexowna, Catharina Livonian woman cited as a model of beauty and virtue by Fum Hoam in a letter to Lien Chi Altangi; captured and enslaved by the Russians, she attracts the notice of Peter the Great, who makes her his wife in Oliver Goldsmith's *The Citizen of the World.*

Alexson, Alex Second husband of Sophia Grieve Ryder in Djuna Barnes's *Ryder.*

Alf, Ferdinand Style-conscious literary acquaintance of Lady Carbury and editor of the *Evening Pulpit;* he stands against Augustus Melmotte as Parliamentary candidate for Westminster and loses in Anthony Trollope's *The Way We Live Now.*

Alfio Young man who is seen as prosperous since he has four mules in his stable in Sicily; marries the pretty girl Lola and thus ignites the jealousy and revenge of Lola's former sweetheart, Turiddu Macca; kills Turiddu in a duel in Giovanni Verga's "Cavalleria Rusticana."

Alfonsa, Duena Matriarchal figure in charge of the La Purisima Ranch, where John Grady Cole and Lacey Rawlins work in Mexico; grandaunt and godmother of Alejandra; pays for the release of both John and Lacey on the condition that John never see Alejandra ever again in Cormac McCarthy's *All the Pretty Horses.*

Alfonso Young man who attends a dinner party hosted by Doña Magdalena and her daughter Amalia, two intriguing women he does not know; compares the two women's illuminated faces in a dark garden as figures in the paintings of

Echave the Elder, fantastic celestial bodies; hears from the two hostesses of his improbable connection—likeness—to a blind military captain of the artillery; runs away in fright and confusion in Alfonso Reyes's "The Dinner."

Alfonso Male canary Birdy buys from Mr. Lincoln to mate with Birdie in William Wharton's *Birdy.*

Alfonso (Fonso) Wife-beater and cousin of Eva Medina Canada in Gayl Jones's *Eva's Man.*

Alfonso, Tertuliano Máximo Nondescript high school history teacher and aimless noncommittal average citizen who discovers his exact duplicate performing in a mediocre film on video in José Saramago's *The Double.*

Alfonso the Good Rightful lord of Otranto, poisoned by Prince Manfred's grandfather for his realm; his ghost, represented by an armor-clad giant in a monstrous plumed helmet, throws down the castle walls and ascends to heaven in a catastrophic revenge finale in Horace Walpole's *The Castle of Otranto.*

Alford, Jeremy Rose Vassiliou's solicitor, who acts promptly to prevent the carrying out of Christopher Vassiliou's threat to take his children out of the country in Margaret Drabble's *The Needle's Eye.*

Alfrado (Frado, Nig) Spirited mulatto girl indentured to the Bellmont family; tells the story of her mistreatment and growth to adulthood in Harriet E. Wilson's *Our Nig.*

Alfred Old professional waiter at Rules restaurant; he knew Sarah Miles and Maurice Bendrix from the days when their affair was active and they met at Rules in Graham Greene's *The End of the Affair.*

Alfred Power-hungry fanatic; he is a leader of the rebellion whose jealousy leads to doubts about his goals in Rex Warner's *The Wild Goose Chase: An Allegory.*

Alfred (Alfy) Bouncer, protector, and watchman of the Bear Flag restaurant, a bar and brothel, in John Steinbeck's *Cannery Row.*

Algernon White mouse used for experiments involving increased intelligence who is treated by Charlie Gordon, another experimental subject, as Gordon's only peer in Daniel Keyes's *Flowers for Algernon.*

Al Hafi Mohammedan begging monk and old acquaintance of Nathan's; interrupts the conversation between Nathan and Daja to tell of the news that he has of late become the treasurer of the sultan; however, Nathan declares that he does not wish to help Al Hafi in his office duties, even though Saladin's generosity has led to a decrease in funds; slanders Nathan's reputation in front of Sultan Saladin to stall the latter's request to take money from Nathan in Gotthold Ephraim Lessing's *Nathan the Wise.*

Alhahuza Head of the rebel faction in Hypotosa that ousts Ochihatou; he aids Eovaai, giving her shelter and magic herbs to prevent Ochihatou's evil intentions toward her in Eliza Haywood's *Adventures of Eovaai, Princess of Ijaveo.*

Ali Arab boy from Biskra befriended by Michel; introduces Michel to his prostitute sister, but then becomes jealous; Michel realizes that he is more interested in Ali than his sister in André Gide's *The Immoralist.*

Ali Baba's Hazara servant and childhood friend; single father of Hassan; suffered from polio as a child and walks with a limp in Khaled Hosseini's *The Kite Runner.*

Ali House steward and manservant of Henry Scobie for fifteen years and brother of Vande; he serves Scobie well but provides Vande and thus Wilson with information about Scobie's affairs; he is murdered after Scobie informs Yusef of this in Graham Greene's *The Heart of the Matter.*

Ali (Eli) Divorced Jewish father; first man Theresa Dunn allows to pick her up in a bar in Judith Rossner's *Looking for Mr. Goodbar.*

Ali, Dubash (Oliver, Ortencio) Handsome but consumptive man of thirty who works as the factory's dubash, or translator; stoned to death when explosives he plants to destroy Gabriel Legge's shipment instead blow up an alley in Bharati Mukherjee's *The Holder of the World.*

Ali, Mahbub Colonel Creighton's faithful adjutant and a horse dealer; thinks about women though he considers them fatal; hates heretics yet compares the values of faith to horses; gives Kim a revolver and teaches him to write reports and maps; becomes responsible for making Kim a colonizer in Rudyard Kipling's *Kim.*

Ali, Mahmoud Pleader for Dr. Aziz's case at the trial in E. M. Forster's *A Passage to India.*

Aliaga, Clara di Wife of Don Francisco di Aliaga and the overbearing, insensitive mother of Isidora (Immalee) and Fernan di Aliaga in Charles Maturin's *Melmoth the Wanderer.*

Aliaga, Fernan di Hot-tempered brother of Isidora (Immalee); he unsuccessfully defends his sister against and is slain by Melmoth the Wanderer in Charles Maturin's *Melmoth the Wanderer.*

Aliaga, Francisco di Father of Isidora and Fernan and husband of Clara; his business ventures keep from the di Aliaga estate during Isidora's reorientation; returning to his family, he is accompanied by Mantilla, to whom he has betrothed Isidora, unaware that Isidora has married Melmoth the Wanderer in Charles Malurin's *Melmoth the Wanderer.*

Aliaga, Isidora (Immalee) di Daughter of Don Francisco di Aliaga; as an infant she is shipwrecked and grows up on an uninhabited island where she is visited by Melmoth the Wanderer and falls in love with him; after she is found and returned to Spain, the Wanderer visits her again and they are married in a non-Christian ceremony; her marriage is discovered and she is turned over to the Inquisition; she dies shortly after giving birth to the Wanderer's child in Charles Maturin's *Melmoth the Wanderer.*

Alibai Indian graduate student in Adam Appleby's department; he is trying to decide on a thesis topic in David Lodge's *The British Museum Is Falling Down.*

Alice Servant at Manderley in Daphne Du Maurier's *Rebecca.*

Alice Lovats' upper-housemaid, not as likeable as Tabitha; she is censorious about Sir Ransome Chace's having an illegitimate daughter in Ivy Compton-Burnett's *Darkness and Day.*

Alice Dalby's secretary; her knowledge of espionage and W.O.O.C.(P.) documents and procedures helps the narrator piece together Dalby's duplicity in Len Deighton's *The Ipcress File.*

Alice Widowed cousin of the Lovatt family; she acts as the children's short-term nanny in Doris Lessing's *The Fifth Child.*

Alice Caroline Knowell's African nurse in Doris Lessing's *A Proper Marriage.*

Alice Daughter of Lady O.; she is considered an acceptable marriage partner for Sebastian, master of Chevron, in Vita Sackville-West's *The Edwardians.*

Alice Attendant to Princess Katherine of France; has some knowledge of the English language and teaches Katherine, upon her request, some English words—many associated with the body; helps translate between Henry V and Katherine when he woos Katherine to be his wife in William Shakespeare's play *Henry V.*

Alice Inquisitive but sensible seven-year-old heroine, who follows a rabbit down a hole and into a fantasy land where her size and shape are subject to surprising changes; she keeps her head, literally and figuratively, throughout encounters with creatures that embody various kinds of tyrannical nonsense, finally triumphantly denouncing the "pack of cards" at the trial which concludes Lewis Carroll's *Alice's Adventures in Wonderland.* Aged "seven and a half, exactly," she climbs through a drawing-room mirror into a world laid out like a gigantic chess board; participating in the game, she reaches the eighth square and is crowned queen in *Through the Looking-Glass.*

Alice Local prostitute in Indochina (now Vietnam); becomes the sexual desire of the teenage female protagonist, in addition to the Chinese man of the book's title in Marguerite Duras's *The Chinese Lover.*

Alice Maid in Mrs. Rachel Arbuthnot's home in Wrockley in Oscar Wilde's play *A Woman of No Importance.*

Alice Maid to Ellinor and Matilda and witness of the marriage of Lord Leicester and Matilda in Sophia Lee's *The Recess.*

Alice Wife of an unnamed sailor stationed in Newport; wants a baby so badly that she urges Theophilus North to impregnate her in Thornton Wilder's *Theophilus North.*

Alice's Sister Elder sister and afternoon companion who listens to Alice's narration of her dream; she envisions it herself and acknowledges her disadvantage of being an adult and part of the "real" world; she reflects that Alice will grow up to share her dream with her own children in Lewis Carroll's *Alice's Adventures in Wonderland.*

Alicia Lover of Cova, with whom she flees into the Colombian jungle in José Eustacio Rivera's *The Vortex.*

Alick Shepherd on the Poyser farm in George Eliot's *Adam Bede.*

Aliena, Vasilia See Fastolfe, Vasilia.

Alina Polish au pair; badly treated by the mother of her charges; seeks revenge by terrifying her charges with horror stories; murders her abusive employer when dismissed in Roddy Doyle's "The Pram."

Alinardo of Grottaferrata One of the oldest of the Benedictine monks; is considered crazy because of his age and strange behavior; gives William of Baskerville the fundamental hint to solve the mysterious murders in Umberto Eco's *The Name of the Rose.*

Aline Wife of Halvard Solness, the master builder; fears that her husband is going mad as he pursues his architectural business to extremes in Henrik Ibsen's *The Master Builder.*

Alingsby, Sophy Tall, weird, intense, colorful, well-connected friend of Lucia Lucas in E. F. Benson's *Lucia in London.*

Alington, Bridget Daughter of Mr. and Mrs. Alington in J. B. Priestley's *Bright Day.*

Alington, David Precocious son of Mr. and Mrs. Alington in J. B. Priestley's *Bright Day.*

Alington, Eva Daughter of Mr. and Mrs. Alington; she is revealed to have been pushed to death by her sister Joan in J. B. Priestley's *Bright Day.*

Alington, Joan Alington daughter responsible for the death of her sister Eva in J. B. Priestley's *Bright Day.*

Alington, Mr. Sophisticated, well-to-do wool merchant of Bruddersford, Yorkshire, who introduces Gregory Dawson to art, music, and literature in J. B. Priestley's *Bright Day.*

Alington, Mrs. Sophisticated, well-to-do wife of Mr. Alington; she and her husband introduce Gregory Dawson to art, music, and literature in J. B. Priestley's *Bright Day.*

Alington, Oliver Mr. and Mrs. Alington's son who dies in World War I in J. B. Priestley's *Bright Day.*

Alis, Lady Wife of the old lord Ansiau de Linnières; curses her son Herbert for his incestuous affair with Eglantine, his half sister, in Zoé Oldenbourg's *The Cornerstone.*

Alison Gerald's married lover; disappears from the party for a while, but reappears dirty and beaten in Robert Coover's *Gerald's Party.*

Alison, Lady Dean Jocelin's "courtesan" aunt, who has sacrificed herself sexually to obtain royal favors so that her nephew can achieve his goal of building a spire on Salisbury cathedral in William Golding's *The Spire.*

Alissa First wife of Don Fairbairn and mother of their four children in John Updike's "How Was It, Really."

Al-Ith Queen of Zone Three who is told by the Providers that she must marry the savage King of Zone Four, whom she learns to love and respect, and with whom she has several children in Doris Lessing's *The Marriages Between Zones Three, Four, and Five.*

Alithea Ellinor's favorite attendant, who helps her mistress escape from Lord Arlington (2) in Sophia Lee's *The Recess.*

Alithea, Mrs. Pinchwife's sister and Sparkish's fiancée; self-assured and honorable; loves Harcourt but refuses to jilt Sparkish because of her sense of duty; informs Sparkish of Harcourt's intentions but is ignored; is delivered to Horner by her abusive brother, but is ultimately freed to marry Harcourt in William Wycherley's play *The Country Wife.*

Aliu Brave, stout brother of Bamu; he bargains with Johnson for his sister's hand in marriage, brings her back home after Johnson loses his government job, and turns Johnson over to the police for the murder of Gollup in Joyce Cary's *Mister Johnson.*

Alix Soon-to-be second wife of Ted in Reynolds Price's *Love and Work.*

Alkahest, John F. Bizarre paraplegic in violent pursuit of drug dealers in *The Smugglers of Lost Souls' Rock,* the interior novel within John Gardner's *October Light.*

Allaby, Mr. Rector of Crampsford; he gives Theobald Pontifex his first job; he is Christina Allaby Pontifex's father in Samuel Butler's *The Way of All Flesh.*

Allaby, Mrs. Mother of Christina Allaby Pontifex; she tries to marry off her other daughters but doesn't know how in Samuel Butler's *The Way of All Flesh.*

Allagash, Tad Drug abuser and womanizing best friend of Jamie Conway who always falls prey to Tad's ploys to party hard and work less in Jay McInerney's *Bright Lights, Big City.*

Allan One of Rob Roy MacGregor's clan in Sir Walter Scott's *Rob Roy.*

Allan Wealthy white radical, now a recluse in Vermont in Nicholas Delbanco's *News.*

Allan, Miss Contented elderly teacher engaged in writing a short *Primer of English Literature* while on vacation at the Santa Marina Hotel; she offers Rachel Vinrace books, ginger, and conversation to no avail in Virginia Woolf's *The Voyage Out.*

Allan, Mrs. Guy Mannering's housekeeper, responsible for the womanly aspects of Julia Mannering's upbringing in Sir Walter Scott's *Guy Mannering.*

Allan-a-Dale Robin Hood's gaily dressed minstrel, who captures Prior Aymer in Sir Walter Scott's *Ivanhoe.*

Allbee, Kirby Anti-Semite and weak-willed drunk who blames Asa Leventhal for his own moral degeneration, persecuting and finally attempting to murder him in retaliation, in Saul Bellow's *The Victim.*

Allberg, Karl Canadian police detective; divorced, middle-aged father of two female college students; investigates murder and finds romance with the town librarian in L. W. Wright's *The Suspect.*

Allbright, Betsy Romantic, much-married, and retired actress in Ludwig Bemelmans's *Dirty Eddie.*

Allchin Grocer's clerk who cannot keep a job but becomes a faithful assistant in Will Warburton's grocer's shop in George Gissing's *Will Warburton.*

Allègre, Henry Millionaire art connoisseur who establishes Doña Rita de Lastaola in Paris society, then dies, willing her his fortune in Joseph Conrad's *The Arrow of Gold: A Story Between Two Notes.*

Alleline, Sir Percy (codename "Tinker") Scottish-born, Cambridge-educated career spy and operational director who takes over as chief after Control's resignation in John le Carré's *Tinker, Tailor, Soldier, Spy.*

Allen Lonely barrister who shares Lewis Elliot's room in Herbert Getliffe's chambers in C. P. Snow's *Time of Hope.*

Allen, Arabella Dark-haired young lady with fur-topped boots, who is an attendant at Isabella Wardle's wedding and the sister of Ben Allen; she elopes with Nathaniel Winkle in Charles Dickens's *The Posthumous Papers of the Pickwick Club.*

Allen, Benjamin Coarse, dissolute medical student, who becomes a medical partner with Bob Sawyer in Bristol; he is Arabella Allen's brother in Charles Dickens's *The Posthumous Papers of the Pickwick Club.*

Allen, Bobbie Waitress and prostitute who is Joe Christmas's first love in William Faulkner's *Light in August.*

Allen, Clara Former sweetheart of Augustus McRae; strong woman, talkative, kind; good horse trainer; has two daughters and had three sons, each of whom died; husband is an invalid; takes in Lorena Woods and July Johnson in Larry McMurtry's *Lonesome Dove.*

Allen, Elisa Henry's independent-minded, 35-year-old wife who finds her married life unfulfilling; preoccupies herself with her flower garden; briefly feels attracted to a traveling tinker; her sense of self-worth is crushed when she finds her gift to him—the chrysanthemum cuttings—deserted on the road in John Steinbeck's "The Chrysanthemums."

Allen, Ethan (Ticonderoga) Enormous prisoner of war in Pendermis Castle, Falmouth, England, whom Israel Potter observes, in Herman Melville's *Israel Potter.*

Allen, Fanny Isaac Allen's daughter, who is courted by Thomas Broad in Mark Rutherford's *The Revolution in Tanner's Lane.*

Allen, George With his father Isaac, a shopkeeper in Cowfold; he marries Priscilla Broad, is politically active in free-trade debate, is falsely accused of infidelity with Marie Pauline Coleman, and emigrates to America with his parents in Mark Rutherford's *The Revolution in Tanner's Lane.*

Allen, Henry Ranch owner in the Salinas Valley of California; husband of Elisa who admires his wife's gift for gardening, especially growing unusually large chrysanthemums; maintains an uneventful relationship with his wife, and the lack of intimacy in their relationship leads his wife to become momentarily attracted to an itinerant tinker in John Steinbeck's "The Chrysanthemums."

Allen, Isaac Ardent Whig, shopkeeper, and deacon in the Reverend Broad's chapel in Cowfold; a friend of Zachariah Coleman, he emigrates to America with his family after confrontation with Broad in Mark Rutherford's *The Revolution in Tanner's Lane.*

Allen, Jim Fellow employee of Falton Harron at Watkins & Company, manufacturer of microscopes in Susan Sontag's *Death Kit.*

Allen, Liddy Maid of Rachel Innes; believes murder and break-ins are the work of ghosts in Mary Roberts Rinehart's *The Circular Staircase.*

Allen, Madge (Kramer) Puma trainer who goes on a short trip to Mexico with Frank Chambers in James M. Cain's *The Postman Always Rings Twice.*

Allen, Miss Nurse at St. Vincent's Hospital; befriends and loves Jason Wheeler in Albert Halper's *Union Square.*

Allen, Mr. Well-to-do, sensible neighbor of the Morland family; his kindness in including Catherine Morland on a visit to Bath raises speculation that she will be his heir in John Thorpe and, consequently, in General Tilney in Jane Austen's *Northanger Abbey.*

Allen, Mrs. Good-humored, indolent, childless matron, fond of fashionable attire, in whose charge Catherine Morland visits Bath in Jane Austen's *Northanger Abbey.*

Allen, Mrs. Isaac Allen's wife, disappointed when her son, George, marries Priscilla Broad in Mark Rutherford's *The Revolution in Tanner's Lane.*

Allen, Reverend Hypocritical minister in Winston Churchill's *Richard Carvel.*

Allen, Risa Woman with whom Edwin Locke becomes romantically obsessed in Joyce Carol Oates's *Cybele.*

Allen, Vera Secretary to Lewis Eliot; she asks Eliot to testify on behalf of the father of her lover, Norman Lacey, in C. P. Snow's *Homecomings.*

Allende Blind older man, passive and permissive husband of María Iribarne, confined to the Buenos Aires apartment in Ernesto Sábato's *The Tunnel.*

Allende's maidservant Polish immigrant in Buenos Aires who is protective of Allende and María's privacy in Ernesto Sábato's *The Tunnel.*

Allerton, Abigail Friend of Hamm Rufe; forced to resign her university history assistantship because of her frankness in writing the political history of the town of Franklin in Mari Sandoz's *Capital City.*

Allerton, Major Guest at Styles; attractive to women, he is detested by Arthur Hastings in Agatha Christie's *Curtain: Poirot's Last Case.*

Allestree, Sir John London acquaintance of Archibald Reeves; he warns Harriet Byron of the mischievous and revengeful character of Sir Hargrave Pollexfen in Samuel Richardson's *Sir Charles Grandison.*

Allewinde, Mr. Erudite Dublin barrister, who leads the Crown case against Thady Macdermot for the murder of Captain Ussher in Anthony Trollope's *The Macdermots of Ballycloran.*

Allgood, Landon Uncle of Mildred Sutton; sleeps in a church pew, waiting for his niece's funeral in Reynolds Price's *A Long and Happy Life.*

Alliluyeva, Svetlana Daughter of Joseph Stalin; neighbor of George Levanter in Princeton in Jerzy Kosinski's *Blind Date.*

Allington, Amy Lonely, depressed, and withdrawn 13-year-old daughter of Maurice Allington by his first marriage; after her father saves her from the green man, a creature sent by Dr. Underhill to kill her, she wants to participate in life again in Kingsley Amis's *The Green Man.*

Allington, Joyce Maurice Allington's second wife, who feels that he has used and neglected her; after Allington arranges an orgy with her, Diana Maybury, and himself as participants, Joyce divorces him and leaves with Diana in Kingsley Amis's *The Green Man.*

Allington, Lucy Maurice Allington's daughter-in-law; she is practical and unemotional but believes that people can see ghosts in Kingsley Amis's *The Green Man.*

Allington, Margaret Maurice Allington's first wife and Amy Allington's mother; she was hit and killed by a car while crossing a street several months after a man with whom she was having an affair refused to leave his wife for her; Maurice's guilt over her death helps him to identify with Dr. Underhill, who killed his wife in Kingsley Amis's *The Green Man.*

Allington, Margaret (Mrs. William Grey) Lower-class, middle-aged married woman; blunt, maternal, practical, sympathetic, sallow-faced and poorly clothed, she is remembered by amnesiac Chris Baldry as beautiful and twenty-one; she reluctantly forces Chris to lose false happiness by recalling him to the reality of his son's death and to his marriage to a demanding and materialistic woman in Rebecca West's *The Return of the Soldier.*

Allington, Maurice Middle-aged proprietor of the Green Man inn and a manipulative, selfish adulterer who drinks excessively; he has difficulty relating to his wife and daughter and is afraid of death; after his encounters with God and the ghost of Thomas Underhill, he learns to be more sensitive to his daughter and accepts death in Kingsley Amis's *The Green Man.*

Allington, Mr. Maurice Allington's common-sensical father; he sees that Joyce is unhappy in her marriage to Maurice and suspects that Maurice is interested in Diana Maybury; he dies of a cerebral hemorrhage after seeing an apparition in Kingsley Amis's *The Green Man.*

Allington, Nick Maurice Allington's son and an assistant lecturer in French literature at a university; he advises his wife, Lucy, to stop encouraging his father's interest in ghosts in Kingsley Amis's *The Green Man.*

Allins, Sigismund Confidential secretary of Thomas Carlyle Craw; he is a rogue and a gambler who boasts of his power with the Craw Press while doublecrossing the Evallonian Monarchists in John Buchan's *Castle Gay.*

Allison Tim Mason's ex-wife; she and Tim have a young daughter, Abby, who plays on the soccer team Tim coaches; after divorcing Tim she marries a wealthy lawyer and moves into a luxury development; she and Tim have a turbulent relationship in Tom Perrotta's *The Abstinence Teacher.*

Allison, Colonel Squeamish Chief Constable of Southbourne, where the murder takes place; he is nauseated by Jacko Jaques's betrayal of his friend Hugo Chesterton in Nicholas Blake's *A Tangled Web.*

Allison, Dick Chief of Haven, Maine, volunteer fire department in Stephen King's *The Tommyknockers.*

Allison, Mrs. Lord Fontenoy's kind, widowed friend, who will not marry him until her son, Lord Ancoats, marries and comes to live at Castle Luton in Mrs. Humphry Ward's *Sir George Tressady.*

Allistoun, Captain Master of the *Narcissus* who survives a great storm off the Cape of Good Hope and confronts the rebellion of his crew in Joseph Conrad's *The Nigger of the "Narcissus."*

Allnutt, Charlie Cockney mechanic in German-occupied Central Africa during World War I; he accompanies Rose Sayer on a boat down the Ulanga River on a doomed mission to torpedo a German ship in C. S. Forester's *The African Queen.*

Allonby, Mrs. Guest attending Lady Jane Hunstanton's party at Hunstanton Chase, outside of London; niece of Lord Brancaster; member of fashionable English society who desires London parties over country estates in Oscar Wilde's play *A Woman of No Importance.*

Allsop, Cassie Visitor who jolts Alvina Houghton into realizing that she herself seems destined to be an old maid in D. H. Lawrence's *The Lost Girl.*

Allston, Anna Cousin and friend of Cornelia Wilton; becomes ill and dies following the disappearance of her husband, Lewis Barnwell, shortly after their wedding in Caroline Gilman's *Recollections of a Southern Matron.*

Allston, Joseph (Joe) Retired literary agent burdened by depression; husband of Ruth Allston and father of a dead son who haunts his thoughts; goes to Denmark to learn about his mother; his journal entries provide much of the first-person narrative for Wallace Stegner's *All the Little Live Things* and *The Spectator Bird.*

Allston, Ruth Loving wife of Joe Allston and mother of a dead son; serves as her husband's confidante and sounding board in Wallace Stegner's *All the Little Live Things* and *The Spectator Bird.*

Allworthy, Thomas Benevolent and generous-spirited squire, who raises as his own the foundling Tom Jones; he is brother to Bridget Allworthy and uncle to Master Blifil, whom he makes his heir until Lawyer Dowling finally reveals the extent of Blifil's hypocrisy; Allworthy is benefactor to many poor and needy individuals throughout Henry Fielding's *The History of Tom Jones.*

Alma Young and troubled white woman who joins an order of nuns serving in the Mairun region of Brazil because she feels the need to redeem herself through sacrifice; meets the young Indian chief Avá but cannot marry him because he must marry an Indian woman; eventually becomes a *mirixorã*, a class of women who do not marry or have children; ironically, she becomes pregnant and is the dead woman in the beginning of the novel in Darcy Ribeiro's *Maíra.*

Almanni Warrior who rules Odo during Media's absence in Herman Melville's *Mardi.*

Almas, The Greek Partner in the Regents Sportsmen's Club, Inc., and loan shark to whom Jerry Doherty owes $18,000; kills Croce Torre in a gun battle in George V. Higgins's *The Digger's Game.*

Almásy, Ladislaus de Hungarian desert explorer and a mapmaker who carries with him a copy of Herodotus's *Histories;* loves Katharine, Geoffrey Clifton's wife; the English soldiers think him a German spy; he sides with the Germans to save Katharine; in a plane crash his body is burned beyond recognition and his identification is lost; saved by Bedouins who heal his burnt skin and benefit from his knowledge of guns and ammunition and then abandon him; becomes the mysterious English patient in Michael Ondaatje's *The English Patient.*

Almaviva, Count Governor of Andalusia; befriends the protagonist, Figaro, and enlists the barber's aid in getting the ward of Dr. Bartholo to marry him; womanizer of great renown; seeks to engage in a tryst with the pretty Suzanne, his wife's lady in waiting; tricked and unmasked when Suzanne and his wife, the countess, exchange clothes and surprise the rogue in Pierre Augustin Caron de Beaumarchais's play *The Marriage of Figaro.*

Almayer, Kaspar Dutch trader who marries Lingard's adopted Malay daughter for her dowry and dreams of finding a gold mine, but loses his daughter to Dain Maroola and ends his days in a half-finished mansion smoking opium in Joseph Conrad's *Almayer's Folly: A Story of an Eastern River.* He enters into an unsuccessful partnership with Peter Willems, who betrays the navigation of the River Pantai to the Arab trader Abdulla in *An Outcast of the Islands.*

Almayer, Mrs. Malayan woman who betrays her husband, Kaspar Almayer, by arranging for their daughter Nina's marriage to a local rajah and deserts her husband in Joseph Conrad's *Almayer's Folly: A Story of an Eastern River.*

Almayer, Nina Beautiful Eurasian daughter of Kaspar Almayer; she rejects the prejudiced society and education of white Europeans, marrying a Malayan rajah, Dain Maroola, and abandoning her father in Joseph Conrad's *Almayer's Folly: A Story of an Eastern River.*

Almitra Seeress of Orphalese who believed in Almustafa before any of her compatriots; entreats Almustafa to speak to the assemblage before boarding his ship; initiates the conversation by introducing the topics of love and marriage before the other townspeople begin participating; concludes the questioning by asking about death; remains in place to remember after Almustafa has sailed off and the crowd has dispersed in Kahlil Gibran's *The Prophet.*

Almond, Elizabeth Aunt of Catherine Sloper; hosts a party at which Catherine meets Morris Townsend in Henry James's *Washington Square.*

Almond, Jackie John Connell's school friend who meets Sarah Bennett at a party and gallantly drives her home; he provides a potential but never an actual romantic affair for Sarah in Margaret Drabble's *A Summer Bird-Cage.*

Almond, Marian Pretty cousin of Catherine Sloper; marries Arthur Townsend and introduces Catherine to Arthur's cousin, Morris Townsend, in Henry James's *Washington Square.*

Almost Soup Humanlike white dog who is rescued as a puppy by Cally Roy and later protects Cally's spirit when she is ill; narrates two chapters in Louise Erdrich's *The Antelope Wife.*

Almsbury See John Randolph, Earl of Almsbury.

Almsbury, Lady Emily Meek and faithful wife of John Randolph, Earl of Almsbury, in Kathleen Winsor's *Forever Amber.*

Almustafa Prophet who has spent 12 years abroad; speaks to the people of Orphalese on the day of his departure for his own land, preaching respect, unity, and balance in all things; speaks in verse, using rhetorical questions and analogies to convey his message of peace; affirms his commitment to the people and promises to return in another form in Kahlil Gibran's *The Prophet.*

Alonso King of Naples, father of Ferdinand; cast ashore in an apparent shipwreck; influenced by Prospero's magic, falsely believes his son Ferdinand to have been killed at sea; plotted against by his brother Sebastian, but saved by Prospero's magic; chastised by Ariel for exiling Prospero, duke of Milan; reunited with his son by Prospero in William Shakespeare's play *The Tempest.*

Alonzo Nephew of the governor of Flanders; he shares a bed with Sylvia at an inn while she is dressed as the Chevalier Bellumere; he boasts that no woman can capture his heart; Sylvia schemes to win him and, with Brilliard's help, succeeds in spending most of his fortune in Aphra Behn's *Love Letters Between a Nobleman and His Sister.*

Alonzo, Don Young lord who loves Arminda and marries her in secret before going to the army; he believes the Duchess and Grizalinda when they claim Arminda betrayed him with Constantine until Augustus the Hermit (Lewis Augustus Albertus) proves Arminda's innocence and they are reunited in Penelope Aubin's *The Life and Adventures of the Lady Lucy.*

Alp, Karl Otto Immigrant and former film star; English-speaking student of the narrator, Martin Goldberg, in Bernard Malamud's "The German Refugee."

Alphones Dapper but cowardly little French cook with enormous black moustachios; he fled to Africa after killing his girlfriend's lover in Marseille; he accompanies Allan Quatermain to the Zu-Vendis and returns to civilization with Quatermain's manuscript narrating their adventures in H. Rider Haggard's *Allan Quatermain.*

Alphonse Character from Frederick Burr Opper's popular comic strip "Alphonse and Gaston"; source of the joke, "After you, my dear Alphonse," by which the two cartoon characters are regularly stymied through their extreme politeness; source of a game played by Johnny and Boyd in Shirley Jackson's "After You, My Dear Alphonse."

Alphonso the Chaste Spanish king and uncle of Julian the Apostate in his incarnation as a king; he educates and trains Julian to be his heir in Henry Fielding's *A Journey From This World to the Next.*

Alpine, Frank Gentile drifter who becomes assistant storekeeper in Bernard Malamud's *The Assistant.*

Alroy, David Jewish "Prince of the Captivity" in thirteenth-century Palestine under the rule of the Turkish caliph; he leads a revolt that is initially successful but ultimately fails because Alroy abandons the altruism that created his initial triumph in Benjamin Disraeli's *The Wondrous Tale of Alroy.*

Alroy, Miriam David Alroy's sister, who is devoted to her brother and stands with him when he falls from power and is thrown into prison in Benjamin Disraeli's *The Wondrous Tale of Alroy.*

Al-Sayyid (Ahmad Abd al-Jawad) Patriarch of his middle-class Muslim family in Cairo; seen as hypocritical due to his nocturnal escapades with women and alcohol, now declining in both health and patriarchal status due to the loss of his son five years earlier in Naguib Mahfouz's *The Cairo Trilogy.*

Alsi Eleven-year-old girl who shows extraordinary courage and willingness to survive the Ice; she assists the older representatives in trying to save the people and in assessing the progress of the glaciers in Doris Lessing's *The Making of the Representative for Planet 8.*

Alsop, Gerald (Jerry) Self-styled moral adviser with deep respect for conventions and clean living whose close friendship with George Webber breaks down at Harvard when Webber begins to question Alsop's values in Thomas Wolfe's *The Web and the Rock.*

Alston, Isaac Elderly town patriarch disabled by a stroke in Reynolds Price's *A Long and Happy Life.*

Alston, Marina (Miss Marina) Elderly and eccentric sister of Isaac Alston in Reynolds Price's *A Long and Happy Life.*

Altamont, Colonel (Johnny Armstrong, J. Amory) Mysterious Indian stranger, who turns out to be Lady Clavering's first husband, J. Amory, transported as a convicted felon and long believed dead; his reappearance invalidates her marriage to Sir Francis Clavering until it is discovered that Altamont had previously, as Johnny Armstrong, been married to Madame Fribsby in William Makepeace Thackeray's *The History of Pendennis.*

Altamont, Lord Duke who is the brother of the recently widowed Lady Matilda Sufton and the eventual spouse of Adelaide Julia Douglas in Susan Ferrier's *Marriage.*

Altemira Woman disguised as a man because she has been seduced by Lord Lofty and wishes to get even with him; she does so by masking herself as Amoranda and marrying Lofty in Mary Davys's *The Reform'd Coquet.*

Altifiorla, Francesca Meddling feminist, who preaches that men on the whole are bad; she persuades Cecilia Holt to break off her relationship with Sir Francis Geraldine; she tries to wreck Cecilia's marriage to George Western by encouraging Sir Francis to tell the husband of his broken engagement with Cecilia in Anthony Trollope's *Kept in the Dark.*

Altmayer One of a group of men who enjoys a drinking night in Goethe's tragedy *Faust.*

Alton, Herbert Famous caricaturist whose drawings of Philip and Lucia Lucas are exhibited at the Rutland Gallery in E. F. Benson's *Lucia in London.*

Alton, Lord Arthur Danvers Brave, noble elder brother of Richard Danvers (Lord Alton) and the real father of Julian Danvers; he challenges Fabroni, who had insulted his wife's family and nation, and dies in the duel that follows in William Godwin's *Cloudesley.*

Alton, Lord Richard Danvers Younger brother of Arthur Danvers, Lord Alton; he cheats his nephew, Julian Danvers, of his name and his inheritance; he later feels compunction at his misdeed and hires William Meadows to locate Julian in William Godwin's *Cloudesley.*

Altringham, Earl of Good-humored man of the world; he regularly welcomes George Hotspur to grouse-shooting at his Scottish estate but will never lend him a penny in Anthony Trollope's *Sir Harry Hotspur of Humblethwaite.*

Altringham, Lady Hearty consort of the Earl; she loves horseracing and regards Goodwood and Ascot as vital days in the calendar; having a soft spot for George Hotspur, she helps him in his pursuit of Emily Hotspur in Anthony Trollope's *Sir Harry Hotspur of Humblethwaite.*

Alva Son of an American mulatto mother and Filipino father; employed as a presser in a costume house; has an affair with Emma Lou Morgan and fathers an illegitimate child by Geraldine in Wallace Thurman's *The Blacker the Berry.*

Alva, Duke of Man who raises military support for the Duke of Norfolk in Sophia Lee's *The Recess.*

Alvan, Sigismund Hungarian-Jewish Socialist leader, lawyer, and free spirit; he falls in love with Clotilde Von Rüediger but fails to overcome the resistance of her family to her marrying such a disreputable figure and is led to fight a duel with a fellow suitor of Clotilde and is killed in George Meredith's *The Tragic Comedians.*

Alvarada, Alphonso d' See Raymond, Marquis de la Cisternas.

Alvarada (de Alvarada) y Moctezuma, Don Julian (El Supremo) Maria de Jesus Tyrannical, crazed leader of Spanish rebel forces with whom Hornblower is to create an alliance and whom he later faces as an enemy in C. S. Forester's *The Happy Return.*

Alvarado, Captain Friend of Madre Maria del Pilar; urges Esteban to go to sea with him as an escape from the loss of Thornton Wilder's *The Bridge of San Luis Rey.*

Alvarado, Francisco Twice widowed father and grandfather of two families; resort analyst for Mexican government; philandering lover of Frances Bowles; leaves her after he reads her badly written travel book about Mexico in Harriett Doerr's *Consider This, Senora.*

Alvarez, Don Governor of Puerto Rico and father to Emanuella in Eliza Haywood's *The Rash Resolve; or, the Untimely Discovery.*

Alvarez, Isora D' Morton Devereaux's young wife, who is murdered by his brother Aubrey Devereaux in Edward Bulwer-Lytton's *Devereaux.*

Alvarez, Madame (Manueleta [Manuelata] Hernandez) Ambitious, aristocratic, Spanish-born wife of President Alvarez of Olancho in Richard Harding Davis's *Soldiers of Fortune.*

Alvarez, Manuel (Manny) Friend of Ruben Fontanez and Marty; dances in the subway for money in Jay Neugeboren's *Listen Ruben Fontanez.*

Alvarez, Maria Child patient at Sacred Heart Hospital, where she is a victim of attempted rape; dies of pneumonia in Edward Lewis Wallant's *The Children at the Gate.*

Alvarez, Pepe Prizefighter once managed by Ed Sansom; former lover of Randolph Lee Skully and the focus of his life in Truman Capote's *Other Voices, Other Rooms.*

Alvarez, President President of Olancho who aspires to establish a dictatorship but is overthrown and executed in Richard Harding Davis's *Soldiers of Fortune.*

Alvarito, Barone Duck-hunting companion of Col. Richard Cantwell in Ernest Hemingway's *Across the River and into the Trees.*

Alvin, Elizabeth Thornwell (Betty) Granddaughter of Cornelia Thornwell; leaves her parents' comfortable home to live modestly with her grandmother; becomes an antiestablishment activist; marries a socialist journalist and fights to save Sacco and Vanzetti from execution in Upton Sinclair's *Boston.*

Alving, Helen Mother of Oswald, who returns from Paris with a deadly inherited disease; finances the construction of the orphanage, a memorial to her licentious husband; hopes the memorial will silence rumors of her husband's profligate life; finds that she and her son are haunted by ghosts, an inheritance of the past; painfully watches her son die in Henrik Ibsen's play *Ghosts.*

Alving, Oswald Prodigal son of Mrs. Helen Alving; returns home to Norway from Paris after a long absence; shows signs of fatigue and illness; falls in love with Regina, a maid in his mother's home who is later revealed to be his half-sister by his licentious father and a maid in the Alving household; reveals that he is mortally suffering from an inherited disease, as the sins of the father are visited on the child; takes his own life in the presence of his mother by an overdose of morphine in Henrik Ibsen's play *Ghosts.*

Alwa Schön's son and Lulu's lover; has an affair with Lulu in *Earth Spirit* and flees with her to London after the death of his father in *Pandora's Box;* also dies at the hands of one of her clients in Frank Wedekind's *Lulu* plays.

al-Wazzan, Hasan Born in the Muslim Spanish city of Granada, the 16th-century Hasan moves to Fez to escape the Christian Inquisition; through his many journeys in the East and Western Africa as an itinerant merchant, Hasan presents an incredible description of Africa and projects the instability of the era; captured by pirates near the island of Jerba and finally taken to Pope Leo X, Hasan is converted to Christianity, freed from slavery, and renamed Johannes Leon, or Leon the African; after serving as emissary of the pope, Hasan reverts to Islam later in life in Amin Maalouf's *Leon the African.*

al-Wazzan, Muhammad Father of Hasan and husband of cousin Salma and the Christian Warda; suffers from Warda's departure and humiliation by his townsmen; gets separated from Hasan after divorcing his mother, Salma, but they reunite after the quarantine of Maryam in Amin Maalouf's *Leon the African.*

Alworth, Mr. Harriot Trentham's cousin and betrothed, who, during their engagement, falls in love with and marries Miss Melman instead; eventually resigned to a bad marriage, he allows Harriot to raise his daughter in Sarah Scott's *A Description of Millenium Hall.*

Alworth, Mrs. Kindly old gentlewoman of large fortune; she raises her grandchildren and hopes for a match between two of them, Harriot Trentham and Mr. Alworth, in Sarah Scott's *A Description of Millenium Hall.*

Alwyn, Blessed (Bles) Favorite pupil of Mary Taylor; lover and later husband of Zora; fails as a Washington politician and returns to Alabama to help blacks free themselves from the sharecropping system in W. E. B. DuBois's *The Quest of the Silver Fleece.*

Alyoshka Prisoner in Gang 104 in a Russian hard labor camp; bunks next to Shukhov; depicted as meek and obedient, and not expecting anything in return for his aid and assistance; as a devout Baptist, he reads a handwritten copy of half the Gospels and urges Shukhov to accept his fate and pray in Alexander Solzhenitsyn's *One Day in the Life of Ivan Denisovitch.*

Alywyn Master of the many-towered Warding Knowe; he foretells his own death in battle in William Morris's *The Sundering flood.*

al-Zarwaly Rich landowner who secures his wealth from taxpayers and is known for his multiple marriages that violate the Islamic marital law as perceived in his harem; secures Muhammad al-Wazzan's promise to bless his marriage to daughter Maryam al-Wazzan as a seal to their partnership; forced to break the engagement, he avenges the shame by quarantining Maryam; murdered by Harun and buried in the mountain of Bin Walid after a humiliating scene masterminded by Harun in Amin Maalouf's *Leon the African.*

Alzire One of the children of Vincent Maheu; crippled and dying of starvation due to the meager wages from the Montsou mine owners in 1884 in Émile Zola's *Germinal.*

Amá Mother of the young female narrator in Helena María Viramontes's "The Moths."

Ama, Maami Devoted mother to her son Kwesi and living in the small village of Bamso in Ghana, West Africa; decides to divorce her brutish husband, Kodjo Fi, a man with three wives; devastated by the news that on the same afternoon of her divorce her son dies from a snake bite in Ama Ata Aidoo's "No Sweetness Here."

Amabel Young, dramatically beautiful French girl Miriam Henderson meets at the women's club she has joined, who shows a decided (even slightly alarming) interest in a relationship with Miriam in Dorothy Richardson's *Dawn's Left Hand.* She moves into Mrs. Bailey's house and becomes the center of Miriam's emotional life, with the result that Miriam begins to feel the need to escape from intense involvements in *Clear Horizon.* Her marriage to Michael Shatov takes place in *Dimple Hill,* and Miriam sees that it is not altogether successful in *March Moonlight.*

Amabel Incredibly rich and beautiful London socialite; she loves Max Adey and, though not asked, joins his fog-delayed holiday party in Henry Green's *Party Going.*

Amadiro, Kelden Prominent theoretical roboticist on the planet Aurora who secretly interrogates Gladia Delmarre's humaniform robot lover to discover its design and who later attempts to kidnap R. Daneel Olivaw for the same purpose; leader of faction opposing space exploration by any world but Aurora; chief political enemy and accuser of Dr. Han Fastolfe in Isaac Asimov's *The Robots of Dawn.*

Amador Laboratory assistant who is the thief of experimental rats in Luis Martin-Santos's *Time of Silence.*

Amadou Youngest child of Noumbe and Mustapha in Sembene Ousmane's "Her Three Days."

Amaechina Ikem and Elewa's daughter whose name means "May-the-path-never-close" in Chinua Achebe's *Anthills of the Savannah.*

Amagüe, Princess Venetia Corona d' Sister of Lord Rockingham and widow of the Spanish nobleman Beltran Corona d'Amagüe; Bertie Cecil strikes his commanding officer to defend her honor; she becomes Bertie's wife when he has been cleared of forgery charges and has the right to the family estates and title in Ouida's *Under Two Flags.*

Amal Cousin of the wealthy Bhupathi; studies at the university in Calcutta and lives with his uncle and Charu, Bhupathi's younger wife; finds that the young woman is falling in love with him and deters her affections; marries another and journeys to London to study law in Rabindranath Tagore's *The Broken Nest.*

Amalia Daughter of Doña Magdalena, the hostess of a dinner party that the protagonist and narrator, Alfonso, attends; relates to Alfonso the strange story of a blind artillery officer who resembles Alfonso in Alfonso Reyes's "The Dinner."

Amalia Maid of Cayo Bermúdez's mistress, "Musa"; woman with whom Ambrosio falls in love in Mario Vargas Llosa's *Conversation in the Cathedral.*

Amalia One of two sisters of Barnabas, the messenger from the castle, in Franz Kafka's *The Castle.*

Amalia (Princess of Schyll-Weilingen), Duchess of Graaetli, Countess of Pohrendorf Austrian aristocrat with affection for Italian patriots; she involves herself in a number of plots involving Vittoria Campa and others in George Meredith's *Vittoria.*

Amalric the Amal Prince, lover of Pelagia, and leader of the band of warrior Goths searching for the holy city of Asgard whom Philammon meets on the Nile; he falls off a parapet to his death during a fight with Philammon over Pelagia in Charles Kingsley's *Hypatia.*

Amalthea, Lady Unicorn who leaves the forest to discover if she is the last of her kind; turned into Lady Amalthea by Schmendrick in order to save her from Red Bull in Peter S. Beagle's *The Last Unicorn.*

Amalu, Joseph Hawaiian cook on the *Currency Lass,* whom Loudon Dodd first meets in a bar in San Francisco; he volunteers to go aloft as lookout after murders on the *Flying Scud* in Robert Louis Stevenson's *The Wrecker.*

Amand, Monsieur Melancholy widower who is attracted to Adeline in Ann Radcliffe's *The Romance of the Forest.*

Amanda Mysterious Flemish young woman, who meets Perry Pickle in a coach from Paris to Ghent; she resists his wooing and finally dismisses him altogether after he embarrasses her in a convent in Tobias Smollett's *The Adventures of Peregrine Pickle.*

Amanda Young woman who falls in love with Peter Pludeck, an intellectual and student who chooses to withdraw from the material and social world in favor of his idealistic ideas in Vaclav Havel's *The Garden Party.*

Amanda's husband Character long absent before the play begins, as he deserted the family; though never seen on stage, this "telephone man who fell in love with long distances" remains a significant influence, referred to throughout and evidenced by his photograph that still hangs over the mantel; symbolizes much, including the failed male provider in a male-dominant society, a role his son also briefly assumes and fails in Tennessee Williams's play *The Glass Menagerie.*

Amaranta Daughter of José Arcadio Buendía and Ursula Iguarán; sister of Colonel Aureliano Buendía and José Arcadio; competes with her step-sister for Pietro Crespi's affections; becomes a spinster in Gabriel García Márquez's *One Hundred Years of Solitude.*

Amaranta, Ursula Daughter of Fernanda del Carpio and Aureliano; mother of Aureliano III; strong-willed and hardworking; becomes friends with her nephew, Aureliano; marries Gastón while in Europe; they separate when she has an affair with Aureliano in Gabriel García Márquez's *One Hundred Years of Solitude.*

Amarantha Good-natured, innocent, and virtuous woman in love with Theanor in Eliza Haywood's *The Perplex'd Dutchess; or, Treachery Rewarded.*

Amaril, Claude Womanizing doctor in Alexandria; he falls helplessly in love with a woman at a masquerade; unmasked, she proves to have lost her nose to disease; he determines to use his surgical skill to construct a nose for her and to make her his wife in Lawrence Durrell's *Mountolive.* The operation and marriage are successful; he also constructs a serviceable mechanical hand for Clea Montis in *Clea.*

Amaril, Semira Wife of the doctor Claude Amaril, whose wedding present to her is a rebuilt nose in Lawrence Durrell's *Mountolive.* She becomes a trained doll surgeon in *Clea.*

Amarylis Art student with whom Stuart Armstrong had an affair that led to his divorce from Kate Fletcher Armstrong in Margaret Drabble's *The Middle Ground.*

Amato, John (Johnny, Squirrel) Compulsive gambler who plans the robbery of a mob-run card game with Frankie and Russell; killed by Jackie Cogan in George V. Higgins's *Cogan's Trade.*

Amaury, Giles de Grand Master of the Templars and a leader of Christian forces on Crusade; he is jealous of King Richard and sends an assassin against the king; he murders his co-conspirator Conrade, Marquis of Montserrat and is beheaded by Saladin in Sir Walter Scott's *The Talisman.*

Ambassadors Arrive from England to tell the Danish royal court that Rosencrantz and Guildenstern have been put to death; appear only in Act 3's final dismal scene in Tom Stoppard's play *Rosencrantz and Guildenstern Are Dead.*

Ambedkar, Stephen Rector of St. Luke's in Ranpur who also serves once a month as chaplain of St. John's Church in Pankot, where Frank Bhoolabhoy and Susy Williams are members; Ambedkar is on the verge of being replaced by Father Sebastian in Paul Scott's *Staying On.*

Ambelas, Hermes Donkey driver who works for Maurice Conchis at Bourani in John Fowles's *The Magus.*

Amber Female healer who befriends Teray in Octavia E. Butler's *Patternmaster.*

Amber See St. Clare, Amber.

Amberley, Gertrude Mark's puritanical wife with intellectual pretensions; Hugo Chesterton points a gun at her when she refuses to apologize for calling his lover a "moronic shop girl" in Nicholas Blake's *A Tangled Web.*

Amberley, Mark Estranged brother of Hugo Chesterton; an extension lecturer at London University and a chaser of lost causes, he wishes to reform his brother in Nicholas Blake's *A Tangled Web.*

Amberley, Mary Promiscuous mother of Helen Ledwidge and first lover of Anthony Beavis; her life is a chronicle of increasing decadence in Aldous Huxley's *Eyeless in Gaza.*

Ambermere, Lady Cornelia Arrogant, patronizing, aristocratic widow; she expects everyone to be silent when she speaks in E. F. Benson's *Queen Lucia.* Only Lucia Lucas dares to assume the task of rejecting her gift to the Riseholme Museum of the stuffed body of her dead lapdog in *Lucia in London.*

Ambermere, Richard (Dicky) Aristocrat and friend of Sebastian in Vita Sackville-West's *The Edwardians.*

Amberson, George Brother of Isabel Amberson Minafer and uncle of George Amberson Minafer; former congressman and a business failure in Booth Tarkington's *The Magnificent Ambersons.*

Amberson, Isabel See Minafer, Isabel Amberson.

Amberson, Major Head of a prominent family whose fortunes dwindle so much that he leaves no estate in Booth Tarkington's *The Magnificent Ambersons.*

Ambien I Ambien II's mate who was on the committee to decide what work the Sirians should be doing on Rohanda (Shikasta); he goes on a spy tour across Rohanda, looking for any information that he can find about Canopian progress on the planet in Doris Lessing's *The Sirian Experiments.*

Ambien II One of the five rulers of the Sirian Empire; before becoming a great expert on Canopian wisdom, she must first learn from the Canopian agent Klorathy to understand that Canopus is not only a planet with high intentions and morals, but one which the Sirians should trust and follow in Doris Lessing's *The Sirian Experiments.*

Ambitoso Son of the duchess by a previous marriage; desires to eliminate his stepbrothers from the line of rulership; pretends to help Lussurioso escape from prison, but miscommunicates to the jailer that their brother was to die by the duke's orders; his own full brother, and not Lussurioso, is executed in Cyril Tourner's play *The Revenger's Tragedy.*

Ambroise French servant of Juliet Granville; he is forced to carry the ransom message to her in England; he marries Margery Fairfield in Frances Burney's *The Wanderer.*

Ambrose Alienated, expatriate, homosexual Englishman who builds a house on a Greek island and tries to establish a homosexual enclave in Christopher Isherwood's *Down There on a Visit.*

Ambrose Margaret Borradale's manservant, who, following her death from a stroke brought on by the shock of witnessing the murder of William, enters the service of Travers in order to assist him in pursuing Margaret's jealous husband, Deloraine, in William Godwin's *Deloraine.*

Ambrose Petty officer aboard the *Renown* in C. S. Forester's *Lieutenant Hornblower.*

Ambrose The Lovats' sententious butler with a gray face and jutting bones; he tries to be the authority to and moral arbiter of the Lovats' servants in Ivy Compton-Burnett's *Darkness and Day.*

Ambrose The 13-year-old protagonist who together with his family goes to the beach at Ocean City on July 4 during World War II; an exceptionally introspective and self-conscious youth who is just becoming aware of his sexuality; enters the funhouse with his friend Magda, age 14, and his older brother Peter; becomes lost in the funhouse in John Barth's "Lost in the Funhouse."

Ambrose, Detective-Sergeant Impassive police investigator who arrests Cliff Sanders for trying to exploit his sister

Julia Delmore's absence by claiming to be a go-between in a kidnapping plot; he is a character in the story novelist Giles Hermitage writes in John Wain's *The Pardoner's Tale.*

Ambrose, Father See Checkley, Father.

Ambrose, Helen Rachel Vincrace's aunt, surrogate mother, dream lover/confidante/friend, and guide; Helen, the "angel of the house," orchestrates the Villa Santa Gervasio and Rachel's world in Santa Marina; vacillating between roles as omniscient, omnipotent visionary deity and human with limited insight evidenced by her rejection of ideal or religion, Helen is the creator of one path to vision for Rachel with enough foresight to foretell her tragic end in Virginia Woolf's *The Voyage Out.*

Ambrose, Ridley Rachel Vinrace's scholarly, self-absorbed uncle, with whom she lives in South America; translating Pindar's odes in his private room/world, Ridley represents single-minded, obsessive devotion to thought and to cold fact in contrast to the imaginative vision embodied by his wife, Helen, in Virginia Woolf's *The Voyage Out.*

Ambrosio Former driver of Don Fermín Zavala, Lima's famous capitalist; meets Santiago Zavala, don Fermín's son, in a bar called The Cathedral years later to recall past years in Peruvian history; hails from a lower-class family with a criminal father; seeks help from his youthhood friend Bermúdez after the latter becomes an official in the Ministry of Internal Affairs of the Odría government; serves as Cayo Bermúdez's driver and hatchet man, directly handling his master's dirty business, such as collecting "protection fees" from the brothels and dispelling political protests in Mario Vargas Llosa's *Conversation in the Cathedral.*

Ambrosio Renowned Capuchin monk with mysterious origins; seemingly incorruptible, pure, virtuous, and charismatic; devoted to his faith, even though it is motivated less by piety than by vanity and pride; proves to be vulnerable and lustful after meeting beautiful Matilda, since he easily succumbs to sexual temptation despite his vows; his wickedness and sexual perversion emerge, leading him to wanton cruelty; condemns Agnes to death, murders Elvira to gain her daughter Antonia, and then, after raping her, murders the young woman in anger; imprisoned, he sells his soul to Satan to escape punishment, but the devil betrays him; dies before he can repent in Matthew Gregory Lewis's *The Monk.*

Ambrosio Rita's first lover and inventor of the scheme of using a billy goat to make men pity her in Juan Carlos Onetti's *A Grave Without a Name.*

Ambrosius See Glendinning, Edward.

Ambrosius Young Franciscan monk who, in 1680, murders Benedicta, the hangman's daughter, to save her from a romance with Rochus in Ambrose Bierce's adaptation of *The Monk and the Hangman's Daughter.*

Ambrosius of Camadoli Friend of the hermit, Serapion, who lives in a dense forest in southern Germany in E. T. A. Hoffmann's "The Story of Serapion."

Amédée Brother of Julius and the character who seeks to intercede to ransom the purportedly kidnapped pope; murdered by the swindler Lafcadio in André Gide's *Lafcadio's Adventures.*

Amedroz, Bernard Apathetic, hypochondriac father of Clara and Charles and proprietor of the Belton estate, to which Will Belton becomes heir; resenting him at first, he comes to value his interest in improving the estate and supports Will's courtship of Clara; his sudden death puts Will in possession of the estate in Anthony Trollope's *The Belton Estate.*

Amedroz, Charles Bernard's son, the heir to die Belton estate until debt drove him to suicide; Will Belton succeeds him as heir in Anthony Trollope's *The Belton Estate.*

Amedroz, Clara Resourceful, proud daughter of Bernard Amedroz; she courageously breaks off her engagement with Captain Aylmer when she realizes he was chiefly interested in what she might inherit from Mrs. Winterfield; her distant cousin Will Belton wants to save her from poverty by handing over Belton Castle to her; his generosity and love win her heart in Anthony Trollope's *The Belton Estate.*

Amelia Amiable cousin and intimate confidante of Felicia; she marries Felicia's rejected suitor Mellifont in Mary Collyer's *Felicia to Charlotte.*

Amelia Beautiful young woman of whom Traffick was enamored and whom Traffick cheated of her fortune; later she marries the Spanish commander of Jamaica in Charles Johnstone's *Chrysal: or, The Adventures of a Guinea.*

Amelia Referred to as "the Mummy"; old woman, shriveled and corpselike, who appears crazy; sits like an entombed body in a cupboard because her eyes cannot stand the light; teasingly called "Pretty Polly"; mother of Adèle in August Strindberg's play *The Ghost Sonata.*

Amelia Second daughter of Bernarda's second marriage; fearful of men, she submits without resistance to the sexual inequality and restrictive morality predicated by her mother in Federico García Lorca's play *The House of Bernarda Alba.*

Amelia Traveling companion of the unnamed narrator in S. J. Pratt's *Travels for the Heart.*

Amelia Wife of a criminal being defended by Mr. Jaggers, who threatens to drop the case if she keeps pestering him about "My Bill" in Charles Dickens's *Great Expectations.*

Amelia ('Melia) Servant at Dr. Blimber's school; she is kind to little Paul Dombey in Charles Dickens's *Dombey and Son.*

Amelia Black maid and youthful friend of the narrator of Aline Bernstein's *The Journey Down.*

Amelie Half-caste servant of Antoinette Cosway after Antoinette's marriage to Mr. Rochester; she brings Daniel Cosway's letters to Rochester and sleeps with Rochester in Jean Rhys's *Wide Sargasso Sea.*

Amelot Damian Lacy's page, who leads soldiers during Damian's convalescence, and who marries Rose Flammock at the end in Sir Walter Scott's *The Betrothed.*

Amenartas Princess of the royal house of Egyptian pharaohs; her exhortation to her son to avenge the death of her husband Kallikrates at the hands of She was passed from generation to generation for two thousand years until it initiated Leo Vincey's and Horace Holly's quest into the African interior in H. Rider Haggard's *She.*

American, The American traveler in Spain who has been living a leisurely, itinerant lifestyle with a female companion; his discussion with her at a train station implies she is pregnant; tense and worried, he tries to persuade her to have an abortion, assuring her the process is simple, while unconvincingly insisting he wants her to do what she chooses in Ernest Hemingway's "Hills Like White Elephants."

"American Dreams" Narrator Child when the action of the story begins and 17 when it ends; works after school and on weekends at his father's petrol station; when he first sees Gleason's hidden model of the city, he thinks it is the most beautiful image he has ever seen and believes that the rest of the townspeople are also filled with wonder; disagrees with his father regarding Gleason's reason for building the model and thinks that Gleason foresaw the consequences in Peter Carey's "American Dreams."

American Horse, Darlene Attractive Native American woman and girlfriend of Cletus Purcel; lover of Dave Robicheaux; killed by Las Vegas hit man hired by Sally Dio; guides Robicheaux in a dream to half-buried bodies of two Native Americans killed by Dio's men in James Lee Burke's *Black Cherry Blues.*

Amerigo, Prince Italian nobleman who marries Maggie Verver and who had a previous attachment to Charlotte Stant in Henry James's *The Golden Bowl.*

Amerson, Alice Rodwell Demanding and unsympathetic wife of Jerrard Amerson and mother of five children; she is condemned by her mother-in-law for killing Jerrard by turning him into a machine to satisfy her demands at the end of Frank Swinnerton's *The Happy Family.*

Amerson, Edward (Teddy) Youngest son of Jerrard and Alice Amerson; he divides his time between his work as an invoice clerk at Tremlett & Grove's, a publishing firm, and his amateur theatricals in Frank Swinnerton's *The Happy Family.*

Amerson, Grace Eldest daughter of Jerrard and Alice Amerson; Grace has made a respectable match with Edwin Gower, son of a prosperous local builder, at the opening of Frank Swinnerton's *The Happy Family.*

Amerson, Jerrard Self-educated and self-reliant manager at the printing firm Dickertons, who began as a messenger boy; his marriage to his cousin Mice, after its first bloom, is joyless; he has thrown himself into his work and dies prematurely in Frank Swinnerton's *The Happy Family.*

Amerson, Mabel Middle daughter of Jerrard and Alice Amerson; she becomes sexually involved with Bert Moggerson, her fiancé, alienating her family in Frank Swinnerton's *The Happy Family.*

Amerson, Mary Youngest of the Amerson children; she gets the brunt of the family criticism; she becomes engaged to Septimus Bright to escape her family, but later chooses Roger Dennett, whom she really loves, in Frank Swinnerton's *The Happy Family.*

Amerson, Mrs. Mother of Jerrard Amerson; she lives with her son and his family in Frank Swinnerton's *The Happy Family.*

Amerson, Tom Eldest of the Amerson children; like his father, he works at Dickertons printing firm; he becomes head of the household after his father's death in Frank Swinnerton's *The Happy Family.*

Amerton, Father Hypocritical, prurient-minded clergyman who denounces the Utopians as promiscuous sinners and becomes a vocal supporter of Rupert Catskill's plan to conquer them in H. G. Wells's *Men Like Gods.*

Ames, Bob Cousin of Mrs. Vance; encourages Carrie Meeber to become an actress in Theodore Dreiser's *Sister Carrie.*

Ames, Cathy See Trask, Cathy Ames.

Ames, Charlotte Wife of Harry Ames and, on one occasion, sexual partner of Max Reddick in John A. Williams's *The Man Who Cried I Am.*

Ames, Charlotte See Emory, Charlotte Ames.

Ames, Dalton Lover of Caddy Compson and the father of Quentin Compson II in William Faulkner's *The Sound and the Fury.*

Ames, Harry Leading African-American novelist of his time; murdered by the CIA in order to suppress publication of a contingency plan, code-named King Alfred, for removing the minority population of the United States to concentration camps in John A. Williams's *The Man Who Cried I Am.*

Ames, Lacey Debney Obese mother of Charlotte Emory and wife of Murray Ames in Anne Tyler's *Earthly Possessions.*

Ames, Mat Youth who leads a group of boys in the snowball fight against the boys led by Jack Harris in Thomas Bailey Aldrich's *The Story of a Bad Boy.*

Ames, Murray Dour photographer father of Charlotte Emory and husband of Lacey Debney Ames in Anne Tyler's *Earthly Possessions.*

Ames, Susan Divorced from Tim Ames; painter and artist; builds a home in Amapolas, Mexico; leaves Mexico but never sells her house there after Tim returns to remarry her in Harriett Doerr's *Consider This, Senora.*

Ames, Tim Former husband of Susan Ames; unsuccessful at various businesses; becomes a successful mountain climber; returns to Sue to remarry her in Harriett Doerr's *Consider This, Senora.*

Amesbury, Catherine See Trask, Cathy Ames.

Ami, David Ben Israeli member of the Palmach; uses biblical passages as military strategies in Leon Uris's *Exodus.*

Amiens One of Duke Senior's men who followed him into exile when the duke was banished by his brother, Frederick; notable for the songs he sings as well as his exchanges with and teasing of the melancholic Jacques in William Shakespeare's play *As You Like It.*

Amigo Mexican cowhand for Major Willard Tetley; convinces the lynch mob to seek the rustlers on a trail different from that pursued by Sheriff Risley in Walter Van Tilburg Clark's *The Ox-Bow Incident.*

Amin, Lieutenant Seemingly mild and controlled police officer who is well liked by Jack Townrow even though he arrests Townrow on charges of espionage and murder; he jumps from a train window and is killed by a British soldier in P. H. Newby's *Something to Answer For.*

Amina Wife and mother in a middle-class Muslim home in Cairo; rises in authority in the home as her husband, al-Sayyad, who has been unmasked as a hypocrite (seeking out women and alcohol), loses his familial power; dies a year following the death of her husband in Naguib Mahfouz's *The Cairo Trilogy.*

Aminadab Beastlike man of low stature and bulky frame; works in the lower depths as a laboratory assistant to the young, possessed, perhaps mad scientist Aylmer in Nathaniel Hawthorne's "The Birth-Mark."

Aminadab Brother of the Portugese Banker; a Jewish stock-jobber and Her Grace's agent, he feels that he must take revenge upon all Christians for the evils done to his race in Charles Johnstone's *Chrysal: or, The Adventures of a Guinea.*

Aminadab, Young Aminadab's son who debases Chrysal of a quarter of his weight and all of the coin's beauty; he gives his Jewish uncle, the Portugese Banker, to the Holy Office and is himself caught by the Holy Office for clipping coins in Charles Johnstone's *Chrysal: or, The Adventures of a Guinea.*

Aminado, Don Attractive Catholic priest of San Seville in Spain; seduced by and has sacrilegious, sadistic sex with the teenage nymphomaniac Simone, during which she strangles him to death in Georges Bataille's *Story of the Eye.*

Amir Protagonist and narrator born in 1963 in Kabul, Afghanistan; privileged son of his widowed father, Baba;

mother dies giving birth to him; escapes to the United States after the Russian invasion and fall of Afghan monarchy;; half-brother of Hassan, also Amir's childhood friend in Khaled Hosseini's *The Kite Runner.*

Amis, Martin Struggling author and screenwriter in Martin Amis's *Money.*

Ammatter German scholar who arranges for Roy Calvert's lecture in Berlin in C. P. Snow's *The Light and the Dark.*

Ammen, Jasper Egoist who, as a study, plots the murder of a stranger in Conrad Aiken's *King Coffin.*

Ammiani, Carlo Merthyr Son of Vittoria Campa and Carlo Ammiani in George Meredith's *Vittoria.*

Ammiani, Count Carlo Ardent revolutionist in the cause of Italian liberation; his traditional ideas concerning female roles hinder his relationship with his sweetheart, later his wife, Vittoria Campa; he is killed after leading a failed revolt in George Meredith's *Vittoria.*

Ammiani, Countess Marcellina Carlo Ammiani's Venetian mother; she initially disapproves of her son's betrothed, Vittoria Campa, for incomplete submission to her son's authority in George Meredith's *Vittoria.*

(Thaumasus) Ammonius Catholic monk who hurls a stone at the prefect Orestes, is crucified, and is subsequently canonized in Charles Kingsley's *Hypatia.*

Ammu Estha and Rahel's mother and a touchable; divorced after refusing to have sex with Mr. Hollick, her husband's boss; victimized by her family and society; makes love to Velutha, an untouchable; stigmatized by society, she dies alone in Bharat Lodge in Arundhati Roy's *The God of Small Things.*

Amoranda Heroine, who is headstrong and very used to having her own way in Mary Davys's *The Reform'd Coquet.*

Amorous La Foole Knight and the subject of Clerimont's and Dauphine's ridicule; arrives to invite both men to a feast at Mistress Otter's house; pitted against Sir John Daw by Clerimont and Dauphine and scared into being blindfolded, giving up his sword, being hit in the mouth, and having his nose tweaked by Dauphine; forced to claim to have successfully wooed Epicoene, only to retract the statement in Ben Jonson's play *Epicoene, or The Silent Woman.*

Amory, Blanche Beautiful, self-centered stepdaughter of Sir Francis Clavering; she jilts Arthur Pendennis to become engaged to Harry Foker, who breaks with her when he learns she has been corresponding with her disreputable father, Colonel Altamont, in William Makepeace Thackeray's *The History of Pendennis.*

Amos Old shepherd of the Essene monastery, who welcomes Jesus back, turning over the flock to him in George Moore's *The Brook Kerith.*

Amos Minister who attempted to burn down his own church; golf partner of Thomas Marshfield at the retreat in John Updike's *A Month of Sundays.*

Amos Prosperous member of the Chicago Stock Exchange who disapproves of his impractical and nonmaterialistic brother, Joseph, in Saul Bellow's *Dangling Man.*

Amos Television character who turns in moochers Kingfish Stevens and Andy Brown to the police for robbing his place in Ishmael Reed's *The Last Days of Louisiana Red.*

Amos, Andrew Loyal Scots patriot and pillar of an intelligence service in World War I; he is Richard Hannay's intelligence contact in Glasgow and the Scottish Highlands in John Buchan's *Mr. Standfast.* He is one of Adam Melfort's instructors and a "watch-dog" in his intelligence training as an undercover agent in World War I in *A Prince of the Captivity.*

Amos, Mr. Valet of Congressman Doolittle; keeps Sara Andrews informed of his employer's failing health in W. E. B. DuBois's *Dark Princess.*

Amram Hebrew father of Aaron and Miriam, and perhaps of Moses as well; slave in Goshen in Zora Neale Hurston's *Moses, Man of the Mountain.*

Amron, Harriet Shippen Philadelphia blue blood married to Saul Amron in Paule Marshall's *The Chosen Place, the Timeless People.*

Amron, Saul American anthropologist who goes to the Caribbean as the leader of a research project designed to improve life for the poor people of Bourne Island; husband of Harriet Shippen Amron in Paule Marshall's *The Chosen Place, the Timeless People.*

Amsden, Mrs. American expatriate and friend of Evalina Bowen; concerned with the affairs of others in William Dean Howells's *Indian Summer.*

Amsel, Eddi Narrator of the years 1917–27; son of a Jewish merchant, Eddi builds scarecrows that resemble the townsfolk; often beaten by anti-Semitic boys in school and also beaten severely by his best friend, Walter Matern, who has become involved with the Nazis; takes on alter egos, such as Mr. Brauxel, after this incident in Günter Grass's *Dog Years.*

Amsterdam, Jack Corrupt construction contractor for the Catholic Church and business and golf partner of Desmond Spellacy; arrested for the murder of Lois Fazenda in John Gregory Dunne's *True Confessions.*

Amthor, Jules Psychic consultant in Raymond Chandler's *Farewell, My Lovely.*

Amula Young woman jealous of the attention Rochus gives Benedicta; comforts Ambrosius before his execution in Ambrose Bierce's adaptation of *The Monk and the Hangman's Daughter.*

Amusa, Sergeant Native African policeman who is offended by the Pilkings' lack of respect for indigenous customs and beliefs of Nigeria; informs Simon Pilkings of Elesin's plan to commit suicide; ordered by Pilkings to arrest Elesin, but when he attempts to he is mocked by the women in the marketplace for doing the European's bidding and sent away humiliated in Wole Soyinka's play *Death and the King's Horseman.*

Amy (Cherry, Mrs. Amy, Madam Collins) Roxana's maid who stays with her after her first husband leaves; she volunteers to sleep with Roxana's landlord to save Roxana from being "undone"; later, she is fired by Roxana for wanting to kill Roxana's daughter Susan, and she has Susan put into debtor's prison falsely; finally, she dies of the "French disease" in Daniel Defoe's *The Fortunate Mistress.*

Amy Sarah and William's youngest child, a Down Syndrome victim, who is loved and cared for by the entire family in Doris Lessing's *The Fifth Child.*

Amy Aunt of Miranda; romanticized by her family as a model of Southern beauty; marries Gabriel Breaux, her longtime suitor, and dies shortly thereafter of tuberculosis in Katherine Anne Porter's *Old Mortality.*

Amyas le Poulet See Clarence.

Amy's Gentleman Messenger for the Prince of —; he becomes Amy's lover in Daniel Defoe's *The Fortunate Mistress.*

Ana Church-going secretary of Dr. Eduardo Plarr in Graham Greene's *The Honorary Consul.*

Ana Nurse who marries Santiago Zavala in Mario Vargas Llosa's *Conversation in the Cathedral.*

Anacã Recently deceased chieftain in the Mairun Indian village in Brazil in Darcy Ribeiro's *Maíra.*

Anacleto Eccentric Filipino manservant excessively devoted to Alison Langdon; disappears shortly after her death in Carson McCullers's *Reflections in a Golden Eye.*

Anaitis, Dame (Lady of the Lake) Ruler of the enchanted island Cocaigne; becomes Jurgen's first wife when he begins a yearlong dalliance in the dream realm in pursuit of his wife Dame Lisa in James Branch Cabell's *Jurgen.*

Analysis, Jack Journalist of Greek parentage and former lover of Molly Calico in Peter De Vries's *The Mackerel Plaza.*

Ana María An 18-year-old girl abused by Linacero six months before her death and who keeps appearing in Linacero's dream in Juan Carlos Onetti's *The Pit.*

Anana Black mistress of Don Pedro de Sylva and benefactress to Mary, Queen of Scots; she arranges Matilda's release from a Jamaican prison in Sophia Lee's *The Recess.*

Anandamoyi Epitome of "Mother India"; a one-time orthodox Brahmin woman who gives shelter to a pregnant British woman and adopts her child, Gora, when the mother dies; gives up Hindu rituals for the sake of Gora; loves Gora's friend Binoy like her own son; holds herself strong despite societal pressures and does not hesitate to bless the interreligious marriages of Gora with Sucharita and Binoy with Lolita in Rabindranath Tagore's *Gora.*

Ananias Anabaptist deacon from Amsterdam who is met with hostility by the character Subtle; leaves and returns with Tribulation; both desire the Philosopher's Stone as a means of accruing more money to further their religion; beaten away by Lovewit at the end of Ben Jonson's play *The Alchemist.*

Anapoupolis, Bettie Mae Friend of Elsinore briefly encountered by Eva Trout in a midwestern American city; her father, who is also present, knows of Willy Trout by reputation; he also delivers a prophetic tirade against the questionable practice of adoption rings on the eve of Eva's adoption of Jeremy in Elizabeth Bowen's *Eva Trout, or Changing Scenes.*

Anarchist, The Brigand that Jack Turner meets in George Bernard Shaw's *Man and Superman.*

Anarchus, King See King Anarchus.

Anatole Tom and Dahlia Travers's French cook, for whose art Bertie Wooster is readily corrupted in P. G. Wodehouse's *The Code of the Woosters* and in *Aunts Aren't Gentlemen.* He appears in four other novels.

Anatole Henry Foker's valet in William Makepeace Thackeray's *The History of Pendennis.*

Anatole Twenty-four-year-old intellectual Congolese schoolteacher in the village of Kilanga; has scarified face; translates Nathan Price's sermons to his congregation; marries Leah Price, fathers four children; imprisoned by the corrupt Mobutu regime; moves with his family to an agricultural station in Angola in Barbara Kingsolver's *The Poisonwood Bible.*

Anatoly Russian son of the farmer-turned-soldier and story's narrator, Andrei Sokolov; finds his mother and sisters killed by German air raids and joins the Soviet army during World War II; quickly rises to a captain and commander of a battery; highly decorated; killed on Victory Day in May in Berlin in Mikhail Sholokhov's "The Fate of a Man."

Ancke, Albert Times Square night person and drug addict in John Clellon Holmes's *Go.*

Ancoats, Lord Edgar Son of Mrs. Allison and heir to Castle Luton; his involvement with an unsuitable actress causes distress to his relations and friends in Mrs. Humphry Ward's *Sir George Tressady.*

Ancrum, Richard Melancholic minister, who befriends David Grieve in Mrs. Humphry Ward's *The History of David Grieve.*

Andemening, Lars Reclusive and overly literary book reviewer orphaned in Poland during World War II, now living in Stockholm; obsessed with and convinced he is the son of a famous Polish author who was murdered by the Nazis in Cynthia Ozick's *The Messiah of Stockholm.*

Anders, Frau Mistress of Hippolyte; sells her into slavery in Susan Sontag's *The Benefactor.*

Anders, John Police captain who investigates the murder of Angela Black in Michael Crichton's *The Terminal Man.*

Anderson See Montrose, Marquis of.

Anderson Young husband of an ailing, pregnant wife and father of several children; he has brought his family to destitution by going bail for a ne'er-do-well brother; in desperation he turns highwayman and tries to rob Tom Jones; he becomes an object of Tom's benevolence in Henry Fielding's *The History of Tom Jones.*

Anderson, Alfred (Al) Proprietor of Al's Lunch Wagon; sympathetic to the Communist labor organizers; helps feed the strikers in John Steinbeck's *In Dubious Battle.*

Anderson, Andy Chief bugler of G Company; feels his position threatened by Robert E. Lee Prewitt; coauthors "The Re-Enlistment Blues" with Prewitt and Sal Clark in James Jones's *From Here to Eternity.*

Anderson, Anne (Sissy) Domineering older sister of Roberta (Bobbi) Anderson; travels to Haven to inform her sister of their father's death and is abducted for use in a macabre experiment in her sister's shed in Stephen King's *The Tommyknockers.*

Anderson, Argustus (Mr. Andy) Father of Mae Douglas; musician and supporter of his grandson, Raymond Douglas, in Herbert Simmons's *Man Walking on Eggshells.*

Anderson, Bess (Bessie) Daughter of Tillie and Ern Anderson and sister of Nonnie and Ed Anderson; college-educated maid in Lillian Smith's *Strange Fruit.*

Anderson, Betty Daughter of mill workers; becomes pregnant by Rodney Harrington and is bought off by his father, Leslie Harrington, in Grace Metalious's *Peyton Place.*

Anderson, Brigham M. (Brig) Senior senator from Utah and chairman of the Senate Foreign Relations Subcommittee on the nomination of Robert Leffingwell in Allen Drury's *Advise and Consent.*

Anderson, Captain Charlotte Grandison's clandestine suitor and the recipient of her rash and regretted written promise not to marry another man without his consent; though the fortune of £10,000 bestowed on her by Sir Charles Grandison is a contrary inducement, Sir Charles's eloquence convinces him of the unmanliness of not releasing her in Samuel Richardson's *Sir Charles Grandison.*

Anderson, Captain Paul Character referred to in the title; rich, decrepit, and moribund bachelor with an ugly, wrinkled face, who looks twice his age of 50; employs the pretty and full-bosomed young Maarja as his maid and cook; longtime morphine addict; desires the young Maarja to share his bed but she refuses; agrees to make her wealthy—so she can marry the young seaman Mait Näkisaar—if she will share his bed; further agrees to make her the heir of his fortune if she will marry him and legitimize their child born out of wedlock; dies on the night of their marriage after Maarja gives him a lethal dose of morphine in Eduard Vilde's "The Skipper's Sleeping-Draught."

Anderson, Charley World War I ace who has a mercurial career as an airplane parts manufacturer after the war; his obsession with the stock market and his lack of moral principles lead to his ruin in John Dos Passos's *U.S.A.* trilogy.

Anderson, Colonel Pessimistic Chief Constable in Agatha Christie's *The A.B.C. Murders.*

Anderson, Crispin (Smog) Son of Bridgitte Appledore's former husband; he attaches himself to Bridgitte and Michael Cullen in Alan Sillitoe's *A Start in Life.*

Anderson, David Kind farmer of AultRigh; he hires Robert Colwan and leads the burial party after his suicide in James Hogg's *The Private Memoirs and Confessions of a Justified Sinner.*

Anderson, Dolly Self-loathing teenage daughter of Viola Anderson; given to flights of fantasy that are a pretext for her murder in Hal Bennett's *The Black Wine.*

Anderson, Donovan Young man from a wealthy family who becomes Martha Quest's first serious romantic interest in Doris Lessing's *Martha Quest.* He also appears in *A Proper Marriage.*

Anderson, Dr. Gilbert Specialist in shell-shock who recognizes that Chris Baldry's unconscious refuses to admit the truth of the last fifteen years; his cure forces Chris into a life of suffering in Rebecca West's *The Return of the Soldier.*

Anderson, Dr. Robert Principal of the racial uplift school where Helga quits her teaching job; resurfaces in New York, where Helga avoids him; becomes engaged to Helga's housemate, Anne Grey, while Helga is in Denmark; kisses Helga in a spontaneous act, and, just as Helga is ready to run off with him, downplays the entire incident in Nella Larsen's *Quicksand.*

Anderson, Ed (Eddie) Son of Tillie and Ern Anderson, brother of Nonnie and Bessie Anderson, and killer of Tracy Deen in Lillian Smith's *Strange Fruit.*

Anderson, Ern Husband of Tillie Anderson and father of Nonnie, Bessie, and Ed Anderson in Lillian Smith's *Strange Fruit.*

Anderson, Heaven Neglected daughter of television star Silver Anderson who goes on to have a prosperous career as a singer in Jackie Collins's *Hollywood Husbands.*

Anderson, Homer Sociologist and factory personnel administrator and neighbor of Gertie and Clovis Nevels in Harriette Arnow's *The Dollmaker.*

Anderson, Hubert Acquaintance of the Westons; he marries Cicely Carmichael in Isabel Colegate's *Statues in a Garden.*

Anderson, Hugh Lovelorn second secretary at the British Legation in Brussels whose courtship of Florence Mountjoy is rebuffed in Anthony Trollope's *Mr. Scarborough's Family.*

Anderson, James Young son of David Anderson; he is the last to speak with Robert Colwan before his suicide in James Hogg's *The Private Memoirs and Confessions of a Justified Sinner.*

Anderson, Jan Strong-willed young protagonist who shoots Uncle Hake Nolan to protect his sister, Timmie Anderson, in Fred Chappell's *The Inkling.*

Anderson, Jaw Buster Neighbor of Nunn Ballew, fox hunter, and owner of a logging truck often used to transport neighbors to town from their isolated community in Harriette Arnow's *Hunter's Horn.*

Anderson, Jenny Nolan Widowed mother of Jan and Timmie Anderson and sister of Hezekiah (Hake) Nolan; gradually loses control of her household and eventually dies of cancer in Fred Chappell's *The Inkling.*

Anderson, Job *Hispaniola's* boatswain, who serves as mate after Arrow goes overboard; he leads the first attack on the stockade, wounds Captain Smollett, tries to stab Jim Hawkins, and is killed by Abraham Gray in Robert Louis Stevenson's *Treasure Island.*

Anderson, Leon Communications expert at nester in Scott Spencer's *Last Night at the Brain Thieves' Ball.*

Anderson, Molly Peggy Anderson's thirteen-year-old daughter, who faithfully nurses her young brother and mother in Henry Fielding's *The History of Tom Jones.*

Anderson, Mr. Silent, morose hypochondriac, who is a past government official in Doris Lessing's *Martha Quest.*

Anderson, Mrs. Donovan Anderson's mother, who knew Martha Quest's mother; she is patronized by Donovan in Doris Lessing's *Martha Quest.*

Anderson, Mrs. Neighbor of Gertie and Clovis Nevels and wife of Homer Anderson; brings Gertie the message that the wife of a factory executive wants dolls to be carved for a Christmas bazaar in Harriette Arnow's *The Dollmaker.*

Anderson, Nick (Nicky) Francis Coldridge's school friend who, after being brutally beaten by police at a demonstration, becomes politically active before his entire family is killed in Doris Lessing's *The Four-Gated City.*

Anderson, Nonnie (Non) Daughter of Tillie and Ern Anderson and sister of Bessie and Ed Anderson; black lover of Tracy Deen and mother of their unborn child in Lillian Smith's *Strange Fruit.*

Anderson, Palmer Anderson An American psychoanalyst of independent means; he is Honor Klein's half brother and lover, the lover of his patient Antonia Lynch-Gibbon, and the protector of Georgie Hands, with whom he leaves for America at the end of Iris Murdoch's *A Severed Head.*

Anderson, Peggy Pregnant wife of Anderson and the mother of several children; the Andersons are cousins of Mrs. Miller, who uses their example as a warning of the hazards of marrying imprudently for love in Henry Fielding's *The History of Tom Jones.*

Anderson, Roberta (Bobbi) Single, fortyish writer of western novels who uncovers an extraterrestrial power source on her property in Haven, Maine; friend and lover of Jim Gardener in Stephen King's *The Tommyknockers.*

Anderson, Silver Famous and vain television soap opera star and neglectful mother of Heaven Anderson; wife of Wes Money in Jackie Collins's *Hollywood Husbands.*

Anderson, Steve Anderson American film star who tries to seduce Jenny McNeil and figures in her fictional account of her experiences in Hollywood in John Fowles's *Daniel Martin.*

Anderson, Tillie Mother of Nonnie, Bessie, and Ed Anderson and wife of Ern Anderson; works in white households as a cook in Lillian Smith's *Strange Fruit.*

Anderson, Timmie Violently insane sister of Jan Anderson; tries to deflect Jan's penetrating gaze by persuading him to wear glasses and hopes to give him insight by cutting eyelike gashes in his hands and feet in Fred Chappell's *The Inkling.*

Anderson, Tommy Peggy Anderson's sick seven-year-old son, who shares a bed with his mother; he is restored to health after his father is aided by Tom Jones in Henry Fielding's *The History of Tom Jones.*

Anderson, Viola Friend of Eloise McLindon; cynical political activist, whorehouse madam, and mother of Dolly Anderson in Hal Bennett's *The Black Wine* and *Seventh Heaven.*

Anderson, Wilbur Son of Argustus Anderson and uncle of Raymond Douglas; trumpet player who buys Douglas his first trumpet and influences his musical style in Herbert Simmons's *Man Walking on Eggshells.*

Anderton, John Allison Commissioner of police and founder of Precrime; nearing retirement, he grows paranoid that his new assistant, Witwer, and his own wife are conspiring against him; intercepts the Precrime report that says he will murder Kaplan, a man he has never met; meets Fleming, who makes accusations against Witwer, Lisa, and Kaplan and gives Anderton a new identity; contacts Walter to examine the minority report; escapes with Lisa and knocks out Fleming; reads the reports and decides to kill Kaplan in order to preserve Precrime; goes to Kaplan's army rally and murders him; sent with his wife to Centaurus X as punishment in Philip K. Dick's "The Minority Report."

Anderton, Lisa John Anderton's wife; earlier his secretary, but now an executive official of Precrime; despite Anderton's suspicions and Fleming's accusation, she is innocent of the plot against Anderton; tries to help Anderton with her ship, and later willingly leaves with Anderton to his exile on Centaurus X in Philip K. Dick's "The Minority Report."

Andieta, Joaquín Chilean lover of the protagonist Eliza Sommers; poor, illegitimate young man with political passion and no real opportunities to improve his social standing; leaves Chile for a new future in California in Isabel Allende's *Daughter of Fortune.*

Andrade Real estate agent in Juan Carlos Onetti's *The Goodbyes.*

André Elder son of the aristocrat M. de Jussat and brother of Charlotte; a physical, strong sort, a direct opposite to the bookish, physically feeble tutor Robert Greslou in Paul Bourget's *The Disciple.*

Andrea Ghost of a Spanish courtier, former lover of Bel-Imperia; the ghost informs the audience of his death in battle and experience in the afterworld, which is disrupted by his joint identity as lover and warrior; sent back accompanied by Revenge to witness Bel-Imperia kill his murderer, Balthazar; empowered by Proserpine, decides the fate of the dead in Thomas Kyd's play *The Spanish Tragedy.*

Andrea Married real estate agent who becomes obsessed with a colorful glass bowl; takes it to all of her open houses, thinking that the cream-tinted bowl is a good luck charm for selling homes; feels a bond, even personal relationship, with the bowl; wants to speak to the object bought for her by her lover some summers before at a crafts fair; finds a new love, even rapture, with the bowl in Ann Beattie's "Janus."

Andrea Polish production secretary with whom Daniel Martin has a two-year affair; she commits suicide several years later in John Fowles's *Daniel Martin.*

Andrea Servant in Count Caloveglia's household in Norman Douglas's *South Wind.*

Andreas Franciscan Superior of the Monastery of Berchtesgaden in Ambrose Bierce's adaptation of *The Monk and the Hangman's Daughter.*

Andreas, Doge Elderly prince who grants Count Rosalvo his niece for ridding Venice of assassins and political conspirators in Matthew Lewis's *The Bravo of Venice.*

Andreeson Federal agent; attempts to find Davy after his escape and in the process earns the disdain of the entire Land family in Lief Enger's *Peace Like a River.*

Andrei Concentration camp worker who, along with the narrator, Tadek, takes food and clothing from the Jews arriving at the camps in Birkenau, a part of Auschwitz, by train; watches as thousands and thousands daily file off to the crematoria; given an extra bowl of soup by Tadek for which Tadek will later receive apples from an orchard in Tadeusz Borowski's *This Way for the Gas, Ladies and Gentlemen.*

Andreich, Leonid Alexandrov Self-effacing Russian professor of engineering blinded by Peter Greene in John Barth's *Giles Goat-Boy.*

Andreiech, Andrei Narrator of the novel; once Nina Bursanov's fiancé, he has enlisted in the Navy and is a friend and frequent guest of the Bursanov family in William Gerhardie's *Futility: A Novel on Russian Themes.*

Andrenyi, Countess Helena (Elena) Beautiful, exotic passenger on the Calais Coach; she is proved to be the daughter of Caroline Martha Hubbard and the aunt of Daisy Armstrong in Agatha Christie's *Murder on the Orient Express.*

Andrenyi, Count Rudolph Hungarian husband of Helena in Agatha Christie's *Murder on the Orient Express.*

Andrés Quintessential Cortazarian protagonist: a man adrift, unsure of his place in the world, yet engaged in constant search to find himself; Argentinean expatriate living in Paris; becomes a member of the Screwery, an unorthodox revolutionary group, through his lover Ludmilla; develops a growing interest in the group's leader Marcos and his protest schemes in Julio Cortázar's *A Manual for Manuel.*

Andrés Member of Pablo's partisan group in Ernest Hemingway's *For Whom the Bell Tolls.*

Andrés Chiliquinga Ecuadorian Indian workman who married the pretty Cunshi against the jealousy of Spanish master Alfonso Pereira and the local priest; sent to build the road that would be used to exploit Ecuador; devastated to find that Alfonso has forced his wife to sleep with him while he was away working in Jorge Icaza's *Huasipungo.*

Andressön, Simon Son of a neighboring landowner at Formo; lives with his sister Sigrid and his illegitimate daughter, Arngjerd; seeks to marry Kristin's youngest sister Ramborg in Sigrid Undset's *Kristin Lavransdatter.*

Andrew Ludovic Lesly's grim and burly yeoman in Sir Walter Scott's *Quentin Durward.*

Andrew Beigh Master's first lover; a self-described untouchable from a Boston Brahmin family who leased a summer home next to the Masters in Bharati Mukherjee's *The Holder of the World.*

Andrew Suitor and spiritual adviser of Mary Pinesett, husband of Doll, elder at Heaven's Gate Church, blacksmith, and carpenter at Blue Brook Plantation in Julia Peterkin's *Scarlet Sister Mary.*

Andrew, Mr. Amiable domestic in the household of Henry Clinton in Henry Brooke's *The Fool of Quality.*

Andrews, Captain Donald Math expert and friend of Captain Nathaniel Hicks; Acting Chief of the Statistical Section in James Gould Cozzens's *Guard of Honor.*

Andrews, Elizabeth Farmer's wife and mother of Pamela Andrews; her religious and moral values inspire her daughter to resist and overcome repeated attempts of seduction and sexual assault; she attends her daughter during childbirth in Samuel Richardson's *Pamela, or Virtue Rewarded.* As "Gammar Andrews" she is mother of Pamela Andrews and Fanny Goodwill; she corroborates the peddler's story that Gypsies switched Joseph Andrews and Fanny while they were infants in Henry Fielding's *The History of the Adventures of Mr. Joseph Andrews and of His Friend Mr. Abraham Adams.*

Andrews, Elizabeth (Polly) Medical technician and first employer of Libby MacAusland; member of the Group in Mary McCarthy's *The Group.*

Andrews, Francis Smuggler on the run from his gang after he has informed on them, having been continually ridiculed for his lack of daring, especially as compared to his father, now deceased; he falls in love with Elizabeth and testifies against the smugglers, but later saves the smugglers' leader, Carlyon, by falsely confessing to the murder of Elizabeth in Graham Greene's *The Man Within.*

Andrews, Gerald Neighbor of Adah Logan and friend of the Mitchells; soldier killed during World War II in Susan Glaspell's *Judd Rankin's Daughter.*

Andrews, Hamish Cambridge student and old boyfriend of Rosamund Stacey; he once attempted to check into a hotel with Rosamund in Margaret Drabble's *The Millstone.*

Andrews, Henrietta Maria Honora Mother of Shamela Andrews; her astute teachings in manipulating men's passions allow her daughter to improve her situation by marrying Squire Booby in Henry Fielding's *An Apology for the Life of Mrs. Shamela Andrews.*

Andrews, John (Goodman, Goody) Farmer and father of Pamela Andrews; his religious and moral values inspire his daughter to resist and overcome repeated attempts of seduction and sexual assault in Samuel Richardson's *Pamela, or Virtue Rewarded.* As "Gaffar Andrews" he is father of Pamela Andrews and Fanny Goodwill; in his youth, he was a sergeant at Gibraltar; he is unaware that while he was overseas, Gypsies switched Fanny, his infant daughter, and Joseph Andrews in Henry Fielding's *The History of the Adventures of Mr. Joseph Andrews and of His Friend Mr. Abraham Adams.*

Andrews, Joseph Virtuous brother of the paragon, Pamela Andrews; as footman to Lady Booby, he refuses her impolite advances out of virtue and loyalty to Fanny Goodwill; as the long-lost son of Mr. Wilson, he can marry Fanny in Henry Fielding's *The History of the Adventures of Mr. Joseph Andrews and of His Friend Mr. Abraham Adams.*

Andrews, Lieutenant Young officer who is attacked by one of his own men after brutally interrogating three black political suspects caught in a military police operation in an African colony experiencing Mau Mau-like activities; he sustains a fractured skull, from which injury he dies in Roy Fuller's *The Father's Comedy.*

Andrews, Miss Isabella Thorpe's off-stage dear friend, frequently mentioned by Isabella for the purpose of showing herself to advantage in Jane Austen's *Northanger Abbey.*

Andrews, Mr. Friend of Henry Fuseli's; a scientist with a haughty and exhausted manner; keeps a skeleton in his closet in Frances Sherwood's *Vindication.*

Andrews, Mr. (Spanking Jack) Friend and schoolmate to Hector Mowbray; he contends with Hugh Trevor for Olivia Mowbray's affection in Thomas Holcroft's *The Adventures of Hugh Trevor.*

Andrews, Pamela (later Pamela B —) Serving maid who, at sixteen, attracts the attentions of her young master and suffers kidnapping and attempted sexual assault before her virtue persuades him to marry her; thereafter she is the virtuous wife who struggles to raise and educate a family of seven, maintain her errant husband's affections, and learn aristocratic behavior without qualifying her own standards; her letters to her parents tell the story in Samuel Richardson's *Pamela, or Virtue Rewarded.* She is Joseph Andrews's supposed sister, whose outstanding virtue sets an example to Joseph and brings about her marriage to rather than ruin by Squire Booby; her influence saves Joseph from Bridewell; she reluctantly accepts Fanny Goodwill as a sibling in Henry Fielding's *The History of the Adventures of Mr. Joseph Andrews and of His Friend Mr. Abraham Adams.*

Andrews, Sara See Towns, Sara Andrews.

Andrews, Shamela Hypocritical heroine, who manipulates Squire Booby into marrying her by feigning maidenhood in Henry Fielding's *An Apology for the Life of Mrs. Shamela Andrews.*

Andrews, Thomas Eldest nephew of Pamela (Andrews) B —; he wishes to live with his grandparents after Pamela's husband provides them with a farm to manage in Samuel Richardson's *Pamela, or Virtue Rewarded.*

Andrews, Thomas T. (Dad) Father of Todd Andrews; commits suicide after the collapse of his personal finances in the stock market crash of 1929; cofounder of the law firm Andrews and Bishop in John Barth's *The Floating Opera.*

Andrews, Todd Fifty-four-year-old lawyer who attempts suicide; narrator and central figure in John Barth's *The Floating Opera.*

Andrews, Walter Man who, seventy years earlier, owned the property and mansion which is the poorhouse in John Updike's *The Poorhouse Fair.*

Andrey One of many ardent and idealistic revolutionary friends of Pavel Vlasov and his mother, Pelagueya; lives in Pelagueya's home until he is arrested by the authorities for protesting the cut in worker wages and then exiled to Siberia in Maxim Gorky's *Mother.*

Andreyev (General) Commander of Soviet 234th Guards Air Assault Regiment; negotiates cease-fire in Iceland when Soviet air support is crippled and the ground situation untenable in Tom Clancy's *Red Storm Rising.*

Andreyevna, Paulina Wife of Ilya Afansyevich Shamrayev; falls in love with Dorn, while she hates her marriage to the uncouth Ilya, who rules her life and whom she cannot escape in Anton Chekhov's play *The Seagull.*

Andreyitch, Vasilya Manager of Babakov's lumber yard; possesses the outward appearance of a landed proprietor; meets the widowed Olinka three months after her husband's death and soon marries her; finds that Olinka's mind becomes dutifully filled with his business and life, as she has no thoughts of her own, in Anton Chekhov's "The Darling."

Andriadis, Milly Often-married society hostess with a cockney accent; said to have been a king's mistress, she is briefly Charles Stringham's in Anthony Powell's *A Buyer's Market.* She is thought to be having an affair with the German Trotskyist Guggenbühl in *The Acceptance World.* Her goings-on are discussed in *Casanova's Chinese Restaurant,* in *The Kindly Ones,* in *The Valley of Bones,* and in *The Military Philosophers.* Her death is mentioned in *Hearing Secret Harmonies.*

Androfski, Andrei Brother of Deborah Bronski, friend of Alexander Brandel and Christopher de Monti, and lover of Gabriela Rak; leads the Warsaw Ghetto Revolt in Leon Uris's *Mila 18.*

Androgyno Hermaphrodite who, along with Nano and Castrone, comes to entertain Volpone; Androgyno's soul is that of Pythagoras, according to the tale Nano tells; part of the group of humorous characters positioned around Volpone and Mosca in Ben Jonson's play *Volpone.*

Andromache Wife of the Trojan military commander Hector; her pregnancy is one of the reasons that Hector desires peace instead of war with the Greeks who have marshaled at the gates of Troy in Jean Giraudoux's *Tiger at the Gates.*

Andros, Nick Deaf-mute chosen to lead The Stand, but who is killed unexpectedly in Stephen King's *The Stand.*

Andrzej Writer of poetry devoid of human problems; sympathizer of the all-powerful state; is shot by the German state in Tadeusz Borowski's *This Way for the Gas, Ladies and Gentlemen.*

Andy Freedman who tells Comfort Servosse about the local chapter of the Union League; caretaker at Warrington Place who tends to the dying Servosse in Albion W. Tourgee's *A Fool's Errand.*

Anerton, Mary Muse of the acclaimed poet Vincent Rendle; the Silvia of the immortal verse; falls in love with the poet even though she is married; later as a widow, she still is denied his love, as she sadly discovers that he has never loved her physically but saw her as a muse; theirs has been an intellectual union rather than an emotional or physical joining; later falls in love with the much younger Danyers, the story's protagonist, who seeks her out because of Rendle's poetry but realizes that too much age separates them in Edith Wharton's "The Muse's Tragedy."

Anerton, Mr. Husband of the beautiful Mary, the muse of Vincent Rendle's verse; infatuated by the poet, as his wife is, in Edith Wharton's "The Muse's Tragedy."

Anfisa Foma's aunt who helps to raise the motherless boy in Maxim Gorky's *Foma Gordyeeff.*

Ange, Miss Drag queen in New Orleans who dresses as Scarlett O'Hara, Desdemona, and Drusilla Duncan in John Rechy's *City of Night.*

Angel Chief of a British broadcasting group that comes to interview Gilbert Pinfold at his home; he is later identified by Pinfold as the leader of the hallucinatory voices in Evelyn Waugh's *The Ordeal of Gilbert Pinfold.*

Angel Seraphic ghost and feathered figure about 20 years old with shoulder-length hair and friendly eyes; member of the last of the Nine Choirs and constantly sent on divine missions; plays a guitar; regular celestial visitor witnessed by the elderly Sophie and her black cat in the old woman's home; brings Sophie a unicorn to play with; becomes romantically involved with the elderly virgin in Dora Alonso's "Sophie and the Angel."

Angel Decrepit old man wearing rags and batlike wings who descends upon the home of Pelayo, Elisenda, and their sick infant; locked up in a chicken coop and, like a circus animal, puts on display for paying gawkers; no one in the town seems to believe that this tried and emaciated figure with wings could be an angel because he does not match the iconic images of the church in Gabriel Garciá Marquez's "A Very Old Man with Enormous Wings."

Angel, Miguel Cara de (Angel Face) President's decision to eliminate these men ushers in the main character of the novel, Miguel Cara de Angel (Angel Face), a young man described as the president's favorite rogue, in that he blindly follows the dictator's orders to lead certain people such as General Canales to their death; later incurs the wrath of the dictator by marrying Camila, the daughter of the president's enemy, General Canales; arrested in a trap for conspiring against the government by no other than Major Farfan, the man he had earlier saved from the president's death sentence; dies in prison in Miguel Angel Asturias's *The President.*

Angel, Stella Bast (Engels) Cousin of Edward Bast; schemes to gain control of her family's General Roll Corporation in William Gaddis's *JR.*

Angela Blonde, beautiful, virtuous Catholic; she marries Dennis after a long engagement and has several children, one of whom has Down syndrome and another of whom is killed by a van; she first breaks with and then forgives Dennis after he has an affair in David Lodge's *How Far Can You Go?*

Angela (d'Arivée) Friend of Ethan and Jacqueline Llewelyn; she recommends that they consider settling on Gabriola Island in Malcolm Lowry's *October Ferry to Gabriola.*

Angela Relative of the Lovatts who is married and has three children in Doris Lessing's *The Fifth Child.*

Angelica Beautiful but unrefined daughter of a rich peasant in southern Italy; marries Tancredi, a nephew of Don Fabrizio Corbera and the prince of Salina, in Giuseppe Tomasi di Lampedusa's *The Leopard.*

Angelica Foresight's niece and Valentine's beloved; independently wealthy, quick witted, and self-possessed; loves Valentine but feigns indifference; sees through Valentine's pretended madness; tests Valentine's devotion by pretending an engagement with his father, Sir Sampson; ultimately chooses Valentine and protects his inheritance by destroying the signed bond in William Congreve's play *Love for Love.*

Angelica, Sister Nun who is Father Trask's apprentice; helps lead the wake for Chalmers Egstrom in William Goyen's *In a Farther Country.*

Angelique Titled pupil at Mme. Beck's boarding school in Charlotte Brontë's *Villette.*

Angélique Discarded mistress of Count Armand de Sacy; courtesan living in forced exile at Bréda in Arna Wendell Bontemps's *Drums at Dusk.*

Angelina Flirtatious 15-year-old beauty who serves as the Duchess's handmaiden in Norman Douglas's *South Wind.*

Angelo As his servant is involved in Marinelli's plan to kill Count Appiani, Angelo is the one who collects information for the plot from Pirro, Galotti's servant, in Gotthold Ephraim Lessing's *Emilia Galotti.*

Angelo Cornelia de Vereza's lover who, denied her hand, joins the army and is believed to be killed; later he becomes a priest in order to be near Cornelia; he witnesses her death in the Saint Augustin monastery in Ann Radcliffe's *A Sicilian Romance.*

Angelo, Dr. Handsome middle-aged Italian physician at the Diamond County Home for the Aged; treats George Lucas's chronic ear infection in John Updike's *The Poorhouse Fair.*

Angelo, Lord Villain of the play; tyrant who rules without mercy; forces difficult dilemmas upon the virtuous Isabella and other characters in William Shakespeare's play *Measure for Measure.*

Angelo, Max Sculptor; sometime lover of Salley Gardens in Susan Cheever's *Looking for Work.*

Angel of Death See Sallow, John.

Angharad Daughter of Seithenyn; she marries Prince Elphin and is the object of Rhûn's lustful pursuit, easily foiled by Taliesin in Thomas Love Peacock's *The Misfortunes of Elphin.*

Angie (Ange) Married woman who claims she is pregnant by her lover, Billy Phelan, in order to test Phelan's love for her in William Kennedy's *Billy Phelan's Greatest Game.*

Angstom, Bertie English teacher of Carter Fisher; complains about his work in Sandra Scofield's *Beyond Deserving.*

Angstrom, Earl Husband of Mary Angstrom and father of Rabbit and Miriam Angstrom; works as a printer in John Updike's *Rabbit, Run* and *Rabbit Redux.*

Angstrom, Harry "Rabbit" Protagonist of John Updike's Rabbit tetralogy about middle-class suburban life from the 1950s through the 1980s, introduced in *Rabbit, Run.* In *Rabbit Is Rich* he is forty-six years old, the successful owner of an automobile dealership in Brewer, Pennsylvania, and caught up in the rampant consumerism of the late 1970s. He reunites with his wife, Janice, from whom he was separated in *Rabbit Redux,* and still as sexually charged as when he was young but increasingly aware of his aging body and his lost youth. Father of Nelson; the birth of his granddaughter drives home Harry's realization that he is now another generation closer to death—which he must confront in *Rabbit at Rest.*

Angstrom, Janice (Jan) Springer Wife of Harry "Rabbit" Angstrom in John Updike's Rabbit tetralogy; first introduced in *Rabbit, Run* as the frustrated housewife who turns to drink and accidentally drowns her infant daughter. In *Rabbit Redux,* has an affair with Charlie Stavros. Reunited with her husband in *Rabbit Is Rich,* she receives an inheritance that makes possible Harry's ability to own the auto dealership; mother of Nelson and grandmother of granddaughter born at end of the novel. Also appears in *Rabbit at Rest.*

Angstrom, Judy Daughter of Nelson and Pru Angstrom, sister of Roy, and granddaughter of Harry "Rabbit" and Janice Angstrom; born at the end of the third novel in John Updike's Rabbit tetralogy, *Rabbit Is Rich;* saved from drowning by her grandfather in *Rabbit at Rest.*

Angstrom, Mary Wife of Earl Angstrom and mother of Rabbit and Miriam Angstrom in John Updike's *Rabbit, Run;* suffers from Parkinson's disease in *Rabbit Redux.*

Angstrom, Miriam (Mim) Younger sister of Rabbit Angstrom in John Updike's *Rabbit, Run* and *Rabbit Redux.*

Angstrom, Nelson Son of Harry "Rabbit" and Janice Angstrom; first introduced as a young child in the first novel in John Updike's Rabbit tetralogy, *Rabbit, Run;* in later novels, husband of Pru and father of Judy and Roy. In *Rabbit at Rest,* he runs and ruins his parents' Pennsylvania auto dealership by embezzling assets to finance his cocaine habit; caught between bitter resentment of and love for his dying father.

Angstrom, Rebecca June Infant daughter of Janice and Rabbit Angstrom; drowns in a bathtub in John Updike's *Rabbit, Run.*

Angstrom, Teresa "Pru" Lubell Wife of Nelson Angstrom; first introduced in *Rabbit Is Rich,* the third novel in John Updike's Rabbit tetralogy; mother of Judy and Roy; attempts to maintain order and stability as her husband's life is falling apart; has a sexual encounter with her father-in-law in *Rabbit at Rest.*

Angustias Only daughter of Bernarda's first marriage and the only one with an inheritance; middle-aged and unattractive, she is betrothed to Pepe el Romano, who is marrying her for her money; her hopes are dashed by the scandal occasioned by Pepe's desire for Adela in Federico García Lorca's play *The House of Bernarda Alba.*

Aniko Sister-in-law of Grusha and married to Lavrenti, on whose farm she has gone to raise the foundling child; her milk money enables Grusha to marry the dying peasant to escape from the community's questions about the child's origins and its father in Bertolt Brecht's play *The Caucasian Chalk-Circle.*

Anisya Daughter of the aging sledge driver Iona Potapov, who is grieving over the sudden death of his son in Anton Chekhov's "Misery."

Anita Father Rentería's niece who is raped by Miguel Páramo; also called Ana in Juan Rulfo's *Pedro Páramo.*

Anitra Dancing girl the Norwegian protagonist Peer Gynt meets in a faraway desert during his journey to distant continents; steals Gynt's money that he has accumulated from his sinful business transactions in Henrik Ibsen's *Peer Gynt.*

Anjou, Duke of French suitor of Queen Elizabeth, who is flattered by his attention in Sophia Lee's *The Recess.*

Ann Eldest daughter of a poor widow; her chronic melancholy attracts her rich, slightly younger neighbor, Mary, to her aid as caretaker and benefactor; after a period of lingering illness Ann's sudden death at their Lisbon retreat casts Mary into despair in Mary Wollstonecraft's *Mary, A Fiction.*

Ann One of three girls from California who, although strangers to Peterson, invade his New York loft in search of a place to spend a few days in Donald Barthelme's "A Shower of Gold."

Ann Traveling companion and supporter of Francis Starwick in Thomas Wolfe's *Of Time and the River.*

Ann Wife who displays incredulity when she learns that her husband would not have married her were she racially different from him, an awareness that leads to an apparently irreparable split in their marriage in Tobias Wolff"s "Say Yes."

Ann, Miss (Our Lady of the Limitless Bladder) Client of C. Card and an accomplished beer drinker; kills the prostitute whose body she hires Card to steal from the morgue in Richard Brautigan's *Dreaming of Babylon.*

Anna Enigmatic and wealthy American who owns the yacht *Gibraltar;* relates to the narrator that her purpose in life is to sail about the world in search of a former lover, a sailor from Gibraltar, who scorned her; sails toward Africa, where she and the narrator will hunt; finds her search fruitless, a patchwork of legend and fantasy; returns from Africa and finds the yacht destroyed by fire in Marguerite Duras's *The Sailor from Gibraltar.*

Anna Girlfriend of the painter and anarchist de Greef; in Georges Simenon's *My Friend Maigret.*

Anna Marriageable daughter of Anton and Maria Dobchinsky; attracted, as is her mother, to the imposter inspector general Ivan; believes that he will marry her and take her to St. Petersburg in high fashion in Nikolai Gogol's "The Inspector General."

Anna Niece of the dying spinster and Irish lady Margaret O'Brien; convinces her dying aunt to tell her her girlhood stories filled with visions of leprechauns, fairies, schoolteachers, and playmates so that Anna can keep them alive to tell her own children in Mary Lerner's "Little Selves."

Anna Wife of Kleshtch, the blacksmith; lingers on the edge of death from consumption; one of the many poor boarders in the lodging owned by the ill-tempered landlord Kostilyoff in Maxim Gorky's play *The Lower Depths.*

Anna Servant in the Hanover school run by Fraulein Pfaff; she is dismissed under a cloud and in a violent scene in Dorothy Richardson's *Pointed Roofs.*

Anna Niece of the Butcher (Giorgio) and lover of and co-terrorist with Robert Leaver in Muriel Spark's *Territorial Rights.*

Anna Traumatized victim of sexual assault who may be the saving love of Lancelot Lamar's new world in Walker Percy's *Lancelot.*

Anna (The Carline) Older woman who cares for Elfhild and whose magical powers save them from danger while they seek for Osberne Wulfsson in William Morris's *The Sundering Flood.*

Anna Annesley Genteel sister-in-law of John Osborne; cares for Mildred and Helen Osborne following their mother's death in Paul Laurence Dunbar's *The Love of Landry.*

Annabel Girlfriend of Carter Fisher; opens a pizza parlor with him; an heiress in Sandra Scofield's *Beyond Deserving.*

Annable, Lady Crystabel Earl's niece once sexually infatuated with the curate Frank Annable; her humiliating indifference after three years of marriage has driven him to flight in D. H. Lawrence's *The White Peacock.*

Annable, Frank Educated ex-parson, now a gamekeeper; he is an embittered misogynist hated by the countryfolk; his "death by misadventure" may be an act of revenge in D. H. Lawrence's *The White Peacock.*

Annable, Poll Frank Annable's second wife and widow, a slatternly but devoted countrywoman and mother of several small children in D. H. Lawrence's *The White Peacock.*

Annable, Sam One of the many young children of the gamekeeper's union to an uneducated countrywoman; after his discovery of his father's body he becomes recklessly delinquent until befriended by Emily Saxton in D. H. Lawrence's *The White Peacock.*

Annaise Young woman with whom the protagonist, Manuel Joseph, falls in love; member of a rival family with a blood feud with Manuel's family; becomes pregnant with his child out of wedlock in Jacques Roumain's *Masters of the Dew.*

Annaly, Florence Lady Annaly's charming daughter, who wins Harry Ormond's heart; after various misunderstandings and adventures Ormond wins her hand in Maria Edgeworth's *Ormond.*

Annaly, Lady Distant relative of Sir Ulick O'Shane's first wife; O'Shane wishes to regain her goodwill; dignified, intelligent, and highly regarded by the public, she sees promise of good character in O'Shane's ward, Harry Ormond, and is proved correct in Maria Edgeworth's *Ormond.*

Annaly, Sir Herbert Honorable but sickly son of Lady Annaly; he befriends Harry Ormond and is an example to him of how a just man can improve the lives of others in Maria Edgeworth's *Ormond.*

Annaple Hobbie (Halbert) Elliot's faithful old nurse in Sir Walter Scott's *The Black Dwarf.*

Annatoo Wife of Samoa; lost at sea in Herman Melville's *Mardi.*

Ann August Daughter of Adele Diamond and Hishan; moves from Bay City, Wisconsin, to Los Angeles at age twelve with her mother; likes to be alone, but rarely is apart from her mother, with whom she fights violently; goes to college in the East, and afterward, rarely visits her mother in Mona Simpson's *Anywhere but Here.*

Anne Married with children; sister of Laird, a young man who has returned to his parents and the home he grew up in to die from AIDs in Alice Elliott Dark's "In the Gloaming."

Anne Woman who is seduced and then abandoned; she educates herself and becomes a famous actress; she is depicted as honorable in Caroline Norton's *The Wife and Woman's Reward.*

Anne Sister of Katie, daughter of Grace and Neil, niece of Dan and Libby, Elinor, May, and Rachel, cousin of Jennie, Celia, Rossie, and Valerie; forever excited or ashamed; develops earlier than her cousins in Joan Chase's *During the Reign of the Queen of Persia.*

Anne The more frankly sexual and less talented of the two girls who live with Henry Breasley, who has nicknamed her "the Freak" in John Fowles's *The Ebony Tower.*

Anne, Princess, Lady of Beaujeau Louis XI's lovely and cherished eldest daughter in Sir Walter Scott's *Quentin Durward.*

Anne, Queen Wife of King James; she scorns her husband and neglects Prince Henry in Sophia Lee's *The Recess.*

Anne, Sister Sister of the young woman who agrees to marry the ugly Blue Beard, a man marked by his blue beard; keeps a lookout for the approach of their brothers, who are coming to save the sister from Blue Beard's deadly sword in Charles Perrault's "Blue Beard."

Annelies Beautiful Indo-European woman whom the protagonist Minke falls in love; daughter of a Javanese concubine and a Dutch factory owner; when her father dies, she becomes the legal property of her Dutch relatives and is taken to the Netherlands, her Islamic marriage having no standing in Pramoedya Ananta Toer's *This Earth of Mankind.*

Anne Marie Young peasant girl friend of Orlando King while he lives with Professor King on the remote French island in Isabel Colegate's *Orlando King.*

Annie Daughter/serving girl in the Collopy household who may be leading a double life in Flann O'Brien's *The Hard Life.*

Annie, Aunt Ferdinand Clegg's aunt, whose stifling moral attitudes have helped to mold him into the repressed deviant he has become in John Fowles's *The Collector.*

Ann-Jules, Count Dark-featured young courtier of Pisuerga and brother of Blanche de Lambese; Olga Blumenghast pines in vain for him in Ronald Firbank's *The Flower Beneath the Foot.*

Anne-Marie Nurse of the three children of Nora and Torvald Helmer in Henrik Ibsen's play *A Doll's House.*

Anne-Marie Student who serves on the Cinema Committee with Hill Gallagher during the student rebellion in James Jones's *The Merry Month of May.*

Annesley, Charles Frivolous but amiable noble dandy; he is a friend of the young Duke of St. James in Benjamin Disraeli's *The Young Duke.*

Annesley, Harriet Gentle daughter of Richard and Harriet Wilkins Annesly; raped by Sir Thomas Sindall, she dies shortly after giving birth to their illegitimate daughter in Henry Mackenzie's *The Man of the World.*

Annesley, Harriet Wilkins Plain but saintly wife of Richard Annesly; she dies giving birth to their third child in Henry Mackenzie's *The Man of the World.*

Annesley, Harry Guileless heir of his uncle Peter Prosper of Burton Hall; innocently caught up in the Scarborough plots concerning property and entail, he begins to lose Prosper's confidence as future squire of Burton; Augustus Scarborough tries to steal his love, Florence Mountjoy, and her mother is set against him; he is restored to favor and marries Florence in Anthony Trollope's *Mr. Scarborough's Family.*

Annesley, Mary Youngest daughter of the Rector of Burton and sister of Harry; she is wooed and won by Joe Thoroughbung, the brewer, in Anthony Trollope's *Mr. Scarborough's Family.*

Annesley, Mr. Cheerful incumbent of a Hertfordshire parish and father of Harry; his brother-in-law, Peter Prosper, chides him with Harry's failings in Anthony Trollope's *Mr. Scarborough's Family.*

Annesley, Mrs. Georgiana Darcy's companion in Jane Austen's *Pride and Prejudice.*

Annesley, Mrs. Peter Prosper's sister and Harry Annesley's mother, a sensible, good-humored woman in Anthony Trollope's *Mr. Scarborough's Family.*

Annesley, Richard Parson who eschews his father's wealth, retires to the country, and dies of a broken heart when his daughter is debauched in Henry Mackenzie's *The Man of the World.*

Annesley, William (Billy) Impetuous, passionate son of Richard; led astray by Sir Thomas Sindall, he falls into fornication, theft, gambling, and eventually criminal transportation in Henry Mackenzie's *The Man of the World.*

Annette Beautiful lover of Alphones; her betrayal and Alphones's killing of her lover in a jealous rage are the subjects of much hilarity in H. Rider Haggard's *Allan Quatermain.*

Annette Madame Montoni's talkative, superstitious maid, who becomes Emily St. Aubert's companion and informant during her captivity in the Castle di Udolpho; she falls in love with Ludovico, the servant who effects Emily's escape; she ultimately marries Ludovico and becomes housekeeper of the St. Aubert estate in Ann Radcliffe's *The Mysteries of Udolpho.*

Annette Discarded mistress of Count Armand de Sacy; courtesan living in forced exile at Bréda in Arna Wendell Bontemps's *Drums at Dusk.*

Annette See Blagovo, Anna Ivanovna.

Annie Wife of the unnamed first-person narrator; in poor health; plans to move with husband from the cold northern Ohio to the warmer climate of North Carolina, where they will harvest grapes on a plantation in Charles Waddell Chesnutt's "The Goophered Grapevine."

Annie Young girl who helps Almeda Joynt Roth with house cleaning in Alice Munro's "Meneseteung."

Annie Anna and Vronsky's little daughter born to an illicit affair; legally christened Karenina; entrusted with Karenin, Anna's husband, after Anna's death and when Vronsky leaves for the Serbian war in Leo Tolstoy's *Anna Karenina.*

Annie Maid of the Wollstonecraft household; sexually abuses Mary in Frances Sherwood's *Vindication.*

Annixter Wheat rancher in the San Joaquin Valley who attempts to influence the state's railroad commission and fails; shot by a railroad agent in Frank Norris's *The Octopus.*

Ann's Husband Man given to the belief that interracial marriages spell trouble; finds himself utterly estranged from his wife when he expresses this view to her in Tobias Wolff's "Say Yes."

Annushka Anna Karenina's maid in Leo Tolstoy's *Anna Karenina.*

Anny Old workhouse woman who helps nurse Old Sally in Charles Dickens's *Oliver Twist.*

Anny Roquentin's former lover whom he has not seen for five years, yet whom he still loves; sends Roquentin a letter asking him to meet her in Paris; has always tried to organize her life around theatrically contrived "perfect moments" and "privileged situations," but when Roquentin meets her, she tells him that she has become disillusioned and, like him, has accepted the random amorphousness of lived experience; cuts her rendezvous with Roquentin short to keep an engagement with one of her many other lovers in Jean-Paul Sartre's *Nausea.*

Anodos Twenty-one-year-old protagonist who, on his birthday, is sent on an eastward journey in Fairyland by his "faerie" grandmother; he is seduced by the Maid of the Alder; Pygmalion-like, he sings the marble lady to life and falls in love with her; he acquires a Shadow, fights the giants with his "brothers," suffers from pride, and loses the Shadow when he learns the true nature of love in George MacDonald's *Phantastes.*

Anonymous Narrator/Killer Man who states that he is sane, although he suffers from a disease which causes an "over-acuteness of the senses"; lives in the home of an old man, one who has a clouded "vulture-like" eye; the narrator becomes so distressed by the man's eye that he plots to murder him; hides the old man's body under the room's wooden flooring; later when the police arrive, the narrator believes he hears the old man's heart beating louder and louder, forcing his spontaneous confession of the crime in Edgar Allan Poe's "The Tell-Tale Heart."

Anonymous Prisoner Horrified victim of the Inquisition, he is sentenced to death and then imprisoned for days in a dark dungeon full of voracious rats and instruments of torture, such as a huge pendulum whose sweeping scimitar is designed to mortally wound him in the chest; he is ultimately rescued by the French army in Edgar Allan Poe's "The Pit and the Pendulum."

Anquetil, Leonard Traveler and explorer invited into the Chevron circle; he becomes the confidant of both Viola and Sebastian, encouraging both to break free of the demands of Chevron and live a wider life; he becomes engaged to Viola in Vita Sackville-West's *The Edwardians.* He and his wife, Viola, visit Miles Vane-Merrick in Kent in *Family History.*

Anquetil, Lesley Daughter of Viola and Leonard Anquetil; she comes with her family to visit Miles Vane-Merrick in Kent; calm and self-contained at eighteen, she is a detached critic of society; Miles is attracted to her and confides in her after the end of his affair with Evelyn Jarrold in Vita Sackville-West's *Family History.*

Anquetil, Paul Son of Viola and Leonard Anquetil; Paul, who is Dan Jarrold's age, comes with his parents to visit Miles Vane-Merrick in Kent in Vita Sackville-West's *Family History.*

Anquetil, Viola See Viola.

Ansaldo, Father (Sacchi) Former suitor to Olivia di Bruno who, upon her rape by and marriage to Ferando di Bruno, becomes a priest; he is the confessor to whom Ferando admits his murder of his brother; later his testimony at Ferando's trial before the Inquisition results in a verdict of death in Ann Radcliffe's *The Italian.*

Ansel, Billy Vietnam veteran who owns the town gas station; widower and father of nine-year-old twins who die in the bus wreck; has an affair with Risa Walker; refuses to join in the lawsuit Mitchell Stephens has filed against the city and the state; becomes an alcoholic in Russell Banks's *The Sweet Hereafter.*

Ansell, Maud Stewart Ansell's kind, helpful sister in E. M. Forster's *The Longest Journey.*

Ansell, Stella Balding lesbian painter who mistakes Daniel Boleyn for a model and forces him to strip and pose; she is a typical illustration of Pierpoint's "Apes of God" theory in Wyndham Lewis's *The Apes of God.*

Ansell, Stewart Rickie Elliott's scholarly Cambridge friend in E. M. Forster's *The Longest Journey.*

Anselm (Arthur, Saint Anselm) Religious poet and bitter friend of Stanley in William Gaddis's *The Recognitions.*

Anselm, Father Sacristan of Salisbury Cathedral and an old friend of Dean Jocelin, although their "rope of friendship has grown thin" in William Golding's *The Spire.*

Anselmo Old man who is Robert Jordan's guide in Ernest Hemingway's *For Whom the Bell Tolls.*

Anselmo Father of the brothel owner Chunga; musician and founder of the first brothel, "The Green House," in Piura city; plays music at local bars and in the streets after the brothel is burned down by members of the higher society of Piura in Mario Vargas Llosa's *The Green House.*

Ansit Wife of Bardia, Captain of the Royal Guard in the land of Glome; she confronts Orual after Bardia's death and castigates Orual for her possessiveness of Bardia; her criticism contributes to Orual's self-knowledge in C. S. Lewis's *Till We Have Faces.*

Ansley, Babs Spirited and dynamic daughter of Grace and Horace Ansley, but whose biological father is Delphi Slade; an American who, while touring Rome, is courted by Campolieri, one of the best eligible bachelors in Rome in Edith Wharton's "Roman Fever."

Ansley, Grace Aging widow and mother of the young and pretty Barbara (Babs); sits and talks with her lifelong friend Alida Slade, also widowed, at a restaurant in Rome; learns that Alida was the secret writer of a long-ago letter that ironically brought Grace and Delphin Slade (future husband of Alida) together one romantic night in the Colosseum, where Babs was conceived, in Edith Wharton's "Roman Fever."

Ansley, Horace Deceased husband of Grace; not the biological father of his daughter Babs in Edith Wharton's "Roman Fever."

Anson, Karen Assistant to Mark Hall in Project Wildfire in Michael Crichton's *The Andromeda Strain.*

Anson, Orestes Paulina Anson's grandfather, who was once considered a literary genius and celebrity, but whose name has become obscure with the passage of time; his granddaughter Paulina attempts to keep his legacy alive by spending her whole life working on a book about him in Edith Wharton's *The Angel at the Grave.*

Anson, Paulina Granddaughter of Orestes Anson, Paulina dedicates her whole adult life to keeping her grandfather's literary name alive; lives alone in the Anson house, having rejected a marriage proposal by Hewlett Winsloe, and spends years working on her grandfather's biography, which no publisher wants, in Edith Wharton's *The Angel at the Grave.*

Anstey, Wilfred Mystically inclined, charismatic, but ultimately shallow warden of Toynton Grange, a private nursing home; he believes himself to have been miraculously cured of multiple sclerosis at Lourdes, although in fact he was misdiagnosed in P. D. James's *The Black Tower.*

Antek Young man in the country around the village of Lipce in central Poland; jealous of his father's new marriage to his lover Jagusia (Jagne) and infuriated that his inheritance is slipping away to the new wife; later kills a man in defending his father and goes to prison in Władysław Stanisław Reymont's *The Peasants.*

Antelminelli, Castruccio Castracani dei Impressively handsome, ambitious, abstemious Italian nobleman, who becomes leader of the Ghibelline party in Lucca, proconsul of Lucca, Lord of Lucca, and Imperial Vicar of Tuscany; high principled at first and naturally ingenuous, he subordinates love to ambition and becomes corrupted by power: a cruel, solitary tyrant in Mary Shelley's *Valperga.*

Antelminelli, Ruggieri dei Ghibeline of Lucca and father of Castruccio; with his family, he is exiled from Lucca by the Guelph party in Mary Shelley's *Valperga.*

Anterrabae Forceful god in Yr, the mental world of Deborah Blau in Hannah Green's *I Never Promised You a Rose Garden.*

Antheil Regulatory agent who forces John Converse to locate Marge Converse, who he believes has the smuggled heroin in Robert Stone's *Dog Soldiers.*

Anthis, Mel Art gallery administrator and secretly a writer; marries Jody; cares for and raises her son as she pursues her career in Ann Beattie's *Picturing Will.*

Anthony Adela Quested's rude servant, who tries to blackmail her in E. M. Forster's *A Passage to India.*

Anthony Coarse English archer in Sir Walter Scott's *Castle Dangerous.*

Anthony Dupe of Cleopatra's cunning wiles; he is forgiven by his saintly wife, Octavia; he commits suicide after hearing the false report of Cleopatra's death that she has sent out to test her power over him in Sarah Fielding's *The Lives of Cleopatra and Octavia.*

Anthony Hospital orderly whom Willie Hall tries to indoctrinate politically in John Edgar Wideman's *The Lynchers.*

Anthony, Alfred (Alfy) Bestwood child who steals a "cobbler" from young William Morel; his mother complains to the Morels that William has retaliated by tearing her son's collar in D. H. Lawrence's *Sons and Lovers.*

Anthony, Campbell Young poet in whom Annabel Paynton is mildly interested; he is editing a volume of love poetry entitled "Doting" in Henry Green's *Doting.*

Anthony, Father Priest and friend of Father Benedict; he aids in the escape of Madam de Beaumont; later he meets Count de Beaumont in Muscovy but is killed by robbers before he can inform him his wife lives in Penelope Aubin's *The Life of Madam de Beaumont.*

Anthony, Father Priest who takes a disliking to Tarry Flynn and urges him to confession, where he recommends that Tarry stop reading Shaw in Patrick Kavanagh's *Tarry Flynn.*

Anthony, Flora de Barral Daughter of the banker de Barral; rescued from suicidal despondency, she marries Captain Roderick Anthony, whom her father attempts unsuccessfully to poison, but loses him in a storm in Joseph Conrad's *Chance: A Tale in Two Parts.*

Anthony, Mrs. Bestwood neighbor of the Morels; she makes money by seaming stockings; after William Morel tears her son Alfy's collar, she complains, triggering a domestic quarrel between Mr. and Mrs. Morel in D. H. Lawrence's *Sons and Lovers.*

Anthony, Mrs. Cook and housekeeper for Godfrey and Charmian Colston in Muriel Spark's *Memento Mori.*

Anthony, Peggy Student at Haddan School who refuses all solid food, supplementing her milk diet with candy bars hidden in a suitcase under her bed in Alice Hoffman's *The River King.*

Anthony, Roderick Ship's captain who rescues Flora de Barral from suicide, marries her, and escapes poisoning by her jealous father, but dies in a shipwreck in Joseph Conrad's *Chance: A Tale in Two Parts.*

Anticant, Dr. Pessimist (caricature of Thomas Carlyle) Disputatious pamphleteer; his journal, *Modern Charity,* attacks Mr. Harding in Anthony Trollope's *The Warden.*

Antigone Daughter of Oedipus and Jocasta and sister to Ismene, Polynices, and Eteocles; defies Creon's law to symbolically bury Polynices; justifies her actions with divine law and family loyalty; buried alive in a cave for her treason and unwavering defiance; remains unrepentant despite sorrow over her sacrifice; hangs herself in Sophocles' play *Antigone.*

Antigone Oedipus's daughter, traveling companion, and caretaker; seized by Creon's men to force Oedipus to return to Thebes, but is saved by Theseus; after her father's death she returns to Thebes to try to prevent her brothers from killing each other in Sophocles' play *Oedipus at Colonus.*

Antigone Young daughter of Oedipus and Jocasta and sister of Oedipus; allowed to say goodbye to her self-mutilated blind father before his exile; condemned to a bitter future without marriage or family because of Oedipus's disgrace and the family curse in Sophocles' play *Oedipus the King.*

Antigonus Sicilian lord; strongly defends Hermione against Leontes' claims of infidelity; charged with carrying Leontes and Hermione's newborn daughter into the wilderness to be left to die; leaves Perdita in the woods near the Bohemian coast, surrounded by gold and jewels; attacked and killed by a bear as he leaves in William Shakespeare's play *The Winter's Tale.*

Antime Befriended by the central character, Stefan; scholar of the works of Partenie; introduces Stefan to an Iron Guardist in Mircea Eliade's *The Forbidden Forest.*

Antiochus King of Antioch who engages in an incestuous affair with his daughter; to keep her for himself, he demands that her suitors solve a riddle or die; all of them fail to solve the riddle, which is about incest, except for Pericles, who, however, refuses to openly declare its meaning; sends Thaliart, a lord, after the escaped Pericles to kill him; burned by a fire from heaven in William Shakespeare's play *Pericles.*

Antiochus's Daughter Beautiful, young daughter of King Antiochus, who, after her mother's death, begins an incestuous affair with her; courted by many suitors whom her father attempts to deflect by forcing them to either solve a riddle about their incestuous affair, or die; all except Pericles fail, but Pericles disavows his claims to the princess because of the incest; burned by a heavenly fire in William Shakespeare's play *Pericles.*

Antipov, Pavel Pavlovich (or Strelnikov) Son of a railway worker who marries Lara; the two move to the Urals to teach school; joins the army but is captured; presumed dead but later returns, using the alias Strelnikov, in Boris Pasternak's *Doctor Zhivago.*

Antiquarian Vain man who has such a desire to collect ancient artifacts that he is easily tricked in Charles Johnstone's *Chrysal: or, The Adventures of a Guinea.*

Antoine, Mr. Fair-haired dancing partner, colleague to the late Paul Alexis Goldschmidt; he consoles Flora Weldon with courtship in Dorothy L. Sayers's *Have His Carcase.*

Antoinette Shallow art student, who introduces Miranda Grey to George Paston and sleeps with Paston in John Fowles's *The Collector.*

Antolini, Mr. Former English teacher of Holden Caulfield at Elkton Hills and a refuge for Holden in New York City; gives Holden a pat on the head, a drunkenly intimate gesture that frightens Holden away, in J. D. Salinger's *The Catcher in the Rye.*

Anton Supervisor of the narrator in a government post at St. Petersburg in the mid-19th century; visited at his home by the spiteful and morbid narrator, but only in the narrator's dream state in Fyodor Dostoevski's *Notes from the Underground.*

Anton (the Quail) Son of Makar and lover of his sister, Ewka, in Jerzy Kosinski's *The Painted Bird.*

Antonapoulos, Spiros Moronic deaf-mute idealized by John Singer; dies of nephritis in an insane asylum in Carson McCullers's *The Heart Is a Lonely Hunter.*

Antone Middle-aged Portuguese sailor flogged for fighting aboard the *Neversink* in Herman Melville's *White-Jacket.*

Antonet Sylvia's maid, who assists and advises her in her amours; she allows Brilliard, whom she loves, to read letters between Octavio and Sylvia; when Brilliard disguises himself as Octavio in order to go to bed with Sylvia, Antonet dupes him by dressing as Sylvia in Aphra Behn's *Love Letters Between a Nobleman and His Sister.*

Antonia Vulnerable virgin who is pious, innocent, and naïve; her goodness blinds her to the world's wickedness; her virginal appearance attracts Ambrosio's attention, and thus he rapes and murders her; finally disclosed that she is his sister in Matthew Gregory Lewis's *The Monk.*

Antonia Irishwoman long in love with her cousin Guy; she inherited not only his estate, Montefort, when he died in France but also responsibility for his fiancée in Elizabeth Bowen's *A World of Love.*

Antonio Perverted philosophical historian; he tries to create his own culture with cruelty and hypocrisy in Rex Warner's *The Wild Goose Chase: An Allegory.*

Antonio Bassanio's friend and a rich Christian merchant; scornful of the Jews, whom he often mistreats, he is nonetheless meek, generous, and beloved of his friends, though inexplicably melancholic; his friendship with Bassanio is so deep that he risks his life for him as he borrows money from Shylock, granting his flesh as security in Shakespeare's play *The Merchant of Venice.*

Antonio Italian nobleman who becomes the evil duke's successor; angered that his wife was raped by one of the sons of the duchess, driving his wife to suicide; succeeds to the throne of the principality after the death of the duke and his son Lussurioso at the hand of Vendice, the revenger; reluctantly orders Vendice to die for his murderous revenge in Cyril Tourner's play *The Revenger's Tragedy.*

Antonio Leonato's brother, who suggests to Leonato that he fake Hero's death in order to discover the truth about Claudio's intentions in William Shakespeare's play *Much Ado About Nothing.*

Antonio Olivia's father, a rich merchant who has business with the English, is arrested by the Inquisition as a spy, and is freed by English sailors in Charles Johnstone's *Chrysal: or, The Adventures of a Guinea.*

Antonio Rescues Sebastian, twin brother to Viola, after his shipwreck and accompanies the young man to Illyria, where he further assists the castaway in William Shakespeare's play *Twelfth Night.*

Antonio Suzanne's uncle and father of Fanchette; the count's castle gardener; screams that he has seen a half-dressed man jump from the countess's window, who was actually C dressed partially in S's clothes; Figaro claims that he was the man to cover up the plot in Pierre Augustin Caron de Beaumarchais's *The Marriage of Figaro.*

Antonio Usurping brother of Prospero and duke of Milan; cast ashore in the apparent shipwreck; plots with Sebastian to kill his brother Alonso, king of Naples; chastised by Ariel for exiling Prospero; at Prospero's demand, surrenders dukedom and is forgiven in William Shakespeare's play *The Tempest.*

Antonio, Brother (Father) Capuchin monk with a mysterious past; model for Miriam's artwork; killed by Donatello in Nathaniel Hawthorne's *The Marble Faun.*

Antonio, Padre (Father Antony) Portuguese ship's Catholic priest, who clears young Bob Singleton of the charge that he is a Turk and a heretic in Daniel Defoe's *The Life, Adventures, and Pyracies of the Famous Captain Singleton.*

Antoniou, Michael He grew up with Milton and Tessie, becoming a Greek Orthodox priest. He was engaged to Tessie until she broke up with him to marry Milton; he then married Milton's sister Zo after much persistence. Zo continually compares him to Milton, creating a growing jealousy that culminates with Michael pretending to be Cal's anonymous kidnapper when Cal runs away to New York. He arranges a ransom with Milton, which leads to a car chase across the Canadian border and results in Milton's death. Michael survives but is incarcerated and gets divorced from Zo in Jeffrey Eugenides' *Middlesex.*

Antonius, Marcus Friend of the Roman ruler Julius Caesar in 44 B.C. in William Shakespeare's play *Julius Caesar.*

Antonovich, Anton Prefect in the small Russian town where the city leaders have profited from bribes and graft; receives an unexpected letter informing the corrupt city officials that the inspector general from St. Petersburg is arriving, perhaps incognito, soon; proceeds quickly to hide signs of graft and bribery and put a general polish on the town; mistakes a mysterious traveler, Ivan, as the inspector; fails to realize his mistake in Nikolai Gogol's "The Inspector General."

Antonovitch, Ivan Town clerk who takes bribes to record the purchases by the protagonist Pavel Ivanovitch Tchitchikov of the names of "dead souls" in Nikolai Gogol's *Dead Souls.*

Antonovna, Pelageya Bosoi's wife in Mikhail Bulgakov's *The Master and Margarita.*

Antony (Mark Antony) One of the triumvirs ruling the Roman Empire; his love for Cleopatra has left him indifferent to his duties and the affairs of Rome; chastened by the news of the death of his wife, Fulvia, and the increasing threat posed by Pompey, he leaves for

Rome; marries Octavius Caesar's sister Octavia in order to cement his bond with Caesar; sends her back and returns to Cleopatra; loses the crucial sea battle at Actium by following Cleopatra's fleeing ship; decides to fight Caesar again, and although initially triumphant, loses once again when the Egyptian fleet defects to Caesar's side; furious, he resolves to kill Cleopatra, but, upon hearing a false report of her suicide, attempts suicide himself and eventually dies from his wounds in William Shakespeare's play *Antony and Cleopatra.*

Antony, Marc Nephew of Julius Caesar; caught attempting to seduce Cleopatra and leaving Rome soon after, in Thornton Wilder's *The Ides of March.*

Antrim, Earl of Kinsman of Alister M'Donnell and commander of the Irish army serving in Montrose's Royalist army in Sir Walter Scott's *A Legend of Montrose.*

Antrobus, Goosie Energetic unmarried daughter of Mrs. Antrobus; she and her sister, Piggy, gambol on the town green in the hope of attracting Colonel Boucher in E. F. Benson's *"Queen Lucia".* She also appears in *Lucia in London,* in *Mapp and Lucia,* and in *Trouble for Lucia.*

Antrobus, Mrs. Hard-of-hearing mother of Goosie and Piggy Antrobus; she wields an ear trumpet in E. F. Benson's *"Queen Lucia"* and in *Lucia in London.* She is called Mrs. Arbuthnot in *Mapp and Lucia.* Mrs. Antrobus has taken up sign language in *Trouble for Lucia.*

Antrobus, Piggy Mrs. Antrobus's unmarried daughter who once pursued Georgie Pillson; she and her sister, Goosie, attempt to attract Colonel Boucher in E. F. Benson's *Queen Lucia.* She also appears in *Lucia in London,* in *Mapp and Lucia,* and in *Trouble for Lucia.*

Antropus, David ("Red Davie") Militant pacifist, nihilist, and Clydeside member of Parliament; he identifies Anton Mastrovin for John Galt, "Jaikie," in John Buchan's *Castle Gay.*

Anulka Local witch who cures the narrator of a kick in the stomach by applying a dead mole to his abdomen in Jerzy Kosinski's *The Painted Bird.*

Anutchkin Bachelor of refined tastes in St. Petersburg in 1830 who calls on Miss Agafya Kooperdyagin for an interview and inspection arranged by Madam Fyokla, the matchmaker; arrives with the other cadre of bachelors including Mr. Omelet in Nikolai Gogol's "The Marriage."

Anville, Madame D' Parisian hostess and one of Henry Pelham's amours during his stay in Paris in Edward Bulwer-Lytton's *Pelham.*

Anya Sheltered and idealistic 17-year-old daughter of the once-wealthy aristocrat Madame Ranevskaya; returns to the ancestral home in a Russian province from a long trip to Paris; becomes romantically tied to the perpetual student Trofimov; returns to Paris with her mother at the end of the drama in Anton Chekhov's *The Cherry Orchard.*

Anya Austrian girl training in the hotel business and acting as nurse to Kate Brown at the London hotel where Kate stays after leaving Spain in Doris Lessing's *The Summer Before the Dark.*

Aoi, Princess Daughter of the powerful Minister of the Left in the emperor's court and Prince Genji's first wife; dies in childbirth in Lady Murasaki Shikibu's *The Tale of Genji.*

Aoife Warrior queen who threatens battle against the Irish kings, particularly Conchubar and Cuchulain; her son, the young champion she has sent to King Cuchulain's lands, is not known to the king to be his son in William Butler Yeats's play *On Baile's Strand.*

Aoife's Son Young champion who arrives at King Cuchulain's seaside castle and fights the enemy of his mother, Aoife; dies in a sword fight with Cuchulain before learning that the Irish king was his father in William Butler Yeats's play *On Baile's Strand.*

Ao Ling Rebellious young Chinese who, having found meaning in Communism and having served in the Red Army, has shipped aboard the *Archimedes* with forged identification to evade capture by the authorities; so informed, Captain Edwardes has him arrested during the hurricane to help quell a mutiny imagined by Mr. Soutar in Richard Hughes's *In Hazard.*

Aonetti (Deer Eyes) Indian maiden enamored of Koningsmarke in James Kirke Paulding's *Koningsmarke.*

Aouda Young and beautiful Parsi woman rescued by the protagonist, Phileas Fogg, from being sacrificed on a funeral pyre by the Brahmins in a religious ceremony in India; accompanies Fogg during the rest of his successful journey around the world; marries the eccentric Brit upon their return to London in 1872 in Jules Verne's *Around the World in Eighty Days.*

Apaecides Unstable brother of Ione; he is raised by Arbaces to be a priest of Isis and is murdered by him after he becomes a Christian in Edward Bulwer-Lytton's *The Last Days of Pompeii.*

Ape, Mrs. Hypocritical American evangelist whose principal interest is financial gain in Evelyn Waugh's *Vile Bodies.*

Apeyahola (Indian Jory) American sailor imprisoned by Tripoli pirates; Creek Indian, trader, pioneer, and cofounder of a town in Oklahoma in H. L. Davis's *Harp of a Thousand Strings.*

Aph-Lin Richest man in a community of the Vril-ya; he serves as host to the Tish in Edward Bulwer-Lytton's *The Coming Race.*

Apjohn, Nicholas Trusted lawyer of Indefer Jones and maker of several of his wills; he tracks down the missing will, which names Isabel Brodrick true heir of Llanfere estate, at the same time unmasking Henry Jones's pathetic hiding of his knowledge of the will's existence so that he might inherit in Anthony Trollope's *Cousin Henry.*

Apley, Catharine Bosworth Boston aristocrat chosen by George Apley's family to be his wife in John P. Marquand's *The Late George Apley.*

Apley, Eleanor (El) Daughter of George and Catharine Apley; rebels against her social class and marries an outsider in John P. Marquand's *The Late George Apley.*

Apley, George William Boston aristocrat and lawyer; son of Thomas Apley, husband of Catharine Apley, and father of John and Eleanor Apley; upholds the family tradition and social convention in John P. Marquand's *The Late George Apley.*

Apley, John Son of George and Catharine Apley; rebels against family tradition but returns to assume his role as head of the family and as a proper Bostonian in John P. Marquand's *The Late George Apley.*

Apley, Thomas Boston aristocrat and textile merchant; molds his son George Apley into a proper Bostonian while maintaining an illegitimate family in New York in John P. Marquand's *The Late George Apley.*

Apley, William Manager of the Apley family textile mills; considers his nephew George incompetent to enter the business in John P. Marquand's *The Late George Apley.*

Apollo Son of Leto and Zeus, god of the oracle at Delphi, and instigator of Orestes' matricide; he clashes with the Furies at the trial, arguing that mothers are not blood relatives of their children, only nurses of an implanted seed, for which he adduces proof in Athena's genesis in Aeschylus's *The Eumenides.*

Apollyon Monster of the Valley of Humiliation; Christian fights him and is wounded but puts him to flight in John Bunyan's *The Pilgrim's Progress from This World to That Which Is to Come.*

Apophis Hyskos leader who sends demands to the Egyptian pharaoh Seqenenra in Thebes, governor of South Egypt; requires that Seqenenra kill the sacred hippopotami in the lake of Thebes, build a temple to the Hyskos god Seth, and take off the White Crown of Egypt; forced into war when his demands are refused; successful in invading Thebes and killing Seqenenra and Kamose in Naguib Mahfouz's *Thebes at War.*

Apothecary Servant of the charity who sells useless medicines to the charity and gets into a disagreement with the Cook in Charles Johnstone's *Chrysal: or, The Adventures of a Guinea.*

Apothecary Unnamed medical man who treats the nearly drowned Mr. Watson; he announces the arrival of the Duke of Monmouth to overthrow King James in Henry Fielding's *The History of Tom Jones.*

Appel, Milton Professor and editor of Jewish cultural monthly, *Inquiry;* Nathan Zuckerman's loudest critic and oldest nemesis; critical of Zuckerman's portrayal of Jewish people; once admired by a college-age Zuckerman for his portrayal of generational strife in Jewish families in Philip Roth's *The Anatomy Lesson.*

Appelfeld, Aharon Real-life Israeli novelist, whose works deal with his childhood experience as a Holocaust survivor; interviewed by his friend, American novelist Philip Roth, in Israel in 1988; advises Roth following his initial encounters with Moishe Pipik, an imposter using Roth's name for possibly nefarious purposes in Philip Roth's *Operation Shylock: A Confession.*

Appiani, Count Emilia's fiancé who is murdered in an attack by Prince Gonzaga's henchmen in their wedding carriage after he refuses to leave Emilia; to avenge his death, and in order not to be bound by marriage to the evil prince, Emilia pleads for her father, Oduardo Galotti, to stab her to death in Gotthold Ephraim Lessing's *Emilia Galotti.*

Appleby Fellow squadron member who reports Yossarian for refusing to take atabrine tablets in Joseph Heller's *Catch-22.*

Appleby, Adam Catholic graduate student in English married to Barbara Appleby; he is having trouble completing his dissertation at the British Museum and lives in fear that his wife is pregnant for the fourth time, since the Safe Method has failed them so far; he resists the temptation of Virginia Rottingdean, causes a fire scare at the British Museum, and is offered a job by Bernie Schnitz in David Lodge's *The British Museum Is Falling Down.*

Appleby, Barbara Catholic wife of graduate student Adam Appleby and a mother of three; she fears that the Safe Method has failed them again and that she may be pregnant a fourth time; she goes in search of Adam at the British Museum when she hears it is on fire in David Lodge's *The British Museum Is Falling Down.*

Appleby, Clare Precocious and talkative three-year-old daughter of Adam and Barbara Appleby in David Lodge's *The British Museum Is Falling Down.*

Appleby, Frank Bank trust officer married to Janet Appleby in John Updike's *Couples.*

Appleby, Janet Seductive wife of Frank Appleby; they couple swap with Marcia and Harold Smith in John Updike's *Couples.*

Appledom, Mr. Fifty-year-old suitor to Violet Effingham; she finds his suit highly comic, but he is unexceptionable in Lady Baldock's eyes in Anthony Trollope's *Phineas Finn.*

Appledore, Bridgitte Dutch au pair girl who becomes Michael Cullen's lover and eventually his wife in Alan Sillitoe's *A Start in Life.*

Applegate, Alf Elderly bachelor neighbor of the Birdwells in Jessamyn West's *The Friendly Persuasion.*

Applegate, Mr. Vicar of Christ Church in St. Botolph's; alcoholic whose weakness is responsible for his colorful sermons in John Cheever's *The Wapshot Scandal.*

Applethwaite Sculptress from whose studio Jeremy Trout is taken by Iseult Arble in a kidnapping scare in Elizabeth Bowen's *Eva Trout, or Changing Scenes.*

Appleton, Corinna Mother of Skippy Appleton, possibly by Louis Zimmerman instead of by Harry Appleton, the husband she abandons in John Updike's *The Centaur.*

Appleton, Harry (Doc) Physician who treats the Caldwell family; belongs to no church and subscribes to no belief system; twin brother of Hester Appleton; abandoned by his wife, Corinna; his son, Skippy, actually may be Louis Zimmerman's in John Updike's *The Centaur.*

Appleton, Hester Spinster sister of Doc Appleton; teacher of Latin and French; harbors longtime fantasies about her colleague George Caldwell in John Updike's *The Centaur.*

Appleton, Mrs. Percy's inflexible, straight-laced mother, who accuses the schoolmaster Anthony Neale of putting ideas into her boy's head; she finally complains to the headmaster about him in C. Day Lewis's *Starting Point.*

Appleton, Percy Aggressive and well-read Communist student who succeeds, with his brother Ted, in persuading his schoolmaster Anthony Neale to join the Party in C. Day Lewis's *Starting Point.*

Appleton, Skippy Son of Corinna Appleton and possibly of Louis Zimmerman in John Updike's *The Centaur.*

Appleton, Stella First girlfriend of Eugene Witla in Theodore Dreiser's *The "Genius."*

Appleton, Ted Percy's brother and fellow Communist in C. Day Lewis's *Starting Point.*

Appleyard Gunner on the flying boat who is shot as the plane ascends with the gold by another treasure hunter on the search for Nazi gold in Alan Sillitoe's *The Lost Flying Boat.*

Appleyard, Nicholas (Nick) Tunstall farmer who had fought at Agincourt and is the first victim of a black arrow in Robert Louis Stevenson's *The Black Arrow: A Tale of Two Roses.*

Apraxine One of the many ill or handicapped people cared for by Chrysis in Thornton Wilder's *The Woman of Andros.*

Apsimar Tyrant who threatens to punish Julian the Apostate, in his incarnation as a monk, when he fails to betray his deposed predecessor, Justinian II, as promised in Henry Fielding's *A Journey From This World to the Next.*

Apt, Rachel (Little Mother) Leader of a group of Jewish resistance fighters battling the Nazis from well-concealed bunkers and in the sewers of occupied Warsaw in John Hersey's *The Wall.*

Aqil One of three soldiers who accompany Robert Winter into the desert in P. H. Newby's *A Journey to the Interior.*

Aqilmund Goth warrior and a particular friend of Amalric the Amal in Charles Kingsley's *Hypatia.*

Aquilanera, Julia d' (Donna Julia) Daughter of Leda Matilda Colonna d'Aquilanera and half sister of Marcantonio d'Aquilanera in Thornton Wilder's *The Cabala.*

Aquilanera, Leda Matilda Colonna, La Duchessa d' Mother of Marcantonio and Julia d'Aquilanera; enlists Samuele's help in curbing Marcantonio's sensual lifestyle in Thornton Wilder's *The Cabala.*

Aquilanera, Marcantonio d' Son of Leda Matilda Colonna d'Aquilanera; adopts a life of dissipation and commits suicide in Thornton Wilder's *The Cabala.*

Aquino Member of Leon Rivas's guerrilla band who has lost two fingers in a Paraguayan prison; he is almost tricked into letting Charley Fortnum escape in Graham Greene's *The Honorary Consul.*

Arab Young Algerian who is being escorted across the desert to the French authorities for his crime of killing his cousin in a family feud over some grain; transferred from the soldier Balducci to the custody of Daru, a schoolmaster and civil servant; offered an opportunity by Daru to flee from being executed, but solemnly decides to proceed alone on his own to the French garrison of Tinguit, where he will be executed in Albert Camus's "The Guest."

Araba Sister of Baako, the novel's central character; bears a son she names after Baako, as he has been educated in the United States and is expected to become prosperous in Ghana; her infant son dies soon after its christening in Ayi Kwei Armah's *Fragments.*

Arabella Title character, who, mistaking French romances for true histories, overestimates both her power and her vulnerability to rape; she loves her cousin Charles Glanville but treats him with queenly disdain; she almost becomes to others what she believes herself to be, but is eventually "cured" (humbled) by a rational clergyman in Charlotte Lennox's *The Female Quixote.*

Arabella Lesbian movie star who acts in Boris Adrian's pornographic movie in Terry Southern's *Blue Movie.*

Arabin, Francis Scholarly clergyman recruited by Archdeacon Grantly in his struggle against Bishop Proudie and Mr. Slope; he marries Eleanor Harding Bold and becomes Dean of Barchester in Anthony Trollope's *Barchester Towers.* He appears in *Framley Parsonage* and in *Doctor Thorne.* His absence in the Holy Land complicates problems for Mr. Crawley in the stolen-cheque scandal in *The Last Chronicle of Barset.*

Arabin, Koré ("Corrie") "Modern" girl; she confides to Sir Edward Leithen her fear of what she must endure as heiress to the Greek island of Plakos with its corrupt House; she and Vernon Milburne survive a test which saves both their lives and makes them aware of their mutual love in John Buchan's *The Dancing Floor.*

Arabin, Mrs. See Harding, Eleanor.

Arabin, Susan (Posy) Younger daughter of Dean Arabin; adored by her grandfather, Mr. Harding, she comforts him in his old age in Anthony Trollope's *The Last Chronicle of Barset.*

"Araby" Narrator Young boy who plays with friends in the neighborhood streets of Ireland; his first love is his friend Mangan's older sister; tells her that he is going to the bazaar at Araby where he will buy her a present; arrives too late at the bazaar at closing time; in a disappointing epiphany, he realizes that he has been "a creature driven and derided by vanity . . . " in James Joyce's "Araby."

Arachnoids Crab-like alien species, most adept at engineering and other activities that involve practical intelligence, who eventually form a telepathic union with the Ichthyoids to create a symbiotic species in Olaf Stapledon's *Star Maker.*

Aragorn (Strider) Young, brave friend of Gandalf who befriends Frodo Baggins and joins the fellowship of the rings; he leads the group after Gandalf is killed in the mines of Moria in J. R. R. Tolkien's *The Fellowship of the Ring.* He helps defeat Sauron's armies and claims his rightful title of King Elessar and marries Lady Arwen in *The Return of the King.*

Arai Younger daughter of Eakahau and Mata, sister of Marama, and servant to Madame de Laage; survives the hurricane in Charles Nordhoff and James Norman Hall's *The Hurricane.*

Aram, Eugene Gentle scholar and scientist, who is arrested on his wedding day and charged with the murder of Geoffrey Lester (Daniel Clarke), uncle of his bride-to-be, Madeline Lester; his post-execution confession (by letter) maintains that the killing was an accident in Edward Bulwer-Lytton's *Eugene Aram.*

Aram, Solomon Wily attorney acting for Lady Mason in her trial; he believes that the forensic skills of Mr. Chaffanbrass will win her case in Anthony Trollope's *Orley Farm.*

Aramis One of the Musketeers of the Guard in the service of Louis XIII in 1625; teams up with Porthos and Athos as the three musketeers; dresses always in black; looks forward to the day when he can give up his sword and enter a monastery in Alexandre Dumas, père's *The Three Musketeers.*

Arana, Ricardo (called "Slave") One of the young cadets at Leoncio Prado, a paramilitary academy in Lim, in the 1950s; always bullied by his peers; punished by the officers of the academy during a cheating scandal; confesses that Cava was the cadet who stole the test questions, information that brings Cava's expulsion and retaliation on Slave by other cadets; mortally shot during a military training exercise in Mario Vargas Llosa's *The Time of the Hero.*

Aranda, Don Alexandro Actual captain of the *San Dominick* who is killed during Babo's slave mutiny; nondisclosed background except that he was friends with Benito Cereno, who is now forced to pretend that he is the ship's captain after the mutiny; killed by Matinqui and Lecbe, both Ashantees; his body is mutilated and his skeleton is put on display to warn the other Spaniards onboard in Herman Melville's "Benito Cereno."

Aranjuez, Second-Lieutenant Son of a Protestant minister; he serves in Major Christopher Tietjens's battalion; his eye is shot out as Tietjens carries him to safety through enemy bullets in Ford Madox Ford's *A Man Could Stand Up.*

Araspes Beautiful captive's protector, who learns that even the most virtuous can be overcome by the bad side of his nature in a parable told by Henry Clinton in Henry Brooke's *The Fool of Quality.*

Arbaces Wicked Egyptian magician, who schemes to win Ione and to destroy Glaucus and Apaecides in Edward Bulwer-Lytton's *The Last Days of Pompeii.*

Arbe, Giles Cousin of Miss Arbe; he befriends the Stranger, Juliet Granville, and helps her to discharge her debts in Frances Burney's *The Wanderer.*

Arbe, Miss Provincial lady of talents; she resigns her part in a play to the Stranger, Juliet Granville, and condescends to patronize Juliet's teaching of the harp in Frances Burney's *The Wanderer.*

Arbelow, Peregrine Alcoholic Irish actor, now playing fat TV villains; he has long concealed his jealous hatred of Charles Arrowby, who broke up his first marriage in Iris Murdoch's *The Sea, the Sea.*

Arblaster, Skipper Thirsty captain of the *Good Hope* who never ceases lamenting Tom; he is cozzened out of his ship by Will Lawless and Dick Shelton and is tricked into releasing them; Dick saves his life from Yorkists at the cost of the favor of Richard of Gloucester in Robert Louis Stevenson's *The Black Arrow: A Tale of Two Roses.*

Arble, Eric Unsuccessful fruit farmer turned garage foreman; he is the husband of Iseult in Elizabeth Bowen's *Eva Trout, or Changing Scenes.*

Arble, Iseult (Smith) Former teacher at Lumleigh, a school for girls, whose special interest in Eva Trout continues after Lumleigh; following the death of Eva's father, she is asked by Eva's guardian, Constantine Ormeau, to take Eva into her house as a paying guest in Elizabeth Bowen's *Eva Trout, or Changing Scenes.*

Arbor, Miss Producer of the absurd and existential TV game show named *Who Am I?,* on which the minor artist Hank Peterson appears in Donald Barthelme's "A Shower of Gold."

Arbour, Miss Old lady who lives in the town where Mark Rutherford receives his first preaching appointment; she tells Mark the secret of her miserable marriage to help him decide about his engagement to Ellen (Butts) in Mark Rutherford's *The Autobiography of Mark Rutherford.*

Arbroath, Lord Impulsive leader of Queen Mary of Scotland's van at Langside in Sir Walter Scott's *The Abbot.*

Arbuthnot, Alexander ("Sandy") (Lord Clanroyden) Effervescent Scot, bold man of genius and action and of chameleonic disguises; recruited by Richard Hannay for an assignment in the Foreign Office, he travels disguised as the leader of the Companions of the Rosy Hours and at Erzerum as the prophet "Greenmantle" leads the Cossack attack which defeats the evil German war machine in John Buchan's *Greenmantle.* Suspicious of the popular Dominick Medina, he investigates Medina's evil past; hearing Medina's plan to conquer the heart of society by controlling human souls, he thwarts Medina and returns the hostages to their families in *The Three Hostages.* As "El Obro Gris" he guides John S. Blenkiron and Blenkiron's niece, Barbara Dasent, in a revolt against the wicked conspirators and then leads the rebel army into Olifa City; he returns to his estates in Scotland with Barbara Dasent as his affianced bride in *The Courts of the Morning.* As husband and father, he assumes with Hannay the protection of Valdemar Haraldsen, and, in disguise as Martel the Belgian, arranges for the children, Anna Haraldsen and Peter John Hannay, to escape from the trawler on which they have been held as hostages in *The Island of Sheep.*

In a last appearance "Sandy" bids farewell to the terminally ill Sir Edward Leithen, who leaves London for New York and a final adventure in *Sick Heart River.*

Arbuthnot, Colonel Only pipe smoker on the Calais Coach; he was the devoted friend of Daisy Armstrong's father in Agatha Christie's *Murder on the Orient Express.*

Arbuthnot, Freddy Lord Peter Wimsey's fellow clubman; he is a suitor of Rachel Levy in Dorothy L. Sayers's *Whose Body?* He is one of the Duke of Denver's houseguests when the Duke is arrested for Denis Cathcart's murder in *Clouds of Witness.* He attends Harriet Vane's first trial with Lord Peter Wimsey in *Strong Poison.*

Arbuthnot, Gerald Innocent and honorable young man of 20 who works as a clerk in a bank; his mother has carefully guarded the secret of his paternity; falls in love with Hester Worsley; offered a coveted secretary's post by Lord Illingworth, who turns out to be Gerald's unknown father; finds himself caught between the past with his mother and the future with his father; discovers that his father is an unrepentant philanderer and disowns him in Oscar Wilde's play *A Woman of No Importance.*

Arbuthnot, Isabella Staveley Judge Staveley's elder daughter, who brings her family to the Christmas celebrations at Noningsby, the Staveley home, in Anthony Trollope's *Orley Farm.*

Arbuthnot, Karen Gracie Tisbourne's friend, who angles for both Richard Pargeter and Sebastian Odmore and marries the latter in Iris Murdoch's *An Accidental Man.*

Arbuthnot, Mrs. Rachel Pious, virtuous, and self-sacrificing woman who has lived the past 20 years in shame; the "Woman of No Importance," as stated in the play's title; as a young girl, she believed George Harford's words that he would marry her, and when he would not, she, with child, left him; has kept the secret of her son's father's identity; by cruel chance, she meets her old lover again and finds that she must tell her son about his reprobate father in Oscar Wilde's play *A Woman of No Importance.*

Arbuthnots Old British couple sailing on the S.S. *Normannia* from Britain to Bombay; acquainted with Captain Lionel March in E. M. Forster's "The Other Boat."

Arcade Guardian angel of Maurice d'Esparvieu; a foolish and lazy young man; suddenly appears in the nude to his mortal charge; steals into Maurice's library to find books to read, as he has nothing else to do because of Maurice's uneventful existence; his reading convinces him to lead the army of angels in a revolt against God; seduces Maurice's mistress, Madame Gilberte des Aubels, in Maurice's bedroom; readies thousands of angels for the revolution and takes them to Satan's throne in Anatole France's *The Revolt of the Angels.*

Arcadio Son born of an affair between José Arcadio and Pilar Ternera; schoolteacher; leads Macondo during Colonel Aureliano Buendía's absence; tyrant who loses control of his leadership to Ursula, who whips him; dies a mysterious death in Gabriel García Márquez's *One Hundred Years of Solitude.*

Arcadio, José First son of José Arcadio Buendía and Ursula Iguarán; has an affair with Pilar Ternera; joins a band of gypsies and leaves Macondo as a young man; returns years later and marries Rebecca in Gabriel García Márquez's *One Hundred Years of Solitude.*

Arcadio, José (II) Raised by Ursula; sent to Rome to become pope; returns to Macondo, where he discovers a treasure; frivolous with his newfound wealth; plans to return to Rome but is murdered in Gabriel García Márquez's *One Hundred Years of Solitude.*

Arcenault, Victory Wanda (Vicki) Thirty-year-old nurse who has moved to New Jersey in the wake of a divorce from an abusive husband; romantically involved with Frank Bascombe; increasingly troubled by Frank's essential lack of deeply felt emotion; finally breaks up with him in Richard Ford's *The Sportswriter.*

Arcenaux, Julius Owner of a grocery store, the central gathering place on the Isle aux Chiens, in Shirley Ann Grau's *The Hard Blue Sky.*

Arch Anker See Clerk, The County.

Archbald, Cora (Mamma) Widowed daughter-in-law of General Archbald; reared on *Little Women,* she tries to rear her daughter, Jenny Blair Archbald, in the same manner in Ellen Glasgow's *The Sheltered Life.*

Archbald, Etta (Aunt Etta) Daughter of General Archbald; invalid, hysterical, and unmarried aunt of Jenny Blair Archbald in Ellen Glasgow's *The Sheltered Life.*

Archbald, General David (Grandfather) Patriarch who idealizes Eva Birdsong in Ellen Glasgow's *The Sheltered Life.*

Archbald, Isabella (Aunt Isabella) Bold and beautiful aunt of Jenny Blair Archbald; marries Joseph Crocker in Ellen Glasgow's *The Sheltered Life.*

Archbald, Jenny Blair Woman who, at age nine, begins keeping a secret with George Birdsong and, at age eighteen, thinks she is in love with him in Ellen Glasgow's *The Sheltered Life.*

Archbishop of Chicago Religious leader who invites Roger Ashley to dinner at the height of Roger's journalistic fame and tells him the parable of the walls in Thornton Wilder's *The Eighth Day.*

Archbold, Captain Red-haired captain of the ship *Sephora;* comes looking for the missing prisoner Leggatt, but the captain does not tell him that the wanted man is aboard; stubborn yet flighty man who will not admit his own faults in Joseph Conrad's *The Secret Sharer.*

Archbold, Edith Matron at Silverton Grove House (asylum), who falls in love with Alfred Hardie and follows him to Drayton House, offering two options: to be made happy by his love or to reduce him to an insane slave in Charles Reade's *Hard Cash.*

Archdale, Alan White counsel for Peter in DuBose Heyward's *Porgy.*

Archdale, Mr. Annabella Richmond's beloved, whom her father finally allows her to many in Charlotte Smith's *The Young Philosopher.*

Archer Colonel Mannering's lieutenant, who lies to him about the relationship between Captain Vanbest Brown (Henry Bertram) and Sophie Wellwood and then confesses the truth on his deathbed in Sir Walter Scott's *Guy Mannering.*

Archer Afghan mujaheddin guerrilla who engages in several attacks on Russian convoys and airfields and launches a major assault (repelled by Bondarenko) on the Bright Star facility in Tom Clancy's *The Cardinal of the Kremlin.*

Archer, Adeline Widowed mother of Newland Archer in Edith Wharton's *The Age of Innocence.*

Archer, Alice Sensitive friend of Sally Manchester and Cecilia Vaughan; dies of a broken heart when Cecilia, her best friend, marries Arthur Kavanagh, Alice's secret love, in Henry Wadsworth Longfellow's *Kavanagh.*

Archer, Charles See Dangerfield, Paul.

Archer, Dallas Son of Newland and May Archer in Edith Wharton's *The Age of Innocence.*

Archer, Helen Friend and lover of Francis Phelan; homeless ex-singer who studied music at Vassar and now spends her days at the public library; is nostalgic and sentimental about Francis and about her life before she became homeless; has a stomach tumor that causes her not to eat in William Kennedy's *Ironweed.*

Archer, Isabel Charming, intellectual, strong-willed heroine who seeks to expand her life experiences in Europe; marries Gilbert Osmond in Henry James's *The Portrait of a Lady.*

Archer, Iva Miles Archer's wife, with whom Sam Spade is attempting to end an affair, in Dashiell Hammett's *The Maltese Falcon.*

Archer, John Doctor who assists Perry Dart in solving a murder case in Rudolph Fisher's *The Conjure Man Dies.*

Archer, Lew California private detective; the hero in eighteen of Ross Macdonald's novels starting with *The Moving Target.*

Archer, May See Welland, May.

Archer, Miles Sam Spade's partner, who is murdered while shadowing Brigid O'Shaughnessy and Floyd Thursby at the beginning of Dashiell Hammett's *The Maltese Falcon.*

Archer, Newland Fiancé of May Welland; falls in love with his cousin, Ellen Olenska, in Edith Wharton's *The Age of Innocence.*

Archer, Sir John Social catch of the season but more interested in racing than in marriage; Miss Vyner successfully pursues him in George Moore's *A Modern Lover.*

Archer, Trudy New to Runnymeade; opens a dance studio; has an affair with Chester; marries the town jeweler, but always believes that Chester loves her in Rita Mae Brown's *Loose Lips.*

Archibald, John Reserved and efficient groom of John, Duke of Argyle, and confidential agent in Sir Walter Scott's *The Heart of Midlothian.*

Archibald, Mrs. Gentleman whose testimony establishes the credibility of Mr. Longfield, a defense witness in the murder-robbery trial of Arabella Clement in Henry Brooke's *The Fool of Quality.*

Archie Absurd vice chancellor at the university where the protagonist, George Moore, lectures as professor of moral philosophy; non-practicing psychiatrist, although he treats Dorothy, George's beautiful neurotic wife, daily in her bedroom; dandy and ladies's man; sees the irrational as rational, and vice versa; calls the Church a monument to irrationality in Tom Stoppard's play *Jumpers.*

Archie One of the conspirators working for the Red-headed League; becomes the target of Sherlock Holmes's investigation in Arthur Conan Doyle's "The Red-headed League."

Archie Richard and Bertha's son; brought up according to Robert's principles; lively and playful, he likes joking with Robert Hand, whereas his relationship with his father, Richard, is more formal in James Joyce's play *Exiles.*

Archie Unemotional sailor on the *Narcissus* in Joseph Conrad's *The Nigger of the "Narcissus."*

Archie, Doctor Howard Small-town doctor who recognizes the musical intelligence of Thea Kronborg; helps her move to Chicago to study music and underwrites her studies in Germany in Willa Cather's *The Song of the Lark.*

Archpriest-Militant Devit Asperamanka Leader of the Church of the Formidable Peace and commander of the Sibornalese forces; he eventually becomes the Supreme Oligarch in Brian W. Aldiss's *Helliconia Winter.*

Arco Mythical son of Perigen and Philella; he murders his father and, with his wife Telamine, founds a cruel race in Robert Paltock's *The Life and Adventures of Peter Wilkins.*

Arcoll, Captain Jim Intelligence officer who traces John Laputa from the Limpopo to a meeting of the Royal Geographical Society in London and back to the kraal; he helps to defeat Laputa in John Buchan's *PresterJohn.* As a police officer in Rhodesia he sends Peter Pienaar, the scout, to warn Richard Hannay of a suspicious group of men converging on Haraldsen's gold claim in *The Island of Sheep.*

Ardan Brother of Naisi and Ainnle who defies the dictates of Conchubor, the high king of Ulster; murdered along with his brothers by Conchubor in John Millington Synge's play *Deirdre of the Sorrows.*

Ardea, Prince Pippino Finds himself in financial straits and must sell his estate; plans, with Catherine Steno's help, to marry the daughter of Justus Hafner, Fannie, a match that would unite Hafner's money with Ardea's noble lineage in Paul Bourget's *Cosmopolis.*

Arden Utopian scientist who dies in the experiment that transports several Earthlings to the perfect world of Utopia in H. G. Wells's *Men Like Gods.*

Arden, Deborah Daughter of John and Patty Arden, with whom she shares a strong love of nature; hysterical after rejection by her husband, Stephen Southernwood, and his desertion of her, she burns down their home in the shadow of an ominous rock formation called Devil's Chair and almost dies wandering in a snowstorm in Mary Webb's *The Golden Arrow.*

Arden, Joe Son of John and Patty Arden and brother of Deborah Arden (Southernwood); he disastrously marries the deceptive and selfish Lily Huntbatch in Mary Webb's *The Golden Arrow.*

Arden, John Shepherd and common countryman; he is husband of Patty Arden and father of Deborah Arden (Southernwood) and Joe Arden; he shares mystic beliefs with Deborah, whom he saves from death in a snowstorm and later unites with her husband, Stephen Southernwood, and their baby in Mary Webb's *The Golden Arrow.*

Arden, Julia Priggish young woman from Torquay, Devonshire, who is Catharine Furze's roommate at school in Abchurch in Mark Rutherford's *Catharine Furze.*

Arden, Patty Midwife; she is wife of John Arden and mother of Joe and Deborah Arden in Mary Webb's *The Golden Arrow.*

Ardenti, Colonel Claims to have decoded the mystery of the Knight Templars' fate in Umberto Eco's *Foucault's Pendulum.*

Ardenvohr, Knight of See Campbell, Sir Duncan.

Ardglass, Bijou, Countess of Fashionable, beautiful, promiscuous divorcée, who is the daughter of theatrical parents in Anthony Powell's *A Buyer's Market.* Her affair with Bob Duport is discussed in *The Acceptance World.* Her war work and her death are mentioned in *The Soldier's Art.*

Ardolph, Count German nobleman who seduces Marchesa (Laurina) di Loredani, forces her daughter into seclusion, and kills her husband in Charlotte Dacre's *Zofloya; or, The Moor.*

Ardworth, John Lawyer and Susan Mivers's kinsman, who is mistakenly believed by Lucretia Clavering to be her lost son, Vincent Braddell, in Edward Bulwer-Lytton's *Lucretia.*

Arentia Female friend to Berentha (Biranthus); she helps with the disguise in Mary Davys's *The Reform'd Coquet.*

Aresby, Mr. Young captain in the militia who flirts with Cecilia Beverley from the time he meets her at Mr. Monckton's in Frances Burney's *Cecilia.*

Arfretee Wife of Deacon Ereemear Po-Po in Herman Melville's *Omoo.*

Argent, Harry Generous, energetic lover of Eliza Quarles; movie producer in Alice Adams's *Listening to Billie.*

Argives Citizens of Argos, complacently repentant for their ruler's crime of regicide and blindly fearing the gods; fail to realize they are set free by Orestes' murderous coup in Jean-Paul Sartre's play *The Flies.*

Argo Sister of Pamphilus in Thornton Wilder's *The Woman of Andros.*

Argus, Jacques d' See Gradus, Jakob.

Argyle, Archibald, Duke of Brother and successor to John, Duke of Argyle and Greenwich, in Sir Walter Scott's *The Heart of Midlothian.*

Argyle, Duchess of Kind and courteous wife of John, Duke of Argyle; she receives Jeanie Deans warmly while she is in London in Sir Walter Scott's *The Heart of Midlothian.*

Argyle, Duke of Chief of the Scottish clan Campbell and present head of the College of Justice during the 1752 Appin murder trial; he is an associate of Prestongrange, Lord Advocate of Scotland, in Robert Louis Stevenson's *Catriona.*

Argyle, James One of Aaron Sisson's friends in Florence, Italy; James, Angus Guest, and Francis Dekker are examples of jaded cosmopolitan travelers in D. H. Lawrence's *Aaron's Rod.*

Argyle, John, Duke of Argyle Powerful Scottish nobleman, who champions his country; his influence at the court of King George II makes him unpopular but allows him to assist Jeanie Deans in Sir Walter Scott's *The Heart of Midlothian.*

Argyle, MacCallum More, Duke of Rob Roy McGregor's protector, who writes letters of reference for Robert Campbell (Rob Roy) in Sir Walter Scott's *Rob Roy.*

Argyle, M'Callum More, Marquis of Lord Justice General of Scotland, and feudal enemy of Montrose; although a coward, he is the potent leader of the Presbyterians; he assumes the name Murdoch Campbell when he visits Dalgetty's cell; the Highlanders dub him Gillespie Grumach (ill-favoured one) in Sir Walter Scott's *A Legend of Montrose.*

Argyll, Mavis Unmarried elder sister of Donna Gibson Grey; after Donna's death she becomes the dutiful caretaker of Austin Gibson Grey, sacrificing her romance with Matthew Gibson Grey in Iris Murdoch's *An Accidental Man.*

Argyle, Mungo Proud, newly wealthy upstart and a widely detested exciseman who shoots Lord Eaglesham in a dispute over hunting rights in John Galt's *Annals of the Parish.*

Arheetoo Tahitian casuist who asks Typee to forge documents in Herman Melville's *Omoo.*

Ariadne Beautiful Neapolitan lady to whom Julian the Apostate, in his incarnation as a wise man, loses his heart; she marries elsewhere when he decides her dowry is insufficient in Henry Fielding's *A Journey from This World to the Next.*

Ariane Young woman of twenty-six who is the shipboard lover of both Allert Vanderveenan and Olaf; disappears mysteriously from the cruise ship in John Hawkes's *Death, Sleep & the Traveler.*

Aricia Royal princess and last descendant of a family annihilated by Theseus; for political expediency, he had prohibited Aricia from falling in love; sworn to silence by Hippolytus, Aricia fails to convince Theseus of his son's innocence; Hippolytus and Aricia then plan to elope for a secret marriage, but Hippolytus is killed on his way; only at the end do Aricia and Theseus share power in Jean Racine's play *Phaedra.*

Aricia, Benny Executive who heads up a division of a company that has received a multibillion-dollar Navy contract; he purposely frames his company and then shows that it overbilled the government $600 million; his role in the fraudulent claim is revealed to the FBI in John Grisham's *The Partner.*

Ariel Passenger on daily train route and attracted to Leticia in Julio Cortázar's "End of the Game."

Ariel Psychotic policeman who interrogates Katurian in Martin McDonagh's *The Pillowman.*

Ariel Spirit, servant to Prospero; freed by Prospero from confinement and bound as his servant; desires freedom from servitude; at Prospero's direction, works magic and illusions, terrifying Alonso, Antonio, and Sebastian and confusing Caliban, Stephano, and Trinculo; freed by Prospero in William Shakespeare's play *The Tempest.*

Ariel Ungainly, feeble-minded cousin of and attendant on Miserrimus Dexter; doglike in her devotion, she dies on his grave not long after his death in Wilkie Collins's *The Law and the Lady.*

Arigof (Negro) Superstitious gambler aided by Vadinho's ghost to win a fortune against the casino's house in Jorge Amado's *Doña Flor and Her Two Husbands.*

Arina Aunt of Agafya Kooperdyagin, a young woman who is interviewing possible suitors; encourages her niece to marry the successful merchant Starikov in Nikolai Gogol's "The Marriage."

Arinbiorn of the Bearings Chief of the Bearings; his fury at the invading Romans leads him to launch a premature attack before the forces of Otter are prepared; he goes mad because of his responsibility for Otter's death in William Morris's *A Tale of the House of the Wolfings.*

Aristides Shrewd organizer of the successful effort to smuggle arms to the Greek Cypriot rebels; because he thought Jack Townrow was a British spy he twice threatened him with death in P. H. Newby's *Something to Answer For.*

Aristo Greek artist and brother of Callista; he tries first to dissuade her from Christianity, then to save her from martyrdom in John Henry Newman's *Callista.*

Arithea Woman of the Bashaw's seraglio who is the beloved of Bellamont in Eliza Haywood's *Philidore and Placentia; or, L'Amour trop delicat.*

Ariyoshi, Robert Japanese fisherman who takes Charlie Stark fishing in Peter Matthiessen's *Raditzer.*

Ariza, Florentino Impassioned poet and romantic letter writer who as a youth falls in love with Fermina Daza; feeds on his unrequited love for more than half a century until Fermina's husband dies; promiscuous with other women; renews his courtship of Fermina, and they begin a cruise down the river in Gabriel García Márquez's *Love in the Time of Cholera.*

Ariza, Tránsito Florentino's mother, the one person to whom he reveals his secret passion for Fermina; prepares for Florentino's marriage, becomes senile, and dies in Gabriel García Márquez's *Love in the Time of Cholera.*

Arkaday, Miss Takes care of the rectory in Mary McGarry Morris's *Songs in Ordinary Time.*

Arkadina, Irina Nikolayevna Fading dowager actress who holds beauty and youth above all else, claiming to look younger than any woman around her; participates in an argument over the nature of art and theater during a visit to the farm of her brother, Sorin; her unwillingness to accept her son's ideas about his own art and her biting criticism of his work contribute to Konstantin's eventual off-stage suicide; desperately manipulative, stingy, and often shallow matriarch in Anton Chekhov's play *The Seagull.*

Arkenholtz Young college student who becomes a hero after helping the injured from a collapsing building; mysteriously sees the Milkmaid and the deceased Consul walking about, characters not visible to others; foolishly befriends the Mephistophelianlike Jacob Hummel; falls in love with Hummel's daughter Adèle, but loses her when she dies because her heart cannot bear the world's wickedness and falsity in August Strindberg's play *The Ghost Sonata.*

Arkie See McClellan, James Parker.

Arkin, Margotte Widowed niece of Artur Sammler's dead wife; earnest and good-hearted but clumsy and verbose woman in whose apartment Sammler is provided a room in Saul Bellow's *Mr. Sammler's Planet.*

Arkos, Abbot Head of the monastery of the Albertian Order of Leibowitz in the 26th century; surprised by the artifacts pertaining to Leibowitz, which Brother Francis discovers, and is concerned that the new material will impede progress on the canonization of Leibowitz; orders Brother Francis to return to the desert to keep his vigil in Walter M. Miller, Jr.'s *A Canticle for Leibowitz.*

Arlen, Madge Friend of India Bridge and member of the Women's Auxiliary in Evan Connell's *Mrs. Bridge* and *Mr. Bridge.*

Arlette Mute orphan of the French revolution who serves the sans-culotte farmer Scevola Bron until Peyrol helps her regain her speech; she marries Lieutenant Eugene Real in Joseph Conrad's *The Rover.*

Arlington, Lord (1) Credulous and jealous dupe of Queen Elizabeth; Ellinor is forced to marry him in Sophia Lee's *The Recess.*

Arlington, Lord (2) Ignorant naval officer who assumes the family title after the death of his brother in Sophia Lee's *The Recess.*

Arlova Nicolas Rubashov's private secretary and former mistress; she is called under suspicion of oppositional conspiracy, falsely confesses, and is sacrificed by Rubashov to save his own position in Arthur Koestler's *Darkness at Noon.*

Armadale, Allan Inheritor of an estate worth £8,000 a year and target of the relentless fortune hunter Lydia Gwilt; he is befriended by Ozias Midwinter, his darker self, and saved by him from a murder attempt by Gwilt; he marries Eleanor Milroy in Wilkie Collins's *Armadale.*

Armand Oldest living vampire who introduces Louis and Claudia to the Théâtre des Vampires in Anne Rice's *Interview with the Vampire.*

Armand-Dubois, Anthime Highly ranked Masonic scientist who has moved to Rome with his wife, Veronica; learns that his wife has been interfering with his experiments out of concern for his animal subjects; after a spiritual vision, he finds that he is cured of his rheumatism; makes a public announcement of his spiritual conversion and is deserted by his many Masonic friends in André Gide's *Lafcadio's Adventures.*

Armatage Gunner on the flying boat; he deserts the treasure hunt because he is sure that they will all be killed and is killed by explosives thrown by another group of treasure hunters in Alan Sillitoe's *The Lost Flying Boat.*

Armbriste, Richie Young pornography magnate in search of a movie erroneously thought to include footage of Hitler at an orgy in Don DeLillo's *Running Dog.*

Armgardson Piccolo and bass-flute player in the orchestra expropriated in wartime by the enemy; he plans to escape in Alan Sillitoe's *The General.*

Armholtz, Elizabeth Eighteen-year-old daughter of Inman Armholtz; alleges she was raped by Fareek Fanon in Tom Wolfe's *A Man In Full.*

Armholtz, Inman Chairman of large chemicals firm; father of Elizabeth in Tom Wolfe's *A Man In Full.*

Arminda Lady of quality disguised as a shepherdess; her reputation has been ruined by the Duchess and Grizalinda, and her husband, Don Alonzo, has deserted her; vindicated by Lewis Augustus Albertus, she is reunited with Alonzo in Penelope Aubin's *The Life and Adventures of the Lady Lucy.*

Armine, Ferdinand Member of an old Roman Catholic family but living in genteel poverty; he falls into debt, and, when his grandfather's entire fortune goes to his cousin, Katherine Grandison, he thinks he must, for the sake of his family, marry her even though he does not love her-even after he falls hopelessly in love with Henrietta Temple-in Benjamin Disraeli's *Henrietta Temple: A Love Story.*

Armine, Lady Constance Grandison Wife of Sir Ratcliffe Armine and mother of Ferdinand Armine in Benjamin Disraeli's *Henrietta Temple: A Love Story.*

Armine, Sir Ratcliffe Father of Ferdinand Armine; that he and his wife live quietly on a heavily mortgaged estate largely motivates Ferdinand's decision to marry his rich cousin even though he is in love with Henrietta Temple in Benjamin Disraeli's *Henrietta Temple: A Love Story.*

Armistead, Lewis (Lew, Lo) Seasoned Confederate general in charge of one of George Pickett's brigades in Michael Shaara's *The Killer Angels.*

Armiston, William (Bill) Activist who betrays the group, brings a bomb into their home, and murders three of the men; murdered by Kam Wright in M. F. Beal's *Amazon One.*

Armitage, Mr. Writer on radical subjects, George Delmont's mentor, and friend of the Glenmorris family in Charlotte Smith's *The Young Philosopher.*

Armitage, Mr. Mill owner who is shot at when there is not enough work in spite of his attempts to conciliate his workers in Charlotte Brontë's *Shirley.*

Armour, Captain Officer of an English army corps quartered in Gudetown; he is discovered to be the brother of a girl hanged for child murder; he rises from stable boy to gentleman in John Galt's *The Provost.*

Armstid, Henry Poor farmer in William Faulkner's *As I Lay Dying, Light in August, The Hamlet, The Town,* and *The Mansion.*

Armstid, Martha (Lula) Wife of Henry Armstid in William Faulkner's *As I Lay Dying, Light in August,* and *The Hamlet.*

Armstrong, Alex Stuart Armstrong's elder brother, who helped Kate Fletcher Armstrong launch her career in journalism in Margaret Drabble's *The Middle Ground.*

Armstrong, Arnold (Aubrey Wallace) Son of Paul Armstrong; as Aubrey Wallace he marries and abandons Lucy Haswell; murdered in Mary Roberts Rinehart's *The Circular Staircase.*

Armstrong, Captain Mrs. March's escort aboard the ship traveling from India to England; valued family adviser to the husbandless Mrs. March in E. M. Forster's "The Other Boat."

Armstrong, Daisy Kidnapped child whose death resulted in a string of tragedies, motivating the action in Agatha Christie's *Murder on the Orient Express.*

Armstrong, David Young British army officer garrisoned in Ireland during the Anglo-Irish War (1919-21); he falls in love with Ascendancy-class Livvy Thompson in Elizabeth Bowen's *The Last September.*

Armstrong, Dr. Edward Eminent physician whose inebriation once caused the death of a patient; he is drowned in Agatha Christie's *And Then There Were None.*

Armstrong, Fanny B. (F. B. A.) Wife of Paul Armstrong; insists that Rachel Innes give up her lease to Sunnyside in Mary Roberts Rinehart's *The Circular Staircase.*

Armstrong, Grace Hobbie (Halbert) Elliot's distant cousin, as well as his betrothed, and a cherished member of the Elliot household; abducted by Willie Graeme, she is soon released, and she and Hobbie are married in Sir Walter Scott's *The Black Dwarf.*

Armstrong, Jackie Young girlfriend of Alec Gooch; because of her love for Alec she sees with new eyes that the world is a dangerous place; she later marries Alec and has a child in John Berger's *Corker's Freedom.*

Armstrong, Joseph Protestant clergyman who helps uncover Barry Lynch's plan to have Doctor Colligan murder Barry's sister, Anty, in Anthony Trollope's *The Kellys and the O'Kellys.*

Armstrong, Kate Young housemaid whose loneliness and jealousy of her friend Edith's romance drive her into the arms of the uncouth Paddy O'Conor in Henry Green's *Loving.*

Armstrong, Kate Fletcher Ex-wife of Stuart Armstrong, mother of their three children, journalist, and feminist; at age forty she is suffering through a midlife crisis, examining her experiences with men, with herself and others; she sees herself as a "marginal person" in Margaret Drabble's *The Middle Ground.*

Armstrong, Louise Daughter of Paul Armstrong; secretly returns to Sunnyside when she discovers her father's plot in Mary Roberts Rinehart's *The Circular Staircase.*

Armstrong, Luisa Wife to Michael Armstrong and mother of their five children; she is a Portuguese Jew; she appears in minor artistic works of the 1930s and 1940s in Margaret Drabble's *The Middle Ground.*

Armstrong, Mark Eighteen-year-old eldest child of Kate (Fletcher) and Stuart Armstrong in Margaret Drabble's *The Middle Ground.*

Armstrong, Michael Husband to Luisa Armstrong and father of their five children; he is half Scottish, half Irish and is an unemployed journalist who had worked as a theatre and art reviewer for a left-wing daily that went out of business in Margaret Drabble's *The Middle Ground.*

Armstrong, Mr. Dean of Winchester and father of Rachel, Viscountess Castlewood, in William Makepeace Thackeray's *The History of Henry Esmond.*

Armstrong, Mr. Sixty-year-old vicar near Cowfold; he teaches astronomy to Didymus Farrow and Miriam Tacchi in Mark Rutherford's *Miriam's Schooling.*

Armstrong, Mr. Armstrong Bigoted Protestant clergyman who takes meat to the Galway poor on Fridays in Anthony Trollope's *The Landleaguers.*

Armstrong, Paul One of the sons of Luisa and Michael Armstrong; he is a writer of a political gossip column for a weekly in Margaret Drabble's *The Middle Ground.*

Armstrong, Paul President of the Traders' Bank who embezzles money and frames John Bailey for the crime in Mary Roberts Rinehart's *The Circular Staircase.*

Armstrong, Reuben Youngest of three children of Kate (Fletcher) and Stuart Armstrong; his parents are divorced and he lives with his mother in Margaret Drabble's *The Middle Ground.*

Armstrong, Ruth Second of the three children of Kate (Fletcher) and Stuart Armstrong; her parents are divorced and she lives with her mother in Margaret Drabble's *The Middle Ground.*

Armstrong, Stella Confidante of Tom Thirkill; she is his chief political adviser in C. P. Snow's *A Coat of Varnish.*

Armstrong, Stuart Ex-husband to Kate Fletcher Armstrong and father of their three children; he is an unsuccessful painter; he was irresponsible with money and unfaithful to his wife, who found him unsatisfactory sexually in Margaret Drabble's *The Middle Ground.*

Armstrong, Superintendant Huge, direct, abrupt police official, who has formidable intelligence in his small eyes; he is an unscrupulous if clumsy tactician in Nicholas Blake's *A Question of Proof.*

Army Chaplain Cleric considered not well bred in England; in America he becomes a leader of polite society and marries the lost European Lady in Charles Johnstone's *Chrysal: or, The Adventures of a Guinea.*

Army Commander Sinner who rapes, murders, and robs his brother's wife and then buys forgiveness and salvation with the stolen gold and jewels, and who, to avoid secular punishment, joins the Jesuits in Charles Johnstone's *Chrysal: or, The Adventures of a Guinea.*

Armytage, Clifford See Gill, Merton.

Arnall, Father Teacher at the Clongowes School in whose class Father Dolan pandies Stephen Dedalus; he delivers the hellfire sermon to the school retreat in James Joyce's *A Portrait of the Artist as a Young Man.*

Arnaud, Claudine Wife of Michel Arnaud; neglected and abused by her husband; suffers from alcoholism and eventual insanity; murders Mouche, her maid, during the slave uprising in 1791; saves herself and several other female refugees from maraudering slaves by cutting off her own finger in order to surrender her wedding ring in Madison Smartt Bell's *All Souls' Rising.*

Arnaud, Michel Brutal master of plantation Habitation Arnaud in the French colony Saint Domingue; uses crucifixions and mutilations as routine punishments for disobedience among his slaves; fathers many children by his slaves but none by his wife, Claudine Arnaud, who is driven to alcoholism by his neglect; in fear of his life during a slave rebellion, he spends several months hiding in the wilderness in Madison Smartt Bell's *All Souls' Rising.*

Arnauti (Child) Young daughter of the first marriage of Justine (Hosnani); she vanished and is the constant object of Justine's searching; she appears, a dying child prostitute, but is not identified in Lawrence Durrell's *Justine.* Financial support of the search is offered as an inducement in Justine's marriage to Nessim Hosnani in *Balthazar.* Justine reveals to Darley her long-past discovery of the dying child; Balthazar has assisted in her denial of the discovery in *Clea.*

Arnauti, Jacob First husband of Justine Hosnani; he has written a novel called *Moeurs* that is a Freudian study of her character in Lawrence Durrell's *Justine.* He is mentioned in *Balthazar,* in *Mountolive,* and in *Clea.*

Arnaz, Desi Bandleader from the same part of Cuba as the Castillo brothers; listens to and likes the Mambo Kings; puts Cesar and Nestor on an *I Love Lucy* episode; married to Lucille Ball; buys the rights to "Beautiful Maria of my Soul"; sends a letter of condolence to Cesar after Nestor dies in Oscar Hijuelos's *The Mambo Kings Play Songs of Love.*

Arnez, Armenta Middle-class high school girl to whom Jake Adams is attracted in Herbert Simmons's *Corner Boy.*

Arnez, Edna Wife of Henry Arnez and mother of Armenta Arnez in Herbert Simmons's *Corner Boy.*

Arnez, Henry Husband of Edna Arnez and father of Armenta Arnez in Herbert Simmons's *Corner Boy.*

Arnheim German businessman (based loosely on the industrialist and statesman Walther Rathenau); an outsider by nationality, he nevertheless becomes a figurehead for the political organization called the Campaign; an adversary to Ulrich and Diotama's love interest in Robert Musil's *The Man Without Qualities.*

Arnobius Jucundus's acquaintance, a young man and student who is interested in his advancement and has no religious beliefs in John Henry Newman's *Callista.*

Arnold Heavyset young man who lives with his parents; eventually goes to live in the house of Christina Goering with his father and Lucie Gamelon in Jane Bowles's *Two Serious Ladies.*

Arnold, Benedict American Revolutionary War colonel who leads an overland attack on Quebec in Kenneth Roberts's *Arundel.*

Arnold, Catherine Sidney Bidulph Daughter of Lady Bidulph, sister of Sir George Bidulph, wife of Mr. Arnold, mother of two daughters, and best friend of Cecilia, to whom this ill-fated heroine writes copiously of her unconsummated love for Orlando Faulkland and her reasons for renouncing him in an ongoing struggle to live virtuously in Frances Sheridan's *Memoirs of Miss Sidney Bidulph.*

Arnold, Cecilia Younger and less beautiful but well-liked daughter of Sidney Bidulph Arnold and Mr. Arnold in Frances Sheridan's *Memoirs of Miss Sidney Bidulph.*

Arnold, Charles Eldest son of a modest country gentleman and a gallant midshipman aboard the *Amputator;* he falls in love with the captured Azemia; he loses her when she is removed from Mrs. Periwinkle's custody; eventually he rescues her from three poachers and marries her in William Beckford's *Azemia.*

Arnold, Charlotte Romantic, loyal servant to Mrs. James Frost and later to her grandson, James; she marries Thomas Madison in Charlotte Yonge's *Dynevor Terrace.*

Arnold, Dolly Elder and beautiful daughter of Sidney Bidulph Arnold and Mr. Arnold in Frances Sheridan's *Memoirs of Miss Sidney Bidulph.*

Arnold, Dr. Imposing and dominating yet kindly headmaster of Rugby School who brings about the moral and spiritual regeneration of Tom Brown in Thomas Hughes's *Tom Brown's Schooldays.*

Arnold, Ida Ample, friendly, determined, life-loving, free and easy, inexorable, early-middle-aged woman; nicknamed "Lily" by the pub's regulars because of her singing, she is loyal and has a strong sense of right and wrong; befriended by Charles Hale as a protective measure against Pinkie Brown's gang, she feels a duty to find out what happened to him; intending to "see justice done," she performs an opposite function and is ultimately responsible for Rose Wilson's marriage to Pinkie, for tracking down Hale's killers, and for Pinkie's exposure and death in Graham Greene's *Brighton Rock.*

Arnold, John Philanderer who inherited from his father the company that owns Captain William Russell's ship; he plans to seduce Sylvia Russell during a sea voyage; she misjudges him as superior to her husband and is later unnerved that she so narrowly escaped his advances; he continues to send her birthday gifts each year and offers her stock in his shipping business, which she declines in Storm Jameson's *Farewell, Night; Welcome, Day.*

Arnold, John Footman on Mr. B—'s Bedfordshire estate; he wins Pamela Andrews's trust by delivering her letters to her parents but betrays that trust by secretly showing the letters to the man who is attempting to seduce her, Mr. B—, before delivering them in Samuel Richardson's *Pamela, or Virtue Rewarded.*

Arnold, Julie Hempel Schoolgirl friend of Selina Peake Dejong; the friendship is renewed later in life in Edna Ferber's *So Big.*

Arnold, Madeline Pretty and determined girl of 19 who pursues and marries Gordon Evans; bears a striking resemblance to Gordon's mother, Nina, in Eugene O'Neill's play *Strange Interlude.*

Arnold, Mr. Genteel and handsome husband of Sidney Bidulph Arnold and owner of Arnold Abbey; estranged from his wife through Mrs. Gerrarde's intrigues, he is happily reunited with Sidney after a long absence; he dies of a wounded skull after a riding accident in Frances Sheridan's *Memoirs of Miss Sidney Bidulph.*

Arnold, Mr. Erroll Another inmate of the home who knows how to build log cabins; Will Barrett will use his skills as he plans his own utopian community with Allie Huger in Walker Percy's *The Second Coming.*

Arnold, Philip Sammy Mountjoy's unscrupulous rival, as child and man, in William Golding's *Free Fall.*

Arnold, Quilt Bodyguard to Jonathan Wild in William Harrison Ainsworth's *Jack Sheppard.*

Arnold, Widow Former wife of Mr. Arnold's deceased elder brother; she marries the attorney she enlists in her effort to gain the Arnold estate by passing off her illegitimate child as the eldest Mr. Arnold's heiress in Frances Sheridan's *Memoirs of Miss Sidney Bidulph.*

Arnot, Andrew Archer for Louis XI's Scottish Guard who relates the king's reaction to the Duke of Burgundy's message of war in Sir Walter Scott's *Quentin Durward.*

Arnott, Mr. Brother of Mrs. Harrel; he constantly pays debts for Mr. Harrel and unsuccessfully loves Cecilia Beverley in Frances Burney's *Cecilia.*

Arnulf of Flanders Treacherous murderer of Duke William of Normandy; he is ultimately forgiven by Duke Richard in Charlotte Yonge's *The Little Duke.*

Aronnax, Professor Pierre Professor of natural history in the museum in Paris; French scientist traveling aboard the American frigate *Abraham Lincoln,* a ship on course to rid the ocean of a reported mysterious but treacherous giant sea creature; survives an attack on the *Abraham Lincoln* when he is rescued from the sea by Captain Nemo of the futuristic submarine *Nautilus;* observes many wonders while riding aboard the underwater craft with Captain Nemo in Jules Verne's *Twenty Thousand Leagues Under the Sea.*

Aronsen Builds a store in the new Norwegian farming settlement where Isak first settled in Knut Hamsun's *Growth of the Soil.*

Arrellano, Carmen Girlfriend of Gerardo Strasser Mendana and later of Antonio Strasser-Mendana in Joan Didion's *A Book of Common Prayer.*

Arrius, Quintus Roman tribune who, while in command of a ship, recognizes the slave Judah Ben-Hur's strength and eminence; is fair-minded, kind, and compassionate; is saved by Ben-Hur when pirates attack their ship and names Ben-Hur his legal heir, providing for him thusly; eventually returns to Rome and becomes a duumvir, bequeathing at his death all his riches to Ben-Hur in Lew Wallace's *Ben-Hur: A Tale of the Christ.*

Arrogant, Lady Arsinoe Woman of rank and the pretentious wife of Colonel Brusque; she finds conversation about poor people distasteful at dinner in William Beckford's *Azemia.*

Arrow Ship's mate on the *Hispaniola* with Long John Silver's sponsorship; drunk most of time and overfamiliar with the crew, he disappears overboard one night before the discovery of the conspiracy in Robert Louis Stevenson's *Treasure Island.*

Arrow, Lady Susannah Wealthy anarchist and bisexual lover in Paul Theroux's *The Family Arsenal.*

Arroway, Eleanor Radio astronomer who first discovers alien palimpsest; believes strongly in the existence of intelligent extraterrestrial life; uses direct and persistent approach to both personal and professional concerns; member of The World Message Consortium, and replaces Drumlin as a member of The Five in Carl Sagan's *Contact.*

Arrowby, Abel Adam's brother, who became a barrister and married an American heiress; James Arrowby is his son in Iris Murdoch's *The Sea, the Sea.*

Arrowby, Adam Charles's now-deceased unambitious, unadventuresome, affectionate father; Charles reflects on his father with respect and affection and still suppresses his resentment of the advantages enjoyed by his richer cousin, James Arrowby, in Iris Murdoch's *The Sea, the Sea.*

Arrowby, Charles Retired actor, director, and playwright, who meets again with unfortunate consequences the girl he loved as a youth; he is narrator of Iris Murdoch's *The Sea, the Sea.*

Arrowby, Estelle James's American mother, now deceased; Charles Arrowby's mother concealed her resentment of Estelle's wealth behind a façade of quiet contempt in Iris Murdoch's *The Sea, the Sea.*

Arrowby, James Charles Arrowby's first cousin and only living kinsman, whose relationship with Charles has always been characterized by tension; a bachelor, a career army officer, and of late a Buddhist, he visits Charles and happens upon an unfolding tragedy; he rescues Charles from drowning in Iris Murdoch's *The Sea, the Sea.*

Arrowby, Marian Charles's puritanical, loving mother, who died before her son achieved professional success in Iris Murdoch's *The Sea, the Sea.*

Arrowhead Untrustworthy Tuscarora Indian who informs the French of the relief party's position in James Fenimore Cooper's *The Pathfinder.*

Arrowpoint, Catherine Sensible heiress, who disturbs her family by marrying her poor Jewish music teacher, Herr Klesmer, in George Eliot's *Daniel Deronda.*

Arrowpoint, Mr. Hospitable owner of Quetcham Hall and father of Catherine Arrowpoint in George Eliot's *Daniel Deronda.*

Arrowpoint, Mrs. Catherine Arrowpoint's mother, who is disappointed at her daughter's marriage to Julius Klesmer in George Eliot's *Daniel Deronda.*

Arrowsmith, Joyce Lanyon See Lanyon, Joyce.

Arrowsmith, Leora Tozer See Tozer, Leora.

Arrowsmith, Martin Medical doctor and researcher frustrated by the commercial and confining aspects of his work in Sinclair Lewis's *Arrowsmith.*

Arroyo, Tomás Self-declared 19th-century revolutionary general in Mexico who reluctantly accepts the American gringo Bierce into his brigade; lingers in Chihuahua at the Miranda hacienda, where he was raised as a worker and illegitimate son; falls into a rivalry with the gringo over the American school teacher Harriet Winslow; fails to have his soldiers join with Poncho Villa in an attack on Mexico City; later executed by Poncho Villa because Arroyo had killed the gringo in Carlos Fuentes's *The Old Gringo.*

Arsat Young powerful native living in a hut among the Malay on the edge of a lagoon in the jungle; on the eve of his wife's death from a fever, he sadly recounts to his friend Tuan how he once rescued her from imprisonment by the island's ruler; also recalls that in choosing to save Diamelen he also chose to leave his brother behind to die at the hands of the pursuing ruler's warriors in Joseph Conrad's "The Lagoon."

Arsella Servant of a contessa; wife of Pipistrello; Adeppi stays with her family in John Hawkes's *The Goose on the Grave.*

Arsene Watt's predecessor as Mr. Knott's servant in Samuel Beckett's *Watt.*

Arsinia Married to Stepan and yet the mistress of many men, including Eugene Listnitsky, a rich Cossack soldier, and Piotra and Gregor Melekhov, two Cossack soldiers; dies under fire from the Red Army as she flees with Gregor in Mikhail Sholokhov's *"The Don Flows Home to the Sea."*

Arsinoé Older woman and pursuer of Alceste; now that she has long lost her attractiveness, she is jealous of Célimène's youth and beauty; she is also bitter that Alceste prefers Célimène to her; to win Alceste's devotion and favor, she betrays her friend Célimène by disclosing to him Célimène's deception in Molière's play *The Misanthrope.*

Art Friend of a friend of the narrator; lives in hotel with a prostitute and a cat in Richard Brautigan's *Trout Fishing in America.*

Art Lillian's husband and father of Adele and Carol; worked for Lillian's father; raises mink in Mona Simpson's *Anywhere but Here.*

Artagnan d' Young Gascon adventurer who travels to Paris to join the Musketeers of the Guard of Louis XIII in 1625; falls in love with Constance, the queen's seamstress; sets out to rescue Constance when she is abducted by Cardinal Richelieu's spies and henchmen; later falls under the sinister spell of the treacherous but beautiful Lady de Winter; helps in exposing Cardinal Richelieu and Lady de Winter for their treasonous acts; at long last, receives a commission in the Musketeers in Alexandre Dumas's, père, *The Three Musketeers.*

Artemia Woman in love with Philamont; Gigantilla discredits her with him; she becomes a Vesta priestess in Eliza Haywood's *The Perplex'd Dutchess; or, Treachery Rewarded.*

Artemis, Melissa Inept dancer and beautiful prostitute; mistress of the dying furrier Cohen, she falls gratefully and slavishly in love with Darley; neglected by him during his affair with Justine Hosnani, she seduces Justine's husband, Nessim, and gives birth to Nessim's daughter before dying of tuberculosis in Lawrence Durrell's *Justine.* Her affair with Cohen resulted in her knowledge of the gunrunning conspiracy, of which she informs Pursewarden in *Mountolive.* She is mentioned in *Balthazar* and in *Clea.*

Artful Dodger See Dawkins, Jack.

Arthur Character who introduces himself as one of two former assistants to the protagonist K., but the story's narrator denies this relationship; looks exactly like Jeremiah, the other purported assistant in Franz Kafka's *The Castle.*

Arthur King of the kings in Britain in Thomas Love Peacock's *The Misfortunes of Elphin.*

Arthur The Black Squire, who helps to rescue three imprisoned damsels; he shifts his affections from Atra to Birdalone, whom he ultimately marries in William Morris's *The Water of the Wondrous Isles.*

Arthur Trustworthy son of Rose Cecil's nurse; he conducts Leicester and Matilda to France in Sophia Lee's *The Recess.*

Arthur (Jones) King of England who, while posing as a peasant with Hank Morgan, is captured and sold into slavery; rescued by Clarence in Samuel Langhorne Clemens's *A Connecticut Yankee in King Arthur's Court.*

Arthur Car captain of the Neighborhood Organization; leads a vigilante group and is shot; member of the American Legion in Bette Pesetsky's *Midnight Sweets.*

Arthur Headmaster of a boys' boarding school and companion of Mrs. Montague; patrols Hill House by night with a revolver in Shirley Jackson's *The Haunting of Hill House.*

Arthur Lifelong naif compromised by his vulnerability but sustained by his idealism; eponymous character in Thomas Berger's *Arthur Rex.*

Arthur, George (Gerdie) Delicate boy, orphaned son of a clergyman who ministered in an industrial parish in the Midlands, who is entrusted to the protection of Tom Brown and thus becomes the means of his moral and spiritual regeneration in Thomas Hughes's *Tom Brown's Schooldays.* Arthur is reported as winning a scholarship to Trinity College, Cambridge, in *Tom Brown at Oxford.*

Arthur, King Legendary founder of Camelot and the Knights of the Round Table; unites England against the Germanic and northern invaders; wins significant victories against Lucius, the Holy Roman Emperor; and establishes the Knightly Code that all knights were sworn to uphold; mortally wounded by Sir Modred, an evil soul who seeks to take the Crown by force, but not before Arthur slays Sir Modred; barge of queens soon appears to take Arthur to Avalon, from where he promises to return some day in England's most dire need at the very end of Thomas Malory's *Le Morte d'Arthur.*

Arthur, Mrs. Bedfordshire neighbor whose sneers and innuendos become pleasantries once Pamela Andrews is raised from the servant class; she and her husband are given to bickering in Samuel Richardson's *Pamela, or Virtue Rewarded.*

Artifoni, Almidano Italian music teacher who befriends Stephen Dedalus in James Joyce's *Ulysses.*

Artworth, Sheila ("Sheikie" Beaker) One of three women in their sixties who at the age of eleven were "best friends" at a school in Kent; now the attractive wife of a successful local businessman and stepmother to his two children, Sheila dreads that gossip will result from the cryptic ads Diana Delacroix has placed to call them all together in Elizabeth Bowen's *The Little Girls.*

Arundel, Clare Beautiful niece of the Catholic patroness Lady St. Jerome; she shares Lothair's desire to alleviate poverty and nurses Lothair after he is hurt fighting for the liberationists in Italy in Benjamin Disraeli's *Lothair.*

Arundel, Earl of Guardian of the young Lord Leicester, for whom he intends Sir Patrick Lineric's daughter as a wife; he introduces Elizabeth Tudor, later Queen Elizabeth, to Leicester in Sophia Lee's *The Recess.*

Arundel, Lady Sister to Lady Pembroke and Sir Philip Sidney and constant ally of Matilda and Ellinor in Sophia Lee's *The Recess.*

Arvanitaki Foreman of the Rasuka oil well; Ford heavily relies on him in P. H. Newby's *A Journey to the Interior.*

Arvey, Curt Head of Arvey Film Studio; lends Vito Orsini money to produce a film and then attempts to take control of it in the middle of production in Judith Krantz's *Scruples.*

Arviragus Cymbeline's younger son; kidnapped at an early age, along with Guiderius, by Belarius, who assigned him the name Cadwal; fights for the British side during the war with Italy and is reconciled with his father and sister, Imogen, after the war in William Shakespeare's play *Cymbeline.*

Arvis, Henry Sixty-year-old manager of the Brooklyn bakery The Cookie Lady in Bette Pesetsky's *Midnight Sweets.*

Arwen, Lady Beautiful young daughter of Elrond and Lady Galadriel; she marries King Elessar (Aragorn) in J. R. R. Tolkien's *The Return of the King.*

Aryaka, Prince Arrested by King Palaka and imprisoned in a dungeon; escapes with the aid of Sarvilaka; later becomes the new king after King Palaka is dethroned in Shudraka's *The Little Clay Cart.*

Asagai, Joseph Nigerian student in love with Beneatha; referred to as Asagai; proud of his African heritage and hopes to return to his home country eventually; desires Beneatha to accompany him as his wife, although he thinks that she is too dependent on the American lifestyle; teaches Beneatha about their African heritage in Lorraine Hansberry's play *A Raisin in the Sun.*

Asalamalakim Long-haired Muslim boyfriend of Dee, whose greeting becomes his name; tells Mrs. Johnson to call him Hakim-a-Barber when she cannot pronounce his real name; shares Dee's opinion of Mrs. Johnson and Maggie as backward and ignorant in Alice Walker's "Everyday Use."

Asano Graham's Japanese valet and guide, who betrays him to the revolutionary leader Ostrog in H. G. Wells's *When the Sleeper Wakes: A Story of the Years to Come.*

Asbella Mother of Valerius; she becomes very ill and loses all her beauty and, therefore, the little female power she had in Jane Barker's *Exilius; or, The Banish'd Roman.*

Asche, Kane Bagley Unemployed paper company manager; married; likes gardening; is fatally shot by Burke Devore in Donald E. Westlake's *The Ax.*

Asche, Stephan See Gwyon, Wyatt.

Aschenbach, Gustave Captured Comanche born in the province of Silesia who comes from a lineage of public officials; tortured by the unnamed narrator in Donald Barthelme's "The Indian Uprising."

Aschenbach, Gustav von Aging writer, repressed but highly regarded by the public; travels to Venice to overcome writer's block and free himself of his inhibitions; falls in love with a 14-year-old Polish boy; tries to model his attraction in terms of Platonic love and Apollonian restraint, but eventually falls prey to Dionysian frenzy and abandons all morality; keeps silent about the cholera epidemic in Venice and eats infected, overripe strawberries; grotesquely rejuvenated at the hands of a hairdresser, he dies at the end while visually following the boy's movements along the beach in Thomas Mann's *Death in Venice.*

Ascher, Alice First murder victim, a tobacconist in Andover, in Agatha Christie's *The A.B.C. Murders.*

Ascher, Franz Drunkard, abusive husband of Alice in Agatha Christie's *The A.B.C. Murders.*

Ascher, Jacob (Jake) Lawyer and friend of the Isaacsons, whom he defends during their espionage trial; his defense is partially responsible for the Isaacsons being convicted and executed in E. L. Doctorow's *The Book of Daniel.*

Ase Mother of the protagonist, Peer Gynt, who upbraids her son for his idleness in Henrik Ibsen's *Peer Gynt.*

Asfur, Captain Police captain who wrongly arrests Edgar Perry for starting a student demonstration in P. H. Newby's *The Picnic at Sakkara.*

Asgill, Mrs. Charlotte Melmoth's friend, who dies and leaves Charlotte her jointure in Thomas Amory's *The Life of John Buncle, Esq.*

Ash Tree ogre, who is always trying to fill the hole in his heart; he follows and threatens Anodos throughout his journey in George MacDonald's *Phantastes.*

Ash, Janice One of the "old guard" at the day-care center where Evelyn Morton Stennett volunteers some of her time in Margaret Drabble's *The Middle Ground.*

Ash, Susan Maid of Beale Farange in Henry James's *What Maisie Knew.*

Ash, Walter Clara Maugham's marginally satisfactory secondary-school boyfriend; she breaks with him before starting her university career in Margaret Drabble's *Jerusalem the Golden.*

Ashalata Young woman and friend of the protagonist, Biondini, in prepartitioned Bengal in Rabindranath Tagore's *Chokher Bali.*

Ashanti Conjurers Group includes Matiluqui, Akim, Lecbe, Yambaio, Mapenda, and Yau; serve as Babo's executioners of the Spanish and most of the whites during the initial mutiny aboard the ship; Matiluqui and Lecbe kill Don Arnada; nondescript except that they are considered warriors; aboard the *Bachelor's Delight,* they spend their time sharpening their hatchets, even when Delano walks by in Herman Melville's "Benito Cereno."

Ashbrook, Lady Madge Old lady in her eighties who disapproves of Lancelot Loseby's relationship with Susan Thirkill; she is murdered, apparently for money, in C. P. Snow's *A Coat of Varnish.*

Ashburnham, Captain Edward English officer and a gentleman; a brave and decorated soldier, the Protestant Ashburnham is married by parental arrangement to a Catholic wife; his predilection for passionate love affairs leads to his mental and emotional bankruptcy and finally to his suicide in Ford Madox Ford's *The Good Soldier: A Tale of Passion.*

Ashburnham, Leonora Beautiful, gracious, Irish-Catholic wife of Edward Ashburnham; she manages his estates and his love affairs in the vain hope that he will return to her in recognition and gratitude; she tortures him and destroys his pride, driving him to suicide in Ford Madox Ford's *The Good Soldier: A Tale of Passion.*

Ashburnham, Lord Wealthy young nobleman who becomes engaged to Lady Beatrix Esmond but grows tired of her demands; he marries Lady Mary Butler in William Makepeace Thackeray's *The History of Henry Esmond.*

Ashburnham, Mrs. Edward's mother, who arranges his marriage to Leonora, daughter of her Irish-Catholic friend Mrs. Powys in Ford Madox Ford's *The Good Soldier: A Tale of Passion.*

Ashby, Beatrice Simon Ashby's unmarried aunt, a professional horse breeder and trainer, who runs the Ashby household with affection and competence in Josephine Tey's *Brat Farrar.*

Ashby, Charles Younger brother of Beatrice Ashby's father; he inherits the estate after Simon Ashby's death in Josephine Tey's *Brat Farrar.*

Ashby, Derek Forty-five-year-old architect; he divorces his wife, Evelyn, to marry Maureen Kirby, with whom his relations progressed from employer to lover in Margaret Drabble's *The Ice Age.*

Ashby, Eleanor Simon Ashby's sister, who realizes as she falls in love with Brat Farrar that he cannot be her brother in Josephine Tey's *Brat Farrar.*

Ashby, Evelyn Wife to Derek Ashby, who divorces her to marry Maureen Kirby; following the divorce she leads an eccentric, solitary existence, refusing to see her children in Margaret Drabble's *The Ice Age.*

Ashby, Jane Ten-year-old sister of Simon and Eleanor Ashby; she is the tomboy of a pair of twins in Josephine Tey's *Brat Farrar.*

Ashby, Lady Mother of Sir Thomas; she is a patrician devoted to a dissolute son and antagonistic toward her new daughter-in-law, Rosalie (Murray), in Anne Brontë's *Agnes Grey.*

Ashby, Patrick Elder Ashby brother, long believed to have committed suicide by drowning in Josephine Tey's *Brat Farrar.*

Ashby, Ruth Jane's dainty, ladylike twin sister in Josephine Tey's *Brat Farrar.*

Ashby, Simon Charming, vicious younger twin brother and heir of Patrick Ashby; he alone knows that the unexpectedly returned Patrick must be an imposter in Josephine Tey's *Brat Farrar.*

Ashby, Sir Thomas Dissolute owner of Ashby Park, who, when he marries Rosalie Murray, adds her to his list of possessions, leaving her in the country while he continues his bachelor ways in town in Anne Brontë's *Agnes Grey.*

Ashe, Edward Illegitimate son of Elias McCutcheon and Ellen Poe Ashe; falls in love with Betsy, fathers a child by her, and flees with them to Canada in Jesse Hill Ford's *The Raider.*

Ashe, Ellen Poe Woman abandoned by her husband; falls in love with Elias McCutcheon and bears their son, Edward Ashe; later marries Colonel Ennis Dalton in Jesse Hill Ford's *The Raider.*

Ashe, Henry Frail, crippled son of Lady Kitty and William Ashe in Mrs. Humphry Ward's *The Marriage of William Ashe.*

Ashe, Herbert Fictional version of Borges's father's friend through whom Borges inherits the 11th volume of an encyclopaedia devoted to Tlön; the volume has, in two places, a blue oval stamp with the inscription *"Orbis Tertius"* in Jorge Luis Borges's "Tlön, Uqbar, Orbis Tertius."

Ashe, Lady Kitty (Bristol) Madcap, unstable wife of William Ashe, cabinet minister; her bizarre behavior is caused by her unhappiness with stifling English society; when she publishes a scurrilous attack on this society and nearly ruins her husband's career, she runs away and dies, reunited at the end with her husband in Mrs. Humphry Ward's *The Marriage of William Ashe.*

Ashe, William Aristocrat, Member of Parliament, and under secretary for foreign affairs; he makes a disastrous marriage with Lady Kitty Bristol after a short acquaintance; his career is nearly ruined by the publication of his wife's book on country-house politics in Mrs. Humphry Ward's *The Marriage of William Ashe.*

Ashe, William (Bill; covername: Murphy) Effeminate GDR intelligence mercenary who makes first contact with Alec Leamas for Abteilung in John le Carré's *The Spy Who Came In from the Cold.*

Ashenden, Brewster (Brew) Millionaire playboy and eligible bachelor who copulates with a bear to save his life; narrator of *The Making of Ashenden,* a novella in Stanley Elkin's *Searches and Seizures.*

Ashenden, William Critical, realistic, cultured novelist and narrator of the story; William meets Edward Driffeld when he is a boy, but as William matures his ties to Driffeld are insignificant compared to his knowledge of Rose Driffeld in W. Somerset Maugham's *Cakes and Ale: Or the Skeleton in the Cupboard.* As a British agent he enjoys the excitement and mystery of his travels yet wishes he could see the result of his work; he relates to people well, using measured amounts of sincerity and falsehood; he sees people as puzzles and tries to decode them in *Ashenden: or The British Agent.*

Ashendyne, Colonel Argall Father of Medway Ashendyne; leads the family's attempt to force traditional womanhood on his granddaughter, Hagar Ashendyne, in Mary Johnston's *Hagar.*

Ashendyne, Hagar Independent girl who grows to overcome her family and culture; becomes a famous author and an advocate for women's rights in Mary Johnston's *Hagar.*

Ashendyne, Medway Father of Hagar Ashendyne; travels to Europe during her childhood; when he is injured, Hagar assumes responsibility for him in Mary Johnston's *Hagar.*

Asher, Luann Half-white, pill-addicted orphan adopted by Simon Asher; rejected by persons of both races in Hal Bennett's *A Wilderness of Vines.*

Asher, Owen Wealthy, fashionable dilettante, an attractive man of forty; he entices Evelyn Innes to Paris, where he has her trained as an opera star; their six-year liaison shapes her life; an atheist, he tries to destroy her Catholicism in George Moore's *Evelyn Innes.* After she rejects him to take the veil, he finds consolation in aestheticism and travel, though he continues to intrude upon her peace, offering marriage in *Sister Teresa.*

Ashfield, Harry "Bevel" Very young boy with a vivid imagination; called "ol' man" by his father; only child in the Ashfield household; makes up names instead of telling people his real name; often beaten by older kids while a babysitter fails to watch over him in Flannery O'Connor's "The River."

Ashfield, Mr. Loving, caring, and meticulous husband and father; although sharply opinionated, he respects the opinion of others; spends most of his time looking after his ill wife in Flannery O'Connor's "The River."

Ashfield, Mrs. Wife and mother who has a very humble and solemn spirit; struck by an illness that leaves her weak and unable to care for herself or her family in Flannery O'Connor's "The River."

Ashford, E. M. Older professor emerita of English literature; earlier mentor of the protagonist, Vivian Bearing, during her graduate studies of John Donne's metaphysical poetry in Margaret Edson's play *Wit.*

Ashford, Reed Lover of Daria Worthington and Eliza Quarles and love object of Evan Quarles; morose about his affair with Daria; takes an overdose of pills and dies in Alice Adams's *Listening to Billie.*

Ashinow, Hamilton Johnny Fortune's good-natured childhood classmate, who came from Lagos to London as a stowaway; he is a hustler and drug addict; he dies of a drug overdose in Colin MacInnes's *City of Spades.*

Ashkenazi, Benish (Rabbi Benish) Revered leader in the Jewish community of Goray, Poland, and father of Levi Ashkenazi; temporarily exiled from Goray after the Chmielnicki massacre of 1648; later returns and remains studiously faithful to the Torah and Jewish tradition, rejecting the Sabbatai Zevi sect as blasphemous, in Isaac Bashevis Singer's *Satan in Goray.*

Ashkenazi, Levi Youngest son of Rabbi Benish Ashkenazi; disdains his father's orthodoxy and leads the followers of Sabbatai Zevi in Isaac Bashevis Singer's *Satan in Goray.*

Ashkenazy, Baron See Tateh.

Ashleigh, Lilian Young heiress and a natural clairvoyant, whose powers are abused by Louis Grayle; she marries Allen Fenwick in Edward Bulwer-Lytton's *A Strange Story.*

Ashleigh, Mrs. Gilbert Kinswoman of Mr. Vigors; she occupies Dr. Lloyd's old house in Edward Bulwer-Lytton's *A Strange Story.*

Ashley, Beata Kellerman See Kellerman-Ashley, Beata.

Ashley, Constance (Constance Ashley-Nishimura) Youngest of the Ashley children; develops sympathy for the downtrodden and becomes internationally acclaimed as a social activist in Thornton Wilder's *The Eighth Day.*

Ashley, John Barrington Wrongly convicted as the murderer of Breckenridge Lansing; stolen from a train by unknown men; flees to Chile and later drowns at sea in Thornton Wilder's *The Eighth Day.*

Ashley, Lady Brett English fiancée of Michael Campbell and former lover of Robert Cohn; has an affair with Pedro Romero in Ernest Hemingway's *The Sun Also Rises.*

Ashley, Lily Scolastica Oldest of the Ashley children; leaves Coaltown to become a world-famous concert singer in Thornton Wilder's *The Eighth Day.*

Ashley, Marie-Louise Scolastique Dubois Grandmother of John Ashley; she is the only member of his early family whose influence he consciously feels; he remembers her prayer to be used in the unfolding of God's plan in Thornton Wilder's *The Eighth Day.*

Ashley, Roger Berwyn (Trent Frazier) Only son of John and Beata Ashley and the first Ashley child to flee Coaltown; becomes a famous journalist in Chicago under the name of Trent Frazier and later as Berwyn Ashley; marries Félicité Lansing in Thornton Wilder's *The Eighth Day.*

Ashley, Senator Godfrey Leading citizen of and chronicler of important social activities in Far Edgerley; junior warden of St. John's Episcopal Church in Constance Fenimore Woolson's *For the Major.*

Ashley, Sophia Daughter of John and Beata Ashley; after her father's disappearance, she takes control of the family's fortune in such enterprises as selling lemonade and books to travelers; insists on turning the family home into a boardinghouse; her hard work leads to a mental breakdown from which she never recovers in Thornton Wilder's *The Eighth Day.*

Ashley-Densley, Dr. Elegantly handsome physician called in to treat a group of nurses; one of them, Eleanor Dear, thereafter assumes him to be on call at demand; he sees through her desperate maneuverings but looks after her anyway in Dorothy Richardson's *The Tunnel.* He becomes Miriam Henderson's friend and potential suitor in *The Trap.* He reports Eleanor Dear's death to Miriam in *Dawn's Left Hand.* Miriam refuses his proposal of marriage in *Clear Horizon.*

Ashley-Nishimura, Constance See Ashley, Constance.

Ashok Eight-year-old Indian boy who is befriended by Barbara Batchelor, the retired missionary teacher, in Paul Scott's *The Towers of Silence.*

Ashton, Colonel Sholto Douglas Ambitious heir of Sir William and Lady Ashton; he challenges Edgar Ravenswood and is killed in a duel in Flanders in Sir Walter Scott's *The Bride of Lammermoor.*

Ashton, Henry Youngest child of Sir William and Lady Ashton; he succeeds to his father's estates and is the last of the Ashtons in Sir Walter Scott's *The Bride of Lammermoor.*

Ashton, Jefferson Inexperienced and opportunistic attorney retained to defend six black men accused of raping a white woman in T. S. Stribling's *Unfinished Cathedral.*

Ashton, Julia American poet in London during World War I and wife of Rafe Ashton in H. D.'s *Bid Me to Live.*

Ashton, Lady Margaret Douglas Wife of Sir William Ashton and a wily politician; in her attempts to ruin Edgar Ravenswood and dismiss him as a suitor for her daughter, Lucy, she unwittingly incurs the enmity of the Marquis of A—, causing her husband's downfall in Sir Walter Scott's *The Bride of Lammermoor.*

Ashton, Lucy Lovely and innocent daughter of Sir William and Lady Ashton; she falls in love with Edgar Ravenswood despite a long-standing feud between their families; her mother's pawn, she eventually breaks with her lover to marry Frank Hayston, Laird of Bucklaw, only to go insane and attack her groom before dying herself in Sir Walter Scott's *The Bride of Lammermoor.*

Ashton, Rafe Poet and soldier married to Julia Ashton but having an affair with Bella Carter in H. D.'s *Bid Me to Live.*

Ashton, Sir Edward Proposed husband for Miss Milner; he is rejected as too old and boring in Elizabeth Inchbald's *A Simple Story.*

Ashton, Sir Harold Determined teetotaller, chartered accountant, and vice-chairman of the Saddleford Building Society in Northern England in Roy Fuller's *Image of a Society.*

Ashton, Sir William Wealthy and politically cunning member of the Scottish Privy Council; he feigns approval of his daughter's romance with Edgar Ravenswood in order to avoid a harmful investigation, but his duplicity loses him his position as well as his daughter in Sir Walter Scott's *The Bride of Lammermoor.*

Ashwood, Mrs. Mrs. Stafford's sister-in-law, who takes Emmeline Mobray into her house near London at Mrs. Stafford's request; there Emmeline meets Humphrey Rochely in Charlotte Smith's *Emmeline: The Orphan of the Castle.*

Asisticus (Scipio) Scipiana's elder brother, who was originally named Scipio but because of his great exploits as a soldier is given a more important name; in love with Clarenthia, he is the hero of Jane Barker's *Exilius; or, The Banish'd Roman.*

Askerton, Colonel Bluff ex-military man whose wife, Mary, he had rescued from a bullying drunkard; he leases the shooting at Belton Castle, avoids social contacts, and refuses to attend church in Anthony Trollope's *The Belton Estate.*

Askerton, Mary Intimate friend of Clara Amedroz, who is bullied by Lady Aylmer over the friendship; Mrs. Askerton is the subject of gossip in the town of Belton concerning her rescue from an abusive husband by Colonel Askerton; her living with him prior to her husband's death casts a shadow over her social position in Anthony Trollope's *The Belton Estate.*

Askew, Joe Army officer who sets up an airplane parts business in partnership with Charley Anderson after the war; when the business is successful, Anderson, who had been living with the Askew family, sells his partner out in a stock exchange deal in John Dos Passos's *U.S.A.* trilogy.

Askew, Mr. Solicitor who represents Mr. Furze during his bankruptcy in Mark Rutherford's *Catharine Furze.*

Askwani White youth reared by the Cherokee of Crow Town; devoted protégé of Ewen Warne; husband of Ruhama Warne in H. L. Davis's *Beulah Land.*

Asmahan Protagonist and an independent Lebanese Muslim woman who opts to remain in Lebanon despite the ravages of the civil war around her; writes a series of letters that remain unsent, correspondence addressed to the narrator's emigrant friend Hanan, her ex-lover Naser, her family's land in a Lebanese village, her grandmother, Billie Holiday, the war, and Beirut itself; wavers between her longing to be with her lover Jawad in Paris, on the one hand, and her inability to renounce her attachment to Beirut, on the other hand, in Hanan al-Shaykh's *Beirut Blues.*

Asmund Ancient Dayling warrior; he foresees the ill effect on Thiodolf of the dwarf-wrought hauberk and penetrates Wood-Sun's disguise as Thorkettle in William Morris's *A Tale of the House of the Wolfings.*

Ason, Grace Young school girl taught by the narrator, Chicha, in the small village of Bamso in Ghana, West Africa, in Ama Ata Aidoo's "No Sweetness Here."

Asper, Constance Wealthy heiress with an impeccable reputation; she pines away for Percy Dacier until his infatuation with Diana Warwick wanes and the two marry in George Meredith's *Diana of the Crossways.*

Asper, Mr. Impecunious second lieutenant of H.M.S. *Harpy;* he is not above sponging on Jack Easy in Captain Frederick Marryat's *Mr. Midshipman Easy.*

Asphalter, Lucas (Luke) Zoologist at the University of Chicago who tells Moses Herzog, his dearest friend, that Madeleine Herzog has cuckolded him with Val Gersbach; stands by Herzog in his time of emotional turmoil in Saul Bellow's *Herzog.*

Aspinall, Connie "Dreary" spinster relation of Edith Liversidge; she plays the harp and pines away in a small village for the scenes of her former glory when she was companion to a lady in Belgrave Square in Barbara Pym's *Some Tame Gazelle.*

Aspinwall, Brian Young teacher at Justin Martyr School and confidant of headmaster Francis Prescott; principal narrator who keeps a journal of various accounts of Prescott's life in Louis Auchincloss's *The Rector of Justin.*

Aspramonte, Knight of Countess Brenhilda's loving but prejudiced Norman father in Sir Walter Scott's *Count Robert of Paris.*

Aspramonte, Lady of Loving but prejudiced Norman mother of Countess Brenhilda in Sir Walter Scott's *Count Robert of Paris.*

Asquith, Robert Diplomat and distant cousin of Isabel Clarendon; he proposes to her when they are young but is refused; he later becomes her friend and adviser and is ultimately accepted in George Gissing's *Isabel Clarendon.*

Asriel, Lord Scholar, inventor, explorer, and father of Lyra Belacqua; former lover of Mrs. Coulter; amasses an army and leads a war against "Heaven" to destroy the "Authority"; kills Lyra's best friend, Roger; forges a bridge between parallel universes; sacrifices himself to destroy the Metatron (the voice of the "Authority") in Philip Pullman's *His Dark Materials.*

Assad One of three Palestinian men who attempt a dangerous border crossing in the 1950s from the refugee camps in southern Iraq into Kuwait; represents the middle generation of Palestinians who are enthusiastic and politically engaged, yet naïve and ineffective at bringing about change in Iraq; decides to flee the refugee camps because the police want to arrest him for his political activities; agrees with the other two men, Abu Qais and Marwan, to be smuggled by Abul Khaizuran through the border posts in the empty tank of his water truck; dies with the other men in the metal tank from the extreme desert heat in Ghassan Kanafani's *Men in the Sun.*

Assad, Jimmy Egyptian in the film business who hosts Daniel Martin and Jane Mallory in Cairo and arranges their trip to Palmyra in John Fowles's *Daniel Martin.*

Assef Neighborhood bully in Amir and Hassan's childhood; child of a German mother and Afghan father; sympathizes with Hitler; as a teenager sodomizes Hassan; as an adult, a Taliban pedophile who terrorizes Hassan's son Sohrab; Sohrab injures Assef's eye when Assef fights Amir in Khaled Hosseini's *The Kite Runner.*

Asselta, John Known as the Ghost, he has an abusive father and an unstable home life; takes the blame and is sent to a psychiatric facility for Daniel Skinner's murder because Ken's father pays his father; psychotic and tortures and kills people for fun; befriended by Julie Miller in high school and never forgets her friendship; tells Katy the truth about her sister's death; reveals to Will that Carly is actually his daughter in Harlan Coben's *Gone for Good.*

Assingham, Col. Robert (Bob) Retired British army officer and husband of Fanny Assingham; listens to his wife's schemes with detachment in Henry James's *The Golden Bowl.*

Assingham, Fanny American-born wife of the retired British army officer Robert Assingham; becomes a confidante of Maggie Verver and breaks the golden bowl in Henry James's *The Golden Bowl.*

Assistant Commissioner Opportunistic police official who oversees the bungling of Chief Inspector Heat in Joseph Conrad's *The Secret Agent: A Simple Tale.*

Assistant Commissioner Police official in his fifties, lately returned from long service in the East; though he sees his job as stopping when the "right man" is caught, he is asked to find out the possible reaction to the execution of Jim Drover and is followed by Conrad Drover, who tries to shoot him, in Graham Greene's *It's a Battlefield.*

Ast, Theodore (Teddy) Women's garment salesman and manufacturer; gets out of his partnership with Harry Bogen in Apex Modes before it goes bankrupt in Jerome Weidman's *I Can Get It for You Wholesale;* starts his own garment firm and steals Martha Mills from Bogen in *What's in It for Me?*

Asta Schnauzer of Nick and Nora Charles in Dashiell Hammett's *The Thin Man.*

Astakhov, Stepan Husband of Aksinia, whom he regularly beats; realizes that his wife has fallen in love with Grigori Panteleimonovich Melekhov, a promising young soldier, in Mikhail Sholokhov's *Quiet Flows the Don.*

Astarte Distinguished calligrapher, who serves as Anna Comnena's slave and Violante's companion in Sir Walter Scott's *Count Robert of Paris.*

Aster, Carter Byron Henry's first submarine commander; brave to the point of recklessness; has a clandestine affair with Byron's sister-in-law after her husband dies; turns command over to Byron and dies heroically when their ship is hit in Herman Wouk's *War and Remembrance.*

Aster, China Candlemaker from Marietta, Ohio, whose attempts to repay loans drive him into poverty in Herman Melville's *The Confidence-Man.*

Aster, Lieutenant Nineteen-year-old female psychiatrist who attempts a therapeutic reprise on Georgie Cornell in Thomas Berger's *Regiment of Women.*

Asterias, Mr. Ichthyologist who spends his life searching for a mermaid in Thomas Love Peacock's *Nightmare Abbey.*

Astill, Laurence Scientist who serves on the advisory committee for nuclear weapons and is included among those investigated for security reasons in C. P. Snow's *Corridors of Power.*

Aston Mick's older brother; committed to an asylum by his mother when he was young; rescues Davies from a pub brawl and cares for him in Harold Pinter's play *The Caretaker.*

Aston, Mack Dance-marathon contestant in Horace McCoy's *They Shoot Horses, Don't They?*

Astor Black hired hand on Mrs. McIntyre's farm in Flannery O'Connor's "The Displaced Person."

Astrid Twenty-six-year-old estranged wife of the nameless narrator of Nicholas Delbanco's *In the Middle Distance.*

Astronomer Learned man whose long solitude has driven him to madness and the delusion that he is in control of the weather; he exemplifies the dangerous prevalence of imagination which preys incessantly on life in Samuel Johnson's *The History of Rasselas, Prince of Abissinia.*

Asya Young woman who falls into a romantic relationship with Dyomka, a trade-school student who is a patient at the Soviet oncology ward; while the doctors want to amputate Dyomka's leg to save his life, Asya wants him to refuse because the operations would rob him of his physical and masculine prowess; she later learns that she has breast cancer and must have the breast removed in Aleksandr Solzhenitsyn's *Cancer Ward.*

Ata. Ben King of Zone Four who is told by the Providers that he must marry Al-Ith; though he does so unwillingly, he learns to love her; later he must leave her behind and marry the savage Queen of Zone Five in Doris Lessing's *The Marriages Between Zones Three, Four, and Five.*

Atamadoul Monkey on a chain who tells her history to Eovaai as a warning against Ochihatou: a woman of the bedchamber to Princess Syllalippe, she wanted Ochihatou for herself and disguised herself as Syllalippe to get him, but then was transformed by Ochihatou into a monkey when he learned that he had been tricked in Eliza Haywood's *Adventures of Eovaai, Princess of Ijaveo.*

Atawel, Sir Ethelbert Honorable English nobleman, to whom Francesco de Guinigi entrusts the eighteen-year-old Castruccio dei Antelminelli; he dislikes Piers Gavaston; he teaches Castruccio honor, horsemanship, arms, dance, and courtly behavior in Mary Shelley's *Valperga.*

Athalfrida Sister of the Gothic king Totila; she is in charge of Veranilda in George Gissing's *Veranilda.*

Athalie Self-centered daughter of Althanas Brasowitsch, a prosperous Hungarian trader; fails in her attempt to murder Timéa, daughter of Ali Tschorbadschi, on her wedding day, and is sent to prison in Maurus Jókai's *A Modern Midas.*

Atheist One of the flatterers warned of by the four Shepherds; he tries to convince Christian and Hopeful that the Celestial City does not exist in John Bunyan's *The Pilgrim's Progress from This World to That Which Is to Come.*

Athel, Philip Egyptologist father of Wilfrid Athel; he disapproves of his son's engagement to the governess in George Gissing's *A Life's Morning.*

Athel, Wilfrid Oxford University student whose ill health forces him to return home; he becomes engaged to a governess, Emily Hood, who cancels the engagement because of family troubles and disappears; he enters Parliament and becomes engaged to another lady but meets Emily again after six years and finally marries her in George Gissing's *A Life's Morning.*

Athelney, Sally Healthy, well-made, practical, and sensible young girl who waits patiently for the maturing Philip Carey to realize her worth in W. Somerset Maugham's *Of Human Bondage.*

Athelney, Thorpe Highly intelligent, well-educated father of nine who toils in a mundane, badly paid job, befriends Philip Carey, and demonstrates what a loving family can be in W. Somerset Maugham's *Of Human Bondage.*

Athelstane the Unready Debauched, slow-witted, drunken direct descendant of Edward the Confessor, revered by the Saxons; Lady Rowena's betrothed, he barely escapes being buried alive in Sir Walter Scott's *Ivanhoe.*

Athena (Athene) Daughter of Zeus, goddess of wisdom, weaving, and war, and patron of Athens; born from her father's skull rather than a woman's womb; presiding over Orestes' trial, she breaks a tie in the defendant's favor by arguing that marriage is more important than motherhood, but also integrates the Furies into the city as protectors; moreover, institutes trial by jury for all time in Aeschylus's play *The Eumenides.*

Athenry, Countess Richard Devereux's aunt, who takes him under her wing when her husband is cruel to him; when she wants to make all his decisions for him they quarrel and he returns to Chapelizod and the Royal Irish Artillery in J. Sheridan Le Fanu's *The House by the Churchyard.*

Athenry, Lewis Sickly son of Lord Roland Athenry and Captain Richard Devereux's cousin; he travels on the Continent with Dan Loftus as his tutor and dies there, bringing Devereux much closer to the family inheritance in J. Sheridan Le Fanu's *The House by the Churchyard.*

Athenry, Lord Roland Selfish, lunatic uncle of Captain Richard Devereux; he shows no fondness for his nephew; he is frequently reported near death in J. Sheridan Le Fanu's *The House by the Churchyard.*

Atherton Boston attorney and friend of Bartley Hubbard in William Dean Howells's *A Modern Instance.*

Atherton, Mrs. Julia Martin's landlady in Jean Rhys's *After Leaving Mr. Mackenzie.*

Athlin, Earl of Scottish nobleman who is slain by a neighboring baron, Malcolm of Dunbayne, in Ann Radcliffe's *The Castles of Athlin and Dunbayne.*

Athos One of the Musketeers of the Guard in the service of Louis XIII in 1625; teams up with Porthos and Aramis as the three musketeers; nobleman by birth and suffers from a great treachery by a woman; also the Count de la Fere who, when married to the Lady de Winter, had hanged her for hiding her criminal past from him, but she survived the death sentence; finds her again and sends her to her execution for her murderous actions in Alexandre Dumas, père's *The Three Musketeers.*

Athy Stephen Dedalus's companion in the school infirmary in James Joyce's *A Portrait of the Artist as a Young Man.*

Atkins Waiter on a train who serves dinner to the boy Carruthers and his chaperone, Miss Fanshawe; bullied by upper-class Carruthers in William Trevor's "Going Home."

Atkins, Captain Emily Atkins's beleaguered father, who failed to instill religious principles in her in Henry Mackenzie's *The Man of Feeling.*

Atkins, Cora Implacable wife of Emerson Atkins; mother of Beulah Madge; devoted to the unending hard work of a depression-era Nebraska farm; dies of a stroke in Wright Morris's *Plains Song for Female Voices.*

Atkins, Emerson Taciturn and stoic Nebraska farmer; husband of Cora; father of Beulah Madge; labors over his farm through the depression and drought in Wright Morris's *Plains Song for Female Voices.*

Atkins, Emily Young prostitute whom Harley rescues from degradation and reunites with her father in Henry Mackenzie's *The Man of Feeling.*

Atkins, Fayrene Dee Third daughter of Belle and Orion, sister of Sharon Rose; plagued by disfiguring acne; marries Avery Dickel, who becomes a successful veterinarian in Wright Morris's *Plains Song for Female Voices.*

Atkins, Harry Sally Atkins's simple and pleasure-loving husband, who drinks too often and beats her in W. Somerset Maugham's *Liza of Lambeth.*

Atkins, (Beulah) Madge (Kibbee) Daughter of Cora and Emerson, Nebraska farmers; plump and placid as a child; dominated by but closely bonded to her cousin Sharon Rose; marries carpenter Ned Kibbee; cares for her three daughters as well as her husband and aging parents in Wright Morris's *Plains Song for Female Voices.*

Atkins, Miss Orphanage dietician whom Joe Christmas sees having sex with an intern in William Faulkner's *Light in August.*

Atkins, Mollie Married woman who runs a money-losing shop and has had affairs with numerous men, including Roger Micheldene; after he admits to her that he loves Helene Bang, Mollie gives him the key to her New York apartment, where he finds Helene with Irving Macher in Kingsley Amis's *One Fat Englishman.*

Atkins, Mr. Clergyman sent for when Mr. Arnold is dying in Frances Sheridan's *Memoirs of Miss Sidney Bidulph.*

Atkins, Mr. Surgeon aboard the *Thunder* when Roderick Random is kidnapped in Tobias Smollett's *The Adventures of Roderick Random.*

Atkins, Orion Outgoing and impetuous brother of Emerson, husband of Belle Rooney, father of Sharon Rose; Nebraska farmer, but more interested in hunting; wife dies during the birth of their third daughter; returns mentally and physically disabled from World War I; dies of a stroke in Wright Morris's *Plains Song for Female Voices.*

Atkins, Sally Liza Kemp's simple, good-hearted friend, who marries Harry Atkins in W. Somerset Maugham's *Liza of Lambeth.*

Atkins, Sharon Rose Oldest daughter of Belle Rooney and Orion Atkins; dominates but is devoted to her older cousin Madge; attends the university in Chicago; never marries and has series of strong attachments to women in Wright Morris's *Plains Song for Female Voices.*

Atkins, Strode New York literary agent and horrible Anglophile, who accompanies Roger Micheldene back to England; he illegally obtained Swinburne's notebooks, which Micheldene steals after finding them in Atkins's New York apartment in Kingsley Amis's *One Fat Englishman.*

Atkins, Will One of three mutineers; he turns against the English Captain but is eventually captured by the captain, Friday, and Robinson Crusoe in Daniel Defoe's *The Life and Strange Surprizing Adventures of Robinson Crusoe of York, Mariner.*

Atkinson Manservant of Colonel Boucher; his engagement to Jane Weston's maid, Elizabeth Luton, poses servant problems that require as solution the marriage of their employers in E. F. Benson's *Queen Lucia.*

Atkinson, Bill Insurance salesman, ex-Army major, and Jim Dixon's dependable friend, who resides in the rooming house where Jim lives; he pretends to faint in order to draw attention away from Jim when Jim has difficulties presenting his "Merrie England" speech in Kingsley Amis's *Lucky Jim.*

Atkinson, George P. Manufacturer of cotton seed products and employer of Mamba in DuBose Heyward's *Mamba's Daughters.*

Atkinson, Joe Foster brother to Amelia Booth; his secret adoration of her prompts his endless friendship and service to both the Booths; he marries Molly Bennet in Henry Fielding's *Amelia.*

Atkinson, Lissa Mulatto daughter of Hagar and granddaughter of Mamba; talented singer who appears in a black folk opera at the Metropolitan Opera House in DuBose Heyward's *Mamba's Daughters.*

Atkinson, Miss Maudie Neighbor who defends Atticus Finch to his children; her house is burned down in Harper Lee's *To Kill a Mockingbird.*

Atkinson, Nurse Mother to Joe Atkinson and wet nurse to Amelia Harris; she shelters Amelia and William Booth after they escape Mrs. Harris before their marriage in Henry Fielding's *Amelia.*

Atlas Son of Poseidon and the Earth; fated to bear the Kosmos on his shoulders; retrieves the golden apples for Heracles, who tricks him into bearing the Kosmos once again; befriended by Laika, the Russian space dog, in Jeanette Winterson's *Weight.*

Atra First love of Arthur and one of the three damsels imprisoned by the Witch-Wife's Sister and released by the three knights in William Morris's *The Water of the Wondrous Isles.*

Atreides, Moneo Serves as Leto II's majordomo and fathers Siona Atreides; originally a rebel against Leto II's reign; dies in the bridge collapse along with Leto II during the assassination by Duncan Idaho in Frank Herbert's *God Emperor of Dune.*

Atreides, Siona Daughter of Moneo; beautiful, headstrong girl who is part of a rebel group that works to overthrow the rule of Leto II; grudgingly agrees to work with the Emperor of Dune; with Duncan Idaho, assassinates Leto II in Frank Herbert's *God Emperor of Dune.*

Atreides II, Leto Son of Paul Muad'Dib; rules the known universe by doling out rations of melange spice he stockpiled when he learned spice would no longer be readily available; his political goal through his tyrannical reign is called the Golden

Path, in which the universe avoids a catastrophic war that would eliminate humankind; is assassinated on the day he will marry Hwi Noree in Frank Herbert's *God Emperor of Dune.*

Atrim, Mary Young woman who died of a fever the day after she accepted George Stranson's marriage proposal; her memory continually haunts George to his dying day in Henry James's "The Altar of the Dead."

***At Swim-Two-Birds,* Narrator** Unnamed college student with literary pretensions who creates the novelist Dermot Trellis and numerous other characters who get out of control in Flann O'Brien's *At Swim-Two-Birds.*

Atta Moneylender, Hashim's son, who is left torn and bleeding after a naïve yet desperate trip to the criminal quarters of Srinagar when a relic of Muhammad causes his father's behavior to become violent and possessive; dies in his attempt to save the family in Salman Rushdie's "The Prophet's Hair."

Attaroa Leader of a fierce tribe of man-hating woman warriors. Strong and cruel, Attaroa plans to kill a wounded Jondalar, and poses the biggest threat to the intertwined destinies of Ayla and Jondalar in Jean Auel's *The Plains of Passage.*

Attendants Servants of the archbishop who at first interpose themselves between the knights and Becket to defend him in T. S. Eliot's play *Murder in the Cathedral.*

Atterbury, Gordon Rejected suitor of Alison Parr in Winston Churchill's *The Inside of the Cup.*

Atti Lioness kept by King Dahfu in the lower reaches of his castle; aids the transformation of Eugene Henderson from pig man to leonine kingly spirit in Saul Bellow's *Henderson the Rain King.*

Attila Strong-minded physician of the Condor; has traveled dangerous regions of the North and acquired a deep understanding of pain and of drugs; silent about the woods, he speaks of the sea; archaic genius in Ernst Jünger's *Eumeswil.*

Attwater, Louise See LOUISE ATTWATER EBORN.

Attwater, William John Steel-hearted but religious fatalist and aristocrat, who commands a small native settlement and pearl export trade on a secluded South Sea island; he successfully repels attack from three outcast sailors, Captain John Davies, Huish, and Robert Herrick in Robert Louis Stevenson's *The Ebb-Tide: A Trio and a Quartette.*

Attwood, Mrs. Widow housekeeper from whom Magdalen Vanstone learns details of the household of Admiral Bartram so that she can insinuate herself there as an employee in Wilkie Collins's *No Name.*

Atufu Big black slave who helps bring about Babo's mutiny on the *San Dominick;* possibly a former king in his homeland, as he carries himself with high regard aboard the *San Dominick;* property of the ship's captain, Don Alexandro; serves as Babo's second in command after the mutiny; falsely portrays himself as a disobedient slave in chains while onboard Delano's vessel in Melville's "Benito Cereno."

Atwater Architect of expensive homes in Henry Blake Fuller's *The Cliff-Dwellers.*

Aubade Young woman, part French and part Annamese, who helps Callisto to perfect the ecological balance in his apartment; finds the temperature outside the apartment a constant 37°F; then breaks the apartment window to bring equilibrium to the inside of the apartment; creates a final absence of all motion in Thomas Pynchon's "Entropy."

Aubels, Madame Gilberte des Maurice's mistress who is seduced by the angel Arcade in Anatole France's *The Revolt of the Angels.*

Auberi Ansiau's young squire in Zoé Oldenbourg's *The Cornerstone.*

Auberry, Mr. Faithful young lover, who, though discharged by Eleanor Grimshaw's father before her marriage, saves her from her wicked husband; they marry, and he joins her father's business in a ghost story interpolated into William Beckford's *Azemia.*

Aubigny, Armand Wealthy Louisianan planter who is the son of a Creole father and French mother; raised in France until his mother's death when he was eight years old; husband of Desirée and father of their son; accuses Desirée of being of African descent when it becomes apparent that their son is mulatto; compels his wife and son to leave their home in order to prevent anyone from discovering his secret; subsequently burns a letter written by his mother to his father that reveals that his mother was of French and African descent and that he is mulatto in Kate Chopin's "Desirée's Baby."

Aubigny, Desirée Young, beautiful adopted daughter of the Valmondés, a wealthy Creole family; wife of Armand Aubigny and mother of his son; notices when their son is three months old that he has the same complexion as one of the mulatto servants; having no knowledge of her biological parents, she accepts Armand's accusation that she must be of African descent if their son is mulatto; leaves her husband in order to spare him embarrassment; unaware that Armand's mother was of French and African descent and that he is mulatto in Kate Chopin's "Desirée's Baby."

Aubineau, Mr. Henpecked host in James Kirke Paulding's *The Dutchman's Fireside.*

Aubineau, Mrs. Shrewish hostess in James Kirke Paulding's *The Dutchman's Fireside.*

Aubrey Ernest Freeman's solicitor; he negotiates with Charles Smithson following the jilting of Ernestina Freeman in John Fowles's *The French Lieutenant's Woman.*

Aubrey, Clare Keith Former well-established concert pianist who met her husband, Piers Aubrey, in Ceylon; thin and nervous and desolate and betrayed in her marriage, she insists on the extraordinary and wonderful possibilities of life to her children, Cordelia, Rose, Mary, and Richard Quin Aubrey; Cordelia's lack of musicianship disappoints her in Rebecca West's *The Fountain Overflows.*

Aubrey, Cordelia Eldest Aubrey child, who resembles her father in appearance and in lack of musical talent; to the chagrin of her mother and of her more gifted sisters, her eccentric teacher, Miss Beevor, insists that she has great talent and must continue to practice her violin in Rebecca West's *The Fountain Overflows.*

Aubrey, Edward Village priest and mentor to Lady Vargrave (Alice Darvil) and Evelyn Templeton; he knows the secret of Evelyn's birth and was the rejected suitor of her grandmother in Edward Bulwer-Lytton's *Alice.*

Aubrey, Mary Second child in the Aubrey family; she is a pianist in Rebecca West's *The Fountain Overflows.*

Aubrey, Piers Father of the four Aubrey children and husband of Clare; a gambler and an attractive and lovable but irresponsible parent, he joins the family in a house on the edge of London about 1900 after they have lived in South Africa and in Edinburgh; he frequently changes jobs because he annoys people, and he gambles in stocks; he sells his wife's furniture in her absence to meet his debts, and he leaves the family and does not communicate for months at a time in Rebecca West's *The Fountain Overflows.*

Aubrey, Richard Quin Youngest and only male Aubrey child, adored by the other members of the family; he is destined to die young in World War I in Rebecca West's *The Fountain Overflows.*

Aubrey, Rose Third child of the Aubrey family; she is ten when her father leaves the family; a pianist, she is the child closest to the mother in understanding; she envies and dislikes Cordelia for her closeness to their father and her inability to achieve musical success; Rose is narrator of Rebecca West's *The Fountain Overflows.*

Auburn, Rose Beautiful, virginal, hard, materialistic "harlot"; she went from one rich lover to the next in W. Somerset Maugham's *Ashenden: or The British Agent.*

Auchenbreck, Knight of See Campbell, Sir Duncan.

Auchtermuchty, John Immoderate and lazy messenger between Kinross and Edinburgh in Sir Walter Scott's *The Abbot.*

Auctioneer Salesman who plays on mankind's desire to buy bargains in Charles Johnstone's *Chrysal: or, the Adventures of a Guinea.*

Auditor, The Dark-clothed and hooded figure who stands silently in the background as the protagonist Mouth talks feverishly alone onstage in Samuel Beckett's play *Not I.*

Audley, Alicia Sir Michael Audley's daughter from his first marriage; she loves her cousin Robert Audley and dislikes her stepmother, is interested in horses, marries Sir Harry Towers, and lives happily in Mary Elizabeth Braddon's *Lady Audley's Secret.*

Audley, Charles Aristocratic young clergyman, who works with Edward Underwood in Bexley and, after his death, becomes guardian of the Underwood children; he eventually goes as a missionary to Australia in Charlotte Yonge's *The Pillars of the House.*

Audley, Lady Socialite English aunt and guardian of Alicia Malcolm (Douglas); she opposes Alicia's marriage to her son, Sir Edmund Audley, in Susan Ferrier's *Marriage.*

Audley, Lady Lucy (Helen Maldon Talboys) Protagonist, who marries wealthy Sir Michael Audley, much her senior, and lives happily with him until her supposedly dead first husband, George Talboys, returns; she tries to cover up her secret by murder but is caught and punished by Robert Audley, Sir Michael's nephew, in Mary Elizabeth Braddon's *Lady Audley's Secret.*

Audley, Monsieur Swiss brother-in-law of Arnand La Luc; he oversees Theodore Peyron's education in Ann Radcliffe's *The Romance of the Forest.*

Audley, Robert Character through whose thoughts the story is told, though not in the first person; suspicious of

Lucy, Lady Audley, his uncle's wife, he hunts for his missing friend, George Talboys, and discovers Lucy's secret; he marries Clara, the sister of George Talboys, in Mary Elizabeth Braddon's *Lady Audley's Secret.*

Audley, Sir Edmund Only child of Lady Audley and the tempestuous suitor of his cousin, Alicia Malcolm, before her marriage to Archibald Douglas in Susan Ferrier's *Marriage.*

Audley, Sir Michael Husband of Lady Audley; he loves her but does not know about her first marriage and her child; he rejects her when he learns the truth from his nephew, Robert Audley, in Mary Elizabeth Braddon's *Lady Audley's Secret.*

Audrey University of London student of history who becomes Arthur Miles's lover for several years; she marries Charles Sheriff and welcomes Miles's offers to help advance Sheriff's scientific career in C. P. Snow's *The Search.*

Audrey Birdalone's mother, from whom she is stolen in babyhood by the Witch-Wife; mother and daughter meet twenty years later in the City of the Five Crafts in William Morris's *The Water of the Wondrous Isles.*

Audrey Goatherd who is wooed by Touchstone, the court jester; agrees to marry him and does so in William Shakespeare's play *As You Like It.*

Audrey Name assumed at majority by the narrator's wife, Aurora, in Peter De Vries's *The Tunnel of Love.*

Audrey Narrates memoir of her childhood; accident at birth causes defect in one eye, which is disfigured and technically blind; at fifteen, seduced by ophthalmologist; wants to be an actress, but becomes writer who fabricates self she might have been as she writes memoir in Lynne Sharon Schwartz's *Leaving Brooklyn.*

Audu, Mallam Road treasurer in Fada who is arrested, without understanding why, for misappropriating funds; he is later rehired by Officer Rudbeck to complete the road in Joyce Cary's *Mister Johnson.*

Auerbach, Eric Wears a football uniform, like his twin and many other men, at a Halloween party thrown during the Pommeroy family reunion at the family's summer place at Laud's Head on the shore in Massachusetts in John Cheever's "Goodbye, My Brother."

Auersperg, Axël d' Romantic hero and young count of Auersberg, Germany, in 1828; decides against becoming an initiate into the Rosicrucian order of metaphysical inquirers; instead decides to leave his vast ancestral castle, but before leaving meets the beautiful Sara de Maupers in the basement of his castle, where the two discover a buried treasure and their new love; soon commits a double suicide with her, as living in ordinary reality now after the bliss they discovered together could only be a disappointment after their imagined life in Auguste Villiers's *Axël.*

Aufidius, Tullus General of the Volscians and Martius's rival; keen and realistic; his hatred for Coriolanus results from the defeat he suffers from the war against Rome; remains aware of Martius's stature; welcomes his coming to Antium to join the Volscians and prepare a new campaign against the Romans; suffers Coriolanus's valor; declares Martinus a traitor and has him murdered after Martius withdraws the Volscian troops from Rome in William Shakespeare's play *Coriolanus.*

(Arsenius) Aufugus Elderly patrician monk, who buys Philammon as a slave before retiring with him from the world to the monastery at the Laura; he returns to Alexandria as a Christian ambassador and watches over the estranged Philammon, with whom he is finally reconciled in Charles Kingsley's *Hypatia.*

Augie (Little Augie, Little Poison) Tiny black jockey born with a caul; succeeds despite a series of setbacks; protagonist of Arna Wendell Bontemps's *God Sends Sunday.*

Augray A sorn, one of the native species of Malacandra (Mars), who meets Ransom on his journey to meet Oyarsa of Malacandra; Augray carries Ransom to Oyarsa's habitation in C. S. Lewis's *Out of the Silent Planet.*

August, Botho Lighthouse keeper; reclusive and rude; has slept with Margaret Handle and has an affair with Alaric; is murdered by Fabian Vas in Howard Norman's *The Bird Artist.*

Augusta (Guster) Mrs. Snagsby's simple-minded maid from the workhouse, who has fits; she is kind to Jo in Charles Dickens's *Bleak House.*

Augusta, Empress Grieves over the loss of her infant daughter and suspects that the foreign princess Lycia bewitched the child in Henryk Sienkiewicz's *Quo Vadis.*

Augusta, Julia Cornelia Wealthy young Roman who befriends the destitute Hipparchia in H. D.'s *Palimpsest.*

Augustin Member of Pablo's partisan group in Ernest Hemingway's *For Whom the Bell Tolls.*

Augustine Sober French maid of Eugenia Münster in Henry James's *The Europeans.*

Augustine, Sister Marie One of the nuns who genuinely care for Antoinette Cosway in the convent in Jean Rhys's *Wide Sargasso Sea.*

Augustine, St. Saint conjured up by De Selby; he voices various complaints and opinions in a Dublin accent in Flann O'Brien's *The Dalkey Archive.*

Augustine of Hippo Celebrated philosopher-monk and Bishop of Hippo, who stays with Synesius at Berenice and influences Raphael Aben-Ezra, eventually converting him to Catholicism in Charles Kingsley's *Hypatia.*

August Person (King) Benevolent and humane monarch, who rewards men who speak and act with honesty and boldness in Charles Johnstone's *Chrysal: or, The Adventures of a Guinea.*

Augustus, Constantius (Constans) Roman emperor who methodically exterminates all other surviving male members of his family with the exception of his cousins Gallus and Julian in Gore Vidal's *Julian.*

Augustus, Julian Roman emperor who struggles unsuccessfully to discredit Christianity and restore worship of the Greek gods; assassinated by Callistus in Gore Vidal's *Julian.*

Augustus Caesar Emperor of Rome; returns with the dying Virgil from Greece to Brundisium (Brindsi, Italy); entreats Virgil not to burn his manuscript of the *Aeneid,* as the celebrated poet has become despondent about the loss of ideals in Rome, in Hermann Broch's *The Death of Virgil.*

Augustus Caesar First emperor of Rome; he rules according to the will of his wife, Livia, who eventually poisons him in Robert Graves's *I, Claudius.*

Auld Baldie the Shepherd Rustic shepherd who introduces the legend of the Black Dwarf in order to impress some tavern mates in Sir Walter Scott's *The Black Dwarf.*

Auld Reekie, Marchioness of Mother of Lord Nidderdale, an aspirant to the hand of Marie Melmotte; her social patronage of the Melmottes assists their climb in Anthony Trollope's *The Way We Live Now.* She appears in *Can You Forgive Her?*

Auld Reekie, Marquis of Uncle and guardian of Lady Glencora MacCluskie (Palliser); he arranges her marriage in Anthony Trollope's *Can You Forgive Her?* He orders his son, Lord Nidderdale, to marry Marie Melmotte in *The Way We Live Now.* He appears in *The Small House at Allington.*

Aulus Military commander sent by Claudius to conquer Britain; following the Roman victory, he nobly offers his friendship to the vanquished Caractacas in Robert Graves's *Claudius, the God and His Wife Messalina.*

Aulus Plautius Roman in whose home the foreign princess Lycia is welcomed as a daughter in Henryk Sienkiewicz's *Quo Vadis.*

Aumerle, Edward, Duke of (See also York, Edward Plantagenet, Duke of) Later known as the Earl of Rutland; son of the Duke and Duchess of York, cousin to Henry Bolingbroke (later Henry IV) and Richard II; warns Richard that overconfidence in his royal prerogative is dangerous; denies that he was responsible for the Duke of Gloucester's death; loses dukedom as punishment for loyalty to Richard; conspires with the Bishop of Carlisle and the Abbot of Westminster, among others, to assassinate Henry; begs successfully for Henry to pardon him once the conspiracy is revealed in William Shakespeare's play *Richard II.*

Aunoy, Jean d' (Louis de St. Pierre) Thief hired by Phillippe de Montalt to capture Henry de Montalt, to pose as Adeline's father, and then to kill her; unable to kill her, he hires du Bosse to do so; his testimony against Phillippe de Montalt results in the marquis's arrest in Ann Radcliffe's *The Romance of the Forest.*

Aunt Woman traveling in a railway carriage with her nephew and nieces; she can hardly manage them and is tired of their difficult and endless questions; in order to still their inquisitive natures, she tells a story but clearly fails as they are not attracted to her didactic tales; when the bachelor tells his story, she considers it an improper one since it goes against all the values taught to the children in Saki's "The Story-Teller."

Aunt Abby (Nab) Maiden sister and ward of John Bellmont; tries to protect Frado from Mrs. Bellmont in Harriet E. Wilson's *Our Nig.*

Aunt Alexandra Sister of Atticus Finch and aunt of Scout and Jem Finch; moves into the Finch home to help turn Scout into a southern lady in Harper Lee's *To Kill a Mockingbird.*

Aunt Arlette Theodora Waite's mother's cousin; jewelry marks the divisions in her life; Theodora stays with her for a while after her mother dies; gives Abner $2,000 to take Theodora off her hands in Bette Pesetsky's *Midnight Sweets.*

Aunt Bessie Insane sister of Sam Evans's father; one of the many Evans family members to suffer from insanity in Eugene O'Neill's play *Strange Interlude.*

Aunt Caroline Relative with whom Henry Miller spends a summer; notable for her kindness to him and her pockmarked face in Henry Miller's *Tropic of Capricorn.*

Aunt Chloe Black nurse of Tom Bailey in New Orleans in Thomas Bailey Aldrich's *The Story of a Bad Boy.*

Aunt Chloe Wife of Uncle Tom and mother of three children; suffers greatly when Tom is sold and attempts to earn the money to buy Tom back by cooking on other plantations in Harriet Beecher Stowe's *Uncle Tom's Cabin.*

Aunt Clara Maternal great aunt of the unnamed male narrator and main character; lives on the margins of both black and white society in Opelika, Alabama; married a doctor, "Uncle Eugene," who was called upon to perform secret abortions on white patients; a landowner with tenants, she is devoted to the isolated dignity of her position in Darryl Pinckney's *High Cotton.*

Aunt Cora Lou Sister of Bertha Ann Upshur, mother of Lil Bits and Mamie, and friend of Mariah Upshur; outcast of Tangierneck in Sarah E. Wright's *This Child's Gonna Live.*

Aunt Cornelia (Cornie) Aunt of Honey Winthrop; takes over Honey's upbringing, allows her to go to Paris for a year, and enrolls her in the Katie Gibbs Secretarial School in New York in Judith Krantz's *Scruples.*

Aunt Escolástica Maiden aunt of Fermina; delivers letters to her niece from Florentino, a youthful admirer; banished penniless from the house by her brother, Fermina's father, in Gabriel García Márquez's *Love in the Time of Cholera.*

Auntie Senile retired theatrical-lodging-house keeper; her boasts of her Czarist-regime past and of her jewels are laughed at by her friend-caretaker-tenant Will Boase, but they unexpectedly enrich him in Iris Murdoch's *Bruno's Dream.*

Aunt Jenny Good-hearted sister of Colonel Sartoris; husband killed at the beginning of the Civil War; cautions Bayard, the colonel's son, not to seek blood revenge against Ben Redmond, his father's killer, in William Faulkner's "An Odor of Verbena."

Aunt Julia Unmarried sister of Mr. Lucas; arrives to take Ethel's role in acting as a caregiver to her father in E. M. Forster's "The Road from Colonus."

Aunt Mamie Boardinghouse proprietor who offers bountiful meals, chaos, and love to the narrator of Aline Bernstein's *The Journey Down.*

Aunt Mandy Wise, matriarchal protector of Mattie Johnson in Countee Cullen's *One Way to Heaven.*

Aunt Martha Cook in Caroline Gordon's "The Last Day in the Field."

Aunt Milly Sister of Bertie Eliot; she urges Lewis Eliot to use his inheritance from Aunt Thirza to pay back his father's debts and lends Lewis money to subsidize his study of law in C. P. Snow's *Time of Hope.*

Aunt of Mildred Pompous and proud woman who serves as an omnipresent chaperone of her spoiled niece Mildred Douglas in Eugene O'Neill's *The Hairy Ape.*

Aunt Ruth Temperamental aunt who cared for Leticia and who brought her to medical "treatments" in Julio Cortázar's "End of the Game."

Aura Beautiful niece of Señora Llorente who seems to be under the spell of Consuelo; Felipe Montero has fallen in love with her and wants her to leave with him when he has finished the translations in Carlos Fuentes's *Aura.*

Aurangzeb, Mughal Emperor Defender of Islam; a frail ascetic, he takes Hannah Legge prisoner and gives her a pearl necklace; his battle against Jadav Singh is his last great victory in Bharati Mukherjee's *The Holder of the World.*

Aurea Beloved of Sir Baudoin, who helps to release her with two other damsels from the prison of the Witch-Wife's Sister; she marries a son of Gerard of the Clee in William Morris's *The Water of the Wondrous Isles.*

Aurelia Estranged daughter of Flavius Anicius Maximus and cousin of Basil; she has married a Goth and become a heretic but agrees to embrace Catholicism secretly in order to inherit her father's property; she is mysteriously spirited away by priests in George Gissing's *Veranilda.*

Aurelia Narrator's grandmother's sister who died in 1939; one of the many family members who appear in the mirror to communicate with the living in Maria Elena Llano's "In the Family."

Aurelia Young noblewoman and daughter of Baron von F—; mysterious woman who resembles the painted image of St. Rosalia; tells Medardus that she loves him, but later, after their marriage, is murdered by Medardus in E. T. A. Hoffmann's *The Devil's Elixir.*

Aurelian Only son of a gentleman of Florence, Don Fabio; after a six-year absence he accompanies his Spanish friend Hippolito di Saviolina to Florence; they attend a masked ball where he meets and falls in love with the mysterious Incognita; he presents himself to her as Hippolito in an effort to delay his father's knowledge of his return; Incognita is later revealed to be the Juliana to whom his betrothal was arranged in William Congreve's *Incognita.*

Aureliano III Child born of an affair between Aureliano Babilonia and Amaranta Ursula; born with the curse of a pig's tale; his mother dies during childbirth and his father is too distracted to care for him in Gabriel García Márquez's *One Hundred Years of Solitude.*

Aureliano Sons (Brothers) Seventeen sons born to Aureliano Buendía during his war campaigns; each has a different mother; all eventually return to the Buendía household; each is marked by permanent ashes on his forehead; all are assassinated in Gabriel García Márquez's *One Hundred Years of Solitude*

Aurelius, Marcus Well-known critic, who thinks Janos Lavin's work is worthy but boring in John Berger's *A Painter of Our Time.*

Auronzo, Concetta Widowed mother of Don Carlo and Domenico Campanati; she is an American transplanted to Europe; intelligent and well-read, she involves herself deeply in the effort to save the Jews from extermination in Nazi Germany in the 1930s in Anthony Burgess's *Earthly Powers.*

Aurora Theodosia's younger sister, who is an agreeable woman of fashion, takes an interest in Pompey, and buys him from Mrs. Wilkins in Francis Coventry's *The History of Pompey the Little.*

Aurora See Audrey.

Austin Professor of physics who directs Arthur Miles's research at King's College, University of London; he chairs the committee that establishes the National Institute for Biophysical Research in C. P. Snow's *The Search.*

Austin, Benny Best friend and business partner of Harry Wyeth in Joan Didion's *Play It As It Lays.*

Austin, Henry (Hank) Father of four children who is fired from his job as truckman by Old Running Water in Albert Halper's *Union Square.*

Austin, Mrs. Wife of Professor Austin; she is hostess for dinner parties attended by Arthur Miles in C. P. Snow's *The Search.*

Austin, Seymour Tory politician; he disappoints Cecilia Halkett when he recommends Blackburn Tuckham to her rather than proposing himself in George Meredith's *Beauchamp's Career.*

Author Middle-class man of sublime sentiments who gives a guinea to a strange woman because she is in distress in Charles Johnstone's *Chrysal: or, The Adventures of a Guinea.*

Authority, The First angel who declares himself the Creator when the next angels appear; acts as the deity worshipped by the church; falls to the ground in his crystal chariot and is released by Lyra and Will; disintegrates upon release into particles of dust in Philip Pullman's *His Dark Materials.*

Author's Friend Competitor for admission into the Mock Monastery who proposes to bring down the minister by attacking his public blunders and his private vices and follies, and who is thrown into jail for his efforts in Charles Johnstone's *Chrysal: or, The Adventures of a Guinea.*

Autolycus Peddler who picks the Clown's pocket; visits the Old Shepherd's house on the day of the sheep shearing to sell ballads; exchanges clothes with Florizel, who wishes to flee to Sicilia unnoticed; decides not to inform Polixenes of his son's escape; sends the unwitting Clown and Old Shepherd into the ship carrying Florizel and Perdita to Sicilia in William Shakespeare's play *The Winter's Tale.*

Autumn, Mr. Mrs. Autumn's long-suffering husband; he feeds his wife's delusion that he is jealous by showing impatience at her imaginary flirtations in Charlotte Lennox's *Henrietta.*

Autumn, Mrs. Henrietta Courteney's elderly but vain and self-deluded employer, who plagues her husband by inventing love intrigues; she falsely accuses Henrietta of having a lover and dismisses her in Charlotte Lennox's *Henrietta.*

Autumn House, The Calls the members of the Family together in different ways throughout the centuries; has a hall carpet embroidered with "make haste to live" in Ray Bradbury's *From the Dust Returned.*

Avá Young Brazilian Mairun man who has symbolically changed his name to Isaías; becomes the Indian successor to Anacã, the recently deceased chieftain in the Mairun village; meets Alma, a white woman who has joined an order of nuns to redeem herself; conforms to the rule of marrying a local woman instead of Alma, feeling he has lost his Mairun soul in Darcy Ribeiro's *Maíra.*

Ava (Delilah Lee) Aspiring dancer and lover of Isolde; names herself after Ava Gardner in Marilyn French's *The Women's Room.*

Avellaneda Short name of the reputed author of the false second part of Don Quixote, which pretends to continue the adventures of Cervantes's *Don Quixote;* often referred to by Cervantes's characters in *Don Quixote Part 2;* full name in false book given as Alonso Fernández de Avellaneda, of Tordesillas, in Miguel de Cervantes Saavedra's *Don Quixote de la Mancha.*

Avellanos, Antonia Costaguanan patriot who falls in love with Martin Decoud but loses him in Joseph Conrad's *Nostromo: A Tale of the Seaboard.*

Avellanos, Don José Costaguanan patriot and father of Antonia in Joseph Conrad's *Nostromo: A Tale of the Seaboard.*

Avenel, Julian Mary Avenel's ruthless uncle, a border baron outlawed by England and Scotland; lawless and formidable, he seizes his niece's inheritance but dies defending the monastery in Sir Walter Scott's *The Monastery.*

Avenel, Lady Alice Mary Avenel's mother; soft-spoken and polite when prosperous, she is treated courteously when misfortune befalls her; she turns to the Protestant Bible for solace and dies holding what the monks term heretical opinions in Sir Walter Scott's *The Monastery.*

Avenel, Leonora Gifted young poet, who secretly marries Audley Egerton, is driven to despair by Baron Levy, and dies giving birth to the boy known as Leonard Fairfield in Edward Bulwer-Lytton's *"My Novel," by Pisistratus Caxton.*

Avenel, Mary Lady Alice's scholarly daughter; deprived of her inheritance, she resides with the Glendinnings; she falls in love with Halbert Glendinning, whom she later marries; born on All-Hallows Eve, she is blessed with intuitive insight and is superstitiously called the Spirit of Avenel in Sir Walter Scott's *The Monastery.* She is Lady of Avenal and wife of Sir Halbert; her childless state causes her to lavish Ronald Graeme with maternal devotion in *The Abbot.*

Avenel, Richard Leonora Avenel's brother, who assists and later quarrels with his nephew Leonard Fairfield in Edward Bulwer-Lytton's *"My Novel," by Pisistratus Caxton.*

Avers, Captain Andrew Father of Raib Avers and Desmond Eden; dies aboard the *Lillias Eden* in Peter Matthiessen's *Far Tortuga.*

Avers, Captain Raib Skilled turtler and captain of the *Lillias Eden;* embittered by changes he has witnessed in the fishery business; attempts to take his crew over Misteriosa Reef at night, but wrecks his boat and dies with all but one of his crew in Peter Matthiessen's *Far Tortuga.*

Avers, Jim Eden (Buddy) Quiet and frightened seventeen-year-old son of Raib Avers; determined to be a turtler even though he gets seasick and lacks ability; dies following the wreck of the *Lillias Eden* in Peter Matthiessen's *Far Tortuga.*

Avery Original owner of the Silver Sun Saloon; tries to persuade Molly Riordan to kill Clay Turner; dies when Turner burns the Silver Sun in E. L. Doctorow's *Welcome to Hard Times.*

Avery, Captain Fellow English pirate, who joins Wilmot and Singleton's group in Madagascar; he persuades Wilmot to split off from Singleton and go with him in Daniel Defoe's *The Life, Adventures, and Pyracies of the Famous Captain Singleton.*

Avery, John Somerton Youthful, unassertive aide to Director Leclerc; he befriends Fred Leiser but ignominiously sacrifices him to Operation Mayfly in John le Carré's *The Looking-Glass War.*

Avery, Megan Caring coworker of Jamie Conway's at a prominent New York magazine who always tries to do her best for him even though she is repeatedly taken advantage of in Jay McInerney's *Bright Lights, Big City.*

Avery, Miss Mysterious old charwoman at the farms attached to Howards End in E. M. Forster's *Howards End.*

Avery, Sarah John Avery's lonely, anxious wife; her bitterness drives her husband further into Leclerc's Neverneverland of outdated espionage threats in John le Carré's *The Looking-Glass War.*

Avery, Shug Singer; loves Celie and teaches her about sex; takes her from her husband to Memphis, Tennessee; leaves to go on singing tour with nineteen-year-old lover; later returns to Celie in Alice Walker's *The Color Purple.*

Avey Independent northern black woman; the narrator mistakes her indifference toward him as indolence in Jean Toomer's *Cane.*

Avila, Daisy Daughter of opposition senator Domingo Avila; wins a government-sponsored beauty contest in the Philippines, then denounces the government in a media interview; falls in love with a rebel leader and joins his guerrilla forces; arrested after coming to her assassinated father's funeral; is tortured, gang-raped, and banished from the country, but returns to become a guerrilla fighter in Jessica Hagedorn's *Dogeaters.*

Avila, Domingo Philippine senator who is critical of the ruling regime's abuses and excesses; champion of human rights who is assassinated by the government; father of Daisy Avila in Jessica Hagedorn's *Dogeaters.*

Avinash Maneck's closest friend at college; teaches Maneck to play chess; president of the student union and chairman of hostel committee; tortured and murdered by police for his political activities in opposition to the emergency in Rohinton Mistry's *A Fine Balance.*

Avis, Buchanan Malt (Malty) West Indian friend of Banjo in Claude McKay's *Banjo.*

Avocatori Four magistrates of the Venetian court; although initially on Celia and Bonario's side, they succumb to Volpone, Mosca, and Voltore's ruse; finally rescind their previous errors after Volpone is forced by Mosca to put an end to their plan; release Celia and Bonario, and deal severe punishments to Volpone, Mosca, Voltore, Corvino, and Corbaccio at the end of Ben Jonson's play *Volpone.*

Avora, Mr. d' Italian master for Louisa Mancel and Miss Melvyn; he later joins the women at Millenium Hall to assist in its management in Sarah Scott's *A Description of Millenium Hall.*

Awad Lawyer hired to take care of Abravanel's and Mrs. Khoury's estates after Abravanel's death in P. H. Newby's *Something to Answer For.*

Awalt, Billy Eighteen-year-old hay baler and resident of a small Nebraska town along the Platt River in Ron Hansen's "Nebraska."

Awberry, Deb Younger and more tender-hearted daughter of Mrs. Awberry; she loves William Wilson and marries him, thanks to the magnanimity of Sir Charles Grandison in Samuel Richardson's *Sir Charles Grandison.*

Awberry, Mrs. Widow with two daughters; Harriet Byron's forced marriage to Sir Hargrave Pollexfen was to have taken place in her house in Samuel Richardson's *Sir Charles Grandison.*

Awberry, Sally Elder and less tender-hearted daughter of the widow Mrs. Awberry in Samuel Richardson's *Sir Charles Grandison.*

'Awkins Argumentative captive soldier held under guard as either a spy or enemy combatant; an English communist and atheist who argues against God's involvement in human life; enjoys playing cards while guarded; unclear which side of the war he is on; learns that he is going to be immediately executed as a reprisal against the enemy's execution of their prisoners in Frank O'Connor's "Guests of a Nation."

Axel Son of Gustav Rask; fathers the illegitimate child of Oscar's daughter; murdered in revenge by Oscar in Carl A. V. Moberg's *Raskens.*

Axël See Auersperg, Axël d'.

Axel Axel (covernames: "Poppy," "Greensleeves," Herr König) Magnus Pym's Czechoslovakian controller and beloved second father-figure; he introduces Magnus to culture, literature, and philosophy; he offers Magnus sanctuary when British Intelligence unearths him, but, even with Mary Pym's help, he is unable to prevent Magnus's suicide in John le Carré's *A Perfect Spy.*

Axelrod, Arthur Father of David Axelrod and a lawyer in Scott Spencer's *Endless Love.*

Axelrod, David (Dave) Obsessive lover of Jade Butterfield; narrator of Scott Spencer's *Endless Love.*

Axelrod, Dr. Marcus J. Boyhood friend of Herman Gold and prosperous Lower East Side physician in Michael Gold's *Jews without Money.*

Axelrod, Rose Wife of Arthur Axelrod and mother of David Axelrod in Scott Spencer's *Endless Love.*

Axelroot, Eeben Disreputable pilot who frequently stays in Kilanga; involved in diamond smuggling and covert CIA operations, apparently has some involvement in the assassination of the prime minister of the Republic of Congo, Patrice Lumumba; takes Rachel to Johannesburg and becomes her lover in Barbara Kingsolver's *The Poisonwood Bible.*

Axwick, Alan Dull and witless Member of Parliament for whom Owen Tuby and Cosmo Sultana form a more exciting image in J. B. Priestley's *The Image Men.*

Axworthy, Samuel Vicious cousin of Leonard Ward; he terrorizes the young Thomas May in Charlotte Yonge's *The Daisy Chain.* He is finally established by Thomas May as the murderer of his uncle in *The Trial.*

Ay, Laintal Yuli's great-great-great grandson, who is destined to become king of Oldorando and lead the country into a new era in Brian W. Aldiss's *Helliconia Spring.*

Ayacanora Indian priestess, actually daughter of John Oxenham; she falls in love with Amyas Leigh during his search for El Dorado; Amyas brings her back to England; her identity is discovered by Salvation Yeo, and she and Amyas finally marry in Charles Kingsley's *Westward Ho!*

Aycock, Willie Duke Sexual rival of Rosacoke Mustian for the affections of Wesley Beavers in Reynolds Price's *A Long and Happy Life.*

Ayesha Mistress of Louis Grayle in Edward Bulwer-Lytton's *A Strange Story.*

Ayesha Pakistani woman with a Danish husband; she works for International Family Planning; she is present at an Evelyn (Morton) and Ted Stennett gathering in Margaret Drabble's *The Middle Ground.*

Ayida, Joe Art historian and sculptor who is Minister of Culture of Adra; Frances Wingate's long-time professional friend, he is her host at the conference from which she is summoned home following the discovery of Constance Ollerenshaw's death in Margaret Drabble's *The Realms of Gold.*

Ayla Strong, resourceful, beautiful Cro-Magnon woman; lives in isolation after her unjust banishment from the Neanderthal Clan that raised her; discoverer of flint and iron pyrite as tools to make fire; expert hunter; skilled healer, eventual lover of Jondular; protagonist of Jean Auel's *The Valley of Horses, The Clan of the Cave Bear, The Plains of Passage,* and *The Mammoth Hunters.*

Aylmer Young man who worships science's ability to alter nature; married to the beautiful Georgiana who has a tiny birthmark—a flaw in her otherwise perfect nature—on her cheek; becomes obsessed with the flaw and desires to remove the mark; the potion he mixes up in his laboratory ends his wife's life in Nathaniel Hawthorne's "The Birth-Mark."

Aylmer, Belinda Meek and adoring sister of Frederick; she is nagged and bullied by her mother in Anthony Trollope's *The Belton Estate.*

Aylmer, Captain Frederick Folliott Cold, egotistical Member of Parliament, who becomes engaged to Clara Amedroz; his snobbish mother snubs her when she visits Aylmer Hall and helps separate the couple; he at last marries Lady Emily Taggmaggert in Anthony Trollope's *The Belton Estate.*

Aylmer, Lady Domineering mother of Frederick; she successfully encourages him to disentangle himself from Clara Amedroz and marry Lady Emily Tagmaggert in Anthony Trollope's *The Belton Estate.*

Aylmer, Sir Anthony Henpecked husband of Lady Aylmer; he advises his son, Frederick, to remain a bachelor; he is the sole member of the family to show kindness to Clara Amedroz when she visits Aylmer Hall in Anthony Trollope's *The Belton Estate.*

Aylmer, Sir William Trustee of Maud Ruthyn's estate in J. Sheridan Le Fanu's *Uncle Silas.*

Aymaro of Alessandria Benedictine monk and copyist in the abbey; fond of gossiping, gives a lot of information to William of Baskerville in Umberto Eco's *The Name of the Rose.*

Aymer Corrupt prior of Jorvaulx Abbey; he brings great grief to the Saxons and so is captured and held for ransom in Sir Walter Scott's *Ivanhoe.*

Aymer, Mr. (alias Mr. Vallance) Evil accomplice of Squire Cranmer in John Buchan's *The Free Fishers.*

Aymeris, Sir Castellan of the Castle of the Quest in William Morris's *The Water of the Wondrous Isles.*

Aymo, Bartolomeo Ambulance driver in the command of Frederic Henry; shot and killed by fellow Italian soldiers in the confusion of a retreat in Ernest Hemingway's *A Farewell to Arms.*

Ayres British army major who attends the yacht party in William Faulkner's *Mosquitoes.*

Ayres, Phoebe Experienced prostitute who, as Fanny Hill's coworker and roommate at Mrs. Brown's bordello, introduces her to lesbian love, voyeurism, and other aspects of life in the professional sisterhood in John Cleland's *Memoirs of a Woman of Pleasure.*

Ayresleigh, Mr. Middle-aged, haggard prisoner for debt in the Fleet prison in Charles Dickens's *The Posthumous Papers of the Pickwick Club.*

Ayscue, Major William ("Willie") Self-doubting chaplain, who is generally ineffective when called upon in professional capacities and more interested in pursuing interests in music in Kingsley Amis's *The Anti-Death League.*

Azar Foot soldier in the Vietnam War and member of Alpha Company; mean-spirited and cruel; makes jokes about enemy corpses and the deaths of his fellow soldiers and mocks traumatized Vietnamese civilians; helps O'Brien play a practical joke on Jorgenson, the unit's medic, after Rat Kiley is removed from combat; forced to help dig Kiowa's body out of the sewage field and finally shows his humanity in Tim O'Brien's *The Things They Carried.*

Azariah Early tutor of Joseph of Arimathea, schooling him in Greek in George Moore's *The Brook Kerith.*

Azarian Rock musician who becomes leader of a band when singer Bucky Wunderlick drops out; ultimately murdered in Don DeLillo's *Great Jones Street.*

Azarina Black servant of Eugenia Münster in Henry James's *The Europeans.*

Azazello One of Woland's band; red-headed with a fang sticking out of his mouth; sent by Woland to persuade Margarita to be a queen at the devil's ball, and also responsible for the chaos created in Moscow in Mikhail Bulgakov's *The Master and Margarita.*

Azazruk Young shaman of Eskimo descent in 12,000 BPE; leads his tribe to start one of the earliest Aleut settlements on island of Lapak in James Michener's *Alaska.*

Azcoitía, D. Jerónimo de Wealthy aristocrat and politician to whom Humberto Peñaloza, the narrator and protagonist of the story, serves as servant and secretary; owns the convent where much of the story takes place and the narrator burns to death in José Donoso's *The Obscene Bird of Night.*

Azdak, Judge Former village employee and recorder who has now been promoted by drunken soldiers to judge of Nuka; friendly to the poor and occasionally breaks laws to get money from the rich; has no proper education but attempts to judge righteously through the famed Chalk-Circle; recognizes Grusha's love and concern for the child during this test of a tug-of-war with the baby and assigns her custody rather than the heartless birth mother in Bertolt Brecht's play *The Caucasian Chalk-Circle.*

Azemia Beautiful Turkish naif captured by a British warship captain; she is intended as a gift for a lecherous duke, but his jealous paramour removes her from the duke's household; she is in the custody of several aristocrats, the last being the good Mrs. Blandford; she eventually marries Charles Arnold in William Beckford's *Azemia.*

Azeredo, Fernande (Nande) Exotic Frenchwoman who has an affair with Sam Dodsworth in Sinclair Lewis's *Dodsworth.*

Azevedo, Daniel Simon Second murdered man who, having been a political tough man and later an ordinary thief, seems very far from any connection to the first murdered rabbi in Jorge Luis Borges's "Death and the Compass."

Azimart, Monsieur D' Famous good shot with a pistol and an old lover of the Duchesse de Perpignan; after she sets up Henry Pelham for his challenge, he is wounded in their duel, having misfired and shot Pelham's hat in Edward Bulwer-Lytton's *Pelham.*

Aziz Mabel Layton's Indian servant who has been with the family for many years; when Mabel dies at Rose Cottage, he returns to his home village in the mountains in Paul Scott's *The Towers of Silence.*

Aziz, Aadam Muslim doctor and Heidelberg graduate; sports a distinguished nose, red beard, dark hair, and sky-blue eyes; feels inferior among Germans during the five years of his studies, and feels alienated and suspected among Indians, including his wife, Naseem, for his European ideologies; ambivalent about God; hates calls for partitioning India and blames foreign countries; permanently scarred by the Amritsar massacre; his son Hanif's suicide makes him rebel against God by refusing to go to Pakistan; accused of stealing Prophet Muhammad's holy hair, thus causing political upheavals; his skeleton disintegrates into powder inside his skin in Salman Rushdie's *Midnight's Children.*

Aziz, Dr. Muslim Indian doctor who is optimistically friendly to the sympathetic English: Henry Fielding, Mrs. Moore, and Adela Quested; Adela's accusation against him of attempted rape in the Marabar Caves he perceives as insulting and maliciously false; he is acquitted when Adela withdraws her accusation at his trial, but he has become hostile to the British in E. M. Forster's *A Passage to India.*

Aziz, Abdul Instigator of the Fouad University student uprising against the British in P. H. Newby's *The Picnic at Sakkara.*

Azureus, President Head of the university who calls a meeting to require the faculty to sign papers of allegiance to the new regime; Adam Krug, whose wife dies only hours before the meeting, alone refuses to sign the declaration in Vladimir Nabokov's *Bend Sinister.*

Azusa Common-law wife of Wolfie, who yearns to return to her in Peter Matthiessen's *At Play in the Fields of the Lord.*

Azvedo, Throat-Cut de Pirate who had been a rabbi's son and a physician in Bharati Mukherjee's *The Holder of the World.*

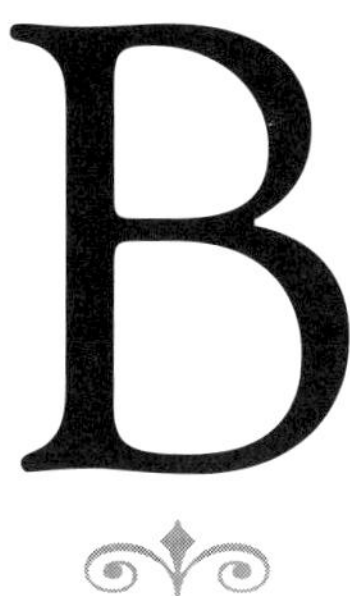

B Artist who is a friend of DeSilva in Doris Lessing's *The Golden Notebook.*

"B" Middle-aged woman and plainly dressed companion of the 90-year-old matriarch named "A"; listens to the old dying woman's life story in Edward Albee's play *Three Tall Women.*

B, Mr. Handsome, confident, and wealthy man who is the middle-aged owner of the Summer Camp, and a teacher at the nearby genteel school attended by a number of the campers in Margaret Atwood's "True Trash."

B., Mr. GESS (Global-Equip Security Services) agent consulted by Anthea Leaver in Muriel Spark's *Territorial Rights.*

B, Mrs. Pressured into supervising the Summer Camp where all the teenagers meet; symbol of the wealthy leisure class seen as an obscure yet ideal adult world in the minds of the teenagers in Margaret Atwood's "True Trash."

B**, Count de** Admirer of Shakespeare and English books; mistakenly believing Yorick is like his namesake, the King's Jester, he promptly acquires the passport Yorick needs to avoid being jailed in the Bastille in Laurence Sterne's *A Sentimental Journey through France and Italy.*

B—, Countess of Lord B—'s mother; impressed with Henrietta Courteney's rejection of her son, she introduces her to her sister in order to find her a good situation in Charlotte Lennox's *Henrietta.*

B—, Earl of Lord B—'s father; he is anxious for his son to marry Jenny Cordwain's money, but sympathetic toward Henrietta Courteney, whom his son prefers, because she is a distressed gentlewoman in Charlotte Lennox's *Henrietta.*

B—, Lord Father of Lady Forester; he raised her to be an atheist and is said to have been highly unpredictable in his treatment of tenants in Richard Graves's *The Spiritual Quixote.*

B—, Lord Jenny Cordwain's betrothed; he conspires with Mrs. Eccles to seduce Henrietta Courteney, hoping to marry her (though she is a servant) if she will convert to Catholicism and thereby inherit her aunt's estate in Charlotte Lennox's *Henrietta.*

B—, William Rake who attempts to seduce but finally marries his mother's young serving maid; his temper, arrogance, and errant behavior as Pamela's husband provide much of the dramatic tension in Samuel Richardson's *Pamela, or Virtue Rewarded.* As Mr. Booby, he is nephew to Lady Booby and husband to Pamela Andrews; his regard for Pamela leads him to rescue successively Joseph Andrews and Fanny Goodwill from his aunt's ire in Henry Fielding's *The History of the Adventures of Mr. Joseph Andrews and of His Friend Mr. Abraham Adams.*

B—, William (Billy) Son of Pamela (Andrews) and Mr. B— in Samuel Richardson's *Pamela, or Virtue Rewarded.*

Baako Central character; young man educated in the United States who returns home to Ghana fearing to face the unrealistic expectations of his family and friends that he will return prosperous; experienced a nervous breakdown from the pressure prior to his return; at home, he seeks the care of Juana, a Puerto Rican psychiatrist practicing in Ghana; also becomes her lover; fails in his attempt to publish his writing that reveals Ghana's social ills; falls into insanity but is guided out of his mental maze by Juana in Ayi Kwei Armah's *Fragments.*

Baba Amir's widowed father; wealthy, successful, and generous businessman in Kabul, Afghanistan, in Khaled Hosseini's *The Kite Runner.*

Bababalouk Chief of Vathek's eunuchs; he likes to bully the women in the harem in William Beckford's *Vathek.*

Babad, Eleazar (Reb Eleazar) Wealthiest man in Goray before the 1648 invasion and massacre; afterward, a widower, wanderer, and father who abandons Rechele Babad to relatives in Isaac Bashevis Singer's *Satan in Goray.*

Babad, Rechele Epileptic daughter of Reb Eleazar Babad, wife of Reb Itche Mates in an unconsummated marriage, and mistress and later wife of Reb Gedaliya; called a prophetess by the people of Goray, she is tormented and impregnated by Satan in Isaac Bashevis Singer's *Satan in Goray.*

Babalatchi Aid to Lakamba, Rajah of Sambir; he helps Kaspar Almayer's daughter elope in Joseph Conrad's *Almayer's Folly: A Story of an Eastern River.* He thwarts Peter Willems and Almayer in *An Outcast of the Islands.*

Babbacombe, Evie Sexual "local phenomenon" of Stilbourne; she makes her body accessible to Oliver as well as to others in William Golding's *The Pyramid.*

Babbacombe, Mrs. Evie's mother and the town of Stilbourne's "only Roman Catholic"; she does not know her place in the social structure of the town and is ridiculed by its inhabitants in William Golding's *The Pyramid.*

Babbacombe, Sergeant Town crier and brutal father of Evie Babbacombe; he has an incestuous relationship with his daughter in William Golding's *The Pyramid.*

Babbalanja Philosopher from Odo and Taji's companion in Herman Melville's *Mardi.*

Babbitt, Eunice Littlefield See Littlefield, Eunice.

Babbitt, George F. (Georgie) Realtor and faithful Zenith civic booster who fails to find happiness upholding community values in Sinclair Lewis's *Babbitt;* also appears in *Elmer Gantry.*

Babbitt, Katherine (Tinka) Daughter of George and Myra Babbitt; adored by her father in Sinclair Lewis's *Babbitt.*

Babbitt, Myra Thompson Patient wife of George Babbitt; mother of Katherine, Theodore, and Verona Babbitt in Sinclair Lewis's *Babbitt.*

Babbitt, Theodore Roosevelt (Ted) Son of George and Myra Babbitt; would-be automobile mechanic who elopes with Eunice Littlefield in Sinclair Lewis's *Babbitt.*

Babbitt, Verona (Rone) Daughter of George and Myra Babbitt; Bryn Mawr graduate who marries Kenneth Escott in Sinclair Lewis's *Babbitt.*

Babbybobby Widower in his early 30s; owns a curragh (boat), which is the only transportation off the island of Inishmaan in Martin McDonagh's *The Cripple of Inishmaan.*

Babchild, Mr. Primitive Methodist pastor whose preference for Hester Limbrick's cooking angers her mother; the pleasant notion of entertaining him in her own home motivates Hester's disastrous marriage to the drunkard Joel Dethridge in Wilkie Collins's *Man and Wife.*

Babcock, Dr. Arthur Amos Cuncliffe Protective English physician to the royal court of Pisuerga and lover of royal governess Aggie Montgomery in Ronald Firbank's *The Flower Beneath the Foot.*

Babcock, Dwight Stodgy member of the Knickerbocker Trust Company who is Patrick Dennis's trustee and Mame Dennis's nemesis in Patrick Dennis's *Auntie Mame* and *Around the World with Auntie Mame.*

Babe Dayton Nickles's wild mare that Rayona Taylor tries to ride in the Havre rodeo in Michael Dorris's *A Yellow Raft in Blue Water.*

Babe See Greene, Beatrice.

Baberton, Anne Resident of the May of Teck Club and owner of a coveted Schiaparelli taffeta evening dress in Muriel Spark's *The Girls of Slender Means.*

Babette, Madame Concierge with whom Virginie de Crequy takes shelter in Elizabeth Gaskell's *My Lady Ludlow.*

Babie Blind Alice Grey's servant, a slovenly and graceless girl, in Sir Walter Scott's *The Bride of Lammermoor.*

Babilonia, Aureliano (Aureliano II) Illegitimate son of Meme and Mauricio Babilonia; sent to Buendía house and raised by Fernanda; carefully studies Melquíades's parchments; has an affair with his aunt Amaranta Ursula in Gabriel García Márquez's *One Hundred Years of Solitude.*

Babington, Anthony Childhood friend of Cecily Talbot; his admiration for Mary, Queen of Scots draws him into a plot against Queen Elizabeth and leads him to a horrible death in Charlotte Yonge's *Unknown to History.*

Babington, Babington Julia Cousin of John Caldigate much in love with him from youth; when he marries Hester Bolton, she becomes his enemy; she marries the Reverend Augustus Smirkie in Anthony Trollope's *John Caldigate.*

Babington, Mary Anne (Aunt Polly) John Caldigate's aunt, who had cared for him when he was little; she turns against him when he declines to marry her daughter, Julia, in Anthony Trollope's *John Caldigate.*

Babington, Nan Suburban middle-class friend of the Henderson girls in Dorothy Richardson's *Backwater.* She makes a brief reappearance in *Clear Horizon.*

Babington, Tommy Nan's brother, also a friend of the Henderson girls, in Dorothy Richardson's *Backwater.*

Babka Orphaned peasant girl who lives in the forest; becomes Grischa Paprotkin's lover and becomes pregnant by him; tries to save him from the death sentence by organizing his escape from prison in Arnold Zweig's *The Case of Sergeant Grischa.*

Babley, Richard (Mr. Dick) Simple-minded man, who was rescued from incarceration in an asylum by Betsey Trotwood, with whom he lives; he is engaged in writing a memorial of the Lord Chancellor, but the subject of King Charles the First's head always gets in the way; Mr. Micawber calls him Mr. Dixon in Charles Dickens's *The Personal History of David Copperfield.*

Babli Twenty-six-year-old single daughter of Mr. Bhowmick, part of a family that moved from India to America years earlier; professional electrical engineer who has modern ideas about sex and marriage; discloses that her pregnancy is the result of artificial insemination and that she has no interest in marrying or having a man in her life in Bharati Mukherjee's "A Father."

Babo Seemingly faithful and attentive slave to his Spanish sea captain, Benito Cereno; turns out to be the ruthless mastermind behind a slave revolt, which, having placed the skeleton of the slave owner Aranda on the prow of the ship, takes as it motto "Follow your leader"; attempts to sail back to Senegal; met by the American whaler *Bachelor's Delight* captained by Amasa Delano, who is fooled by the story Babo forces Cereno to relate; Babo tries to kill Cereno in a dingy but fails; captured, Babo refuses to speak again and is "dragged to the gibbet" and decapitated in Herman Melville's "Benito Cereno."

Babu, Paresh True humanist and guru of many; has brought up Sucharita and her brother Satish like his own children; a Brahmo but respects all religions; has given freedom of choice to all his own as well as adopted children; blesses Gora's union with Sucharita without any fear of society or Samaj in Rabindra Nath Tagore's *Gora.*

Babushkin, Meyer Partner of Harry Bogen in Apex Modes, a women's garments manufacturing company; goes to jail because of Bogen's stealing from the firm in Jerome Weidman's *I Can Get It for You Wholesale.*

Baby Sneezing, howling, squirming infant of the Duchess; encumbered with its care, Alice releases it into the wood after it has undergone improvement by turning into a pig in Lewis Carroll's *Alice's Adventures in Wonderland.*

Baby Igor See Metzger.

Baby Thor Son of Amanda Ziller conceived during an electrical storm in Tom Robbins's *Another Roadside Attraction.*

Baca, Jesus de Old, poor priest of Isleta whose sole worldly possession is a wooden parrot in Willa Cather's *Death Comes for the Archbishop.*

Baccani, Mr. Italian scientist who was Nathan Benjulia's friend in his youth; Mr. Mool gets from him information correcting Benjulia's mistaken evidence impugning the character of Carmina Graywell's mother in Wilkie Collins's *Heart and Science.*

Bach Crippled ex-Nazi married to a woman who is half-Jewish in Thomas Berger's *Crazy in Berlin.*

Bach, Richard Biplane-flying narrator of *Illusions: The Adventures of a Reluctant Messiah,* whose brief summer encounter with enigmatic Donald Shimoda sparks Bach's rocky journey to spiritual self-discovery.

Bache, Richard Son-in-law of Benjamin Franklin; gets Thomas Paine a job as a tutor when Paine first arrives in America in Howard Fast's *Citizen Tom Paine.*

Bachelor, The Sexton of the old church in the village where Nell Trent dies; he converses with her and shows her the old well in the church in Charles Dickens's *The Old Curiosity Shop.*

Bachelor, The Young man who is traveling in the same railway carriage compartment with three children and their aunt; he notices how the aunt fails to control the children and especially tests their patience with her boring moral story; he then tells the young tots a funny story that is rather different from usual stories since it flouts the convention of conveying a moral; in fact, it outrageously shows punishment being meted out for goodness; he tells the story of a good girl, Bertha, who is privileged to take a stroll in the prince's park as an acknowledgment of her peerless goodness but is eaten by a wolf who finds her an easy prey in that lonely place; the aunt highly disapproves of his tale, but he defends himself by saying that he at least has succeeded in keeping the three children quiet for 10 minutes in Saki's "The Story-Teller."

Bacheron, Octave White pharmacist who supports the civil rights efforts of the Reverend Phillip Martin in Ernest J. Gaines's *In My Father's House.*

Bachir Cheerful, hardworking young Tunisian manager of the Duchess of Varna's exotic but discreet flower shop "Haboubet of Egypt" in Ronald Firbank's *The Flower Beneath the Foot.*

Bachofen, Linda (Lin) Beautiful blonde government enforcer and sister of Mariette Bachofen; comes with her fiancé to arrest Mr. Ember and later appears with another fiancé, Doctor Alexander, to arrest Adam and David Krug; executed for her mistakes in Vladimir Nabokov's *Bend Sinister.*

Bachofen, Mariette (Mariechen) Young sister of Linda Bachofen who becomes David Krug's nurse; probably informs on Adam Krug; dies after being raped by forty soldiers in Vladimir Nabokov's *Bend Sinister.*

Bacon, Abra Young woman engaged to marry Aron Trask but who feels unworthy of his extreme virtue and trapped by his narrow view of life and love; realizes that Caleb Trask is the one she truly loves in John Steinbeck's *East of Eden.*

Bacon, Felix Man who lives with Jonathan Swift, dances with him, and sits on his knee; he becomes a drawing master at Josephine Napier's school and marries Helen Keats after his father, Sir Robert, dies in Ivy Compton-Burnett's *More Women Than Men.*

Bacon, Francis Very intelligent eleven-year-old pupil at Lucius Cassidy's school in Ivy Compton-Burnett's *Two Worlds and Their Ways.*

Bacon, Lillian Dance-marathon partner of Pedro Ortega; violently attacked by Ortega when he learns that Rocky Gravo attempted to seduce her in Horace McCoy's *They Shoot Horses, Don't They?*

Bacon, Mr. Personal enemy and rival publisher of his former friend and partner, Mr. Bungay, in William Makepeace Thackeray's *The History of Pendennis.*

Bacon, Mrs. Mr. Bungay's sister and Mr. Bacon's wife in William Makepeace Thackeray's *The History of Pendennis.*

Bacon, Reginald Reverend who heads many political, social, and religious organizations in the Bronx; behind-the-scenes orchestrator of the case against Sherman McCoy in Tom Wolfe's *The Bonfire of the Vanities.*

Bacon, Sir Francis Writer and courtier in George Garrett's *Death of the Fox.*

Bacon, Sir Robert Felix's father, who disapproves of his way of life; when he is dying, he makes Felix promise to marry and continue the family and protect the estate in Ivy Compton-Burnett's *More Women Than Men.*

Badcock Ugly and deformed fellow student of Ernest Pontifex at Cambridge; a leader of the despised Simonites, he invites Ernest to hear Gideon Hawke speak; after the session, Badcock tells Ernest that Hawke enquired after him in Samuel Butler's *The Way of All Flesh.*

Baddeley, Father Michael Chaplain at Toynton Grange, a private home for the disabled; he writes to Adam Dalgliesh, whom he knew as a child, requesting a visit, but is murdered before Dalgliesh can arrive in P. D. James's *The Black Tower.*

Baddely, Sir Philip Shallow, oath-using false friend of Clarence Hervey; he asks Belinda to marry him; when she refuses, he circulates malicious rumors about her in Maria Edgeworth's *Belinda.*

Baddlestone, Captain Rude merchant captain of the "Princess"; he is good in battle alongside Hornblower but shows contempt for the navy in C. S. Forester's *Hornblower and the Crisis: An Unfinished Novel.*

Bader, Miriam Wife of Shmuel Bader; helps David Lurie with his German studies in Chaim Potok's *In the Beginning.*

Bader, Shmuel Torah teacher of David Lurie and European field director of an organization that brings Polish Jews to the United States in Chaim Potok's *In the Beginning.*

Badger Kindly and wise creature, experienced in the ways of both the Wild Wood and the Wide World; with the help of Water Rat and Mole he decides to take the irresponsible Toad in hand and make him learn the error of his ways in Kenneth Grahame's *The Wind in the Willows.*

Badger, Bayham Medical man in Chelsea, with whom Richard Carstone lodges while training to be a surgeon; he is proud to be the third husband of Laura Badger in Charles Dickens's *Bleak House.*

Badger, Hugh Gamekeeper at Rookwood Place in William Harrison Ainsworth's *Rookwood.*

Badger, Laura Youthfully dressed woman of fifty, who was married twice before marrying Mr. Badger; she speaks fondly of her former husbands, Captain Swosser and Professor Dingo, and has their portraits displayed in Charles Dickens's *Bleak House.*

Badger, Ray Ne'er-do-well first husband of Melissa Scaddon Wapshot; jewel thief and rival to Moses Wapshot in John Cheever's *The Wapshot Chronicle.*

"Bad Glazier, The" Narrator Contemplative, indolent, and bored Parisian who, seldom known for taking action in life or acting with spontaneity, suddenly seizes the moment when he looks down from his apartment balcony to see a poor elderly glazier carrying his clear panes of glass along the drab streets; an overwhelming hatred for this poor soul fills the narrator; invites the window seller to his apartment, where the resident finds the panes drab and lacking color; shoves the glazier from the apartment and then throws a flower pot down on the man, shattering his glass wares; attributes his actions to the caprices of malicious demons, housed within him and others, that force him to "carry out their most absurd wishes" in Charles Baudelaire's "The Bad Glazier."

Badsen, Miss Thin, dark lady, who teaches music and French at Mr. Herrick's school; she is a feminist in Ivy Compton-Burnett's *Pastors and Masters.*

Baffin, Arnold Successful and prolific novelist, who is the father of Julian Baffin; his wife, Rachel Baffin, murders him out of sexual jealousy in Iris Murdoch's *The Black Prince.*

Baffin, Julian Arnold and Rachel Baffin's student daughter, with whom the fifty-eight-year-old Bradley Pearson falls joyously and disastrously in love in Iris Murdoch's *The Black Prince.*

Baffin, Rachel Wife of Arnold and mother of Julian; her unimportance to both her husband and to Bradley Pearson so enrages her that she kills the former with a poker and frames the latter for the murder in Iris Murdoch's *The Black Prince.*

Bagarag, Shibli Wandering barber; he is the brave but vain hero of numerous adventures leading up to his successful attempt to shave the head of Shagpat, particularly a single hair, the Identical, which has rendered the people of the city of Oolb subject to Shagpat; his adventures lead him to shed his vanity in George Meredith's *The Shaving of Shagpat.*

Bagchi, Mrs. Meenakshi Self-reliant widow and the "girlfriend" of Ruma's father; independent-minded woman who no longer wants to share her life with any man; meets and remains friendly with Ruma's father only during the tours; it is to her he has written a postcard, which Ruma posts in the end in Jhumpa Lahiri's *Unaccustomed Earth.*

Bagenhall, James Extravagant and treacherous employer of William Wilson; his indebtedness makes him a conspirator with Solomon Merceda in Sir Hargrave Pollexfen's kidnapping of Harriet Byron; he acts as Sir Margrave's agent in attempting to force a duel upon Sir Charles Grandison in Samuel Richardson's *Sir Charles Grandison.*

Baggart, Proctor (Proc) Bigoted and disreputable magistrate charged with keeping blacks subservient and with maintaining law and order in the district outside Charleston where Charles Raymond's Phosphate Mining Company is located in DuBose Heyward's *Mamba's Daughters.*

Baggett, Mrs. Domineering housekeeper of William Whittlestaff; once her master has become engaged to his young ward, Mary Lawrie, she is determined that the marriage take place in Anthony Trollope's *An Old Man's Love.*

Baggett, Sergeant Drunken, one-legged husband of William Whittlestaff's housekeeper; he reappears to plague her with care in Anthony Trollope's *An Old Man's Love.*

Baggins, Bilbo Formerly comfort-loving, unambitious hobbit who travels with Gandalf to rescue the Mountain and its treasure from the dragon and finds the One Ring in J. R. R. Tolkien's *The Hobbit; or There and Back Again.* He leaves his home and the ring to his nephew Frodo Baggins in *The Fellowship of the Ring.* He and Frodo depart over the Sea for eternity in *The Return of the King.*

Baggins, Frodo Young, brave hobbit who accepts the responsibility for the One Ring from his uncle Bilbo Baggins in J. R. R. Tolkien's *The Fellowship of the Ring.* He manages to take the ring to the Mountain of Doom; paralyzed by the spider Shelob, he is left for dead by his companion Sam Gamgee in *The Two Towers.* Reunited with Sam, he destroys Sauron's power in *The Return of the King.*

Baggs, Alderman Prominent Tory canvasser, who decides to support Aubrey Bohun when the Tory candidate, Mr. Vavasour, resigns in Benjamin Disraeli's *A Year at Hartlebury; or, The Election.*

Bagillard, M. Lecherous Frenchman who cultivates William Booth to seduce Booth's wife, Amelia; Colonel Bath kills Bagillard in a duel in Henry Fielding's *Amelia.*

Baginut, Archpriest Branza Borlienese priest who interrogates Billy Xiao Pin in Brian W. Aldiss's *Helliconia Summer.*

Bagley, Dr. President of Polycarp College in Peter De Vries's *Let Me Count the Ways.*

Bagley, Harry British explorer who symbolizes his homeland's sense of masculinity and courage; hides his homosexuality; falls into a sexual relationship with Edward, the son of Clive and Betty, in Caryl Churchill's play *Cloud 9.*

Baglione, Father Battista Catholic priest and member of the Common Sense Committee in Robert Coover's *The Origin of the Brunists.*

Baglioni, Professor Adviser and mentor to Giovanni; prying and intrusive, he cautions Giovanni to avoid Beatrice and her father and concocts an antidote for Beatrice's poisonous breath that ultimately kills her in Nathaniel Hawthorne's "Rappaccini's Daughter."

Bagnet, Matthew Ex-artilleryman who is the good friend of Trooper George (Rouncewell) in Charles Dickens's *Bleak House.*

Bagnet, Mrs. Soldierly-looking wife of Matthew Bagnet and the decision maker of the family; she advises Trooper George and reunites him with his mother, Mrs. Rouncewell, in Charles Dickens's *Bleak House.*

Bagnoli, Mrs. Woman expert at running farm machinery such as balers and tractors; visits the narrator's nearby farm where Floyd Dey works in Janet Kauffman's "Patriotic."

Bagot Favorite of Richard II; at the beginning of Henry Bolingbroke's rebellion, he observes that the common people will revolt against Richard for financial reasons; fears the common people will pursue him, as well as Green and Bushy, for their complicity in Richard's taxation of them; flees to Ireland to alert Richard of the nobles' rebellion; prophesies that he, Bushy, and Green will never see each other again; accuses Aumerle of conspiring to kill the duke of Gloucester and wishing Henry dead in William Shakespeare's play *Richard II.*

Bagot, Billy (Little Billie) Young, brilliant painter who goes to Paris to study painting and discovers the model and singer Trilby O'Ferrall; naive and sensitive, he falls in love with Trilby to the point of obsession; he is the tragic hero in George Du Maurier's *Trilby.*

Bagot, Blanche Younger, caring sister of Little Billie (Billy Bagot); she nurses him and quietly watches his life slip by; after his death, she marries his friend Taffy Wynne in George Du Maurier's *Trilby.*

Bagot, Mrs. Possessive mother unable to see her son Billy Bagot marry beneath his social position; she manipulates him and divides him and Trilby O'Ferrall; finally, she recognizes the tragedy she creates by meddling in George Du Maurier's *Trilby.*

Bagradian, Gabriel Armenian patriot who returns in 1915 with his family to his ancestral village of Yoghonoluk in Turkey after living in Paris for more than two decades; travels home to escape the European hostilities and to settle his dying brother's affairs; finds that Armenians are persecuted in Turkey; takes a community of people and freedom fighters to the mountain plateau Musa Dagh, where they defend themselves from the government troops for 40 days; dies after heroically helping his refuges to safety in Franz Werfel's *The Forty Days of Musa Dagh.*

Bagradian, Juliette Wife of Gabriel, the leader of the small freedom force that defends an encampment of Armenians who have fled to the mountain plateau Musa Dagh; seduced by the Greek-American adventurer Gonzague Maris but decides against fleeing with him under the protection of his passport; dies of fever during the defense of the mountain siege by Turkish soldiers in Franz Werfel's *The Forty Days of Musa Dagh.*

Bagradian, Stephan Son of Gabriel; heroic defender with his father of the mountain plateau Musa Dagh in Turkey;

runs raids on the Turkish gun fortifications; soon killed by the Turkish soldiers as the young man seeks to bring reinforcements to defend the mountain plateau in Franz Werfel's *The Forty Days of Musa Dagh.*

Bagration Russian military commander in Leo Tolstoy's *War and Peace.*

Bags (Bad Giants) Lovers (Little Ones) who have grown in body but whose depravity keeps them spiritually and emotionally brutal and underdeveloped in George MacDonald's *Lilith.*

Bagshaw, Lindsay ("Books-Do-Furnish-a-Room") Seedy left-wing journalist given to drink and rows; his nickname derives from an apocryphal statement attributed to him at University; he is a founder of the progressive weekly *Fission* in Anthony Powell's *Books Do Furnish a Room.* He is a television personality with a house and a large family in *Temporary Kings.*

Bagshaw, Mr. English gentleman who reveals to John Dowell that Florence Dowell had an affair before their marriage; his arrival in Bad Nauheim precipitates Florence's suicide in Ford Madox Ford's *The Good Soldier: A Tale of Passion.*

Bagshot, Bob Ingenuous acquaintance whom Jonathan Wild easily persuades to rob Count La Ruse and who, in turn, becomes Wild's victim in Henry Fielding's *The Life of Mr. Jonathan Wild the Great.*

Bagster, Florence (Florrie) Young servant of Carolyn Lessways; she joins Hilda Lessways in George Cannon's Brighton boarding house, where her physical charms soon make her the mistress of the newly widowed boarder Mr. Boutwood in Arnold Bennett's *Hilda Lassways.*

Bagster, Freddie Young man with a crush on Helen Rolt in Graham Greene's *The Heart of the Matter.*

Bagstock, Major Joseph (Joey B.) Retired, conceited military man, who lives opposite Miss Tox; he believes that she loves him; insulted when her interest fades, he strikes up a friendship with Paul Dombey, introducing him to Mrs. Skewton and Edith Granger in Charles Dickens's *Dombey and Son.*

Bagwax, Samuel Dedicated Post Office official, whose detective work proves a forged postmark on a letter involved in a court case which has led to the false imprisonment for bigamy of John Caldigate; he marries Jemima Curlydown in Anthony Trollope's *John Caldigate.*

Bahadur, Sir Ahmed All Gaffus Kasim The Nawab of Mirat, a Muslim Prince, in Paul Scott's *The Jewel in the Crown.* He graciously offers a guest house on his estate to Susan Layton and her family so that she may be married to Edward Bingham in Mirat in *The Day of the Scorpion.* His presence continues to be felt in *The Towers of Silence* and in *A Division of the Spoils.*

Bailey Beleaguered father of three children who takes his mother and his family on a trip to Florida; they are murdered by an escaped convict called The Misfit and his two accomplices in Flannery O'Connor's "A Good Man Is Hard to Find."

Bailey, Benjamin (Bailey Junior, Uncle Ben, Young Brownrigg, Collars) Assertive servant at Todgers's Commercial Boarding House and later groom to Tigg Montague (formerly Montague Tigg); he is physically "an undersized boy" and behaviorally "an ancient man" in Charles Dickens's *The Life and Adventures of Martin Chuzzlewit.*

Bailey, Brandy Student at Jane Addams High School who is suspended from school for making off-color remarks about a homosexual relationship between another student named Lorrie and a teacher, Mr. D'Angelo, in Carolyn Ferrell's "Proper Library."

Bailey, Captain One of Miss Larkins's dance partners at the ball where she dances with David Copperfield in Charles Dickens's *The Personal History of David Copperfield.*

Bailey, Edward (Neddy) Young clerk in a London office who is a friend of Richard in Thomas Hughes's *The Scouring of the White Horse.*

Bailey, Henry Hired man who helps the narrator's father with the fox farm and with shooting Mack and Flora, the old horses; found intriguing by the young girl narrator and her brother Laird; remarks one day when the young girl and her brother are fighting that the day will come when Laird will be able to beat his older sister, suggesting the profound difference between boys and girls in Alice Munro's "Boys and Girls."

Bailey, Isadora Prim schoolteacher from Boston who attempts to blackmail Rutherford Calhoun into marriage; is about to marry Papa Zeringue when Rutherford disrupts the ceremony; accepts Rutherford's proposal of marriage and the responsibility of raising Baleka in Charles Johnson's *Middle Passage.*

Bailey, John (Alex, Alexander Graham, Jack) Bank cashier accused of murdering Arnold Armstrong and of causing the Traders' Bank to fail; disguises himself as a gardener in order to clear his name in Mary Roberts Rinehart's *The Circular Staircase.*

Bailey, Kenneth Private detective that helps main character Jennifer Parker in her struggle as a young lawyer in Sidney Sheldon's *Rage of Angels.*

Bailey, Mrs. Miriam Henderson's widowed landlady on the edge of London's Bloomsbury in Dorothy Richardson's *The Tunnel.* She has decided to take boarders rather than merely lodgers but allows Miriam to stay on as lodger, with the option of paying for a meal when she wishes in *Interim.* She astonishes Miriam by agreeing to marry a young man half her age in *Deadlock.*

Bailey, Polly Sissie Bailey's sister in Dorothy Richardson's *Interim.*

Bailey, Sissie One of two young daughters on whose behalf Mrs. Bailey has decided to convert 7 Tansley Street to a boarding-house, in the hope of providing social opportunities for them in Dorothy Richardson's *Interim.* Sissie grows "from an elderly schoolgirl into a young housekeeper" and disapproves of Amabel's flirtatious behavior in *Clear Horizon.*

Bailey, Thomas (Tom) Youth who has numerous adventures in Rivermouth; narrator of Thomas Bailey Aldrich's *The Story of a Bad Boy.*

Bailie Portly, bustling, and impatient official in Sir Walter Scott's *The Monastery.*

Baillet, Raymond Obliging Parisian taxi driver; may have inspired Jean-Louis Lebris de Kérouac's satori, or sudden illumination, in Jack Kerouac's *Satori in Paris.*

Baillie, General Skillful Presbyterian officer and Covenanter, who briefly joins his army with Argyle's in Sir Walter Scott's *A Legend of Montrose.*

Bailly, Nanette de Dark, high-colored Frenchwoman, of good family, from Provence; her engagement to Colonel Stanley Levin is announced in Ford Madox Ford's *No More Parades.*

Baily, Eva Sister of Minna Baily; lives with Minna and their nephew in a 70th Street apartment building managed by Norman Moonbloom in Edward Lewis Wallant's *The Tenants of Moonbloom.*

Baily, Joe Rival of Augie; a bad nigger who contends with Tom Wright for the affection of Florence Dessau in Arna Wendell Bontemps's *God Sends Sunday.*

Baily, Minna Sister of Eva Baily; lives with Eva and their nephew in a 70th Street apartment building managed by Norman Moonbloom in Edward Lewis Wallant's *The Tenants of Moonbloom.*

Bailzou, Annaple Fortune-telling beggar, who buys the Whistler, the illegitimate son of Effie Deans and George Staunton, and later sells him to an outlaw in Sir Walter Scott's *The Heart of Midlothian.*

Bainbridge, Blair Wealthy male model, he has an affair with Sarah Vane-Tempest in Rita Mae Brown's *Cat on the Scent.*

Bainbridge, Vesta Glamorous, opportunistic features editor of a women's magazine who attempts to reform F. X. Enderby as well as capitalize on his literary reputation in Anthony Burgess's *Inside Mr. Enderby* and in *Enderby Outside.*

Baines, Constance Placid, custom-bound oldest daughter of John Baines; she spends her life maintaining her parents' standards in her marriage to their clerk Cyril Povey, in her parenthood of Samuel Povey, and in her attitude toward her wayward sister, Sophia, in Arnold Bennett's *The Old Wives Tale.*

Baines, Hattie Anthony Keating's first girlfriend, whom he sees years later at the Mike Morgan comedy performance in Margaret Drabble's *The Ice Age.*

Baines, John Long-paralyzed and bed-ridden proprietor of Bursley's best dry-goods store; his death by his daughter Sophia's negligence precipitates her renunciation of a teaching career and her repentant clerking in the store where she meets the traveling salesman Gerald Scales, with whom she disastrously elopes to Paris in Arnold Bennett's *The Old Wives Tale.*

Baines, Miss Timberwork secretary who is somewhat incompetent in Isabel Colegate's *Orlando King.*

Baines, Mrs. Salvation Army commissioner in the soup kitchen where Major Barbara works to convert the sinful to the righteous; to do God's work, she is forced to accept large financial donations from the wealthy arms manufacturer Andrew Undershaft, Major Barbara's father, in George Bernard Shaw's play *Major Barbara.*

Baines, Mrs. John Widow of John Baines and confident mother of Constance and Sophia; she finds she cannot control the circumstances of her maturing daughters' lives and withdraws in defeat to live with her widowed sister in her birthplace, Axe, in Arnold Bennett's *The Old Wives Tale.*

Baines, Sophia Beautiful, intelligent, impetuous younger daughter of John Baines; by deceiving her family and negligently causing her father's death, she is precipitated into an elopement and psychically wounding experiences in Paris with her insensitive husband, Gerald Scales, and she is abandoned there; she ruthlessly sets up the Bursley standards she had run from and lives a repressed life in the Paris commune until age and strain force her return to her birthplace, where she struggles with her sister's customs and dies of the shock sustained by having to view her late husband's body in Arnold Bennett's *The Old Wives Tale.*

Bains, Guitar Best friend of Macon (Milkman) Dead III and member of a racial revenge group called the Seven Days in Toni Morrison's *Song of Solomon.*

Bains, Lulu Daughter of a church deacon; Elmer Gantry narrowly escapes having to marry her, although he later has an affair with her, in Sinclair Lewis's *Elmer Gantry.*

Bains, Rosemary Elderly ex-school mistress who is deeply inspired by one of Charles Watkins's lectures; she very much wants to meet him in Doris Lessing's *Briefing for a Descent into Hell.*

Baird, Jeff Director of comedy films who gives Merton Gill his first starring role, in Harry Leon Wilson's *Merton of the Movies.*

Baird, Marie Wife of Vincent Baird; a member of Margaret's church; owns a gift shop, The Gilded Peacock, in Gail Godwin's *Evensong.*

Baird, Vincent Husband of Marie Baird; has a styling shop above his wife's shop; cuts Margaret's and what is left of Adrian's hair in Gail Godwin's *Evensong.*

Baise-la-main, Monsieur Art collector and banker; he becomes patron of Jeremy Watersouchy, who earns immediate success with the precise rendering of the coins in the financier's countinghouse in William Beckford's *Biographical Memoirs of Extraordinary Painters.*

Bakaleyev Owner of house where Razumihin arranges for Raskolnikov's mother and sister to lodge in Fyodor Dostoevsky's *Crime and Punishment.*

Bakayoko, Ibrahima Protagonist and railroad strike leader in a bitter dispute between the African workers and the French owners of the Dakar-Niger line of the West African Company; faces the railroad officials in Dakar and through a dramatic, nationally publicized speech, succeeds in expanding the strike into a general strike across West Africa, forcing the railroad to capitulate in Ousmane Sembène's *God's Bits of Wood.*

Baker Friend who visits Anne and Phil Sorenson to recover from a divorce and clumsily seduces Anne in Frederick Busch's *Manual Labor.*

Baker, Antoinette (Tony) Pretty and flirtatious neighbor of the Eberhardts; has an affair with David Eberhardt and eventually marries him many years later in Sue Miller's *Family Pictures.*

Baker, April Spaced-out teenage sister of Nicole Baker Barrett; innocent companion of Gary Gilmore during his first murderous spree in Norman Mailer's *Executioner's Song.*

Baker, Colonel Orthopedic surgeon at Kilrainey Army Hospital who wants to amputate the right leg of Bobby Prell in James Jones's *Whistle.*

Baker, Corporal Cruel, spiteful N.C.O. at the Basic Training camp; he is hostile to Jonathan Browne; he is assaulted by Mike Brady for having hounded Percy Higgins to his death; he is demoted in David Lodge's *Ginger, You're Barmy.*

Baker, Dorris Father of a boy who accidentally drowns on the day Glen Davis returns from prison in Larry Brown's *Father and Son.*

Baker, Dr. Physician whom Rebecca de Winter visited the day of her death, according to her journal; his surprising evidence concludes the investigation into Rebecca's death in Daphne duMaurier's *Rebecca.*

Baker, Helen Friend of Larry Donovan; works at a hot dog stand in Jack Conroy's *The Disinherited.*

Baker, Hermione Slightly less sinister of the two evil principals of the state educational institution for women in Henry Green's *Concluding.*

Baker, Jordan Dishonest friend of Daisy Buchanan; romantically involved with Nick Carraway in F. Scott Fitzgerald's *The Great Gatsby.*

Baker, Lizzie Music-hall barmaid, who becomes Frank Escott's mistress; he nurses her back to health in George Moore's *Spring Days.* He persuades her to marry him, and their happy home is envied by Mike Fletcher in *Mike Fletcher.*

Baker, Lou Garbo (Left Bank, Montana Lou) Bohemian and writer; mistress of Jesse Proctor in Wright Morris's *The Huge Season.*

Baker, Mary Niece of George Bertram; she is pursued for her money by Sir Lionel Bertram in Anthony Trollope's *The Bertrams;* also she comforts Margaret Mackenzie who is upset by gossip in *Miss Mackenzie.*

Baker, Miss Elderly woman who falls in love with Old Grannis in Frank Norris's *McTeague.*

Baker, Mr. Beleaguered first mate of the *Narcissus* in Joseph Conrad's *The Nigger of the "Narcissus."*

Baker, Mr. Pawnbroker who runs Silverton Grove House asylum entirely for profit in Charles Reade's *Hard Cash.*

Baker, Mr. President of the First National Bank in New Baytown who tries to use Ethan Allen Hawley to gain additional wealth and power for himself in John Steinbeck's *The Winter of Our Discontent.*

Baker, Mrs. Insensitive widow, who laments the burden of supporting the six-year-old orphan, Elizabeth Raby, in Mary Shelley's *Falkner.*

Baker, Mrs. Samuel Widow of a Washington lobbyist and client of John Carrington, to whom she reveals the improper dealings of Senator Ratcliffe, in Henry Adams's *Democracy.*

Baker, Nancy May Lover of Marshall Pearl; ornithologist studying eagles in New Mexico for the University of Chicago in Mark Helprin's *Refiner's Fire.*

Baker, Nicole See Barrett, Nicole Kathryne Baker.

Baker, Rena Baker Dying sanitorium patient beloved and mourned by Don Wanderhope in Peter De Vries's *The Blood of the Lamb.*

Baker, Steve Actor on the Cotton Blossom who leaves the showboat with his wife Julie Dozier in Edna Ferber's *Show Boat.*

Baker, Sue Mother of a boy who accidentally drowns on the day Glen Davis returns from prison in Larry Brown's *Father and Son.*

Baker, Tracy Ex-pupil of Romley Fourways', the school Kate Fletcher (Armstrong) attended; years later she is seen in Majorca in Margaret Drabble's *The Middle Ground.*

Bakewell, Gus Thug and associate of Donald Washburn in Thomas Berger's *Who Is Teddy Villanova?*

Bakewell, Tom Loyal but somewhat dull-witted laborer Richard Feverel pays to burn Farmer Blaize's hayricks; he becomes Richard's servant and assists Richard and Lucy Desborough before and after their marriage in George Meredith's *The Ordeal of Richard Feverel.*

Bakon, Bello Son of Bello in Djìbrìltamsìr Niane's *Sundiata: An Epic of Old Mali.*

Balaban, Daniel Cryptanalyst working for the United States during World War II; he is Louise Kahan's lover during the war; marries Abra Scott after the war, and they travel together to Japan in Marge Piercy's *Gone to Soldiers.*

Balbino Peasant who suffers mistreatment as a gum tree laborer in the Amazon region in José Eustacio Rivera's *The Vortex.*

Balcairn, Earl of Young aristocrat whose financial difficulties force him to become a newspaper gossip writer; he eventually commits suicide when he is ostracized by the high-society set in Evelyn Waugh's *Vile Bodies.*

Balch, Annabel Fiancée of Lucius Harney and rival of Charity Royall in Edith Wharton's *Summer.*

Balchristie, Janet The Laird of Dumbiedikes's lazy housekeeper, who terrorizes Jeanie Deans in Sir Walter Scott's *The Heart of Midlothian.*

Balderick Retired rear-admiral who lost a leg in the service; he amuses Matthew Bramble with his recovered friendship at Bath in Tobias Smollett's *The Expedition of Humphry Clinker.*

Balderini, Agostino Old Italian poet who has suffered much in the cause of liberation; the librettist of the opera *Camilla,* he proposes-despite the male chauvinism of other revolutionaries-that when Vittoria Campa sings the disguised revolutionary songs in it, she signal the beginning of the Milanese revolt in George Meredith's *Vittoria.*

Balderson, Caleb Edgar Ravenswood's devoted servant, who fiercely protects his master and loves to talk of the ancient glory of the Ravenswood family in Sir Walter Scott's *The Bride of Lammermoor.*

Baldini, Guiseppe Well-known perfumer; knows the art of creating perfume but lacks true talent; recognizes Grenouille's gift and buys him from Grimal; teaches Grenouille the art of mixing and creating perfumes and cosmetics in Patrick Süskind's *Perfume.*

Baldino, Guiseppe (Pepino) Italian patient in Clive Ward who loses his right hand after a fiery bus crash; unable to speak or understand English, he frantically tries to find out if his pregnant wife in Italy has borne him a son in John Berger's *The Foot of Clive.*

Baldock, Lady Violet Effingham's outspoken aunt, who promotes the claims of suitors Lord Fawn and Mr. Appledom and is strongly opposed to Lord Chiltern and Phineas Finn; she is an inveterate supporter of good causes, such as emigration for unmarried women in Anthony Trollope's *Phineas Finn.* She visits Violet and Lord Chiltern in *Phineas Redux.*

Baldock, Lord George (or Gustavus) Lady Baldock's son, who corrects her assessments of Violet Effingham's suitors in Anthony Trollope's *Phineas Finn.*

Baldoni, Nina Close friend and confidante of Ayala Dormer; she marries Lord George Bideford in Anthony Trollope's *Ayala's Angel.*

Baldry, Christopher (Chris) Thirty-six-year-old amnesiac soldier and successful businessman; he returns from service in World War I to his fine country estate and his wife, Kitty, and cousin, Jenny, who pride themselves on having provided him with a "gracious life"; he recalls only the sweetheart of his youth, Margaret Allington, daughter of an innkeeper, and he blocks out fifteen years of memory in Rebecca West's *The Return of the Soldier.*

Baldry, Kitty Wife of amnesiac Chris Baldry; she is a rich, materialistic woman who thinks Chris should remember her because he gave her the beautiful necklaces she fingers as she welcomes him home; she expresses anger at his refusal to recall their marriage and at his pursuit of a dowdy, uneducated, and unattractive woman, Margaret Allington, whom he met at an inn fifteen years earlier in Rebecca West's *The Return of the Soldier.*

Balducci Soldier in the French army who transports an Arab prisoner to the watchful eye of Daru, the local schoolteacher and government overseer; an aging, good-natured soldier, he follows military codes and orders in minute detail; leaves a revolver with Daru for protection from the prisoner in Albert Camus's "The Guest."

Baldwin, Archbishop Archbishop of Canterbury, successor of Thomas á Becket; he insists that Hugo de Lacy honor his pledge to go on Crusade in Sir Walter Scott's *The Betrothed.*

Baldwin (Bawley), Benedict Unmarried uncle of Bick Benedict; runs a small cattle operation in Edna Ferber's *Giant.*

Baldwin, Count Crusader and brother to Godfrey of Bouillon in Sir Walter Scott's *Count Robert of Paris.*

Baldwin, George Unscrupulous attorney who rises to the top of his profession and becomes the third husband of Ellen Thatcher in John Dos Passos's *Manhattan Transfer.*

Baldwin, Mr. Mysterious British financier who travels to Ishmaelia and helps defeat the Russian coup d'état in Evelyn Waugh's *Scoop.*

Baldwin, Ted Also known as Hargrave, a suitor of Ettie Shafter; he served time for crimes as a member of the Scowrers gang in America; he is shot dead in England in Arthur Conan Doyle's *The Valley of Fear.*

Baldy Scotch sailor aboard the *Neversink* whose life is saved by Cadwallader Cuticle in Herman Melville's *White-Jacket.*

Bale, Leonard Chief Inspector who is the senior policeman working with Frank Briers investigating the murder of Lady Ashbrook; he travels to New York for evidence in C. P. Snow's *A Coat of Varnish.*

Bale, Mr. Merchant and friend of Henrietta Courteney's late father; as guardian of the orphaned Henrietta, he is kindly and generous but is ill and abroad during most of her adventures; he ultimately returns to arrange settlements to enable her to marry the Marquis of—with his father's consent in Charlotte Lennox's *Henrietta.*

Bale, Mr. (the younger) Son of Henrietta Courteney's guardian; he falls for Henrietta and plots to abduct her while pretending to help her on his father's behalf in Charlotte Lennox's *Henrietta.*

Bale, Mrs. Shrewish wife of the younger Mr. Bale; she finds out her husband has been helping Henrietta Courteney and confronts her, thus exposing Mr. Bale's designs on her in Charlotte Lennox's *Henrietta.*

Bale, Simon Religious fanatic whose wife dies in their burning house; accidentally killed by Henry Soames in John Gardner's *Nickel Mountain.*

Baleia Family dog that hunts a preá (small rodent), which serves to feed the others; plays with the two boys; gets hydrophobia and is sacrificed by Fabiano in Graciliano Ramos's *Barren Lives.*

Baleka Eight-year-old Allmuseri slave on the *Republic;* is rescued along with Squibb and Rutherford and taken aboard the *Juno,* where she nurses Rutherford back to health; is "adopted" by Rutherford and Isadora and raised by them once they are married in Charles Johnson's *Middle Passage.*

Baley, Elijah (Lije) Agoraphobic Earth detective assigned to solve a politically sensitive case of roboticide and clear Dr. Han Fastolfe's name on the planet Aurora; founder of Earth's fledging movement to colonize unsettled worlds; investigative partner of R. Daneel Olivaw in Isaac Asimov's *The Robots of Dawn.*

Balfour Merchant who rescues Constantia Dudley from a group of ruffians; Constantia rejects him after a subsequent courtship in Charles Brockden Brown's *Ormond.*

Balfour, Alan Son of David and Catriona (Drummond) Balfour in Robert Louis Stevenson's *Catriona.*

Balfour, Alexander Deceased father of young David Balfour and elder brother of Ebenezer Balfour; he exchanged his claim to his estate for the right to court and wed the brothers' hotly contested lover, Grace Pitarrow, in Robert Louis Stevenson's *Kidnapped.*

Balfour, Barbara Daughter of David and Catriona (Drummond) Balfour in Robert Louis Stevenson's *Catriona.*

Balfour, David Young, courageous, and principled Scottish heir to the "Shaws" estate; he is kidnapped, befriends the Jacobite Alan Breck Stewart, and is subsequently involved in the political imbroglio of the 1752 "Appin" murder of Colin Ray Campbell in Robert Louis Stevenson's *Kidnapped.* He attempts to exonerate alleged murderer James Stewart and falls in love with Catriona Drummond in *Catriona.*

Balfour, Ebenezer David Balfour's miserly and hateful uncle, who tries to cheat his young nephew from any rightful claim to the "Shaws" estate by having him kidnapped and taken aboard the Scottish brig *Covenant,* which is destined for colony slave plantations (and slavery for David) in Robert Louis Stevenson's *Kidnapped.*

Balfour, Grace Pitarrow David Balfour's deceased mother, who married Alexander Balfour after being courted by both Alexander and his brother, Ebenezer, in Robert Louis Stevenson's *Kidnapped.*

Balfour, John (Burley) Renegade rebel soldier, who was a comrade of Henry Morton's father and is a leader of the Cameronian rebels against King James II; later he refuses to accept William as his king; he becomes increasingly fanatic, merciless, and treacherous and at last drowns while attempting to escape after the ambush and murder of Lord Evandale (William Maxwell) in Sir Walter Scott's *Old Mortality.*

Balfour of Pilrig Edinburgh Laird and kinsman to David Balfour; he writes David a letter of introduction to Prestongrange, Lord Advocate of Scotland, in Robert Louis Stevenson's *Catriona.*

Balham, Lord Englishman and commissioner for refugees of the Society of Nations; Mary Douglas solicits his aid in blocking the expulsion order for German and Austrian refugees in Martha Gellhorn's *A Stricken Field.*

Balich, Drenka Wife of Matija Balich and hostess at inn he owns; adulterous lover of Mickey Sabbath; dies of cancer in Philip Roth's *Sabbath's Theater.*

Balkiz Mercedes owned and worshipped by the protagonist, Bayram; also referred to as "Honey Girl" and the "virgin" lover; its horn sounds more beautiful than a woman's voice; gives Bayram a sense of power and sexual ecstasy while he drives it in Adalet Agaoglu's *The Slender Rose of My Desire.*

Ball, Denise (Scooter) Schoolmate of Kate Fletcher (Armstrong); she worked hard to become a nurse; she becomes Terry Ball's wife; her story is used by Kate in the television film Kate is making in Margaret Drabble's *The Middle Ground.*

Ball, John Hedge priest prominent in Wat Tyler's Rebellion of 1381; he discusses with the Scholar the future of England when feudal slavery will be replaced by wage slavery in William Morris's *A Dream of John Ball.*

Ball, John Margaret Mackenzie's cousin, a widower short of cash and with nine children to look after; urged by his mother to set his cap at his spinster cousin, he gradually finds he is in love with her; when it is discovered that he in fact is true heir to the Mackenzie fortune, she agrees to marry him in Anthony Trollope's *Miss Mackenzie.*

Ball, Jonathan Brother of Sir John Ball; he causes an uproar by leaving his money to his Mackenzie cousins in Anthony Trollope's *Miss Mackenzie.*

Ball, Lady Disagreeable wife of Sir John Ball and mother of John Ball; she begrudges Margaret Mackenzie's coming into a fortune; her approval of her son's courtship of Margaret is contingent on Margaret's possession of the fortune in Anthony Trollope's *Miss Mackenzie.*

Ball, Professor Headmaster of an academy for boys and a leader of the Free Farmers' Brotherhood of Protection and Control, a vigilante organization designed to control tobacco prices by any means necessary, in Robert Penn Warren's *Night Rider.*

Ball, Sir John Grouchy baronet, a kinsman of Margaret Mackenzie and the owner of an estate in Twickenham; he and his wife resolve a long-standing rift between the families by inviting Margaret to stay at their home in Anthony Trollope's *Miss Mackenzie.*

Ball, Terry Electrical engineer, married to Denise (Scooter); their story is used by Kate Fletcher Armstrong in the television film she is making in Margaret Drabble's *The Middle Ground.*

Ballard, Eliza Daughter of Judge and Mary Ballard; worked as a professional secretary for Rausch Cordage Company; local gossip in Helen Hooven Santmyer's "*. . . And Ladies of the Club.*"

Ballard, Gregory (Greg) Black fisherman from Cape Cod who fights for the loyalists in the Spanish civil war and against the racial hatred of Hitler; friend of Jake Starr in William Herrick's *Hermanos!*

Ballard, Mary Married to a judge in Waynesboro, Ohio; crusader for progressive causes such as temperance and women's suffrage in Helen Hooven Santmyer's "*. . . And Ladies of the Club.*"

Ballerina, The Physically gifted performer whom Harrison strips of her handicaps; he names her his empress so that he can have a partner to dance with, displaying the pinnacle of human athletic achievement; Diana Moon Glampers also murders her in Kurt Vonnegut's "Harrison Bergeron."

Ballew, John (Old John, Uncle John) Second cousin of Nunn Ballew; prosperous, highly respected farmer in Harriette Arnow's *Hunter's Horn;* sells land to Gertie Nevels in *The Dollmaker.*

Ballew, Lee Roy Eldest son of Nunn and Milly Ballew; assumes responsibilities as man of the house while his father fox hunts in Harriette Arnow's *Hunter's Horn.*

Ballew, Lucy Youngest daughter of Nunn and Milly Ballew in Harriette Arnow's *Hunter's Horn.*

Ballew, Milly Long-suffering, hardworking wife of Nunn Ballew and mother of five living children and two others who died young in Harriette Arnow's *Hunter's Horn.*

Ballew, Nunnely Danforth (Nunn) Kentucky fox hunter obsessed with chasing the fox called King Devil; husband of Milly Ballew in Harriette Arnow's *Hunter's Horn.*

Ballew, Suse Intelligent, sensitive adolescent daughter of Nunn and Milly Ballew; longs to escape her family's poverty in Little Smokey Creek, Kentucky, in Harriette Arnow's *Hunter's Horn.*

Ballew, William Danforth (Bill Dan) Baby son of Nunn and Milly Ballew in Harriette Arnow's *Hunter's Horn.*

Balliere, Francis Thief hired by Phillippe de Montalt to ambush his half brother Henry de Montalt in Ann Radcliffe's *The Romance of the Forest.*

Ballindine, Lord, Francis (Frank) O'Kelly Impecunious aristocrat addicted to gambling; he finally wins Fanny Wyndham over her guardian's opposition in Anthony Trollope's *The Kellys and the O'Kellys.*

Ballinger, Drew Sales supervisor for a large soft-drink company; spokesman for the laws of civilization who is killed during the three-day canoe trip on the Cahulawassee River in James Dickey's *Deliverance.*

Balloon (Baloon), Old Bull (Old Bull Lewis, Smiley Bull Balloon) Alcoholic gambler who sells flyswatters door-to-door with Cody Pomeray, Sr., in Jack Kerouac's *Visions of Cody;* plays pool with Doctor Sax in *Doctor Sax;* appears as W. C. Fields in *Book of Dreams;* drinks with Emil Duluoz in *Visions of Gerard.*

Balloon, The Object that hovers over a 45-block section in Manhattan; cannot be removed by authorities and changes quotidian life of the city; is at last stored in West Virginia by its maker, waiting for some other time of unhappiness to prevail in society in Donald Barthelme's "The Balloon."

"Balloon, The" Narrator Creates the balloon, a "spontaneous autobiographical disclosure," as a consequence of lover's trip to Bergen, Norway; observes and describes the reactions of other characters as they interact with the spherical orb; removes the giant inflated sphere when the lover returns in Donald Barthelme's "The Balloon."

Ballou, Mick Unofficial owner of "Grogan's" bar and much else; career criminal, soulmate, and former drinking partner of Matt Scudder in Lawrence Block's *A Dance at the Slaughterhouse.*

Balmforth, Rozina (Rozzie) Strong-willed, independent, life-long friend of Sara Monday; she advises Sara on how to handle Gulley Jimson's advances in Joyce Cary's *Herself Surprised* and in *The Horse's Mouth.*

Balmy, Mr. Elderly gentleman of kindly aspect, who looks like an early Christian and explains the history of Sunchildism; he had been a professor of hypothetical languages when forced out because he urged adoption of Sunchildism in Samuel Butler's *Erewhon Revisited Twenty Years Later.*

Balou French character who feels alienated and constrained in the poverty of the ghettos of Paris in Mehdi Charef's *Tea in the Harem.*

Balsam, Mr. Mild, respectable barrister, very learned on points of law, brought in to represent Henry Jones in his libel case against Gregory Evans in Anthony Trollope's *Cousin Henry.*

Baltazar Narrator's cousin who died in 1940; one of the many family members who appear in the mirror to communicate with the living in Maria Elena Llano's "In the Family."

Balterghen, Joseph Small, moustached, Armenian-born, conscienceless man; chairman of Pan-Eruasian Petroleum and a shareholder in Cator and Bliss munitions firm, he employs Stefan Saridza to steal the B2 plans in Eric Ambler's *Uncommon Danger.*

Balthamos Rebel angel and lover of Baruch; vows to accompany and protect Will Parry on his journey; runs away in shame after he is unable to fulfill his vow; returns at the end of the trilogy and is killed by Father Gomez, a priest working for the Magisterium in Philip Pullman's *His Dark Materials.*

Balthasar Egyptian companion of Sheik Ilderim and friend of Judah Ben-Hur; father of the lovely but cunning Iras; helps Ben-Hur defeat his enemy, the Roman Messala, and helps Ben-Hur find his imprisoned mother and sister; after the miracle of curing the female Hurs' leprosy, becomes a follower of Jesus Christ in Lew Wallace's *Ben-Hur: A Tale of the Christ.*

Balthazar Julian the Apostate's incarnation as a Jewish miser in Henry Fielding's *A Journey From This World to the Next.*

Balthazar Patriarch of the Gypsies and friend of Dick Turpin in William Harrison Ainsworth's *Rookwood.*

Balthazar Prince of Portugal, captured by Don Horatio and Prince Lorenzo; the killer of Don Andrea, Balthazar courts Andrea's lover, Bel-Imperia, and with her brother Lorenzo murders her new lover Horatio and imprisons Bel-Imperia; killed by Bel-Imperia during Hieronimo's revenge playlet in Thomas Kyd's play *The Spanish Tragedy.*

Balthazar, Frere Capuchin friar, who horrifies Roderick Random with his lust and theft on the road to Paris in Tobias Smollett's *The Adventures of Roderick Random.*

Balthazar, S. Homosexual physician and a leading student of the Cabala; he is a friend of L. G. Darley, of Justine Hosnani, and of Clea Montis in Lawrence Durrell's *Justine.* He expands upon Darley's version of Justine's private life in *Balthazar.* He helplessly attends the dying Narouz Hosnani in *Mountolive.* He recovers from a passion for a Greek actor in *Clea.*

Baltimore Black cook aboard the *Julia* who delivers the round robin to the English consul on Tahiti in Herman Melville's *Omoo.*

Baltimore, Lord See Charles Calvert, Lord Baltimore.

Balue, Cardinal John Lord Bishop of Auxerre and Grand Almoner of France; as Louis XI's favorite, he rose quickly from the lower ranks; a vain and presumptuous meddler, he betrays Louis to the Duke of Burgundy when the king insults him; he is subsequently imprisoned in Sir Walter Scott's *Quentin Durward.*

Baluzzo Assassin brought to justice by Abellino/Flodoardo (Count Rosalvo) in Matthew Lewis's *The Bravo of Venice.*

Balwhidder, Micah Presbyterian minister from 1760 to 1810 of the parish of Dalmailing (Ayrshire); at first rebuffed, he overcomes the congregation's resentment at his appointment; he writes the parish annals which include mentions of individuals and significant events and developments such as the American War of Independence, the French Revolution, and the agricultural and industrial revolutions in John Galt's *Annals of the Parish.*

***Balzac and the Little Chinese Seamstress,* Narrator** Young man sent along with his friend Luo to be punished and reeducated in China's remote mountain region known as "Phoenix of the Sky" during the Cultural Revolution in the 1960s; forced to work in coal mines; befriends and falls in love with the Little Seamstress, daughter of the local tailor; discovers a horde of Western novels hidden in a suitcase belonging to Four Eyes; devours the books and finds aesthetic transcendence despite cultural deprivation in Dai Sijie's *Balzac and the Little Chinese Seamstress.*

Bambarella, Rocco (Bullets) Macho gambler and police detective in Joseph Wambaugh's *The Black Marble.*

Bamber, Jack Elderly, shriveled regular at the Magpie and Stump, who tells a story about a queer client in Charles Dickens's *The Posthumous Papers of the Pickwick Club.*

Bamboo Cheerful young fisherman in the village of Mediaville and lover of Miami Mouth; he is eaten by a shark after Miami moves away to the city in Ronald Firbank's *Sorrow in Sunlight.*

Bambridge, Mr. Horse dealer who is owed money by Fred Vincy; he overhears John Raffles discussing his information against Bulstrode and later realizes that Raffles was murdered in George Eliot's *Middlemarch.*

Bamman, Hugo World War I ambulance driver, freelance journalist and documentary novelist, communist, and former schoolmate of the narrator in Edmund Wilson's *I Thought of Daisy.*

Bamu Beautiful daughter of Brimah; she becomes Johnson's wife, serves him faithfully but will not adopt his civilized nature, and later leaves him after he loses his job in Joyce Cary's *Mister Johnson.*

Banahan, Catherine Fiancée of Studs Lonigan; conceives their child, although he dies before they can wed, in James T. Farrell's *Judgment Day.*

Banascalco, Joseppi Captain of the Europe-bound *Castel Felice,* on which most of the action centers in Calvin Hernton's *Scarecrow.*

Band, George R. (Brass Band, Tall George) First lieutenant in C-for-Charlie Company who replaces James Stein as company commander; his lust for heroism earns him the hatred of his men, and he is eventually relieved of command for failing to communicate with headquarters in James Jones's *The Thin Red Line.*

Bandele Principled, quiet, and resourceful Nigerian who helps the other characters to be reconciled to their own lives, while at other times drawing attention to their internal conflicts and contradictions in Wole Soyinka's *The Interpreters.*

Bandello, Cesare (Rico) Ambitious and ruthless gang leader who takes over Sam Vettori's gang; enjoys seven years of success and fame before he is forced to flee Chicago and is killed in Toledo, Ohio, in William Riley Burnett's *Little Caesar.*

Bandicott, Acheson American millionaire and amateur archaeologist, who discovers the Viking burial barrow and treasure of "Harold Blacktooth"; he behaves in a sportsmanlike manner when "John Macnab" succeeds in killing a salmon in Strathlarrig waters in John Buchan's *John Macnab.*

Bandicott, Junius Theodore Son of a wealthy American who has rented Strathlarrig, a great house and estate bordering the property of Sir Archibald Roylance; he meets and falls in love with Agatha Raden, elder daughter of Colonel Alastair Raden and Janet's sister, in John Buchan's John *Macnab.*

Bandinelli, Guilio One of the Italian revolutionists who meet atop Monte Motterone to plan the initial uprising of the Milanese revolt in George Meredith's *Vittoria.*

Bando, Dai Disreputable former prizefighter who teaches Huw Morgan to box, attacks Mr. Jonas when he beats Huw, and, despite his blindness, helps Huw to search the mine for his father's body in Richard Llewellyn's *How Green Was My Valley.*

Bane Chair of Absurdist Drama in Adam Appleby's department; he has been promoted over the head of Briggs, Adam's supervisor, in David Lodge's *The British Museum Is Falling Down.*

Banford, Isabel (Bell) Apparently the illegitimate daughter of Pierre Glendinning II; she and Pierre Glendinning III pretend to be married in Herman Melville's *Pierre.*

Banford, Jill Moralistic, selfishly dependent, tiny woman, who lives with her Lesbian lover Nellie March on an unproductive Berkshire farm during World War I; she is deliberately killed by a tree felled by Henry Grenfel in D. H. Lawrence's *The Fox.*

Bang, Arthur Seven-year-old son of Helene and Ernst Bang; his presence makes it difficult for Roger Micheldene to get together with Helene; Micheldene mistakenly blames him for taking his lecture notes, and after Arthur beats Micheldene at Scrabble, Micheldene reveals his childishness by breaking one of Arthur's toys in Kingsley Amis's *One Fat Englishman.*

Bang, Dr. Ernst Danish philologist who comes to an American college for one year as a Visiting Fellow from the University of Copenhagen; he knows and accepts the fact that his wife, Helene, has meaningless affairs and plans to move with her to Chicago, where he has been offered a job in the linguistics department in Kingsley Amis's *One Fat Englishman.*

Bang, Helene Danish wife of Ernst Bang; she renews her affair with Roger Micheldene while he is in Pennsylvania and then has an affair with Irving Macher during the weekend she promised to spend with Micheldene; she realizes that Micheldene is hostile and loves her but does not like her in Kingsley Amis's *One Fat Englishman.*

Bangham, Mrs. Charwoman who attended Mrs. Dorrit at the birth of Amy Dorrit in the Marshalsea Prison in Charles Dickens's *Little Dorrit.*

Bangles, Peter Wine merchant whom Madalina Demolines marries after Johnny Eames's escape in Anthony Trollope's *The Last Chronicle of Barset.*

Bangrove, Mr. Worthy curate in the parish of Arabella Bloomville in William Beckford's *Modern Novel Writing; or, the Elegant Enthusiast.*

Bangs, Thomas Buckminster (Tommy) Sociable, mischievous boy in Louisa May Alcott's *Little Men.*

Banham, Father John Zealous Catholic priest at Beccles; he dines with Roger Carbury and cannot resist trying to convert his host in Anthony Trollope's *The Way We Live Now.*

Banion, Joe Black hired hand on Mat Feltner's Kentucky tobacco farm; husband of Nettie Banion in Wendell Berry's *A Place on Earth* and *The Memory of Old Jack.*

Banion, Nettie Black housekeeper and cook on Mat Feltner's Kentucky tobacco farm; wife of Joe Banion in Wendell Berry's *A Place on Earth* and *The Memory of Old Jack.*

Banion, William Hays (Will) Kentuckian who leads the Liberty covered wagon train in Emerson Hough's *The Covered Wagon.*

Banister Man who becomes Oroonoko's executioner after his failed uprising; he has Oroonoko burned at the stake and subjected to mutilation in Aphra Behn's *Oroonoko.*

Banjo See Agrippa Daily, Lincoln.

Bank Clerk Moll Flanders's fifth husband, who divorces his previous wife to marry Moll; after five years of marriage, he dies and leaves Moll and their two children penniless in Daniel Defoe's *The Fortunes and Misfortunes of the Famous Moll Flanders.*

Bankes, William Long-time bachelor friend of the Ramsays; he walks with Lily Briscoe, and Mrs. Ramsay tries to match them romantically in Virginia Woolf's *To the Lighthouse.*

Bank Porter Edinburgh guide who rudely chastises his employer, David Balfour, for talking with Catriona Drummond in the streets in Robert Louis Stevenson's *Catriona.*

Banks, Alonzo (Lonnie) Younger brother of the black councilman Randolph Banks; dedicated Communist expelled from the party for opposing its stand on domestic issues in Julian Mayfield's *The Grand Parade.*

Banks, Billy School friend of Terry Wilson, whom he tries to help get off drugs in Donald Goines's *Dopefiend.*

Banks, Freddie Twelve-year-old boyfriend of Jane Baxter in Booth Tarkington's *Seventeen.*

Banks, Joe Husband of Missie May; hard working man who worships his wife; comes home early one day from work to discover his wife with Otis D. Slemmons, a charlatan and womanizer; later reunites with Missie May in Zora Neale Hurston's "The Gilded Six-Bits."

Banks, Joey Enervated society woman, who is described by Miriam Henderson as "an Oriental princess" in Dorothy Richardson's *Honeycomb.*

Banks, Joseph President of the Royal Society who secures Roger Byam a midshipman's berth on HMS *Bounty* so Byam can compile a dictionary of the Tahitian language; provides for Byam's defense after he is returned to England as a mutineer in Charles Nordhoff and James Norman Hall's *Mutiny on the Bounty.*

Banks, Major Douglas Knowell's superior who confirms that Douglas can no longer serve in active duty because of his ill health in Doris Lessing's *A Proper Marriage.*

Banks, Margaret Wife of Michael Banks; kidnapped and beaten by a group of killers and thieves who want to benefit from her husband's theft of a horse, Rock Castle, which they expect to win one race in John Hawkes's *The Lime Twig.*

Banks, Michael Husband of Margaret Banks, who is convinced by his lodger, William Hencher, to steal a horse, Rock Castle, to win one race, but becomes entangled in a group of killers and thieves who want to benefit from his theft in John Hawkes's *The Lime Twig.*

Banks, Nanse Exemplary schoolmistress of Dalmailing who is admired by Micah Balwhidder for her "Christian submission of spirit" in John Galt's *Annals of the Parish.*

Banks, Randolph (Randy) Black city councilman and Harvard Law School graduate; brother of Lonnie Banks and lover of Patty Speed in Julian Mayfield's *The Grand Parade.*

Banks, Si Leftist writer and friend of the narrator in Edmund Wilson's *Memoirs of Hecate County.*

Banks, Sir Gerald Intelligent, wealthy aristocrat with impeccable taste and a fabulous art collection who offends Janos Lavin with his cold, "dead" art collection; he later buys one of Lavin's paintings in John Berger's *A Painter of Our Time.*

Banks, Wallace Obsequious friend of William Baxter; usually gets the unenviable jobs of master of ceremonies and money taker for the jaunts of the young townspeople in Booth Tarkington's *Seventeen.*

Bankwell, Michael Virtuous contrast to the wicked Mr. Sedley in S. J. Pratt's *Pupil of Pleasure.*

Banmann, Baroness Bavarian campaigner for women's rights, a very formidable speechmaker invited to address members of the Rights of Women Institute in the Marylebone Road in Anthony Trollope's *Is He Popenjoy?*

Banner, Judge Goodwill Owner of the New York Knights baseball team in Bernard Malamud's *The Natural.*

Bannet, Asa Heshel Prodigal son and grandson of rabbis in Tereshpol Minor, a village distant from the urban chaos of Warsaw; comes to Warsaw to find his intellectual fortune, squandering his material, familial, and spiritual fortune to pay for that quest; meets two women—Adele, Rose's daughter, and Hadassah, Abrams's niece—at the Moskat family's Chanukah celebration; runs off in disgrace with Hadassah to Switzerland; later marries Adele but continues his love affair with Hadassah; has children by both women in Isaac Bashevis Singer's *The Moskat Family.*

Banning, Ethel Instructor of Spanish and French and one of Jacob Horner's interviewers at Wicomico State Teachers College in John Barth's *The End of the Road.*

Bannister Thomas Carlyle Craw's butler and a born organizer who loves mystery and secrecy in John Buchan's *Castle Gay.*

Bannister, Auriol Bookstore proprietor and employer of Agatha (King) Field in Isabel Colegate's *Agatha.*

Bannister, Thomas Barrister who represents Abe Cady in Leon Uris's *QB VII.*

Bannon, Homer Lisle (Granddad) Second husband of Jewel Bannon and grandfather of Lonnie Bannon; ranch owner with a diseased cattle herd; killed by his stepson Hud in Larry McMurtry's *Horseman, Pass By.*

Bannon, Jewel Second wife of Homer Bannon, mother of Hud, and stepgrandmother of Lonnie Bannon in Larry McMurtry's *Horseman, Pass By.*

Bannon, Lonnie Stepnephew of Hud; leaves the ranch after the death of his grandfather, Homer Bannon; narrator of Larry McMurtry's *Horseman, Pass By.*

Bannon, Roger Ambitious building contractor who attracts Grace Caldwell Tate in John O'Hara's *A Rage to Live.*

Bannon, Scott (Hud, Huddie) See Hud.

Banquo Macbeth's wise, noble friend, and his antithesis; seen as a Renaissance man; respectable, balanced person; as a rationalist, he finds it difficult to trust the mysterious three witches, although they foretell that his progeny will inherit the Scottish throne; after his murder, his ghost haunts Macbeth in William Shakespeare's play *Macbeth.*

Banta, Henry (Hank) Mean boy, a compound of deceit and resentment, who causes Ralph Hartsook trouble in Edward Eggleston's *The Hoosier School-Master.*

Bantam, Angelo Cyrus Aging dandy and master of the ceremonies at the Pump Room in Bath, where Samuel Pickwick and friends go to socialize in Charles Dickens's *The Posthumous Papers of the Pickwick Club.*

Banter, Mr. One of die London tavern boys; he leads the "roast" of Dr. Wagtail, becomes a companion of Roderick Random after his return from France, helps Roderick get revenge against Melinda Goosetrap, and leads him to success in gambling; he advises Roderick on a scheme to marry Miss Snapper for her money and Banter's own benefit and refuses Don Rodriguez's offer to buy him a commission in the army in Tobias Smollett's *The Adventures of Roderick Random.*

Bantry, Dolly Jane Marple's closest friend in St. Mary Mead; she appears in Agatha Christie's *Sleeping Murder* and in two other novels.

Banu Prophet who lives in a cave and is an associate of John the Baptist in George Moore's *The Brook Kerith.*

Banubula, Count Decrepit nobleman; he is in the employ of Countess Hippolyta, sporadically cataloguing her library in Lawrence Durrell's *Tunc.*

Bao, Miss One of two Chinese beauties the protagonist, Fang Hong-jian, meets aboard a French liner sailing to China; lured the protagonist to her cabin during the trip and then forgot him before the liner docked in Hong Kong, as her fiancé was waiting for her at the Hong Kong harbor in Qian Zhong-shu's *Fortress Besieged.*

Baobabs On Earth, Baobabs are simply giant African trees, no more significant than other trees; on smaller, more fragile planets, Baobabs represent danger; they can extend their roots throughout a planet's structure, crushing the planet; the Little Prince makes a morning ritual of finding and digging out Baobab seeds on his home planet before they can grow into adult trees and destroy his home in Antoine de Saint Exupéry's *The Little Prince.*

Baps, Mr. Professor of dancing at Dr. Blimber's boarding school in Charles Dickens's *Dombey and Son.*

Baps, Mrs. Wife of Mr. Baps; she accompanies him to the dance at Dr. Blimber's boarding school in Charles Dickens's *Dombey and Son.*

Baptista Servant who informs the evil Marquis de Mazzini that his wife, Maria de Vellorno, is having an affair in Ann Radcliffe's *A Sicilian Romance.*

Baptiste Male servant in Rochester's island home who serves Antoinette Cosway rum which contributes to her ultimate decline into madness in Jean Rhys's *Wide Sargasso Sea.*

Baptiste Rapacious bandit killed by his wife Marguerite as he is about to murder Alphonso d'Alvarada (Raymond, Marquis de la Cisternas) and Rodolpha, Baroness Lindenberg in Matthew Lewis's *The Monk.*

Baptiste, Jean (The Homesteader, St. John the Baptist) Black homesteader; would-be lover of Agnes Stewart and husband of Orlean McCarthy in Oscar Micheaux's *The Homesteader.*

Baptistin One of the confederates of Protos and a member of the group perpetrating the swindle involving the kidnapping of the pope in André Gide's *Lafcadio's Adventures.*

Barabo, Antonina Elder daughter of Signor Barabo; fascinated by the power of Il Gufo, she declares her love and offers herself to him in John Hawkes's *The Owl.*

Barabo, Ginevra Younger sister of Antonina Barabo; attacked by Il Gufo's pet owl in John Hawkes's *The Owl.*

Barabo, Signor Father of Antonina and Ginevra Barabo; tries to obtain the release of a prisoner to marry Antonina in John Hawkes's *The Owl.*

Barach Blind man who belatedly tells his master, King Cuchulain, that the young foreign champion he has killed is his own son by the warrior queen Aoife in William Butler Yeats's play *On Baile's Strand.*

Baracoa (Indian) Loyal kitchen maid and only trusted servant allowed in the Menchaca household in Carlos Fuentes's *The Death of Artemio Cruz.*

Barak El Hadgi Fakir and secret agent of Prince Hyder Ali Khan Bahauder; he gives Dr. Adam Hartley friendship in return for his medical attention and arranges an interview with the monarch on Menie Gray's behalf in Sir Walter Scott's *The Surgeon's Daughter.*

Baranov, Aleksandr Visionary, steadfast Russian merchant sent to found and manage fur company affairs in Kodiak, Alaska; creates ordered settlement and establishes capital at Sitka; ultimately dishonored through bureaucratic harassment in James Michener's *Alaska.*

Barasi, Senor Unctuous, wealthy Gibraltar businessman who marries Richard Ennis's mistress, Conception Gomez, while still remaining on friendly terms with Ennis himself in Anthony Burgess's *A Vision of Battlements.*

Barbacela (Queen of Emmets) Sorceress who appears to Prince Bonbennin bonbobbin-bonbobbinet as an old woman and promises him the white mouse he covets provided he will marry her; later in the shape of the white mouse she is destroyed by Queen Nanhoa, in an oriental fable told by Lien Chi Altangi in Oliver Goldsmith's *The Citizen of the World.*

Barban, Tommy Soldier of fortune who becomes Nicole Warren Diver's second husband in F. Scott Fitzgerald's *Tender Is the Night.*

Barbanel, Joseph Former lumber dealer; member of Kovno ghetto council; keeps secret record of all actions and regulations by Gestapo; lists names of members; records fate of Jews killed or transported; lover of Greta Margolin; uses Yehoshua Mendelssohn to smuggle manuscript in E. L. Doctorow's *City of God.*

Barbara Derba's granddaughter, whose child nature helps the king overcome his nightmares; she becomes his ward in George MacDonald's *The Princess and Curdie.*

Barbara Orlando King's secretary; Judith (Gardner) King finds out about Barbara's affair with him in Isabel Colegate's *Orlando King.*

Barbara Pretty and shy servant girl of the Garlands; she eventually marries Kit Nubbles in Charles Dickens's *The Old Curiosity Shop.*

Barbara Servant at Lowood School, the boarding school attended by Jane Eyre; she serves the headmistress, Miss Temple, in Charlotte Brontë's *Jane Eyre.*

Barbara (the witch) Depressingly wholesome and efficient secretary who is one of Billy Fisher's three fiancées in Keith Waterhouse's *Billy Liar.*

Barbara Attorney and agent of Henry Wiggen in Mark Harris's *It Looked Like For Ever.*

Barbara Runs the pressers at Kolditis Cleaners in Mary McGarry Morris's *A Dangerous Woman.*

Barbara Sexual conquest of Carol Severin Swanson in Jim Harrison's *Wolf.*

Barbara, Lady Daughter of the Earl of Huntingdon and one of Queen Eleanor's favorites; she marries Gaston de Blondeville only to see him killed by the ghost of Reginald de Folville within days of their marriage in Ann Radcliffe's *Gaston de Blondeville.*

Barbara's Mother Kindhearted woman, who becomes a good friend to Mrs. Nubbles and assists her when Kit Nubbles is in prison in Charles Dickens's *The Old Curiosity Shop.*

Barbarsa Duplicitous minister of the king Georigetti; he seduces Yaccombourse and, with her, is executed for sedition in Robert Paltock's *The Life and Adventures of Peter Wilkins.*

Barbary, Miss Godmother (actually aunt) to Esther Summerson and sister to Lady Dedlock; she is grave, strict, and forbidding; she raised Esther in a repressive way from birth, telling her that it would have been far better if she had never lived, in Charles Dickens's *Bleak House.*

Barbatov, Captain Russian military martinet outsmarted by George Levanter in Jerzy Kosinski's *Blind Date.*

Barbazon, Mrs. Stella Mathews's mother who interferes in her daughter's life after the baby is born in Doris Lessing's *A Proper Marriage.*

Barbecue-Smith, Mr. Pretentious writer of popular philosophy; briefly joining the houseparty at Crome estate, he attempts to offer his hackneyed advice on writing to Denis Stone in Aldous Huxley's *Crome Yellow.*

Barbedienne, Master Florian Deaf judge in Paris who condemns the hunchback Quasimodo to torture in Victor Hugo's *The Hunchback of Notre Dame.*

Barber Drops cryptic hints about the cholera epidemic; later glibly dyes Gustav von Aschenbach's hair and paints his face; depicted as a mysterious and devilish character in Thomas Mann's *Death in Venice.*

Barber, Arthur Student council president who tries to convince Dr. Charles Osman to change his mind about failing Raymond Blent in Howard Nemerov's *The Homecoming Game.*

Barber, Helen Van Vleck First love of Nelson Dewey; marries Joel Barber and dies in childbirth in August Derleth's *The Shadow in the Glass.*

Barber, Joel Law partner of Nelson Dewey; successfully competes with Dewey for Helen Van Vleck in August Derleth's *The Shadow in the Glass.*

Barber, Solomon Physically large professor of history who, when younger, seduced one of his students, Emily, who eventually turns out to be Marco's long-lost mother; as fat as Marco, the narrator, is thin; represents the author Auster's contempt for academics, as opposed to those inspired by the muse of creative endeavor; produces a huge corpus of scholarly writing but never creates great fiction; his sole attempt at originality, a novel entitled *Keppler's Blood,* is a hodgepodge of every clichéd situation and stock character of popular literature; visits Emily's grave with Marco, where Solomon slips and falls into an empty grave, breaking his back; represents part of the past that Marco strives to uncover and discard in his quest for self-identification in Paul Auster's *Moon Palace.*

Barber, The One of the representatives of the mortal world who enters the mountain world filled with elemental spirits in Gerhart Hauptmann's play *The Sunken Bell.*

Barber at the Inn One of the men talking in a tavern in Engsng when the funeral procession of the poor young clerk Hans Schönschreiber passes by in August Strindberg's "A Funeral."

Barbon, Frederick ("Freddy") Thomas Carlyle Craw's confidential secretary in John Buchan's *Castle Gay.*

Barbon, Nosy Aspiring young artist who worships Gulley Jimson and later helps Gulley paint the Creation in Joyce Cary's *The Horse's Mouth.*

Barboulis, Stephanie Jill's roommate her senior year; Greek girl who likes Howie and later marries him in Marge Piercy's *Braided Lives.*

Barbro Brede Olsen's daughter who lives with Axel, a farmer, and helps him with his farm work in Knut Hamsun's *Growth of the Soil.*

Bárcenas, Márgara Beautiful daughter of a fugitive of the Revolution and lover of Domingo Vizquez de Anda in Josefina Niggli's *Step Down, Elder Brother.*

Barclay, Adam Young soldier from Texas who quickly falls in love with the protagonist, Miranda; second lieutenant in the engineers corps and soon to be shipped overseas in World War I; takes care of Miranda when she suffers from the plague; tragically dies of influenza at the end of the war in 1918 in Katherine Anne Porter's "Pale Horse, Pale Rider."

Barclay, Edith Secretary to Frank Hirsh; later becomes his second mistress but leaves for Chicago after Agnes Hirsh discovers their affair in James Jones's *Some Came Running.*

Barclay, Elizabeth Long-suffering wife of Wilfred Barclay; she sees him clearly for what he is in William Golding's *The Paper Men.*

Barclay, Emily Daughter of Elizabeth and Wilfred Barclay; she has little more than contempt for her father, who sees himself as the protagonist of his own religious tragedy but whom she sees as an egocentric monster in William Golding's *The Paper Men.*

Barclay, Jane Mason Wife of John Barclay and mother of Jeanette Barclay; her death from typhoid fever is indirectly caused by her husband's greed in William Allen White's *A Certain Rich Man.*

Barclay, Jeanette Daughter of John and Jane Barclay; marries Neal Dow Ward after her father is rid of his fortune in William Allen White's *A Certain Rich Man.*

Barclay, John (Johnnie) Capitalist who founds the Golden Belt Wheat Company monopoly; husband of Jane Barclay and father of Jeanette Barclay; after his wife's death, he dismantles his fortune and returns to Sycamore Ridge in William Allen White's *A Certain Rich Man.*

Barclay, Wilfred Townsend Dipsomaniac novelist and narrator; he believes he is a penitent undergoing a religious crisis but is simply a sadistic prig experiencing a kind of literary delirium tremens in William Golding's *The Paper Men.*

Barcroft, Amanda (Miss Manda) Jilted lover of Harley Drew in Shelby Foote's *Love in a Dry Season.*

Barcroft, Florence (Miss Flaunts) Invalid sister of Amanda Barcroft in Shelby Foote's *Love in a Dry Season.*

Barcroft, Major Malcolm Cotton factor in Bristol, Mississippi, and father of Amanda and Florence Barcroft in Shelby Foote's *Love in a Dry Season.*

Bard Grim but wise man of Lake-town Esgaroth who kills Smaug the dragon after he is chased out by Bilbo Baggins and his companions in J. R. R. Tolkien's *The Hobbit; or There and Back Again.*

Bardamu, Ferdinand Young medical student who enlists in the French army in 1914; wounded and disillusioned by the horrors of war; manages a trading post in Equatorial Africa; bored with the regimentation and sick with fever, he escapes to America; works in a Ford plant in Detroit and lives with prostitute before returning to France to finish his medical degree; sets up practice among the poor and later works in a psychiatric institute, satirizing the medical profession and scientific research; encounters the even more disillusioned and amoral antihero, Leon Robinson, whose experiences parallel his own in Louis-Ferdinand Céline's *Journey to the End of the Night.*

Bardell, Martha Samuel Pickwick's middle-aged landlady, who sues him for breach of promise in Charles Dickens's *The Posthumous Papers of the Pickwick Club.*

Bardell, Tommy Martha Bardell's son, who likes to kick people in Charles Dickens's *The Posthumous Papers of the Pickwick Club.*

Bardi, Bardo de' Blind father of Romola, descendant of a great family but poor because he has devoted his life to scholarship and used his money collecting rare books for his library; he allows Tito Melema to marry Romola only because he wants help with his studies in George Eliot's *Romola.*

Bardi, Dino de' (Fra Luca) Brother of Romola; he leaves his father's scholarly work to become a Dominican monk; he warns Romola against marriage before he dies in the monastery, but he does not tell her that Tito has left his adopted father in slavery in George Eliot's *Romola.*

Bardi, Romola de' Intellectual and beautiful woman raised in Florence to help her blind, scholarly father; she marries Tito Melema before she realizes his evil nature; the novel ends with Tito's mistress and illegitimate children living with and being taught by Romola in George Eliot's *Romola.*

Bardia Captain of the Royal Guard in the land of Glome; he teaches Orual swordsmanship and becomes a trusted counsellor after her ascension to the throne; he is the object of Orual's possessiveness which is revealed to her after his death in C. S. Lewis's *Till We Have Faces.*

Bardianni Sage who influences Babbalanja in Herman Melville's *Mardi.*

Bardolph Tavern companion of Prince Hal's; takes part in the robbery at Gad's Hill with Falstaff, Gadshill, and Peto in William Shakespeare's *Henry IV, Part One;* delivers a letter to Prince Hal from Falstaff; accepts bribes from Mouldy and Bullcalf to be released from duty; accompanies Falstaff at the coronation of Henry V; as a member of Falstaff's company, banished from the king's presence; arrested, along with Falstaff and others, by the lord chief justice after Henry V rejects Falstaff in William Shakespeare's *Henry IV, Part Two;* mourns Falstaff's death with Pistol, Nym, Hostess Quickly, and the Boy; leaves for France to fight in the war; appears to be brave in battle, but is truly a coward; steals a pix in France, and Exeter orders his execution by hanging; despite Pistol's efforts to have him freed, executed in William Shakespeare's play *Henry V.*

Bardolph, Lord Allied to the earl of Northumberland; tells Northumberland the false report that the rebels have beaten Henry IV at the Battle of Shrewsbury; contradicted by Travers and Morton, who report the loss of Shrewsbury; rallies with Northumberland about reorganizing the rebellion; meets with the archbishop of York regarding a new rebellion; asks Hastings if York's army will be ready without the aid of Northumberland because, he implies, Northumberland is not trustworthy; advises that if Northumberland is essential to their plot they should be careful how deeply involved they become without absolute confirmation that Northumberland will not abandon them; points out that Hotspur believed Northumberland (his father) would provide reinforcements for him, but that Northumberland's abandonment caused not only Hotspur's death but also the deaths of many others and the failure of the rebellion; ironically, though a voice of reason to the other rebels, flees with Northumberland to Scotland; captured by the sheriff of Yorkshire in William Shakespeare's play *Henry IV, Part Two.*

Bardolph, Mrs. Card-playing gossip at Bath who speaks favorably of Geoffry Wildgoose to Lady Sherwood in Richard Graves's *The Spiritual Quixote.*

Bareacres, Countess of Impecunious aristocrat, who is condescending towards Becky Sharp except when she needs her horses at Waterloo in William Makepeace Thackeray's *Vanity Fair.*

Bareacres, Earl of Impoverished nobleman, whose daughter is the despised daughter-in-law of Lord Steyne in William Makepeace Thackeray's *Vanity Fair.*

Bareau, Carbon Mountaineer who identifies Arnaud du Tilh as his nephew in Janet Lewis's *The Wife of Martin Guerre.*

Barefoot, Juanita Collins Harmeyer (Mother Goddam) Madam and friend of Perry in James Leo Herlihy's *Midnight Cowboy.*

Barefoot, Tombaby (Princess) Son of Juanita Barefoot in James Leo Herlihy's *Midnight Cowboy.*

Barfield, Arthur (Ginger) Gentleman rider and trainer, son and inheritor of Woodfield estate; he rarely visits his mother and dislikes her middle-class, Dissenter associates in George Moore's *Esther Waters.*

Barfield, Margaret (Peggy) Daughter of a rich brewer and cousin of the Barfields; she is attracted physically to William Latch, who marries her to spite Esther Waters; the marriage ends in divorce in George Moore's *Esther Waters.*

Barfield, Mary Pleasant, attractive daughter of the Barfields; she shows a preference for Esther Waters among the servants; because of ill health, she is taken to Egypt, where she dies in George Moore's *Esther Waters.*

Barfield, Mr. (the Gaffer) Bluff retired soldier, devoted to horses and gambling; one of the new landed gentry, he is owner of an estate, Woodfield; though he wins big at gambling, he finally loses the estate in George Moore's *Esther Waters.*

Barfield, Mrs. (the Saint) Mistress of the Barfield estate; well-loved and unassuming, she is a member of the Plymouth Brethren and abhors the family gambling; she respects and likes a fellow worshipper, the cook's helper Esther Waters; in old age and widowhood she invites Esther to return to the estate as servant; the two share common interests in religion and in their sons in George Moore's *Esther Waters.*

Barfoot, Everard Footloose and irresponsible fellow, who believes in freedom and equality between husband and wife; he offers the feminist Rhoda Nunn an unconventional union but refuses to marry her when she decides she wants marriage in George Gissing's *The Odd Women.*

Barfoot, Mary Feminist of moderate aims who runs a school that trains girls to earn their living at various occupations in George Gissing's *The Odd Women.*

Bargeman Anonymous fellow who makes an unsuccessful sexual assault on Catharine Furze while she is staying at Chapel Farm in Mark Rutherford's *Catharine Furze.*

Bargetta Described as the only black friend the unnamed male narrator had in college; a tall, striking young woman from Memphis who remains aloof to the social and racial politics among other young blacks in the college set; dates only white men; follows a French artist to Paris, where she is eventually abandoned by him and expelled from his apartment by his disapproving mother in Darryl Pinckney's *High Cotton.*

Bargrove, Mr. Kindly country gentleman, who agrees to help Eleanor Grimshaw in a ghost story interpolated into the narrative of William Beckford's *Azemia.*

Bargrove, Mrs. Benevolent wife of Mr. Bargrove in a ghost story interpolated into the narrative of William Beckford's *Azemia.*

Barham, Mr. English visitor to Kentucky in James Kirke Paulding's *Westward Ho!*

Baring, Dr. Margaret Warden of Shrewsbury College, Oxford University; she wants to expose the anonymous mischief maker without embarrassing the college in Dorothy L. Sayers's *Gaudy Night.*

Barkeeper Saloon owner who refuses to force his guests to drink with the Swede; later accused of not preventing the fight; the prominent merchants and district attorney rush out of his bar after the Swede is killed; finds himself hanging on to a chair and staring at the murderer, who tells him he will be home if anyone wants to prosecute him; goes outside to look for help and companionship in Stephen Crane's "The Blue Hotel."

Barker Former chauffeur to Lilian Portway and Canon Portway; he blackmailed the Canon with knowledge of Gilbert Stokesay's practical joke in the Melpham discovery; he dies after years as a mute in the care of his daughter, Alice Cressett, in Angus Wilson's *Anglo-Saxon Attitudes.*

Barker, Betty One of the Cranford ladies; her cow has a flannel coat in Elizabeth Gaskell's *Cranford.*

Barker, Cecil James Former partner of John Douglas in a gold mine in California and an important witness in the Birlstone Manor case; he is attentive to Douglas's wife in Arthur Conan Doyle's *The Valley of Fear.*

Barker, Damon Lost father of Agnes Deming and loyal father-surrogate to Jo Erring and Ned Westlock in E. W. Howe's *The Story of a Country Town.*

Barker, Israel Walter Morel's "fellow-butty" in the mines in D. H. Lawrence's *Sons and Lovers.*

Barker, James Government official who becomes Lord High Provost of South Kensington and spokesman for the other borough leaders; their desire to build a road through Notting Hill leads to war with the borough of Notting Hill in G. K. Chesterton's *The Napoleon of Notting Hill.*

Barker, Jean Communist Party member, married to a minor party official and considered a "clown" by other party members because she never thinks before speaking in Doris Lessing's *The Golden Notebook.*

Barker, Ned Bullying, blundering boy in Louisa May Alcott's *Little Men.*

Barker, Penny Former girlfriend of Clyde Stout, whose grammar she corrects in Jack Matthews's *Hanger Stout, Awake!*

Barker, Phil Drunken customer at the Three Cripples public house in Charles Dickens's *Oliver Twist.*

Barker, Rolfe Boy who takes Anne into a back room and puts his hands on her in Joan Chase's *During the Reign of the Queen of Persia.*

Barkis, Mr. Carrier who proposes to Clara Peggotty by sending through young David Copperfield the message that "Barkis is willin'"; he eventually marries her in Charles Dickens's *The Personal History of David Copperfield.*

Barkley, Catherine English volunteer hospital worker in Italy at the beginning of World War I; falls in love with Frederic Henry and dies of hemorrhaging after the Caesarean delivery of their stillborn son in Ernest Hemingway's *A Farewell to Arms.*

Barkley, Wilbur New husband of the divorcee Leila in Edith Wharton's "Autres Temps . . . ."

Barley, Clara Daughter and nurse of Old Bill Barley and Herbert Pocket's bride-to-be in Charles Dickens's *Great Expectations.*

Barley, Old Bill (Gruffandgrim) Drunken, bedridden father of Clara Barley and a resident with Abel Magwitch (who has assumed the name Provis) at Mrs. Whimple's house in Charles Dickens's *Great Expectations.*

Barleymoon, Bessie English captain's widow with means and resident of Pisuerga who, in the opinion of her friend Mrs. Bedley, doesn't get enough respect for her noble background in Ronald Firbank's *The Flower Beneath the Foot.*

Barlo, King Charismatic black preacher and field laborer famous for his cane-cutting and his attractiveness to women in Jean Toomer's *Cane.*

Barlow Mugger turned cabdriver who works for Edward Pierce in Michael Crichton's *The Great Train Robbery.*

Barlow Vampire and owner, with his partner Richard Straker, of Marsten House in Stephen King's *'Salem's Lot.*

Barlow, Anthea Emissary from the pastorate whose repeated efforts to see the new rector, Carel Fisher, are blocked by Pattie O'Driscoll; recognized by Marcus Fisher, she is revealed to have been the girl with whom he, Carel, and their late brother Julian were simultaneously in love in Iris Murdoch's *The Time of the Angels.*

Barlow, Citizen African-American young man (late 20s to early 30s); feels guilt since he was responsible for the death of another man; comes to Aunt Ester to have his soul washed by Aunt Ester in August Wilson's play *Gem of the Ocean.*

Barlow, Dennis Young, cynical English author who comes to Hollywood to write films; lack of success forces him to take a job at a pet cemetery; he courts Aimée Thanatogenos, but after her death he returns to England with money obtained from Mr. Joyboy for secretly cremating Aimée at the pet cemetery in Evelyn Waugh's *The Loved One.*

Barlow, Elder Joseph African American recently returned to the Hill District of Pittsburgh; down on his luck; owner of a house slated for demolition by Hammond Wilks and Roosevelt Hicks in August Wilson's play *Radio Golf.*

Barlow, Eli Elderly director of the Saddleford Building Society who finds it convenient to turn off his hearing device in Roy Fuller's *Image of a Society.*

Barlow, Frankie Roadhouse owner ruthlessly murdered by Glen Davis after his release from prison in Larry Brown's *Father and Son.*

Barlow, Frank X. See Fender, Dr. Robert.

Barlow, Joel American expatriate in France who helps arrange for the publication of Thomas Paine's *The Age of Reason* in Howard Fast's *Citizen Tom Paine.*

Barlow, Mr. Alderman who is reminded by everything of his obligations to General Barton in William Beckford's *Modern Novel Writing; or, the Elegant Enthusiast.*

Barlow, Polly (Mary) Waiting maid to Pamela (Andrews) B—; unheedful of her mistress's example, she agrees to enter into a common-law alliance with the silly, thoughtless gentleman Jackey H—; the affair is thwarted before it is consummated-and Polly's honor ruined-by Pamela's inadvertent discovery of them in flagrante delicto; she ultimately marries a clergyman in Samuel Richardson's *Pamela, or Virtue Rewarded.*

Barman Brighton bartender who supplies information to Ida Arnold about Kite, Colleoni, and Pinkie Brown in Graham Greene's *Brighton Rock.*

Barmby, Samuel Vulgar advocate of materialistic culture; he is in love with Nancy Lord and is made a trustee of the will that deprives her of her inheritance because she is married in George Gissing's *In the Year of Jubilee.*

Barnabas Kind, young man and a messenger who delivers a note from Klamm, a chief at the castle, to the protagonist K.; lives with his two sisters—Olga and Amalia; befriends K. by inviting the young wanderer to stay at his home in Franz Kafka's *The Castle.*

Barnabas, Mr. Clergyman called to Joseph Andrews's apparent deathbed; he prefers visiting with the Towwouses to ministering to a penniless nobody in Henry Fielding's *The History of the Adventures of Mr. Joseph Andrews and of His Friend Mr. Abraham Adams.*

Barnack, Eustace Epicurean patron of the arts whose scandalous enjoyment of life's many pleasures is an embarrassment to his relations; himself childless, he dotes on his nephew Sebastian Barnack, on whom he showers expensive gifts; after his sudden death he hovers in the after-life bemused by his random memories and observations of the living in Aldous Huxley's *Time Must Have a Stop.*

Barnack, John Sebastian's often-absent father, an upper-class Socialist whose politics cause Sebastian many unnecessary embarrassments in Aldous Huxley's *Time Must Have a Stop.*

Barnack, Sebastian Sensitive and socially insecure youth who writes clever verse chiefly for the amusement of his Uncle Eustace Barnack; his immaturity leads him into various intrigues at his uncle's Florentine home and though aided in his difficulties after Eustace's death by Bruno Rontini, he fails to develop a sense of equanimity until after many years of unhappiness in Aldous Huxley's *Time Must Have a Stop.*

Barnacle, Clarence Tite Barnacle's weak-minded son, who sports a monocle, works in the Circumlocution Office, and does his best not to help Arthur Clennam in his inquiries regarding William Dorrit and Daniel Doyce's patent in Charles Dickens's *Little Dorrit.*

Barnacle, Ferdinand Sprightly young Barnacle who works in the Circumlocution Office and advises Arthur Clennam to give up his inquiries, stating that the Office's goal is "to be left alone" in Charles Dickens's *Little Dorrit.*

Barnacle, Jessie ("Granny") Noisy, cantankerous resident patient of the old women's hospital ward; when the transfer of the bullying nurse, Sister Burstead, removes the stimulation of her hatred, she dies in Muriel Spark's *Memento Mon.*

Barnacle, Lord Decimus Tite Revered head of the Barnacle family and uncle of Tite Barnacle in Charles Dickens's *Little Dorrit.*

Barnacle, Mrs. Tite (née Stilt-stalking) Expensive and well-connected wife of Tite Barnacle in Charles Dickens's *Little Dorrit.*

Barnacle, Tite Pompous member of the highborn Barnacle family; he has high standing in the inefficient and cumbersome Circumlocution Office; he perpetuates its creed of "how not to do it" and its goal of being left alone and hinders Arthur Clennam in his inquiries in Charles Dickens's *Little Dorrit.*

Barnacle, William Lord Decimus Tite Barnacle's connection who is a Member of Parliament and well versed in the art of "how not to do it" in Charles Dickens's *Little Dorrit.*

Barnadine Prisoner who is sentenced to be executed together with Claudio, Isabella's brother; saved from the death sentence when the Duke commutes his sentence in William Shakespeare's play *Measure for Measure.*

Barnard, Augustus Spirited friend of Arthur Gordon Pym; arranges Pym's stowaway on the *Grampus;* wounded in the retaking of the ship from mutineers; dies from exposure and malnutrition in Edgar Allan Poe's *The Narrative of Arthur Gordon Pym.*

Barnard, Dr. Thomas Rector of St. Philip's Church, Winchelsea; he assists the French Protestants and is the staunch protector of Denis Duval's interests in William Makepeace Thackeray's *Denis Duval.*

Barnard, Elizabeth (Betty) Young woman murdered on a beach at Bexhill-on-Sea in Agatha Christie's *The A.B.C. Murders.*

Barnard, Harold Constance Ollerenshaw's solicitor, an agreeable, sensible, happily married man whom Frances Wingate admires and likes in Margaret Drabble's *The Realms of Gold.*

Barnard, Henry D. See Bryant, Chalmers.

Barnard, Megan Betty's intelligent, observant sister; she joins forces with Hercule Poirot to find her sister's killer in Agatha Christie's *The A.B.C. Murders.*

Barnard, Mr. Father of Augustus Barnard and captain of the *Grampus;* set adrift when the ship's crew mutinies in Edgar Allan Poe's *The Narrative of Arthur Gordon Pym.*

Barnard, Mrs. Kindly wife of the rector and supporter of Denis Duval in his childhood romance with Agnes de Saverne in William Makepeace Thackeray's *Denis Duval.*

Barnardini Porter at Castle di Udolpho, who betrays Montoni by participating in Count Morano's attempt to kidnap Emily St. Aubert in Ann Radcliffe's *The Mysteries of Udolpho.*

Barnby, Ralph Third-generation painter of talent; he is Edgar Deacon's tenant in Anthony Powell's *A Buyer's Market.* He is a well-known womanizer, involved amicably with Lady Anne Stepney, among others, in *The Acceptance World.* He is discussed in *Casanova's Chinese Restaurant,* in *The Kindly Ones,* and in *The Valley of Bones.* His murals for the Donners-Brebner building are destroyed by a bomb, and he is killed when his plane is shot down in *The Soldier's Art.*

Barnes Barnabas Tyrre's steward, who assists in the harassing of the Hawkinses and in the imprisonment of Emily Melville; he objects strongly to Emily's being removed from her sickbed to jail but does as he is ordered by the angry Tyrrel in William Godwin's *Caleb Williams.*

Barnes Maid to Olive and Alice Barton; she connives to help Olive by carrying messages in George Moore's *A Drama in Muslin.*

Barnes Soldier who thinks "The Lady of the Lake" is "good po'try", and tells Mike Brady and Jonathan Browne the story of his brother-in-law, the Jehovah's Witness, in David Lodge's *Ginger, You're Barmy.*

Barnes, Betty Chambermaid first to Arabella Harlowe and then to her younger sister Clarissa; she is rude and insolent to Clarissa and a spy for other members of the family in Samuel Richardson's *Clarissa: or, The History of a Young Lady.*

Barnes, Cissie General Curzon's abandoned but not forgotten old flame in C. S. Forester's *The General.*

Barnes, Djuna Literary figure, portrayed here in advanced age in her apartment at Patchin Place in New York's Greenwich Village; asks the narrator to hand-wash a blouse, followed by an observation about the "touchiness" of blacks, which causes a fatal rupture in their friendship in Darryl Pinckney's *High Cotton.*

Barnes, Dr. Elderly surgeon now angry that he has to deliver news to Dr. Benjamin that Dr. Benjamin has been replaced as the surgeon of a poor woman in the charity ward by Dr. Leeds, the son of a senator, in Clifford Odets's play *Waiting for Lefty.*

Barnes, Etta Daughter of Solon and Benecia Barnes; disregards her parents' wishes and attends the University of Wisconsin; mistress of Willard Kane; returns home following the suicide of her brother Stewart Barnes in Theodore Dreiser's *The Bulwark.*

Barnes, George Lord Kew's younger brother in William Makepeace Thackeray's *The Newcomes.*

Barnes, Hannah and Rufus Quaker parents of Solon Barnes in Theodore Dreiser's *The Bulwark.*

Barnes, Jacob (Jake) American newspaperman in Paris rendered impotent by a war wound; narrator of Ernest Hemingway's *The Sun Also Rises.*

Barnes, Joe Marshall in the small town where Whitey's barbershop sits; summoned to prevent Jim Kendall from harassing and assaulting Julie Gregg in her home in Ring Lardner's "Haircut."

Barnes, June Barnes Schoolmate of Kate Fletcher (Armstrong); upon leaving school, she took a lackluster position in an estate office in Margaret Drabble's *The Middle Ground.*

Barnes, Lady Julia Lady Kew's unmarried daughter, dominated by her sharp-tongued mother in William Makepeace Thackeray's *The Newcomes.*

Barnes, Lett Poet and friend of Julia Ashton in H. D.'s *Bid Me to Live.*

Barnes, Lieutenant Barney Black CIA agent who warns the narrator about bureaucratic traps being set for him; he is murdered for his loyalty in Len Deighton's *The Ipcress File.*

Barnes, Mattie Original dance-marathon partner of Kid Kamm; collapses and is eliminated from the competition in Horace McCoy's *They Shoot Horses, Don't They?*

Barnes, Mr. London secondhand bookseller, 65 years old, who employs Clara Hopgood as a clerk in Mark Rutherford's *Clara Hopgood.*

Barnes, Osella Childhood nurse of Gavin Hexam and later a maid for Gavin and N. Hexam; quits her job as maid because she believes N. Hexam is a witch in Diane Johnson's *The Shadow Knows.*

Barnes, Sergeant Ruby Sailing master on Earth who pilots the raft with which the explorers get to the Raman island and with which they rescue Lieutenant Pak in Arthur C. Clarke's *Rendezvous with Rama.*

Barnes, Solon Quaker farmer and businessman who attempts to be both successful and a good Quaker in Theodore Dreiser's *The Bulwark.*

Barnes, Stewart (Stew) Son of Solon and Benecia Barnes; commits suicide following his involvement in the death of Psyche Tanzer in Theodore Dreiser's *The Bulwark.*

Barnes, Will Local swain who took up with (among others) Betty and Molly Seagrim and probably fathered Molly's child in Henry Fielding's *The History of Tom Jones.*

Barnet, John Scots-speaking servant of the Reverend Wringhim; he reproves Robert Colwan for conceit and hypocrisy and is provoked into leaving his post through Robert's scheming in James Hogg's *The Private Memoirs and Confessions of a Justified Sinner.*

Barnet, Mr. Mrs. Barnet's brother-in-law, secretly married to Miss Groves, proving how far she has fallen socially in Charlotte Lennox's *The Female Quixote.*

Barnet, Mrs. Attends Clarissa Dolloway's fashionable evening party at which the protagonist, Mabel Waring, is present in Virginia Woolf's "The New Dress."

Barnet, Mrs. Sister of Miss Groves's former maid; she provides Miss Groves a place to give birth to an illegitimate child in Charlotte Lennox's *The Female Quixote.*

Barnevelt, Miss Harriet Byron's London acquaintance, a lady of masculine mind and features, who holds her own sex in contempt; her chief pleasure in being a woman derives from the impossibility of her marrying a woman, but she is much taken with Harriet in Samuel Richardson's *Sir Charles Grandison.*

Barney Dwarf member of Nick Ollanton's magic act who grows more and more irresponsible; enticed and then insulted by Nonie Colmar, he strangles her but escapes the clutches of the law through an elaborate scheme devised by Nick, who has his own sense of justice in J. B. Priestley's *Lost Empires.*

Barney Waiter at the Three Cripples who speaks through his nose; he is Fagin's confederate in Charles Dickens's *Oliver Twist.*

Barnhelm, Minna von Rich young German woman of 21 years; goes in search of Major von Tellheim, her betrothed, who has been discharged from the German army and is financially destitute; learns that he will not marry her due to his fallen monetary state; forms a scheme with her maid Franziska to recapture her betrothed in Gotthold Ephraim Lessing's play *Minna von Barnhelm.*

Barnington, Mrs. Social leader in Robert Surtees's *Handley Cross.*

Barnstaple, William Disillusioned Victorian socialist and journalist who crosses into another dimension, the perfect world of Utopia, where he resists attempts by other Earthlings to overthrow the Utopian system; in Utopia he learns that humanity's only hope of developing an equally mature society is through the persistence of ethical men like himself in H. G. Wells's *Men Like Gods.*

Barnstorff, Edith Dewar Grandmother of Jane Clifford in Gail Godwin's *The Odd Woman.*

Barnwell, Anna Allston See Allston, Anna.

Barnwell, Lewis Girlhood boyfriend of Cornelia Wilton; disappears shortly after his marriage to Anna Allston in Caroline Gilman's *Recollections of a Southern Matron.*

Baron Danna of Mameha; orders Sayuri to attend a party without Mameha and forcibly undresses and observes her; this issue is never discussed between Mameha and Sayuri, serving a twofold purpose of exhibiting the position of weakness and power of geisha and illustrating the bond of women who can form friendships rather than rivalries over the acts of men in Arthur Golden's *Memoirs of a Geisha.*

Baron, Arthur (Art) Company division head responsible for replacing Andy Kagle with Bob Slocum in Joseph Heller's *Something Happened.*

Baron, The Former nobleman now reduced to menial labor; one of the many poor boarders in the lodging owned by the ill-tempered landlord Kostilyoff in Maxim Gorky's play *The Lower Depths.*

Baroness Bredow (née Tolstoy) Extraordinary aunt of Vadim Vadimovich, who exhorted him as a child to quit moping and use his imagination to invent reality by looking at the harlequins in Vladimir Nabokov's *Look at the Harlequins!*

Baronet ("handsome Sir—") Heavy drinker who is robbed by Moll Flanders but who later has an affair with her for a year in Daniel Defoe's *The Fortunes and Misfortunes of the Famous Moll Flanders.*

Baroni Extremely intelligent and able Jew, who was persecuted in his European home but was given a place in Sidonia's circle of talented associates; he is sent by Sidonia to be the companion of Tancred, Lord Montacute during his travels in Palestine in Benjamin Disraeli's *Tancred; or The New Crusade.*

***Baron in the Trees, The,* Narrator** Brother of the protagonist and eccentric Cosimo, the title character who lives in the upper branches of tall trees; converses with Voltaire in Paris during the Age of Reason in the 18th century in Italo Calvino's *The Baron in the Trees.*

Barons Drinking partners of King Henry's and general mediocrities who take Henry at his word and kill Becket in Canterbury Cathedral in Jean Anouilh's play *Becket.*

Baroque, Amadeus Mill worker who finds and reads the only extant manuscript of Doctor Sax, written under the pen name Adolphus Asher Ghoulens, in Jack Kerouac's *Doctor Sax.*

Barr, Augustus M. Unscrupulous ex-minister; steals Peter Kaden's beloved in Oscar Micheaux's *The Homesteader.*

Barr, Lilli See Tolliver, Ellen.

Barraclough, Moses Methodist and a hypocritical preacher, who leads the machine breakers; he is eventually transported under Robert Moore's orders in Charlotte Brontë's *Shirley.*

Barraclough, Robbie Academic sociologist in his late twenties; he is a resident in the West Oxfordshire village where Emma Howick has come to stay in Barbara Pym's *A Few Green Leaves.*

Barraclough, Tamsin Academic sociologist wife of Robbie; she is a resident in the West Oxfordshire village where Emma Howick has come to stay in Barbara Pym's *A Few Green Leaves.*

Barraglioul, Julius de Prominent author and husband of Marguerite, Veronica's sister; becomes involved with the notorious Lafcadio in André Gide's *Lafcadio's Adventures.*

Barralonga, Lord Gnomish land baron whose automotive rampage across Utopia confounds its peaceful inhabitants and who supports Rupert Catskill's plan to overthrow Utopian rule in H. G. Wells's *Men Like Gods.*

Barralty, Joseph Bannatyne "Half-adventurer, half squire" but "ugly as sin"; he proposes to Lancelot Troth the enterprise to seek revenge on Valdemar Haraldsen in John Buchan's *The Island of Sheep.*

Barras Belgian soldier and friend of Pierre Lavendie; he is a painter driven near to madness by his experiences on the battlefield in World War I in John Galsworthy's *Saint's Progress.*

Barre, Celestine Wife of Raoul Barre in Allen Drury's *Advise and Consent.*

Barre, Raoul French ambassador to the United States; with his wife, Celestine Barre, and the British ambassador, expresses the NATO countries' viewpoint in Allen Drury's *Advise and Consent.*

Barreaux, Monsieur Reclusive botanist, who is a friend of the St. Aubert family in Ann Radcliffe's *The Mysteries of Udolpho.*

***Barren Lives,* Older Boy** Laughs at the younger brother, who falls from a goat; asks Sinha Vitória what hell is and is punished by her for his curiosity; then sadly mopes around hugging Baleia; during the family Christmas celebration in the city, he feels threatened by the great concentration of people in Graciliano Ramos's *Barren Lives.*

***Barren Lives,* Younger Boy** During the family march he is carried by Fabiano; tries to impress the older brother by riding a goat, but falls down a cliff; during the family Christmas celebration in the city, he feels threatened by the great concentration of people in Graciliano Ramos's *Barren Lives.*

Barrett, Captain Paul Decorated older army veteran of the European theater in World War II; no-nonsense C.O. at Camp Crowder, Missouri; short, gruff, and crisp commander of the trainee boot camp in Philip Roth's "Defender of the Faith."

Barrett, Charlie Singer for whom Bertram Verren provides piano accompaniment on a twenty-week provincial tour in Frank Swinnerton's *The Young Idea: A Comedy of Environment.*

Barrett, Daisy Tim Reede's lover, a fiercely honest, vituperative, harmless painter who no longer paints; after Tim returns to Gertrude Openshaw, she leaves for California in Iris Murdoch's *Nuns and Soldiers.*

Barrett, Ed Father of Will Barrett; his suicide haunts Will in Walker Percy's *The Last Gentleman.*

Barrett, Jennifer Cavilleri (Jenny) Daughter of Philip Cavilleri; working-class Radcliffe graduate who marries Oliver Barrett IV against his family's wishes; dies of leukemia in Erich Segal's *Love Story.*

Barrett, Joshua Little bully who sustains a head injury after Martha Horgan hits him with an iron ladle in Mary McGarry Morris's *A Dangerous Woman.*

Barrett, Mabel Wife of the singer Charlie Barrett; she has an affair with Bertram Verren, her husband's piano accompanist, in Frank Swinnerton's *The Young Idea: A Comedy of Environment.*

Barrett, Marion Peabody Homely northern woman of wealth whom Will Barrett marries because he likes to see her happy; a fervent "social Christian" who eats herself to death in Walker Percy's *The Second Coming.*

Barrett, Mrs. Housekeeper and Lucy Snowe's former nurse, who suggests Lucy might teach English abroad in Charlotte Brontë's *Villette.*

Barrett, Nicole Kathryne Baker (Nicole Kathryne Gilmore, Nucoa Butterball) Girlfriend of Gary Gilmore in Norman Mailer's The *Executioner's Song.*

Barrett III, Oliver (Old Stonyface) Olympic rower, textile mill owner, and father of Oliver Barrett IV; disapproves of his son's wife in Erich Segal's *Love Story;* brings his son into the family firm in *Oliver's Story.*

Barrett IV, Oliver (Ollie) Wealthy Harvard graduate who marries Jennifer Cavilleri, a working-class woman, against his family's wishes in Erich Segal's *Love Story;* falls in love with Marcie Binnendale Nash but finds that she is shallow and unethical in *Oliver's Story.*

Barrett, Pamela (Pam) Television reporter in William Bayer's *Peregrine;* witnesses a fatal Peregrine falcon attack on a girl; becomes the object of the falconer's obsession.

Barrett, Sir Justinian Purcell Barren's father, who dies, leaving his son a title but denying him his inheritance because his mother ran away with another man in George Meredith's *Emilia in England.*

Barrett, Sir Purcell Male sentimentalist; his aristocratic poverty endears him to the Poles, and he and Cornelia Pole fall in love, but her abstract ideals lead him to suicide, deserted by her and disinherited by his father in George Meredith's *Emilia in England.*

Barrett, Sonny Troubled high school teen and chum of Donny Coble; helped by Donny to break into a freshman's locker in Anne Tyler's "Teenage Wasteland."

Barrett, Sylvia (Syl) First-year teacher who learns the intricacies of life at Calvin Coolidge High School; finds herself buried in meaningless paperwork with little time or support to teach in Bel Kaufman's *Up the Down Staircase.*

Barrett, Will Seeker of love and divine truth; a successful lawyer, Will is less good as a husband and father; he must comprehend his history with his own father before he can begin to live a genuine life in Walker Percy's *The Second Coming.*

Barrett, Willston Bibb (Billy, Will) Humidification engineer who crosses America, trying to live as the epitome of southern honor in Walker Percy's *The Last Gentleman.*

Barringer, Paul Glamour boy of the Calvin Coolidge High School English faculty; unpublished writer who composes a poem for every occasion; pursues Sylvia Barrett; responds to a love letter from a student by correcting it grammatically in Bel Kaufman's *Up the Down Staircase.*

Barrios Brave Costaguanan general in Joseph Conrad's *Nostromo: A Tale of the Seaboard.*

Barron, Delia Unrelenting flirt whose interest in George Birdsong causes one of Eva Birdsong's early attacks of neuralgia in Ellen Glasgow's *The Sheltered Life.*

Barron, Grace Wife of Virgil Barron and friend of the Bridges; commits suicide in Evan Connell's *Mrs. Bridge* and *Mr. Bridge.*

Barron, Homer Yankee foreman who works in the southern town of Jefferson; although not the marrying type, publicly courts the reclusive and lonely Emily Grierson; comes and goes from her home until one day he is seen no more; his long decomposed body is discovered in Emily's bed upon her death in William Faulkner's "A Rose for Emily."

Barron, Virgil Bank executive, husband of Grace Barron, and friend of the Bridges in Evan Connell's *Mrs. Bridge* and *Mr. Bridge.*

Barron, Wilkie Acquaintance of Jeremiah Beaumont in law school and successful politician; preserves Beaumont's manuscript and shoots himself tidily through the heart in Robert Penn Warren's *World Enough and Time.*

Barronneau, Henri Innkeeper with whom Rigaud lodged while in Marseilles in Charles Dickens's *Little Dorrit.*

Barronneau, Madame Henri Barronneau's widow, who married Rigaud and was murdered by him in Charles Dickens's *Little Dorrit.*

Barrow Friend of Berkeley (Howard Tracy) in Samuel Langhorne Clemens's *The American Claimant.*

Barrow, G. H. Randy labor lobbyist whom J. Ward Morehouse uses to forge a cooperative spirit between management and labor; lover of Mary French in John Dos Passos's *U.S.A.* trilogy.

Barrow, Mr. Bedfordshire apothecary in Samuel Richardson's *Pamela, or Virtue Rewarded.*

Barrow, Mr. Discretionary associate of Mr. Marsden; he is good at deception and convinces Hornblower to spy in C. S. Forester's *Hornblower And the Crisis: An Unfinished Novel.*

Barrows, Mrs. Ulgine Loud-speaking and domineering woman who finagles her way into the employment of Mr. Fitweiler at F & S; employed as the president's personal assistant and efficiency expert; brings a myriad of changes to F & S, including threats to change Mr. Martin's filing department; tricked into looking mentally unstable by Mr. Martin in James Thurber's "The Catbird Seat."

Barry, Bell Brady Energetic, handsome widowed mother of Redmond Barry; she helps him guard his wife, and at last, when he is destitute, she cares for him in prison in William Makepeace Thackeray's *The Luck of Barry Lyndon.*

Barry, Cornelius (the Chevalier de Balibari) Sixty-year-old, tall, gaudily dressed, one-eyed Irish adventurer and Redmond Barry's uncle; sent to spy on him, the nephew discovers the uncle's identity; the two become partners in card-sharping in high society on the Continent; eventually the uncle, a lifelong Catholic, retires to a convent in William Makepeace Thackeray's *The Luck of Barry Lyndon.*

Barry, Dr. Hall family's well-meaning neighbor, whose attempts to play the role of father and advisor to Maurice Hall are unsuccessful in E. M. Forster's *Maurice.*

Barry, Felicia Arthur Ronald's beautiful aunt, who is to Christopher Kirkland the ideal woman in Mrs. Lynn Linton's *The Autobiography of Christopher Kirkland.*

Barry, Fred T. Wealthy businessman and arts patron in Kurt Vonnegut's *Breakfast of Champions.*

Barry, Major Tiresome storyteller with an abnormal interest in gossip in Agatha Christie's *Evil Under the Sun.*

Barry, Mr. John Grey's not over-scrupulous younger partner, who proposes marriage for reasons of self-interest to Grey's daughter, Dorothy, and is rejected; he eventually takes over the firm in Anthony Trollope's *Mr. Scarborough's Family.*

Barry, Redmond (later Barry Lyndon) Narrator and protagonist, a braggart and an unscrupulous Irish adventurer; having fought a duel at sixteen, he is shipped off to Dublin, where he escapes the consequences of his debt by joining the army as a private soldier; he deserts, is impressed into the Prussian army, and deserts again; his career as a card-sharp is capped by his marriage to Honoria, Countess of Lyndon, whose name he takes; his dissipation and profligacy worsen; eventually his wife escapes his control, and he becomes an inmate of Fleet Prison in William Makepeace Thackeray's *The Luck of Barry Lyndon.*

Barry, "Roaring" Harry Redmond Barry's late father, a scoundrel, in William Makepeace Thackeray's *The Luck of Barry Lyndon.*

Barrymoore, Eliza Housekeeper at Baskerville Hall and wife of John in Arthur Conan Doyle's *The Hound of the Baskervilles.*

Barrymoore, John Butler at Baskerville Hall, husband of Eliza, and beneficiary of a sum of money from the death of Sir Charles Baskerville in Arthur Conan Doyle's *The Hound of the Baskervilles.*

Barrymore Servant at the Baskervilles Hall who is suspected by Dr. Watson when he is seen with a candle at the window; refuses to answer the questions asked by Dr. Watson; becomes upset when he learns that Dr. Watson and Sir Henry have tried to capture Selden, his brother-in-law, who has escaped from prison in Sir Arthur Conan Doyle's *The Hound of the Baskervilles.*

Barrymore, Mrs. Barrymore's wife, who tries to help her brother, Selden, who has escaped from prison in Sir Arthur Conan Doyle's *The Hound of the Baskervilles.*

Barsad, John See Solomon, Pross.

Barstow, Clyde British consul at Wallacia who represents Jane Murray at her trial; she is convicted, and he is assassinated later in Margaret Drabble's *The Ice Age.*

Bart Ellie O'Grady's fiancé in Mary Lavin's *Mary O'Grady.*

Bart Hangman who executes Ben Harper in Davis Grubb's *The Night of the Hunter.*

Bart Son of Utch Thalhammer and the unnamed narrator, brother of Jack, and playmate and friend of Fiordiligi and Dorabella Winter; favored by Severin Winter, who thinks that Bart will be an excellent 177-pound wrestler in John Irving's *The 158-Pound Marriage.*

Bart, Lily Well-bred but poor New York socialite whose futile attempts to arrange a suitable marriage for herself initiate the central plot of Edith Wharton's *The House of Mirth.*

Barter, Hussell Rector of Worsted Skeynes who opposes Gregory Vigil's efforts to secure a divorce for Helen Bellew in John Galsworthy's *The Country House.*

Barter, Rose Wife of the Rector Hussell Barter; she delivers her eleventh child in John Galsworthy's *The Country House.*

Barter, Tom Employee of Philip Crow and, later, of Johnny Geard; his profligacy produces twins and then marriage to their mother, Tossie Stickles; his homosexual love for John Crow culminates in his death, defending John, at the hands of Finn Toller in John Cowper Powys's *A Glastonbury Romance.*

Barthé, Euclides Chemist and counsellor in Santa María; influences a law that will approve of Junta's brothel and asks for a monthly 500-peso kickback; maintains a relationship with a young man to whom he unofficially leaves his pharmacy at his death in Juan Carlos Onetti's *The Body Snatcher;* helps Moncha with her esoteric inquiries in Juan Carlos Onetti's "The Stolen Bride;" editor for *El Liberal* in Juan Carlos Onetti's *Past Caring.*

Bartholo, Dr. Doctor from Seville and unknowingly Figaro's father; former guardian of the Countess Rosine Almaviva; seeks revenge on Figaro because the young barber had aided Count Almaviva in getting his ward to marry the aristocrat in Pierre Augustin Caron de Beaumarchais's play *The Marriage of Figaro.*

Bartholomew, Mr. Ninety-year-old, eccentric, well-traveled gentleman with excellent manners; living on a Caribbean island, he gives parties in the kitchen and on the beach for all visitors and residents in Rosamond Lehmann's *A Sea-Grape Tree.*

Bartholomew/The Page Servant of the lord; dresses as a woman and pretends to be Christopher Sly's wife when he awakens in William Shakespeare's *The Taming of the Shrew.*

Bárthory, Erzebeth Hungarian woman Juan compares to a vampire in Julio Cortázar's *62: A Model Kit.*

Bartle Seventeen-year-old irrepressible "boy" servant of the Lovats; he eavesdrops on the servants to discover the latest gossip in Ivy Compton-Burnett's *Darkness and Day.*

Bartleby Enigmatic man whose life story is never revealed; works as a copyist for the narrator; never displays emotions, certainly not frustration or anger; answers each work request from his employer with "I would prefer not to," which ultimately produces consternation in the narrator and his staff; starts living in the office building, to the chagrin of his employer; ultimately dismissed by the narrator; later ends up in the Tombs, a prison, where his refusal to eat costs him his life in Herman Melville's "Bartleby, The Scrivener."

"Bartleby the Scrivener," Narrator Industrious, hardworking, and very practical in his business affairs and life; consummate name dropper and ambitious socialite; at a loss as to how to deal with his employee Bartleby's refusal to work; entranced by the forlorn Bartleby and with each refrain of "I would prefer not to" by Bartleby; becomes fixated on trying to figure out Bartleby; this curiosity turns into frustration, as he tries to fire Bartleby on multiple occasion and is unsuccessful; finally, frustration turns into compassion, as the narrator is the only one who cares about what happens to Bartleby in the Tombs, a prison, in Herman Melville's "Bartleby, The Scrivener."

Bartlett The Westons' butler in Isabel Colegate's *Statues in a Garden.*

Bartlett Rancher who sways the mob to the idea of lynching the rustlers in Walter Van Tilburg Clark's *The Ox-Bow Incident.*

Bartlett, Arlene Mother of Laney Bartlett; poor but vital widow who takes several lovers and is frequently pregnant in Joyce Carol Oates's *Childwold.*

Bartlett, Charlotte Lucy Honeychurch's well-meaning but troublesome cousin and chaperone on a trip to Italy; she tries to keep Lucy and George Emerson apart, only to turn around and unite them in E. M. Forster's *A Room with a View.*

Bartlett, Dickie Teenage helper of Clem Streeter; held prisoner and then released by Legs Diamond in William Kennedy's *Legs.*

Bartlett, Dr. Ambrose Virtuous tutor who accompanies the vicious young Mr. Lorimer on a European tour; to remove the curb on his licentiousness, Lorimer has Dr. Bartlett imprisoned by the Turkish authorities in Athens, where Sir Charles Grandison rescues him from execution; he becomes Sir Charles's revered companion and is the source of much of Harriet Byron's information about Sir Charles's Italian adventures in Samuel Richardson's *Sir Charles Grandison.*

Bartlett, Edith Nineteenth-century fiancée of Julian West in Edward Bellamy's *Looking Backward.*

Bartlett, Edward Artist from Los Angeles hired to draw Nicole for a Stephanie Sykes doll; is caught naked with Nicole in the woods and is sent back to California in Ann Beattie's *Love Always.*

Bartlett, Evangeline Ann (Laney) Teenager from an impoverished rural area who becomes the focus of the eccentric Fitz John Kasch's obsession; daughter of Arlene Bartlett in Joyce Carol Oates's *Childwold.*

Bartlett, Evie Mousey wife of the vicar in E. F. Benson's *Miss Mapp,* in *Mapp and Lucia,* in *The Worshipful Lucia,* and in *Trouble for Lucia.*

Bartlett, Hector Hanger-on of the novelist Emma Loy, member of a radionics-blackmail group, and "pisseur de copie" according to Nancy Hawkins in Muriel Spark's *A Far Cry from Kensington.*

Bartlett, Kenneth (Padre) Card-playing vicar of Tilling; though he comes from Birmingham, he speaks in a distinctive combination of Elizabethan English and Scottish dialect in E. F. Benson's *Miss Mapp,* in *Mapp and Lucia,* in *The Worshipful Lucia,* and in *Trouble for Lucia.*

Bartlett, Paul A. Large, self-confident scientist of about forty who is appointed leader of the group of scientists who will populate a new colony in space; his brittle inflexibility leads to an intense conflict with his group in Anthony Burgess's *The End of the World News.*

Bartlett, Vale Embittered Vietnam veteran and son of Arlene Bartlett in Joyce Carol Oates's *Childwold.*

Bartley Last surviving son of Maurya; intent on going by horse and then boat to the nearby Irish town of Connemara on a fateful day; an unexpected strong wave sweeps him off his horse and into the sea, where he is lost; joins his father and five brothers who have perished in the treacherous sea in John Millington Synge's play *Riders to the Sea.*

Bartley Teenage boy who is obsessed with telescopes and sweets in Martin McDonagh's *The Cripple of Inishmaan.*

Bartley, Calvin LeRoy Youngest son of Lizzie Bartley; rejected by Darlene Mosby, he commits suicide by covering himself with pitchlime in Hal Bennett's *A Wilderness of Vines.*

Bartley, Jack Unhappily married and impoverished man whose alcoholic wife deserts him and who becomes involved in a forgery ring and is arrested in George Gissing's *The Nether World.*

Bartley, Lizzie Matriarch of the Bartley clan noted for dark-skin good looks and virility; also mother by Blessed Belshazzar of Birchie Bartley in Hal Bennett's *A Wilderness of Vines* and *The Black Wine.*

Bartley, Robert Father of 13 children and lover of Neva Stapleton and Eloise McLindon; responsible for the death of Otha Manning during World War I in Hal Bennett's *A Wilderness of Vines* and *The Black Wine.*

Bartolomé, Count Attractive, courtly man who allows the difficult child Robin Empson to ride on his palomino mare in Gail Godwin's *The Perfectionists.*

Bartolomeu, Fray Invents the "passarola," or "great bird," a flying machine, the lifelong occupation of the visionary monk whom he has been befriended in José Saramago's *Baltasar and Blimunda.*

Barton Twenty-first-century minister who preaches to thousands via telephone in Edward Bellamy's *Looking Backward.*

Barton, Alice Neglected and unhappy daughter of Mrs. Barton; she dislikes the marriage market and admires two intellectuals, both socially undesirable; without parental blessing she marries Edward Reed and escapes to London; she becomes a novelist and has a happy home, providing sanctuary for her sister, Olive, and her schoolgirl friends in George Moore's *A Drama in Muslin.*

Barton, Arthur Father of Alice and Olive and an aesthete usually dismissed as boring; he is ineffectual in practical matters and selfishly inadequate in responding to his daughters' needs in George Moore's *A Drama, in Muslin.*

Barton, General Rakish owner of a mansion near the cottage of Arabella Bloomville; he is among the casualties of a fatal banquet in William Beckford's *Modern Novel Writing; or, the Elegant Enthusiast.*

Barton, Ivy Twenty-year-old country girl who was a model for Bianca Dallison; she copies old Mr. Stone's book manuscript and unsuccessfully tries to persuade Hilary Dallison to take her with him when he leaves in John Galsworthy's *Fraternity.*

Barton, John Factory worker and Trade Unionist father of Mary Barton; he is embittered by the deaths of his wife and son and by the conditions of his life as a Manchester worker; his shooting of Harry Carson is catastrophic in Elizabeth Gaskell's *Mary Barton.*

Barton, Johnny Twenty-year-old carpenter, whose love for a young girl is thwarted by poverty until Robert Lovelace provides a modest marriage settlement in Samuel Richardson's *Clarissa: or, The History of a Young Lady.*

Barton, Lady General Barton's grandmother, who writes poetry and has occasional bouts with insanity; her death nearly unhinges her grandson in William Beckford's *Modern Novel Writing; or, the Elegant Enthusiast.*

Barton, Mary John Barton's daughter, who is in danger of being tempted like her "fallen" Aunt Esther Fergusson; when Jem Wilson is accused of murdering her would-be seducer, Harry Carson, she proves his alibi and realizes she loves him in Elizabeth Gaskell's *Mary Barton.*

Barton, Miss Fellow at Shrewsbury College, Oxford; her book attacking the subjugation of women is burnt in Dorothy L. Sayers's *Gaudy Night.*

Barton, Miss Lavinia Mother of Odessa Barton Market and disapproving mother-in-law of Joe Market in Hal Bennett's *Lord of Dark Places.*

Barton, Mr. Young, simple-minded rustic convinced by Mrs. Howard that he loves and should marry Sophia Darnley despite her poverty in Charlotte Lennox's *Sophia.*

Barton, Mrs. Aggressive, foolish mother of Alice and Olive; her entire interest is in society; she neglects her husband and keeps company with Lord Dungory; she fails to understand either her intelligent daughter, Alice, or her beautiful daughter, Olive, who submits to her match-making schemes in George Moore's *A Drama in Muslin.*

Barton, Mrs. Mr. Barton's mother; resenting Mrs. Howard's attempt to marry the penniless Sophia Darnley to her son, she informs her that young Mr. Howard also loves Sophia; she conspires to brand Sophia as a man-trap in Charlotte Lennox's *Sophia.*

Barton, Mrs. Mrs. Allen's friend, who nurses Priscilla (Broad) Allen in childbirth in Mark Rutherford's *The Revolution in Tanner's Lane.*

Barton, Mrs. Mary Mother of Mary Barton; her early death deprives her daughter of guidance and her husband of a softening influence in Elizabeth Gaskell's *Mary Barton.*

Barton, Odessa See Market, Odessa Barton.

Barton, Olive Cameo beauty with "nothing wanting but a mind"; through her mother's scheming she becomes the belle of the Dublin social season; though she loves Captain Hibbert, her mother is ambitious for her to catch a title; she is both outschemed by a rival classmate and thwarted in her plans to elope in George Moore's *A Drama in Muslin.*

Barton, Ralph London politician and an acquaintance of Jery Melford; he unsuccessfully courts Liddy Melford; Tabith Bramble, misunderstanding him, thinks she is the object of his amours in Tobias Smollett's *The Expedition of Humphry Clinker.*

Bartram Rough and heavy-looking lime-burner who spends his time watching his kiln with his son Joe; described as middle aged and obtuse; believes his son to be a timid coward like his mother, yet also proves to be frightened by Ethan Brand and his Unpardonable Sin; visited by the stranger Ethan Brand and learns his story despite his unwillingness to welcome Ethan Brand's presence; becomes the first witness to Ethan Brand's tale, then sends his son to fetch the townspeople from the tavern; heads the inquisitive conversation between characters and allows Ethan Brand to oversee his furnace for the duration of the night; afterwards comments on Ethan Brand's value as a corpse on his marble in Nathaniel Hawthorne's "Ethan Brand."

Bartram, Admiral Arthur Lusty ex-seafaring owner of St. Crux who has a soft spot for ladies; he employs as parlour maid the disguised Magdalen Vanstone in Wilkie Collins's *No Name.*

Bartram, George Rich cousin of Norah Vanstone; he inherits the Vanstone family fortune from his uncle, Admiral Bartram, and marries Norah in Wilkie Collins's *No Name.*

Bartram, Joe Sensitive, extraordinarily perceptive boy who lives with his father in the mountains; has lost his mother to some unknown cause; sent to the tavern to get the townsfolk, and subsequently his father perceives him as a barrier between the guest, Ethan Brand, and himself; becomes frightened when he is glimpsed in the diorama by Ethan Brand; cries when apprehending the latter's deep-seated loneliness and despair; finally becomes a witness to finding Ethan Brand's remains in the furnace in Nathaniel Hawthorne's "Ethan Brand."

Bartram, May Young woman who, by accident, again meets John Marcher after many years; carries on a lifetime friendship with him, without romance or passion, in which they meet in drawing rooms to talk politely about why John feels that he is awaiting some significant event in his life, a beast in the jungle that is tracking him; May knows this secret but will not disclose it until John realizes it on his own; at an elderly age she dies after a lengthy and painful blood disease; her gravesite is visited by John, who then realizes that what he was to discover was that he had never felt passionately about anyone or life itself in Henry James's "The Beast in the Jungle."

Bartram, Mistress Teacher who bears a child by Portius Wheeler; the child is named Rosa Tench after Bartram marries Jake Tench in Conrad Richter's *The Fields;* becomes a recluse in *The Town.*

Baruch Rebel angel and lover of Balthamos; brother of Enoch, the Regent of Heaven and the Metatron; is killed in the War against Heaven after revealing key information to Lord Asriel in Philip Pullman's *His Dark Materials.*

Barvile, Mr. Young gentleman deviant, who introduces Fanny Hill to flagellation, active and passive, in John Cleland's *Memoirs of a Woman of Pleasure.*

Baryton, Dr. Administrator of a madhouse where Léon takes a job in Louis-Ferdinand Céline's *Journey to the End of the Night.*

Bascom, Chaplain Baptist chaplain and friend of Father Donovan; rushes to save Donovan but is crushed by the same lorry that kills his friend in John Horne Burns's *The Gallery.*

Bascombe, Clarissa Twelve-year-old daughter of Frank Bascombe, who is as grounded as her older brother, Paul, is troubled; lives with her mother and stepfather in upscale Deep River, Connecticut; is fiercely loyal to her brother and surreptitiously refuses to offer her parents any insight to his problems or their solutions; describes herself as "thirty-twelve" in Richard Ford's *Independence Day.*

Bascombe, Frank Divorced 44-year-old writer turned real estate agent in Haddam, New Jersey, first introduced in Richard Ford's *The Sportswriter.* Offers detached yet detailed descriptions of the ordinary concerns that make up his life while he takes his troubled teenage son on a July 4th weekend trip to the basketball and baseball halls of fame; faced with a serious accident that will potentially cause him to become reengaged in his own life in *Independence Day.*

Bascombe, Lena Actress playing the mother in the film version of Osgood Wallop's *The Duchess of Obloquy* in Peter De Vries's *Mrs. Wallop.*

Bascombe, Paul Troubled 15-year-old-son of Frank Bascombe, who is awaiting trial for shoplifting three boxes of condoms; accompanies his father on a July 4th trip to visit the basketball and baseball halls of fame and has an encounter with a seventy-five-mile-per-hour baseball in Richard Ford's *Independence Day.*

Basellecci Elderly teacher of Italian; afflicted with cancer of the bowel; lives in the Mott Street building managed by Norman Moonbloom in Edward Lewis Wallant's *The Tenants of Moonbloom.*

Bashele Wife of Koppel, a once-trusted caretaker for the patriarch Meshulam Moskat; divorced and left penniless by her husband, as he runs off with Leah, one of Meshulam's married daughters, and much of Meshulam's fortune to America; later remarries in Isaac Bashevis Singer's *The Moskat Family.*

Bashele Wife of Zelig, mother of Shosha, and mother-in-law of Aaron Greidinger in Isaac Bashevis Singer's *Shosha.*

Bashkirs Nomadic Russian people who bargain with Pahom, a Russian peasant, for all the land he can walk around in a day in Leo Tolstoy's "How Much Land Does a Man Need?"

Bashti Island chief who leads the destruction of the Arangi and is Jerry's keeper in Jack London's *Jerry of the Islands.*

Bashuto Cigar-smoking old man who realizes that the stone toad found in a field is an old relic crafted by his ancestors, and tells the story that countless jugs filled with silver coins can be unearthed while digging on a farm in Salarrué's "The Vessel."

Bashwood, Felix Broken-down, nervous steward engaged by Allan Armadale to assist Ozias Midwinter through the good offices of the elder Mr. Pedgift; Bashwood is captivated by Lydia Gwilt and seeks unsuccessfully to stop her marrying Midwinter in Wilkie Collins's *Armadale.*

Bashwood, James (Jemmy) Churlish, uncouth son of Felix; his skills as professional private detective are called upon by his father, besotted with Lydia Gwilt, to spy on her and Allan Armadale in Wilkie Collins's *Armadale.*

Basie, Harold Lawyer hired to represent Oscar Crease in his suit against Erebus Entertainment who provides competent representation but is found to have lied about his credentials and must flee the law before the case is won in William Gaddis's *A Frolic of His Own.*

Basil Fictional character in the writing of the Unnamable; he is later called Mahood in Samuel Beckett's *The Unnamable.*

Basil Second son of an unnamed widower of fortune and ancient family; having agreed to Mr. Sherwin's demand that Basil's marriage to Margaret Sherwin take place a year before its consummation, the love-sick husband is deranged to discover her unchastity with Robert Mannion; hounded by Mannion after Basil has disfigured him in a beating, Basil narrowly escapes death in Cornwall in Wilkie Collins's *Basil: A Story of Modern Life.*

Basil Young Roman patrician in love with the Gothic princess Veranilda; he searches for her after she is abducted and suspects her of infidelity when he finds her with his false friend Marcian, whom he kills; he regrets his actions after instruction from St. Benedict at the Abbey of Cassino, is reunited with Veranilda, and receives the Gothic king's promise that they will be married in George Gissing's *Veranilda.*

Basil, Mrs. Wife of an officer in Burma; her prolonged affair with Edward Ashburnham leads to her husband's blackmailing Edward for years in Ford Madox Ford's *The Good Soldier: A Tale of Passion.*

Basil's Father Unnamed widower whose austere pride motivates the secrecy of Basil's attachment and marriage to a linen draper's daughter in Wilkie Collins's *Basil: A Story of Modern Life.*

Basini Young classmate of the protagonist, Törless, in an exclusive academy on the outskirts of the Austro-Hungarian Empire; discovered by Törless and other boys to have stolen money from student lockers; forced to become the object of brutal sexual experiments by the other boys; eventually turns himself in to the headmaster for his thefts in Robert Musil's *Young Törless.*

Baske, Miriam Wealthy young widow, whose long residence in Italy enables her to escape her repressed Puritanical tendencies and makes her attractive to Ross Mallard, whom she marries in George Gissing's *The Emancipated.*

Baskelett, Captain Cecil Successful challenger of his cousin Nevil Beauchamp for Parliament; he incites Dr. Shrapnel and Everard Romfrey to great enmity in George Meredith's *Beauchamp's Career.*

Baskerville, Herman Homosexual mentor of Bill Kelsey and student of racial mythology and revolution in Hal Bennett's *Seventh Heaven.*

Baskerville, Sir Charles Baronet and landowner whose recent death from terror is brought to Sherlock Holmes's attention by James Mortimer in Arthur Conan Doyle's *The Hound of the Baskervilles.*

Baskerville, Sir Henry Baskerville heir who comes from Canada to London; appears to be disturbed by the effect of the mysterious murder of Sir Charles; receives a note that warns him to stay away from the moor, where he finally goes, accompanying Dr. Watson and Dr. Mortimer, Sir Charles's best friend; falls in love with Mrs. Stapleton; finally used as a bait by Sherlock Holmes to solve the mystery of the Baskerville's curse in Sir Arthur Conan Doyle's *The Hound of the Baskervilles.*

Baso, George Japanese Zen master suffering from tuberculosis; friend visited by Jack Duluoz and Dave Wain in Jack Kerouac's *Big Sur.*

Bason, Wilfred Fussy, spinsterish, gossipy housekeeper and gourmet cook for the celibate priests in the St. Luke's clergy house in Barbara Pym's *A Glass of Blessings.* His menus are still remembered and discussed in *A Few Green Leaves.*

Basque Manservant in Célimène's household who announces the arrival of her visitors in Moliere's play *The Misanthrope.*

Bass, Jethro Devious political boss who is personally a kind and genuinely concerned leader; loves Cynthia Ware;

guardian of Cynthia Wetherell in Winston Churchill's *Coniston.*

Bass, Jonathan Staunch Son of Pourty F. Bloodworth; half brother of Amos-Otis Thigpen, LaDonna Scales, Regal Pettibone, and Noah Grandberry; minister who counsels Thigpen and Abraham Dolphin in Leon Forrest's *The Bloodworth Orphans.*

Bassanio Wealthy Venetian nobleman who has squandered his money; to court the beautiful Portia of Belmont, he gets money from Shylock, but it is Antonio who vouches for him; worthy suitor who chooses the right casket and finds Portia's portrait, thus winning her hand, in Shakespeare's play *The Merchant of Venice.*

Bassart, Lucy Nelson Granddaughter of Willard Carroll and daughter of Myra and Duane Nelson; her dreams of independence are thwarted by premarital pregnancy; marriage to Roy Bassart and motherhood bring her no happiness in Philip Roth's *When She Was Good.*

Bassart, Roy Dreamy World War II veteran who becomes a photographer and marries his pregnant girlfriend Lucy Nelson in Philip Roth's *When She Was Good.*

Bassett Worker on the country estate of Chevron in Vita Sackville-West's *The Edwardians.*

Bassett Gardener working for Paul's family; becomes Paul's partner in horserace betting; bets on the boy's behalf and keeps the money won thereby safe and secret; trusts his little master's amazing conjectures about the winning horse; the one who finally brings the news that Paul has made 80,000 pounds in betting on the night of the boy's death in D. H. Lawrence's "The Rocking-Horse Winner."

Bassett, Claude Educated orphan and drifter; seasonal husband of Maggie Moore who returns every winter and leaves every spring until his death in Betty Smith's *Maggie-Now.*

Bassett, Ethel First wife of Will Brady; spends their wedding night rolled in a sheet and later abandons him in Wright Morris's *The Works of Love.*

Bassett, Georgie (The Little Gentleman) Boy whose excellent behavior and refined ways irritate Penrod Schofield in Booth Tarkington's *Penrod, Penrod and Sam,* and *Penrod Jashber.*

Bassett, Henry Wears a football uniform, like many other men, at a Halloween party thrown during the Pommeroy family reunion at the family's summer place at Laud's Head on the shore in Massachusetts in John Cheever's "Goodbye, My Brother."

Bassett, Madeline Golden-haired, baby-talking girl who perceives Bertie Wooster as an acceptable fall-back suitor in P. G. Wodehouse's *The Code of the Woosters* and in four other novels.

Bassett, Sir Watkyn Madeline's father, who competes with Tom Travers for possession of a silver cow-creamer and for the services of the French cook Anatole in P. G. Wodehouse's *The Code of the Woosters.* He appears in two other novels.

Bassianus Brother of Saturninus and husband of Lavinia; lured into a trap and murdered by Aaron and Tamora in William Shakespeare's play *Titus Andronicus.*

Bassingfield, Myra Frank Dawley's girlfriend and mother of his infant son, Mark; she left her husband to live with Frank in Algeria until Frank left on an idealistic gun-running mission for the Algerian guerillas in Alan Sillitoe's *The Death of William Posters.* She returns to England and becomes involved with the family of Frank's best friend, Albert Handley; when their house burns down she invites them to live with her on the large estate left to her when her husband died in *A Tree on Fire.*

Bast, Edward Young composer who reluctantly becomes JR's business representative in William Gaddis's *JR.*

Bast, Jacky Leonard's uncultured wife; brought with Leonard to a Wilcox family event by the restitution-seeking Helen Schlegel, Jacky recognizes Henry Wilcox as her old lover; Helen's sympathetic but extreme response brings more disaster upon the Basts in E. M. Forster's *Howards End.*

Bast, Leonard Poor clerk whose aspirations for culture lead to his involvement with the Schlegel sisters and consequently, through a series of misunderstandings and mishaps, to his economic ruin and death; he is the father of Helen Schlegel's baby and is killed by Charles Wilcox in E. M. Forster's *Howards End.*

Bastaki Son of a Rumanian industrialist; a corrupt businessman, he is Stefan Saridza's contact man in Prague in Eric Ambler's *Uncommon Danger.*

Bastard of Burgundy Military leader; his troop encounters Denys, who is on leave and has nearly reached home for the first time in three years, and impresses him into service in Charles Reade's *The Cloister and the Hearth.*

Bas-Thornton, Edward Younger brother of Emily Bas-Thornton; he enjoys being aboard the pirate ship in Richard Hughes's *A High Wind in Jamaica.*

Bas-Thornton, Emily Ten-year-old girl who, en route with her siblings to the safety of England after a hurricane in Jamaica, is accidentally captured by pirates; in mistaken fear she kills another captive, a Dutch captain who wants her to help him escape; though her hysterical testimony condemns the pirate captain, Jonsen, to hang, she retains the savage innocence of childhood throughout her adventures in Richard Hughes's *A High Wind in Jamaica.*

Bas-Thornton, Frederick Emily's father, who understands his daughter enough to be afraid of her in Richard Hughes's *A High Wind in Jamaica.*

Bas-Thornton, John Eldest of the Bas-Thornton children; he is killed in an accidental fall, and his name is never again mentioned by his siblings in Richard Hughes's *A High Wind in Jamaica.*

Bas-Thornton, Laura Three-year-old youngest of the Bas-Thornton children; she, Edward, and Rachel are the "Liddlies", for whom John and Emily are expected to be responsible in Richard Hughes's *A High Wind in Jamaica.*

Bas-Thornton, Mrs. Well-read, well-intending woman incapable of understanding her children or of being an object of interest to them in Richard Hughes's *A High Wind in Jamaica.*

Bas-Thornton, Rachel Younger sister of John and Emily Bas-Thornton in Richard Hughes's *A High Wind in Jamaica.*

Bastock Driver for Huguenine's circus who trains Caroline Trid to be Carolina, lady high rider, in Walter D. Edmonds's *Chad Hanna.*

Basu, Jay Partner of Venn at the Massachusetts Institute of Technology; works on constructing virtual reality; a fan of *Murder, She Wrote* in Bharati Mukherjee's *The Holder of the World.*

Bat Motion picture mechanic who lives at Queenie's Boarding House; part of the group that sings with George Brush in Thornton Wilder's *Heaven's My Destination.*

Bat, Obed (Dr. Battius) Naturalist full of book knowledge but deficient in common sense; accompanies Ishmael Bush and clan onto the prairie; serves as a comic foil to Natty Bumppo in James Fenimore Cooper's *The Prairie.*

Batch, Clarence Katie's young brother, who returns home to describe the drowning of the Duke of Dorset and the other undergraduates in Max Beerbohm's *Zuleika Dobson; or An Oxford Love Story.*

Batch, Katie Landlady's daughter whose silent love for the Duke of Dorset is rewarded by his giving her, just before his suicide, the earrings Zuleika Dobson gave him in Max Beerbohm's *Zuleika Dobson; or An Oxford Love Story.*

Batch, Mrs. Boarding-house landlady who likes to mother her Oxford-undergraduate tenants, especially the Duke of Dorset, in Max Beerbohm's *Zuleika Dobson; or An Oxford Love Story.*

Batchelor, Barbara Retired missionary teacher and companion to Mabel Layton at Rose Cottage; her presence in Rose Cottage is a continuing irritation to Mabel's daughter-in-law, Mildred Layton, who would like to live there herself; within days of Mabel's death, Barbara is forced to find other accommodations in Paul Scott's *The Towers of Silence.* After having been injured in a fall from a small cart, she ends up in hospital unable, or unwilling, to communicate with anyone but Sarah Layton in *A Division of the Spoils.*

Batchford, Miss Lucilla Finch's maternal aunt, whose dislike of Madame Pratolungo's revolutionary politics creates a barrier of communication which endangers Lucilla in Wilkie Collins's *Poor Miss Finch.*

Batelle, Carole (C. B.) Single mother of Dawn Batelle; activist and only member of the group to be captured; serving an indeterminate prison sentence at the end of M. F. Beal's *Amazon One.*

Batelle, Dawn Melody (Dawn Melody Topp) Illegitimate daughter of Carole Batelle; reared to age seven by Topper; after her mother's arrest, sent to live with foster parents in M. F. Beal's *Amazon One.*

Bateman Student of Nun's College, Oxford, an Anglo-Catholic ritualist, and an early influence on Charles Reding in John Henry Newman's *Loss and Gain.*

Bateman, Glen Sociology professor and fourth lead in The Stand in Stephen King's *The Stand.*

Bateman, Latimer Peter's son, constantly humiliated by his father and by Sophia Stace's wounding comments; he obtains a partnership-apprenticeship with the "little house agent" in Ivy Compton-Burnett's *Brothers and Sisters.*

Bateman, Matilda (Tilly) Peter's daughter, who adores her Stace cousins but agrees to marry the "little house agent" so that she and Latimer Bateman can have a future in Ivy Compton-Burnett's *Brothers and Sisters.*

Bateman, Patrick Handsome, well-educated twenty-six-year-old; works by day on Wall Street earning a fortune to add to the money that he was born with; spends his nights committing acts of violence against women as a psychopathic serial killer in Bret Easton Ellis's *American Psycho.*

Bateman, Peter Cousin of the Staces; a neighborhood doctor with no tact or discretion, he spreads the news of Christian and Sophia Stace's incest in Ivy Compton-Burnett's *Brothers and Sisters.*

Bates Colonel Calloway's man who is shot by Harry Lime, whom he is tracking in the sewer beneath Vienna in Graham Greene's *The Third Man and the Fallen Idol.*

Bates Miranda Hume's maid who tells Miss Burke of the vacant housekeeper position in the neighborhood in Ivy Compton-Burnett's *Mother and Son.*

Bates, Amy Young maid who grows old in service to the Baines family; she becomes unprecedentedly critical of old Constance and Sophia and loses her place in Arnold Bennett's *The Old Wives Tale.*

Bates, Annie Daughter of Walter and Elizabeth; enamored of the chrysanthemums in her mother's apron; complains about being sent to bed before her father has come home; awakens when Walter's body is brought home, forcing her mother to put her back to bed before she sees her father's body in D. H. Lawrence's "Odour of Chrysanthemums."

Bates, Charley Sprightly boy who works for Fagin; he is shocked by Nancy's murder and reforms at the end of Charles Dickens's *Oliver Twist.*

Bates, Digby Deputy chief of the Los Angeles Police Department; publicity hound in Joseph Wambaugh's *The Black Marble.*

Bates, Eliza Sociable elderly woman in Maudie Fowler's neighborhood; her social rank is better than Maudie's in Doris Lessing's *The Diaries of Jane Somers.*

Bates, Elizabeth Wife of coal miner Walter Bates, pregnant with their third child; disapproves of her widower father's early remarriage; angrily suspects her husband of staying out drinking after his shift in the coal mine, but discovers that he has, in fact, died of asphyxiation in a mining accident; washes Walter's body with his mother when it is brought home; the sight and touch of her husband's body causes her to realize the stark divide between life and death in D. H. Lawrence's "Odour of Chrysanthemums."

Bates, Henrietta (Hetty) Good-natured spinster aunt of Jane Fairfax; her inability to stop talking of trivialities causes Emma Woodhouse to be cruelly rude to her in Jane Austen's *Emma.*

Bates, Henry Mulatto lover of Teresa Cary; forced away on the day of their elopement by Teresa's mother, Olivia Cary, in Jessie Redmon Fauset's *Comedy, American Style.*

Bates, Ildiko Oxford friend of Sarah Bennett; he joins David Vesey and Simon Rathbone in throwing a party, at which Sarah meets Jackie Almond in Margaret Drabble's *A Summer Bird-Cage.*

Bates, James Dance-marathon contestant who, with his wife, Ruby, is Robert Syverten's and Gloria Beatty's best friend in the marathon in Horace McCoy's *They Shoot Horses, Don't They?*

Bates, Joe Coal workers' union leader in Benditch; D. cannot persuade him to refuse to work for enemy agent L.'s contract in Graham Greene's *The Confidential Agent.*

Bates, John Companion of Alexander Court and Michael Williams on the night before the Battle of Agincourt; says the English have no reason to wish for day to come since the odds of winning against the French are so slim; meets Henry V in disguise; says the king can show outward courage, but wishes he were up to his neck in the Thames; wishes they were not in France; wishes the king were in France alone so the king could ransom himself and English lives could be saved; claims that, as subjects of the king, if they sin in doing service for the king in battle, the fact that they were obeying orders absolves them of sin in William Shakespeare's play *Henry V.*

Bates, John Five-year-old son of Walter and Elizabeth; fetched from playing outside at dusk by his mother; enjoys the beauty of fire, but protests that he cannot see when his mother temporarily darkens the room by putting fresh coals on the fire in D. H. Lawrence's "Odour of Chrysanthemums."

Bates, Josep New England tutor of Cornelia Wilton and her brothers in Caroline Gilman's *Recollections of a Southern Matron.*

Bates, Louis Unsophisticated, unconventional, maladroit, self-important student with a possible poetic gift; he falls in love with Emma Fielding, attempts suicide, and ends up in a mental hospital in Malcolm Bradbury's *Eating People Is Wrong.*

Bates, Miss Teacher who suggested a job possibility to Kate Fletcher (Armstrong) when she was age sixteen in Margaret Drabble's *The Middle Ground.*

Bates, Mr. Doctor who treats the patients at Lowood School in Charlotte Brontë's *Jane Eyre.*

Bates, Mrs. Elderly, deaf mother of the good Miss Bates and grandmother of Jane Fairfax in Jane Austen's *Emma.*

Bates, Prudence Twenty-nine-year-old London spinster, who shares her romantic woes and triumphs with Jane Cleveland, her friend and former English tutor at Oxford; she is Arthur Grampian's research assistant and hopelessly devoted lover in Barbara Pym's *Jane and Prudence.* Her "love affairs" are mentioned again in *A Glass of Blessings.*

Bates, Ruby Dance partner and wife of James Bates; her participation in a marathon while pregnant is protested by the Mothers' League for Good Morals in Horace McCoy's *They Shoot Horses, Don't They?*

Bates, Sue Lathrop Head of Chicago society in Henry Blake Fuller's *With the Procession;* also appears in *The Cliff-Dwellers.*

Bates, Theodora Friend of Orlando King in Italy; she lives near Orlando's villa and takes Agatha King under her protection in Isabel Colegate's *Orlando at the Brazen Threshold.*

Bates, Walter Coal miner, husband of Elizabeth, and father of Annie and John; dies of asphyxiation in a mining accident at the end of the day; his body is brought home and washed by his wife, Elizabeth, and mother in D. H. Lawrence's "Odour of Chrysanthemums."

Bateshaw, Hymie Mad pseudoscientist who studies boredom and thus claims to have discovered how to generate life; survives the shipwreck of the Sam MacManus with Augie March, whom he attacks viciously, in Saul Bellow's *The Adventures of Augie March.*

Bath, Colonel Pugnacious brother of Jenny Bath; his exaggerated sense of honor propels him into duels on the slightest pretext in Henry Fielding's *Amelia.*

Bath, Lady Pedantic lady, whose learning only Frank Leigh can match in Charles Kingsley's *Westward Ho!*

Bath, Paulette Librarian; raised in London; helps Fabian by paying for his art supplies in Howard Norman's *The Bird Artist.*

Bathgate, Billy Young man, once known as Billy Behan, from the Bronx (Bathgate Avenue) who impresses the mobster Dutch Schultz enough to join his gang though Dutch's influence is waning; Bathgate survives Dutch's demise in E. L. Doctorow's *Billy Bathgate.*

Bathilde, Amédée Marcel's loving grandmother; constantly concerned for Marcel's physical and moral well-being; after her death, Marcel dreams about her; Marcel inherits from her his sense of having no great personal importance in Marcel Proust's *In Search of Lost Time* (also known as *À la recherche du temps perdu*).

Bathilde de Chasteller Beautiful and rich widow in Nancy in the years following the failed revolution of 1830 in France; aristocratic lady who draws the romantic desires of the protagonist and commoner Lucien Leuwen; loses the young Lucien through the subterfuge of Dr. du Poirer in Stendhal's *Lucien Leuwen.*

Bathkaarnet-she Half-human Madi who is Sayren Stund's wife and queen of Oldorando in Brian W. Aldiss's *Helliconia Summer.*

Bathsheba Beautiful woman with whom King David falls passionately and permanently in love; eighth wife of David's harem who insists on being made his queen; doting mother who continually attempts to advance their son Solomon by asking David to name him as heir to the throne in Joseph Heller's *God Knows.*

Batsby, Captain Benjamin Fox-hunting half brother of Sir Harry Albury; he fancies himself a lady-killer and pursues Ayala Dormer and Gertrude Tringle, whom he persuades to elope with him to Ostend; his gamble pays off when Sir Thomas Tringle makes a generous wedding settlement in Anthony Trollope's *Ayala's Angel.*

Batson, Billy Leader of the warrior faction of the Indians; committed to fighting government troops head-on and dying rather than dispersing peacefully throughout the United States in Marge Piercy's *Dance the Eagle to Sleep.*

Batt, Albert Elevator operator at the residence of Marguerite Vandemeyer; he becomes Tuppence and Tommy Beresford's office boy in Agatha Christie's *The Secret Adversary.* He becomes their butler, appearing in the remaining three Beresford novels, ending with *Postern of Fate.*

Batt, Elsie Mrs. Craddock's chambermaid; she supplies information about Mrs. Craddock's association with Dr. Roberts in Agatha Christie's *Cards on the Table.*

Battacharya, Mrs. Indian woman who invites Mrs. Moore and Adela Quested to her home in E. M. Forster's *A Passage to India.*

Battaglia, Santa Native New Orleanian and aunt of patrolman Angelo Mancuso; a widow who dotes on the memory of her departed mother; meets Mrs. Reilly through her nephew; helps Mrs. Reilly leave her abusive son and find a new love in John Kennedy Toole's *A Confederacy of Dunces.*

Batte, Miss Priscilla Majestic teacher at Dinwiddie Academy for Young Ladies, guardian of the old order, and matchmaker in Ellen Glasgow's *Virginia.*

Battersby, Mr. Baker from Dollington who aids Mrs. Page in the food preparations for the Hunt Ball in J. Sheridan Le Fanu's *Wylder's Hand.*

Batterson, Camille Turner Retired teacher of writing and symbol of civilized behavior in Randall Jarrell's *Pictures from an Institution.*

Battiloro, Cynthia Former love of William Demarest, whom she meets unexpectedly aboard ship in Conrad Aiken's *Blue Voyage.*

Battisfore, Max Sheriff of Iron Cliffs County in Robert Traver's *Anatomy of a Murder.*

Battle Hyperactive, tap-dancing black man, an ex-sailor committed to a psychiatric hospital after knocking out his second engineer's tooth; he threatens others with "treatment 63" in Malcolm Lowry's *Lunar Caustic.*

Battle, John Brand Hellfire and brimstone revival preacher in Harriette Arnow's *Hunter's Horn* and *The Dollmaker.*

Battle, Mr. Burly solicitor from London engaged by Dean Lovelace to probe the circumstances of the marriage of the Marquis of Brotherton and the legitimacy of his heir in Anthony Trollope's *Is He Popenjoy?*

Battle, Superintendent Careful, relentless Scotland Yard man, who works with Hercule Poirot and Ariadne Oliver to solve the murder of Mr. Shaitana in Agatha Christie's *Cards on the Table.* He appears in four other novels.

Battle, Vance Town doctor and Will Barrett's golf partner who takes great pride in curing his patients' physical ills in Walker Percy's *The Second Coming.*

Battleax, Captain Commander of the British gunboat which comes to end the presidency of John Neverbend over the independent island of Britannula near New Zealand by training its 250-ton cannon on the capital in Anthony Trollope's *The Fixed Period.*

"Battle Royal," Narrator Naïve black youth who is affected by his grandfather's dying words that the young man must keep up the fight and act as a spy in the white enemy's camp; delivers an oration with humility on social responsibility on his graduation from high school; praised by the whites in his community; invited to repeat the speech at a gathering of the town's elite white citizenry; takes part with nine other young men in a battle royal, a fighting match with blindfolds, as part of the event's entertainment; experiences shame, confusion, and bitterness from the spectacle in Ralph Ellison's "Battle Royal."

Batts, Mr. Member of Truth Society [Unitarian], who gives Charles Reding a pamphlet to deter him from becoming Roman Catholic in John Henry Newman's *Loss and Gain.*

Batty Colin Saville's childhood friend, who does not escape the poverty of the coalmine family in David Storey's *Saville.*

Batulcar, William American proprietor in 1872 in Japan of a circus troupe made up of jugglers, clowns, and acrobats; employs the destitute traveler Passepartout, Phileas Fogg's manservant, as a gymnast in Jules Verne's *Around the World in Eighty Days.*

Baucis Male slave on the Sawyer plantation; accompanies the Laceys to Beulah and returns with them to the Tidewater in Mary Lee Settle's *Beulah Land.*

Baudoin, Sir The Golden Knight, who helps to free the three imprisoned damsels; he is killed by the Red Knight when rescuing Birdalone in William Morris's *The Water of the Wondrous Isles.*

Baudolino Title character who rescues the hapless historian and Byzantine court official Niketas from the marauding knights of the Fourth Crusade during the sack of Constantinople in April 1204; carries out a quest for the mythical kingdom of Prester John; recalls being adopted by Frederick the Great and stealing historical parchments to write his life story; attracted to Empress Beatrice, the young wife of Frederick the Great; constructs elaborate lies about his life and his involvement in historical events, intoxicating readers by the sheer innovation of his implausible narration in Umberto Eco's *Baudolino.*

Baudouin, Father Jesuit confessor and ally of Sister Alexandra in Muriel Spark's *The Abbess of Crewe.*

Bauersch, Mr. Well-dressed book buyer from New York; he deplores Henry Earlforward's refusal to provide even the minimum services for customers, but acknowledges he will continue to seek rarities in the shop in Arnold Bennett's *Riceyman Steps.*

Bauerstein, Dr. German spy disguised as a convalescent; he is an expert on poisons in Agatha Christie's *The Mysterious Affair at Styles: A Detective Story.*

Baum, Eva (Greek) Femme fatale of Earl Horter in Wright Morris's *Love among the Cannibals.*

Baum, Ingrid Trudi's devout Catholic friend who wants to become a missionary; challenged by Trudi about her beliefs; suffers a breakdown as an adult and kills one of her children because she was sexually molested by her father as child; sent to a mental asylum in Ursula Hegi's *Stones from the River.*

Bäumer, Paul Protagonist and narrator of the novel, a young German soldier fighting in the trenches of World War I; the brutalities of the war leave him devoid of feelings in Erich Maria Remarque's *All Quiet on The Western Front.*

Baumgartner, Karl Alcoholic lawyer from Mexico City traveling with his abused wife and fearful son in Katherine Anne Porter's *Ship of Fools.*

Bauvillers, Count French nobleman who criticizes Valancourt to Emily St. Aubert in Ann Radcliffe's *The Mysteries of Udolpho.*

Baviaan Trickster character who is a dog-headed baboon and the wisest animal in South Africa; the Ethiopian and the Leopard question him about the disappearance of the animals from the High Veldt; knowing where the animals have gone, he winks and gives the Leopard and the Ethiopian a cryptic answer to their question in Rudyard Kipling's "How the Leopard Got His Spots."

Bawd Woman who supplies Pander with prostitutes; repeatedly but unsuccessfully attempts to convince Marina, Pericles' lost daughter who is sold to Pander by pirates, to give up her virginity in William Shakespeare's *Pericles.*

Bawwah, Fritz German cutter for Mr. Neefit, the breeches-maker; his employer sends him to Ralph Newton (the heir) to collect money owed to him in Anthony Trollope's *Ralph the Heir.*

Baxendale, Mr. Wealthy mayor of Dunfield, a man of great practical intelligence and a Member of Parliament in George Gissing's *A Life's Morning.*

Baxendale, Mrs. Gracious wife of the town's mayor; she once employed Emily Hood as a governess and advises her and her lover, not always wisely, in George Gissing's *A Life's Morning.*

Baxter Puritan preacher whose attempts to eliminate heresy and anarchic distemper in Cromwell's army force the soldiers to begin meeting secretly in order to obtain privacy in Mary Lee Settle's *Prisons.*

Baxter See Hagar.

Baxter, Abner Violent coal miner who succeeds Ely Collins as the pastor of the Nazarene church in Robert Coover's *The Origin of the Brunists.*

Baxter, Charlie Ryan Writer of experimental novels in Alison Lurie's *Real People.*

Baxter, Ezra Ezekial (Pa, Penny) Honest and hardworking man who affectionately oversees the boyhood of his son, Jody Baxter, in Marjorie Kinnan Rawlings's *The Yearling.*

Baxter, Frances (Black Piggy, Franny) Daughter of Abner and Sarah Baxter in Robert Coover's *The Origin of the Brunists.*

Baxter, Jane (Little Jane) Ten-year-old sister of William Baxter; pesters her brother while he is suffering the pangs of adolescent love in Booth Tarkington's *Seventeen.*

Baxter, Jody Adolescent who adopts an orphaned fawn; matures when his mother shoots the fawn to save the family food supply in Marjorie Kinnan Rawlings's *The Yearling.*

Baxter, Mr. English pharmaceutical salesman, former air-raid warden, and passenger on the *Medea;* he dies of a heart attack in Graham Greene's *The Comedians.*

Baxter, Mrs. Methodist whose interview with Ernest Pontifex causes him again to question his faith in Samuel Butler's *The Way of All Flesh.*

Baxter, Mrs. Patient, sympathetic, and long-suffering mother of William Baxter; tries to cope with her son's infatuation with Miss Lola Pratt during his seventeenth summer in Booth Tarkington's *Seventeen.*

Baxter, Nathan (Black Hand, Nat) Son of Abner and Sarah Baxter in Robert Coover's *The Origin of the Brunists.*

Baxter, Ory (Ma) Hardworking mother of Jody Baxter in Marjorie Kinnan Rawlings's *The Yearling.*

Baxter, Paul (Black Peter, Paulie) Son of Abner and Sarah Baxter in Robert Coover's *The Origin of the Brunists.*

Baxter, Rupert Lord Emsworth's suspicious secretary, whose investigations are interpreted as evidence of derangement in P. G. Wodehouse's *Something New.* His dismissal is mourned by Lady Constance Keeble; she hires him to steal and destroy the manuscript of Galahad Threepwood's almost-completed memoirs in *Fish Preferred.* He appears in three other novels.

Baxter, Sarah Devoted friend of Constantia Dudley; reveals to Constantia a connection between Ursula Monrose and Ormond; loses her husband and their two daughters to yellow fever in Charles Brockden Brown's *Ormond.*

Baxter, Sarah Intimidated wife of Abner Baxter in Robert Coover's *The Origin of the Brunists.*

Baxter, Timothy Squire Thornhill's agent in the abduction of Sophia Primrose in Oliver Goldsmith's *The Vicar of Wakefield.*

Baxter, William Sylvanus (Silly Bill) Seventeen-year-old who makes a fool of himself when he falls in love with Miss Lola Pratt in Booth Tarkington's *Seventeen.*

Bay, Pelly Teenage portrait artist who lives in Quill, a small Canadian village, with his aunt Hettie and uncle Sam; dies when his unicycle falls through the ice as he performs stunts for the village in Howard Norman's *Northern Lights.*

Bay, Turget Businessman from Istanbul; known for running guns to the Middle East; his beautiful daughter, Lale, drowns with the other students; his tragedy is very graphically described in Mary Lee Settle's *Blood Tie.*

Bayard Son of Colonel Sartoris; 24 years old and studying law near his Mississippi home; learns that his stern father has been murdered by his old nemesis, Ben Redmond; smells the scent of verbena in the hair of his stepmother Drusilla; pressed by his stepmother to seek revenge against the killer; rides to Jefferson, Mississippi, where, unarmed, he confronts Redmond; unharmed, he watches Redmond run out of town for good in William Faulkner's "An Odor of Verbena."

Bay Boy Boy Claudia MacTeer challenges to defend Frieda MacTeer in school playground fight in Toni Morrison's *The Bluest Eye.*

Bayer, Ludwig Communist Party leader who tells William Bradshaw of Arthur Norris's intrigues and is later assassinated in Christopher Isherwood's *Mr. Norris Changes Trains.*

Bayham, Fred ("F. B.") Gifted mimic and a good-humored Bohemian; assisted in need by Colonel Newcome, he campaigns for the colonel's election to Parliament and is ever ready with helpful advice in a crisis in William Makepeace Thackeray's *The Newcomes.*

Baylen Police detective who interrogates the salesmen in the high-pressure Chicago real estate sales office where a group of hungry salesmen lie, cheat, bribe, and even steal to make sales; questions the salesmen in the theft of sales leads and office equipment at the firm in David Mamet's play *Glengarry Glen Ross.*

Bayles, Walter Danny's partner of eight years; lawyer who lives in the suburbs; is addicted to pornography and is thinking of leaving Danny in David Leavitt's *Equal Affections.*

Bayliss, Jim Successful doctor whose real desire is to work in medical research; friend of the Keller family in Arthur Miller's play *All My Sons.*

Bayliss, Mr. Penniless, skeleton-like, tubercular young man with costly tastes, the protégé of Mrs. Satterthwaite in Ford Madox Ford's *Some Do Not. . . .*

Bayliss, Sue Wife of Jim, a physician; she is a friend of the Keller family, although she believes that Joe Keller, the owner of a manufacturing company, is guilty of shipping faulty airplane parts to the government during World War II, an act that caused the deaths of more than 20 U.S. pilots in Arthur Miller's play *All My Sons.*

Bayliss, Tommy Young son of Jim and Sue; friends with Bert, another youth in Arthur Miller's play *All My Sons.*

Baynard Old friend of Matthew Bramble; driven toward bankruptcy by the excesses of his wife, he is rescued by the interference of Bramble when his wife dies in Tobias Smollett's *The Expedition of Humphry Clinker.*

Baynes, Charlotte General Baynes's daughter, who marries Philip Firmin in spite of her mother's implacable opposition; she is an affectionate and devoted wife but unreasonably jealous of Caroline Brandon in William Makepeace Thackeray's *The Adventures of Philip on His Way through the World.*

Baynes, Eliza Shrewish, domineering wife of General Baynes; their seven children include Charlotte, whose engagement to Philip Firmin is bitterly opposed by the mother when his money has been lost; the marriage estranges mother and daughter in William Makepeace Thackeray's *The Adventures of Philip on His Way through the World.*

Baynes, General Charles Retired Indian officer, timid everywhere but in military action; as trustee of Philip Firmin's fortune, he allows Dr. Firmin to embezzle it; his subjugation to his wife makes him a weak and vacillating friend to Philip's engagement to his daughter Charlotte in William Makepeace Thackeray's *The Adventures of Philip on His Way through the World.*

Baynes, Louisa Philip Bosinney's aunt, who cannot tell June Forsyte about Bosinney's relationship with Irene Forsyte in John Galsworthy's *The Man of Property.*

Bayoumi Owner of a coffee shop and a Janus man whom the young woman Firdaus meets after she escapes from her husband's physical abuse; acts kindly toward Firdaus initially, but then he begins to beat her; locks her in his apartment and allows his friends to have sex with her in Nawal El Saadawi's *Woman at Point Zero.*

Bayram Young man who seeks to regain respect in his small Turkish village; spends all his time and energy working to save money to buy a Mercedes and, in the process, sacrifices everything that is good in him for the automobile; driving from Germany, where he has worked in exile, back to his village, finds himself mesmerized by the idea that the coffeehouse men in his village will admire his car and respectfully call him Bey (Mister); ironically, finds in the village upon his return no one left from his previous social network, not even his girlfriend, Kezban, in Adalet Agaoglu's *The Slender Rose of My Desire.*

Bayson, Arthur Ineffectual husband of Betty Starr Bayson in Thomas Berger's *Killing Time.*

Bayson, Betty Starr Venal woman whose mother and sister were murdered by Joseph Detweiler in Thomas Berger's *Killing Time.*

Bayton, Mr. Workhouse inhabitant who ordered medicine for his sick wife; he dies in Charles Dickens's *Oliver Twist.*

Bayton, Mrs. Woman who dies shortly after coming to the workhouse in Charles Dickens's *Oliver Twist.*

Bazarov, Evgeny Vasilich Protagonist and student of modern science whose radical ideas shock the country gentry and his parents; returns to his home to practice medicine, but dies of an infection incurred through his own carelessness; affected by the presence of Russian nature represented in Anna Odintsova and Fenechka, although the narrative is unclear to what extent Bazarov is changed by them, in Ivan Turgenev's *Fathers and Sons.*

Bazarov, Vasily Ivanich Father of Evgeny Bazarov; country doctor who mixes contemporary science with folk beliefs; tries to understand his son, but Evgeny's radicalism confuses him; simple, honest man who wants the best for everyone and is deeply pained by his son's death; represents a naïve liberalism among the Russian country gentry in Ivan Turgenev's *Fathers and Sons.*

Bazarova, Arina Vlasaevna Mother of Evgeny Bazarov who is suffocating in her love for her son and represents the superstitions of the Russian country gentry; unlike her husband, does not even attempt to understand the new ideas in Russia; trusts to the old traditions as a way of dealing with change; both Vasily and she put all their hopes for the future in their son and are crushed by his death in Ivan Turgenev's *Fathers and Sons.*

Bazhakuloff (Messiah) Russian ex-monk who moves to Nepenthe; his disciples record his words in the *Golden Book* in Norman Douglas's *South Wind.*

Bazile Music master to Countess Rosine Almaviva; unscrupulous character who aids the countess's husband, Count Almaviva, in his design to seduce the pretty virgin Suzanne, a chambermaid in the castle and engaged to Figaro; desires to marry Marceline, but is disappointed when she marries Bartholo, the father of her newly discovered grown son Figaro in Pierre Augustin Caron de Beaumarchais's play *The Marriage of Figaro.*

Bazin, Mr. Large, ill-favored French keeper of the inn at which James MacGregor and his daughter Catriona Drummond stay in exile in Robert Louis Stevenson's *Catriona.*

Bazzard, Mr. Hiram Grewgious's sharp-tongued clerk, who has written a tragedy titled *The Thorn of Anxiety* that reflects Rosa Bud's anxious sexual feelings about John Jasper in Charles Dickens's *The Mystery of Edwin Drood.*

B-e, W-m Old shepherd who guides the Editor and his companions in an expedition to dig up the suicide's grave in James Hogg's *The Private Memoirs and Confessions of a Justified Sinner.*

Bea Operator and mistress of ceremonies in the Hippodrome; mother of Iris; dies of a heart attack in Cyrus Colter's *The Hippodrome.*

Beach, Alice (Alie) Younger sister of Lucy Beach; at forty-three, senses that her life lacks meaning but ignores her sister's encouragement to leave their mother in William Maxwell's *Time Will Darken It.*

Beach, Lucy Older sister of Alice Beach; given musical training but denied a career by her mother; expresses her frustration near the end of William Maxwell's *Time Will Darken It.*

Beach, Sebastian Blandings Castle butler, whose appearance bodes imminent apoplexy but who is merely a hypochondriac in P. G. Wodehouse's *Something New.* Endebted to Ronnie Fish for profitable horse-racing tips, he assists Ronnie in kidnapping Lord Emsworth's prize sow, the Empress of Blandings, in *Fish Preferred.* He appears in nine other novels.

Beaconsfield, Lord Influential member of the Marquess of Carabas's political party; he helps cause Vivian Grey's political downfall by withdrawing his support of Frederick Cleveland, the candidate for Parliament whom Grey had advised the Marquess to nominate in Benjamin Disraeli's *Vivian Grey.*

Beadle Arrests Doll Tearsheet for accessory to murder in William Shakespeare's play *Henry IV, Part Two.*

Beadle, Calvin Tutor and self-schooled psychologist who accepts the challenge to help the troubled teen Donny Coble; his hippie-style approach of "live and let live," rock music, and "blame the establishment" fails Donny in Anne Tyler's "Teenage Wasteland."

Beadle, Harriet (Tattycoram) Ill-tempered and jealous maid of Minnie (Pet) Meagles; she runs away to Miss Wade and later returns to Mr. Meagles with the iron box which holds the information about Arthur Clennam's birth in Charles Dickens's *Little Dorrit.*

Beads, Deanna Whiteheart Mostly Ojibwa girl; daughter of Rozina Roy and Richard Whiteheart Beads and twin sister of Cally Roy; dies as a result of her father's suicide attempt in Louise Erdrich's *The Antelope Wife.*

Beads, Richard Whiteheart Urban, mostly Ojibwa trash contractor whose obsessive love for his wife, Rozina Roy, alienates her and whose suicide attempt results in the death of his daughter Deanna in Louise Erdrich's *The Antelope Wife.*

Beal, Major General Ira N. (Bus) Commander at Ocanara Army Air Base whose leadership is tested when black officers attempt to use the officers' club in James Gould Cozzens's *Guard of Honor.*

Beale Cabinet minister who wishes to find out what the popular reaction will be to Jim Drover's execution in Graham Greene's *It's a Battlefield.*

Beale, Miss Temperance and religious activist who teaches Patience Sparhawk about people's obsessive roles in Gertrude Atherton's *Patience Sparhawk and Her Times.*

Beale, Mrs. See Farange, Mrs. Beale.

Beamish Richard Butler's friend and Catherine Butler's betrothed in Anne Thackeray Ritchie's *The Village on the Cliff.*

Beamish, Mary "Excellent" woman, devoted to church and social work, who becomes landlady to Father Ransome and considers a vocation in a religious community, once freed from caring for her elderly mother in Barbara Pym's *A Glass of Blessings.*

Beamish, Tommy A born comic who is at the top of the bill on the variety circuit; he cannot fully control his sadistic streak and a touch of madness in J. B. Priestley's *Lost Empires.*

Bean, Elizabeth (Lizzie) Psychological counselor at a college in upstate New York; pregnant by Horace L'Ordinet, she gives birth to the baby boy later adopted by Annie and Phil Sorenson; lover of Eli Silver in Frederick Busch's *Rounds.*

Bean, "Granny" Resident patient so old as to seem androgynous; her hundredth birthday is celebrated in the old women's hospital ward in Muriel Spark's *Memento Mori.*

Bean, Old Solicitor who locates Art Kipps through a newspaper announcement and who handles his inheritance and finances in H. G. Wells's *Kipps: The Story of a Simple Soul.*

Bean, Sidney Good friend of Henry's; fails to stop Henry from diving off a bridge over the Mississippi River the night before Henry was to marry Karen; blames himself and tries to help Karen get over her anger toward him for Henry's death; works on farms where he breaks horses in Rick Bass's "Wild Horses."

Bean, Titus Journalist and friend of Mabry Jenkins; writes scripts for pornographic movies in addition to writing stories about a chemical company's illicit activities in Peter Gent's *Texas Celebrity Turkey Trot.*

Bean Lean, Alice Daughter of Donald Bean Lean; Edward Waverly mistakes her for a serving girl while held in the robber's cave; she helps Waverly recover important letters in Sir Walter Scott's *Waverly.*

Bean Lean, Donald Chieftain of a group of Highland robbers; he rescues Edward Waverly from jail and smuggles him to the Highlands; it is his interception of Waverly's letters which brings charges against Waverly in Sir Walter Scott's *Waverly.*

Bear, John Deaf-mute Pawnee Indian who helps Molly Riordan when she is burned; flees town when Clay Turner appears for a second time in E. L. Doctorow's *Welcome to Hard Times.*

Bear, Petal First wife of Quoyle; killed in car accident after selling their two daughters, who are later recovered, to a maker of pornographic videos in E. Annie Proulx's *The Shipping News.*

Beard, Ceridwen Welsh sister of Leonora Beard and sister-in-law of Ronald Beard; she nurses and comforts Beard after the death of his wife in Anthony Burgess's *Beard's Roman Women.*

Beard, Dr. Shakespeare Agamemnon Black founder of the National Social Equality League in George S. Schuyler's *Black No More.*

Beard, Leonora Alcoholic, tart-tongued wife of Ronald Beard; she dies of cirrhosis of the liver but remains very much alive in his memory, even to making phantom phone calls to him in Rome in Anthony Burgess's *Beard's Roman Women.*

Beard, Ronald Fiftyish film-script writer and heavy drinker; he is a Briton living in Rome more or less permanently; he deludes himself only about important matters, including his love for Paola Belli in Anthony Burgess's *Beard's Roman Women.*

Beardon, Maudie Tall, thin, 28-year-old fellow chorus girl with yellow hair and white skin; she is Anna Morgan's early roommate in Jean Rhys's *Voyage in the Dark.*

Beardsall, Cyril ("Sybil," "Pat") Lettie Beardsall's self-effacing bachelor brother; his slow-maturing avowed love is for Emily Saxton, but his most deeply felt affection is for Emily's brother George; he is narrator of D. H. Lawrence's *The White Peacock.*

Beardsall, Frank Unkempt, dying father of Lettie and Cyril; he does not identify himself to them when he encounters them after an 18-year absence in D. H. Lawrence's *The White Peacock.*

Beardsall, Lettice Mother of Lettie and Cyril; her husband left her 18 years earlier; finding him dead, she regrets that she kept his children from him for so many years in D. H. Lawrence's *The White Peacock.*

Beardsall, Lettie Romantic, selfish, charming girl; after considerable vacillation, she marries the more eligible but the less physically compelling of two devoted suitors; the happiness of her successful marriage comes from maternity in D. H. Lawrence's *The White Peacock.*

Bearing, Vivian Middle-aged doctor of philosophy and professor of 17th-century poetry who specializes in the Holy Sonnets of John Donne and the poet's tools of wit; hospitalized for advanced metastatic ovarian cancer at University Hospital, where, surrounded by doctors of medicine, she undergoes lengthy and painful chemotherapy; divines that only a comma separates life from life everlasting before succumbing in Margaret Edson's play *Wit.*

Bearn, Madame Companion to the Countess de Villefort in Ann Radcliffe's *The Mysteries of Udolpho.*

Beasley, Mabel Norma Jean's doting and critical mother who spends a great deal of time in her daughter's house; successfully urges her daughter and son-in-law to drive off by themselves to Shiloh to see the Civil War battlefield in Bobbie Ann Mason's "Shiloh."

Beast Eccentric mysterious creature that lives in a remote castle; resembles a huge lion with a broad mane and long claws; catches Beauty's father stealing a white rose for his poor daughter, then compels the old man to bring Beauty to the castle; falls in love with Beauty, and, after she departs the castle, begins to pine away toward death; saved from death when Beauty returns and shows her compassion and love for him; revealed to have the name Mr. Lyon in Angela Carter's "The Courtship of Mr. Lyon."

Beast, The Prince condemned to exist inside of a hideous monster's body until he is broken from his curse; disturbed and vengeful creature who then develops into a kind and gentle soul, especially toward the Beauty in the play, a young woman in Jean Cocteau's *Beauty and the Beast.*

Beata Israeli lawyer who pleads for Jamil's release after he had been imprisoned and tortured in Carlos Fuentes's *The Hydra Head.*

Beaton, Angus Arrogant art director of the magazine *Every Other Week* in William Dean Howells's *A Hazard of New Fortunes.*

Beaton, Mr. Secretary and general counsel for Typon International, whose admiration for Amy Joubert leads him to plot for her control of the company in William Gaddis's *JR.*

Beatrice Cynthia, Lady Weston's personal maid, who carries the news of Cynthia's affair with Philip Weston to Sir Aylmer Weston after she is rejected by Ralph Moberly in Isabel Colegate's *Statues in a Garden.*

Beatrice Elderly housekeeper at Villa Altieri, who witnesses Ellena Rosalba's abduction and later identifies Sister Olivia as the Countess di Bruno and Ellena's mother in Ann Radcliffe's *The Italian.*

Beatrice Rosamund Stacey's sister, an Oxford graduate; a pacifist, she is a housewife living with her atomic-scientist husband and her three children in the Midlands in Margaret Drabble's *The Millstone.*

Beatrice Sharp-tongued maiden beyond the traditional age of marriage; lives with her uncle Leonato and cousin Hero; sworn enemy of the soldier Benedick but is gulled into loving and marrying him; denies Don Pedro's proposal; forces Benedick to avenge the feigned death of Hero in William Shakespeare's play *Much Ado About Nothing.*

Beatrice (Prophetess of Ferrara, Ancilla Dei) Daughter of the executed heretic Magfreda and the adopted daughter of Bishop Marsilio of Ferrara; a rivetingly beautiful innocent, she has an exalted imagination and is victimized by the Church, the Paterins, and Castruccio dei Antelminelli; she goes mad from henbane poisoning in Mary Shelley's *Valperga.*

Beatrice (Trissie) Reuben Egerton's fiancée; the daughter of a clergyman, she is pursued sexually by Hereward Egerton, Reuben's father, in Ivy Compton-Burnett's *A God and His Gifts.*

Beatrice, Empress Frederick the Great's new young wife; beauty to whom the young title character, Baudolino, is attracted in Umberto Eco's *Baudolino.*

Beatrice, Marchesa D' Baldoni Outgoing wife of an Italian marquis; she introduces Ayala Dormer to her cousin, Colonel Stubbs, in Anthony Trollope's *Ayala's Angel.*

Beatty, Captain Enforces the rules of the era in which he lives by burning dangerous books; represents authority; provides exposition about when political correctness encouraged censorship of dangerous intellectualism; uses quotations from literature to demonstrate that books are dangerous because they confuse people with their divisive positions; lives in a dystopic post-1990 America; killed by Montag in Ray Bradbury's *Fahrenheit 451.*

Beatty, Gloria Cynical aspiring actress who convinces Robert Syverten to enter the dance marathon with her; killed by Syverten at her request in Horace McCoy's *They Shoot Horses, Don't They?*

Beatty, Ken Coroner who died of the flu in the town where Whitey's barber shop sits near Centerville in Ring Lardner's "Haircut."

Beauchamp Poet occasionally entertained at the Sneaze household and closely observed by the narrator, an alley cat adopted by the Sneaze family, in Natsume Soseki's *I Am a Cat.*

Beauchamp, Bobo Groom in William Faulkner's *The Reivers.*

Beauchamp, Caroline Handsome and wealthy young woman, considered somewhat coarse by some; Stanley Lake tells his sister, Rachel, he might marry Caroline in order to allay Rachel's suspicions about his designs on Dorcas Brandon in J. Sheridan Le Fanu's *Wylder's Hand.*

Beauchamp, Elizabeth Mary Aunt of both Nevil Beauchamp and Blackburn Tuckham; she divides her estate between them in George Meredith's *Beauchamp's Career.*

Beauchamp, Emily Crayton Daughter of Colonel Crayton and only true friend of Charlotte Temple among the gentility in the United States; writes to Charlotte's parents in England to explain the plight of their daughter in Susanna Rowson's *Charlotte.*

Beauchamp, Henry Son of Lucas and Mollie Beauchamp in William Faulkner's *Go Down, Moses.*

Beauchamp, Hubert Plantation owner and uncle of Ike McCaslin in William Faulkner's *Go Down, Moses.*

Beauchamp, James Thucydides (Tennie's Jim, Thucydus) Son of Tomey's Turl and Tennie Beauchamp in William Faulkner's *Go Down, Moses;* grandfather of Bobo Beauchamp in *The Reivers.*

Beauchamp, Lady Woman who, disappointed in her romantic attraction to Edward Beauchamp, takes revenge by marrying his widowed father and having the son's income in exile greatly reduced; she is talked out of her meanness by Sir Charles Grandison; her stepson treats her generously when she is widowed in Samuel Richardson's *Sir Charles Grandison.*

Beauchamp, Lucas Quintus Carothers McCaslin Son of Tomey's Turl and Tennie Beauchamp; accused of murdering Vinson Gowrie; appears in William Faulkner's *Go Down, Moses; Intruder in the Dust;* and *The Reivers.*

Beauchamp, Matilda Daughter of Sir Benjamin and cofounder of Shenstone-Green; she marries the reformed spendthrift Danvers Davies in S. J. Pratt's *Shenstone-Green.*

Beauchamp, Molly (Mollie) Wife of Lucas Beauchamp in William Faulkner's *Go Down, Moses* and *Intruder in the Dust.*

Beauchamp, Mrs. Landlady who watches visitors to Lewis Eliot's rooms where he lives alone after his wife's suicide and who gossips with him about them in C. P. Snow's *Homecomings.*

Beauchamp, Nevil Patriotic and idealist hero of the Crimean War; he campaigns for Parliament as a Liberal, aided by Dr. Shrapnel, estranging his Tory uncle; his involvement with a Frenchwoman and the radical Dr. Shrapnel loses him the campaign, his beloved, and his health; though he reconciles with his family and marries Shrapnel's ward, Jenny Denham, he dies in an act of heroism in George Meredith's *Beauchamp's Career.*

Beauchamp, Philip Manigault Soldier who helps execute General Gragnon in William Faulkner's *A Fable.*

Beauchamp, Samuel Worsham Grandson of Lucas and Molly Beauchamp; executed for killing a Chicago policeman in William Faulkner's *Go Down, Moses.*

Beauchamp, Sir Benjamin Founder of a Utopian community who watches it disintegrate under the pressure of human frailties in S. J. Pratt's *Shenstone-Green.*

Beauchamp, (Sir) Edward Sir Charles Grandison's friend and European traveling companion; Sir Charles persuades Edward's father and stepmother to drop their unkind treatment of him; Edward is discouraged by Sir Charles from courting Emily Jervois because of her youth, but their eventual union is anticipated at the end of Samuel Richardson's *Sir Charles Grandison.*

Beauchamp, Sir Harry Baronet who is influenced by his young second wife to withdraw support from his son and heir, Edward; Sir Charles Grandison's good-humored intercession restores family harmony, and when Sir Harry dies, Sir Edward treats his stepmother magnanimously in Samuel Richardson's *Sir Charles Grandison.*

Beauchamp, Sophonsiba See McCaslin, Sophonsiba Beauchamp.

Beauchamp, Tennie Wife of Tomey's Turl and mother of James Thucydides (Tennie's Jim, Thucydus), Lucas, and Sophonsiba Beauchamp in William Faulkner's *Go Down, Moses;* great-grandmother of Bobo Beauchamp in *The Reivers.*

Beauchamp, Tomey's Turl Husband of Tennie Beauchamp and father of James Thucydides (Tennie's Jim, Thucydus), Lucas, and Sophonsiba Beauchamp in William Faulkner's *Go Down, Moses;* a character of the same name appears in *The Town.*

Beauclair Honest and gullible lover of Montamour; he disguises himself as a friar in order to get her in Eliza Haywood's *The Injur'd Husband; or, the Mistaken Resentment.*

Beauclere Gambler murdered by Charles Archer (Paul Dangerfield); Lord Dunoran is convicted of the crime on Archer's testimony in J. Sheridan Le Fanu's *The House by the Churchyard.*

Beaudair, Count de Nephew of Count de Vinevil; left in charge of the family holdings in France when the count takes his family to Constantinople, he faithfully restores the estate to Ardelisa de Vinevil when she returns in Penelope Aubin's *The Strange Adventures of the Count De Vinevil and His Family.*

Beaudreau, Bob Football fanatic and financier who loses his girlfriend to Phil Elliott in Peter Gent's *North Dallas Forty.*

Beaudry, Clair Abusive, wife-beating landlord who rents an apartment to Yolanda Garcia in Julia Alvarez's *Yo!*

Beaudry, Marie Abused wife of Clair Beaudry; rents an apartment to Yolanda Garcia; encouraged by Yo to permanently separate from Clair in Julia Alvarez's *Yo!*

Beaufils, Justin Childhood friend of Ursa Mackenzie; defeats Primus Mackenzie in election in Paule Marshall's *Daughters.*

Beaufort, Julius Husband of Regina Beaufort; wealthy banker of mysterious origins and dissipated habits in Edith Wharton's *The Age of Innocence.*

Beaufort, Lucia Cousin of the Coventry family; promised to Gerald and loves him deeply, until Gerald falls for Jean Muir; quite perceptive and never trusts Muir, who calls her the "icicle," in Louisa May Alcott's novella *Behind a Mask.*

Beaufort, Maria McInnis Banker's daughter who marries a university professor-psychiatrist after an affair with Jed Tewksbury in Robert Penn Warren's *A Place to Come To.*

Beaufort, Regina Dallas Wife of Julius Beaufort and ostentatious hostess of old New York society in Edith Wharton's *The Age of Innocence.*

Beaujeu, de Keeper of a gambling house in Sir Walter Scott's *The Fortunes of Nigel.*

Beaujolais, Henri de Patient, concerned, observant military man and storyteller; he belongs to the Spahis XIXth (African) Army Corps; he uses his reasoning to solve a mystery he narrates to his friend George Lawrence while traveling; he is an inspiration to the Geste brothers in Percival Christopher Wren's *Beau Geste.*

Beauly, Helena Eustace Macallan's cousin, with whom he was in love and whose marriage helped propel him into marriage with his first wife; a widow and houseguest at the time of Sara Macallan's death, she is important as both suspect and motive for Eustace as suspect in Wilkie Collins's *The Law and the Lady.*

Beaumanoir, Duchess of Dignified and accomplished wife of the duke and mother of Henry Sidney in Benjamin Disraeli's *Coningsby; or, The New Generation.*

Beaumanoir, Duke of Well-meaning but politically uninformed father of Harry Coningsby's friend Henry Sidney in Benjamin Disraeli's *Coningsby; or, The New Generation.*

Beaumanoir, Lucas Grand Master of the Templars; he accuses Rebecca of sorcery and is later banished by King Richard in Sir Walter Scott's *Ivanhoe.*

Beaumanoir, Marquis of, Percy Elder brother of Henry Sidney and Harry Coningsby's frivolous rival for Edith Millbank during her brief estrangement from Coningsby in Benjamin Disraeli's *Coningsby; or, The New Generation.*

Beaumont, Belinda, Madam de Protestant orphan, the virtuous daughter of a French nobleman and an English lady; she marries Catholic Count de Beaumont, with whom she has a daughter before they are separated by her father-in-law's objections to her religion; she lives in a cave in Wales for 14 years, whereupon she meets Mr. Lluelling, who loves her daughter and finds the count, reuniting the family in Penelope Aubin's *The Life of Madam de Beaumont.*

Beaumont, Count de Son of the governor of Normandy; he elopes with the Protestant Belinda; separated from her by his father because of her religion, he joins the Swedish Army, is taken prisoner, has several adventures, and refuses women who want to love him; he finally remarries but cannot forget Belinda; he is reunited with her and his daughter after 14 years in Penelope Aubin's *The Life of Madam de Beaumont.*

Beaumont, Duke of One of the French nobles in William Shakespeare's play *Henry V.*

Beaumont, Hortensia Friend whom Lady Clementina della Porretta visits in Rome and who reveals to the family Clementina's love for Sir Charles Grandison; she believes that only marriage to Sir Charles will cure Clementina's affliction in Samuel Richardson's *Sir Charles Grandison.*

Beaumont, Jeremiah (Jerry, William K. Grierson) Altruist and author of the manuscript that provides the plot of the novel; kills Colonel Cassius Fort, escapes from jail, but is caught and decapitated in Robert Penn Warren's *World Enough and Time.*

Beaumont, Lady de Count de Beaumont's second wife, a young widow with a daughter; she dies from grief after two years because he cannot forget his first wife in Penelope Aubin's *The Life of Madam de Beaumont.*

Beaumont, Miss Principal in Dick Lennox's acting company until she is replaced by Kate Ede in leading roles; she is mollified by the attention she gets from admirers in high society in George Moore's *A Mummer's Wife.*

Beaumont, Mrs. Kinswoman of Lord Orville; she is the Bristol hostess for Orville and Louisa Larpent in Frances Burney's *Evelina.*

Beaumont, Ned Beaumont Gambler who investigates murder charges against his friend, political boss Paul Madvig, in Dashiell Hammett's *The Glass Key.*

Beaumont, Rachel Jordan Wife of Jeremiah Beaumont and former lover of Colonel Cassius Fort, father of her first child, in Robert Penn Warren's *World Enough and Time.*

Beaunoir, Count de Whimsical, extravagant Frenchman, who engages in a duel with Coke Clifton, later becoming Coke's friend and a suitor of Anna St. Ives in Thomas Holcroft's *Anna St. Ives.*

Beauplaisir Accomplished man who approaches Fantomina—a woman whose reputation for virtue and chastity kept him from attempting to seduce her—when she disguises herself as a prostitute; to keep his interest, Fantomina repeatedly transforms her costume and her identity; she becomes pregnant; Beauplaisir promises to serve as the child's custodian after Fantomina is sent to live in a monastery in France in Eliza Haywood's *Fantomina; Or, Love in a Maze.*

Beauséant, Madame de Eugéne de Rastignac's cousin in Honoré de Balzac's *Father Goriot.*

Beauseigneur, Pussy (Mrs. Beau) Example of encroaching commuters in Woodsmoke, Connecticut; employs Frank Spofford as a handyman in Peter De Vries's *Reuben, Reuben.*

Beauty Girlfriend of Trevor Lomas in Muriel Spark's *The Ballad of Peckham Rye.*

Beauty Lovely and innocent daughter of a financially imperiled father; compelled to visit the remote castle of the Beast, a huge creature in the form of a lion; accepts living at the Beast's estate in order to help save her father from financial and legal ruin; grows to feel compassion and then love for the Beast; comes to the bedside of the dying Beast, and through her love, he is saved from death and transformed into a human mortal who marries her; his name is revealed to be Mr. Lyon in Angela Carter's "The Courtship of Mr. Lyon."

Beauty Young girl who lives and gets pleasure out of helping those in need; heroine of this romantic play; works off her father's debt to the Beast; her kind spirit and patience are her qualities that help the Beast trust and respect her in Jean Cocteau's *Beauty and the Beast.*

Beauty (Chips) Ugly carpenter aboard the *Julia* in Herman Melville's *Omoo.*

Beauvais, Martinette de (Ursula Monrose) Purchaser of the lute Constantia Dudley sells to alleviate her family's financial distress; revealed to be the sister of Ormond, from whom she was separated during adolescence, in Charles Brockden Brown's *Ormond.*

Beauvaris Savillon's epistolary intimate, who eventually dies in Henry Mackenzie's *Julia de Roubigné.*

Beaver, John Brenda Last's parasitic lover, who deserts her when she is no longer able to finance their affair in Evelyn Waugh's *A Handful of Dust.*

Beaver, Mrs. John Beaver's unprincipled mother; she is the proprietor of a London interior-decorating business whose sole interest is making money in Evelyn Waugh's *A Handful of Dust.*

Beaver, Ollie Totem Head Water Guide on the Alaskan hunting expedition in Norman Mailer's *Why Are We in Vietnam?*

Beavers, Myrlene Elderly resident of the solidly black, working-class neighborhood of Wallace Hill in Haddam, New Jersey; in a moment of forgetfulness, calls the police on her old acquaintance, Frank Bascombe, as he tries to collect rent from her neighbors in Richard Ford's *Independence Day.*

Beavers, Tug Poor-white teamster on a railroad construction gang who is murdered by Peck Bradley in T. S. Stribling's *Teeftallow.*

Beavers, Wesley Sexually magnetic protagonist in Reynolds Price's *A Long and Happy Life.*

Beavis, Anthony Directionless intellectual who attempts to sort out his spiritual growth in a series of fragmented diary entries, at the center of which are his relationships with Helen Ledwidge, his longtime lover, and with Dr. Miller, an ardent pacifist from whom he discovers something about human decency in Aldous Huxley's *Eyeless in Gaza.*

Bebreuilh, Anne Psychoanalyst and esteemed wife of the celebrated writer Robert Debrueih; represents the author Simone de Beauvoir, as her husband represents Jean-Paul Sartre, de Beauvoir's lifelong friend, lover, and intellectual companion; admits only to herself her emotional vulnerability; conducts her exterior life with practicality and careful precision, always internally assessing the feelings of others; maintains a loyal marriage in France while also conducting a passionate love affair overseas with a Chicago writer, Lewis Bogan, who in the novel represents the American writer Nelson Algren, in Simone de Beauvoir's *The Mandarins.*

Becca Wife of Howie, daughter of Nat, older sister of Izzy; late 30s to early 40s; lives in Larchmont (suburban New York City); grieving the death of her son Danny in David Lindsay-Abair's *Rabbit Hole.*

Bech, Hannah Mother of Henry Bech; dies in a Riverdale nursing home in John Updike's *Bech: A Book.*

Bech, Henry Middle-aged Jewish writer from New York; experiences writer's block after publishing two novels, *Travel Light* and *The Chosen,* the novella *Brother Pig,* and two collections, *When the Saints* and *The Best of Bech;* his travels take him to Russia, Romania, Bulgaria, London, Martha's Vineyard, and Virginia in John Updike's *Bech: A Book.*

Beck Crossing sweeper who baffles Lucretia Clavering's plot against Helen Mainwaring and Percival St. John and is murdered by Lucretia before she discovers he is her lost son, Vincent Braddell, in Edward Bulwer-Lytton's *Lucretia.*

Beck, Alfons School friend of Emil Sinclair; initiates Emil into the world of evil and alcohol in Hermann Hesse's *Demian.*

Beck, Desiree Mme. Beck's eldest child, who is brought up according to a system of spying to be sly and destructive in Charlotte Brontë's *Villette.*

Beck, Fifine Mme. Beck's second child, who has her father's honest nature, and who, when she breaks her arm, brings Dr. John Bretton to the school for the first time in Charlotte Brontë's *Villette.*

Beck, Georgette Mme. Beck's youngest child, who is attached to Lucy Snowe in Charlotte Brontë's *Villette.*

Beck, Modeste Maria Determined, cunning headmistress of a boarding school in Villette, Labassecour, who hires Lucy Snowe without references as a nursery governess, promotes her to English teacher, and actively interposes when her cousin, M. Paul Emanuel, becomes interested in Lucy in Charlotte Brontë's *Villette.*

Beckendorff, Mr. Eccentric, Machiavellian prime minister of Austria, whose political intrigues include arranging the marriage of Baroness Sybilla to the Prince of Reisenburg, thereby preventing her marriage to Vivian Grey in Benjamin Disraeli's *Vivian Grey.*

Becker Old, fat Jew in the concentration camp at Birkenau, near Auschwitz; once was a senior at the Jewish camp outside Poznań; for the Germans, he killed other Jews in the death camps; hanged one of his two sons for stealing bread; his other son wants to murder the father for this offense; later beaten by Ivan for stealing food and sent to the crematorium in Tadeusz Borowski's *This Way for the Gas, Ladies and Gentlemen.*

Becker, David Fiancé of Susan Fletcher and a linguist; he travels to Seville, Spain, to find the reason for the death of the Japanese cryptographer Ensei Tankado in Dan Brown's *Digital Fortress.*

Becker, Gadi ("the Steppenwolf," Jose; covernames: Peter Richthoven, Joseph) Disillusioned Israeli military hero and skeptical Mossad (Israeli intelligence) operative, who is manipulated by Marty Kurtz into seducing Charlie; he scripts her infiltration into Khalil's inner circle, murders Khalil in her bed, and, after finally rejecting Kurtz's moral uncertainty, returns to Charlie to try to repair their shattered psyches in John le Carré's *The Little Drummer Girl.*

Becker, Ralph Wealthy banker acquaintance of Theodora Bates in Isabel Colegate's *Orlando at the Brazen Threshold.*

Beckerman, Craig Electrode implantation volunteer at Neuropsychiatric Research Unit in Michael Crichton's *The Terminal Man.*

Beckerman, Dr. Senior teacher at Petersons School who falls into an insane fit at seeing Bryan Morley's statue of a nude Fay Corrigan exhibited at the school in David Storey's *A Prodigal Child.*

Becket Saxon raised through the church to become King Henry II's confidant, chancellor, and friend. The integrity that Henry admires in Becket is turned against him when the interests of the church Becket is sworn to protect come into conflict with his relationship to and need to serve King Henry, a conflict that ultimately leads to Becket's murder in Jean Anouilh's play *Becket.*

Becket, Archbishop Thomas Formerly the chancellor of England and close friend of King Henry II, now the archbishop of Canterbury; dutiful to his religious calling, he refuses to obey the king and lives in France in exile for seven years after opposing the premature crowning of the king's son; returns to England knowing he may be assassinated; tempted four times but preaches a sermon on accepting Christian martyrdom as God's will; killed by four knights in his own cathedral in T. S. Eliot's play *Murder in the Cathedral.*

Beckett, Beautiful Joe Cynical, manipulative young thug loved by Cato Forbes; when Joe, who has kidnapped both Cato and his sister, Colette Forbes, in an extortion scheme, is attempting to rape Colette, Cato kills him in Iris Murdoch's *Henry and Cato.*

Beckford, William Second cousin of the Cavaliere, twenty years old, stupendously rich, the author of a slim ironic book of imaginary biographies; homosexual; becomes a misanthropic recluse in his forties in Susan Sontag's *The Volcano Lover.*

Becky White southerner who bears two black sons; dies alone, rejected by both black and white religious communities, in Jean Toomer's *Cane.*

Beddoes, Mrs. Tom Mallow's wealthy aunt from Belgravia who expresses the family's concern about Tom's living with Catherine Oliphant and gives a coming-out party for her daughter attended by Mark Penfold in Barbara Pym's *Less Than Angels.*

Bede, Adam Authoritative and rigidly moral man, whose fixed ideas of right and wrong are challenged and softened when his betrothed, Hetty Sorrel, deserts her newborn child of another father; ultimately he finds peace through his marriage to Dinah Morris, the Methodist preacher, in George Eliot's *Adam Bede.*

Bede, Adam (the younger) Son of Adam and Dinah (Morris) Bede in George Eliot's *Adam Bede.*

Bede, Belinda Elder of two middle-aged spinsters whose lives center on church activities in a small village; she is harmlessly devoted to the local vicar, with whom she fell in love at Oxford while studying seventeenth-century poetry in Barbara Pym's *Some Tame Gazelle.*

Bede, Harriet Plump spinster sister of Belinda; she plays the piano, flirts with young curates, and has an affinity for colorful clothes in Barbara Pym's *Some Tame Gazelle.*

Bede, Lisbeth Adam Bede's anxious, nagging mother, who depends upon this favorite son completely; when her husband drowns, the importance of mourning rites and traditions in calming a grieving loved one are clear in George Eliot's *Adam Bede.*

Bede, Lisbeth (the younger) Daughter of Adam and Dinah (Morris) Bede in George Eliot's *Adam Bede.*

Bede, Matthias Adam Bede's hard-drinking father, who drowns; this begins his son's regeneration because Adam feels guilty for his ill-feelings towards the old alcoholic in George Eliot's *Adam Bede.*

Bede, Seth Gentle, pious younger brother of Adam Bede; he loves Dinah Morris, but his suit is unsuccessful; when Adam falls in love with Dinah, Seth kindly steps aside to allow his brother full joy in marriage in George Eliot's *Adam Bede.*

Bedford Bankrupt businessman and fledgling playwright who assists Cavor in developing Cavorite and in building the space ship with which they explore the moon; when they become separated there, he is forced to return to Earth alone, where he settles in Italy to write his account of their adventures in H. G. Wells's *The First Men in the Moon.*

Bedford, Duncan Son of Malcolm and Sarah Bedford; after serving in the Confederate army, he returns to Portobello plantation and marries Julia Valette Somerville in Stark Young's *So Red the Rose.*

Bedford, Earl of English envoy to Mary, Queen of Scots and supporter of the Duke of Norfolk's plan to free the pregnant Mary in Sophia Lee's *The Recess.*

Bedford, John, Duke of (see also Lancaster, John, Prince of) Aware of the conspiracy against Henry V and Henry's plan to foil the conspirators; accompanies Henry throughout the action in William Shakespeare's play Henry V.

Bedford, Lieutenant Platoon leader in France during World War I who is killed at the battle of Soissons in Thomas Boyd's *Through the Wheat.*

Bedford, Malcolm (Mac) Husband of Sarah Tate Bedford, father of Duncan Bedford, and owner of Portobello plantation in Natchez; joins the Confederate army and dies of typhus in Stark Young's *So Red the Rose.*

Bedford, Sarah Tate (Sallie, Tait) Wife of Malcolm Bedford and mother of Duncan Bedford; widowed during the Civil War, she manages Portobello plantation until Duncan returns from the army in Stark Young's *So Red the Rose.*

Bedley, Mrs. Venerable "Mother of the English Colony" of Kairoulla, the capital of Pisuerga, who operates a combined circulating library and tea-room, provides information to tourists, and resents her lack of social status relative to the Court society of Pisuerga in Ronald Firbank's *The Flower Beneath the Foot.*

Bedloe, Bee Mother of Claudia, Danny, and Ian and wife of Doug; unkempt, but believes every part of her life is wonderful; becomes disabled from arthritis in Anne Tyler's *Saint Maybe.*

Bedloe, Danny Middle child of Bee and Doug Bedloe and brother of Claudia and Ian; husband of Lucy Dean and father of Daphne; works at the post office; commits suicide after he hears that Lucy may be having an affair in Anne Tyler's *Saint Maybe.*

Bedloe, Daphne Daughter of Lucy Dean and Danny Bedloe; after her mother's death, is raised by her uncle, Ian; does not want to move out of the home that she occupies with Ian and her grandparents Dee and Doug in Anne Tyler's *Saint Maybe.*

Bedloe, Doug Father of Claudia, Danny, and Ian and husband of Bee; quiet high school baseball coach who retires and assists the neighbors with home repairs; helps take care of Agatha, Thomas, and Daphne in Anne Tyler's *Saint Maybe.*

Bedloe, Ian Youngest child of Bee and Doug Bedloe and brother of Claudia and Danny; feels responsible for Danny's suicide; finds guidance through The Church of the Second Chance, where he feels welcome; drops out of college at nineteen and becomes a carpenter; marries Rita DiCarlo in Anne Tyler's *Saint Maybe.*

Bedloe-Daley, Claudia Oldest child of Bee and Doug Bedloe and sister of Danny and Ian; wife of Macy Daley and mother of Abbie, Barney, Cindy, Davey, and Francis; dropped out of college her senior year to get married in Anne Tyler's *Saint Maybe.*

Bednar, Record Head (Bednarski) Veteran Chicago police captain who bears the guilt of the criminals with whom he has dealt in Nelson Algren's *The Man with the Golden Arm.*

Bedonebyasyoudid, Mrs. See Queen of the Fairies.

Bedos Henry Pelham's inestimable French valet; he high-mindedly resists all Pelham's offers to effect a reunion with his wife by providing her with employment in Edward Bulwer-Lytton's *Pelham.*

Bedwin, Mrs. Mr. Brownlow's housekeeper, who nurses Oliver Twist when he is ill in Charles Dickens's *Oliver Twist.*

Beebe, Arthur Understanding rector of Summer Street who observes and sympathizes with Lucy Honeychurch's dilemma in E. M. Forster's *A Room with a View.*

Beeber, Dr. Mark Title character; elderly man who now prefers poverty and simplicity to his former life of wealth and acclaim for his novels; humble and proud; poorly chooses to marry the rich Saltsche, an admirer of his writing, who now tries to force him to return to his writing by daily locking him in his study; retaliates by gambling away her money; thrown from Saltsche's house, returns to the old neighborhood of his poverty in Isaac Bashevis Singer's "Dr. Beeber."

Beeblebrox, Zaphod Hails from a planet in Betelgeuse; semi-cousin to Ford; has two heads and three arms; elected president of Imperial Galactic Government; steals the *Heart of Gold,* which is a spaceship that possesses the capability to effectively operate the ground-breaking Infinite Improbability Drive; involved with Trillian; likes to have fun and does not appear to be very bright; usually able to talk his way out of the trouble he attracts in Douglas Adams's *The Hitchhiker's Guide to the Universe.*

Beech Maternal tree-woman, who wants to progress to womanhood; she helps protect Anodos in George MacDonald's *Phantastes.*

Beech, Mrs. President of the Women's City Club interested in political reform in Chicago; in an attempt to join forces with others who share her reform interests, she is one of the white guests at Sara Andrews Towns's dinner party in W. E. B. DuBois's *Dark Princess.*

Beecham, Beulah See Renfro, Beulah Beecham.

Beecham, Frances Forty-eight-year-old aunt of Martha Horgan; sister of Floyd Horgan; widow of Horace Beecham, at one time the wealthiest man in southern Vermont, whom she married when she was 21 and he was 61; longtime lover of Steve Bell in Mary McGarry Morris's *A Dangerous Woman.*

Beecham, John Former enlisted army trooper with history of violent acts; also known as Japheth Dury; suspected by Dr. Lazlo Kriezler of committing grisly New York City serial murders in Caleb Carr's *The Alienist.*

Beechum, Clara See Pettit, Clara Beechum.

Beechum, Jack (Old Jack) Subsistence farmer and representative patriarch of Port William, Kentucky; overextending his farm to please his wife, Ruth Lightwood, he becomes estranged from her and has an affair with Rose McInnis; central presence whose thoughts organize Wendell Berry's *The Memory of Old Jack;* also appears in *Nathan Coulter* and *A Place on Earth.*

Beechum, Nancy See Feltner, Nancy Beechum.

Beechum, Ruth See Lightwood, Ruth.

Beeder, Lady Sir William's wife, an aspiring artist in Joyce Cary's *The Horse's Mouth.*

Beeder, Sir William Wealthy art collector and a benefactor of Gulley Jimson; he wishes to obtain one of Gulley's nudes; Gulley ransacks his apartment while staying there and then sells him a reproduction of one of his nudes in Joyce Cary's *The Horse's Mouth.*

Beekman, Cyrus U. (Beeky) Cunning and devious opportunist and Union army officer who exploits southern whites and blacks; carpetbag candidate for governor of Alabama who advocates a New South commercial ethic in T. S. Stribling's *The Forge and The Store.*

Beekman, Gracie See Vaiden, Gracie.

Beekman, Sir Francis (Piggie) Wealthy man attracted to Lorelei Lee; she is affectionate to him long enough to gain a diamond tiara that his wife desires for herself in Anita Loos's *Gentlemen Prefer Blondes.*

Beeler, Old Man Retired pharmacist living with his daughter Sheryl Beeler in a Mott Street apartment managed by Norman Moonbloom in Edward Lewis Wallant's *The Tenants of Moonbloom.*

Beeler, Sheryl Daughter of Old Man Beeler; exchanges sexual favors with Norman Moonbloom for rent cuts in Edward Lewis Wallant's *The Tenants of Moonbloom.*

Beerbohm, Max Writer who was once seated next to Zuleika Dobson at a dinner; the literary flavor of her speech was picked up from his example in Max Beerbohm's *Zuleika Dobson; or An Oxford Love Story.*

Beers, Alma Marries Ennis del Mar and soon has two children: Alma, Jr., and Francine; spots Ennis embracing Jack Twist in their home; later divorces him and marries the town grocer in Annie Proulx's "Brokeback Mountain."

Beers, Hiram Horse trainer and menial-for-hire for Norwood; serves as an ambulance driver during the Civil War and becomes Reuben Wentworth's stable hand in Henry Ward Beecher's *Norwood.*

Beery, Shep Accomplice of Gerry Kells in Paul Cain's *Fast One.*

Beesley, Alfred Member of the university English Department and a resident in the rooming house where Jim Dixon lives; he gives Jim notes on "The Age of Chaucer" to use in Jim's "Merrie England" lecture in Kingsley Amis's *Lucky Jim.*

Beeswax, Sir Timothy Astute, devious Conservative politician and political enemy of the (younger) Duke of Omnium in Anthony Trollope's *The Prime Minister.* He is a protégé of Mr. Daubeny and rises to become Leader of the House of Commons; a falling out with his chief, Lord Drummond, causes his downfall in *The Duke's Children.* He appears in *The American Senator.*

Beetle, Agony Meriam's normal, civil father in Stella Gibbons's *Cold Comfort Farm.*

Beetle, Meriam Simple, rural hired girl who gives birth once a year as the natural result of springtime passions; she is finally captured by Urk Starkadder as an earthy alternative to the ethereal Elfine Starkadder in Stella Gibbons's *Cold Comfort Farm.*

Beetle, Mrs. First normal, civil person that Flora Poste meets at Cold Comfort Farm; she is in contrast with the Starkadder family in Stella Gibbons's *Cold Comfort Farm.*

Beevor, Miss Violin teacher who becomes obsessed with the conviction that the untalented Cordelia Aubrey will become a great musician; she wears huge feathered hats, and she becomes roguish and plump, supposedly because she gains nourishment from her hopes for Cordelia in Rebecca West's *The Fountain Overflows.*

Beffa Man who works at Lazzaro Scacerni's mill on the Po River, near the city of Ferrara; dislikes his master and works secretly with smugglers who rob Lazzaro; joins Raguseo, the leader of a smuggling ring, and is soon killed by a rival band of outlaws in Riccardo Bacchelli's *The Mill on the Po.*

Befies, Maria Daughter of the designer of a black housing development and married lover of Bill Kelsey; dispatching black rivals, she proves the strength of white Juju in Hal Bennett's *Seventh Heaven.*

Beg, Arif One of the overseers in the construction of the Drina Bridge in Ivo Andrić's *The Bridge on the Drina.*

Beg, Callum Young Highlander of the MacIvor clan; he guides Edward Waverly through much of Scotland in Sir Walter Scott's *Waverly.*

Beg, Nawab Haider The underling of the Mughal emperor Aurangzeb in Bharati Mukherjee's *The Holder of the World.*

Beggar Charlatan beggar Harley meets on the way to London; he tells pleasing fortunes to people to earn his living in Henry Mackenzie's *The Man of Feeling.*

Beggarmaster Controls a network of beggars whom he protects; collects a portion of their wages in return; protects Dina Dalal from *goondas* (thugs) who, on behalf of her landlord, want to evict her from her apartment; discovers he is a half-brother of Shankar, "Worm," in Rohinton Mistry's *A Fine Balance.*

Begsurbeck Pious king of Normnbdsgrsutt and revered ancestor of Georigetti; he receives prophetic notice of Peter Wilkins's mission in Robert Paltock's *The Life and Adventures of Peter Wtikins.*

Beguildy Wizard and an aggressive atheist; Jancis Beguildy's father, he destroys the property of the Sarn family in vengeance against Gideon Sarn's sleeping with Jancis prior to marriage in Mary Webb's *Precious Bane.*

Beguildy, Jancis Daughter of the village wizard, Beguildy; she is beautiful and greatly loved by the Sarn family and by her own; after Beguildy burns Gideon Sarn's crops and Gideon refuses to support her and their baby, Jancis drowns herself and the infant in Mary Webb's *Precious Bane.*

Beguildy, "Missus" Wife of the wizard, Beguildy, and mother of Jancis Beguildy; in her husband's absence she permits Jancis and Gideon Sarn's unlawful wedding night with tragic consequences in Mary Webb's *Precious Bane.*

Behari Close friend of Mahendra in prepartitioned Bengal; studies medicine in India in Rabindranath Tagore's *Chokher Bali.*

Behemoth Huge black cat who talks, pays his trolley fare, drinks brandy, fires guns, and creates havoc in Moscow, as he mostly accompanies Korovyev and Azazello; finally presented as a page demon in the scene of Woland's departure in Mikhail Bulgakov's *The Master and Margarita.*

Behgin, Michel Overweight, intelligent, middle-aged, masterful French agent; a member of the Secret Generale attached to the French Department of Naval Intelligence, he blackmails Josef Vadassy into discovering the identity of the spy who took the photographs, acts as his control, and ultimately corners the real spy and is responsible for his death in Eric Ambler's *Epitaph for a Spy.*

Behm, Joseph First casualty of Paul Bäumer high school classmates to die in the German army during World War I in Erich Maria Remarque's *All Quiet on the Western Front.*

Behr-Bleibtreau, Edmond (Sordino) Psychologist and hypnotist who disrupts a radio talk show hosted by Dick Gibson in Stanley Elkin's *The Dick Gibson Show.*

Behrens, Dr. Hofrat Cynical director of the hospital, now a widower who lost his wife to tuberculosis; physically repellent with massive extremities; enjoys having power over his patients and is nicknamed Rhadamanthys ("judge of the dead"); his medical decisions are often questionable; at one point, cruelly tells a patient in his death throes not to fuss so much; paints in oil, with Chauchat as one of his sitters in Thomas Mann's *The Magic Mountain.*

Behrman, S. Railroad agent in the San Joaquin Valley who manipulates the law to the disadvantage of the wheat growers in Frank Norris's *The Octopus.*

Beidaoui, Thami Family outcast; Moroccan friend and victim of Nelson Dyar in Paul Bowles's *Let It Come Down.*

Beilby, Mr. Senior partner in the engineering firm of Beilby and Burton, in which Harry Clavering becomes apprenticed in Anthony Trollope's *The Claverings.*

Beineberg Young classmate of Törless in an exclusive academy on the outskirts of the Austro-Hungarian Empire; one of three boys who sexually abuse and torture fellow student Basini in Robert Musil's *Young Törless.*

Beineke, Dr. Fantasy leader of an expedition with which Margaret Reynolds travels to the interior of the Amazon to study the primitive Itwo tribe in Anne Richardson Roiphe's *Up the Sandbox!*

Beizmenne, Erwin Detective inspector responsible for the arrest of Katharina Blum and Ludwig Götten in Heinrich Böll's *The Lost Honor of Katharina Blum.*

Bel See Isabel.

Belacqua, Lyra Ward of Jordan College, Oxford; daughter of Marisa Coulter and Lord Asriel; owns and reads the alethiometer; journeys north to save the children or Bolvangar; walks among parallel universes; teaches Mary Malone to talk to "shadow" particles; discovers the nature of Dust; leads the trapped souls out of the Underworld; kills the Authority; falls in love with Will Parry and reprises the role of Eve in the Second Temptation, restoring Dust to the Universe in Philip Pullman's *His Dark Materials.*

Belaine, Clair Annabel Paynton's close friend and confidante, who becomes involved with Charles Addinsell, in whom Annabel is also interested, in Henry Green's *Doting.*

Belarab Ousted successor to the rule of Wajo; he leads the settlement of "vanquished fanatics, fugitives, and outcasts" living on the Shore of Refuge in Joseph Conrad's *The Rescue: A Romance of the Shallows.*

Belarius British lord unfairly banished by Cymbeline from the court; in revenge, kidnapped Cymbeline's two young sons, Guiderius and Arviragus, raising them as his own in the forests of Wales; assumes the name of Morgan; fights valiantly along with Cymbeline's two sons for Britain against Rome; reveals his real identity and that of the two sons in order to prevent Guiderius from being punished by Cymbeline for Cloten's murder; forgiven by the king in William Shakespeare's play *Cymbeline.*

Belbo In league with the narrator-protagonist and Diotellevi, becomes immersed in an international conspiracy that encompasses the Knights Templar, the Holy Grail, and the Milanese publishing community; exposed to the Diabolicals, a group of self-financing occult writers; combines computer technology with the numerology of the kabbalah to create the Plan, a system that uses a computer program to generate random connections between seemingly unconnected facts and thus to rewrite history; this enterprise endangers his life in Umberto Eco's *Foucault's Pendulum.*

Belbo Large slave who serves as a bodyguard and doorman for Gordianus, a Roman private investigator; remains unimaginative but utterly loyal to Gordianus in Steven Saylor's Rome Sub-Rosa series.

Belcampo, Pietro Old hairdresser who rescues Medardus from an angry mob in Frankenburg in E. T. A. Hoffmann's *The Devil's Elixir.*

Belch, Sir Toby Lady Olivia's rowdy and heavy drinking uncle who lives at her estate; tries unsuccessfully to marry Olivia off to his friend Sir Andrew Aguecheek; plays a cruel trick on Malvolio, Olivia's manservant; matched up later in love with Maria, Olivia's witty servant and a woman who desires to rise above her social class, in Shakespeare's *Twelfth Night.*

Belcher Big, good-natured Englishman held as a captured enemy spy or combatant during war; joyfully helps the old woman in whose house he is guarded by carrying water and chopping wood; enjoys playing cards and talking with his guards; unclear which side of the war he is on; learns that he is going to be immediately executed by the guards as a reprisal against the enemy's execution of their prisoners in Frank O'Connor's "Guests of a Nation."

Belcher, Carl Incompetent night foreman at the Past Bay Manufacturing Company factory who precipitates the strike in Robert Cantwell's *The Land of Plenty.*

Belcour Unscrupulous friend of Jack Montraville; convinces Montraville to desert Charlotte Temple on the claim that she is faithless; dies at the hands of Montraville when Montraville learns of the deception in Susanna Rowson's *Charlotte.*

Belcredi, Baron Tito Wealthy simpleton who accompanies the beautiful widow Marchioness Donna Matilda Spina; seeks an audience with the madman who believes himself to be Henry IV, the German king who reigned from 1065 to 1106; dresses in the period costume of a Benedictine monk, wearing the habit of the Abbey of Cluny in Luigi Pirandello's play *Henry IV.*

Belden, Amy Widow who helps Mary Leavenworth and Henry Clavering elope, and who hides the maid Hannah Chester after the murder of Horatio Leavenworth, in Anna Katharine Green's *The Leavenworth Case.*

Belden, Gilbert Partner with David Marshall in a wholesale grocery in Henry Blake Fuller's *With the Procession.*

Belden, Judy See Denton, Jennie.

Belfield, Duke of Admirer of Caroline Strike in George Meredith's *Evan Harrington.*

Belfield, Henrietta Sister of Mr. Belfield; she nurses him during his illness after his duel; she is befriended by Cecilia

Beverley; she secretly loves Mortimer Delvile but marries Mr. Arnott in the end in Frances Burney's *Cecilia.*

Belfield, Mr. Proud though poor brother of Henrietta; he changes his enthusiasms from literature to field labor, is seriously wounded in a duel with Sir Robert Floyer for Cecilia Beverley's attention, and is viewed by Mortimer Delvile as a rival in Frances Burney's *Cecilia.*

Belford, John ("Jack") Rakish principal confidant and chief correspondent of Lovelace but never an accessory to Lovelace's machinations; attending Clarissa Harlowe in her decline helps to effect his reformation; he becomes executor for both Clarissa and Lovelace in Samuel Richardson's *Clarissa: or, The History of a Young Lady.*

Belfounder, Hugo Entrepreneur businessman and patron of the performing arts who befriends Jake Donaghue at a common-cold research establishment and inspires *The Silencer,* Jake's philosophical treatise in dialogue; Hugo's disappointing romantic involvement with the sisters Anna and Sadie Quentin ends in his giving up his theatrical pursuits to become a watchmaker in Iris Murdoch's *Under the Net.*

Belfrage, Sir Henry The British ambassador to Argentina; he would like to be rid of Charley Fortnum, the Honorary Consul, but he offers some help to Dr. Eduardo Plarr when Charley is kidnapped in Graham Greene's *The Honorary Consul.*

Belgian Doctor with cold, hard eyes who works for Spain's republican army during that country's civil war (1936–39); takes copious notes of the condemned men's physical reactions and comments in the hours before their execution by a firing squad; questions the narrator and protagonist Pablo Ibbieta about his thoughts of death in Jean-Paul Sartre's "The Wall."

Belgrave, Lord Nobleman who dismisses Mr. Gifford as tutor to his bear when Mr. Gifford unwittingly lets the animal eat the latest delivery of butter in William Beckford's *Modern Novel Writing; or, the Elegant Enthusiast.*

Bel-Imperia Niece of the Spanish king and sister to Lorenzo; defies her father and brother by taking lower-status lovers; seeks revenge for the death of her lover Don Andrea by first taking a new lover, Don Horatio, then attempting to urge Hieronimo on to vengeance while she is imprisoned by Balthazar and Lorenzo, finally stabbing her lovers' killer, Balthazar, prince of Portingale, in a playlet created by Hieronimo in Thomas Kyd's play *The Spanish Tragedy.*

Belinda Subject of a letter from Cynthia to Camilla (Simple); she loves the married Philander; after inheriting money she supports him and his wife and then marries him after his wife dies in Sarah Fielding's *Familiar Letters between the Principal Characters of David Simple and Some Others.*

Belinda (Marie O'Neill) Movie star at Olympia Studios; married to Maurice Cassard in Ludwig Bemelmans's *Dirty Eddie.*

Belinda, Lady Jealous woman of fashion; she removes the beautiful Azemia from the duke's clutches because her matrimonial plans for the noble are threatened; she takes her to the house of Mr. and Mrs. Wildcodger in William Beckford's *Azemia.*

Belknap American man who manages the mill on the narrator's farm in Africa; his gun is found by the young boys, which, after a tragic accident, results in a death and serious injury in Isak Dinesen's *Out of Africa.*

Bell Proprietor of a sugar plantation in Taloo; married to a beautiful woman from Sydney in Herman Melville's *Omoo.*

Bell, Angelica Pretty five-year-old daughter of Vanessa Bell in Michael Cunningham's *The Hours.*

Bell, Anita Alcoholic wife of Steve Bell in Mary McGarry Morris's *A Dangerous Woman.*

Bell, Clara (Claribel) Anna Donne's older cousin, who has been part of the family since Anna's mother died in Ivy Compton-Burnett's *Elders and Betters.*

Bell, Clinton Harkavy Advertising executive and father of David Bell; figures prominently in his son's extended flashback in Don DeLillo's *Americana.*

Bell, David New York television producer who travels west with friends to make a documentary about the Navaho but becomes obsessed with a zany film of his own creation; narrator of Don DeLillo's *Americana.*

Bell, Diana Older daughter of a prominent Newport family who is about to elope with Hilary Jones, a married man, until Theophilus North manages to halt them in Thornton Wilder's *Theophilus North.*

Bell, Edwin Former headmaster of a foundling boys' school in Greenfield; he is one of the three men who provide commentary on the events in William Golding's *Darkness Visible.*

Bell, Francis Clergyman prevented by a rash youthful engagement from marrying his cousin, Helen Thistlewood (later Pendennis), to whose care he bequeaths his daughter, Laura (later Pendennis), in William Makepeace Thackeray's *The History of Pendennis.*

Bell, Gracie Baby half-sister of the young boys Cato and Emerson, who freeze to death, in Elizabeth Bishop's "The Farmer's Children."

Bell, Irene Actress who leaves Willie Spearmint for Harry Lesser in Bernard Malamud's *The Tenants.*

Bell, Jan Oldest daughter of Steve Bell; recently divorced and moved back in with her parents in Mary McGarry Morris's *A Dangerous Woman.*

Bell, Joe Lexington Avenue bartender who takes messages for Holly Golightly in Truman Capote's *Breakfast at Tiffany's.*

Bell, John Private, then sergeant, stationed in the Pacific; haunted by memories of his wife; receives news of his promotion to lieutenant the same day he learns of his wife's intention to leave him for another man in James Jones's *The Thin Red Line.*

Bell, Julian Grave, handsome 15-year-old son of Vanessa Bell; bluff, sturdy, and gracefully muscular in Michael Cunningham's *The Hours.*

Bell, Margaret Full professor of English at Moo University, the youngest full professor and most heavily recruited; African American; friends with Helen Levy and Timothy Monahan in Jane Smiley's *Moo.*

Bell, Mary Ann Fresh and innocent high school sweetheart of Mark Fossie, a medic in the Vietnam War; arrives in Vietnam to visit Fossie; becomes even more formidable than the Green Berets after accompanying them on several ambushes; eventually disappears into the Vietnam jungle in Tim O'Brien's *The Things They Carried.*

Bell, Mr. Old friend of Mr. Hale and godfather to Margaret Hale; her inheritance of his wealth enables her to save John Thornton and marry him in Elizabeth Gaskell's *North and South.*

Bell, Patsy Youngest daughter of Steve Bell; recently divorced; a high-school French teacher in Hanover, New Hampshire, who has sublet her apartment and moved back in with her parents in Mary McGarry Morris's *A Dangerous Woman.*

Bell, Quentin Ruddy young son of Vanessa Bell in Michael Cunningham's *The Hours.*

Bell, Steve Husband of Anita Bell, longtime attorney and lover of Frances Beecham; always eager to smooth out any discord in Mary McGarry Morris's *A Dangerous Woman.*

Bell, Vanessa Loving sister of Virginia Woolf; voluptuous and spirited in Michael Cunningham's *The Hours.*

Bella Dark-haired lesbian prostitute who enthusiastically tattoos and tortures Peter Leland in Fred Chappell's *Dagon.*

Bella (Belle) Brill Daughter of Clothilde Wright and cousin of Jim Calder; makes opportunistic marriages with Joe Stowe and Allen Southby in John P. Marquand's *Wickford Point.*

Belladonna Female piglet in Ludwig Bemelmans's *Dirty Eddie.*

Bellagambia Former fascist and now a café and hotel keeper in Ferrara, Italy, in Giorgio Bassani's *The Heron.*

Bellair, Lady Great society hostess in Benjamin Disraeli's *Henrietta Temple: A Love Story.*

Bellairs, Harry D. Disreputable San Francisco attorney, who bids against Jim Pinkerton as agent for Norris Carthew; he becomes friends with Loudon Dodd on a ship to Europe as he tracks Carthew in Robert Louis Stevenson's *The Wrecker.*

Bellairs, Mrs. Member of the spy ring "The Free Mothers"; fronting as a fortune teller and medium, she passes along information through specific clients in Graham Greene's *The Ministry of Fear.*

Bellairs, Mrs. Wife of Harry D. Bellairs and daughter of the man who ruined Bellairs's family; she is still supported by Bellairs though she ran off with a drummer after two years of marriage in Robert Louis Stevenson's *The Wrecker.*

Bellamont Placentia's brother, who was thought to be dead but instead was castrated by the Bashaw, thus becoming the Christian Eunuch; he is rescued by Philidore in Eliza Haywood's *Philidore and Placentia; or, L'Amour trop delicat.*

Bellamont, George, Duke of Doting but unworldly and socially reclusive father of Tancred, Lord Montacute; he and his wife have spent most of their lives on their country estate and do not understand their son's need to find spiritual fulfillment during a tour through the Holy Land in Benjamin Disraeli's *Tancred; or, The New Crusade.*

Bellamont, Katherine, Duchess of Wife of the duke and mother of Tancred, Lord Montacute in Benjamin Disraeli's *Tancred; or, The New Crusade.*

Bellamy, Camilla Divorced wife of Edward Bellamy; she is a femme fatale who pursues Sir Godfrey Haslem when his wife dies, but she becomes engaged to the richer lawyer Dominic Spong in Ivy Compton-Burnett's *Men and Wives.*

Bellamy, Edward Rector of the Haslams' parish; he is a nervous, self-dramatizing man, who divorces Camilla, proposes to Griselda Haslam and, after the Haslam family scandals, proposes to Kate Dabis in Ivy Compton-Burnett's *Men and Wives.*

Bellamy, Mr. Farmer, friend, and customer of Mr. Furze; he is owner of Chapel Farm, where Catharine Furze likes to visit, in Mark Rutherford's *Catharine Furze.*

Bellamy, Mrs. Childless wife of Mr. Bellamy and friend of Catharine Furze; she nurses Catharine in her mortal illness in Mark Rutherford's *Catharine Furze.*

Bellamy, Tessa Ailing upper-class Englishwoman who, accompanied by her young cousin, Sydney Warren, is wintering at a resort in northern Italy favored by the British in Elizabeth Bowen's *The Hotel.*

Bellantoni, Alice Daughter of Polina Bellantoni in Rita Mae Brown's *Rubyfruit Jungle.*

Bellantoni, Polina Columbia University professor, mother of Alice Bellantoni, and lover of Paul Digita and Molly Bolt in Rita Mae Brown's *Rubyfruit Jungle.*

Bellarmin, Cardinal Works in Rome; critical of Galileo for his heresy against the Catholic church; charged by the pope to caution Galileo to abandon his unorthodox teachings; calls Galileo's writings that the Earth revolves around the Sun, thus displacing humankind from the center of God's creation, foolish in Bertolt Brecht's play *Galileo.*

Bellarmine French lord whose European dress and manners capture Leonora's heart away from Horatio; Bellarmine abandons her when her father refuses to offer an advantageous dowry in Henry Fielding's *The History of the Adventures of Mr. Joseph Andrews and of His Friend Mr. Abraham Adams.*

Bellaston, Lady Sophia Western's distant relative, with whom Sophia takes shelter in London; having started an affair with Tom Jones, and wanting to dispose of Sophia, she encourages Lord Fellamar to rape her so she will more readily accept his marriage proposal; Tom's proposal of marriage to Lady Bellaston has the desired effect of causing her to break with him in outrage; she actively plots his ruin in Henry Fielding's *The History of Tom Jones.*

Bellby, Mr. Junior barrister who works with Dreamer, Q.C., on Winifred Dartie's divorce case in John Galsworthy's *In Chancery.*

Belle Dowerless sweetheart of Ebenezer Scrooge; she releases him from their engagement because of his "master passion, Gain," and is later seen as a comely matron with a loving family in Charles Dickens's *A Christmas Carol.*

Belle, Blondy Former moll and girlfriend of Little Arnie Worch; takes up with Rico Bandello and alerts him to Arnie's cheating on Rico in William Riley Burnett's *Little Caesar.*

Belle, La Isold Lover of Tristram; dies when his body is found in Thomas Berger's *Arthur Rex.*

Bellegarde, Celestine Raised politician Primus Mackenzie; has little regard for his wife in Paule Marshall's *Daughters.*

Bellegarde, Claire de See Cintré, Claire de Bellegarde de.

Bellegarde, Emmeline de Murderer of her husband and mother of Claire de Cintré; opposes the marriage of Claire and Christopher Newman in Henry James's *The American.*

Bellegarde, Henri-Urbain de Husband of Emmeline de Bellegarde and father of Claire, Urbain, and Valentin de Bellegarde; murdered by his wife and Urbain because he opposed Claire's first marriage in Henry James's *The American.*

Bellegarde, Madame Urbain de Unhappily married wife of Urbain de Bellegarde; encourages Christopher Newman's suit of Claire de Cintré in Henry James's *The American.*

Bellegarde, Urbain de Eldest son of Emmeline de Bellegarde, with whom he plots to kill his father; despises Christopher Newman in Henry James's *The American.*

Bellegarde, Valentin de Younger brother of Urbain de Bellegarde and friend of Christopher Newman; killed by Stanislas Kapp in a duel over Noémie Nioche in Henry James's *The American.*

Bellenden, Edith Granddaughter of Lady Margaret Bellenden; she loves Henry Morton, becomes engaged to Lord Evandale (William Maxwell) after she believes Morton is dead, and marries Morton after the death of Lord Evandale in Sir Walter Scott's *Old Mortality.*

Bellenden, Lady Margaret Mistress of Tillietudlem and a strong Jacobite, whose castle is the site of battles between Cameronian rebels and Royalist soldiers; driven out during the wars, she loses her estate to her villainous turncoat cousin Basil Olifant and lives on charity until his death in Sir Walter Scott's *Old Mortality.*

Bellenden, Major Miles Uncle of Edith Bellenden and brother-in-law of Lady Margaret Bellenden; he pleads to Francis Stewart, Sergeant Bothwell, for the life of Henry Morton and leads in the defense of Tillietudlem against the Cameronian rebels in Sir Walter Scott's *Old Mortality.*

Beller, Harry Former toastmaster converted to temperance, mentioned in the "Report of the Committee of the United Grand Junction Ebeneezer Temperance Association," in Charles Dickens's *The Posthumous Papers of the Pickwick Club.*

Bellerophon King of Lycia and slayer of the Chimera; must leave his city and assume an artificial identity in the *Bellerophoniad,* a novella in John Barth's *Chimera.*

Bellette, Amy (Anne Frank) Librarian and former student of E. I. Lonoff; wants Lonoff to leave his wife and live with her in Italy; becomes the second wife, and later widow, of Lonoff; urges Zuckerman to stop the publication of Lonoff's biography; imagined by Nathan Zuckerman to be Anne Frank in Philip Roth's *The Ghost Writer.*

Bellew, Captain Jaspar Landowner and neighbor of the Pendyces; he sues his wife for divorce, naming George Pendyce as co-respondent, and drops his suit after appeal from Margery Pendyce in John Galsworthy's *The Country House.*

Bellew, Clare (Kendry) Irene's childhood friend; passes for white and travels widely with her wealthy and racist white husband and their white-appearing daughter; has a "having" way about her and courts danger in her desire to be reunited with fellow African Americans while her husband is away on business; ingratiates herself into Irene's family and social circle; dies when she falls, jumps, or is pushed out a window after her husband discovers her true identity in Nella Larsen's *Passing.*

Bellew, Helen Wife of Captain Bellew; she is separated from her husband and is sued for divorce with George Pendyce as co-respondent; she ceases to care for George and leaves him in John Galsworthy's *The Country House.*

Bellew, John (Jack) Clare's husband and a wealthy businessman; racist who claims not to know any African Americans; jokingly and ironically calls his wife "Nig"; discovers the truth when he surprises Clare at a Harlem party, where she subsequently dies in Nella Larsen's *Passing.*

Bellew, Margery Daughter of John Bellew and Clare Kendry; attends boarding school in Switzerland in Nella Larsen's *Passing.*

Bellfield, Captain Gustavus Flashy suitor of Mrs. Greenow, who chooses his raffish charm over the stolidity of Samuel Cheesacre and marries him in Anthony Trollope's *Can You Forgive Her?*

Bellfleur, Count de Fickle Venetian lover of Melanthe; he transfers his affections to Louisa just as he wins Melanthe in Eliza Haywood's *The Fortunate Foundlings.*

Belli, Paola Lucrezia Beautiful, thirtyish, Italian still photographer; separated from her Jamaican husband, she meets Ronald Beard at a Hollywood party and becomes his lover in Anthony Burgess's *Beard's Roman Women.*

Bellinetti, Arturo Effusive office assistant to Sidney Arthur Ferning, later to Nick Marlow; an agent of OVRA (Italian secret police), he spies on Marlow and is responsible for the assault on him in Eric Ambler's *Cause for Alarm.*

Belling, Oscar Julian Baffin's art-student boyfriend; Julian destroys his letters but eventually marries him in Iris Murdoch's *The Black Prince.*

Bellingham Governor of Massachusetts Bay who wants to take Pearl from her mother, Hester Prynne, in Nathaniel Hawthorne's *The Scarlet Letter.*

Bellingham, Henry Upper-class seducer of Ruth Hilton; he is maneuvered by his mother into abandoning her while he is ill and she is pregnant; having taken the name Donne as a condition of inheriting wealth, he becomes Member of Parliament for Ecclestone; he reencounters Ruth, who repulses him but nurses him during a cholera epidemic; he recovers, but Ruth is infected and dies in Elizabeth Gaskell's *Ruth.*

Bellingham, Mrs. Mother of Henry Bellingham; she takes advantage of his illness to drive the pregnant Ruth Hilton away in Elizabeth Gaskell's *Ruth.*

Bellini, Louis (Schemer) Family man who leads a double life; dies from a gunshot wound suffered in a robbery in William Riley Burnett's *The Asphalt Jungle.*

Bellipine Jemmy Jessamy's best friend, who is very poor; he has no honor and manipulates everyone in Eliza Haywood's *The History of Jemmy and Jenny Jessamy.*

Bellman, Christopher Scholar and antiquarian; the widowed father of Frances, he is in love with Millie Kinnard, whom he assists financially and to whom he becomes briefly engaged; though apolitical, he is killed by a sniper in the 1916 Easter Rising in Iris Murdoch's *The Red and the Green.*

Bellman, Frances Anglo-Irish girl, Christopher Bellman's daughter; though everyone expects her to marry Andrew Chase-White, when his proposal comes she turns it down, being in love with her first cousin Pat Dumay in Iris Murdoch's *The Red and the Green.*

Bellmann, John R. (Boss) Politician elected on a reform platform and later murdered in Paul Cain's *Fast One.*

Bellmont, James Abolitionist sympathizer who befriends Frado; business associate of his brother, Lewis Bellmont, and husband of Susan Bellmont; dies after a lingering illness in Harriet E. Wilson's *Our Nig.*

Bellmont, Jane Invalid daughter of John and Mrs. Bellmont; marries George Means against her mother's will in Harriet E. Wilson's *Our Nig.*

Bellmont, Jenny Young woman from a poor family in the West; marries Jack Bellmont and suffers the hatred and lies of her mother-in-law, Mrs. Bellmont, in Harriet E. Wilson's *Our Nig.*

Bellmont, John Kind patriarch of the Bellmont family who tries to protect Frado from the cruelty of Mrs. Bellmont in Harriet E. Wilson's *Our Nig.*

Bellmont, John (Jack) Youngest son of John and Mrs. Bellmont; befriends Frado (Alfrado), a girl of mixed race indentured to his family, and defies his mother and sister on her behalf, claiming her as his protegé; husband of Jenny Bellmont in Harriet E. Wilson's *Our Nig.*

Bellmont, Lewis Son of John and Mrs. Bellmont; lives in Baltimore, where he is associated in business first with his brother James and later with his brother Jack in Harriet E. Wilson's *Our Nig.*

Bellmont, Mary Younger daughter of John and Mrs. Bellmont; follows her mother's example in tormenting Frado, whom Mary attempts to kill by hurling a knife at her, in Harriet E. Wilson's *Our Nig.*

Bellmont, Mrs. Tyrannical and sadistic persecutor of Frado; professed Christian and wife of John Bellmont in Harriet E. Wilson's *Our Nig.*

Bellmont, Susan Descendant of a wealthy Baltimore family; wife of James Bellmont in Harriet E. Wilson's *Our Nig.*

Bellmour, Sir George Charles Glanville's rakish friend; loved by Charlotte Glanville, he competes with Glanville in wooing Arabella by inventing romances; he reforms when Glanville stabs him nearly to death in a jealous rage; he buys the Glanvilles' forgiveness by agreeing to marry Charlotte in Charlotte Lennox's *The Female Quixote.*

Bello Humpbacked ruler of Dominora in Herman Melville's *Mardi.*

Bello Son of M'Bali Nènè in *Sundiata: An Epic of Old Mali.*

Belloni, Emilia Alessandra (Sandra) A pure, half-Italian singer; her friends the Poles, her patron Pericles, and even her father try to exploit her financially and socially; only Merthyr Powys remains true, rescuing her from suicide and arranging for her to go to Italy to study music; she vows to grow to love him in George Meredith's *Emilia in England.* Involved with the struggle for Italian liberation from Austria, she changes her name to Vittoria Campa; her revolutionary efforts are hindered by her loyalties to the Poles and by Pericles; she marries a patriot, Carlo Ammiani, who dies in a failed revolt; she names their son after him and Merthyr, whom she perhaps marries at last in *Vittoria.*

Belloni, Mr. Emilia Belloni's father, an Italian revolutionary and a violinist, who tries to arrange a mercenary marriage for Emilia, causing her to run away; he later tries to help Pericles send her to Italy to study music in George Meredith's *Emilia in England.*

Belloni, Mrs. Emilia Belloni's good-hearted mother in George Meredith's *Emilia in England* and in *Vittoria.*

Belloussovsky-Dommergues, Mildred Often-married writer seated next to Henry Bech at his induction ceremony in John Updike's *Bech: A Book.*

Bellows, Alf and Mrs. Couple who run the boardinghouse where Aleck Maury resides while he is in Florida in

Caroline Gordon's "To Thy Chamber Window, Sweet" and *Aleck Maury, Sportsman.*

Bellows, Dr. Director of the Entrenationo Language Centre in London, where D. meets his contact in Graham Greene's *The Confidential Agent.*

Bellozane, Chevalier de George Godolphin's Swiss cousin, who is attracted to Emmeline Mobray during her stay with Lord and Lady (Augusta Delamere) Westerhaven at his father's chateau; no rebuff can check his importunities; he follows Emmeline to England, where a liaison with Lady Frances Crofts ends when he kills Frederic Delamere in a duel in Charlotte Smith's *Emmeline: The Orphan of the Castle.*

Belmont, Evelina Anville Seventeen-year-old daughter of Sir John Belmont; she is not acknowledged by her father until he is forced to recognize her mother in her features; she falls in love with Lord Orville, saves Mr. Macartney from suicide, and marries Orville after her reconciliation with Sir John in Frances Burney's *Evelina.*

Belmont, Lady Lady Julia Belmont's devoted and well-meaning mother in Frances Brooke's *The History of Lady Julia Mandeville.*

Belmont, Lady Julia Beautiful heroine of wealth, virtue, and sensibility; her mutual love for Henry Mandeville is supported by her parents and all seems well, but grief at the sudden death of Henry causes her immediate death from fever in Frances Brooke's *The History of Lady Julia Mandeville.*

Belmont, Lady Mary Elderly relative of both Belmonts and Mandevilles, once a member of Queen Mary's court; she bequeaths a fortune to Henry Mandeville, which facilitates jointure arrangements made secretly by their parents for Henry's marriage to Lady Julia Belmont in Frances Brooke's *The History of Lady Julia Mandeville.*

Belmont, Lord Descendant of ancient English nobility, a benevolent patriarch concerned with the Belmont lineage and securing fitting jointure arrangements for its continuance; he realizes the disastrous effects of his over-solicitude with the deaths of his daughter Julia and her beloved Henry Mandeville in Frances Brooke's *The History of Lady Julia Mandeville.*

Belmont, Sir John English baronet and the father of Evelina Anville Belmont, whom he refuses to acknowledge until he is forced to meet her; he joyously bestows an inheritance upon her when she marries in Frances Burney's *Evelina.*

Belmour, Miss Lady D-'s relation and Henrietta Courteney's employer; she confides to Henrietta her passion for a married man; she takes her advice to run away to Paris, where she promotes Henrietta to companion; there she resumes her illicit intrigue, forcing Henrietta to leave her service in Charlotte Lennox's *Henrietta.*

Beloe, Mr. Author of Arabian stories, who, though he likes to criticize the work of others, gets angry when his works are attacked in William Beckford's *Modern Novel Writing; or, the Elegant Enthusiast.*

Beloff, Esther Leonie Sensual daughter of the Reverend Marian Miles Beloff and the object of religious leader Nathan Vickery's tormented sexual attraction in Joyce Carol Oates's *Son of the Morning.*

Beloff, Reverend Marian Miles Exploitative, materialistic religious leader who employs the young Nathan Vickery in his ministry; father of Leonie Beloff in Joyce Carol Oates's *Son of the Morning.*

Belovar Faithful friend of the protagonist; epitomizes proximity to nature and its powers; follows his emotions and joins the protagonist's fight against the Oberförster in Ernst Jünger's *On the Marble Cliffs.*

Beloved Sethe's dead baby; returns eighteen years after her death and exhibits characteristics of a young child; occupies all of Sethe's time and energy; forces Paul D out of the house and seduces him; is exorcised by the women in the community in Toni Morrison's *Beloved.*

Belrose, Charles Hearty wholesaler of cheeses; he discovers the body of the miser Henry Earlforward by his open safe on the evening of his wife's death in hospital, and he discovers Earlforward's servant Elsie Sprickett hiding her beloved Joe upstairs in Arnold Bennett's *Riceyman Steps.*

Belrose, Mrs. Charles Large, jolly, compassionate wife of a cheesemaker; she willingly calls the hospital for news of Violet Earlforward for the servant Elsie Sprickett and is informed of Violet's death from undernourishment in Arnold Bennett's *Riceyman Steps.*

Belses, Lord Harry Eldest son of Lord Snowdoun, Minister of Scotland; he is made prisoner by Squire Cranmer, escapes, is injured, and finds succor in the home of the minister Mr. Blackstocks; he joins the Free Fishers and Wyse in saving the lives of the Prime Minister and Gabriel Cranmer, whom he loves and who, one day, will love him and marry him in John Buchan's *The Free Fishers.*

Belsey, Howard Liberal academic who specializes in Rembrandt and teaches art history at Wellington College; white male of British descent; lives in Wellington, Massachusetts, a small college town, with his family; his affair with his friend and colleague Claire Malcom leads to tension in his family in Zadie Smith's *On Beauty.*

Belsey, Jerome Belsey's eldest son; an undergraduate student at Brown; sensitive, intellectual, and inexperienced; a series of e-mails to his father after his brief engagement to Victoria Kipps results in an even greater enmity between the Kippses and the Belseys in Zadie Smith's *On Beauty.*

Belsey, Levi Belsey's youngest child; named after Primo Levi; embraces hip-hop culture and speaks with a Brooklyn accent; his interest in "low culture" as represented by hip-hop is at odds with the aesthetic sensibilities of the academic circle in which he was raised in Zadie Smith's *On Beauty.*

Belsey, Zora Intelligent and earnest young student at Wellington College who emulates her father; highly driven young woman; befriends Carl Thomas and encourages him to join Claire Malcom's poetry class in order to further her own agenda in Zadie Smith's *On Beauty.*

Belshazzar, Blessed Escaped rapist, leader of the sect of the Blessed Belshazzar, and father of Birchie Bartley in Hal Bennett's *A Wilderness of Vines.*

Belshue, A. M. Atheistic and freethinking jeweler and husband of Nessie Sutton; commits suicide in T. S. Stribling's *Teeftallow.*

Belsize (later Lord Highgate), Charles ("Jack") Aristocratic but impoverished suitor of Lady Clara Pulleyn, with whom he subsequently elopes after her unhappy marriage to Barnes Newcome and after he has succeeded to the title of Lord Highgate in William Makepeace Thackeray's *The Newcomes.*

Belt (Alonzo Fiber) Master of the dojo at the Sun N Fun motel in Florida in Harry Crews's *Karate Is a Thing of the Spirit.*

Beltane, Mrs. Blue-haired, smug suburban widow who fancies her grey poodle more than her grown children; she lives next door to Dulcie Mainwaring in Barbara Pym's *No Fond Return of Love.*

Beltane, Paul Shy young owner of a florist's shop who lives next door to Dulcie Mainwaring and becomes romantically interested in her niece Laurel in Barbara Pym's *No Fond Return of Love.*

Beltham, Dorothy Beautiful, sought-after, wealthy aunt of Harry Richmond; she consistently intercedes with her brother, Squire Beltham, in Harry's favor; it is revealed that she loves and supports Harry's profligate father, Richmond Roy, in George Meredith's *The Adventures of Harry Richmond.*

Beltham, Squire Rich, traditional grandfather of Harry Richmond and the direct opposite of his enemy Richmond Roy, the father of his grandson; he attempts to mold Harry in the Beltham image, but, losing patience with his grandson, disinherits him in George Meredith's *The Adventures of Harry Richmond.*

Belton, Bill Local pilot and neighbor to Spence and Lila Culpepper; expands Spence's horizons by planting marijuana in his cornfields and by taking Spence into his plane to fly over Spence's farm in Bobbie Ann Mason's *Spence and Lila.*

Belton, Mary Beloved crippled sister of Will, whose household she manages; she tries to befriend Clara Amedroz, with whom her brother is much in love, in Anthony Trollope's *The Belton Estate.*

Belton, Thomas Robert Lovelace's libertine friend, who is cruelly treated by his common-law wife and dies of consumption; his death helps to effect John Belford's reformation in Samuel Richardson's *Clarissa: or, The History of a Young Lady.*

Belton, Will Prosperous, industrious, unsophisticated landowner and farmer, who inherits Belton estate; meeting Clara Amedroz he instantly falls in love, but she keeps him at arm's length; when her fortunes decline he offers to give her Belton Castle; his loyalty and generosity finally win her heart in Anthony Trollope's *The Belton Estate.*

Beltrán, Irene Young, idealistic, and naïve journalist in revolutionary Chile; goes with Franciso Leal in search of the saintly young Evangelina, who has mysteriously disappeared; engaged to a military officer, a man described by Francisco as "the Bridegroom of Death"; leaves him, as she now loves Francisco; later discovers Evangelina's body in a mass grave, people murdered by brutal government officials; gunned down in the street for her discovery, but does not die despite her grave injuries; with Francisco is then forced to flee their country in Isabel Allende's *Of Love and Shadows.*

Beltrán, Lina Mother of Rafael; is sick and self-centered; monopolizes her son's time and does not like his teaching her cook how to read; enjoys being doted on in Sandra Benítez's *A Place Where the Sea Remembers.*

Beltrán, Rafael Forty-one-year-old schoolteacher; son of Lina, with whom he has lunch every day; teaches his mother's cook how to read; falls in love with and marries Esperanza Clemente in Sandra Benítez's *A Place Where the Sea Remembers.*

Belvawney, Miss Member of the Vincent Crummles Theatrical Company who seldom speaks in Charles Dickens's *The Life and Adventures of Nicholas Nickleby.*

Belvedere, Count of Unexceptionable suitor to Lady Clementina della Porretta; not suspecting her infatuation for himself, even Sir Charles Grandison pleads Belvedere's case; recovered from depression and madness, partly induced by cruel treatment, Clementina is looking at Belvedere with some favor and resignation at the end of Samuel Richardson's *Sir Charles Grandison.*

Belville, Colonel Recipient of Lady Anne Wilmot's correspondence and eventually of her hand in Frances Brooke's *The History of Lady Julia Mandeville.*

Bembo (Mowree) New Zealand harpooner who, as temporary captain of the *Julia,* tries to wreck the ship near Tahiti in Herman Melville's *Omoo.*

Bemis, Elijah Westlake (Lige) County attorney, federal judge, and protector of John Barclay's monopoly in William Allen White's *A Certain Rich Man.*

Bemis, Luther (Lute) Former partner of Jud Clasby; convicted and hanged for his part in the Indian massacre in Jessamyn West's *The Massacre at Fall Creek.*

Bemis, Ora (Ory) Wife of Luther Bemis in Jessamyn West's *The Massacre at Fall Creek.*

Bemish, Karl Amiable sixty-five-year-old operator of Franks, a birch beer stand outside of Haddam, New Jersey; runs a tight ship and enjoys offering advice to Frank Bascombe in Richard Ford's *Independence Day.*

Ben Drug supplier and friend of Arthur Ketcham in John Clellon Holmes's *Go.*

Ben Financier; European Jewish immigrant to the United States; Harvard educated; formerly married to Rachel, who divorced him; falls in love with Veronique Decaze, a married French woman who is the cousin of his best friend Jack; communicates his ambiguity about marrying her to Veronique; rejected by her, he commits suicide in Louis Begley's *The Man Who Was Late.*

Ben First husband of Deirdre in Bette Pesetky's *Midnight Sweets.*

Ben Large and menacing gangster whom Christina Goering meets in a bar; he deserts her in Jane Bowles's *Two Serious Ladies.*

Ben Mentally handicapped man who lives near the cottage to which Rebecca de Winter used to bring her lovers in Daphne Du Maurier's *Rebecca.*

Ben Name used for two slaves, designated big Ben and little Ben, who are opossum hunters in John Pendleton Kennedy's *Swallow Barn.*

Ben Phoebe's husband, who is the caretaker of Daniel Martin's country house, Thorncombe, in John Fowles's *Daniel Martin.*

Ben Refugee who has been rescued by Jahor from a whirlpool; afterwards he is unable to emerge from his state of shock in Doris Lessing's *Re: Colonised Planet 5, Shikasta.*

Ben Rough but straightforward sailor and Sir Sampson's younger son and intended heir; returns from sea to marry Miss Prue, Foresight's daughter; refuses to marry Prue, which spurs his father to pursue Angelica; rejected by Mrs. Frail when it appears he will not inherit in William Congreve's play *Love for Love.*

Ben Tough-talking hit man waiting for orders to kill; works with Gus in Harold Pinter's play *The Dumb Waiter.*

Ben Underling vociferously ordered by Long John Silver in pursuit of Black Dog, whom Jim Hawkins has spotted at the Spy Glass tavern in Robert Louis Stevenson's *Treasure Island.*

Ben (Old Ben) Slave and house servant of Moseley Sheppard in Arna Wendell Bontemps's *Black Thunder.*

Benally, Ben Friend and roommate of Abel in N. Scott Momaday's *House Made of Dawn.*

Benbacaio, Benboaro Disciple of Og of Basan; he follows his master into the deepest wilds but is abandoned by the tormented Og, who is reported dead by peasants shortly afterward in William Beckford's *Biographical Memoirs of Extraordinary Painters.*

Benbow, Albert Vulgar opportunist who marries Clara Clayhanger; he juggles false camaraderie and reluctant deference to her brother, Edwin, in Arnold Bennett's *Clayhanger.* His treatment of his children, his attempts to be noticed socially, and his financial incompetence cause Edwin to despise him in *These Twain.*

Benbow, Belle Mitchell Mother of Titania Mitchell, divorced from Harry Mitchell, and married to Horace Benbow; appears in William Faulkner's *Sartoris (Flags in the Dust)* and *Sanctuary.*

Benbow, Bert Cowed eldest son of Albert Benbow in Arnold Bennett's *These Twain.*

Benbow, Horace Attorney in William Faulkner's *Sartoris* (*Flags in the Dust*) and *Sanctuary.*

Benbow, Narcissa See Sartoris, Narcissa Benbow.

Bencomb, Marcia Young woman who meets Jocelyn Pierston when she is running away from her father; he immediately falls in love with her and jilts his betrothed, Avice Caro; perceiving that he is growing tired of her also, Marcia leaves him to return to her father; she eventually marries and, widowed, raises her husband's son, Henri Leverre; she nurses Jocelyn through a serious illness and they marry comfortably but without love in old age in Thomas Hardy's *The Well-Beloved.*

Bender, Cassie Much married and divorced art dealer; has affairs with painters in her shows; once lover of Major Wedburn in Dawn Powell's *The Golden Spur.*

Bender, George James Excellent wrestler who injures his knee as a sophomore at Iowa State and fails to win the Big Eight championship; beaten by Willard Buzzard because Edith Winter tries to seduce and humble Bender in John Irving's *The 158-Pound Marriage.*

Bendham, John, Viscount Neighbor of the elder William Norwynne; he dies from overindulgence in food and drink in Elizabeth Inchbald's *Nature and Art.*

Bendham, Lady Childless wife of Lord Bendham; after her husband's death she ruins herself by gambling in Elizabeth Inchbald's *Nature and Art.*

Bendish, Mr. Art dealer who collects indiscriminately, paying little but aiding young artists in George Moore's *A Modern Lover.*

Benditch, Lord Rose Cullen's father, an English coal magnate whom D. attempts to persuade into providing coal for his government in Graham Greene's *The Confidential Agent.*

Bendix, Albert F. Brother of H. W. and R. N. Bendix; famous for giving large tips in Henry Miller's *Black Spring.*

Bendix, H. W. Brother of Albert F. and R. N. Bendix; wealthy merchant who complains about the quality of merchandise and services in Henry Miller's *Black Spring.*

Bendix, R. N. Brother of Albert F. and H. W. Bendix; unable to visit the tailor shop because he has had his legs amputated in Henry Miller's *Black Spring.*

Bendrix, Maurice Middle-aged, jealous, cynical, self-absorbed, materialistic, intellectual, sexually proficient bachelor and professional writer; a former lover of Sarah Miles, he attempts to resurrect the affair after a two-year hiatus and after engaging a detective to follow Sarah; he asks the dead Sarah to help him avoid starting an affair with Sylvia Black; after the funeral, he moves in with Henry Miles and gradually begins to take care of him just as Sarah did as a means of expiation of guilt in Graham Greene's *The End of the Affair.*

Bend-the-Bow Courteous English archer in Sir Walter Scott's *Castle Dangerous.*

***Beneath the Red Banner,* Narrator** Story is told from the perspective of a Manchu boy in 1898 in the time of the Qing dynasty; born on a lucky day because that was the opportune day that the God of the Stove left for heaven to report the business of the household he had supervised during the whole year; his father serves as a soldier of the Chinese Red Banner, and the book's narrator is the youngest child of a poor family in Lao She's *Beneath the Red Banner.*

Benecia Wallin Barnes Wife of Solon Barnes and mother of five children, including Etta and Stewart Barnes, in Theodore Dreiser's *The Bulwark.*

Benecke, Father Priest excommunicated for his book and a friend of Edward Manisty; he befriends Eleanor Burgoyne and Lucy Foster in their self-imposed exile at Torre Amiata in the Italian hill country in Mrs. Humphry Ward's *Eleanor.*

Benedetto, Don Liberal priest and a former Catholic teacher in the Italian village of Rocca dei Marsi; prepares to celebrate his 75th birthday, but war with the Abyssinians was in the wind; poisoned at a mass he was officiating when he drank the sacramental wine in Ignazio Silone's *Bread and Wine.*

Benedick Braggart soldier in Don Pedro's company; spars verbally with Beatrice before being gulled into loving and proposing to her; vows revenge against his companion Claudio for besmirching Hero's reputation; pursues justice for Hero in William Shakespeare's play *Much Ado About Nothing.*

Benedict Saint and abbot of Cassino who takes the sick Basil into his monastery and gives him religious instruction in George Gissing's *Veranilda.*

Benedict, Alan Doctor in Piedmont, Arizona, who opens the Scoop VII satellite and unleashes the Andromeda Strain in Michael Crichton's *The Andromeda Strain.*

Benedict, Alice Kitty Weston's companion/governess, who falls in love with Edmund Weston and is disliked by Cynthia, Lady Weston; Alice is the third-person narrator of Isabel Colegate's *Statues in a Garden.*

Benedict, Father Priest in France who, when he hears how Maintenon has imprisoned Madam de Beaumont because of her religion, helps her escape and pays for her passage back to England in Penelope Aubin's *The Life of Madam de Beaumont.*

Benedict, Juana Wife of Jordy Benedict in Edna Ferber's *Giant.*

Benedict, Leslie Lynnton (Les) Wife of Bick Benedict and mother of Jordy Benedict and Luz Benedict II; forsakes her pleasant Virginia homestead for the rigors of rural Texas and the husband she loves in Edna Ferber's *Giant.*

Benedict (I), Luz Sister of Bick Benedict; manages the Reata household and helps oversee the ranch in Edna Ferber's *Giant.*

Benedict (II), Luz Daughter of Bick and Leslie Benedict in Edna Ferber's *Giant.*

Benedicta Apparently the illegitimate daughter of a hangman but actually the daughter of the Saltmaster and the hangman's wife; secretly loves Ambrosius, a monk, who murders her in Ambrose Bierce's adaptation of *The Monk and the Hangman's Daughter.*

Benedictine, Salvatore Monk and ex-member of the Dulcinian heresy; speaks a mixture of Latin and different vulgar languages; tried, tortured, and condemned by the inquisitor Bernard Gui in Umberto Eco's *The Name of the Rose.*

Benedict the Fourth, Jordan (Jordy) Son of Jordan and Leslie Benedict and husband of Juana Benedict; becomes a physician in Edna Ferber's *Giant.*

Benedict the Third, Jordan (Bick) Husband of Leslie Lynnton Benedict and father of Jordy Benedict and Luz Benedict II; manages Reata, the huge family cattle estate, in Edna Ferber's *Giant.*

Benefactor The Leader of society; elected unanimously every year in public ceremony; causes D-503 to confess his crimes to him in Evgeny Zamyatin's *We.*

Benenck, Laird Scottish neighbor and friend of Laird Douglas in Susan Ferrier's *Marriage.*

Benengeli, Cid Hamete Fictional Moorish writer and learned Arabic historian invented by Cervantes and listed as the author of the adventures of Don Quixote; serves as buffer to the real author of a "novel, a concept and a literary form not fully orthodox" in 1605 and 1615, when the book was written, in Miguel de Cervantes Saavedra's *Don Quixote de la Mancha.*

Benevento, Dr. Dr. Eduardo Plarr's only medical colleague in the northern Argentine city; he regularly "inspects" the girls at Senora Sanchez's brothel in Graham Greene's *The Honorary Consul.*

Benevolent Army Officer Elder brother of the Benevolent Naval Captain; he uses his own money to support his men and demonstrates that moral virtue is the best foundation for true heroism in Charles Johnstone's *Chrysal: or, The Adventures of a Guinea.*

Benevolent Naval Captain Virtuous and compassionate captain of a Man of War, who, concerned with his sailors and ship, runs his ship with interesting rules: no gaming, no cursing or swearing, no drunkenness in Charles Johnstone's *Chrysal: or, The Adventures of a Guinea.*

Benévolo, João Member the poor class who receives the frequent visit of the down-to-earth Ponciano; unemployed character who represents the great many have-nots in the society; offers a contrast to other characters through his dreamy romanticism in Erico Verissimo's *Crossroads.*

Bengston French character who feels alienated and constrained in the poverty of the ghettos of Paris in Mehdi Charef's *Tea in the Harem.*

Bengtsson Colonel's devoted servant who exposes the manipulative and sinister Jacob Hummel as a murderer and fraud in August Strindberg's play *The Ghost Sonata.*

Benham, Cleo Wife of Elmer Gantry and mother of their two children in Sinclair Lewis's *Elmer Gantry.*

Ben-Hur, Judah Young Jewish son of the deceased Prince Ben-Hur of Jerusalem; handsome, strong, devoted to his family; wrongly enslaved for a supposed assassination attempt by Messala, a friend-turned-enemy, who is a Roman subject; is delivered from slavery years later by a Roman tribune who was friends with his father, eventually becoming the man's legal heir; exacts revenge on Messala by defeating him in a chariot race; through much effort finds his long-lost mother and sister and has them cured of their lately-acquired leprosy by the young Jesus Christ, who he tries to save from death in Lew Wallace's *Ben-Hur: A Tale of the Christ.*

Ben-Hur, Tirzah Beautiful Jewish sister of Judah Ben-Hur; kind and guileless in her youth; is imprisoned with her mother by the Roman Messala after an unfortunate accident involving her brother; is stricken with leprosy while imprisoned for eight years; is eventually saved by agents of her brother and is cured of leprosy by a young Jesus Christ in Lew Wallace's *Ben-Hur: A Tale of the Christ.*

Beniform, Flora Howard Kirk's current lover; she makes a habit of going to bed with men who have troubled marriages in Malcolm Bradbury's *The History Man.*

Benignus Virtuous hero thwarted in his benevolence; he retires to a forest hermitage, where he dies, in S. J. Pratt's *Liberal Opinions upon Animals, Man, and Providence.*

Ben Israel, Nathan Jewish physician who lives near Templestowe; he helps Isaac of York gain entrance to Templestowe to try to ransom Rebecca in Sir Walter Scott's *Ivanhoe.*

Benito, Gabriel Ishmaelian governmental official engaged in an unsuccessful coup to overthrow the ruling Jackson family and set up a Soviet state in Evelyn Waugh's *Scoop.*

Benjamin See Eliezer, Benjamin.

Benjamin Well educated, formal post office clerk in Fada and friend of Johnson; although he tries to bring excitement to his life by stealing stamp monies, he rebukes Johnson for stealing from Gollup in Joyce Cary's *Mister Johnson.*

Benjamin, Abie Mary's husband and a retail magnate in Carlos Fuentes's *The Hydra Head.*

Benjamin, Dr. Practiced surgeon who is informed by Dr. Barnes that he has been replaced as the surgeon of a charity case by Dr. Leeds, the son of a senator; further learns that he is being fired due to cutbacks at the hospital, even though he has seniority; dismissed because he is Jewish; vows that he may get a job as a taxi driver to learn more about American ways in Clifford Odets's play *Waiting for Lefty.*

Benjamin, Little See Partridge, Mr.

Benjamin, Mr. Clerk to Valeria Brinton's late father; he gives her away at her marriage to Eustace Woodville (really Macallan), assists her in her investigations, and performs the important task of piecing together the scraps of the torn-up and long-discarded last letter of the poisoned Sara Macallan in Wilkie Collins's *The Law and the Lady.*

Benjamin, Mr. Junior partner in the firm of shady jewelers Harter and Benjamin, with whom Lady Eustace had dealings before her marriage; he engineers the theft of the Eustace necklace and is convicted of the crime in Anthony Trollope's *The Eustace Diamonds.*

Benjamin, Mrs. Maid at Wood Hill from Mount Sorrel in Isabel Colegate's *Agatha.*

Benjamin, Owen Married to Rose; father of Philip; director of admissions at private boys' school; hidden homosexual whose only outlet is pornographic movies; eventually reveals self to wife and gay son in David Leavitt's *The Lost Language of Cranes.*

Benjamin, Philip Son of Rose and Owen; edits romance novels; unsophisticated homosexual; falls in love with Eliot Abrams; later becomes lover of former college friend Brad Robinson; sympathetic when father reveals hidden homosexuality; becomes Brad's lover in David Leavitt's *The Lost Language of Cranes.*

Benjamin, Rose Married to Owen; mother of Philip; copy editor; comfortable marriage without passion leads to five-year affair with coworker; shocked by son's revelation of homosexuality; realizes before husband tells her he is hidden homosexual in David Leavitt's *The Lost Language of Cranes.*

Benjie School caretaker who informs the headmaster about the sexual acts committed by Miss Manning and Mr. Carew on school property in William Golding's *Free Fall.*

Benjulia, Dr. Nathan Specialist in diseases of the brain and nervous system; a gaunt, gloomy scientist, he performs secret chemical experiments on animals, expecting to achieve immortality through the publication of the fruits of his experiments; his only human affection is for the child Zoe Gallilee, whom he likes to tickle and in whose favor he makes his will; he commits suicide when his discoveries are pre-empted by Ovid Vere's book in Wilkie Collins's *Heart and Science.*

Benjulia, Lemuel Publisher's clerk with a reputation as a lazy sensualist; an antivivisectionist, he hates his brother, Nathan, who in turn holds him in contempt in Wilkie Collins's *Heart and Science.*

Benkowski, Casimir (Casey) Washed-up Polish boxer, minor hood, and Bruno (Lefty) Bicek's boxing manager in Nelson Algren's *Never Come Morning.*

Benlow, Judge Arranged the dissolution of the business partnership between Colonel Sartoris and Ben Redmond in William Faulkner's "An Odor of Verbena."

Benlow, Mrs. Mathematician of Maria Spence's caliber and even superior to Azora Burcot and Antonia Fletcher in Thomas Amory's *The Lift of John Buncle, Esq.*

Benn Young man who, while he appreciates the beauty of a woman, he does not understand the sexual pretexts he encounters in Saul Bellow's *More Die of Heartbreak.*

Benn, Martin Retired journalist; friend of Carlos Rueda; skeptic and realist; finds it difficult to believe in Carlos's gift of vision; narrates Carlos's story in Lawrence Thornton's *Imagining Argentina.*

Benner, Peaches (or Benez) Young neglected daughter of a prostitute in Maureen Howard's *Natural History.*

Bennerley, Lady Eva Sir Clifford Chatterley's imperious, elderly aunt; she is one of the Wragby Hall "mental-lifers" who condemn the "life of the body" and the "love-business" in D. H. Lawrence's *Lady Chatterley's Lover.*

Bennet, Carola Exploited woman of London who is forced into prostitution by her aunt, Mrs. Hunfleet, and sold to the rapist Cantalupe; she lives with the wealthy Irishman Frederic Dancer and is converted to Christianity by, and married to, Mr. Tench, a clergyman, in Thomas Amory's *The Life of John Buncle, Esq.*

Bennet, Catherine (Kitty) Silly, fretful Bennet sister, fourth of the five; she thinks of nothing but handsome officers in Jane Austen's *Pride and Prejudice.*

Bennet, Charley Molly Bennet's infant son; the Noble Lord feigns to dote on him in order to win Molly's trust in Henry Fielding's *Amelia.*

Bennet, Elizabeth Witty, intelligent, and clear-sighted heroine, second of the five Bennet sisters; she attracts the proud Mr. Darcy, refuses his first proposal of marriage, but eventually loses her initial prejudice against him and grows to love him in Jane Austen's *Pride and Prejudice.*

Bennet, Issachar Shaker missionary who helps Jerry Fowler rescue Norah Sharon in Walter D. Edmonds's *Erie Water.*

Bennet, Jane Sweet, good, and beautiful elder sister of Elizabeth; she loves and eventually marries the pleasant Mr. Bingley in Jane Austen's *Pride and Prejudice.*

Bennet, Lydia Vain, foolish, headstrong youngest of the Bennet sisters; at sixteen she elopes with George Wickham to London, where Mr. Darcy finds her and bribes Wickham to marry her in Jane Austen's *Pride and Prejudice.*

Bennet, Mary Bookish and pedantic, the plain Bennet sister, third of the five, in Jane Austen's *Pride and Prejudice.*

Bennet, Miss Head nurse to the Clare children; she is kind and interested in others in Ivy Compton-Burnett's *The Present and the Past.*

Bennet, Miss Servant of Mr. Monckton; her objection stops Cecilia Beverley's first attempt at marriage in Frances Burney's *Cecilia.*

Bennet, Molly Sorrowful young woman, friend to Mrs. Ellison; she reveals her history to Amelia Booth to warn her to shun the Noble Lord's masquerade; she marries Joe Atkinson and restores her fortunes in Henry Fielding's *Amelia.*

Bennet, Mr. Scholarly, ironic, and detached father of Elizabeth and her four sisters in Jane Austen's *Pride and Prejudice.*

Bennet, Mrs. Silly mother, whose goal in life is to marry off her five daughters in Jane Austen's *Pride and Prejudice.*

Bennet, Tom Impoverished clergyman and husband of Molly Bennet; he dies in financial ruin and misery after discovering Molly's seduction in Henry Fielding's *Amelia.*

Bennett Henry Carr's manservant who often expresses his opinions concerning world affairs during World War I in Tom Stoppard's play *Travesties.*

Bennett Communist Party leader who thinks Conder is following him, while Conder thinks the same of him in Graham Greene's *It's a Battlefield.*

Bennett Ship's boy who recovers from an attack of terror to become wholly possessed by his task of pouring out oil to quiet the waves engulfing the *Archimedes* during the hurricane in Richard Hughes's *In Hazard.*

Bennett, "Benny" Aging servant whose deranged religiosity is supposed harmless; she kills Freddy Hamilton's mother in Muriel Spark's *The Mandlebaum Gate.*

Bennett, Captain Captain of the flying boat who plans to retrieve a hoard of gold left hidden by Nazis at the end of World War II; he goes crazy when the money is found and shoots one of his crew as they load the gold; he is killed when the plane crashes in Alan Sillitoe's *The Lost Flying Boat.*

Bennett, Cuthbert (Couth) Friend of Fred Trumper; catches a venereal disease from Elsbeth Malkas; caretaker at the Pillsbury Estate, who eventually marries Sue Kunft Trumper and cares for Colm Trumper in John Irving's *The Water-Method Man.*

Bennett, Elizabeth Married woman who is separated from her husband; she has an affair with Colin Saville in David Storey's *Saville.*

Bennett, F. W. Industrialist and a patron to Warren Penfield whose house on Loon Lake brings Warren, Joe Patterson, and Clara Lukaks together and who remains an ambiguous symbol of glory and greed in E. L. Doctorow's *Loon Lake.*

Bennett, George Former army buddy of Jack Sellars; persuades Jack and Bebe Sellars to manage his property at Pickerel Beach in Doris Betts's *The River to Pickle Beach.*

Bennett, Lucinda Bailey Wife of F. W. Bennett and lover of Warren Penfield; she is a celebrated aviatrix but crashes into the ocean with Penfield after they have planned to fly away together in E. L. Doctorow's *Loon Lake.*

Bennett, Mr. Father of Sarah and of Louise Halifax in Margaret Drabble's *A Summer Bird-Cage.*

Bennett, Mrs. Mother of Sarah and of Louise Halifax in Margaret Drabble's *A Summer Bird-Cage.*

Bennett, Mrs. Rose Cullen's childhood nurse; she refuses to help D. when he seeks her out in Benditch in Graham Greene's *The Confidential Agent.*

Bennett, Sarah (Sal) Intellectual and pretty sister of the bride Louise Bennett Halifax; she is at loose ends after graduating from Oxford and waiting for her fiancé to return from America; she finally acquires a sense of self separate from the personality and powers of her sister in Margaret Drabble's *A Summer Bird-Cage.*

Bennett, Sue Kunft Trumper (Biggie) Mother, by her husband Fred Trumper, of Colin Trumper; divorces Trumper and marries Cuthbert Bennett in John Irving's *The Water-Method Man.*

Bennett, Ward Arctic explorer who courts Lloyd Searight, contributing to the death of Richard Ferriss as he does so, in Frank Norris's *A Man's Woman.*

Benno of Uppsala Benedictine monk from Scandinavia; a copyist of rhetoric texts appointed assistant librarian after Berengar's death in Umberto Eco's *The Name of the Rose.*

Benoit, Charles Blue-eyed daredevil who is up to every trick; traveled the Far East on merchant ships and smoked opium; knows many novels and relates them in fascinating ways; remains unperturbed when his and Herbert's escape from the training camp is discovered and he is arrested in Ernst Jünger's *Afrikanische Spiele.*

Bensey, Lov Railroad coal chute worker whose child wife, Pearl Lester Bensey, abandons him in Erskine Caldwell's *Tobacco Road.*

Bensey, Pearl Lester Daughter of Ada Lester; abandons her husband, Lov Bensey, in Erskine Caldwell's *Tobacco Road.*

Bensheng Shuyu's brother and Lin Kong's greedy brother-in-law; lives in Goose Village in Ha Jin's *Waiting.*

Bensington, Mr. Timid, nervous scientist, who is both hailed and reviled as the inventor of herakleophorbia, the growth-inducing compound commonly called Boomfood; he first enjoys and then endures his notoriety, and he retires to a Tunbridge Wells sanitorium after a mob attempts to assassinate him in H. G. Wells's *The Food of the Gods, and How It Came to Earth.*

Benskin, Ted Barrister who leads in the defense of Cora Ross in C. P. Snow's *The Sleep of Reason.*

Benson Butler for the Huntingdons at Grassdale Manor, who is loyal to the family despite Arthur Huntingdon's abuses in Anne Brontë's *The Tenant of Wildfell Hall.*

Benson, Bob Friend of Jule Jackson in New York; helps Jule become a printer's apprentice in George Wylie Henderson's *Jule.*

Benson, Faith Thurstan Benson's sister, who helps him rescue Ruth Hilton; she is the practical support of the household during Ruth's progress and later trouble in Elizabeth Gaskell's *Ruth.*

Benson, George Murderer of Folded Leaf; convicted and hanged in Jessamyn West's *The Massacre at Fall Creek.*

Benson, Harold Franklin (Harry) Computer scientist upon whom the stage-three operation is performed in Michael Crichton's *The Terminal Man.*

Benson, Mrs. Disagreeable employer of Anne Meredith; she dies after consuming hat paint instead of Syrup of Figs in Agatha Christie's *Cards on the Table.*

Benson, Sir Harry Miss Walton's purported betrothed, according to a rumor that proves to be false in Henry Mackenzie's *The Man of Feeling.*

Benson, Steven (Chuckie, Dandy, Steve, Stevie) Narrator and central character in Ed Bullins's *The Reluctant Rapist.*

Benson, Thurstan Crippled dissenting minister of Ecclestone, who provides a home for Ruth Hilton and her son by Henry Bellingham; he stands by her when her past is discovered and the wealthy Mr. Bradshaw withdraws the financial support for his ministry; his help when Bradshaw's son gets into trouble assists the reconciliation in Elizabeth Gaskell's *Ruth.*

Benson, Walter Arlis See Boyle, Walter.

Bent, Bill Husband of Karen Michaelis's Aunt Violet in Elizabeth Bowen's *The House in Paris.*

Bent, Elkanah Officer in the Union Army; has a grudge against Orry Main and George Hazard that reaches back to their days together at West Point and will do anything to exact his revenge in John Jakes's *Love and War.*

Bent, Elspeth (Aunt Jetty) Granddaughter of Jess and Eliza Birdwell and daughter of Mattie Birdwell and Gardiner Bent in Jessamyn West's *The Friendly Persuasion* and *Except for Me and Thee.*

Bent, Gardiner (Gard) Fiancé and then husband of Mattie Birdwell in Jessamyn West's *The Friendly Persuasion* and *Except for Me and Thee.*

Bent, Mattie See Birdwell, Martha Truth.

Bent, Violet Cork relative with whom Karen Michaelis takes refuge while she tries to sort out her ambivalent feelings about her engagement to Ray Forrestier; Violet's serious illness and pending surgery increase Karen's feeling that before she marries she must know more about life in Elizabeth Bowen's *The House in Paris.*

Bentein Sira Eirik's grandson who accosts the 15-year-old protagonist, Kristin Lavransdatter, but fails to sexually harm her; later kills Arne Grydson, a friend of Kristsin's, in Sigrid Undset's *Kristin Lavransdatter.*

Bentham, Julia Divorced distant relative and companion of Emily Watson; beautiful and intelligent, she attracts Hubert Price but refuses his proposals out of loyalty to Emily; in desperation at Emily's tyranny, she and Hubert flee to London, where their marriage is shadowed by news of Emily's suicide in George Moore's *Vain Fortune.*

Bentham, Lucy Wealthy landowner who decides to sponsor Lewis Seymour's career; she is discreetly but deeply in love with him and jealous of Lady Helen Seely, who marries him; she becomes friends with the couple and later shares Lady Helen's recognition of Seymour's weak character in George Moore's *A Modern Lover.*

Bentham, Mr. Lucy Bentham's caddish husband, who lives in Paris and will not give her a divorce; hearing Paris gossip, he blackmails her in George Moore's *A Modern Lover.*

Bentham, Mr. Justice Judge who decides the case brought by Soames Forsyte against Philip Bosinney in John Galsworthy's *The Man of Property.*

Bentinck, Lord William British Minister in Palmero in C. S. Forester's *Hornblower and the Atropos.*

Bentley, Delia Thirty-year-old daughter of Henry; she is kind to her younger stepbrothers in Ivy Compton-Burnett's *Pastors and Masters.*

Bentley, Henry Father of two boys at Mr. Herrick's school; he berates and badgers his sons and daughter Delia in Ivy Compton-Burnett's *Pastors and Masters.*

Bentley, Horace Generous friend of the poor after being ruined by Eldon Parr in Winston Churchill's *The Inside of the Cup.*

Bentley, Jesse Son of Tom Bentley; assumes responsibility for the Bentley farm after his father's retirement; injured by his grandson David Hardy in Sherwood Anderson's *Winesburg, Ohio.*

Bentley, Katherine Wife of Jesse Bentley; dies giving birth to Louise Bentley in Sherwood Anderson's *Winesburg, Ohio.*

Bentley, Louise See Hardy, Louise Bentley.

Benton, Henry Young neighbor boy who tells Elizabeth that she has remained a child far too long in Peter Taylor's "A Spinster's Tale."

Benton, John Older cousin of the 10-year-old Robert Josiah Benton; while studying at Harvard, looks in on his young relative in a nearby boarding school; writes Josiah's father that the boy is in ill health and at his young age should be given a reprieve from his studies so that he might return home to see his mother in Mary Ladd Gavell's "The Rotifer."

Benton, Josiah Patriarch and state treasurer in the 1840s in the South; rigid, stern, and ambitious scion who dominates his wife and son in Mary Ladd Gavell's "The Rotifer."

Benton, Lizzie Wife of Josiah; frail woman who lacks the fortitude to speak her own mind in the home due to her husband's domineering nature in Mary Ladd Gavell's "The Rotifer."

Benton, Nat Stockbroker who advises Charley Anderson, allowing him to garner enough of stock in Askew-Merritt to sell out his senior partner, Joe Askew; Benton supplies Anderson with tips throughout the market boom in John Dos Passos's *U.S.A.* trilogy.

Benton, R. B. "Arby" Short, eleven-year-old African-American seventh-grader and computer genius; best friend of Kelly Curtis; student assistant of Richard Levine; stowaway onboard RV laboratory trailer destined for dinosaur-infested Costa Rican jungle in Michael Crichton's *The Lost World.*

Benton, Robert Josiah Son of Josiah and Lizzie; at age 10 he is sent away by his father from his home in the South to a school in Massachusetts to become a scholar and gentleman; through letters, the boy relates his hard work in Latin and other studies and that he greatly misses his mother and sister in Mary Ladd Gavell's "The Rotifer."

Benton, Sheila Health and beauty editor for *Vogue* magazine who is obsessed by her passion for Ambrose Clay in Gail Godwin's *Violet Clay.*

Bentson, Billy Small-time Dallas gambler and friend of Mabry Jenkins; reaches the big time by taking Junior Everett for several hundred thousand dollars in Peter Gent's *Texas Celebrity Turkey Trot.*

Bentwich, Jasper Rather cynical esthete who spends time at Lady Nelly Staveley's Venetian palazzo; he befriends Eustace Cherrington and provides commentary on the characters in L. P. Hartley's *Eustace and Hilda.*

Bentworth, Wilfred Old Squire who accepts the chairmanship of Michael Mont's committee for slum clearance in John Galsworthy's *Swan Song.* He is chairman of Hilary Cherrell's slum-conversion committee in *Maid in Waiting.*

Benvolio Cousin of Romeo; acts as his friend and advocate; his name suggests good will, even though he is allegedly as quick to quarrel as most of the other young men in Verona in William Shakespeare's play *Romeo and Juliet.*

Benvolio, Madame la Duchesse French countess, who makes her living preying on male travelers; John Jorrocks becomes a victim of her charms in Robert Surtees's *Jorrocks's Jaunts and Jollities.*

Benway, Dr. (Doc) Mad scientist and surgeon; manipulator and coordinator of symbol systems and expert in all phases of interrogation, brainwashing, and control; director of the Reconditioning Center in William S. Burroughs's *Naked Lunch;* also appears in *Nova Express, The Soft Machine,* and *Exterminator!*

Benwick, Captain James Shy poetry lover, mourning the death of his betrothed; Anne Elliot's suspicion that he is not immune to consolation is borne out by his engagement to Louisa Musgrove in Jane Austen's *Persuasion.*

Benyon, Tegwen Oldest of seven children of impoverished parents; she encourages Huw Morgan to witness the birth of her mother's child in Richard Liewehlyn's *How Green Was My Valley.*

Benziger, Natalie See Eaton, Natalie Benziger.

Beppo Merthyr Powys's servant, who ministers to the wounded Powys in George Meredith's *Emilia in England.* He acts also on behalf of Vittoria Campa in *Vittoria.*

Ber, Zeydel (Reb Zeydel) Ritual slaughterer, widower, uncle of Rechele Babad, and son-in-law of Granny; provides food, clothing, and shelter for Rechele until his death in Isaac Bashevis Singer's *Satan in Goray.*

Beragon (Bergoni), Montgomery (Monty) Polo-playing lover and later husband of Mildred Pierce; wastes Mildred's money and betrays her by sleeping with her daughter, Veda Pierce, in James M. Cain's *Mildred Pierce.*

Berbelang Leader of the Third World group that returns art from Western museums to its true owners; killed by Biff Musclewhite in Ishmael Reed's *Mumbo Jumbo.*

Bercy, Marquis René-Victor de French nobleman engaged to Thérèse de Fontenay in H. L. Davis's *Harp of a Thousand Strings.*

Berczynskas, Marija Cousin of Ona Rudkus; lends money to Jurgis Rudkus to buy a house; becomes a prostitute to support the family in Upton Sinclair's *The Jungle.*

Berdoe, Robert London ironmonger and relative of Mrs. Cardew; he employs Tom Catchpole upon the Reverend Theophilus Cardew's recommendation in Mark Rutherford's *Catharine Furze.*

Bere Old farmer who is a distant relative of the Forsyte family in John Galsworthy's *Swan Song.*

Beregond Human friend whom Pippin Took rescues in J. R. Tolkien's *The Two Towers.*

Bereket, Agha Rifaat Mohammadan friend of the protagonist Gabriel Bagradian in Turkey in 1915; warns Gabriel that rich Armenians will be persecuted by the government in Franz Werfel's *The Forty Days of Musa Dagh.*

Berengar of Arundel Benedictine monk and assistant librarian who knows the secrets of the forbidden manuscripts kept in the abbey's library; has a homosexual affair with fellow monk Adelmo; is found dead in Umberto Eco's *The Name of the Rose.*

Berengaria, Queen Queen of England, wife of King Richard; on pilgrimage to the Holy Land while he fights in the Crusade, she joins in the pranks to tease Lady Edith Plantagenet about Sir Kenneth in Sir Walter Scott's *The Talisman.*

Berenger Protagonist who works in an office and is in love with a secretary, Daisy; unkempt, aimless, bored, and apathetic, he drowns his alienation in alcohol; after a fight, Daisy leaves him; the only human being left at the end, he first unsuccessfully tries, then refuses, to change into a rhinoceros in Eugène Ionesco's play *Rhinoceros.*

Berenger, Eveline Only child of Sir Raymond Berenger; she is rescued from Gwenwyn's siege of Garde Doloureuse Castle by Hugo de Lacy; betrothed to him, she is faithful to him while he is on the Crusades; she comes to love his nephew Damian de Lacy, who was left behind to protect her, and she marries Damian with Hugo's blessing after his return from the Holy Land in Sir Walter Scott's *The Betrothed.*

Berenger, Sir Raymond Norman knight who, lured onto the open plain by insinuations against his honor, dies in battle to defend his castle, Garde Doloureuse, against the attack of Gwenwyn in Sir Walter Scott's *The Betrothed.*

Berenza, Il Conte Venetian nobleman who marries Victoria di Loredani and is later poisoned by her in Charlotte Dacre's *Zofloya; or, The Moor.*

Beresford, Mrs. Passenger returning to England aboard the *Agra* with her son; both are saved by the heroism of David Dodd in Charles Reade's *Hard Cash.*

Beresford, Prudence Cowley (Tuppence) Spirited, ingenious young wife and partner in adventure of Tommy Beresford in Agatha Christie's *The Secret Adversary.* The mysteries continue and the family increases and ages through two other novels before the last, *Postern of Fate.*

Beresford, Thomas (Tommy) Red-haired, unimaginative, twice-wounded lieutenant; jobless after World War I, he becomes involved in preventing a plot to take over Britain in Agatha Christie's *The Secret Adversary.* He and his wife, Tuppence, establish the International Detective Agency and continue to solve crime in two other novels before they appear, retired and in their seventies, in *Postern of Fate.*

Bérété, Mandjan Brother of Sassouma Bérété; does not wish to follow Dankaran in *Sundiata: An Epic of Old Mali.*

Bérété, Sassouma First wife of Maghan Kon Fatta in *Sundiata: An Epic of Old Mali.*

Berg, Mack Volunteer in an American battalion in the Spanish civil war; killed and mutilated in the loyalists' efforts to raise the siege of Madrid in William Herrick's *Hermanos!*

Berg, Miriam See Stone, Miriam Berg.

Berg, Theodore (Teddy) Famous American composer in Alison Lurie's *Real People.*

Bergan, Alf Assistant to the Dublin sub-sheriff's office; he is among the patriotic drinkers in Barney Kiernan's Pub in James Joyce's *Ulysses.*

Bergdahl, P. O. Mysterious character; possibly the father of O. P. Dahlberg or possibly Dahlberg himself in Wright Morris's *The Fork River Space Project.*

Bergen, Minna Spoiled neighbor of Ada Fincastle and Ralph McBride; pursues Ralph in Ellen Glasgow's *Vein of Iron.*

Bergenstrohm, Helga Wife of Swede Bergenstrohm; washerwoman and cook for the miners; fights with Molly Riordan over feeding Jimmy Fee in E. L. Doctorow's *Welcome to Hard Times.*

Bergenstrohm, Swede Hardworking husband of Helga Bergenstrohm; killed by Clay Turner in E. L. Doctorow's *Welcome to Hard Times.*

Berger, Astrid (covernames: Helga, Edda, Maria Brinkhausen) German national and a calculating Palestinian mercenary; she sadistically threatens Charlie should she fail the Palestinian cause, and she suspects Charlie as a double agent in John le Carré's *The Little Drummer Girl.*

Berger, Herbert Dreamy adolescent who runs away from his bourgeois north German home to enlist in the French foreign legion, where he experiences various disenchanting incidents; his attempt to escape with Charles Benoit into the Sahara fails; is eventually summoned home by his father in Ernst Jünger's *Afrikanische Spiele.*

Berger, Tyrone C. Psychiatrist who counsels Conrad Jarrett after Conrad's suicide attempt in Judith Guest's *Ordinary People.*

Bergerac, Cyrano de Skillful French swordsman and poet with an uncommonly long nose; loves his cousin Roxanne, but his ugliness prevents him from pursuing her; regrettably helps the good-looking but clumsy and reticent Christian de Neuvillette to woo Roxanne; composes love letters for Christian that win the lady's heart; later, mortally wounded, receives Roxanne's pledge of love when she discovers that he wrote the tender letters in Edmond Rostand's play *Cyrano de Bergerac.*

Bergerac, Hogo (Roy) de Loathsome troublemaker and anti-prince in Donald Barthelme's *Snow White.*

Bergerac, Vinny Madcap boyhood friend of Jack Duluoz; known for cursing in Jack Kerouac's *Doctor Sax, Maggie Cassidy,* and *Book of Dreams.*

Bergeron, George Harrison's father; so gifted intellectually that he needs a sonic disrupter to keep him from having a coherent train of thought; witnesses his son's televised death, but his sonic disrupter quickly stops him from contemplating it too thoroughly in Kurt Vonnegut's "Harrison Bergeron."

Bergeron, Harrison Young man of super heroic strength and agility living in a dystopian future that handicaps exceptionally gifted people in an attempt to create equality; eventually breaks free of his impediments and has one glorious moment of physical performance, only to be destroyed by government enforcers in Kurt Vonnegut's "Harrison Bergeron."

Bergeron, Hazel Harrison's mother, who, unlike George, is not gifted intellectually; has natural difficulties remembering what she has just watched on television in Kurt Vonnegut's "Harrison Bergeron."

Bergfeld, Anna Austrian living in Michael Mont's parliamentary district; after her husband kills himself she becomes cook for Nora Curfew in John Galsworthy's *The Silver Spoon.*

Bergfeld, Fritz German actor who is married to Anna; he is given work on a poultry farm by Michael Mont; he hangs himself in John Galsworthy's *The Silver Spoon.*

Bergmann, Clara South German pupil in the Hanover school in Dorothy Richardson's *Pointed Roofs.*

Bergmann, Emma Younger sister of Clara and, at fourteen, the youngest pupil in the Hanover school; her piano-playing exemplifies German freedom of emotional expression as contrasted with English restraint in Dorothy Richardson's *Pointed Roofs.*

Bergner, Father Catholic priest from Santa María; makes a deal with Augusto Goerdel to work for him administrating, renting, buying, and selling land; arranges the marriage between Goerdel and Helga Hauser in Juan Carlos Onetti's "Death and the Girl;" also the priest at Moncha Insurralde and at Marcos Bergner's marriage ceremony in Juan Carlos Onetti's "The Stolen Bride."

Bergner, Julita Marcos's sister and Father Bergner's niece; marries Federico Malabia and has an affair after her husband's death with her brother-in-law, Jorge; feels guilty and commits suicide in Juan Carlos Onetti's *The Body Snatcher.*

Bergner, Marcos Moncha's fiancé in Juan Carlos Onetti's "The Stolen Bride."

Bergotte Decadent author whose intricate writing style has great influence; admired by most but equally despised by others; a close friend to Gilberte; Madame Swann's salon is based around him in Marcel Proust's *À la recherche du temps perdu.*

Bergson, Alexandra Smart, ambitious, but lonely farmer who becomes successful because she plans for the future in Willa Cather's *O Pioneers!*

Bergson, Emil Restless, college-educated brother of Alexandra Bergson; loves Marie Shabata and is killed by her husband, Frank Shabata, in Willa Cather's *O Pioneers!*

Bergson, John Swedish immigrant; hardworking but unsuccessful farmer who leaves his farm to his daughter, Alexandra Bergson, in Willa Cather's *O Pioneers!*

Bergson, Lou Greedy and bigoted brother of Alexandra Bergson; becomes a populist agitator in Willa Cather's *O Pioneers!*

Bergson, Mrs. Wife of John Bergson; longs for Sweden in Willa Cather's *O Pioneers!*

Bergson, Oscar Greedy and bigoted son of Mr. and Mrs. John Bergson; resents his brother Emil Bergson's intellectual tendencies and his sister Alexandra Bergson's farming success in Willa Cather's *O Pioneers!*

Bergstein, Mrs. A convert to Judaism from Unitarianism whom Miriam Henderson visits at the urging of Michael Shatov in Dorothy Richardson's *Deadlock.*

Berilla, Donna Hypocrite who pretends to like Emanuella but is malicious and plots against her in Eliza Haywood's *The Rash Resolve; or, the Untimely Discovery.*

Bering, Vitus Unassuming but decisive Danish sea captain of several expeditions commissioned by Tsar Peter Romanoff in the waters east of Siberia; one of the first Russian explorers to reach Alaska in James Michener's *Alaska.*

Berinthia (Berry) Good-natured niece of Mrs. Pipchin; she works in the boarding establishment from dawn to dusk and plays with the child boarders in Charles Dickens's *Dombey and Son.*

Berkeley, Kirkcudbright Llanover Marjoribanks Sellers (Howard Tracy), Viscount Son of the Earl of Rossmore; wishes to renounce his title and live in America; falls in love and marries Sally Sellers in Samuel Langhorne Clemens's *The American Claimant.*

Berkeley, Thomas, Fifth Baron Loyal to Richard II; comes to Henry Bolingbroke to learn the reason for his rebellion in William Shakespeare's play *Richard II.*

Berkeley-Tyne Obnoxious editor of an art monthly; on the pretense of interviewing Janos Lavin at his exhibition, he delivers his own opinions on the modern artist, infuriating Lavin, who brushes him off in John Berger's *A Painter of Our Time.*

Berkely, Lady Augusta de (Augustine) Fair English heiress, who promises to marry Sir John de Walton if he holds Castle Douglas for a designated period; she adopts the masculine disguise of Augustine and is captured by Sir James Douglas; after de Walton loses in combat and concedes the castle, she marries him in Sir Walter Scott's *Castle Dangerous.*

Berkins, Mr. Boorish and ridiculed city magnate, who was born a gentleman but came up through poverty; he marries Grace Brookes in George Moore's *Spring Days.*

Berkley, Maurice Middle-aged, married, bitter manager of the Palladium cinema and former owner of the theater when it was a vaudeville house; he has an affair with the young usher Doreen Higgins, who becomes pregnant by him in David Lodge's *The Picturegoers.*

Berlew, Lightning Hired hand of Mat Feltner and husband of Sylvania Berlew; alienated from the land in Wendell Berry's *The Memory of Old Jack.*

Berlew, Sylvania (Smoothbore) Wife of Lightning Berlew in Wendell Berry's *The Memory of Old Jack.*

Berlin, Paul Army infantry specialist stationed in Vietnam; compelled to imagine the diverse realities of the war in Tim O'Brien's *Going After Cacciato.*

Berlingier, Chevalier de Second to Don Pedro de Gonzales in a farcical duel with Lord Mahogany in William Beckford's *Modern Novel Writing; or, the Elegant Enthusiast.*

Berlioz, Mikhail Alexandrovich Editor of a Moscow magazine and a member of the MASSOLIT (literary association) committee; discusses religion with Ivan Bezdomny; meets Woland, who prophesies that Berlioz will not make it to a meeting since he will have his head cut off by a Russian woman; not taking the prophecy seriously, Berlioz slips and falls under a trolley bus, fulfilling the prophecy; buried in Moscow with honors, but his head disappears and later turns up on a platter at Woland's ball in Mikhail Bulgakov's *The Master and Margarita.*

Berman, Benjamin Samson (Ben) Jewish father of Samuel Paul Berman; retired cabdriver and former radio actor in Jay Neugeboren's *Sam's Legacy.*

Berman, Morrie Former pimp, gambler, and backer of Billy Phelan's bowling and pool games; involved in Charlie Boy McCall's kidnapping in William Kennedy's *Billy Phelan's Greatest Game.*

Berman, O. J. Hollywood agent who helps change Holly Golightly from a hillbilly to a potential starlet in Truman Capote's *Breakfast at Tiffany's.*

Berman, Otto "Abbadabba" Right-hand man and accountant to Dutch Schultz who shows particular favor to Billy Bathgate in E. L. Doctorow's *Billy Bathgate.*

Berman, Samuel Paul (Sam) Son of Benjamin Samson Berman, professional gambler, and lover of Stella; moves to California to escape paying gambling debts in Jay Neugeboren's *Sam's Legacy.*

Bermúdez, Cayo Heads the Peruvian dictator Odría's brutal secret service; lives a scandalous life, as he abandons his wife, Rosa, has a mistress "Musa" at Lima, and tries to seduce other men's wives; uses his power to collect protection fees from local merchants; eventually forced from office by Odría and flees Peru with a cache of money in Mario Vargas Llosa's *Conversation in the Cathedral.*

Bernab, Commendatore Italian Ordnance Office's go-between for payment and for the Spartacus machinery information exchange between General Vagas and Nicholas Marlow in Eric Ambler's *Cause for Alarm.*

Bernadet, Jacques Stephan Zelli's former jailmate who, after Stephan's release from jail, is Stephan's "benefactor"; Marya Zelli immediately dislikes him in Jean Rhys's *Postures.*

Bernal, Don Gamaliel Father of Gonzalo and Catalina in Carlos Fuentes's *The Death of Artemio Cruz.*

Bernal, Gonzalo Prisoner killed in Perales prison for revolutionary activities in Carlos Fuentes's *The Death of Artemio Cruz.*

Bernard Character in the 20th-century story line of the play that is divided into two distant time periods; in his late 30s, he teaches at Sussex University and is extremely literary; seen also as pompous and solipsistic; tries to prove through his research that Lord Byron killed Mr. Chater in a duel at Sidley Park in 1809 in Tom Stoppard's play *Arcadia.*

Bernard Charley's son who earlier in school tried to warn Biff that he must focus more on his studies; becomes a successful lawyer and achieves a measure of prosperity, unlike Willy Loman's two sons, Biff and Happy, in Arthur Miller's *Death of a Salesman.*

Bernard Phrasemaker and novelist, who as a child unable to distinguish between the knob of the dresser ("a loop of light") and the horizon, awakens to sensation with Nanny's sponge and fears to lose his self; he attempts to hang on with his beautiful, wise, witty words and to tell the "true" story of his friends' lives; after experiencing a dreaded loss of self during a solar eclipse, he regains his identity and is able at last to write the perfect novel, no longer merely collecting phrases in Virginia Woolf's *The Waves.*

Bernard Young monk who helps Miles to accept his homosexuality in David Lodge's *How Far Can You Go?*

Bernard Student who serves on the Cinema Committee with Hill Gallagher during the student rebellion in James Jones's *The Merry Month of May.*

Bernard 1 First son of Salter; age 40; given up by his father and reared in a juvenile institution; professional criminal in Caryl Churchill's *A Number.*

Bernard 2 Second son of Salter; created by cloning Bernard 1, at Salter's request; age 35; raised by Salter; murdered by Bernard 1 in Caryl Churchill's play *A Number.*

Bernard, Jefferson (Jeff) Aged recluse whose explanation of Mildred Latham's past to Sidney Wyeth causes Wyeth to return to her in Oscar Micheaux's *The Forged Note.*

Bernard, John Physician who attends the disfigured Robert Mannion and the dying Margaret Sherwin; he is recognized as an old friend by Basil's brother, Ralph, and provides important information in Wilkie Collins's *Basil: A Story of Modern Life.*

Bernarda Authoritarian mother in Federico García Lorca's play *The House of Bernarda Alba.*

Bernardin Faithful former servant of Reginald de St. Leon and his family; he provides them with money which eases the hunger and penury they suffer near Lake Constance in William Godwin's *St. Leon.*

Bernardo Cornelia's kind and generous lover, whose faithfulness is tested by several scheming women and a domineering stepmother in Sarah Scott's *The History of Cornelia.*

Bernarr, Jesse (Jess) Active telepath who joins the Pattern, a vast network of mental links in Octavia E. Butler's *Mind of My Mind.*

Bernay, Mr. Pawnbroker who sells Conrad Drover the rusty gun with blank cartridges with which Conrad tries to kill the Assistant Commissioner in Graham Greene's *It's a Battlefield.*

Bernice Marjorie Harvey's socially awkward ugly duckling cousin from Eau Claire, Wisconsin; pretty, dark-haired, but shy and boring at parties; poor conversationalist and nervous until Marjorie tutors her in how to be popular; becomes clever and witty and develops charm; gains enough confidence to attract Warren, Marjorie's boyfriend; socially embarrassed and ostracized after Marjorie traps her into having her hair bobbed; leaves town, but before going cuts off a sleeping Marjorie's blonde braids and tosses them onto Marjorie's porch in F. Scott Fitzgerald's "Bernice Bobs Her Hair."

Bernice See Stockton, Bernice.

Bernini, Louisa Sweet-tempered wife of the Marquis de Mazzini; she is imprisoned in a cave beneath the castle so that the Marquis can remarry; she is discovered twenty years later by her daughter Julia and is freed in Ann Radcliffe's *A Sicilian Romance.*

Bernis, Jacques Pilot who loves the freedom of flying and the romantic lifestyle of French airmail pilots; falls in love with Genevieve, but this long sought after romantic liaison with an earthly being cannot compensate for life in the air; the couple are romantically reunited as a consequence of sorrowful events in Genevieve's life, but their past links them together in a way that their future cannot endure; their constructions of each other cannot conquer harsh reality in Antoine de Saint-Exupéry's *Southern Mail.*

Bernstein, Aaron M. Physicist at Massachusetts Institute of Technology; one of the many voices of identity in the race riots in Crown Heights, Brooklyn, in 1991, in Anna Deavere Smith's play *Fires in the Mirror: Crown Heights, Brooklyn and Other Identities.*

Bernstein, Baron Beatrix Esmond's second husband, now deceased, a disreputable German nobleman in William Makepeace Thackeray's *The Virginians.*

Bernstein, Baroness See Esmond, Lady Beatrix.

Bernstein, Madame Anna Member of the Cabala and the power behind the German banking house in Thornton Wilder's *The Cabala.*

Bernstein, Professor Award-winning economics professor and analyst of the Mexican economy in Carlos Fuentes's *The Hydra Head.*

Berowne, Sir Paul Government minister and baronet; he is murdered in an old church in P. D. James's *A Taste for Death.*

Berquist, Mark Former senior foreign policy aide; becomes a senator unwilling to admit any knowledge of the cold war intrigue that led to the death of Elena McMahon in Joan Didion's *The Last Thing He Wanted.*

Berr, Porfirio Ilyitch (Poor Berr) Blind servant in the household of the exiled Count Nikolai Diakanov in Paris; Gorin (Monsieur Komensky) almost convinces Vassili Iulievitch Chubinov that Berr is guilty of spying on his master in Rebecca West's *The Birds Fall Down.*

Berrendo, Lieutenant Paco Member of Captain Mora's fascist group in Ernest Hemingway's *For Whom the Bell Tolls.*

Berri, Duke of One of the French nobles in William Shakespeare's play *Henry V.*

Berrisfort, Bob Learned, well-bred owner of Yeoverin-Green; John Buncle first meets him on a passenger boat; he goes hunting with Buncle and discusses theology and literature with him in Thomas Amory's *The Life of John Buncle, Esq.*

Berrisfort, Juliet Bob Berrisfort's sister, whose daring at hunting leads to a harmless accident in Thomas Amory's *The Life of John Buncle, Esq.*

Berry Crewman aboard the *Renown* in C. S. Forester's *Lieutenant Hornblower.*

Berry Timid maker of inconsequential remarks during conversations among the Wragby Hall intellectuals who surround Sir Clifford Chatterley in D. H. Lawrence's *Lady Chatterley's Lover.*

Berry, Bob Grandfather of the Berry children; an aging wrestling coach and confidante to his grandson, John Berry in John Irving's *The Hotel New Hampshire.*

Berry, Egg Youngest child in the Berry family; dies in a plane accident when the Berry family flies from the United States to Vienna in John Irving's *The Hotel New Hampshire.*

Berry, Frank Oldest child of the Berry family; a closeted homosexual who leads his siblings with a quiet authority in John Irving's *The Hotel New Hampshire.*

Berry, Franny Oldest daughter in the Berry family; devoted sister and best friend of John Berry in John Irving's *The Hotel New Hampshire.*

Berry, John Narrator who details the wild experiences of his family as they live in the United States and abroad in John Irving's *The Hotel New Hampshire.*

Berry, John Pathologist and narrator; former law student and military policeman (MP); husband of Judith and good friend of Dr. Arthur Lee; investigates the murder charges against Dr. Lee in Jeffery Hudson's *A Case of Need.*

Berry, Lilly Youngest daughter in the Berry family; possesses a talent for writing and publishes a best-seller before her suicide in John Irving's *The Hotel New Hampshire.*

Berry, Mary Matriarch of the Berry family; is killed with her youngest son, Egg, in a plane accident that occurs while the family is flying from the United States to Vienna in John Irving's *The Hotel New Hampshire.*

Berry, Win Patriarch of the Berry family; rears his children in Vienna after his wife and son's deaths in John Irving's *The Hotel New Hampshire.*

Berryl, Arthur Admirable friend of Lord Colambre; he takes care of his penniless family and later marries the heiress Miss Broadhurst in Maria Edgewordi's *The Absentee.*

Berryl, Sir John Arthur's father, who borrows from Mr. Mordicai and leaves his family penniless at his death in Maria Edgeworth's *The Absentee.*

Berson, Dolek Member of the Nazi-dominated Judenrat forced to coordinate the so-called resettlement of Polish Jews; becomes the strategic leader of the final battle against total Nazi destruction of the Warsaw ghetto in John Hersey's *The Wall.*

Bert Lazy, completely amoral member of the IRA, highly attracted to terrorist activities as well as to women; Alice Mellings dislikes him in Doris Lessing's *The Good Terrorist.*

Bert Working-class neighbor and father of five who helps Dan Graveson try to start a small grassroots peace movement in Alan Burns's *Buster.*

Bert Young boy who lives in the Kellers' neighborhood; frequently visits the Kellers' home, where he plays "jail" with Joe Keller, in Arthur Miller's play *All My Sons.*

Bert Youngest man of four who are on a long bicycle ride in England, where they encounter Roman roads; seeking a pub for refreshment, comes across the Tavern, a place where tea is served but no beer, in V. S. Pritchett's "Many Are Disappointed."

Bertha See Chatelaine of La Trinité.

Bertha Heart of the play and Richard Rowan's wife; beautiful, vital creature, intellectually inferior to Richard but throbbing with life; her name recalls both the Earth and the mystery of birth, linking her to the physical world (thus, akin to Robert Hand, whose name suggests the lexeme *birth,* too), to sexual maturity, and to motherhood; suffering from the unbridgeable spiritual gap, which is the hallmark of her relationship with Richard, whom she loves wholeheartedly, does not reject Robert's wooing, but seems to yield to his advances in order to arouse her husband's jealousy; although the doubts about their affair are never removed, Bertha's soul remains faithful to her husband, Richard, in James Joyce's play *Exiles.*

Bertha Kind and caring maid in the Tesman villa's household in Henrik Ibsen's play *Hedda Gabler.*

Bertha Wife of "Fido" in Olaf Stapledon's *Odd John: A Story Between Jest and Earnest.*

Bertha Wife of the unnamed first-person narrator; encourages her husband to pay bribe money to Mr. Zumpen in order to be awarded a contract for construction work in Heinrich Böll's "Like a Bad Dream."

Bertha Young daughter of the captain and Laura; sits at the center of the war between her parents over the legitimacy of her parentage; at first, sides with her father about going away to study, but ultimately turns against him in favor of her domineering mother, who wants her to study in the family home, in August Strindberg's play *The Father.*

Bertha (Agatha) Hereward's betrodied, a Saxon captured by the Norman Knight of Aspramonte, rebaptized and renamed Agatha; she is the Countess Brenhilda's efficient squire and trusted friend; she accompanies Brenhilda on the crusade and marries Hereward at its conclusion in Sir Walter Scott's *Count Robert of Paris.*

Bertha Mae Teenaged lover of Jule Jackson; eventually moves with him from Alabama to New York in George Wylie Henderson's *Jule.*

Berthe Charles and Emma's daughter; her mother refuses her because she is not a boy; ends up working in a cotton mill as an orphan in Gustave Flaubert's *Madame Bovary.*

Berthelin, Edward Idealistic French patriot who believes that after World War II is over a Christian society will be established; he remains in the army for ten years after the war because he thinks the army represents a positive and strong "gathering of men"; he later becomes the manager of Cousin Honoré's ironworks in Storm Jameson's *Cousin Honoré.*

Berthelin, Robert Strongly pro-English son of Edward Berthelin; he lost his mother when he was two years old; now 17, he loves Fanny Siguenau and enlists in the French army in Storm Jameson's *Cousin Honoré.*

Berthold Also named Fino; new member of the four private counselors to the mad character dressed as the German king Henry IV, the great and tragic emperor who reigned from 1065 to 1106; to play his new role skillfully, he must learn the historical period in Luigi Pirandello's play *Henry IV.*

Berthold, Louis French journalist with ever-changing politics; colleague of Mary Douglas in Martha Gellhorn's *A Stricken Field.*

Bertie Victim of Harry Cresswell's sexual abuse and mother by him of a mulatto child, Emma, in W. E. B. DuBois's *The Quest of the Silver Fleece.*

Bertie, Sir Husband of Lady Diana and a good and helpful friend of the Brooks family in Caroline Norton's *Lost and Saved.*

Bertilia (Bert) Daughter of Suzanne Winograd, who behaves more maturely than her mother in Mark Harris's *It Looked Like For Ever.*

Bertin, Werner Soldier in the German army and writer; drafted into the military and marries his girlfriend, Lenore Wahl, during WWI in Arnold Zweig's *Young Woman of 1914;* involved in the private war between two officers in Arnold Zweig's *Education before Verdun;* works as clerk in Posnanski's office and assists him in the efforts to save Grischa Paprotkin's life in Arnold Zweig's *The Case of Sergeant Grischa.*

Bertolini, Signor Young Venetian gambler, who is a partner in Montoni's plan to use Udolpho as a fortress for mercenaries in Ann Radcliffe's *The Mysteries of Udolpho.*

Bertolt Young man studying to be a judge in the court system; forces a young married woman to be his lover; becomes one of Joseph K's foes in Franz Kafka's *The Trial.*

Bertram Lady Augusta de Berkely's loyal attendant; an enthusiastic minstrel, he obtains permission to study the old lays in Douglas Castle's library; though imprisoned and threatened with torture, he refuses to betray his mistress in Sir Walter Scott's *Castle Dangerous.*

Bertram, Augusta Henry Pulling's supposed aunt, who although in her late seventies continues to live as she always has, traveling from country to country and taking new lovers as she goes; upon the death of Henry's stepmother she takes Henry traveling with her and regales him with many stories about her past lovers and about his family; she winds up settling in Paraguay happily reunited with one of her lovers, Mr. Visconti, and is joined by Henry, who discovers that Aunt Augusta is actually his mother in Graham Greene's *Travels with My Aunt.*

Bertram, Edmund Responsible, kindhearted, clever, somewhat pedantic younger son of Sir Thomas Bertram; his bent for instruction makes him an ideal mentor to his young cousin Fanny Price, who loves him wholeheartedly; his intended profession of clergyman is distasteful and unacceptable to the worldly Mary Crawford, whom he loves in spite of himself; eventually he recognizes Fanny's superiority and marries her in Jane Austen's *Mansfield Park.*

Bertram, George Intelligent but aimless son of feckless Sir Lionel Bertram; he falls in love with Caroline Waddington, who refuses to marry him until he acquires wealth; their engagement broken off, she marries, but some time after her husband's death they become reconciled in Anthony Trollope's *The Bertrams.*

Bertram, George (the elder) Rich and disagreeable uncle of George Bertram and grandfather of Caroline Waddington; he leaves his fortune to a college for the children of fishmongers in Anthony Trollope's *The Bertrams.*

Bertram, Godfrey, Laird of Ellangowan Henry and Lucy Bertram's father; seventeen years after the kidnapping of Henry, he dies from the shock of losing the family fortune, leaving Lucy an impoverished orphan in Sir Walter Scott's *Guy Mannering.*

Bertram, Henry (Harry; Captain Vanbest Brown) Godfrey Bertram's heir, who is kidnapped at the age of five and renamed Vanbest Brown; while serving under Colonel Mannering in India, he falls in love with Julia Mannering; his true identity is discovered through the efforts of Meg Merriles in Sir Walter Scott's *Guy Mannering.*

Bertram, Julia Youngest of the Bertram children; she vies with her sister, Maria, for the attentions of Henry Crawford; humiliated and disappointed by his preference for Maria, she admits the attentions of Tom Bertram's friend Mr. Yates, eventually eloping with and marrying him in Jane Austen's *Mansfield Park.*

Bertram, Lady Maria Ward Handsome and kindhearted but self-centered and indolent wife of Sir Thomas Bertram and mother of Thomas, Edmund, Maria, and Julia; she is a sister of Mrs. Norris and Mrs. Price; she is loved by her niece Fanny Price in Jane Austen's *Mansfield Park.*

Bertram, Lewis Godfrey Bertram's prudent father in Sir Walter Scott's *Guy Mannering.*

Bertram, Lucy Dutiful daughter of Godfrey Bertram; she remains loyal to her father and her eccentric tutor, Dominie Abel Sampson, and marries Charles Hazelwood in Sir Walter Scott's *Guy Mannering.*

Bertram, Margaret Godfrey's selfish, cantankerous relative, who refuses to assist him but leaves her property to his son, Henry Bertram, in Sir Walter Scott's *Guy Mannering.*

Bertram, Maria Proud and self-consequential handsome elder daughter of Sir Thomas Bertram; she becomes engaged to an immensely wealthy and stupid young neighbor, Mr. Rushworth, but readily responds to Henry Crawford's attentions by falling in love with him; upon his departure she marries Rushworth out of wounded pride and determination to escape paternal restraint; she runs away with Crawford and is eventually doomed to a life of social isolation in Jane Austen's *Mansfield Park.*

Bertram, Mrs. Widowed, refined, money-borrowing mother of Sarah Miles; after Sarah's cremation, she confesses to Maurice Bendrix that she had Sarah baptized (secretly) a Roman Catholic, thereby reinforcing the significance of Sarah's desire to convert in Graham Greene's *The End of the Affair.*

Bertram, Mrs. Godfrey Mother of Henry and Lucy Bertram; she is a depressed and superstitious invalid, who dies giving birth to Henry in Sir Walter Scott's *Guy Mannering.*

Bertram, Sir Lionel Minor diplomatic official in the Middle East whose charm hides his feckless nature; in Jerusalem he meets his son, George, with whom he has had no contact for many years; he retires to the English countryside and pursues two single ladies for their money in Anthony Trollope's *The Bertrams.*

Bertram, Sir Thomas Stern and repressive, though just, parent of Tom, Edmund, Maria, and Julia; he takes on the guardianship of his wife's niece Fanny Price, for whom he is a source of terror but who eventually grows to love him in Jane Austen's *Mansfield Park.*

Bertram, Tom Eldest of Sir Thomas Bertram's four children; extravagant and careless of responsibility, he is oblivious to the emotional hazards which threaten his sisters; his triviality is diminished by serious illness at the conclusion of Jane Austen's *Mansfield Park.*

Bertram, Uncle Dulcie Mainwaring's ostentatiously High-Church relation who contemplates entering a monastery in Barbara Pym's *No Fond Return of Love.*

Bertrand Friend of the young man Joachim von Pasenow, who has left the German army; takes an interest in the young woman Ruzena, Joachim's mistress, and helps her get a chorus part on the stage; later distrusted by Ruzena and Joachim in Hermann Broch's *The Sleepwalkers.*

Bertrand One of two thugs hired by Montoni to transport Emily St. Aubert from Udolpho to Tuscany in Ann Raddiffe's *The Mysteries of Udolpho.*

Bertrand, Cecile Aristocratic woman living in isolation; she aids Gabrielle di Montmorency by raising her child Agnes D'Albini, only to lose Agnes when she marries the tyrant Pierre Bouffuet in Charlotte Dacre's *The Libertine.*

Bertrand, Solange (Walker) Beautiful Frenchwoman living in France during the German occupation of World War II; loving mother of three children; wife of Sam Walker in Danielle Steel's *Kaleidoscope.*

Bertrandin, Agilulf Emo, of the Guildivern Model knight in Charlemagne's army who is an empty suit of white armour; his rigid devotion to rules and regulations allows him to maintain his existence; he is assigned Gurduloo as his squire, and earns his knighthood by saving Sophronia, the King of Scotland's virgin daughter, but his knighthood is contested by Sophronia's son Torrismund, who claims that his mother was not a virgin at the time of the deed; this accusation prompts Agilulf's quest; before the truth about Sophronia is revealed, Agilulf believes that he does not deserve to be a knight, and leaves behind his armour for Raimbaut in Italo Calvino's *The Nonexistent Knight.*

Besamitikahl, Besi Eedam Mun Odin's mistress, who has an affair with Harbin Fashnalgid and eventually dies of the Fat Death in Brian W. Aldiss's *Helliconia Winter.*

BeShears, Alexander (Alex) Store owner and neighbor of the Vaidens; father of Ponny BeShears and victim of the Leatherwood gang's violence in T. S. Stribling's *The Forge and The Store.*

BeShears, Ponny Daughter of Alex BeShears, lover of Polycarp Vaiden, and first wife of Miltiades Vaiden; dies during childbirth; appears in T. S. Stribling's *The Forge and The Store.*

Bess Beautiful, gregarious lover, who makes herself ill over the past in Rex Warner's *The Aerodrome: A Love Story.*

Bess Mistress of Crown, who deserts her; taken in by Porgy, from whom she runs away, in DuBose Heyward's *Porgy.*

Bess, Aunt (Bessie) Wife of Uncle Clyde; boards Dandy Benson at her Maryland farm during summers in his boyhood in Ed Bullins's *The Reluctant Rapist.*

Bess, Edgeworth One of Jack Sheppard's loyal mistresses in William Harrison Ainsworth's *Jack Sheppard.*

Bessas Byzantine commander of Rome whom Heliodora, at Marcian's suggestion, tries to corrupt in George Gissing's *Veranilda.*

Bessemer, Travis (Blix) Friend of Condé Rivers; helps Rivers become a writer and falls in love with him in the process in Frank Norris's *Blix.*

Bessie Daughter of the farmer and his wife; she introduces Sylvie and Bruno to her doll, Matilda Jane, and sings a song for the doll that Sylvie taught her in Lewis Carroll's *Sylvie and Bruno Concluded.*

Bessie Employee at the women's lodging where the nurses live in Margaret Drabble's *The Millstone.*

Bessie Streetwalker who is asked to model for Dick Heldar; she falls in love with his best friend, Torpenhow, and, to revenge herself for Dick's sending Torpenhow away from her, destroys Dick's masterpiece painting, completed just before he goes blind in Rudyard Kipling's *The Light That Failed.*

Bessie Girlfriend of Van Norden; obsessed with technique in Henry Miller's *Tropic of Cancer.*

Besso, Adam Father of Eva, the "Rose of Sharon"; he is the banker to whom Tancred, Lord Montacute presents the letters of credit secured from Sidonia in Benjamin Disraeli's *Tancred; or, The New Crusade.*

Besso, Eva Called the "Rose of Sharon," the daughter of the banker Adam Besso; she enchants Tancred, Lord Montacute with her beauty as well as her passionate and highly intelligent explanations of the mysteries of ancient Judaism in Benjamin Disraeli's *Tancred; or, The New Crusade.*

Bessy Mae Sister of Teddy, who steals Bessy Mae's ADC check to support his heroin addiction in Donald Goines's *Dopefiend.*

Best, Ann Attractive woman serving in the Wrens whom Alan Percival meets during a radio and radar training course and later marries in Roy Fuller's *The Perfect Fool.*

Best, Dr. Insane psychiatrist in his forties with shining blue eyes and black-edged teeth; he typically diagnoses his patients as having problems with same-sex-sexual-attraction repression; suspected of being a spy, he comes to believe he is a member of the Anti-Death League in Kingsley Amis's *The Anti-Death League.*

Best, Jack Publicist who attempts to blackmail Gordon Walker and Lee (LuAnne) Verger with a compromising photo in Robert Stone's *Children of Light.*

Best, Mr. Librarian from the Irish National Library who criticizes Stephen Dedalus's interpretation of Shakespeare in James Joyce's *Ulysses.*

Best, Mrs. Housekeeper at Donnithorne Chase in George Eliot's *Adam Bede.*

Best Beloved Presumably a child to whom the story is narrated in Rudyard Kipling's "How the Leopard Got His Spots."

Beste-Chetwynde, Margot Wealthy socialite who controls a white-slavery ring; deciding to marry to boost her sagging social reputation, she becomes engaged to Paul Pennyfeather and sends her innocent fiancé on a risky mission connected with her business; after Paul's arrest she uses her influence with Humphrey Maltravers, her new husband and head of the prison system, to have Paul freed by faking his death in Evelyn Waugh's *Decline and Fall.*

Beste-Chetwynde, Peter Margot's son, who is Paul Pennyfeather's student at Llanabba School; Peter takes a strong liking to Paul and is pleased that Paul may become his stepfather; he is an Oxford student drinking heavily at the end of Evelyn Waugh's *Decline and Fall.*

Bester, Samuel Chairman of the language arts department at Calvin Coolidge High School; observes teachers and leaves extensive memos; believes all students should read Charles Dickens and Shakespeare in Bel Kaufman's *Up the Down Staircase.*

Bestudik, Wilfrid (Wilf) Dimwitted priest, rector of St. Clement's Hill Retreat House, and superior of Father Urban in J. F. Powers's *Morte D'Urban.*

Bestwick, Gordon Cambridge student from a poor background who is a friend of Charles Eliot; he is implicated in the national-security incident in C. P. Snow's *Last Things.*

Bethel, Erasmus Lionel Desmond's former guardian and correspondent, who advises him to extricate himself from involvement with the Verney family, although he assists Geraldine Verney in Desmond's absence; letters exchanged by him and Desmond are vehicles for notions about the French Revolution that inform a large part of Charlotte Smith's *Desmond.*

Bethesda Born in Roman Egypt, her mother was killed; was sold into slavery and bought by Gordianus, who took her to Rome, where they married and she helped him in his detective work, later taking ill and returning to Alexandria with him in Steven Saylor's *Roman Blood* and other books in the Rome Sub-Rosa series.

Bethia Middle-aged maid of the Edgeworths; she declines the family invitation to go to church in Ivy Compton-Burnett's *A House and Its Head.*

Bethune, John Highland cotter and poet, frequently cited by Alton Locke as a source of inspiration in Charles Kingsley's *Alton Locke.*

Bethune, Lydia Wife of Bart Bethune, a prominent member of Mt. Ephraim Country Club; informs Corinne that Marianne is no longer attending school and is spending her days in the isolated St. Ann's Catholic Church, which ultimately leads Corinne to know that her daughter was raped in Joyce Carol Oates's *We Were the Mulvaneys.*

Betina Daughter of the well-to-do capitalist Roberto Regules, a man who undermined Robles's financial empire; considered Mexico City's "golden girl"; falls in love with the brilliant young lawyer Jamie Ceballos in Carlos Fuentes's *Where the Air Is Clear.*

Beto Good-natured cabdriver with a questionable past in Carlos Fuentes's *Where the Air Is Clear.*

Betonie The old Dine (Navajo) medicine man who guides Tayo through the ceremony that sets into motion his quest for the cattle and healing in Leslie Marmon Silko's *Ceremony.*

Betsy Prostitute friend of Nancy; she works for Fagin in Charles Dickens's *Oliver Twist.*

Betsy Serving girl who works for Mrs. Raddle in Charles Dickens's *The Posthumous Papers of the Pickwick Club.*

Betsy Slave owned by Ellen Ashe and sold after Edward Ashe falls in love with her; Edward finds Betsy and their child and moves with them to Canada in Jesse Hill Ford's *The Raider.*

Betsy The Jorrockses' cook in Robert Surtees's *Jorrocks's Jaunts and Jollities.*

Betsy Troubled teenager who is first seen as a member of the Huron Street Ann Arbor Consciousness Raising Rap Group; later becomes Scoop's editor in Wendy Wasserstein's *The Heidi Chronicles.*

Betsy Wholesome friend of Esther Greenwood and her fellow guest editor at a New York fashion magazine; she and Esther suffer ptomaine poisoning at a *Ladies' Day* magazine banquet in Sylvia Plath's *The Bell Jar.*

Betsy ("Rosebud") Seventeen-year-old maid whom, as an act of conceit, Robert Lovelace vows not to seduce; instead he provides a marriage settlement for her so that she can marry her beloved in Samuel Richardson's *Clarissa: or, The History of a Young Lady.*

Bett, Lulu Spinster sister of Ina Bett Deacon; released from domestic drudgery when she marries, inadvertently, Ninian Deacon, a man already married; marries Neil Cornish in Zona Gale's *Miss Lulu Bett.*

Bett, Mrs. Mother of Ina and Lulu Bett and mother-in-law of Dwight Deacon, in whose house she lives, in Zona Gale's *Miss Lulu Bett.*

Betteredge, Gabriel Garrulous family retainer in the Verinder household; he prides himself on his common sense but uses random texts from Robinson Crusoe as guides to conduct; he helps Sergeant Cuff investigate the theft of a yellow diamond willed to Rachel Verinder by her wicked uncle, John Herncastle, in Wilkie Collins's *The Moonstone. A Romance.*

Betteredge, Penelope Pert, outspoken daughter of Gabriel Betteredge and servant in the Verinder household; she is protective of Rosanna Spearman and furious at the blundering investigation by Superintendent Seegrave into the loss of a diamond willed to Rachel Verinder in Wilkie Collins's *The Moonstone. A Romance.*

Bettersworth, Thomas (Tommy) Small-town businessman who is killed in a fight over his wife's reputation in Mary Austin's *A Woman of Genius.*

Betterton, Miss Nottingham tradesman's daughter tricked into flight with Robert Lovelace, who rapes her eighteen months before he tricks Clarissa Harlowe; she dies delivering his son in Samuel Richardson's *Clarissa: or, The History of a Young Lady.*

Betty Booth family maid, who stole Amelia's last possessions to make her own fortune in Henry Fielding's *Amelia.*

Betty Compassionate chambermaid at the Dragon Inn who provides clothing for the sick, naked Joseph Andrews; she is fired after Mrs. Tow-wouse discovers her in bed with Mr. Tow-wouse in Henry Fielding's *The History of the Adventures of Mr. Joseph Andrews and of His Friend Mr. Abraham Adams.*

Betty Haggard, vulgar girl who supports herself and her lover Edwin Froulish and pays for the apartment they share with Charles Lumley by prostituting herself to hypocritical Robert Tharkles in John Wain's Hurry *On Down.*

Betty Nurse who cared for Gyp Winton (Fiersen) from infancy and then cared for Little Gyp (Fiersen) in John Galsworthy's *Beyond.*

Betty Privileged old servant of the Holmans, who counsels Paul Manning and later Phillis Holman in Elizabeth Gaskell's *Cousin Phillis.*

Betty Unfortunate chambermaid, whom Mrs. Slipslop unjustly accuses of being pregnant by Joseph Andrews; jealousy provokes Lady Booby to dismiss her in Henry Fielding's *The History of the Adventures of Mr. Joseph Andrews and of His Friend Mr. Abraham Adams.*

Betty Wife of the proper British aristocrat and protagonist Clive; character played onstage by a man in act 1 and by a woman in act 2; finds difficulty in making decisions and defers to her husband's power; finds her duty as wife and mother sometimes suffocating and dreams of romance with Harry, who does not return her desires; rejects the hints of sexual desire by her son's governess, Ellen; later finds independence and freedom, even divorce, from Clive in Caryl Churchill's play *Cloud 9.*

Betty Fiancée of Miss Lonelyhearts in Nathanael West's *Miss Lonelyhearts.*

Betty Owner and operator of a dive called The Melody Coast, where the unnamed male narrator becomes a regular in Darryl Pinckney's *High Cotton.*

Betty Window designer for Saks who does layouts for Renate's planned magazine in Anaos Nin's *Collages.*

Betty, Lady Friend of Lady Davers; her expectations of Mr. B— are dashed when he marries Pamela Andrews; she becomes an admirer of Pamela through reading her letters in Samuel Richardson's *Pamela, or Virtue Rewarded.*

Betty, Mrs. Lady Maria Esmond's maid, who gets drunk with Gumbo and Case in William Makepeace Thackeray's *The Virginians.*

Betty Chambermaid Servant at Robin's inn who, fearing Tom Jones's ghost, refuses to answer his bell until the drawer accompanies her in Henry Fielding's *The History of Tom Jones.*

Betty Jean Niece of Mrs. Wickam in Charles Dickens's *Dombey and Son.*

Betty Jean Older black woman and mother of O. E. Parker; works in a laundry; worries that her son, who has a fetish to cover his body in tattoos, will not turn out well in life in Flannery O'Connor's "Parker's Back."

Betu Uncastrated billy goat with a red collar studded with bells; a voracious pet that swallows whatever piece of paper he finds lying around in Gopinath Mohanty's "The Solution."

Beulah Robert's recently deceased wife who died from cancer; assumed the role as the reader for the "blind man" after the narrator's wife stopped working for him; pitied by the narrator since she was married to a blind man in Raymond Carver's "Cathedral."

Beutler, Herbert Georg One of three physicists confined to the Les Cerisiers insane sanatorium run by Mathilde von Zahnd; believes himself to be Sir Isaac Newton; earlier killed one of the female nurses, a crime being investigated by the police onstage; later reveals that he and the other scientist, Ernst Heinrich Ernesti, are not really insane but are killing the nurses to fake their mental derangement; actually, he is a spy, like Heinrich Ernesti, who has penetrated the asylum to secure Möbius's secret scientific discoveries in Friedrich Dürrenmatt's play *The Physicists.*

Bevan, Mr. The only American young Martin Chuzzlewit and Mark Tapley meet who objectively views the failings of his country; he befriends them by advancing money for their return from Eden to New York and offers further assistance in Charles Dickens's *The Life and Adventures of Martin Chuzzlewit.*

Bever, Mr. Dishonest steward of Sir Thomas Grandison's English estate; he conspires with Mr. Filmer to try to establish Miss Obrien as Sir Thomas's mistress in Samuel Richardson's *Sir Charles Grandison.*

Beveridge, Ben ("Old") Longtime Jago dweller, who accurately observes to Dicky Perrott that the only ways out of the Jago are to join the High Mob, to go to prison, or to die in Arthur Morrison's *A Child of the Jago.*

Beverley, Cecilia Young woman whose estate is in the trust of three London gentlemen; an heiress about to come of age, she is pursued by many admirers in London and in her home county of Suffolk; she deliberately gives away most of her wealth to help the poor and sick; she loves Mortimer Delvile and secretly marries him, but loses her mind for a while when she thinks he has deserted her in London; she is reconciled to his father in the end in Frances Burney's *Cecilia.*

Beverley, Frank An earl's nephew, made into a servant of all work at Drayton House, who sets the fires that free the inmates in Charles Reade's *Hard Cash.*

Bevill, Thomas Tory government minister who chairs committees in charge of atomic-energy research, loses his appointment during the war, and returns to government after the war to continue atomic-energy development; he offers to appoint Martin Eliot as head of research in C. P. Snow's *The New Men.* He becomes Lord Grampound before his death in *Corridors of Power.*

Beville, Captain Dashing officer murdered by the jealous Don Pedro de Gonzales in William Beckford's *Modern Novel Writing; or, the Elegant Enthusiast.*

Bevis Attractive young man, who makes love to the married Monica (Madden) Widdowson, causing a crisis in her marriage in George Gissing's *The Odd Women.*

Bevis, Mrs. Widow at the boarding house in Hampstead where Clarissa Harlowe first hides from Robert Lovelace, who charms her into betraying Clarissa in Samuel Richardson's *Clarissa: or, The History of a Young Lady.*

Bevys, Sir Ghostly victim of murder in a story read by Ludovico as he stands watch in the bedroom of the dead Marchioness de Villeroi in Ann Radcliffe's *The Mysteries of Udolpho.*

Bewick, Valentine Working-class labor-union leader who opposes Sir George Tressady during the strike at Tressady's coal mines in Mrs. Humphry Ward's *Sir George Tressady.*

Bey, Muzaffer Bashaw of Buda and favorite of the Turkish sultan; Reginald de St. Leon, in the guise of the Sieur de Chattilon, petitions him to provide aid to the Christian inhabitants of the province in William Godwin's *St. Leon.*

Beye, Lillian Woman always fighting inner turmoil and seeking self-fulfillment; pianist in Anaïs Nin's *Ladders to Fire, Children of the Albatross,* and *Seduction of the Minotaur.*

Beynon, Butcher Member of the colorful and fanciful community of Llaregyb, a mythical seaside village in Wales in Dylan Thomas's play *Under Milk Wood.*

Beynon, Gossomer Schoolteacher who dreams of a lover; member of the colorful and fanciful community of Llaregyb, a mythical seaside village in Wales in Dylan Thomas's play *Under Milk Wood.*

Beynon, Mrs. Wife of Butcher Beynon in the colorful and fanciful community of Llaregyb, a mythical seaside village in Wales in Dylan Thomas's play *Under Milk Wood.*

Beynon, O. Killa Candidate for the same job that John Lewis wants; he is older than Lewis and has written pamphlets on Welsh antiquities in Kingsley Amis's *That Uncertain Feeling.*

"Beyond the Wall," Narrator Man who passes a week in San Francisco on the way to New York to visit an old schoolmate, with whom he had corresponded years earlier; has become wealthy during his business ventures in the Orient; wants to renew the old friendship; perceives his old friend as melancholic, older, and somewhat uncanny; hears a mysterious tapping noise and is told the tale of a young girl, who was his friend's neighbor; leaves him later that night feeling sympathetic toward him in Ambrose Bierce's "Beyond the Wall."

Bezdomny, Ivan (Ivan Nikolayevich Ponyrov) Young and well-known poet in Moscow; becomes a witness to Woland's prediction that Berlioz will have his head cut off by a woman; unsuccessfully tries to catch the devil; ends up in a mental asylum where he meets the Master; these events change Ivan's life, making him realize that the poetry he wrote was inferior; decides he will never write again and instead becomes a historian in Mikhail Bulgakov's *The Master and Margarita.*

Bezoni, Signer Learned Italian, whose materialistic philosophy temporarily plunges Morton Devereux into deep despair in Edward Bulwer-Lytton's *Devereux.*

Bezukhov, Pierre Socially awkward and illegitimate son of an old Russian grandee; educated abroad; returns to Russia as misfit; unexpectedly inherits a large fortune and thus becomes socially desirable, despite his misfit character; falls prey to the fortune-seeking Helene Kuragina, whose deception marks Pierre with confusion; sets out on a spiritual odyssey that spans the epic novel; eventually weds Natasha Rostova in Leo Tolstoy's *War and Peace.*

Bezzemelny, Princess Purported by Katerina Ivanovna to have given a blessing to her and Marmeladov's marriage in Fyodor Dostoevsky's *Crime and Punishment.*

Bhaer, Friedrich (Fritz) Kindly, eccentric German tutor who marries Jo March in Louisa May Alcott's *Little Women;* also appears in *Little Men.*

Bhaer, Jo March See March, Jo.

Bhaer, Robin (Rob, Robby) Enthusiastic chatterbox at Plumfield; son of Jo and Friedrich Bhaer in Louisa May Alcott's *Little Men.*

Bhagirathi Praneshacharya's ill wife; marriage with her has brought no physical joy for the great scholar; the sexual instincts of the scholar are suppressed due to this marital bond with her in U. R. Ananthamurthy's *Samskara: A Rite for a Dead Man.*

Bhagmati Born with the name of Bindu Bashini into a Hindu merchant family; works for Henry Hedges, and he falls in love with her; after he dies, she becomes a serving girl for Hannah in Fort St. Sebastian; accompanies Hannah on her journeys and dies in the battle between Emperor Aurangdev and Jadav Singh; is buried under the name Hester Hedges in Bharati Mukherjee's *The Holder of the World.*

Bhatice Old Indian man and close friend and neighbor of Varma's; listens sympathetically to Varma's flood of complaints about how poorly he is being treated by his son, a medical doctor, in Anita Desai's "A Devoted Son."

Bhave, Mithum Ten-year-old Indo-Canadian boy; dies when Sikh terrorists bomb his plane; Shaila Bhave, his mother, floats a half-painted model B-52 in the Irish Sea where his plane went down in Bharati Mukherjee's "The Management of Grief."

Bhave, Shaila Thirty-six-year-old Indian émigré living in Toronto, narrates the story of her husband and two sons who are killed when Sikh terrorists bomb their airplane; wracked internally by grief, yet appears composed; enlisted by social worker Judith Templeton to mediate between traditional Indian and progressive Western cultures; travels to Ireland in an unsuccessful attempt to identify her family members' bodies, but maintains hope that they are alive; travels to India, begins to hear the voices of her husband and sons; returns to Toronto, becomes politically active, and bravely walks into the future at the unresolved but hopeful end of Bharati Mukherjee's "The Management of Grief."

Bhave, Vikram Indo-Canadian husband of Shaila Bhave; anglicizes his name to "Vik" in his workplace; dies when Sikh terrorists bomb his plane; returns to Shaila in a vision; encourages and comforts her throughout Bharati Mukherjee's "The Management of Grief."

Bhave, Vinod Fourteen-year-old son of Shaila Bhave; dies when Sikh terrorists bomb his plane; because he is a strong swimmer, his mother floats a pocket calculator in the Irish Sea, hoping he has survived; Irish officials incorrectly identify his body in Bharati Mukherjee's "The Management of Grief."

Bhoolabhoy, Frank Husband of the owner of Smith's hotel in Pankot; though he is hotel manager, Frank is kept in the dark about most of the hotel's business; he reluctantly composes the letter instructing Colonel and Mrs. Smalley to vacate the Lodge, also owned by Lila Bhoolabhoy; Frank is a devoted member of St. John's Church, where he is an assistant warden, in Paul Scott's *Staying On.*

Bhoolabhoy, Lila Wife of Frank Bhoolabhoy and owner of Smith's Hotel in Pankot; Lila dreams of great financial schemes to transform Smith's into a center of commerce;

since part of her current scheme is to tear down The Lodge, where "Tusker" and Lucy Smalley have lived for many years, she makes her husband Frank write the eviction letter which precipitates "Tusker's" death in Paul Scott's *Staying On.*

Bhowmick, Mr. Protagonist who, under his wife's insistence, moved from his homeland in Bihar, India, to Detroit to find economic prosperity; metallurgist who studies rust in automobiles; devout man who prays daily in Sanscrit to Kali-Mata, patron goddess of the family; becomes infuriated when he learns that his single daughter is pregnant by artificial insemination and wants nothing to do with marriage in Bharati Mukherjee's "A Father."

Bhowmick, Mrs. Wife of the protagonist and mother of the grown daughter Babli; acted as the catalyst years earlier to push her husband to leave India for America; a woman of progressive ideas; agnostic toward God, unlike her highly religious husband; becomes infuriated when she learns that her single daughter is pregnant by artificial insemination and wants nothing to do with marriage in Bharati Mukherjee's "A Father."

Bhryeer Phagor who steers the sledge while Uuundaamp drives the dogs; it is he who throws Harbin Fashnalgid from the sledge in Brian W. Aldiss's *Helliconia Winter.*

Bhupathi Wealthy businessman in 19th-century Calcutta; married to the younger Charulata; pursues his newspaper enterprise with total zeal, leaving little time for his wife; later finds that Charu and he have nothing in common, even as his business fails from his financial neglect in Rabindranath Tagore's *The Broken Nest.*

Biaggi, Bella See Dehn, Bella Biaggi.

Bianca Baptista's youngest daughter; beautiful, kindhearted, and more subdued than her vociferous sister, Katherina; pursued by several potential suitors; shows a preference for her tutor, Lucentio (in disguise), and agrees to marry him; later suggested not to be as obedient as she appears after her sister is tamed in William Shakespeare's *The Taming of the Shrew.*

Bianca Courtesan and Cassio's mistress in William Shakespeare's play *Othello.*

Bianca Former lover of Bill Agatson and former fiancée of Arthur Ketcham in John Clellon Holmes's *Go.*

Bianca Servant-confidante of Princess Matilda in Horace Walpole's *The Castle of Otranto.*

Bianchi, Signora Ellena Rosalba's aunt and guardian, who approves of Ellena's engagement to Vincentio di Vivaldi, only to die and leave Ellena vulnerable to the schemes of the Marchesa di Vivaldi in Ann Radcliffe's *The Italian.*

Bianco, Count Ricardo Gentle, sad bachelor, hopelessly devoted to the middle-aged Harriet Bede in Barbara Pym's *Some Tame Gazelle.*

Biasse, Billy Friend of Jake Brown and host to the longshoremen's gaming rendezvous in Claude McKay's *Home to Harlem.*

Bib, Julius Washington Merryweather American "gentleman in the lumber line" and a member of the delegation that greets Elijah Pogram in Charles Dickens's *The Life and Adventures of Martin Chuzzlewit.*

Bibbit, William (Billy, Club) Stuttering, mother-dominated mental patient who slits his throat in response to the domination of Big Nurse in Ken Kesey's *One Flew Over the Cuckoo's Nest.*

Biberkopf, Franz Ex-convict and transportation worker; after serving a sentence for manslaughter, returns to Berlin to start a new life but gets involved in criminal activities; as result, loses his arm, and his new girlfriend, Mieze, is murdered; ends up in a prison and a psychiatric ward; finally goes through spiritual rebirth in Alfred Döblin's *Berlin Alexanderplatz.*

Bibi Four-year-old son of Calixta and Bobinôt; away from home running errands with his father during a thunderstorm in Kate Chopin's "The Storm."

Bibi, Lila Chand Name assumed by Arista Prolo on tour in Tokyo in Carlene Hatcher Polite's *Sister X and the Victims of Foul Play.*

Bibokov, B. A. Investigating magistrate for Cases of Extraordinary Importance; tries to help clear Yakov Bok of murder charges in Bernard Malamud's *The Fixer.*

Bicek, Bruno (Lefty) Polish hood and boxer who betrays his girlfriend Steffi Rostenkowski into prostitution and who commits a senseless murder in Nelson Algren's *Never Come Morning.*

Bick, Fanny Young woman who has an intense affair with the much older William Dubin in Bernard Malamud's *Dubin's Lives.*

Bickerton, Margo Wild, indiscreet, outgoing, once-married aunt of Rita; she does as she pleases; she blames Nellie and Jack for ruining her chances for happiness; though she is fond of Rita, she wants a man and seizes upon Ira when the occasion arises in Beryl Bainbridge's *The Dressmaker.*

Bickerton, Miss Parlor boarder at Mrs. Goddard's school; taking a country walk with Harriet Smith, she runs away in fright, abandoning Harriet to the importunities of a group of Gypsies in Jane Austen's *Emma.*

Bickerton, Mrs. Prejudiced Scotswoman afflicted with gout; Jeanie Deans's landlady in York, she also befriends her in Sir Walter Scott's *The Heart of Midlothian.*

Bicket, Anthony (Tony) Young worker who is sacked for stealing copies of Wilfred Desert's book to sell; he plans to emigrate to Australia in John Galsworthy's *The White Monkey.* He writes to Michael Mont to complain about Australia in *The Silver Spoon.*

Bicket, Victorine (Vic) Collins Wife of Tony; she models nude to earn money for passage to Australia in John Galsworthy's *The White Monkey.*

Biddenhurst, Alexander English visitor to Virginia by way of Philadelphia; proponent of liberty and agitator of the revolt against planter-aristocrats in Henrico County, Virginia, in Arna Wendell Bontemps's *Black Thunder.*

Biddle, John Captain of the ship by which Lemuel Gulliver travels back to England after leaving Blefuscu in Jonathan Swift's *Travels into Several Remote Nations of the World. In Four Parts. By Lemuel Gulliver.*

Biddlebaum, Wing Adolph Myers gained this nickname from the townsfolk of Winesburg, Ohio, due to his uncontrollable fluttering hands; paroxysms resulted from narrowly escaping being lynched to death after being wrongly accused of child molestation in a Pennsylvania small town; a former schoolteacher, now works as a farm hand picking berries since he arrived in Winesburg 20 years earlier; lives in a decayed house near a ravine on the outskirts of town, ostracized from the community, prematurely old at 40, and condemned to be lonely in Sherwood Anderson's "Hands." Morbidly obsessed with his hands because of a scandal that nearly resulted in his lynching in Sherwood Anderson's *Winesburg, Ohio.*

Biddlepen, Sprigge Meek, dapper little clergyman, a guest at a house party given by Lady Monica Knollys; he eventually marries Milly Ruthyn in J. Sheridan Le Fanu's *Uncle Silas.*

Biddy Orphan who lives with her harsh grandmother, Mr. Wopsle's great aunt; later she takes care of Mrs. Joe Gargery during her illness and, after Mrs. Joe's death, marries Joe Gargery; Biddy critically observes the development of Pip Pirrip's snobbish attitude toward Joe and his pretentions of gentility; she tells Pip that Estella is not worth having if she does not like him as he is in Charles Dickens's *Great Expectations.*

Bideawhile, Mr. Junior partner in the firm of Slow and Bideawhile; he breaks with Louis Trevelyan over Trevelyan's planned abduction of his son in Anthony Trollope's *He Knew He Was Right.* Bideawhile appears in *Framley Parsonage,* in *Orley Farm,* and in *Miss Mackenzie.* He tells Frank Gresham of Louis Satcherd's death in *Doctor Thorne.* His firm is consulted by the Longestaffes in *The Way We Live Now.*

Bideford, Lord George Hearty, good-natured squire, who marries Nina Baldoni in Anthony Trollope's *Ayala's Angel.*

Bidet French commander in William Faulkner's *A Fable.*

Bide-the-Bent, Peter Strict Presbyterian minister, whose religious prejudices lead him to assist Lady Ashton in dissolving the engagement between Edgar Ravenswood and Lucy Ashton in Sir Walter Scott's *The Bride of Lammermoor.*

Bidlake, John Robust artist of great renown and father of Walter Bidlake and Elinor Quarles; a life-long philanderer, he returns to his third wife when he learns of his fatal illness, selfishly demanding the attention of the entire household in Aldous Huxley's *Point Counter Point.*

Bidlake, Mrs. Aloof and vague mother of Walter Bidlake and Elinor Quarles and the third wife of John Bidlake, by whom she was abandoned early in their marriage; content with his long absence, she accepts him back for his final illness in Aldous Huxley's *Point Counter Point.*

Bidlake, Walter Ineffectual literary critic and son of John Bidlake; bored with his mistress Marjorie Carling, he is briefly the object of Lucy Tantamount's amorous interest; he is devastated when she moves on to new amusements in Aldous Huxley's *Point Counter Point.*

Bidulph, Lady Sensible, strict, and sometimes interfering mother of Sidney Bidulph and Sir George Bidulph; she educates her daughter according to the highest standards of virtue, and her death numbers among her daughter's misfortunes in Frances Sheridan's *Memoirs of Miss Sidney Bidulph.*

Bidulph, Lady Sarah Monied and materialistic daughter of a newly created peer; she marries Sir George Bidulph and behaves coldly and condescendingly toward Sidney Bidulph Arnold while affecting kindness and consolation in Frances Sheridan's *Memoirs of Miss Sidney Bidulph.*

Bidulph, Sidney See Arnold, Catherine Sidney Bidulph.

Bidulph, Sir George Elder brother of Sidney Bidulph Arnold; he wants his sister to marry his friend Orlando Faulkland; he separates from his wife, Lady Sarah; finally he reconciles with his wife and his sister and gives the report of Falkland's death in Frances Sheridan's *Memoirs of Miss Sidney Bidulph.*

Bidwell Servant who is shared by Lewis Eliot and Roy Calvert in their Cambridge rooms; he is made to answer for his thefts by Calvert in C. P. Snow's *The Light and the Dark.*

Bidwell, Harry Grandfather of Pinky; stalks a Fifth Avenue apartment dressed for business when there is no business to go to in the 1930s; reads British murder mysteries in Maureen Howard's *Expensive Habits.*

Bidwell, Mrs. Grandmother of Pinky; of missionary descent; as sweet and cold as the Schrafft's lemon sherbet she invariably serves with one cream wafer for dessert in Maureen Howard's *Expensive Habits.*

Biedenhorn Influential leader of a group of mercenaries; rather than doing what he is paid for by the Marina's rulers, waits for a chance to assume higher offices in the Oberförster's rising regime in Ernst Jünger's *On the Marble Cliffs.*

Biederman, Arnold Swiss magistrate who has been disinherited in favor of his brother, the Count of Geierstein; he has cared for his niece, Anne of Geierstein, for seven years; he leads an embassy to negotiate with Charles, Duke of Burgundy, and declares war with the duke on behalf of the Swiss cantons in Sir Walter Scott's *Anne of Geierstein.*

Biederman, Rudiger One of Arnold Biederman's sons; he becomes a companion of Arthur Philipson (Arthur de Vere) and is killed during the battle in which Charles, Duke of Burgundy, is killed in Sir Walter Scott's *Anne of Geierstein.*

Biederman, Sigismund One of Arnold Biederman's sons; he offers safe haven to Arthur de Vere and his father after the death of Charles, Duke of Burgundy, in Sir Walter Scott's *Anne of Geierstein.*

Biegánska, Dr. Zbigniew (Papa) Polish professor, author of an anti-Semitic pamphlet, and father of Sophie Zawistowska; executed by the Nazis in William Styron's *Sophie's Choice.*

Biegler, Paul (Polly) Lawyer from Michigan's Upper Peninsula who defends Frederic Manion; narrator of Robert Traver's *Anatomy of a Murder.*

Bierce American gringo of the title; at first befriended in Mexico by the revolutionary general Tomás Arroyo but later shot in the back by Arroyo because of a perceived rivalry over the American schoolteacher Harriet Winslow in Carlos Fuentes's *The Old Gringo.*

Biff Disillusioned grown son of Willy Loman; started off as a fanciful youth, a champion footballer in high school; once idolized his father until he discovered his father's clandestine love affair; shattered by Willy's disloyalty, ends any drive for a career or future prospects and instead becomes a kleptomaniac; the only Loman who dares to break the success myth that all the others in the family have so foolishly and carefully built up; stops hating Willy only toward the end when he realizes that he has also been as fake as his father was in Arthur Miller's play *Death of a Salesman.*

Biffen, Harold Impoverished writer, who devotes himself to a realistic novel about slum life, saves his manuscript from a fire, falls hopelessly in love with Edwin Reardon's widow, and takes his own life when his novel is a failure in George Gissing's *New Grub Street.*

Biffin, Major Boring fellow traveller with George Bertram and Arthur Wilkinson on their return journey from the Middle East in Anthony Trollope's *The Bertrams.*

Big, Daddy Cousin of Bindy McCall; former gambler and pool hustler; jailed for two years for a crime he did not commit; assisted by Billy Phelan in William Kennedy's *Billy Phelan's Greatest Game.*

Big, Mr. Smuggler who considers himself the "first of the great Negro criminals"; he is James Bond's adversary in Ian Fleming's *Live and Let Die.*

Big Bertha Black cook on the wandering island in John Hawkes's *Second Skin.*

Big Bertha of Heaven See Blackman.

Big Boy One of the four African-American boys caught swimming in Jim Harvey's pool; protagonist who watches his friends Bobo, Buck, and Lester killed because of their skin color; ultimately kills Jim Harvey and flees to Chicago in Richard Wright's "Big Boy Leaves Home."

Big Daddy Patriarch of the Pollitts; momentarily deceived into believing that his illness is inconsequential, but recovers his self-confidence during his 65th birthday party and feels disposed to remain in charge of his cotton plantation and to make his favorite son, Brick, give up alcohol; then discovers that his illness is a deadly cancer; believes that Maggie is pregnant and decides to bequeath his possessions to Brick's supposed child instead of to Gooper and his six descendants in Tennessee Williams's play *Cat on a Hot Tin Roof.*

Bigears, Nancy Native Tlingit Indian; daughter of Sam Bigears; has brief affair with Tom Venn; after a few weeks at the university in Seattle returns to Alaska to defend native rights; marries Chinese immigrant Ah Ting; has daughter Tammy Bigears Ting in James Michener's *Alaska.*

Bigears, Sam Native Tlingit; loses land and fishing rights to cannery near Juneau; passionate defender of native rights; father of Nancy Bigears in James Michener's *Alaska.*

Big Elk, Ruby Daughter of the former chief of the Osage nation, wife of Cimarron Cravat, and mother of two children in Edna Ferber's *Cimarron.*

Big Ellis Kentucky farmer and drinking partner of Burley Coulter in Wendell Berry's *Nathan Coulter* and *A Place on Earth.*

Bigelow, Reverend Doctor James Traveling evangelist who shocks George Brush in Thornton Wilder's *Heaven's My Destination.*

Biggers, Roxie Sister of Perry Northcutt; pietistic busybody and gossip who is opposed to Sunday baseball in T. S. Stribling's *Teeftallow.*

Biggs, Chester Trainer and handler of Victoria Regina, a miniature schnauzer stolen in Joseph Wambaugh's *The Black Marble.*

Biggs, Lyde (Little) Cynical, swaggering swindler in E. W. Howe's *The Story of a Country Town.*

Biggs, Martha Ingratiating, fawning friend of Mrs. Furnival; she revels in the supposed infidelities of Mr. Furnival, who loathes her spying in Anthony Trollope's *Orley Farm.*

Biggs, Miriam Kitchenmaid for the Lambs who is at the bottom of the house's pecking order; she grew up in an orphanage; she offers to teach Miss Buchanan to read in Ivy Compton-Burnett's *Manservant and Maidservant.*

Biggs, Mr. Boatswain of H.M.S. *Harpy;* he is the butt of Jack Easy's practical jokes in Captain Frederick Marryat's *Mr. Midshipman Easy.*

Biggs, Sir Impey Council for the Duke of Denver in his trial for murder in Dorothy L. Sayers's *Clouds of Witness.* He defends Harriet Vane in *Strong Poison.*

Big Laura Leader of a group of ex-slaves heading north after the Civil War; killed while defending them from vengeful whites in Ernest J. Gaines's *The Autobiography of Miss Jane Pittman.*

Biglin, Luther Jailer in William Faulkner's *The Mansion.*

Big Lot Young man who spends the night with Charlie and causes the breakup in the relationship between Charlie and the male narrator of Tennessee Williams's *Moise and the World of Reason.*

Big Mama Big Daddy's lifelong companion, her devotion to him makes her disregard his mockeries and snubs; news of his cancer leaves her desolated, although she keeps enough fortitude to defy Gooper in his dogged self-appointment as Big Daddy's legatee in Tennessee Williams's play *Cat on a Hot Tin Roof.*

Big Mama Ruler over the kingdom of Macondo; loved and hated at the same time by her family and the peasants of the kingdom; repents and makes her last requests before passing away; never married, nor had children; offers to leave her possessions and position as ruler to her niece, Magdalena, who refuses the offer in Gabriel García Márquez's "Big Mama's Funeral."

Big Nurse See Ratched, Nurse.

Bigoness, Theresa (Theresa Haug) Coworker of Martha Reganhart; becomes pregnant by a man other than her husband, passes herself off as single, bears a daughter, gives the child up for adoption, and returns to her harsh marriage in Philip Roth's *Letting Go.*

Big Sally Black woman who drives a Mercedes and talks of her oppression in Ishmael Reed's *The Last Days of Louisiana Red.*

Big-Tooth Mid-Pleistocene ancestor of the narrator, member of a race about to make evolutionary gains in Jack London's *Before Adam.*

Big Tub Leader of the Rastas in Mark Helprin's *Refiner's Fire.*

Big Turtle Shawnee Indian who captures Salathiel Albine and gives him the name of Little Turtle in Hervey Allen's *The Forest and the Fort.*

Bigwell, Mr. Master at Lucius Cassidy's school who did not attend Oxford or Cambridge; he teaches the boys Latin and Greek in Ivy Compton-Burnett's *Two Worlds and Their Ways.*

Bigwig (Thlayli) Junior member of the Sandleford Owsla (rabbit-warren militia) who joins Hazel's pioneers; he plays a critical role in the infiltration of the Efrafa Warren and in the subsequent defense of the new warren from General Woundwort in Richard Adams's *Watership Down.*

Bijoy Chatterjee Kind man and the father Anju never knows; believes that Gopal is the harbinger of good luck because the monsoon arrives, after a long drought, on the day that he arrives at the Chatterjee residence; trusts people without question; mortgages his property in order to finance the trip, with Gopal, to find rubies in a secret cave; finds out near the ruby caves that Gopal is actually his uncle's illegitimate son; killed in an accident near the ruby caves in Chitra Banerjee Divakaruni's *Sister of My Heart.*

Bilbo, Mr. Agitated divine, who cries out in original Greek in William Beckford's *Modern Novel Writing; or, the Elegant Enthusiast.*

Bildad An owner of the *Pequod* in Herman Melville's *Moby-Dick.*

Biles, Hezekiah Rustic, gossiping chorister in Thomas Hardy's *Two on a Tower.*

Bilham, John Little Aspiring artist who is a friend of Chad Newsome and a confidant of Lambert Strether; becomes engaged to Mamie Pocock in Henry James's *The Ambassadors.*

Bill Aggressive, cruel, confident farmer in Rex Warner's *The Wild Goose Chase: An Allegory.*

Bill City editor of the *Blue Mountain News,* where the protagonist, Miranda, works in 1918 in Katherine Anne Porter's "Pale Horse, Pale Rider."

Bill Clerk in Mr. Dabb's London shop, who gives Andrew Tacchi a critical unwelcome in Mark Rutherford's *Miriam's Schooling.*

Bill Editor of Miranda in Katherine Anne Porter's *Pale Horse, Pale Rider.*

Bill "Enlightenment leader" and yin-yang adherent who pursues Lise in Muriel Spark's *The Driver's Seat.*

Bill Former enlisted man and friend of Gerry; he participates in the kidnaping and firebombing masterminded by Sophy Stanhope in William Golding's *Darkness Visible.*

Bill Gamekeeper at Knowl who helps protect Maud Ruthyn from a coach of rough intruders (one of whom is her cruel cousin, Dudley Ruthyn) in J. Sheridan Le Fanu's *Uncle Silas.*

Bill Grave digger in Charles Dickens's *Oliver Twist.*

Bill Inebriated boyfriend of a young pregnant woman; they are discovered squatting in Anthony Keating's uninhabited London home by Keating; Bill is arrested and the woman dies later in Margaret Drabble's *The Ice Age.*

Bill Leader of the seven impotent capitalists who live with Snow White, wash windows, and make Chinese baby food; hanged for throwing two six-packs of beer through a windshield in Donald Barthelme's *Snow White.*

Bill Lizard whose pathetic willingness and helplessness are exploited by the other creatures; after Alice has grown so large as to fill the White Rabbit's house, blocking doors and windows, Bill is sent down the chimney to investigate but is kicked up and out by Alice; Bill later acts as a juror in the trial of the Knave of Hearts in Lewis Carroll's *Alice's Adventures in Wonderland.*

Bill Mean, jealous husband of Winnie; he gets his buddies to help him beat up Arthur Seaton several times for having an affair with his wife in Alan Sillitoe's *Saturday Night and Sunday Morning.*

Bill Palace of Pleasure shooting-booth attendant; he unwittingly provides an alibi for Pinkie Brown in Graham Greene's *Brighton Rock.*

Bill Reporter for *Field and Stream* and lover of Lisa in Anaïs Nin's *Collages.*

Bill (Commanding Officer, Colonel) Efficient, careful, gruff friend of McKechnie; overstrained, he becomes drunk and is locked up by Christopher Tietjens, to whom he later confides that he has a fatal cancer in Ford Madox Ford's *A Man Could Stand Up—.*

Bill (Comrade Bill) Young, cynical, and wary man in charge of culture in the British Communist Party; he interviews Anna Wulf and admits her into the Party in Doris Lessing's *The Golden Notebook.*

Bill (My Bill) Amelia's husband, a criminal whom Mr. Jaggers is defending in Charles Dickens's *Great Expectations.*

Bill, Aunt Malicious, resentful woman who lived on National Assistance until her death; she took in her orphaned niece and nephew, Crystal and Hilary Burde, but soon sent the troublesome Hilary to an orphanage in Iris Murdoch's *A Word Child.*

Bill, M. A. (Medium Asshole) Personnel director for Pure Pores Filters Company; goes on the Alaskan hunting expedition in Norman Mailer's *Why Are We in Vietnam?*

Bill, Old One of the Gorbals Die-Hards; he guides Dickson McCunn to Sakskia, the Russian princess, in John Buchan's *Huntingtower.*

Billali White-bearded, patriarchal, venerable "Father" or head of an Amahagger tribe; kindly disposed toward the Englishmen Leo Vincey and Horace Holly, he saves their lives from his cannibalistic fellow tribesmen and escorts them into the presence of She in H. Rider Haggard's *She.*

Bill Barnwell Slave beaten by his master Lewis Barnwell in Caroline Gilman's *Recollections of a Southern Matron.*

Bill Collector Irate and surly man, who presents Colonel Jack with a payment; he threatens to become violent in Daniel Defoe's *The History and Remarkable Life of the Truly Honourable Colonel Jacques, Commonly Call'd Colonel Jack.*

Billickin, Mrs. Sharp-tongued British woman, who provides lodgings for Rosa Bud after she flees John Jasper and leaves Miss Twinkleton's academy in Charles Dickens's *The Mystery of Edwin Drood.*

Billie, Miss Friend of Marie Canada and mother of Charlotte; gives a wooden bracelet to Eva Medina Canada in Gayl Jones's *Eva's Man.*

Billings, George Former astronaut who serves as Jace Everett's troubleshooter; hires Mabry Jenkins to work for Everett's radio station but fires him when the ratings slip in Peter Gent's *Texas Celebrity Turkey Trot.*

Billins, Roe College roommate of Jerry Payne; spring house-party date of Nancy Putnam in John Nichols's *The Sterile Cuckoo.*

Billows, Isobel Rich widow and doting paramour of Martin Bowles in Muriel Spark's *The Bachelors.*

Billson Biggest operator at Muskegon Commercial Academy; he becomes Loudon Dodd's clerk when a bad stock deal bankrupts him in Robert Louis Stevenson's *The Wrecker.*

Billson Misanthropic, hysterical parlormaid of the Jenkins family who is mentally unhinged by unrequited passion for Creech, the cook, in Anthony Powell's *The Kindly Ones.*

Billy Captain Nares's friend, who was wrecked in the *Navigators* and decided to stay in Robert Louis Stevenson's *The Wrecker.*

Billy Gentleman loafer and errand boy for Douglas Longhurst in Robert Louis Stevenson's *The Wrecker.*

Billy Judy's blind, older husband; a member of Pinkie Brown's mob, he owns a boarding house where Pinkie, Spicer, Dallow, and other mob members live in Graham Greene's *Brighton Rock.*

Billy Son of Martin and Stevie; has recently come out as gay in Edward Albee's play *The Goat, or, Who is Sylvia.*

Billy Retarded and abandoned sweeper of a pool hall who is employed and protected by Sam the Lion; butt of practical jokes; killed by a truck while sweeping the streets in Larry McMurtry's *The Last Picture Show.*

Billy Vietnam veteran who is impatient with passive Civil Rights-era methods of the Reverend Phillip Martin in Ernest J. Gaines's *In My Father's House.*

Billy, Uncle Thief and drunkard who steals the mules and provisions from the destitute outcasts who have sheltered in a cave during a severe snowstorm in the Rocky Mountains in Bret Harte's "The Outcasts of Poker Flat."

Billy, Uncle Belly-bumping champion whom Skipper defeats and from whom Skipper receives the crucifix he later gives to Catalina Kate in John Hawkes's *Second Skin.*

Billy Bocksfuss See Giles, George.

Billyboy Fat, brutal thug a few years older than Alex; a rival gang leader, he becomes a police officer in order to enable him to even the score with Alex for past humiliations in Anthony Burgess's *A Clockwork Orange.*

Bilson Maid for Soames and Irene Forsyte; she quietly understands their tensions in John Galsworthy's *The Man of Property.*

Bilson, Mr. Profligate reclaimed by his wife's virtue; released from prison after Lady Dently pays his debts, he retires to the country to exercise his philanthropic impulses in Sarah Fielding's *The History of the Countess of Dellwyn.*

Bilson, Mrs. Exemplar of domestic virtues who reclaims her husband from a life of frivolous excess and then extends her beneficence to public acts of generosity in Sarah Fielding's *The History of the Countess of Dellwyn.*

Bilton Foreman at Andrew Understhaft's munitions factory in George Bernard Shaw's play *Major Barbara.*

Bim Russian clown; paired with Bom he comments critically on English Society in the Epilogue to Richard Aldington's *The Colonel's Daughter.*

Bimbister, Margery Neil Rolandson's praiseworthy wife in Sir Walter Scott's *The Pirate.*

Binde, Harold Chancellor of Euphoric State University; he tries to handle student protest in David Lodge's *Changing Places: A Tale of Two Campuses.*

Binder, Rabbi Rigid and absolutist young Hebrew schoolteacher who responds to excessive questioning and perceived misbehavior with corporal punishment; experiences severe classroom management problems when pupil Ozzie Freedman flees to the roof and refuses to come down until he is assured that no one will hit anyone else and that all things—even immaculate conception—are possible for God in Philip Roth's "The Conversion of the Jews."

Bindloose, Mr. Sheriff-clerk and banker, who introduces Meg Dods to Peregrine Touchwood in Sir Walter Scott's *St. Ronan's Well.*

Bindo (Albinois) Albino fool of Euthanasia dei Adimari's court; he predicts the downfall of Valperga and brings Beatrice to the witch of the Luccan forest (Fior de Mandragola) in Mary Shelley's *Valperga.*

Binford, Lucius Common-law husband of Reba Rivers in William Faulkner's *Sanctuary, The Mansion,* and *The Reivers.*

Bingham, Captain Edward (Teddie) Arthur David Young British officer of the Muzzafirabad Guides Regiment stationed in Pankot; he marries Susan Layton at the Nawab's palace in Mirat and returns to duty after only a three-day honeymoon; Captain Bingham is killed shortly afterward while trying to locate and restore to duty an Indian soldier of his regiment who has gone over to the INA (the "Indian National Army", a collection of renegade soldiers who allied themselves with the Japanese) in Paul Scott's *The Day of the Scorpion.*

Bingham, Doc Disreputable book peddler who hires Mac in Chicago and, after being caught in bed with a farmer's wife, flees, leaving Mac stranded in rural Michigan in John Dos Passos's *U.S.A.* trilogy.

Bingham, Emily Wealthy ward in Chancery; after attempting unsuccessfully to attract Harry Lorrequer, she becomes engaged to Tom O'Flaherty in Charles Lever's *The Confessions of Harry Lorrequer.*

Bingham, Jo-Lea Pregnant daughter of Timothy Bingham in Robert Penn Warren's *The Cave.*

Bingham, Thomas (Tom) Architect who encourages his friend David Marshall to endow a college building in Henry Blake Fuller's *With the Procession.*

Bingham, Timothy Father of Jo-Lea Bingham and chief stockholder, president, and cashier of the People's Security Bank of Johntown, Tennessee; arranges for Jo-Lea to have an abortion in Robert Penn Warren's *The Cave.*

Bingley, Caroline Proud, conceited sister of Mr. Bingley; hoping to marry Mr. Darcy, she views his growing attraction to Elizabeth Bennet with alarm and schemes to separate her brother from Jane Bennet in Jane Austen's *Pride and Prejudice.*

Bingley, Charles Handsome, agreeable, rich, and young newcomer to the Bennets' neighborhood; he falls in love with Jane Bennet; too easily persuaded that Jane does not return his affections, he is separated from her by the joint efforts of his sisters and Mr. Darcy but eventually marries her in Jane Austen's *Pride and Prejudice.*

Binks, Sir Bingo Quarrelsome English baronet, who challenges Francis Tyrrell to a duel and publicizes Tyrrell's shame for not appearing in Sir Walter Scott's *St. Ronan's Well.*

Binky, Craig Unintelligent and unintelligible but extremely rich owner of *The Ghost* newspaper, competitor of Harry Penn's *The Sun* in Mark Helprin's *Winter's Tale.*

Binnendale, Marcie See Nash, Marcie Birmendale.

Binnie, James Mrs. Mackenzie's brother and Colonel Newcome's old friend, who, by leaving his money to Rosey Mackenzie, precipitates her marriage to Clive Newcome in William Makepeace Thackeray's *The Newcomes.*

Binny, Mr. Curate who proposes to the widowed Amelia (Sedley) Osborne in William Makepeace Thackeray's *Vanity Fair.*

Binodia Storekeeper of the *math,* a decent man of humble origins who becomes wealthy after Madha's death in Fakir Mohan Senapati's "The Brideprice."

Binodini Key character in prepartitioned Bengal; vivacious and educated young girl in India; forced to marry an old man and soon must live the hard and traditional life of a widow; referred to as the "chokher bali," or the "grain of sand that causes disruption to eyes," the pet name given her by Ashalata; later contemplates two options open to her—suicide or exile to the holy city of Benares—and cleverly chooses Benares in Rabindranath Tagore's *Chokher Bali.*

Binu Ramesh's *chaprasi,* or "aide"; dark and strong, a man in his mid 50s, balding and with six teeth less, unable to understand the officer's restless urge to catch thieves and even less his final decision to let them go; longing to get back home to see his third wife, Gori, left under the care of his older wives, dreams of having a son as soon as possible, maybe because of fears he might be abandoned by Gori in Gopinath Mohanty's "Ants."

Binz, Beansy Young left-handed pitcher who replaces Henry Wiggen on the New York Mammoths in Mark Harris's *It Looked Like For Ever.*

Bion Timothy's brother; very strong; works as an undertaker in Ray Bradbury's "Homecoming."

Biondello Lucentio's servant; agrees to help Lucentio and Tranio with their plan to woo Bianca in William Shakespeare's *The Taming of the Shrew.*

Biondo, Jimmy Gangster who threatens to kill Legs Diamond in William Kennedy's *Legs.*

Biranne, Edward Henrietta's twin brother; the children are fond of watching flying saucers in Iris Murdoch's *The Nice and the Good.*

Biranne, Henrietta Nine-year-old daughter of Richard and Paula; she is Edward's twin sister in Iris Murdoch's *The Nice and the Good.*

Biranne, Paula Divorced schoolteacher who is at last reconciled with her errant husband, Richard, in Iris Murdoch's *The Nice and the Good.*

Biranne, Richard Civil servant and colleague of Octavian Gray; before his divorce from Paula he was an unfaithful and violently jealous husband; he and Paula are ultimately reconciled, to the satisfaction of their twins in Iris Murdoch's *The Nice and the Good.*

Biranthus (Berentha) Character who disguises himself as a woman, Berentha, to get close to Amoranda; he tries to rape her but instead shoots her coachman in Mary Davys's *The Reform'd Coquet.*

Birch, Colonel Frank Friend of Lord Charles Oakley in William Beckford's *Modern Novel Writing; or, the Elegant Enthusiast.*

Birch, Constance Moves from Ohio to Greenwich Village in 1927; secretary and typist for artists and writers; becomes pregnant; returns to Ohio and marries Johnathan Jaimison in Dawn Powell's *The Golden Spur.*

Birch, Harvey Mysterious peddler thought to be a spy for the British army but who is, in fact, George Washington's most trusted agent; his actions are marked by a selfless devotion to his country in James Fenimore Cooper's *The Spy.*

Birchem, Master Lazarus Schoolmaster in James Kirke Paulding's *Koningsmarke.*

Birchfield, Marilyn Kindhearted social worker who tries to befriend Sol Nazerman in Edward Lewis Wallant's *The Pawnbroker.*

Birchie Bartley Insane twelve-year-old daughter of Lizzie Bartley and Blessed Belshazzar; her trial for murder is used by the state of Virginia to punish blacks for the crime of pretending to be white in Hal Bennett's *A Wilderness of Vines.*

Bird Introverted, 27-year-old cram-school teacher wrestling with a moral dilemma brought on by the birth of his son, who suffers from a suspected brain hernia; feels fear, remorse, guilt, pain, and denial as he struggles to accept the imperfect child; all the while his wife lies bedridden in a hospital after the birth; escapes into the arms of his ex-girlfriend, Himiko, and tries to lose himself in sex and alcohol; dreams of escaping to Africa; finally realizes that he must accept the child in Kenzaburo Oe's *A Personal Matter.*

Bird, Harriet Beautiful woman who shoots athletes with silver bullets in Bernard Malamud's *The Natural.*

Bird, Henry Employee of the Free Press who fights with Bartley Hubbard over Hannah Morrison in William Dean Howells's *A Modern Instance.*

Bird, Janet Ollerenshaw Young mother who derives little satisfaction from the intelligence and clarity of her perceptions, being ridiculed by a sarcastic husband and suppressed by the conditions of her marriage; her chief solace comes from an emotional readiness for catastrophe until the arrival of her distant cousin, Frances Wingate, brings some diversion in Margaret Drabble's *The Realms of Gold.*

Bird, Jem The one-hundred-year-old pride of the village; he tells the history of Deerbrook and the origins of its name in Harriet Martineau's *Deerbrook.*

Bird, Loretta Nosy, brash neighbor of the Peebles; mimics their middle-class sensibilities, trying to make herself more important than Edie, the Peebles's housekeeper; has seven children and a husband with a drinking problem; often invites herself over to the Peebles; eggs on the confrontation between Alice Kelling and Edie after she confesses to kissing Alice's fiancé in Alice Munro's "How I Met my Husband."

Bird, Luke (Preacher) Temperance reformer and dejected pursuer of Jenny Bunce; he believes that only beasts possess souls worthy of divine recitation; he seeks out the wine merchant Weston to fill his well with wine in order to get the approval of Thomas Bunce in T. F. Powys's *Mr. Weston's Good Wine.*

Bird, Mark Janet's mean-spirited, sarcastic, bullying husband in Margaret Drabble's *The Realms of Gold.*

Bird, Miss Iris (Aunt Iris) Crippled biology teacher; a spinster who chaperones a beach house party for Cress Delahanty and friends in Jessamyn West's *Cress Delahanty.*

Bird, Pete Unemployed, debt-plagued amateur poet and friend of Daisy Meissner in Edmund Wilson's *I Thought of Daisy.*

Bird, Senator and Mrs. Ohio couple who aid Eliza and Harry Harris as they flee the Shelby estate in Harriet Beecher Stowe's *Uncle Tom's Cabin.*

Birdalone Young woman who was stolen from her mother, Audrey, as a baby by the evil Witch-Wife; after her escape and her adventures involving the Castle of the Quest, she marries Arthur in William Morris's *The Water of the Wondrous Isles.*

Birdie Birdy's canary persona in his fantasy bird life in William Wharton's *Birdy.*

Birdseye, Miss Elderly philanthropist and leader of New England reform movements who dies at Marmion, the summer cottage of Olive Chancellor, in Henry James's *The Bostonians.*

Birdsong, Dabney Brilliant engineer and architect who becomes the lover of Annabel Upchurch, his childhood friend, after she marries Judge Honeywell in Ellen Glasgow's *The Romantic Comedians.*

Birdsong, Eva Howard Famous Queensborough beauty of the 1890s who gives up a career in opera for the great passion of loving the unfaithful George Birdsong in Ellen Glasgow's *The Sheltered Life.*

Birdsong, George Charming but struggling attorney who marries Eva Howard; lover of Memoria and other women, including Jenny Blair, in Ellen Glasgow's *The Sheltered Life.*

Birdwell, Eliza Cope Recorded Quaker minister and wife of Jess Birdwell in Jessamyn West's *The Friendly Persuasion* and *Except for Me and Thee.*

Birdwell, Jane Younger daughter of Jess and Eliza Birdwell in Jessamyn West's *The Friendly Persuasion.*

Birdwell, Jesse Griffith (Jess) Quaker nurseryman and husband of Eliza Birdwell in Jessamyn West's *The Friendly Persuasion* and *Except for Me and Thee.*

Birdwell, Joshua (Josh) Son of Jess and Eliza Birdwell in Jessamyn West's *The Friendly Persuasion* and *Except for Me and Thee.*

Birdwell, Laban (Labe) Son of Jess and Eliza Birdwell in Jessamyn West's *The Friendly Persuasion* and *Except for Me and Thee.*

Birdwell, Little Jess Youngest child of Jess and Eliza Birdwell in Jessamyn West's *The Friendly Persuasion* and *Except for Me and Thee.*

Birdwell, Martha Truth (Mattie) Daughter of Jess and Eliza Birdwell; marries Gardiner Bent; appears in Jessamyn West's *The Friendly Persuasion* and *Except for Me and Thee.*

Birdwell, Sarah Daughter of Jess and Eliza Birdwell who dies young; appears in Jessamyn West's *The Friendly Persuasion* and *Except for Me and Thee.*

Birdwell, Stephen (Steve) Youngest son of Jess and Eliza Birdwell; marries Lidy Cinnamond in Jessamyn West's *The Friendly Persuasion.*

Biren, John Ernest See Courland, John Ernest Biren, Duke of.

Biris Philosopher and teacher who serves as Stefan's confidante and is able to shed light on Stefan's preoccupation with history; realizes that Stefan is horrified by historical events and that the young man longs for "the paradise of his childhood"; eventually dies at the hands of communist intelligence agents in Mircea Eliade's *The Forbidden Forest.*

Birkebeba Azemia's judicious and sensible paternal grandmother in William Beckford's *Azemia.*

Birkin London bookseller who loses a pair of boots to the author Tim Cropdale, whom he beats in a footrace, in Tobias Smollett's *The Expedition of Humphry Clinker.*

Birkin, Rupert School inspector who looks for and finds "star-equilibrium" (togetherness without merging) in his relationship with Ursula Brangwen, but is frustrated in his quest for "Bluterbrüderschaft" (sworn blood-brotherhood) with Gerald Crich; he is given to apocalyptic condemnations of the modern world in D. H. Lawrence's *Women in Love.*

Birkman, Kareen Young girlfriend and lover left behind by Joe Bonham in Dalton Trumbo's *Johnny Got His Gun.*

Birkman, Mike Father of Kareen Birkman in Dalton Trumbo's *Johnny Got His Gun.*

Birnbaum, Jacob (Ikey Mo) Short, fair, stout, and very wealthy admirer of Albert Sanger; Birnbaum loves Sanger's daughter Antonia and after suffering some rejection at her hands eventually marries her in Margaret Kennedy's *The Constant Nymph.*

Biron, Lord Commander of military forces besieged by the Parliamentary Army at Chester during the reign of Charles I in J. Henry Shorthouse's *John Inglesant, A Romance.*

Birt, Sebastian Young economics tutor having an affair with the mentally disturbed Elizabeth Rock in Henry Green's *Concluding.*

Birtley, Norman Lillian Matfield's suitor in J. B. Priestley's *Angel Pavement.*

Bisbee, B. D. Friend of Chad Hanna, advance man for Huguenine's circus, and eventually part-owner of the circus in Walter D. Edmonds's *Chad Hanna.*

Bisch Prison cellmate of Leo Feldman; tailor who creates Feldman's fool suit in Stanley Elkin's *A Bad Man.*

Bishop Fat, immoral London bishop, who preaches a sermon written by Hugh Trevor and who publishes Hugh's *Defense of the Thirty-nine Articles* under his own name in Thomas Holcroft's *The Adventures of Hugh Trevor.*

Bishop Man who enjoys eating and has great faith in dreams in Charles Johnstone's *Chrysal: or, The Adventures of a Guinea.*

Bishop One of the clients at The Grand Balcony, a brothel, who assumes the role of a bishop during a fantasy role-playing game and who, when the play begins, overstays his welcome and is forced to stop by Irma, the Queen and brothel manager; assumes the role of the actual bishop at the end of Jean Genet's *The Balcony.*

Bishop Titular head of the Order which serves the leproserie in Graham Greene's *A Burnt-Out Case.*

Bishop, Bernice Welfare worker who with Mr. Rayber attempts to get Francis Marion Tarwater away from his great-uncle; failing, she marries Rayber but deserts him after bearing their idiot son, Bishop Rayber, in Flannery O'Connor's *The Violent Bear It Away.*

Bishop, Clare Former mistress and secretary of Sebastian Knight during the six years in which he wrote his first two novels; eventually marries someone else and dies without ever speaking to V. in Vladimir Nabokov's *The Real Life of Sebastian Knight.*

Bishop, Ephraim (Eef) Sheriff in William Faulkner's *The Mansion.*

Bishop, Jesse Congressional Medal of Honor winner and member of the 918th Bomb Group; dies in battle in Beirne Lay, Jr., and Sy Bartlett's *Twelve O'Clock High!*

Bishop, Mary Frances Daughter of Eliza and Mr. Bishop; she dies of dysentery after Eliza flees her abusive husband and leaves her, with the idea that she will go back to get her in the care of others in Frances Sherwood's *Vindication.*

Bishop, Meg Judgmental journalist who accuses Mrs. Karen Stone of escapism as a way to forget her husband in Tennessee Williams's *The Roman Spring of Mrs. Stone.*

Bishop, Mr. Husband of Eliza Bishop and father of Mary Frances Bishop; beats Eliza until she leaves him in Frances Sherwood's *Vindication.*

Bishop, The High-ranking church official who listens to the priest's sincere confession that what the old women saw was no more than a father's demonstration of love for his daughter in Salarrué's "The Priest."

Bishop of Digne Priest who befriends the protagonist, Jean Valjean, by giving him food and shelter; discovers that the house's silverware has been stolen by Valjean, but, upon the thief's arrest, does not prosecute him but adds silver candle sticks to the sack of loot in Victor Hugo's *Les Misérables.*

Bishop of El Toboso Father Quixote's regional bishop; he is the immediate superior to the humble parish priest; when the letter arrives from the Vatican promoting Father Quixote to monsignor, the Bishop informs Father Quixote in a rather uncomplimentary letter, suggesting that his rank is now too great for such a small parish; when word of Father Quixote's escapades reaches El Toboso, the Bishop arranges to have Father Quixote kidnapped and returned to El Toboso; Father Quixote, however, escapes and continues his journey in Graham Greene's *Monsignor Quixote.*

Bishop of Glasgow Kindly, peaceful prelate, who performs the services on Palm Sunday in the kirk of Douglas in Sir Walter Scott's *Castle Dangerous.*

Bishop of Motopo Cleric sent from Rome on special assignment to Spain; when his car apparently breaks down near El Toboso, he is aided by Father Quixote and invited to lunch; after lunch, Father Quixote "fixes" the car by adding a little petrol to the tank and sends the Bishop on his way; the Bishop is so impressed with Father Quixote that he recommends his promotion to monsignor in Graham Greene's *Monsignor Quixote.*

Bishop of Norchester Oliver Green's superior; he is a shy man who discourages easy intimacy but has time for everyone and is universally confident and clear visioned in C. Day Lewis's *Child of Misfortune.*

Bishop Otto Historian and uncle of the 12th-century ruler Frederick the Great in Umberto Eco's *Baudolino.*

Bishopriggs, Mr. Inn employee who testifies as a witness to the "Scotch marriage" of Anne Silvester and Arnold Brinkworth; he sells Anne the letter he stole from her in Wilkie Collins's *Man and Wife.*

Bishops Catholic bishops who preside in the illicit crowning of Henry II's son as heir to the throne of England; excommunicated for usurping Becket's role as the archbishop of Canterbury, which eventually leads to his murder, in T. S. Eliot's play *Murder in the Cathedral.*

Bishop's Lady Card player who believes in dreams in Charles Johnstone's *Chrysal: or, The Adventures of a Guinea.*

Bisi Senior lecturer, an affectionate, happy person, with whom Kamala seems to get on well but whose visits are soon interrupted by egocentric, jealous Sura in Gopinath Mohanty's "Bed of Arrows."

Bisland, Leota B. Sixth-grade classmate and first lover of Molly Bolt in Rita Mae Brown's *Rubyfruit Jungle.*

Bismark Winifred Crich's pet rabbit in D. H. Lawrence's *Women in Love.*

Bissell, Agate Strong-willed servant-for-hire who does her Christian duty for all the citizens of Norwood; serves as a hospital administrator and member of the Sanitary Commission during the Civil War and marries Parson Buell after his first wife dies in Henry Ward Beecher's *Norwood.*

Bisset, Alexandra (Biscuit) Beautiful half-Pakistani servant of Lady Kitty Jopling; she has invented an exotic Indian identity but is in fact a cockney; she carries messages to Hilary Burde from Kitty and attracts his playful amorous attentions; she marries Christopher Cather, who is promoting her career as a model at the end of Iris Murdoch's *A Word Child.*

Bissonnette, Joe (Iddiboy, Iddyboy) Muscular boyhood friend of Jack Duluoz in Jack Kerouac's *Doctor Sax* and *Maggie Cassidy.*

Biswanger, Grace One-half of an uncouth couple, according to Neddy; terse to Neddy after he crashes her outdoor pool party; gossips to another guest about Neddy's financial woes in John Cheever's "The Swimmer."

Bitherstone, Master Little Paul Dombey's fellow boarder at Mrs. Pipchin's establishment; he wants to run away to his parents in India in Charles Dickens's *Dombey and Son.*

Bitters, Billy (Extra) Mary's beau and later husband; has a bad reputation in Runnymeade and is thought of as "white trash"; handsome; fights in World War II in Rita Mae Brown's *Six of One* and *Loose Lips.*

Bittesch, Rudi Collector of authors' handwritten letters and one of Jane Wright's part-time employers in the period following Germany's surrender in 1945 in Muriel Spark's *The Girls of Slender Means.*

Bittlebrains, Lady Lady who is uneasy with her newly acquired title and is eager to attain the friendship of her neighbors, the Ashtons, in Sir Walter Scott's *The Bride of Lammermoor.*

Bittlebrains, Lord Quick-witted man who has a flair for earning money; he has used his wealth and power to grant political services and gain his title in Sir Walter Scott's *The Bride of Lammermoor.*

Bitts, Roderick Magsworth (Roddy), Junior Scion of a snobbish, well-to-do family; his infrequent encounters with Penrod Schofield usually come to disastrous conclusions in Booth Tarkington's *Penrod, Penrod and Sam,* and *Penrod Jashber.*

Bitzenko Former Russian landowner who acts as Otto Kreisler's second in a duel with Louis Soltyk; he insists on the dignity of the duel and flees the country after Soltyk's accidental shooting in Wyndham Lewis's *Tarr.*

Bitzer Colorless student in Thomas Gradgrind's school; he mechanically adheres to his utilitarian training to be without imagination or sentiment in Charles Dickens's *Hard Times.*

Bivens, Jimmy White grocer beaten by Sonny Boy Mosby; his death convinces the town of Somerton that blacks have set out to kill all the white people in Jesse Hill Ford's *The Liberation of Lord Byron Jones.*

Bixby, Luella Aunt of Serena Lindley; member of numerous church societies and organizations for social improvement in Mary Austin's *Santa Lucia.*

B. J. Character addressed by William Lee in William S. Burroughs's *The Ticket That Exploded;* consultant to the CIA on the fate of the British monarchy in *Exterminator!*

Björgulf One of the seven sons of Erlend and Kristin; along with his sibling Björgulf, he enters the brotherhood at Tautra in Sigrid Undset's *Kristin Lavransdatter.*

Björgulfsön, Lavrans Kristin Lavransdatter's father, owner of the estate Jörundgaard; descendent of powerful landowners; much later relinquishes his family estate to Kristin and sails to Iceland with Bishop Skaalholt in Sigrid Undset's *Kristin Lavransdatter.*

Bjorn, Sir Husband of Lady Aashild, a woman who deserts him for Erlend Nikulaussön and later commits suicide when she is spurned by Erlend in favor of the protagonist, Kristin Lavransdatter, in Sigrid Undset's *Kristin Lavransdatter.*

Bjornstam, Bea Sorenson See Sorenson, Bea.

Black Seaman who gets drunk during the advance to Scotchman's Bay in C. S. Forester's *Lieutenant Hornblower.*

Black (Kara) Miniaturist artist and manuscript binder recently returned from 12 years in Persia; nephew of Enishte, in love with his daughter Shekure, and one of the recurring narrators in Orhan Pamuk's *My Name Is Red.*

Black, Angela (Doris Blankfurt) Stripper killed by Harold Benson in Michael Crichton's *The Terminal Man.*

Black, Capitola See Le Noir, Capitola.

Black, Captain Squadron intelligence officer who spearheads the Glorious Loyalty Oath Campaign in Joseph Heller's *Catch-22.*

Black, Colin Margorie Pratt's suitor, later husband, a civil servant who makes Anton Hesse quite jealous in Doris Lessing's *A Ripple from the Storm.*

Black, Harry Machinist, union shop steward, and strike leader who resents the sexual demands of his wife and who, despite his apparent total masculinity, becomes intrigued by, then infatuated with, and later scorned by a series of male homosexuals and transvestites; ultimately sexually molests a ten-year-old boy and is beaten by a mob in Hubert Selby, Jr.,'s *Last Exit to Brooklyn.*

Black, Iris Beautiful sister of Ivor Black and first wife of Vadim Vadimovich; killed by a crazed lover in front of her brother and husband, who claims that Iris and his unnamed fourth wife were the only women he truly loved in Vladimir Nabokov's *Look at the Harlequins!*

Black, Ivor Brother of Iris Black and Cambridge friend of Vadim Vadimovich, whom he offhandedly invites to his Riviera villa, where Vadim meets Iris in Vladimir Nabokov's *Look at the Harlequins!*

Black, James (J. B.) Community storyteller who takes pride in his African roots in George Cain's *Blueschild Baby.*

Black, Josina Kugler Owner of the Black Motor Company in Mari Sandoz's *Capital City.*

Black, Lem Native nemesis of the emperor Brutus Jones on a jungle island in the West Indies; leads a band of rebel soldiers who dethrone and kill the puppet despot who has stolen vast wealth from the poor island natives in Eugene O'Neill's play *The Emperor Jones.*

Black, Michael Created by cloning Bernard 1, without the knowledge of Salter; age 35; mathematics teacher; married with three children in Caryl Churchill's *A Number.*

Black, Miss Lady O'Shane's companion and "evil genius," who, disliking Sir Ulick O'Shane's son, Marcus, and his ward, Harry Ormond, constantly works mischief by persuading Lady O'Shane to thwart the two whenever possible; she continues to spread malicious gossip and to scheme in opposition to Ormond as Mrs. M'Crule after her marriage in Maria Edgeworth's *Ormond.*

Black, Mr. Ironside minister; usually humane man and a saint of misery until World War I unleashes his sermons on God's righteous wrath in Ellen Glasgow's *Vein of Iron.*

Black, Peggy Richard Hardie's servant and mistress, who lures Alfred Hardie away from his wedding day with a letter of assignation for important information in Charles Reade's *Hard Cash.*

Black, Sirius Nicknamed Padfoot, James Potter's closest friend, Harry Potter's godfather, and an Animagus, a wizard who can take the shape of an animal; falsely accused of betrayal and murder and imprisoned in Azkaban; member of the Order of the Phoenix; killed by his cousin Bellatrix Lestrange in J. K. Rowling's Harry Potter series.

Black, Sylvia Young, intelligent aspiring writer and girlfriend of Peter Waterbury; she accompanies Maurice Bendrix to Sarah Miles's cremation and is ready to be seduced by him, but the attempt is aborted when Sarah's mother speaks to Bendrix at Sarah's cremation in Graham Greene's *The End of the Affair.*

Black, Willis B. See Will, Black.

Black Antler Seneca Indian and follower of a Seneca prophet in Jessamyn West's *The Massacre at Fall Creek.*

Blackavar Efrafan rabbit mutilated by Council Police for attempting to emigrate; rescued by Bigwig, he becomes a valued member of the band, proving his worth in the defense of the new warren in Richard Adams's *Watership Down.*

Blackberry Clever rabbit in Hazel's band of pioneers; he is responsible for devising and implementing important stratagems, including the use of boats in Richard Adams's *Watership Down.*

Black Bess Celebrated horse on which the highwayman Dick Turpin rides nonstop from London to York in William Harrison Ainsworth's *Rookwood.*

"Blackbird Pie," Narrator Male speaker who receives a letter slipped under his door from his wife of 23 years; reads in the letter an outline of his wife's grievances of all she finds wrong with him and their marriage; reacts incredulously, as he finds the "charges" to be "outrageous" and not within his wife's usual character in Raymond Carver's "Blackbird Pie."

Black Cat Guitar player who plays while Ideal, as a little girl, is implored to dance on a big brass bed in Carlene Hatcher Polite's *The Flagellants.*

Black Dog One of Flint's crew; he is pale and missing two fingers; he threatens Billy Bones and is stabbed in the shoulder by him; he deserts Pew in the rout at the Admiral Benbow Inn; spotted by Jim Hawkins at Long John Silver's pub, he eludes the pursuit Silver has ostentatiously directed in Robert Louis Stevenson's *Treasure Island.*

Black Donald Wily chief of a bandit gang and supposed henchman of the villain Gabriel Le Noir; befriended by Capitola Le Noir in E.D.E.N. Southworth's *The Hidden Hand.*

Blackenhurst, Paul English, upper-middle-class pilot (later killed) in Doris Lessing's *The Golden Notebook.*

Blackett, Mrs. Aged but cheerful and self-reliant widowed mother of Mrs. Almira Blackett Todd and William Blackett in Sarah Orne Jewett's *The Country of the Pointed Firs.*

Blackett, William Neat, handsome, and shy farmer/fisherman who is the brother of Mrs. Almira Todd; marries Esther Hight, whom he has secretly courted for forty years, in Sarah Orne Jewett's *The Country of the Pointed Firs.*

Blackford, Jerry Tenant farmer, husband of Judith Pippinger, and father of three children in Edith Summers Kelley's *Weeds.*

Blackford, Judith Pippinger (Judy) Daughter of Bill and Annie Pippinger, wife of Jerry Blackford, and mother of three children in Edith Summers Kelley's *Weeds.*

Blackford, Wyeth Feckless best friend of Anson Page and curator of a hunt club in Hamilton Basso's *The View from Pompey's Head.*

Black Guinea (Ebony, Guinea) Crippled blackman who catches coins in his mouth in Herman Melville's *The Confidence-Man.*

Black Herman Noted occultist in Ishmael Reed's *Mumbo Jumbo.*

"Black Hoodie," Narrator Irish teenager who discovers civil rights through his love for a Nigerian girl in Roddy Doyle's "Black Hoodie."

Blackie Leader of the Wormsley Common Gang of young boys who, after tiring of playing ball games in the London streets, decide to maliciously demolish a historic home that had only recently survived the London bombings of World War II in Graham Greene's "The Destructors."

Blackingson, Lawyer Farmer who loves oppressing the poor and beating his maids; he circulates cruel rumors that Dr. Sanderson has adopted democratic principles in William Beckford's *Modern Novel Writing; or, the Elegant Enthusiast.*

Black Kitten Offspring of the cat, Dinah; Alice's playful scolding of the kitten leads to her investigation of the world beyond the drawing-room looking-glass; the Red Queen turns into the kitten at the conclusion of Lewis Carroll's *Through the Looking-Glass.*

Blackledge, Rosie Repressed and misunderstood wife of the successful Stuart Blackledge; she has an affair with the aspiring writer and company lawyer Philip Witt in Roy Fuller's *Image of a Society.*

Blackledge, Stuart Mortgage manager of the Saddleford Building Society; a flashy, ambitious man who is considered the executive most likely to succeed the General Manager, he is later detected in what proves to have been a somewhat shady property deal in Roy Fuller's *Image of a Society.*

Blacklow, Mrs. Superficially unimpressive employee; with her husband a prisoner of war, she becomes pregnant by another soldier and impresses Lord Raingo with her attitude toward her situation and condition so that he provides funds for her care in Arnold Bennett's *Lord Raingo.*

Blackman (Big Bertha of Heaven) Itinerant fundamentalist preacher who conducts a revival in Irontown, Tennessee, in T. S. Stribling's *Teeftallow.*

Blackman, Captain Abraham Black career soldier cut down by snipers in Vietnam; in delirium, imagines he participates in outstanding moments of black military history, from the Battle of Bunker Hill in the American Revolution to the Abraham Lincoln Brigade in the Spanish civil war, in John A. Williams's *Captain Blackman.*

Blackman, Mr. Middle-aged client of the London procuress Mrs. Skelton; he sexually harasses Julia Townsend but goes away unsatisfied in Richard Graves's *The Spiritual Quixote.*

Black Masseur Gigantic, resolute, and nameless character; Anthony Burns's clear antithesis and the instrument for the fulfillment of his masochistic pleasure; through his massages he gives free rein to his sadistic vein in a sort of symbiotic relationship that culminates with his devouring Burns in a perverse reenactment of the Christian Eucharist in Tennessee Williams's "Desire and the Black Masseur."

Blackmore, Honour Sophia Western's maid, who escapes with Sophia to London, calling herself Mrs. Abigail at the Upton Inn; she switches allegiance to Lady Bellaston after Squire Western discharges her in Henry Fielding's *The History of Tom Jones.*

Black One Six-year-old narrator who, beginning in 1939, wanders throughout eastern Europe and experiences the cruelty and barbarity of those who shun him in Jerzy Kosinski's *The Painted Bird.*

Blackpool, Mrs. Stephen Slovenly, alcoholic wife of the good Stephen; she will not free him to marry the loving Rachel in Charles Dickens's *Hard Times.*

Blackpool, Stephen Mistreated but uncomplaining worker in Josiah Bounderby's factory; he is wrongly accused of being a thief; he falls down an abandoned mine shaft and dies in Charles Dickens's *Hard Times.*

Black Rabbit of Inlé Mythological rabbit responsible for death and disease; El-ahrairah turns to him in desperation in Richard Adams's *Watership Down.*

Blacksmith Trainer of George Pendyce's horse Ambler in John Galsworthy's *The Country House.*

Blacksmith Freed African slave from New Amsterdam with an independent mind and body; ventures to Jacob Varrk's estate in 1680s and 1690s Virginia and amazes Florens, the young black girl, with his dignity and self-confidence; sought by Florens during a smallpox epidemic for his knowledge of herbal medicines; abhors servitude and slavery of every kind; wants nothing of Florens's submission to him in Toni Morrison's *A Mercy.*

Blackstone, Garrett Roger Unemployed man with 26 years' experience in the paper industry; has a wife and four sons; Burke Devore decides not to kill him when he finds out that Garrett has already been hired at a paper company in Donald E. Westlake's *The Ax.*

Blackthorn, Rufus Once the dark-skinned gamekeeper in the Black Woods; bold, handsome flirt who enticed the married Dinah Lock and Rose Olliver into romantic relationships; remains a fond memory to both women in A. E. Coppard's "The Field of Mustard."

Black Warrior Primitive Indian philosopher in James Kirke Paulding's *Westward Ho!*

Blackwater, Lord Dissolute late father of Lady Kitty Bristol (Ashe); he married two heiresses in succession, spending the fortunes of both and wasting the dowry of his elder daughter before dying, survived by his second wife and both daughters in Mrs. Humphry Ward's *The Marriage of William Ashe.*

Blackwell, Alexandra Very attractive, pleasant woman who half-heartedly inherits a family fortune and business; people pleaser; twin sister of Eve Blackwell in Sidney Sheldon's *Master of the Game.*

Blackwell, David American from Oregon who works his way up to the head of an international conglomerate in South Africa and marries into it; husband of Kate Blackwell in Sidney Sheldon's *Master of the Game.*

Blackwell, Eve Very attractive, conniving woman who spends her life trying to make the world hers and finds only suffering; twin sister of Alexandra Blackwell in Sidney Sheldon's *Master of the Game.*

Blackwell, Kate Strong, successful, beautiful woman who parlays her inheritance into an international conglomerate; grateful daughter, manipulative wife, mother, grandmother and great-grandmother; daughter of Jamie McGregor in Sidney Sheldon's *Master of the Game.*

Blackwell, Melaine Widowed Irish-American painter who befriends and attempts to seduce Dan Boleyn in Wyndham Lewis's *The Apes of God.*

Blackwell, Tony Artistic dreamer who goes insane after not being aloud to follow his lifelong dream of being a painter; son of Kate Blackwell in Sidney Sheldon's *Master of the Game.*

Black Will (Willis B. Black) Well traveled African American and confidant of Abyssinia in Carlene Hatcher Polite's *Sister X and the Victims of Foul Play.*

Black Wolf College-educated Sioux Indian who is a friend of Aaron Gadd; murdered and scalped by the Ojibway Indians in Sinclair Lewis's *The GodSeeker.*

Blackwood, Carrie Religiously doctrinaire, argumentative wife of Herbert; she is competitive with her sister, Sophia Hutton, in Ivy Compton-Burnett's *Dolores.*

Blackwood, Charles Brother of Julian Blackwood and cousin of Constance and Mary Katherine Blackwood; enters the Blackwood home to secure the family fortune for himself and brings about the destruction of house and family in Shirley Jackson's *We Have Always Lived in the Castle.*

Blackwood, Constance Older sister of Mary Katherine Blackwood and nominal head of the household; accused but acquitted of the Blackwood family poisoning; never leaves the house and grounds because she is feared and hated in the village in Shirley Jackson's *We Have Always Lived in the Castle.*

Blackwood, Elsa Elder daughter of Herbert and Carrie; more independent and worldly than her sister, she secretly marries Bertram Hutton and waits while he is educated at Oxford in Ivy Compton-Burnett's *Dolores.*

Blackwood, Herbert Hospitable man, the Wesleyan minister, who is an evangelist for temperance; he invites the Huttons to dinner parties in Ivy Compton-Burnett's *Dolores.*

Blackwood, Herbert (the younger) Quiet-mannered son of Herbert and Carrie; he marries Evelyn Hutton in Ivy Compton-Burnett's *Dolores.*

Blackwood, Julian Elderly invalid uncle of Constance and Mary Katherine Blackwood; sole survivor of the Blackwood family poisoning, about which he is writing a book in Shirley Jackson's *We Have Always Lived in the Castle.*

Blackwood, Lettice Younger daughter of Herbert and Carrie; she gives her parents no trouble and is converted at a young age to Wesleyanism in Ivy Compton-Burnett's *Dolores.*

Blackwood, Mary Katherine (Merricat) Reclusive, psychotic 18-year-old who lives in the family manse with her older sister, Constance Blackwood, and her uncle, Julian Blackwood; as a child, poisoned most of her family in Shirley Jackson's *We Have Always Lived in the Castle.*

Blade, Harlow, Jr. Teenage author of a book on masturbation, which he delivers to the narrator's library in Richard Brautigan's *The Abortion.*

Blade, Harold Artist who paints portraits of Anne Forsyte, Jon Forsyte, and Fleur Mont in John Galsworthy's *Swan Song.*

Bladud, Prince Young prince featured in "True Legend of Prince Bladud" as legendary founder of Bath, recounted by Samuel Pickwick in Charles Dickens's *The Posthumous Papers of the Pickwick Club.*

Blagovo, Anna Ivanovna (Annette) Typist for Vadim Vadimovich; becomes his second wife and the mother of their daughter, Isabel; leaves Vadim under the influence of Ninel Langley, with whom she drowns in floods resulting from a hurricane in Vladimir Nabokov's *Look at the Harlequins!*

Blaikie, Captain Robert Old friend of Richard Hannay in Rhodesia; he is in a shell-shock hospital at Isham, where Hannay visits him and first sees Mary Lamington in John Buchan's *Mr. Standfast.*

Blain, Maggie Overtalkative cook at the state educational institution for women in Henry Green's *Concluding.*

Blaine, Amory Romantic egotist in and hero of F. Scott Fitzgerald's *This Side of Paradise.*

Blaine, Beatrice O'Hara Extravagant and alcoholic mother of Amory Blaine in F. Scott Fitzgerald's *This Side of Paradise.*

Blair High school girlfriend of Clay who enjoys life in Los Angeles and wants Clay to remain on the West Coast, though he intends to attend college in New Hampshire in Bret Easton Ellis's *Less Than Zero.*

Blair, Bartholomew Scott (Barley; covername: Mr. Brown) Individualistic but feckless London publisher and gifted amateur jazz musician; he becomes a reluctant spy, betraying his country for his love, Katya Orlova, when he gives Soviet K.G.B. agents the questions about Soviet military readiness that British Intelligence wants Russian dissident "Goethe" (Yakov Savelyev) to answer in John le Carré's *The Russia House.*

Blair, Edith Lawrence Childhood friend of Ruth Holland; stops seeing her after Ruth runs away with Stuart Williams, a married man, in Susan Glaspell's *Fidelity.*

Blair, Harriet Aging actress and the neglectful mother of Theodore Follett; she is an artificial, self-absorbed partygoer and giver; she needs the love and peace which she unexpectedly finds with her son's friend Henry Voyce; in a moment of derangement during an untoward and violent confrontation, Theodore kills her and himself in C. Day Lewis's *Starting Point.*

Blair, Hugh Editor in chief of *The Townsman* in Peter De Vries's *The Tunnel of Love.*

Blair, James Friend of Samuele; graduate of Harvard University in classical studies who travels to Europe as an archaeological adviser to a film company in Thornton Wilder's *The Cabala.*

Blair, Jenny See Archbald, Jenny Blair.

Blair, Robert Solicitor employed in the defense of Marion Sharpe and her mother; his investigative efforts, deductive powers, and belief in his clients triumph over his inexperience with criminal cases in Josephine Tey's *The Franchise Affair.*

Blaise Son of King Peter and successful merchant in Whitwall in William Morris's *The Well at the World's End.*

Blaize, Giles Uncle of Lucy Desborough and owner of a farm adjacent to Raynham Abbey; he horsewhips Richard Feverel and Ripton Thompson when they trespass on his land, which impells them to pay Tom Bakewell to set fire to the farmer's hayricks; Blaize thinks poorly of Richard and opposes his marriage to Lucy, to no avail in George Meredith's *The Ordeal of Richard Feverel.*

Blake Beigh Masters's lover during her freshman year in Bharati Mukherjee's *The Holder of the World.*

Blake, Alice Student at Calvin Coolidge High School who throws herself out of a window because of her unreturned love for English teacher Paul Barringer, whose response to her love letter was to correct it grammatically in Bel Kaufman's *Up the Down Staircase.*

Blake, Ben Aspiring law student and first serious boyfriend of Francie Nolan in Betty Smith's *A Tree Grows in Brooklyn.*

Blake, Betty Daughter of Rachel Colbert Blake; dies in an outbreak of diphtheria in Willa Cather's *Sapphira and the Slave Girl.*

Blake, Blacky Forest ranger who supervises and befriends Glacier District lookouts Jarry Wagner and Jack Duluoz in Jack Kerouac's *Desolation Angels.*

Blake, Catherine Wife of William Blake; has a ménage à trois with William and Mary in Frances Sherwood's *Vindication.*

Blake, Charlie The Blakes's 14-year-old son who is only referred to in the story; prefers spending time away from his parents' cold, estranged household and has practically moved into the neighbors' house in John Cheever's "The Five-Forty-Five."

Blake, Franklin Energetic amateur sleuth, who helps solve the mystery of the yellow diamond stolen from Rachel Verinder, with whom he is wildly in love; when it is established that he removed the diamond from her room, she will have no more to do with him; Ezra Jennings proves that Blake took the diamond while under the influence of a drug administered by Dr. Candy as a joke; the true thief, Godfrey Ablewhite, is unmasked, and the lovers are united in Wilkie Collins's *The Moonstone. A Romance.*

Blake, Hagar Weylin Great-grandmother of Dana Franklin in Octavia E. Butler's *Kindred.*

Blake, Harry Boyhood friend of Tom Bailey; inveterate carver of his initials in Thomas Bailey Aldrich's *The Story of a Bad Boy.*

Blake, Honor One of the village girls very much smitten with Christy Mahon, the newly arrived playboy; brings him a slice of cake in J. M. Synge's play *The Playboy of the Western World.*

Blake, James Suitor favored by Emma Flather until she becomes convinced she is sought by James, Earl of Bray in Robert Surtees's *Hillingdon Hall.*

Blake, Louise Main character's wife, a lonely and emotionally abused woman, for whom Mr. Blake feels no attraction or concern; only referred to in the story; through her absence, she reveals her husband's perspective on women and marriage, as he holds little respect for either in John Cheever's "The Five-Forty-Five."

Blake, Mabel Widowed mother of Tony Blake; stabbed to death by Erskine Fowler in Richard Wright's *Savage Holiday.*

Blake, Macijah Citizen of New Economy; informs Preacher of Pearl and John Harper's presence in the town in Davis Grubb's *The Night of the Hunter.*

Blake, Mary (Baby) High-spirited cousin of Charles O'Malley; she endeavors to attract him after his uncle's death but eventually marries Sparks in Charles Lever's *Charles O'Malley.*

Blake, Mary (Molly) Daughter of Rachel Colbert Blake; survives a diphtheria epidemic in Willa Cather's *Sapphira and the Slave Girl.*

Blake, Meredith Sensitive herbalist, apparently in love with Caroline Crale but actually in love with Elsa Greer; he is suspected of the poisoning of Amyas Crale in Agatha Christie's *Five Little Pigs.*

Blake, Michael United States congressman from Virginia; husband of Rachel Colbert Blake; dies of yellow fever during an epidemic in Willa Cather's *Sapphira and the Slave Girl.*

Blake, Miss Third governess of Muriel Ponsonby; she quits her post after Dr. Chaucer proposes to her in Ivy Compton-Burnett's *Daughters and Sons.*

Blake, Montagu Garrulous young curate, who had been at Oxford with John Gordon; completely absorbed by Kattie Forrester, he constantly sings her praises and has a grand wedding in Winchester Cathedral in Anthony Trollope's *An Old Man's Love.*

Blake, Mr. Judgmental, misogynistic, and superficial protagonist who considers himself both perceptive and sensitive, though he is neither; seems to blend in with all the other business commuters on Madison Avenue, and at the men's bar, and on the 5:45 train; treats women with total disregard, firing Miss Dent after their evening of intimacy and refusing to speak to his wife for two weeks after she forgets to prepare dinner one night; ironically, finds himself terrified and at the mercy of a woman's death threat, literally with his "face in the dirt," by the story's end; seems affected by Miss Dent's hostile confrontation in John Cheever's "The Five-Forty-Five."

Blake, Mr. Supposed friend of Benignus; he tricks him into suing his wife and then forces him to pay £2,500 damages in S. J. Pratt's *Liberal Opinions upon Animals, Man, and Providence.*

Blake, Mrs. Employment agency worker; advises Emma Lou Morgan to return to school and helps her find temporary work in Wallace Thurman's *The Blacker the Berry.*

Blake, Nathaniel (Nat) Orphaned street musician who is sent to Plumfield in Louisa May Alcott's *Little Men.*

Blake, Philip Meredith Blake's brother and Amyas Crale's best friend; he was in love with Caroline Crale, although seeming to hate her in Agatha Christie's *Five Little Pigs.*

Blake, Philip Relative and neighbor of the O'Malleys and father of Mary (Baby) Blake in Charles Lever's *Charles O'Malley.*

Blake, Rachel Colbert Daughter of Sapphira and Henry Colbert; widow of Michael Blake; helps her mother's slave Nancy escape to Canada in Willa Cather's *Sapphira and the Slave Girl.*

Blake, Ron Teenage beatnik and singer; admirer of Evelyn Pomeray and companion of Jack Duluoz during a retreat to a remote cabin in Jack Kerouac's *Big Sur.*

Blake, Sid One of four men on a long bicycle tour in England, where they encounter Roman roads; seeking a pub for refreshment; comes across the Tavern, a place where tea is served but no beer; lanky and cocksure young man who makes friends with the woman proprietor and her daughter; thinks romantically about the married woman in V. S. Pritchett's "Many Are Disappointed."

Blake, Thomas Protestant gentleman in County Galway who sympathizes with Philip Jones in the troubles among the tenantry in Anthony Trollope's *The Landleaguers.*

Blake, Tony Young son of Mabel Blake; accidentally falls from the balcony of his apartment after being frightened by the sudden appearance of Erskine Fowler in Richard Wright's *Savage Holiday.*

Blake, Walter (Dot) Gambler and horsetrainer, who encourages the courtship by Frank O'Kelly (Lord Ballindine) of Fanny Wyndham in Anthony Trollope's *The Kellys and the O'Kellys.*

Blake, William English poet and illustrator who helps Thomas Paine flee from England after Paine's *The Rights of Man* creates a furor in Howard Fast's *Citizen Tom Paine.*

Blake, William Thursday-night dinner guest of Joseph Johnson; has a ménage à trois with Catherine and Mary in Frances Sherwood's *Vindication.*

Blakely, Captain Presiding officer at the courtmartial of Lieutenant Steve Maryk for mutiny in Herman Wouk's *The Caine Mutiny.*

Blakely, Laura Actress who is falsely characterized in a story made up by Tim and told to Anthony Keating; the story proves to Keating that his suspicions about Tim's credibility are true in Margaret Drabble's *The Ice Age.*

Blakesley, Roger Rival of Charles Gray; loses the bank vice-presidency to Gray in John P. Marquand's *Point of No Return.*

Blakeston, Jim Big, strong married man with whom Liza Kemp enjoys the passionate love she denies Tom; however, the lovers can control neither their physical passion nor events in their lives in W. Somerset Maugham's *Liza of Lambeth.*

Blakeston, Mrs. Large, strong, blowsy, wronged wife of Jim; she physically fights the pregnant Liza Kemp for her husband in W. Somerset Maugham's *Liza of Lambeth.*

Blakey School boarder at Seaforth House whose parents live in Jamaica in Roy Fuller's *The Ruined Boys.*

Blalock, Clinton W. Friend who tries to get Lee Youngdahl a teaching position at Harvard in Mark Harris's *Wake Up, Stupid.*

Blamington, Mr. Frobisher dinner-party guest; eighteen years earlier, when he proposed marriage to the Provincial Lady, he was called Bill Ransom in E. M. Delafield's *The Provincial Lady Goes Further.*

Blamington, Mrs. The Provincial Lady's old flame's wife, whose look—lovely hair, Paris frock—the Provincial Lady "does not like at all" in E. M. Delafield's *The Provincial Lady Goes Further.*

Blanc, Estel Abyssinian mortician and an eccentric; first person Malcolm visits on his journey through life in James Purdy's *Malcolm.*

Blanc, Mr. (Man from the East) Quiet and reserved; does not understand The Swede's theories about the West and believes his vision is skewed because he has read too many dime novels; is frequently standing in the background, analyzing and evaluating but rarely contributing; stands up after the Swede is killed and confesses that he saw Johnnie cheating; feels guilty for not calling Johnnie out; believes that The Swede's death was a collaboration and that all the men are partly responsible for it in Stephen Crane's "The Blue Hotel."

Blanc, Pere Mission priest in Cameroon who befriends the young protagonist, Toundi Ondoua; teaches the youth to read and write, and keep a journal, a written record that will later expose tragedies in Cameroon in Ferdinand Oyono's *Life of a Houseboy.*

Blanca Daughter of the central figure, Esteban Trueb; persists against her father's violent disapproval in a relationship with a peasant, Pedro Tercero García, in Isabel Allende's *The House of the Spirits.*

Blanca Shrewish wife of Alfonso Pereira in Ecuador; seeks a wet nurse for her baby from the native Indian mothers; picks the unfortunate married Cunshi, for Alfonso forces the young girl to sleep with him in Jorge Icaza's *Huasipungo.*

Blanca, Dona Mother of Dr. Juvenal Urbino and mother-in-law of Fermina; forces Fermina to take harp lessons and to eat eggplant; dies while Dr. Urbino and Fermina are in Europe in Gabriel García Márquez's *Love in the Time of Cholera.*

Blanch, Mrs. Woman detective assigned by Claude Polteed to spy on Irene Forsyte for Soames Forsyte in John Galsworthy's *In Chancery.*

Blanchard, Augusta Young American painter who belongs to the artistic fraternity of Rome; fiancée of Mr. Leavenworth in Henry James's *Roderick Hudson.*

Blanchard, Bobby Mary and Virgil's son; the county sheriff and a sensitive and caring man who falls in love with Jewell Coleman in Larry Brown's *Father and Son.*

Blanchard, Emmy Elder sister of Jenny; she has spent the last ten years taking care of the household and caring for her ailing father; she feels she has lost her youth and her chance for romance, but she finds happiness with Alf Rylett, who originally courted her sister in Frank Swinnerton's *Nocturne.*

Blanchard, Jane Allan Wrentmore's bride-elect, stolen from him by a subterfuge involving forged letters and other trickery by Fergus Ingleby as prelude to events in Wilkie Collins's *Armadale.*

Blanchard, Jenny Millinery-shop worker who dreams of romance; at nearly twenty-six, she has begun to feel that life is passing her by until she meets Keith Reddington, captain of a small private yacht, whose rebellious and romantic temperament matches her own in Frank Swinnerton's *Nocturne.*

Blanchard, Mary Virgil's lover before he goes off to fight in World War II; she marries another man while pregnant with Virgil's child; later she becomes a teacher and successfully raises her son in Larry Brown's *Father and Son.*

Blanchard, Mr. Minister who preaches morality, warns Robert Colwan against Gil-martin, and becomes Robert's first murder victim in James Hogg's *The Private Memoirs and Confessions of a Justified Sinner.*

Blanchard, Mrs. Former mistress of Thorpe-Ambrose, the Norfolk estate which comes into the possession of Allan Armadale in Wilkie Collins's *Armadale.*

Blanchard, Pa Semi-invalid who, though he depends on his daughters Emmy and Jenny for his care, is financially stable, having provided for income in addition to his retirement through membership in various beneficent societies in Frank Swinnerton's *Nocturne.*

Blanchard, Rita Paramour of Walter Knight and onetime owner of a ranch coveted by Joe Templeton in Joan Didion's *Run River.*

Blanchard-White, Mr. Uni-European zealot who forces Emile Englander to use the zoo as a source for animal torture and human contests after the victory of the Uni-Europeans in Angus Wilson's *The Old Men at the Zoo.*

Blanche Common-law wife of Albert Shore; he nurses her with great care through a terminal illness in Roy Fuller's *My Child, My Sister.*

Blanche Prostitute with Jake Jackson when he is robbed by a pickpocket in Richard Wright's *Lawd Today.*

Blanche, Anthony Brilliantly cultured aesthete who is, for a time, a student at Oxford with Charles Ryder and Sebastian Flyte; he leaves Oxford to carry on a homosexual relationship in Munich and later gives a clever and dismissive analysis of Charles Ryder's recent series of paintings in Evelyn Waugh's *Brideshead Revisited.*

Blanche, Sir Carte Comic, ostentatious architect, who undertakes excessive and ruinously expensive renovations of the Duke of St. James's London residence (Hauteville House) and country seat (Hauteville Castle) in Benjamin Disraeli's *The Young Duke.*

Blancove, Algernon Cousin of Edward Blancove, Dahlia Fleming's seducer; Algernon arranges to pay Nic Sedgett to marry Dahlia and delays Dahlia's letters to Edward, which restore his love for her, until it is too late for Edward to prevent her marriage to Sedgett in George Meredith's *Rhoda Fleming.*

Blancove, Edward Sir William Blancove's son, who seduces Dahlia Fleming, tires of her, asks his cousin to pay someone to marry her, realizes he loves her and rushes back to England but is unable to stop the marriage; although it proves invalid, he is unable to convince Dahlia to marry him because she has lost all taste for life in George Meredith's *Rhoda Fleming.*

Blancove, Sir William Edward Blancove's father, a banker who marries Mrs. Lovell, once courted by his son in George Meredith's *Rhoda Fleming.*

Bland Master-at-arms who runs an alcohol-smuggling ring aboard the *Neversink* in Herman Melville's *White-Jacket.*

Bland, Daisy Extremely naïve and beautiful nineteen-year-old from the Cotswold hills working in a London millinery shop when she meets Hugo Chesterton, a suave criminal, and is soon pregnant with his child; passive and not particularly bright, this "child of nature" is treated as a white goddess among savages in her lover's underworld; she is tricked into giving evidence against him in Nicholas Blake's *A Tangled Web.*

Bland, Gerald Harvard classmate of Quentin Compson I in William Faulkner's *The Sound and the Fury.*

Bland, Roy (codename "Soldier") Working-class Oxford don, ex-Marxist dialectical materialist, and British Intelligence officer who is Bill Haydon's second in command of the London Station; he creates and runs European espionage networks Aggravate, Contemplate, and Plato in John le Carré's *Tinker, Tailor, Soldier, Spy.* He appears in *The Honourable Schoolboy.*

Blandeville, Lady Emily Youngest daughter of a noble peer; she is wooed by Sir Everard Waverly before marrying Colonel Talbot; her loss of their child causes Edward Waverly to gain Talbot's freedom, placing them in Edward's debt in Sir Walter Scott's *Waverly.*

Blandford, Mrs. Benevolent, rich widow, unsympathetic to the aristocratic defense of an economic and political system that forces the majority of the English to live at a subsistence level; she assumes the care and instruction of Azemia, who loves her benefactress dearly; she gives Azemia a dowry in William Beckford's *Azemia.*

Blandford Carteret's Mother Southern widow who writes a letter informing Blandford Carteret that her deceased husband's old vassal and bodyguard during the Civil War is traveling to New York to hand him a relic gold watch that belonged to his father's family in O. Henry's "Thimble, Thimble."

Blandish, Lady Widow and neighbor of Sir Austin Feverel; she attempts to reconcile Sir Austin and Richard Feverel; she falls in love for a time with Sir Austin but, after seeing the tragic end of his system, rejects both the man and the system in George Meredith's *The Ordeal of Richard Feverel.*

Blandish, Madame Sisseretta (Mrs. Sari Blandine) Owner of a Harlem hair-straightening parlor; when the Black-No-More process makes all blacks white, she develops a process to stain white skin light brown in George S. Schuyler's *Black No More.*

Blandly Squire Trelawney's old friend, who finds the schooner *Hispaniola* and Captain Smollett for him; he is to send a consort if the *Hispaniola* fails to return by end of August in Robert Louis Stevenson's *Treasure Island.*

Blane, Julie Actress in Tommy Beamish's act who lives with him in a loveless relationship; she seeks solace from the much younger Dick Herncastle, but is thrown out by Beamish, who discovers them together; she continues her second-rate career in South Africa in J. B. Priestley's *Lost Empires.*

Blane, Niel Town piper and taverner, who helps Henry Morton find Burley (John Balfour) after Morton returns home from exile in Sir Walter Scott's *Old Mortality.*

Blaney, Alexander Homosexual man killed accidentally by Los Angeles policeman Sam Niles in Joseph Wambaugh's *The Choirboys.*

Blaney, Ethel Teacher and sister of Elizabeth Blaney Morison in William Maxwell's *They Came Like Swallows.*

Blankenship, Jim Chief minister of the Pine Street Methodist Church; initiator of extravagant fund-raising schemes for building a large nonsectarian cathedral in T. S. Stribling's *Unfinished Cathedral.*

Blankenship, Mrs. Wife of the mill owner in Hopewell, Kentucky; after James and Christianna Wheeler's quintuplets die, Mrs. Blankenship helps arrange for the Wheelers' to tour with the remains of the quints in Bobbie Ann Mason's *Feather Crowns.*

Blankfurt, Doris See Black, Angela.

Blarney, Lady Strumpet posing as a town lady; she is an acquaintance of Squire Thornhill in Oliver Goldsmith's *The Vicar of Wakefield.*

Blasillo el bobo The "town idiot" loyal unto death to his pastor in Miguel de Unamuno's *Saint Manuel the Good, Martyr (San Manuel Bueno, mártir).*

Blaskin, Gilbert Novelist who befriends Michael Cullen and is discovered to be his father in Alan Sillitoe's *A Start in Life.*

Blathers, Mr. Bow Street runner who comes to Mrs. Maylie's house to investigate the burglary in Charles Dickens's *Oliver Twist.*

Blatherwick, Bill Professional beggar who employs the young Arthur Golding in George Gissing's *Workers in the Dawn.*

Blatherwick, Mrs. Slum landlady who takes in the wandering Arthur Golding in George Gissing's *Workers in the Dawn.*

Blatt, Horace Intrusive, irritating vacationer; his snapshot-taking is annoying but helpful to Hercule Poirot in Agatha Christie's *Evil Under the Sun.*

Blatt, Sister Deaconess resident of the Malorys' parish and an "excellent" woman acquaintance of Mildred Lathbury in Barbara Pym's *Excellent Women.* She makes a brief appearance in *A Glass of Blessings.*

Blattergowl, Mr. Minister and friend of Oldbuck (Jonathan Oldenbuck); he visits the ruins of St. Ruth's Priory with Oldbuck and others in Sir Walter Scott's *The Antiquary.*

Blau, Bernice Museum curator Jack Flood consults about the fan Yin-Li sends him; a virginal thirty-five; not noticeably pretty except when she is aroused by the fan in Maureen Howard's *Expensive Habits.*

Blau, Deborah (Deb) Mentally ill teenage Jewish heroine committed to a mental hospital in Hannah Green's *I Never Promised You a Rose Garden.*

Blau, Esther Distraught, yet strong mother of Deborah Blau; has to fight herself and her family to help her daughter by committing her to a mental hospital in Hannah Green's *I Never Promised You a Rose Garden.*

Blau, Jacob Accountant whose family emigrated from Poland; father of Deborah Blau; feels the pressures of guilt, failure, and love in Hannah Green's *I Never Promised You a Rose Garden.*

Blau, Susan (Suzy) Younger sister of Deborah Blau; has to live in the shadow of a sister who is not present in Hannah Green's *I Never Promised You a Rose Garden.*

Blazo, Colonel Sir Thomas Bowler in a cricket match in the West Indies, in an anecdote by Alfred Jingle in Charles Dickens's *The Posthumous Papers of the Pickwick Club.*

Blazon, Padre Eccentric, aged Spanish member of the Bollandists, a Jesuit association of scholars of hagiography, the study of saints and sainthood, whom Dunstan Ramsay meets in Austria during the course of his scholarly mission to prove Mary's sainthood; convinces Dunstan of the subjective nature of sainthood, allowing him to reach an ambivalent closure to his quest in Robertson Davies's *Fifth Business.*

Blearney, Arthur Amicable and well-travelled entertainment promoter who introduces Charles Lumley to Bernard and Veronica Roderick and later gives Charles a job as a bouncer in an all-night club in John Wain's *Hurry On Down.*

Bledlow, Lady Constance Rich, orphaned daughter of Lord and Lady Risborough; she enriches the lives of the family of her uncle, Ewen Hooper, an Oxford don; she marries the financially ruined, aristocratic Douglas, Lord Falloden in Mrs. Humphry Ward's *Lady Connie.*

Bledsoe, A. Hebert President of a southern black college who expels the narrator and sends him to New York in Ralph Ellison's *Invisible Man.*

Bledsoe, Chris Nephew of Lee Buck Cal; attracted to Louisa Sheridan, who feels herself falling in love with him; killed in a feud in Harriette Simpson Arnow's *Mountain Path.*

Bledsoe, Jerry Sawyer's and Sloat's electrician and handyman; electrocuted in Stephen King's and Peter Straub's *The Talisman.*

Bledyard Landscape painter and art master at St. Bride's School and the voice of William Mor's moral conscience in Iris Murdoch's *The Sandcastle.*

Bleecker Host of the party at which George Kelcey gets drunk in Stephen Crane's *George's Mother.*

Bleedham, Mr. Deaf director for the New Collier Company who participates in the General Meeting in John Galsworthy's *The Man of Property.*

Bleeding Nun See Cisternas, Beatrice de las.

Bleeding Nun, The Female ghost of one of Raymond's relatives, Beatrice de las Cisternas; takes the veil against her will and breaks her vows; beautiful and voluptuous, gives free impulse to her passions; her sexual licentiousness leads her both to murder and death; as she is doomed to suffer from remorse and her bones go unburied, she continues to haunt the castle of Lindenberg until Raymond buries her skeleton in Matthew Gregory Lewis's *The Monk.*

Blefuscu, Emperor of Ruler of the Lilliputians' neighbors and enemies; he welcomes Lemuel Gulliver when he escapes from Lilliput to Blefuscu by wading in Jonathan Swift's *Travels into Several Remote Nations of the World. In Four Parts. By Lemuel Gulliver.*

Blekensop, Lady Shallow and money-conscious friend of Lady Ashton, with whom she schemes to bring about the marriage of Lucy Ashton and Frank Hayston, Laird of Bucklaw, in Sir Walter Scott's *The Bride of Lammermoor.*

Blemont, Caroline de Beautiful but heartless pupil at Mlle. Reuter's school, who sits in the front row in Charlotte Brontë's *The Professor.*

Blenda, Queen Mother of Charles Xavier, the last king of Zembla; erects a tasteless monument on the site of her husband's death in Vladimir Nabokov's *Pale Fire.*

Blenkinsop Chauffeur to the Pattersons in Frank Swinnerton's *Some Achieve Greatness.*

Blenkinsop, Barbara Daughter of Old Mrs. Blenkinsop; she repeatedly breaks her engagement to Crosbie Carruthers to placate her dominating mother; she then marries just before he leaves for India in E. M. Delafield's *The Diary of a Provincial Lady.*

Blenkinsop, Cousin Maud Elderly spinster who comes to the village to be companion of Old Mrs. Blenkinsop; both are cheered as she recklessly drives her tiny Austin about the village in E. M. Delafield's *The Provincial Lady Goes Further.*

Blenkinsop, Heather Bossy 59-year-old librarian; she has always taken her holidays with and planned to retire with her old school friend Daphne Dagnall in Barbara Pym's *A Few Green Leaves.*

Blenkinsop, Mrs. Possessive woman who bitterly opposes the marriage of her daughter in E. M. Delafield's *The Diary of a Provincial Lady.* A year later she proudly displays her daughter's baby and insists that the grandchild is an exact replica of her picture of herself as an infant in *The Provincial Lady Goes Further.*

Blenkiron, John Scantlebury Wealthy American engineer industrialist with a duodenal complaint and the habit of playing Patience in times of stress; gifted with the cool nerve of the ideal counterespionage agent, he moves across enemy lines to solve the cryptic puzzle and defeat the German war machine in John Buchan's *Greenmantle.* He works with Richard Hannay and Mary Lamington under the direction of Sir Walter Bullivant of the Foreign Service in destroying the secret organization of a dangerous German agent in *Mr. Standfast.* Officially dead, but in disguise as "Senor Rosas", he uncovers a new threat against civilization brought by Mr. Castor in Olifa in South America and ends Castor's dictatorship in *The Courts of the Morning.* He urges Sir Edward Leithen to search for the missing Francis Galliard, without knowing that Leithen is terminally ill in *Sick Heart River.*

Blent, Raymond (Ray) Star football player who purposely fails two courses to cover up accepting a bribe to lose a game; boyfriend of Lily Sayre in Howard Nemerov's *The Homecoming Game.*

Blessing, Shenandoah Army lieutenant and friend of Sean O'Sullivan; heads police services in Rombaden in post-World War II Germany in Leon Uris's *Armageddon.*

Blessingbourne, Lady, Duchess of Dounderdale Woman who appears as a parody of aristocratic snobbery in S. J. Pratt's *Tutor of Truth.*

Blessingbourne, Lord, Duke of Dounderdale Male character portrayed in hyperbole as a parody of aristocratic snobbery in S. J. Pratt's *Tutor of Truth.*

Bletchley, Ian Lifelong friend of Colin Saville; he gets an education and manages to escape the almost inevitable poverty of a coalmine family in David Storey's *Saville.*

Bletheram, Colonel Rakish octogenarian in Ellen Glasgow's *The Romantic Comedians;* also appears in *They Stooped to Folly.*

Blethyn Husband of Ceridwen Morgan in Richard Llewellyn's *How Green Was My Valley.*

Bletson, Joshua Intellectual politician who is privately an atheist; he is one of the parliamentary commissioners sent to take possession of Woodstock in Sir Walter Scott's *Woodstock.*

Bleu, Deni Seaman and friend of Jack Duluoz in New York in Jack Kerouac's *Visions of Cody;* also appears in *Book of Dreams* and *Desolation Angels.*

Blevins, Jimmy Young boy whom John Grady Cole and Lacey Rawlins encounter while traveling to Mexico. He fears God will take his life during a rain storm, and during one such storm he loses his horse, which he steals from the person who recovered it. Blevins is eventually killed after being tortured by the police captain in Cormac McCarthy's *All the Pretty Horses.*

Blewitt, Mr. Benevolent but financially indiscreet acquaintance of the hero Benignus in S. J. Pratt's *Liberal Opinions upon Animals, Man, and Providence.*

Blicero, Captain Dominus See Weissmann, Lieutenant.

Blick, Calvin Blackmailer and an evil manipulator, disliked and feared by others in Iris Murdoch's *The Flight from the Enchanter.*

Blick, Danny Boyfriend to Kate Fletcher (Armstrong) during her sexual-awakening year of sixteen; he is a naïve, small-time con man; Kate includes him on her list of possible "marginal people" in Margaret Drabble's *The Middle Ground.*

Blick, Dr. Hypocitical clergyman who receives his post because of special favors he did for Lord Grondale in Robert Bage's *Hermsprong.*

Blifil, Bridget Allworthy Sister to Thomas Allworthy, mother to Master Blifil and clandestinely to Tom Jones; her obvious preference for Tom arouses Allworthy's pity for Blifil; Blifil intercepts and conceals her deathbed revelation that Tom is her child in Henry Fielding's *The History of Tom Jones.*

Blifil, Captain Avaricious brother of Dr. Blifil; having married Bridget Allworthy, he fathers Master Blifil; his untimely death forestalls his plan to inherit Squire Allworthy's estate in Henry Fielding's *The History of Tom Jones.*

Blifil, Dr. Ill-trained, impoverished medical man, who encourages his brother to court Bridget Allworthy; the match secure, he is cast out by his brother and dies of a broken heart in Henry Fielding's *The History of Tom Jones.*

Blifil, Master Hypocrite and villain, who schemes to ruin his half brother, Tom Jones; he is son to Bridget Allworthy Blifil and nephew to Squire Allworthy; he is undone when circumstance reveals his villainy to Allworthy in Henry Fielding's *The History of Tom Jones.*

Bligh, Mr. Mr. Weston's predecessor as Mr. Hatfield's curate at Horton in Anne Brontë's *Agnes Grey.*

Bligh, Sergeant Member of the Royal Irish Artillery, in charge of transporting Dr. Sturk back to his house when he is found badly beaten in the woods in J. Sheridan Le Fanu's *The House by the Churchyard.*

Bligh, William Captain of the HMS *Bounty* whose harsh treatment of his men leads them to rebel in Charles Nordhoff and James Norman Hall's *Mutiny on the Bounty;* set adrift with eighteen men in a small boat and brings all but one of them to safety in *Men Against the Sea.*

Blight, Young Solicitor Mortimer Lightwood's clerk, who invents imaginary clients in Charles Dickens's *Our Mutual Friend.*

Blimber, Cornelia Dr. Blimber's daughter and teacher of dead languages at the school; a serious scholar who wears spectacles and cuts her hair short, she marries Mr. Feeder in Charles Dickens's *Dombey and Son.*

Blimber, Dr. Pompous head of the boys' boarding school in Brighton that little Paul Dombey attends; his unfortunate method of education is to force learning into the boys' heads and overfeed them academically, but he grows very fond of Paul in Charles Dickens's *Dombey and Son.*

Blimber, Mrs. Dr. Blimber's wife; not as learned as her husband or daughter, she pretends to appreciate the classical and the classics in Charles Dickens's *Dombey and Son.*

Blimin, Mr. Member of the Communist Party's Central Committee in New York; questions Lionel Lane about his true identity and political beliefs and about the murders of Langley Herndon, Gilbert Blount, and Jack Hilton in Richard Wright's *The Outsider.*

Blimunda Wise female protagonist who possesses a second sight that perceives the wills of others; sees others leaving their souls to the church in José Saramago's *Baltasar and Blimunda.*

Blind Beggar Artist of begging, who lives well on alms and who takes Pompey to Bath in Francis Coventry's *The History of Pompey the Little.*

Blind Beggar Hideously deformed and afflicted with scrofula and blindness, accosts travelers on the road from Yonville to Rouen with trashy songs of love; already bankrupt, Emma gives him all her change; when Homais fails to cure his disease, he has him locked up in an asylum in order to distract from his medical quackery in Gustave Flaubert's *Madame Bovary.*

Blinder, Mrs. Landlady of the Necketts, who works in a chandler's shop; she generously forgives the children the rent of their lodging after their father dies in Charles Dickens's *Bleak House.*

Blind George Observer of dock life who tries to use his knowledge for self gain; he blinds Dan Ogle with lime in Arthur Morrison's *The Hole in the Wall.*

Blind Pig (Piggy-O) Blind, filthy drug deliverer and later drug dealer in Nelson Algren's *The Man with the Golden Arm.*

Blind White Devil (King of San Francisco) Blind party boss, who confers with Black Tom and is sketched by Loudon Dodd in Robert Louis Stevenson's *The Wrecker.*

Blint, Mr. Member of the Ververs' social circle who is the object of Lady Castledean's romantic interest in Henry James's *The Golden Bowl.*

Bliss Boyhood name of Senator Adam Sunraider in Ralph Ellison's *Juneteenth.*

Bliss Native of Gaia who joins Golan Trevize and Janov Pelorat in order to teach them about Gaia, is suspected by Trevize of being a robot; paramour of Pelorat in Isaac Asimov's *Foundation's Edge.*

Bliss, Betty Plump, earnest graduate student of Russian; writes a paper on Dostoyevski for Professor Pnin in Vladimir Nabokov's *Pnin.*

Bliss, Dorothy Elderly Jewish widow who lives in the Towers condominium complex in Miami, Florida; mother of Ellen, Marvin, and Frank in *Mrs. Ted Bliss,* by Stanley Elkin.

Bliss, Ellen Dorothy Bliss's daughter-in-law; widow of Marvin Bliss; health food fanatic and shoe salesperson; marries Milton Yellin in *Mrs. Ted Bliss,* by Stanley Elkin.

Bliss, Frank Dorothy Bliss's son; sociology professor; doesn't like Manny Tressler helping Mrs. Bliss; lives in Pittsburgh, and later in Providence in *Mrs. Ted Bliss,* by Stanley Elkin.

Bliss, Marvin Dorothy Bliss's deceased son; dies in his thirties of leukemia in *Mrs. Ted Bliss,* by Stanley Elkin.

Bliss, Mattie See Carrington, Nina.

Bliss, Maxine Dorothy Bliss's daughter; lives in Cincinnati in *Mrs. Ted Bliss,* by Stanley Elkin.

Bliss, Ted Deceased husband of Dorothy; dies in his early seventies of cancer and is returned to Chicago to be buried; was a butcher and sold meat on the black market during World War II in *Mrs. Ted Bliss,* by Stanley Elkin.

Blitch, Mabel See Lipscomb, Mabel Blitch.

Blix See Bessemer, Travis.

Blixen, Karen Famous writer whom the Allstons meet on their journey to Denmark; introduces the possibility that Joe Allston's peasant mother may have immigrated to America to escape the sexual advances of Astrid's father, an experimenter in genetic purity in Wallace Stegner's *The Spectator Bird.*

Bloch, Albert Marcel's school friend; recommends Bergotte to Marcel; speaks in neo-Homeric jargon; an indiscreet Jewish snob; rival writer to Marcel who ignores Marcel's article in *Le Figaro;* changes his name to Jacques de Rozier and adopts English mannerisms in Marcel Proust's *Á la recherche du temps perdu.*

Bloch, Shifrah Puah Polish concentration camp survivor and mother of Masha Tortshiner in Isaac Bashevis Singer's *Enemies, A Love Story.*

Block, the Tradesman Grain merchant named Rudi, who, like Joseph K., is a client of the defense lawyer Huld, though for already more than five years and without any indication of advancement or success concerning the defense of the charges against him, in Franz Kafka's *The Trial.*

Block Elder Big, red-headed woman who oversees a group of female prisoners at the Nazi concentration camp; against her better judgment, answers the women's pleadings to learn the fate of their husbands and children, who have been gassed to death and burned in pits in Tadeusz Borowski's *This Way for the Gas, Ladies and Gentlemen.*

Blockitt, Mrs. Florence Dombey's nurse in Charles Dickens's *Dombey and Son.*

Blodgett, Doremus (Reme) Hosiery salesman who is the first of many people to be shocked by George Brush's unusual theories in Thornton Wilder's *Heaven's My Destination.*

Bloeckman (Black), Joseph Movie producer in F. Scott Fitzgerald's *The Beautiful and Damned.*

Blofeld, Ernst Stavro Powerful, two-hundred-eighty-pound leader of the international terrorist organization SPECTRE; he steals two atomic bombs in an extortion plot against England and the United States in Ian Fleming's *Thunderball.* Thwarted, he devises a biological-warfare scheme against England from his Alpine fortress in *On her Majesty's Secret Service.* He has become "Dr. Shatterhand", the owner of a Japanese island property stocked with poisonous tropical plants; James Bond succeeds in his mission to kill him in *You Only Live Twice.*

Blois, Chevalier de Young Tom Newcome's French tutor, an emigré of ancient family; his daughter marries Comte de Florac but retains a lifelong innocent affection for Newcome in William Makepeace Thackeray's *The Newcomes.*

Blok, Hafen Hessian deserter and Indian fighter; heavy drinking, storytelling vagrant in John Pendleton Kennedy's *Swallow Barn.*

Blok, Nikkel Crude and brutal butcher of Liège; he kills the Bishop of Liège with his cleaver at William De la Marck's command in Sir Walter Scott's *Quentin Durward.*

Blomburg, Dr. Jules First of John Wilder's psychiatrists; Wilder calls him a dead-silent bullshit artist in Richard Yates's *Disturbing the Peace.*

Blonay, Moll (Mother Blonay) Poor, elderly, potion-selling woman living in a hovel near Dorchester, South Carolina; assists her son Ned Blonay in betraying Major Singleton's partisan band to the British in William Gilmore Simms's *The Partisan.*

Blonay, Ned (Goggle) Son of Moll Blonay; betrays Major Singleton's partisan band to the British in William Gilmore Simms's *The Partisan.*

Blondel of Nesle Minstrel who sings to entertain King Richard in Sir Walter Scott's *The Talisman.*

Blondeville, Gaston de French knight favored by Henry III and accused by Hugh Woodreeve of robbing and murdering Reginald de Folville; he marries Lady Barbara only to be haunted by the ghost of Folville; upon winning in a tournament, he is struck dead by Folville's ghost in Ann Radcliffe's *Gaston de Blondeville.*

Blondie Margarito Sadistic soldier in the Mexican Revolution (1910–17) in Mariano Azuela's *The Underdogs.*

Blood, Colonel Soldier who is employed as a henchman by the Duke of Buckingham to prevent Edward Christian's return to London in Sir Walter Scott's *Peveril of the Peak.*

Blood, Fanny Friend of Mary Wollstonecraft since childhood; quick with numbers; marries Hugh Skeys and moves to Portugal; dies a few months after she miscarries in Frances Sherwood's *Vindication.*

Blood, Jewell Mother of Loyal, Marvin (Dub), and Mernelle Blood and wife of Mink Blood; sells the farm after Mink's death; learns how to drive; makes money by working for a vegetable canning company and knitting for a ski shop; while on a drive, dies of an aneurysm, although her body is never found; wedding ring is buried in her place in E. Annie Proulx's *Postcards.*

Blood, Loyal Oldest child of Mink and Jewell Blood and brother of Marvin (Dub) and Mernelle Blood; kills his girlfriend, Billy Handy, then tries to cover up his murder by moving away; keeps a journal and sends postcards to his family; becomes a uranium prospector; is almost blinded in one eye by a splinter, and in the hospital meets Bullet Wulff; becomes a fossil hunter with Wulff; buys a farm in North Dakota and raises beans, but the farm burns down; traps coyotes for their pelts; as an old man, reflects on his itinerant life and collects hats in E. Annie Proulx's *Postcards.*

Blood, Lydia (Lily, Lurella, Lyddy) Niece of Maria Latham and the Erwins and granddaughter of Deacon Latham; becomes, on her trip to Venice, the Lady of the Aroostook; marries James Staniford in William Dean Howells's *The Lady of the Aroostook.*

Blood, Marvin (Dub) Son of Mink and Jewell Blood and brother of Loyal and Mernelle Blood; lost an arm in a train accident; dates Myrtle, who leaves him; burns his father's barn at his father's request and goes to jail for a year; moves to Miami and initially makes his money by swindling people through a bogus letter written from a Mexican jail; becomes a realtor, then meets and marries Pala Suarez in E. Annie Proulx's *Postcards.*

Blood, Mernelle Daughter of Mink and Jewell Blood and sister of Loyal and Marvin (Dub) Blood; as a child, has pen pals and enjoys receiving mail; answers an advertisement in the newspaper for a wife from Ray MacWay; marries Ray; visits her mother often and takes care of her in E. Annie Proulx's *Postcards.*

Blood, Minkton (Mink) Father of Loyal, Marvin (Dub), and Mernelle and husband of Jewell Blood; has arthritis, but works hard on the dairy farm; asks Dub to burn their barn for the insurance money; the arson is found out and he goes to jail for two years; hangs himself in his cell in E. Annie Proulx's *Postcards.*

Bloodworth, Arlington, Sr. Plantation and slave owner who adopts and rears Pourty Bloodworth in Leon Forrest's *The Bloodworth Orphans.*

Bloodworth, Pourty Ford Worthy Bloodworthy Foundling reared by Arlington Bloodworth, Sr.; father of LaDonna Scales, Regal Pettibone, Amos Otis Thigpen, Noah Grandberry, and Jonathan Bass; kills his foster father in Leon Forrest's *The Bloodworth Orphans.*

Bloodworth III, Arlington Father, by Rachel Rebecca Carpenter Flowers, of Industrious Bowman and Carl-Rae Bowman in Leon Forrest's *The Bloodworth Orphans.*

Bloom, Ellen Deceased mother of Leopold Bloom; she is remembered by her son in James Joyce's *Ulysses.*

Bloom, Isaac Nathan Army private who boxes for the regimental team; commits suicide after being implicated in a military investigation of homosexual activity in James Jones's *From Here to Eternity.*

Bloom, "Lady" Collaborator with the gamester Pliant in a scheme to cheat George Edwards of his fortune; she feigns love for George in John Hill's *The Adventures of Mr. George Edwards, a Creole.*

Bloom, Leopold Apparently insignificant middle-aged Jewish advertising man whose wanderings in Dublin on June 16th, 1904, parallel the homecoming of Homer's Odysseus; he suffers the prejudice of Dublin's Roman Catholic citizens, avoids confronting the infidelity of his wife, Molly, with whom he has not had sex for ten years, and rescues Stephen Dedalus from British soldiers in the brothel district in James Joyce's *Ulysses.*

Bloom, Marion (Molly) Leopold Bloom's voluptuous wife, who has an affair with Blazes Boylan; her stream-of-consciousness monologue, recalling all the men she has ever loved, is the final episode in James Joyce's *Ulysses.*

Bloom, Milly Leopold Bloom's adolescent daughter working in a Mullingar photo shop whose letter home appears in James Joyce's *Ulysses.*

Bloom, Rudy Son whose death in infancy initiated Leopold and Molly Bloom's decade of celibacy in James Joyce's *Ulysses.*

Bloomacre One of the greatest libertines in Eliza Haywood's *The History of Miss Betsy Thoughtless.*

Bloomberg, Anatole Tackle for the Logos College football team and philosophizing roommate of Gary Harkness in Don DeLillo's *End Zone.*

Bloomfield, Fanny Pretty but willful four-year-old child, who has already learned to be deceitful in Anne Brontë's *Agnes Grey.*

Bloomfield, Harriet Only Bloomfield child still untainted; since she is only two, she is still looked after by a nurse in Anne Brontë's *Agnes Grey.*

Bloomfield, Mary Ann Naughty, intractable child, almost six years old, who has discovered that throwing tantrums is the easiest method of getting her way in Anne Brontë's *Agnes Grey.*

Bloomfield, Mr. Irascible owner of Wellwood House and Agnes Grey's first employer; he harangues both his wife and the governess in Anne Brontë's *Agnes Grey.*

Bloomfield, Mrs. Severe, taciturn woman, blind to her children's faults; she is wife and mother in the family where Agnes Grey is first employed; she renders futile Agnes's efforts at disciplining the children in Anne Brontë's *Agnes Grey.*

Bloomfield, Tom Seven-year-old eldest child of the Bloomfields; he delights in torturing small animals and birds, especially in front of his governess in Anne Brontë's *Agnes Grey.*

Bloomguard, Harold Los Angeles policeman and organizer of off-duty meetings in MacArthur Park; one of ten protagonists in Joseph Wambaugh's *The Choirboys.*

Bloomville, Arabella Lady Fairville's daughter, who was thought to have died as a child; she lives in a pastoral cottage but comes into contact with much of London society; she dresses as a shepherdess, including crooked staff and pocketful of turnips, to search for her missing Henry Lambert; eventually reunited with the mother she thought dead, she marries Henry and becomes Lady Laughable in William Beckford's *Modern Novel Writing; or, the Elegant Enthusiast.*

Blore Butler for Sir Lawrence Mont and Aunt Emily Mont; he helps Dinny Cherrell find a pawnbroker in John Galsworthy's *Maid In Waiting.*

Blore District Officer in Fada who is ready to press charges against Johnson for stealing government funds; he is released before a trial begins and is replaced by Rudbeck in Joyce Cary's *Mister Johnson.*

Blore, Sammy Rustic, gossiping chorister in Thomas Hardy's *Two on a Tower.*

Blore, William Henry Retired police detective whose perjured testimony resulted in the prison death of an innocent man in Agatha Christie's *And Then There Were None.*

Blorna, Hubert Successful lawyer, employer, and friend of Katharina Blum; when he remains loyal to Katharina, he and his wife, Trude, become targets for attacks by the tabloid press in Heinrich Böll's *The Lost Honor of Katharina Blum.*

Blossom, Pear Young slave who becomes Wang Lung's mistress in Pearl Buck's *The Good Earth;* after Wang Lung's death, she cares for his and O-lan's retarded daughter; following the daughter's death, she enters a nunnery in *Sons.*

Blotton, Mr. Member of the Pickwick Club and quarrelsome rival of Samuel Pickwick in Charles Dickens's *The Posthumous Papers of the Pickwick Club.*

Blount, Angus Young scamp who jilts Annabel Upchurch in Ellen Glasgow's *The Romantic Comedians.*

Blount, Colonel Nina's eccentric father, who supports a movie being filmed on his estate; he purchases the film when it cannot find a commercial outlet and shows it for his own pleasure in Evelyn Waugh's *Vile Bodies.*

Blount, Eva Artist married to Gilbert Blount; becomes involved in an affair with Lionel Lane after Blount's death; commits suicide by jumping from a window of an apartment building in Richard Wright's *The Outsider.*

Blount, Gilbert (Gil) Communist Party official married to Eva Blount; attempts to recruit Lionel Lane; murdered by Lane in Langley Herndon's apartment in Richard Wright's *The Outsider.*

Blount, Jake Itinerant labor organizer who confides his dreams to the deaf-mute John Singer in Carson McCullers's *The Heart Is a Lonely Hunter.*

Blount, Nina Fiancée of Adam Fenwick-Symes; she eventually marries Eddy Littlejohn; while her husband is away in the army, she renews her relationship with Adam in Evelyn Waugh's *Vile Bodies.*

Blout, Sir Nicolaus Older follower of Thomas Ratcliffe, Earl of Sussex; he is Walter Raleigh's friend and sparring partner in Sir Walter Scott's *Kenilworth.*

Blow, William Merchant at Bristol on whom Mr. Warner depends for help with benevolent actions on behalf of Mr. Price and his daughter in Frances Sheridan's *Memoirs of Miss Sidney Bidulph.*

Blower, Mrs. Widow of a smuggler; she unsuccessfully woos the Earl of Etherington (Valentine Bulmer) when he moves through the social circle of St. Ronan's Well in Sir Walter Scott's *St. Ronan's Well.*

Bloxham, Eliza Ridd John Ridd's youngest sister, who is a smart, sassy, and sarcastic bookworm; she can be agreeable but has no desire to exercise charm; Eliza and John don't get along well in R. D. Blackmore's *Lorna Doone.*

Bluck, Bully Stentorian leader of the Darlford conservatives who supports Nicholas Rigby's election to Parliament in Benjamin Disraeli's *Coningsby; or, The New Generation.*

Blue Islamic fundamentalist who is having an affair with Kadife, daughter of the hotel keeper of the Snow Palace Hotel; strong and well-spoken with a formidable charisma; encourages young women to commit suicide in the name of religion in Orhan Pamuk's *Snow.*

Blue Self-appointed mayor and chronicler of Hard Times; marries Molly Riordan and cares for Jimmy Fee; ambushes and mortally wounds Clay Turner; narrator of E. L. Doctorow's *Welcome to Hard Times.*

Blue, Billy Gangster who attempts to assassinate Legs Diamond and is eventually killed by Diamond in William Kennedy's *Legs.*

Blue, Mr. Short, aging aluminum siding salesman who befriends Frederick Exley in the apartment of the Counselor and recruits him to work as his canvasser; talks incessantly about oral sex; dominated by his common-law wife, Deborah, he is a pathetic figure of frustration and missed opportunities in Frederick Exley's *A Fan's Notes.*

Blue, Walden Tenor saxophonist in John Clellon Holmes's *The Horn.*

Blue Back Old Oneida Indian and friend of Gil Martin in Walter D. Edmonds's *Drums along the Mohawk.*

Blue Beard Wealthy but monstrous looking figure with a blue beard; desires to marry again but finds no one will wed such an ugly creature; finally convinces one of two sisters to share his bed; grants his new bride access to the many chambers filled with gold, silver, and jewels in his vast home but forbids her entry into a locked closet; returns from a trip to discover that his wife has entered the closet and discovered the many bodies of his previous wives—hanging with their throats cut; decides to kill his new wife as punishment but is slain instead by her brothers in Charles Perrault's "Blue Beard."

Blue Beard's New Wife One of two beautiful sisters who agrees to marry the ugly but wealthy figure who has a blue beard; curiosity compels her to open a forbidden closet in her vast castle where she discovers the bloody bodies of her husband's previous wives—hanging with their throats cut; barely escapes the same fate when her brothers arrive in time to slay Blue Beard in Charles Perrault's "Blue Beard."

Bluebell Rabbit jokester and storyteller who escapes with Captain Holly from the doomed Sandleford Warren and joins Hazel's new colony in Richard Adams's *Watership Down.*

Blue Billie Childhood foe and later ally of Jimmie Johnson in Stephen Crane's *Maggie: A Girl of the Streets;* hoodlum whose impending fight with George Kelcey is interrupted by news of Kelcey's mother's illness in *George's Mother.*

Blue Fairy Godmother See Wirtanen, Frank.

Blue Jack Only supportive figure in Cholly's life; taught him about history, life, and family in Toni Morrison's *The Bluest Eye.*

Blue Juice Pimp who assaults Jake Jackson after Jackson accuses the prostitute Blanche of picking his pocket in Richard Wright's *Lawd Today.*

Bluemits, Nancy Shaw Bluestocking daughter of a Scottish friend of the Laird Douglas family; she now resides in Bath and entertains Miss Grizzy Douglas and Mary Douglas in Susan Ferrier's *Marriage.*

Blue Prairie Woman Nineteenth-century Ojibway woman whose infant daughter is carried away on the back of a dog during a U.S. Cavalry raid; grandmother of Zosie and Mary Shawano in Louise Erdrich's *The Antelope Wife.*

Blues Berry Prisoner in the stockade; beaten to death by guards led by Fatso Judson in James Jones's *From Here to Eternity.*

Blueskin Captain of Jonathan Wild's gang who refuses to give Wild a stolen gold watch; he foments rebellion until Wild has him arrested in Henry Fielding's *The Life of Mr. Jonathan Wild the Great.* He is a swarthy-faced, immensely strong criminal crony of Jonathan Wild; he shifts his allegiance to Jack Sheppard and dies trying to save him from the gallows in William Harrison Ainsworth's *Jack Sheppard.*

Bluestone, Alice Youngest daughter of Serjeant Bluestone and close friend of Lady Anna Lovel; she advises Lady Anna not to marry Daniel Thwaite, die tailor, because of the social gulf between them in Anthony Trollope's *Lady Anna.*

Bluestone, Mrs. Good-hearted wife of the eminent lawyer Serjeant Bluestone; she takes care of Lady Anna Lovel when her mother, the Countess Lovel, turns her out of her home for refusing to marry the young earl, Frederick Lovel, in Anthony Trollope's *Lady Anna.*

Bluestone, Serjeant Eminent barrister, loud in the courtroom and docile at home, who acts for the Countess Lovel in Anthony Trollope's *Lady Anna.*

Blum, Andrei Antonovich von Von Lembke's secretary; raids Stepan's residence and confiscates political papers in Fyodor Dostoevsky's *The Possessed.*

Blum, Freddy Randy resident of Emma Lazarus Retirement Home; believed by Mandy Dattner to be the father of her unborn child in Alan Isler's *The Prince of West End Avenue.*

Blum, Katharina Industrious housekeeper at Dr. Blorna's; accused of helping the alleged criminal Ludwig Götten escape from the police; kills Werner Tötges, the journalist responsible for slanderous attacks on her and her family, in Heinrich Böll's *The Lost Honor of Katharina Blum.*

Blum, Minna One of the well-to-do German pupils in the Hanover school; her conventional future life as middle-class wife and mother is pictured by young Miriam Henderson with a mixture of envy and pity in Dorothy Richardson's *Pointed Roofs.*

Blumberg, Julian Weak, struggling novelist and screenwriter who unwittingly becomes a ghostwriter for Sammy Glick in Budd Schulberg's *What Makes Sammy Run?*

Blumenfeld, Monroe First child to have his bar mitzvah in the temple David Dehn builds; announces at his bar mitzvah that as an adult he will live in Israel in Jerome Weidman's *The Temple.*

Blumenghast, Olga Young lady of the court of Pisuerga and friend of Laura de Nazianzi; her "exotic, sexless" nature attracts the amorous interest of the Countess Violet of Tolga, despite Olga's love for the aloof Count Ann-Jules in Ronald Firbank's *The Flower Beneath the Foot.*

Blumenthal, Sarah Rabbi at Synagogue of Evolutionary Judaism; married to Rabbi Joshua Gruen; daughter of man known as Yehoshua Mendelssohn; continues to run synagogue after husband's death; falls in love with and marries Thomas Pemberton in E. L. Doctorow's *City of God.*

Blundell Joseph Balterghen's innocuous second secretary; he provides insight into Balterghen's character in Eric Ambler's *Uncommon Danger.*

Blundell, Superintendent Official in charge of the investigation into the death of an unknown man; he welcomes Lord Peter Wimsey's assistance in Dorothy L. Sayers's *The Nine Tailors: Changes Rung on an Old Theme in Two Short Touches and Two Full Peals.*

Blunderbussiana Sixteenth-century painter admired for correctness of anatomical rendering and wild scenes; the son of a bandit, he learns anatomy by dissecting his father's victims; his early life with outlaws provides subjects for paintings; he dies of fever and his body is given to surgeons for dissection in William Beckford's *Biographical Memoirs of Extraordinary Painters.*

Blunderbussiana, Rouzinski Father of sixteenth-century painter Blunderbussiana and leader of a murderous gang of bandits; his mountain hideouts and exploits provide images for his son's later paintings; his murder victims provide the youngster with opportunities to study anatomy in William Beckford's *Biographical Memoirs of Extraordinary Painters.*

Blunket, Lady Sir Paul Blunket's wife, a confirmed invalid with a surprising appetite; she is one of the houseguests at Marlowe in J. Sheridan Le Fanu's *Guy Deverell.*

Blunket, Miss Daughter of Sir Paul and Lady Blunket and a houseguest with them at Marlowe; although she is in her thirties, she giggles and acts very girlish in J. Sheridan Le Fanu's *Guy Deverell.*

Blunket, Sir Paul Great agriculturalist and eminent authority on liquid manures; he is a stolid guest at Marlowe in J. Sheridan Le Fanu's *Guy Deverell.*

Blunt, Captain J. K. Affected American supporter of the Spanish royalists who deceitfully wounds Monsieur George in a duel fought over Doña Rita de Lastaola in Joseph Conrad's *The Arrow of Gold: A Story Between Two Notes.*

Blunt, Jack "Irish cockney" sailor aboard the Highlander who uses hair darkener and tries to interpret his dreams in Herman Melville's *Redburn.*

Blunt, Major Hector Taciturn big-game hunter visiting at Fernly Park; he becomes engaged to Flora Ackroyd in Agatha Christie's *The Murder of Roger Ackroyd.*

Blunt, Sir John Nonspeaking role; son of Sir Walter Blunt; ally of King Henry IV; mentioned in William Shakespeare's play *Henry IV, Part Two.*

Blunt, Sir Walter Member of Henry IV's court; announces that Hotspur, Mortimer, and the Earl of Douglas have gathered a force against Henry and are assembled at Shrewsbury; comes to Hotspur's camp to parley before the battle; comes to learn of the rebels' quarrels with the king; disguises himself as King Henry in order to act as a decoy; killed by Douglas in William Shakespeare's play *Henry IV, Part One.*

Bluntschli, Captain A 34-year-old professional soldier from Switzerland who fought for the Serbian army; climbs into Raina's bedroom through a window to escape possible death; his cynicism clashes with Raina's idealism, as he thinks it is better to carry chocolate than ammunition; later visits the Petkoff household to return Major Petkoff's coat, which Raina lent him so he could escape; a skilled businessman; his pragmatic and worldly attitude contrasts with most of the other characters' idealism; receives notice that his father died, with Bluntschli inheriting a highly successful hotelier business; able to see through Raina's posturing as they try to hide evidence of their previous acquaintance; reveals himself to be a secret romantic; finally becomes engaged to Raina in George Bernard Shaw's play *Arms and the Man.*

Bluton, Gilly (Prince) Sensuous, hedonistic, aggressive mulatto who attempts to seduce Lissa Atkinson; employee of and informer for Proctor Baggart; murdered by Hagar in DuBose Heyward's *Mamba's Daughters.*

Bluvard, Terrence (Terry) Writer and wealthy white lesbian lover of Renay Davis in Ann Allen Shockley's *Loving Her.*

Bly, Cornelia Abstract artist and mistress of Augie Poole; bears a child by Poole that Poole unwittingly adopts in Peter De Vries's *The Tunnel of Love.*

Bly, Mr. Man who tried to do something to Kate Fletcher (Armstrong) that was embarrassing for her when she was eleven years old in Margaret Drabble's *The Middle Ground.*

Blyth, Lavinia-Ada (Lavvie) Valentine's invalid wife, cheerful despite her suffering, whose childlessness is relieved by the adoption of the ten-year-old deaf-mute "Madonna" (Grice); when Madonna's parentage is revealed, Mrs. Blyth wisely encourages Zack Thorpe to travel with Mat Grice, knowing that Madonna is attracted to Zack, her half brother, in Wilkie Collins's *Hide and Seek.*

Blyth, Mr. Mr. Goodworth's friend and Valentine's father, a businessman whose support of his son's artistic ambitions produces a good man, though not a great artist in Wilkie Collins's *Hide and Seek.*

Blyth, Valentine Whole-hearted man, whose dedication to painting results in some professional success in spite of limited talent; he is devoted to his invalid wife and to his adopted deaf-mute daughter, "Madonna" (Grice), in Wilkie Collins's *Hide and Seek.*

Blythe, Pevensey Editor of *The Outpost* who persuades Michael Mont to accept Foggartism in John Galsworthy's *The Silver Spoon.* He is distressed when Michael turns his attention to slum clearance in *Swan Song.* He writes the preface for Hubert Cherrell's diary in *Maid In Waiting.*

Bo, Karl Marx Law student from Sierra Leone in Colin MacInnes's *City of Spades.*

Boa One of the young cadets at Leoncio Prado, a paramilitary academy in Lima; belongs to a secret organization called the "Circle" at the school in which the boys carry out pranks and other mischievous acts in Mario Vargas Llosa's *The Time of the Hero.*

Boam, Major Frequent visitor to the Wandrous home; his pedophiliac behavior traumatizes Gloria Wandrous in John O'Hara's *Butterfield 8.*

Boanerges, Lord Old friend of the (old) Duke of Omnium; he teaches Martha Dunstable to blow soap bubbles on scientific principles in Anthony Trollope's *Framley Parsonage. He appears briefly in The Bertrams* and in *Orley Farm.*

Board, Mr. Rich, drunken bachelor mayor of Maidenbridge who is loved by Nancy Gipps in T. F. Powys's *Mr. Weston's Good Wine.*

Boardman, Milly Teenaged daughter of Quincy Boardman and student at a Massachusetts boarding school in Albert Halper's *Union Square.*

Boardman, Quincy (Boardie) Widower father of Milly Boardman; executive who lives, with his mistress Margie, in the Glen Cove Apartments in Albert Halper's *Union Square.*

Boarham, Mr. Fashionable suitor of Helen Lawrence (later Huntingdon); he is undaunted in his pursuit of her, notwithstanding her outright refusal in Anne Brontë's *The Tenant of Wildfell Hall.*

Boase, Nigel Bruno Greensleave's mystical nurse-companion; he is Will Boase's twin and Adelaide de Crecy's cousin in Iris Murdoch's *Bruno's Dream.*

Boase, Wilfred (Will) Professional actor long enamored of his cousin, Adelaide de Crecy; his duel with Danby Odd results in his marriage to Adelaide; his marriage and career prove unexpectedly successful in Iris Murdoch's *Bruno's Dream.*

Boatwright, Alma Sister of Anney and aunt of Bone and Reese; wife of Wade; leaves Wade after discovering his affairs; has nervous breakdown when her husband claims not to love her; eventually reconciles with Wade in Dorothy Allison's *Bastard Out of Carolina.*

Boatwright, Anney See Waddell, Anney Boatwright Parson.

Boatwright, Carr Only woman in her family to marry an outsider and leave South Carolina; rumored to have been in love with Wade and jealous of her sisters' good looks as a teenager in Dorothy Allison's *Bastard Out of Carolina.*

Boatwright, Earl (Black) Brother of Anney and favorite uncle of Bone and Reese; fighting and infidelities cost him his happiness; tries to kill Glen Waddell for beating Bone in Dorothy Allison's *Bastard Out of Carolina.*

Boatwright, Fay Wife of Nevil; reported to be the fattest as well as most quiet woman in Greenville County in Dorothy Allison's *Bastard Out of Carolina.*

Boatwright, Granny Granddaughter of a Cherokee; matriarch of the Boatwright family; the family storyteller; first in the family to express her distrust of Glen Waddell in Dorothy Allison's *Bastard Out of Carolina.*

Boatwright, Moses Lincoln Black, Harvard-educated philosopher who murdered and cannibalized his victim; interviewed in prison by Max Reddick in John A. Williams's *The Man Who Cried I Am.*

Boatwright, Nevil Husband of Fay; heavy drinker; overhears his mother compare him and his wife to furniture (taking up space and shedding dust); vows to kill Glen Waddell after discovering the rape in Dorothy Allison's *Bastard Out of Carolina.*

Boatwright, Raylene Sister of Anney and aunt of Bone and Reese; discovers bruises and belt welts on Bone; asks her brother Earle to kill Glen Waddell; Bone moves in with her after Anney leaves; she is a lesbian and the most stable member of the family in Dorothy Allison's *Bastard Out of Carolina.*

Boatwright, Ruth Sister to Anney and aunt to Bone and Reese; married to Travis; mother of eight children; works in a factory; when she becomes ill with cancer, Bone moves in to help care for her; on her deathbed Ruth is the first adult to discuss Bone's abuse, which validates the problem for her niece in Dorothy Allison's *Bastard Out of Carolina.*

Boatwright, Ruth Anne (Bone) Thirteen-year-old daughter of Anney Boatwright; rejects religion as a salvation from the violence of her stepfather, Glen Waddell; moves in with her aunt to escape her stepfather, who rapes and beats her; rejected by her mother, who chooses Glen over her in Dorothy Allison's *Bastard Out of Carolina.*

Boaz Martian army sergeant in Kurt Vonnegut's *The Sirens of Titan.*

Bob Boyish man who is Don Dubrow's errand boy in Don's Resale Shop, a junk store; wants to take part in the heist of a coin collection, including American Buffalo nickels, in David Mamet's play *American Buffalo.*

Bob Frightened, silly musician; George thinks of Bob as a friend but realizes Bob is afraid of being alone in Rex Warner's *The Wild Goose Chase: An Allegory.*

Bob Husband of Constance Marlow; the Logan brothers mistake Bob and Constance for bowling trophy thieves and shoot them in Richard Brautigan's *Willard and His Bowling Trophies.*

Bob Ines's brother who does not want an older man to marry his sister because he believes in youth as the paradigm of beauty and purity; unfortunately, later discovers that he will also become old in Juan Carlos Onetti's "Welcome, Bob."

Bob Milly's husband, who informs May Quest that her daughter, Martha, is employed in England by a communist writer in Doris Lessing's *The Four-Gated City.*

Bob Old friend of Emma Evans; he helped Emma when she first started modeling and has recently offered her a job on a television news program in Margaret Drabble's *The Garrick Year.*

Bob Son of Torvald and Nora Helmer in Henrik Ibsen's play *A Doll's House.*

Bob Turnkey of the Marshalsea debtors' prison when William Dorrit was first imprisoned; he was a good friend to Amy Dorrit and assisted her in her effort to support her family in Charles Dickens's *Little Dorrit.*

Bob, Little Jen's two-year-old brother in Isabel Colegate's *Orlando King.*

Bob and Gertrude American Protestant missionaries in the Brazilian village of Mairun in Darcy Ribeiro's *Maíra.*

Bobbe, Comrade-Editor (satirical portrait of D. H. Lawrence) Vain, class-conscious Socialist political writer whom George Winterbourne meets at a London literary evening in Richard Aldington's *Death of a Hero.*

Bobbie Homosexual friend of Alva in Wallace Thurman's *The Blacker the Berry.*

Bobby German bartender and boarder at Fraulein Schroeder's in Christopher Isherwood's *Goodbye to Berlin.*

Bobby Lee Accomplice of The Misfit; carries out the murder of Bailey and other members of his family in Flannery O'Connor's "A Good Man Is Hard to Find."

Bobchinsky One of two squires in a small Russian town who announces that a mysterious stranger has arrived; believes the traveler to be the expected inspector general from St. Petersburg in Nikolai Gogol's "The Inspector General."

Bober, Helen Twenty-three-year-old daughter of Morris and Ida Bober; pursued by Frank Alpine in Bernard Malamud's *The Assistant.*

Bober, Ida Wife of Morris Bober in Bernard Malamud's *The Assistant.*

Bober, Morris Jewish storekeeper in Bernard Malamud's *The Assistant.*

Bobinôt Acadian farmer who is in love with Calixta, although the latter is romantically attracted to Alcée Laballière; proposes marriage to Calixta several times and is rejected; attends the Acadian ball, where he is distracted by Calixta's presence; finally secures Calixta's consent to marry him after Alcée abandons her at the ball in Kate Chopin's "At the 'Cadian Ball."

Bobinôt Acadian farmer; husband of Calixta and father of four-year-old Bibi; waylaid by a thunderstorm while out doing errands with his son; unaware that Calixta has had a sudden sexual encounter with her former romantic interest Alcée Laballière while he is away in Kate Chopin's "The Storm."

Bobo One of the four African-American boys caught swimming in the Harvey's pool; watches his friends Buck and Lester get shot by Jim Harvey; beaten and hanged from a tree; then burnt with tar, feathered, and set on fire by a white mob in Richard Wright's "Big Boy Leaves Home."

Bobo Party host whose gatherings include an ecletic mix of the old aristocrats, nouveau riche, intellectuals, artists, and stylish youths in Carlos Fuentes's *Where the Air Is Clear.*

Bobochka Soviet Writers' Union official in charge of Henry Bech's itinerary in Russia in John Updike's *Bec h: A Book.*

Bobynin (zek) Boss of Laboratory Number Seven at the Marfino gulag prison camp located in the Moscow suburbs in Aleksandr Solzhenitsyn's *The First Circle.*

Bocage Dishonest caretaker at Michel's Norman estate, La Morinière; father of Charles and Alcide in André Gide's *The Immoralist.*

Bocage, Alcide Younger son of the dishonest caretaker at Michel's Norman estate, La Morinière; poaches on the estate at night in André Gide's *The Immoralist.*

Bocage, Charles Older son of the dishonest caretaker at Michel's Norman estate, La Morinière; at first befriended by Michel, but later their friendship cools in André Gide's *The Immoralist.*

Bocanegra Dog who attacks Guzmán, loyal to its sire, and appears to el Señor in a vision in Carlos Fuentes's *Terra Nostra.*

Bocastle, Lady Doris Wife of Lord Bocastle; she makes Lewis Eliot her confidant in C. P. Snow's *The Light and the Dark.*

Bocastle, Lord Hugh Brother of Lady Muriel Royce; he is crushed by the death of his only child in World War II in C. P. Snow's *The Light and the Dark.*

Boccadolce, Andrea President of Venice art society; his pronouncement that nut oil is a canvas varnish superior to egg whites leads to the decline of Sucrewasser and the ascent of Og of Basan and Andrew Guelph in William Beckford's *Biographical Memoirs of Extraordinary Painters.*

Bodach Glas Foreboding apparition which has warned the MacIvors of imminent death or captivity for three hundred years in Sir Walter Scott's *Waverly.*

Bodden, Junior (Speedy, Speedy-Boy) Tough and determined crew member of the *Lillias Eden* and only survivor of its wreck in Peter Matthiessen's *Far Tortuga.*

Boddick, Henry Ex-serviceman, out of work, who accepts Michael Mont's offer to start a poultry farm in John Galsworthy's *The Silver Spoon.*

Boddy, Mr. Feeble but cheerful old man with a wooden leg; he entertains by playing his fiddle and dies pathetically as a derelict in George Gissing's *Thyrza.*

Bode, Almeric Young man in love with Alison Edgeworth; he runs away with her when Grant Edgeworth is discovered to be the father of her son, Richard, in Ivy Compton-Burnett's *A House and Its Head.*

Bode, Dulcia Almeric's sister, a friend of Nance and Sibyl Edgeworth; she is outspoken but warm and cheerful in Ivy Compton-Burnett's *A House and Its Head.*

Bode, Else David Parker's housekeeper, who loves Gordon Paget; she leaves the nursery for a while after Meg Eliot arrives to convalesce from her nervous breakdown in Angus Wilson's *The Middle Age of Mrs. Eliot.*

Bode, Father Nondescript, good, selfless assistant priest to the parish of St. Luke's, who makes a contrast with the well-heeled connoisseur vicar, Father Thames, in Barbara Pym's *A Glass of Blessings.* His scheduled succession to the retiring Father Thames is mentioned in Edwin Braithwaite's reminiscences about the parish in *Quartet in Autumn.*

Bode, Mr. Almeric's father, who has money through his wife's inheritance in Ivy Compton-Burnett's *A House and Its Head.*

Bode, Mrs. Almeric's mother; she is embarrassed when he and Alison Edgeworth run away together in Ivy Compton-Burnett's *A House and Its Head.*

Bodeen, Gabriella Glamorous actress with whom Lee Youngdahl believes himself in love in Mark Harris's *Wake Up, Stupid.*

Bodger Dean of students at Steering School and friend of Jennie Fields and Garp in John Irving's *The World According to Garp.*

Bodien Disbarred plumber employed by Norman Moonbloom in Edward Lewis Wallant's *The Tenants of Moonbloom.*

Bodine, Pig Former shipmate of Benny Profane; involved with the Whole Sick Crew in Thomas Pynchon's *V.;* possibly Seaman Bodine in *Gravity's Rainbow.*

Bodine, Seaman AWOL seaman who befriends Tyrone Slothrop and Roger Mexico in Thomas Pynchon's *Gravity's Rainbow;* possibly Pig Bodine in *V.*

Bodine, William Yancey Organizer of a secret association to advance Americanism and to persecute Jews, blacks, and Catholics in T. S. Stribling's *Unfinished Cathedral.*

Bodkin, Peter Eldest son of Sir Nicholas and supporter of Tom Daly in opposing the guerillas and revolutionaries struggling against the Irish landowners in Anthony Trollope's *The Landleaguers.*

Bodkin, Sir Boreas Windbag secretary of the Post Office; he rebukes the clerk, Samuel Crocker, for bad behavior in Anthony Trollope's *Marion Fay.*

Bodkin, Sir Nicholas Conservative landowner in County Galway and opponent of Home Rule; he believes tenants must be kept in their place and that nothing must get in the way of hunting in Anthony Trollope's *The Landleaguers.*

Bodle, Betty Daughter of the Laird of Kilmarkeckle; Claud Walkinshaw arranges her marriage to his son Walter, and she dies in childbirth without producing the male heirs Claud had wanted in John Galt's *The Entail.*

Bodle, Laird of Kilmarkeckle Betty Bodle's father, who is obsessed with snuff in John Galt's *The Entail.*

Body (Bloodworth), William S. (Willie) Lover of Lavinia Masterson and father, by his half sister Carrie Trout, of Abraham Dolphin in Leon Forrest's *The Bloodworth Orphans.*

Bodyagin, Ignat Twenty-year-old local food commissar in a Russian district; communist and member of the Red Party; encounters his father, who has been arrested for leading a Cossack insurrection; although he holds the power to save his father from the firing squad, he and his father cannot reconcile their bitter differences; later, while fleeing the Cossack army, saves a young orphaned boy from freezing to death; soon dies at the hands of the pursuing Cossacks in Mikhail Sholokhov's "The Food Commissar."

Boeffleurs, Chevalier De Corrupt French nobleman, who forces Baron Julius von Konigstein to be his accomplice in cheating Albert St. George at the gambling house in Benjamin Disraeli's *Vivian Grey.*

Boeuf, Madame Having been pursued by a rhinoceros, rushes into the office and reports her husband sick; when she realizes the rhinoceros waiting at the staircase is her spouse, joins him by jumping on his back in Eugène Ionesco's play *Rhinoceros.*

Boeuf, Monsieur Another colleague of Berenger's; one of the first to transform into a rhinoceros; his name means "ox" in Eugène Ionesco's play *Rhinoceros.*

Boffin, Henrietty Noddy Boffin's plump, cheerful wife, who aims to be a "high-flyer" of fashion; she wishes to adopt an orphan to replace John Harmon, and, after the child dies, adopts Sloppy in Charles Dickens's *Our Mutual Friend.*

Boffin, Mr. Arch conservative left out of the (younger) Duke of Omnium's coalition government; he allies himself with Sir Orlando Drought to bring the duke's administration down in Anthony Trollope's *The Prime Minister.*

Boffin, Nicodemus (Noddy) Large, child-like, benevolent foreman of the mounds, who inherited Harmon's estate after John Harmon was presumed dead; he invites Bella Wilfer to live with him and his wife, and gradually changes into a miser, but only to teach Bella the danger of becoming too mercenary in Charles Dickens's *Our Mutual Friend.*

Bogan, Charles Senior partner at Bogan, Rapley, Vitrano, and Havarac; cousin to the Senator who assists Aricia in obtaining his reward for being a whistle blower; his role in the conspiracy against the government is revealed by Patrick Lanigan, and he is indicted by the federal government in John Grisham's *The Partner.*

Bogan, Lewis Chicago writer who carries on a love relationship with the married Anne Bebreuilh, a character based on author Simone de Beauvoir's own life; his character is based on the American writer Nelson Algren in Simone de Beauvoir's *The Mandarins.*

Bogard, Léry Scholar who accompanies Samuele to the Villa Horace for a week visit as the guest of Marie-Astrée-Luce de Morfontaine in Thornton Wilder's *The Cabala.*

Bogardes, Jack (Jackie, Jacques) Wealthy but neurotic journalist who lives with his mother on Park Avenue; friend of Eric Eisner and lover of Marie Curtin in Phillip Lopate's *Confessions of Summer.*

Bogardus, Peter Orderly in a Chicago hospital where Roger Ashley works briefly; the first to expose Ashley to the concept of reincarnation in Thornton Wilder's *The Eighth Day.*

Bogart, Dr. Dominie Clergyman and longtime friend of Aaron Burr; officiates at Burr's marriage to Eliza Bowen Jumel in Gore Vidal's *Burr.*

Bogart, Marin Daughter of Charlotte Douglas and Warren Bogart; runs off with leftist revolutionaries in Joan Didion's *A Book of Common Prayer.*

Bogart, Mrs. Strict Baptist and neighbor of the Kennicotts in Sinclair Lewis's *Main Street.*

Bogart, Warren Wandering ne'er-do-well; first husband of Charlotte Douglas and later her lover; father of Marin Bogart in Joan Didion's *A Book of Common Prayer.*

Bogen, Harry (Heshalle, Heshie) Women's garment manufacturer who steals from his own firm, Apex Modes, and makes his partner, Meyer Babushkin, take the blame and go to jail; narrator of Jerome Weidman's *I Can Get It for You Wholesale;* enters into partnership with and steals from Hrant Yazdabian; has his own money stolen by Martha Mills, his girlfriend; narrator of *What's in It for Me?*

Bogen, Mrs. Mother of Harry Bogen in Jerome Weidman's *I Can Get It for You Wholesale;* becomes ill and dies while Harry is trying to escape to Europe in *What's in It for Me?*

Bogger, George Epileptic who lives with his parents and works as a roadman with the highway department; dies of a seizure while hunting frogs in Mark Steadman's *A Lion's Share.*

Bogle, Benjamin ("Fish Benjie") Scots ragamuffin, an impudent urchin who becomes the resourceful ally and coconspirator in "John Macnab's" plot to poach the two stags and salmon in John Buchan's *John Macnab.*

Bogolepov, Elizaveta Innokentievna See Wind, Dr. Elizaveta Innokentievna Bogolepov Pnin.

Bogrov, Michael (Prisoner No. 38) Former sailor on the Battleship Potemkin and Nicolas Rubashov's broken-spirited friend; he is imprisoned, viciously tortured, and executed as a political extremist for opposing No. 1's naval construction plans in Arthur Koestler's *Darkness at Noon.*

Bogsby, J. G. Landlord of the Sol's Arms in Cook's Court in Charles Dickens's *Bleak House.*

Bohack Leader of Happy Valley Commune in Don DeLillo's *Great Jones Street.*

Bohemian Petitioner Brother of the Jesuit from Peru; he petitions the King of Bulgaria for the return of his wife in Charles Johnstone's *Chrysal: or, The Adventures of a Guinea.*

Bohemond Prince and Count of Tarentum; he is a crafty Norman-Italian crusader, who becomes Emperor Alexius Comnenus's ally only after receiving several large bribes in Sir Walter Scott's *Count Robert of Paris.*

Bohl, Jimmy Argus, North Dakota, steakhouse owner briefly married to Sita Kozka in Louise Erdrich's *The Beet Queen.*

Böhm, Arno Old-time Block Elder, Kapo, and Camp Kapo; kills men for selling tea on the black market and whips others for minor offenses in Tadeusz Borowski's *This Way for the Gas, Ladies and Gentlemen.*

Böhm, Lotte Lover of Igor Karlovy in Leon Uris's *Armageddon.*

Bohn, Harry Friend of Luke Lampson; born of his dead mother's body; helps to bury Hattie Lampson in John Hawkes's *The Beetle Leg.*

Bohr, Margrethe Wife of Danish physicist Niels Bohr; disapproves of his meeting with German physicist Werner

Heisenberg in Nazi-occupied Copenhagen in Michael Frayn's *Copenhagen*.

Bohr, Niels Danish physicist and pioneer of quantum mechanics; winner of the 1922 Nobel Prize in physics; director of the Institute of Theoretical Physics at the University of Copenhagen; married to Margrethe Bohr; half-Jewish man working in Nazi-occupied Copenhagen when he is visited by his younger German colleague Werner Heisenberg in September 1941 in Michael Frayn's *Copenhagen*.

Bohun, Aubrey Charming, wealthy, influential, but unprincipled owner of Bohun Castle; he is drawn back to his home in Hartlebury after 10 years' absence by the political turmoil of the Reform Bill and decides to contest the borough seat of Fanchester as a liberal-independent; he wins by one vote (that of the Whig, Mr. Gainsborough) and makes a great impact in London; at the same time, he courts Helen Molesworth, who accepts his advances but later discovers his unprincipled nature in Benjamin Disraeli's *A Year at Hartlebury; or, The Election*.

Bohun, Aveline de Lady-prize of the tournament held by Henry III in Ann Radcliffe's *Gaston de Blondeville*.

Boilermaker, The Friendly mechanic who helps the protagonist, Marlow, refit the damaged steamer in central Africa; often speaks of his children and pet pigeons in Joseph Conrad's *Heart of Darkness*.

Bois, Monsieur Du French gentleman who accompanies Madame Duval to England; he speaks only French and returns to France without her in Frances Burney's *Evelina*.

Boisbelle, Josephine de Sister of the Marquis de Montfleuri; forced into an early marriage, she is estranged from her husband when she meets Lionel Desmond, whose child she bears and commits to his care and Geraldine Verney's while secluded in England; her reputation thus untarnished when her husband dies, she hopes to marry her first love in Charlotte Smith's *Desmond*.

Boise (Boy) Cat that is Thomas Hudson's companion in Ernest Hemingway's *Islands in the Stream*.

Bois-Guilbert, Brian de Proud Norman Templar and famed crusader; he is an adherent of Prince John; he falls in love with and kidnaps Rebecca the Jewess, taking her to Templestowe; when she is sentenced to death for witchcraft, he is commanded to fight as the Temple's champion; she spurns his offer to sacrifice his ambitions and escape with her; he is defeated by her champion, Ivanhoe, in Sir Walter Scott's *Ivanhoe*.

Boissec Scoffing, pompous professor from M. Paul Emanuel's college; he suggests that Lucy Snowe's compositions are plagiarized and forces her to take an examination in Charlotte Brontë's *Villette*.

Bojanus, Mr. Cockney tailor of socialist sympathies who helps the younger Theodore Gumbril perfect his pneumatic pants in Aldous Huxley's *Antic Hay*.

Bok, Yakov Shepsovitch (Yakov Ivanovitch Dologushev) Jewish handyman arrested for the murder of a young boy and sent to prison in Bernard Malamud's *The Fixer*.

Boke, Miss Fat and friendly newcomer whose monopolization of William Baxter at Miss Lola Pratt's going-away party almost induces him to commit mayhem in Booth Tarkington's *Seventeen*.

Bokonon See Johnson, Lionel Boyd.

Bokum, Mrs. Widow who is Mrs. MacStinger's bridesmaid at her marriage to John Bunsby in Charles Dickens's *Dombey and Son*.

Bolam, Enid Abrasive administrative head of Steen Psychiatric Clinic; she is murdered in P. D. James's *A Mind to Murder*.

Bolam, Marion Self-effacing cousin of Enid Bolam in P. D. James's *A Mind to Murder*.

Boland Bully from the Belvedere School who interrogates Stephen Dedalus in James Joyce's *A Portrait of the Artist as a Young Man*.

Boland, Miss Middle-aged academic who becomes involved romantically with F. X. Enderby; she is shy but friendly and masks her self doubts with a confident manner in Anthony Burgess's *Enderby Outside*.

Bold, Eleanor See Harding, Eleanor.

Bold, John Zealous surgeon and town councilor, who leads the attack on Septimus Harding for alleged abuse of a charitable trust; he marries Eleanor, Mr. Harding's daughter, in Anthony Trollope's *The Warden*.

Bold, Johnny Baby son of the widowed Eleanor Harding Bold; Mr. Slope coos over the child in order to flatter his mother, whom he hopes to marry in Anthony Trollope's *Barchester Towers*.

Bold, Mary Sister of John Bold and friend and later sister-in-law of Eleanor Harding Bold in Anthony Trollope's *The Warden.* She is Johnny Bold's adoring aunt in *Barchester Towers.*

Boldero, Mr. Diminutive financier and partner of the younger Theodore Gumbril in the marketing of his pneumatic pants in Aldous Huxley's *Antic Hay.*

Boldieu, Paul (Kid Faro, Scot, Scotch, Scotcho, Scotty) Baseball pitcher and boyhood friend of Jack Duluoz in Jack Kerouac's *Doctor Sax, Maggie Cassidy,* and *Book of Dreams.*

Boldini, Francesco Tricky, dishonest, experienced Legionnaire; he is a source of information for the Geste brothers; he plots to steal the jewel Michael Geste supposedly took; he is a spy for Color Sergeant Lejaune in Percival Christopher Wren's *Beau Geste.*

Boldwig, Captain Fierce little man, who catches Samuel Pickwick sleeping on his property in a wheelbarrow and puts him in the stocks in Charles Dickens's *The Posthumous Papers of the Pickwick Club.*

Boldwood, John Gentleman farmer obsessively in love with but rejected by Bathsheba Everdene; expecting at last to win her after the extended absence of her deceitful husband, Frank Troy, Boldwood is deranged by Troy's reappearance and kills him; his death sentence is commuted in Thomas Hardy's *Far from the Madding Crowd.*

Boleo, Joe Skilled woodsman and courier for the American forces in the Mohawk Valley; instrumental in saving Gil Martin's family from destruction in Walter D. Edmonds's *Drums Along the Mohawk.*

Boles, Terence Mark Coldridge's publisher in Doris Lessing's *The Four-Gated City.*

Boleyn, Anna Spirit of the ill-fated second wife of Henry VIII; she recounts her experiences to Judge Minos to gain entry to Elysium; her sufferings from her own ambition, as well as at the hands of her scheming father and the king, form the last chapter of Henry Fielding's *A Journey From This World to the Next.*

Boleyn, Daniel Nineteen-year-old homosexual Irish naïf, who has written "one most lovely poem"; under Horace Zagreus's tutelage, he undergoes a course of instruction in the ways of apery; his innocence and naïveté highlight the hypocracies and pretensions of bohemian society in Wyndham Lewis's *The Apes of God.*

Bolgolam, Skyresh High Admiral of Lilliput; his malice toward Lemuel Gulliver is increased when Gulliver seizes the Blefuscu fleet; he acts for the wishes of the Empress of Lilliput in trying to gain the capital penalty when Gulliver is impeached in Jonathan Swift's *Travels into Several Remote Nations of the World. In Four Parts. By Lemuel Gulliver.*

Bolin, Lester Scientist who assists Robert Softly in developing a cosmic language based on mathematical principles in Don DeLillo's *Ratner's Star.*

Bolingbroke, Henry Duke of Hereford, son of John of Gaunt in William Shakespeare's play *Richard II.*

Bolkonskaya, Lise Andrew's good-natured wife who dies in childbirth in Leo Tolstoy's *War and Peace.*

Bolkonskaya, Marya Sad and suffering daughter of the crudely stern Prince Bolkonski, a retired military commander; endures her father's cruel treatment and her isolated life in the country; later marries Nicholas Rostov, who rescues the princess from a lonely solitude after her father dies in the war with Napoleon in Leo Tolstoy's *War and Peace.*

Bolkonsky, Andrei Ambitious and intelligent son of Prince Bolkonsky, a retired military commander; seen as coldly analytical and lacking emotion; despairs after the death of his wife, Lise; falls in love with Natasha Rostova, but cannot overlook her earlier love for Anatole in Leo Tolstoy's *War and Peace.*

Bolkonsky, Prince Andrei's old-fashioned father; lives as a recluse in the country after retiring as a military commander from the army; stern in general and often cruel toward his daughter Marya in particular; cynical about the changes that modern life is bringing to Russia; forced to return to his military duties in the war with Napoleon; dies as the French advance toward his country estate in Leo Tolstoy's *War and Peace.*

Bollens, Farmer Prosperous, middle-aged country man with whom Adelaide Hinton elopes, freeing Edward Springrove from his engagement in Thomas Hardy's *Desperate Remedies.*

Bolling, Dr. Romantic and restless father of Binx Bolling; joins the R.C.A.F. and dies during World War II in Walker Percy's *The Moviegoer.*

Bolling, Emily See Cutrer, Emily Bolling.

Bolling, John Bickerson (Binx, Jack) New Orleans stockbroker and film buff who pursues money, women, and God; narrator of Walker Percy's *The Moviegoer.*

Bolling, Kate Cutrer See Cutrer, Kate.

Bollum, Richard Nefarious partner of Timothy Crinkett; he persuades John Caldigate to pay Crinkett back part of the purchase price for a gold mine in New South Wales; the payment looks like a bribe and further increases Caldigate's troubles in Anthony Trollope's *John Caldigate.*

Bolo, Miss Lady Snuphanuph's card-playing companion, with whom Samuel Pickwick plays whist in a cut-throat match in Charles Dickens's *The Posthumous Papers of the Pickwick Club.*

Bologna, Antonio de The duchess's steward and later husband; flees to Ancona with his eldest son on the Duchess's orders; optimistic about reconciliation with her; haunted by the duchess's echo in a graveyard; approaches the cardinal about a truce but is stabbed by Bosola in John Webster's *The Duchess of Malfi.*

Bolowski, Lazarus London music publisher who prints but does not distribute Hugh Firmin's songs in Malcolm Lowry's *Under the Volcano.*

Bolsover, Gwen Real-estate secretary who unwittingly helps Michael Cullen in a shady real-estate deal while becoming his lover in Alan Sillitoe's *A Start in Life.*

Bolster, Bridget Key witness, along with John Kenneby, at Lady Mason's trial for forgery; she withstands a withering examination from Mr. Chaffanbrass in Anthony Trollope's *Orley Farm.*

Bolt Chauffeur at Rudge Hall, the estate for which Lester Carmody is trustee in P. G. Wodehouse's *Money for Nothing.*

Bolt Master's mate of the English sloop *Amelia* captured by Peyrol while spying for the English in Joseph Conrad's *The Rover.*

Bolt Pander's servant; ordered to rape Marina in order to bring an end to her virtuous talk, which has had an adverse effect on Pander's brothel business; succumbs to Marina's virtuous speech as well, however, and agrees to find her a more suitable place to work and live in William Shakespeare's play *Pericles.*

Bolt, Cameron Husband of Francesca Fox Bolt; district attorney seeking election as attorney general of California in Gail Godwin's *Glass People.*

Bolt, Carl Adoptive father of Molly Bolt in Rita Mae Brown's *Rubyfruit Jungle.*

Bolt, Carrie Adoptive mother of Molly Bolt in Rita Mae Brown's *Rubyfruit Jungle.*

Bolt, Francesca Fox Wife of Cameron Bolt and, briefly, seeker of her own identity in Gail Godwin's *Glass People.*

Bolt, Molly (Moll) Illegitimate child, adopted daughter of Carl and Carrie Bolt, lesbian heroine, and narrator of Rita Mae Brown's *Rubyfruit Jungle.*

Bolt, Mrs. Extortionate landlady of the lodging house where Bernard Kingcote and his sister stay in George Gissing's *Isabel Clarendon.*

Bolt, Myra University student who is defended by Lewis Eliot when she is threatened with expulsion for sexual misconduct in C. P. Snow's *The Sleep of Reason.*

Bolt, Rachel Confidante and New York guide of Hagar Ashendyne; recovers from her husband's abuse in Mary Johnston's *Hagar.*

Bolt, Sir Simon Longtime Master of the Brotherton Hunt known far and wide for his expertise with horse and hound in Anthony Trollope's *Is He Popenjoy?*

Boltby, John Family lawyer of Sir Harry Hotspur; he learns of George Hotspur's debts and actress mistress, Lucy Morton, and advises his client to forbid his daughter, Emily, to marry the rogue in Anthony Trollope's *Sir Harry Hotspur of Humblethwaite.*

Bolter, The Youngest sister of Sadie Radlett and Emily Warbeck and mother of Fanny Logan; married at least three times and the veteran of many love affairs, she has been almost entirely absent from Fanny's life until she returns to England from Europe at the outbreak of World War II in Nancy Mitford's *The Pursuit of Love.*

Bolton Defrauding steward of the Mansfield family in Samuel Richardson's *Sir Charles Grandison.*

Bolton Third lieutenant of the *Indefatigable* in C. S. Forester's *Mr. Midshipman Hornblower.* He has been promoted and is captain of the *Caligula,* though he lacks the manners and elegance that are usually requisite for his station in life in *Ship of the Line.*

Bolton, Bolton Oliver Farmer and caretaker of the Kilburn estate in William Dean Howells's *Annie Kilburn.*

Bolton, Chick Black racketeer obsessed with hatred for all whites; counterpart of Hank Dean in Julian Mayfield's *The Grand Parade.*

Bolton, Fanny Daughter of the porter at Shepherd's Inn; Arthur Pendennis is enamored of her until his mother rescues him, fearing a dishonorable liaison; Fanny then marries Samuel Huxter in William Makepeace Thackeray's *The History of Pendennis.*

Bolton, Harry Sir Thomas Sindall's virtuous cousin, heir apparent to the Sindall estate and lover of Lucy Sindall in Henry Mackenzie's *The Man of the World.*

Bolton, Harry (Bury) Mysterious friend of Redburn; crushed to death between a whale and a ship in Herman Melville's *Redburn.*

Bolton, Ivy Gossipy Tevershall parish nurse, who comes to Wragby Hall to care for the crippled Sir Clifford Chatterley; still loving her husband, who died in a mine accident, she inspires Lady Chatterley with her remarks on the lasting value of "touch" between lovers; she enters into "an intimacy of perversity" with Chatterley, who gives over full control to her as a "Magna Mater" figure at the end of D. H. Lawrence's *Lady Chatterley's Lover.*

Bolton, Jackie Founder of the first "true" Communist Party in Martha Quest's town; he scoffs at people like Boris Kruger for organizing ineffective groups like Sympathizers for Russia in Doris Lessing's *A Proper Marriage* and in *A Ripple from the Storm.*

Bolton, Margaret Sympathetic wife of Robert Bolton; she joins with her husband in urging Hester Bolton to escape from her repressive mother by marrying John Caldigate in Anthony Trollope's *John Caldigate.*

Bolton, Mary Religious fanatic obsessed by the idea of dominating her daughter, Hester, and saving her from John Caldigate; when the young people marry, she becomes nearly deranged, and after a scandal erupts around the husband, she locks Hester up in Puritan Grange; even when Caldigate is cleared of a bigamy charge, she remains implacable towards him in Anthony Trollope's *John Caldigate.*

Bolton, Mr. Fanny Bolton's father, porter of Shepherd's Inn in William Makepeace Thackeray's *The History of Pendennis.*

Bolton, Mrs. Fanny Bolton's mother, portress of Shepherd's Inn in William Makepeace Thackeray's *The History of Pendennis.*

Bolton, Mrs. Plain and dowdy wife of Captain Bolton; her appearance somewhat comforts Maria Hornblower in C. S. Forester's *Ship of the Line.*

Bolton, Nicholas Cambridge banker devoted to his only daughter, Hester, and deeply pained by her mother's cruel treatment of her; he turns against Hester's husband, John Caldigate, when the young man is said to have committed bigamy in Anthony Trollope's *John Caldigate.*

Bolton, Nicholas (the younger) Narrow-minded son of a successful Cambridge banker; he shares his parents' religious bigotry in Anthony Trollope's *John Caldigate.*

Bolton, Pauliny Wife of Oliver Bolton and proud housekeeper of the Kilburns in William Dean Howells's *Annie Kilburn.*

Bolton, Robert Easy-going, gregarious Cambridge attorney and son of Nicholas by his first marriage; observing his stepmother's tyranny towards her daughter, Hester, he advises Hester to marry John Caldigate in Anthony Trollope's *John Caldigate.*

Bolton, Ruth Philadelphia Quaker; medical student and girlfriend of Philip Sterling in Samuel Langhorne Clemens and Charles Dudley Warner's *The Gilded Age.*

Bolton, Stawarth Brusque but chivalrous captain in the English army; he provides protection for the Glendinning house and family in Sir Walter Scott's *The Monastery.*

Bolton, William Successful London barrister son of Nicholas Bolton; he succeeds in reconciling his parents to the marriage of their daughter, Hester, and John Caldigate in Anthony Trollope's *John Caldigate.*

Boltwood Church Bishop who is the father of Tess; he is pleased by her announcement of marriage with Stephen Freer in C. P. Snow's *The Malcontents.*

Boltwood, Bella-Lenore Associate of Nathaniel Turner Witherspoon and lover of fairy tales in Leon Forrest's *The Bloodworth Orphans.*

Boltwood, Tess University student who is a member of a Marxist group planning political action; she believes the death of Bernard Kelshall was martyrdom and accepts Stephen Frer's proposal of marriage in C. P. Snow's *The Malcontents.*

Bom Russian clown; paired with Bim he comments critically on English society in the Epilogue to Richard Aldington's *The Colonel's Daughter.*

Bom Tormentor created by and identified with the "I"; his arrival is awaited in the third section of Samuel Beckett's *How It Is.*

Bomba, Kalabi Son of Lahilatoul Kalabi and brother of Kalabi Dauman in *Sundiata: An Epic of Old Mali.*

Bombie of the Frizzled Head (Snow Ball) Witchlike black servant of Heer Peter Piper in James Kirke Paulding's *Koningsmarke.*

Bomerer, David Bookkeeper in San Francisco, a loner who is unable to change his empty life and who spends his days trapped in the demands of paperwork, the tragedies he reads about in the newspaper on his way home, and the ecstasy of the movies he watches in the evening in William Saroyan's "Secrets in Alexandria."

Boms, Mr. Clergyman and an obsequious shareholder, who attends the General Meeting of the New Collier Company in John Galsworthy's *The Man of Property.*

Bomston, Lord Edward Briton living in Switzerland; meets with Juliet and Saint-Preux to discuss their lovers' plight, even though he himself has fallen in love with Juliet; pleads the lovers' case to Juliet's father, Baron d'Etange, but his words are ignored; finally suggests that the couple elope but finds that Juliet will not go against her father's decision that she marry the older de Wolmar in Jean Jacques Rousseau's *The New Héloïse.*

Bon, Charles Probably the son of Thomas Sutpen and his first wife, Eulalia Bon; engaged to his probable half sister Judith Sutpen in William Faulkner's *Absalom, Absalom!*

Bon, Charles Etienne Saint-Valery Son of Charles Bon and his octoroon mistress; father of Jim Bond in William Faulkner's *Absalom, Absalom!*

Bon, Eulalia See Sutpen, Eulalia Bon.

Bonacieux D'Artagnan's landlord who seeks the young musketeer's aid in rescuing his daughter Constance, the Queen's seamstress; agrees to forgive the back rent owed by the swordsman for his lodgings in repayment in Alexandre Dumas, père's *The Three Musketeers.*

Bonacieux, Constance Queen's young and loyal seamstress; daughter of Bonacieux, D'Artagnan's landlord; abducted on Cardinal Richelieu's orders in order to pry from her information regarding the romance between the Queen and the Duke of Buckingham; imprisoned in a convent where the villainous Lady de Winter poisons her in Alexandre Dumas, père's *The Three Musketeers.*

Bonali, Angela (Angie) Daughter of Vince Bonali; necks in a car during a high school basketball game while the mine accident occurs in Robert Coover's *The Origin of the Brunists.*

Bonali, Charlie Disaffected wastrel son of Vince Bonali; goes AWOL from the marines in Robert Coover's *The Origin of the Brunists.*

Bonali, Etta Fat, long-suffering wife of Vince Bonali in Robert Coover's *The Origin of the Brunists.*

Bonali, Vince Supervisor at the Deepwater Mine who becomes involved in efforts to stop the Brunist cult in Robert Coover's *The Origin of the Brunists.*

Bonamo Vincentio di Vivaldi's cowardly friend and confidant in Ann Radcliffe's *The Italian.*

Bonamy, Richard (Nick) Jacob Flanders's counterpart, who is attracted to the same women; he is sullen, opportunistic, and meaty where Jacob is bright, beautiful, idealistic, and diaphanous; Jacob writes the saga of his life in letters to Nick in Virginia Woolf's *Jacob's Room.*

Bonaparte Narrator and young soldier who is guarding two enemy spies; quickly grows to like the prisoners, Belcher and 'Awkins; surprised when he is ordered immediately to execute the prisoners as a reprisal against the enemy's execution of their soldiers in Frank O'Connor's "Guests of a Nation."

Bonaparte, Napoleon French dictator who seeks Thomas Paine's support to add legitimacy to his regime in Howard Fast's *Citizen Tom Paine.*

Bonaparte, Napoleon French ruler and lover of Angela Guessippi in Hervey Allen's *Anthony Adverse.*

Bonaparte, Napoleon ("Boney") French emperor and enemy with whose forces the English navy engages battle in C. S. Forester's *Hornblower and the Hotspur.*

Bonaparte, Pauline Licentious wife of General Leclerc; enjoys male attention, especially that of Soliman, the masseur, and becomes a believer in voodoo under his influence; flees Santo Domingo after her husband's death of cholera in Alejo Carpentier's *The Kingdom of This World.*

Bonario Young gentleman and Corbaccio's son; upon encountering Mosca, he initially refuses to speak to him but eventually gives in, only to be informed that his father has disinherited him; ordered to hide and observe Corbaccio and Volpone; instead, observes Volpone's failed seduction of Celia and rescues her after Volpone threatens to rape her; framed by Volpone, Mosca, and Voltore before the Venetian court and accused of kidnapping Celia; finally released and accorded his father's entire property after Volpone ends his ruse in Ben Jonson's play *Volpone.*

Bonbennin bonbobbin-bonbobbinet Exemplary prince, whose name means "Enlightener of the Sun"; he chooses Nanhoa out of seven hundred candidates to be his bride, but then barters her for a white mouse with green eyes in an oriental fable by Lien Chi Altangi in Oliver Goldsmith's *The Citizen of the World.*

Bonbon, Louise Childish wife of Sidney Bonbon; ignored by her husband, she becomes romantically involved with Marcus Payne in Ernest J. Gaines's *Of Love and Dust.*

Bonbon, Sidney Cajun plantation overseer who kills Marcus Payne in Ernest J. Gaines's *Of Love and Dust.*

Boncassen, Ezekiel Forthright American scholar engaged in research at the British Museum; proud of his humble origins, he nonetheless has reservations about his daughter, Isabel, entering British aristocracy through marriage to Lord Silverbridge; seeing the young man's devotion, he gives permission for his daughter's marriage in Anthony Trollope's *The Duke's Children.*

Boncassen, Isabel Comely, charming, and outspoken American, the novelty and belle of the season, and daughter of Ezekiel Boncassen; she enchants Lord Silverbridge but is deemed an inappropriate wife by his father, the (younger) Duke of Omnium, because of her antecedents; she charms the duke, who at last gives consent to the wedding in Anthony Trollope's *The Duke's Children.*

Boncassen, Mrs. Reticent and awkward American mother of Isabel; she is somewhat overawed at the prospect of her daughter's entering the highest ranks of British society by marrying Lord Silverbridge in Anthony Trollope's *The Duke's Children.*

Boncoeur, Remi Prep school friend of Sal Paradise; works as a barracks guard in Jack Kerouac's *On the Road.*

Bond, Hamish (Old Man Bond, 'Sieur' Amsh, Alec Hinks, Captain Strike-down-then-make-the-Palaver) Slave runner turned New Orleans plantation owner who buys the mulatto Amantha Starr and takes her as a mistress; hangs himself while a captive of Rau-Ru and black rioters in 1866 in Robert Penn Warren's *Band of Angels.*

Bond, James (Code 007) British Secret Service agent whose 00 code designation gives him a license to kill; he duels LeChiffre at baccarat in Ian Fleming's *Casino Royale.* He pursues Mr. Big, a USSR agent who is running a gold-smuggling scheme in *Live and Let Die.* He foils Hugo Drax's plot to destroy London in *Moonraker.* He uses the name Francs during his investigation of "The Spangled Mob" in *Diamonds Are Forever.* He is the intended victim of an assassination that he foils, but he is perhaps fatally wounded by a poison-tipped blade in Rosa Klebb's shoe in *From Russia, With Love.* Recovering, he acts as a freelance agent in his investigation into mysterious deaths on Crab Key in *Dr. No.* He blocks a plot to rob Fort Knox in *Goldfinger.* He thwarts Ernst Stavro Blofeld's atomic-bomb extortion plot in *Thunderball.* He is seen through the eyes of Vivienne Michel, whom he rescues from professional arsonists in *The Spy Who Loved Me.* He poses as Sir Hilary Bray to infiltrate Blofeld's Alpine fortress; his marriage to Tracy di Vicenzo ends with her murder by Blofeld in *On Her Majesty's Secret Service.* He takes the identity Taro Todoroki on his Japanese mission; he kills Blofeld but loses his memory in *You Only Live Twice.*

Bond, Jim Idiot son of Charles Etienne Saint-Valery Bon and a black woman in William Faulkner's *Absalom, Absalom!*

Bond, May Aspiring actress, Oxford student, and part-time lover of the younger Tom Nimmo; she plans to open a burlesque acting company with Tom, but their plans go awry in Joyce Cary's *Prisoner of Grace.*

Bond, Miss Mr. Bond's daughter, who loves Major Smyth in Frances Sheridan's *Memoirs of Miss Sidney Bidulph.*

Bond, Mr. Gentleman with a wife, several daughters, and a son home from college; the Faulklands stay with them while their country house is being built in Frances Sheridan's *Memoirs of Miss Sidney Bidulph.*

Bondarenko, Gennady Iosifovich Soviet colonel assigned to evaluate Bright Star, an antiballistic-missile defense laser; takes command of the security forces to defend the project from an Afghan assault; is eventually given command of the facility in Tom Clancy's *The Cardinal of the Kremlin.*

Bondelmonti, Francesco Italian nobleman who heads the Florentine army; a cousin of Euthanasia dei Adimari, he urges her to join the conspiracy to overthrow Castruccio dei Antelminelli in Mary Shelley's *Valperga.*

Bondorlonganon, Father Priest of Wutra, the god worshipped in Oldorando; he conducts the funeral for Laintal Ay's grandfather in Brian W. Aldiss's *Helliconia Spring.*

Bondum, Mr. Corrupt bailiff, who tricks William Booth to arrest him and tries to multiply the suits against him in Henry Fielding's *Amelia.*

Bondy, Mr. London pawnbroker who lends money to Dinny Cherrell on Jean Tasburgh Cherrell's pendant in John Galsworthy's *Maid In Waiting.*

Bone, Everard Handsome, clever, churchgoing anthropologist with an eccentric mother; he tries to use Mildred Lathbury to extricate him from a nebulous relationship with his married colleague Helena Napier, and then seems to be interested in Mildred herself in Barbara Pym's *Excellent Women.* His further career is mentioned in *Less Than Angels.*

Bone, Mrs. Eccentric, energetic, elderly widow whose near-madness takes the form of obsessions about dangerous birds and proselytizing Jesuits; she is the agnostic mother of the devout Everard Bone in Barbara Pym's *Excellent Women.* She is briefly mentioned in *Less Than Angels.*

Bonello, Aldo Italian ambulance driver in the command of Frederic Henry during the retreat from Caporetto; wanders off with the hope of being taken prisoner by the Germans in Ernest Hemingway's *A Farewell to Arms.*

Bones, Billy Seaman with a sabre cut who spends his last violent and frightened days as a drunken guest at the Admiral Benbow Inn; Flint's first mate on the *Walrus,* he has possession of Flint's treasure map and is hiding from his *Walrus* shipmates in Robert Louis Stevenson's *Treasure Island.*

Bones, Brom Rough and strong young man of Sleepy Hollow; popular and athletic; given the name Abraham (Brom) Van Brunt at birth, but is known to everyone as Brom Bones because of his strong frame; courts Katrina Van Tassel, though perhaps not earnestly enough to suit her; views Ichabod Crane as a rival for Katrina's affections, an idea encouraged by her; according to some, chases Ichabod Crane in the guise of the Headless Horseman in order to scare off his main rival; finally marries Katrina in Washington Irving's "The Legend of Sleepy Hollow."

Bones, Inspector Middle-aged, carelessly dressed policeman who investigates the murder of the Jumper and Professor Duncan McFee at George and Dorothy's apartment; dogmatic yet absurd; arrives to arrest Dorothy for murder, but is dissuaded by his admiration for Dorothy's past as a beautiful actress and his fallible logic; his brother was a patient of the absurd psychiatrist Archie in Tom Stoppard's play *Jumpers.*

Boneyard, Blanche Lebanon Timberlane First wife of Cass Timberlane in Sinclair Lewis's *Cass Timberlane.*

Bongiorno, Ann Chapin See Chapin, Ann.

Bongiorno, Charley Jazz saxophonist and Ann Chapin's first husband in John O'Hara's *Ten North Frederick.*

Bongo, Alfy Young homosexual who was raised by Mr. Obo-King; he performs sexual favors in Colin MacInnes's *City of Spades.*

Bonham, Al Expert skin diver and small businessman in Ganado Bay, Jamaica; teaches Ron Grant to skin-dive in James Jones's *Go to the Widow-Maker.*

Bonham, Joe American soldier who suffers nearly complete physical incapacitation as the result of wounds received in World War I; his dreams and reminiscences comprise Dalton Trumbo's *Johnny Got His Gun.*

Bonham, Letta Jamaican schoolteacher and wife of Al Bonham; divorces Bonham and moves to Kingston in James Jones's *Go to the Widow-Maker.*

Bonhome Steward and secretary to Count de Vinevil; he accompanies the family to Turkey and is killed with the count in Penelope Aubin's *The Strange Adventures of the Count de Vinevil and His Family.*

Boniface (Father Blinkhoolie) Ineffectual abbot of the Monastery of St. Mary's of Kennaquhair; he is kindly and hospitable, though pompous and insecure; incapable of dealing with the Reformation, he is sent a capable subprior whom he resents but to whom he is ultimately forced to relinquish his miter in Sir Walter Scott's *The Monastery.* After his abdication he acts as mail-gardener at Kinross; he unwillingly aids the rescuers of Queen Mary of Scotland, after which he disguises himself as Blinkhoolie and enters the Abbey of Dundrennan in *The Abbot.*

Boniface, Barnaby Tenant whose offer to permit a neighbor to decide on the merit of the proprietary claims of Walter Warmhouse is rejected; the ensuing lawsuit has gone thirteen years without progress in an anecdote told by Mr. Fielding in Henry Brooke's *The Fool of Quality.*

Bonifacia Aguaruna Indian girl abducted by Spanish nuns to be converted at their jungle mission; frees indigenous girls kidnapped by the colonists; marries Lituma and moves to the coastal region; enticed by Lituma's friend when Lituma is imprisoned; becomes a prostitute in the brothel The Green House owned by Chunga in Mario Vargas Llosa's *The Green House.*

Bonifante, Eunice Aunt of Lester Stoner; widow of Al Bonifante, who committed suicide; lover of Sonny, her sister-in-law's husband; finds a new boyfriend; owns a restaurant in Mary McGarry Morris's *Songs in Ordinary Time.*

Bonita Eleven-year-old sister of the two main characters, Lyman and Henry, known as the "Crazy Lamartine boys"; lives with her family on a Chippewa Indian reservation in Louise Erdrich's "The Red Convertible."

Bonita, María Prostitute who works in Larsen's brothel in Juan Carlos Onetti's *The Body Snatcher.*

Bonkers (Bonkie) Newfoundland retriever who bites off part of Garp's left ear; Garp bites off one of Bonkers's ears in John Irving's *The World According to Garp.*

Bonnac, Monsieur French nobleman rescued from debtor's prison by Valancourt; later he is given die Castle di Udolpho by Emily St. Aubert in Ann Radcliffe's *The Mysteries of Udolpho.*

Bonnard, Dr. Gerard French child-care expert; because of his handicap, Jeremy Trout is placed in Dr. Bonnard's care in Elizabeth Bowen's *Eva Trout, or Changing Scenes.*

Bonnard, Mrs. Gerard Dr. Bonnard's wife, who assists with Jeremy Trout's education in Elizabeth Bowen's *Eva Trout, or Changing Scenes.*

Bonne-chance, Père Good-hearted priest of a country parish in the French colony Saint Domingue; lives with a mistress, Fontelle, by whom he has many children; is executed after a slave rebellion for crimes he did not commit in Madison Smartt Bell's *All Souls' Rising.*

Bonner, Adrian Husband of Margaret; chaplain and headmaster at Fair Haven School; dies of lung problems in Gail Godwin's *Evensong.*

Bonner, Benny Psychology student and older maternal cousin who practices analysis on Joe Sandwich in Peter De Vries's *The Vale of Laughter.*

Bonner, Carl Attorney who represents Hanna Trout in her divorce from Paris; married to Leslie Morgan Bonner; was the youngest Eagle Scout in the history of Georgia and feels he has to live up to his "Eagle Scout" image; is shot and killed by Paris Trout in Pete Dexter's *Paris Trout.*

Bonner, Dolly Mistress of Milton Loftis in William Styron's *Lie Down in Darkness.*

Bonner, Evette Mother of Adrian, wife of Joseph; deserts Adrian at an orphanage when he is six; dies eight months later of cancer in Gail Godwin's *Evensong.*

Bonner, Joseph Anthony (Tony) Bonner Father of Adrian, husband of Evette; leaves Adrian at an orphanage when he is six; later confesses to Margaret that he is Adrian's father and has served time in prison; lives in a house near Margaret and Adrian; outlives his son Adrian and dies at ninety-six in Gail Godwin's *Evensong.*

Bonner, Julianna Ill-tempered, sickly heiress who dies, leaving Beckley Court to Evan Harrington, with whom she had fallen in love, in George Meredith's *Evan Harrington.*

Bonner, Margaret Thirty-three-year-old wife of Adrian, an Anglican pastor at the parish of All Saints High Balsam; her church burns down; she has a daughter; moves to New York after Adrian's death in Gail Godwin's *Evensong.*

Bonner, Mary Sir Thomas Underwood's lovely niece, who arrives from the West Indies needing a home, much to her uncle's initial irritation; the philandering Ralph Newton, heir of Newton Priory, makes up to her, but she falls in love with the other Ralph Newton, who plucks up courage finally to propose to her in Anthony Trollope's *Ralph the Heir.*

Bonner, Mrs. Source of the Countess of Saldar's financial ambitions; she dies, leaving Beckley Court to her granddaughter Julianna in George Meredith's *Evan Harrington.*

Bonneville, Nicholas de French newspaper editor who helps shelter Thomas Paine in Paris and who later sends his family to Paine in America during the Napoleonic regime in Howard Fast's *Citizen Tom Paine.*

Bonnicastle, Miss Robust artist who tries to arrange Olga Hannaford's love affairs in George Gissing's *The Crown of Life.*

Bonnie Girlfriend of Lyons Maxsom; works in a laundry at a hospital in August Wilson's play *Fences.*

Bonnycastle, Mr. Cool, elegant private-school headmaster in Holy Orders, who uses the cane to give Jack Easy his first reason for abandoning the absurd egalitarianism of his father, Nicodemus, in Captain Frederick Marryat's *Mr. Midshipman Easy.*

Bonnyfeather, John Prominent Leghorn merchant; maternal grandfather of Anthony Adverse, whom he gives a surname and educates, in Hervey Allen's *Anthony Adverse.*

Bonnyfeather, Maria (Marquise da Vincitata) Mother, by Denis Moore, of Anthony Adverse in Hervey Allen's *Anthony Adverse.*

Bonnyrigg, Rachel New wife of Sir Bingo Binks; she helps to spread gossip among the visitors to St. Ronan's Well in Sir Walter Scott's *St. Ronan's Well.*

Bono, Jim Friend of the chief character Troy Maxsom; married to Lucielle; lives in the black tenements of Pittsburg in the 1950s in August Wilson's play *Fences.*

Bonteen, Mr. Loquacious party underling, who mocks Phineas Finn for going against party discipline in Anthony Trollope's *Phineas Finn.* He staunchly supports Plantagenet Palliser in reforming the coinage in *The Eustace Diamonds.* He befriends Lizzie Eustace and tries to help her escape from her marriage to Mr. Emilius; he is murdered in *Phineas Redux.*

Bonteen, Mrs. Busybody wife of a political hack; she tries to bolster his career by denigrating his rivals in Anthony Trollope's *Phineas Finn.* When her husband is murdered, she is vociferous in accusing Phineas Finn of the crime in *Phineas Redux.*

Bonthron Drunken thug, who is a henchman of John Ramorny and Henbane Dwining; he is defeated in a fight with Henry Smith to adjudicate Bonthron's murder of Oliver Proudfute; he undergoes a mock hanging; he helps to murder the Duke of Rothsay and is summarily executed by Archibald, Earl of Douglas, in Sir Walter Scott's *The Fair Maid of Perth.*

Booby, John Naive young squire, whose lust for Shamela Andrews allows him to believe she is a virgin and to be manipulated into a marriage settlement with her in Henry Fielding's *An Apology for the Life of Mrs. Shamela Andrews.*

Booby, Lady Thomas Booby's widow, who assuages her grief through fickle but prolonged pursuit of Joseph Andrews; her passion turns to hatred, and she abuses her aristocratic power to block Joseph's marriage to Fanny Goodwill in Henry Fielding's *The History of the Adventures of Mr. Joseph Andrews and of His Friend Mr. Abraham Adams.*

Booby, Mr. See B—, William.

Booby, Mrs. Wealthy woman who seeks spiritual guidance from Geoffry Wildgoose at Bath, ostensibly because of her estrangement from her husband but actually because she has been snubbed by her former lover's wife in Richard Graves's *The Spiritual Quixote.*

Booby, Thomas Status-conscious lord of the estate and husband to Lady Booby; he employs both Joseph Andrews and Fanny Goodwill before his death early in Henry Fielding's *The History of the Adventures of Mr. Joseph Andrews and of His Friend Mr. Abraham Adams.*

Booch, Mrs. Pensioned servant who visits Bladesover; her stereotypical remarks make her disgusting to young George Ponderevo in H. G. Wells's *Tono-Bungay.*

Boodle, Captain (Doodles) Dimwitted friend of Archibald Clavering, similarly engrossed in the turf; he counsels Archie in wooing Lady Ongar via her friend Sophie Gordeloup; he becomes fascinated by Sophie and follows her to the Continent in Anthony Trollope's *The Claverings.* He appears in *Phineas Redux.*

Booker Middle-aged pool hall owner who allows his customers—mostly corner boys—to play dice in the back room in Herbert Simmons's *Corner Boy.*

Booker One of the many illegal workers at the pancake house owned by the Chinese American Ralph Chang; flees his job to avoid prosecution by the immigration authorities in Gish Jen's "In the American Society."

Booker White man who has recently joined the Communist Party, lacks knowledge of the names of others in the party and when they are planning their next meeting; helps Sue, who has just been beaten by police, by giving her a cool, wet cloth to ease her pain in Richard Wright's "Bright and Morning Star."

Booker, Alfred Shrewd editor of the *Literary Chronicle,* who knows all the tricks of his trade and writes book reviews without troubling himself to read the books through in Anthony Trollope's *The Way We Live Now.* He appears in *The Prime Minister.*

Booker, Craig Nine-year-old twin of Scott and brother of Joe; son of Frank and Diane Booker; grandson of Daniel and Ellen Booker; pestiferous source of comic relief in Nicholas Evans's *The Horse Whisperer.*

Booker, Diane Wife of Frank Booker; mother of Joe, Scott, and Craig Booker; daughter-in-law of Ellen Booker; sister-in-law and possessive caretaker of Tom Booker; jealous observer of Annie Graves Maclean's relationship with Tom; alerts Grace Maclean to her mother's affair in Nicholas Evans's *The Horse Whisperer.*

Booker, Ellen Quiet but strong widow of rancher Daniel Booker; mother of Tom, Rosie, and Frank Booker and grandmother of Joe, Craig, and Scott Booker in Nicholas Evans's *The Horse Whisperer.*

Booker, Frank Brother, partner, and friend of Tom Booker; co-owner of the Booker ranch; father of Joe, Scott, and Craig Booker; son of Ellen Booker; brother of Rosie Booker; arranges Grace's celebration and going-home party at the ranch in Nicholas Evans's *The Horse Whisperer.*

Booker, Joe Twelve-year-old son of Frank and Diane Booker; nephew of Tom Booker; helps Grace Maclean to ride again following her amputation; heir apparent to Tom Booker's talent as a trainer and friend of horses in Nicholas Evans's *The Horse Whisperer.*

Booker, Knobby Informer for Bumper Morgan against Timothy Landry in Joseph Wambaugh's *The Blue Knight.*

Booker, Mr. Director for the New Collier Company who participates in the General Meeting in John Galsworthy's *The Man of Property.*

Booker, Rose Mother of two young daughters; daughter of Daniel and Ellen Booker, the latter of whom lives with her; sister of Frank and Tom Booker; assistant at the ranch in Nicholas Evans's *The Horse Whisperer.*

Booker, Scott Nine-year-old twin of Craig and brother of Joe; son of Frank and Diane Booker; source of comic relief in Nicholas Evans's *The Horse Whisperer.*

Booker, Tom Son of Daniel and Ellen Booker; brother of Rosie and Frank Booker; uncle to Joe, Scott, and Craig Booker; partner in the Booker ranch, where he manages the horses; ex-husband of cellist Rachel Feinerman Booker and father of Hal Booker; lover of Annie Graves Maclean; sacrifices himself to protect the Maclean family in Nicholas Evans's *The Horse Whisperer.*

Bookseller Man of business who usually buys poetry by quantity rather than quality in Charles Johnstone's *Chrysal: or, The Adventures of a Guinea.*

Bookwright, Calvin (Uncle Cal) Bootlegger in William Faulkner's *The Town, The Mansion,* and *The Reivers.*

Bookwright, Odum Wealthy farmer and one of the buyers of Old Frenchman's Place; appears in William Faulkner's *The Hamlet* and *The Mansion.*

Boomer, Father Nondescript priest who baptizes the dying Jamie Vaught in Walker Percy's *The Last Gentleman.*

Boon, Charles Eccentric, self-confident English graduate student from Rummidge; now at Euphoric State University, he hosts a wildly popular radio talk show in Plotinus; he moves in with Melanie Byrd, Morris Zapp's daughter, and during his on-air interview with Philip Swallow, Hilary Swallow calls and discusses the Swallows' sex life in David Lodge's *Changing Places:*

Boon, Danny Comedian to whom Billy Fisher has sent material and for whom he hopes to work in London in Keith Waterhouse's *Billy Liar.*

Boon, Lord Edward Ponderevo's nemesis; he uses his newspaper to spread rumors concerning Edward in H. G. Wells's *Tono-Bungay.*

Boone, Avery He runs a successful fishing business in Moray Key; hires Bob Dubois as his assistant; smuggles drugs in Russell Banks's *Continental Drift.*

Boone, Daniel Frontiersman who marries Diony Hall Jarvis and Evan Muir in Elizabeth Madox Roberts's *The Great Meadow.*

Boone, Hugh Mysterious figure in Arthur Conan Doyle's "The Adventure of the Norwood Builder."

Boone, Pete Idealistic young assistant to the cynical scientist Dr. Obispo; in love with the beautiful Virginia Maunciple and unable to reconcile his idealistic view of the world with its sordid reality, he contemplates suicide but is murdered by a jealous Jo Stoyte in Aldous Huxley's *After Many a Summer.*

Boot, John Courteney Popular author who desires to be a war correspondent in Ishmaelia; by mistake another writer with the same last name is chosen; later John becomes a correspondent in Antarctica in Evelyn Waugh's *Scoop.*

Boot, Mr. Proprietor of an old, charming sweets factory which is forced out of business by modern property developers in Margaret Drabble's *The Ice Age.*

Boot, Theodore William Boot's elderly uncle, who takes William's place at the banquet honoring William's journalistic achievement in Evelyn Waugh's *Scoop.*

Boot, William Timid nature writer who, because of mistaken identity, is sent to Ishmaelia to cover the war for a London newspaper; he discovers a Russian plot, reports the scoop, and returns to acclaim in England; he resumes his old position as a rural commentator in Evelyn Waugh's *Scoop.*

Bootersac, Mynheer Maternal grandfather of Jeremy Watersouchy; his gifts of engravings inspire the child's first efforts at drawing in William Beckford's *Biographical Memoirs of Extraordinary Painters.*

Booth Bulky bosun aboard the *Renown* in C. S. Forester's *Lieutenant Hornblower.*

Booth, Amelia (Emily) Harris William Booth's virtuous and loving wife, who supports her husband despite his vices, spurns temptations to sacrifice her virtue to sustain her family, does what virtuous things she can to preserve her family, and patiently waits for her husband to grow up in Henry Fielding's *Amelia.*

Booth, Billy Oldest son of William and Amelia Booth; he charms Dr. Harrison with his Christian notions of revenge in Henry Fielding's *Amelia.*

Booth, Elizabeth With William and Adolph, a beneficiary of the Vorakers' fortune who is loyal to her husband, Paul Booth, though he is absorbed by his attempts to earn capital in William Gaddis's *Carpenter's Gothic.*

Booth, Emily Second child of William and Amelia Booth; she becomes the favorite and heir of Dr. Harrison in Henry Fielding's *Amelia.*

Booth, James Gardener at Fieldhead, the Keeldar home in Charlotte Brontë's *Shirley.*

Booth, John Wilkes Underdog in the play; historical character and the assassin of the play's "Topdog" Abraham Lincoln in Suzan-Lori Parks's play *Topdog/Underdog.*

Booth, Nancy William Booth's cherished sister, whose death removes Booth from Amelia Harris long enough for Mrs. Harris to approve his rival for Amelia's hand in Henry Fielding's *Amelia.*

Booth, Paul Conniving businessman who schemes to take advantage of the wealth of Elizabeth Booth, his wife in William Gaddis's *Carpenter's Gothic.*

Booth, William (Billy) Good-hearted but weak husband of Amelia Booth; his belief that dominant passions rule man's behavior allows him to justify infidelity and gambling debts; he discovers true faith after reading sermons while imprisoned, eschews his bad habits and company, and, with Amelia's fortune restored, builds his family a contented life in Henry Fielding's *Amelia.*

Boothby, June Mr. and Mrs. Boothby's adolescent daughter, who is sexually aware of the men around her; she eventually meets and marries a man in Mashopi in Doris Lessing's *The Golden Notebook.*

Boothby, Mr. Owner of a successful hotel in Mashopi; his distrust of Anna Wulf's group of socialist friends is due to their subtle criticisms of him as a colonist in Doris Lessing's *The Golden Notebook.*

Boothby, Mrs. Plain woman who is pleasant and polite but unable to understand why Paul Blackenhurst and Jimmy tease her, or to realize that their maliciousness towards her is due to her treatment of the Africans in Doris Lessing's *The Golden Notebook.*

Boothby, Mrs. Widowed housekeeper/companion who joins the Sindall household after the death of Mrs. Selwyn and who acts as a pander for Sir Thomas Sindall with his ward Lucy Sindall in Henry Mackenzie's *The Man of the World.*

Booth-Henderson, Lieutenant Pudgy, pimply, stupid, nervous, pompous officer in charge of intake at Catterick; he interviews Jonathan Browne as a potential officer candidate during Basic Training in David Lodge's *Ginger, You're Barmy.*

Boothroyd, Gran Aged grandmother of Billy Fisher; her death leads to a partial and temporary easing of family problems in Keith Waterhouse's *Billy Liar.*

Boothroyd, Major Head of the weapons branch of the British Secret Service; he advises James Bond to change guns in Ian Fleming's *Dr. No.*

Boots, Mr. Young man who functions as a buffer at the Veneering dinner parties in Charles Dickens's *Our Mutual Friend.*

Borabolla Fat king of Mondoldo in Herman Melville's *Mardi.*

Borak, Akbil Friendly, conscientious professor of English at the University of Ankara; he and his wife Oya Borak are Philip Swallow's hosts at Ankara in David Lodge's *Small World.*

Borak, Oya Turkish wife of Akbil Borak in David Lodge's *Small World.*

Borden, Mr. Impudent auctioneer of wrecked ships who auctions off the *Flying Scud* in Robert Louis Stevenson's *The Wrecker.*

Bordenave Manager of the Théâtre des Variétés, a dancing hall he calls a brothel, in Paris in 1867; brings the devastatingly beautiful and 15-year-old Nana to the stage for her premiere performance in *The Blonde Venus;* remarks that Nana, even though she cannot sing or act, possesses other rare feminine qualities in Émile Zola's *Nana.*

Boreal, Lord Carlo, or Sir Charles Latrom Gentleman who lives in both Lyra's and Will's worlds; friend of Mrs. Coulter; attempts to steal the alethiometer from Lyra in exchange for the subtle knife; murdered by Mrs. Coulter in Philip Pullman's *His Dark Materials.*

Boreham, Augusta Lady Baldock's unmarried daughter, who manages her mother by indirection in Anthony Trollope's *Phineas Finn.* She has converted to Roman Catholicism and become Sister Veronica John to the dismay of her mother in *Phineas Redux.*

Borg, Dolly von Granddaughter of Russian friends of Vadim Vadimovich, the object of a childhood crush and later her lover in Vladimir Nabokov's *Look at the Harlequins!*

Borg, Paul R. Self-satisfied lawyer and friend of John and Janice Wilder in Richard Yates's *Disturbing the Peace.*

Borgé, Isabelle First love of Amory Blaine while he is at Princeton in F. Scott Fitzgerald's *This Side of Paradise.*

Borges First-person narrator and fictive version of the author Jorge Luis Borges in many of his stories, including "Borges and I," "The Aleph," "Twenty-fifth of August, 1983," "Funes, the Memorius," "Tlön, Uqbar, Orbis Tertius," and "The Other Borges."

Borgesius, Katje (Domina Nocturna) Agent of Dutch descent with no fixed allegiance; involved in various sexual liaisons with Lieutenant Weissmann, Tyrone Slothrop, Gottfried, Pirate Prentice, and Brigadier Ernest Pudding in Thomas Pynchon's *Gravity's Rainbow.*

Boris Editor of *Lilith* during the 50s; he is supposed to represent "the new wave", but he actually turns out to be highly inefficient in Doris Lessing's *The Diaries of Jane Somers.*

Boris Illegitimate grandson of the music teacher La Pérouse; La Pérouse's son died estranged from his father, and Boris's mother moved to Russia; accompanied by his Russian psychiatrist, who intimates that Boris suffers from mental illness related to precocious sexual activity; moves to Paris, arranged by Edouard, to board at the academy where his grandfather teaches in André Gide's *The Counterfeiters.*

Boris Maurice Castle's humane communist controller and confessor, who helps arrange Maurice's defection in Graham Greene's *The Human Factor.*

Boris Moscow Centre agent; investigating him, Ricki Tarr becomes the lover of his common-law wife, Irina, and is told of the existence of a double agent high in British Intelligence in John le Carré's *Tinker, Tailor, Soldier, Spy.*

Boris Russian POW in Germany in World War II; falls in love with the protagonist, Leni; conceives a child with her named Leni; at war's end, Boris, carrying a German identification, is arrested by U.S. forces, handed over to the French, and dies soon in a coal mine in Heinrich Böll's *Group Portrait with Lady.*

Boris Weather prophet living with Henry Miller at the Villa Borghese in Henry Miller's *Tropic of Cancer.*

Boris the Mankiller World War II nemesis of Lieutenant Mamiya in Haruki Murakami's *The Wind-Up Bird Chronicle.*

Bork, Thaddeus (Ned) Effeminate assistant minister to Thomas Marshfield; sleeps with Alicia Crick; professes liberal political and social ideas in John Updike's *A Month of Sundays.*

Bornier, Leonie Housekeeper and foster sister of Julie Le Breton in Mrs. Humphry Ward's *Lady Rose's Daughter.*

Boromir Ambitious member of the fellowship whose mission is to destroy the One Ring and its evil power; Boromir desires the power of the ring and attempts to take the ring from Frodo Baggins; he repents of his actions but is killed in a battle with Orcs in J. R. R. Tolkien's *The Fellowship of the Ring.*

Boronai Leader of the tribe of Niaruna Indians into which Lewis Moon comes as a spirit leader in Peter Matthiessen's *At Play in the Fields of the Lord.*

Borowski Accordion-playing friend of Henry Miller; gives Miller lunch on Wednesdays in Henry Miller's *Tropic of Cancer.*

borracho ("drunkard") Unnamed man who beats a blind woman and her dead dog in Malcolm Lowry's *Dark as the Grave Wherein My Friend Is Laid.*

Borradale, Lord Rich, cultured, and worldly elder brother of Maurice Borradale and sole heir to their deceased father's estate; he seeks to marry Maurice's daughter, Margaret, to his undesirable son; to this end, he provides Margaret and her parents with a cottage on his estate in northern England in William Godwin's *Deloraine.*

Borradale, Margaret Ethereal beauty who loves William, who, she fears, has been lost at sea, but marries Deloraine; at her unexpected reunion with William her obsessively jealous husband murders him, and she suffers a stroke and dies in William Godwin's *Deloraine.*

Borradale, Maurice Father of Margaret; as a result of the prevailing system of primogeniture, he is impoverished and dependent on his elder brother, Lord Borradale, but he resists the latter's plans for marriage between Margaret and her first cousin in William Godwin's *Deloraine.*

Borre German baron who controls Värend, a region in the Swedish countyside of Småland; resides in the manor house Ubbetorp, situated next to the village Brändebol; represents the foreign noblemen who were brought in to control parts of Sweden during the reign of Queen Kristina (1644–54); arrogant ruler who heavily taxes and physically punishes the poor farmers and villagers in Vilhelm Moberg's *Ride This Night!*

Borrero, Louie Disabled Vietnam War veteran who leads a group for fellow vets suffering from post-traumatic stress disorder, from walking them through the experience of eating in a Chinese restaurant to bringing them to visit "The Moving Wall," if not the actual Vietnam War Memorial, in Washington, D.C.; takes Les Farley under his wing, albeit without the desired results, in Philip Roth's *The Human Stain.*

Borrioboola-Gha, King of African ruler whose enthusiastic participation in the slave trade jeopardizes Mrs. Jellyby's charitable project of establishing a settlement in his country in Charles Dickens's *Bleak House.*

Borrisoff, Helen Unconventional woman who has married for interest rather than love and recommends this policy to the heroine of George Gissing's *The Crown of Life.*

Borromeo Veteran of many years' imprisonment in Algeria; he is blunt, indifferent to danger, and considers himself an outcast among men; these qualities awaken sympathy in Gloudesley, who befriends him and trusts him with the secret of Julian Danvers's true parentage in William Godwin's *Cloudesley.*

Borroughs, Cousin Cousin to John Andrews; he wants Andrews to employ his son as farm help after Mr. B— provides his parents-in-law with a farm to manage in Samuel Richardson's *Pamela, or Virtue Rewarded.*

Bors, Sir One of the French knights in Arthur's court and a cousin to Sir Lancelot; one of the three Knights of the Round Table to fully accomplish the quest for the Holy Grail; best characterized as the knight of wisdom, since his trials on the quest deal with the mind, in Thomas Malory's *Le Morte d'Arthur.*

Borsagrass, King of Rival who invades Gwyntystorm at the urging of the traitorous lord chancellor and is defeated there by Curdie Peterson and the king in George MacDonald's *The Princess and Curdie.*

Borth, Sergeant Leonard Fearless M.P. in charge of security during the Allied occupation of Adano in John Hersey's *A Bell for Adano.*

Borthwick, Lieutenant Young officer in General Curzon's regiment; his knowledge of modern weaponry is in contrast to the general's deliberate ignorance of it in C. S. Forester's *The General.*

Bortz, Emory Professor of English and editor of the Lectern Press edition of Richard Wharfinger's *The Courier's Tragedy* in Thomas Pynchon's *The Crying of Lot 49.*

Bory, Manding (Manding Bakary) Son of Maghan Kon Fatta and Namandjé Kamara in *Sundiata: An Epic of Old Mali.*

Boryna, Maciej Rich and respected farmer in the country around the village of Lipce in central Poland; though he has been widowed twice and has grown-up children, he decides to marry again, choosing the 19-year-old Jagusia

(Jagne) despite her bad reputation, in Władysław Stanisław Reymont's *The Peasants.*

Bosanquet, Clive Barrister who leads the prosecution in the trial of Cora Ross and Kitty Pateman in C. P. Snow's *The Sleep of Reason.* Now a judge, he decides in favor of Jenny Rastall's challenge to her father's will in 1970; his decision is overturned on appeal in 1972 in *In Their Wisdom.*

Boscenos, Prince des Nobleman penguin of Penguinia on the mythical island of Alca; seeks to restore the king of Alca to the throne in Anatole France's *Penguin Island.*

Bosco, Dr. Boston surgeon who becomes so fascinated with the hints that Theophilus North effects cures with his hands that he urges North to become associated with Bosco's medical practice in Thornton Wilder's *Theophilus North.*

Bose, Dr. Ambassador from Mars to the United Planets and chairman of the Rama committee; he approves the expedition in Arthur C. Clarke's *Rendezvous with Rama.*

Bosenby, Joe Agent for many variety artists, including Nick Ollanton, in J. B. Priestley's *Lost Empires.*

Bosinney, Philip (The Buccaneer) Architect engaged to June Forsyte but in love with Irene Forsyte; he loses a lawsuit to Soames Forsyte over the country house he builds; he dies when he is run over by a London omnibus in John Galsworthy's *The Man of Property.*

Bosoi, Nikanor Ivanovich His last name means "barefooted"; chairman of the tenants' association of Sadovaya Street, building 302-bis, where Berlioz and Likhodeyev shared an apartment; accepts a bribe and signs a contract letting Woland take the rooms where the late Berlioz lived; after hiding foreign currency received from Woland in an air duct in his bathroom, is arrested because Woland gives him up to the police in Mikhail Bulgakov's *The Master and Margarita.*

Bosola, Daniel de Convicted criminal and paid henchman of Ferdinand; provider of Duchess's horses; discovers the Duchess's pregnancy and Antonio's identity; tortures and murders the Duchess but vows to avenge her death; accidentally kills Antonio; murders Ferdinand, the Cardinal; stabbed by Ferdinand in John Webster's *The Duchess of Malfi.*

Boss, Robin Drunken town drummer whose public conduct often causes trouble; he is dismissed after striking up the "firebeat" in the middle of the night in John Galt's *The Provost.*

Boss, Sugar (Hornbuckle) Second cousin of Alice; married a Cherokee; her picture appears in *Life* magazine with the sign "Welcome to Heaven"; serves as the connection between Turtle's white foster family and her Cherokee tribe in Barbara Kingsolver's *Pigs in Heaven.*

Bosse, de Criminal hired by Jean d'Aunoy to murder Adeline; instead he releases her to La Mott; his testimony in La Mott's trial incriminates Phillippe de Montalt, resulting in his arrest in Ann Radcliffe's *The Romance of the Forest.*

Bossenberger, Herr Music master in the Hanover school in Dorothy Richardson's *Pointed Roofs.*

Bossnowl, Lady Clarinda Young woman who decides to marry for money and is betrothed to young Crotchet; she is converted to romance by the true love of Captain Fitzchrome when Crotchet goes bankrupt in Thomas Love Peacock's *Crotchet Castle.*

Bostock, Captain Billy Rugged proprietor of a public house and tea garden named Currency Lass; he had sailed on the brig *Jolly Roger* in Robert Louis Stevenson's *The Wrecker.*

Bostock, Miss Alan Percival's teacher at school in Garside in Roy Fuller's *The Perfect Fool.*

Boswell, James Professional strongman and collector of great men; yearns for immortality and authors a diary in Stanley Elkin's *Boswell.*

Boswell, Joe Darkly handsome Gypsy; he is the social outcast who causes "something [to take] fire" in the breast of Yvette Saywell; he rescues her from raging flood waters and spends the night with her, but his caravan departs at the end in D. H. Lawrence's *The Virgin and the Gipsy.*

Boswell, Margaret See Medici, Principessa Margaret dei.

Bosworth ("Boz") Went to law school with Lexi and lived with her in Elizabeth Benedict's *Slow Dancing.*

Bosworth, Catharine See Apley, Catharine Bosworth.

Bosworth, Dr. James McHenry Former diplomat and author of several books on American architecture; elderly resident of Newport who is a virtual captive in his home because of incontinence, a problem Theophilus North helps alleviate in Thornton Wilder's *Theophilus North.*

Bosworth, Sarah Daughter of Dr. James Bosworth; because she dislikes Theophilus North, she seeks to hinder his efforts to aid her father in Thornton Wilder's *Theophilus North.*

Botard Senior archivist past his prime; cynical and jealous; resents the professional advancement of younger coworkers; always skeptical, tries to rationalize the presence of the rhinoceros, but conformity wins him over in the end in Eugène Ionesco's play *Rhinoceros.*

Botchan Young male Tokyoite who takes a teaching job in a middle school in Shikoku, the smallest of the four main Japanese islands; the "little master" quickly falls into disputes with students and fellow teachers, as he lacks social skills and is too honest and blunt in his remarks; quarrels with the slimy, hypocritical Redshirt, so named because he always wears a red flannel shirt, and Clown, another scheming teacher; eventually driven from the school, along with his fellow teacher Porcupine, by false accusations from Redshirt and Clown back to Tokyo, but not before giving Redshirt and Clown a sound thrashing in Natsume Sôseki's *Bochan.*

Botcher, Jacob (Jake) Behind-the-scenes political manipulator and dispenser of bribes in Winston Churchill's *Mr. Crewe's Career.*

Bothwell Husband of Mary, Queen of Scots; he is presumed dead but is found to be alive after the marriage of Mary and the Duke of Norfolk in Sophia Lee's *The Recess.*

Botot, Doctor Wealthy widower and physician who cares for the residents of St. Médard parish in Grace King's *The Pleasant Ways of St. Médard.*

Botsford, Loretta See Wendall, Loretta Botsford.

Bott, Mr. Toadying supporter in Parliament of the rising Plantagenet Palliser; he is heartily disliked by Glencora Palliser, who rightly suspects him of spying on her and telling tales about her and Burgo Fitzgerald; he finally marries another busybody, Mrs. Masham, in Anthony Trollope's *Can You Forgive Her?*

Bottesford, Alfie Foundry office clerk and childhood friend of Michael Cullen; Michael seduces his girlfriend in Alan Sillitoe's *A Start in Life.*

Botting, Mrs. Bindon Garrulous Folkestone society matron who hosts the crucial Anagram Tea at which Art Kipps discovers his childhood sweetheart Anne Pornick working as her maid in H. G. Wells's *Kipps: The Story of a Simple Soul.*

Bottom, Happy Buxom nurse, letter writer extraordinaire, and bedmate of Justin Miller in Robert Coover's *The Origin of the Brunists.*

Bottom, Lord (Jemmy) Insolent son of Lord Mansfield; he fights with and makes fun of young Harry Clinton in Henry Brooke's *The Fool of Quality.*

Bottom, Nick Weaver and amateur actor; egotistical and hungry for attention; assigned the role of Pyramus in the rude mechanicals' play; magically given the head of an ass by Puck; wooed by the enchanted Titania; disenchanted by Puck and returns to Athens; performs at Theseus's wedding feast in William Shakespeare's *A Midsummer Night's Dream.*

Bouc, Monsieur Hercule Poirot's long-time professional friend; he hires Poirot to investigate the murder of Samuel Edward Ratchett in Agatha Christie's *Murder on the Orient Express.*

Bouc, Pierre See Piotr.

Boucher, Colonel Jacob Elderly bachelor whose friendship with the widow Jane Weston is of years' standing; the engagement of their servants prompts their own in E. F. Benson's *"Queen Lucia".* He is her husband in *Lucia in London* and in *Mapp and Lucia.*

Boucher, John Mill worker, discontented with a cautious union policy; a leader in the irresponsible strike riot when Margaret Hale is injured, he later commits suicide in despair at not being able to cope with his family's poverty in Elizabeth Gaskell's *North and South.*

Boucher, Lady Misinformed, "purblind dowager" and gossip, who frequently visits Lady Delacour in Maria Edgeworth's *Belinda.*

Boucher, Mrs. John Boucher's wife, who is left with starving children after his suicide in Elizabeth Gaskell's *North and South.*

Bouckman Jamaican slave who gives the call to arms in the wake of the news that France has decreed all its slaves free; killed when the French colonists quell the uprising in Alejo Carpentier's *The Kingdom of This World.*

Boudrault, Sulie Longtime servant in the Peck household; widow of a ragtime pianist in Anne Tyler's *Searching for Caleb.*

Boudreau, Hal Hired hand and tenant on the Sherbrooke estate; drunkard and possible lover of Maggie Sherbrooke in Nicholas Delbanco's *Sherbrookes.*

Bouffuet, Pierre Tyrant who marries Cecile Bertrand for her money and property and drives away her adopted daughter, Agnes D'Albini, by his cruelty in Charlotte Dacre's *The Libertine.*

Bouie, Angelina (Nanane) Aged godmother of the Reverend Phillip Martin in Ernest J. Gaines's *In My Father's House.*

Bouilloux, Michelle Longtime secret lover of Harry Ames entrusted to deliver his message from beyond the grave to Max Reddick in John A. Williams's *The Man Who Cried I Am.*

Boukman Ugly, menacing black leader of a group of rebel slaves in Arna Wendell Bontemps's *Drums at Dusk.*

Boulanger, Rodolphe Shrewd, wealthy landowner and renowned womanizer; Emma's first lover who injects new life into her romantic fantasies; manipulates Emma into eloping with him, only to dump her at the last minute; in exchange for sex, Emma seeks financial help from him at the end, but he turns her down, in Gustave Flaubert's *Madame Bovary.*

Boularis, Yves Versatile, strong, middle-aged Tunisian bodyguard and electronics and demolition expert; Paul Firman's right-hand man and instrumental in saving Paul Firman, he is murdered by Mathew Williamson Tuakana's men in Eric Ambler's *Send No More* Roses.

Boulger, Charlotte Wynn Young woman and daughter of Mrs. Lorin Boulger; unlike others in high society, she does not shun the protagonist Mrs. Lidcote for the latter's long ago divorce and perhaps other moral shortcomings in Edith Wharton's "Autres Temps. . . ."

Boulger, Mrs. Lorin New York City socialite who shuns Mrs. Lidcote for being divorced and other moral lapses in Edith Wharton's "Autres Temps. . . ."

Boultby, Dr. Thomas Rector of Whinbury, a hotheaded Welshman who is doted on by his wife in Charlotte Brontë's *Shirley.*

Boultby, Grace Thomas's wife, who spends much of her time pampering her husband in Charlotte Brontë's *Shirley.*

Bounama, Bilali Servant of Muhammad, ancestor of Sundiata in *Sundiata: An Epic of Old Mali.*

Bouncer, Mr. Novelist and member of a London club, the Universe, haunt of politicians; he is present during the quarrel between Phineas Finn and Mr. Bonteen on the night Bonteen is murdered; he testifies at Finn's trial in Anthony Trollope's *The Eustace Diamonds.*

Bound, Bob Naive lieutenant, who advises William Booth to pay touch money instead of repaying George Trent's debt in Henry Fielding's *Amelia.*

Bounderby, Josiah Blustery, selfish factory owner, who hypocritically brags about being "self-made," and who marries Louisa Gradgrind in Charles Dickens's *Hard Times.*

Bourbon, John, Duke of One of the French nobles; taken prisoner in William Shakespeare's play *Henry V.*

Bourggraff, Raoul de Masterful art department head at Olympia Studios in Ludwig Bemelmans's *Dirty Eddie.*

Bourienne, Mademoiselle French companion of Russian princess Mary; lives on the Bolkonski estate with the princess; becomes the object of the aging Prince Bolkonski's love shortly before his death in a battle with Napoleon's army in Leo Tolstoy's *War and Peace.*

Bourke, Garan New York lawyer who rescues his lover Patience Sparhawk from execution for murder in Gertrude Atherton's *Patience Sparhawk and Her Times.*

Bourne, Catherine Young wife of David Bourne; jealous of husband's writing life; introduces David to unusual sexual practices; falls in love with Marita; burns David's manuscripts, press clippings, and reviews; grows progressively more psychotic; leaves David in Ernest Hemingway's *The Garden of Eden.*

Bourne, David American writer of two successful novels; living in Europe with wife, Catherine; acquiesces to wife's sexual experiments; falls in love with Marita; loses ability to write as a result of emotional and sexual relationships with Catherine and Marita; regains it when wife leaves and he stays with Marita in Ernest Hemingway's *The Garden of Eden.*

Bourne, Ursala (Mrs. Ralph Paton) Secret wife of Roger Ackroyd's estranged stepson; employed as parlormaid at Fernly Park, she is fired on the day of Ackroyd's death in Agatha Christie's *The Murder of Roger Ackroyd.*

Bournisien, Abbé Inadequate town priest who dismisses Emma's plight as a physical or worldly ailment rather than a spiritual crisis; uncritical, dogmatic, and old fashioned, better at exorcising a cow than helping his parishioners in Gustave Flaubert's *Madame Bovary.*

Boutts, Dolly Flirt interested in John Gwynne; rival of Isabel Otis in Gertrude Atherton's *Ancestors.*

Boutwell, Breckenridge (Breck) Bad boy and brother of Honey Boutwell; born with an inverted thumb, growing toward the wrist; sexually active young man who attracts the notice of the vice society; joins the Marines and later dies heroically in World War I; memorialized through a nude sculpture of him as a war monument to be erected in the town of Reedyville in William March's "A Memorial to the Slain."

Boutwell, Honey Bad girl run out of Reedyville by the same vice committee that also later objects to erecting a nude war memorial in the town; years later turns up in Boston in a murder scandal; now a celebrated and rich singer in Paris, who finances the surprise nude sculpture for the provincially minded townspeople in Reedyville in William March's "A Memorial to the Slain."

Boutwood, Mr. Newly widowed boarder; his taking as mistress the flirtatious servant Florrie Bagster disgusts Hilda Lessways as they all try to survive in George Cannon's Brighton boarding house in Arnold Bennett's *Hilda Lessways.*

Bouverie, Colonel Devoted friend of William; he receives an appointment under General Murray, Governor of Canada, and proposes that William join him there in William Godwin's *Deloraine.*

Bovary, Berthe Charles and Emma's daughter; her mother refuses her because she is not a boy; ends up working in a cotton mill as an orphan in Gustave Flaubert's *Madame Bovary.*

Bovary, Charles An *officier de santé,* or country doctor; passionately loves his wife, Emma, but she finds him dull and unsophisticated; well-meaning and kind, fails as both husband and doctor, especially when he botches a clubfoot operation that results in the patient's amputation and, symbolically, Charles's castration; remains clueless about his wife's adultery; only after her death does he discover her infidelities and dies a broken man in Gustave Flaubert's *Madame Bovary.*

Bovary, Charles Senior Disgraced former army officer who once harbored romantic illusions but degenerates into an alcoholic and womanizer; his wife hates him, but he does not seem to care, in Gustave Flaubert's *Madame Bovary.*

Bovary, Emma Country girl educated in a Catholic convent, where she read romantic novels; marries Charles Bovary but soon finds wedded life disappointing; looking for passion, ecstasy, sublimity, she has affairs with Léon and Rodolphe; convinced that the grass is always greener, she finds in adultery all the platitudes of marriage; her mounting financial debt and increasing depression lead her to swallow arsenic; dies a decidedly unromantic death in Gustave Flaubert's *Madame Bovary.*

Bovary, Madame Senior Charles's mother, who is disappointed in her own marriage; projects all her hopes on her son and thus repeatedly conflicts with Emma, of whose excessive spending she disapproves; has a falling out with Charles after Emma's death in Gustave Flaubert's *Madame Bovary.*

Bovey, Miles One of the men whom Charles Watkins remembers as having been aboard his ship (in his alternate reality); he was the only person who Charles felt understood him in Doris Lessing's *Briefing for a Descent into Hell.*

Bowater, Herbert Julius Charnock's muscular young curate, who neglects his duties until brought to a more serious frame of mind by illness in Charlotte Yonge's *The Three Brides.*

Bowater, Joanna Sister of Herbert Bowater; she has rejected Raymond Charnock Poynsett's offer of marriage before the novel opens and is ultimately reunited with her long-lost lover in Natal in Charlotte Yonge's *The Three Brides.*

Bowden, Hortense Mother of Clara (Bowden) Jones and grandmother of Irie Jones, Hortense Bowden is the daughter of a black Jamaican mother, Ambrosia, and a white English father, Captain Charlie Durham, an officer stationed in Jamaica early in the 20th century who took advantage of his position to seduce the adolescent Ambrosia. Born during the Kingston earthquake of 1907, Hortense devotes her life to waiting for the end of the world, whose imminence is promised repeatedly by the elders of her church, the Jehovah's Witnesses, in Zadie Smith's *White Teeth.*

Bowden, Matt Opportunist who pursues Major Grumby in William Faulkner's *The Unvanquished.*

Bowdoin, Antoine Musician Miriam Henderson meets through Bernard Mendizabal, one of Mrs. Bailey's boarders;

he invites her to hear him play on his own piano in a setting that strikes her as really "bohemian" in Dorothy Richardson's *Interim.*

Bowen, Charles Elderly friend of Laura Fairford; philosophizes about the male passion for moneymaking that relegates women to the periphery of men's lives in Edith Wharton's *The Custom of the Country.*

Bowen, Dr. Physician who oversees the care of Helen Chichester-Redfern during her physical decline and who Giles Hermitage resentfully suspects is engaged sexually with Dinah Redfern at the same time he is himself in John Wain's *The Pardoner's Tale.*

Bowen, Effie Daughter of Evalina Bowen and admirer of Theodore Colville in William Dean Howells's *Indian Summer.*

Bowen, Evalina Ridgely (Lina) Widow who marries her friend Theodore Colville; mother of Effie Bowen and temporary guardian of Imogene Graham in William Dean Howells's *Indian Summer.*

Bowen, Jack Brother of Marie Ann Bowen and friend of Steve Benson from summers in Maryland in Ed Bullins's *The Reluctant Rapist.*

Bowen, Lora See Nolan, Lora Bowen.

Bowen, Marie Ann Sister of Jack Bowen and girlfriend of Dandy Benson in Ed Bullins's *The Reluctant Rapist.*

Bower, Eden Aspiring opera singer who rents the room next to Hedger for a few months en route to Paris; confident and adventurous, she encourages Hedger to expand his boundaries; returns to New York 18 years later as a successful opera star, pleased to hear of Hedger's success, if only to confirm that her youthful affair was not in embarrassingly bad taste, in Willa Cather's "Coming Aphrodite."

Bower, Mary Pious working-class girl, who is intolerant of nonbelievers in George Gissing's *Thyrza.*

Bower, Mr. Prosperous shop foreman, who helps organize lectures to workmen but becomes alienated in George Gissing's *Thyrza.*

Bower, Mrs. The Morels' neighbor who comes to assist during Gertrude Morel's labor and childbirth and seems antagonistic toward Walter Morel on that occasion in D. H. Lawrence's *Sons and Lovers.*

Bowers, Frederika Chief mistress of Prince Cabano; helps her rival Estella Washington escape from Cabano in Ignatius Donnelly's *Caesar's Column.*

Bowers, Humphrey Capstone Big-game-hunting pukka chap whom Elizabeth Barclay takes on, briefly, as either lover or husband in William Golding's *The Paper Men.*

Bowers, James (Jim) Employee at a funeral home owned by Tyree Tucker; proposes marriage to Emma Tucker after Tyree Tucker's death in Richard Wright's *The Long Dream.*

Bowers, Madison Fashionable but excellent Chicago voice teacher with whom Thea Kronborg studies in Willa Cather's *The Song of the Lark.*

Bowker, Norman Foot soldier in the Vietnam War and member of Alpha Company; quiet and unassuming, feels guilty because he survived the war while several of his friends died in battle; cannot adjust to civilian life after the war; asks O'Brien to write a story about a young man like him who has difficulty talking about the trauma he experienced during the war; eventually commits suicide by hanging himself at his hometown's YMCA in Tim O'Brien's *The Things They Carried.*

Bowker, William Impeccably dressed but penniless friend of John Jorrocks; he is owner of a snuff and cigar shop, a critic of the theater, and a Whig party candidate for a seat in Parliament; his candidacy is bought off by the Duke of Donkeyton to ensure election for James, Marquis of Bray, who then loses to Jorrocks in Robert Surtees's *Hillingdon Hall.*

Bowlegs, George Fourteen-year-old Navajo Indian who lives on the Zuni reservation in New Mexico; steals artifacts from Chester Reynolds's anthropological dig site; believes he must make reparation to the Zuni spirits for his attempt to learn secrets of Zuni religion; killed by Reynolds in Tony Hillerman's *Dance Hall of the Dead.*

Bowles Master who gives classes in navigation to the mates and to the midshipmen aboard the *Justinian* in C. S. Forester's *Mr. Midshipman Hornblower.*

Bowles, Frances Twice-divorced travel writer; builds a house in Mexican town of Amapolas; left by boyfriend Francisco Alvarado; meets an archaeologist in Yucatán while researching a book; sells her home in Amapolas and leaves permanently in Harriet Doerr's *Consider This, Senora.*

Bowles, Magnus Blaise Gavender's patient, a painter whose neurotic compulsion prevents his leaving home in the daytime; he is in fact the invention of Monty Small, created as a believable alibi for Blaise's evening absences; he is so real to Harriet Gavender that Monty makes him a suicide to forestall her attempts to consult him in Iris Murdoch's *The Sacred and Profane Love Machine.*

Bowles, Martin Bachelor barrister who lives with his mother and exploits his professional and personal relationship with Isobel Billows in Muriel Spark's *The Bachelors.*

Bowles, Mrs. Friend of Mildred Montag, representative of the status quo of anti-intellectualism; lives in a dystopic post-1990 America in Ray Bradbury's *Fahrenheit 451.*

Bowles, Sally Naïve, promiscuous expatriate English cabaret singer, who takes Christopher Isherwood under her wing in Christopher Isherwood's *Goodbye to Berlin.*

Bowles, Ursula Widowed mother of Frances Bowles; revisits childhood home in Mexico before her death in Harriett Doerr's *Consider This, Senora.*

Bowley, Lady Sir Joseph Bowley's young wife, who shares his patronizing view of the working classes in Charles Dickens's *The Chimes.*

Bowley, Master Twelve-year-old son of Sir Joseph Bowley in Charles Dickens's *The Chimes.*

Bowley, Sir Joseph Baronet and Member of Parliament, who styles himself "the Poor Man's Friend and Father," but whose contributions to the welfare of the working class are limited to pontifical speech making in Charles Dickens's *The Chimes.*

Bowling, Bat Charles Arnold's faithful servant, who discusses his difficulty understanding the logic of customs, excises, and taxes in William Beckford's *Azemia.*

Bowling, George Fat, unhappy insurance man, who decides to go back to his old home town and reclaim his youth and memories, telling his wife he is on business; finding that his old love has grown old and fat and his little town has become industrialized and polluted, he decides that his regular life and marriage are really what he wants in George Orwell's *Coming Up for Air.*

Bowling, Hilda Wife of George Bowling; she recognizes when he is trying to get away with something but loves him in spite of her anger in George Orwell's *Coming Up for Air.*

Bowling, Tom Roderick Random's sailor uncle, who helps punish the schoolmaster, sends Roderick to university, and jumps his ship after a fight with his captain; found in France and helped to return to England by Roderick, he commands a ship to South America, where he and Roderick discover Roderick's long-lost father in Tobias Smollett's *The Adventures of Roderick Random.*

Bowls, Mr. Stately butler to Miss Matilda Crawley; he marries Mrs. Firkin in William Makepeace Thackeray's *Vanity Fair.*

Bowlsby, Florence Cochran (Mrs. Ralph) Divorcée and friend of Garp; teaches English at a university where she has affairs with senior faculty members in John Irving's *The World According to Garp.*

Bowman, Carl-Rae Son of Arlington Bloodworth III and Rachel Rebecca Carpenter Flowers; brother of Industrious Bowman in Leon Forrest's *The Bloodworth Orphans.*

Bowman, David Astronaut and captain of the space ship *Discovery;* he is the only crew member to escape HAL's murder attempt; he destroys HAL's intellectual capacity, goes through the star gate, and becomes the star child in Arthur C. Clarke's *2001: A Space Odyssey.*

Bowman, Industrious Son of Arlington Bloodworth III and Rachel Rebecca Carpenter Flowers; brother of Carl-Rae Bowman; associate of Nathaniel Turner Witherspoon in Leon Forrest's *The Bloodworth Orphans.*

Bowman, Ramelle Celeste and Curtis Chalfonte's lover; has a daughter by Curtis; moves in with Celeste at twenty-one; plays bridge with Celeste, Fairy, and Fannie; dies of lung cancer at seventy-four in Rita Mae Brown's *Six of One.* Also appears in *Loose Lips.*

Bow-may Huntress and "damsel at arms," whose accurate archery is effective in peace and in battle; she marries Hart of Highcliff in William Morris's *The Roots of the Mountains.*

Bows, Mr. Crippled fiddler, friend, and mentor of Miss Fotheringay (Emily Costigan) and Fanny Bolton; he resents Arthur Pendennis's love for both women in William Makepeace Thackeray's *The History of Pendennis.*

Bowshot Randall Peronett's head gardener in Iris Murdoch's *An Unofficial Rose.*

Bowshot, Nancy The Peronetts' head gardener's wife; yearning for Randall Peronett, she is Ann Peronett's constant companion and silent enemy in Iris Murdoch's *An Unofficial Rose.*

Bowyer, Dick Sly but slow servant of Sir Daniel Brackley; he outfits Brackley's troops at Moat House and volunteers to take Brackley's letter to Wensleydale in Robert Louis Stevenson's *The Black Arrow: A Tale of Two Roses.*

Bowyer, Mr. Kindly, weak, dissenting minister, who frequently drinks tea with Alton Locke's mother and Mr. Wiglinton; he responds sympathetically to the young Alton's questions in Charles Kingsley's *Alton Locke.*

Boxall, Nelly Ever-indignant servant of the Woolfs; competent and precise, treats Virginia with exasperation in Michael Cunningham's *The Hours.*

Boxe, Lady Rich woman who flaunts her knowledge of drama, art, and literature; she arrives at parties with an entourage of fashionable friends and waves whitegloved hands as she drops her jeweled bag, lace parasol, and embroidered handkerchief in E. M. Delafield's *The Diary of a Provincial Lady.*

Boxer (satiric representation of the proletariat) Large cart horse; the hardest and most loyal worker in the cooperative of animals, he dies in the midst of his work in George Orwell's *Animal Farm.*

Boxer, Henry Ray Mary McNutt's oldest son (twenty-one); is short-tempered; works as a cleaner at the state asylum; buys a 1949 Chevrolet and car insurance from Paris Trout, but wrecks the car immediately; leaves the car at Trout's store when Trout refuses to honor the insurance in Pete Dexter's *Paris Trout.*

Boxer, Mrs. Charwoman employed by Kitty Friedman, who worries that she will not be paid while Mrs. Friedman is in hospital in Margaret Drabble's *The Ice Age.*

"Boxes," Mother Clinging 70-year-old mother of the story's male narrator; complains constantly about every detail of her life, including the weather, her landlord, and the infrequent visits by her son and his live-in girlfriend, Jill; has moved residences repeatedly over the decades and now lives across town in Longview from where her son moved years earlier; threatens to move back to California, and has been living out of packed boxes until the eventual day comes in Raymond Carver's "Boxes."

"Boxes," Narrator Married, divorced, and now living with Jill, a woman he met a year earlier; finds it difficult to break loose from his aging mother's clinging nature, especially after she has moved to the town in which he lives; finally watches with relief and regret as she moves back to California and realizes that he will never see her again in Raymond Carver's "Boxes."

Boy Nonspeaking part; an adolescent youth who remains largely invisible on the stage for much of the play until the end, when, in a reenactment, it is revealed that he watched passively as his sister drowned in the fountain; commits suicide and dies on stage by shooting himself; one of the titular six characters in Luigi Pirandello's *Six Characters in Search of an Author.*

Boy The man's only companion in the postapocalyptic environment and the man's only reason to live; was born shortly after the catastrophe that caused the end of the world occurred and has no memories of the preapocalyptic world; feels pity and sympathy for people such as Ely and the thief, but is dissuaded from helping or comforting them by his father's stoic survivalism; is taken in after the death of his father by a small vagrant family in Cormac McCarthy's *The Road.*

Boy Unnamed youth on the same bus as Ethan and Jacqueline Llewelyn; he has an uncertain command of Latin but firm opinions of Calgary girls and of Americans; he calls Ethan "Old Somebody" in Malcolm Lowry's *October Ferry to Gabriola.*

Boy Young black servant at the narrator's banana plantation; the narrator is frustrated by the boy's inability to carry out his requests and orders properly and seemingly irritated by the boy's contrastingly capable subservience to the narrator's wife, A . . .; effectively the only character of any significance outside the love triangle in the narrative proper in Alain Robbe-Grillet's *Jealousy.*

Boy (see also Page, Falstaff's) Announces that Falstaff is ill and then mourns Falstaff's death with Bardolph, Pistol, Nym, and Hostess Quickly; leaves for France to fight in the war; in battle, wishes he were still safely in London; describes each of his companions and points out their ironic qualities; acts as an ethical counterpoint to the tavern men; translates between Pistol and a French soldier during the Battle of Agincourt; calls Pistol a braggart and a mercenary; says that Bardolph and Nym have both been hanged for stealing; guards the "luggage" in the king's camp and is killed in William Shakespeare's play *Henry V.*

Boy, The Frail and timid boy who appears at the end of both acts of the play, announcing that Godot will not be coming that day; bullied by Estragon in the first act and does not remember meeting Estragon and Vladimir the night before when he appears in the second act in Samuel Beckett's play *Waiting for Godot.*

Boy, The Startled by the photographer, young teen fled the scene in Julio Cortázar's "Blow-Up."

Boyce, Deighton Free-spirited father of Selina Boyce; commits suicide within sight of the coast of Barbados after trying to find himself in New York in Paule Marshall's *Brown Girl, Brownstones.*

Boyce, Evelyn Upper-class mother of Marcella; her husband's financial misdeeds shame and humiliate her in Mrs. Humphry Ward's *Marcella.*

Boyce, Humphrey Sixtyish widower owner of an antiques shop near Sloan Square who is initiating his nephew into the business; he takes a decided interest in Leonora Eyre in Barbara Pym's *The Sweet Dove Died.*

Boyce, Ina Sister of Selina Boyce; quiet, soft-spoken young woman who is devoted to her church; settles into an uneventful life and a dull marriage in Paule Marshall's *Brown Girl, Brownstones.*

Boyce, James Twenty-four-year-old recent university graduate; the orphan nephew of Humphrey, he works in his uncle's antiques shop while deciding on his sexual preference; he becomes romantically entangled with two women and one man in Barbara Pym's *The Sweet Dove Died.*

Boyce, Marcella Beautiful, upper-class defender of the rights of the urban and rural poor; she escapes county social life to take a yearlong course in nursing, after which she works with the urban poor and eventually marries Aldous Raeburn, Lord Maxwell in Mrs. Humphry Ward's *Marcella.* As Lady Maxwell she helps the passage of her husband's Factory Bill through her emotional and moral influence on Sir George Tressady in *Sir George Tressady.*

Boyce, Richard Upper-class Member of Parliament and father of Marcella; his misuse of funds leads to the ostracism of his family in Mrs. Humphry Ward's *Marcella.*

Boyce, Rupert Extremely wealthy collector of books on the occult in which the Overlords are interested; he holds a séance in which Jean Morrel's psychic powers are revealed in Arthur C. Clarke's *Childhood's End.*

Boyce, Selina (Deighton Selina) Daughter of Silla and Deighton Boyce and sister of Ina Boyce; unsettled heroine who returns to the Caribbean after becoming disillusioned with America in Paule Marshall's *Brown Girl, Brownstones.*

Boyce, Silla (Silla-gal) Wife of Deighton Boyce and mother of Selina and Ina Boyce; driven woman determined to control the lives of those in her family in Paule Marshall's *Brown Girl, Brownstones.*

Boyd Black youth who plays with Johnny and eats lunch at the Wilson house one afternoon; his father is a factory foreman and his older sister hopes to become a teacher; completely puzzled by Mrs. Wilson's racist assumptions that he and his family are poor and need her help in Shirley Jackson's "After You, My Dear Alphonse."

Boyd, Beverly (Bev) Homosexual college instructor rejected by Peter Gale in Louis Adamic's *Grandsons.*

Boyd, Gordon Wild boyhood friend of Walter McKee; writer and self-proclaimed failure in Wright Morris's *The Field of Vision* and *Ceremony in Lone Tree.*

Boyd, Kenneth Sefton (Kenny) Aristocratic ne'erdo-well who, as a student, is viciously betrayed by Magnus Pym; as a dissolute adult, he is one of the few who understand and forgive Magnus's duplicity in John le Carré's *A Perfect Spy.*

Boyd, Lorimer Friend of Sir Douglas Ross; he acts as narrator when he describes events through his thoughts; he brings Sir Douglas and Gertrude Ross together at the end in Caroline Norton's *Old Sir Douglas.*

Boyd, Mrs. See Daughter.

Boyer Rich man from whom the Kern family has repurchased the family farm they sold years earlier in John Updike's "Pigeon Feathers."

Boyer, J. Accomplished clergyman attracted to Eliza Wharton in Hannah Webster Foster's *The Coquette.*

Boyes, Philip Novelist whose love affair with Harriet Vane lasted two years and ended when he proved the insincerity of his principles by wanting her to marry him; Harriet narrowly escapes being convicted of his death by arsenic poisoning in Dorothy L. Sayers's *Strong Poison.*

Boykin, Miss Tee (Auntee) Loving presence and mother of Scooter in Albert Murray's *Train Whistle Guitar.*

Boylan, Hugh (Blazes) Advertising agent and Casanova who has an affair with Molly Bloom in James Joyce's *Ulysses.*

Boyle, Captain "New on the job" police captain who investigates Robert Halliday's bomb-threat report and reception in Eric Ambler's *The Care of Time.*

Boyle, Mary Rose ("Mizz Bee") Roommate of Catherine Bray; union official's daughter in her early forties; former nun, now a social worker; has a brief affair with James Bray in Maureen Howard's *Natural History.*

Boyle, Orren Failing industrialist who seeks government protection against free market competition in Ayn Rand's *Atlas Shrugged.*

Boyle, Walter (Walter Arlis Benson) Salesman, sometimes sanctimonious, sometimes involved in petty crimes; lives separate lives under different names in John Gardner's *The Sunlight Dialogues.*

Boynton, Jim Friend who encourages Clyde Stout to stop letting people take advantage of him; owns a 1963 Corvette in Jack Matthews's *Hanger Stout, Awake!*

Boyo, Nogood Fisherman and professed agnostic; member of the colorful and fanciful community of Llaregyb, a mythical seaside village in Wales, in Dylan Thomas's play *Under Milk Wood.*

"Boys and Girls," Narrator Young girl who narrates her journey from childhood into girlhood; fancies herself as strong and courageous; tomboy on the farm who works with her father on a fox farm where one of her jobs is to take water to the fox pens in the summer; prefers helping her father with the farm work than doing domestic tasks inside the house with her mother; hopes her father will be proud of her ability to help him; starts to become less of a tomboy as she grows older, but even so wants to work the farm and not perform domestic chores; later intentionally allows the horse Flora to escape its pen and run free, although the narrator does not know why she did this in Alice Munro's "Boys and Girls."

Boy Staunton Lifelong friend of Dunstan Ramsay; accidentally strikes Mary Dempster with a stone, causing her insanity; alienates himself from the act and the possibility of guilt; marries Leola Cruickshank but eventually pushes her to suicide through neglect and infidelity; enjoys public success, thriving financially during the Great Depression and joining the federal cabinet during World War II; eventually confronted with his dormant guilt by Dunstan and found dead in a car in Lake Ontario in Robertson Davies's *Fifth Business.*

Boythorn, Lawrence John Jarndyce's ferocious, loud, and warmhearted friend, who feuds with Sir Leicester Dedlock over their boundary lines; he once loved Miss Barbary but was rejected by her; he makes his home available to Esther Summerson for her recuperation from smallpox in Charles Dickens's *Bleak House.*

Boy with the Squint Blinded early in the epidemic and loyal to the core group of those interned in José Saramago's *Blindness.*

Bozzari Erstwhile friend of the Greek warlord Colocotroni, whom he betrays to the Turks; when Colocotroni escapes from prison, Bozzari murders him in order to have free access to his daughter, Irene Colocotroni, in William Godwin's *Cloudesley.*

Bozzle, Mrs. Samuel Bozzle's wife and confidante, who takes Emily Trevelyan's part when her child is kidnapped in Anthony Trollope's *He Knew He Was Right.*

Bozzle, Samuel Disreputable private detective engaged by Louis Trevelyan to spy on his wife, Emily, and to arrange the kidnapping of his young son in Anthony Trollope's *He Knew He Was Right.*

Bra Aph-Lin's wife, who likes to read the ancient literature of the Vril-ya, which resembles stories of life in our own world in Edward Bulwer-Lytton's *The Coming Race.*

Brabantio Senator of Venice and Desdemona's father; welcomes Othello at first, then narrow-mindedness and superstition induce him to believe in the Moor's supposed black magic; disapproves of his daughter's marriage to Othello; frustrated by the Duke's approval of the marriage in William Shakespeare's play *Othello.*

Brabner, Janice Volunteer social worker who comes to check on Marcia Ivory in the aftermath of her operation, ineffectually suggesting a number of activities and improvements for Marcia's life in *Quartet in Autumn.*

Brace, Eloisa Resident at the fourth address to which Mr. Cox sends Malcolm; painter who often invites musicians to her house in James Purdy's *Malcolm.*

Brace, Jerome Ex-convict and husband of Eloisa Brace; because he sees Malcolm as the spirit of life, begs Malcolm for his friendship in James Purdy's *Malcolm.*

Bracegirdle Horatio Hornblower's shipmate aboard the *Indefatigable* in C. S. Forester's *Mr. Midshipman Hornblower.* He has become Admiral Lord St. Vincent's flag lieutenant; he sympathizes with Hornblower but refuses entry to retrieve his watch in C. S. Forester's *Hornblower and the Atropos.*

Bracegirdle, Mary Sexually frustrated but naïve guest at the Crome estate; she offers herself to Ivor Lombard but is disappointed by his aloof indifference in Aldous Huxley's *Crome Yellow.*

Bracely, Olga Good-natured, popular, refreshingly unconventional, sophisticated woman and an acclaimed and gifted opera star; she settles in Riseholme, makes an immediate conquest of Georgie Pillson, and inadvertently unseats Lucia Lucas as the cultural leader of Riseholme; she is the wife of George Shuttleworth in E. F. Benson's *"Queen Lucia".* She is Lucia's neighbor and cheerfully allows herself to be used in Lucia's social campaign in *Lucia in London.* She introduces the Duchess of Sheffield to Georgie and Lucia in *Trouble for Lucia.*

Braceweight, Samuel P. Wealthy chocolate tycoon who befriends Charles Lumley in the hospital and hires Charles briefly as a chauffeur in John Wain's *Huny On Down.*

Braceweight, Walter Spoiled, mature-looking adolescent hot-rod enthusiast whom George Hutchins unsuccessfully attempts to tutor and whom Charles Lumley shields from Mr. Braceweight's wrath by taking the blame for an auto accident and forfeiting his chauffeur job in John Wain's *Hurry On Down.*

Bracey Captain Jenkins's smartly turned-out, melancholic soldier-servant, who loves the emotionally unstable maid Billson; he is killed in 1914 in Anthony Powell's *The Kindly Ones.*

Bracher, Gerald Sensitive boy attending Seaforth House, a second-rate English public school on the brink of financial collapse; consigned to the school after the break up of his parents' marriage, Bracher changes gradually from conformist to rebel in Roy Fuller's *The Ruined Boys.*

Brack, Judge Manipulative and scheming rake of the coarse rising middle class who attempts to blackmail the married aristocratic Hedda Gabler into a love affair in Henrik Ibsen's play *Hedda Gabler.*

Brackenshaw, Lady Leader of the Pennicote society in George Eliot's *Daniel Deronda.*

Brackenshaw, Lord Husband of Lady Brackenshaw in George Eliot's *Daniel Deronda.*

Brackley, Lady Tall, remote wife of Sir Daniel Brackley; Goody Hatch waits upon her in Robert Louis Stevenson's *The Black Arrow: A Tale of Two Roses.*

Brackley, Sir Daniel Villainous guardian of Dick Shelton; he killed Sir Henry Shelton, stole Ellis Duckworth's lands, and tries to marry Joan Sedley to Lord Shoreby; his allegiance to Lancaster or York follows his convenience, not his conscience in Robert Louis Stevenson's *The Black Arrow: A Tale of Two Roses.*

Bracknell, Lady Algernon's authoritarian and high-minded; aunt; Gwendolen's mother; wants to see her daughter married well to a man with high social standing; does not consider Jack Worthing a proper match, since his ancestry is that of an orphan baby found in a cloakroom; eventually revealed as Jack's aunt; a pompous and satiric figure whose role is to mock the British aristocracy in Oscar Wilde's play *The Importance of Being Earnest.*

Bracknell, Sarah See Hazlett, Sarah Bracknell.

Bracton, Len Stage comedian for whom Owen Tuby and Cosmo Sultana form a marketable image in J. B. Priestley's *The Image Men.*

Bracton, Sir Harry Noisy, good-looking landowner; he attends the Hunt Ball, where he courts Dorcas Brandon and then badly wounds Stanley Lake in a duel; later he enters Gylingden to canvass for votes against Lake in the upcoming election in J. Sheridan Le Fanu's *Wylder's Hand.*

Bracy, Earl Old friend of Dr. Wortle, at whose preparatory school his son Lord Carstairs had been taught prior to attending Eton; when Carstairs falls in love with Mary, the headmaster's daughter, Lord Bracy gives his blessing to the match in Anthony Trollope's *Dr. Wortle's School.*

Bracy, Maurice de Vain leader of a band of mercenaries; he captures Lady Rowena and attempts to force her into marrying him in Sir Walter Scott's *Ivanhoe.*

Bradamante Young female knight who has excellent skill on the battlefield; saves Raimbaut, who later espies her bathing and falls in love; she is in love with Agilulf; mistakenly sleeps with Raimbaut when he wears Agilulf's armour; is actually Sister Theodora, and leaves the abbey to resume her identity as Bradamante when Raimbaut comes in Italo Calvino's *The Nonexistent Knight.*

Bradbourne, Lilias Favorite attendant of the Lady of Avenel (Mary Avenel); jealous of her mistress's attention, she is responsible for the dismissal of Roland Graeme in Sir Walter Scott's *The Abbot.*

Bradbury, Nelson Goodfellow (Big Nellie) American journalist who first reports the Berlin airlift in Leon Uris's *Armageddon.*

Braddell, Vincent See Beck.

Braddock, General Leader of the forces against the French in America; young George Warrington serves in his expedition and, captured by Indians, is believed killed in William Makepeace Thackeray's *The Virginians.*

Braddock, Mr. Barrister who defends the smugglers and makes a mockery of Francis Andrews and his crucial testimony during cross-examination in Graham Greene's *The Man Within.*

Braddock, Mr. Diana Warwick's solicitor; he defends her successfully when Augustus Warwick sues her for divorce in George Meredith's *Diana of the Crossways.*

Braden, Jellie Wife of James Lee Braden III; married twenty years earlier in India to Dhiren Velayudum, a revolutionary separatist and poet killed in an ambush, with whom she had a daughter, Jaya; while married to Braden and living in Cedar Bend, has an affair with Michael Tillman; then flees to India in Robert James Waller's *Slow Waltz In Cedar Bend.*

Bradfield, Hazel Rawley Bradfield's beautiful wife and Leo Harting's mistress; she gives Harting the key to an unused basement office of the Bonn Embassy where Harting stores pilfered documents confirming Karfeld's guilt in John le Carré's *A Small Town in Germany.*

Bradfield, Rawley Condescending, dishonest Head of Chancery at the Bonn Embassy; he hides information about Klaus Karfeld's concentration camp experiments on humans from British diplomatic politicians to demean Leo Harting, repress his subordinates, divert and officially terminate Alan Turner's investigation, and compromise democratic principles to current political expediencies in John le Carré's *A Small Town in Germany.*

Bradford, Henry Saloon owner who nearly beats Adolph Myers (Wing Biddlebaum) to death because Myers supposedly molested Bradford's son in Sherwood Anderson's *Winesburg, Ohio.*

Bradford, Hilkiah Pious, straight-laced, and kindly protector (and, later, tutor) of the child Charles Mandeville on his perilous journey from Dublin to London during the Irish Uprising in 1641 in William Godwin's *Mandeville.*

Bradford, Joe Life-saver who recalls all the people he has pulled from the sea around Cape Cod; pulls a drowned man from the sea and takes him, out of habit, to the old life-saving station, which has been converted to the home of Mrs. Patrick in Susan Glaspell's play *The Outside.*

Bradish New York artist friend and studio mate of Richard Dale in Sarah Orne Jewett's *A Marsh Island.*

Bradley Creditor whose bill for $200 wrecks Jim Pinkerton's firm in Robert Louis Stevenson's *The Wrecker.*

Bradley, Ardis Wife of Tuck Bradley in Joan Didion's *A Book of Common Prayer.*

Bradley, Austin Owner of Happy's Café, following Tadpole McCormick's ownership of it in Gayl Jones's *Corregidora.*

Bradley, Isabel Radiantly healthy young girl who is engaged to marry Larry Darrell; being completely unable to understand Larry's changed thinking after his experiences in World War I, she marries the mundane Gray Maturin although she covertly hankers after Larry; Isabel can love only selfishly, never realizing that Larry will always be out of her reach in W. Somerset Maugham's *The Razor's Edge.*

Bradley, Jessie First wife of George Ogden; her spending ruins Ogden financially in Henry Blake Fuller's *The Cliff-Dwellers.*

Bradley, Louisa Isabel's pleasant, practical mother, who is perfectly content with her middle-class values that approve of the Gray Maturins of this era but would never comprehend the philosophy of a Larry Darrell in W. Somerset Maugham's *The Razor Edge.*

Bradley, Luke See Rookwood, Luke.

Bradley, Peck Poor-white hill man who is lynched for murdering Tug Beavers in T. S. Stribling's *Teeftallow.*

Bradley, Peter See Rookwood, Alan.

Bradley, Susan See Rookwood, Susan.

Bradley, Thorne Friend of Forrest Mayfield; refuses to continue their friendship after Forrest elopes in Reynolds Price's *The Surface of Earth.*

Bradley, Tuck American ambassador to Boca Grande in Joan Didion's *A Book of Common Prayer.*

Bradly, Colonel Member of the expedition against the wild boys; later joins them and shoots a movie of them in William S. Burroughs's *The Wild Boys.*

Bradshaw Footman to Dr. Henry Jekyll and fellow servant of Poole, Jekyll's butler, in Robert Louis Stevenson's *The Strange Case of Dr. Jekyll and Mr. Hyde.*

Bradshaw, Elizabeth Daughter of Mr. Bradshaw and pupil of Ruth Hilton in Elizabeth Gaskell's *Ruth.*

Bradshaw, Jacob Strong-minded provincial silk manufacturer who travels in Italy in George Gissing's *The Emancipated.*

Bradshaw, Jemima Spirited daughter of Mr. Bradshaw; she befriends Ruth Hilton but unwittingly learns about and reveals the secret of Ruth's past; she marries Walter Farquhar in Elizabeth Gaskell's *Ruth.*

Bradshaw, Laura Gregory Dawson's friend from youth who liberates him to live in the present when she tells him that Joan Alington had been responsible for Eva Alington's death in J. B. Priestley's *Bright Day.*

Bradshaw, Mary Daughter of Mr. Bradshaw and pupil of Ruth Hilton in Elizabeth Gaskell's *Ruth.*

Bradshaw, Mr. Wealthy, self-important businessman, and a Dissenter who is the main financial support of Thurstan Benson's chapel; after learning about Ruth Hilton's past and Benson's role in concealing it he harshly rejects them; the misconduct of his son plays a major part in changing his own attitudes in Elizabeth Gaskell's *Ruth.*

Bradshaw, Mrs. Conventional-minded wife of Jacob Bradshaw in George Gissing's *The Emancipated.*

Bradshaw, Mrs. Wife of Mr. Bradshaw; her more generous nature is dominated by his rigid attitudes in Elizabeth Gaskell's *Ruth.*

Bradshaw, Richard Mr. Bradshaw's son, who reacts against his rigid upbringing; he forges Benson's signature to get money, and the discovery of this shatters Mr. Bradshaw's complacency in Elizabeth Gaskell's *Ruth.*

Bradshaw, Sir George Dissolute companion of Casimir Fleetwood's revels who introduces him to the bewitching Mrs. Comorin in William Godwin's *Fleetwood.*

Bradshaw, Sir William Dr. Holmes's mentor and superior; he is a didactic, sanctimonious medical doctor; his tardy appearance at Clarissa Dalloway's party forges another superficial link between the Dostoevskian doubles, Septimus Smith and Mrs. Dalloway; to her dismay, Bradshaw describes Septimus's gory impalement in Virginia Woolf's *Mrs. Dalloway.*

Bradshaw, Thomas Minister of the London meetinghouse attended by the Colemans; his sermons inspire Zachariah Coleman in Radical political views; he warns Coleman to escape London in Mark Rutherford's *The Revolution in Tanner's Lane.*

Bradshaw, William Young, gullible English writer who travels to Germany to tutor English and narrates the story of how he became embroiled in Arthur Norris's schemes; he demonstrates how the desire for experience may blind one to reality in Christopher Isherwood's *Mr. Norris Changes Trains.*

Bradstreet, Inspector Police inspector investigating the case of the disappearance of Neville St. Clair; helps Sherlock Holmes perform his investigation in Sir Arthur Conan Doyle's "The Man with the Twisted Lip."

Bradwardine, Cosmo Comyne Verbose Baron of Bradwardine, whose speech is full of Latin misnomers; a great friend of Sir Everard Waverly, he entertains Edward Waverly on his Scottish estate before joining Prince Charles Stuart's army and sharing many military adventures; as Rose's father, he eventually becomes Edward's father-in-law in Sir Walter Scott's *Waverly.*

Bradwardine, Rose Beautiful but shy daughter of the baron; she loves Edward Waverly and writes to Prince Charles Stuart to arrange his escape; after she nurses him to health and obtains the papers which will clear him, her friendship with Flora MacIvor guarantees his safety in the Highlands in Sir Walter Scott's *Waverly.*

Bradwardine of Inch-Grabbit, Malcolm The Baron of Bradwardine's distant heir, who receives Bradwardine's forfeited estate and then sells it unknowingly to Duncan Macwheeble in Sir Walter Scott's *Waverly.*

Brady Irish schoolmaster who cares for Morton Goodwin and Kike Lumsden; marries Lumsden's mother in Edward Eggleston's *The Circuit Rider.*

Brady, Benjamin John Jorrocks's young and clever but slothful groom in Robert Surtees's *Jorrocks's Jaunts and Jollities* and in *Handley Cross.*

Brady, Caithleen (Cait) Clever and intelligent daughter of Mr. Brady; after her mother's tragic death, she goes to a convent on scholarship; she is later expelled, along with Bridget Brennan, for misconduct, and eventually she follows Bridget to Dublin, where she works as a shop assistant and pursues her affair with the married Mr. Gentleman in Edna O'Brien's *The Country Girls.*

Brady, Cecilia Daughter of Pat Brady; her love for Monroe Stahr is unrequited; narrator of F. Scott Fitzgerald's *The Last Tycoon.*

Brady, Charlotte Captain Maurice's "ward," who discovers that she is in fact his daughter; she is raised and educated by Mrs. Darnford in Clara Reeve's *Plans of Education.*

Brady, Honoria (Nora) First cousin and first love of Redmond Barry when he is 16 and she 23; she is the subject of his duel with Captain Quin, whom she later marries in William Makepeace Thackeray's *The Luck of Barry Lyndon.*

Brady, Michael Redmond Barry's maternal uncle and Nora and Ulick's father; he is a good-humored Irish squire in William Makepeace Thackeray's *The Luck of Barry Lyndon.*

Brady, Mick Michael Brady's eldest son, who resents and persecutes Redmond Barry in William Makepeace Thackeray's *The Luck of Barry Lyndon.*

Brady, Mike Rebellious, fiercely principled Irish Catholic friend of Jonathan Browne, who shares his hatred of National Service; Brady befriends Percy Higgins and avenges his death by assaulting Corporal Baker; later he joins the Irish Republican Army and is arrested in a raid on Jonathan's camp; he dates Pauline Vickers and introduces her to Jonathan, who later marries her in David Lodge's *Ginger, You're Barmy.*

Brady, Molly Young, fleshy, sensual farm girl; she plays flirtatious games with Tarry Flynn and catches his interest, but he later refuses to associate with her in Patrick Kavanagh's *Tarry Flynn.*

Brady, Mr. Drunken, abusive father of Caithleen Brady; through his reckless behavior, he loses his wife, his farm, and his daughter's affections in Edna O'Brien's *The Country Girls.*

Brady, Mrs. Mother of Caithleen Brady; she tragically drowns on her way to her father's house while trying to escape her abusive, drunken husband in Edna O'Brien's *The Country Girls.*

Brady, Mrs. Quarrelsome wife of Michael Brady; she and her sister-in-law, Bell Barry, are on bad terms in William Makepeace Thackeray's *The Luck of Barry Lyndon.*

Brady, Mysie Younger sister of Nora Brady in William Makepeace Thackeray's *The Luck of Barry Lyndon.*

Brady, Pat Broken-nosed manager for Thady Macdermot; he is suborned by Hyacinth Keegan into helping ruin his master in Anthony Trollope's *The Macdermots of Ballycloran.*

Brady, Pat Father of Cecilia Brady and treacherous partner of Monroe Stahr in F. Scott Fitzgerald's *The Last Tycoon.*

Brady, Ray Graduate student in charge of devising a test that can measure people's Irishness in Roddy Doyle's "57% Irish."

Brady, Susan One of the village girls very much smitten with Christy Mahon, the newly arrived playboy; brings him a pat of butter in J. M. Synge's play *The Playboy of the Western World.*

Brady, Ulick Redmond Barry's first cousin and friend; Barry helps him kidnap the heiress Amelia Kiljoy, whom he marries by force in William Makepeace Thackeray's *The Luck of Barry Lyndon.*

Brady, Will Jennings Unsuccessful entrepreneur, hotel lobby dweller; dies while dressed for the role of Santa Claus in Wright Morris's *The Works of Love.*

Brady, Willy, Jr. Son of Mickey Ahearn adopted by Will Brady in Wright Morris's *The Works of Love.*

Bragg, Clinton Early suitor and second husband of Mateel Shepherd, whose first husband, Jo Erring, kills him in E. W. Howe's *The Story of a Country Town.*

Braggioni Leader of the Mexican Revolution; his love of luxury, particularly apparent in his expensive clothing, betrays his revolutionary ideals; temporarily abandons his wife to pursue Laura, a young American who supports the revolution; returns to his wife when Laura spurns his advances in Katherine Anne Porter's "The Flowering Judas."

Bragwell, Mr. One of the London tavern boys who participate in the "roast" of Dr. Wagtail in Tobias Smollett's *The Adventures of Roderick Random.*

"Brahms Four" See Munte, Dr. Walter von.

Braid-Beard See Mohi.

Brailstone, Lord Lord Fleetwood's friend, whose failed attempt to seduce Henrietta (Fakenham) Kirby causes her to faint and burn her face in George Meredith's *The Amazing Marriage.*

Brainard, Abbie Daughter of Abigail and Erastus Brainard; second wife of George Ogden in Henry Blake Fuller's *The Cliff-Dwellers.*

Brainard, Abigail Wife of Erastus Brainard and mother of Abbie, Burton, and Marcus Brainard in Henry Blake Fuller's *The Cliff-Dwellers.*

Brainard, Burton Tillinghast (Burt) Son of Abigail and Erastus Brainard and vice president of his father's bank; his financial schemes drive the family into poverty in Henry Blake Fuller's *The Cliff-Dwellers.*

Brainard, Cornelia McNabb Tillinghast (Nealie) Waitress and then stenographer in the Clifton; wife of Burt Brainard in Henry Blake Fuller's *The Cliff-Dwellers.*

Brainard, Erastus M. Husband of Abigail Brainard and father of Abbie, Burton, and Marcus Brainard; president of the Underground National Bank; killed by his son Marcus in Henry Blake Fuller's *The Cliff-Dwellers.*

Brainard, Marcus Son of Abigail and Erastus Brainard; frustrated artist who kills his father, strangles his brother, Burt, and commits suicide in Henry Blake Fuller's *The Cliff-Dwellers.*

Brainerd, Marigold Shoemaker Philadelphian living in Paris; rival of Aileen Cowperwood for the affections of Bruce Tollifer in Theodore Dreiser's *The Stoic.*

Braithwaite, Cecil Otis Black lawyer, janitor, and hairdresser who travels to Europe and Africa before returning to his wife in John Edgar Wideman's *Hurry Home.*

Braithwaite, Edwin Sixtyish widower clerk who lives alone in a semi-detached house but vacations with his daughter and her family; his life revolves around his church, where he is Master of Ceremonies, and vague speculation about his co-workers in Barbara Pym's *Quartet in Autumn.*

Braithwaite, Esther Brown Wife of Cecil Braithwaite, whom she supports through law school, only to have him desert her in John Edgar Wideman's *Hurry Home.*

Braithwaite, Maurice Star player on the Rugby League team who plays with Arthur Machin, becomes his friend, gets married, and tries to get Arthur to go into business with him in David Storey's *This Sporting Life.*

Braithwaite, Mr. Cashier at the colliery who pays out miners' wages when Paul Morel goes to collect his father's pay in D. H. Lawrence's *Sons and Lovers.*

Braithwaite, Simon Stillborn son of Esther Brown and Cecil Braithwaite in John Edgar Wideman's *Hurry Home.*

Braller, Linda A student in Benjamin Fermoyle's class in Mary McGarry Morris's *Songs in Ordinary Time.*

Bramber, Earl of Proprietor of Ongar Castle, where John Jorrocks sleeps in the bathhouse in Robert Surtees's *Handley Cross.*

Bramber, Mr. Justice Judge in the bigamy case brought against John Caldigate; he directs the jury to convict and gives Caldigate a two-year prison sentence in Anthony Trollope's *John Caldigate.*

Bramble, Matthew Loyd Welsh bachelor landowner, who leads a family expedition through Bristol, Bath, London, Edinburgh, and Glasgow; he sends his correspondent Dr. Lewis reports on scenes, manners, and customs of places visited; he discovers his footman Humphry Clinker is really his natural son; he arranges the affairs of his friend Baynard after the death of Baynard's wife, and he agrees to marriages by his sister, his niece, and his natural son in Tobias Smollett's *The Expedition of Humphry Clinker.*

Bramble, Tabitha Forty-five-year-old sister of Matthew Bramble; she flirts with every available gentleman she encounters during the family expedition; she is forced by Matthew to choose between her dog, Chowder, and continuing on the expedition; she finally marries in Tobias Smollett's *The Expedition of Humphry Clinker.*

Brambledown, Dowager Countess of Eccentric patron of Valentine Blyth in Wilkie Collins's *Hide and Seek.*

Brame, Della Young black woman whose several sexual encounters with Buck Russell may have produced her son in Reynolds Price's *A Generous Man.*

Bran Huge British mastiff, beloved pet of Raphael Aben-Ezra; she travels with her despairing master and leads him back to a belief in human nature in Charles Kingsley's *Hypatia.*

Bran See Sirius.

Branch, Kate Helen Mother of Burley Coulter's bastard son in Wendell Berry's *Nathan Coulter.*

Brancher, Miriam Body model for art students; short-term lover/fiancée of Warren in Joyce Carol Oates's *You Must Remember This.*

Branco, Joseph Illegitimate Trotta cousin; peddler and country bumpkin who describes the fate of the people in the dual monarchy of Austria-Hungary in the sequel to *The Radetzky March* in Joseph Roth's *Emperor's Tomb.*

Brand, Bertha Brittle, sharp-faced elderly spinster who after working all her life solicits a job at Corker's employment agency in order to stay out of a home for the elderly; desperate to continue working and briefly hopeful that Corker will hire her as his housekeeper, she ends up in an "Old People's Home" in John Berger's *Corker's Freedom.*

Brand, Bobby Vietnam veteran and former junkie who accompanies David Bell and friends on a trip west to make a documentary film in Don DeLillo's *Americana.*

Brand, Charles K. L. Secretary to the mayor of New York; trips Pal Smurch, causing the crude mechanic turned heroic aviator to plunge from a high office tower window; his trickery cements Smurch's status forever as a hero before his actual crude self can besmirch his reputation in James Thurber's "The Greatest Man in the World."

Brand, Charlotte Wentworth See Wentworth, Charlotte.

Brand, Dinah Golddigger who provides information and companionship to the Op in Dashiell Hammett's *Red Harvest.*

Brand, Ellas Credulous, pedantic parson, whose disparaging, false report of Clarissa Harlowe's behavior at the Smiths' boardinghouse keeps the family from relenting in Samuel Richardson's *Clarissa: or, The History of a Young Lady.*

Brand, Ellen Nineteen-year-old Danish girl with uncanny abilities; hears voices and sees dead people; Krokowski then trains her to make contact with the otherworld; at one séance and with the help of a mysterious medium named Holger, conjures up Ziemßen's ghost, which unsettles Hans so much that he turns on the electric light and ends the session once and for all in Thomas Mann's *The Magic Mountain.*

Brand, Ethan Former lime-burner who has spent 18 years searching for his Unpardonable Sin—god-like egotism and conceit; has lost his morals as his intellectual powers have increased; possesses no remarkable physical aspects yet has an undefinable and questionable air about him; slowly discloses some details of his long, agonizing story; known for his appalling laugh and his implied connection with Satan and his powers; finds evil within his own heart; despises the townspeople who greet him as a friend; sees no escape from his suffering and sinful passions and finally commits suicide in Nathaniel Hawthorne's "Ethan Brand."

Brand, Gala Undercover policewoman who helps James Bond avert the destruction of London; she is engaged to be married and has no sexual interest in Bond in Ian Fleming's *Moonraker.*

Brand, Mr. Unitarian minister who courts Gertrude Wentworth but who ultimately marries Charlotte Wentworth in Henry James's *The Europeans.*

Brand, The (Individual Four) A female, once kept in a concentration camp, with whom Individual Five has sexual relations in Doris Lessing's *Re: Colonised Planet 5, Shikasta.*

Brandel, Alexander (Alex) Father of Wolf Brandel and friend of Andrei Androfski; historian of the Warsaw ghetto and leader of the Bathyran Zionist Executive Council; scholar and pacifist turned activist; diarist/journalist in Leon Uris's *Mila 18.*

Brandel, Wolf Son of Alexander Brandel and lover of Rachel Bronski; leads survivors from the Warsaw ghetto in Leon Uris's *Mila 18.*

Brander One of a group of men who enjoys a drinking night in Goethe's tragedy *Faust.*

Brander, George Sylvester Ohio senator who dies before he can marry his lover Jennie Gerhardt in Theodore Dreiser's *Jennie Gerhardt.*

Brandir, Lord Alan Lorna Doone's relative, murdered by Carver Doone in R. D. Blackmore's *Lorna Doone.*

Brandler, Mark California Superior Court judge who presides at the first trial of Gregory Powell and Jimmy Smith in Joseph Wambaugh's *The Onion Field.*

Brandley, Mrs. Woman in whose house in Richmond Estella lives after returning from the Continent; many of

Estella's suitors call there, exasperating Pip Pirrip, in Charles Dickens's *Great Expectations.*

Brandon, Augustus (Gussie) Arrogant, competitive, aggressive nephew of Sir Hector Brandon; he is too much like his brutal uncle; Michael Geste dislikes but tolerates Augustus in Percival Christopher Wren's *Beau Geste.*

Brandon, Backwater Tidewater gentleman living in Fluvanna County; never adapts to frontier ways and so is always at odds with his neighbors in Mary Lee Settle's *O Beulah Land.*

Brandon, Caroline Gentle, loving professional nurse known as the Little Sister; lured into a false marriage by "Dr. Brandon" (Doctor Firmin) in her youth, she expiates this sin and compensates for the death of her infant son by consistently protecting the interests of Dr. Firmin's legitimate son, Philip Firmin, in William Makepeace Thackeray's *The Adventures of Philip on His Way through the World.*

Brandon, Colonel Worthy man of thirty-five and the survivor of an unhappy romance; he punishes John Willoughby for the seduction of his ward, Miss Williams, and offers the disinherited Edward Ferrars a living so that Edward may marry; he falls in love with and eventually marries Marianne Dashwood in Jane Austen's *Sense and Sensibility.*

Brandon, Constancia Brown (Constance, Lady Macbeth, Mrs. Shakespeare) Garrulous, pretentious hostess of a salon in Harlem's Striver's Row; satirized, along with an outrageous assortment of her guests, in Countee Cullen's *One Way to Heaven.*

Brandon, Cousin Annie See O'Neill, Annie Brandon.

Brandon, Dorcas Grave beauty, proud and solemn, who believes that the family tradition of wicked men and brave and suffering women continues in her generation; engaged to marry Mark Wylder, she loves Stanley Lake, whom she marries when Wylder disappears, in spite of Rachel Lake's warning of Stanley's corruption; Stanley confesses his crime to her in order to coerce her into giving him money to pay blackmail to the lawyer Josiah Larkin; after Stanley dies, she and Rachel travel abroad together in J. Sheridan Le Fanu's *Wylder's Hand.*

Brandon, Dr. George Husband of Constancia Brandon in Countee Cullen's *One Way to Heaven.*

Brandon, Emma Heiress who nearly yields to the twin temptations represented by the Roman Catholic church and the reprobate Mark Gardner in Charlotte Yonge's *Heartsease.*

Brandon, Gregory Sir Walter Ralegh's executioner in George Garrett's *Death of the Fox.*

Brandon, Julius (Uncle Lorne) Elderly relative who must, according to the will, be kept at Brandon Hall; he is mistaken by the narrator of the story, Charles de Cresseron, for the ghost of Uncle Lorne; he believes himself a prophet; he predicts the death and the return of Mark Wylder in J. Sheridan Le Fanu's *Wylder's Hand.*

Brandon, Lady Mary Dorcas's mother, beautiful and kind but sad because of an unhappy marriage; she died young before the action of the story begins in J. Sheridan Le Fanu's *Wylder's Hand.*

Brandon, Lady Patricia Refined, abused wife of Sir Hector; she cares for her nieces and nephews, including the Geste brothers; she tries to handle the finances of Brandon Abbas; she is the beloved friend of George Lawrence; she is the owner of the sapphire called the "Blue Water" in Percival Christopher Wren's *Beau Geste.*

Brandon, Lucy William Brandon's niece, who believes in the virtue of Paul Clifford and helps him escape from an Australian penal colony to America in Edward Bulwer-Lytton's *Paul Clifford.*

Brandon, Mrs. Owns the variety store and phones mothers if kids take a pack of gum in Alice Hoffman's *Local Girls.*

Brandon, Oliver Black companion and employee of William Howland; helps Abigail Tolliver fight a mob and save the Howland home in Shirley Ann Grau's *The Keepers of the House.*

Brandon, Sir Hector Brutal, cruel husband to Patricia; he is hated for squandering money while his estate collapses in Percival Christopher Wren's *Beau Geste.*

Brandon, Stuart Wastrel brother of Mamie Brandon Catlett and father of Annie Brandon O'Neill in Mary Lee Settle's *Know Nothing.*

Brandon, William Hanging judge and uncle of Lucy Brandon; he condemns Paul Clifford to death despite his knowledge that Clifford is his son in Edward Bulwer-Lytton's *Paul Clifford.*

Brandreth, Percy Petitioner for Mrs. Munger; male lead in *Romeo and Juliet* in William Dean Howells's *Annie Kilburn.*

Brandt, Hannah Historical character Margaret is writing about; once active in the American Communist Party and the National Woman's Party; is senile and bitter in her old age when Margaret interviews her in Maureen Howard's *Expensive Habits.*

Brandt, Margaret Daughter of Peter the Magician; she is betrothed but not wed to Elias's son Gerard; she bears his son and works in Rotterdam as a doctor's assistant, then washerwoman; hearing Gerard preach, she lures him out of his hermit cave and establishes him as pastor of Gouda; she rescues their son from the plague at Deventer School and dies of the plague in Gerard's arms in Charles Reade's *The Cloister and the Hearth.*

Brandt, Peter "the Magician" Pedantic old scholar of Sevenbergen, who plots Gerard's escape from a prison tower, suffers a paralytic stroke, and dies after a vision of Gerard sore-disfigured, in a boat on a great river in Charles Reade's *The Cloister and the Hearth.*

Brandwhite, Thomas Wealthy financier who gossips about Captain and Mrs. Bellew in John Galsworthy's *The Country House.*

Brandybuck, Meriadoc (Merry) Young, unadventurous hobbit who is a member of the fellowship who travel with Frodo Baggins to destroy the One Ring in J. R. R. Tolkien's *The Fellowship of the Ring.* He fights with Theoden, King of the Mark, and kills Ringwraith in battle in *The Two Towers.* He is reunited with the fellowship to join the rebellion against the invading men in *The Return of the King.*

Brane, Mr. Justice Judge in the libel case brought by Marjorie Ferrar against Fleur Mont in John Galsworthy's *The Silver Spoon.*

Branghton, Biddy Eldest daughter of Mr. Branghton; she is a 19-year-old silly woman of fashion who pursues Mr. Smith for a husband in Frances Burney's *Evelina.*

Branghton, Mr. Forty-year-old nephew of Madame Duval; he is contemptuous of all foreigners in Frances Burney's *Evelina.*

Branghton, Polly Younger daughter of Mr. Branghton; aged seventeen, she is ignorant but good-natured; she pursues Mr. Brown for a husband in Frances Burney's *Evelina.*

Branghton, Tom Eldest son of Mr. Branghton; 20 years old, he is foolish and spends his time tormenting his sisters in Frances Burney's *Evelina.*

Brangwen, Anna Daughter of Lydia Brangwen's first marriage; Anna marries her stepfather's nephew, Will Brangwen; her sensuality is in conflict with his spirituality in D. H. Lawrence's *The Rainbow.*

Brangwen, Gudrun Ursula Brangwen's little sister; she is closest to Ursula in D. H. Lawrence's *The Rainbow.* She emerges, now grown up, as a nihilistic artist and becomes Gerald Crich's demonic and destructive lover and later Loerke's lover in *Women in Love.*

Brangwen, Lydia (Lynsky) Exotic widowed Polish immigrant in England who marries Tom Brangwen, alleviating his sexual repression in D. H. Lawrence's *The Rainbow.*

Brangwen, Tom (the elder) Farmer troubled by conflicts of sensuality and religious fervor; his marriage to Lydia is both liberating and tormented; in old age he drowns in a flood in D. H. Lawrence's *The Rainbow.*

Brangwen, Tom (the younger) Son of Lydia and the elder Tom Brangwen; a colliery manager and Ursula Brangwen's uncle, he marries Winifred Inger in D. H. Lawrence's *The Rainbow.*

Brangwen, Ursula Daughter of Will and Anna; she becomes a teacher who urgently strives for independence and meaning in her life; she has a Lesbian affair with another teacher, Winifred Inger; she has an intense love affair with Anton Skrebensky in D. H. Lawrence's *The Rainbow.* She provides a realistic balance to her lover Rupert Birkin in *Women in Love.*

Brangwen, Will Carpenter and wood-carver with artistic yearnings for the spirituality in church architecture; he becomes submissive and resigned in the warfare engendered by his and his wife Anna's passions in D. H. Lawrence's *The Rainbow.*

Branley, Jimmy Architect who lives with Ellen Proctorr; a cheerful, amiable man; nearly fifty, with two grown kids in Donald E. Westlake's *The Hook.*

Branney, Mrs. Homer See Lipscomb, Mabel Blitch.

Brannigan, Biddy Maid of John Melmoth's uncle; she recounts the Melmoth family's complicity in Cromwell's carnage against the Irish in Charles Maturin's *Melmoth the Wanderer.*

Branno, Harla Ambitious Mayor of Terminus who exiles Councilman Golan Trevize from Terminus and sends him to search for the rival Second Foundation in order to destroy it and found a second Galactic Empire during her administration in Isaac Asimov's *Foundation's Edge.*

Brannom, Bob Corrupt district attorney who is killed by Dix Handley in William Riley Burnett's *The Asphalt Jungle.*

Brannon, Alice Little-mourned wife of Biff Brannon; dies following surgery in Carson McCullers's *The Heart Is a Lonely Hunter.*

Brannon, Bartholomew (Biff) Methodical and observant café owner who is fond of freaks; husband of Alice Brannon in Carson McCullers's *The Heart Is a Lonely Hunter.*

Branston Butler at Knowl in J. Sheridan Le Fanu's *Uncle Silas.*

Braquemart Witty, fickle, and cruel member of the Mauretanian order; nihilist and technocrat; murdered soon after he begins to organize a resistance movement against the Oberförster in Ernst Jünger's *On the Marble Cliffs.*

Bras-Coupé Former African prince; tortured and dies following an attempted escape from slavery in George Washington Cable's *The Grandissimes.*

Brashear, Etta Cincinnati working woman who befriends Susan Lenox; marries a rich brewer in order to avoid a life of poverty and prostitution in David Graham Phillips's *Susan Lenox.*

Brasi, Luca Close friend of Don Corleone; killed by rival gangsters in Mario Puzo's *The Godfather.*

Brasowitsch, Athanas Prosperous Hungarian trader in Komorn; owner of the *Saint Barbara,* a cargo ship on which Ali Tschorbadschi and his daughter Timéa are fleeing Turkish court pursuers; declares that the young girl become a servant in his home after her father's death in Maurus Jókai's *A Modern Midas.*

Brass, Sally Tall, gaunt sister of Sampson Brass; she is hard and merciless, lacking Sampson's cowardice; she conspires in the plot to frame Kit Nubbles and is cruel to her servant girl, the Marchioness, in Charles Dickens's *The Old Curiosity Shop.*

Brass, Sampson Tall, angular, and cowardly lawyer, who is at Daniel Quilp's beck and call, assists Quilp in his villainy and constantly sings his praises, hires Dick Swiveller as a clerk, and frames Kit Nubbles for theft in Charles Dickens's *The Old Curiosity Shop.*

Bratch Planet 6 Representative of Health who must decide how the miraculous blue flowering summer plant can be divided among the millions of hungry people and animals in Doris Lessing's *The Making of the Representative for Planet 8.*

Brattle, Carry Beloved daughter of Jacob Brattle; victim of a seducer, she is turned out of her home and becomes a prostitute; aided by Frank Fenwick, she is at last restored to her father, and they are reconciled in Anthony Trollope's *The Vicar of Bullhampton.*

Brattle, Fanny Younger daughter of Jacob Brattle; she supports her parents loyally when her brother Sam is accused of murder in Anthony Trollope's *The Vicar of Bullhampton.*

Brattle, George Prosperous, tight-fisted son of Jacob Brattle; he reluctantly puts up bail for his brother, Sam; he refuses to give shelter to his sister Carry in Anthony Trollope's *The Vicar of Bullhampton.*

Brattle, Jacob Cross-grained, moody, but hard-working miller at Bullhampton sorely beset by troubles when his son Sam is accused of murdering Farmer Trumbull; the Marquis of Trowbridge demands that the Brattles be evicted from the mill; Brattle also endures shame and sorrow for his seduced daughter, Carry, abandoned to a life of prostitution; father and daughter are finally reunited in Anthony Trollope's *The Vicar of Bullhampton.*

Brattle, Maggie Heroic, self-sacrificing mother of Carry, the daughter seduced and turned out of the house; she also bravely endures the anguish of having her son Sam wrongly accused of murder in Anthony Trollope's *The Vicar of Bullhampton.*

Brattle, Sam Youngest son of the miller, Jacob Brattle; he is the prime suspect in the murder of Farmer Trumbull, hounded, imprisoned and brought to trial; he is found not guilty thanks to the efforts and testimony of the vicar, Frank Fenwick, in Anthony Trollope's *The Vicar of Bullhampton.*

Braun, Anna German teacher to Lucy Snowe and Paulina Home in Charlotte Brontë's *Villette.*

Braun, Carlton See Brown, Carl.

Braun, Mr. Multiligual brooding captain's clerk and translator to Hornblower; he steals guns from Hornblower and tries to commit an assassination at the Imperial Palace of Peterhof in C. S. Forester's *Commodore Hornblower.*

Braunbeck-Corcoran, Thalia Corky's stepdaughter from Charlotte's first marriage; wild, neurotic, and a hippy; friend of Mailee Plummer in Joyce Carol Oates's *What I Lived For.*

Brausen, Juan María Gertrudis's husband, who experiences the unfortunate consequences of his wife's breast amputation and the downfall of their marriage; creates in a screenplay a parallel world called Santa María and slowly becomes part of it, redeeming himself through the act of writing in Juan Carlos Onetti's *The Brief Life;* appears in later novels as the founder of Santa María and as God-Brausen in many narrations in Juan Carlos Onetti's "The Stolen Bride" and *Past Caring.*

Brauxel, Mr. One of the adult alter-egos of Eddi Amsel; designs robotic versions of his childhood scarecrows that offer oaths of allegiance to Brauxel & Co.; latest master of Prinz, Hitler's German shepherd, in Günter Grass's *Dog Years.*

Bravassa, Miss Member of the Vincent Crummles Theatrical Company in Charles Dickens's *The Life and Adventures of Nicholas Nickleby.*

Braverman, Inez Widow of Leslie Braverman in Wallace Markfield's *To an Early Grave.*

Braverman, Leslie Deceased writer who is the subject of recollections by several of his friends in Wallace Markfield's *To an Early Grave.*

Brawl, Baron Loud and arrogant but eminent judge who deigns to dine at Sir Henry Harcout's splendid house in Anthony Trollope's The Bertrams. He appears briefly as the (old) Duke of Omnium's guest in *Framley Parsonage.*

Braxley, Richard Lawyer for Major Roland Forrester; tries to cheat Edith Forrester of her inheritance in Robert Montgomery Bird's *Nick of the Woods.*

Braxton Unemployed gambler and hustler; shares an apartment with Alva in Wallace Thurman's *The Blacker The Berry.*

Bray, Catherine "Cath" Daughter of Nell Bray and sister of James Bray; in adulthood works as a copy editor in New York, has affairs with married men, attempts suicide twice; returns to Bridgeport, becomes a spinner and weaver; keeps the secret that her father had an affair with Isabelle Poole in Maureen Howard's *Natural History.*

Bray, Eamonn James Bray's son by his first marriage, becomes a banker in London in Maureen Howard's *Natural History.*

Bray, Harold (Harry) Protean figure; the false Grand Tutor whom George Giles drives out of the college in John Barth's *Giles Goat-Boy.*

Bray, James Son of Nell Bray and brother of Cath Bray; becomes an actor in Los Angeles and New York; married twice, the second time to Lilah Lee Hulburt; father of two, his second child is Jen Bray in Maureen Howard's *Natural History.*

Bray, James, Marquis of Flirtatious, flamboyantly dressed son of the Duke and Duchess of Donkeyton; he runs for a seat in Parliament against John Jorrocks and loses in Robert Surtees's *Hillingdon Hall.*

Bray, Jen Daughter of James and Lilah Lee Bray in Maureen Howard's *Natural History.*

Bray, Lilah Lee Second wife of James Bray and mother of Jen Bray; the only beautiful one of seven children; has affair with Morty Ziff; loves her Arabian horse, Falada, in Maureen Howard's *Natural History.*

Bray, Madeline Loving daughter of Walter Bray; she is willing to sacrifice herself in marriage to Arthur Gride in order to save her father; the plot is foiled by Nicholas Nickleby, who learns of it in his work for the Cheeryble brothers; she marries Nicholas in Charles Dickens's *The Life and Adventures of Nicholas Nickleby.*

Bray, Nell Mother of Catherine and James Bray; former teacher; dreamy and distant; naturally grand though unaffected in Maureen Howard's *Natural History.*

Bray, Sir Bernard Member of Parliament and cousin to Mr. Evelyn; he takes Hugh Trevor under his wing and later deserts him to join his previous political opponents in Thomas Holcroft's *The Adventures of Hugh Trevor.*

Bray, Walter Old man who owes money to Arthur Gride and is willing to sell his daughter to the miser in a marriage arranged by Ralph Nickleby in order to retire his debts and be released from prison in Charles Dickens's *The Life and Adventures of Nicholas Nickleby.*

Bray, William Aloysius "Bill" or "Billy" Husband of Nell Bray and father of Catherine and James Bray; county detective in the state's attorney's office; former soldier in Normandy; dies in 1955 in Maureen Howard's *Natural History.*

Bread, Catherine Servant of the de Bellegardes; reveals to Christopher Newman that Emmeline and Urbain de Bellegarde killed Urbain's father in Henry James's *The American.*

Breakspeare Editor of a provincial newspaper who supports Dyce Lashmar's political campaign in George Gissing's *Our Friend the Charlatan.*

Breasley, Henry English painter now in old age, living in the French countryside with two young girls as companions; he rejects abstract art as a retreat from human reality; he alternately berates and befriends David Williams in John Fowles's *The Ebony Tower.*

Breaux, Gabriel (Gabe) Drinker and gambler who courts and marries Amy in Katherine Anne Porter's *Old Mortality.*

Breck, Angus Member of Rob Roy MacGregor's clan in Sir Walter Scott's *Rob Roy.*

Breckbridge, Gavin Dursilla's fiancé before she married Colonel Sartoris in William Faulkner's "An Odor of Verbena."

Breckbridge, Gavin Fiancé of Drusilla Hawk; killed at Shiloh in William Faulkner's *The Unvanquished.*

Breckinridge, Myra (Myron) Female transsexual, born Myron Breckinridge, seeking to destroy traditional sex roles; rapes Rusty Godowsky and tries to seduce Mary-Ann Pringle; reverts to her original sex and marries Mary-Ann in Gore Vidal's *Myra Breckinridge.*

Breda, Madame Sinister colleague of Dominick Medina and Dr. Newhover; she purports to be a Swedish masseuse to whom Richard Hannay is sent by Dr. Newhover for "treatment", to determine and increase Hannay's sensitivity to Medina's hypnotic powers in John Buchan's *The Three Hostages.*

Bredahl, Andersen ("Andy") Marathon Chinless ship's cook aboard the *Oedipus Tyrannus* who becomes Dana Hilliot's chief tormenter but eventually accepts him in Malcolm Lowry's *Ultramarine.*

Bredalbane, Edmonia Honeywell Liberated, promiscuous, oft-married twin sister of Judge Gamaliel Bland Honeywell in Ellen Glasgow's *The Romantic Comedians.*

Bredalbane, Ralph Young and poor fourth husband of Edmonia Bredalbane, on whose money he lives, in Ellen Glasgow's *The Romantic Comedians.*

Brederhagan, Nathan Profligate rake who stabs Christina Jansen during an attempted rape in Ignatius Donnelly's *Caesar's Column.*

Breedlove, Cholly Husband of Pauline; father of Sammy and Pecola; unemployed alcoholic; rapes Pecola and burns his storefront house down; beats Pauline and gets arrested in Toni Morrison's *The Bluest Eye.*

Breedlove, Hallie Mulatto prostitute with a fierce sense of independence in Nelson Algren's *A Walk on the Wild Side.*

Breedlove, Monica Neighbor and friend of Christine Penmark; senses fear and worry in Christine, but is oblivious to the evil in Rhoda Penmark, in William March's *The Bad Seed.*

Breedlove, Pauline Williams (Polly) Wife of Cholly; mother of Sammy and Pecola; has a deformed foot; marries Cholly because he is the first man to ever talk to her; works as a cleaning woman for a white family and considers them more desirable than her own in Toni Morrison's *The Bluest Eye.*

Breedlove, Pecola Daughter of Cholly and Pauline Breedlove and sister of Sammy; is named after a mulatto character in the movie *Imitation of Life;* considers the three whores who live above her as family over her own; wishes for blue eyes as a remedy to her problems; raped and impregnated by her father, she goes insane in Toni Morrison's *The Bluest Eye.*

Breedlove, Sammy Son of Cholly and Pauline Breedlove and brother of Pecola; reacts to his parent's fighting by cursing and trying to hurt Cholly; runs away to escape his parents and his legacy in Toni Morrison's *The Bluest Eye.*

Breedlove, Yancey Young deputy who is second-in-command of the hunt for Rato Mustian, the dog, and the snake in Reynolds Price's *A Generous Man.*

Breen, Denis Dublin eccentric obsessed with discovering the sender of an anonymous, cryptic postcard in James Joyce's *Ulysses.*

Breen, Josie Powell Wife of crazy Denis; she was formerly attracted to Leopold Bloom in James Joyce's *Ulysses.*

Breene, Charlie Wealthy suitor of Dorothy Shaw; their marriage is cruelly opposed by his parents; when he is penniless and her husband is dead, they marry in Anita Loos's *But Gentlemen Marry Brunettes.*

Brehgert, Ezekiel Influential city banker, a Jewish widower with grown children; despite her parents' horror and his much-dyed hair, Georgiana Longestaffe accepts his proposal of marriage; caught up in the financial whirlwind of Augustus Melmotte's downfall, he finds he can no longer promise her a London house, and she breaks the engagement in Anthony Trollope's *The Way We Live Now.*

Brempong, Lawrence Ghanian government official and a writer like the protagonist, Baako; materialist seeker whom Baako meets on his flight home to Ghana from the United States, where he was educated, in Ayi Kwei Armah's *Fragments.*

Brenda Operator of a nursery group that includes Jane Gray's son, Laurie; Jane is critical of Brenda's methods; the women are afraid of each other in Margaret Drabble's *The Waterfall.*

Brenda Well-brought-up, quiet, shy, directionless woman; denominated a "born victim" by Freda, she feels inadequate in coping with the role reversal forced on her by the discovery of Freda's murdered corpse in Beryl Bainbridge's *The Bottle Factory Outing.*

Brenda Winnie's sister, who is married to Arthur Seaton's friend Jack; she becomes pregnant by Arthur and aborts in Alan Sillitoe's *Saturday Night and Sunday Morning.*

Brendan Young member of the Northern Irish contingent of the INLA (Irish National Liberation Army) intending to kill Padraic; killed by Padraic in Martin McDonagh's *The Lieutenant of Inishmore.*

Brenhilda, Countess Beloved daughter of the Knight and Lady of Aspramonte and the large, handsome, loving, Amazonian wife of Count Robert of Paris; trained early in arms, she accompanies her husband on the crusade; she is endangered by Caesar Nicephorus Briennius's pursuit at Constantinople in Sir Walter Scott's *Count Robert of Paris.*

Brennan, Bridget (Baba) Beautiful, coy, and malicious daughter of Mr. Brennan; she gets herself and Caithleen Brady expelled from the convent so that they can lead wild, free lives in Dublin in Edna O'Brien's *The Country Girls.*

Brennan, Gladys, Zoe, and Emily Unmarried ladies in their 30s; they are laughed at for their yearly trips to the Sherbourne to be in society in George Moore's *A Drama in Muslin.*

Brennan, Martha Beautiful mother of Bridget Brennan; she desires drink and admiration in life; she is a good friend to Caithleen Brady, especially after Cait's mother dies in Edna O'Brien's *The Country Girls.*

Brennan, Mr. Hard-working veterinary surgeon and father of Bridget Brennan; he watches over Caithleen Brady after her mother's death and tries to protect her from her abusive father in Edna O'Brien's *The Country Girls.*

Brennan, Ned New captain of the Irish Citizen Army, as he has taken over Jack Clitheroe's rank; tells Jack that he now has the title of commandant and is to report to the night's meeting; arrested by British soldiers in a roundup of all Irish men during the Easter Rebellion of 1916 in Sean O'Casey's *The Plough and the Stars.*

Brenner, Dr. Important chemist working for a company that makes poisonous gas for chemical warfare; works for Fayette, a man who is suspicious of the scientist's loyalties, in Clifford Odets's play *Waiting for Lefty.*

Brent, Captain Elijah (Lige) Riverboat captain and devoted friend of Colonel Carvel, and therefore of the South, in Winston Churchill's *The Crisis.*

Brent, Ellen Pregnant wife of Henry Brent; scared into her grave by her husband's mad delusions in Andrew Lytle's *A Name for Evil.*

Brent, Emily Self-righteous Puritan who was accused of causing the death of an unfortunate servant girl; Miss Brent is the fatal victim of an apparent bee sting in Agatha Christie's *And Then There Were None.*

Brent, Frederick (Fred, Freddie) Ward of Hester Prime; Baptist pastor in Dexter, Ohio, who leaves his post in disgrace and migrates to Cincinnati, where he meets his father, a born-again Christian, in Paul Laurence Dunbar's *The Uncalled.*

Brent, Henry Haunted man who undertakes the restoration of his ancestor's farm; narrator of Andrew Lytle's *A Name for Evil.*

Brent, Jimmy Peter Templer's fat, high-voiced City friend, who is immediately disliked by Nicholas Jenkins in Anthony

Powell's *A Question of Upbringing.* Jenkins is dismayed to learn that Jean (Templer) Duport ended her affair with him to pursue one with Brent in *The Kindly Ones.* Brent tells Jenkins about his affair with Jean in *The Valley of Bones.*

Brent, Major Former owner of The Grove and felt to be its ghostly inhabiter by his descendant Henry Brent in Andrew Lytle's *A Name for Evil.*

Brent, Margaret (Mag, Margar't) Wife of Tom Brent and mother of Frederick Brent; dies from alcoholism in Paul Laurence Dunbar's *The Uncalled.*

Brent, Mrs. Mistress of Sir George Tufto in William Makepeace Thackeray's *Vanity Fair.*

Brent, Robert New York playwright who helps Susan Lenox become an actress and dies through the plotting of her jealous lover, Freddie Palmer, in David Graham Phillips's *Susan Lenox.*

Brent, Sophy Beautiful and talkative young actress, who has recently finished drama school and is part of the ensemble gathered at Hereford; she has an affair with David Evans in Margaret Drabble's *The Garrick Year.*

Brent, Tom Drunkard who abuses and later abandons his wife, Margaret Brent, and son, Frederick Brent; becomes a born-again Christian and is reunited with his son in Paul Laurence Dunbar's *The Uncalled.*

Brentford, Earl of One-time Privy Seal and now backroom political power, at whose townhouse Phineas Finn meets eminent people; when the marriage of his daughter, Lady Laura (Standish), to Robert Kennedy breaks down, he is desolate and takes her abroad; his long quarrel with his headstrong son, Lord Chiltern, is healed by Chiltern's marriage to Violet Effingham in Anthony Trollope's *Phineas Finn.* He protects Lady Laura further from her husband in *Phineas Redux.*

Brentham, Duchess of Wife of the duke and mother of Lady Corisande Brentham and Lord Bertram Brentham in Benjamin Disraeli's *Lothair.*

Brentham, Duke of Father of Lady Corisande Brentham and Lord Bertram Brentham in Benjamin Disraeli's *Lothair.*

Brentham, Lady Corisande Daughter of the Duke and Duchess of Brentham; Lothair falls in love with her soon after their meeting; she represents the true England that Lothair finally chooses in Benjamin Disraeli's *Lothair.*

Brentham, Lord Bertram Oxford friend of Lothair and heir to the dukedom of Brentham in Benjamin Disraeli's *Lothair.*

Brenzo, Tony Liberal white policeman, friend of Joe Market, and eloquent foe of narcissism and nihilism in Hal Bennett's *Lord of Dark Places.*

Bressac, Count de Young aristocrat filled with vices: wickedness, vindictiveness, cruelty, atheism, and debauchery; extreme libertine; detests and hates his aunt, who tries to reform him; decides to enlist the aid of the maid Thérèse in killing the woman; tortures the pretty young maid when she betrays him by informing the aunt of his plan; virtue in his mind fails to triumph over evil in Marquis de Sade's *Justine: Or the Misfortunes of Virtue.*

Bressac, Marquise de Attempts to reform her libertine and wicked nephew Count de Bressac; becomes the object of his murderous intentions; informed by Thérèse of the count's intention to poison her in Marquis de Sade's *Justine: Or the Misfortunes of Virtue.*

Bret, Frank Good-looking tenor in Dick Lennox's acting company; he becomes Lucy Leslie's love after Dick becomes interested in Kate Ede in George Moore's *A Mummer's Wife.*

Breteuil, Jean Pierre French novelist who, to the surprise of his English translator Jake Donaghue, wins the Prix Goncourt; *The Wooden Nightingale,* Jake's translation of an earlier novel, is appropriated by Sammy Starfield in Iris Murdoch's *Under the Net.*

Bretlev, Ivan Ivanovitch Moscow Centre agent who probably recruited Nelson Ko for Karla in John le Carré's *The Honourable Schoolboy.*

Brett, Colonel Humphrey Husband of Mary Brett and father of Lise Brett; the reckless, talkative commandant of a Prisoner of War camp in Northern Scotland, he is disturbed by trials and executions and suffers guilt for the deaths of six German prisoners killed in an attempted escape and also for the anticipated execution of Emil Gerlach in Storm Jameson's *The Black Laurel.*

Brett, Dr. Harriet Lovatt's extremely conventional doctor, who will not admit that something is indeed "wrong" with her fifth child, Ben Lovatt, in Doris Lessing's *The Fifth Child.*

Brett, Lise Twelve-year-old neglected child, who cries all night for her mother and is comforted by her eighteen-year-old neighbor, Arnold Coster, in Storm Jameson's *Before* *the Crossing.* An eighteen-year-old girl in 1945, she lives at a Scottish military installation with her father, Colonel Humphrey Brett, and in London and Berlin with her mother, Mary Brett, and falls in love with Arnold in Storm Jameson's *The Black Laurel.*

Brett, Mary Unfaithful wife of Colonel Brett and neglectful mother of Lise Brett in 1939; she is an actress and musician who arranges concerts for charities, dines with Julian Swan, and frequently has her picture in the London *Tatler* in Storm Jameson's *Before the Crossing.* She has been the mistress of Lieutenant Edward West for four years when she discovers he is attempting to seduce her eighteen-year-old daughter, Lise, in Storm Jameson's *The Black Laurel.*

Brett, Nina Chic young woman who interviews Francesca Bolt at an employment agency in Gail Godwin's *Glass People.*

Bretton Political agent for Miles Vane-Merrick in Kent; the son of the local blacksmith, he is described by Miles as "a raging communist" in Vita Sackville-West's *Family History.*

Bretton, Dr. Mrs. Bretton's husband and father to John Graham; he dies young in Charlotte Brontë's *Villette.*

Bretton, Dr. John Graham Physician attending Mme. Beck's pupils; Lucy Snowe has known him in her youth as Graham Bretton; he falls in love with Ginevra Fanshawe but later is happily married to Paulina Home in Charlotte Brontë's *Villette.*

Bretton, Louisa Devoted mother of John Graham Bretton and godmother to Lucy Snowe; she is a sensible and kind woman, who takes care of Lucy when she becomes ill during a summer vacation from teaching in Villette in Charlotte Brontë's *Villette.*

Brewer Elderly, overweight man; a lower-middle-class pony player, he is behind in "subscription" payments on horse-racing bets to Pinkie Brown's mob; he is roughed up by Pinkie in Graham Greene's *Brighton Rock.*

Brewer Husband of Roxana for eight years; he is a jolly but weak and empty-headed man, who lets his business go to ruin; he abandons Roxana but later emerges in the French military, only to die in the Battle of Mons in Daniel Defoe's *The Fortunate Mistress.*

Brewer, Dr. Cambridge-educated physician, whose unprofitable practice has led him to innkeeping in Richard Graves's *The Spiritual Quixote.*

Brewer, Mr. Young man who functions as a buffer at the Veneering dinner parties in Charles Dickens's *Our Mutual Friend.*

Brewer, Mrs. Amiable wife of the innkeeper Dr. Brewer in Richard Graves's *The Spiritual Quixote.*

Brewer's Brother-In-Law Husband of the brewer's sister; he is a charitable man who is moved to pity over the condition of Roxana's children and gets family members to help provide support for them in Daniel Defoe's *The Fortunate Mistress.*

Brewer's Sister Sister-in-law to Roxana; she refuses to take in Roxana and the brewer's children after the brewer abandons his family in Daniel Defoe's *The Fortunate Mistress.*

Brewster, Emily Gruff and hearty spinster; she and Patrick Redfern are the apparent discoverers of Arlena Marshall's body in Agatha Christie's *Evil Under the Sun.*

Brewster, Maud Shipwrecked woman rescued by the *Ghost;* assists Hump Van Weyden in navigating the ship to the United States in Jack London's *The Sea Wolf.*

Brewster, Rev. Evan Minister of the Ebenezer Baptist Church in Sinclair Lewis's *Kingsblood Royal* and *Cass Timberlane.*

Brewton, Brock (Brock Chamberlain) Son of Lutie Brewton and Brice Chamberlain, although Colonel James B. Brewton refuses to accept this fact; becomes a gambler and then an outlaw; killed by a posse in Conrad Richter's *The Sea of Grass.*

Brewton, Colonel James B. (Jim) Powerful cattle baron and rancher who battles against nester settlements until government laws restrain his actions; welcomes the return of his errant wife Lutie in Conrad Richter's *The Sea of Grass.*

Brewton, Harry (Hal) Nephew of Colonel James Brewton; becomes a medical doctor; narrator of Conrad Richter's *The Sea of Grass.*

Brewton, Lutie Cameron Wife of Colonel James B. Brewton; has an affair with Brice Chamberlain and has a son by him; deserts her family because of boredom with pioneer life, but returns home fifteen years later in Conrad Richter's *The Sea of Grass.*

Briac, Alphonse Pupil of Chopin who is a monk at Shangri-la and teaches Hugh "Glory" Conway an unknown song by Chopin in James Hilton's *Lost Horizon.*

Brian Car salesman with a wealthy family in Isabel Colegate's *Orlando at the Brazen Threshold.*

Brian Foul-smelling, marginally human boy whose whole experience is limited to the goings-on in a slaughterhouse; he resists Norah's well-meant but fleeting attempts to improve him in Richard Hughes's *The Wooden Shepherdess.*

Brian Group leader of the rebellious teenagers by whom Kate wants to be accepted in Doris Lessing's *The Diaries of Jane Somers.*

Brian, Peter Gardener at Belmont who reports to the other servants he has seen Lieutenant Puddock and Becky Chattesworth kiss in the garden in J. Sheridan Le Fanu's *The House by the Churchyard.*

Brice, Captain Lady Croom's brother and a house guest at the manor Sidley Park; not particularly intelligent and follows the lead of Lady Croom; engages in an affair with Mrs. Chater, the wife of his supposed friend Chater in Tom Stoppard's play *Arcadia.*

Brice, Father Haitian slave trader; works for the Worthingtons; is killed by the Worthingtons in Herbert Gold's *Slave Trade.*

Brice, Margaret Mother of Stephen Brice in Winston Churchill's *The Crisis.*

Brice, Stephen Atterbury (Steve) Antislavery lawyer who marries Virginia Carvel in Winston Churchill's *The Crisis.*

Brice, Torn Groom at Bartram-Haugh who Maud Ruthyn erroneously thinks has betrayed her by giving her uncle, Silas Ruthyn, her letter meant for Lady Monica Knollys; Bryce helps Maud escape from Bartram-Haugh the night of Mme. de la Rougierre's murder; later he marries Meg Hawkes in J. Sheridan Le Fanu's *Uncle Silas.*

Brice, Virginia Carvel See Carvel, Virginia.

Brick Disgusted with mendacity and dependent on drink until he gets an awakening "click" in his head; has dodged away from life after the suicide of his friend Skipper, for which Brick feels responsible since he hung up on Skipper when he tried to confess his real feelings; breaks the news to Big Daddy that the old man actually has cancer, as a retort to Big Daddy's suggestion that his friendship with Skipper was homosexual, in Tennessee Williams's *Cat on a Hot Tin Roof.*

Brick, Jefferson War correspondent for the *New York Rowdy Journal,* who is exceedingly youthful in appearance in Charles Dickens's *The Life and Adventures of Martin Chuzzlewit.*

Brick, Mrs. Jefferson Child in appearance but a matron with two children in Charles Dickens's *The Life and Adventures of Martin Chuzzlewit.*

Brickmaker, The One of the "Pilgrims" who spies on the others for the General Manager; never produces bricks, as he is always waiting for a necessary component to arrive from Europe; possesses a painting made by Kurtz of a blindfolded woman holding a torch in Joseph Conrad's *Heart of Darkness.*

Bride Daughter of Hall-ward; when the affections of her betrothed, Face-of-god, shift to Sun-beam, and after she is wounded during the war in Silver-dale, she marries Folk-might in William Morris's *The Roots of the Mountains.*

Bride, Constance Secretary to Lady Ogram; she likes Dyce Lashmar and pretends to be engaged to him at Lady Ogram's command but manifests her independence by rejecting him when she comes into an inheritance in George Gissing's *Our Friend the Charlatan.*

Bride, The Silent and respectful, hides an ardent passion for her past suitor Leonardo but consents to be married to the Bridegroom in the hope of thus forgetting her former love; nonetheless, after the wedding, readily elopes with Leonardo into the woods, from where she will return alone and dishonored in Federico Garcia Lorca's *Blood Wedding.*

Bridé, Joberlin One of two schoolmasters who find no progress in Gargantua's education in François Rabelais's *Gargantua and Pantagruel.*

Bridegroom, The Vigorous and hard-working young man who wants only to marry the Bride and lead a peaceful life, but after her elopement with Leonardo Felix has no choice but to avenge not only this affront to him, but also the blood feud for his father and brother, in a confrontation with Leonardo that will lead both of them to death, in Federico Garcia Lorca's *Blood Wedding.*

Bridegroom's Messengers Men who bring the nonexistent groom's marriage proposal and agree to pay the outrageous brideprice demanded by Madha Mohanty on the wedding day in Fakir Mohan Senapati's "The Brideprice."

Bridegroom's Mother, The After having lost her husband and eldest son in a clan dispute with the Felix family, abominates knives and other weapons and detests anything that has to do with the Felixes; however, her utter love for her only remaining son, the Bridegroom, is too strong for her to oppose his desire to marry a girl whose former suitor had been a Felix, the fatal consequences of which fulfill her utmost fears, in Federico Garcia Lorca's *Blood Wedding.*

Bridegroom's Party Relatives who testify that the wedding was celebrated in Fakir Mohan Senapati's "The Brideprice."

Bridehead, Sue Intelligent but emotionally immature cousin and lover of Jude Fawley; she marries the aging schoolmaster Richard Phillotson out of a misguided sense of duty, then later leaves him to live with Jude, by whom she bears two children; after the tragic deaths of the children, she returns to Phillotson although still in love with Jude in Thomas Hardy's *Jude the Obscure.*

Brideshead, Lord (Bridey) Lord and Lady Marchmain's oldest son; strait-laced and humorless, he is a strict Roman Catholic who eventually marries a middle-aged widow and enlists in the British army in World War II in Evelyn Waugh's *Brideshead Revisited.*

Bridesman Flight commander in William Faulkner's *A Fable.*

Bridewell First lieutenant aboard the *Neversink* in Herman Melville's *White-Jacket.*

Bridewell, Hannah See Catlett, Hannah Bridewell.

Bridge, Arthur Works Manager at the Dupret Foundry; his approach to the workers makes him very unpopular with them and with Richard Dupret in Henry Green's *Living.*

Bridge, Carolyn (Corky) Daughter of Walter and India Bridge; marries and moves to Parallel, Kansas, in Evan Connell's *Mrs. Bridge* and *Mr. Bridge.*

Bridge, Douglas Son of Walter and India Bridge; frequently in trouble as a child; later joins the army in Evan Connell's *Mrs. Bridge* and *Mr. Bridge.*

Bridge, India Wife of Walter Bridge and mother of Ruth, Carolyn, and Douglas Bridge in Evan Connell's *Mrs. Bridge* and *Mr. Bridge.*

Bridge, Ma'am Washerwoman for Clarissa Packard's mother in Caroline Gilman's *Recollections of a Housekeeper.*

Bridge, Ruth Daughter of Walter and India Bridge; moves to New York City and takes a job with a women's magazine in Evan Connell's *Mrs. Bridge* and *Mr. Bridge.*

Bridge, Walter Husband of India Bridge and father of Ruth, Carolyn, and Douglas Bridge; dies in his Kansas City law office in Evan Connell's *Mrs. Bridge* and *Mr. Bridge.*

Bridgebane, Dr. Psychoanalyst who tells the married Hollywood film director Miles Calman that the reason he cheats on his wife is that he suffers from a mother complex in F. Scott Fitzgerald's "Crazy Sunday."

Bridgenorth, Alice Major Bridgenorth's daughter, who is cared for in the household of Lady Peveril until removed by her father during the Restoration years; taken to London by her uncle, Edward Christian, she is intended as part of a political plot to be made the mistress of King Charles II; rescued by Julian Peveril, she marries Julian in Sir Walter Scott's *Peveril of the Peak.*

Bridgenorth, Major Ralph Presbyterian friend and neighbor of Sir Geoffrey Peveril; he was a justice of the peace during the Protectorate and pursues Charlotte de la Tramouille, the Countess of Derby, for revenge in Sir Walter Scott's *Peveril of the Peak.*

Bridger, Jim Mountaineer who aids the wagon train and Molly Wingate in Emerson Hough's *The Covered Wagon.*

Bridges, Cicily Carver See Lancaster, Cicily Carver Bridges.

Bridges, James (John) One of three Englishmen, sympathetic to the American cause, who send Israel Potter as courier to Benjamin Franklin in Herman Melville's *Israel Potter.*

Bridges, Katherine (Kathie) "New Woman of the nineties" with radical political views and leanings toward Bernard Shaw and William Morris; she meets Mr. Chips on a rock-climbing expedition at Great Gable; the older Mr. Chips and the beautiful young woman fall in love, marry, and take up residence at Brookfield, where she is well liked by students and staff and has a rejuvenating, tempering effect on Mr. Chips's character; she and her newly born child die on April 1 in James Hilton's *Good-bye, Mr. Chips.*

Bridges, Ronald Roman Catholic epileptic assistant curator of a handwriting museum whose expertise leads to the downfall of Patrick Seton in Muriel Spark's *The Bachelors.*

Bridget Ex-abbess of St. Catherine Nunnery; she becomes a conspirator for Queen Mary of Scotland and the Catholic church in Sir Walter Scott's *The Abbot.*

Bridget Loyal, loving fiancée of Len; she has to walk home alone after the movies and is attacked by Harry but escapes him; she marries Len in David Lodge's *The Picturegoers.*

Bridget Mistress of Sir Stephen Penrhyn both before and after his marriage to Eleanor Raymond; she hates Eleanor and her children; she marries Sir Stephen after Eleanor's death in Caroline Norton's *Stuart of Dunleath.*

Bridget One of the Irish living in the quiet community of Baile Beag in County Donegal in 1833 in Brian Friel's play *Translations.*

Bridget Widow Wadman's maid, courted by Corporal Trim (James Butler) simultaneously with Captain Toby Shandy's courtship of her mistress in Laurence Sterne's *The Life and Opinions of Tristram Shandy, Gentleman.*

Bridgett Overworked social worker for the elderly in Doris Lessing's *The Diaries of Jane Somers.*

Bridgett Schoolgirl from a broken family who takes refuge on her holidays with Harriet and David Lovatt's family until Ben Lovatt is born in Doris Lessing's *The Fifth Child.*

Bridgitte Aunt of Ruprecht, the young man accused in court of breaking Marthe Rull's cherished jug, in Heinrich von Kleist's *The Broken Jug.*

Bridgnorth, Mr. Lawyer who undertakes Jem Wilson's defense and counsels his family and Mary Barton in Elizabeth Gaskell's *Mary Barton.*

Bridle, Francis Protagonist in Partridge's story proving the existence of ghosts in Henry Fielding's *The History of Tom Jones.*

Brid'Oison, Don Guzman Judge who, along with Bartholo, comes to inform Figaro that the lawsuit against him by Marceline over money owed to the woman is starting in Pierre Augustin Caron de Beaumarchais's play *The Marriage of Figaro.*

Bridwell, Charley Reclusive father of Jed Bridwell in Vardis Fisher's *In Tragic Life.*

Bridwell, Jed Untamed boy who lives across Snake River from Vridar Hunter in Vardis Fisher's *In Tragic Life;* also appears in *Orphans in Gethsemane.*

Bridwell, Lela Mother of Jed Bridwell and friend of Prudence Hunter; leaves her husband, Charley Bridwell, after years of suffering with him in Vardis Fisher's *In Tragic Life.*

Briennius, Nicephorus Anna Comnena's handsome husband; though he became Caesar through his marriage, he is indifferent to his wife and pursues Brenhilda at Constantinople; haughty and ambitious, he conspires to become emperor in Sir Walter Scott's *Count Robert of Paris.*

Brierly, Father Austin The Catholic curate of Our Lady and St. Jude's, where the student group attends morning mass; he marries Angela and Dennis, is transferred several times because of his changing attitudes towards doctrine, studies first Biblical scholarship and then psychology, and ends up leaving the priesthood and pairing up with Lynn, Dennis's secretary, in David Lodge's *How Far Can You Go?*

Brierly, Henry (Harry) College friend of Philip Sterling, with whom Brierly goes west to make money in railroads; business partner of Beriah Sellers; loves but is rejected by Laura Hawkins in Samuel Langhorne Clemens and Charles Dudley Warner's *The Gilded Age.*

Briers, Betty Wife of Frank; she is slowly dying of a debilitating disease in C. P. Snow's *A Coat of Varnish.*

Briers, Frank Detective Chief Superintendent who believes that Ralph Perryman is the murderer of Lady Ashbrook but cannot prove it; he asks Humphrey Leigh to work for him in anti-terrorism in C. P. Snow's *A Coat of Varnish.*

Brigada, Monna Cousin of Bardo de' Bardi; she reveals to Romola de' Bardi that her brother is not dead but a Dominican friar in George Eliot's *Romola.*

Brigadier One of the many corpses that has responded to the invitation of Adrian Prokhoroff to attend a celebration of the coffin maker in Alexander Pushkin's "The Coffin-Maker."

Brigge, Malte Laurids Protagonist living in Paris who witnesses the ubiquitous squalor and disease in the City of Lights; threat of contagion, psychological and spiritual, more than physical, is one of Malte's dominant fears; fear becomes a motive for the character becoming a poet, for transforming his life into art, in Rainer Maria Rilke's *The Notebooks of Malte Laurids Brigge.*

Brigginshaw, H. W. Colleague of Cornelius Cardew; he amuses Cardew's wife while Cardew is away in Isabel Colegate's *The Shooting Party.*

Briggs Adam Appleby's thesis supervisor at the university; he has been working on the same book for twenty years; he halfheartedly tries to help Adam obtain a position in the department in David Lodge's *The British Museum Is Falling Down.*

Briggs Stony young roommate of little Paul Dombey at Dr. Blimber's boarding school in Charles Dickens's *Dombey and Son.*

Briggs, Arabella Faithful companion to Miss Matilda Crawley, who ridicules her but leaves her a legacy; Becky (Sharp) Crawley retains her as a companion to aid in maintaining a façade of respectability and defrauds her of her money in William Makepeace Thackeray's *Vanity Fair.*

Briggs, Hortense Shop employee admired by Clyde Griffiths in Theodore Dreiser's *An American Tragedy.*

Briggs, Jack Previously worked as a journalist on the *Times,* who became involved in leftist politics, found a low-paying job working for a left newspaper, and was forced to resign because of rumors that he was communist, in Doris Lessing's *The Golden Notebook.*

Briggs, John Nicholas Urfe's successor at the Lord Byron School on Phraxos in John Fowles's *The Magus.*

Briggs, Mr. London solicitor who accompanies Richard Mason to interrupt the wedding of Mr. Rochester and Jane Eyre in Charlotte Brontë's *Jane Eyre.*

Briggs, Mr. One of Cecilia Beverley's trustees; a miser who has made money from a life of business, he insults Cecilia with a shabby room when she seeks refuge with him in Frances Burney's *Cecilia.*

Brigham, Professor English department head at Brockshire University in J. B. Priestley's *The Image Men.*

Bright, Agatha Stepmother of Viola and Septimus; a young and attractive widow, Agatha becomes involved with and ultimately engaged to Robson Joyce, a sales representative for Tremlett & Grove's, the publishing firm where her stepson Septimus works, in Frank Swinnerton's *The Happy Family.*

Bright, Septimus Junior clerk at the publishing house Tremlett & Grove's; engaged to Mary Amerson, he becomes jealous of her attentions to Roger Dennett and conspires to get Dennett dismissed from the publishing firm; the failure of his plan results in his own dismissal in Frank Swinnerton's *The Happy Family.*

Bright, Viola Sister of Septimus Bright; she strives to attract Roger Dennett but loses him to Mary Amerson in Frank Swinnerton's *The Happy Family.*

Brightling, Carol Presidential science adviser and radical environmentalist in Tom Clancy's *Rainbow Six.*

Brightling, John Businessman, founder of the Horizon Group, and radical environmentalist in Tom Clancy's *Rainbow Six.*

Brightman, A. M. Retired major who initially tries to help James Latter so that he will file suit against Chester Nimmo; the plan fails, and Jim later realizes that Brightman is out only for personal gain during the General Strike in Joyce Cary's *Not Honour More.*

Brightwalton, Mrs. Society matron at whose dinner party Jocelyn Pierston improves his acquaintance with Nichola Pine-Avon in Thomas Hardy's *The Well-Beloved.*

Brightwell Educated and artistic young man, who befriends Caleb Williams while the two are in jail; his death while awaiting trial demonstrates the unfairness of the British system of holding people in jail for extended periods of time without trial in William Godwin's *Caleb Williams.*

Brigid Old servant of the Rowan family in James Joyce's play *Exiles.*

Brigitta Impudent seven-year-old bastard daughter of the whiskey priest; growing up in poverty and violence, she is worldly and mature beyond her years and, to her father's grief, is lost utterly in Graham Greene's *The Power and the Glory.*

Brigitte Wife of Octave Pian and stepmother to Louis and Michelle; spends her lifetime trying to be a saint; highly critical and suspicious of others; commits acts that disrupt many lives; finally gains painful insight when her husband, Octave Pian, drinks himself to death, realizing that "her way of life was not the only way"; spends her last days with a handsome widower, Dr. Gellis, and befriends Calou, in François Charles Mauriac's *A Woman of the Pharisees.*

Brigstock Member of Benditch's coal board, which votes for L. rather than for D. in Graham Greene's *The Confidential Agent.*

Brigstock, Mona Owen Gereth's vulgar and domineering fiancée and, finally, wife in Henry James's *The Spoils of Poynton.*

Brigstock, Mrs. Mother of Mona Brigstock and mistress of the Waterbath estate in Henry James's *The Spoils of Poynton.*

Brill, Clothilde See Wright, Clothilde Brill.

Brill, Harry Parasitical son of Clothilde Wright and cousin of Jim Calder; preoccupied with maintaining his social position in John P. Marquand's *Wickford Point.*

Brill, Joseph Principal and founder of Edmond Fleg Primary School; Holocaust survivor; is infatuated by Hester Lilt; father of Naphtali in Cynthia Ozick's *The Cannibal Galaxy.*

Brill, Miss Principal character; a portrait of modernist isolation and self-delusion; aging single woman whose sole pleasures in life are experienced in a public garden watching other people and experiencing vicarious joy through her imagined stories of their lives, which she believes to be happy, despite the evidence that most of these lives are as unhappy and lonely as she is; her fragile illusion of happiness is casually crushed by a young woman whom Miss Brill overhears mocking her and her treasured but worn fur; suddenly seeing her sad life through another's eyes, the disheartened woman retreats to her "little dark room . . . like a cupboard" in Katherine Mansfield's "Miss Brill."

Brill, Naphtali Son of Joseph and Iris Brill; initially wants to be a teacher, but in college decides he wants to go into business in Cynthia Ozick's *The Cannibal Galaxy.*

Brilliard Friend of Philander and a penniless cadet, who marries Sylvia in order to bar her father's interference in her affair with Philander; he falls in love with her himself, accuses Octavio of treason to prevent him from marrying her, and eventually assists her in duping Octavio and Alonzo out of their money in Aphra Behn's *Love Letters Between a Nobleman and His Sister.*

Brimah Bamu's father; a shrewd bargainer, he continually raises the price Johnson must pay to marry his daughter in Joyce Cary's *Mister Johnson.*

Brimblecombe, John (Jack) Schoolmaster's fat son, who is intimidated in his schooldays by young Amyas Leigh; he loves Rose Salterne and is invited by Frank Leigh to join the Brotherhood of the Rose, of which he finally proves to be a worthy member, sailing to rescue Rose from Don Guzman de Soto in Charles Kingsley's *Westward Ho!*

Brimblecombe, Vindex Stern yet kindhearted master of Bideford grammar school who flogs Amyas Leigh as a way of caring for the fatherless boy, and whose head Amyas breaks in Charles Kingsley's *Westward Ho!*

Brimley, Alisa Adrian Fielding's wartime secretary and George Smiley's Intelligence colleague; she edits and writes as Barbara Fellowship the *Christian Voice* before enlisting Smiley's aid to help Stella Rode in John le Carré's *A Murder of Quality.* She operates a safehouse for Smiley in *Tinker, Tailor, Soldier, Spy.*

Brimmer Communist labor organizer in F. Scott Fitzgerald's *The Last Tycoon.*

Brink, Dr. Myron T. Second psychiatrist of John Wilder; prescribes large quantities of drugs to treat Wilder's emotional breakdowns in Richard Yates's *Disturbing the Peace.*

Brinklow, Roberta Missionary of the Eastern mission who is aboard the highjacked plane and taken to the Tibetan monastery, Shangri-La, with Hugh "Glory" Conway, Henry D. Barnard, and Captain Charles Mallison in James Hilton's *Lost Horizon.*

Brinkworth, Arnold Naive youth who, because Geoffrey Delamayn saved him from drowning, trusts him; he represents himself as Anne Silvester's husband when he meets her at an inn, bringing Geoffrey's excuses; charged with being Anne's husband by "Scotch marriage," Arnold finds his later marriage to Blanche Lundie in jeopardy in Wilkie Collins's *Man and Wife.*

Brinsley Narrator's friend and fellow student, who is a voice of common sense in Flann O'Brien's *At Swim-Two-Birds.*

Brinville, Miss Young pupil of Juliet Granville on the harp; she is dropped by Sir Lyell Sycamore in favor of Juliet in Frances Burney's *The Wanderer.*

Brisbane-Brown, Harriet Westwater Alison Westwater's clannish and devoted aunt; she falls in love with Thomas Carlyle Craw, the newspaper magnate, in John Buchan's *Castle Gay.* She has married Craw in the beginning of *The House of the Four Winds.*

Briscoe, Colonel Jimmy Dahlia Travers's friend and host, through whom Bertie Wooster rents a seaside cottage; owner of a racing stable, he is Mr. Cook's chief rival in P. G. Wodehouse's *Aunts Aren't Gentlemen.*

Briscoe, Lily Self-described "peevish, ill-tempered dried-up old maid", who represents the questing artist; she brings her androgynous vision as a means to redemptive reunion between conflicting forces; she finally completes her long-unfinished painting, in which Mrs. Ramsay is a "wedge of darkness" in Virginia Woolf's *To the Lighthouse.*

Briscoe, Mr. Marie Fermoyle's employer; catches Benjy shoplifting in Mary McGarry Morris's *Songs in Ordinary Time.*

Brisdine, Judge Comical judge who loses his coat and shoes during the Confederate raid on Chambersburg in Hervey Allen's *Action at Aquila.*

Brisk Would-be seducer of Mercy; he pretends to love her in John Bunyan's *The Pilgrim's Progress from This World to That Which Is to Come.*

Brissenden, Grace Gossip married to Guy Brissenden, a man nearly half her age, in Henry James's *The Sacred Fount.*

Brissenden, Guy (Briss) Young man married to Grace Brissenden, a woman nearly twice his age; acts as a front for the affair between Gilbert Long and Lady John in Henry James's *The Sacred Fount.*

Brissenden, Russ Socialist poet who encourages and inspires Martin Eden; commits suicide in Jack London's *Martin Eden.*

Bristol, Cecile Daughter of William and Julia; student at Berkeley; elopes to Las Vegas to be married in Susan Cheever's *The Cage.*

Bristol, Julia Wife of William; mother of Cecile; imprisons her husband in a cage at their vacation home; shoots him, perhaps accidentally, while waiting to shoot the deer who destroyed her vegetable garden in Susan Cheever's *The Cage.*

Bristol, Louise British commoner living off Los Angeles coast; is engaged to and then left by crown prince Lawrence Mayfair; writes tongue-in-cheek exposé in Stanley Elkin's *Van Gogh's Room at Arles.*

Bristol, William Writer and editor for a weekly magazine; married to Julia; father of Cecile; after wife has imprisoned him in a cage at their vacation home, realizes he can live only by asserting himself; escapes and is shot, perhaps accidentally, by his wife in Susan Cheever's *The Cage.*

Bristow, Arthur Good-looking dreamer and ethereal young man in Pittsburgh who writes to his lover, Shirley, that he cannot marry her because he has not made his way in life yet; tells her that he has taken a job as an overseer of a coffee plantation in Java; dates other girls behind Shirley's back in Theodore Dreiser's "The Second Choice."

Bristow, Wellington (Don Velantén Bristé) American businessman who keeps a list of wanted men in Thornton Wilder's *The Eighth Day.*

Britain, Benjamin (Little Britain) Doctor Jeddler's cheerful manservant, who marries Clemency Newcome for friendship; they become owners of the public house The Nutmeg Grater in Charles Dickens's *The Battle of Life.*

Britain, Duke of One of the French nobles; claims the English are bastards of the Normans; focuses on the inferiority of the English, all the while recognizing the two countries have blood ties; agrees with the Dauphin that the French women scorn the lack of prowess of the French soldiers in William Shakespeare's play *Henry V.*

Britannicus Claudius's son, whose proud refusal to flee incognito to Britain, as Claudius suggests, costs him his life in Robert Graves's *Claudius, the God and His Wife Messalina.*

Britannicus Teenage son of the dead emperor Claudius and Néron's stepbrother; naive, credulous, and blinded by love and youth, gets caught up in a power struggle between Néron and Agrippine and is ruthlessly poisoned at a banquet of fraternal reconciliation in Jean Racine's play *Britannicus.*

Britling, Edith Scientific wife of Mr. Britling; she offsets her husband's Hellenistic qualities, yet cannot relate to him on an emotionally intimate level in H. G. Wells's *Mr. Britling Sees It Through.*

Britling, Hugh Bumbling but distinguished philosopher and writer, who questions the Hellenistic attitudes of England in the face of German threat; he views his home, Dower House, as a pampered microcosm of England; he attempts to justify and later condemns the war through his writing; he discovers God and a mutuality with Germany through his son's death in H. G. Wells's *Mr. Britling Sees It Through.*

Britling, Hugh (the younger) Oldest Britling son by a previous marriage; his plans to study science at Oxford are interrupted by World War I; he lies about his age and joins the war at seventeen; his letters home inspire pride and anxiety before he is killed in the trenches in H. G. Wells's *Mr. Britling Sees It Through.*

Britling, Sunny Jim One of two minor Britling sons; he reads American comics and, like his brother, lives the war through toy soldiers in H. G. Wells's *Mr. Britling Sees It Through.*

Briton, Jules Friend of Conder and lover of Kay Rimmer; he thinks anxiously about trying to help Jim Drover, receives a small inheritance from his father, and decides to propose to Kay, taking her for a country outing in Graham Greene's *It's a Battlefield.*

Britt, Bill (Billy) Stepson of Helen and son of Paul Britt in Gail Godwin's *Evensong.*

Britt, Helen Stepmother of Bill Britt, widow of Paul Britt in Gail Godwin's *Evensong.*

Britt, Paul Husband of Helen Britt, father of Bill Britt; owned newspapers; dies of a heart attack in Gail Godwin's *Evensong.*

Brittain, Cora Surreptitious racial avenger emulated by her grandson Kevin Brittain in Hal Bennett's *Wait Until the Evening.*

Brittain, Dolores Adopted daughter of Grandpa Brittain and wife of Henry Robinson, who murders her as she gives birth to her lover's child in Hal Bennett's *Wait Until the Evening.*

Brittain, Kevin Son of Minnie and Percy Brittain; narrator of Hal Bennett's *Wait Until the Evening.*

Brittain, Minnie Wife of Percy Brittain and mother of eight; frees her family from the despotism of her father-in-law in Hal Bennett's *Wait Until the Evening.*

Brittain, Paul Son of Minnie and Percy Brittain; tricked into hanging himself by his brother Kevin Brittain in Hal Bennett's *Wait Until the Evening.*

Brittain, Percy Philandering husband of Minnie Brittain and father of eight; marked for death by his son Kevin Brittain in Hal Bennett's *Wait Until the Evening.*

Brittain, Shadrach (Grandpa, Mr. Brittain) Former slave and tyrannical owner of the farm on which his family works as sharecroppers; husband of Cora Brittain in Hal Bennett's *Wait Until the Evening.*

Britten, Mr. Employee of Henry Dalton; questions Bigger Thomas about the disappearance of Mary Dalton in Richard Wright's *Native Son.*

Brittle, Mr. Tea and china merchant to Lady Juliana Douglas after her return from Scotland to London; he is eager to relieve her of her new wealth in Susan Ferrier's *Marriage.*

Brittlereed, Mr. Skillful cricketeer who joins Jack Neverbend at the crease and helps the Britannula side beat the British in an epic struggle in Anthony Trollope's *The Fixed Period.*

Britton, Nan Faithful maid and confidante of Amber St. Clare in Kathleen Winsor's *Forever Amber.*

Brittson, Sergeant English borderer entrusted by Captain Stawarth Bolton with the care of Elspeth Glendinning and her home in Sir Walter Scott's *The Monastery.*

Brixham, Mrs. Major Pendennis's landlady, who is cheated by his valet Morgan in William Makepeace Thackeray's *The History of Pendennis.*

Brixton, Lady Adele American cousin of Agnes Sandeman; she becomes the first of many "Luciaphiles", a group of London elite who are captivated by Lucia Lucas's social maneuvers in E. F. Benson's *Lucia in London.* She purchases Lucia's house in Riseholme in *Mapp and Lucia.*

Broad, John Minister of Tanner's Lane Chapel in the village of Cowfold in 1840, who rules his community with his hypocritical opinions; he is paralyzed when he tries to eject George and Isaac Allen from the chapel in Mark Rutherford's *The Revolution in Tanner's Lane.*

Broad, Mrs. Wife of the Reverend Broad; she is socially ambitious for her children in Mark Rutherford's *The Revolution in Tanner's Lane.*

Broad, Priscilla The Reverend and Mrs. Broad's daughter, aged seventeen in 1840, who marries George Allen despite her parents' opposition in Mark Rutherford's *The Revolution in Tanner's Lane.*

Broad, Thomas The Reverend and Mrs. Broad's eldest child, aged eighteen in 1840, who is sent to London to remove him from Fanny Allen, and who attempts to seduce Marie Pauline Coleman in Mark Rutherford's *The Revolution in Tanner's Lane.*

Broad, Tryphosa Youngest child of the Reverend and Mrs. Broad in Mark Rutherford's *The Revolution in Tanner's Lane.*

Broadbent, Donald R. Inept counsel for the State Senate Standing Committee on Education, Welfare, and Public

Morality investigating the propriety of an attempt to purchase a brilliant child in John Hersey's *The Child Buyer.*

Broadbent, Dr. Kind man and an eloquent speaker at a Bible Society meeting in Charlotte Brontë's *Shirley.*

Broadbury, Colonel Gentleman who meets Richard Hannay in the Highlands of Scotland where Hannay is again on the run; after checking Hannay's credentials, he takes Hannay home for a civilized twenty-four hours in the company of Broadbury's son, Ted, maimed in the war, in John Buchan's *Mr. Standfast.*

Broaden, Thomas Prosperous, college-educated mulatto banker who promotes high culture in the upper echelon of the black community in DuBose Heyward's *Mamba's Daughters.*

Broadfoot, Bailie Alderman of Leith, Scotland, and town guide to Archibald Douglas and his niece and foster daughter, Mary Douglas, on her trip to be reunited with her mother in Susan Ferrier's *Marriage.*

Broadhurst, Miss Intelligent, sensible English heiress and friend to Grace Nugent; she is intended as a wife for Lord Colambre but marries Mr. Berryl instead in Maria Edgeworth's *The Absentee.*

Brobdingnag, King of Enlightened monarch, who questions his guest and plaything, Lemuel Gulliver, about English institutions in Jonathan Swift's *Travels into Several Remote Nations of the World. In Four Parts. By Lemuel Gulliver.*

Broc, Marie Imbecile pupil at Mme. Beck's school, a cretin who is looked after during the long summer vacation by Lucy Snowe and partially personifies her own mental state in Charlotte Brontë's *Villette.*

Brochio, Signor Italian mercenary hired by Montoni; he tries to seduce Emily St. Aubert in Ann Radcliffe's *The Mysteries of Udolpho.*

Brock, Decimus Somerset rector who takes as pupil Allan Armadale and witnesses the strange friendship between Allan and Ozias Midwinter in Wilkie Collins's *Armadale.*

Brock, Dorothy (Dotty) American Red Cross worker in Luxembourg and lover of Lieutenant Colonel John Dawson Smithers in Martha Gellhorn's *Wine of Astonishment.*

Brock, Lord Prime Minister succeeded by Lord de Terrier in Anthony Trollope's *Framley Parsonage.* He is the illustrious leader of the Liberal party in *Can You Forgive Her?* Mrs. Finn recalls him as a model statesman in *The Prime Minister.*

Brock, Mr. Effete weekend guest of Margy Stuart; he thinks Georgie Smithers a "fantastic frump" in Richard Aldington's *The Colonel's Daughter.*

Brockie, Mrs. Widow who runs an inn whose name attracts Dickson McCunn on the first stage of his journey in John Buchan's *Huntingtower.*

Brocklehurst, Augusta Mr. Brocklehurst's second daughter, who amazes the pupils of Lowood School with the finery of her clothes in Charlotte Brontë's *Jane Eyre.*

Brocklehurst, Broughton Mr. Brocklehurst's youngest child, whose piety is amply rewarded with treats in Charlotte Brontë's *Jane Eyre.*

Brocklehurst, Miss Mr. Brocklehurst's eldest daughter, whose elegant dress contrasts sharply with the homespun smocks of the pupils at Lowood School in Charlotte Brontë's *Jane Eyre.*

Brocklehurst, Mrs. Mr. Brocklehurst's nosy wife, who comes to inspect Lowood School in her best lace and linen in Charlotte Brontë's *Jane Eyre.*

Brocklehurst, Naomi Mr. Brocklehurst's mother, whose memory is commemorated in a stone inscription over the door of Lowood School in Charlotte Brontë's *Jane Eyre.*

Brocklehurst, Robert Humorless clergyman and treasurer of Lowood School, a semi-charity institution which, in the name of humility and fortitude, he controls in a severely parsimonious fashion in Charlotte Brontë's *Jane Eyre.*

Brocklehurst, Theodore Mr. Brocklehurst's third child in Charlotte Brontë's *Jane Eyre.*

Brockway, Lucius Supervisor at Liberty Paints in Ralph Ellison's *Invisible Man.*

Brod (covernames: Ivlov, Lapin) Moscow Centre operative; during an adulterous affair with Moscow Centre agent Irma, he revealed to her the existence of Karla's double agent Gerald; he is executed with Irma for his betrayal in John le Carré's *Tinker, Tailor, Soldier, Spy.*

Broder, Andrew Forty-something journalist and author from Florida who moves to Boulder, Colorado, to be closer to his young daughter, Sara; published one book as a cathartic measure after the death of his son in a car accident; is the ex-husband of Francine "B. B." Brady Broder; develops a deep relationship with Margo Sampson in Judy Blume's *Smart Women.*

Broder, Francine "B. B." Brady Successful forty-something realtor in Boulder, Colorado; has one daughter, Sara; marries an older lover on a whim; blames ex-husband for the death of their son, has a mental breakdown in Judy Blume's *Smart Women.*

Broder, Herman Member of a well-to-do Polish family who survived World War II by hiding in a hayloft after hearing that the Nazis had killed his wife and children; later marries the servant who hid him and immigrates to America, where he poses as a traveling book salesman in order to have time to spend with his mistress and serve as a ghostwriter for a successful rabbi in Isaac Bashevis Singer's *Enemies, A Love Story.*

Broder, Sara Eleven-year-old daughter of Francine "B. B." Brady Broder and Andrew Broder in Judy Blume's *Smart Women.*

Broder, Tamara Luria Polish upper-class activist and first wife of Herman Broder; shot and left to die by Nazis but survives her wounds and, subsequently, Russian work camps; learns after the war that her husband is alive and follows him to New York in Isaac Bashevis Singer's *Enemies, A Love Story.*

Broder, Yadwiga Pracz Polish Catholic; former servant and later wife of Herman Broder; immigrates with him to America, where she gives birth to a daughter named after his mistress in Isaac Bashevis Singer's *Enemies, A Love Story.*

Brodeshaw, Colonel Wealthy Tory Member of Parliament who appears sympathetic to Anton Hesse's desire to become a citizen in Doris Lessing's *A Proper Marriage* and in *Landlocked.*

Brodhag, Mrs. Devoted housekeeper of Don and Carol Wanderhope in Peter De Vries's *The Blood of the Lamb.*

Brodie Tattooed bomber and anorexic teenage girl in Paul Theroux's *The Family Arsenal.*

Brodie, Bennett Medical student and fiancé of Sarah Henderson in Dorothy Richardson's *Backwater.* He marries Sarah and provides a home for his bankrupt father-in-law in *Honeycomb.*

Brodie, Ian Officious and censorious doctor, brother-in-law of January Marlowe, and sometime double for Robinson in Muriel Spark's *Robinson.*

Brodie, Jean Charismatic, unorthodox teacher at the Marcia Blame School in Edinburgh; she manipulates the girls who form "the Brodie set" to fulfill her political and sexual fantasies until one of her girls is moved to betray her in Muriel Spark's *The Prime of Miss Jean Brodie.*

Brodie, Marian Miriam Henderson's young niece in Dorothy Richardson's *March Moonlight.*

Brodie, Valentine Professor of literature in twenty-first-century North America and a writer of science fiction; he is the philandering, shallow, and self-absorbed but charming husband of Vanessa Frame Brodie in Anthony Burgess's *The End of the World News.*

Brodie, Vanessa Frame Brilliant, beautiful, unemotional scientist, daughter of Hubert Frame; she is one of the top theoretical physicists of her time; she remains inexplicably in love with Valentine Brodie even after divorcing him in Anthony Burgess's *The End of the World News.*

Brodie, William Miriam Henderson's nephew, Marian Brodie's brother, in Dorothy Richardson's *March Moonlight.*

Brodribb Middle-aged secretary of the dock workers' union who encourages Chester Nimmo to start a farm laborers' union in Joyce Cary's *Except the Lord.*

Brodrick, Isabel Favorite niece of Indefer Jones, who leaves his estate to her in the last of several wills; the will being lost, his nephew Henry Jones inherits; she refuses to marry Henry, but at last the missing will establishes her as rightful heir, and she marries her true love, William Owen, in Anthony Trollope's *Cousin Henry.*

Brodrick, Mrs. Stepmother of Isabel Brodrick; caught up in caring for her own large family, she is anxious to see Isabel married and well out of sight in Anthony Trollope's *Cousin Henry.*

Brodsky, Dr. Social scientist and the developer of a method of criminal reform using behavioral conditioning; superficially friendly and possibly well-meaning, he is also coldly scientific and is able to deal ruthlessly with Alex to prove his theory in Anthony Burgess's *A Clockwork Orange.*

Brody, Ellen Wife of Martin Brody; unsympathetic toward her husband's concerns about the Great White Shark;

becomes so bored that she has an affair with Matt Hooper in Peter Benchley's *Jaws.*

Brody, Martin Chief of police in Amity determined to protect people from the Great White Shark; sole survivor of the attempt to hunt the shark in Peter Benchley's *Jaws.*

Brodzinski, Michael Polish scientist who serves on the advisory committee for nuclear weapons; he opposes Roger Quaife's policy on disarmament and impugns the loyalty of scientists and civil servants in C. P. Snow's *Corridors of Power.*

Brogley, Mr. Bill-broker and owner of a second-hand furniture shop; creditor to Solomon Gills, he is about to execute on the overdue debt but is forestalled by Paul Dombey's payment of the bill in Charles Dickens's *Dombey and Son.*

Broke, Sally Snobbish young society woman in Winston Churchill's *Coniston.*

Broken-girth-flow, Laird of Jacobite who complains that the Union has ruined Scottish agriculture, though his is a barren district, in Sir Walter Scott's *The Black Dwarf.*

Bromberg, Austin (Irwin Swenson) Erudite essayist and owner of an impressive private library; host of Leo Percepied in Jack Kerouac's *The Subterraneans;* mentioned in *Book of Dreams.*

Bromden, Chief Broom (Big Chief) Large, half Native American inmate of a mental hospital who hallucinates and pretends to be deaf and mute before Randle McMurphy restores his self-confidence; narrator of Ken Kesey's *One Flew Over the Cuckoo's Nest.*

Brome Crazed woman who is after Chester Nimmo for supposedly causing her son's death by not exempting him from war service; after numerous incidents she is committed to an asylum in Joyce Cary's *Not Honour More.*

Bromley Surviving member of the crew of the jolly boat in C. S. Forester's *Mr. Midshipman Hornblower.*

Bromley, Mr. Burly, kindly medical student, who tends to Alton Locke, paying for a bed for him when Alton collapses after having been thrown out of his mother's house in Charles Kingsley's *Alton Locke.*

Bron, Scevola Bloodthirsty sans-culotte farmer who forces Arlette to participate in the Terror and is killed with Peyrol carrying the false papers to the British blockaders in Joseph Conrad's *The Rover.*

Bronk, Louie Convicted murderer on death row in Texas; admits guilt before being executed, though the validity of the admission is called into question in Mary Willis Walker's *The Red Scream.*

Bronowsky, Dmitri White-Russian emigre who serves as secretary to the Nawab of Mirat, Sir Ahmed Bahadur, a local prince; Bronowsky's network of informants and his participation or connection with events make him an informed commentator in Paul Scott's *The Jewel in the Crown,* in *The Day of the Scorpion,* in *The Towers of Silence,* and in *A Division of the Spoils.*

Bronski, Charlie Young Los Angeles vice detective in the Red Scalotta case in Joseph Wambaugh's *The Blue Knight.*

Bronski, Deborah Androfski Sister of Andrei Androfski, wife of Paul Bronski, and lover of Christopher de Monti; becomes active in the Warsaw ghetto resistance in Leon Uris's *Mila 18.*

Bronski, Jan Cousin and lover of Oskar's mother and possible father of Oskar; Polish national whom the Nazis execute as a suspected member of the resistance in Günter Grass's *The Tin Drum.*

Bronski, Paul Husband of Deborah Bronski; heads the Jewish Civil Authority for Warsaw after the Nazi occupation; commits suicide in Leon Uris's *Mila 18.*

Bronski, Rachael Daughter of Paul and Deborah Bronski and lover of Wolf Brandel; resistance fighter in the Warsaw ghetto in Leon Uris's *Mila 18.*

Bronson, George H. Newly elected prosecuting attorney who sees the trial of Ralph Hartsook as an opportunity to distinguish himself in Edward Eggleston's *The Hoosier School-Master.*

Bronstein, Lev Davidovich (Leon Trotsky) Russian-Jewish politician, one of the intellectual leaders of the Bolshevik wing of the Russian Communist party in the early twentieth century; he seems uncharacteristically frivolous in Anthony Burgess's *The End of the World News.*

Bronzebeard Faithful colonel of the guards; he helps the king defeat the King of Borsagrass in George MacDonald's *The Princess and Curdie.*

Bronzini, Albert Retired science teacher and chess tutor living in a decaying neighborhood in New York City; formerly married to Klara Sax; perceives every loss as an echo of

Klara's departure; dies himself in the summer of 1992 in Don DeLillo's *Underworld.*

Brood, Mackey Friend and lover of Jack Curran; gives birth to a son nine months after her last night with Curran before his death in Mark Steadman's *A Lion's Share.*

Brook, Rhoda Milkmaid and mother of Farmer Lodge's son; believes that her actions in a dream cause the disfigurement of Gertrude Lodge's arm; introduces Gertrude to Conjuror Trendle in Thomas Hardy's "The Withered Arm."

Brooke, Arthur Old uncle of Celia and Dorothea Brooke; he is a typical English squire and the owner of Tipton Grange; he invites Will Ladislaw to visit Lowick without consulting Dorothea and asks Will to remain in the area to help with his unsuccessful campaign for Parliament in George Eliot's *Middlemarch.*

Brooke, Celia (Kitty) Pretty younger sister of Dorothea; she does not understand her sister's intellect or effort to help the poor; after she marries Sir James Chettam and they have a son, Celia is totally enraptured by her child in George Eliot's *Middlemarch.*

Brooke, Daisy (Posy, Mrs. Shakespeare Smith) Twin sister of Demijohn Brooke in Louisa May Alcott's *Little Women;* also appears in *Little Men.*

Brooke, Dorothea (Dodo) Intelligent, idealistic heroine bent on improving the lives of those in need, originally through the construction of cottages for the poor; she marries Edward Casaubon, a much older man who she mistakingly assumes will teach her about his studies in classical learning; after Casaubon's death, she marries his cousin, Will Ladislaw, a man closer to her own age and temperament in George Eliot's *Middlemarch.*

Brooke, John (Demi, Demijohn) Twin brother of Daisy Brooke and son of Meg and John Brooke in Louisa May Alcott's *Little Women;* also appears in *Little Men.*

Brooke, John Sensible tutor of Theodore Laurence; marries Meg March in Louisa May Alcott's *Little Women;* also appears in *Little Men.*

Brooke, Lisa Seventy-three-year-old woman of wealth, viciousness, and legendary promiscuity; after her death, her estate prompts discord and discovery among her aged relatives, housekeeper, and old lovers in Muriel Spark's *Memento Mori.*

Brooke, Lord Friend of Sir Philip Sidney; he delivers letters from Lord Leicester to Matilda in Sophia Lee's *The Recess.*

Brooke, Margaret March See March, Margaret.

Brooke, Miss Daughter of the dissenting former Birmingham baker; she marries Captain James, to the distress of Lady Ludlow in Elizabeth Gaskell's *My Lady Ludlow.*

Brooke, Mr. Dissenter and a Birmingham baker, who buys a neighboring estate where he builds "Yeast House"; his religion is more distressing than his former trade to Lady Ludlow in Elizabeth Gaskell's *My Lady Ludlow.*

Brooke, Sir James English officer stationed in Ireland; he befriends Lord Colambre and warns him to stay away from the conniving Lady Dashfort and her daughter Lady Isabella in Maria Edgeworth's *The Absentee.*

Brookenham, Fernanda (Nanda) Daughter of Mrs. Brookenham; loves Van Vanderbank; lives in London with her godfather, Mr. Longdon, in Henry James's *The Awkward Age.*

Brookenham, Mrs. Edward (Mrs. Brook) Daughter of Lady Julia and leader of a social group; ambitious mother of Nanda Brookenham in Henry James's *The Awkward Age.*

Brooker Formerly a clerk to Ralph Nickleby; he acts as Smike's father in order to have the boy confined at Squeers's Dotheboys Hall and out of Ralph's life; Brooker's evidence helps prove that Smike is Nickleby's illegitimate son when Nickleby will not help him financially in Charles Dickens's *The Life and Adventures of Nicholas Nickleby.*

Brookes, Aunt Hester Spinster sister of James Brookes; she counsels his daughters with religious advice in George Moore's *Spring Days.*

Brookes, Grace Eldest daughter of James Brookes, whose disapproval of her young officer drives her to marry their wealthy neighbor Mr. Berkins; she entertains for her sister in George Moore's *Spring Days.*

Brookes, James Wealthy, self-pitying widower, who worries about his three marriageable daughters but has not cultivated society; he objects to "villa" commoners' associating with his daughters; he is unable to keep money from dominating their marriage arrangements; he finally sells his house to keep his daughters from becoming subjects of scandal in George Moore's *Spring Days.*

Brookes, Maggie James Brookes's youngest daughter, who falls in love with Frank Escott, among others; her jealousy of Frank's model and her father's awkward insistence on marriage settlements with Lord Mount Rorke derail the marriage plans in George Moore's *Spring Days.*

Brookes, Mary Wife and former mistress of Willy Brookes; she has a crippled child, not Willy's, who charms Frank Escott in George Moore's *Spring Days.*

Brookes, Sally Brookes James Brookes's second daughter, a headstrong flirt who likes Jimmy Measons, one of the "villa" persons her father dislikes in George Moore's *Spring Days.*

Brookes, Willy James Brookes's only son, who is too methodical to work with his father; he fails in several businesses; he considers himself unlucky but has a happy secret marriage with his former mistress; he is a school friend and confidant of Frank Escott in George Moore's *Spring Days.*

Brooklyn, Reggie Young friend of Eleanor Burgoyne and Edward Manisty; he is fondly protective of Eleanor's well-being in Mrs. Humphry Ward's *Eleanor.*

Brooks, Beatrice Heroine, who loves Montague Treherne when she is still a child and later marries him in a secret ceremony because his inheritance hinges on secrecy; she is unaware that the ceremony is also a mock one; Treherne leaves her pregnant and alone; she works to support herself and her child, who dies at the age of two; she returns to success and marries a rich marquis in Caroline Norton's *Lost and Saved.*

Brooks, Captain Father of Beatrice and Owen Brooks and guardian of Mariana, the daughter of his wife, Leonora Aldi; a good, kind man, he keeps up a happy home for the children after his wife dies; he rejects Beatrice when he thinks she has married without his permission in Caroline Norton's *Lost and Saved.*

Brooks, Mr. Pieman who used cats in sausages in an anecdote by Sam Weller in Charles Dickens's *The Posthumous Papers of the Pickwick Club.*

Brooks, Mr. Rag-and-bottle merchant in the last stages of dropsy, who is fearful of death and a tenant of Mrs. Jupp; Ernest Pontifex, as clergyman, attempts to help him in Samuel Butler's *The Way of All Flesh.*

Brooks, Mrs. Bedfordshire neighbor whose sneers and innuendos become pleasantries once Pamela Andrews is raised by marriage from the servant class in Samuel Richardson's *Pamela, or Virtue Rewarded.*

Brooks, Mrs. (Tacchi) Forty-year-old widow with no children, who becomes Giacomo Tacchi's second wife in Mark Rutherford's *Miriam's Schooling.*

Brooks, Owen Brother of Beatrice and son of Captain Brooks; he joins the navy; he loves and helps his sister in Caroline Norton's *Lost and Saved.*

Brooks, Pierce R. (P. R.) Los Angeles homicide detective sergeant; investigating officer in the death of Ian Campbell in Joseph Wambaugh's *The Onion Field.*

Broom, Florence One of a pair of sisters who are day-pupils at Wordsworth House, the school in north London where Miriam Henderson teaches in Dorothy Richardson's *Backwater.* They make friendly overtures to Miriam and continue to invite her to their comfortable home for restorative weekends in *Interim* and in *The Trap.* Miriam goes to the Broom sisters from her Swiss holiday before returning to her job in the dental surgery in *Dawn's Left Hand.* Miriam travels on holiday with them to Sussex in *Dimple Hill.*

Broom, Grace Florence Broom's sister in Dorothy Richardson's *Backwater,* in *Interim,* in *The Trap,* in *Dawn's Left Hand,* and in *Dimple Hill.*

Brophy, J. Jerome (Jerry) District attorney who offers to dismiss a rape charge against Ralph Detweiler if Arthur Winner will support his quest for a judgeship in James Gould Cozzens's *By Love Possessed.*

Broscomin Ruler of a small principality who wants to be king of Ginsky; he is unorthodox and sleazy in Eliza Haywood's *Adventures of Eovaai, Princess of Ijaveo.*

Brosnan, Father Firebrand sympathizer with the tenantry in Galway involved in struggles with the landlords; he makes Florian Jones swear not to tell his father what he knows of the conspirators in Anthony Trollope's *The Landleaguers.*

Brother Narrates physical and symbolic displacement from ancestral home, recounting the Nazi invasion and occupation of France in Julio Cortázar's "House Taken Over."

Brother, "A Spinster's Tale" Older brother of the child narrator, Elizabeth; his drinking, like her father's, frightens Elizabeth in Peter Taylor's "A Spinster's Tale."

Brother Bethune Baptist minister at the Beecham family reunion in Eudora Welty's *Losing Battles.*

Brother Bolo Priest who smuggles religious artifacts out of Castiglione; friend of Dolce, with whom he made a hair shirt out of rat skins for Arsella's mother, in John Hawkes's *The Goose on the Grave.*

Brotherhood, Jack (covername: Marlow) Senior British Intelligence officer; he recruits young Magnus Pym, grooms him for high honors in the "Firm", and becomes one of the two father figures Magnus betrays in John le Carré's *A Perfect Spy.*

Brothers (Two) Knights who, with Adonos, overthrow the giants tyrannizing their father's kingdom; they teach Anodos brotherhood and courage in George Macdonald's *Phantasies.*

Brothers, Jeremy Rich host of the annual posh pool party attended by Ralph Chang and his family; inebriated and foolish, he insults Mr. Chang by assuming that he is a servant; finds that his apologies are not accepted in Gish Jen's "In the American Society."

Brotherton, Bishop of Mild and urbane bishop greatly perplexed by the wild stories circulating about the dean, Henry Lovelace; he is especially bewildered when the dean throws the Marquis of Brotherton into a fireplace in Anthony Trollope's *Is He Popenjoy?*

Brotherton, Dowager Marchioness of Ill-tempered defender of her long-absent, malicious eldest son against the claims of her five dutiful children in Anthony Trollope's *Is He Popenjoy?*

Brotherton, Marchioness of Aging Italian widow who speaks no English; the date of her marriage to the marquis is the object of speculation and investigation in Anthony Trollope's *Is He Popenjoy?*

Brotherton, Marquis of, Frederick Augustus Idle and self-indulgent landowner, who returns from Europe with an Italian widow he claims is his wife and a son and heir, Lord Popenjoy; he summarily evicts his brother, Lord George Germain, from the family estate, Manor Cross; the eventual deaths of the child and of the marquis enable Lord George and his own child to succeed to the titles and estate in Anthony Trollope's *Is He Popenjoy?*

Broud Brutal, brutish youth groomed to be leader of Neanderthal Clan; obsessively vengeful leader who puts his petty dreams of revenge before the interests of the Clan and whose banishment of Ayla devastates the Clan; father of Ayla's son; son of Brun in Jean M. Auel's *The Clan of the Cave Bear.*

Brough, Belinda Affected daughter of John Brough in William Makepeace Thackeray's *The History of Samuel Titmarsh and the Great Hoggarty Diamond.*

Brough, Isabella Blindly devoted wife of John Brough in William Makepeace Thackeray's *The History of Samuel Titmarsh and the Great Hoggarty Diamond.*

Brough, John Head of the Independent West Diddlesex Fire and Life Insurance Co.; reputedly of vast wealth, he is a swindler who decamps, leaving his dupe Samuel Titmarsh to answer for the collapse of the association in William Makepeace Thackeray's *The History of Samuel Titmarsh and the Great Hoggarty Diamond.*

Brough, Mr. Barrister who represents Sir Gerald Corven in his divorce suit in John Galsworthy's *Over the River.*

Broughton, Dobbs Unsavory partner of Augustus Musselboro and Mrs. Van Siever in a moneylending business; he kills himself after bankruptcy in Anthony Trollope's *The Last Chronicle of Barset.*

Broughton, Maria Wife of the shady stockbroker Dobbs Broughton, after whose death she marries his partner, Augustus Musselboro, in Anthony Trollope's *The Last Chronicle of Barset.*

Broum, Paul Louis ("Johnnie Vulkan", "King", "Mr. Angle") Prague-born, half-Jewish agricultural biologist who served as a wartime interpreter for Britain; believed killed at Treblinka, he escaped by impersonating the concentration-camp guard John August Vulkan; as Vulkan he works as Dawlish's Berlin contact and occasional operative; he tries unsuccessfully to collect £250,000 of the Broum family securities by obtaining his true identification from British intelligence and an endorsed claim from the Israeli government; he accidentally dies in a fight with the narrator in Len Deighton's *Funeral in Berlin.*

Broun, Jessie Mother of the bastard child of the Master (James Durie); she stones Henry Durie for betraying the Master; she is supported by a pension delivered on Henry's authority in Robert Louis Stevenson's *The Master of Ballantrae: A Winter's Tale.*

Broune, Nicholas Influential newspaper editor, who assists the literary career of Lady Carbury; although he recognizes her faults of character and fears her profligate son, he becomes fascinated and proposes marriage; her generous refusal cements the friendship and leads later to a marriage of mutual affection in Anthony Trollope's *The Way We Live Now.* The Brounes appear briefly as guests it Gatherum Castle in *The Prime Minister.*

Brovik, Knut Architect employed by Halvard Solness, the Norwegian master builder; once a successful, independent architect, but now works under Solness's crushing business tactics in Henrik Ibsen's *The Master Builder.*

Brovik, Ragnar Son of the architect Knut Brovik and now employed as a draftsman by Halvard Solness, the ruthless master builder; engaged to Kaia Fosli, Solness's bookkeeper, in Henrik Ibsen's *The Master Builder.*

Browborough, Mr. Tory Member for Tankerville for three Parliaments, unseated by Phineas Finn and later tried for bribery in Anthony Trollope's *Phineas Redux.*

Browder, Bo Childhood acquaintance of Thomas Eborn; policeman who investigates the break-in at the house of Louise Eborn in Reynolds Price's *Love and Work.*

Browdie, John Miller from Yorkshire who marries Matilda Price and who helps Nicholas Nickleby break up Dotheboys Hall school run by Wackford Squeers in Charles Dickens's *The Life and Adventures of Nicholas Nickleby.*

Brower Insurance adjuster and roommate of George Ogden in Henry Blake Fuller's *The Cliff-Dwellers.*

Brower, Theodore Settlement house resident who courts Jane Marshall in Henry Blake Fuller's *With the Procession.*

Brown Burly, vulgar, lower-class coxswain, who eventually shows his more reserved, compassionate side in his service to Horatio Hornblower and William Bush in C. S. Forester's *The Happy Return,* in *Ship of the Line,* and in *Flying Colours.* He is the intelligent, resourceful, masterful coxswain and companion who anticipates and fulfills Hornblower's needs in *Commodore Hornblower* and in *Lord Hornblower.*

Brown Narrator, owner of the Trianon, a hotel above Port-au-Prince, and a lapsed Catholic who distrusts everyone and is committed to no one and nothing; he is the lover of Martha Pineda, an ambassador's wife; he befriends Major Jones and helps him to join Haitian rebels; he becomes an undertaker in Santo Domingo in Graham Greene's *The Comedians.*

Brown One of the female servants of the Murrays of Horton Lodge in Anne Brontë's *Agnes Grey.*

Brown One of three English road laborers mistaken by John Lavender for German prisoners of war in John Galsworthy's *The Burning Spear: Being the Experiences of Mr. John Lavender in Time of War.*

Brown, Abe Rich, self-driven businessman, who loves his daughter, Susan; he makes family and business decisions with brutal force in John Braine's *Room at the Top.* He rules his employees according to his ideas and disregards other opinions in *Life at the Top.*

Brown, Andy Radio character jailed for robbing Amos's place; freed from jail by Minnie Yellings in Ishmael Reed's *The Last Days of Louisiana Red.*

Brown, Annie McGairy Eighteen-year-old bride of Carl Brown; budding writer and heroine of Betty Smith's *Joy in the Morning.*

Brown, Arthur Fellow of the Cambridge college; a Junior Tutor, he helps organize support for the election of Roy Calvert to his college; he informs Lewis Eliot that Calvert is killed in C. P. Snow's *The Light and the Dark.* He helps Chrystal woo an endowment from Sir Horace Timberlake, refuses to stand as a compromise candidate for new Master, and supports Paul Jago to the very end in *The Masters.* He casts the deciding vote for reinstatement of Howard's fellowship in *The Affair.* He delivers the eulogy for Sir Francis Getliffe in *Last Things.*

Brown, Benson Light-skinned black man attracted to Emma Lou Morgan; eventually marries Gwendolyn Johnson in Wallace Thurman's *The Blacker the Berry.*

Brown, Berenice Sadie Black cook and confidante of Frankie Addams in Carson McCullers's *The Member of the Wedding.*

Brown, Betty See Swain, Eliza Mellon.

Brown, Biglow (Papa Biglow) Magnificent ginger-colored giant and rival of Augie for the affection of Della Green in Arna Wendell Bontemps's *God Sends Sunday.*

Brown, Bobby See Swain, Wilbur Rockefeller Daffodil-11.

Brown, Bo-Jo Harvard football hero and classmate of Harry Pulham; organizes their twenty-fifth class reunion in John P. Marquand's *H. M. Pulham, Esquire.*

Brown, Bubber Comical friend of Jinx Jenkins in Rudolph Fisher's *The Walls of Jericho* and *The Conjure-Man Dies.*

Brown, Buddy Rival of Tom More; doctor who defends the use of euthanasia with the elderly in Walker Percy's *Love in the Ruins.*

Brown, Bunny Harlem friend of Max Disher; becomes white through the Black-No-More process and helps Disher run the Knights of Nordia in George S. Schuyler's *Black No More.*

Brown, Captain Retired officer, whose honest and generous spirit despite his lack of means overcomes the Cranford prejudice toward men; he dies saving a young girl from a train and is mourned by all in Elizabeth Gaskell's *Cranford.*

Brown, Carl (Carlton Braun) Struggling law student at a midwestern university in 1927; husband of Annie McGairy Brown in Betty Smith's *Joy in the Morning.*

Brown, Charles Beloved of Mary Conant banished from New England because he is an Episcopalian; returns to wed Conant and adopt her half-Indian son in Lydia Maria Child's *Hobomok.*

Brown, Cicely Ian Bedloe's high school girlfriend; refuses to marry Ian and moves to California in Anne Tyler's *Saint Maybe.*

Brown, Corporal Union soldier who befriends the black child Ticey and renames her Jane in Ernest J. Gaines's *The Autobiography of Miss Jane Pittman.*

Brown, Cyril Marine killed on Saipan in Leon Uris's *Battle Cry.*

Brown, Dan Loving husband of Laura Brown, father of Richie; World War II veteran in Michael Cunningham's *The Hours.*

Brown, Dick Humpbacked, cheerful boy in Louisa May Alcott's *Little Men.*

Brown, Dick Second-rate commercial artist; married man and first lover of Dorothy Renfrew in Mary McCarthy's *The Group.*

Brown, Dr. Exemplary ex-carpenter, who rises above his proletarian beginnings to become a rich and respected Cambridge man, mentioned by Dean Winnstay in Charles Kingsley's *Alton Locke.*

Brown, Eileen Twenty-two-year-old only daughter of Kate and Michael Brown; she accompanies her father to Boston for the summer and is attempting to decide if she will want her mother's life style for herself, or if she will become radically different in Doris Lessing's *The Summer Before the Dark.*

Brown, Esther See Braithwaite, Esther Brown.

Brown, Fats Bartender at the Grove in Richard Wright's *The Long Dream.*

Brown, Fran College friend of Renay Davis and babysitter for Denise Davis in Ann Allen Shockley's *Loving Her.*

Brown, Frederick (Steely) Ten-year-old son of Paul and Mae Brown; reader sees ghetto life from his viewpoint in Julian Mayfield's *The Long Night.*

Brown, Gentleman Rapacious pirate who raids Patusan and, while fleeing, murders Dam Warns in retribution for Jim's resistance in Joseph Conrad's *Lord Jim.*

Brown, George, Sheriff of Calstoun One of the four Scottish counsels to James Stewart; he is doubtful of the advantages of David Balfour's testifying in the Appin murder trial in Robert Louis Stevenson's *Catriona.*

Brown, Goody Envious villager, who was thrashing Molly Seagrim in the churchyard brawl when Tom Jones interceded in Henry Fielding's *The History of Tom Jones.*

Brown, Hattie Wife of Heck Brown, daughter of Ma Sigafoos, and client of Billy Bumpers in Peter De Vries's *I Hear America Swinging.*

Brown, Helen See Sterling, Angela.

Brown, Herkimer (Heck) Renegade farmer, husband of Hattie Brown, son-in-law of Ma Sigafoos, and client of Billy Bumpers in Peter De Vries's *I Hear America Swinging.*

Brown, Herman (Wimpy) Heroin addict and informer for Bumper Morgan in Joseph Wambaugh's *The Blue Knight.*

Brown, Hillman (Hilly) Accident-prone 10-year-old son of Bryant and Marie Brown and grandson of Everett (Ev) Hillman; makes younger brother David disappear; then slips into a coma in Stephen King's *The Tommyknockers.*

Brown, Honey Camden Foster brother of Berenice Sadie Brown; imprisoned for breaking into a drugstore in Carson McCullers's *The Member of the Wedding.*

Brown, Jackie Hard-bitten gun dealer who acts as middleman for those who sell guns and those who want them for illegal reasons in George V. Higgins's *The Friends of Eddie Coyle.*

Brown, Jake Longshoreman who returns to Harlem longing to embrace friends and familiar places; meets the girl of his dreams, Felice, his first night home, loses her the next day, therefore spending the rest of the novel trying to find his "little brown" in Claude McKay's *Home to Harlem;* expatriate returning to the United States from Marseilles in *Banjo.*

Brown, James British prime minister who is forced to resign as a consequence of his daughter's giving a party at No. 10 Downing Street in Evelyn Waugh's *Vile Bodies.*

Brown, James Second son of Michael and Kate Brown; he will begin at the university after a summer spent on an archaeological "dig" in the Sudan with his friends in Doris Lessing's *The Summer Before the Dark.*

Brown, Jane See Pittman, Miss Jane.

Brown, Jayhu (Jehu) Union man whose cough keeps him from being drafted into the Confederate army; assists Union prisoners of war who escape from Salisbury prison in Albion W. Tourgee's *A Fool's Errand.*

Brown, Jenny (Jane, Jenny Angel, Johanna Engel) American painter traveling with David Scott, with whom she has a tumultuous relationship in Katherine Anne Porter's *Ship of Fools.*

Brown, Jessie Younger daughter of Captain Brown; she marries her early love, Major Gordon, after the deaths of her father and elder sister in Elizabeth Gaskell's *Cranford.*

Brown, Joe See Burch, Lucas.

Brown, John Harmless, drunk Scottish *Flying Scud* sailor killed by Captain Joe Wicks; Mac assumes his identity in Robert Louis Stevenson's *The Wrecker.*

Brown, John Sturdy Berkshire squire and justice of the peace, who sends his son Tom to Rugby School to learn to become a Christian gentleman in Thomas Hughes's *Tom Brown's Schooldays.* He watches over his son's progress anxiously in *Tom Brown at Oxford.*

Brown, John Villager whose son, Charley, is injured by Lord Froth's coach and restored to health by Bryan Perdue, Patrick Mac Neale, Alexander Gordon, and Henry Fairman in Thomas Holcroft's *The Memoirs of Bryan Perdue.*

Brown, John Christian abolitionist devoted to freeing slaves and helping already freed blacks find work and learn to farm; fathers twenty children, only eight of whom reach adulthood; gets his family deeper into debt with each scheme to sell wool or buy land; hanged when he is captured at Harpers Ferry in Russell Banks's *Cloudsplitter.*

Brown, Johnny Sales executive under Andy Kagle in Joseph Heller's *Something Happened.*

Brown, Kate Ferreira Middle-aged, married woman—the nurturer to her four children, her husband, and her coworkers—who is alone for the first time since she can remember when her husband and children go their separate ways one summer; she begins a deep examination into her past life and her present self in Doris Lessing's *The Summer Before the Dark*

Brown, Kate's Grandfather Kindly, tyrannical man from Lourenço Marques with whom Kate Brown spent a year while a teenager learning Portuguese; expected Kate to grow up and become only a wife and mother in Doris Lessing's *The Summer Before the Dark.*

Brown, Laura Restless, discontented homemaker in 1949 Los Angeles who is reading *Mrs. Dalloway;* wife of Dan, mother of Richie; meets Clarissa Vaughan after her adult son Richard commits suicide in Michael Cunningham's *The Hours.*

Brown, Laurence Frail, hypersensitive tutor of Josephine and Eustace Leonides; he and Brenda Leonides are arrested for the murder of her husband in Agatha Christie's *Crooked House.*

Brown, Lieutenant Vanbest Smuggler who is involved in Francis Kennedy's murder and Henry Bertram's kidnapping and is killed in a smuggling raid; Henry is given his name by the kidnappers in Sir Walter Scott's *Guy Mannering.*

Brown, Mae Long-suffering wife of Paul Brown, by whom she is temporarily deserted, and mother of Steely Brown in Julian Mayfield's *The Long Night.*

Brown, Man of the Moors Legendary character, the sighting of whom is an omen of bad tidings; Hobbie (Halbert) Elliot and Patrick Earnscliff mistake Elshender (Sir Edward Mauley) for this character and return from hunting to find Hobbie's farm destroyed in Sir Walter Scott's *The Black Dwarf.*

Brown, Margaret Overcritical, socially busy wife of Abe and mother of Susan in John Braine's *Room at the Top* and in *Life at the Top.*

Brown, Mary Sickly elder daughter of Captain Brown; her care is the cheerfully borne burden of her father and sister in Elizabeth Gaskell's *Cranford.*

Brown, Maureen Sophomore at Haddan School who lights black candles on her windowsill and alarms her roommates with the wicked things she says in her sleep in Alice Hoffman's *The River King.*

Brown, Michael Kate Brown's wealthy husband, a neurologist, who has comfortable but increasingly uninvolved relationships with his wife and children; he has had numerous affairs and has grown apart from his wife in Doris Lessing's *The Summer Before the Dark.*

Brown, Mike Revolutionary War veteran; drunken farmer and blacksmith whose family deserts him in John Pendleton Kennedy's *Swallow Barn.*

Brown, Mr. Grave, elderly gentleman in Brussels, who finds William Crimsworth, with his letter of introduction from Hunsden, a teaching post at M. Pelet's school in Charlotte Brontë's *The Professor.*

Brown, Mr. London haberdasher who is the object of Polly Branghton's marital designs in Frances Burney's *Evelina.*

Brown, Mr. Master criminal and propagandist for peace during World War I in Agatha Christie's *The Secret Adversary.*

Brown, Mr. White missionary respected by the Ibo clan because he preaches against excessive zeal in Chinua Achebe's *Things Fall Apart.*

Brown, Mrs. London madam who hires the newly arrived innocent country girl Fanny Hill and lures her into prostitution in John Cleland's *Memoirs of a Woman of Pleasure.*

Brown, Mrs. Maid at Beech Park, the residence of Frederick, Lord Lindore and his sister, Lady Juliana Douglas, in Susan Ferrier's *Marriage.*

Brown, Nancy Old widow, afflicted with religious melancholy and nearly blind, living on the grounds of Horton Lodge; she is befriended by Agnes Grey in Anne Brontë's *Agnes Grey.*

Brown, Ned See Douglass, Edward Stephen.

Brown, Owen Third son of John Brown and an atheist; tells the story of his father's raid on Harpers Ferry in Virginia in 1859; responsible for Lyman Epp's death; escapes to the California mountains in Russell Banks's *Cloudsplitter.*

Brown, Parson Minister to whom Gregory Grooby entrusts the care of his illegitimate son, Gregory Glen, in Robert Bage's *Hermsprong.*

Brown, Paul Father of Steely Brown and husband of Mae Brown; defeated by ghetto life in Julian Mayfield's *The Long Night.*

Brown, Pinkie (The Boy) Seventeen-year-old, cold, frigid, amoral, calculating bookmakers' extortion-mob leader and killer of Charles Hale; haunted by his lower-class background and Roman Catholic upbringing, he seduces and marries Rose Wilson to keep her from identifying Spicer as posing as Charles Hale in Snow's restaurant; after Rose refuses to kill herself and the police come, he douses himself with vitriol and drowns himself in order to avoid police capture in Graham Greene's *Brighton Rock.*

Brown, Puggy Hypocritical, adulterous Benjamite preacher who marries Lucy Wilcher in Joyce Cary's *To Be a Pilgrim.*

Brown, Recktall Corrupt businessman who talks Wyatt Gwyon into forging paintings in William Gaddis's *The Recognitions.*

Brown, Richard (Richie) As a child, sensitive and adores his mother; as an adult, a talented poet and novelist; former lover of Clarissa Vaughan and Louis; dying of AIDS, he commits suicide before Clarissa's party in Michael Cunningham's *The Hours.*

Brown, Robert Tom Wilcher's nephew; he is a scientific farmer who wants to assume control of Tolbrook Manor; he marries Ann Wilcher but has an affair with Molly Panton in Joyce Cary's *Herself Surprised* and in *To Be a Pilgrim.*

Brown, Sergeant William (Willie) Misogynistic soldier in Norman Mailer's *The Naked and the Dead.*

Brown, Sheldon Los Angeles deputy district attorney; co-prosecutor in the second murder trial of Gregory Powell and Jimmy Smith in Joseph Wambaugh's *The Onion Field.*

Brown, Sir Ferdinando New governor of Britannula, an ex-British colony off New Zealand, who takes the reins of office from John Neverbend when the British navy combined with the local populace puts an end to Neverbend's compulsory euthanasia program for 68-year-olds in Anthony Trollope's *The Fixed Period.*

Brown, Sister Creepy neighbor of the Bray family; has a sickly, clever daughter in Maureen Howard's *Natural History.*

Brown, Stephen Oldest son of Kate and Michael Brown; he is in his last year at the university in Doris Lessing's *The Summer Before the Dark.*

Brown, Sue Diminutive, adorable chorus girl of resourcefulness and spirit; she is in love with Ronnie Fish in P. G. Wodehouse's *Fish Preferred* She appears in two other novels.

Brown, Susan Young, immature, beautiful, rich girl; although Joe Lampton does not love her, he woos her successfully to win her from her childhood sweetheart, Jack Wales, in John Braine's *Room at the Top.* She proves to be smarter and more passionate than her husband knew in *Life at the Top.*

Brown, Ted Working-class Englishman who had won scholarships to Oxford, and who was the only genuine socialist of Anna Wulf's group of friends in Mashopi in Doris Lessing's *The Golden Notebook*

Brown, Tiger Chief of police; old friend of Macheath, the notorious criminal, from the military and his unofficial protector; blackmailed by Jonathan Jeremiah Peachum, the leader of London's gang of thieves and beggars, into arresting Macheath in Bertolt Brecht's play *The Threepenny Opera.*

Brown, Tim Nineteen-year-old problem son of Kate and Michael Brown; he causes an emotional crisis in the family by shouting that his mother was suffocating him in Doris Lessing's *The Summer Before the Dark.*

Brown, Tom Eldest child of Squire Brown; he goes to Rugby School in the 1830s and becomes a scapegrace but reforms morally and spiritually under the influence of George Arthur and Doctor Arnold in Thomas Hughes's *Tom Brown's Schooldays.* He learns much about the problems of society while at St. Ambrose's College, Oxford, before marrying Mary Porter in *Tom Brown at Oxford.*

Brown, Tommy Young, highly sensitive and sincere member of the Communist Party whom the rest of the members, especially Andrew McGrew, watch out for and protect in Doris Lessing's *A Ripple from the Storm.*

Brown, William Young Englishman stationed in Martha Quest's town who leads her to want to become a communist, and who has an extended affair with her in Doris Lessing's *A Proper Marriage* and in *A Ripple from the Storm.*

Brown, Young Goodman Puritan who sets off on a nighttime journey into the dark woods despite the fervent pleas of his young wife, Faith; meets the devil; resists the attraction of evil until he sees pink ribbons, which are like the ribbons worn by Faith, and thereupon loses his faith; after either dreaming of or actually participating in a satanic baptism attended by many of the town's church elders, becomes a bitter, distrustful man in Nathaniel Hawthorne's "Young Goodman Brown."

Brown, Yvette (the Comtesse de Lascot-Villiers) Narrator's mother, who left him at a Jesuit school in Monaco; a colorful figure who may have fought in the French resistance, she acquires the Trianon, a Haitian hotel, and leaves it to Brown in Graham Greene's *The Comedians.*

Browne, Edward Maggie Browne's selfish brother, who forges Mr. Buxton's name; he dies in a shipwreck when fleeing to America in Elizabeth Gaskell's *The Moorland Cottage.*

Browne, Elizabeth See Rogers, Elizabeth Browne.

Browne, Jonathan Conforming, pragmatic, agnostic narrator; he clings to Mike Brady during the Basic Training portion of his National Service stint out of need for intelligent companionship and moral support; he tries to neither help nor hurt Mike, but feels in the end that he has betrayed him; he marries Mike's former girlfriend, Pauline Vickers, in David Lodge's *Ginger, You're Barmy.*

Browne, Leonard Talis Browne's irascible ailing father, who lives with him; Tallis is unable to tell the old man that he is fatally ill in Iris Murdoch's *A Fairly Honourable Defeat.*

Browne, Maggie Heroine, who marries Frank Buxton; her courage, loyalty, and selflessness set the example in Elizabeth Gaskell's *The Moorland Cottage.*

Browne, Morgan Browne Hilda Foster's younger sister, a linguistics professor; she is the discarded lover of Julius King, whose child she aborted on finding herself pregnant; estranged from her husband, Tallis Browne, she is the supposed lover of Rupert Foster in an elaborate punitive practical joke engineered by Julius in Iris Murdoch's *A Fairly Honourable Defeat.*

Browne, Mrs. Self-pitying widow, who spoils her worthless son and disregards her selfless daughter in Elizabeth Gaskell's *The Moorland Cottage.*

Browne, Nosey Bankrupt Cockney owner of a hunting establishment; John Jorrocks hires him as huntsman; his disregard for land boundaries leads Jorrocks onto Squire Cheatum's property in Robert Surtees's *Jorrocks's Jaunts and Jollities.*

Browne, Sam Browne Stereotypic Public School Englishman without intelligence or character; he is Isabel Winterbourne's "sheik" in Richard Aldington's *Death of a Hero.*

Browne, Tallis Adult-education lecturer, who is a morally upright person; he is Julius King's inadequate adversary in Iris Murdoch's *A Fairly Honourable Defeat.*

Brownell, Katherine Morley (Kitty) American visitor to Schloss Riva and friend of Warren Howe; possibly (and briefly) Etienne Dulac's mistress in Wright Morris's *Cause for Wonder.*

Browning, Clarissa Academy Award-winning actress with a troubled past and secret history in Jackie Collins's *Hollywood Husbands.*

Browning, Hank Buys a field from Gram in Joan Chase's *During the Reign of the Queen of Persia.*

Browning, Phoebe Younger and less stern of two spinster sisters; she defends Molly Gibson when appearances are against her in Elizabeth Gaskell's *Wives and Daughters.*

Browning, Sally Senior of the two Browning sisters; she represents local custom and moral tradition in judging Molly Gibson's conduct in Elizabeth Gaskell's *Wives and Daughters.*

Browning, Yvonne (Velvet) Pretty accomplice of her beloved houseburglar-boyfriend, Wolf; she goes to Corker's employment agency posing as a jobseeker to case the place; she deceives Corker but winds up in jail unjustly accused of hitting Irene Corker over the head in John Berger's *Corker's Freedom.*

Brownjohn, Mr. Corrupt lawyer, who, because as a married man he cannot himself get Medora Glenmorris's inheritance through forced marriage, kidnaps her as a bride for his half brother, Dicky Darnell, in Charlotte Smith's *The Young Philosopher.*

Brownleigh, Charles Rational, no-nonsense attorney for the prosecution in Hugo Chesterton's trial; he is susceptible to Daisy Bland's charm in Nicholas Blake's *A Tangled Web.*

Brownlie, Mr. Banker, the nephew of Lord Port Scatho; he harbors a gloomy passion for Sylvia Tietjens; convinced that she will marry him if she can be got to divorce her husband, he juggles accounts at the bank so that Christopher Tietjens overdraws in Ford Madox Ford's *Some Do Not. . . .*

Brownlow, Edith Elegant, carefree companion since childhood of sickly Gregory Marrable, whose father has always planned on their marrying in Anthony Trollope's *The Vicar of Bullhampton.*

Brownlow, Mr. Housemaster at Westminster who encourages the theatrical abilities of young Piers Mosson in Angus Wilson's *Setting the World on Fire.*

Brownlow, Mr. Old gentleman who takes Oliver Twist home with him after theft charges are dropped against the boy; an old friend of Oliver's father, he had long been searching for Oliver's mother and the boy in Charles Dickens's *Oliver Twist.*

Brownlow, Mrs. Tactful mother of Edith; she helps ease Sir Gregory Marrable's pain when his long-cherished plan to see Edith marry his son is thwarted when the son dies in Anthony Trollope's *The Vicar of Bullhampton.*

Brownly, Sue Ann Elementary school student who has a crush on Joseph, a classmate, who, slow-minded, is also past 30 years of age; Joseph sprains his ankle over a note she tries to pass in class, then feels pride that he is limping; catches her older "sweetheart" and the teacher Miss Mandible making love during recess in a cloakroom and tattletales in Donald Barthelme's "Me and Miss Mandible."

Brownside, Dr. Dean of Nottingham, whose shallow preaching disillusions Charles Reding with liberal Anglicanism in John Henry Newman's *Loss and Gain.*

Brownwell, Adrian Pericles Owner and editor of the Sycamore Ridge *Banner* whose modest wealth saves John Barclay's bank early in Barclay's career and who, with Barclay's help, marries Molly Culpepper in William Allen White's *A Certain Rich Man.*

Brownwell, Molly Culpepper Daughter of Martin Culpepper and wife of Adrian Brownwell; loves Bob Hendricks in William Allen White's *A Certain Rich Man.*

Bruce Pan-like bisexual friend and lover of Renate, who travels with her through Mexico and periodically lives with her in Anaïs Nin's *Collages.*

Bruce, Colonel Commander of the station outpost in Robert Montgomery Bird's *Nick of the Woods.*

Bruce, Dr. (Doc) Black physician and business partner of Tyree Tucker in Richard Wright's *The Long Dream.*

Bruce, John Tutor at Trinity College, Dublin; he teaches John Buncle his Unitarian beliefs in Thomas Amory's *The Life of John Buncle, Esq.*

Bruce, Rev. Calvin Chicago minister in Charles M. Sheldon's *In His Steps.*

Bruch, Walter Sixty-year-old musicologist and baritone who likes to enact his own funeral and is a compulsive masturbator when excited by women's arms, a weakness he confesses regularly to Artur Sammler in Saul Bellow's *Mr. Sammler's Planet.*

Bruchsal, Count von Wealthy uncle of Minna von Barnhelm; sanctions the marriage between Minna and Major von Tellheim in Gotthold Ephraim Lessing's play *Minna von Barnhelm.*

Brudegher, Joseph A Vineyard native and Vix's first lover; eventually marries Caitlin and has a daughter with her in Judy Blume's *Summer Sisters.*

Bruder, Cécile Wife of Ernest Bruder and mother of Dora; housewife born in Budapest and sent to Auschwitz five months after her husband and daughter in Patrick Modiano's *Dora Bruder.*

Bruder, Dora Jewish girl born in Paris to immigrant parents; runs away from a Catholic boarding school, gets arrested, is interned at Tourelles prison, is moved to Drancy camp, and finally is deported with her father to Auschwitz in 1942 in Patrick Modiano's *Dora Bruder.*

Bruder, Ernest Father of Dora; an ex-Austrian unskilled laborer and former French legionnaire; places an ad about his missing daughter in December 1941; is deported to Auschwitz in 1942 in Patrick Modiano's *Dora Bruder.*

Bruff, Matthew Kindhearted family lawyer of the Verinders; he follows up the whereabouts of the stolen diamond lodged with Septimus Luker; he shows Rachel Verinder that Godfrey Ablewhite's interest in her is entirely mercenary in Wilkie Collins's *The Moonstone. A Romance.*

Bruge, Victor Friend of Stewart Barnes; gives Psyche Tanzer a fatal dose of a drug he believes is an aphrodisiac in Theodore Dreiser's *The Bulwark.*

Bruges, General Military leader of the "Mary Anne" secret societies pledged to promote liberation movements in Europe; he is Lothair's commander when the young heir is convinced to take part in some of the fighting in Italy in Benjamin Disraeli's *Lothair.*

Brumpton, Lady Lady Mary Jones's sister-in-law, who has a weakness for public admiration and cultivates learned company; fatal illness makes her realize her mistaken priorities in Sarah Scott's *A Description of Millenium Hall.*

Brun Stern but fair leader of Neanderthal Clan that adopts the orphaned Cro-Magnon child Ayla; proud father whose love for his son Broud blinds him to Broud's unfitness to succeed him as leader; brother of Creb and Iza in Jean M. Auel's *The Clan of the Cave Bear.*

Brundige, Joe Author of a story in the *Evening News* reporting his scientific body transfer with a Mayan so he can destroy the Mayan control machine in William S. Burroughs's *The Soft Machine.*

Brune, Pamela Goddaughter of Sir Edward Leithen; affirming her love and courage, both by precept and example, she overcomes a dangerous illness and is rewarded by joyful union with Charles Ottery in John Buchan's *The Gap in the Curtain.*

Brunel, Toto de Homosexual socialite given to inappropriate word substitutions when speaking English; he wears Justine Hosnani's identifiable ring—at her request—at a masked ball and is murdered in error by Narouz Hosnani in Lawrence Durrell's *Balthazar.*

Brunelda Obese and despotic woman for whom the protagonist, Karl Rossman, works; smothers the young man in her capacious breasts; also the scoundrel Delamarche's mistress in Franz Kafka's *Amerika.*

Brunne, Baron de Character to whom a ghost appears in the story Ludovico reads while watching in the bedroom of the dead Marchioness de Villeroi in Ann Radcliffe's *The Mysteries of Udolpho.*

Brunner, Eddie Platonic friend of Gloria Wandrous; struggles to find work as a commercial artist while working as a night man in a brothel in John O'Hara's *Butterfield 8.*

Bruno Manuel Venator's unsystematic but precise philosophical mentor; looks at the world like a knowledgeable magician in Ernst Jünger's *Eumeswil.*

Bruno Warden of Oudand's precocious five-year-old son, the younger brother of Sylvie; good and kind, he is the rightful heir of the ruler of Outland; he is sometimes seen as an

Outlander, sometimes as a fairy, sometimes as a human child; he is the counterpart of Arthur Forester in Lewis Carroll's *Sylvie and Bruno.* He returns to Outland for Uggug's banquet and is reunited with his father but remains a fairy in *Sylvie and Bruno Concluded.*

Bruno, Antonio Father of Giovanni and Marcella Bruno; dies in front of a television set in Robert Coover's *The Origin of the Brunists.*

Bruno, Count di Olivia di Bruno's husband, murdered by his brother Ferando di Bruno in Ann Radcliffe's *The Italian.*

Bruno, Emilia Mother of Giovanni and Marcella Bruno in Robert Coover's *The Origin of the Brunists.*

Bruno, Ferando di (Father Schedoni) Lascivious younger son who kills his brother, Count di Bruno, out of jealousy and greed; he rapes and then marries his sister-in-law, Olivia; mistakenly thinking he murdered Olivia, he takes refuge in the Church as Father Schedoni, the politically ambitious confessor to the Marchesa di Vivaldi; he plots with her to abduct, imprison, and finally kill Ellena Rosalba, who he mistakenly comes to believe is his daughter; imprisoned by the Inquisition, he is poisoned and dies in Ann Radcliffe's *The Italian.*

Bruno, Giordan Distinguished Italian Renaissance thinker who was burned at the stake for heresy against the Catholic Church in Bertolt Brecht's play *Galileo.*

Bruno, Giovanni Catholic coal miner who, during a mine disaster, claims to have been visited by the Virgin Mary, thereby inaugurating the chiliastic cult of the Brunists in Robert Coover's *The Origin of the Brunists.*

Bruno, Marcella Innocent sister of Giovanni Bruno and Justin Miller's object of infatuation; hit and killed by a car in Robert Coover's *The Origin of the Brunists.*

Bruno, Olivia di (Sister Olivia) Widow of the Count di Bruno; she is raped by, forced to marry, and believed to be killed by her brother-in-law Ferando di Bruno; she escapes his murder attempt to become a nun in the San Stefano convent, where she befriends Ellena Rosalba and helps her to escape with Vincentio di Vivaldi; she retires to a Neapolitan convent, where she is reunited with Ellena and discovered to be her mother in Ann Radcliffe's *The Italian.*

Brunoni, Signor Stage name of the conjuror Sam Brown; he provides the link with Miss Matty Jenkyns's long-lost brother in Elizabeth Gaskell's *Cranford.*

Brunoni, Signora Purveyor of the information that sets in motion the return of Matilda Jenkyns's brother in Elizabeth Gaskell's *Cranford.*

Brunskill, Irene Woman whose marriage to Martin Eliot is discouraged by Lewis Eliot; she flirts with other men after her marriage, has a son named for Lewis, and breaks with her lover Edgar Hankins to settle into her marriage in C. P. Snow's *The New Men.* She encourages Martin in his advocacy of Donald Howard's reinstatement in *The Affair.* She worries about the financial future of her son, Pat Eliot, in *The Sleep of Reason.*

Brury, Alice Young, spirited hotel housekeeper; having quit her post because of a contretemps with a thieving guest, she begs to be reinstated but is placed in another hotel in Arnold Bennett's *Imperial Palace.*

Brush, Bascom Political manipulator and dispenser of bribes in Winston Churchill's *Mr. Crewe's Career.*

Brush, Elizabeth Martin See Martin, Elizabeth.

Brush, George Marvin (George Busch, James Bush, Jim) Innocent, religiously and socially conservative representative of a textbook company in Thornton Wilder's *Heaven's My Destination.*

Brusque, Colonel Military man whose elegant entertainment attracts guests of every kind in William Beckford's *Azemia.*

Brussels Courtier Number One Son of a low-born father who purchased a title; he is welcome in all the fashionable places in Charles Johnstone's *Chrysal: or, The Adventures of a Guinea.*

Brussels Courtier Number Two Well-born man whose life of pleasure distresses his fortune and debases his principles in Charles Johnstone's *Chrysal: or, The Adventures of a Guinea.*

Brute-men Alien species whose worship of irrationalism, instinct, and ruthlessness travesties fascism in Olaf Stapledon's *Star Maker.*

Bruton, James English fiancé, for a brief period, of Jane Clifford in Gail Godwin's *The Odd Woman.*

Bruton, Lady Millicent Duchess and a powerful meddler, with whom Richard Dalloway frequently has intimate lunches; Clarissa Dalloway is jealous of her on the day of her party in Virginia Woolf's *Mrs. Dalloway.*

Brutt, Major Eric E. J. Retired British army officer of modest means and no property who lives in inexpensive residential hotels; to Anna Quayne's discomfort, he emerges from her indiscreet past; in his blustering avuncular manner, he becomes an understanding and trusted friend to Portia Quayne in Elizabeth Bowen's *The Death of the Heart.*

Brutus Brutal enemy of the reformed Tom Robinson; he becomes a tool of Peter Crawley in attempts to kill Tom and George Fielding in Charles Reade's *It Is Never Too Late to Mend.*

Brutus, Junius Lucrece's kinsman; vows revenge for her rape and suicide; leads the Roman people against the Tarquins, unseating their dynasty; founds and serves as first leader of the Roman Republic in William Shakespeare's play *The Rape of Lucrece.*

Brutus, Junius Roman tribune who is clever, opportunistic, and a good politician; regards Coriolanus as a danger to the people and foments sedition in William Shakespeare's play *Coriolanus.*

Brutus, Marcus One of the conspirators against Caesar in William Shakespeare's play *Julius Caesar.*

Brutus, Marcus Junius Former enemy of Caesar; recalled from Gaul by Caesar to become Praetor; one of Caesar's assassins in Thornton Wilder's *The Ides of March.*

Bry, Lou Laintal Ay's grandmother, a sorceress in Brian W. Aldiss's *Helliconia Spring.*

Bryanston, Mr. Rose Vassiliou's abject, irritating, hard father; a self-made man of great wealth, he speaks primarily to impress or be approved of in Margaret Drabble's *The Needle's Eye.*

Bryant, Bobby Alcoholic friend of Bill Kelsey; committed to winning government money by becoming the first male to bear a child in Hal Bennett's *Seventh Heaven.*

Bryant, Chalmers American banker who is traveling under the alias Henry D. Barnard because of business crimes amounting to millions of dollars; he is abducted on a highjacked plane and taken to the Tibetan monastery, Shangri-La, along with Hugh "Glory" Conway, Roberta Brinklow, and Captain Charles Mallinson in James Hilton's *Lost Horizon.*

Bryant, Clarke Charismatic white supremacist and political leader against school integration in Julian Mayfield's *The Grand Parade.*

Bryant, Elsie Mrs. Wilbraham's maid, who was under suspicion when her employer's necklace was stolen some fifteen years earlier in Dorothy L. Sayers's *The Nine Tailors: Changes Rung on an Old Theme in Two Short Touches and Two Full Peals.*

Bryant, Inspector Scotland Yard officer who uncovers a plot by terrorists using Ralph Tucker's play production as a front and makes arrests during its presentation at Tothill House in Angus Wilson's *Setting the World on Fire.*

Bryant, Malcolm (Malc) Anthropologist-sociologist who analyzes the class structure of the town of Clyde in John P. Marquand's *Point of No Return.*

Bryant, Thomas English R.A.F. pilot stationed in Martha Quest's town; she takes a strong romantic interest in him in Doris Lessing's *A Proper Marriage.*

Bryant, William Cullen Poet and editor of the *Evening Post* in Gore Vidal's *Burr.*

Brydehaven, Lady Sara Macallan's aunt; her testimony tended to incriminate Eustace Macallan in his murder trial that precedes the opening of Wilkie Collins's *The Law and the Lady.*

Brydon, Spencer Rich American who leaves New York and returns 30 years later, when he has inherited his family's wealth; finds New York much changed and obsesses over what he would have been had he remained in the city; searches his family's mansion to find the Form of his alter ego; in a dream, meets the Form, is mortally frightened, loses consciousness, and is revived the next afternoon by Alice Staverton in Henry James's "The Jolly Corner."

Bryerly, Dr. Hans Emmanuel Swedenborgian friend of Austin Ruthyn and trustee of Maud Ruthyn's estate; he attempts but fails to remove her from Silas Ruthyn's guardianship; he is somewhat mysterious and intimidating, but a true friend to Maud; later he becomes manager of her estate in J. Sheridan Le Fanu's *Uncle Silas.*

Brykin, Vassya Youth who is an ironmonger's apprentice whom Yury meets on a train bound for Varykino in Boris Pasternak's *Doctor Zhivago.*

"Bub" Unnamed narrator who is referred to as "Bub" by Robert; gruff and judgmental protagonist who is a heavy drinker and a serious pot smoker; honest, semicurious, and rather emotionless for most of the story except for the frequent jealousy he reveals over his wife's ex-husband and her intimate past friendship with Robert in Raymond Carver's "Cathedral."

Bubb, Mrs. Landlady of a lodging house in George Gissing's *The Town Traveller.*

Bubble, Madam Witch who tries to tempt Stand-fast and the other pilgrims in Christiana's party to commit various sins in John Bunyan's *The Pilgrim's Progress from This World to That Which Is to Come.*

Bubbles See Wiggins, Richard.

Buch Owner of the house where Raskolnikov lodges in Fyodor Dostoevsky's *Crime and Punishment.*

Buchan, Lacy Gore Fifteen-year-old son of Major Lewis Buchan; friend of George Posey and in love with Jane Posey; tries to understand both the Buchan and Posey families; joins the Confederate army after the death of his father; narrator of Allen Tate's *The Fathers.*

Buchan, Major Lewis Father of Semmes, Susan, and Lacy Buchan; member of an old Virginia family; remains loyal to the Union but is killed by the Union army in Allen Tate's *The Fathers.*

Buchan, Semmes (Brother Semmes) Son disowned by Major Lewis Buchan; Virginia native who Joins the Confederate army against his father's wishes; loves and plans to marry Jane Posey; killed by George Posey in Allen Tate's *The Fathers.*

Buchan, Susan See Posey, Susan Buchan.

Buchanan, Daisy Fay Wife of Tom Buchanan and treacherous lost love of Jay Gatsby in F. Scott Fitzgerald's *The Great Gatsby.*

Buchanan, Doctor Golf partner and doctor of Judge Honeywell in Ellen Glasgow's *The Romantic Comedians.*

Buchanan, Father Bede College chaplain who officiates at the Paschal Festival which occurs at the end of David Lodge's *How Far Can You Go?*

Buchanan, Miss Woman with a dry sense of humor; she keeps a general shop and conceals the fact that she cannot read in Ivy Compton-Burnett's *Manservant and Maidservant.*

Buchanan, Rosemarie (Rosie) Friend of Ray Smith and mistress of Cody Pomeray; leaps off an apartment building to her death during an attack of paranoia in Jack Kerouac's *The Dharma Bums;* also appears in *Book of Dreams* and *Big Sur.*

Buchanan, Tom Unfaithful millionaire husband of Daisy Buchanan in F. Scott Fitzgerald's *The Great Gatsby.*

Buchwald Army private who helps execute General Gragnon in William Faulkner's *A Fable.*

Buck Dog who leads a dog team and twice saves the life of John Thornton, whose death Buck mourns, in Jack London's *The Call of the Wild.*

Buck One of the four African-American boys caught swimming in the Harvey's pool; tells Big Boy to stay in the pool until Bertha leaves instead of going to retrieve their clothes; shot in the head by Jim Harvey while he is still in the pool in Richard Wright's "Big Boy Leaves Home."

Buck, Billy Tiflins' cowhand with strong, thick hands whose well-publicized knowledge of horses earns Jody's respect; connects and emphasizes with Jody, who grapples with the death of his pony, in John Steinbeck's *The Red Pony.*

Buck, Joe (Cowboy, Tex) Would-be hustler and grandson of Sally Buck; travels from Albuquerque to Houston and New York, where he befriends Ratso Rizzo in James Leo Herlihy's *Midnight Cowboy.*

Buck, Mr. Draper who becomes Lord High Provost of North Kensington; he is killed by Adam Wayne during the last battle in G. K. Chesterton's *The Napoleon of Notting Hill.*

Buck, Rachel Daughter of Gram and Grandad, sister of Libby, Grace, Elinor, and May; mother of her son, Rossie, aunt of Valery, Jenny, Celia, Anne, and Katie; married for a short, miserable spell at eighteen, remarried to Tom Buck in Joan Chase's *During the Reign of the Queen of Persia.*

Buck, Sally Grandmother of Joe Buck; dies while Joe is in the army in James Leo Herlihy's *Midnight Cowboy.*

Buck, Tom Second husband of Rachel, divorces his wife to marry her; stepfather of Rossie; years before was in love with Grace and wanted to marry her in Joan Chase's *During the Reign of the Queen of Persia.*

Bucket, Mr. Steady detective officer, who first investigates the death of Nemo (Captain Hawdon), then pursues Mr. Gridley, and then cleverly finds Lady Dedlock and solves the murder of Mr. Tulkinghorn in Charles Dickens's *Bleak House.*

Buckhurst, Lord Generous but impulsive aristocratic friend of Harry Coningsby at Eton; he becomes a member of the "New Generation" of young English politicians in Benjamin Disraeli's *Coningsby; or, The New Generation.*

Buckingham See Villiers, George.

Buckingham, Duke of British noble who meets secretly with his lover, the married Queen of France in 1625; finds his life in peril in Paris and returns to London; stabbed to death by an admirer of Lady de Winter's, at her urging, as she has convinced her agent that Buckingham has harmed her reputation in Alexandre Dumas, père's *The Three Musketeers.*

Buckingham (Henry Stafford, Duke of Buckingham) Supporter of Richard III; assists Richard III in consolidating power, deposing Edward V, and killing Lord Hastings; rejects Richard's plan to kill the two princes; turns against Richard, raising an army to assist Richmond in deposing him; captured by Richard and put to death in William Shakespeare's play *Richard III.*

Buckingham, Duke of, George (Steenie) Villiers Companion of Prince Charles and a public enemy of Nigel Olifaunt; he witnesses the king's interrogation of Lord Dalgarno on the matter of his marital obligations in Sir Walter Scott's *The Fortunes of Nigel.*

Buckingham, Second Duke of, Charles Villiers Nobleman in the court of King Charles II; he conspires with Edward Christian to seize control of the Isle of Man and kidnap Alice Bridgenorth for the king; he is tricked by the allure of Zarah in Sir Walter Scott's *Peveril of the Peak.*

Buckland First lieutenant of the *Renown;* he is a capable seaman, who assumes command and is taken captive during the Spanish prisoners' revolt; he is angered by Hornblower's promotion in C. S. Forester's *Lieutenant Hornblower.*

Buckle, Helen Outspoken wife of Slim Buckle in Jack Kerouac's *Visions of Cody.*

Buckle, Slim (Ed Buckle) Cross-country traveling companion of Cody Pomeray and Jack Duluoz; husband of Helen Buckle in Jack Kerouac's *Visions of Cody;* also appears in *Book of Dreams.*

Buckley, David A. State's attorney who prosecutes Bigger Thomas for the murder of Mary Dalton in Richard Wright's *Native Son.*

Buckley, Ezra Eccentric millionaire and disciple of the sect responsible for inventing the country Uqbar who proposes the invention of a planet, Tlön, with the provisos that the project be kept secret and that an encyclopedia of the imaginary planet Tlön be written by the sect in Jorge Luis Borges's "Tlön, Uqbar, Orbis Tertius."

Buckley, Father Military chaplain of the Royal Dublin Fusiliers; accompanies Willie Dunne and his company in Flanders; supports home rule for Ireland; dies in an aid post while giving the last rites to dying soldiers in Sebastian Barry's play *A Long Long Way.*

Buckner, Asher Maternal uncle of Paul Herz; lives an unattached life as a painter in Philip Roth's *Letting Go.*

Buckram Horse trader who provides vicious mounts in Robert Surtees's *Mr. Sponge's Sporting Tour.*

Buckram, Mr. Lawyer hired to draft and administer the conveyance of Sir Sampson's estate from Valentine to Ben; refuses to let Valentine sign the deed when Valentine is not in his right mind; flees from Valentine's chamber when Valentine threatens him with violence in William Congreve's play *Love for Love.*

Buckray, Lady Lady of fashion and former friend of Mrs. Blandford; she gives a masquerade ball in William Beckford's *Azemia.*

Buckton, Ned Former geography teacher turned warden of the local youth hostel; he is the husband of Sally Buckton and the father of their two children; he meets Anthony Keating at Mrs. Bunney's pub, and they become friends in Margaret Drabble's *The Ice Age.*

Buckton, Sally Wife of Ned Buckton and mother of their two children in Margaret Drabble's *The Ice Age.*

Bucktrout, Gervaise Estate agent who sells Lady Slane the house in Hampstead and becomes her true companion in Vita Sackville-West's *All Passion Spent.*

Bud, Rosa Pretty heroine, who lives in Miss Twinkleton's boarding school and is engaged to Edwin Drood, also orphaned like herself; Rosa has taken music lessons from John Jasper but is afraid of him, as she admits to Edwin in Charles Dickens's *The Mystery of Edwin Drood.*

Budd, Eleanor Apley See Apley, Eleanor.

Budd, Irma Barnes Wealthy American heiress and wife of Lanny Budd in Upton Sinclair's *Dragon's Teeth.*

Budd, Lady Frederica Lord Warminster's eldest daughter, a distinguished-looking, self-controlled, highly respectable widow in Anthony Powell's *The Acceptance World* and in *Casanova's Chinese Restaurant.* Her sister Isobel (Tolland) Jenkins stays with Frederica during the war when she is pregnant in *The Kindly Ones.* Frederica becomes Dicky Umfraville's fifth wife in *The Valley of Bones.* The marriage endures through *Hearing Secret Harmonies.*

Budd, Lanning Prescott (Lanny) Wealthy American son of an arms manufacturer; helps secure the release of Johannes and Freddi Robin from the Nazis in Upton Sinclair's *Dragon's Teeth.*

Budd, William (Baby, Beauty, Billy) Handsome sailor aboard the *Rights-of-Man* impressed into service on the *Indomitable;* when falsely accused of planning a mutiny, he accidentally kills his accuser John Claggart in Herman Melville's *Billy Budd.*

Budda Ben Crippled son of Maum Hannah and adviser to Mary Pinesett; banished from Heaven's Gate Church for cursing, but later reinstated, in Julia Peterkin's *Scarlet Sister Mary.*

Buddenbrook, Antonie Referred to as Tony and sister of Thomas; marries twice through the prompting of her family, yet both marriages end in divorce; represents one of the family members who must sacrifice personal happiness for the family's business success in Thomas Mann's *Buddenbrooks.*

Buddenbrook, Christian Only brother of Thomas; crippled by hypochondria and psychopathic tendencies, fails to contribute to the success of the family business in Thomas Mann's *Buddenbrooks.*

Buddenbrook, Johann Genial patriarch and a practical and serious businessman who leaves his wealthy grain business to his family-oriented son, Jean; also leaves a tradition in the family firm that requires different generations to work together to secure the success of the business in Thomas Mann's *Buddenbrooks.*

Buddenbrook, Thomas Son of Johann; cunning businessman who finds life progressively tiresome; his marriage produces a son, Hanno, and an increase in fortunes through his wife's dowry, but lacks the ability to manage and prosper in his business affairs; successful businessman who breaks every record in the firm's history despite numerous obstacles and becomes a senator in government activities; the decline of the Buddenbrooks relies not as a result of financial trouble but stems from physical and mental weakness; the Buddenbrook's fortune dwindles under his leadership and is liquidated upon his death at the premature age of forty-nine in Thomas Mann's *Buddenbrooks.*

Buddhist priest Traveler who reports meeting a man and woman, each on horseback, on the road the day before the murder; says the man was carrying a sword, a bow, and a black quiver; his testimony is one of seven varying accounts of the murder of a samurai, Kanazawa no Takehiro, whose corpse is found in a bamboo forest near Kyoto in Akutagawa Ryūnosuke's "In a Grove," the basis for the film *Rashomon.*

Buddle, Doctor Village doctor called in to treat Stanley Lake after his duel with Sir Harry Bracton; later he treats Fairy Wylder in J. Sheridan Le Fanu's *Wylder's Hand.*

Buddy Smart, sly good friend to the Geste brothers; inseparable from his friend Hank, he is an American soldier in the French Foreign Legion in Percival Christopher Wren's *Beau Geste.*

"Buddy" Grown up narrator looking back on himself as a seven-year-old and best friend to his elderly cousin, who names him "Buddy" in memory of another boy of the same name she knew who died young; spends more time with his elderly cousin than with his family; remembers their childhood with innocence and idyllic simplicity; recalls in a wistful tone their yearly pre-Christmas ritual during "fruitcake weather" of the fun and pleasure of shopping and making fruitcakes; gave each other handmade paper kites for Christmas; hears news of her death in a letter while away at military school; symbolizes the fragile and ephemeral memories of their Christmases together as kites flying overhead in Truman Capote's "A Christmas Memory."

"Buddy"'s Cousin Buddy's unnamed, 60-something elderly cousin and best friend and guardian; small, sprightly, white-haired, and craggy yet delicate-faced woman who is an innocent dreamer; reclusive, spontaneous, and childlike, tells Buddy stories and prefers his company to that of her family; confuses Buddy with another boy of the same name who died young; a religious Christian whose real adult life is judgmental and harsh, prefers to be with Buddy; shares her universe of pleasure with him in Truman Capote's "A Christmas Memory."

Bude, Duchess of Domineering mother of Lady Emily Winter-Willoughby; she is an intrusive mother-in-law to General Curzon in C. S. Forester's *The General.*

Bude, Duke of Father-in-law to General Curzon; his amiable, gentle nature is in contrast to his wife's in C. S. Forester's *The General.*

Budgen, Martin Son of Mrs. Budgen; he makes cynical observations on the visits of the upper crust in John Galsworthy's *Fraternity.*

Budgen, Mrs. Lame caretaker for the house where Ivy Barton, Joshua Creed, and the Hugheses live in John Galsworthy's *Fraternity.*

Budger, Mrs. Wealthy widow courted by Dr. Slammer; she attends the ball at the Bull Inn in Rochester and is pursued by Alfred Jingle in Charles Dickens's *The Posthumous Papers of the Pickwick Club.*

Budstock, Sir Henry Lord Raingo's predecessor as Minister of Records; he recognizes the status of a "mushroom" Ministry in Arnold Bennett's *Lord Raingo.*

Buell Intelligent, unemotional minister of Norwood whose sermons are filled with carefully crafted scholarship and who marries Agate Bissell after the death of his first wife in Henry Ward Beecher's *Norwood.*

Buell, Elgin Spy and personal cinematographer in Lancelot Lamar's quest to see sin in Walker Percy's *Lancelot.*

Buell, Miss Kind elementary teacher with a grayish face who teaches the 12-year-old protagonist, Paul Hasleman; notices Paul's new habit of daydreaming and drifting into himself in Conrad Aiken's "Silent Snow, Secret Snow."

Buendía, Colonel Aureliano Second son of José Arcadio Buendía and Ursula Iguarán; first person born in Macondo; said to have wept in the womb and was born with his eyes open; studies in his father's lab; said to have premonitions; both an artist and a soldier in Gabriel García Márquez's *One Hundred Years of Solitude.*

Buendía, José Arcadio Founder and patriarch of Macondo, husband of Ursula Iguarán and father of Colonel Aureliano Buendía, José Arcadio, and Amaranta; takes a deep interest in the mysteries and inventions introduced by Melquíades; known to have a lab where he experiments in alchemy until he goes insane in Gabriel García Márquez's *One Hundred Years of Solitude.*

Buffalo Wallow Woman Wife of Old Lodge Skins in Thomas Berger's *Little Big Man.*

Buffle, Sir Raffle Snobbish and authoritarian head of the Income Tax Office and Johnny Eames's chief in Anthony Trollope's *The Small House at Allington.* He suffers from Eames's quick wit in *The Last Chronicle of Barset.*

Buffles (The Stink Merchant) Pale, lean, and medically unfit science master at Brookfield in James Hilton's *Goodbye, Mr. Chips.*

Buford, John Adept cavalry officer who is the first Northern general to arrive at Gettysburg in Michael Shaara's *The Killer Angels.*

Buggerie, Dr. Samuel White statistician who discovers that over half the Anglo-Saxon population of the United States has black ancestors; eventually lynched in George S. Schuyler's *Black No More.*

Buggins, Mr. Friend of Art Kipps from the Folkestone Drapery Bazaar who warns Kipps against answering Old Bean's inheritance announcement but whom Kipps later sets up in business as a gentlemen's clothier in H. G. Wells's *Kipps: The Story of a Simple Soul.*

Buggins, Mrs. Margaret Mackenzie's old servant, at whose house Margaret faces up to the formidable Lady Ball in Anthony Trollope's *Miss Mackenzie.*

Buggit, Beety Dennis's wife; often takes care of Bunny and Sunshine; has comedy act that is big hit at annual Christmas pageant in E. Annie Proulx's *The Shipping News.*

Buggit, Dennis Jack Buggit's youngest son; married to Beety; does carpentry work; loves to fish in E. Annie Proulx's *The Shipping News.*

Buggit, Jack Started newspaper to get out of the nonlucrative fishing business; had one son, Jesson, drown and a second son, Dennis, almost drown; assumed dead from drowning until he sits up in his coffin in E. Annie Proulx's *The Shipping News.*

Bukuwky, Herr Ottokar Employee of the von Studenitz family and husband of Frau Natalie Schuschnigg; instrumental in arranging restoration of Rudolf Stanka to family position in Louis Adamic's *Cradle of Life.*

Bulder, Colonel Head of the garrison stationed in Rochester who attends the ball at the Bull Inn in Rochester in Charles Dickens's *The Posthumous Papers of the Pickwick Club.*

Bulder, Miss Daughter of Colonel and Mrs. Bulder in Charles Dickens's *The Posthumous Papers of the Pickwick Club.*

Bulder, Mrs. Wife of Colonel Bulder in Charles Dickens's *The Posthumous Papers of the Pickwick Club.*

Bulgaraux, Professor Leader of the Autogenists in Susan Sontag's *The Benefactor.*

Bulgarian Soldier Clergyman who was happily married but who loses everything and everyone in a French attack, and who is wounded in the course of the battle in Charles Johnstone's *Chrysal: or, The Adventures of a Guinea.*

Bulic Gullible, conceited clerk in the Yugoslav Submarine Defence Department; befriended by Wladyslaw Grodek and Dimitrios Makropoulos, who later force him to steal secret information, he is roughed up by Dimitrios and when Grodek informs on him is sent to prison for life in Eric Ambler's *The Mask of Dimitrios.*

Bulic, Madame Amiable, pretty, stupid wife of Bulic; her gambling losses as manipulated by Wladyslaw Grodek serve as the means for Bulic's downfall in Eric Ambler's *The Mask of Dimitrios.*

Bulkaen Fellow inmate imprisoned with the book's narrator in France's Fontervault penitentiary, a monastery converted to a prison after the French Revolution in 1789; homosexual lover of the narrator and viewed as a sublimated, virile version of the narrator in Jean Genet's *The Miracle of the Rose.*

Bulkington Popular crewman from the *Grampus* who signs aboard the *Pequod* in Herman Melville's *Moby-Dick.*

Bull KolobEktofer's aide; he advises against attacking the Draits in Brian W. Aldiss's *Helliconia Summer.*

Bull Tattooed gunner on the flying boat who gets lost in a fog on the first night of the treasure hunt, falls off a cliff, and is decapitated in Alan Sillitoe's *The Lost Flying Boat.*

Bull, Dr. Saturday of the General Council of the Anarchists of Europe who is entrusted with the plans to assassinate the Czar and the King of France; he reveals himself to Gabriel Syme and Professor de Worms as a Scotland Yard Detective and travels with them to France to prevent the assassination; he joins with the other Council members in the pursuit of Sunday in G. K. Chesterton's *The Man Who Was Thursday: A Nightmare*

Bull, Mrs. Fat gossip who tells everyone about Arthur Seaton's various affairs and then is shot in the buttocks with an air rifle by Arthur in Alan Sillitoe's *Saturday Night and Sunday Morning.*

Bullamy Solemn and imposing porter, whose presence lends credibility to his employer, the Anglo-Bengalee Disinterested Loan and Life Assurance Company, in Charles Dickens's *The Life and Adventures of Martin Chuzzlewit.*

Bullbean, Mr. George Hotspur's card-playing associate, who is willing to testify before a magistrate that George cheats in Anthony Trollope's *Sir Harry Hotspur of Humblethwaite.*

Bullcalf, Peter Ill man recruited for the army by Falstaff; bribes Bardolph to avoid service in the army in William Shakespeare's play *Henry IV, Part Two.*

Bullen, Mrs. Farmer's wife of Mr. Armstrong's parish who criticizes her vicar for his interest in astronomy in Mark Rutherford's *Miriam's Schooling.*

Buller Maurice Castle's trusting dog that Castle kills before he defects so his wife Sarah and adopted son Sam can live with his prejudiced mother in Graham Greene's *The Human Factor.*

Bullford, Sir Thomas Neighbor of Baynard; he plays a practical joke on Obadiah Lishmahago and is himself a victim of Lishmahago's revenge in Tobias Smollett's *The Expedition of Humphry Clinker.*

Bullfry Barrister who represents Marjorie Ferrar in her libel suit against Fleur Mont in John Galsworthy's *The Silver Spoon.*

Bullingdon, Viscount Proud, mistreated stepson of Barry Lyndon; he runs away to volunteer in the British army and is reported killed in America; he returns to his mother and horsewhips his stepfather in William Makepeace Thackeray's *The Luck of Barry Lyndon.*

Bullitt, Joe Friend of William Baxter; one of Baxter's rivals for the affections of Miss Lola Pratt in Booth Tarkington's *Seventeen.*

Bullivant Butler to the Lambs; he has witty talks with Mortimer Lamb but speaks sententiously to the other servants in Ivy Compton-Burnett's *Manservant and Maidservant.*

Bullivant, Mr. Sculptor and poet, a friend of Valentine Blyth in Wilkie Collins's *Hide and Seek.*

Bullivant, Mr. Shop assistant who courts Monica Madden ineffectively in George Gissing's *The Odd Women.*

Bullivant, Sir Walter (Lord Artinswell) Permanent Secretary at the Foreign Office who aids Richard Hannay in subverting the villainous plot of enemy agents to steal British naval plans in John Buchan's *The Thirty-Nine Steps.* He recruits Hannay as an intelligence officer to prevent the forming of a jehad in the Near East in *Greenmantle.* He seeks Hannay's undercover abilities to locate and destroy an enemy spy network headed by Moxton Ivery (Graf von Schwabing) in World War I in *Mr. Standfast.* He appeals to Hannay to solve the mysterious disappearance of the three kidnap victims in *The Three Hostages.*

Bull Nosy Brother of Bull Shockhead; he abducts Ursula but is slain by the lustful Gandolf, King of Utterbol in William Morris's *The Well at the World's End.*

Bullock, Frederick Augustus Member of a banking family who marries Maria Osborne for her money in William Makepeace Thackeray's *Vanity Fair.*

Bullock, Major Rupert Close friend of Judge Clinton McKelva; informs Fay McKelva's family that the judge has died in Eudora Welty's *The Optimist's Daughter.*

Bullock, Tennyson Close friend of Becky McKelva; wife of Major Bullock and mother of Tish Bullock in Eudora Welty's *The Optimist's Daughter.*

Bullock, Tish Bridesmaid and close friend of Laurel McKelva Hand; daughter of Major and Tennyson Bullock in Eudora Welty's *The Optimist's Daughter.*

Bulls-Eye Bill Sikes's much kicked and battered dog; Sikes's attempts to drown the dog to keep it from leading pursuers to him after he murders Nancy are unsuccessful in Charles Dickens's *Oliver Twist.*

Bull Shockhead Wild mountain man, who becomes the thrall of Ralph; he later revenges his brother's murder by slaying Gandolf, King of Utterbol and becomes Lord of Utterbol and marries the queen in William Morris's *The Well at the World's End.*

Bulmer, Valentine Illegitimate half brother of Francis Tyrrel; he claims the title of Earl of Etherington, pursues Clara Mowbray to make their mock marriage legitimate, uses John Mowbray's gambling and need of money to gain his consent for marriage to his sister, and is killed by Mowbray in a duel in Sir Walter Scott's *St. Ronan's Well.*

Bulrush, Absalom Poor white man whose farm is mortgaged to Frank Meriwether in John Pendleton Kennedy's *Swallow Barn.*

Bulstrode, Harriet Sister of Walter Vincy and wife of a powerful banker; she attempts unsuccessfully to arrange a marriage between Rosamond Vincy and Ned Plymdale and is so angry when this match fails that she arranges a meeting with Dr. Lydgate to question his intentions toward Rosamond in George Eliot's *Middlemarch.*

Bulstrode, Nicholas Power-mad banker of Middlemarch; he was once married to a wealthy widow whose daughter was Will Ladislaw's mother; wanting all the family money, he kept the daughter hidden; this secret is carefully guarded, as is the one that he was dealing in stolen goods, until John Raffles arrives in George Eliot's *Middlemarch.*

Bulteel Elderly government Resident who helps Rudbeck complete his road by secretly diverting funds from other treasury accounts in Joyce Cary's *Mister Johnson.*

Bumble, Mr. Fat, choleric beadle of the parish workhouse where Oliver lives; he marries Mrs. Corney in Charles Dickens's *Oliver Twist.*

Bumfrett, Ethel Devoted assistant to Mary Taylor, matron of a teaching hospital in P. D. James's *Shroud for a Nightingale.*

Bummer, Emil (Satire) German dope dealer and former cat burglar in Thomas Pynchon's *Gravity's Rainbow.*

Bumpas, Stanley Policeman who thirteen years before beat Sonny Boy Mosby; an accomplice of Willie Joe Worth in the murder of Lord Byron Jones in Jesse Hill Ford's *The Liberation of Lord Byron Jones.*

Bump Baily Outfielder for the Knights, practical joker, and lover of Memo Paris; dies going after a fly ball in Bernard Malamud's *The Natural.*

Bumpers, William (Billy) Marriage counselor who earned a doctorate by submitting a rejected sociology dissertation to the English department as an experimental novel; narrator of Peter De Vries's *I Hear America Swinging.*

Bumppo, Nathaniel (Deerslayer, Hawkeye, Leatherstocking, la Longue Carabine, Natty, Pathfinder) White woodsman and guide with knowledge of Indian ways; helps Chingachgook rescue Wah-ta!-Wah and protects the Hutter family in James Fenimore Cooper's *The Deerslayer;*

guide and escort to Major Heyward and the Munro sisters in *The Last of the Mohicans;* experiences love for Mabel Dunham in *The Pathfinder;* comes into conflict with the settlers of Templeton in *The Pioneers;* dies on the prairie in *The Prairie.*

Bumptious, Sergeant Overzealous counsel on behalf of Squire Cheatum; he wins the court case against John Jorrocks, who is found guilty of trespassing his big toe on Squire Cheatum's property in Robert Surtees's *Jorrocks's Jaunts and Jollities.*

Bumpus, Richard (Dickie) Little, dark man who had meant romance for William Masson in youth; he pretends that a book he wrote years ago is a second, new creation in Ivy Compton-Burnett's *Pastors and Masters.*

Bumstead, Dr. Father of Harriet Bumstead Alden; briefly cares for Peter Alden in George Santayana's *The Last Puritan.*

Bumstead, Harriet See Alden, Harriet Bumstead.

Bunce Aged bedesman at Hiram's Hospital sorely perplexed by squabbles over alleged misuse of the charity in Anthony Trollope's *The Warden.* He appears in *Barchester Towers.*

Bunce, Bessy Thomas Bunce's wife, who pickles onions and supplies the Angel Inn with a grandfather clock in T. F. Powys's *Mr. Weston's Good Wine.*

Bunce, Jacob Journeyman copyist in a legal stationer's office; he provides Phineas Finn with lodgings and educates him in rights of labor with realistic estimates of political chicanery among the legislators in Anthony Trollope's *Phineas Finn.* He proclaims his belief in Finn's innocence in the murder case in *Phineas Redux.*

Bunce, Jane Stout-hearted wife of Jacob, at whose house Phineas Finn lodges; she loathes politics, her husband's consuming interest, in Anthony Trollope's *Phineas Finn.* She is distressed by Finn's ordeal in being tried for murder in *Phineas Redux.*

Bunce, Jenny Thomas Bunce's playful daughter, who admires Tamar Grobe, narrowly averts being raped by the Mumby brothers, and marries Luke Bird in T. F. Powys's *Mr. Weston's Good Wine.*

Bunce, Jo Workingman of vulgarly radical tastes and fiercely antireligious sentiments who nevertheless cares faithfully for his orphaned children in George Gissing's *Thyrza.*

Bunce, John (Frederick Altamont) Captain Clement Cleveland's lieutenant and devoted friend; a gaudy rake, he despises his plebeian name and wishes to be addressed as Frederick Altamont; arrested for piracy, he is spared hanging because of a past humane deed and gains employment in government service in Sir Walter Scott's *The Pirate.*

Bunce, Thomas (Landlord) Proprietor of the Angel Inn who believes God is to be blamed for everything and sets out to prove God is to blame for the ruin of Folly Down's maidens in T. F. Powys's *Mr. Weston's Good Wine.*

Bunch, Byron Mill worker who befriends Lena Grove in William Faulkner's *Light in August.*

Bunch, Colonel Tom General Baynes's friend, who is challenged by the General to a duel because he takes the side of Philip and Charlotte (Baynes) Firmin in William Makepeace Thackeray's *The Adventures of Philip on His Way through the World.*

Bunch, Mrs. Colonel Bunch's wife in William Makepeace Thackeray's *The Adventures of Philip on His Way through the World.*

Buncombe, Mr. Man whose wife has left him for a career but who lives in a large house, hoping she will return in George Gissing's *The Whirlpool.*

Buncombe, Pauline (Polly) Wife of Willis Buncombe; helps her husband in their grocery store at Pickerel Beach and hides Bible verses among the vegetables in Doris Betts's *The River to Pickle Beach.*

Buncombe, Willis Husband of Pauline Buncombe; proprietor of a small grocery store at Pickerel Beach in Doris Betts's *The River to Pickle Beach.*

Bunde, John Self-conscious autobiographer, who is estranged from his father because of his Unitarian beliefs; he wanders through the mountains of Ireland and Northern England; he marries seven wives whose premature deaths spur on his alpine and philosophical wanderings; he is at length reconciled with his father, a newly converted Unitarian, in Thomas Amory's *The Life of John Buncle, Esq.*

Bunde, John (the elder) Wealthy and educated father of John Buncle; he is generous to his son until he throws him out after a disagreement over a daily prayer, an estrangement aggravated by the selfishness of his recently wedded young wife and her nephew; he is ultimately converted to Unitarianism by his son's writing in Thomas Amory's *The Life of John Buncle, Esq.*

Bunder, Teddy Flashy, gangling automobile-export delivery driver who recruits co-worker Charles Lumley for a subsidiary drug-smuggling operation and who shoves Charles from a moving, stolen car while fleeing the police in John Wain's *Hurry On Down.*

Bundle, Nat Press agent for Harry Mercury in Peter De Vries's *Through the Fields of Clover.*

Bundren, Addie First wife of Anse Bundren and mother of five children, one of whom, Jewel, is fathered by the minister Whitfield; following Addie's death, the family carries her body to Jefferson in William Faulkner's *As I Lay Dying.*

Bundren, Anse Husband of Addie Bundren and father of four children; honors his wife's request to be buried in Jefferson, Mississippi; remarries soon after Addie's funeral in William Faulkner's *As I Lay Dying.*

Bundren, Cash Son of Anse and Addie Bundren; carpenter who builds his mother's coffin in William Faulkner's *As I Lay Dying.*

Bundren, Darl Son of Anse and Addie Bundren; committed to an asylum in William Faulkner's *As I Lay Dying.*

Bundren, Dewey Dell Daughter of Anse and Addie Bundren; impregnated by Lafe in William Faulkner's *As I Lay Dying.*

Bundren, Jewel Son of Addie Bundren and her lover Whitfield in William Faulkner's *As I Lay Dying.*

Bundren, Vardaman Son of Anse and Addie Bundren in William Faulkner's *As I Lay Dying.*

Bundy (Old Bundy) Aging, bald, and extremely thin slave with a predilection for alcohol; dies as a result of a whipping administered by Thomas Prosser in Arna Wendell Bontemps's *Black Thunder.*

Bunfit, Mr. Plodding detective in the case of the stolen diamonds whose theory turns out to be less reliable than that of his police colleague Gager in Anthony Trollope's *The Eustace Diamonds.*

Bungall, Mrs. The late part owner of a Devon brewery; her one-third interest in the company passes to her great-nephew, Luke Rowan, but is insufficient to assure him the partnership he wants in Anthony Trollope's *Rachel Ray.*

Bungay, Mr. Publisher of the *Pall Mall Gazette;* he is the enemy of his former friend and partner, Mr. Bacon, in William Makepeace Thackeray's *The History of Pendennis.*

Bungay, Mrs. Sister of Mr. Bacon and wife of Mr. Bungay in William Makepeace Thackeray's *The History of Pendennis.*

Bungs Cooper aboard the *Julia* in Herman Melville's *Omoo.*

Bunkin, Mrs. Neighbor of Mrs. Susannah Sanders in Charles Dickens's *The Posthumous Papers of the Pickwick Club.*

Bunn, Jenny Slender 20-year-old beauty with long black hair and darkish coloring who is a grade-school teacher; she falls in love with rake Patrick Standish and after prolonged resistance loses her prized virginity to him on his terms in Kingsley Amis's *Take a Girl Like You.*

Bunney, Mrs. Proprietress of a pub Anthony Keating finds a pleasant escape from various pressures at his home, High Rook House, in Margaret Drabble's *The Ice Age.*

Bunny Indo-Chinese hairdresser and associate of William Holmes in Isabel Colegate's *Orlando at the Brazen Threshold.*

Bunny First daughter of Quoyle and Petal Bear; imaginative and fearful; stands up for her friend, Wavy's son, Herry, by pushing a teacher who mimics him in E. Annie Proulx's *The Shipping News.*

Bunsby, Captain John (Jack) Captain Cuttle's nautical, mahogany-faced friend, who is regarded by Cuttle as an oracular sage and marries Mrs. MacStinger in Charles Dickens's *Dombey and Son.*

Bunsby, John Pilot of the *Tankadere,* a ship carrying the protagonist, Phileas Fogg, to Shanghai during his circumnavigation of the globe in Jules Verne's *Around the World in Eighty Days.*

Bunshaft, Gloria Featherbrained wife of Wally Hines and paramour of Joe Sandwich in Peter De Vries's *The Vale of Laughter.*

Bunt, Irma A "toad-like," brutal woman, who is Ernst Stavro Blofeld's secretary and mistress in Ian Fleming's *On Her Majesty's Secret Service.* She has become "Mrs. Shatterhand" in *You Only Live Twice.*

Bunter, Mervyn Lord Peter Wimsey's imperturbable, resourceful manservant, whose photography hobby, observation, and adaptability are useful to Lord Peter in Dorothy L. Sayers's *Whose Body?*, in *Clouds of Witness*, in *Unnatural Death*, in *The Unpleasantness at the Bellona Club*, in *Strong Poison*, in *Have His Carcase*, and in *The Nine Tailors: Changes Rung on an Old Theme in two Short Touches and Two Full Peals*.

Bunting, Jacob Retired soldier who accompanies Walter Lester on his travels and helps him collect the evidence that leads to the indictment for murder against Eugene Aram in Edward Bulwer-Lytton's *Eugene Aram*.

Bunting, Mr. Iping vicar whom Griffin burgles to get needed rent money and whose clothes he later steals in H. G. Wells's *The Invisible Man: A Grotesque Romance*.

Buntline, Amanita Wealthy lesbian friend of Caroline Rosewater in Kurt Vonnegut's *God Bless You, Mr. Rosewater*.

Bunyan, Dorothea Muriel Ponsonby's first governess; she leaves insulted by Sabine Ponsonby; she is the niece of the Reverend Dr. Chaucer in Ivy Compton-Burnett's *Daughters and Sons*.

Buonarotti Venetian saved from an assassin by Abellino (Count Rosalvo); his ingratitude encourages Abellino to join the bravos in Matthew Lewis's *The Bravo of Venice*.

Burbridge, Agatha Lady Clementina Burbridge's daughter and Margaret Roehampton's cousin in Vita Sackville-West's *The Edwardians*.

Burbridge, Lady Clementina Sister to George, Earl of Roehampton; she upholds the traditional values and standards of aristocratic Edwardian society in Vita Sackville-West's *The Edwardians*.

Burch, Agatha Housekeeper at the Tennant estate who is disturbed and offended when Charley Raunce becomes head butler in Henry Green's *Loving*.

Burch, Doctor Young New York doctor who loves Dorinda Oakley and guides her emotional recovery and intellectual development in Ellen Glasgow's *Barren Ground*.

Burch, Lucas (Joe Brown) Braggart mill worker and bootlegger who fathers Lena Grove's child in William Faulkner's *Light in August*.

Burchell, Miss (Miss B., Mrs. Jefferis, Mrs. Faulkland) Mrs. Gerrarde's niece, whom Sidney Bidulph Arnold wants Orlando Faulkland to marry in order to legitimize his unborn child; under the name Jefferis, she reveals her true name (Burchell) and delivers a son; when married to Orlando Faulkland, she is shot by him for adultery; finally she dies an unloved wretch in Frances Sheridan's *Memoirs of Miss Sidney Bidulph*.

Burchell, Mr. See Thornhill, Sir William.

Burckheim, Caroline Second wife of Honoré Burckheim; considered completely unmanageable by her husband, she struggles to be accepted as a French woman rather than as the daughter of an American senator; the jealous Anne-Marie Eschelmer and later Honoré himself taunt her for her inability to conceive children; she finally returns to America, disillusioned by her husband's intrigues but loyal to France in Storm Jameson's *Cousin Honoré*.

Burckheim, Genevieve Lighthearted first wife of Honoré Burckheim, whom she married at age nineteen and who remembers her as very young when he is over eighty; he also remembers her as a woman who constantly contradicted herself and was the only love of his life in Storm Jameson's *Cousin Honoré*.

Burckheim, Honoré Lusty, cunning, greedy, elderly egoist; he is the independent and self-centered owner of an ancient vineyard in an Alsatian valley and of an ironworks; husband of first Genevieve and then Caroline, he is also the father of an illegitimate daughter, Anne-Marie Eschelmer; he is fiercely anti-German just before the fall of France in World War II; he loves France but is an unheroic and often heartless figure, who is betrayed by relatives who see the financial success of the ironworks as dependent upon covert cooperation with German industrialists in Storm Jameson's *Cousin Honoré*.

Burcot, Azora Head of the female republic at Burcot Lodge, a self-sufficient colony of one hundred deeply religious women remarkably advanced in mathematics; she takes up lengthy religious discussions with John Buncle in Thomas Amory's *The Life of John Buncle, Esq.*

Burcot, Mr. Wealthy gentleman, who squanders his fortune in search of the philosopher's stone; reformed by his daughter, Azora, he sets up a colony in Stanemore in Thomas Amory's *The Life of John Buncle, Esq.*

Burde, Crystal Hilary Burde's beloved unmarried sister, a dressmaker; she cherishes a selfless, hopeless passion for Gunnar Jopling in Iris Murdoch's *A Word Child*.

Burde, Hilary Orphanage-reared illegitimate child who became a brilliant linguist but is now working as a civil-service clerk in Whitehall; he becomes involved in an emotional triangle that repeats the tragedy that destroyed his career as an Oxford don years before; he is narrator of Iris Murdoch's *A Word Child.*

Burden (I), Calvin Father of Nathaniel Burden; John Sartoris kills Burden and Calvin Burden II in William Faulkner's *Light in August.*

Burden (II), Calvin Son of Nathaniel and Juana Burden; John Sartoris kills Burden and Calvin Burden I in William Faulkner's *Light in August.*

Burden, Ellis (Scholarly Attorney) Lawyer who marries Jack Burden's mother and moves her from Arkansas to Burden's Landing; leaves her when Jack is about six years old in Robert Penn Warren's *All the King's Men.*

Burden, Jack (Jackie, Jackie-Bird, Jackie-Boy) Student of history, friend of Anne and Adam Stanton, son of Judge Irwin, and cynical right-hand man for Willie Stark; narrator of Robert Penn Warren's *All the King's Men.*

Burden, Jim Lawyer for a railroad company who recalls his friendship with Ántonia Shimerda; narrator of Willa Cather's *My Ántonia.*

Burden, Joanna Daughter of Nathaniel Burden and his second wife; lover of Joe Christmas, who murders her, in William Faulkner's *Light in August;* also appears in *The Mansion.*

Burden, Juana First wife of Nathaniel Burden and mother of Calvin Burden II in William Faulkner's *Light in August.*

Burden, Martha White New York artist friend of Angela Murray in Jessie Redmon Fauset's *Plum Bun.*

Burden, Milly Defiant and unsettling secretary of Virginius Littlepage; seduced, impregnated, and abandoned by Martin Welding in Ellen Glasgow's *They Stooped to Folly.*

Burden, Nathaniel Father of Calvin Burden II (by Juana Burden) and Joanna Burden (by his second wife) in William Faulkner's *Light in August.*

Burden, Simon Ancient coastal-village rustic and beacon watchman during the period of concern over an invasion in the Napoleonic War in Thomas Hardy's *The Trumpet-Major.*

Burdick, Alberta Ross See Ross, Alberta.

Burdock, Squire Matthew Bramble's friend at whose house Bramble meets the Count de Melville (Renaldo de Melvil) and Seraphina Melvilia Grieve in Tobias Smollett's *The Expedition of Humphry Clinker.*

Burdon, Clark Gunman and homesteader who befriends Clay Clavert in H. L. Davis's *Honey in the Horn.*

Burdon, Lester Deputy sheriff for San Mateo County, California; serves the eviction notice to Kathy; feels sorry for her and helps her move out of the house; exists in a loveless marriage; visits the evicted Kathy at her motel and tells his wife he wants a divorce; takes Kathy to his friend's fishing cabin; has admitted to tampering with evidence in the past in order to ensure a guilty verdict when he believed the defendant was guilty; feels enraged on Kathy's behalf over the situation she has been put into; plans to intimidate the Behranis by showing up in uniform to imply that he has the power to deport them if they do not give the house back to her; drives to a fishing cabin to see Kathy, but does not find her there; later breaks into the house where he finds the Behrani family trying to rouse her from an overdose of sleeping pills; threatens the family and is jailed for multiple felonies in Andre Dubus's *House of Sand and Fog.*

Burgan, Wally Shady lawyer and former business partner of Herbert Pierce; lover of Mildred Pierce in James M. Cain's *Mildred Pierce.*

Burge Arrogant college acquaintance and physician-in-training whom Charles Lumley encounters at a hospital staff party, where Charles attacks Burge's snobbery head-on in John Wain's *Hurry On Down.*

Burge, Jonathan Owner of a carpentry firm in Hayslope; he employs Adam Bede and eventually makes Adam his partner in George Eliot's *Adam Bede.*

Burge, Mary Daughter of Adam Bede's employer, Jonathan Burge; she wants to marry Adam and thus insure that she will inherit her father's carpentry business in George Eliot's *Adam Bede.*

Burgess, Bartholomew Sour, discontented uncle of Brooke Burgess; a long-time resident of Exeter, his strongest passion is his hatred of Miss Jemima Stanbury in Anthony Trollope's *He Knew He Was Right.*

Burgess, Becky Daughter of a poor fisherman who married into the middle class; found guilty of killing her husband with the assistance of teen lover, Sam; first in family to go to college in Marge Piercy's *The Longings of Women.*

Burgess, Bessie Vitriolic and coarse woman in the crowded Irish tenement building; engages in a verbal battle with Mrs. Gogan in a pub after a demonstration for Irish independence in 1916; goes out to loot stores during the fighting in the Easter Rebellion; shot dead by English soldiers as she stands in the window of her room, mistaken for a sniper, in Sean O'Casey's play *The Plough and the Stars.*

Burgess, Brooke Clerk in the Ecclesiastical Record Office and Jemima Stanbury's chosen heir; he courts and marries Dorothy Stanbury in Anthony Trollope's *He Knew He Was Right.*

Burgess, Milton Owner of a general store and rival merchant of Jasper Lathrop in Wendell Berry's *A Place on Earth* and *The Memory of Old Jack.*

Burgess, Mr. Undermaster who teaches the older boys in Mr. Herrick's school; he is retained for his image as a man with a degree in Ivy Compton-Burnett's *Pastors and Masters.*

Burgess, Rev. Mr. One of the "virtuous" townspeople in Hadleyburg; oversees the determination of the true identity of the benevolent soul who befriended the mysterious stranger; finally selects Mr. Robinson as the one worthy of receiving the bag of gold coins in Samuel Langhorne Clemens's "The Man That Corrupted Hadleyburg."

Burgess, Richard Guard for the South Eastern Railway who is bribed into helping Edward Pierce in Michael Crichton's *The Great Train Robbery.*

Burgess, Ted Handsome, vital tenant farmer identified with Aquarius who has a clandestine love affair with Marian Maudsley, the wealthy daughter of the resident family at Brandham Hall; he kills himself following discovery of their union in L. P. Hartley's *The Go-Between.*

Burgh, Sir Thomas Aristocratic college friend of Charles Smithson; he accompanies him on a night of debauchery in John Fowles's *The French Lieutenant's Woman.*

Burgomaster of Riva Referred to as Salvatore by his wife; a dignitary who receives the body of the Hunter Gracchus into the German port town of Riva; as the Burgomaster anticipates, the long dead hunter reawakens to tell the story of his life, death, and endless wandering aboard a rudderless death ship in Franz Kafka's "The Hunter Gracchus."

Burgos, Beto Son of César Burgos; student of Rafael Beltran; feels responsible for his mother's death; keeps his mother's shawl after her death; helps his father decorate a roadside altar for his family with shells and sea glass in Sandra Benítez's *A Place Where the Sea Remembers.*

Burgos, César Fisherman and father of Beto Burgos; his wife and two other sons are killed in a bus accident; builds a roadside altar for his family in Sandra Benítez's *A Place Where the Sea Remembers.*

Burgoyne, Colonel Chief Constable of the village in Kent where the actress Christine Clay was murdered in Josephine Tey's *A Shilling for Candles.*

Burgoyne, Eleanor Widowed cousin of Edward Manisty; she acts as his secretary for the writing of his book; she loves Manisty but loses him to Lucy Foster, a young American whom she has befriended in Mrs. Humphry Ward's *Eleanor.*

Burgoyne, Erica Daughter of Colonel Burgoyne; she befriends Robin Tisdall and clears him as a suspect by recovering an important piece of evidence in Josephine Tey's *A Shilling for Candles.*

Burgundy, Duke of, Charles the Bold Louis XI's kinsman, who hates his overlord and frets against his feudal bonds; Louis in turn hates and fears the powerful duke, who presides over an extravagant but well-fortified court in Sir Walter Scott's *Quentin Durward.* He negotiates with John de Vere for an alliance with Margaret of Anjou, refuses peace terms with Swiss cantons, and dies in battle in *Anne of Geierstein.*

Burgundy, Philip the Good, Duke of Part of the French nobility; later a character in *Henry VI, Part One;* hopes that the peace brought by the Treaty of Troyes will restore France to its former greatness in William Shakespeare's play *Henry V.*

Burhan, Mirza Known as "Firebeard" because of his fiery beard; clerk and philosopher riding with a caravan in the Iran desert bound for Tehran; contemplates the camel as a prophet but fails to interpret the camel's eyes in Derenik Demirjyan's "Chargah: A Poem."

Burke, Carlyle Retired schoolteacher who provokes his former brother-in-law into killing him in L. R. Wright's *The Suspect.*

Burke, Colonel Francis (Crowding Pat) Irish occasional confederate of the Master (James Durie) in Scotland, America, and France; he announces the Master's survival of both Scottish campaign and India; Mackellar uses parts of his laudatory autobiography to forward the narrative in Robert Louis Stevenson's *The Master of Ballantrae: A Winter's Tale.*

Burke, Dan Old farmer and shepherd who pretends to be dead to test his much younger wife, Nora, in the matter of fidelity after noting her fondness for conversation with any passing shepherd or traveler; suddenly arises from his false death upon hearing a neighbor, Micheal, propose to Nora, and banishes her into the night before sitting down for a drink with the neighbor in J. M. Synge's play *The Shadow of the Glen.*

Burke, Elizabeth (Betty) Servingwoman at the Nutters' who tries to protect her mistress from Mary Matchwell in J. Sheridan Le Fanu's *The House by the Churchyard,*

Burke, Father Catholic priest and gifted orator who speaks at a retreat to cure the protagonist, Tom Kernan, of his drinking problem in James Joyce's "Grace."

Burke, Frederick David Lovatt's stepfather, an academic who lives in a large, shabby house in Oxford with David's mother in Doris Lessing's *The Fifth Child.*

Burke, Lord The Marquis of Kilcarney, social catch of the season; he favors Olive Barton for much of the season but selects Violet Scully in George Moore's *A Drama in Muslin.*

Burke, Mary Former suburban housewife; goes through a bitter divorce; is injured in a fire and later goes to live in California with Leila Landsman's sister in Marge Piercy's *The Longings of Women.*

Burke, Matthew (Matt) Teacher who befriends Ben Mears; assists in destroying the evil that surrounds the Marsten House in Stephen King's *'Salem's Lot.*

Burke, Miss Woman not hired as a companion by Miranda Hume but hired as a housekeeper by Emma Greatheart; Rosebery Hume proposes to her in Ivy Compton-Burnett's *Mother and Son.*

Burke, Molly David Lovatt's mother, who can never forgive Harriet Lovatt for going to take Ben Lovatt out of the institution where she and her husband had put him in Doris Lessing's *The Fifth Child.*

Burke, Mr. Catholic husband who cruelly abuses his newly wedded, Protestant wife to convert her to Catholicism in Thomas Amory's *The Life of John Buncle, Esq.*

Burke, Mr. Reformist agent of the town Colambre (a part of Lord Clonbrony's estate); he is promoted to be the agent of Colambre and Clonbrony (another part of Lord Clonbrony's Irish estate) when Nicholas Garraghty is fired in Maria Edgeworth's *The Absentee.*

Burke, Nancy Assistant costume designer and friend of Delia Poole in Janet Flanner's *The Cubical City.*

Burke, Nora Young, lonely wife of the old man Dan Burke; enjoys speaking with any stranger or neighbor who passes the isolated farm; when a tramp arrives in the night she thinks her husband has suddenly died, she takes him in, also fetching her friend and neighbor, Micheal Dara; when Micheal proposes marriage to her, Dan arises from his feigned death to banish Nora from their home; leaves in the company of the tramp, who at least promises her some sense of freedom; echoes of Henrik Ibsen's *A Doll's House* sound in Nora in J. M. Synge's play *The Shadow of the Glen.*

Burke, O'Madden Newspaperman in James Joyce's *Ulysses.*

Burke, Sadie Private secretary to and mistress of Willie Stark; her jealousy leads to Stark's assassination in Robert Penn Warren's *All the King's Men.*

Burke, Studsy Ex-convict, owner of the speakeasy The Pigiron Club in Dashiell Hammett's *The Thin Man.*

Burke, Teddy Pickpocket who pretends to pick Edgar Trent's pocket, thus permitting Edward Pierce to gain information on safe keys in Michael Crichton's *The Great Train Robbery.*

Burke, Tim Irishman, goldsmith, and close friend of the Mor family in Iris Murdoch's *The Sandcastle.*

Burkette, Toonker Dentist who tells of Eleanor Fite's murder and Thomas McCutcheon's suicide in Jesse Hill Ford's *Mountains of Gilead;* mentioned in *The Liberation of Lord Byron Jones.*

Burkhalter, Johnnie Price Hardware dealer in Somerton and tennis partner of Steve Mundine in Jesse Hill Ford's *The Liberation of Lord Byron Jones.*

Burkin High school teacher who has accompanied his friend, Ivan Ivanovitch, on his walk in the country and takes shelter with him in the country house of their friend, Alehin; bathes with the other men and then listens to Ivan Ivanovitch's story about his brother; has trouble sleeping, as he is preoccupied with the "oppressive" smell of a tobacco pipe in Anton Chekhov's "Gooseberries."

Burkin, George Fellow inmate of George Brush in an Ozarksville, Missouri, jail in Thornton Wilder's *Heaven's My Destination.*

Burkin-Jones, Clare ("Mumbo") One of three women in their sixties who at the age of eleven were "best friends" at a school in Kent; now divorced, childless, and the successful owner of a chain of gift shops, she assumes a half-cynical, half-amused pose toward Diana Delacroix's cryptic ads designed to call them all together in Elizabeth Bowen's *The Little Girls.*

Burl Brother of Molly, uncle of Lil; travels to California and New York; his favorite sister was Lil's mother in Joan Chase's *During the Reign of the Queen of Persia.*

Burlap, Denis Pompous editor of a small literary magazine; his pious devotion to Christian charity is overshadowed by his indifference to his employee Walter Bidlake's financial problems and his calculated seduction of the vulnerable Beatrice Gilray in Aldous Huxley's *Point Counter Point.*

Burleigh Lawyer who gains acquittal for Royal Earle Thompson in Katherine Anne Porter's *Noon Wine.*

Burleigh, Cecil Conservative politician and supposedly eminent philosopher who first explains human society to the Utopians and who later succumbs to Rupert Catskill's plan to overthrow Utopian rule in H. G. Wells's *Men Like Gods.*

Burleigh, Dr. Ed Family doctor who warns Rosicky not to overexert himself; poor local boy who returns to serve his community; reflects on the completeness and beauty of Rosicky's life and death in Willa Cather's "Neighbour Rosicky."

Burleigh, Lord Commander of the Covenanters; he is defeated under the walls of Aberdeen in Sir Walter Scott's *A Legend of Montrose.*

Burleigh, Lord Cunning minister to Queen Elizabeth and implacable enemy to the Earl of Essex (2); he forces Ellinor to marry Lord Arlington (1) and to renounce her ties to the Stuart line in Sophia Lee's *The Recess.*

Burleson, John Friend of Melville Gurney and chief of the county Ku Klux Klan; speaks out against murdering Comfort Servosse and tends to the dying Servosse; ultimately denounces the Klan in Albion W. Tourgee's *A Fool's Errand.*

Burley See Balfour, John.

Burling, Jean Lover of Nicholas Delbanco in Nicholas Delbanco's *In the Middle Distance.*

Burlingame III, Henry Gifted tutor who gives Ebenezer Cooke an unusually comprehensive education in John Barth's *The Sot-Weed Factor.*

Burlingham, Robert Showboat owner and Susan Lenox's protector in David Graham Phillips's *Susan Lenox.*

Burlington One of the partners in Burlington and Smith, a London law firm which conspires with Lawyer Larkin in his plot to take the property of William Wylder in J. Sheridan Le Fanu's *Wylder's Hand.*

Burman, Mrs. Elderly legal wife of Victor Radnor; she married the young Radnor when she was already advanced in years, a disparity that led Victor to abandon her; she refuses to grant a divorce and frustrates Victor's designs of entering society in George Meredith's *One of Our Conquerors.*

Burnecker, Johnny Well-meaning Iowa farm youth who joins the army and is inspired by the example of Noah Ackerman in Irwin Shaw's *The Young Lions.*

Burnell, Nichole Fourteen-year-old paralyzed survivor of a bus accident; before the accident was frequently molested by her father; lies during her deposition in order to stop the accident victims' lawsuit and get revenge on her father in Russell Banks's *The Sweet Hereafter.*

Burner, Father Young ambitious priest who, through ridicule and intrigue, tries to push out Father Malt, the older priest in charge of the parish, so he can advance his own career; hypocritical and falsely pious, engages in torturing the story's narrator, a cat named Fritz, to rid the parish of one so well liked by Father Malt; he fails to remember that a cat has more than one life in J. F. Powers's "Death of a Favorite."

Burnet, Mr. Hubert Price's wealthy uncle, who disinherits him in favor of Emily Watson, then reinstates Hubert when Emily refuses his marriage proposal in George Moore's *Vain Fortune.*

Burnham, Alistair Australian neighbor; lives in a hippie commune with his wife, Julie, and his son, Chen-Yu, in Diane Johnson's *Lying Low.*

Burnham, Frank Stunt pilot killed in an airplane crash in William Faulkner's *Pylon.*

Burnham, Julie Neighbor who lives with her husband, Alistair, and son, Chen-Yu; creates and sells false identities; makes explosives and stores them in jars in Diane Johnson's *Lying Low.*

Burnham, Mr. White-haired older man who owns the Burnham Hall rented by the Pocahontas Drill Team in the town of Los Robles in Jessamyn West's "Love, Death, and the Ladies' Drill Team."

Burns, Anthony Timid, childlike man who frequents a Turkish bath in search of a soothing massage for his aching back; finds there the realization of his hidden masochistic desire at the pounding hands of a black masseur; undergoes an increasingly violent though satisfying treatment until he offers his emaciated body to be devoured by the masseur in Tennessee Williams's "Desire and the Black Masseur."

Burns, Helen Pensive and intelligent pupil at Lowood School, who befriends Jane Eyre and becomes Jane's spiritual guide through the example of her stoicism and selflessness in spite of her consumptive condition in Charlotte Brontë's *Jane Eyre.*

Burns, Mr. Employment manager at the Cosmodemonic Telegraph Company of North America in Henry Miller's *Tropic of Capricorn.*

Burns, Thomas Dublin shopkeeper who gives Caithleen her job as a shop assistant in Edna O'Brien's *The Country Girls.*

Burnside, Beauregard Jackson Pickett (Beau) Southern millionaire who marries Mame Dennis after she sells him twenty pairs of roller skates; dies thirteen months after their wedding in Patrick Dennis's *Auntie Mame.*

Burnside, Elmore Jefferson Davis Obnoxious southerner, ladies' underwear salesman, and cousin of Mame Dennis's dead husband; tries to court Mame until her nephew arranges to have him arrested by Fascists in Patrick Dennis's *Around the World with Auntie Mame.*

Burnside, Mame Dennis See Mame, Dennis.

Burnside, Reggie Rich young snob engaged in atomic research at Cambridge; he is first Fanny Welford's lover and then Elizabeth Paston's in Richard Aldington's *Death of a Hero.*

Burr, Aaron Conspirator to conquer and rule in Mexico; opponent of Thomas Jefferson; acquitted at a trial for treason in Mary Johnston's *Lewis Rand.*

Burr, Col. Aaron Third vice president of the United States; accused of killing Alexander Hamilton in a duel and arrested for treason in Gore Vidal's *Burr.*

Burr, Theodosia Daughter of Aaron Burr and wife of Joseph Alston; believed to have drowned in Gore Vidal's *Burr.*

Burra Little, demonstrative girl at the north London school, whose affection Miriam Henderson tries to keep within bounds in Dorothy Richardson's *Backwater.*

Burrage, Henry Son of Mrs. Burrage; Harvard student who proposes marriage to Verena Tarrant in Henry James's *The Bostonians.*

Burrage, Mrs. Society hostess who entertains Verena Tarrant in New York in Henry James's *The Bostonians.*

Burrard, Harry G. Variety artist whose day has passed; billed as an "Eccentric Comedian", he sings idiotic songs made up in white face with a red nose and topped with a ginger wig in an embarrassingly bad act; a victim of paranoia, he commits suicide in J. B. Priestley's *Lost Empires.*

Burrell, Alice Friend of Martha Quest and Stella Mathews; she works as Dr. Stern's nurse in Doris Lessing's *A Proper Marriage.*

Burrell, Willie Alice's husband, a friend of Martha Quest's husband, Douglas Knowell, in Doris Lessing's *A Proper Marriage.*

Burrhus Tutor to Néron (together with Sénèque, who has been exiled and is absent in the play); unlike his colleague Narcisse, he caters to Néron's morality and honesty, including marital fidelity; he also reminds Agrippine that Néron is now master of the world and later informs her of Britannicus's death in Jean Racine's *Britannicus.*

Burrington, Nathaniel Father of Calvin Burden I in William Faulkner's *Light in August.*

Burrows, Anne Sullen and sickly wife of John Burrows; she refuses to cooperate with Constable Toffy over her husband's activities or whereabouts in respect to the murder of Farmer Trumbull in Anthony Trollope's *The Vicar of Bullhampton.*

Burrows, John (the Grinder) Jailbird and prime mover in the murder of Farmer Trumbull in Anthony Trollope's *The Vicar of Bullhampton.*

Burrows, Mrs. Ribald crone, mother of John Burrows; she shelters Sam Brattle for a while in her cottage at Pycroft Common where Mr. Fenwick finds Sam's sister Carry in Anthony Trollope's *The Vicar of Bullhampton.*

Bursanov, Magda Nikolaevna Nikolai Bursanov's wife; she is the gentle-natured mother of Sonia, Nina, and Vera Bursanov and the lover of, successively, Eisenstein and Cecedek in William Gerhardie's *Futility: A Novel on Russian Themes.*

Bursanov, Nikolai Vasilievich Father to Sonia, Nina, and Vera Bursanov; he is married to Magda Bursanov but lives with his long-time mistress Fanny Ivanovna and wishes to marry his new mistress, Zina; he is handsome and somewhat honorable, yet weak and sloppy; he is not rich but owns gold mines in Siberia and another home and is the source of income for his extended family in William Gerhardie's *Futility: A Novel on Russian Themes.*

Bursanov, Nina Second eldest of the three Bursanov sisters; she is irresistibly attractive and charming, yet cold, sarcastic, and often childish; she was once the fiancée of Andrei Andreiech in William Gerhardie's *Futility: A Novel on Russian Themes.*

Bursanov, Sonia Eldest of the three Bursanov sisters and wife of Baron Wunderhausen; she is very attractive and well-mannered, yet unmotivated to do anything significant with her life in William Gerhardie's *Futility: A Novel on Russian Themes.*

Bursanov, Vera Youngest of the three Bursanov sisters; very attractive like her sisters, she is in other ways quite different from them; she is thought to be the natural daughter of Eisenstein, and she is apparently hated by her sisters and putative father, Nikolai Bursanov, in William Gerhardie's *Futility: A Novel on Russian Themes.*

Burstead, Sister ("Sister Bastard") Wrathful, hostile, middle-aged nurse in the old women's hospital ward; her fear of her own approaching old age has made her malicious in Muriel Spark's *Memento Mori.*

Bürstner, Fräulein Typist who lives in the same building as the accused Joseph K; Joseph K., on the night after his arrest, kisses her like an animal, perhaps even a vampire, upon her throat—an advance she rebuffs in Franz Kafka's *The Trial.*

Burt, Charles Social climber with a veneer of friendliness who attends a fashionable evening party at which the protagonist, Mabel Waring, appears; speaks to Mabel about her dress as old-fashioned in Virginia Woolf's "The New Dress."

Burt, Tom Thieving Maidenbridge child who tries to steal from Mr. Weston's Ford and discovers a lion in T. F. Powys's *Mr. Weston's Good Wine.*

Burtenshaw, Alexander Rosamund's father, a man who followed no calling in Ivy Compton-Burnett's *A House and Its Head.*

Burtenshaw, Rosamund Woman retired from missionary work, active in Oscar Jekyll's church; she is closest to her cousin Beatrice Fellowes in Ivy Compton-Burnett's *A House and Its Head.*

Burt-Jones, Poppy White English music teacher of Magid and Millat Iqbal and Irie Jones, with whom the Iqbal boys' father, Samad, has a brief extramarital affair; in addition to providing the pretext for Samad's crisis of faith and identity, which results in his sending Magid back to Bangladesh to be raised as a good Bengali Muslim, Poppy provides comic moments with her attempts to draw clear lines between cultures amid the cultural confusion of Zadie Smith's *White Teeth.*

Burton, Anthony (Tony) President of the Stuyvesant Bank who awards the vice-presidency of the bank to Charles Gray in John P. Marquand's *Point of No Return.*

Burton, Bertrand Manservant of Ebenezer Cooke; temporarily becomes a king in John Barth's *The Sot-Weed Factor.*

Burton, Cecilia Stouthearted wife of Theodore and staunch ally of Harry Clavering and supporter of his match with Florence Burton; she calls on Lady Ongar in a brave effort to dissuade her from continuing to draw Harry away from Florence in Anthony Trollope's *The Claverings.*

Burton, Charles (Barton) Baylor University pathologist and member of the scientist group at Project Wildfire in Michael Crichton's *The Andromeda Strain.*

Burton, Detective Policeman investigating the murders in Donald E. Westlake's *The Ax.*

Burton, Doc Physician who treats the migrant workers and supports their strike in John Steinbeck's *In Dubious Battle.*

Burton, Florence Devoted bride-to-be of Hairy Clavering; she suffers great sorrow when she learns of his renewed attention to Lady Ongar; she sends a parcel of his love letters to Mrs. Clavering, and Harry, thoroughly shamed, begs forgiveness; they finally marry in Anthony Trollope's *The Claverings.*

Burton, Hannah Clarissa Harlowe's favored chambermaid, who is discharged by the Harlowe family as a means of punishing Clarissa; bad health and Robert Lovelace's machinations stop her from joining Clarissa after the latter escapes from Lovelace in Samuel Richardson's *Clarissa: or, The History of a Young Lady.*

Burton, Jack Salesman for a firm selling chair covers; he is an enthusiastic theater goer and culture seeker who falls hopelessly in love with Alan Percival in Roy Fuller's *The Perfect Fool.*

Burton, Mr. Junior partner in a firm of civil engineers and father of Florence; he trains Harry Clavering, who falls in love with Florence; he shares the family's dismay when Clavering neglects her for a while in Anthony Trollope's *The Claverings.*

Burton, Mrs. Practical and unselfish wife of a civil engineer and mother of Theodore, three married daughters, and Florence; she suffers with her husband when Florence seems to be in danger of losing her betrothed, Harry Clavering, in Anthony Trollope's *The Claverings.*

Burton, Ralph English officer friendly to Johnny Lacey; brings Lacey news of Braddock's death after the defeat outside Fort Duquesne in Mary Lee Settle's *O Beulah Land.*

Burton, Ted Member of the Henderson girls' social circle who is understood to be "sweet" on Miriam Henderson in Dorothy Richardson's *Backwater.*

Burton, Theodore Unpretentious, good-natured eldest son of a civil engineer; he is destined to take over the firm; he injures his standing with his future brother-in-law, Harry Clavering, by dusting his boots with his handkerchief in Anthony Trollope's *The Claverings.*

Burton, Thomas One-legged purveyor of cats' meat, converted to temperance, mentioned in the "Report of the Committee of the United Grand Junction Ebeneezer Temperance Association" in Charles Dickens's *The Posthumous Papers of the Pickwick Club.*

Burton, Thomas One of the soldiers who tries to make a deal with Richard Mast for the pistol Mast possesses in James Jones's *The Pistol.*

Burwell, Tom Coarse young black man, also called Big Boy, who is known for his violent actions; works as a field hand on the Stone estate; kills young Bob Stone in a knife fight over their romantic pursuit of Louisa; is killed by an angry mob in retaliation in Jean Toomer's "Blood-Burning Moon."

Burwell, Tom (Big Boy) Southern black laborer who resents white Bob Stone's advances toward his girlfriend Louisa; in self-defense he cuts Stone's throat and is lynched by a white mob in Jean Toomer's *Cane.*

Bury, Caroline Wealthy, generous old friend of both Philip Surrogate and the Assistant Commissioner; Surrogate persuades her to ask the Assistant Commissioner to help obtain a reprieve for Jim Drover in Graham Greene's *It's a Battlefield.*

Bury, Sir Wilfrid Trustee of Lady Henry's estate and her valued friend; he attempts to mediate the quarrel between Lady Henry and Julie Le Breton in Mrs. Humphry Ward's *Lady Rose's Daughter.*

Buryan, John Thomas Farmer in Cornwall; Richard Lovat Somers helps him harvest corn and do other tasks in D. H. Lawrence's *Kangaroo.*

Busby, Bob English lecturer at the University of Rummidge in David Lodge's *Changing Places: A Tale of Two Campuses.* He organizes the University Teachers of English conference at the University of Rummidge and agonizes over arrangements and entertainment in *Small World.*

Busco, Bobby Large 16-year-old boy in Mary McGarry Morris's *Songs in Ordinary Time.*

Bush One of the Homo sapiens tribe given metaphoric names based on botanical resemblances by Lok and Fa as they observe their opponents from up in a tree in William Golding's *The Inheritors.*

Bush, Asa Firstborn son of Ishmael and Esther Bush; shot in the back by his uncle, Abiram White, who tries to blame Natty Bumppo for Asa's murder, in James Fenimore Cooper's *The Prairie.*

Bush, Esther (Eester) Powerful and fearless wife of Ishmael Bush; concurs with Ishmael in imposing a death sentence on her brother, Abiram White, in James Fenimore Cooper's *The Prairie.*

Bush, Ike (Al Kennedy) Fighter dissuaded from taking a dive by the Op in Dashiell Hammett's *Red Harvest.*

Bush, Ishmael (the Great Buffalo) Squatter, patriarch, and law unto himself; husband of Esther Bush and brother-in-law of Abiram White; with White, kidnapper of Inez de Certavallos in James Fenimore Cooper's *The Prairie.*

Bush, William Innately cautious lieutenant aboard the *Renown;* he is injured during a prisoner break in C. S. Forester's *Lieutenant Hornblower.* He is Horatio Hornblower's battle-ready lieutenant in *Hornblower and the Hotspur.* His capability as a seaman and his loyalty continue to be of service to his country and to Captain Hornblower in *The Happy Return* and in *Ship of the Line.* He has lost a foot during battle before they return home in *Flying Colours.* He is an aggressive, out-for-bloodshed captain under Hornblower's command in *Commodore Hornblower,* in *Lord Hornblower,* and in *Hornblower And the Crisis: An Unfinished Novel.*

Bushel, Brother Tory farmer, deacon in the Reverend Broad's chapel, who opposes George Allen on the issue of free trade, and who dies vexed by the railroad survey on his lands in Mark Rutherford's *The Revolution in Tanner's Lane.*

Bushfield, Ambrose Frontiersman in James Kirke Paulding's *Westward Ho!*

Bushman Self-proclaimed son of an African chief; he illegally sells government-issued goods on the streets of London in Colin MacInnes's *City of Spades.*

Bushy Favorite of Richard II; announces to Richard II that John of Gaunt, Richard's uncle, is grievously ill and entreats Richard to visit him; comforts Queen Isabella when Richard goes to Ireland; when informed of the nobles' rebellion, asks why rebel nobles have not been proclaimed traitors; balks at the task of raising an army against Henry Bolingbroke and his followers; flees to Bristol Castle with Green; executed by Henry in William Shakespeare's play *Richard II.*

Businessman The fourth planet the Little Prince visits acquaints him with the Businessman, a powerful individual who owns all the stars over which the King rules; daily counts the number of stars he possesses, and every evening locks the list in a drawer; says that being wealthy allows him to acquire even more stars, yet never inquires about the names of stars he already has in Antoine de Saint Exupéry's *The Little Prince.*

Buskbody, Martha Young dressmaker, who persuades the schoolteacher Mr. Pattieson to complete his narration in Sir Walter Scott's *Old Mortality.*

Buss, Mrs. Senior secretary for the Robinson, Cohen legal firm; she is completely devoted to mothering Jasper Cohen in Doris Lessing's *Martha Quest,* in *A Proper Marriage* and in *A Ripple from the Storm.* After his departure she transfers her devotion to Mr. Robinson until she and her husband leave the city in *Landlocked.*

Bussen, Otto Mathematics student at the University of Berlin; roomer in Rosa Reichl's boardinghouse in Katherine Anne Porter's *The Leaning Tower.*

Bussie, Jeanne Wet nurse to baby Jean-Baptiste Grenouille; recognizes that the child has no scent; refuses to nurse the unnatural child; leaves him with the local priest, Father Terrier, in Patrick Süskind's *Perfume.*

Bustamente, Senor Manager of the cinema in Malcolm Lowry's *Under the Volcano.*

Buster (Bus) Friend and playmate of Sandy Rodgers; passes for white in Langston Hughes's *Not Without Laughter.*

Buster, Lucky Retarded man who falls into the spillway of the Hoover Dam and is saved by Turtle and Taylor in Barbara Kingsolver's *Pigs in Heaven.*

Bustos, Baltasar Protagonist who writes a series of letters to Manuel Varela, a friend in Buenos Aries; young man and son of a wealthy Argentinean land owner deeply influenced by the Enlightenment, including Voltaire, Rousseau, and Diderot; faces a collision of ideas with the Catholic Church and his secular readings; involved in a campaign to remedy the contradictions and pacify the struggles regarding Spanish America's fight for independence in Carlos Fuentes's *The Campaign.*

Bustrófedon Deceased poet who, according to the story, was the creator of the tongue twister "tres tristes tigres" in Guillermo Cabrera Infante's *Three Trapped Tigers.*

Buswell, Seth Owner and editor of the *Peyton Place Times* who gives Allison MacKenzie her first job in Grace Metalious's *Peyton Place.*

Butch One of four young white men who are intent on harming Will Mayes for the accusation that he molested Minnie Cooper, a white, middle-aged spinster in William Faulkner's "Dry September."

Butcher One of the few compassionate men who, being aware of Mrs. Grimes's harsh life, gives her extra things such as soup bones or livers while she is selling her eggs; seems to hate Jake Grimes and his son for maltreating the poor woman in Sherwood Anderson's "Death in the Woods."

Butcher, Dr. Eastthorp doctor who is considered second-rate but socially superior in Mark Rutherford's *Catharine Furze.*

Butcher, Guy Businessman who is sympathetic to Frederick Tarr, listens to his sermon on English humor and its effect on reality, and advises him against marrying Bertha Lunken in Wyndham Lewis's *Tarr.*

Butcher, Mrs. Wife of a doctor in Eastthorp; Mrs. Furze wishes to move into her social circle in Mark Rutherford's *Catharine Furze.*

Butcher, Samuel (Long Sam) Head night porter of giant size; he appreciates Evelyn Orcham's notice in Arnold Bennett's *Imperial Palace.*

Butcher, Sir Ryland Senior Council for the defense of Giles Colmore in Roy Fuller's *The Father's Comedy.*

Buteo Native of South America and king-to-be when the revolution is won; fights alongside Ramón Cordes and feels brotherhood with him in William Herrick's *The Last to Die.*

Butler Mysterious stranger who abducts Ellen Langton; falls from a cliff and dies while fighting Fanshaw in Nathaniel Hawthorne's *Fanshawe.*

Butler, Aileen (Ai) See Cowperwood, Aileen Butler.

Butler, Arthur Patriot hero captured by the Tories; rescued by Horse Shoe Robinson in time to fight at King's Mountain; husband of Mildred Lindsay in John Pendleton Kennedy's *Horse Shoe Robinson.*

Butler, Bonnie Rhett Butler and Scarlett O'Hara's only child; brings parents together and is spoiled by both of them; dies riding a pony; Scarlett blames Rhett for the loss; her death provokes the end of her parents' marriage in Margaret Mitchell's *Gone with the Wind.*

Butler, Catherine Eldest daughter of the Butler family; her brilliant marriage to Beamish of the Foreign Office contrasts to the dreary career of Catherine George in Anne Thackeray Ritchie's *The Village on the Cliff.*

Butler, David Son of Reuben and Jeanie (Deans) Butler in Sir Walter Scott's *The Heart of Midlothian.*

Butler, Deb (Dorcas Wykes, Dorcas Martindale) Deceitful servant and Robert Lovelace's spy in the London brothel where Lovelace lodges the unsuspecting Clarissa Harlowe; she uses the names Dorcas Wykes and Dorcas Martindale in Samuel Richardson's *Clarissa: or, The History of a Young Lady.*

Butler, Donald Son of Reuben and Jeanie (Deans) Butler in Sir Walter Scott's *The Heart of Midlothian.*

Butler, Edward Malia (Eddie) Father of Aileen Butler; uses his political influence to ruin Frank Cowperwood in Theodore Dreiser's *The Financier.*

Butler, Eugenie Victoria (Bonnie Blue) Daughter of Scarlett O'Hara and Rhett Butler; killed in a horse-riding accident in Margaret Mitchell's *Gone with the Wind.*

Butler, Euphemia Daughter of Reuben and Jeanie (Deans) Butler in Sir Walter Scott's *The Heart of Midlothian.*

Butler, James (Corporal Trim) Uncle Toby Shandy's lanky, devoted servant, voluble but respectful, and like his master a retired soldier with a war wound (in the knee); he helps design and execute re-creations of famous military sieges on Toby's bowling green in Laurence Sterne's *The Life and Opinions of Tristram Shandy, Gentleman.*

Butler, Judith Reuben Butler's grandmother, who fights against age and poverty to procure Reuben an education in the ministry in Sir Walter Scott's *The Heart of Midlothian.*

Butler, Lady Mary The Duke of Ormonde's daughter, who marries Lord Ashburnham in William Makepeace Thackeray's *The History of Henry Esmond.*

Butler, Michael X. (Butty) First husband of Rozelle Hardcastle; dies in a yachting accident in Robert Penn Warren's *A Place to Come To.*

Butler, Miss Lecturer in classics with a sense of humor who teaches Dolores Hutton; she is later replaced by Dolores at the women's college in Ivy Compton-Burnett's *Dolores.*

Butler, Mrs. Elizabeth's cleaning woman, whose testimony at the trial of the smugglers reveals to them Elizabeth's role in sheltering Francis Andrews in Graham Greene's *The Man Within.*

Butler, Reuben Kind and scholarly man, who is somewhat vain about his learning; once educated, he becomes an assistant schoolmaster and is forced to officiate as clergyman at the hanging of John Porteous; he marries Jeanie Deans and receives a comfortable living from the kirk of Knocktarlities in Sir Walter Scott's *The Heart of Midlothian.*

Butler, Rhett A social outcast from Charleston, S.C.; makes a fortune as a blockade runner during the Civil War; falls in love with Scarlett O'Hara; becomes her third husband; leaves her after years of waiting for her to forget Ashley Wilkes and love him in Margaret Mitchell's *Gone with the Wind.*

Butler, Richard Kind but lazy painter, who is loved by Catherine George and later aided by her to overcome his social pride and recognize his deep love for Reine Chretien in Anne Thackeray Ritchie's *The Village on the Cliff.*

Butler, Sarah Young pupil of Catherine George in Anne Thackeray Ritchie's *The Village on the Cliff.*

Butler, Sophia Wife of one of Albert's stepsons; sent to jail for slapping the mayor's wife; released on parole as servant to mayor and his family; serves as a role model for Celie in Alice Walker's *The Color Purple.*

Butler, Stephen (Bible Butler, Stephen Scripture) Reuben Butler's Bible-thumping grandfather; as a soldier, he saved Argyle's grandfather, a debt John, Duke of Argyle repays to Reuben and Jeanie Deans in Sir Walter Scott's *The Heart of Midlothian.*

Butler, Walter Damned soul and British Loyalist; handpicked member of the jury by the Devil, Mr. Scratch; decides the fate of Jabez Stone's soul in Stephen Vincent Benét's "The Devil and Daniel Webster."

Butler, Widow Invalid mother of Butler; lives with her sister in Nathaniel Hawthorne's *Fanshawe.*

Butt Fellow convict, who wants Robert Penfold to give poison to the dog so that he can rob General Rolleston in Charles Reade's *Foul Play.*

Butt, Admiral Officer who accompanies Andrei Andreiech during the revolution; he is a man of sweeping movements and a war-winning air of confidence in William Gerhardie's *Futility: A Novel on Russian Themes.*

Buttall, Mr. Barrister who prosecutes the case against Hubert Cherrell for extradition to Bolivia in John Galsworthy's *Maid In Waiting.*

Butte, John British Communist Party member with whom Anna Wulf has an antagonistic, if not dubious, friendship, in Doris Lessing's *The Golden Notebook.*

Butterfield Insurance corporation clerk who, fired by Robert Elderson, is employed by Michael Mont as a bookseller in John Galsworthy's *The White Monkey.* He helps Soames Forsyte in the libel case against Fleur Forsyte Mont in *The Silver Spoon.* Soames plans for Butterfield to replace old Gradman in *Swan Song.*

Butterfield, Ann Wife of Hugh Butterfield and mother of Jade, Sam, and Keith Butterfield in Scott Spencer's *Endless Love.*

Butterfield, Hugh Doctor and father of Jade, Sam, and Hugh Butterfield; killed by a taxi while pursuing David Axelrod in Scott Spencer's *Endless Love.*

Butterfield, Jade Object of David Axelrod's obsessive love in Scott Spencer's *Endless Love.*

Butterfield, Keith Son of Hugh and Ann Butterfield in Scott Spencer's *Endless Love.*

Butterfield, Mr. Small butcher who is unwittingly used by Orkid Jim to make Tom Catchpole look like a thief in Mark Rutherford's *Catharine Furze.*

Butterfield, Sam (Sammy) Son of Hugh and Ann Butterfield in Scott Spencer's *Endless Love.*

Butterfly One of three miniaturists and illuminators who are suspects in the murders, the result of artistic and religious conspiracies in 16th-century Ottoman Turkey; paints figures in the book of Death, the Melancholy Woman; recurrent narrator in Orhan Pamuk's *My Name is Red.*

Butterfly See Song Liling.

Butterfly Catcher Nameless man of fifty, whom Mark Rutherford encounters during his lonely walks while preaching at the Unitarian chapel, and who renews Mark's acquaintance in London after Mary Mardon's death in Mark Rutherford's *The Autobiography of Mark Rutherford.*

Buttermead, Mabella Young society woman who banters with Jocelyn Pierston and whom he does not mistake for the "well-beloved" in Thomas Hardy's *The Well-Beloved.*

Buttermere Sir Godfrey Haslam's butler, who always overhears the family secrets in Ivy Compton-Burnett's *Men and Wives.*

Butterwell, Mr. Secretary of the General Committee Office; on his promotion Adolphus Crosbie is given his job in Anthony Trollope's *The Small House at Allington.* He lends Crosbie £500 in *The Last Chronicle of Barset.*

Butterworth, Clara Daughter of Tom Butterworth and student at Ohio State University; thoughtful young woman who marries Hugh McVey in Sherwood Anderson's *Poor White.*

Butterworth, Tom Ohio farmer and father of Clara Butterworth; invests in the factory that produces Hugh McVey's inventions in Sherwood Anderson's *Poor White.*

Button Lucy's hairdresser at the country estate of Chevron in Vita Sackville-West's *The Edwardians.*

Buttrick, Elsie Spirited independent officer in the Rhode Island Natural Resources Department and lover of Dick Pierce; she chooses him to be the father of her child in John Casey's *Spartina.*

Butts, Ben Easygoing, homily-quoting Texan; husband of Sophie Butts in Aaron Elkins's *Old Bones.*

Butts, Clement (Clem) Son of the marriage of Miss Leroy and George Butts; Mark Rutherford's boyhood friend who drifts apart from him, he becomes a successful schoolmaster and marries Ellen after her engagement to Mark is broken; he emigrates to Australia with her after he is discovered making love to another woman in Mark Rutherford's *Mark Rutherford's Deliverance.*

Butts, Ellen (Mrs. Clem) Mark Rutherford's betrothed, whom he met while they taught Sunday school before he went to college and to whom he tells his religious doubts to break their engagement in Mark Rutherford's *The Autobiography of Mark Rutherford.* He finally marries her after she is widowed and he lives as a journalist in London in *Mark Rutherford's Deliverance.*

Butts, George Placid miller who marries Miss Leroy and provides her with respectability for her eccentric ways in Mark Rutherford's *Mark Rutherford's Deliverance.*

Butts, Harold The Coldridges' gardener who, like his wife, Mary, helps out the family when they need to escape London for the countryside in Doris Lessing's *The Four-Gated City.*

Butts, Marie Ten-year-old crippled daughter of Clem and Ellen Butts; her selfless nursing of Ellen wins Mark Rutherford's profound love after his marriage to Ellen in her widowhood in Mark Rutherford's *Mark Rutherford's Deliverance.*

Butts, Mary Mark Coldridge's former nanny, who is often called to take care of his children when he is under stress in Doris Lessing's *The Four-Gated City.*

Butts, Red Sammy Proprietor of The Tower, a rundown highway barbecue restaurant; he laments the way of the world in clichés with the grandmother in Flannery O'Connor's "A Good Man Is Hard to Find."

Butts, Sophie Plain-spoken wife of Ben Butts and aunt of Ray Schaefer in Aaron Elkins's *Old Bones.*

Butz, Earl White Landrace boar that is the subject of Dr. Bo Jones's animal science experiment at Moo University; escapes from his pen when the building where he is housed is demolished, and dies while in flight in Jane Smiley's *Moo.*

Buxley, Edward Suitor of two of the icy Pole sisters in George Meredith's *Emilia in England.*

Buxton, Frank Son of the wealthy Mr. Buxton; he saves the life of Maggie Browne, to whom he is engaged, during the shipwreck in Elizabeth Gaskell's *The Moorland Cottage.*

Buxton, Mr. First mate of the hurricane-tossed ship *Archimedes;* the experience makes him understand, after twenty-five years of seagoing, that his virtue as a man and his profession are inextricable in Richard Hughes's *In Hazard.*

Buxton, Mr. Wealthy landowner, who disapproves of his son's engagement to Maggie Browne; her conduct wins him over in Elizabeth Gaskell's *The Moorland Cottage.*

Buxton, Mrs. Ailing wife of Mr. Buxton; her death removes a softening influence in Elizabeth Gaskell's *The Moorland Cottage.*

Buz Bold and honest but utterly unintelligent son of a local administrator; admires the Hussars and everything equestrian; natural-born follower who serves Teo in Ernst Jünger's *Die Zwille.*

Buzfuz, Serjeant Fat, red-faced lawyer, who represents Martha Bardell in her breach of promise suit against Samuel Pickwick in Charles Dickens's *The Posthumous Papers of the Pickwick Club.*

Buzhardt, Marvell A "small owlish American, postgraduate in psychology, anthropology, and environment at Columbia University, underground journalist, film-maker, and cultural entrepreneur", who is the guest of Quentin Villiers and the dispenser of exotic drug combinations in Martin Amis's *Dead Babies.*

Buzzard, Justice London judge who hears the trial of Humphrey Clinker, accused of highway robbery; he knows Clinker did not do it and that Edward Martin did in Tobias Smollett's *The Expedition of Humphry Clinker.*

Buzzard, Willard Iowa State wrestler who beats his former teammate George Bender in the championship for the one-hundred-fifty-eight-pound division in John Irving's *The 158-Pound Marriage.*

Buzzy Boyhood tormentor of the unnamed male narrator in Darryl Pinckney's *High Cotton.*

Bvalltu One of the Other Men; he is a philosopher who allows his mind and body to serve as a host to the disembodied narrator in Olaf Stapledon's *Star Maker.*

Byam Deputy-governor of the colony; he is wounded by an arrow from Imoinda's bow; he urges Oroonoko to surrender after the failed insurrection, then has him brutally whipped in Aphra Behn's *Oroonoko.*

Byam, Roger Midshipman on the HMS *Bounty* who narrates the events of the voyage to Tahiti, his efforts to compile a dictionary of the Tahitian language, the mutiny, his return to England in chains, and his narrow escape from being hanged as a mutineer in Charles Nordhoff and James Norman Hall's *Mutiny on the Bounty.*

Byass, Bessie Samuel Byass's wife, who is lively and amusing like her husband and his partner in benevolence; they quarrel and become estranged in George Gissing's *The Nether World.*

Byass, Samuel Lively and amusing benefactor to various people; he and his wife and partner in benevolence, Bessie, eventually quarrel and become alienated in George Gissing's *The Nether World.*

Bycliffe, Maurice Christian Real father of Esther Lyon and heir to the Transome estate; just before his death the scheming servant Henry Scaddon usurps his identity in George Eliot's *Felix Holt, the Radical.*

Bydel, Miss Local gossip who mishears the initials on a letter to give the Stranger, Juliet Granville, the name of Ellis in Frances Burney's *The Wanderer.*

Bye, Peter Doctor of mixed racial heritage; husband of Joanna Marshall in Jessie Redmon Fauset's *There Is Confusion.*

By-ends Traveler from Fair-speech who professes whatever will profit him the most; he hides selfish motives beneath apparent religiosity in his conversations with Christian and Hopeful in John Bunyan's *The Pilgrim's Progress from This World to That Which Is to Come.*

Byers, Eileen Wife of Pete Byers in Alice Hoffman's *The River King.*

Byers, Pete Husband of Eileen Byers; as the pharmacist, privy to more personal matters than anyone else in Haddan; doesn't gossip or judge in Alice Hoffman's *The River King.*

Byers, Sean Nephew of Pete Byers; handsome seventeen-year-old who has stolen two cars; friend of Gus Pierce; falls in love with Carlin Leander in Alice Hoffman's *The River King.*

Byfield, Mr. Track coach of Homer Macauley at Ithaca High School; prejudiced against students from immigrant families in William Saroyan's *The Human Comedy.*

Bygrave, Theresa Maud Enderby's aunt with whom Maud is sent to live after her parents separate in George Gissing's *The Unclassed.*

Byng, Stephanie ("Stiffy") Madeline Bassett's forthright cousin, whose engagement to "Stinker" Pinker is opposed by Sir Watkyn Bassett in P. G. Wodehouse's *The Code of the Woosters.* She is referred to as Mrs. Pinker in *Aunts Aren't Gentlemen.* She appears in *Stiff Upper Lip, Jeeves.*

Byrd, Anthony Florist, aspiring writer, and friend of Annie Brown in Betty Smith's *Joy in the Morning.*

Byrd, Crowell Father of Susan Byrd and son of Heddy Byrd in Toni Morrison's *Song of Solomon.*

Byrd, Heddy Indian woman who finds and rears Jake (Macon Dead I) when he is dropped by his father, the flying African; mother of Sing and Crowell Byrd and grandmother of Susan Byrd in Toni Morrison's *Song of Solomon.*

Byrd, Jessica John Ducane's lover, who proves to be the only possible girl for Willy Kost in Iris Murdoch's *The Nice and the Good.*

Byrd, Melanie Morris Zapp's free-spirited daughter from a former marriage; she lives on the ground floor of the house in which Philip Swallow lives in Plotinus, and Philip sleeps with her once; thereafter, she moves in with Charles Boon in David Lodge's *Changing Places: A Tale of Two Campuses.*

Byrd, Sing Wife of Macon Dead I, daughter of Heddy Byrd, and mother of Pilate Dead and Macon Dead II; dies in childbirth in Toni Morrison's *Song of Solomon.*

Byrd, Susan Granddaughter of Heddy Byrd and cousin of Macon (Milkman) Dead III; tells Milkman during his visit to Shalimar, Virginia, of the flying powers of his great-grandfather in Toni Morrison's *Song of Solomon.*

Byril, Emily Described as a "weak intelligent woman" in love with Mike Fletcher, but too possessive, in George Moore's *Mike Fletcher.*

Byring Young, handsome, well-bred diplomat for the British government; Byring could have been ambassador if he had not fallen in love with Rose Auburn in W. Somerset Maugham's *Ashenden: or The British Agent.*

Byrne, Joe Bushranger and lieutenant of the Kelly Gang who participates in the murders in Stringybark Creek; is killed during the siege of Glenrowan in Peter Carey's *True History of the Kelly Gang.*

Byrne, Joe Itinerant tinker who lives with his two beautiful wives in a tent by the wild moor; receives the stranger Carney into his tent during a storm; offers the traveler food and drink, but becomes incensed when Carney seeks to make love to one of the wives in Liam O'Flaherty's "The Tent."

Byrne, Michael Dublin patron of the arts who invites students and budding artists to his home in Flann O'Brien's *At Swim-Two-Birds.*

Byrne, Raymond Los Angeles deputy district attorney; co-prosecutor in the second murder trial of Gregory Powell and Jimmy Smith in Joseph Wambaugh's *The Onion Field.*

Byrnison, Iorek Exiled king of the talking armored bears of Svalbard; enslaved by men in a northern town until Lyra saves him and shows him how to retrieve his armor; saves Lyra and the children from Bolvangar; returns to Svalbard to fight and kill the usurper Iofur Raknison; gives Lyra the name "Silvertongue"; mends the subtle knife after Will shatters it trying to find Lyra; leads his bears south in search of colder climes after the ice on Svalbard begins to melt in Philip Pullman's *His Dark Materials.*

Byron, Harriet Beautiful heroine, a universally admired and courted orphan, raised by her grandmother; she is kidnapped by a rejected suitor, Sir Hargrave Pollexfen, and foils a secret marriage ceremony with him; Sir Charles Grandison rescues her, falls in love, and, after some trials, marries her in Samuel Richardson's *Sir Charles Grandison.*

Bywaters, Mrs. Frederick County postmistress who helps Nancy escape to Canada in Willa Cather's *Sapphira and the Slave Girl.*

BZ Homosexual film producer and husband of Helene; commits suicide in Joan Didion's *Play It As It Lays.*

Bzik, Jan Sickly Polish peasant, father of Wanda Bzik, and owner of the slave Jacob Eliezer in Isaac Bashevis Singer's *The Slave.*

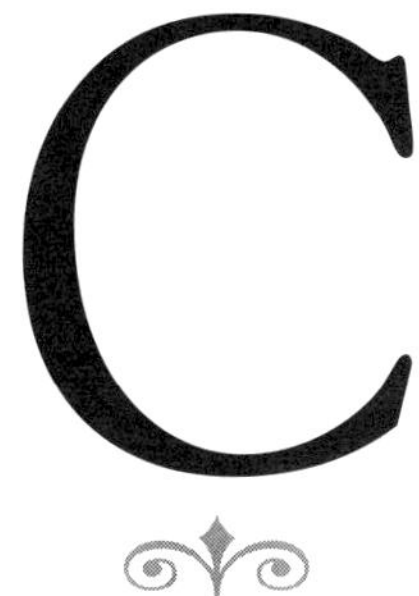

"C" Young female lawyer who has arrived at A's bedside during the latter's final hours before death; hopes to put A's legal affairs in order before the old woman's demise; listens in on A's life stories filled with marriage, wealth, and illicit romance in Edward Albee's play *Three Tall Women.*

C., Emma Object of Stephen Dedalus's unrequited love; she is admired on the tram at Harold's Cross by Stephen, who ultimately sees her as representing the conformity that he must reject in James Joyce's *A Portrait of the Artist as a Young Man.*

C—, Countess of Aristocratic confidante of Lady Davers; she reads Pamela Andrews's letters with much excitement and sympathy in Samuel Richardson's *Pamela, or Virtue Rewarded.*

C—, Mr. Recipient of Mrs. E—'s letter, which takes him to a rendezvous with Syrena Tricksy, who, though expecting Mr. E—, succumbs to his ardor in Eliza Haywood's *Anti-Pamela: or, Feign'd Innocence Detected.*

C—, Mrs. Jealous wife who surprises her husband and Syrena Tricksy together and has Syrena arrested, in accordance with Mrs. E—'s plot in Eliza Haywood's *Anti-Pamela: or, Feign'd Innocence Detected.*

Cabano, Prince (Jacob Isaacs) Jewish banker and a leader in the Oligarchy who attempts to deflower Estella Washington; killed during an apocalyptic revolution in Ignatius Donnelly's *Caesar's Column.*

Cabascango, Juancho Ecuadorian Indian with prosperous land; refuses to pay Padre Loma's extortion money for a mass; soon beaten to death by his suspicious neighbors after a flash flood brings God's wrath on them in Jorge Icaza's *Huasipungo.*

Cabinet, Count "Fallen" minister of the Pisuergan Court who lives in exile with his servant Peter Passer on the secluded island of St. Helena; he is visited by the pious Countess Yvorra with religious tracts during his stay at the nearby Summer-Palace in Ronald Firbank's *The Flower Beneath the Foot.*

Cable, Mannon Prolific movie star and womanizer; husband of Melanie-Shanna in Jackie Collins's *Hollywood Husbands.*

Cable, Melanie-Shanna Forgiving wife of womanizing movie-star husband Mannon Cable in Jackie Collins's *Hollywood Husbands.*

Cabot, Eben Twenty-five-year-old passionate son of the elderly patriarch Ephraim Cabot; blames his father for his mother's death and feels that the farm rightfully belongs to him and not his two half-brothers; at first, rejects Abbie Putnam, the beautiful young wife his father has brought to the farmstead, as an interloper, but soon falls in love with her; has a child with her; assumes responsibility for Abbie's murder of the infant and is arrested by the sheriff in Eugene O'Neill's play *Desire Under the Elms.*

Cabot, Ephraim Seventy-five-year-old widower who briefly abandons his New England farm to his three sons, who detest him; later returns to the farmstead with a beautiful wife, Abbie Putnam, half his age; fails to recognize that the new infant born to Abbie under his roof was fathered not by him but his son Eben; after Abbie kills the child, he turns his wife over to the sheriff; finds himself all alone to run the farm in Eugene O'Neill's play *Desire Under the Elms.*

Cabot, Lionel Best friend of Ulysses Macauley in William Saroyan's *The Human Comedy.*

Cabot, Peter Thirty-seven-year-old half-brother of Eben's, who despises his father; sells his future prospect of any inheritance of the family farmstead to Eben and strikes out with his brother Simeon for California in Eugene O'Neill's play *Desire Under the Elms.*

Cabot, Simeon Thirty-nine-year-old half-brother of Eben who despises his father; sells his future prospect of any inheritance of the family farm to Eben and strikes out with his brother Peter for California in Eugene O'Neill's play *Desire Under the Elms.*

Cabrini, Mrs. Teacher at Jane Addams High School who shows confidence in the protagonist, Lorrie's, intelligence and future in Carolyn Ferrell's "Proper Library."

Cacambo Faithful servant to Candide when they travel to South America; practical, smart, savvy, devoted; bails out Candide numerous times and eventually brings him and Cunégonde together; ends up cultivating the soil on Candide's farm in Voltaire's *Candide.*

Cacciato American infantryman who goes AWOL to travel from Vietnam to Paris and is pursued by his own squad in Tim O'Brien's *Going After Cacciato.*

Cacilda Whore who mingles with people in the monied class, including Leitão Leiria and Pedro, in Erico Verissimo's *Crossroads.*

Cacoethes, Rheinhold San Francisco literary critic in Jack Kerouac's *The Dharma Bums.*

Cacopardo, Matteo Sulfur processor who advises Major Joppolo to secure a bell for the town in John Hersey's *A Bell for Adano.*

Caddies, Mr. Albert Edward's bumpkin father, the perennial butt of Lady Wondershot's snobbish contempt; she considers him the archetypal selfish, indolent serf in H. G. Wells's *The Food of the Gods, and How It Came to Earth.*

Caddies, Albert Edward Boomfood baby from the village of Cheasing Eyebright who lives in ignorance of the other Giants, grows dissatisfied with his serfdom, and travels to London; there he becomes the first giant to be killed by the fearful Little People in H. G. Wells's *The Food of the Gods, and How It Came to Earth.*

Caderousse, M. Innkeeper who conceals the plot against the young protagonist, Edmond Dantès, in France in 1815; greed eventually destroys him, gratifying the revengeful Dantès, now disguised as the Count of Monte-Cristo, in Alexander Dumas, père's, *The Count of Monte-Cristo.*

Cadiga Prudent mistress of Nourjahad and sister of Cozro (Schemzeddin); named for the favorite wife of Mahomet, she is identified by a natural rosebud birthmark later painted on by an impersonator who feigns Cadiga's death when Nourjahad stabs her; she transfers Nourjahad's secret to Cozro in Frances Sheridan's *The History of Nourjahad.*

Cadman Lucia Lucas's chauffeur, who marries Georgie Pillson's housemaid, Foljambe, in E. F. Benson's *Mapp and Lucia.* He appears in *The Worshipful Lucia.*

Cadman, Emily Godwin Peak's aunt, who helps Godwin obtain financial support for his studies when he is a boy in George Gissing's *Born in Exile.*

Cadman, Mr Minor partner and manager of the publishing house Tremlett & Grove's; though he has no literary training, Cadman knows what sells books and is a good judge of character in Frank Swinnerton's *The Happy Family.*

Cadmus Legendary founder and the former king of Thebes; grandfather to both Cadmus and Dionysus; joins Teiresias in affirming Dionysus's divinity; unsuccessfully capitalizes upon his age and experience to incite Pentheus to honor Dionysus in Euripides' play *The Bacchants.*

Cadogan, Mrs. Mother of Emma; widow of Lyon the blacksmith, lover of Joe Hart the brewer and the Welshman Cadogan in Susan Sontag's *The Volcano Lover.*

Cadurcis, Captain George Plantagenet Cadurcis's loyal and noble cousin, who encourages Venetia Herbert's marriage to Plantagenet though he loves her himself, but who finally does become her husband after Plantagenet's death in Benjamin Disraeli's *Venetia.*

Cadurcis, Lady Katherine Bitter, unrefined widowed mother of Plantagenet Cadurcis, with whom she has an increasingly volatile relationship until her death in Benjamin Disraeli's *Venetia.*

Cadurcis, Lord Plantagenet (characterization of George Gordon, Lord Byron) Renowned, aristocratic poet, whose childhood affection for Venetia Herbert grows into an adult love, tragically ended by his untimely death by drowning in Benjamin Disraeli's *Venetia.*

Cadwalader, Mr. Leader of the Progressive group and official head of the Farmer-Labor Party in Chicago with whom Mrs. Beech seeks an alliance in W. E. B. DuBois's *Dark Princess.*

Cadwallader Long-dead giant whose skull Mr. Escott acquires from a sexton and with which he bribes Mr. Cranium's consent to his marriage to Cephalis Cranium in Thomas Love Peacock's *Headlong Hall.*

Cadwallader, Elinor Busybody matchmaking wife of the Rector of Tipton Grange and Freshitt Hall in George Eliot's *Middlemarch.*

Cadwallader, Humphrey Rector of Tipton Grange and Freshitt Hall; he refuses to interfere with Dorothea Brooke's plans to marry Edward Casaubon, although Sir James Chettam begs him to do so in George Eliot's *Middlemarch.*

Cadwallon (Renault Vidal) Welsh bard; he swears vengeance for the death of Gwenwyn, serves Hugo de Lacy under the assumed name of Renault Vidal, murders Randal de Lacy, whom he mistakes for Hugo, and is hanged by King Henry II in Sir Walter Scott's *The Betrothed.*

Cady, Abraham (Abe) American Jewish author of *The Holocaust,* a book that charges Adam Kelno with sterilizing healthy Jewish patients without the use of an anaesthetic in the Jadwiga concentration camp; defendant in a libel suit; lover of Sarah Wydman in Leon Uris's *QB VII.*

Cady, Alex Bigoted and violent poor-white tenant farmer who persecutes blacks; destroys a wagon belonging to Miltiades Vaiden and leads a mob that lynches Toussaint Vaiden in T. S. Stribling's *The Store.*

Cady, Ben Son of Abe Cady; Israeli pilot killed during the Arab-Israeli conflict in Leon Uris's *QB VII.*

Cady, Dr. Benjamin Nobel Prize winner, one of Jesse Vogel's medical heroes, and father of Helene Cady Vogel in Joyce Carol Oates's *Wonderland.*

Cady, Eph Son of Alex Cady; assassinates Miltiades Vaiden in T. S. Stribling's *Unfinished Cathedral.*

Cady, Helene See Vogel, Helene Cady.

Caecilius [St. Cypriian] Bishop of Cardiage, who reconverts Agellius to Christianity and saves him from persecution, converts Callista and visits her in prison, and relieves Juba's madness in John Henry Newman's *Callista.*

Caesar III Prize-winning Boston bull terrier; Hedger's constant companion; serves as a register for Hedger's resistance to change; resents Eden Bower's intrusion into their lives in Willa Cather's "Coming Aphrodite."

Caesar, Augustus (Gus) Former slave of Richard Cameron; rapes Marion Lenoir and is lynched by the Ku Klux Klan in Thomas Dixon's *The Clansman.*

Caesar, Gaius Julius Dictator of Rome whose death occurs on the Ides of March in Thornton Wilder's *The Ides of March.*

Caesar, Julius Ruler of Rome and its empire in 44 B.C. in William Shakespeare's play *Julius Caesar.*

Caesarina Former prostitute and now wife of Ulderico Cavaglieri, the older cousin of the middle-aged protagonist Edgardo Limentano in Giorgio Bassani's *The Heron.*

Caesarini, Castruccio Idealistic poet, who is betrayed by Lumley Ferrers, his rival for the hand of Florence Lascilles, and lapses into madness in Edward Bulwer-Lytton's *Ernest Maltravers.* He hunts down and kills Ferrers before drowning himself in *Alice.*

Caffrey, Brian (Art) Grandson of Katherine Brownell and heir apparent to Etienne Dulac's audacity in Wright Morris's *Cause for Wonder.*

Caffrey, Cissy Companion of Gerty MacDowell observed by Leopold Bloom on the beach in James Joyce's *Ulysses.*

Caffyn, Mrs. Widow of 50 who befriends Madge Hopgood during her pregnancy in Mark Rutherford's *Clara Hopgood.*

Cafour Princess Carathis's Negress attendant, who forms love relationships with ghouls and enjoys romping in graveyards and other strange activities in William Beckford's *Vathek.*

Cage, Mr. Intelligent, humorous teacher and friend; he is Ann Veronica Stanley's lover, and he makes a life for Ann and himself in H. G. Wells's *Ann Veronica: A Modern Love Story.*

Cage, Rollo Loyal white friend of Jule Jackson and son of a store owner in George Wylie Henderson's *Jule.*

Cagertown, Liam Boyfriend of Jean Warner; British psychology professor; Dara makes a pass at him, and he tells Jean about it in Ann Beattie's *My Life, Starring Dara Falcon.*

Cahel, Delia Young fiancée of Michael Gillane who must stand by and watch her betrothed leave on the eve of their upcoming marriage day to go off to fight for Ireland in William Butler Yeats's play *Cathleen ni Houlihan.*

Cahill, Percy Dolly Wilcox's uncle, who marries Evie Wilcox in E. M. Forster's *Howards End.*

Cahn, Matthew (Matt) Handsome Arab; second husband of Rachel Farrell in William Herrick's *The Itinerant.*

Cahow, Eddie Ubiquitous barber with genealogical genius in Wright Morris's *The Man Who Was There* and *The Home Place.*

Caillard, Colonel Jean-Baptiste Proud, cruel aide-de-camp to Napoleon who is ordered to escort Horatio Hornblower, William Bush, and Brown to Paris; they escape, leaving him bound and gagged in C. S. Forester's *Flying Colours.*

Caillaud, Jean (John Kaylow) French shoemaker, a leading member of the London radical political club Zachariah Coleman joins; he is executed for killing a soldier to defend Major Maitland during the march of Manchester Blanketeers in 1817 in Mark Rutherford's *The Revolution in Tanner's Lane.*

Caillaud, Pauline Illegitimate child of Victorine and Dupin and the foster daughter of Jean Caillaud; an intellectual, free-thinking dancer, she marries Zachariah Coleman after his release from prison in 1821, bears his daughter, and dies in 1822 in Mark Rutherford's *The Revolution in Tanner's Lane.*

Caillet, Anna Oliver Beautiful and artistic older daughter of Thomas Oliver; marries Oliver's adopted son, Robert Caillet, and bears a son to carry on the family name in Shirley Ann Grau's *The Condor Passes.*

Caillet, Anthony Son of Anna and Robert Caillet destined to carry on the family name; commits suicide, driving his parents to despair in Shirley Ann Grau's *The Condor Passes.*

Caillet, Aurelie Mother of Joan Mitchell and four other daughters from five successive marriages in Shirley Ann Grau's *The House on Coliseum Street.*

Caillet, Robert Adopted son of Thomas Oliver; unfaithful husband of Anna Oliver Caillet and father of Anthony Caillet in Shirley Ann Grau's *The Condor Passes.*

Cain, Amanda (Mandy) Adulteress whose infidelity, discovered by Ellen Chesser, causes the suicide of Cassie Beal MacMurtrie in Elizabeth Madox Roberts's *The Time of Man.*

Cain, George (Georgie, Daddy George, Junior) Harlem basketball star and community hero unable to handle the pressure in a private school, which he attends as a token black; becomes a drug addict and ex-convict; narrator of George Cain's *Blueschild Baby.*

Cain, Keith (Raschid) Brother of George Cain; involved in urban street violence; becomes a Muslim in George Cain's *Blueschild Baby.*

Cain, Mom Deeply religious mother of George Cain in George Cain's *Blueschild Baby.*

Cain, Pop (Grandad) Ambitious government worker and father of George Cain in George Cain's *Blueschild Baby.*

Cain, Woodrow Boy Frieda MacTeer fights at the school playground to defend Pecola Breedlove in Toni Morrison's *The Bluest Eye.*

Caird, Ephraim ("Chasehope") Influential elder of the Kirk in the parish of Woodilee, but also the high priest of the coven in depraved Satanic revels in the Black Wood in John Buchan's *Witch Wood.*

Cairn American writer of short stories; he is an ugly drinking companion to Marya Zelli and an honest appraiser of the Heidlers in Jean Rhys's *Postures.*

Cairo, Joel Homosexual pursuer of the jewel-encrusted statuette who forms a temporary alliance with Brigid O'Shaughnessy in Dashiell Hammett's *The Maltese Falcon.*

Caius Lucius Roman ambassador to Britain; attempts to negotiate a continuation of Britain's payment of tribute to Rome without success; assumes the position of general of the Roman army that invades Britain during the ensuing war in William Shakespeare's play *Cymbeline.*

Cal Favorite student of Thomas Eborn; Eborn dreams that Cal has died on the evening Eborn's mother actually dies in Reynolds Price's *Love and Work.*

Cal, Corie See Calhoun, Corie.

Cal, Haze See Calhoun, Haze.

Cal, Rie See Calhoun, Rie.

Calac Argentinean acquaintance Juan meets in "the City" who resembles the author Cortázar in Julio Cortázar's *62: A Model Kit.*

Calamity Jane (Martha Jane Canary) Childhood friend of Morissa Kirk; drunkenly taunts Morissa about being illegitimate in Mari Sandoz's *Miss Morissa.*

Calamy, Mr. Rich, handsome amorist, who is a houseguest at Lillian Aldwinkle's Italian villa; after a passionate affair with Mary Thriplow, he retires to a cottage in the mountains to contemplate life in Aldous Huxley's *Those Barren Leaves.*

Calary Aoz Roon's human slave, who is made a ceremonial sacrifice in Brian W. Aldiss's *Helliconia Spring.*

Calash, Joseph P. (Gentleman Joe) Highwayman who helps Daniel Harrow escape a beating and who is later helped to escape by Harrow and Molly Larkins, only to be shot by a posse, in Walter D. Edmonds's *Rome Haul.*

Caldecott Previous captain of the *Atropos* who stripped the captain's quarters bare in C. S. Forester's *Hornblower and the Atropos.*

Calder Mining leader who wants very much to overthrow the tyrannous Volyen Empire but is extremely distrustful of Klorathy's advice; he does heed his suggestion to grow a food source that ultimately gives the planet the power to overthrow both Volyen and Sirius in Doris Lessing's *Documents Relating to the Sentimental Agents in the Volyen Empire.*

Calder, Jim Successful writer of magazine fiction and cousin of the Brills; alternately drawn to and repelled by Wickford Point; narrator of John P. Marquand's *Wickford Point.*

Calderone, Jessica Terence's mother, who loves him best; she is a deeply meditative, ethical woman, who kills herself when her niece Anna Donne tells her that she is blighting her family's life in Ivy Compton-Burnett's *Elders and Betters.*

Calderone, Julius Thomas and Jessica's eleven-year-old son, who is closest to his sister Dora; he gives his father conventional answers when Thomas wants conventional children in Ivy Compton-Burnett's *Elders and Betters.*

Calderone, Terence Elder son of Jessica and Thomas; he tutors his cousin Reuben Donne and proposes to his cousin Anna Donne; he is not willing to make his own living in Ivy Compton-Burnett's *Elders and Betters.*

Calderone, Theodora (Dora) Thomas and Jessica's ten-year-old daughter who, with her brother Julius, has her own religion, praying to the Great God Clung in Ivy Compton-Burnett's *Elders and Betters.*

Calderone, Thomas Journalist and critic, married to Jessica; after Jessica's death he proposes to Florence Lacey, but he loves his daughter Tullia best in Ivy Compton-Burnett's *Elders and Betters.*

Calderone, Tullia Elder daughter of Jessica and Thomas; she is closest to her father and jealous of his proposed marriage to Florence Lacey in Ivy Compton-Burnett's *Elders and Betters.*

Caldicote, Dora School friend of Mildred Lathbury, with whom she has shared a flat; now a resident schoolteacher, she visits to comment on Mildred's life in Barbara Pym's *Excellent Women.*

Caldicote, William Fussy, epicene civil servant, brother to Dora; his purported passion for Mildred Lathbury has become almost a joke in Barbara Pym's *Excellent Women.* He makes an appearance in *Jane and Prudence.*

Caldigate, Daniel Just, hard, outwardly unsympathetic father of John, and squire of Folking, near Cambridge; angered by his son's debts, he disinherits him, but when John returns from Australia having made his fortune in gold mines, the pair are reconciled in Anthony Trollope's *John Caldigate.*

Caldigate, George Reliable nephew of Daniel Caldigate; at one point he seems likely to become his uncle's heir in Anthony Trollope's *John Caldigate.*

Caldigate, Hester Bolton Only daughter of Nicholas Bolton; she suffers persecution by her mother, who does all she can to separate her from John Caldigate; when scandal breaks out concerning his allegedly bigamous marriage to her, she stands by him; eventually his name is cleared and they are reunited in Anthony Trollope's *John Caldigate.*

Caldigate, John Restless, improvident son of Daniel Caldigate; he falls in love with Hester Bolton and seeks his fortune gold-mining in Australia; a foolish relationship with an adventuress, Euphemia Smith, almost wrecks his marriage when she turns up later in England; he is jailed on a trumped-up bigamy charge but is finally cleared and released from prison in Anthony Trollope's *John Caldigate.*

Caldwell Midshipman aboard the *Goliath* in C. S. Forester's *Mr. Midshipman Hornblower.*

Caldwell, Brock Idle, sarcastic older brother of Grace Caldwell Tate; gradually matures and becomes head of the Caldwell family in John O'Hara's *A Rage to Live.*

Caldwell, Catherine Kramer (Cassie, Chariclo) Wife of George Caldwell, mother of Peter Caldwell, and daughter of Pop Kramer in John Updike's *The Centaur.*

Caldwell, Dr. Edward (Ned) Father of William Caldwell; beloved country doctor injured in a buggy accident in Mary Austin's *Santa Lucia.*

Caldwell, Duck Hired worker for the Crooms; represents a high manifestation of ordinary life in Lionel Trilling's *The Middle of the Journey.*

Caldwell, Elias (Old Man) Dying neighbor of the Holbrooks, who tries to tell Mazie Holbrook what he has learned about life and wills her his books, which her father sells for fifty cents in Tillie Olsen's *Yonnondio.*

Caldwell, Emily Wife of Duck Caldwell and lover of John Laskell; her unreality distances the Crooms in Lionel Trilling's *The Middle of the Journey.*

Caldwell, George W. (Chiron, Sticks) Husband of Cassie Caldwell and father of Peter Caldwell; high school general science teacher and swimming coach preoccupied with death and mythic delusions that he is the perpetually wounded Chiron, noblest of all centaurs; narrates part of John Updike's *The Centaur.*

Caldwell, Grace Brock See Tate, Grace Brock Caldwell.

Caldwell, Maude West Indian neighbor of the Coffin family and twelve-year-old best friend of Francie Coffin in Louise Meriwether's *Daddy Was a Number Runner.*

Caldwell, Peter Son of George and Cassie Caldwell; cares deeply about his father but is often embarrassed by him; longs to be an artist; narrates part of John Updike's *The Centaur.*

Caldwell, Professor Professor of English who helps Martin Eden expand his interests in Jack London's *Martin Eden.*

Caldwell, Rebecca (Becky) Sixteen-year-old sister of Maude Caldwell and neighbor and friend of Francie Coffin in Louise Meriwether's *Daddy Was a Number Runner.*

Caldwell, Sally Divorced mother, "lady friend" of Frank Bascombe; owns Curtain Calls, a business that finds Broadway theater tickets for people with terminal illnesses in Richard Ford's *Independence Day.*

Caldwell, Sam Railroad man in William Faulkner's *The Reivers.*

Caldwell, Susan Daughter of Duck and Emily Caldwell; John Laskell becomes friendly with her in Lionel Trilling's *The Middle of the Journey.*

Caldwell, Vallejo (Vallie) Neighbor of Francie Coffin; arrested and sentenced to die for the robbery and murder of a shoe salesman in Louise Meriwether's *Daddy Was a Number Runner.*

Caldwell, William (Billy) Ebullient daughter of Doctor Caldwell; loved by Edward Jasper and successfully courted by George Rhewold in Mary Austin's *Santa Lucia.*

Cale, Sally Aging homosexual Hong Kong antiques dealer who introduces Lizzie Worthington to Drake Ko in John le Carré's *The Honourable Schoolboy.*

Calendar Captain of the fleet who puts on military airs despite his lower-class origin in C. S. Forester's *Flying Colours.*

Calenus Venal priest of Isis; he attempts to blackmail Arbaces in Edward Bulwer-Lytton's *The Last Days of Pompeii.*

Calhoun, Bud Lazy genius inventor who joins revolutionaries in Kurt Vonnegut's *Player Piano.*

Calhoun, Corie (Corie Cal) Wife of Lee Buck Calhoun and mother of Rie Calhoun and five other children in Harriette Simpson Arnow's *Mountain Path.*

Calhoun, Gerald (Bull's-eye, Jerry) Former college quarterback ashamed of his father; in love with Sue Murdock, daughter of his employer, Bogan Murdock, in Robert Penn Warren's *At Heaven's Gate.*

Calhoun, Haze (Haze Cal) Brother, neighbor, and moonshining partner of Lee Buck Calhoun in Harriette Simpson Arnow's *Mountain Path.*

Calhoun, Jackson Rutherford's older brother and father figure who cares for their master, Peleg Chandler; asks Chandler to divide his inheritance among the slaves instead of taking all for himself and Rutherford in Charles Johnson's *Middle Passage.*

Calhoun, Lee Buck Calhoun family patriarch, farmer, school trustee, moonshiner, fiddler, and landlord of Louisa Sheridan in Harriette Simpson Arnow's *Mountain Path.*

Calhoun, Mabel Daughter of Haze Calhoun; cousin and schoolmate of Rie Calhoun in Harriette Simpson Arnow's *Mountain Path.*

Calhoun, Noah Hardworking lover of poetry, the North Carolina outdoors, and Allie Nelson; his adoration of Allie survives fourteen years of separation, Allie's engagement to Lon Hammond, and Allie's battle with Alzheimer's disease in Nicholas Sparks's *The Notebook.*

Calhoun, Professor Seth Bigot and author of *The Menace of the Negro to Our American Civilization;* invited by Constancia Brandon to speak at a soiree in her salon in Countee Cullen's *One Way to Heaven.*

Calhoun, Rie (Rie Cal) Oldest daughter of Lee Buck and Corie Calhoun; student of Louisa Sheridan in Harriette Simpson *Arnow's Mountain Path.*

Calhoun, Riley Rutherford's father; leaves his family to escape from Peleg Chandler's farm; is caught and killed in Charles Johnson's *Middle Passage.*

Calhoun, Rutherford Freed slave from southern Illinois who works as petty thief; travels to Louisiana once freed; works on a slave clipper, the *Republic,* to avoid creditor Philippe "Papa" Zeringue and marriage to Isadora Bailey; survives mutiny and shipwreck to be rescued by luxury ship, the *Juno;* rediscovers Isadora and saves her from marriage to Zeringue by marrying her himself; raises Baleka as his own daughter in Charles Johnson's *Middle Passage.*

Caliban Slave to Prospero; son of the former owner of the island, the witch Sycorax, desires to claim the island and Miranda for himself; in a comic subplot, encounters Trinculo and Stephano, who give him wine, convincing him that they are gods; ineffectively colludes with Stephano and Trinculo to overthrow Prospero and establish Stephano as king of the island; punished but forgiven by Prospero in William Shakespeare's play *The Tempest.*

Calico, Molly Clerk of the zoning board and later parish secretary; clandestinely courted and affianced by Andrew Mackerel during the period of mourning for his late wife; finally marries Mike Todarescu in Peter De Vries's *The Mackerel Plaza.*

Calico, Pippa Mother of Molly Calico and temporary housekeeper for Andrew Mackerel in Peter De Vries's *The Mackerel Plaza.*

Caligula Grandnephew and successor of Tiberius, whose murder he oversees; he eventually goes mad and is assassinated by conspirators in Robert Graves's *I, Claudius.*

Calista, Lady of Mountfaçon Lady in waiting to Queen Berengaria and a leader in the prank that lures Sir Kenneth from his sentry post in Sir Walter Scott's *The Talisman.*

Calixta Young, beautiful Acadian woman who is the focus of romantic attraction by Bobinôt; romantically attracted to Alcée Laballière, with whom she is reputed to have had a brief affair; attends the Acadian ball and enjoys a secluded moment with Alcée; consents to marry Bobinôt when Alcée abandons her at the ball to go home with Clarisse in Kate Chopin's "At the 'Cadian Ball."

Calixta Acadian woman; wife of Bobinôt and mother of four-year-old son, Bibi; former romantic interest of Alcée Laballière; offers her home as a refuge to Alcée during a thunderstorm while her husband and son are away from home; has a sexual encounter with Alcée during the storm; acts as if nothing has happened when Bobinôt and Bibi return home in Kate Chopin's "The Storm."

Calkin, Agatha Sixty-year-old widow, who tries to be a mother to Gregory Haslam; she takes over Harriet Haslam's place in the charity sewing circle in Ivy Compton-Burnett's *Men and Wives.*

Calkin, Chief Constable Detective-Sergeant Mather's weak, place-hunting, bullying superior in Graham Greene's *A Gun for Sale.*

Call, Woodrow F. Former Texas Ranger captain; partner with Augustus McCrae in the Hat Creek Cattle Company; father of Newton Dobbs; gives Newton responsibility over cattle operations in Larry McMurtry's *Lonesome Dove.*

Callaghan, Christine Intelligent, sensitive woman who leaves Bertrand Welch and becomes romantically involved with Jim Dixon in Kingsley Amis's *Lucky Jim.*

Callahan, Deedee (Dolores) Wife of Jack Callahan; heavy marijuana user; has sex with Pablo Tabor on the *Cloud* and is killed by him in Robert Stone's *A Flag for Sunrise.*

Callahan, Donald Pastor of Jerusalem's Lot, who seeks to help Matt Burke destroy vampires in Stephen King's *'Salem's Lot.*

Callahan, Jack Owner of the *Cloud,* a shrimp boat Pablo Tabor works on; sells guns to the rebels; married to Deedee; is killed by Pablo Tabor in Robert Stone's *A Flag for Sunrise.*

Callahan, Thomas Recovering alcoholic, middle-aged law professor at Tulane University; former law clerk of one of the Supreme Court justices who is murdered in John Grisham's *The Pelican Brief;* boyfriend of Darby Shaw, a law student at Tulane; killed in a car bombing.

Callan, Robert Servant of Lord Stivers; he assists in the robbery of the nobleman's corpse and accuses Arabella Clement of the crime in Henry Brooke's *The Fool of Quality.*

Callander, Mrs. Inquisitive passenger aboard the ship taking John Caldigate to Australia; she reprimands him for his flirtatious behavior towards Euphemia Smith in Anthony Trollope's *John Caldigate.*

Callas, Maria Singer and girlfriend of Trout Fishing in America in Richard Brautigan's *Trout Fishing in America.*

Callcott, Jack Former soldier and now a workman; he tries to lure Richard Lovat Somers into the secret, fascistic "Diggers Clubs" that plans a revolution and a seizing of power in Australia; Callcott shows his pathological mentality when he kills three Socialists during a political rally in D. H. Lawrence's *Kangaroo.*

Callcott, Victoria Bright, attractive wife of Jack Callcott; she seems willing to become Richard Lovat Somers's lover, but Somers typically holds back and does not commit himself in D. H. Lawrence's *Kangaroo.*

Callendar, Major British officer stationed in Chandrapore, India, in E. M. Forster's *A Passage to India.*

Callendar, Mark Troubled son of Ronald Callendar; he takes a job as a gardener and is murdered in P. D. James's *An Unsuitable Job for a Woman.*

Callendar, Miss Recently hired faculty member of the English Department at Howard Kirk's university; she finds herself added to the list of his sexual conquests in Malcolm Bradbury's *The History Man.*

Callendar, Ronald Prominent, cold-hearted scientist; he hires Cordelia Gray to investigate the death of his son, Mark, in P. D. James's *An Unsuitable Job for a Woman.*

Callender, Mindy Young and pregnant girlfriend of Jake Simms in Anne Tyler's *Earthly Possessions.*

Calles, Plutarco Elías One of the acclaimed revolutionary leaders in the Mexican revolution (1910–17) in Mariano Azuela's *The Underdogs.*

Callicchio, Dante Former boxer and wrestler and father of three children; severely beats the federal men in New York so Fred Trumper can flee them in John Irving's *The Water-Method Man.*

Callid One of Amoranda's suitors, who wants only her money in Mary Davys's *The Reform'd Coquet.*

Callipus Charmides's friend who tries to warn him about consorting with Christians in the Reverend Theophilus Cardew's story in Mark Rutherford's *Catharine Furze.*

Callis, Max Seedy middle-aged Bohemian who is found shot with Harry Sinton's revolver in Roy Fuller's *Fantasy and Fugue.*

Callista Greek sculptress and singer, converted by her suitor Agellius and Bishop Caecilius; she denies being a Christian when shown instruments of torture but refuses to sacrifice to Roman gods and undergoes martyrdom following instruction and baptism by Caecilius in John Henry Newman's *Callista.*

Callister, Dutt Neighbor who accompanies Elias McCutcheon on the raid of the Horse Pens and later to the Civil War in Jesse Hill Ford's *The Raider.*

Callister, Fancy Wife of Dutt Callister; bears several children and constantly complains in Jesse Hill Ford's *The Raider.*

Callisto Middle-aged man who sees his life as running down, following the laws of thermodynamics and entropy; gives comfort and warmth to a sick bird by transferring his body heat to the bird's; has perfected the ecological balance in his apartment as a hothouse, compared to the constant 37°F outside in Thomas Pynchon's "Entropy."

Callistus Servant and bodyguard assigned to Julian Augustus by a cabal of Christian military officers; assassinates Julian at the height of a military skirmish with the Persians in Gore Vidal's *Julian.*

Call-me-Cobber Vain television personality constantly looking for new faces for his television show, *Junction!;* he films the racial riots in Napoli in Colin MacInnes's *Absolute Beginners.*

Callonby, Earl of Irish landowner and father of Lady Jane Callonby in Charles Lever's *The Confessions of Harry Lorrequer.*

Callonby, Lady Jane Daughter of the Irish landowner the Earl of Callonby; her love is sought by Guy Lorrequer but won by Harry Lorrequer in Charles Lever's *The Confessions of Harry Lorrequer.*

Calloway Manservant to Sir Ronald, minister at the British legation in Stockholm; Minty tries to get information on Krogh from him in Graham Greene's *England Made Me.*

Calloway, Caroline Intellectual mother of Louisa Calloway; suffers from periods of depression in Alice Adams's *Families and Survivors.*

Calloway, Colonel British officer, formerly of Scotland Yard, who for a time erroneously believes Harry Lime to be dead; in charge of the investigation into Lime's racketeering, he is the wary narrator of Graham Greene's *The Third Man and the Fallen Idol.*

Calloway, Corrine Stockbroker who desperately wishes to leave professional life to start a family; suffers a miscarriage and separates from her husband, Russell, after he has an affair; feels guilty when Jeff Pierce, the couple's mutual friend and her onetime lover, dies; remains in love with Russell after a divorce in Jay McInerney's *Brightness Falls.*

Calloway, Jack Tobacco-rich father of Louisa Calloway; vocal in his prejudice against Franklin Delano Roosevelt, unions, blacks, and Jews; spends life in and out of sanitoriums in Alice Adams's *Families and Survivors.*

Calloway, Louisa (Lou, Louisa Jeffreys, Louisa Wasserman) Modern southern belle rebelling against family wealth and tradition; protagonist of Alice Adams's *Families and Survivors.*

Calloway, Russell (Crash) Rising young editor at a New York publishing house who lives with his wife, Corrine, in a tiny Manhattan apartment; seeks to overthrow his former mentor; fails, and destroys his marriage; out of a job and divorced, he lands in Los Angeles, working for a movie studio and developing scripts in Jay McInerney's *Brightness Falls.*

Calloway, Zeb See Caudill, Boone.

Calman, Miles Famous Hollywood film director who lives in Beverly Hills; although married, lives a care-free life, including a two-year love affair with Eva Goebel, his wife's best friend; sees an analyst for depression and anxiety; thinks he suffers from a mother complex; intensely jealous of men who talk to his beautiful wife; dies in a plane crash in F. Scott Fitzgerald's "Crazy Sunday."

Calman, Stella Beautiful wife of the famous Hollywood film director Miles Calman; often referred to as Stella Walker; hosts a cocktail party at which the young film writer Joel Coles begins to fall in love with her; depressed over her husband's affair with her best friend, Eva Goebel; learns that Miles has died in a plane crash in F. Scott Fitzgerald's "Crazy Sunday."

Calomel, Mr. Social-climbing apothecary, who is duped by Lady Riot into wearing his pajamas to a high-toned party in an anecdote told by Mr. Rouvell in Richard Graves's *The Spiritual Quixote.*

Calou, Monsieur Curé who lives alone with his many books, waiting for God to drop into his life a soul that he can rescue; Jean is that soul; shows the unruly boy infinite patience and understanding; sees the relationship among Jean, Michelle, and Louis as beneficial, apt to keep a rascal like Jean out of trouble in François Charles Mauriac's *A Woman of the Pharisees.*

Caloveglia, Count Polite but poor Italian who forges the *Locri Faun* sculpture to provide a dowry for his daughter in Norman Douglas's *South Wind.*

Calphurnius Tribune whose intervention Jucundus seeks; it comes too late to save Callista from martyrdom in John Henry Newman's *Callista.*

Calpurnia Benevolent Roman widow who becomes a close friend of Helena in Evelyn Waugh's *Helena.*

Calpurnia Black woman who maintains the attorney Atticus Finch's household in a quiet southern Alabama town in Harper Lee's *To Kill a Mockingbird.*

Calpurnia Caesar's wife in William Shakespeare's play *Julius Caesar.*

Calpurnia Housekeeper for the Finch family and mother substitute for Scout and Jem Finch in Harper Lee's *To Kill a Mockingbird.*

Calpurnia Last wife of Caesar; they are married weeks before his death in Thornton Wilder's *The Ides of March.*

Calvert Newspaper owner who is the father of Roy; he drops his financial support of Jack Cotery to learn printing when he learns that Roy has a romantic attachment to Jack in C. P. Snow's *Strangers and Brothers.*

Calvert, Arabella (Bell) Prostitute who is eyewitness to young George Colwan's murder and who assists Arabella Logan in seeking evidence against Robert Colwan in James Hogg's *The Private Memoirs and Confessions of a Justified Sinner.*

Calvert, Charles, Lord Baltimore Lord Proprietary of the Province of Maryland in John Barth's *The Sot-Weed Factor.*

Calvert, Clay Orphan adopted by Uncle Preston Shiveley in H. L. Davis's *Honey in the Horn.*

Calvert, Herbert Commission agent; his pressure for rent on Ruth Earp involves Denry Machin in saving her from the runaway pantechnicon (furniture van) in which she tries to slip out of town at night in Arnold Bennett's *The Card: A Story of Adventure in the Five Towns.*

Calvert, Miss Jake Richardson's student whom he holds in contempt for her lack of intellectual ability and interest in seeking knowledge in Kingsley Amis's *Jake's Thing.*

Calvert, Lieutenant Joe Pilot of the *Endeavor* and member of the Rama expeditionary group; he first discovers the nature of Rama's propulsion system in Arthur C. Clarke's *Rendezvous with Rama.*

Calvert, Muriel Daughter of Roy and Rosalind (Wykes) Calvert; she is pregnant and engaged to marry Pat Eliot in C. P. Snow's *The Sleep of Reason.* She divorces him after the birth of their daughter; she lives with Charles Eliot as his mistress in *Last Things.* She is a spectator of the court challenge by Jenny Rastahl of her father's will and is a guest at Jenny's wedding in *In Their Wisdom.*

Calvert, Olive Roy's cousin, who breaks her relationship with Arthur Morcom, is seduced by Jack Cotery, and is one of the three tried and acquitted for fraud in C. P. Snow's *Strangers and Brothers.* Divorced from Jack Cotery, she is remarried; she hates Lewis Eliot for his political past in *The Sleep of Reason.*

Calvert, Roy Son of a newspaper owner; his romantic attachment to Jack Cotery causes the elder Calvert to drop his financial support for Jack's schooling in C. P. Snow's *Strangers and Brothers.* A scholar learned in ancient Asian languages, he is elected to a fellowship in a Cambridge college, suffers from mania and depression, and demonstrates some enthusiasm for the Nazis in Germany; he marries Rosalind Wykes in order to have a child and dies during a bombing mission during World War II in *The Light and the Dark.* He is active in support of Paul Jago for election as new college Master in *The Masters.*

Calvin Black gay man who befriends Molly Bolt on her arrival in New York City in Rita Mae Brown's *Rubyfruit Jungle.*

Calvo, Baldassare Tito Melema's benefactor, who raised the boy as a father but is abandoned by Tito and left to remain a slave of the Turks; he frees himself and kills Tito for revenge in George Eliot's *Romola.*

Calwell, Robert Author and homosexual neighbor of Daniel House; he fought in the Spanish civil war and, with a number of others, is a guest at House's island retreat soon after the arrival there of James Ross in Roy Fuller's *The Carnal Island.*

Calyxa Mythical figure who is also a student writing a thesis on *Perseus in the Perseid,* a novella in John Barth's *Chimera.*

Camaldoli, Frederigo, Count of Esteemed friend of Franceso Perfetti; he is admired by Julian Danvers; he is considered the very embodiment of the Renaissance ideal in William Godwin's *Cloudesley.*

Camara (Princess) Six-year-old daughter of Truman Held and Lynne Rabinowitz; dies as the result of a violent, unspecified crime in Alice Walker's *Meridian.*

Camber, Joe Owner of Cujo, who neglects to take the dog to the vet for his rabies shots. An independent and alcoholic backwoods mechanic, he offers to fix Donna Trenton's car in Stephen King's *Cujo.*

Cambray, Dr. New parson at Sir Ulick O'Shane's home; his benevolence, intelligence, and understanding make him an excellent adviser to Harry Ormond after Cornelius O'Shane's death in Maria Edgeworth's *Ormond.*

Cambridge, Earl of Son of the duke of York; brother of the duke of Aumerle; bribed by France to conspire to assassinate Henry V with Lord Scroop and Sir Thomas Grey; confronted by Henry about the conspiracy; arrested and sent to execution in William Shakespeare's play *Henry V.*

Cambridge, Thomas Maternal uncle of Clara and Theodore Wieland; reveals to Clara that Theodore killed his own wife and children at Carwin's instigation in Charles Brockden Brown's *Wieland.*

Cambujo Thief who stole Professor Bernstein's ring in Coatzacoalcos in Carlos Fuentes's *The Hydra Head.*

Camel Sardonic perpetual graduate student in English, who has been working on his doctoral thesis at the British Museum for years; he amuses Adam Appleby with a game called "When We Are in Power," and is the intended recipient of a job in the English department mistakenly offered to Adam in David Lodge's *The British Museum Is Falling Down.*

Camerando, Hector Resident of the Towers, a seniors' condominium complex where Mrs. Bliss lives; gives Mrs. Bliss a ride after one of her therapist meetings; afterward, places bets on the greyhound races and jai alai games for her in Stanley Elkin's *Mrs. Ted Bliss.*

Cameron Principal of the school where George Passant teaches nights; he presides at the board meeting at which Calvert drops his subsidy for Jack Cotery; he dismisses Passant from the faculty during the trial in C. P. Snow's *Strangers and Brothers.*

Cameron Professional killer, companion of Greer, habitual counter, and destroyer of the Hawkline Monster; plans to but does not marry Susan Hawkline in Richard Brautigan's *The Hawkline Monster.*

Cameron, Alec Letty Green's brother, down from Oxford; he is a veteran who needs violence, a militant of the Society of Ancient Britain who believes the only way to waken democrats is to kill them in C. Day Lewis's *Child of Misfortune.*

Cameron, Ben Confederate colonel who organizes the Ku Klux Klan to overthrow the black-dominated government of Reconstruction in Thomas Dixon's *The Clansman.*

Cameron, Dr. Lemuel (Bracciani) Site director of Talifer Missile Base known for his ruthlessness and brilliance; discredited in a congressional hearing in John Cheever's *The Wapshot Scandal.*

Cameron, Evelyn See Templeton, Evelyn.

Cameron, Henry Pioneer in modern architecture; defies mediocrity but finally is crushed by it in Ayn Rand's *The Fountainhead.*

Cameron, Kenneth New York producer who marries Kim Ravenal in Edna Ferber's *Show Boat.*

Cameron, Kim Ravenal Daughter of Magnolia and Gaylord Ravenal; New York actress who marries Kenneth Cameron in Edna Ferber's *Show Boat.*

Cameron, Margaret Sister of Ben Cameron; loves Phil Stoneman in Thomas Dixon's *The Clansman.*

Cameron, Richard Father of Ben and Margaret Cameron; physician who identifies Augustus Caesar as Marion Lenoir's assailant in Thomas Dixon's *The Clansman.*

Camila General Canales's daughter with whom Miguel Cara de Angel (Angel Face) falls in love and marries; her serious illness and their marriage help transform Angel Face from a traitorous rogue into a benevolent doer of charitable acts in Miguel Angel Asturias's *The President.*

Camilla Governess of Rosabella of Corfu in Matthew Lewis's *The Bravo of Venice.*

Camilla Governess to Lady Clementina della Porretta in Samuel Richardson's *Sir Charles Grandison.*

Camilla Sister of Matthew Pocket, wife of Cousin Raymond, and one of Miss Havisham's disappointed relatives in Charles Dickens's *Great Expectations.*

Camilla Sweet-tempered nurse of Julian Danvers in William Godwin's *Cloudesley.*

Camilla, Mother Nun of St. Clare and harsh jailer of Agnes de Medina in Matthew Lewis's *The Monk.*

Camille Second wife of Dean Moriarty; following a third marriage, he returns to her in Jack Kerouac's *On the Road.*

Camillo Sicilian lord; ordered by Leontes to poison Polixenes; refuses to oblige, opting instead to escape to Bohemia with Polixenes; after 16 years in Bohemia, requests to return to Sicilia, which Polixenes disapproves of; advises Florizel to escape with Perdita to Sicilia in the hope that Polixenes will follow them with Camillo in his company; upon his return to Sicilia, following his reconcilement with Leontes, is betrothed by him to Paulina in William Shakespeare's play *The Winter's Tale.*

Camillo, Don Valerio Venetian scholar and philosopher in Carlos Fuentes's *Terra Nostra.*

Camish, Mrs. Simon's intelligent, grindingly self-driven mother; the wife of an invalid, she became a radio-script writer to enable her son to escape the poverty of his background in Margaret Drabble's *The Needle's Eye.*

Camish, Julie Simon's socialite wife, whose unhappiness finds expression in scathing criticism of her husband; she improves in cheerfulness and goodwill after she and Rose Vassiliou become friends in Margaret Drabble's *The Needle's Eye.*

Camish, Simon Constrained, self-effacing, embittered barrister; he feels dead inside until he meets Rose Vassiliou; her plight and character rouse his respectful, unconsummated love in Margaret Drabble's *The Needle's Eye.*

Camp, Flora Youngest daughter of Tom Camp; abducted and killed, apparently by Dick, in Thomas Dixon's *The Leopard's Spots.*

Camp, Reuben (Reub) Unsuccessful farmer who agrees with many of Homos's criticisms of America in William Dean Howells's *A Traveler from Altruria.*

Camp, Tom Poor, crippled Confederate veteran who becomes insane after his daughters are killed by blacks in Thomas Dixon's *The Leopard's Spots.*

Campa, Vittoria See Emilia Alessandra (Sandra) Belloni.

Campanati, Domenico Self-indulgent younger brother of Don Carlo Campanati, brother-in-law of Kenneth Toomey, and husband of Hortense Toomey Campanati; he is a successful composer of Hollywood film scores, as well as a successful womanizer in Anthony Burgess's *Earthly Powers.*

Campanalti, Don Carlo (Pope Gregory XVII) Aggressive, worldly Catholic priest with a large appetite for food and drink; he befriends Kenneth Toomey when both are in their thirties; Don Carlo ascends to the top of the Church hierarchy by shrewd and subtle machinations and a stroke of luck in Anthony Burgess's *Earthly Powers.*

Campanati, Hortense Toomey Beautiful, willful younger sister of Kenneth Toomey and later wife of Domenico Campanati; she bears twins adulterously; after her divorce from Domenico, she forms a longstanding Lesbian alliance in Anthony Burgess's *Earthly Powers.*

Campbell Awe-struck crofter who discovers Pincher Martin's body on the Hebrides beach in William Golding's *Pincher Martin.*

Campbell, Adah Former Las Vegas showgirl; wife of Ian Campbell in Joseph Wambaugh's *The Onion Field.*

Campbell, Alan Once a good friend, maybe lover, of Dorian, he is a gifted musician but has turned to chemistry; helps dispose of Basil's murdered body when Dorian blackmails him; shoots himself in his laboratory, probably over remorse of conscience in Oscar Wilde's *The Picture of Dorian Gray.*

Campbell, Chrissie Mother of Ian Campbell in Joseph Wambaugh's *The Onion Field.*

Campbell, Colin Ray (the Red Fox, Glenure) Government factor to King George and member of the clan Campbell; he is shot by an unidentified man, supposedly a member of the Jacobite Appin Stewarts; David Balfour meets his road party by chance and witnesses the shooting; afterwards, David is wanted as an accessory to his murder in Robert Louis Stevenson's *Kidnapped.*

Campbell, Colonel Kind friend to the orphaned Jane Fairfax; she is brought up and educated in his home; the Campbells' departure for Ireland to visit their daughter, lately married to Mr. Dixon, causes Jane to return to her grandmother's home near Hartfield in Jane Austen's *Emma.*

Campbell, Dougal Scottish landlord who is host for Matthew Bramble's entourage at Inverary; he dislikes bagpipe music in Tobias Smollett's *The Expedition of Humphry Clinker.*

Campbell, General Colin Commander of loyal forces; he captures the Pretender Charles Stewart with Jacobite conspirators and gives all their freedom at the command of King George in Sir Walter Scott's *Redgauntlet.*

Campbell, Howard W., Jr. American playwright turned Nazi propagandist and U.S. spy; narrator of Kurt Vonnegut's *Mother Night,* and the "American Quisling" in *Slaughterhouse-Five.*

Campbell, Ian James Los Angeles policeman killed by Gregory Powell and Jimmy Smith in Joseph Wambaugh's *The Onion Field.*

Campbell, Kay (Kay-Kay, The Pumpkin) English literature major from Iowa and lover of Alex Portnoy; her refusal to convert to Judaism prompts Portnoy to end their relationship in Philip Roth's *Portnoy's Complaint.*

Campbell, Lady Sir Duncan's wife and Annot Lyle's grieving mother in Sir Walter Scott's *A Legend of Montrose.*

Campbell, Michael (Mike) Heavy-drinking British fiancé of Lady Brett Ashley in Ernest Hemingway's *The Sun Also Rises.*

Campbell, Milly Wife of Shep Campbell and mother of their four sons; contented with her suburban life in Richard Yates's *Revolutionary Road.*

Campbell, Mr. Kindly Scottish minister who is the long-time family friend and mentor of young David Balfour in Robert Louis Stevenson's *Kidnapped.*

Campbell, Mr. Young Anglo-Catholic rector, who tries to convince Charles Reding to remain Anglican in John Henry Newman's *Loss and Gain.*

Campbell, Mrs. Colonel Campbell's wife and Mrs. Dixon's mother in Jane Austen's *Emma.*

Campbell, Mungo Colin Ray Campbell's kinsman and lawyer, who is with him when he is shot, and who draws up and prints the placards advertising David Balfour and Alan Breck Stewart as the wanted criminals in Robert Louis Stevenson's *Kidnapped.*

Campbell, Murdoch See Argyle, Marquis of.

Campbell, Nicholas First love of Phebe Grant and the husband of one of her friends in Jessie Redmon Fauset's *Comedy, American Style.*

Campbell, Sheppard Sears (Shep) Well-educated and affluent engineer who adopts a self-created mask of boorish masculinity; secretly in love with April Wheeler in Richard Yates's *Revolutionary Road.*

Campbell, Sir Duncan Knight of Ardenvohr, Knight of Auchenbreck; he is the stately old kinsman of the Marquis of Argyle and principal commander of his army; fatally wounded in battle while trying to rally his men, he is taken prisoner and dies shortly after being reunited with his long-lost daughter, Annot Lyle, in Sir Walter Scott's *A Legend of Montrose.*

Campbell, Terrence (Terry) Ward of Adam Kelno and friend of Stephan Kelno; medical doctor in Leon Uris's *QB VII.*

Campbell, Tunis G. Antislavery activist, author of a memoir, and subject of Sam's research in Nicholas Delbanco's *News;* mentioned in *In the Middle Distance.*

Campbell, Virgil Owner and operator of Bound for Hell Grocery and Dry Goods on the outskirts of Tipton, North Carolina; discovers that a child rescued from a roadside creek is a relative of a state official and, with the help of a reporter, declares the rescuer a hero in Fred Chappell's *Brighten the Corner Where You Are.*

Campbell, Virgil Wily country storekeeper and school board member who gives David Christopher the job as principal of Cornhill Grammar School in Fred Chappell's *It Is Time, Lord.*

Campbell-Ward, Mrs. Professional beauty, the sensation of one of Lucy Bentham's balls; she arrives discreetly with her card-playing husband but is obviously admired by the Marquis of Worthing in George Moore's *A Modern Lover.*

Camper Traveler who helped to build the dam originally and who witnessed the mud slide that killed Mulge Lampson; helps to bury Hattie Lampson in John Hawkes's *The Beetle Leg.*

Camper, Lady Wealthy, attractive, intelligent widow who becomes acquainted with General Ople when she detects the romance developing between her nephew and his daughter; General Ople misconstrues her friendliness, forcing her to subject him to trial by ridicule before she eventually marries him in George Meredith's *The Case of General Ople and Lady Camper.*

Camperdine, Dorabella Young woman of propertied family who is insolently attracted to the handsome Gideon Sarn; his dreams of vengeance fuel his lust for wealth in Mary Webb's *Precious Bane.*

Camperdine, Mr Young squire who Beguildy hopes will fall in love with his daughter, Jancis, in Mary Webb's *Precious Bane.*

Camperdown, John Samuel Camperdown's son, the junior member of the firm of Camperdown and son in Anthony Trollope's *The Eustace Diamonds.* An energetic attorney, he establishes the existence of Mr. Emilius's first wife in Anthony Trollope's *Phineas Redux.*

Camperdown, Samuel Thoroughly trusted lawyer of the Eustace family; incensed by Lizzie Eustace's claim that diamonds from her late husband were an outright gift, he insists that as an heirloom they belong to the estate; he is consistently frustrated by her lies and maneuvers in Anthony Trollope's *The Eustace Diamonds.*

Campian, Theodora Mysterious inspiration of the "Mary Anne" movements; her father and brothers died with Garibaldi, and she tries to win Lothair over to the cause of the revolutionary liberals in Benjamin Disraeli's *Lothair.*

Campinet, Caroline Charles Hermsprong's love interest and cousin, Lord Grondale's daughter, and Maria Garnet's grandniece, who, with her friend Maria Fluart, plots to escape from an arranged betrothal to Sir Philip Chestrum in Robert Bage's *Hermsprong.*

Campion Efrafan rabbit, captain of Woundwort's Owsla (rabbit-warren militia) who succeeds Woundwort as Chief Rabbit of Efrafa in Richard Adams's *Watership Down.*

Campion, Dan T. Corrupt contractor and important member of the Catholic Church in John Gregory Dunne's *True Confessions.*

Campion, Lord Bryan Perdue's rival for Henrietta Saville's affections; he finally marries Henrietta and becomes Bryan's friend in Thomas Holcroft's *The Memoirs of Bryan Perdue.*

Campion, Lord, General Edward White-haired, red-checked, lame friend of Christopher Tietjens and an admirer of Christopher's wife, Sylvia, in Ford Madox Ford's *Some Do Not. . . .*He believes Sylvia's slander about Christopher until his interrogation of Christopher in *No More Parades.* He distinguishes himself during World War I, and lives at Groby with Sylvia after the war in *A Man Could Stand Up* and in *The Last Post.*

Campion, Luis Homosexual expatriate in F. Scott Fitzgerald's *Tender Is the Night.*

Campley, Mr. Married seducer of Miss Belmour; he follows her to Paris and carries on with her there, endangering the reputation of her companion, Henrietta Courteney, in Charlotte Lennox's *Henrietta.*

Camplin, Old Hard-hearted attorney, who is part of Sir Thomas Sindall's circle in Henry Mackenzie's *The Man of the World.*

Camplin, Young Witty friend of Sir Thomas Sindall; the son of the attorney Old Camplin, he is a reluctant soldier who furthers Sindall's evil schemes in Henry Mackenzie's *The Man of the World.*

Campo-Basso, Count de Italian nobleman and the Duke of Burgundy's nefarious favorite; the duke vainly commands Isabella de Croye to accept him as her husband in Sir Walter Scott's *Quentin Durward.* He proves to be a traitor to the duke in the battle with the Swiss in *Anne of Geierstein.*

Campolieri Young Italian aviator and highly sought-after bachelor; pursued by Babs Ansley in Edith Wharton's "Roman Fever."

Campos, Lieutenant Social agent of the Guardia Nacional in Tecan; kills a young hippie girl and confesses to Father Egan about it; watches Sister Justin and later tortures and kills her and confesses it to Father Egan in Robert Stone's *A Flag for Sunrise.*

Canaan, Akiva Ben Brother of Barak Ben Canaan and uncle of Ari and Jordana Ben Canaan; heads illegal terrorist activities against the British forces in Palestine in Leon Uris's *Exodus.*

Canaan, Ari Ben Lover of Kitty Fremont; soldier in the Israeli War of Independence and smuggler of Jews into Palestine, his home, in Leon Uris's *Exodus.*

Canaan, Barak Ben Father of Ari and Jordana Ben Canaan and brother of Akiva Ben Canaan; political head of Palestine in Leon Uris's *Exodus.*

Canaan, Jordana Ben Sister of Ari Ben Canaan and lover of David Ben Ami; Israeli sabra and fighter in Leon Uris's *Exodus.*

Canada, Eva Medina (Eve, Sweet) Narrator who, as a young woman, is sentenced to a reformatory for having stabbed Moses Tripp in the hand; married for two years to James Hunn; murders her lover, Davis Carter, and is imprisoned in a psychiatric prison in Gayl Jones's *Eva's Man.*

Canada, John Husband of Marie Canada and father of Eva Medina Canada in Gayl Jones's *Eva's Man.*

Canada, Marie Wife of John Canada, mother of Eva Medina Canada, and lover of Tyrone in Gayl Jones's *Eva's Man.*

Canales, General One of two men who becomes the target of the president's plot for murdering those suspected of being enemies of the government; initially escapes the president's scheme, only to later be poisoned in Spain; his daughter Camila marries Angel Face, a man who had earlier befriended the general in Miguel Angel Asturias's *The President.*

Canary Unusual avian purchased by Macedo from a secondhand shop; speaks fluently and philosophically only to its new owner in Machado de Assis's "A Canary's Ideas."

Canary, Martha Jane See Calamity Jane.

Canby Eponymous owner of the only saloon in the town of Bridger's Wells in Walter Van Tilburg Clark's *The Ox-Bow Incident.*

Candide Naïve, gullible, good-natured young man who travels the world to find out whether he lives in the best of all possible worlds; ejected from his home, faces numerous hardships and misfortunes, comes to question his tutor Pangloss's optimism, and stubbornly pursues the woman he loves, Cunégonde; finally realizes that "we must cultivate our garden," that is, focus on the small picture in Voltaire's *Candide.*

Candoe, John (Johnny) Puritan soldier and follower of Johnny Church and Thankful Perkins; condemned to death for mutiny but spared in Cromwell's blanket pardon in Mary Lee Settle's *Prisons.*

Candy Aging ranch hand who dreams of making a new start with George Milton and Lennie Small in John Steinbeck's *Of Mice and Men.*

Candy See Christian, Candy.

Candy, Maria Slum mother addicted to drink; she lives with her son and daughter in desperate poverty in George Gissing's *The Nether World.*

Candy, Mrs. Housekeeper and cook for Doremus Jessup; quiet supporter of the New Underground in Sinclair Lewis's *It Can't Happen Here.*

Candy, Pennyloaf Vigorous girl of the slums; she has an alcoholic mother, marries a cruel and irresponsible husband, and is left a poor widow in George Gissing's *The Nether World.*

Candy, Stephen Maria's son, who lives in poverty with his mother in George Gissing's *The Nether World.*

Candy, Thomas Fussy local physician, who takes offence at Franklin Blake's disparaging the medical profession; by secretly dosing him with laudanum, he unwittingly sets off a chain of events involving the loss of a yellow diamond and the eventual solving of its theft in Wilkie Collins's *The Moonstone. A Romance.*

Cane, Lucy Child who rescues Hazel from the cat during his last expedition to Nuthanger farm; driven in Dr. Adams's car, she brings Hazel back to the down in Richard Adams's *Watership Down.*

Caneback, Major Sporting chum of Lord Rufford; he has a nasty accident while fox hunting, and the ensuing drama enables Arabella Trefoil to come closer to her own quarry, Lord Rufford, in Anthony Trollope's *The American Senator.*

Canford, Peggy Older and less attractive of two concert-party girls performing in Blackpool; intelligent but cynical, she has a brief relationship with the younger Dick Herncastle in J. B. Priestley's *Lost Empires.*

Canidius One of Antony's generals; defects to Octavius Caesar's side after Antony's shameful loss in the crucial sea battle at Actium in William Shakespeare's *Antony and Cleopatra.*

Canino, Lash Killer in Raymond Chandler's *The Big Sleep.*

Cann, Billy Diminutive professional thief, who gives evidence against his associates Mr. Smiler and Mr. Benjamin in Anthony Trollope's *The Eustace Diamonds.*

Cann, Miss Teacher and former governess, who lodges with the Ridleys and is kind to young J. J. Ridley in William Makepeace Thackeray's *The Newcomes.*

Cannibal, Jimmy Former champion boxer who is beaten by Billy Whispers and knifed by Ronson Lighter because they suspect he is a police informant in Colin MacInnes's *City of Spades.*

Cannibal King Alcoholic drifter whose seedy and enigmatic presence inspires Joe to include his adversarial persona in the fantasy game "Africa" in Wolf Mankowitz's *A Kid for Two Farthings.*

Cannister, Martin Sexton who becomes an innkeeper and marries the maidservant Unity in Thomas Hardy's *A Pair of Blue Eyes.*

Cannon, Audrey Assistant professor of dance and theater arts who limps because of an accident with a lawnmower; has an affair with Severin Winter in John Irving's *The 158-Pound Marriage.*

Cannon, George Thirty-six-year-old hopeful hotel entrepreneur; he loves Hilda Lessways and draws her into his Bursley newspaper project, which fails, then into his Brighton boarding-house venture, and then into a marriage, the bigamous nature of which a servant reveals to her in Arnold Bennett's *Hilda Lessways.* He is an innocent prisoner for theft in Dartmoor; he is discovered there by Hilda and Edwin Clayhanger, and Edwin helps him to a new life in America in *These Twain.*

Cannon, George Edwin Illegitimate young son of Hilda Lessways; he charms Edwin Clayhanger before Edwin becomes his stepfather in Arnold Bennett's *Clayhanger.* He adores his stepfather and hopes to become the architect Edwin always wanted to be in *These Twain.*

Canon High-ranking priest; one of two Catholic fathers hearing confessions late one afternoon; oddly, has only two women in his single confessional line, while Father Deeley has two long lines of penitents; agitated and disturbed as he thinks about the confessions he has heard because he thinks the penitents are not sincere; many of them, such as Madgie, whose confession he is about to hear, lie during their confessions; jaundiced by his long years of hearing sinners sin even in the confessional in Seán O'Faoláin's "The Sinners."

Cantabile, Rinaldo (Ronald) Flashy criminal and would-be mafia operator who smashes Charlie Citrine's Mercedes over a welched bet and tries to exploit Citrine's writings for personal profit in Saul Bellow's *Humboldt's Gift.*

Cantacuzene, Michael Emperor Alexius Comnenus's grand sewer, or household officer, in Sir Walter Scott's *Count Robert of Paris.*

Cantalupe Villainous male who drugs Carola Bennet at a brothel and rapes her in Thomas Amory's *The Life of John Buncle, Esq.*

Canterbury, Arundel, Archbishop of Mentioned in *Richard II,* in alliance with Henry Bolingbroke; crowned Henry IV in 1399 in William Shakespeare's play *Richard II.*

Canterbury, Henry Chicheley, Archbishop of Announces to the bishop of Ely that a bill is being considered by Parliament that would confiscate church lands and give monetary and property provisions to the Crown; recounts Henry V's redemption and reformation; says that the time of miracles is over and that Henry's reformation must have been somewhat calculated; dodges the threat of confiscation of property by offering to finance an invasion of France; recounts four examples in which the lineage of the crown of France inherits from females; famously compares the duties and stations of the government and its people to honey bees; advises that England should invade France with one quarter of its army and leave the other three-quarters at home to defend against the Scots in William Shakespeare's play *Henry V.*

Cantle, Christian Elderly grandson of Granfer Cantle and like him a commentator on Egdon Heath folk customs in Thomas Hardy's *The Return of the Native.*

Cantle, Grandfather Aged, comic rustic figure who seems to know or intuit the proceedings and behavior of those outside his social sphere in Thomas Hardy's *The Return of the Native.*

Cantley, Gerald (Chief) White chief of police who receives kickbacks from Tyree Tucker's illegal businesses; murders Tyree Tucker and arrests Fish Tucker for attempted rape in Richard Wright's *The Long Dream.*

Cantor, Davey Fellow student and friend of Reuven Malter in Chaim Potok's *The Chosen.*

Cantrip, Hughie Manipulative young artist who plans to marry Lady Franklin without giving up his mistress, Constance Copthorne, until his plan is foiled through an anonymous note sent to Lady Franklin by her car-hire driver, Steven Leadbitter; during a chauffeured drive after this note has been received, Leadbitter crashes his for-hire car, killing both himself and Hughie with Constance alone surviving in L. P. Hartley's *The Hireling.*

Cantrip, Lady Wife of an eminent Liberal statesman in Anthony Trollope's *Phineas Finn,* in *Phineas Redux,* and in *The Prime Minister.* She acts as adviser to Lady Mary Palliser and reluctantly assists Lord Popplecourt's suit with Mary in *The Duke's Children.*

Cantrip, Lord Wise senior statesman friend of Plantagenet Palliser and Phineas Finn's chief at the Colonial Office; he begs Finn not to resign over Irish tenant rights in Anthony Trollope's *Phineas Finn.* He is one of the Whig inner circle in *Phineas Redux.* He adds to the problems of the Duke of Omnium (Palliser) by declining to take office in *The Prime Minister.* He makes a brief appearance in *The Duke's Children.*

Cantwell, Richard (Dick, Ricardo) American army officer who, fatally ill, returns to Venice to visit a lover and hunt for ducks in Ernest Hemingway's *Across the River and into the Trees.*

Canty, John Cruel father of Tom Canty; introduces Edward Tudor, disguised as Tom Canty, to thieves and beggars in Samuel Langhorne Clemens's *The Prince and the Pauper.*

Canty, Tom Boy from the London slums who looks exactly like Edward Tudor; exchanges identity with Edward and learns the burdensome duties of royal life in Samuel Langhorne Clemens's *The Prince and the Pauper.*

Cao, Mr. Professor who employs the young Xiang Zi in his home after the latter has fled from the romantic trap set by Hu Niu; later allows the young man to continue his old job as a manservant in Lao She's *Camel Xiang Zi.*

Cao Yuan-lang Poet whom Miss Su Wen-wan marries in Qian Zhong-shu's *Fortress Besieged.*

Cap, Charles Sea captain who is uneasy on land and inland waters in James Fenimore Cooper's *The Pathfinder.*

Caparra, Nicolò Weapons maker of Florence who sells Tito Melema a chain mail vest for protection against knife thrusts in George Eliot's *Romola.*

Cape, Benjamin (Ben) Son of Caleb and Lizzie Cape; witnesses the murder of his friend Folded Leaf in Jessamyn West's *The Massacre at Fall Creek.*

Cape, Caleb (Cale) Husband of Lizzie Cape and unordained preacher to the settlement in Jessamyn West's *The Massacre at Fall Creek.*

Cape, Hannah (Hannay) Daughter of Caleb and Lizzie Cape; courted by Charles Fort and Oscar Dilk in Jessamyn West's *The Massacre at Fall Creek.*

Cape, Lizzie Wife of Caleb Cape in Jessamyn West's *The Massacre at Fall Creek.*

Capece, Count Nobleman of Florence and father of Cavaliere di Guardino and Lauretta Capece in J. Henry Shorthouse's *John Inglesant, A Romance.*

Capece, Lauretta Beautiful daughter of Count Capece of Florence; she is betrayed by her brother, Cavaliere di Guardino; she marries John Inglesant and dies of the plague with their son in J. Henry Shorthouse's *John Inglesant, A Romance.*

Capello, Luigi and Angelo Italian twins blamed for the murder of York Driscoll in Samuel Langhorne Clemens's *Pudd'nhead Wilson.*

Capetenakis, Johnny Aging Greek who owns a restaurant where Martha Quest and her colleagues often eat and discuss politics in Doris Lessing's *Landlocked.*

Capodistria, Paul ("Da Capo") Rich lecher whose rape of Justine Hosnani when she was a girl has resulted in her troubled promiscuity; his apparently accidental death during a shooting party frees her to leave husband and lover in Lawrence Durrell's *Justine.* Evidence that his death was faked is supplied in *Balthazar.* He is proved to be a co-conspirator with Justine and Nessim Hosnani in gunrunning in *Mountolive.* He writes to Balthazar from his hideout in *Clea.*

Capon, Mrs. Woman with whom Frado leaves her son until she can regain strength and find a livelihood in Harriet E. Wilson's *Our Nig.*

Cappadocian, The Guest at Herod's palace; skeptical about the invisible God of the Jews in Oscar Wilde's *Salomé.*

Capper, John One of Ellis Duckworth's men; he goes to summon help to the cottage; he fails to recognize the begging friars Will Lawless and Dick Shelton in their disguises in Robert Louis Stevenson's *The Black Arrow: A Tale of Two Roses.*

Cappone Tall, graceful, melancholic manager of the hotel restaurant; he delights in creating unique menus for wealthy patrons and brings an orchid to Gracie Savotte when she first dines in the restaurant in Arnold Bennett's *Imperial Palace.*

Caprio, Barry Brother of Steve Caprio and former navy boxer; hired by Jackie Cogan to beat a confession out of Mark Trattman in George V. Higgins's *Cogan's Trade.*

Caprio, Steve Mafia thug and brother of Barry Caprio; hired by Jackie Cogan to beat a confession out of Mark Trattman in George V. Higgins's *Cogan's Trade.*

Captain Nameless narrator of the sea tale; young man commanding his first ship, to which he was appointed only a fortnight before; racked with feelings of inadequacy, as he seems like a stranger on his own ship; while on watch finds the nearly drowned Leggatt hanging on to the ship's ladder and secretes him into his quarters; perceiving a startling similarity between himself and Leggatt, decides to help the admitted murderer escape prosecution; at the point of obsession with Leggatt, whom he calls his "double," nearly wrecks the ship while helping him escape in Joseph Conrad's *The Secret Sharer.*

Captain Career army soldier whose real interest lies in the scientific study of elements in meteorites; referred to as Adolf, finds himself in a household filled with domineering women; wants his daughter Bertha to leave the home to prepare herself for the teaching profession; becomes embroiled with his wife, Laura, over his decision, as she wants the women of the house to educate the daughter in the new ways; is the target of his wife's acrimonious actions to render him insane with her declaration that no man can be certain that he is the father of his children; finally placed in a straightjacket and dies from a heart attack in August Strindberg's play *The Father.*

Captain Friendly and easily bribed man who makes Jemy E. and Moll Flanders's voyage to America more comfortable by providing them with special amenities in Daniel Defoe's *The Fortunes and Misfortunes of the Famous Moll Flanders.*

Captain Man who is attracted to Charlotte Woodville but who behaves honorably and rescues her from other potential molesters when he learns dial she is engaged to Mr. Rivers in Richard Graves's *The Spiritual Quixote.*

Captain Seasoned leader of "The Bars" life-saving station at Cape Cod; has saved and lost many lives to the sea; tries but fails to revive a drowned man who has been brought to Mrs. Patrick's home in Susan Glaspell's play *The Outside.*

Captain Sinner from Peru; he joins the Jesuits to save his life and is the man in charge of the assassination of the king of Portugal in Charles Johnstone's *Chrysal: or, The Adventures of a Guinea.*

Captain Unnamed officer who, following the orders of his master, the unnamed squire, abducts Fanny Goodwill from the inn in Henry Fielding's *The History of the Adventures of Mr. Joseph Andrews and of His Friend Mr. Abraham Adams.*

Captain Lover of Ida Farange while she is married to Sir Claude in Henry James's *What Maisie Knew.*

Captain, The Stalwart captain whose ship sinks in the Atlantic, leaving him injured in a small lifeboat with three others; despite profound indignation at the loss of his ship, crew, and passengers, remains calm, patient, and stoic; maintains his unquestioned authority in the lifeboat, still advising the other three, for whom he serves as a father figure; after the boat is swamped, manages to reach shore safely while remaining mindful of the others in Stephen Crane's "The Open Boat."

Captain, The Forty-year-old prisoner surnamed Buynovsky who is a well-educated former naval captain and is arrested because of a friendship with a British admiral; works hard but has trouble adjusting to prison camp life in Alexander Solzhenitsyn's *One Day in the Life of Ivan Denisovitch.*

Captain/Priest Middle-aged, non-English-speaking priest appointed by the Order to supervise the ship's crew, cargo, and infrequent passengers to and from the leproserie in Graham Greene's *A Burnt-Out Case.*

Captain, *Woyzeck* Woyzeck's superior who comments on Woyzeck's lack of moral fiber; teases him about the infidelity of his wife, Marie, in Georg Büchner's play *Woyzeck.*

Captain Bob Tahitian jailer and linguist in Herman Melville's *Omoo.*

Captain of Attacking Vessel Cruel man who proves the maxim "cowardice is the inseparable companion of cruelty" and who is granted a trial in Charles Johnstone's *Chrysal: or the Adventures of a Guinea.*

Captain of English Man of War Miser who is bribed by the Spanish to avoid the Spanish treasure ships and who also avoids attacking any ship sighted so that he can get his gold back to England; later, he disobeys orders by leaving his station in order to get to England with his newfound wealth in Charles Johnstone's *Chrysal: or The Adventures of a Guinea.*

Captain of the Artillery Military officer who becomes the topic of conversation by Doña Magdalena and her daughter Amalia; left for Berlin with the hope of seeing the Parisian sights on his way, but was blinded in a boiler explosion accident before reaching the French capital in Alfonso Reyes's "The Dinner."

Captain of the Gendarmes Man in exile on a mission; mercilessly hunts down Timur in a graphic, labyrinthine chase and ensuing brutal murder; shows no remorse for his actions in Mary Lee Settle's *Blood Tie.*

Captain of the *Sainte-Marie-des-Anges* Irish captain of the ship on which the Master (James Durie) and Colonel Francis Burke leave Scotland; he is made to walk the plank by Teach in Robert Louis Stevenson's *The Master of Ballantrae: A Winter's Tale.*

Captain's Widow Moll Flanders's friend, who takes Moll in and tries to help her find a husband; she succeeds in marrying a captain herself in Daniel Defoe's *The Fortunes and Misfortunes of the Famous Moll Flanders.*

Capulet, Lady Wife of Capulet; proud, severe woman; distant when interacting with her daughter, compelling her to marry despite her youth and inexperience with men; justifies her severe behavior by noting she bore Juliet when only a teenager herself; sides with her husband in domestic matters, even though he exhibits little regard for anyone's interest but his own in William Shakespeare's play *Romeo and Juliet.*

Capulet, Lord Affluent, powerful, and domineering man, head of the Capulet household; engaged in a longstanding feud with Montague that leads to public altercations among members of both households; despite his age, purportedly wants to fight in the streets alongside other members of his clan; aggressively pushes his daughter to marry Paris, not knowing of her love for Romeo; makes peace with Montague only after he has lost his daughter in William Shakespeare's play *Romeo and Juliet.*

Cara Lord Marchmain's likeable middle-aged mistress in Evelyn Waugh's *Brideshead Revisited.*

Cara Bansity, Bardol Dealer in bodies and anatomical specimens; he gives JandolAngand the alien watch and becomes for a short time the king's chancellor in Brian W. Aldiss's *Helliconia Summer.*

Carabas, Sidney Lorraine, Marquess of Stupid and pompous political leader, whom young Vivian Grey successfully manipulates for his own political ends until the Marquess and his party repudiate him in Benjamin Disraeli's *Vivian Grey.*

Caracciolo, Admiral Forty-seven-year-old Neapolitan prince who gives decades of service to the Bourbon monarchs; put to death by a verdict requested by The Hero in Susan Sontag's *The Volcano Lover.*

Caractacas Noble British king defeated by Claudius's invading army; he is allowed to live freely in Rome as the city's guest in Robert Graves's *Claudius, the God and His Wife Messalina.*

Caradoc Famous architect who designs projects for the Firm; he gives a mighty, drunken lecture on proportion in front of the Parthenon, and escapes to the Cook Islands but is recaptured by the Firm in Lawrence Durrell's *Tunc.*

Carádoc, Lady Barbara (Babs) Daughter of Lord and Lady Valleys; she is torn between her love for Charles Courtier and her love for Lord Harbinger; when Courtier leaves England, she marries Harbinger in John Galsworthy's *The Patrician.*

Carádoc, Hubert (Bertie) Younger son of the Earl of Valleys; he follows adventure around the world in John Galsworthy's *The Patrician.*

Caradoc of Menwygent Young Welsh bard, who competes with Cadwallon for fame in Sir Walter Scott's *The Betrothed.*

Caraher Anarchist saloon keeper in the San Joaquin Valley who influences Presley to bomb S. Behrman's home in Frank Norris's *The Octopus.*

Caramel, Richard (Dick) Successful novelist and friend of Anthony Patch in F. Scott Fitzgerald's *The Beautiful and Damned.*

Carathis Vathek's Greek mother who teaches him astrology and is adept in witchcraft; engages freely in acts of murder, and communicates with afrits (subterranean genies) to achieve her goals, thus destroying herself and Vathek in the process; when her heart is set on fire, starts twirling until she becomes invisible in William Beckford's *Vathek.*

Carathis, Princess Vathek's cunning, wicked mother, whose ambition causes her to go to extraordinary lengths to encourage and aid her son's attempt to obtain the treasures offered by the Giaour; she also suffers Vathek's fate in William Beckford's *Vathek.*

Caravaggio Restless Italian thief who serves the Allies in the Secret Intelligence; has lost his thumbs as a result of torture by the German Ranuccio Tommasoni; appears partially shell shocked; determined to reveal the true identity of the English patient, and warns Kip that the English are using him to fight their wars in Michael Ondaatje's *The English Patient.*

Caravaneer Sullen man who leads a caravan of camels across the Iran desert enroute to Tehran; mistrusts the deceitful Riza; tries to intercede to save the camel's life after the animal killed Ali Nizam, but is beaten back by the angry caravan attendants in Derenik Demirjyan's "Chargah: A Poem."

Carballino, Ángela Young narrator who recounts the history of Don Manuel in Miguel de Unamuno's "Saint Manuel the Good, Martyr."

Carberry Insensitive master aboard the *Renown;* he is wounded in C. S. Forester's *Lieutenant Hornblower.*

Carberry, Judge Darwin Judge who ultimately frees George Brush from an Ozarksville, Missouri, jail in Thornton Wilder's *Heaven's My Destination.*

Carbottle, Mr. Liberal candidate in the election at Polpenno, Cornwall, in which Frank Tregear triumphs in Anthony Trollope's *The Duke's Children.*

Carbuncle, Jane Domineering aunt of Linda Roanoke; living alone and with a dubious past, she is noted for her technicolor complexion; she forces her niece to accept the proposal of Sir Griffin Tewett, bringing the young girl to a mental breakdown in Anthony Trollope's *The Eustace Diamonds.*

Carbury, Henrietta (Hetta) Lady Carbury's lovely, high-minded daughter, who defies her mother's insistence that she marry her devoted cousin, Roger Carbury, because she loves Paul Montague; she becomes Montague's wife and Carbury's heir in Anthony Trollope's *The Way We Live Now.*

Carbury, Lady Matilda Romantic, foolish, hard-pressed widow of a baronet without property; she works arduously for financial and critical success as a writer, for the marriage of her son to an heiress, and for the marriage of her daughter to the owner of the family property; she succeeds at none of these endeavors but makes an unlooked-for successful marriage of her own to the newspaper editor Nicholas Broune in Anthony Trollope's *The Way We Live Now.*

Carbury, Roger Morally upright, unbending head of the Carbury family; he warns his friend Paul Montague against dealings with Augustus Melmotte; he is deeply in love with his cousin, Hetta Carbury, but loses her to Paul Montague; he resigns himself to a lonely bachelor life, gives the bride away at her wedding to Paul, and makes her heir to his property in Anthony Trollope's *The Way We Live Now.*

Carbury, Sir Felix Wastrel son of Lady Carbury, on whom he sponges unmercifully; to extricate himself from debts he follows his mother's advice by persuading Marie Melmotte to elope; he gambles away the money she has stolen from her father and fails to keep their tryst; his mother is reluctantly persuaded to make him a remittance-man in Prussia with a clergyman in attendance in Anthony Trollope's *The Way We Live Now.*

Card, C. (Eye, Stew Meat) Spanish civil war veteran and down-and-out private detective given to daydreaming about Babylon; hired to steal a corpse in Richard Brautigan's *Dreaming of Babylon.*

Card, Robert African-American man known as Bobby; joins Civil Rights movement; undergoes horrors in Mississippi while working on voter registration campaign; helped by John Calvin Marshall; lives with African-American woman and has daughter with her; leaves for a white lover; reconciles with mother of his child in Julius Lester's *And All Our Wounds Forgiven.*

Card, Tert Managing editor for *Gammy Bird* newspaper in E. Annie Proulx's *The Shipping News;* hires Quoyle; leaves newspaper to write newsletter for oil rig suppliers.

Cardan, Mr. Elderly guest and one-time lover of Lillian Aldwinkle; a social parasite, he proposes marriage to the dull-willed Grace Elver, but her death thwarts his designs in Aldous Huxley's *Those Barren Leaves.*

Carde, Jimmy Intelligent, supercilious St. Bride's classmate and closest friend of Donald Mor; when the two boys attempt a forbidden climb of the school tower, Carde is seriously injured in a fall in Iris Murdoch's *The Sandcastle.*

Cardew, Ada Cornelius Cardew's wife, who divorces him in Isabel Colegate's *The Shooting Party.*

Cardew, Cecily Jack Worthing's ward; granddaughter of the man who found and cared for Jack when Jack was a baby; intent on marrying a man named Earnest; interested in wicked men, which leads her to construct an imaginary romance with Jack's equally imaginary profligate brother, whose name is Earnest; a pupil of Miss Prism; gets engaged to Algernon after she forgives him for deceiving her with his fabricated name of Earnest in Oscar Wilde's play *The Importance of Being Earnest.*

Cardew, Cornelius Radical activist attempting to win Sir Randolph Nettleby's support in his goals of obtaining animals' rights and "free landowning" in Isabel Colegate's *The Shooting Party.*

Cardew, Jane Wife of the Reverend Theophilus Cardew; she loves her husband but feels rejected by him in Mark Rutherford's *Catharine Furze.*

Cardew, Mabel Mrs. Crankshaw's niece, to whom Eustace Cherrington is introduced at the wedding of his sister Barbara to Jimmy Crankshaw; Eustace finds her too inclined to wince and wiggle during their exchange of "almost passionate civilities" in L. P. Hartley's *The Sixth Heaven.*

Cardew, Theophilus Thirty-five-year-old rector in Abchurch, son of a London merchant; he is married already when he falls in love with Catharine Furze in Mark Rutherford's *Catharine Furze.*

Cardiff, Lady Wealthy, reclusive, and eccentric noblewoman, who marries John Inglesant's twin brother, Eustace, in J. Henry Shorthouse's *John Inglesant, A Romance.*

Cardigan, Imogen Dartie Daughter of Montague and Winifred Dartie; she comes out into society in John Galsworthy's *In Chancery.* Fleur Forsyte visits Imogen before meeting her father at the gallery in *To Let.* Imogen goes to the race track to watch Val Dartie's horse in *Swan Song.*

Cardigan, Jack Husband of Imogen Dartie; he is devoted to health and physical fitness in John Galsworthy's *To Let.* He introduces Soames Forsyte to golf in *The Silver Spoon.* He tries to interest Soames in betting on horses in *Swan Song.*

Cardinal Brother of Ferdinand and the Duchess; keeps a mistress (Julia) and endorses Ferdinand's plots against their sister, although questioning his motives; elected to the papacy; leads an army against the Duchess; murders Julia with a poisoned Bible; stabbed by Bosola in John Webster's *The Duchess of Malfi.*

Cardinal Commercial traveler in the cloth trade, who lives in London and who is rescued from his despair by Mark Rutherford and M'Kay in their mission in Mark Rutherford's *Mark Rutherford's Deliverance.*

Cardinal, Mrs. Cardinal's wife; she cares nothing for him, but her jealousy makes him miserable until she wins self-esteem with help from Mark Rutherford and M'Kay in Mark Rutherford's *Mark Rutherford's Deliverance.*

Cardinal, Ric Referred to as the saint; dedicated to his job as a social worker; father of a troubled youth, Sam; third narrator; counsels Tala and supports Roya in her endeavors in Farnoosh Moshiri's *Against Gravity.*

Cardinal Spring Daughter of Chia Cheng and Madame Wang; Pao-yu's sister; imperial concubine who is advanced to the rank of an imperial consort in Ts'ao Hsueh-chin's *Dream of the Red Chamber.*

Cardiole, Don Fernando de Spanish aristocrat who kills his rival for the affections of Donna Corina, then leaves for Turkey, where he leads a life of plunder and debauchery until his conscience awakens and he lives out his years as a hermit; he is found on his deathbed by Father Francis in Penelope Aubin's *The Strange Adventures of the Count de Vinevil and His Family.*

Cardona, Marie Mersault's lover and former coworker; committed to marrying the loner and existential protagonist despite his total detachment other than physical pleasure; visits during Mersault's imprisonment for murder, but then breaks off the connection, in Albert Camus's *The Stranger.*

Cardonnel, Mary Daughter of Guilielmina De Verdon Cardonnel; she is her grandmother Lady Mary De Verdon's heir; she refuses all suitors until she comes of age because of her honorable determination to divide her fortune with her first cousin, Medora Glenmorris Delmont; she feels morally bound to acknowledge a just claim stalled by legal machinations in Charlotte Smith's *The Young Philosopher.*

Cardonnel, Mr. Wealthy young man who becomes Lord Daventry when his family purchases an Earldom for him on the occasion of his marriage to Guilielmina De Verdon; he survives his wife and remarries, leaving his daughter, Mary, in the care of her grandmother, Lady Mary De Verdon, in Charlotte Smith's *The Young Philosopher.*

Cardoso, Manuel Nineteenth-century Uruguayan gaucho who has a lifelong hate for his neighbour Silveira and with whom, during war, is condemned to death in Jorge Luis Borges's "The Other Duel."

Cardoso & Sa Mystical philosopher and astrologer sought by Flor in Jorge Amado's *Doña Flor and Her Two Husbands.*

Carella, Gino Impulsive, good-looking, sexually compelling, jovial young Italian of no background or education; he marries the visiting English widow Lilia Herriton in E. M. Forster's *Where Angels Fear to Tread.*

Careri, Antonio Venetian autodidact and physician who claims he is following in the footsteps of his uncle, Gemelli Careri, who had experienced many marvels in the Indian jungles in Bharati Mukherjee's *The Holder of the World.*

Caretaker Employee of the nursing home where the protagonist and existential Mersault's mother dies; chats with him at her funeral and then testifies against him, saying that Mersault showed no emotion toward the loss of his mother, at his trial for the murder of a stranger—an Arab young man—in Albert Camus's *The Stranger.*

Carew, Kitty Wealthy and witty popular "courtesan," who is a friend of Mike Fletcher, the young lords, and the aesthetes in George Moore's *Mike Fletcher.*

Carew, Mr. Latin teacher and rugby coach who, although married, becomes the lover of Miss Manning in William Golding's *Free Fall.*

Carew, Sir Danvers Well-mannered, kindly, and aristocratic white-haired gentleman, who is clubbed to death in Robert Louis Stevenson's *The Strange Case of Dr. Jekyll and Mr. Hyde.*

Carey Slave of Frank Meriwether; coachman and butler in John Pendleton Kennedy's *Swallow Barn.*

Carey, Fiona Macfarlane Former teacher of Kate Fletcher Armstrong; years afterward Kate interviews her in Margaret Drabble's *The Middle Ground.*

Carey, Louisa Philip Carey's shy, gentle aunt, who is the only person who genuinely loves the lonely boy during his isolated childhood in W. Somerset Maugham's *Of Human Bondage.*

Carey, Mother See Queen of the Fairies.

Carey, Mr. Head of the English and Drama department at a new school at Camden; he is husband to Fiona Macfarlane Carey, long-time teacher at the school that had been attended by Kate Fletcher (Armstrong) in Margaret Drabble's *The Middle Ground.*

Carey, Philip Intelligent, shy boy who is dreadfully sensitive about his club foot; he seeks self-knowledge and worldly experience by attempting to study art in Paris; realizing his own mediocrity, he turns to medicine in London, simultaneously becoming disastrously involved with the deceitful Mildred Rogers; finally, after dire poverty, he finds a gentle peace with Sally Athelney in W. Somerset Maugham's *Of Human Bondage.*

Carey, Widow Fanny Matthews's rival for Cornet Hebbers's affection; her superior fortune gains her the prize in Henry Fielding's *Amelia.*

Carey, Will Carey Squire of Clovelly Court and member of the Brotherhood of the Rose who sails with Amyas Leigh to Ireland and sails again to rescue Rose Salterne from Don Guzman de Soto in Charles Kingsley's *Westward Ho!*

Carey, William Weakly hypocritical and mediocre clergyman; convention expects him to bring up his dead sister-in-law's child, Philip Carey, to whom he is neither kind nor cruel but indifferent in W. Somerset Maugham's *Of Human Bondage.*

Cargill A novice who assists in ship operation; later, promoted to officer of the watch, he proves his worth to his commander as he navigates the ship in rough weather in C. S. Forester's *Hornblower and the Hotspur.*

Cargill, Colonel Former marketing executive famed for failure; now troubleshooter for General Peckem in Joseph Heller's *Catch-22.*

Cargill, Josiah Absentminded minister, who, having presided over the mock marriage of Valentine Bulmer and Clara Mowbray, is in possession of the secret in Sir Walter Scott's *St. Ronan's Well.*

Cariola Chambermaid and confident of the Duchess; witness of the Duchess's marriage to Antonio; warns her against her sham pilgrimage; imprisoned with the Duchess; pleads for her life before being strangled on Bosola's orders in John Webster's *The Duchess of Malfi.*

Carker, Harriet Sister of James and John Carker; she chose to live with John after his disgrace, separating from James, and is loved by Mr. Morfin in Charles Dickens's *Dombey and Son.*

Carker, James Manager at Paul Dombey's firm; he pretends subservience to Dombey but plots against him and is successful in wooing Edith (Granger) Dombey away from Dombey; his passion destroys him, and he dies when he falls under a train in Charles Dickens's *Dombey and Son.*

Carker, John Older brother of James Carker; he works for Dombey and Son; he had once stolen money from the firm and was forgiven but never allowed to be promoted; now gray and worn, he takes an interest in Walter Gay but wishes to be left alone in Charles Dickens's *Dombey and Son.*

Carl Fire-tender who was cast from the clan when he let the fire die out; flees alone to the cold regions of the north; learns how to hunt and plant by the changing seasons; meets a woman, Mam, who becomes his wife; rediscovers fire and its uses in Johannes V. Jensen's *The Long Journey.*

Carl (Joe) Writer who has written no book; hates Paris in Henry Miller's *Tropic of Cancer.*

Carl Farm boy who is the first love of Rose Dutcher in Hamlin Garland's *Rose of Dutcher's Coolly.*

Carl Former lover from whom the narrator receives a bottle of brandy she later gives to her new suitor, a talented and passionate young writer, in Aline Bernstein's *The Journey Down.*

Carl Husband of Vera; kills her lover, E. L. Fletcher in Jerry Bumpus's *Anaconda.*

Carl Navy combat veteran whose plan to murder Raditzer is thwarted in Peter Matthiessen's *Raditzer.*

Carla Mental patient who becomes Deborah Blau's friend in Hannah Green's *I Never Promised You a Rose Garden.*

Carle Guard who sleeps through Hugh Woodreeve's escape and later testifies in Woodreeve's trial in Ann Radcliffe's *Gaston de Blondeville.*

Carle Old man who lives alone on the shore where a storm drives the ship of Walter Golden; he warns Walter against entering the lands beyond the high rock wall in William Morris's *The Wood beyond the World.*

Carlé, Rolf Native Austrian who comes to South America; scarred by his father, whose favorite pastimes included sexually humiliating his wife and abusing his children; witnessed the human bodies left behind at a German prison camp during World War II; meets Eva Luna at a party, during which Eva tells one of her stories, a story that has the dual effect of convincing the director of National Television to give her a contract and of attracting Rolf's love interest in Isabel Allende's *Eva Luna.*

Carleton-Robbins, Clare Flamboyant art gallery owner; divorced with one daughter, Puffin; is caught in the middle of a conflict between her friends Margo Sampson and Francine "B. B." Brady Broder; attempts a cautious reconciliation with her husband, Robin, in Judy Blume's *Smart Women.*

Carlin, Basil Married tenant in Milly Sanders's house in Muriel Spark's *A Far Cry from Kensington.*

Carlin, Eva Basil's wife; they are childless and secretive tenants in Milly Sanders's house in Muriel Spark's *A Far Cry from Kensington.*

Carlin, Jemmy Unsuccessful farmer whose land is supposedly purchased by Mrs. Flynn; he later tells Tarry Flynn that his good fields were not part of the sale, and as a result the Flynns lose money and prestige in Patrick Kavanagh's *Tarry Flynn.*

Carlin, Tom Unsuccessful farmer who loses his land, which turns out to be very poor land, to Mrs. Flynn in Patrick Kavanagh's *Tarry Flynn.*

Carling, Marjorie Clinging mistress of Walter Bidlake, by whom she is impregnanted after abandoning her husband; insecure in her relationship, she eventually finds some solace in acquaintance with Rachel Quarles in Aldous Huxley's *Point Count Point.*

Carlisle, Captain Clement Conventional, virtuous hero, who overcomes many obstacles to marry his beloved Lucia de Grey in S. J. Pratt's *Tutor of Truth.*

Carlisle, Darlene Mosby Best friend of Neva Manning and former lover of Calvin Bartley in Hal Bennett's *A Wilderness of Vines.*

Carlisle, Ida (Cordelia) Powerful preserver of a social system based on differences in skin color among blacks in Burnside, Virginia; convicted of pretending to be white; dies in a home for the criminally insane; appears in Hal Bennett's *A Wilderness of Vines, The Black Wine,* and *Wait Until Evening.*

Carlisle, Thomas Merks, Bishop of Advises Richard II not to be afraid of the rebellion led by Henry Bolingbroke but to defend his divine right to the throne; tells Richard that his fear will add strength to his enemy; defends Richard's right to the throne when Henry is told of Richard's abdication; gives a clear summary of the theory of divine right to rule; calls Henry a traitor; prophesies that the result of the usurpation will be civil war for generations to come; arrested for treason after he shows his loyalty to Richard; banished after Rutland's conspiracy is revealed in William Shakespeare's play *Richard II.*

Carlo Garage owner and pursuer of Lise in Muriel Spark's *The Driver's Seat.*

Carlo Left-wing terrorist kidnapper of Morris Zapp; he negotiates with Desiree Zapp for Morris's release in David Lodge's *Small World.*

Carlo Servant ordered to prevent Julia de Mazzini from escaping her forced marriage to Duke de Luovo in Ann Radcliffe's *A Sicilian Romance.*

Carlo Steward of the Castle di Udolpho who, though kind to Emily St. Aubert, remains faithful to the evil Montoni in Ann Radcliffe's *The Mysteries of Udolpho.*

Carlo William Fielding's dog that goes with George Fielding to Australia and saves him and his friends several times from their enemies before being killed by one of the thugs in Charles Reade's *It Is Never Too Late to Mend.*

Carlo Handsome, teenaged hand-organ player aboard the *Highlander* in Herman Melville's *Redburn.*

Carlo, King Alberto (Charles Albert) Italian king leading the forces on the side of Italian liberation, despite his association with Austria, which causes his co-revolutionists some unease; Vittoria Campa's faith in him angers Carlo Ammiani in George Meredith's *Vittoria.*

Carloman Sickly son of King Louis of France; he is pitied and protected by the young Duke Richard of Normandy in Charlotte Yonge's *The Little Duke.*

Carlos Neighbor of Harry Meyers; often beats his wife, Nydia, and threatens Meyers in Jay Neugeboren's *Listen Ruben Fontanez.*

Carlos Proprietor of a wine cellar in John Edgar Wideman's *Hurry Home.*

Carlotta Mother of BZ; gives BZ and Helene money to stay married in Joan Didion's *Play It As It Lays.*

Carlson, Bob Sophomore at Moo University; caretaker of Earl Butz, the porcine subject of Dr. Bo Jones's experiment in Jane Smiley's *Moo.*

Carlson, Christina See Jansen, Christina.

Carlstadt, Claudia Woman hired by Frank Cowperwood to seduce the mayor of Chicago so Cowperwood can blackmail him in Theodore Dreiser's *The Titan.*

Carlton, Lady (Corinna) Beautiful wife of Bruce Carlton; her faithfulness eventually persuades him to give up his relationship with Amber St. Clare in Kathleen Winsor's *Forever Amber.*

Carlton, Lord (Bruce) Dashing cavalier, privateer, only real love of Amber St. Clare, and father of two of her children; begins a King's grant plantation in Virginia with his wife, Corinna, in Kathleen Winsor's *Forever Amber.*

Carlton, Mr. Fellow of Leicester College, Oxford, who defends Anglican diversity and makes a last-ditch effort to dissuade Charles Reding from becoming Roman Catholic in John Henry Newman's *Loss and Gain.*

Carlton, Mr. Gentleman who shares business with Mr. B— and whose death persuades Mr. B— to write his own will in Samuel Richardson's *Pamela, or Virtue Rewarded.*

Carlton, Mrs. Henrietta Courteney's maternal grandmother, the widow of a bankrupt army officer; her petition for her husband's pension is turned down by the Earl of—in Charlotte Lennox's *Henrietta.*

Carlyle, Mr. Lawyer who is made joint trustee of Scottish estates with Ephraim Mackellar when Henry Durie's family moves to New York in Robert Louis Stevenson's *The Master of Ballantrae: A Winter's Tale.*

Carlyon Intelligent, charismatic successor to Francis Andrews's father as leader of a smuggling gang; he is protective and compassionate towards Andrews until Andrews informs on and testifies against the gang, whereupon Canyon seeks revenge against him; he attempts to save Elizabeth from other members of the gang and is himself saved from arrest by Andrews in Graham Greene's *The Man Within.*

Carma Muscular black southerner whose denial of adultery results in her husband's being sentenced to a chain gang in Jean Toomer's *Cane.*

Carmelo Hired hand of Sparicio; works the tiller and sings a Mediterranean ballad in Lafcadio Hearn's *Chita.*

Carmen Worker at The Grand Balcony, a brothel, and the favorite of the queen and brothel manager, Irma; appears during fantasy games twice a week in the dress and role of the Immaculate Conception of Lourdes to a bank clerk; has a daughter in the countryside with whom she yearns to be reunited; oversees the bookkeeping at the brothel in Jean Genet's play *The Balcony.*

Carmen Partner of Winston; lived with Ursula and Michael for a year; always preferred exotic men from foreign countries before Winston in Sandra Scofield's *Beyond Deserving.*

Carmichael, Augustus Poet guest stoned on opium and liquor at the Ramsays' summer house in the Hebrides; eventually, during World War I and after Mrs. Ramsay's death, he publishes an acclaimed volume of poetry, much to Mr. Ramsay's chagrin in Virginia Woolf's *To the Lighthouse.*

Carmichael, Cicely Friend of the Westons and of Ida; she hopes to attract Edmund Weston in Isabel Colegate's *Statues in a Garden.*

Carmichael, Frank Chief of police in Peter De Vries's *Comfort Me with Apples.*

Carmichael, John Hard-drinking executive of a meatpacking firm in Robert Herrick's *The Memoirs of an American Citizen.*

Carmichael, Margaret See Howland, Margaret Carmichael.

Carmichael, Robert See Howland, Robert Carmichael.

Carmine, Captain Lawrence Authority on Indian and oriental studies and frequentor of Dower House; he is emotionally scarred by the war in H. G. Wells's *Mr. Britling Sees It Through.*

Carmody, Frank Writer and drug addict; companion of Adam Moorad and Leo Percepied in Jack Kerouac's *The Subterraneans.*

Carmody, George Student who stands up to Howard Kirk and is forced out of the university by Howard in Malcolm Bradbury's *The History Man.*

Carmody, Hugo Nephew of Lester Carmody, upon whose parsimonious trusteeship he depends; he wants to invest in a nightclub with Ronnie Fish in P. G. Wodehouse's *Money for Nothing.* He is Lord Emsworth's secretary and is in love with Millicent Threepwood in *Fish Preferred.* He appears in *Heavy Weather.*

Carmody, Jersey Single mother, writer, and helper of the other activists in M. F. Beal's *Amazon One.*

Carmody, Lester Uncle of both John Carroll and Hugo Carmody; he is the parsimonious trustee of Hugo's estate; he hopes to raise money from inalienable family heirlooms by arranging their theft in conspiracy with "Soapy" Molloy in P. G. Wodehouse's *Money for Nothing.*

Carmody, Lucette Crippled child evangelist whose preaching fascinates both Mr. Rayber and young Francis Marion Tarwater in Flannery O'Connor's *The Violent Bear It Away.*

Carmona, Manuel Romantic, mystical, vain, self-reliant spy, who fascinates Ashenden with his brutal and exotic stories; Ashenden does not trust Carmona but respects his survival instincts in W. Somerset Maugham's *Ashenden: or The British Agent.*

Carn, Mr. Attorney who represents Mr. Eggleston's claim against Cecilia Beverley's estate in Frances Burney's *Cecilia.*

Carnaby, Earl of Wealthy, elderly aristocrat who is Beatrice Normandy's rich lover, much to George Ponderevo's disgust in H. G. Wells's *Tono-Bungay.*

Carnaby, Hugh Well-traveled outdoorsman who kills a man he thinks is seducing his wife and goes to prison in George Gissing's *The Whirlpool.*

Carnaby, Sybil Superior lady of much self-control and luxurious tastes who exposes a rival lady's infidelity in George Gissing's *The Whirlpool.*

Carnashan Alcoholic messenger hired by Henry Miller in Henry Miller's *Tropic of Capricorn.*

Carnehan, Peachey Taliaferro English scam artist and loafer; somewhat more sensible than his fellow conman Dravot; travels to Kafiristan with Dravot in the hope of becoming kings; once in Kafiristan, takes over the training and drilling of the native people as commander in chief; after it is revealed that he and Dravot are not gods, the tribal people attempt to crucify him; surviving the crucifixion for a day, is released by the Kafir; begging his way back to India, finds the narrator and relays the past year's events, showing the narrator the head of Dravot, which he has kept in a bag; exhausted, dies the next day; no belongings are found on his body in Rudyard Kipling's "The Man Who Would Be King."

Carney Tall, sturdily built man with dark eyes and a fighter's face; sergeant-major in army two months ago and now tramping the roads in search of a night's shelter out of the storm; meets Joe Byrne, an itinerant tinker with two beautiful wives living in a tent; seeks to make love with the golden-haired mate of the tinker; ends up in a fight with the tinker and cast back on the road from which he started in Liam O'Flaherty's "The Tent."

Carney, Cassius P. (Cash) Boyhood friend of John Wickliff Shawnessy; financier in Ross Lockridge, Jr.'s *Raintree County.*

Caro, Ann Avice Avice Caro's daughter; immediately following her mother's burial she meets Jocelyn Pierston, the man who once jilted her mother; he promptly falls in love with her, but she, like Pierston himself when younger, is inconstant in her affections; she accompanies him to London as a housemaid; when he surprises her by proposing marriage, she reveals that she secretly married a young man before her mother's death; Jocelyn helps her establish a household with her husband and does not see her again until, widowed, she writes to him, intending to promote a match between him and her daughter, Avice Pierston, in Thomas Hardy's *The Well-Beloved.*

Caro, Avice Young, ingenuous, pretty woman whom Jocelyn Pierston meets when he returns to the peninsular village of his family origins; she falls in love with him and accepts his proposal, but meeting Marcia Bencomb, he abandons her; she marries a cousin of the same name and has a daughter, Ann Avice Caro; she dies when the daughter has grown up in Thomas Hardy's *The Well-Beloved.*

Carol Student roommate of Melanie Byrd in David Lodge's *Changing Places: A Tale of Two Campuses.*

Carol Rational secretary for Leclerc's incompetent Department; though ignored by her condescending employers, she accurately diagnoses Leclerc's intelligence operations as chauvinistic fantasies in John le Carré's *The Looking-Glass War.*

Carol Twelve-year-old white girl who attends a black church with her best friend, Parialee; haunted for a long time after witnessing several church members displaying their religious fervor through screams and writhing on the floor; discovers that she no longer can be friends with Parialee because of their different races and hidden class differences in her school and society in Tillie Olsen's "O Yes."

Carol Young blond girl at Ruth's evening party, where Tom Harris, a traveling salesman, shows up; comes to his hotel room, but finds that Tom maintains a safe distance from human relationships in Eudora Welty's "The Hitch-Hikers."

Carola Lafcadio's mistress and a confederate in the scheme to swindle money based on a rumor of the kidnapped pope in André Gide's *Lafcadio's Adventures.*

Caroline Plump young student with whom Robin Meadowes is having an affair in David Lodge's *How Far Can You Go?*

Caroline Alice Mellings's close friend who later comes to despise the rest of the house members when she is told about their plans to leave a time bomb in a car parked near a busy pavement in Doris Lessing's *The Good Terrorist.*

Caroline Friend of Agatha King and Imogene King; she is a model who has an affair with Orlando King in Isabel Colegate's *Orlando at the Brazen Threshold.*

Caroline First bride-elect of Lord Lowborough; she breaks with him when he loses his fortune through gambling in Anne Brontë's *The Tenant of Wildfell Hall.*

Caroline Wife of one of Ebenezer Scrooge's debtors; she is relieved at news of Scrooge's death in Charles Dickens's *A Christmas Carol.*

Caroline Young woman who aborts her child by Ernesto in Maria Virginia Estenssoro's "The Child That Never Was."

Caroline Wife of Uncle Alex; nurses Ollie from wounds received in a knife fight in George Wylie Henderson's *Ollie Miss;* appears also in *Jule.*

Caroline, Queen King George II's wife and a power unto herself; she assists Jeanie Deans through the intercession of John, Duke of Argyle, in Sir Walter Scott's *The Heart of Midlothian.*

Carolo Violinist and former child prodigy once married to Matilda Wilson; he boards with the Machinticks and runs away with Audrey Maclintick in Anthony Powell's *Casanova's Chinese Restaurant.* Long parted from Audrey, he appears as a white-haired stand-in violinist at a party in *Temporary Kings.*

Caron, Monsieur Old printer and comrade of Max du Parc; he tries to apply socialist principles in his paper mill but is killed in the battle of the Commune in Anne Thackeray Ritchie's *Mrs. Dymond.*

Carp, Joe Bakery worker with Charlie Gordon in Daniel Keyes's *Flowers for Algernon.*

Carpenter Character in Tweedledee's poem; his participation in the deception played on the oysters is not so hypocritical as the Walrus's but he eats as many as he can in Lewis Carroll's *Through the Looking-Glass.*

Carpenter, Belle Employee in a millinery shop who allows herself to be courted by George Willard because of her distrust of Ed Handby in Sherwood Anderson's *Winesburg, Ohio.*

Carpenter, David (Davey) Infant son of Patsy and Jim Carpenter in Larry McMurtry's *Moving On.*

Carpenter, Edmund Playwright and friend of Wyndham Farrar in Margaret Drabble's *The Garrick Year.*

Carpenter, Jack Detective-constable who annoys Billy Fisher and ends up in bed with Helen Lightfoot in Keith Waterhouse's *Billy Liar on the Moon.*

Carpenter, James (Jim) Husband of Patsy White Carpenter and father of Davey Carpenter; leaves Patsy for fellow Rice University graduate student Clara Clark in Larry McMurtry's *Moving On.*

Carpenter, Mrs. Secretary to Dr. Bellows at the Entrenationo Language Centre in Graham Greene's *The Confidential Agent.*

Carpenter, Mrs. Mother of Sybil; lives with Sybil in Whirly Wood, Connecticut; is friends with Mrs. Hubbel, a woman vacationing at the Florida resort, in J. D. Salinger's "A Perfect Day for Bananafish."

Carpenter, Patsy White Wife of Jim Carpenter and mother of Davey Carpenter; takes Hank Malory as a lover and loses her husband to Clara Clark in Larry McMurtry's *Moving On.*

Carpenter, Sybil Young girl on vacation with her mother, Mrs. Carpenter; midway through the story, approaches Seymour; appears that the two have met previously; tells Seymour that her mother and she live in Whirly Wood, Connecticut, in J. D. Salinger's "A Perfect Day for Bananafish."

Carpenter, The One of the lesser described members of the religious pilgrimage to Canterbury in Geoffrey Chaucer's *The Canterbury Tales.*

Carper, Carl Youngest son of Hildie Carper, half brother of Blue and Peter in Mary McGarry Morris's *Songs in Ordinary Time.*

Carper, Hildie Mother of Blue; sells alcohol to minors in Mary McGarry Morris's *Songs in Ordinary Time.*

Carper, Peter Son of Hildie Carper, half brother of Blue and Carl in Mary McGarry Morris's *Songs in Ordinary Time.*

Carpio, Fernanda del Known for her beauty; comes to Macondo to compete against Remedios to be crowned Queen of the Carnival; marries Aureliano Segundo; mother of José Arcadio, Renata Remedios, and Amaranta Ursula; follows Ursula as leader of the Buendía family in Gabriel García Márquez's *One Hundred Years of Solitude.*

Carr, Antonio Desperate and bankrupt man who narrates in his diary how he leaves Monte, where he had worked in a hopper, to go to Santa María and accept a job in a dam to do nothing but let do (smuggle), for which he receives good money and where he secretly loves the girl Elvirita, a relationship which will never flourish, in Juan Carlos Onetti's last novel, *Past Caring.*

Carr, Arthur See Thorpe, Zachary.

Carr, Carey Minister who presides at the funeral of Peyton Loftis; confidant of Helen Loftis in William Styron's *Lie Down in Darkness.*

Carr, Cecily Librarian in the Zurich library; becomes the wife of the English consul Henry Carr; she expresses doubts as to whether Carr actually ever met the Dada poet Tristan Tzara or the Russian revolutionary Lenin in Switzerland during World War I in Tom Stoppard's play *Travesties.*

Carr, Dr. Edward Physician whose reiterated puzzlement over Agatha Dawson's premature death costs him the loss of his practice; his story initiates Lord Peter Wimsey's investigation, which motivates two additional murders and several attempted murders in Dorothy L. Sayers's *Unnatural Death.*

Carr, Henry English consular official living in Zurich, Switzerland, during World War I; recalls his perceptions and experiences with such early 20th-century influential figures as Lenin, James Joyce, and Tristan Tzara in Tom Stoppard's play *Travesties.*

Carr, Private Pugnacious cockney soldier who strikes Stephen Dedalus in the brothel district in James Joyce's *Ulysses.*

Carradine, Brent Young American scholar who helps Detective Inspector Alan Grant, bedridden with a broken leg, resurrect the reputation of King Richard III by doing the research to prove that Henry Tudor (later King Henry VII) had more to gain by the death of the two Princes in the Tower than did Richard in Josephine Tey's *The Daughter of Time.*

Carranza, President President during Artemio's early years in Carlos Fuentes's *The Death of Artemio Cruz.*

Carranza, Venustiano Famous Mexican revolutionary leader fighting federal forces; bickers with Pancho Villa, an action that divides the rebel army, in Mariano Azuela's *The Underdogs.*

Carrasco, Dona Carlota Don Ramon's Catholic first wife, who dies of fever and shock in D. H. Lawrence's *The Plumed Serpent (Quetzalcoatl).*

Carrasco, Don Ramon Leader of a religious and political revolution in Mexico resurrecting the old Aztec gods; he assumes the persona of Quetzalcoatl (the "plumed serpent") in D. H. Lawrence's *The Plumed Serpent (Quetzalcoatl).*

Carraway, Nick Neighbor and befriender of Jay Gatsby; narrator of F. Scott Fitzgerald's *The Great Gatsby.*

Carre, Sir Robert Military leader for Governor Lovelace in James Kirke Paulding's *Koningsmarke.*

Carreño, Tomás Lituma's assistant; engages in a love relationship with Mercedes, a young prostitute from Lituma's hometown, Piura; before coming to the Andes, was a fugitive who killed a drug dealer to save Mercedes's life in Mario Vargas Llosa's *Death in the Andes.*

Carreon, Oswaldo "Pepe" Protégé and possibly son of General Nicasio Ledesma; member of the Philippine security forces that assassinate Senator Domingo Avila; woman-hater who marries into the wealthy Alacran family and neglects his wife, Baby Alacran, in Jessica Hagedorn's *Dogeaters.*

Carreras, Senor Former member of Mr. Castor's Bodyguard in Olifa, now in league with the evil Jacques D'Ingraville and the plot against Valdemar Haraldsen in John Buchan's *The Island of Sheep.*

Carricker, Lieutenant Colonel Benny Young fighter pilot and war hero whose punching of a black pilot is partly responsible for triggering unrest among black officers in James Gould Cozzens's *Guard of Honor.*

Carrie Waitress at the boardinghouse where Aleck Maury stays while he is in Florida in Caroline Gordon's "To Thy Chamber Window, Sweet."

Carrie Mute slave who befriends Dana Franklin and marries Nigel in Octavia E. Butler's *Kindred.*

Carrington, Henry, M.A. New Vicar of Cleeve, a widower with a private income; he disappoints as a possible husband for Georgie Smithers in Richard Aldington's *The Colonel's Daughter.*

Carrington, James Lawford Nashville sculptor and second husband of Rozelle Hardcastle; dies of a heroin overdose in Robert Penn Warren's *A Place to Come To.*

Carrington, John Washington lawyer whom Senator Ratcliffe sends to Mexico in order to get him away from Madeleine Lee in Henry Adams's *Democracy.*

Carrington, Louisa George Uploft's betrothed; she is prevented from revealing the Harringtons' class origin by her own secret, a skin disease, in George Meredith's *Evan Harrington.*

Carrington, Lukey London science teacher and algae specialist who barely survives an attack by giant water-beetle larvae in H. G. Wells's *The Food of the Gods, and How It Came to Earth.*

Carrington, Nina (Mattie Bliss) Chambermaid at the hotel where Paul Armstrong fakes his death; tries to blackmail Frank Walker in Mary Roberts Rinehart's *The Circular Staircase.*

Carrington, Rebecca See Jones-Talbot, Rebecca Carrington.

Carrington, Rico Sophisticated but effeminate would-be artist, the husband of Rachel Witt; he is injured by the great stallion St. Mawr in D. H. Lawrence's *St. Mawr.*

Carrington, Rozelle Hardcastle Butler (Beauty Queen of Dugton High, Miss Pritty-Pants, Rose) Wife successively of Michael X. Butler, J. Lawford Carrington, and a black man posing as a swami; lover of Jed Tewksbury in Robert Penn Warren's *A Place to Come To.*

Carrington, Sir William Boyd Recent possessor of a large inherited estate; Hercule Poirot finds him a stupid bore in Agatha Christie's *Curtain: Hercule Poirot's Last Case.*

Carrino, Iulo Fiercely loyal young Gentleman in the Apostolic Chamber whose desire to kill the blackmailers Hadrian VII quells in Frederick William Rolfe's *Hadrian the Seventh.*

Carrol, Judy Servingwoman at Lieutenant O'Flaherty's quarters; she angers O'Flaherty by showing Major O'Neill and Magnolia Macnamara up to his room when he is half-dressed and hung over in J. Sheridan Le Fanu's *The House by the Churchyard.*

Carroll, Amelia Eldest of John Grey's six vulgar nieces, who are all looked after and detested by their cousin, Dolly Grey; her engagement to Mr. Jumper broken, Amelia is enabled by Mr. Grey's dowry of £500 to marry the widower Mr. Matterson in Anthony Trollope's *Mr. Scarborough's Family.*

Carroll, Brenda One of John Grey's six vulgar nieces in Anthony Trollope's *Mr. Scarborough's Family.*

Carroll, Captain Patrick Raffish, improvident Irish brother-in-law of John Grey, upon whom he sponges for the maintenance of his wife and six silly daughters in Anthony Trollope's *Mr. Scarborough's Family.*

Carroll, Georgina Third of John Grey's six vulgar nieces and a noisy, romping 16-year-old in Anthony Trollope's *Mr. Scarborough's Family.*

Carroll, John Cousin of Hugo Carmody and nephew of Lester Carmody, whose estrangement from his old friend Colonel Wyvern complicates John's romantic attachment to Patricia Wyvern; John wins Patricia by proving himself intrepid and resourceful when necessary in P. G. Wodehouse's *Money for Nothing.*

Carroll, Madam Marion More Morris Second wife of Major Carroll, stepmother of Sara Carroll, and mistress of the Carroll Farms; forced by her husband's mental decline to protect him and the community from each other in Constance Fenimore Woolson's *For the Major.*

Carroll, Major Scarborough Owner of the Carroll Farms, first citizen of Far Edgerley, and senior warden of St. John's Episcopal Church; subject of protective attention from his wife Marion More Carroll and daughter, Sara Carroll, as senility and blindness threaten his position in the community in Constance Fenimore Woolson's *For the Major.*

Carroll, Minna One of John Grey's six vulgar nieces in Anthony Trollope's *Mr. Scarborough's Family.*

Carroll, Moriarty Lower-class man shot by Harry Ormond during a quarrel in which Ormond tries to defend Marcus O'Shane; Carroll generously refuses to blame Ormond and becomes his friend in Maria Edgeworth's *Ormond.*

Carroll, Mrs. John Grey's sister, married to an impecunious inebriate; Mr. Grey maintains in respectability the Carroll family, including their six daughters; only Mrs. Carroll has feelings of gratitude in Anthony Trollope's *Mr. Scarborough's Family.*

Carroll, Pat Ringleader of the tenantry engaged in mayhem throughout Galway; he refuses to pay rents to Philip Jones and leads a gang to flood some fields in Anthony Trollope's *The Landleaguers.*

Carroll, Potsey One of John Grey's six vulgar nieces; her openly acknowledged plainness is the despair of the Carroll family in Anthony Trollope's *Mr. Scarborough's Family.*

Carroll, Sara Daughter of Major Carroll and beloved of Frederick Owen; responds diplomatically to the needs of both her father and stepmother, Marion More Carroll, in Constance Fenimore Woolson's *For the Major.*

Carroll, Scar Son of Major Carroll and Marion More Carroll and stepbrother of Sara Carroll in Constance Fenimore Woolson's *For the Major.*

Carroll, Sophy Second of John Grey's six vulgar nieces; her status as the beauty of the family does not make her less odious to her cousin Dolly Grey in Anthony Trollope's *Mr. Scarborough's Family.*

Carroll, Terry Ruffian brother of Pat; he is shot in the Galway courtroom as he is about to testify against his brother and the terrorists in Anthony Trollope's *The Landleaguers.*

Carroll, Willard Paterfamilias and grandfather of Lucy Nelson Bassart in Philip Roth's *When She Was Good.*

Carruthers Sharp-faced bad boy of 13; traveling by train with Miss Fanshawe, a middle-aged school matron, at the end of the school term; likes to drink and smoke, although he is underaged; acts older than his years; bullies the train's waiter, Atkins; reveals to his chaperone that he has been expelled from Ashleigh Court Preparatory School for Boys for stealing the president's cigarette lighter in William Trevor's "Going Home."

Carruthers, Amy Wealthy North Carolina socialite who becomes Harley Drew's lover in Shelby Foote's *Love in a Dry Season.*

Carruthers, Crosbie Impatient fiancé of Barbara Blenkinsop; he spends much of his time reading *The Times of India;* he finally asserts himself, proposing at the zoo, and Barbara chooses to follow him rather than her mother in the struggle for power that has supplied village gossip for months in E. M. Delafield's *The Diary of a Provincial Lady.*

Carruthers, Jeff Husband and cousin of Amy Carruthers in Shelby Foote's *Love in a Dry Season.*

Carruthers, Lord George de Bruce Horse-faced confidence trickster, who becomes a suspect in the Eustace necklace theft; he approaches Lizzie Eustace's romantic ideal of a corsair lover, but he eludes her grasp, finding her too unscrupulous even for his relaxed standards in Anthony Trollope's *The Eustace Diamonds.* His pecuniary embarrassments may have lowered his standards sufficiently at the end of *Phineas Redux.* His escape is apparent from Lizzie's unchanged marital condition in *The Prime Minister.*

Carruthers, Lowell Tense, paranoid boyfriend of Ursa Mackenzie; hates his job and his boss at an electronics company in Paule Marshall's *Daughters.*

Carruthers, Mr. Lawyer who saves Mr. Furze by making with full payment of his debts in Mark Rutherford's *Catharine Furze.*

Carshot, Mr. Fat, nagging window dresser who supervises Art Kipps at the Folkestone Drapery Bazaar in H. G. Wells's *Kipps: The Story of a Simple Soul.*

Carslake Young inexperienced purser of the *Atropos* who finally proves himself capable of his duties in C. S. Forester's *Hornblower and the Atropos.*

Carson Sympathetic Communist agent who helps Sarah Castle escape South Africa and whose death, allegedly from pneumonia, in a British-South African prison provokes

Maurice Castle into betraying Operation Uncle Remus and himself in Graham Greene's *The Human Factor.*

Carson Crewman aboard the *Indefatigable* and the *Marie Galante* in C. S. Forester's *Mr. Midshipman Hornblower.*

Carson, Christopher (Kit) Mountaineer and scout who brings news of the discovery of gold in California in Emerson Hough's *The Covered Wagon.*

Carson, Edward (Ed, Kit, Pimples) Acne-ridden seventeen-year-old apprentice mechanic to Juan Chicoy; interested in the electrifying Camille Oaks in John Steinbeck's *The Wayward Bus.*

Carson, Frederic Augustus Suitor of Nina Gordon, whom he loses to Edward Clayton, in Harriet Beecher Stowe's *Dred.*

Carson, Grondine Garbage man; engaged to Jozia, but she breaks up with him in Mary McGarry Morris's *Songs in Ordinary Time.*

Carson, Harry Son of the mill owner John Carson; his shooting death at the hands of John Barton is blamed on Jem Wilson, the honorable rival of Harry's dishonorable pursuit of Mary Barton in Elizabeth Gaskell's *Mary Barton.*

Carson, John Mill owner whose son is murdered by John Barton; his desire for vengeance finally gives way to recognition that conditions make men desperate in Elizabeth Gaskell's *Mary Barton.*

Carson, Jonah Dean (J. D.) Powerful political ally of Angus Cleveland under indictment for theft of political funds; manipulator of anti-school integration demonstrations in Julian Mayfield's *The Grand Parade.*

Carson, Kit (Christóbal) Explorer, trapper, and Indian hunter; friend of Bishop Latour in Willa Cather's *Death Comes for the Archbishop.*

Carson, Marvin (Marv) Banker who encourages Larry Cook to transfer his farm, Harold Clark to buy his tractor, and Tyler Smith to buy the Slurrystore and Harvestore for raising hogs; his refusal to lend Ty the money to plant, coupled with a downturn in agricultural prices, ultimately leads to the demise of the farm in Jane Smiley's *A Thousand Acres.*

Carson, Sonny Social activist; one of the many voices of identity in the race riots in Crown Heights, Brooklyn, in 1991, in Anna Deavere Smith's play *Fires in the Mirror: Crown Heights, Brooklyn and Other Identities.*

Carson, Widow Martha Quest's landlady, who is petrified of the Africans' breaking into her house and stealing from her in Doris Lessing's *A Ripple from the Storm.*

Carsons, Audrey American child who becomes a wild boy in William S. Burroughs's *The Wild Boys;* creates his lover Jerry in his story, *The Autobiography of a Wolf,* and participates in the attempt to blow up the nerve-gas train in *Exterminator!*

Carstairs Servant to Lord Glenalmond in Robert Louis Stevenson's *Weir of Hermiston: An Unfinished Romance.*

Carstairs, Lord Eldest son of Earl Bracy; returning to Bowick School as an old boy, he falls in love with Mary Wortle, the headmaster's daughter, in Anthony Trollope's *Dr. Wortle's School.*

Carstone, Richard Handsome young man, who is John Jarndyce's ward; he falls in love with his cousin, Ada Clare, and tries to pursue a profession but always loses interest after a few months; he becomes obsessed with the Jarndyce and Jarndyce Chancery case, which eventually kills him, in Charles Dickens's *Bleak House.*

Cartaret, Alice (Ally) Youngest sister who, pregnant, marries a local farmer, James Greatorex; her confrontation with her sister Mary and her father results in her father's severe stroke and Mary's refusal to associate with her in May Sinclair's *The Three Sisters.*

Cartaret, Gwendolen (Gwenda) Middle sister, who leaves Garth in the hope that her lover, Steven Rowcliffe, will marry her younger sister Alice and thereby cure Alice's hysteria; her sacrifice backfires and she remains unmarried and the caretaker of her father in May Sinclair's *The Three Sisters.*

Cartaret, James Twice-widowed vicar of Garth, abandoned by his third wife; the tyrannical father of Mary, Gwendolen, and Alice, he mellows when a stroke destroys his memory in May Sinclair's *The Three Sisters.*

Cartaret, Mary Eldest sister, who manipulates Steven Rowcliffe into marriage although he loves her sister Gwendolen; she secures her marriage by becoming the perfect Victorian wife and mother in May Sinclair's *The Three Sisters.*

Cartaret, Robina James Cartaret's third wife, who leaves him; she later uses her influence to obtain a position for Gwendolen Cartaret when she leaves Garth in May Sinclair's *The Three Sisters.*

Carteloise, Alisande de la See Sandy.

Carter Edwin Reardon's friend who holds a position as an administrator in a hospital and gives Reardon a job there in George Gissing's *New Grub Street.*

Carter Mentally incompetent prisoner, who tries to solve his problem with "hard labor" by destroying the gauge on the weighted crank he is set to turn; he is then punished by the torturing "jacket," bites Hawes's fingers, and becomes brutish in Charles Reade's *It is Never Too Late to Mend.*

Carter Third witness of the forged will that disinherited Amelia Booth in favor of her sister, Betty Harris, in Henry Fielding's *Amelia.*

Carter Colonel Calloway's young assistant who first suggests that Harry Lime's body be exhumed in Graham Greene's *The Third Man and the Fallen Idol.*

Carter Second officer of the *Hermit,* the stranded schooner that interferes with Lingard's plans to reestablish native succession in Wajo; he attempts to remain dutiful to Mr. and Mrs. Travers but proves to have greater allegiance to Lingard in Joseph Conrad's *The Rescue: A Romance of the Shallows.*

Carter, A. Chief of British Intelligence; he commissions Tommy and Tuppence Beresford to find Jane Finn in Agatha Christie's *The Secret Adversary.* Tommy discovers that he is Lord Easterfield in *N or M?.*

Carter, Ardis See Ross, Ardis.

Carter, Bella Mistress of Rafe Ashton in H. D.'s *Bid Me to Live.*

Carter, Cyrus President of a railroad, employer of Oliver Tappan, and uncle of Madeline Carter in Hjalmar Hjorth Boyesen's *The Golden Calf.*

Carter, Davis (Davy) Kentuckian who is murdered by his lover, Eva Medina Canada in Gayl Jones's *Eva's Man.*

Carter, Dr. Harry Teacher of psychology and one of Jacob Horner's interviewers at Wicomico State Teachers College in John Barth's *The End of the Road.*

Carter, Faron Fishing guide who works out of Key West in Thomas McGuane's *Ninety-Two in the Shade.*

Carter, Gil Rowdy best friend of Art Croft in Walter Van Tilburg Clark's *The Ox-Bow Incident.*

Carter, Hattie (Hattie Starr) Proprietor of a Louisville brothel; mother of Berenice Fleming in Theodore Dreiser's *The Stoic* and *the Titan.*

Carter, John Sir Daniel Brackley's servant; wounded, he lies moaning for a priest; Bennet Hatch tells Dick Shelton to ask him about Harry Shelton's murder, but he won't talk in Robert Louis Stevenson's *The Black Arrow: A Tale of Two Roses.*

Carter, John T. Southern gentleman serving in the Union army during the Civil War who marries Lillie Ravenel despite the objections of her father; dies in battle shortly after the discovery of his affair with Lillie's aunt, Mrs. Larue, in John William DeForest's *Miss Ravenel's Conversion from Secession to Loyalty.*

Carter, Joseph Tenant farmer of Indefer Jones; he and his son witness Jones's last will and by their testimony lead Mr. Apjohn to where Jones had hidden it in Anthony Trollope's *Cousin Henry.*

Carter, Lillie Ravenel Louisiana belle who, through a series of adventures and marriages, becomes firmly attached to the Union cause in the Civil War in John William DeForest's *Miss Ravenel's Conversion from Secession to Loyalty.*

Carter, Madam Fannie Rosalie de Neighbor of Aunt Hager Williams; fights for women's suffrage and prohibition in Langston Hughes's *Not Without Laughter.*

Carter, Madeline Aristocratic New Yorker and niece of Cyrus Carter; marries Oliver Tappan and inspires his corruption in Hjalmar Hjorth Boyesen's *The Golden Calf.*

Carter, Martha Wife of Simon; a wealthy half American, she takes their children to California to be safe during the war; she tries to leave Simon when she learns how the zoo animals are tortured under the administration of Emile Englander in Angus Wilson's *The Old Men at the Zoo.*

Carter, Mr. Surgeon who quietly treats Mr. Rochester's mad wife, Bertha, and any victims of her attacks in Charlotte Brontë's *Jane Eyre.*

Carter, Mr. Tutor hired by Sir Boyvill Neville to prepare his son, Gerald Neville, to testify against his mother, Alithea Neville, in divorce proceedings in Mary Shelley's *Falkner.*

Carter, Mrs. Fellow lodger with the Colemans in Manchester; she nurses Jane Coleman during her illness in Mark Rutherford's *The Revolution in Tanner's Lane.*

Carter, Mrs. Widow "in the ripe September of her life" who pursues Aleck Maury and attempts to reform him in Caroline Gordon's "To Thy Chamber Window, Sweet."

Carter, Rain Young painter, commissioned to paint Demoyte's portrait, who falls in love with William Mor but refuses to break up his marriage and run away with him, so saving the quality of her art in Iris Murdoch's *The Sandcastle.*

Carter, Ravenel (Ravvie) Son of John and Lillie Ravenel Carter; his presence and need for attention occupies Lillie after her husband's infidelity is discovered in John William DeForest's *Miss Ravenel's Conversion from Secession to Loyalty.*

Carter, Simon Secretary of the zoological gardens; a young administrator, he helps implement the plan of the removal of animals to the Welsh reserve, takes practical charge of the London zoo during the war, is imprisoned by the conquering Uni-Europeans, and survives to compete for the directorship of the zoo after the fall of the conquerors in Angus Wilson's *The Old Men at the Zoo.*

Carter, Ted Young man who, to the chagrin of his social-climbing family, loves the socially unacceptable Selena Cross in Grace Metalious's *Peyton Place.*

Carter, William Communist agent posing as a slick British representative of Nucleaners Ltd.; he gives James Wormold poisoned whiskey at a vacuum-cleaner convention in Graham Greene's *Our Man in Havana.*

Carter, William See Yeager, Jackson.

Carteret, Blandford Cousin of the Carterets of Virginia who has been living in New York since he was 15; fortifies himself to marry Olivia de Ormond rather than take back his word in O. Henry's "Thimble, Thimble."

Carteret, Charles Friend of Nick Dormer; urges Dormer to enter politics in Henry James's *The Tragic Muse.*

Carteret, John Cousin of the Carterets of the North, a group of shrewd businessmen who worship money and practical matters rather than Southern chivalry and honor; being very similar in appearance to Blanford Carteret, proposes playing with Uncle Jake to see if the old servant can still make out the true descendant of the South; advises his look-alike, Blanford, to pay Olivia de Ormond the $10,000 she demands to end their engagement in O. Henry's "Thimble, Thimble."

Carteret, Major Philip Aristocratic white newspaper owner and adversary of Dr. William Miller in Charles W. Chesnutt's *The Marrow of Tradition.*

Carteret, Miss Daughter of the Dowager Viscountess Dalrymple in Jane Austen's *Persuasion.*

Cartero Unnamed postman with a goatee beard who delivers to Geoffrey Firmin a postcard that Yvonne Firmin had mailed to him nearly a year earlier in Malcolm Lowry's *Under the Volcano.*

Carthew, Henry Norris Carthew's brother and Lady Ann Carthew's favorite, killed in a hunting accident in Robert Louis Stevenson's *The Wrecker.*

Carthew, Lady Ann Dignified, exacting mother of Norris Carthew, who tells her the story of the *Flying Scud* before leaving for France in Robert Louis Stevenson's *The Wrecker.*

Carthew, Lord Singleton Vain, stupid father of Norris Carthew; after frequent fights he finally banishes Norris to Australia; he dies one year before Loudon Dodd's visit to the Carthew estate in Robert Louis Stevenson's *The Wrecker.*

Carthew, Mrs. Admiral Fakenham's housekeeper, so blinded by the romance of Carinthia Kirby's marriage to wealthy Lord Fleetwood that she doesn't notice his rudeness and lack of affection in George Meredith's *The Amazing Marriage.*

Carthew, Norris (Norrie) (Goddedaal, Dickson, Madden) Bored, disenchanted English gentleman, whose misfortunes in life and aboard the *Currency Lass* lie behind the mystery of the wreck of the *Flying Scud;* he uses various aliases in his bidding for wrecked ships in Robert Louis Stevenson's *The Wrecker.*

Cartlett Second husband of Arabella Donn in Thomas Hardy's *Jude the Obscure.*

Cartographer, The Cowardly war-time mapmaker left behind when his colleagues were captured by the enemy; he takes shelter for several months in a greenhouse where he tends to the plants obsessively; he becomes embroiled in the petty rivalries of his enemies and, becoming an embarrassment to them, is eventually reunited with his countrymen, who regard him as a hero in Nigel Dennis's *A House in Order.*

Carton, Sydney Dissolute London barrister, whose identical appearance to Charles Darnay (Charles St. Evrémonde) is decisive for both of their lives; he falls in love with Lucie Manette and dies on the scaffold in place of Darnay out of love for Lucie in Charles Dickens's *A Tale of Two Cities.*

Cartright, Emily Child most likely severely neglected as a baby; she is left to go through puberty while living with the narrator in Doris Lessing's *Memoirs of a Survivor.*

Cartucho Violent figure from Madrid's shanty world and Florita's boyfriend; blames the protagonist, Pedro, for her pregnancy and death, and kills Dorita, Pedro's lover, in revenge in Luis Martin-Santos's *Time of Silence.*

Cartwright Fourteen-year-old boy who helps Sherlock Holmes track down information and brings the detective food on the moor in Arthur Conan Doyle's *The Hound of the Baskervilles.*

Cartwright Artist who explains, at the dinner table, the mystery of the ancient god Pan in D. H. Lawrence's *St. Mawr.*

Cartwright, Althea Upper-class bluestocking, who allows Christopher Kirkland to be her escort in society in his first year in London in Mrs. Lynn Linton's *The Autobiography of Christopher Kirkland.*

Cartwright, Elijah J. (Hookworm) Sex-driven Tennessee mountain boy who is a member of Big Red Smalley's traveling gospel show in George Garrett's *Do, Lord, Remember Me.*

Cartwright, Joanna Freddy Hamilton's friend and frequent hostess in Jordan in Muriel Spark's *The Mandlebaum Gate.*

Cartwright, Lettie Midwife of Tangierneck in Sarah E. Wright's *This Child's Gonna Live.*

Cartwright, Matt Joanna's husband and Freddy Hamilton's frequent host in Jordan in Muriel Spark's *The Mandlebaum Gate.*

Cartwright, Mr. Father of five girls who has been forced to adopt a reduced style of living in George Gissing's *A Life's Morning.*

Cartwright, Mrs. Dominating mother of five girls in George Gissing's *A Life's Morning.*

Caruso, Paul Ruth Ramsey's friend and next-door neighbor while she was growing up; the first person with whom Ruth, had sexual intercourse as a teenager; after her divorce and the uproar over her teaching methods, finds Paul on classmates.com and arranges a romantic rendezvous in Tom Perrotta's *The Abstinence Teacher.*

Carvajal, Licenciado One of two men who becomes the target of the president's plot for murdering those suspected of being enemies of the government in Miguel Angel Asturias's *The President.*

Carvel, Colonel Comyn Grandson of Dorothy Manners and Richard Carvel; father of Virginia Carvel; proslavery aristocrat in Civil War St. Louis in Winston Churchill's *The Crisis.*

Carvel, Dorothy Manners See Manners, Dorothy.

Carvel, Grafton Deceitful, unprincipled uncle of Richard Carvel in Winston Churchill's *Richard Carvel.*

Carvel, Lionel Kindly man who rears the orphaned Richard Carvel in Winston Churchill's *Richard Carvel.*

Carvel, Philip Ne'er-do-well son of Grafton Carvel in Winston Churchill's *Richard Carvel.*

Carvel, Richard (Dick) Manly Marylander who suffers greatly as an American supporter during the Revolutionary War; husband of Dorothy Manners; narrator of Winston Churchill's *Richard Carvel.*

Carvel, Virginia (Jinny) Descendant of Richard Carvel; spirited and high-minded supporter of her Maryland ancestors and of slavery; marries Stephen Brice in Winston Churchill's *The Crisis.*

Carver, Alden, Jr. Bachelor brother of Stephen Carver; succeeds his father as a bank president; appears in Margaret Ayer Barnes's *Years of Grace* and *Wisdom's Gate.*

Carver, Betsy Middle-aged Memphis eccentric and oldest daughter of George and Minta Carver; prevented from marrying her Nashville sweetheart, Wyant Brawley; opens a real estate business in Memphis; never marries and carries on an indiscreet social life in Memphis nightclubs in Peter Taylor's *A Summons to Memphis.*

Carver, Captain Jonathan Officer in Rogers' Rangers who later betrays Major Robert Rogers in Kenneth Roberts's *Northwest Passage.*

Carver, Cicily (Silly) Unmarried sister of Stephen Carver in Margaret Ayer Barnes's *Years of Grace.*

Carver, Cicily See Lancaster, Cicily Carver Bridges.

Carver, General Insipid friend and visitor of Lady Matilda Sufton and a guest at the home of Lord Altamont and Adelaide Douglas after their marriage in Susan Ferrier's *Marriage.*

Carver, George, Jr. Youngest son of George and Minta Carver; described as an unimaginative and insensitive boy as he seems undisturbed by the family's relocation from Nashville to Memphis; after briefly working in his father's law firm, he lies about being drafted into the army in order to establish his independence from his domineering parent; killed in World War II in Peter Taylor's *A Summons to Memphis.*

Carver, George, Sr. Husband of Minta Carver and father of George, Phillip, Betsy, and Josephine; takes his family from Nashville to Memphis after being betrayed by a friend and business partner; becomes a successful lawyer; he earns the resentment of his family, who address their emotions when he is older and wants to remarry in Peter Taylor's *A Summons to Memphis.*

Carver, Jane Ward (Mumsy) Daughter of John and Lizzie Ward, wife of Stephen Carver, and mother of three children, including Cicily Carver; despite her education and opportunities, she accepts a conventional life in Margaret Ayer Barnes's *Years of Grace* and *Wisdom's Gate.*

Carver, Josephine Youngest daughter of George and Minta Carver; prevented from marrying Clarkson Manning; opens a real estate business in Memphis with her sister, Betsy; submits to her father's control as a young woman; eventually rebels and evolves into an independent woman in Peter Taylor's *A Summons to Memphis.*

Carver, Lawyer Attorney who reads Peregrine Lacey Catlett's will to the Catlett family in Mary Lee Settle's *Know Nothing.*

Carver, Maury Loudmouth member of Johnny Catlett's militia unit in Mary Lee Settle's *Know Nothing.*

Carver, Minta Wife of George Carver, Sr. and mother of Betsy, Josephine, Phillip, and George; tries to maintain the family's spirits when it leaves Nashville for Memphis, but eventually loses her health in Peter Taylor's *A Summons to Memphis.*

Carver, Mother Wise old frontier woman who settles with her family at Beulah; tries to help Sally Lacey adapt to frontier life but is scorned in Mary Lee Settle's *O Beulah Land.*

Carver, Mr. Art dealer who introduces Lewis Seymour to Lucy Bentham; he accepts a secret annual commission from her to buy Seymour's pictures in George Moore's *A Modern Lover.*

Carver, Phillip Son of George, Sr., and Minta Carver and brother of Josephine, Betsy, and George, Jr., whose life in New York City is interrupted by his sisters' determination that he become involved in family matters in Memphis. The interruption allows him to address issues he has ignored in Peter Taylor's *A Summons to Memphis.*

Carver, Preston Eighteen-year-old dandy and subordinate officer in Johnny Catlett's Confederate army unit in Mary Lee Settle's *Know Nothing.*

Carver, Stephen Boston banker married to Jane Ward Carver; father of three children, including Cicily Carver, in Margaret Ayer Barnes's *Years of Grace* and *Wisdom's Gate.*

Carwin, Francis Biloquist who wreaks havoc on the lives of Clara Wieland, her family, and her friends in Charles Brockden Brown's *Wieland.*

Cary, Christopher Blanchard, Jr. (Chris) Son of Olivia Cary; saved from her influence by his father and his wife's claiming of their black heritage in Jessie Redmon Fauset's *Comedy, American Style.*

Cary, Christopher Fidele Husband of Olivia Cary; a doctor who refuses to pass for white in Jessie Redmon Fauset's *Comedy, American Style.*

Cary, Edward Son of Warwick Cary, brother of Judith Cary, nephew of Fauquier Cary, and husband of Désirée Gaillard; fights with the Confederate navy in Virginia and Mississippi in Mary Johnston's *The Long Roll* and *Cease Firing.*

Cary, Fairfax Brother of Ludwell Cary; postpones engagement to Unity Dandridge to pursue his brother's murderer in Mary Johnston's *Lewis Rand.*

Cary, Fauquier Uncle of Judith and Edward Cary and cousin of Richard Cleave; Whig veteran of the Mexican War who wants to preserve the Union, until the battle at Fort Sumter; promoted to the rank of general and loses an arm at Sharpsburg; appears in Mary Johnston's *The Long Roll* and *Cease Firing.*

Cary, Judith Jacqueline Daughter of Warwick Cary, sister of Edward Cary, and niece of Fauquier Cary; attends wounded Confederate troops in Richmond, and marries

Richard Cleave; appears in Mary Johnston's *The Long Roll* and *Cease Firing.*

Cary, Lucy Aunt of Judith and Edward Cary and sister of Fauquier Cary; makes shirts, from family curtains, for Confederate troops in Mary Johnston's *The Long Roll.*

Cary, Ludwell Brother of Fairfax Cary; rival in politics and romance of Lewis Rand, by whom he is murdered, in Mary Johnston's *Lewis Rand.*

Cary, Oliver Dark-skinned son of Olivia Cary; driven to suicide by his mother's treatment of him in Jessie Redmon Fauset's *Comedy, American Style.*

Cary, Olivia Blanchard Upper-class, light-skinned woman who eventually destroys two of her children by her obsession with skin color in Jessie Redmon Fauset's *Comedy, American Style.*

Cary, Teresa (Tess, Treesa) Light-skinned mulatto daughter of Olivia Cary; forced by her mother to give up her dark-skinned lover to marry the white Aristide Pailleron in Jessie Redmon Fauset's *Comedy, American Style.*

Caryle, Mrs. Wife eloped from her husband; she takes a room above the Milliner's shop in Francis Coventry's *The History of Pompey the Little.*

Carysbroke, Lady Mary Well-bred, kindly, engaging sister of Lord Ilbury; she befriends Maud Ruthyn at Elverston in J. Sheridan Le Fanu's *Uncle Silas.*

Carysbroke, Mr. See Ilbury, Lord.

Casabianca Competent, likable, ingenious holiday tutor who accompanies the Provincial Lady's family on a Brittany tour in E. M. Delafield's *The Provincial Lady Goes Further.*

Casamassima, Prince Young and exceedingly wealthy Italian prince married to Christina Light in Henry James's *Roderick Hudson;* pursues his runaway wife in an attempt to convince her to return home in *The Princess Casamassima.*

Casamassima, Princess See Light, Christina.

Casares, Bioy Fictive version of Borges's friend Adolfo Bioy Casares, who recalls that a heresiarch in Uqbar had declared that mirrors and copulation were abominable, since they both multiplied the number of men; this triggers fictional Borges's curiosity concerning its source, and Bioy Casares refers him to an article on Uqbar in the *Anglo-American Cyclopedia* in Jorge Luis Borges's "Tlön, Uqbar, Orbis Tertius."

Casaubon Narrator-protagonist who, with his colleagues Belbo and Diotellevi, becomes immersed in an international conspiracy that encompasses the Knights Templar, the Holy Grail, and the Milanese publishing community; exposed to the Diabolicals, a group of self-financing occult writers; combines computer technology with the numerology of the kabbalah to create "the Plan," a system that uses a computer program to generate random connections between seemingly unconnected facts, and thus to rewrite history; this enterprise endangers his life in Umberto Eco's *Foucault's Pendulum.*

Casaubon, Edward Clergyman and scholar, who has been writing and researching his text "A Key to All Mythologies" for many years; although he is fifty and she is nineteen, he marries Dorothea Brooke in order to have company when he is not studying; the two can never understand each other, for he is cold-hearted while she is loving; he dies in his garden before he can force a promise from Dorothea that she will compile and publish his notes in George Eliot's *Middlemarch.*

Casby, Christopher Patriarchal landlord of the Bleeding Heart Yard with long, flowing white hair; he is Flora Finching's father; he appears benevolent but is greedy and hard-hearted to his tenants; he is eventually humiliated by his collection agent, Mr. Pancks, in the Bleeding Heart Yard in Charles Dickens's *Little Dorrit.*

Case, Mr. Confidential servant of the Baroness Bernstein (Beatrix Esmond) in William Makepeace Thackeray's *The Virginians.*

Case, Tiffany James Bond's neurotic American ally and eventual lover in Ian Fleming's *Diamonds Are Forever.* She lives with Bond in his London flat but leaves to marry an American serviceman in *From Russia, With Love.*

Casement, Catherine Thirty-two-year-old beauty with fair skin, hazel eyes, and dark blond hair who falls in love with Captain James Churchill; she recovers from a cancer operation; she is divorced from her first husband and separated from her second and is a patient of Dr. Best in Kingsley Amis's *The Anti-Death League.*

Casement, Dolly Lesbian guest at Margy Stuart's weekend party who embarrasses Georgie Smithers by her attentions in Richard Aldington's *The Colonel's Daughter.*

Casey, Captain Jack Emma Newcome's first husband, who was abusive and died of drink in William Makepeace Thackeray's *The Newcomes.*

Casey, Jem Poet of the Pick and Bard of Booterstown who writes "A Pint of Plain is Your Only Man" and "The Gift of God is a Working Man" in Flann O'Brien's *At Swim-Two-Birds.*

Casey, Jock Imaginary pitcher who kills Damon Rutherford with a bean ball in Robert Coover's *The Universal Baseball Association, Inc., J. Henry Waugh, Prop.*

Casey, John Old Fenian who bitterly argues politics with Stephen Dedalus's Aunt Dante Riordan in James Joyce's *A Portrait of the Artist as a Young Man.*

Casey, Margaret Manipulative Irish-Catholic housekeeper to whom Isabel Moore makes a final conscience payment in Mary Gordon's *Final Payments.*

Casey, Mrs. Patient of Jack Flood who dies; ran a smoke shop for forty years in Maureen Howard's *Expensive Habits.*

Casey, Violet Shrinking, melancholy, penitential Irish Catholic, prone to nervous breakdowns; she is seduced by her college tutor, Robin Meadowes, and marries him; she is continually troubled by religious doubt and marital difficulties; she becomes first a Jehovah's Witness and then a Sufist in David Lodge's *How Far Can You Go?*

Cashel, Lady Weak-minded aunt of Fanny Wyndham; she supports her niece's loyalty to Frank O'Kelly (Lord Ballindine) in Anthony Trollope's *The Kellys and the O'Kellys.*

Cashel, Lord Uncle and guardian of Fanny Wyndham; he tries to enforce her marriage to his son, Lord Kilcullen, in Anthony Trollope's *The Kellys and the O'Kellys.*

Cashmore, Dr. Overworked physician; his initial mistake in identifying the master as the valet allows the famous artist Priam Faril to pose as Henry Leek after Leek's death in Arnold Bennett's *Buried Alive: A Tale of These Days.*

Caspar Bastard mulatto child of Sophia Willoughby's uncle; he is sent to England to become Sophia's ward, follows Sophia to Paris where he becomes a member of the Gardes Mobiles, and is slain by Sophia after he bayonets Minna Lemuel in Sylvia Townsend Warner's *Summer Will Show.*

Cass, Dunston Drinking, gambling, second son of Squire Cass; he imagines himself to be a lucky fellow who is able to rely on chance; he steals Silas Marner's gold and drowns still clutching the heavy money bags in George Eliot's *Silas Marner.*

Cass, Godfrey Oldest son of Squire Cass; he allows his wife Molly to die and makes no attempt to claim Eppie as his daughter until many years after his childless marriage to Nancy Lammeter in George Eliot's *Silas Marner.*

Cass, Leni Unemployed actress living with her son in a Second Avenue apartment managed by Norman Moonbloom in Edward Lewis Wallant's *The Tenants of Moonbloom.*

Cass, Miss Evelyn Orcham's trusted, authoritative, efficient, well-dressed personal secretary; she believes that men lack a sense of actuality; she is considered sufficiently eminent to be invited to the celebratory dinner of the male officials who created the merger of eight luxury hotels in Arnold Bennett's *ImperialPalace.*

Cass, Molly First wife of Godfrey Cass, but unrecognized as such by anyone except Dunston Cass; she is an opium addict, who dies outside in the snow with her child, Eppie, in her arms in George Eliot's *Silas Marner.*

Cass, Squire Wealthiest man in Ravenloe; he is renowned more for his ill-temper and irresponsible nature than for any kindness toward the townspeople; he is the father of Godfrey and Dunston Cass in George Eliot's *Silas Marner.*

Cassandra Homer's prophetess, Cassandra, reflects on her life, the walled city of Troy, and the long war that leads to Troy's destruction at the hands of the Greeks; this story, written in the 20th century, is mostly told as a first-person interior monologue, using Homer's events as a basis; Cassandra is a prisoner of war and awaiting her execution, with her children at her side; recalls the sequence of events that led up to the war and the events during the war; her forewarning of the fall of Troy went unheeded by the Trojans in Christa Wolf's *Cassandra.*

Cassandra Trojan princess and now Agamemnon's slave and concubine; the god Apollo had given her the gift of prophecy, but when she refused to make love to him, he made sure no one would believe her knowledge of the future; thus futilely predicts Agamemnon's and her own murders; also recounts the story of the curse of the House of Atreus and predicts the return of the son of Agamemnon and Clytemnestra in Aeschylus's *Agamemnon.*

Cassandra Trojan princess and sister to the military commander Hector; seer whose prediction that war cannot be avoided between the Trojans and the Greeks proves correct even to those that doubt her prophecy; offers Hector's wife Andromache the picture of a tiger prowling at the palace gates and waiting for the moment to strike in Jean Giraudoux's *Tiger at the Gates.*

Cassandra Woman of uncertain origin who appears regularly at the Forum in Rome; tries to learn information on enemies of Julius Caesar; has an affair with Gordianus, a Roman private investigator; and is murdered in Steven Saylor's *A Mist of Prophecies.*

Cassandra (Candy) Daughter of Skipper and Gertrude, mother of Pixie, and wife of Fernandez; commits suicide by jumping from the top of a lighthouse in John Hawkes's *Second Skin.*

Cassard, Maurice (Joe) French screenwriter who marries Belinda in Ludwig Bemelmans's *Dirty Eddie.*

Cassell, Dr. Physician of the village, who preaches on religious subjects in the building in the field; he regales people with anecdotes he has read in Ivy Compton-Burnett's *Dolores.*

Cassell, Margarita Beautiful, well-dressed performer at the poetry reading that introduces Clara Maugham to Clelia Denham in Margaret Drabble's *Jerusalem the Golden.*

Cassell, Mrs. Slender, comely, affectionate wife of Dr. Cassell; she knows little about housekeeping in Ivy Compton-Burnett's *Dolores.*

Casse-tête Thief executed with Stefan in William Faulkner's *A Fable.*

Cassewary, Miss Elderly companion to Lady Mabel Grex and a distant cousin of the family; she constantly fears that the country is steadily declining in Anthony Trollope's *The Duke's Children.*

Cassiani, Leona Determined, intelligent black woman whom Florentino meets on a trolley and mistakes for a whore; asks him for a job, not sex; becomes indispensable in the river company; nurtures Florentino's career and cares for him in his old age in Gabriel García Márquez's *Love in the Time of Cholera.*

Cassidy, Aldo Successful and overgenerous pram manufacturer and emotionally repressed, naïve lover; he seeks love and escape from his safe, middle-class world through a doubtful affair with a charismatic, failed novelist, Shamus, and Shamus's abused, sexually provocative wife, Helen, but destroys all his loving relationships through inertia and betrayal in John le Carré's *The Naive and Sentimental Lover.*

Cassidy, Eusebius Cassidy Sentimental poet, farmer, and horse-breeder; Tarry Flynn's best friend, he loves to spread gossip no matter who gets into trouble, including Tarry, in Patrick Kavanagh's *Tarry Flynn.*

Cassidy, Hugo Aldo Cassidy's seven-year-old son; he manipulates his father as obviously and successfully as does the grandfather for whom he is named in John le Carré's *The Naive and Sentimental Lover.*

Cassidy, Hugo ("Old Hugo") Aldo Cassidy's manipulative father; he lives off his son's largesse while draining away Aldo's emotional reserves in John le Carré's *The Naive and Sentimental Lover.*

Cassidy, Juliet Sister of Lesbia Firebrace and of the late Mary Shelley; she is married to Lucius Cassidy; she kindly conceals Maria Shelley's theft of an earring belonging to her father, Oliver Firebrace, and replaces it in Ivy Compton-Burnett's *Two Worlds and Their Ways.*

Cassidy, Lucius Juliet's husband, who runs a school for boys; he reproves Oliver Shelley and Oliver Spode for their conspicuous friendship in Ivy Compton-Burnett's *Two Worlds and Their Ways.*

Cassidy, Maggie (M. C.) First love of Jack Duluoz; ultimately rejects him in Jack Kerouac's *Maggie Cassidy;* mentioned in *Book of Dreams* and *Desolation Angels.*

Cassidy, Mark Aldo Cassidy's eleven-year-old son; he is isolated at Sherborne School because he never receives his father's secret confessional letters in John le Carré's *The Naive and Sentimental Lover.*

Cassidy, Sandra Aldo Cassidy's uncommunicative wife; she refuses to comfort Aldo but overlooks his affairs with Shamus and Helen and accepts him back after his psychic breakdown for the sake of her children in John le Carré's *The Naive and Sentimental Lover.*

Cassie Fiancée of Bumper Morgan and teacher of French at Los Angeles City College in Joseph Wambaugh's *The Blue Knight.*

Cassio Othello's friend who is appointed lieutenant rather than Iago; kind, loyal, and trusted, often manipulated by others; becomes the target of Iago's revenge and jealousy, as Iago tricks Othello into thinking that his wife, Desdemona, is having an affair with Cassio in William Shakespeare's play *Othello.*

Cassius, Caius One of the conspirators against Caesar in William Shakespeare's play *Julius Caesar.*

Casson, Mr. Fat, satisfied owner of the Donnithorne Arms, a tavern in Hayslope, which he opens after being the rich Donnithorne family's butler for 15 years in George Eliot's *Adam Bede.*

Cassy (Miss Cassy) Mysterious, unwilling slave mistress to Simon Legree; manages the escape of herself and Emmeline, her daughter, with the help of Uncle Tom and is reunited by chance with Eliza Harris in Harriet Beecher Stowe's *Uncle Tom's Cabin.*

Castagnet, Jacqueline French prostitute who is one-hundred-sixty-five years old but appears under thirty; she is a supernormal being discovered telepathically by John Wainwright in Olaf Stapledon's *Odd John: A Story Between Jest and Earnest.*

Castaldo, Gian-Battasta (Count of Piadena) Persevering, indefatigable general in the army of the Emperor Charles IV and generous patron of the Chevalier de Damville (Charles de St. Leon) in William Godwin's *St. Lean.*

Castel, Dr. Old medical doctor in the French Algerian city of Oran who has worked on plague outbreaks during his visits to China and Paris, enabling him to correctly diagnose the disease in Albert Camus's *The Plague.*

Castel, Juan Pablo Self-alienated artist whose inability to connect with his society contributes to his murder of an impassive woman in Ernesto Sábato's *The Tunnel.*

Castelluci, Lou Former student of Yolanda Garcia; discovers a collection of short stories by Professor Garcia that contains a story strikingly similar to one he wrote in a creative writing class; husband of Penny Ross Castelluci in Julia Alvarez's *Yo!*

Casterley, Lady Elderly mother of Lady Valleys; she prevents her grandson, Lord Miltoun, from ruining his political future by persuading Audrey Noel to leave England in John Galsworthy's *The Patrician.*

Castevet, Minnie Wife of Roman Castevet; prepares the mysterious daily drinks for Rosemary Woodhouse during Rosemary's pregnancy with Satan's son in Ira Levin's *Rosemary's Baby.*

Castevet, Roman Warlock who poses as a kindly old neighbor of Rosemary and Guy Woodhouse; orchestrates Satan's seduction of Rosemary Woodhouse in Ira Levin's *Rosemary's Baby.* See also Steven Marcato.

Casti, Julian Bookish, culture-loving chemist's assistant and aspiring writer; he becomes the friend of Osmond Waymark by answering an advertisement and contracts a miserable marriage with his cousin, Harriet Smales, in George Gissing's *The Unclassed.*

Castiglione Italian knight who assists Castruccio dei Antelminelli in the siege of Valperga in Mary Shelley's *Valperga.*

Castiglione, Joe Miner who initiates a new recruit by sodomizing him with an air hose in Robert Coover's *The Origin of the Brunists.*

Castillo, Alejandro Younger son of the valley's richest man and lover of the beautiful Maria de las Garzas; friend of Bob Webster; married to a woman he does not love; dies tragically in Josefina Niggli's *Mexican Village.*

Castillo, Cesar Older brother of Nestor Castillo and son of Maria and Pedro Castillo; moves to New York from Cuba to become a famous bandleader; drinks himself to death in a hotel room surrounded by his old recordings and photographs in Oscar Hijuelos's *The Mambo Kings Play Songs of Love.*

Castillo, Consuela Twenty-four-year-old gorgeous daughter of Cuban émigrés who now live in New Jersey; glossy black haired beauty with a pale complexion, is busty and uses her body to its advantage in her affair with her teacher David Kepesh; tries too hard at first to impress him; nonetheless uses her sensual beauty to enthrall and then dominate Kepesh; receives master's degree, whereupon Kepesh ends their one-and-a-half-year affair; calls him after seven years in distress because she is suffering from breast cancer; unable to cope with a lost future, visits Kepesh because she knows he once loved her body; asks him to photograph her and caress her before she soon undergoes surgery in Philip Roth's *A Dying Animal.*

Castillo, Eugenio Son of Nestor and Delores Castillo; as a child, is close to his uncle Cesar, but as an adult, is distant; calls Desi Arnaz to tell him about Cesar's death in Oscar Hijuelos's *The Mambo Kings Play Songs of Love.*

Castillo, Joaquín Older son of the valley's richest man; leaves Hidalgo to fight in the Revolution of 1910; returns incognito as an actor with a wandering troupe and reclaims his position in the village, eventually becoming a close friend of Bob Webster, in Josefina Niggli's *Mexican Village.*

Castillo, Maria Wife of Pedro and mother of Cesar and Nestor Castillo; dejected by Nestor's death; thinks Cesar has become a drunkard; lives in Cuba in Oscar Hijuelos's *The Mambo Kings Play Songs of Love.*

Castillo, Nestor Younger brother of Cesar Castillo and son of Maria and Pedro Castillo; moves to New York to play in a band with his brother; writes their most famous song, "Beautiful Maria of My Soul"; marries Delores Fuentes and has two children; never gets over his love for Maria Rivera; dies in a car accident in Oscar Hijuelos's *The Mambo Kings Play Songs of Love.*

Castillo, Pablo Cousin and immigration sponsor of Cesar and Nestor; works at a meatpacking plant; worries about Cesar after Nestor's death in Oscar Hijuelos's *The Mambo Kings Play Songs of Love.*

Castillo, Pedro Husband of Maria and father of Cesar and Nestor Castillo; beats Cesar until he moves to Havana; believes musicians are effeminate; works hard on his farm in Cuba; is not compassionate or kind toward anyone in Oscar Hijuelos's *The Mambo Kings Play Songs of Love.*

Castillonnes, Victor (Cabasse) de Young poet who has improved on his name and is a hanger-on of the Duchesse d'lvry, who instigates his duel with Lord Kew in William Makepeace Thackeray's *The Newcomes.*

Castiza Sister of Vendice and Hippolito; nearly falls victim to Lussurioso's lustful trap; proves her virtue to Vendice in Cyril Tourner's play *The Revenger's Tragedy.*

Castle, James Elkton Hills student who commits suicide rather than retract his statement accusing another student of conceit in J. D. Salinger's *The Catcher in the Rye.*

Castle, Julian Operator of a jungle hospital; Albert Schweitzer-figure in Kurt Vonnegut's *Cat's Cradle.*

Castle, Maurice Emotionally drained espionage analyst; he betrays South Africa maneuvers, particularly the genocidal Operation Uncle Remus, to Soviet Intelligence as emotional repayment for a communist agent's help freeing his African wife from her government's apartheid oppression; he defects without being able to protect her or her young son in Graham Greene's *The Human Factor.*

Castle, Mr. Sexually molests Jill Harrington after she baby-sits for him; won't let his wife drive his new Lincoln to the store in Alice Hoffman's *Local Girls.*

Castle, Mrs. Maurice Castle's prejudiced mother; she chides Maurice for forgetting his deceased wife and belittles his African family but takes them into her home after Maurice defects in Graham Greene's *The Human Factor.*

Castle, Mrs. Wife of Mr. Castle; hires Jill Harrington to baby-sit her children Pearl and Amy in Alice Hoffman's *Local Girls.*

Castle, Philip Son of Julian Castle; hotelkeeper and author of a book on San Lorenzo in Kurt Vonnegut's *Cat's Cradle.*

Castle, Sam Sarah Castle's seven-year-old son, whose love for Arthur Davis and naïve questions torture his adoptive father, Maurice Castle, in Graham Greene's *The Human Factor.*

Castle, Sarah MaNkosi Former M.I.6 agent and Maurice Castle's African wife who, while pregnant, escapes South Africa, marries Maurice despite his family's ostracism, and is trapped without support in Britain after Maurice defects in Graham Greene's *The Human Factor.*

Castledanes, Lord Childless earl, who, after the death of his long-insane wife, marries in old age a young half sister of his nephew's wife and has two sons, apparently ruining Adolphus Delmont's hope of inheritance in Charlotte Smith's *The Young Philosopher.*

Castledean, Lady Member of the Ververs' social circle who is romantically interested in Mr. Blint in Henry James's *The Golden Bowl.*

Castlemaine See Palmer, Barbara, Lady Castlemaine.

Castlemaine, Mr. Irving Macher's college friend who informs Roger Micheldene that Macher is in New York City, leading Micheldene to find Macher with Helene Bang in Kingsley Amis's *One Fat Englishman.*

Castlemallard, Lord Nobleman who resides near Chapelizod; he is Mervyn's guardian and a very dull conversationalist in J. Sheridan Le Fanu's *The House by the Churchyard.*

Castleton, Betty Jenny James's aristocratic friend, at whose card party Amelia Booth encounters the Noble Lord while William Booth becomes reacquainted with George Trent in Henry Fielding's *Amelia.*

Castleton, Marquess of Aging nobleman, who marries Fanny Trevanion to ensure heirs to his estate in Edward Bulwer-Lytton's *The Caxtons.*

Castlewell, Lord Eloquent suitor of Rachel O'Mahony, the opera singer; he secures a singing engagement for her at Covent Garden and becomes briefly engaged to her in Anthony Trollope's *The Landleaguers.*

Castlewood Anna, Dowager Countess of Second wife, now widow, of Frank, fifth Viscount and first Earl of Castlewood; she is mother of the Hon. William and Lady Fanny Esmond in William Makepeace Thackeray's *The Virginians.*

Castlewood, Clotilda de Wertheim, Viscountess of Lady from Brussels who marries the very young Frank, fifth Viscount Castlewood, converts him to Roman Catholicism, and rules over him in William Makepeace Thackeray's *The History of Henry Esmond.* Her children are Lady Maria Esmond and Eugene, Earl of Castlewood in *The Virginians.*

Castlewood, Edward Esmond, Earl and Marquis of Father of Lady Dorothea Esmond, who is heir to his property and ancestress of the Viscounts Castlewood in William Makepeace Thackeray's *The History of Henry Esmond.*

Castlewood, Eugene, second Earl of No friend of the Virginian Warringtons, his cousins; he gambles with Harry, fleecing him, and tries to deprive both brothers of their inheritance after his marriage to the wealthy Lydia Van den Bosch in William Makepeace Thackeray's *The Virginians.*

Castlewood, Francis, first Viscount of Son of Lady Dorothea and Henry (Poyns) Esmond; he is made baronet by King James I, and later viscount; his eldest son is the second viscount; his two younger sons are fathers of the third and fourth viscounts in William Makepeace Thackeray's *The History of Henry Esmond.*

Castlewood, Francis, fourth Viscount of Vain, good-natured first cousin of Henry Esmond's father, Thomas, the third viscount; he inherits the title after Thomas's death; he marries Rachel Armstrong and fathers Beatrix and Frank (later the fifth viscount); angry at Lord Mohun's attentions to his wife, he fights a duel with him and is killed; dying, he confesses to his protegé Henry Esmond that he knows Henry is legitimate and the rightful fourth Viscount Castlewood in William Makepeace Thackeray's *The History of Henry Esmond.*

Castlewood, Francis James (Frank), fifth Viscount of Henry Esmond's cheerful and charming young second cousin, who serves with him in Marlborough's wars before he marries the Catholic Clotilda Wertheim; he is Beatrix Esmond's brother in William Makepeace Thackeray's *The History of Henry Esmond.* His children are Lady Maria Esmond and Eugene, Earl of Castlewood (by Clotilda) and the Hon. William and Lady Fanny Esmond (by his second wife, Anna) in *The Virginians.*

Castlewood, George, second Viscount of Nobleman ruined by his loyalty to the Stuarts; his daughter, Lady Isabel, marries his nephew and heir, Thomas, in William Makepeace Thackeray's *The History of Henry Esmond.*

Castlewood, Lady Isabel, Viscountess of Daughter of George, the second Viscount Castlewood; she marries her first cousin, Thomas, the third viscount; vain and ridiculous as she ages, she is nevertheless kind to her supposedly illegitimate stepson, Henry Esmond, bequeathing him her modest fortune in William Makepeace Thackeray's *The History of Henry Esmond.*

Castlewood, Rachel Armstrong, Viscountess of Wife of the fourth viscount, who is intellectually and morally her inferior; beautiful and high-minded, she is a warm friend to the boy Henry Esmond; after her husband's death following a duel, she is for a time estranged from Esmond; she becomes a supporter of his courtship of her daughter, Lady Beatrix Esmond, and after Beatrix's flight consoles him by marrying him herself; they emigrate to America in William Makepeace Thackeray's *The History of Henry Esmond.*

Castlewood, Thomas, third Viscount of Colonel Thomas Esmond's son; he is a dissipated soldier whose marriage to Gertrude Maes goes unrecognized; he marries his cousin, Lady Isabel; he brings his son, Henry Esmond, to Castlewood but does not acknowledge him as his legitimate heir before he dies in Ireland in William Makepeace Thackeray's *The History of Henry Esmond.*

Castor Referred to as Uncle Castor; one of Grandfather Eustace's brothers; visits the unnamed male narrator and main character at boyhood Capital Avenue home; jazz musician; travels with bands across the United States and Europe until his fortunes decline and he relies on relatives for his support in Darryl Pinckney's *High Cotton.*

Castor, Senor Olifa's dictatorial Gubernado and president of the Gran Seco; when forced by Lord Clanroyden to command the rebel troops, he is captured by a new dream and discovers a more wholesome allegiance to Olifa before he sacrifices his life to save the life of Lady Roylance (Janet Raden) in John Buchan's *The Courts of the Morning.*

Castor, Stephanos Celebrated wrestler, who possesses a magnificent shape but clownish features and a surly disposition; he is a conspirator against Emperor Alexius Comnenus in Sir Walter Scott's *Count Robert of Paris.*

Castorp, Hans Twenty-three-year-old, middle-class naval engineer from Hamburg who travels to a tuberculosis sanatorium in Davos, Switzerland, to visit his cousin; in rapid succession, had lost his mother, father, and grandfather and hence had a morbid sympathy with death; believing he his healthy, is proved otherwise and stays for seven years rather than three weeks; instructed in matters philosophical, medical, musical, supernatural, and sexual, loses his illusions; finally descends from the mountain to fight in World War I in Thomas Mann's *The Magic Mountain.*

Castra, Agnes de Cousin to Antonia Cranmer in Thomas Amory's *The Life of John Buncle, Esq.*

Castro, Benito Indian soldier and gaucho who returns to the Peruvian village of Rumi after the beloved mayor is murdered; organizes the people to build a new homestead higher in the Andes, but is killed when government forces pursue the villagers to decimate them in Ciro Alegria's *Broad and Alien Is the World.*

Castro, Fidel Cuban dictator who, in Margaret Reynolds's fantasy, is really a woman disguised as a man in Anne Richardson Roiphe's *Up the Sandbox!*

Castrone Eunuch who joins Nano and Androgyno in entertaining Volpone, and who, along with them, forms a consistent group of Volpone's humorous followers in Ben Jonson's play *Volpone.*

Casy, Jim Former preacher who baptized the infant Tom Joad (II); inspires Tom to correct some social wrongs in John Steinbeck's *The Grapes of Wrath.*

Cat Narrator and alley cat who recounts in disarming candor the details of his life; saved from starvation by adoption into the Sneaze middle-class family, comments in a learned and quizzical manner on his dealings with humans; muses on the irrationality of human actions compared to the superiority of cats; introduces various eccentric and engaging human personalities in Natsume Soseki's *I Am a Cat.*

Cat, Captain Retired and blind sea captain who, as he sits in Llaregyb—a mythical seaside village in Wales—recalls many men lost at sea; member of the colorful and fanciful community in Dylan Thomas's play *Under Milk Wood.*

Cata, Ernesto Twelve-year-old Zuni Indian in Tony Hillerman's *Dance Hall of the Dead;* chosen to represent Shulawitsi, the Little Fire God, in an important annual religious ceremony; killed by Chester Reynolds, disguised as a Salamobia, or death spirit, because he stole falsified artifacts from Reynolds's dig site.

Catafago, Dr. Pompous doctor who examines Jack Townrow when he becomes delirious in P. H. Newby's *Something to Answer For.*

Catalina Kate See Kate.

Catau Signora di Modena's servant girl, who aids the escape of her prisoner in Charlotte Dacre's *Zofloya; or, The Moor.*

Catchpole Former boyfriend of Margaret Peel; he reveals to Jim Dixon that Margaret is a liar and a manipulator in Kingsley Amis's *Lucky Jim.*

Catchpole, Michael (Mike) Former employee of Mr. Furze; blinded in his work, he is forced to sell shoelaces until his son, Tom, is employed by Furze in Mark Rutherford's *Catharine Furze.*

Catchpole, Tom Son of Mike Catchpole; Mr. Furze's assistant, he falls in love with Catharine Furze after she rescues him from a fire; he helps prevent the Reverend Theophilus Cardew from committing adultery with Catharine; the victim of a plot to drive him away from Eastthorp, he goes to London with a reference from Cardew in Mark Rutherford's *Catharine Furze.*

Caterham, John Conservative politician who sees the dangers of Boomfood; his failure to block its development or to effect its containment is due largely to the meddling Dr. Winkles in H. G. Wells's *The Food of the Gods, and How It Came to Earth.*

Caterina Servant in the Castle di Udolpho in Ann Radcliffe's *The Mysteries of Udolpho.*

Caterina Servant who helps Julia de Mazzini to escape her father's castle the night before her forced marriage to Duke de Luovo in Ann Radcliffe's *A Sicilian Romance.*

Caterpillar Arrogant and patronizing creature, who sits on a mushroom, smoking a hookah; after his interrogation of Alice he requires her to recite "You Are Old, Father William" as a test of her memory and then advises her to use the mushroom to control her size in Lewis Carroll's *Alice's Adventures in Wonderland.*

Cates, Governor John (Blackjack) Head of Typhon International; great-uncle of Amy Joubert in William Gaddis's *JR.*

Cates, John Vernon African-American professor of chemistry at Moo University; married to a woman from Ghana; has one son; discovers the plans for Loren Stroop's machine, thereby saving the university from financial ruin in Jane Smiley's *Moo.*

Cates, Molly Headstrong investigative reporter; author of recent crime book based on true-life accounts of Texas death row inmate Louie Bronk; discovers that her book contains potentially false information based on recent evidence, and fights in vain to overturn Bronk's conviction in Mary Willis Walker's *The Red Scream.*

Catesby One of the attendants on Richard of Gloucester, who explains to him why he is so hungry for glory; Catesby tells Dick Shelton he would be an earl tomorrow if his name were Richard in Robert Louis Stevenson's *The Black Arrow: A Tale of Two Roses.*

Catesby, Monsignore Jesuit of noble family; he is more forceful and cunning than Father Coleman in trying to convince Lothair to become a Catholic in Benjamin Disraeli's *Lothair.*

Catfield, Mr. Deacon at Mark Rutherford's first chapel; he distributes the hymns and is ignorant of most things outside a few verses of the Bible in Mark Rutherford's *The Autobiography of Mark Rutherford.*

Catharina Wife of painter Johannes Vermeer in Tracy Chevalier's *Girl with a Pearl Earring.*

Catharines, Marmaduke Elderly clergyman who writes a character reference clearing the woman accused of kidnapping Ned Fielding; he performs the marriage of young Harry Clinton and Abenaide in Henry Brooke's *The Fool of Quality.*

Cathcart, Abiah Stolid New Englander who rises from poverty to become a leading citizen of Norwood, owning the best set of matched horses in town and fathering an enormous family, in Henry Ward Beecher's *Norwood.*

Cathcart, Alice Friend of Rose Wentworth; joins Wentworth and Agate Bissell in Northern hospital duty during the Civil War, only to see her true love, Thomas Heywood, die fighting for the South at Gettysburg, in Henry Ward Beecher's *Norwood.*

Cathcart, Barton Son of Abiah and Rachel Cathcart; practical yet mystical graduate of Amherst who becomes the Norwood schoolmaster; rises to a Union generalship in the Civil War despite being wounded and captured several times; marries Rose Wentworth in Henry Ward Beecher's *Norwood.*

Cathcart, Colonel Air force officer whose desire for personal glory causes him to keep raising the number of bombing missions Yossarian's squadron must fly in Joseph Heller's *Catch-22.*

Cathcart, Denis Fiancé of Lady Mary Wimsey; he is found dead of a gunshot wound in the garden of the Duke of Denver's country place in Dorothy L. Sayers's *Clouds of Witness.*

Cathcart, Lydia Disapproving aunt of Denis Cathcart in Dorothy L. Sayers's *Clouds of Witness.*

Cathcart, Rachel Liscomb Sensitive wife of Abiah Cathcart; passes on some of her mystical spirit to her son Barton Cathcart in Henry Ward Beecher's *Norwood.*

Cather, Andrew (Andy) Husband of Bertha Cather; at age twelve he found the body of his drowned mother; narrates part of Conrad Aiken's *Great Circle.*

Cather, Bertha (Berty) Wife of Andrew Cather; has an affair with Tom Crapo in Conrad Aiken's *Great Circle.*

Cather, Christopher Handsome bisexual young man whose defunct rock group boasted one hit; he rents a room in Hilary Burde's apartment; after affairs with both Clifford Larr and Laura Impiatt he marries Biscuit Bisset in Iris Murdoch's *A Word Child.*

Cather, David Uncle of Andrew Cather and brother of John Cather; drowns with his lover Doris Cather in Conrad Aiken's *Great Circle.*

Cather, Doris Mother of Andrew Cather; drowns with her lover David Cather in Conrad Aiken's *Great Circle.*

Cather, John Father of Andrew Cather in Conrad Aiken's *Great Circle.*

Catherick, Anne Poor, demented woman, whose resemblance to Laura (Fairlie), Lady Glyde makes her the victim of Sir Percival Glyde's plan to defraud his wife of her fortune; she dies and is buried under Laura's name while Laura is incarcerated; Walter Hartright discovers that she was the illegitimate daughter of Laura's father in Wilkie Collins's *The Woman in White.*

Catherick, Mrs. Mother of Anne, the girl with an uncanny likeness to Laura Fairlie; she reveals that Laura's father had been the father of the illegitimate Anne in Wilkie Collins's *The Woman in White.*

Catherina, Donna Mother of Violetta and wife of Don Manuel in Penelope Aubin's *The Strange Adventures of the Count de Vinevil and His Family.*

Catherine Aunt of Arlette in Joseph Conrad's *The Rover.*

Catherine Jane Gray's younger sister, who is believed by Jane to be their parents' favorite in Margaret Drabble's *The Waterfall.*

Catherine Age 25; gave up her mathematical career to care for her father, Robert; lives in the family home in Hyde Park, Chicago; uncertain of her sanity and mathematical abilities; sister of Claire in David Auburn's *Proof.*

Catherine Daughter, wife, and mother of 32 years who keeps an emotional barrier between herself and others in her family; desires to break down this self-imposed defense; an unnamed fear thwarts her attempt, and so the isolation against her mother, husband, and young son persists; intimacy through conversation is difficult, as many personal thoughts are left unsaid; ultimately, instills the same neurosis for emotional distance in her son in Clarice Lispector's "Family Ties."

Catherine Employee of the Countess of Somerset (2) and attendant to the imprisoned (younger) Mary, whom she poisons in Sophia Lee's *The Recess.*

Catherine Julian Avenel's beautiful mistress and the mother of his illegitimate son; often ill-treated by him, she is nonetheless devoted, and she dies of grief upon discovering his body in Sir Walter Scott's *The Monastery.*

Catherine Sixteen-year-old daughter of Vincent Maheu; works in the infamous Montsou mine pits; meets Chaval one night and allows him to seduce her, then leaves home to live with her lover; also attracted to the socialist labor strike leader Étienne Lantier; trapped in a mine shaft explosion in 1884 and dies along with Chaval, but Etienne survives, in Émile Zola's *Germinal.*

Catherine Wife of Elias; the mother of nine, she is foolish, obstinate, and ignorant, but completely devoted to her family in Charles Reade's *The Cloister and the Hearth.*

Catherine Asthmatic wife of the Cavaliere; the only child of a wealthy Pembrokeshire squire in Susan Sontag's *The Volcano Lover.*

Catherine Wife of Hugh, lover of Cyril, and mother of Meredith, Dolores, and Eveline; once forced by Hugh to wear a chastity belt in an attempt to stop her affair with Cyril; collapses at Hugh's funeral and spends time in a village sanctuary in John Hawkes's *The Blood Oranges.*

Catherine—, Lady Clever, enthusiastic young Irish baroness, who attends Frances (Henri) Crimsworth's school in Brussels in Charlotte Brontë's *The Professor.*

Catherine, Little Crippled, saintly daughter of Elias; she aids Gerard in his escape from the burgomaster's prison tower and befriends Margaret Brandt in Charles Reade's *The Cloister and the Hearth.*

Catherine, Mère Madam of a Haitian brothel where Brown encounters Captain Concasseur and Major Jones in Graham Greene's *The Comedians.*

Catherine, Queen (Infanta Catherine of Portugal) Barren queen of Restoration England's Charles II; tolerates his many mistresses out of love for him and the hope that she will eventually give him a legitimate heir to the English throne in Kathleen Winsor's *Forever Amber.*

Catherwood, George Brother of Tom Catherwood; Confederate soldier in a divided family in Winston Churchill's *The Crisis.*

Catherwood, Tom Brother of George Catherwood; Union soldier in a divided family in Winston Churchill's *The Crisis.*

Cathey, Doc Physician and small-town philosopher; long-term companion and comforter to Henry Soames in John Gardner's *Nickel Mountain.*

Cathie, Alfred Emery Solicitor given power of attorney when Jack Higgs leaves for Erewhon in Samuel Butler's *Erewhon Revisited Twenty Years Later.*

Cathleen Daughter of Maurya, an old woman who has seen her husband and six sons killed at sea; attempts to comfort her mother when they must prepare for the burial of the two sons Michael and Bartley in John Millington Synge's play *Riders to the Sea.*

Cathleen Maid in the Tyrone family home who appears flirtatious and drunk in Eugene O'Neill's play *Long Day's Journey into Night.*

Cathy Bookkeeper at Ullswater Press and friend of Nancy Hawkins in Muriel Spark's *A Far Cry from Kensington.*

Cathy Boarder at the Geronimo Hotel and a student at the local teacher's college; alternately spies on and flirts with Paco in Larry Heinemann's *Paco's Story.*

Catiline Based on the Roman politician Lucius Sergius Catalina, appears to be a truthful and mistrusted figure heading toward his destiny of rebellion in Steven Saylor's *Catilina's Riddle.*

Catlett, Andy Oldest son of Bess and Wheeler Catlett in Wendell Berry's *A Place on Earth* and *The Memory of Old Jack.*

Catlett, Bess Feltner Daughter of Mat and Margaret Feltner; wife of Wheeler Catlett and mother of Andy and Henry Catlett in Wendell Berry's *A Place on Earth* and *The Memory of Old Jack.*

Catlett, Ezekiel (Zeke) Eldest son of Jeremiah and Hannah Catlett; marries Sara Lacey and becomes Johnny Lacey's heir; kills Witcikti, using the English tomahawk once stolen from Witcikti himself, in Mary Lee Settle's *O Beulah Land.*

Catlett, Hannah Bridewell London pickpocket transported to Virginia; as a captive of Shawnee Indians, she is the first white settler to see Beulah land; killed by Witcikti in the last Indian raid at Beulah; wife of Jeremiah and mother of Ezekiel and Rebecca Catlett in Mary Lee Settle's *O Beulah Land.*

Catlett, Henry Youngest son of Bess and Wheeler Catlett in Wendell Berry's *A Place on Earth* and *The Memory of Old Jack.*

Catlett, Jeremiah Illiterate farmer and New Light preacher led to escape his indentures, travel west, rescue Hannah Bridewell Catlett, his future wife, in the wilderness, and move to Beulah, where he is killed in the last Indian raid; father of Ezekiel and Rebecca Catlett in Mary Lee Settle's *O Beulah Land.*

Catlett, Johnny Younger son of Leah and Peregrine Lacey Catlett; leaves Beulah to avoid commitment to Melinda Lacey; goes to Missouri and Kansas, but returns to take over Beulah from his father; eventually enlists in the Confederate army but without believing in the southern position or the possibility of success in Mary Lee Settle's *Know Nothing.*

Catlett, Leah Cutwright Descendant of Doggo Cutwright; Ohio-born wife of Peregrine Lacey Catlett and mother of Lewis, Johnny, and Lydia Catlett; an outsider who is initially an abolitionist, she becomes willing to sell slaves and more approving of slavery than is her husband in Mary Lee Settle's *Know Nothing.*

Catlett, Lewis Elder son of Leah and Peregrine Lacey Catlett; inherits his mother's antislavery attitudes, religious piety, and sense of being an outsider; becomes a preacher and an abolitionist; leaves Beulah and eventually enlists in the Union army in Mary Lee Settle's *Know Nothing.*

Catlett, Lydia See Neill, Lydia Catlett.

Catlett, Mamie Brandon Descendant of Backwater Brandon and the Kreggs; daughter-in-law of Ezekiel Catlett and mother of Peregrine Lacey Catlett in Mary Lee Settle's *Know Nothing.*

Catlett, Peregrine Lacey Grandson of Ezekiel Catlett, proprietor of Beulah, husband of Leah Cutwright Catlett, and father of Lewis, Johnny, and Lydia Catlett and of the slave Toey; deplores the responsibilities of being a slave owner and supports the Union in Mary Lee Settle's *Know Nothing.*

Catlett, Rebecca (Becky) Daughter of Jeremiah and Hannah Catlett and sister of Ezekiel Catlett in Mary Lee Settle's *O Beulah Land.*

Catlett, Sara Lacey (Mrs. Ezekiel Catlett) Daughter of Johnny and Sally Lacey, sister of Peregrine and Montague Lacey, and wife of Ezekiel Catlett; only child of Johnny Lacey to share his love for Beulah land and his egalitarian ideas, she eventually inherits Beulah in Mary Lee Settle's *O Beulah Land.*

Catlett, Sara Lacey (Mrs. Lewis Catlett) Daughter of Brandon and Sally Lacey; beautiful child who, as an adult, becomes gawky, religious, and conscious of being a poor relation; marries Lewis Catlett and adopts his attitudes in Mary Lee Settle's *Know Nothing.*

Catlett, Wheeler Lawyer in Port William, Kentucky, and son-in-law of Mat Feltner; husband of Bess Catlett and father of Andy and Henry Catlett in Wendell Berry's *A Place on Earth* and *The Memory of Old Jack.*

Catlin, Debby Daughter of John and Marian Catlin in Wallace Stegner's *All the Little Live Things.*

Catlin, Henry (Hank) Depression-era newcomer to California from the Midwest; defeats Walter Knight for a seat in the state legislature in Joan Didion's *Run River.*

Catlin, Jeremiah Union soldier from Lane County, Tennessee, who is imprisoned by the Confederates; husband of Marcia Vaiden in T.S. Stribling's *The Store.*

Catlin, John Husband of Marian Catlin in Wallace Stegner's *All the Little Live Things.*

Catlin, Marcia Vaiden See Vaiden, Marcia.

Catlin, Marian Neighbor of the Allstons; dies of cancer while pregnant in Wallace Stegner's *All the Little Live Things.*

Catlin the Second, Jerry Son of Jerry and Marcia Catlin; seduces Pammy Lee Sparkman; Methodist minister infatuated with Sydna Crowninshield Vaiden but who marries Aurelia Swartout; appears in T. S. Stribling's *The Store* and *Unfinished Cathedral.*

Cato Young, good-natured son of a farmer and stepmother; loves his father but finds that his stepmother dotes on her three girls and neglects him and his brother; sent on a winter night with his brother, Emerson, to the farm's distant barn to sleep the night and keep watch on the farm implements; denied blankets by his stepmother and finds no blankets in the cold barn; curls up with his brother in the hay for warmth; found frozen to death the next day in Elizabeth Bishop's "The Farmer's Children."

Cato, Angela Black youth who is injured when an auto strikes her and her cousin, two pedestrians; her cousin Gavin dies at the scene of the accident; the incident sparks the riots between Jews and blacks in Crown Heights, Brooklyn, in 1991, in Anna Deavere Smith's play *Fires in the Mirror: Crown Heights, Brooklyn and Other Identities.*

Cato, Carmel Character originally from Guyana; one of the many voices of identity in the race riots in Crown Heights, Brooklyn, in 1991, in Anna Deavere Smith's play *Fires in the Mirror: Crown Heights, Brooklyn and Other Identities.*

Cato, Gavin Black youth of seven years of age; killed in an auto accident, with his death sparking the Crown Heights riots in Brooklyn in 1991 in Anna Deavere Smith's play *Fires in the Mirror: Crown Heights, Brooklyn and Other Identities.*

Caton, Dr. L S. Editor of a scholarly journal; he accepts Jim Dixon's article for publication, becomes evasive when Jim asks when it will be published, and publishes it as his own in Kingsley Amis's *Lucky Jim.*

Caton, Miss Colorless, middle-aged assistant in Humphrey Boyce's antiques shop in Barbara Pym's *The Sweet Dove Died.*

Cator Head clerk at the Rasuka oil well; he is a tense man with a prejudice against the Rasuka natives; he is stabbed by Hebechi Effendi but survives in P. H. Newby's *A Journey to the Interior.*

Cator, Mrs. Excitable wife of Cator in P. H. Newby's *AJourney to the Interior.*

Cat-piano Player Mysterious and sinister-looking man with a switchblade who walks uninvited into Hank Peterson's New York loft in Donald Barthelme's "A Shower of Gold."

Catskill, Rupert Britain's Secretary of State for War who plots to overthrow Utopia, arguing that its inhabitants are a decadent race who should be dominated by the more vital Earthlings in H. G. Wells's *Men Like Gods.*

Cattarina, Mademoiselle French ballet dancer who charms Harry Warrington for a time in William Makepeace Thackeray's *The Virginians.*

Catterick Snobbish gentleman of the Royal Court in C. S. Forester's *Hornblower and the Atropos.*

Catterick, Mrs. Unwilling jailer of Thomas Carlyle Craw; she agrees to provide room and board for Dougal Crombie and John Galt, "Jaikie", in John Buchan's *Castle Gay.*

Cattermole, Miss Shrewsbury College undergraduate who is resentfully dissatisfied with her academic program and social life in Dorothy L. Sayers's *Gaudy Night.*

Cattle, Carry Younger sister of Elder Miss Cattle; she adds to gossip about Mr. Cutts in Mark Rutherford's *Miriam's Schooling.*

Cattle, Elder Miss Daughter of Mr. and Mrs. Cattle; she leads the gossip about Mr. Cutts in Mark Rutherford's *Miriam's Schooling.*

Cattle, Mr. and Mrs. Giacomo Tacchi's visitors, who gossip about Mr. Cutts burning his house in Mark Rutherford's *Miriam's Schooling.*

Cattleman, Katherine Wife of Paul Cattleman; becomes the lover of Iz Einsam, a psychiatrist for whom she works as a research assistant at UCLA in Alison Lurie's *The Nowhere City.*

Cattleman, Paul History researcher, husband of Katherine Cattleman, and lover of Ceci O'Connor in Alison Lurie's *The Nowhere City.*

Catullus, Gaius Valerius Young poet with great potential; first an enemy of Caesar and then a friend; loves Clodia Pulcher, who rejects him, in Thornton Wilder's *The Ides of March.*

Caudill, Boone (Zeb Calloway) Fledgling mountain man who leaves his Kentucky home to trap furs in the Rocky Mountains in A. B. Guthrie's *The Big Sky.*

Caulder, Charlotte Ann Former girlfriend of Bob Beaudreau, who shoots her after she becomes Phil Elliott's lover in Peter Gent's *North Dallas Forty.*

Caulfield, Allie Sensitive younger brother of Holden Caulfield; dies of leukemia in J. D. Salinger's *The Catcher in the Rye.*

Caulfield, D. B. Older brother of Holden Caulfield; writer of sensitive short stories who now writes movie scripts in Hollywood in J. D. Salinger's *The Catcher in the Rye.*

Caulfield, Holden Seventeen-year-old prep school dropout who recounts the events leading to his confinement in a sanitorium; narrator of J. D. Salinger's *The Catcher in the Rye.*

Caulfield, Lord William Convivial and trustful English Lord Governor of the province of Ulster and resident at Charlemont; he is tricked and taken captive along with his officers and men by the treacherous Sir Phelim O'Neile, leader of the Irish conspiracy, in William Godwin's *Mandeville.*

Caulfield, Phoebe Josephine Ten-year-old sister of Holden Caulfield; writes short stories about Hazle Weatherfield in J. D. Salinger's *The Catcher in the Rye.*

Cava One of the young cadets at the paramilitary academy in Lima, Peru; belongs to a secret organization called the "Circle" at the school in which the boys carry out pranks and other mischievous deeds; assisted by other members of the "Circle," steals the questions of an exam; soon expelled from the academy for the theft and breaking the honor code in Mario Vargas Llosa's *The Time of the Hero.*

Cavaglieri, Ulderico Older cousin of the middle-aged protagonist Edgardo Limentano; seeks to reestablish friendship with his younger cousin after their relations were strained when Edgardo objected to Ulderico's marriage to Caesarian, a former prostitute, in Giorgio Bassani's *The Heron.*

Cavalier Second son of a Shropshire gentleman; his father tries to settle him with a marriage and an annual income, but he wishes to travel; at the instigation of John Hepburn, he joins the forces of King Gustavus Adolphus of Sweden; upon returning home to England, he joins the Loyalists in fighting for Charles I and details the adventures of his life in Daniel Defoe's *Memoirs of a Cavalier.*

Cavaliere II (Sir William Hamilton) Husband of Catherine and, later, of Emma; grandson of a duke, youngest son of a lord, and childhood companion of the king; has a front-rank diplomatic posting abroad in Naples; wherever he is, prone to cast himself in the role of guide or mentor; flees the French army and ends up in Palermo; returns to London with Emma Hart and The Hero; passes away in Susan Sontag's *The Volcano Lover.*

Cavalier's Father Shropshire gentleman, who wishes to settle his son with a wife but consents to allow him to travel and join the military; he too is among the Loyalists in Daniel Defoe's *Memoirs of a Cavalier.*

Cavalleto, Jean Baptist Small Italian imprisoned with Rigaud in Marseilles; he later works for Daniel Doyce in the Bleeding Heart Yard and is instrumental in hunting down Rigaud in Charles Dickens's *Little Dorrit.*

Cavalojos, Duchess (Her Gaudiness) Gossipy "Mistress of the Robes" for Queen Lois of Pisuerga and aunt of Laura de Nazianzi, whose court debut she helps to make in Ronald Firbank's *The Flower Beneath the Foot.*

Cavanagh, Mary Commonplace, uneducated woman, whose marriage to Morton Cavanagh causes him to be socially ostracized and ultimately ruined in Mrs. Lynn Linton's *The Autobiography of Christopher Kirkland.*

Cavanagh, Morton Upper-class bohemian artist and best friend of Christopher Kirkland; he sinks into alcoholic depravity because of his unfortunate marriage to a woman beneath him in Mrs. Lynn Linton's *The Autobiography of Christopher Kirkland.*

Cavanagh, Rita Actress turned lyric poet and Greenwich Village celebrity in Edmund Wilson's *I Thought of Daisy.*

Cavanaugh, Melissa Lover of Tommy Douglas in Scott Spencer's *Preservation Hall.*

Cavanaugh, Theodore (Ted) President of West Condon's First National Bank who is behind the efforts of the Common Sense Committee to disband the Brunists in Robert Coover's *The Origin of the Brunists.*

Cavanaugh, Tommy (Kit, Kitten) Son of Ted Cavanaugh; follows in the footsteps of Justin Miller as a high school basketball star in Robert Coover's *The Origin of the Brunists.*

Cave, Mary Wife of the Reverend Mr. Helstone; also loved by Hiram Yorke, she dies after five years of marriage amid rumors of neglect in Charlotte Brontë's *Shirley.*

Cave, Montagu (Monty) Conservative member of Parliament who serves in a ministry with Roger Quaife; he is a competitor with Quaife for high office; his wife leaves him in C. P. Snow's *Corridors of Power.*

Cavely, Martha Unpleasant widowed sister of Martin Tinman; she assists her brother in his pursuit of Annette Smith in George Meredith's *The House on the Beach.*

Cavendish Proud first lieutenant of the *Pluto* in C. S. Forester's *Ship of the Line.*

Cavendish, Elizabeth (Bess of Hardwicke) Formidable wife of Lord Shrewsbury and grandmother of Arabella Stewart in Charlotte Yonge's *Unknown to History.*

Cavendish, John Childhood friend whom the convalescing Captain Arthur Hastings visits; he is accused of poisoning his stepmother, Emily Inglethorp, in Agatha Christie's *The Mysterious Affair at Styles: A Detective Story.*

Cavendish, Lawrence John's younger brother, an unsuccessful publisher of poetry in Agatha Christie's *The Mysterious Affair at Styles: A Detective Story.*

Cavendish, Mary John's wife, who is admired by Dr. Bauerstein and Captain Hastings in Agatha Christie's *The Mysterious Affair at Styles: A Detective Story.*

Cavendish, Robert Left-wing professor of political science at Columbia University; uses women sexually and domestically; has an affair with Felicitas Taylor in Mary Gordon's *The Company of Women.*

Cavidge, Anne Gertrude Openshaw's old friend, who has for fifteen years been a nun in a closed convent; she leaves the order just before Guy Openshaw's death; she falls unrequitedly in love with "Count" Szczepanski; she leaves for Chicago when it is clear that his dogged devotion to Gertrude will endure despite Gertrude's happy marriage to Tim Reede in Iris Murdoch's *Nuns and Soldiers.*

Cavigni Robber chieftain who captures Megalena de Metastasio and is killed by Wolfstein in Percy Bysshe Shelley's *St. Irvyne.*

Cavigni, Signor Italian gallant who helps the evil Montoni in his suit to marry Madame Cheron in Ann Radcliffe's *The Mysteries of Udolpho.*

Cavilleri, Jennifer (Jenny) See Barrett, Jennifer Cavilleri.

Cavilleri, Philip (Phil) Rhode Island pastry chef and father of Jennifer Cavilleri Barrett; approves of his daughter's marriage to Oliver Barrett IV in Erich Segal's *Love Story;* consoles Barrett after Jenny's death in *Oliver's Story.*

Cavor Brilliant, eccentric scientist who develops the gravity-repelling alloy Cavorite, with which he builds a spherical spaceship and journeys to the Moon; there he becomes the permanent prisoner of the native Selenites, whose hierarchical, ant-like culture he at first admires, and to whom he appears the ambassador of a savage, dangerous race in H. G. Wells's *The First Men in the Moon.*

Cawthorne, Bridget Author of an innocuous letter given to Henry Lambert by mistake in William Beckford's *Modern Novel Writing; or, the Elegant Enthusiast.*

Caxon, Jacob Old barber, who dresses the only three wigs in the parish of Fairmont and sometimes serves as a messenger for Oldbuck (Jonathan Oldenbuck) in Sir Walter Scott's *The Antiquary.*

Caxton, Austin Father of Pisistratus Caxton; an unworldly, futile scholar, he is absorbed in writing a history of human error in Edward Bulwer-Lytton's *The Caxtons* and in *"My Novel," by Pisistratus Caxton.*

Caxton, Blanche Caxton Roland Caxton's daughter, who is groomed by her father and her uncle, Austin Caxton, to be the ideal wife for Pisistratus Caxton in Edward Bulwer-Lytton's *The Caxtons.* She provides commentary in *"My Novel," by Pisistratus Caxton.*

Caxton, Herbert Roland Caxton's lost son, who is the rival of Pisistratus Caxton for Fanny Trevanion; he farms sheep with Pisistratus in Australia and dies as a soldier in India in Edward Bulwer-Lytton's *The Caxtons.*

Caxton, Katharine (Kitty) Young ward and later wife of Austin Caxton; she is a model of domestic insipidity in Edward Bulwer-Lytton's *The Caxtons.* She provides commentary in *"My Novel," by Pisistratus Caxton.*

Caxton, Pisistratus Austin Caxton's son, who tells the story of his birth and youth, marries his cousin Blanche, and becomes a novelist in Edward Bulwer-Lytton's *The Caxtons.* He is a novelist in *"My Novel," by Pisistratus Caxton* and in *What Will He Do With It? by Pisistratus Caxton.*

Caxton, Roland Brother of Austin Caxton and a Waterloo veteran; he is obsessed with the family honor in Edward Bulwer-Lytton's *The Caxtons* and in *"My Novel," by Pisistratus Caxton.*

Cayce, Dorinda (D'rindy) Attractive daughter of John Cayce; scorns the suit of Rick Tyler and believes that Hiram Kelsey is similar to an Old Testament prophet in Mary Noailles Murfree's *The Prophet of the Great Smoky Mountains.*

Cayce, John Moonshiner and father of Dorinda Cayce in Mary Noailles Murfree's *The Prophet of the Great Smoky Mountains.*

Cayenne, Mr. American Tory who establishes the first cotton-weaving mill in the area and builds the town of Cayenneville to house the workers; he rivals in power the older aristocracy of the parish in John Galt's *Annals of the Parish.*

Caypor, Grantley Energetic, vibrant, cheerful, devoted Englishman who is a British and a German spy; Caypor loves his wife more than anything else and works side by side with her; his good-natured side competes with his cold-heartedness in W. Somerset Maugham's *Ashenden: or The British Agent.*

Caypor, Mrs. Cold, quiet, loyal German wife of Grantley; she sees World War I Germany as the greatest nation in the world; she has a scholarly background, but she discusses only her German speech lesson with Ashenden; her passion is her husband in W. Somerset Maugham's *Ashenden: or The British Agent.*

Ceballos, Jaime Young protagonist filled with rebellious ideals; must choose between being at peace with the prestige and comfort of his family's wealth and the fiery idealism of his youth; lives in the provincial town of Guanajuato, where his struggle is heightened by the narrowness of the community; fails in his struggle for individualism against his repressive family and the social restraints; loses his idealistic and individualistic spark, and gives way to conformity in Carlos Fuentes's *The Good Conscience.*

Ceballos, Jamie Brilliant young lawyer who falls in love with Betina Regules, daughter of the well-known capitalist Roberto Regules, in Carlos Fuentes's *Where the Air Is Clear.*

Ceccone, Ser Underhanded informer who gives information to the party willing to pay the most; he is jealous of Tito Melema's ability to receive and pass information more quickly in George Eliot's *Romola.*

Cecedek Magda Bursavov's latest lover, an Austrian; he is an extraordinarily wealthy man until the Bolshevik Revolution in William Gerhardie's *Futility: A Novel on Russian Themes.*

Cecelia Wishes to open a car rental office in the town of Prester; is looking for a place to live; is shown several places and asked to live in the city, where the only buildings are churches, by Mr. Phillips; declines Mr. Phillips's offer in Donald Barthelme's "A City of Churches."

Ceci See O'Connor, Cecile.

Cecil, Berkeley Younger brother of Bertie Cecil; he forges the Duke of Rockingham's name to pay a gambling debt but escapes punishment when his brother is blamed instead; he inherits the family estates and title when Bertie is presumed dead in Ouida's *Under Two Flags.*

Cecil, Bertie Second-eldest son of the Viscount Royallieu and a member of the elite English guard; accused of forgery and disgraced, he joins the French Foreign Legion under the name of Louis Victor and is stationed in Algiers for twelve years in Ouida's *Under Two Flags.*

Cecil, Lady Sophia Wife of Lord Cecil and the charming stepsister of Gerald Neville; she introduces Elizabeth Raby to English society and narrates her brother's story in Mary Shelley's *Falkner.*

Cecil, Lord English aristocrat and husband of Lady Cecil in Mary Shelley's *Falkner.*

Cecil, Peter Englishman who shows up at Alice Mellings's door wanting information about Andrew Connors, and to whom, in her hurry, Alice gives incriminating evidence in Doris Lessing's *The Good Terrorist.*

Cecil, Rose Lord Burleigh's daughter, who selflessly suppresses her love for Lord Leicester and arranges his and Matilda's escape from England; abducted by Mr. Mortimer, she takes her own life rather than submit to a forced and degrading marriage in Sophia Lee's *The Recess.*

Cecil, William, Lord Burleigh Elisabeth I's treasurer and first adviser; consistently argues in favor of the state and his queen; sees beheading Mary, the Queen of Scotland, as the only right act according to reasons of state; assesses Mary as a danger to convert England to Catholicism again and to begin a civil war; typical Machiavellian representing the English-Protestant perspective in Friedrich Schiller's *Mary Stuart.*

Cécile Daughter of M. Grégoire, owner of the Montsou mines, where the poor work for starvation wages; betrothed to Négrel by her father in Émile Zola's *Germinal.*

Cecilia Best friend of Sidney Bidulph Arnold since childhood; while living abroad with her husband, who has a station in the court of Vienna, she receives the correspondence containing Sidney's vicissitudes, and upon arriving in London she supplements the correspondence with a narrative describing Sidney's later years in Frances Sheridan's *Memoirs of Miss Sidney Bidulph.*

Cecilia Eladio Linacero's wife, who leaves him due to frustration over their exhausted love relationship, in Juan Carlos Onetti's *The Pit.*

Cecilia Young Christian in Rome; it is in her house that Marius becomes enamoured of the Christian religion in Walter Pater's *Marius the Epicurean.*

Cecy Timothy's sister who can send her mind far away and travel in the minds of others; controls those in whom her mind travels; goes into Timothy's mind to let him do things he normally cannot, such as drink blood, but pulled out of his mind in the midst of making him think he has wings in Ray Bradbury's "Homecoming"; also known as the Sleeper who Dreams, decides to be in love, and learns that she cannot always compel people to go against their natures when she tries to compel Ann Leary to love Tom; compels Ann to give Tom the address of the Autumn House, so he can see Cecy someday, in Ray Bradbury's "The Wandering Witch" and "The April Witch"; causes great cathedral bells to ring in John the Unjust's ears to keep him from betraying the Family; sends a warning to the Family members when it is time for them to evacuate the House in Ray Bradbury's *From the Dust Returned.*

Cedar Utopian scientist who houses the infectious Earthlings at Quarantine (Coronation) Crag and is wounded in their attempt to take him hostage in H. G. Wells's *Men Like Gods.*

Cedarquist, Mr. Wealthy manufacturer and shipbuilder who sees a great future in grain exports to the Far East in Frank Norris's *The Octopus.*

Cedarquist, Mrs. Wife of Mr. Cedarquist and supporter of the arts, including artists of dubious merit, in Frank Norris's *The Octopus.*

Cederberge Chief inspector in the international marine police; investigates the disappearance of Hellos in Calvin Hernton's *Scarecrow.*

Cedric the Saxon of Rotherwood Wealthy, blustering Saxon, Ivanhoe's father and Lady Rowena's guardian; he longs for the ascendancy of his race, plotting the marriage of Rowena and Athelstane and disinheriting his son because of his love for the lady; eventually, King Richard wins him over in Sir Walter Scott's *Ivanhoe.*

Cee Cee Cousin of the young homosexual Lorrie; makes fun of his nickname, when his real name is Lawrence Lincoln Jefferson Adams, in Carolyn Ferrell's "Proper Library."

Celadine Self-imagined lady-killer; he chases Jenny Jessamy in Eliza Haywood's *The History of Jemmy and Jenny Jessamy.*

"Celebrated Jumping Frog of Calaveras County, The" Narrator Young man who complies with the request of a friend to inquire into the history of Leonidas W. Smiley, but instead hears the tall tale from Simon Wheeler of the infamous gambler Jim Smiley, in Samuel Clemens's "The Celebrated Jumping Frog of Calaveras County."

Celedonio Well-pampered coachman of the Marques de Torres-nobles de Fuencar's farm estate; decides to leave abruptly his employer once news arrives that the servants have won a share in a popular lottery, from a ticket purchased by the Marques; talks of setting up his own tavern with his winnings in Emilia Pardo Bazan's "The First Prize."

Céleste Meursault's friend, racetrack partner, and owner of a café where they dine; one of the few who support the loner and existentialist Mersault at his murder trial in Albert Camus's *The Stranger.*

Celestial Bill Cosey's mistress whom May calls a sporting woman and considers capable of anything; has a scar across her face but holds her head high; eyes described as cold and scary, but she can also smile; compared to a prostitute in a brothel by Christine; remains a mystery in the novel, since no one seems to know her true identity or character in Toni Morrison's *Love.*

Celestina Lover of Philip the Beautiful in Carlos Fuentes's *Terra Nostra.*

Celestina (in another era) Sorceress who trains a younger Celestina, who becomes her protégée in Carlos Fuentes's *Terra Nostra.*

Celia Daughter of Dan and Libby, sister of Jennie; cousin of Anne, Jenny, Rossie, and Valerie; niece of Grace, Rachel, May, and Elinor; engaged to Philip Masterson, but breaks it off when she discovers he has gotten Louanne Price pregnant; marries her old beau, Jimmy; tries to commit suicide with an overdose of pills and loses her baby in Joan Chase's *During the Reign of the Queen of Persia.*

Celia Duke Frederick's daughter; Rosalind's cousin and close friend; volunteers to go into exile along with Rosalind and Touchstone when Rosalind is banished by the duke; disguises herself as Aliena, a simple shepherdess, while in the forest of Arden; falls in love with Oliver upon first sight; marries him at the end of William Shakespeare's *As You Like It.*

Celia Friend of Hélène who is later victimized by her in Julio Cortázar's *62: A Model Kit.*

Celia Merchant Corvino's wife; jealously guarded by her husband; throws her handkerchief to Volpone, who arrives before her house disguised as a mountebank; unsuccessfully attempts to reason with her husband thereafter; instead, is reproved by him; begs of him not to force her to sleep with Volpone, to no avail; rebuffs Volpone's advances and is consequently threatened with rape; rescued by Bonario; framed by Volpone, Mosca, and Voltore, with support from Corvino; arrested by the court, but eventually released after Volpone's con game is revealed at the end of Ben Jonson's play *Volpone.*

Celia Sensitive young woman who attends a cocktail party at Edward and Lavina Chamberlayne's London flat; wants Edward to divorce Lavina so she can marry him, but soon laughs at her own ridiculous infatuation with the older married man; dies two years later as a nurse on a tropical island, killed in a native rebellion in T. S. Eliot's play *The Cocktail Party.*

Celia Vindictive and jealous neighbor who discloses Vadinho's scurrilous habits before his wedding to Doña Flor in Jorge Amado's *Doña Flor and Her Two Husbands.*

Celia Woman who recounts how she has devoted her life to the pursuit of pleasure to her correspondent Sophronia, whose obsession is philosophy in Sarah Fielding's *Familiar Letters between the Principal Characters of David Simple and Some Others.*

Celia-of-the-Woods Country girl; Jemmy Jessamy is enamored of her, but she becomes the haughty Lady Handy, who loves intrigues in Eliza Haywood's *The History of Jemmy and Jenny Jessamy.*

Celie Wife of Albert; older sister of Nettie; writes letters to God and later to Nettie; raped by man she believes to be her father, later discovered to be her stepfather, bears two children by him; loves Shug Avery; discovers sexuality with her; becomes active and independent in Alice Walker's *The Color Purple.*

Célimène Young and beautiful widow who is admired by many men, particularly Alceste; her open display of coquettish humor and wit drives the misanthrope Alceste to demand that she publicly denounce all other suitors in his favor; ultimately Alceste's escalating demands on her—that she leave with him so they can live away from society as hermits—prove too much for the love she has for him in Molière's play *The Misanthrope.*

Celinda Fifteen-year-old English girl, who is seduced by Ferdinand in the guise of music master and is abandoned by him to dissipation in addiction to drugs in Tobias Smollett's *The Adventures of Ferdinand Count Fathom.*

Cennini, Menico Florentine goldsmith and moneylender in George Eliot's *Romola.*

Centaur, Madam One of the collegiate ladies who invites Epicoene into their ranks; much like Madam Haughty and Mistress Mavis, is shocked to discover that Epicoene is actually a man, in Ben Jonson's play *Epicoene, or The Silent Woman.*

Centavos, Cinquo (Sinker) Young Mexican horse wrangler with the Del Sol trail herd in Emerson Hough's *North of 36.*

Centeville, Astride (Fru Astrida) de Nurse to Duke Richard of Normandy; she maintains his knowledge of the old Norse language and of the sagas in Charlotte Yonge's *The Little Duke.*

Centeville, Eric de Norman baron and guardian of young Duke Richard in Charlotte Yonge's *The Little Duke.*

Centeville, Osmond de Loyal, quick-witted squire of Duke Richard of Normandy; he contrives to escape from the court of King Louis in Charlotte Yonge's *The Little Duke.*

Cereno, Benito Member of the ship's company when the *San Dominick* is overtaken by mutinous slaves aboard; forced under threat of death by the slaves to act as the new ship's captain when the vessel is boarded by Captain Amasa Delano of the *Bachelor's Delight;* carries on this masquerade until he leaps from the ship to reveal that the *San Dominick* has been taken by slaves and its captain and crew killed; later put on trial for his actions in Herman Melville's "Benito Cereno."

Ceres, M. Cabinet minister in Anatole France's *Penguin Island.*

Ceria Brilliant manager of the grill-room; he is counted among Evelyn Orcham's finest employees; his wistful, appealing smile involves Violet Powler in her second romantic difficulty in Arnold Bennett's *Imperial Palace.*

Cerillo, Juan Zapotecan Indian in the employ of the Banco Ejidal who taught Hugh Firmin how to whinney like a horse; he is a symbol of generosity and self-sacrifice in Malcolm Lowry's *Under the Volcano.* He is associated with Juan Fernando Martinez in *Dark as the Grave Wherein My Friend Is Laid.*

Cerimon Physician in Ephesus who revives Thaisa, Pericles' wife, when she lands onshore after being thrown overboard by the seamen on Pericles's ship, who presumed her dead, in William Shakespeare's play *Pericles.*

Certavallos, Inez de Sixteen-year-old daughter of a wealthy Spanish nobleman in Louisiana and bride of Duncan Uncas Middleton; kidnapped on her wedding night by Abiram White and Ishmael Bush; later rescued by Middleton, with the help of Natty Bumppo, in James Fenimore Cooper's *The Prairie.*

Cervantes Cockfighter, friend of Geoffrey Firmin, and bartender from whom Geoffrey orders mescal at the Salon Ofelia in Malcolm Lowry's *Under the Volcano.*

Cervantes, Luis Member of Demetrio Macías's band of rebels in the Mexican revolution (1910–17); federal deserter and opportunist who fights on the side he thinks will profit him the most in Mariano Azuela's *The Underdogs.*

Cesarini, Princess Claelia Gerard's patroness, who, because he does not return her love, hires the assassin Lodovico to slay him; she relents and orders the assassin killed; upon a pilgrimage of penitence to Loretto, she washes the feet of Friar Clement (Gerard) and confesses her wicked plot to the proposed victim in Charles Reade's *The Cloister and the Hearth.*

Cesario Gallant young prince and a plotter against the king of France; he is emasculated by his love for Hermione and defeated by his dealings with the sorcerer Fergusano; the king, who can forgive Cesario's treason but not his slander of the king's reputation, executes him in Aphra Behn's *Love Letters Between a Nobleman and His Sister.*

Cesario Servant to Count Morano; he assists in an attempt to kidnap Emily St. Aubert in Ann Radcliffe's *The Mysteries of Udolpho.*

Chabot, Marian Low-born, remarkably gifted friend of Marguerite de St. Leon (Marguerite de Damville), who is similar to her in appearance and gesture in William Godwin's *St. Leon.*

Chace, Ann Sir Ransome's middle daughter, shorter and fairer than Emma; she tries to be friendly to Mildred Hallam in Ivy Compton-Burnett's *Darkness and Day.*

Chace, Emma Sir Ransome's eldest daughter, who did not want her father to adopt Brigit Hallam (later Brigit Lovat) when Brigit was young; she is never proposed to in Ivy Compton-Burnett's *Darkness and Day.*

Chace, Jack Young man about town who has the ambition to be thought a man of consummate debauch and who marries Daughter Frippery in Francis Coventry's *The History of Pompey the Little.*

Chace, Sir Ransome Man eighty years old, chivalrous and affectionate to his daughters Emma and Ann; Brigit Lovat is his secret daughter in Ivy Compton-Burnett's *Darkness and Day.*

Chacha, Ashraf Muslim tailor; family friend of the Darjis; takes in Dukhi Darjis sons, Ishvar and Narayan, at Dukhi Darji's request so they do not have to be cobblers; family is saved by the Darjis during Hindu riots against Muslims; later murdered on the street in Rohinton Mistry's *A Fine Balance.*

Chadband, Mr. Large, oily, dissenting minister with great oratorical skill, who marries Mrs. Rachael, is patronized by Mrs. Snagsby, and tries to "convert" Jo by discoursing on the "human boy" in Charles Dickens's *Bleak House.*

Chadd Lieutenant aboard the *Indefatigable* and commander of the first gig in the *Indefatigable's* surprise attack of the *Papillin* in C. S. Forester's *Mr. Midshipman Hornblower.*

Chaddy Brother of the narrator, Pommeroy; lives in Manhattan with Odette and their children; attends a family reunion at his family's summer place at Laud's Head on the shore in Massachusetts in John Cheever's "Goodbye, My Brother."

Chadwick, Bernard William China buyer for a wholesale firm; his evidence at the Sharpe women's trial contradicts their accuser, Betty Kane, in Josephine Tey's *The Franchise Affair.*

Chadwick, Dr. Black general practitioner who comforts John Wilder during Wilder's last emotional breakdown in Richard Yates's *Disturbing the Peace.*

Chadwick, Jocelyn English land-agent who watches over Major Jack Thompson's estate; he is ruthless and unkind to the tenant farmers and eventually meets his death at their hands in Liam O'Flaherty's *Famine.*

Chadwick, John Steward of the Bishop of Barchester in charge of Hiram's Hospital accounting in Anthony Trollope's *The Warden.* He appears briefly in *Barchester Towers* and in *Framley Parsonage.* He is called on for legal advice in the Crawley case in *The Last Chronicle of Barset.*

Chadwick, Mary Francis Bernard's wife; her evidence supports his, explains Betty Kane's injuries, and exonerates the Sharpe women at their trial in Josephine Tey's *The Franchise Affair.*

Chaeras Genteel but ugly middle daughter of Maladie Alamode; her name is explained as a translation of "king's evil" in Henry Fielding's *A Journey From This World to the Next.*

Chaffanbrass, Mr. Scruffy Old Bailey barrister, who specializes in defending criminals and scourging witnesses; he takes on Alaric Tudor's case in Anthony Trollope's *The Three Clerks.* He defends Lady Mason with his customary ferocity in *Orley Farm.* He similarly defends Phineas Finn in a murder trial in *Phineas Redux.*

Chagny, Raoul Becomes transfixed by Christine Daae, as he remembers her from his youth, having once chased into the sea after her scarf; overhears her in her dressing room arguing with a man who mysteriously disappears; declares his love for Christine, drawing the jealousy of the phantom, Erik; imprisoned by the fiend but manages his escape; weds Christine in Gaston Leroux's *The Phantom of the Opera.*

Chaikin, Freddy Agent for Maria Wyeth in Joan Didion's *Play It As It Lays.*

Chain, Jud Professional gambler and business associate of Bo Mason in Wallace Stegner's *The Big Rock Candy Mountain.*

Chainmail, Mr. Young man who believes in the complete superiority of the 12th century over the 19th; he marries Susanna Touchandgo in Thomas Love Peacock's *Crotchet Castle.*

Chairman Love interest of Sayuri, the geisha; gives Chiyo, as a child, a few coins for shaved ice which she instead offers in prayer and soon decides for herself to become a geisha; encourages Mameha to become Chiyo's mentor; encourages Chiyo/Sayuri's relationship with Nobu, his friend and partner, which would forever curtail a physical relationship between the Chairman and Sayuri; discovering Sayuri with another man, which Nobu is meant to witness, Nobu gives up his claim to Sayuri and the Chairman becomes her danna; entertained by Sayuri exclusively thereafter, first in his resort home, and after her move to New York in Arthur Golden's *Memoirs of a Geisha.*

Chairman Mao's Robot Chinese woman delegate to a youth festival in Moscow; kidnapped and sexually exploited by George Levanter and Romarkin in Jerzy Kosinski's *Blind Date.*

Chairman of the Bench Official who convicts the errant Toad of stealing a motor car, of furious driving, and of the more serious offence of checking the police in Kenneth Grahame's *The Wind in the Willows.*

Chakravati, Ramlochan Respected pillar of the Indian village and chief source of legal advice; spreads the false rumor that Chandara had killed her sister-in-law named Radha, when, in fact, he knows the murderer to be Dukhiram, the victim's husband; his well-regarded status in the town is key to the innocent Chandara's conviction and execution in Rabindranath Tagore's "Punishment."

Chakravorti, Conrad Indian who rents the Adirondack cabin inhabited by Ambrose Clay; mishap prevents his discovery of Clay's suicide in Gail Godwin's *Violet Clay.*

Chalfen, Joshua Eldest of the four sons of Marcus and Joyce Chalfen, a precocious, self-confident youth who, in the confusion of a drug raid on the Glenard Oak School, finds himself charged along with the young rebel Millat Iqbal and Irie Jones; the incident brings Irie Jones and Millat Iqbal into the sphere of Joshua's influential parents, a circumstance which, in turn, contributes to the alienation of Joshua; later joins a radical animal protection group called FATE (Fighting Animal Torture and Exploitation), which plans to rescue Marcus Chalfen's famous test subject, FutureMouse, in Zadie Smith's *White Teeth.*

Chalfen, Joyce Wife of Marcus Chalfen and mother of Joshua and three other Chalfen sons; primary target of the critique of middle-class Englishness in the novel; overwhelmingly assured of her own enlightenment and remains blithely unaware of both her own class privilege and of the conservative notions of gender that inform her books on gardening, which are thinly veiled lessons about family life and proper social organization; defines herself as a mother, one seeking to nurture plants and children alike; regarded by the book's narrator as a latter-day frontier missionary, full of self-confidence and good intentions, but blind to the negative consequences of her actions, in Zadie Smith's *White Teeth.*

Chalfen, Marcus Geneticist whose research involves the creation of mice genetically programmed to develop cancer at the time and in the form of Chalfen's choosing; hopes through his research to "eliminate the random" and thereby firmly establish human dominion over nature; however, sorely lacks both imagination and a knowledge of history; despite his own family's German and Polish Jewish roots, fails to make a connection between his research and the early work of his mentor, a French eugenicist who served the Nazi cause in the World War II, in Zadie Smith's *White Teeth.*

Chalfont, Mrs. Giles Peters's old, elegant ex-mother-in-law; she attends the Mike Morgan comedy performance with Giles and Anthony Keating in Margaret Drabble's *The Ice Age.*

Chalfonte, Celeste Cora's employer and friend; sister of Curtis, Spottiswod, and Carlotta; lesbian lover of Ramelle-kills Brutus Rife; dies at sixty-seven of a fall from a horse in Rita Mae Brown's *Six of One.* Also appears in *Loose Lips.*

Chalfonte, Curtis Brother of Celeste Chalfonte; lives in California; has an affair with Ramelle and is father of her daughter in Rita Mae Brown's *Six of One.*

Chalfonte, Spottiswood (Spotty) Celeste's youngest brother; is in the army and dies in World War I in Rita Mae Brown's *Six of One.*

Chalk Lieutenant of the *Goliath* in charge of impressing men into the navy in C. S. Forester's *Mr. Midshipman Hornblower.*

Challee, Lieutenant Commander Jack Navy judge advocate who prosecutes Lieutenant Steve Maryk for mutiny in Herman Wouk's *The Caine Mutiny.*

Challenger, Mark Tailor and friend of Arthur Golding; he is a member of a workingmen's club and arouses Arthur's interest in social problems in George Gissing's *Workers in the Dawn.*

Challenger, Professor Irascible scientist who defies public and scholarly opinion and leads an expedition to the region of dinosaurs in Arthur Conan Doyle's *The Lost World.*

Challenor, Beryl Childhood friend and playmate of Selina Boyce; values prestige and material gain in Paule Marshall's *Brown Girl, Brownstones.*

Challenor, Percy Father of Beryl Challenor and a leader of the Association of Barbadian Homeowners and Businessmen in Paule Marshall's *Brown Girl, Brownstones.*

Challice, Alice Endearing, practical Putney widow; seeking a new husband by advertising, she contacts Henry Leek; she accepts the great artist Priam Farll as Leek, and she insouciantly copes with the series of comical crises the double identity of her new husband brings in Arnold Bennett's *Buried Alive: A Tale of These Days.*

Challoner, Claude Youngest son of Simon and Fanny (Graham); he is a charming little boy who wants to marry his sister Emma in Ivy Compton-Burnett's *A Heritage and Its History.*

Challoner, Emma Younger daughter of Simon and Fanny (Graham); she copies the actions of her brother Claude; she is forgotten by her parents after Sir Edwin's funeral in Ivy Compton-Burnett's *A Heritage and Its History.*

Challoner, Graham Son of Simon and Fanny (Graham); intelligent and ironic, he is kept under constraint by Simon, who begrudges him his financial support in Ivy Compton-Burnett's *A Heritage and its History.*

Challoner, Hamish Brother to Sir Edwin, who is always the center of Hamish's life; Hamish dies in his sixties in Ivy Compton-Burnett's *A Heritage and Its History.*

Challoner, Hamish (the younger) Sir Edwin's legal son; when his wife, Marcia, wants to leave the house, Hamish gives up his inheritance to Simon Challoner, his natural father, in Ivy Compton-Burnett's *A Heritage and Its History.*

Challoner, Julia Hamish's wife, who feels that she gave him up to his elder brother, Sir Edwin; she is shocked that Simon is the father of the younger Hamish in Ivy Compton-Burnett's *A Heritage and Its History.*

Challoner, Marcia Wife of the younger Hamish; she is charmed by Simon Challoner to influence Hamish to relinquish his claim to the family estate in Ivy Compton-Burnett's *A Heritage and Its History.*

Challoner, Naomi Elder daughter of Simon and Fanny (Graham); she falls in love with and wants to marry her supposed cousin, the younger Hamish Challoner; their mothers are sisters, but his father is not her father's uncle, as publicly believed, but her own father in Ivy Compton-Burnett's *A Heritage and Its History.*

Challoner, Ralph Son of Simon and Fanny (Graham); he is always threatened by his disappointed father with the workhouse as his future in Ivy Compton-Burnett's *A Heritage and Its History.*

Challoner, Simon Hamish's son, reared in expectation of inheriting his uncle's title and estate; he is supplanted by his own natural son, the younger Hamish, when Sir Edwin, married to the mother, Rhoda Graham, assumes paternity; Simon feels his life is ruined and brings up his legitimate children in harsh preparation for penury in Ivy Compton-Burnett's *A Heritage and Its History.*

Challoner, Sir Edwin Baronet who evicts his nephew, Simon Challoner, from his house when he discovers that Simon has impregnated Rhoda Graham; married to Rhoda, Sir Edwin rears her son, the younger Hamish, as his own in Ivy Compton-Burnett's *A Heritage and Its History.*

Challoner, Walter Younger brother of Simon; he does not earn a degree at Oxford and remains in the family home as a dependent in Ivy Compton-Burnett's *A Heritage and Its History.*

Chalmers Schoolmaster with a Glasgow M.A., who is jealous of Clement Butt's greater success with lesser education in Mark Rutherford's *Mark Rutherford's Deliverance.*

Cham, Oiseau de Also known as Word Scratcher; character who appears as the author himself in the shantytown dwellings near the oil refinery on the outskirts of Fort-de-France, Martinique's capital city, in Patrick Chamoiseau's *Texaco.*

Chama Young woman in Fatima's family who expresses rebellious theories against the harem system and helps the harem women discover their talents and develop self-confidence; stages plays about the lives of heroines of literature and history and important feminists in the Arab world; her unfamiliar embroidery is a significant tactic that mocks the traditionalism of the proharem women in Fatima Mernissi's *Dreams of Trespass.*

Chamar, Madame Charles (Anastasia Petrovna Potapov) Russian mother of Armande Chamar Person; product of a noble family ruined by the revolution in Vladimir Nabokov's *Transparent Things.*

Chamberlain Reports to Gadshill that the travelers he hopes to rob will have 300 marks in gold; helps to arrange the robbery in William Shakespeare's play *Henry IV, Part One.*

Chamberlain, Brice Prominent lawyer who supports the nesters; paramour of Lucie Brewton and father of Brock Brewton; becomes judge of the district court in Conrad Richter's *The Sea of Grass.*

Chamberlain, Joshua Lawrence Brilliant Union colonel who defends a rocky hill called Little Round Top against a rebel onslaught at Gettysburg in Michael Shaara's *The Killer Angels.*

Chamberlaine, Henry Fitzackerly Handsome, affable, utterly self-centred prebendary of Salisbury Cathedral and uncle of Harry Gilmore; his goal in life is not to become involved, but he is reluctantly drawn into the controversy over the chapel built on glebe land in Anthony Trollope's *The Vicar of Bullhampton.*

Chamberlayne, Edward Middle-aged husband of Lavina; hosts a cocktail party with his wife in their London flat; desires another woman when his wife is under his roof, but after she leaves him he wants her back; meets his wife at a therapist's office in T. S. Eliot's play *The Cocktail Party.*

Chamberlayne, Lavina Wife of Edward Chamberlayne; intended to hostess a cocktail party with her husband but left their London flat without explanation; feels drained due to marital turbulence; domineering wife to a husband who cannot make up his mind; becomes infatuated with the young man Peter in T. S. Eliot's play *The Cocktail Party.*

Chamberlin, Anne Daughter of Colonel Chamberlin and sweetheart of Marse Chan; finds her love for Marse threatened by family differences, politics, and the Civil War in Thomas Nelson Page's "Marse Chan."

Chamberlin, Colonel Father of the young girl Anne who is the sweetheart of Marse Chan; decides to run for Congress but is opposed by his friend Mr. Channing and Marse's father; wins the election but finds a wedge has been driven between the two families in Thomas Nelson Page's "Marse Chan."

Chamber Maid at Inn Player of a trick on the Disguised Gentleman by sending him to the wrong room, starting all the other travelers in a merry game of accusation and counter accusation in Charles Johnstone's *Chrysal: or, The Adventures of a Guinea.*

Chambers, Frank Drifter who works for Nick Papadakis and is the lover of Cora Papadakis; with Cora, he murders Nick, but is acquitted; later convicted of murdering Cora, who dies accidentally, in James M. Cain's *The Postman Always Rings Twice.*

Chambers, Ishmael Owner, publisher, and sole reporter of the *San Piedro Review;* childhood sweetheart of Hatsue Imada; discovers evidence that could exonerate Kabuo Miyamoto of the murder of Carl Heine in David Guterson's *Snow Falling on Cedars.*

Chambrolet, Edith de Wealthy expatriate American who takes in McKenna Gallagher after Louisa Gallagher's suicide attempt in James Jones's *The Merry Month of May.*

Champfort Lord Delacour's deceitful, conceited servant, who turns him against Lady Delacour and circulates lies about Lord Delacour's relationship with Belinda Portman in Maria Edgeworth's *Belinda.*

Champfort, Marchioness Parisian widow of dubious character, whose parties Valancourt frequents during his separation from Emily St. Aubert in Ann Radcliffe's *The Mysteries of Udolpho.*

Champion, Steve Stylish, flamboyant British agent perceived as an anachronism by his superiors; he is suspected of planning to supply the Arabs with massively destructive weapons in Len Deighton's *Yesterday's Spy.*

Champneis, Lord Edward Famous explorer and writer who is Christine Clay's husband; he smuggles a well-known Eastern European radical into England under circumstances which suggest opportunity and alibi for the murder of his wife in Josephine Tey's *A Shilling for Candles.*

Chan, Marse Young man of a prosperous Virginia family—Channing—during the Civil War era; falls in love with Anne Chamberlin, daughter of Colonel Chamberlin; finds his love for Anne threatened by family differences, politics, and war; goes off after college to fight for the South in the Civil War where he is killed just after receiving a letter announcing Anne's eternal love in Thomas Nelson Page's "Marse Chan."

Chanca, Demetrio Highway construction foreman whose mysterious disappearance is investigated by Sergeant Lituma in Mario Vargas Llosa's *Death in the Andes.*

Chance (Chauncey Gardiner) Gardener, idiot, and hero who is propelled to fame in Jerzy Kosinski's *Being There.*

Chance, George (Fat) Portly inspector and chief of detectives in Peter De Vries's *The Mackerel Plaza.*

Chance, Vic Airplane builder in William Faulkner's *Pylon.*

Chanceller, Kate Feminist, socialist, and student at Ohio State University; becomes a good friend of Clara Butterworth in Sherwood Anderson's *Poor White.*

Chancellor Conspirator in the scheme to usurp the Warden of Outland and create a Vice-Warden in Lewis Carroll's *Sylvie and Bruno.* He attends Uggug's birthday banquet and escorts in the beggar in *Sylvie and Bruno Concluded.*

Chancellor, Miss Mistress who teaches history at Lesbia Firebrace's school; she accompanies the four girls to visit Clemence Shelley at her home in Ivy Compton-Burnett's *Two Worlds and Their Ways.*

Chancellor, Olive Radical Boston spinster who opposes the marriage of her protégée Verena Tarrant in Henry James's *The Bostonians.*

Chancey and Mrs. Shortley Poor white couple who are shiftless hired workers on Mrs. McIntyre's farm in Flannery O'Connor's "The Displaced Person."

Chand, Hamijolli Wife of the owner of the Hotel Phoenix in Delhi; becomes Lieutenant Corson's lover in Tim O'Brien's *Going After Cacciato.*

Chandara Beautiful and independent-thinking young wife of the traditional-minded Indian Chidam; displeased with her arranged marriage and domineering husband; reluctantly follows her husband's hasty strategy that she falsely confess to his brother's crime of killing his wife in a fit of rage; when asked by the police for a true account of the crime, ultimately chooses death over living a life with Chidam in Rabindranath Tagore's "Punishment."

Chandler, Cathie See Finer, Cathie Chandler.

Chandler, Mr. Farmer who is a friend and customer of Mr. Furze in Mark Rutherford's *Catharine Furze.*

Chandler, Reverend Peleg Rutherford's master; a tobacco planter, cared for until his death by Rutherford's brother Jackson; frees Rutherford and Jackson upon his death; gives Rutherford about forty dollars and the family Bible as his share of inheritance in Charles Johnson's *Middle Passage.*

Chandler's-Shopkeeper Woman who explains how she came by the manuscript in Charles Johnstone's *Chrysal: or, The Adventures of a Guinea.*

Chandri Naranappa's low-caste concubine; Praneshacharya, the great scholar of theology, sleeps with this mistress of Naranaappa; through her, Praneshacharya participates in the situation of his opposite, Naranappa; the renowned priest's sudden sexual experience with her awakens him to the fact that salvation is as possible through indulgence as by self-control in U. R. Ananthamurthy's *Samskara: A Rite for a Dead Man.*

Chaney, Tom Hired hand and outlaw who kills two men and who is pursued by Mattie Ross, Rooster Cogburn, and LaBoeuf in Charles Portis's *True Grit.*

Chang Polite citizen of Shangri-La whose monkhood is pending; he is a diligent and compassionate host to his unwilling guests at the Tibetan monastery in James Hilton's *Lost Horizon.*

Chang, Callie Narrator and one of two young Chinese-American daughters of Ralph Chang; desires to join a posh country club in Gish Jen's "In the American Society."

Chang, Cho Ravenclaw student one year above Harry, Quidditch Seeker, and member of Dumbledore's Army, dates Cedric Diggory, Harry Potter, and Roger Davies; later attends the Yule Ball with Cedric Diggory in J. K. Rowling's Harry Potter series.

Chang, Helen Gentle, frail daughter of an aristocratic Shanghai family that secures a student visa for her to flee to the United States during the Chinese revolution in 1949; wife of Ralph Chang in Gish Jen's *Typical American.* In *Mona in the Promised Land,* she is a strict parent whose American-born children's attempts to determine their individual identities often challenge her sense of propriety and her belief that the concerns of family are paramount.

Chang, Mona One of two young Chinese-American daughters of Ralph Chang; desires to join a posh country club in Gish Jen's "In the American Society."

Chang, Mona Chinese-American teenager living in an upscale, largely Jewish New York suburb; intelligent and witty daughter who rebels against her immigrant parents by adopting the new popular ideals of late-1960s and early-1970s America; converts to Judaism in Gish Jen's *Mona in the Promised Land.*

Chang, Mrs. Mother of the household run by the Chinese man Ralph; has two daughters, Callie and Mona; desires to get the family admitted to a posh country club in Gish Jen's "In the American Society."

Chang, Ralph Chinese man who heads an American household filled with his wife and two daughters; owns a profitable pancake house, where his daughters, Callie and Mona, work; uses his workers as servants as well as employees, as they run all sorts of personal errands for him; gets into trouble with immigration authorities over illegal workers in his restaurant; offended that the host of an upscale pool party he attends as a guest mistakenly treats him as a servant in Gish Jen's "In the American Society."

Chang, Ralph Chinese graduate student stranded in the United States by the 1949 Chinese revolution; dissatisfied engineering professor who becomes an entrepreneur; domineering in times of family crisis; husband of Helen Chang, brother of Theresa Chang in Gish Jen's *Typical American.*

Chang, Theresa Studious independent-minded woman who arrives with her friend Helen in the United States during the 1949 Chinese revolution and finds her brother, Ralph, despairing over his poverty and his uncertain status as a foreign student; postpones her medical career to encourage Ralph to complete his doctorate; lonely and unmarried; her affair with Ralph's married colleague estranges her from Ralph and her sister-in-law Helen in Gish Jen's *Typical American.*

Chang Hi-tang (Chang-hi-tang) Beautiful 16-year-old girl who is sold into a house of prostitution by her impoverished family after her father's death; becomes the second wife of Ma Chun-shing, a wealthy but childless tax collector in the Chinese district; bears a son, Shoulang, a birth that triggers the jealousy and wrath of Ma's first wife, Ah-Siu, a barren woman; falsely accused of poisoning Ma, an act of revenge perpetrated by Ah-Siu; learns that Ah-Siu now claims motherhood of the infant son; later forced to a test of true motherhood, as she, the real mother of the infant, and Ah-Siu are positioned in a chalk circle with the baby between them; declines to harm the child in a tug of war for the baby and is thus awarded the child in Li Hsing-tao's *The Circle of Chalk.*

Chang-ling Brother of the young girl Chang-hi-tang; poor scholar who opposes the sale of his sister to a teahouse in Nanking, although he receives part of the proceeds; joins a secret society whose manifesto is to strike down the oppressors of the poor; arrested but later set free by the new emperor in Li Hsing-tao's play *The Circle of Chalk.*

Chankery, Young Barrister who represents Philip Bosinney in court in John Galsworthy's *The Man of Property.*

Channelcliffe, Countess of Hostess at whose assembly Jocelyn Pierston hopes for a glimpse of the "well-beloved" in Thomas Hardy's *The Well-Beloved.*

Channell, Luke Disgusting rogue and secret first husband of Amber St. Clare in Kathleen Winsor's *Forever Amber.*

Channell, Mrs. Luke See Clare, Amber St.

Channing, Christina Singer with a symphony orchestra and mistress of Eugene Witla in Theodore Dreiser's *The "Genius."*

Channing, Elizabeth Rockbridge Stunningly beautiful artist who moves to the small village of Chatham, Massachusetts; begins a tragic affair with one of the school's married teachers, Leland Reed; is charged with attempted murder and adultery and is convicted and imprisoned for three years for the latter offense in Thomas H. Cook's *The Chatham School Affair.*

Channing, Judy Mistress of the special school that Molly Murray attends; Channing writes to Molly's mother, Alison Murray, of Molly's unusual, hard-to-control behavior in Margaret Drabble's *The Ice Age.*

Channing, Mr. Head of a wealthy Virginia family during the Civil War era; father of Marse Chan, the young protagonist who has fallen in love with Anne Chamberlin; declares himself a candidate for Congress in opposition to Colonel Chamberlin, the father of Anne; loses the election, an action that results in a wedge between the two families in Thomas Nelson Page's "Marse Chan."

Channing, Nancy Dupree (Bugsy) Bay Area socialite who marries and divorces Ryder Charming in Joan Didion's *Run River.*

Channing, Ryder Entrepreneur and real estate developer; seducer of Martha McClellan and Lily Knight McClellan; murdered by Everett McClellan in Joan Didion's *Run River.*

Chant, Mercy Young lady devoted to church work and seen by Angel Clare's parents as a suitable bride for him; she marries his brother Cuthbert in Thomas Hardy's *Tess of the D'Urbervilles.*

Chantal Female worker at The Grand Balcony, a brothel, who is stolen away by Roger and is positioned by the rebels outside as the symbol of their insurrection; assassinated on the orders of the bishop, who wishes to transform her into a martyr to his cause, in Jean Genet's *The Balcony.*

Chantal French character who feels alienated and constrained in the poverty of the ghettos of Paris in Mehdi Charef's *Tea in the Harem.*

Chantal Daughter of Papa and Honorine, older sister of Pascal, and lover of Henri for five years; with Henri, an unwilling passenger in the car in John Hawkes's *Travesty.*

Chantal, Mademoiselle Strong-willed and self-centered daughter of the count; ridicules and embarrasses the young parish priest, then later convinces the clergyman to speak to her mother, the countess, about the girl's unhappiness at the prospect of being sent to England to live with her mother's cousin in Georges Bernanos's *The Diary of a Country Priest.*

Chantelle, Madame de Mother-in-law of Anna Leath; represents aristocratic French propriety in spite of her American origins in Edith Wharton's *The Reef.*

Chantrey, Lady Rose Deceased mother of Julie Le Breton; she chose to flout tradition and bear a daughter out of wedlock rather than live with a husband she no longer loved in Mrs. Humphry Ward's *Lady Rose's Daughter.*

Chapa, Mateo Mestizo chauffeur whose entrepreneurial ambitions and intelligence accelerate his rise in the

Monterrey business world; marries Sofia Vázquez de Anda in Josefina Niggli's *Step Down, Elder Brother.*

Chapin, Ann Daughter of Edith and Joe Chapin I in John O'Hara's *Ten North Frederick.*

Chapin, Benjamin Father of Joe Chapin I in John O'Hara's *Ten North Frederick.*

Chapin, Charlotte Hofman Wife of Benjamin Chapin and mother of Joe Chapin I in John O'Hara's *Ten North Frederick.*

Chapin, Edith Stokes Wife and widow of Joe Chapin I in John O'Hara's *Ten North Frederick.*

Chapin, Joseph (Joe) Benjamin Gibbsville, Pennsylvania, lawyer who aspires to be president of the United States in John O'Hara's *Ten North Frederick.*

Chapin, Joseph Benjamin, Jr. (Joby, Joe) Son of Edith and Joe Chapin I; jazz pianist unappreciated by his parents; works for the OSS in John O'Hara's *Ten North Frederick.*

Chaplain Religious adviser to the Swedish Army; at first, promotes the idea of "holy war"; later captured by the Catholic army, but Mother Courage helps him disguise his identity to escape; travels with Mother Courage's canteen cart for several years; competes with The Cook for Mother Courage's affections; intends to return to clerical life after the war in Bertolt Brecht's *Mother Courage and Her Children.*

Chaplain of the Charity Person of some learning; he places his abilities in a conspicuous light in Charles Johnstone's *Chrysal: or, The Adventures of a Guinea.*

Chaplain of the Man of War Libertine who is reformed by the Benevolent Naval Captain in Charles Johnstone's *Chrysal; or, The Adventures of a Guinea.*

Chaplin, Mr. Teacher and house master at Seaforth House school in Roy Fuller's *The Ruined Boys.*

Chaplitsky Professional gambler who has squandered millions of rubles in card games; Countess Anna Fedotoona once took pity on his misfortunes by disclosing to him the secret of a certain winning strategy at card games in Alexander Pushkin's "The Queen of Spades."

Chapman Landing-party member who suffers a sprained ankle in C. S. Forester's *Lieutenant Hornblower.*

Chapman Ill-disposed traveling merchant, who lusts after Elfhild but sells her to Sir Mark (the Blue Knight) in William Morris's *The Sundering Flood.*

Chapman Traveling merchant from the Westland Cities of the Plain; he had once been held to ransom by Folkmight for dastardly deeds in William Morris's *The Roots of the Mountains.*

Chapman, Celia Eighteen-year-old cleaning woman who loves Leon Fisher in Albert Halper's *Union Square.*

Chapman, John Friend of Thomas Keene and Fanny Cooper; grows apples and is nicknamed Appleseed John; admirer of Emanuel Swedenborg; townspeople think he is a lunatic, but they tolerate him in Hugh Nissenson's *The Tree of Life.*

Chapman, John Lawyer and prestigious private investigator; lonely man who finds solace in his work in Danielle Steel's *Kaleidoscope.*

Chapman, Mr. Bedfordshire neighbor whose love and tenderness toward his wife are a foil to the behavior of aristocratic couples in Samuel Richardson's *Pamela, or Virtue Rewarded.*

Chapman, Mr. Henry Lambert's friend in William Beckford's *Modern Novel Writing; or, the Elegant Enthusiast.*

Chapman, Mr. Fiery and independent Labour Member of Parliament; he rescues Edward Leithin from two murderous plots of the "Power-House" until he himself is hospitalized after being run down by a car in John Buchan's *The Power-House.*

Chapman, Mrs. Bedfordshire neighbor whose kindness to and love of her husband are a foil to the behavior of aristocratic couples in Samuel Richardson's *Pamela, or Virtue Rewarded.*

Chapman, Nat Rustic, gossiping chorister in Thomas Hardy's *Two on a Tower.*

Chapman, Richard Fifteen-year-old boy sentenced to hang on charges of murder and attempted rape; Ethan Llewelyn imagines himself unsuccessfully defending the boy against the charges in Malcolm Lowry's *October Ferry to Gabriola.*

Chapron, Florent Brother of Lorent; also brother of Lincoln Maitland's wife, Lydia, in Paul Bourget's *Cosmopolis.*

Chapter Eleven Cal's older brother, he is scientifically inclined and helps family business by designing hot dogs. He goes to University of Michigan for engineering but gets caught up by hippie counterculture and turns to anthropology. He destroys the business when he takes over after Milton's death in Jeffrey Eugenides' *Middlesex.*

Chapultepec, Ali Juan (God of Street Boys) Street boy in William S. Burroughs's *The Soft Machine;* as Clinch Smith's houseboy, he runs amok and is killed in *Exterminator!;* appears also in *Nova Express, The Ticket That Exploded,* and *The Wild Boys.*

Chapy, Mr. North American developer and exploiter working in league with Don Julio; seeks to build a road in rural Ecuador to drill for oil; plans to drive the poor native Indians from their homes and land in Jorge Icaza's *Huasipungo.*

Charaiambos, Anna-Maria Sister of Orsetta Procopirios in Nicholas Delbanco's *The Martlet's Tale.*

Chardin, Simone Jacques Bernadet's sluttish paramour, who ends up with Stephan Zelli after he deserts Marya Zelli in Jean Rhys's *Postures.*

Charette, M. de Wealthy officer who is attempting to raise armies to turn back rebels in C. S. Forester's *Mr. Midshipman Hornblower.*

Charge, Major Henry Pulling's politically conservative and gruff next-door neighbor, who occasionally watches Pulling's dahlias when he is away in Graham Greene's *Travels with my Aunt.*

Chargut One of the supernormals of John Wainwright's Pacific island colony; he sacrifices himself to prevent dissolution of the colony in Olaf Stapledon's *Odd John: A Story Between Jest and Earnest.*

Charibon, Lambert Friend of Orkney Vas; owns a trout camp; burly, large, and nervous around women in Howard Norman's *The Bird Artist.*

Charisma, John F. (Jack) Martyred United States president and rival of Trick E. Dixon in Philip Roth's *Our Gang.*

Charitas Conventional neighbor of Helen; shocked by Helen's views of love and morality; forces her son Damastor to leave home after he impregnates Helen's maid Adraste in John Erskine's *The Private Life of Helen of Troy.*

Charity One of three virgins of the Palace Beautiful who catechize Christian and later his sons; she shows them the house and its contents in John Bunyan's *The Pilgrim's Progress from This World to That Which Is to Come.*

Charity Wife of Lazarus and nurse to Johnny Church, his mother, and his aunt, Nell Lacy, in Mary Lee Settle's *Prisons.*

Charity Supporter Number Eight Large athletic and deprived man, who cheats his ward out of her estate and gives everything to his daughter in Charles Johnstone's *Chrysal: or, The Adventures of a Guinea.*

Charity Supporter Number Five (Attorney) Man who is beyond reproach, knowledgeable in his profession, honest, and generous in Charles Johnstone's *Chrysal: or, The Adventures of a Guinea.*

Charity Supporter Number Four Low-bred avaricious wretch, who marries his pupil's mother and turns her against her son, whom she disinherits in Charles Johnstone's *Chrysal: or, The Adventures of a Guinea.*

Charity Supporter Number Nine (Man-Midwife) Man who becomes a midwife through a desire to alleviate the suffering of the poor but neglects to appreciate the force of public opinion in Charles Johnstone's *Chrysal: or, The Adventures of a Guinea.*

Charity Supporter Number One (Scrivener) Huge man who is the principal support of every public charity founded on the principle of the feast; he acquires the money he gives to charity from vice in Charles Johnstone's *Chrysal: or, The Adventures of a Guinea.*

Charity Supporter Number Seven Superannuated fop, who in his own home is a perfect cypher for his wife in Charles Johnstone's *Chrysal: or, The Adventures of a Guinea.*

Charity Supporter Number Six Man of such indolence of mind that he completely submits to his wife's capricious tyranny in Charles Johnstone's *Chrysal: or, The Adventures of a Guinea.*

Charity Supporter Number Three (Clergyman) Venerable and happy man, who is a true supporter of charity and a blessing to mankind in Charles Johnstone's *Chrysal: or, The Adventures of a Guinea.*

Charity Supporter Number Two (Almoner) Hypocrite who dispenses other people's charity because of his pious demeanor in Charles Johnstone's *Chrysal: or, The Adventures of a Guinea.*

Charke, Tom Gambler associated with the young Silas Ruthyn; his death in a locked room during a visit to Bartram-Haugh is believed to be a suicide until Maud Ruthyn's experiences reveal how he was murdered in J. Sheridan Le Fanu's *Uncle Silas.*

Charlane Tough-talking chef at the Deerslayer Inn in Richard Ford's *Independence Day.*

Charlecote, Honora Wealthy, devout spinster, who adopts the orphaned children of Owen Sandbrook, the man who jilted her, and is bitterly disappointed in them in Charlotte Yonge's *Hopes and Fears.*

Charlecote, Humfrey Worthy, high-minded country squire, who finally wins Honora Charlecote but dies before they can marry in Charlotte Yonge's *Hopes and Fears.*

Charlecote, Humfrey (the younger) Canadian and the heir to Honora Charlecote's estate; he marries Phoebe Fulmort in Charlotte Yonge's *Hopes and Fears.*

Charlemagne Parodic version of the historical king of the Franks and the Holy Roman Empire; has a casual view of the war and indulges himself with food, drink, and the occasional joke on his knights in Italo Calvino's *The Nonexistent Knight.*

Charlemont St. Louis merchant who bankrupts himself to help a needy friend in Herman Melville's *The Confidence-Man.*

Charles Nephew of the Cavaliere; mineralogy is the ruling passion of his life; manages Catherine's estate in Wales; compulsively washes his hands; never marries in Susan Sontag's *The Volcano Lover.*

Charles Son of Clara, brother of Susan, and stepson of Pete; in love with Laura, a married woman who eventually leaves her husband in Ann Beattie's *Chilly Scenes of Winter.*

Charles Young street hustler and drug addict; sent to a school for delinquent boys at age fourteen for stealing; homeless after his release because his mother is hospitalized and his father has disappeared in Alexis Deveaux's *Spirit in the Street.*

Charles Friend and narrator of Harley's story in Henry Mackenzie's *The Man of Feeling.*

Charles Lucy Snowe's uncle whom she apparently resembles in Charlotte Brontë's *Villette.*

Charles Schoolfriend to whom William Crimsworth writes the letter that forms the first chapter of Charlotte Brontë's *The Professor.*

Charles Son of an aristocratic family; he marries the heiress Mary by parental arrangement and then leaves for an extended absence on the Continent, fueling the young wife's already active aversion to the empty union in Mary Wollstonecraft's *Mary, A Fiction.*

Charles Known as Uncle Charles; Curate of Chapelizod and the narrator's uncle and godfather; his attendance at the funeral of Lady Darby and the finding of the skull of Barney Sturk precipitate the telling of the story of events in Chapelizod in 1767 in J. Sheridan Le Fanu's *The House by the Churchyard.*

Charles Wrestler at Duke Frederick's court; concerned by the prospect of defeating Orlando and thereby falling out of favor with the court; approaches Orlando's brother Oliver to encourage him to dissuade Orlando from participating in the match, to no avail; soundly defeated by Orlando in their match at the beginning of William Shakespeare's *As You Like It.*

Charles, Uncle Stephen Dedalus's granduncle who smokes in the outhouse and exercises in the park with him in James Joyce's *A Portrait of the Artist as a Young Man.*

Charles I, King Prince Charles and son of King James I in Sir Walter Scott's *The Fortunes of Nigel.* He is the reigning monarch during the English civil war for whom John Inglesant is messenger and courtier in J. Henry Shorthouse's *John Inglesant, A Romance.* As monarch of England he enlists the Cavalier to fight for him in the civil war; he is dejected and constantly plagued with poor advice from his counselors in Daniel Defoe's *Memoirs of a Cavalier.*

Charles II See Stuart, Charles.

Charles II See Vseslav, Charles Xavier.

Charles II, King British monarch who orders the release of the Peverils from the Tower and tricks Zarah into revealing her identity to Charlotte de la Tremouille, the Countess of Derby, in Sir Walter Scott's *Peveril of the Peak.* He is king of Scotland and deposed king of England; using the names Charles Stewart and Louis Kerneguy he is in hiding at Woodstock Lodge while escaping to the Continent; he attempts to seduce Alice Lee and narrowly escapes a duel with her lover, Markham Everard, in *Woodstock.*

Charles V Emperor of Germany; welcomes Faustus to his court as a renowned magician; requests to see the long-dead Alexander the Great and his lover; Faustus obliges the emperor's wishes by conjuring two spirits akin to the pair desired by Charles in Christopher Marlowe's play *Dr. Faustus.*

Charles VI King of France (1380–1422); when confronted with Henry's claim to the throne, begins to prepare for war; recalls the Battles of Crecy (1346) and Poitiers (1356), during which the French underestimated the forces of Edward III and Edward the Black Prince; believes that Henry V is a strong king and that the French must arm strongly against him; offers Henry marriage with Princess Katherine and to hand over "some petty and unprofitable dukedoms" instead of the Crown; calls for Montjoy to address Henry with firm defiance; sends Montjoy to ask Henry what he is willing to pay for his ransom; stays at Roan with the Dauphin while the French prepare to fight; after the Battle of Agincourt, meets with Henry and his counsel to negotiate the terms of the Treaty of Troyes, accepting all Henry's demands in William Shakespeare's play *Henry V.*

Charles, Anatole Art dealer who sponsors a show of Eugene Witla's work in Theodore Dreiser's *The "Genius."*

Charles, Helena Actress, socialite, and friend of Alison Porter who comes to stay in Alison and Jimmy's apartment; despised by the working-class Jimmy because of her upper-class background; sends a telegram to Alison's father telling him that Alison needs to be rescued from her abusive husband; after Alison flees the apartment, Helena surprisingly becomes Jimmy's lover, taking Alison's role; later forced from the apartment when Alison returns to rejoin Jimmy in John Osborne's play *Look Back in Anger.*

Charles, Leo Handsome black Londoner in his late 20s who works for the city council; Nick Guest's first lover and responsible for Nick's sexual awakening; acts as Nick's guide to London's gay subculture; race and class pose an insurmountable barrier in his relationship with Nick in Alan Hollinghurst's *The Line of Beauty.*

Charles, Mrs. Leo Charles's mother; a West Indian immigrant; her home is the first black home into which Nick Guest is invited; unaware of her son's homosexual orientation; her open love of Jesus is compared to Nick's closeted love for Leo in Alan Hollinghurst's *The Line of Beauty.*

Charles, Nick Out-of-retirement private detective in Dashiell Hammett's *The Thin Man.*

Charles, Nora Wealthy wife of Nick Charles in Dashiell Hammett's *The Thin Man.*

Charles, Prince (Stuart) See Stewart, Charles Edward.

Charles, Rosemary Leo Charles's sister, who informs Nick that Leo has died of AIDS, in Alan Hollinghurst's *The Line of Beauty.*

Charles, Vera Famed actress and best friend of Mame Dennis in Patrick Dennis's *Auntie Mame* and *Around the World with Auntie Mame.*

Charlesbois, Inez Dresden Piano and accordion teacher idealized by Cress Delahanty until Cress learns of her affair with Don Rivers in Jessamyn West's *Cress Delahanty.*

Charlesbois, Luther Husband of Inez Charlesbois in Jessamyn West's *Cress Delahanty.*

Charles the Simple King of France, son of Louis III; he was the butt of many of Julian the Apostate's jokes in his incarnation as court jester in Henry Fielding's *A Journey From This World to the Next.*

Charlesworth, Alfred Colliery manager in Bestwood; he hears Walter Morel mimicking his "squeaky voice" in a pub and then retaliates by assigning Morel unprofitable mine "stalls" to work in D. H. Lawrence's *Sons and Lovers.*

Charley Inexperienced sailor on the *Narcissus* in Joseph Conrad's *The Nigger of the "Narcissus".*

Charley Adolescent who is in love with Eustacia Vye and mourns her death in Thomas Hardy's *The Return of the Native.*

Charley Owner of a second-hand marine store in Chatham to whom David Copperfield sells his jacket on the way to Dover in Charles Dickens's *The Personal History of David Copperfield.*

Charley Potboy at the Magpie and Stump in Charles Dickens's *The Posthumous Papers of the Pickwick Club.*

Charley Willy Loman's neighbor who is sympathetic to the troubles the aging salesman faces in Arthur Miller's play *Death of a Salesman.*

Charley, Lester Bookstore owner and later a canaller who rents a room to Jerry and Mary Fowler in Walter D. Edmonds's *Erie Water.*

Charlie Large, kind, black male nurse on the Men's Violent Ward of Bellevue Mental Hospital, where John Wilder is a patient in Richard Yates's *Disturbing the Peace.*

Charlie Painter from Texas whose affair with Big Lot inspires the male narrator, Charlie's lover, to write in Tennessee Williams's *Moise and the World of Reason.*

Charlie Reactivated reluctant American World War II spy; he returns to service impersonating a burnedout field agent to investigate his close wartime friend Steve Champion's suspicious liaisons with Egypt but ends up killing his one-time comrade in Len Deighton's *Yesterday's Spy.*

Charlie Fellow voyager who, in Charles Watkins's hallucination, was snatched up by the Crystal Disc in Doris Lessing's *Briefing for a Descent into Hell.*

Charlie Inebriated boatman-postilion whose concussion forces Hornblower to assist the crew of the canal boat in C. S. Forester's *Hornblower and the Atropos.*

Charlie Hard-drinking member of the Alpha and Omega Club in Norman Douglas's *South Wind.*

Charlie New, lazy, good-natured editor of *Lilith* whom many of the magazine's employees feel to be a disappointment; he later marries Jane Somers's coworker Phyllis in Doris Lessing's *The Diaries of Jane Somers.*

Charlie (Charmian, "Charlie the Red"; covernames: Comrade Leila, Fräulein Palme, Imogen Boastrup, Joan, Margaret) Chameleon-like red-haired British actress, naïve political radical, and Palestinian sympathizer manipulated by the Israelis into espionage; at Marty Kurtz's orders, she infiltrates a Palestinian train-ing camp and, by a supreme performance in the "theatre of the real", sets up the Israeli assassination of Palestinian bomb-maker Khalil and her own psychic death in John le Carré's *The Little Drummer Girl.*

Charlock, Felix Inventor and the central consciousness of the narrative; after an affair with Iolanthe Samiou he marries Benedicta Merlin; he strives to resist the machinations of the Firm in Lawrence Durrell's *Tunc.* He ultimately becomes the Firm's puppet, even after rising to its directorship in *Nunquam.*

Charlock, Mark Young son of Benedicta Merlin and Felix Charlock; he is killed accidentally by a shotgun booby trap Felix plants within the Abel computer in Lawrence Durrell's *Tunc.*

Charlot Full-time professional criminal in Porquerelles, an island paradise located off the southern French coast in the Mediterranean, in Georges Simenon's *My Friend Maigret.*

Charlot Idiot groom assigned to Quentin Durward by Louis XI in Sir Walter Scott's *Quentin Durward.*

Charlotta Charming young woman, who is insensible of her attractions; she is no coquette in Eliza Haywood's *Life's Progress Through the Passions: or, the Adventures of Natura.*

Charlotta Governess of Anya on Madame Ranevskaya's estate in a Russian province in Anton Chekhov's *The Cherry Orchard.*

Charlotte Pretty young daughter of the aristocrat M. de Jussat and a student of the tutor Robert Greslou; becomes the love interest of Robert, but as the teacher's philosophical experiment; a lovers' suicide pact by Charlotte and Greslou goes awry when she carries through with her death act but Robert reneges in Paul Bourget's *The Disciple.*

Charlotte Sowerberrys' kitchenmaid, who feeds Noah Claypole oysters and later robs the till and runs off with Noah to London in Charles Dickens's *Oliver Twist.*

Charlotte London friend and recipient of Felicia's letters; she possesses fashionable society's conventional views about male-female relationships and the virtues of country living, but a visit to Felicia changes her mind in Mary Collyer's *Felicia to Charlotte.*

Charlotte Daughter of Miss Billie in Gayl Jones's *Eva's Man.*

Charlotte French trainee PaPa LaBas hires to replace Berbelang; becomes an assistant in a stage show and, because she helps Berbelang return art stolen by Western museums to the original owners, is killed by Biff Musclewhite in Ishmael Reed's *Mumbo Jumbo.*

Charlotte Mina and Anatole Krainik's niece; orphaned by an accident in the salmon-canning factory where her parents worked; moves to Toronto; becomes more independent; meets Martha and Bernice, waitresses at a diner she frequents, and invites them to her birthday party in Howard Norman's *Northern Lights.*

Charlotte Viennese prostitute questioned about lust by Jenny Fields; has sex with Garp, becomes a close friend of his, and dies of uterine cancer in John Irving's *The World According to Garp.*

Charlotte American nun who runs an institute for retarded adults in southern California; she takes Ruth (Sister Mary Joseph) to a meeting of charismatic Catholics in David Lodge's *How Far Can You Go?*

Charlotte (Charley) George and Jim's friend who allows George to express his grief in Christopher Isherwood's *A Single Man.*

Charlton, Mrs. Suffolk neighbor of Cecilia Beverley; until her death she provides hospitality to Cecilia as desired in Frances Burney's *Cecilia.*

Charlus, Baron de Decadent aesthete and dilettante aristocrat; reputedly a womanizer and lover of Odette; friend of Swann; develops his homosexual character and becomes socially isolated due to his sexual indiscretions; latterly a pederast in Marcel Proust's *In Search of Lost Time* (also known as *Á la recherche du temps perdu*).

Charmian One of Cleopatra's maids; suggests to Cleopatra that she retreat to her monument and send Antony a false report that she has committed suicide; joins her mistress in committing suicide at the end of William Shakespeare's *Antony and Cleopatra.*

Charmides Greek sculptor in Rome who becomes a Christian martyr with a woman he loves in a story written by the Reverend Theophilus Cardew and given to Catharine Furze in Mark Rutherford's *Catharine Furze.*

Charmolue, Master Jacques One of Claude Frollo's associates; tortures the young street woman Esmerelda to force her to confess to killing Phoebus de Chateaupers; later directs her execution in Victor Hugo's *The Hunchback of Notre Dame.*

Charmond, Felice Beautiful former actress, now a lonely widow, who has a love affair with Edred Fitzpiers which costs him his wife and his medical practice; she is killed by a former lover in Thomas Hardy's *The Woodlanders.*

Charney, Ed Gibbsville bootlegger and keeper of Helene Holman in John O'Hara's *Appointment in Samarra.*

Charnock, Anne South African colonist who comes to England as the bride of Commander Miles Charnock; her rigid, repressive brand of Evangelicalism comes into conflict with the practices of her worldly new relations in Charlotte Yonge's *The Three Brides.*

Charnock, Commander Miles Second son of Julia Charnock Poynsett; he sends home from South Africa his rigidly Evangelical bride, Anne, in Charlotte Yonge's *The Three Brides.*

Charnock, Frank Fourth son of Julia Charnock Poynsett; he gains the hand of Eleonora Vivian after many vicissitudes and succeeds as a literary man in Charlotte Yonge's *The Three Brides.*

Charnock, Julius Albino and Rector of Compton Poynsett; he introduces High Church practices to his parishioners and reconciles Anne Charnock to her in-laws in Charlotte Yonge's *The Three Brides.*

Charnock, Lady Rosamond (Lady Rose) Daughter of an impoverished Irish earl and the warmhearted wife of Julius Charnock; she is held in contempt by her sister-in-law Cecil but overcomes her natural indolence to become a pattern wife and mother in Charlotte Yonge's *The Three Brides.*

Charnock Poynsett, Cecil Priggish young bride of Raymond Charnock Poynsett; she chafes at living in her mother-in-law's house, dabbles in feminism, and recognizes her passion for her husband only as he is dying in Charlotte Yonge's *The Three Brides.*

Charnock Poynsett, Julia Widowed mistress of a large estate and mother of Raymond Charnock Poynsett and of Miles, Julius, and Frank Charnock (the younger sons bear the patronymic alone); she has been crippled in a riding accident; her abnormally strong hold on her eldest son is partly responsible for the failure of his marriage in Charlotte Yonge's *The Three Brides.*

Charnock Poynsett, Raymond Eldest son of Julia Charnock Poynsett and Member of Parliament, who marries his young cousin Cecil Charnock largely for his mother's sake and suffers for his mistake until he dies of typhoid in Charlotte Yonge's *The Three Brides.*

Charo Miss Mary's gun bearer and tracker; protective of her; aware of her deficiencies as a marksman in Ernest Hemingway's *True At First Light.*

Charoba Compassionate and independent daughter of Totis, king of Egypt; she becomes Queen of Egypt when her father is poisoned and rids herself of her unwanted suitor and would-be conqueror, the giant Gebirus, by poisoning him in the appended romance "The History of Charoba, Queen of Egypt" in Clara Reeve's *The Progress of Romance.*

Charolois, Countess Belated patroness of Gerard; at the reminder of his brother, the dwarf Giles, she fulfils an old promise by bestowing Gouda parsonage upon him in Charles Reade's *The Cloister and the Hearth.*

Charon Ferryman who carries the dead across the River Styx to the underworld in Tom Stoppard's *The Invention of Love.*

Charon, Mark Corrupt police detective who works with Henry Tucker; arranges the murder of one of Tucker's contacts, Eddie Morello, is killed by Tucker's associate Tony Piaggi during the final confrontation between Tucker and Kelly in Tom Clancy's *Without Remorse.*

Charpentier, Arthur Royal Navy sublieutenant initially arrested for the murder of Enoch Drebber in Arthur Conan Doyle's *A Study in Scarlet.*

Charrington Old man who runs an antiques store in the prole section of Oceania when he is in disguise and is actually part of the Thought Police; he sets up the environment where Smith and Julia get caught in George Orwell's *Nineteen Eighty-Four.*

Charskaya, Princess Betsy Penniless Russian princess, incomparably plain but chic; she must attach herself to others to subsist; she receives favors from Mr. Rivers for bringing wealthy women such as Martha Denman to his dress shop in Vita Sackville-West's *Family History.*

Charteris, Anna Nineteen-year-old daughter of a schoolmaster; she communes with her only friend, a tree, until Steve Hallem appears; though attracted to Steve's rebelliousness, she fears the consummation of love; she marries Steve in spite of her father's opposition in C. Day Lewis's *The Friendly Tree.*

Charteris, Edward Anna's gracelessly and rigidly moral father, a schoolmaster, who claims to be a "bit of a socialist himself"; believing that he has devoted his life to Anna and worrying that she will leave him, he plans strategies against her marrying in C. Day Lewis's *The Friendly Tree.*

Charteris, Sir Patrick Provost of Perth, who offers himself as champion of Henry Smith, Simon Glover, and other burgesses in their quarrel with the Duke of Rothsay and John Ramorny in Sir Walter Scott's *The Fair Maid of Perth.*

Chartersea, Duke of Degenerate, immoral suitor of Dorothy Marmaduke and rival of Richard Carvel in Winston Churchill's *Richard Carvel.*

Charudatta Brahmana who devotes himself to the gods and pledges to help the poor in Ujjayini in India; married and has a son, but is enamored with Vasantasena, a wealthy courtesan, who loves him in return; mistakenly accused of her murder and sentenced to execution; saved from death when Vasantasena, surviving the attack on her, appears to reveal that the evil Samsthanka had accosted her; his wealth is restored and is made a member of the new king's court in Shudraka's *The Little Clay Cart.*

Charulata Affectionately called Charu; young, intelligent woman in 19th-century Calcutta, married to the older and wealthy Bhupathi, whose business pursuits leave little time for her; enjoys the friendship of Amal, a university student living in her home, especially since they talk about the novels they are reading; begins to fall in love with Amal, but the young man shuns her affections; finds that she can no longer love her husband, Bhupathi, in Rabindranath Tagore's *The Broken Nest.*

Charvill, Robin Oxford undergraduate and rugby star; he joins Dougal Crombie and John Galt, "Jaikie", in saving Prince John of Evallonia from the Republican conspirators determined to keep him off the throne in John Buchan's *Castle Gay.*

Charwoman Cleaning lady with a pronounced bone structure and predilection for feather hats; shows no repugnance for Gregor's transformation into a giant beetle; morbidly fascinated by the insect; cheerfully inspects Gregor's carcass and disposes of it; is then given immediate leave in Franz Kafka's *The Metamorphosis.*

Charwoman, Laundress, and Undertaker's Man Three thieves who steal from the dead Scrooge, thus illustrating his friendless state at the time of his death in Charles Dickens's *A Christmas Carol.*

Chase Brief flirtation of Beigh's from a summer archaeology dig in Harvard Yard, with a knack for finding fragments; the first of her friends to win a genius grant in Bharati Mukherjee's *The Holder of the World.*

Chase, Adelia (née Montfort) Iris and Laura's grandmother; assumes the role of the submissive wife; finds an outlet in architecture, interior design, and art; means of self-expression include sculpture, decorations, and poems on Christmas cards in Margaret Atwood's *The Blind Assassin.*

Chase, Benjamin Adelia's husband, Iris and Laura's grandfather; builds the button factory in the early 1870s in Margaret Atwood's *The Blind Assassin.*

Chase, Betsy Fiancée of Eric Herman, the new photography instructor at Haddan School and houseparent at St. Anne's dormitory; is used to life in the city rather than life in a small town, continually gets lost; orphaned, she possesses a survivor's guilt; becomes the lover of Abel Gray and runs away with him in Alice Hoffman's *The River King.*

Chase, Elyot Passionate and fiery by nature; newly married to Sibyl, and formerly married to the combustible and explosive Amanda, who is now married to the even-tempered Victor Prynee; meets Amanda by coincidence at a hotel in which the two couples are staying; affirms his old love for Amanda and suddenly runs off to Paris with her, leaving his wife and Amanda's new husband behind in Noel Coward's play *Private Lives.*

Chase, Jack Respected British captain of the main-top aboard the *Neversink;* deserts ship to fight for Peru; secures liberty for the crew in Rio in Herman Melville's *White-Jacket.*

Chase, Jasper Local society novelist in love with but rejected by Rachel Winslow in Charles M. Sheldon's *In His Steps.*

Chase, Joseph Raymond (Joe, Joey) Brother of Orpha Chase; Quaker minister and faith healer charged with manslaughter in the death of Marie Griswold in Jessamyn West's *The Life I Really Lived.*

Chase, Mary Eliza Niece of Eliza Bowen Jumel; marries Nelson Chase in Gore Vidal's *Burr.*

Chase, Nelson Nephew by marriage of Eliza Bowen Jumel and husband of Mary Eliza Chase in Gore Vidal's *Burr.*

Chase, Orpha (Mrs. Dudley, Mrs. Hesse, Tumbleweed) Novelist; sister of Joseph Chase; wife of Alonzo Dudley, Jacob Hesse, and Ralph Navarro; lover of Tom O'Hara and Gregory McGovern; adoptive mother of Wanda; narrator of Jessamyn West's *The Life I Really Lived.*

Chase, Sibyl Young woman newly married to Elyot, and loves being in a state of matrimony; takes pride in knowing how to handle a husband; fears that the passionate and fiery Elyot still loves the combustible and explosive Amanda, his ex-wife, more than her; only morally disturbed when Elyot and Amanda fall into each other's warring arms again and run off together, leaving the other spouses merely looking on, in Noel Coward's play *Private Lives.*

Chase, Warrender Central and title character in Fleur Talbot's novel in Muriel Spark's *Loitering with Intent.*

Chasen, Dean Bond trader on Wall Street who dreams of retiring so that he can become a full-time writer; begins a promising relationship with Alison Poole that is eventually sabotaged by infidelity and the excesses of Alison's lifestyle in Jay McInerney's *Story of My Life.*

Chase-White, Andrew Young, virginal, and decent British cavalry officer stationed in Ireland in 1916; stunned after his proposal of marriage is rejected by Frances Bellman, he becomes briefly involved with his sexually magnetic aunt, Millie Kinnard; the inglorious part he plays in the Easter Rising is redeemed by his hero's death later at Passchendaele in Iris Murdoch's *The Red and the Green.*

Chase-White, Hilda Andrew's widowed Anglo-Irish mother, pleased with her recent purchase of a picturesque house in Ireland; oblivious to the political and familial chaos around her, she is euphoric on the eve of the Easter Rising in Iris Murdoch's *The Red and the Green.*

Chastain, Darryl Louise (DL) Ninja warrior who was trained in Japan while her parents were stationed at a military base; serves as an assassin in a failed attempt to murder Brock Vond; protects Prarie Wheeler from Brock Vond and informs the girl of the political acts of her parents during the 1960s in Thomas Pynchon's *Vineland.*

Chastinet Meticulous Bahia Casino croupier who dropped his chips in Jorge Amado's *Doña Flor and Her Two Husbands.*

Chasuble, Rev. Canon, D.D. Reverent man responsible for the Manor House residents' salvation; approached by both Jack and Algernon with the hasty request to be christened "Earnest"; harbors secret romantic feelings for Miss Prism, Cecily's governess, in Oscar Wilde's *The Importance of Being Earnest.*

Chatach, Maire Young Irish woman in the quiet community of Baile Beag, in the County Donegal, in 1833; falls in love with the British orthographer lieutenant Yolland, a soldier who has come to translate the Irish place names into English for modern British maps; contemplates emigration to America; finds herself caught in a love triangle: She loves the Briton Yolland but is pursued by her childhood friend and Irishman Manus O'Donnell in Brian Friel's play *Translations*.

Chateaupers, Phoebus de Captain of the king's archers and the man to whom the beautiful street dancer Esmerelda dedicates her heart; saves La Esmerelda from Quasimodo but is stabbed by the archdeacon Claude Frollo out of the latter's jealousy; wrongly believed by everyone to have died from his wounds; later fails to come forward when La Esmerelda is hanged for his supposed murder; later marries Fleur-de-Lys de Gondelaurier in Victor Hugo's *The Hunchback of Notre Dame*.

Châteauroy, Colonel Raoul de Colonel in the French Foreign Legion who is called "the Black Hawk"; his jealousy, hatred and maltreatment of Louis Victor (Bertie Cecil) lead to a scuffle and a charge of insubordination against Victor in Ouida's *Under Two Flags*.

Chatelaine of La Trinité (Bertha) Chatelaine of a community in the High Alps; travels through Europe with Aurelia West, dilettantes, and minor nobles in Henry Blake Fuller's *The Chatelaine of La Trinité*.

Chater, Ezra Flawed poet and amateurish biologist; seems oblivious that his wife has cuckolded him with most of the men at the Sidley Park manor; friend of Captain Bryce, a man who engages in an affair with Mrs. Chater; later dies in Malta of a spider bite in Tom Stoppard's play *Arcadia*.

Chatillion, Denise Early settler of Fort Hill and wife of Pettecasockee in Jesse Hill Ford's *The Raider*.

Chatillon Admiral of the navy of Penguinia on the mythical island of Alca; seduced by the Viscountess Olive in her attempt to prevent the admiral from defending the republic against revolutionary forces in Anatole France's *Penguin Island*.

Chattaway, Mrs. The mistress for English literature in Josephine Napier's school; she is a widow whose chatter is not discreet in Ivy Compton-Burnett's *More Women Than Men*.

Chatter, Billy One of the London tavern boys, who becomes a companion of Roderick Random after his return from France and suggests that Roderick court Miss Biddy Gripewell in Tobias Smollett's *The Adventures of Roderick Random*.

Chatteris, Mr. Successor to Mr. Ralston at Brookfield; diabetic and visually impaired, he is unfit for military duty when the war breaks out; the shortage of masters at the school forces him to call back Mr. Chips from retirement; Chatteris dies shortly thereafter, and Mr. Chips serves as Acting Head until the end of the war in James Hilton's *Good-bye, Mr. Chips*.

Chatterjee, Anju Impetuous, willful heir to the famous Chatterjee name and dwindling fortune; considers Sudha almost a twin and is protective and possessive of her; intelligent, smart, and used to being considered unattractive; decides to study English literature in college so that she can run her family's bookshop; falls deeply in love with Sunil, her arranged-marriage bridegroom; discovers, on her wedding day, that Sunil is infatuated with Sudha; instrumental in having Sudha move to America to start a new life in Chitra Banerjee Divakaruni's *Sister of My Heart*.

Chatterjee, Bijoy Kind man who is the father Anju never knows; believes that Gopal is the harbinger of good luck because the monsoon arrives, after a long drought, on the day that he arrives at the Chatterjee residence; trusts people without question; mortgages all his property in order to finance the trip, with Gopal, to find rubies in a secret cave; finds out near the ruby caves that Gopal is actually his uncle's illegitimate son; finally is killed in an accident near the ruby caves in Chitra Banerjee Divakaruni's *Sister of My Heart*.

Chatterjee, Lady Lili Widow of the late Sir Nello Chatterjee; she is part of that small segment of educated and often Anghicized Indians who form the civil-servant and professional class throughout the Raj; an old friend of Lady Manners, Lady Chatterjee becomes a surrogate "auntie" to Daphne Manners, welcoming her to her home and looking after her interests in Paul Scott's *The Jewel in the Crown*. Lady Chatterjee comments on events, especially in *The Day of the Scorpion*. She appears in *The Towers of Silence* and in *A Division of the Spoils*.

Chatterley, Sir Clifford Constance's husband, who is paralyzed and rendered impotent during World War I; he returns home to run his prosperous Midlands mines and to host gatherings of "highly mental" friends at Wragby Hall in D. H. Lawrence's *Lady Chatterley's Lover*.

Chatterley, Lady Constance (Connie) Daughter of artists and intellectuals whose husband returns from World War I paralyzed and impotent; her sufferings induced by his "life of the mind" are not sufficiently alleviated by a brief sexual affair with a young writer; an affair with the estate's gamekeeper, Mellors, brings her into vital life and closer contact with nature; pregnant by Mellors, she abandons Clifford and plans a life with the gamekeeper at the end of D. H. Lawrence's *Lady Chatterley's Lover.*

Chatterley, Sir Geoffrey Baronet and a wealthy mine owner; he is Clifford's father in D. H. Lawrence's *Lady Chatterley's Lover.*

Chatterly, Simon Dandified prelate who visits St. Ronan's Well for its waters and gossiping society in Sir Walter Scott's *St. Ronan's Well.*

Chattesworth, General Gertrude's father and Rebecca's brother, the jovial leader of the Royal Irish Artillery and owner of the Belmont estate in J. Sheridan Le Farnu's *The House by the Churchyard.*

Chattesworth, Gertrude Graceful daughter of General Chattesworth; she falls in love with Mervyn, but they keep their engagement a secret until his family's name is cleared; Paul Dangerfield tries to marry her but she resists in J. Sheridan Le Fanu's *The House by the Churchyard.*

Chattesworth, Rebecca (Aunt Becky) Kind-hearted but dictatorial sister of General Chattesworth and thus the matriarch of the Royal Irish Artillery; she administers her benevolences somewhat tyrannically; she opposes Mervyn and promotes Paul Dangerfield as a husband for Gertrude until the truth comes out; she finally confesses a long-standing affection for Lieutenant Puddock and marries him in J. Sheridan Le Fanu's *The House by the Churchyard.*

Chaucer Chief writer for comedian Harry Mercury in Peter De Vries's *Through the Fields of Clover.*

Chaucer, Dr. Herbert Maternal uncle of Dorothea Bunyan; a clergyman, he proposes to two governesses (Edith Hallam and Miss Blake) and finally successfully to Henrietta Ponsonby in Ivy Compton-Burnett's *Daughters and Sons.*

Chauchat, Clawdia Twenty-eight-year-old Russian femme fatale and repeat patient in the sanatorium; her name combines English "claws" and French "hot cat"; married but refuses to wear a wedding band; notorious for being lascivious, slamming doors, and biting her nails; as Hans's mistress, initiates him into erotic mysteries and leaves the next day; he keeps an X-ray of her as a memento, but then she returns two years later in the company of another man, in Thomas Mann's *The Magic Mountain.*

Chauffeur L.'s unnamed employee, who beats D. at the behest of Captain Currie in Graham Greene's *The Confidential Agent.*

Chauncey, Ellen Pleasant young woman Ellen Montgomery meets at the Marshmans' Christmas dinner; they become bosom friends in Susan Warner's *The Wide, Wide World.*

Chaval Workman in the Montsou mine pits; seduces Catherine, the 16-year-old daughter of Vincent Maheu, and then lives with her; jealous that Étienne Lantier shows interest in Catherine; dies along with Catherine in a cave in Émile Zola's *Germinal.*

Chavez, Domingo (Ding) Light-infantry sergeant who volunteers for a covert operation against Colombian drug-smuggling operations; is stranded in Colombia with members of other teams when Cutter cuts off support for their mission; fends off Colombian assaults long enough for Jack Ryan and John Clark to effect their rescue; transfers to CIA at Clark's suggestion in Tom Clancy's *Clear and Present Danger.* Later appears as a CIA field officer and son-in-law to Clark in *Rainbow Six.*

Chayne Private detective who spies on Clare Corven and her activities with Tony Croom to supply evidence for Gerald Corven's divorce proceedings in John Galsworthy's *Over the River.*

Chayo Director General's aloof secretary in Carlos Fuentes's *The Hydra Head.*

Cheap, Mary Elderly Jewish store owner who insists Joe Market end her life as he did his son's in Hal Bennett's *Lord of Dark Places.*

Cheatum, Squire Landowning neighbor of John Jorrocks; he is jealously vigilant against trespassing on his property in Robert Surtees's *Jorrocks's Jaunts and Jollities.*

Cheche Half-brother of Santiago, the middle-aged owner of a cigar factory in Tampa, Florida, in 1929; half-Cuban and half-American male in his early 40s; loses his wife to another man and then sets his eyes on Marela, his half-brother's younger daughter in Nilo Cruz's *Anna in the Tropics.*

Checkley, Father Sinister Catholic priest, who officiates at the secret wedding of Sir Piers Rookwood and Susan Bradley and subsequently murders Susan Bradley; later (as Father Ambrose) he attends the Mowbray family; he is finally strangled to death in William Harrison Ainsworth's *Rookwood.*

Cheekey, John Abrasive London lawyer known for his powers of cross-examination; he acts for Gregory Evans in the libel action Henry Jones brings against Evans in Anthony Trollope's *Cousin Henry.*

Cheeryble, Charles Twin brother of Edwin Cheeryble and a kindhearted philanthropist, who gives Nicholas Nickleby a job as a clerk and later makes him a partner in Charles Dickens's *The Life and Adventures of Nicholas Nickleby.*

Cheeryble, Edwin Twin brother of Charles and also a philanthropist; the two help Madeline Bray resolve her father's debt problems with Arthur Gride and work to bring Ralph Nickleby's schemes to a halt in Charles Dickens's *The Life and Adventures of Nicholas Nickleby.*

Cheeryble, Frank Nephew of the Cheerybles, who marries Kate Nickleby after he and Nicholas Nickleby foil Ralph Nickleby's plans to marry Madeline Bray to Arthur Gride in Charles Dickens's *The Life and Adventures of Nicholas Nickleby.*

Cheesacre, Samuel Stolid Norfolk farmer, who pays court to the rich widow, Arabella Greenow, but loses to his rival, Captain Bellfield; he marries Charlotte Fairstairs in Anthony Trollope's *Can You Forgive Her?*

Cheeseman Disreputable old acquaintance of James Hood; he extracts money from him in George Gissing's *A Life's Morning.*

Cheeseman, Mr. Money-tight bookseller; he starts a two-penny library of cheap paperback books and hires Gordon Comstock after he gets arrested in George Orwell's *Keep the Aspidistra Flying.*

Cheeseman, Maria Retired actress and singer whose biography Dougal Douglas is supposed to be writing in Muriel Spark's *The Ballad of Peckham Rye.*

Cheggs, Alick Market gardener who is Dick Swiveller's rival for Sophy Wackles; he wins Sophy after Dick breaks with her in Charles Dickens's *The Old Curiosity Shop.*

Cheggs, Miss Alick Cheggs's sister, who is present at the party where Dick Swiveller breaks with Sophy Wackles and Alick wins Sophy in Charles Dickens's *The Old Curiosity Shop.*

Chekalinsky Wealthy and celebrated gambler among the Moscow and St. Petersburg elite class; loses a great fortune in two games to the young military officer Hermann before soundly defeating the young man in Alexander Pushkin's "The Queen of Spades."

Chekhtaryova, Mrs. State councillor's wife and supposed acquaintance of the snobbish, low-level government assessor major Kovalyov in Nikolai Gogol's "The Nose."

Chekov Character taken from the television series and movie *Star Trek;* dispatched by the Indian House to look into the mystery of the disappearance of his old school friend Zulu in Birmingham in 1984 in Salman Rushdie's "Chekov and Zulu."

Chekov, Anton Moribund character in the final days of life; recalls his past, his career, and his interactions with other writers like Leo Tolstoy; fondly remembers times good and bad before drawing his final breath in Raymond Carver's "Errand."

Chela Maid of honor at Cleófilas's wedding in Sandra Cisneros's "Woman Hollering Creek."

Chelford, Lady Mother of Lord Chelford and a rich, strict, old-fashioned dowager, who often lectures the young people around her; she arranges the engagement between Mark Wylder and Dorcas Brandon in J. Sheridan Le Fanu's *Wylder's Hand.*

Chelford, Lord Respected, intelligent, courteous son of Lady Chelford; he loves Rachel Lake, who loves him in return but refuses him because of her secret knowledge of her brother Stanley's crimes; he helps save William Wylder from the machinations of Lawyer Larkin; he hears Stanley Lake's deathbed confession in J. Sheridan Le Fanu's *Wylder's Hand.*

Chelifer, Francis Romantic but aloof poet who after being rescued from near drowning by Lillian Aldwinkle holds off her pointed advances; the story of his life is recorded in a series of tedious fragments which he writes before escaping to London to work as editor for the *Rabbit Fancier's Gazette* in Aldous Huxley's *Those Barren Leaves.*

Chelles, Comte Raymond de Third husband of Undine Spragg; enraged when Undine attempts to sell his family's Louis Quinze tapestries hanging in his chateau de Saint Désert in Edith Wharton's *The Custom of the Country.*

Chelles, Countess Raymond de See Spragg, Undine.

Chelnov, Vladimir Erastovich Professor of mathematics in Aleksandr Solzhenitsyn's *The First Circle.*

Chelsea, Annie Billy Chelsea's five-year-old daughter in Mary McGarry Morris's *A Dangerous Woman.*

Chelsea, Billy Widower whom Martha Horgan has a crush on; has two small daughters in Mary McGarry Morris's *A Dangerous Woman.*

Chelsea, CeeCee Billy Chelsea's four-year-old daughter in Mary McGarry Morris's *A Dangerous Woman.*

Chelyustnikov Anti-Stalinist who presents a fake religious service for a dignitary from the West in Kiev in "The Mechanical Lions" in Danilo Kiš's *A Tomb for Boris Davidovich.*

Ch'en Chinese terrorist and killer in Shanghai; member of the Red revolutionaries; seizes a secret document listing arms aboard a ship in the harbor; tries twice but fails to assassinate Chiang Kai-shek; killed in the second failed car bombing attempt in André Malraux's *Man's Fate.*

Chenal, Albert White merchant in protest of whom the Reverend Phillip Martin is organizing the black community in Ernest J. Gaines's *In My Father's House.*

Chen Hao Revered teacher and mentor of the younger teacher Wang Ta-nien in Taiwan in the 1960s; referred to as "Sage"; once a rival for Wen-chin, who eventually married Wang Ta-nien; mocks his younger colleague's idea of corporate fish farming, as he fears the enterprise's failure and that he, if he joins it, will lose his stable teaching job in Hua-ling Nieh's "The Several Blessings of Wang Ta-nien."

Ch'en Ta Erh Chinese Communist assassin living in Shanghai who commits a murder at the start of the novel; only revolutionary who is Chinese in André Malraux's *Man's Fate.*

Chentshiner, Celia Intellectual wife of Haiml Chentshiner and lover of Morris Feitelzohn and Aaron Greidinger in Isaac Bashevis Singer's *Shosha.*

Chentshiner, Haiml Well-to-do husband of Celia Chentshiner and friend and benefactor of Aaron Greidinger in Isaac Bashevis Singer's *Shosha.*

Chépé, Coralie Governess for the Talbot family before the Civil War; strips their abandoned house of its remaining valuables and refuses to help them when they return to New Orleans destitute after the war in Grace King's *The Pleasant Ways of St. Médard.*

Cheri (Fred Pelous) Spoiled 25-year-old young man who is having an affair with the wealthy Lea de Lonval, a woman twice his age; at first, was a poor lover, but Lea's experienced guidance improved his art in love and romance; habitually dependent on wealthy women; soon leaves Lea and marries Edmée, an 18-year-old heiress; argues with her and leaves her, to return to Lea; sees Lea's aging body and is filled with disgust; returns to Edmée in Colette's *Cheri.*

Chernyshevsky, Alexander Friend of Russian émigré writer Fyodor Gudunov-Cherndyntsev in Berlin, Germany; goes insane after his son Yasha commits suicide in Vladimir Nabokov's *The Gift.*

Chernyshevsky, Nikolai Gavrilovich Subject of Russian émigré writer Fyodor Gudunov-Cherndyntsev's irreverent biography; 19th-century Russian political writer and novelist; major influence on Russian liberals and Bolsheviks; represents for Fyodor the decline of 19th-century Russian literature into didacticism in Vladimir Nabokov's *The Gift.*

Chernyshevsky, Yasha Russian émigré writer who commits suicide in Berlin, Germany; subject of Fyodor Gudunov-Cherndyntsev's writing in Vladimir Nabokov's *The Gift.*

Cheron, Madame, later Madame Montoni Superficial French gentlewoman and guardian to her niece Emily St. Aubert; her marriage to the evil Montoni leads to her and Emily's confinement in the Castle di Udolpho and ultimately to her own death in Ann Radcliffe's *The Mysteries of Udolpho.*

Cherrell, Adrian Fiftyish museum curator who is in love with Diana Ferse; he finds Ronald Ferse's body in John Galsworthy's *Maid In Waiting.* He is critical of Wilfred Desert's conversion to Islam in *Flowering Wilderness.* He writes his wife a description of Dinny Cherrell's wedding in *Over the River.*

Cherrell, Cuthbert (Cuffs) Canon, aged eighty-two, whose death occasions the gathering of his nieces and nephews in John Galsworthy's *Maid In Waiting.*

Cherrell, Elizabeth (Dinny) Twenty-four-year-old daughter of General Sir Conway and Elizabeth Cherrell; she uses her brother Hubert's diary to prevent his extradition and gives evidence to protect her Uncle Adrian at the coronor's inquest in John Galsworthy's *Maid In Waiting.* She plans to marry Wilfred Desert in 1930, surrenders to him when he decides to leave England again, and returns to her parents in sorrow in John Galsworthy's *Flowering Wilderness.* She helps her sister Clare during the divorce from Sir Gerald Corven; she learns that her dream of Wilfred Desert's death is true, and in 1932 she marries Eustace Dornford, the new Member of Parliament from Oxfordshire, in *Over the River.*

Cherrell, General Sir Conway Sixty-year-old eldest brother of his family, who worries over the fate of his son, Hubert, in John Galsworthy's *Maid In Waiting.* Sixty-two in 1930, he is grieved by Dinny Cherrell's engagement to a man branded as a coward in *Flowering Wilderness.* He stands by his daughter Clare (Corven) during her divorce in John Galsworthy's *Over the River.*

Cherrell, Hilary (Charwell) Vicar who persuades his nephew Michael Mont to take up the cause of slum clearance in John Galsworthy's *Swan Song.* He performs the marriage ceremony for his nephew Hubert Cherrell and Jean Tasburgh, and he helps his brother Adrian search for Ronald Ferse in *Maid In Waiting.* He sticks by his niece, Dinny Cherrell, when she decides to marry Wilfred Desert in *Flowering Wilderness.*

Cherrell, Hubert Son of General Conway Cherrell; he is a British Army Officer and is liable to extradition to Bolivia for the murder of a half-caste Bolivian Indian in John Galsworthy's *Maid In Waiting.* He attends a family conference on his sister Dinny's problems with Wilfred Desert before taking a foreign post in John Galsworthy's *Flowering Wilderness.*

Cherrell, Jean Tasburgh Daughter of the rector near Sir Lawrence Mont's estate; at twenty-one she marries Hubert Cherrell; she plans for him to escape extradition in John Galsworthy's *Maid In Waiting.* She fails to make Wilfred Desert surrender his affections for Dinny Cherrell in *Flowering Wilderness.*

Cherrell, Lady Alison (Charwell) Wife of Michael Mont's young uncle Lionel; she helps Fleur Forsyte Mont with social arrangements in John Galsworthy's *The White Monkey.* She helps Fleur communicate with the Bolivian ambassador on behalf of Dinny and Hubert Cherrell in *Maid In Waiting.*

Cherrell, Lady Elizabeth Frensham Wife of General Sir Conway Cherrell in John Galsworthy's *Maid In Waiting.* She hears her daughter Dinny's problems of love without help for her in John Galsworthy's *Flowering Wilderness.* She offers kindly advice to her daughters Clare (Corven) and Dinny in *Over the River.*

Cherrell, Lionel (Charwell) Michael Mont's uncle in John Galsworthy's *The White Monkey.* As a new judge he avoids involvement in Hubert Cherrell's legal problems in *Maid In Waiting.* He joins in family conference about Dinny Cherrell and Wilfred Desert in *Flowering Wilderness.*

Cherrell, May (Charwell) Wife of Hilary; she supports her husband's slum-clearance project in John Galsworthy's *Swan Song.* She helps her niece Dinny Cherrell keep in touch with Hilary during the trials of Hubert Cherrell in *Maid In Waiting.* She criticizes Wilfred Desert's conversion in *Flowering Wilderness.*

Cherrington, Alfred Widower and rather weak father of Eustace, Hilda, and Barbara; his wife died in childbirth with the latter child in L. P. Hartley's *The Shrimp and the Anemone.*

Cherrington, Barbara Youngest sibling in L. P. Hartley's *The Shrimp and the Anemone.* She is the nubile younger sister of Eustance and Hilda when she marries Jimmy Crankshaw in *The Sixth Heaven.* As Barbara Crankshaw, she gives birth to her first child, a boy named after her brother Eustace, as an act of renewal in *Eustace and Hilda.*

Cherrington, Eustace Neurotic, sister-dominated boy who becomes the recipient of an old woman's financial largesse in L. P. Hartley's *The Shrimp and the Anemone.* He is an Oxford undergraduate who has refined his earlier capacity to render himself agreeable but possesses an interior life rich in romantic fantasy in *The Sixth Heaven.* As a sensitive young man in Venice, he writes a novella which is accepted for publication; he plunges into the Adriatic sea as a ritual baptism, aids in the recovery of his sister Hilda, and undergoes transfiguration and death in *Eustace and Hilda.*

Cherrington, Hilda Eustace's older sister, who is largely responsible for creating his senses of reality and morality in L. P. Hartley's *The Shrimp and the Anemone.* She administers Highcross Hill for Crippled Children with money from Eustace's inheritance and becomes romantically involved with Dick Staveley in *The Sixth Heaven.* Notwithstanding her own rejection of Dick Staveley, she is shocked by the announcement of his engagement and suffers psychosomatic paralysis, only to recover as a result of a shock imposed by Eustace to benefit her; she resumes care of him in *Eustace and Hilda.*

Cherrington, Sarah (Aunt) Strict, puritanical mother-substitute, who presides over the household at Anchorstone and warns the family about presuming beyond one's social and economic class in L. P. Hartley's *The Shrimp and the Anemone.* Resuming her care over her nieces and nephew, she calls Eustace back to England from Venice at the behest of Hilda in *Eustace and Hilda.*

Cherry Brian's girlfriend in Isabel Colegate's *Orlando at the Brazen Threshold.*

Cherry See Melanie, Cherry.

Cherry, Mary Opinionated spinster who moves from family to family in the Natchez plantation society; during the Civil War, sneaks messages and medicines through the picket lines in Stark Young's *So Red the Rose.*

Cherry-Marvel, Mr. Garrulous English socialite in Paris from whom the writer-narrator learns that his friend Iris Storm is ill and under the obstetric care of Conrad Masters in Michael Arlen's *The Green Hat.*

Cherson, Mrs. Ferdinand Woman whose gossip about financial matters encourages Diana Warwick to invest and lose a great deal of money in George Meredith's *Diana of the Crossways.*

Cherubin Young page of Count Almaviva; enamored with many women; informs Suzanne that he has just been fired by the count for being caught hiding in the bedroom of Fanchette; banished from the castle, although later returns to the castle to be matched in marriage with a maid in Pierre Augustin Caron de Beaumarchais's *The Marriage of Figaro.*

Cheryl Speech therapist; teaches Theodora not to hiss her s's in Bette Pesetsky's *Midnight Sweets.*

Cheshire, Pete (The Smoothie) Ex-convict and attempted blackmailer in Peter De Vries's *Comfort Me with Apples.*

Cheshire-Cat Unperturbed creature first encountered in the Duchess's chaotic kitchen; it carries on a conversation with Alice full of logical fallacies about madness; its power to appear and disappear at will annoys the King of Hearts at the croquet party in Lewis Carroll's *Alice's Adventures in Wonderland.*

Chesney, Stella Beautiful actress, fugitive from a jealous lover in Mexico, and finally wife of Augie March and starlet in the French movie *Les Orphelines* in Saul Bellow's *The Adventures of Augie March.*

Chesnokov, Ivan War-seasoned leader in the Russian Cossack army; the young narrator who becomes assigned to his military unit in Isaac Babel's "My First Goose."

Chesser, Ellen (Ellie) Daughter of an itinerant farmer; engaged to Jonas Prather but marries Jasper Kent and has many children in Elizabeth Madox Roberts's *The Time of Man.*

Chesser, Henry Itinerant farmer who is the husband of Nellie Chesser and the father of Ellen Chesser in Elizabeth Madox Roberts's *The Time of Man.*

Chesser, Nellie Wife of Henry Chesser and mother of Ellen Chesser in Elizabeth Madox Roberts's *The Time of Man.*

Chessman, Hattie Old friend of Swithin Forsyte in John Galsworthy's *The Man of Property.*

Chester, Edward Frenchman and new companion of the divorced Diana; attends his paramour's family reunion at the family's summer place at Laud's Head on the shore in Massachusetts in John Cheever's "Goodbye, My Brother."

Chester, Edward Sir John Chester's son, disinherited when he refuses to marry a rich heiress; he falls in love with Emma Haredale, niece of his father's hated enemy, marries her, and leaves England to live abroad in Charles Dickens's *Barnaby Rudge.*

Chester, Hannah Maid to Eleanore and Mary Leavenworth; discovered to be missing following the murder of Horatio Leavenworth in Anna Katharine Green's *The Leavenworth Case.*

Chester, Sir John Refined but vicious gentleman, who has wronged Geoffrey Haredale and plots to wreck the relationship between his son, Edward, and Emma Haredale because of his hatred of the Haredales in Charles Dickens's *Barnaby Rudge.*

Chesterton, Hugo (born Chester Hugo Amberly) Quick-witted, self-assured young man of the public-school type, but a violent-tempered natural anarchist incapable of responding to social values; a manic-depressive thief, he falls totally in love with Daisy Bland's innocence; he is sentenced to die for killing a police inspector in Nicholas Blake's *A Tangled Web.*

Chestle, Mr. Hop grower in Ashford who marries Miss Larkins in Charles Dickens's *The Personal History of David Copperfield.*

Chestnut-head Red-haired Homo sapiens man, metaphorically designated by Lok and Fa; he is the father of Tanakil in William Golding's *The Inheritors.*

Chestrum, Sir Philip Foppish character who loves Caroline Campinet and convinces his mother to arrange their betrothal in Robert Bage's *Hermsprong.*

Cheswick, Charles (Cheswickle) Blustering but insecure mental patient who apparently drowns himself in Ken Kesey's *One Flew Over the Cuckoo's Nest.*

Chettam, Arthur Celia (Brooke) and Sir James's baby boy, who is the joy of his mother's existence in George Eliot's *Middlemarch.*

Chettam, Lady Dowager Mother of Sir James Chettam in George Eliot's *Middlemarch.*

Chettam, Sir James Baronet and owner of Freshitt Hall, who, when he is rejected as a suitor of Dorothea Brooke, marries her younger sister, Celia; for many years he does not forgive Dorothea for marrying Will Ladislaw in George Eliot's *Middlemarch.*

Chetty, Kashi Trader at Fort St. Sebastian in Bharati Mukherjee's *The Holder of the World.*

Chetwynd, Alyn Favorite teacher of Sophia Baines; she encourages Sophia to follow her desire to be a teacher in defiance of her parents' wish in Arnold Bennett's *The Old Wives Tale.*

Chetwynd-Smythe, Mrs. Intemperate woman of means who waddles in a big house; Daisy Bland is delivering her hat when she encounters Hugo Chesterton in Nicholas Blake's *A Tangled Web.*

Chevalley Representative of Savoia's government; arrives to offer Don Fabrizio Corbera, a prominent figure on the island and an aristocrat in southern Italy, a seat in the new senate in Rome in Giuseppe Tomasi di Lampedusa's *The Leopard.*

Chevez, Madame Rich, overbearing Turkish woman; she introduces Charles Latimer to Colonel Zia Haki at a party at her villa in Eric Ambler's *The Mask of Dimitrios.*

Cheviot, Charles Headmaster of the Stoneborough school; he marries Mary May in Charlotte Yonge's *The Trial.*

Chew, Jacob American Indian trader who guides the Master (James Durie) and Colonel Francis Burke through the wilderness; he dies, poisoned, in a canoe in Robert Louis Stevenson's *The Master of Ballantrae: A Winter's Tale.*

Cheyne, Harvey Spoiled 15-year-old son of a millionaire; he falls out of an ocean liner and is rescued by the members of the cod-fishing boat *We're Here;* they gradually help him to mature and discard his mannerisms in Rudyard Kipling's *"Captains Courageous": A Story of the Grand Banks.*

Cheyne, Romola Clever woman who maintains a difficult social position as mistress to the King; Sebastian recognizes her great soul despite her materialism and hardness in Vita Sackville-West's *The Edwardians.*

Chia Cheng Younger son of Madame Shih, the matriarch, in Ts'ao Hsueh-chin's *Dream of the Red Chamber.*

Chia Gen Master of the Ningkuofu compound outside Peking (Beijing) in Ts'ao Hsueh-chin's *Dream of the Red Chamber.*

Chia Ging Prince of the Ningkuofu who has retired to a Taoist temple, leaving his son Chia Gen as master in his place of the family compound outside Peking (now Beijing) in Ts'ao Hsueh-chin's *Dream of the Red Chamber.*

Chia Huan Chia Cheng's son by his concubine in Ts'ao Hsueh-chin's *Dream of the Red Chamber.*

Chia Jung Son of Chia Gen and Yu-shih in Ts'ao Hsueh-chin's *Dream of the Red Chamber.*

Chiang (Elder Gull, The Elder) Leader of the flock of seagulls who are perfecting their flying skills; helps Jonathan Livingston Seagull become a better flyer in Richard Bach's *Jonathan Livingston Seagull.*

Chiang Kai-shek Chinese general and leader of the Blues in Shanghai in 1927 in André Malraux's *Man's Fate.*

Chia Sheh Older son of Madame Shih, the matriarch; master of the Yungkuofu, the western compound of the aristocratic family's rich land holdings, in Ts'ao Hsueh-chin's *Dream of the Red Chamber.*

Chicago, Bebe (Francois Parmentier) West Indian homosexual with political connections to the guerrilleros and to Gerardo Strasser-Mendana in Joan Didion's *A Book of Common Prayer.*

Chicester, Sir Arthur Lord Governor legendary for his success in pacifying Ireland and a contemporary of Charles Mandeville's great-uncle in William Godwin's *Mandeville.*

Chicha Narrator and female schoolteacher in the small village of Bamso in Ghana, West Africa; visits Maami Ama, the mother of the handsome young boy Kwesi; relates the story of Maami's divorce and little Kwesi's tragic death from a snakebite that both occur in one brief afternoon in Ama Ata Aidoo's "No Sweetness Here."

Chichester, Mr. Member of the Brotherhood of the Rose in Charles Kingsley's *Westward Ho!*

Chichester-Redfern, Dinah (Diana) Redfern Strong and sensual but ruthlessly independent and controlling professional guitarist, who shares her passions for music, sex, and superficial religious ritual with novelist Giles Hermitage while she lives with and cares for her dying mother in John Wain's *The Pardoner's Tale.*

Chichester-Redfern, Helen Terminally ill matron and avid reader of the novels of Giles Hermitage; she asks him to come visit her at her home to help her "make sense of' them and ultimately to indict, in his fiction, her own abandonment years ago by her husband in John Wain's *The Pardoner's Tale.*

Chichester-Redfern, Richard Scientist husband who leaves his homemaker-wife Helen and unborn daughter Diana for a more fulfilling relationship with a younger woman colleague; Helen struggles to come to terms with the desertion years later on her deathbed in John Wain's *The Pardoner's Tale.*

Chick, Frederick Son of John and Louisa Chick in Charles Dickens's *Dombey and Son.*

Chick, George One of John and Louisa Chick's sons in Charles Dickens's *Dombey and Son.*

Chick, John Stout and bald husband of Louisa Chick; slightly vulgar, he likes to whistle and hum tunes at inappropriate times and is animated by bickering with his wife in Charles Dickens's *Dombey and Son.*

Chick, Louisa Paul Dombey's sister; she supports him in his pride of Dombey and Son, schemes to have him marry Miss Tox, is active in his household, and drops Miss Tox after Dombey marries Edith Granger in Charles Dickens's *Dombey and Son.*

Chicken Little Young boy who, during a child's game, slips from Sula's hands and drowns in Toni Morrison's *Sula.*

Chicken Number Two Lifetime convict who, in his dying days, evokes a transforming sympathy in Zeke Farragut that results in Farragut's escape in John Cheever's *Falconer.*

Chickenstalker, Anne Proprietress of a grocery shop where Trotty Veck owes money in Charles Dickens's *The Chimes.*

Chickerel, Joey Ethelberta Petherwin's younger brother, infatuated with the lady's maid Menlove; by revealing to Menlove his relationship he jeopardizes Ethelberta's social position and influences her choice of husband and her clandestine marriage; Joey's studying for the clergy is an effect of Lord Mountclere's general benevolence to his young wife's family in Thomas Hardy's *The Hand of Ethelberta.*

Chickerel, Mrs. Invalid mother of numerous and variously capable children, including Ethelberta Petherwin; she is the nominal keeper of a lodging house established by Ethelberta after Lady Petherwin's death in Thomas Hardy's *The Hand of Ethelberta.*

Chickerel, Picotee Ethelberta Petherwin's younger sister; she marries Ethelberta's rejected suitor Christopher Julian in Thomas Hardy's *The Hand of Ethelberta.*

Chickerel, R. Father of heroine Ethelberta Petherwin; he hides his relationship to his daughter because of his position as servant in Thomas Hardy's *The Hand of Ethelberta.*

Chickerel, Sol Carpenter and Ethelberta Petherwin's brother; his concern over Lord Mountclere's character causes him to accompany Mr. Mountclere in an unsuccessful effort to prevent the viscount's marriage to Ethelberta in Thomas Hardy's *The Hand of Ethelberta.*

Chickering, Crystal Fiancée, then wife of Chick Swallow in Peter De Vries's *Comfort Me with Apples.*

Chickweed, Conkey Clever robber who kept a public house as related by Mr. Blathers of the Bow Street runners in Charles Dickens's *Oliver Twist.*

Chiclitz, Clayton (Bloody) American industrialist and president of Yoyodyne, Inc. in Thomas Pynchon's *V.* and *The Crying of Lot 49;* toy manufacturer involved in black-marketeering with Major Duane Marvy in *Gravity's Rainbow.*

Chico Highly touted, brainy W.O.O.C.(P). agent; he bungles every assignment and has to be rescued by agents working with the narrator in Len Deighton's *The Ipcress File.*

Chicoy, Alice Querulous, bored, and alcoholic wife of Juan Chicoy; helps at her husband's diner and fears that Juan will leave her in John Steinbeck's *The Wayward Bus.*

Chicoy, Juan Irish-Mexican mechanic, bus driver, and owner of a gas station/diner; considers abandoning his mud-stuck bus and his troublesome passengers to start a carefree life away from his gas station and his alcoholic wife in John Steinbeck's *The Wayward Bus.*

Chief (codename: C) Bureaucratic-minded head of the Secret Service; he recalls James Wormold to England and rewards his incompetence with a promotion, an O.B.E. (Officer of the Order of the British Empire), and a substantial raise in Graham Greene's *Our Man in Havana.*

Chief, The Brigand; strong man with black hair and a pointed beard and upturned moustache; favorite orator to the other brigands in George Bernard Shaw's play *Man and Superman.*

Chief, The Leader of Italian revolutionaries who meet atop Monte Motterone; he supports Vittoria Campa's involvement despite objections about her sex in George Meredith's *Vittoria.*

Chief Accountant, The First European met by Marlow at the Central Station; appears to be exact in his perfect accounting files and in his clean and tidy appearance, both of which are rarities in the African Congo; frustrated by a dying agent whose moaning distracts him in Joseph Conrad's *Heart of Darkness.*

Chief Broom See Bromden, Chief Broom.

Chief Captain of the Romans Ambitious and inexperienced officer, who is cornered with his remaining troops in the Wolfing homestead; he kills Thiodolf and is slain by Wolfkettle in William Morris's *A Tale of the House of the Wolfings.*

Chief Clerk High-powered businessman who comes to the Samsa's flat just minutes after Gregor fails to show up for work; when Gregor refuses to open the door to his room, the chief clerk accuses him of embezzling the firm's money; upon seeing his employee's transformation, flees in horror in Franz Kafka's *The Metamorphosis.*

Chief Clerk of the Court Enigmatic dark and threatening figure in Franz Kafka's *The Trial.*

Chief Mate Rather crude, whiskered seagoer for whom the Captain, the story's protagonist, has a mild distaste; suspicious of some of the Captain's strange behaviors in Joseph Conrad's *The Secret Sharer.*

Chief of Police Irma's erstwhile lover; strives for a position of complete authority, which he achieves when Roger, an insurrectionist, decides to play his part in The Grand Balcony, a brothel, thereby allowing the chief to be aligned with other subjects of role-playing such as the Bishop, General, and Judge in Jean Genet's play *The Balcony.*

Chief of Rostrums Along with the Chief of Gardens (Fructuoso Sanabria) and the Chief of the Municipality (Zuzugoitea), one of the three fascist militiamen who persecute Geoffrey Firmin at the Farohito; it is he who actually shoots Geoffrey in Malcolm Lowry's *Under the Volcano.*

Chief of Staff Leader of the Russian Cossack army; issues orders for Ivan Chesnokov and his soldiers to destroy the enemy at Chugunov-Dobryvodka; the narrator, a young and unproven new recruit, is part of this platoon in Isaac Babel's "My First Goose."

Chielo Widow with two children and the priestess of Agbala, the Oracle of the Hills and the Caves, in Chinua Achebe's *Things Fall Apart.*

Chiffinch (Will Smith) Servant of King Charles II; he conspires with the Duke of Buckingham and Edward Christian to kidnap Alice Bridgenorth; he also steals letters from Julian Peveril to implicate him in the Popish Plot in Sir Walter Scott's *Peveril of the Peak.*

Chigi, Cardinal di Cardinal elected Pope upon the death of Pope Innocent X; he is uncle of Don Agostino di Chigi and patron of John Inglesant in J. Henry Shorthouse's *John Inglesant, A Romance.*

Chigi, Don Agostino di Friend and traveling companion of John Inglesant in *John Inglesant, A Romance.*

Chihani, Simone Young, striking, intense Algerian (Berber) woman; a trained terrorist, undercover agent, and security officer for Karlis Zander, she is also his daughter; she protects Robert Halliday and is instrumental in the success of the Ruler-NATO negotiations in Eric Ambler's *The Care of Time.*

Chikako Former mistress of Kikuji's father; introduces Kikuji to the Inamura girl, a prospective bride, in Yasunari Kawabata's *Thousand Cranes.*

Chilcox, Humphrey Political opponent who loses Parliamentary election to Lord Miltoun in John Galsworthy's *The Patrician.*

Child Pretty, blond, over-indulged adolescent and Red Riding Hood figure who knows how to use a knife and is afraid of nothing, but is seduced by the wolfish young man; submits to the wolf's embrace and to his wild and savage way of life in Angela Carter's "The Company of Wolves."

Child, The Youth who is malnourished and trapped alone in a basement; people of Omelas must all, at least once, look at the child so that they know their happiness is possible only through the child's suffering in Ursula Le Guin's "Those Who Walk Away from Omelas."

Childe, Joanna Rector's daughter, elocution teacher, and resident of the May of Teck Club; virginal and ritualistic, she is deficient in the self-centered, life-affirming drives that variously characterize her fellow residents; she dies in the fire after an unrecovered German bomb belatedly explodes in Muriel Spark's *The Girls of Slender Means.*

Childers, E. W. B. Horseback rider and trainer in Sleary's circus; he marries Sleary's daughter, Josephine, in Charles Dickens's *Hard Times.*

Childish, Lady Stereotypical lady of quality who acts thirty years younger than her age in Henry Brooke's *The Fool of Quality.*

Children of Crake/Crakers Genetically engineered humanlike beings created by Crake to repopulate the Earth; cared for after Crake's death by Jimmy/Snowman in Margaret Atwood's *Oryx and Crake.*

Chiliquinga Andrés Ecuadorian Indian workman who married the pretty Cunshi against the jealousy of Spanish master Alfonso Pereira and the local priest; sent to build the road that would be used to exploit Ecuador; devastated to find that Alfonso has forced his wife to sleep with him while he was away working in Jorge Icaza's *Huasipungo.*

Chilleywater, Harold First attache to the English Embassy in Pisuerga whose successful diplomatic career becomes less certain when his wife begins publishing "lurid stories of low life" under her maiden name in Ronald Firbank's *The Flower Beneath the Foot.*

Chilleywater, Victoria Gellybone Frinton Aristocratic, Kentish-born wife of an English Embassy official in Pisuerga and a vain, popular romantic novelist in Ronald Firbank's *The Flower Beneath the Foot.*

Chillingsworth, Lady Charlotte Emilia Belloni's rival for Wilfrid Pole; she believes, rightly, that Pole's feelings for Emilia are superficial in George Meredith's *Emilia in England.*

Chillingworth, Doctor Reverend Wesley Augustus Professor of ethics at the divinity school Thomas Marshfield attended; father of Jane Chillingworth Marshfield in John Updike's *A Month of Sundays.*

Chillingworth, Roger Name assumed by the husband of Hester Prynne; conceals his identity, with Hester's help, in order to seek revenge on Arthur Dimmesdale, his wife's lover, in Nathaniel Hawthorne's *The Scarlet Letter.*

Chillip, Mr. Doctor who delivers David Copperfield in Charles Dickens's *The Personal History of David Copperfield.*

Chilon Traitorous Greek sycophant who, for a reward, helps Vinicius and Petronious find the young princess Ligia, who has gone into hiding with other Christians, in Henryk Sienkiewicz's *Quo Vadis.*

Chiltern, Lord Oswald Standish Earl of Brentford's savage son, much given to gambling at cards and on horses; his sister, Lady Laura Standish, has used her fortune to pay his debts; he quarrels with his father; repeatedly rejected by Violet Effingham, he fights a duel with Phineas Finn, who refuses to promise not to court her; he wins Violet at last because of the unchanged intensity of his love in Anthony Trollope's *Phineas Finn.* He becomes a passionately committed Master of Foxhounds, angry with both Dukes of Omnium for failing to be considerate of his foxes in *The Eustace Diamonds,* in *Phineas Redux,* in *The Prime Minister,* and in *The Duke's Children.* He is Lord Mistletoe's guest in *The American Senator.*

Chilton, Fredrick Experienced FBI agent who supervises the young agent Clarice Starling; assigns Starling to the "Buffalo Bill" case, that of a serial killer; directs her to work and seek advice from Dr. Hannibal Lecter in Thomas Harris's *Silence of the Lambs.*

Chilton, Teresa Woman who rejects Ninian Middleton, rejects Hugo Middleton, and finally accepts Ninian as a husband, saying that she has little feeling for her life in Ivy Compton-Burnett's *The Mighty and Their Fall.*

Chilvers, Bruno Pretentious and hypocritical clergyman, who advocates a union of science and religion and has a successful career in George Gissing's *Born in Exile.*

Chin Mid-level member of the Communist Party; comrade who receives military intelligence from Song Liling, who has gathered the information from her lover, Rene Gallimard, in David Henry Hwang's play *M. Butterfly.*

China Thinnest of the three prostitutes who live above the Breedloves; so named for her makeup choices; like her roommates, she hates men in Toni Morrison's *The Bluest Eye.*

Chinaman, Jack Keeper of an opium den in Charles Dickens's *The Mystery of Edwin Drood.*

China Mary Longtime housekeeper for the McClellan family in Joan Didion's *Run River.*

Chinatown See Moss, Chinatown.

Chinese Lover, The Rich and older Chinese man (unnamed) of the book's title living in Indochina (now

Vietnam); meets a teenage French girl with whom he begins a long sexual affair; ultimately leaves her, as he is engaged to a beautiful Chinese woman through an arranged marriage, so the French girl must return with her family to her homeland, in Marguerite Duras's *The North China Lover.*

Ching Honest and industrious farmer and overseer of Wang Lung's land in Pearl Buck's *The Good Earth.*

Chingachgook (Great Serpent, Indian John, John Mohegan) Noble Indian who is the last of his tribe, the father of Uncas, and the companion of Natty Bumppo; enlists Bumppo's help in rescuing Wah-ta!-Wah in James Fenimore Cooper's *The Deerslayer;* helps Bumppo fight Magua in *The Last of the Mohicans;* helps Bumppo guide Mabel Dunham to her father in *The Pathfinder;* converted to Christianity, he lives in a cabin near Templeton, where he dies in a fire, in *The Pioneers.*

Ching-wen (Bright Design) Pao-yu's serving maid who is dismissed from her role in the household due to gossip that she was carrying on a secret affair; soon kills herself out of loss of honor in Ts'ao Hsueh-chin's *Dream of the Red Chamber.*

Chinita Daughter of the nouveau riche Coronel Zé Maria Pedrosa; provincial girl who, aspiring to a better and more glamorous life, imitates Hollywood artists in Erico Verissimo's *Crossroads.*

Chink Keeper of the clockworks, shaman of Siwash Ridge, and impregnator of Sissy Hankshaw Gitche in Tom Robbins's *Even Cowgirls Get the Blues.*

Chinney, Joseph Railway porter whose belated evidence that Eunice Manston survived the fire convinces Cytherea Graye that her marriage to Aeneas Manston is illegal in Thomas Hardy's *Desperate Remedies.*

Chinnock, Bet (Mad Bet) Madwoman whose unrequited passion for John Crow motivates her conspiracy with Finn Toller to murder him; she kills Toller after his murder attempt goes awry, and her plot is never discovered in John Cowper Powys's *A Glastonbury Romance.*

Chin-shih Wife of Chia Jung and daughter-in-law of Chia Gen; dies following a long illness; given an elaborate funeral after her husband is made a chevalier of the Imperial Dragon Guards in Ts'ao Hsueh-chin's *Dream of the Red Chamber.*

Chipande Intelligent black man who returns home to South Africa from exile as the confidential secretary to the country's new president after majority rule has been won; friends with the white liberal lawyer and his wife in Nadine Gordimer's "A Soldier's Embrace."

Chipley, Elly (Lenore La Verne) Actress on the *Cotton Blossom* in Edna Ferber's *Show Boat.*

Chippering, Thomas Professor of linguistics; compulsive womanizer and liar; boyhood friend of Herbie and Lorna Sue Zylstra; serves in Vietnam; marries Lorna Sue; after she leaves, seeks revenge on her and new husband; begins affair with Donna Kooshof; loses his job; agrees to marry Donna Kooshof in Tim O'Brien's *Tomcat in Love.*

Chipping, Mr. (Mr. Chips) Classics teacher at Brookfield School who devotes a lifetime to teaching generations of British boys; he witnesses the upheavals in the world and the changes in masters and headmasters through his decades at Brookfield, yet strives for balance between the old world and the new, the young and the old, and earns the love and respect of all with his wisdom and keen sense of humor in James Hilton's *Good-bye, Mr. Chips.*

Chippo See Simon, Erin.

Chipps, Edith English radio and television writer; wife, then widow of Gowan McGland and paramour of Alvin Mopworth in Peter De Vries's *Reuben, Reuben.*

Chips See Beauty.

Chirk, Mrs. Muddleheaded patient taken by Beaufort Mallet from Dr. Towzer's waiting room; "Captain Mallet" recasts her as his own overzealous maid, who also responds to the name of "Mrs. Finch" in Nigel Dennis's *Cards of Identity.*

Chiroc, Monsieur Sensitive, courteous newsman and adventurer; he befriends Sophia Baines after her husband abandons her, falls in love with her, and, after her refusal of him, purposely goes on a dangerous mission from which he never returns in Arnold Bennett's *The Old Wives Tale.*

Chiron Brother of Demetrius and son of Tamora; encouraged by Aaron to rape Lavinia; cuts off her tongue and hands to prevent her from revealing his crime; disguises himself to fool Titus; captured by Titus and cooked into a pie; fed to Tamora in William Shakespeare's play *Titus Andronicus.*

Chisholm, Deputy Warden Unsympathetic supervisor at Falconer prison whose denial of drugs to Zeke Farragut gives the convict periods of extreme agony in John Cheever's *Falconer.*

Chit, Miss Ensnarer of Jemmy Jessamy in Bellipine's plan that fails in Eliza Haywood's *The History of Jemmy and Jenny Jessamy.*

Chitling, Tom Young man who comes to Fagin's after being released from prison in Charles Dickens's *Oliver Twist.*

Chitral, Alcibiades Buys Mrs. Bliss's deceased husband's Buick LeSabre; Mrs. Bliss testifies against him; he is convicted of dealing drugs and is sentenced to one hundred years in prison; Mrs. Bliss later visits him in prison in Stanley Elkin's *Mrs. Ted Bliss.*

Chitterlow Aggressive, overwhelming playwright who befriends Art Kipps and recognizes him as the missing heir in Old Bean's inheritance announcement, and whose play *Pestered Butterfly* is a great success, making Kipps, one of its investors, independently wealthy in H. G. Wells's *Kipps: The Story of a Simple Soul.*

Chiverly, Mrs. Woman of rank, proud of her family connections in William Beckford's *Azemia.*

Chivery, John Weak-eyed and slight son of the Marshalsea turnkey and tobacco shop proprietor; he loves Amy Dorrit although she rejects his marriage proposal; he serves Arthur Clennam when the latter is a prisoner in the Marshalsea, and he reveals Amy's love to Clennam in Charles Dickens's *Little Dorrit.*

Chivery, Mr. Turnkey of the Marshalsea debtors' prison and tobacco-shop proprietor; he is the concerned father of John Chivery in Charles Dickens's *Little Dorrit.*

Chivery, Mrs. Prudent and watchful mother of John Chivery in Charles Dickens's *Little Dorrit.*

Chiyo/Sayuri Narrator and main character; named Chiyo as a child and given her new name, Sayuri, when she becomes an apprentice geisha; demonstrates the limits of a geisha, but also the power that can be exercised even within a position of seeming inferiority; Sayuri's choices culminate in her own greatest desire being fulfilled—freedom from a geisha house and love in Arthur Golden's *Memoirs of a Geisha.*

Chlegen, Lady Former Lady Fanny Fashion; she competes with Lady Dellwyn for social preeminence in Sarah Fielding's *The History of the Countess of Dellwyn.*

Chlestakon Covernamed K.G.B. agent who enlists Giles Trent as a minor K.G.B. mole to cover for the real mole, Fiona Samson, in Len Deighton's *Berlin Game.*

Chloe Barmaid at Yandaemonium Club in Hampstead in Muriel Spark's *The Bachelors.*

Chloris Denizen of the enchanted forest Leuke; becomes Jurgen's second wife after his apotheosis as a solar legend and subsequent exile from Cocaigne following the vernal equinox in James Branch Cabell's *Jurgen.*

Choang Korean husband who dies, then revives to find his wife Hansi about to remarry; he survives her himself lo marry again in a cynical parable on marital faithlessness told by Lien Chi Altangi in Oliver Goldsmith's *The Citizen of the World.*

Choape, Sir Trevor London doctor favored by the Duchess of Bude; he assumes Lady Emily (Winter-Willoughby) Curzon's obstetrical care in C. S. Forester's *The General.*

Choate, Chief Full-blooded Indian corporal who boxes on the regimental team in James Jones's *From Here to Eternity.*

Choh Artisan and Tehkohn wife of Gehnahteh; fosters Tien in Octavia E. Butler's *Survivor.*

Chojnacki, Count Nonchalant Polish count in Joseph Roth's *The Radetzky March.*

Choke, General Cyrus Arrogant and nationalistic American military officer, who insists the Queen of England lives in the Tower of London, and who is a member of the Eden Land Corporation, by which young Martin Chuzzlewit and Mark Tapley are cheated in Charles Dickens's *The Life and Adventures of Martin Chuzzlewit.*

Chokee, Bill Pawnbroker from whom Edward Pierce buys guns and bullets in Michael Crichton's *The Great Train Robbery.*

Chollop, Major Hannibal Migratory, tobacco-spitting proponent of liberty, whom Mark Tapley meets in Eden; he carries a host of weapons which he delights to use on anyone who disagrees with him; he advocates slavery and lynch law in Charles Dickens's *The Life and Adventures of Martin Chuzzlewit.*

Cholly, Luzana (Old Luze) Legendary bluesman idolized by Scooter in Albert Murray's *Train Whistle Guitar.*

Cholmley, Lionel Young boarder in Mrs. Bailey's house who in the past would have attracted Miriam Henderson, especially with his ambition "to disseminate poetry," but whom she resists taking up in Dorothy Richardson's *Clear Horizon.*

Cholmondely, Mrs. Fashionable lady in Villette, who chaperons Ginevra Fanshawe in society in Charlotte Brontë's *Villette.*

Chon María's silent mother in Salarrué's (Salvador Salazar Arrué's) "La petaca."

Chong, Mr. "Old Chong"; the narrator Jing-mei's deaf piano teacher; has poor eyesight and is deaf; feels the rhythm of the music, but cannot hear it; because he has poor eyesight, cannot visually keep up with the notes the narrator plays; thus, so long as the narrator plays in rhythm, she can play a cacophony and he will find her music to be lovely; can hear only the music that he has in his own mind, as he says, "like Beethoven," in Amy Tan's *The Joy Luck Club.*

Chong, Mrs. Wife of the young girl narrator's deaf piano teacher and neighbor in Amy Tan's *The Joy Luck Club.*

Choo One of many Haitian immigrants who call Wellington home; proudly embraces his African heritage; provides Levi with a link to lower-class blacks and a kind of black culture that Levi has been unable to access for most of his life in Zadie Smith's *On Beauty.*

Chopper Member of the regular fire brigade; he is assigned to Richard Roe's auxiliary fire service unit in Henry Green's *Caught.*

Chorsoman Hunnish governor of Cumae who is persuaded by Marcian to allow Veranilda to leave the city and then comes to occupy and pillage Aurelia's villa in George Gissing's *Veranilda.*

Chorus Women on pilgrimage who make offerings to a shrine and chant the glories of motherhood in Federico García Lorca's play *Yerma.*

Chorus Unlike classical choruses, which use many people in a group that interacts with fellow players, Shakespeare's in *Henry V* consists of a single character who does not interact with other characters, and, instead, narratologically frames the play; gives a prologue to each act; announces setting of coming events, though this mapping is sometimes inconsistent; praises Henry V with patriotic warmth; in epilogue, admits that though Henry V was a successful warrior king, his success was not long lasting, in William Shakespeare's play *Henry V.*

Chorus Ancient chorus upset with Antigone for taking away its lines; shoots Minnie Yellings aboard an airplane she is hijacking; the airplane captain, mistaking Chorus for a hijacker, shoots it to death in Ishmael Reed's *The Last Days of Louisiana Red.*

Chorus, *Agamemon* Twelve wise elder citizens of Argos; too old to fight in the war and now act as advisers to Queen Clytemnestra; provide background information on the Trojan War; generally, as in Greek tragedy, comment on the action and have been referred to as the ideal spectator or moral voice in Aeschylus's play *Agamemnon.*

Chorus, *Prometheus Bound* Comprised of the daughters of Oceanus, whose rivers surround the world; visit Prometheus in friendship and encourage him to seek moderation in his relation to Zeus, which Prometheus rejects; in their exchanges with him, lead Prometheus to divulge his entire history, which arouses sympathy in them; make the extraordinary decision to voluntarily share in the suffering that is heaped upon Prometheus at the end of Aeschylus's play *Prometheus Bound.*

Chorus, *The Eumenides* Made up of the Furies, or Erinyes; chthonic, or primal, goddesses, predate the Olympian gods; harbor great resentment against the new system of justice; kindred bloodshed is more abhorrent to them than murder of a spouse; terrifying, savage, brutal, have snakelike hair, black skin, bloodshot eyes, and vile breath; at the end of the play, are escorted by a second chorus to their new honorable home under the soil of Athens; from now on, named Eumenides, or "Kind Ones," in Aeschylus's play *The Eumenides.*

Chorus, *The Libation Bearers* Captive Trojan women bearing offerings, or libations, to Agamemnon's grave; conspire with Orestes and Electra in Aeschylus's play *The Libation Bearers.*

Chorus, *Romeo and Juliet* Traditional intermediary figure who helps audiences appreciate the drama; uses a sonnet, a traditional form associated with love, to introduce the tragedy of Romeo and Juliet in William Shakespeare's play *Romeo and Juliet.*

Chorus of Men Twelve angry and stubborn old men who vainly attempt to put the women in their place by conjuring up the most grotesque misogynistic scenarios, thus offering high comedy; fail to lay siege to the Acropolis, which the women have occupied, but are reconciled in the end in Aristophanes' play *Lysistrata.*

Chorus of Old Men from Colonus Elders of Colonus who investigate the interloper of their sacred grove; promise to protect him if he leaves the grove, but revoke their promise when they discover who he is; interrogate Oedipus about his past; require him to perform purification rites to appease the Furies in Sophocles' play *Oedipus at Colonus.*

Chorus of Old Theban Men Group of Theban elders who advise the king and comment critically and sympathetically on unfolding events; initially side with Creon, but Tiresias's prophecy urges them to intercede; convince Creon to free Antigone and bury Polynices, but their help comes too late to save Antigone in Sophocles' play *Antigone.*

Chorus of Satyrs Comic, unindividuated collective common to all satyr plays; a race of wild humanoids with the lower body of a goat and a horse's tail; crude, lecherous, unrestrained, cowardly, and inordinately alcoholic; former servants of Dionysus, the god of wine; currently stranded in Sicily and enslaved by the Cyclops; oscillates treacherously between the Ithacans and the Cyclops, depending on the balance of power, in Euripides' play *The Cyclops.*

Chorus of Theban Citizens Theban delegation that petitions their king, Oedipus, to save them from the plague; initially rejects the possibility that Oedipus is the murderer of King Laius and the source of the plague, but eventually and despairingly accepts the truth that Oedipus is the source of evil in Sophocles' play *Oedipus the King.*

Chorus of the Women of Canterbury Group of townswomen loyal to Becket; rejoice at his return from France after seven years of exile, but know Henry II will kill Becket and try to persuade him to flee; mourn Becket's death but thank God for strengthening the church with another saint in T. S. Eliot's play *Murder in the Cathedral.*

Chorus of Women Though physically frail, outwit the men with jars of water; under the pretense of sacrifice, seize the Acropolis, Athens's political and religious center; by appropriating the treasury, immediately terminate warfare and join in a grand celebration of love and peace in Aristophanes' play *Lysistrata.*

Choucoune Tiny mulatto modiste who sometimes sews at Bréda in Arna Wendell Bontemps's *Drums at Dusk.*

Choufleur Free mulatto; son of Sieur Maltrot, a wealthy planter of the French colony Saint Domingue; when his father is captured during the slave rebellion of 1792–1802, Choufleur murders him and saves his father's severed penis in a snuff box as a gift for his father's former mistress, Nanon; attempts to seduce Nanon in Madison Smartt Bell's *All Souls' Rising.*

Chow Official of Justice in Nanking; paramour of Mrs. Ma; deprived of his office as punishment for his duplicity in Mrs. Ma's murder of her husband in Li Hsing-tao's play *The Circle of Chalk.*

Chrabotzky, Emilia Catholic widow of a professor and mother of Halina Chrabotzky; beloved friend of Yasha Mazur in Isaac Bashevis Singer's *The Magician of Lublin.*

Chrabotzky, Halina Sickly daughter of Emilia Chrabotzky; her youth, beauty, and precocity sexually attract Yasha Mazur, unbeknown to Emilia, and to Yasha's admitted shame, in Isaac Bashevis Singer's *The Magician of Lublin.*

Chremes Father of Philumena; does not understand why Simo does not insist that Pamphilus marry Philumena in Thornton Wilder's *The Woman of Andros.*

Chretien, Reine Beautiful, capable woman, who manages her father's farm in Normandy; she loves Richard Butler but hesitates to marry him because of his family's contempt for her social position in Anne Thackeray Ritchie's *The Village on the Cliff.*

Chris Friend of Gwen Murray in Jenkintown; seriously pretty, with a rope of blond hair and creamy, pale skin in Alice Hoffman's *Here on Earth.*

Chrissy Blond receptionist at a large corporation; joins in a lunchroom conversation with other women employees about their rape fantasies in Margaret Atwood's "Rape Fantasies."

Christabel Schoolgirl who finds the young Alfred Polly's impassioned attempts to woo her merely a source of entertainment for herself and her friends; her rejection drives him to marry Miriam Larkins (Polly) in H. G. Wells's *The History of Mr. Polly.*

Christémio Paquita's obedient mulatto foster-brother; adores and protects his sister as he transports de Marsay to and from her boudoir in Honoré de Balzac's "The Girl with the Golden Eyes."

Christian Pilgrim who journeys from the City of Destruction to the Celestial City, aided by his faith and the spiritual guides sent to help him; he errs and helps others avoid error along the way; he fights and defeats the demon Apollyon; he is accompanied by Faithful, then by Hopeful; he is welcomed by the King of the Celestial City in Part 1 of John Bunyan's

The Pilgrim's Progress from This World to That Which Is to Come.

Christian, Bill Member of the board of directors of the Association of Growers of Dark Fired Tobacco, an organization designed to influence tobacco prices; supporter of the night riders in Robert Penn Warren's *Night Rider.*

Christian, Candy Innocent who, in her search for love, has a number of bizarre sexual encounters in Terry Southern and Mason Hoffenberg's *Candy.*

Christian, Edward (Ganlesse, Simon Canter) Hypocritical enemy of Charlotte de la Tremouille, the Countess of Derby; he conspires with the Duke of Buckingham to kidnap Alice Bridgenorth for King Charles II and confesses that he is the father of the mysterious Zarah in Sir Walter Scott's *Peveril of the Peak.*

Christian, Fletcher Master's mate on HMS *Bounty* who marries Maimiti and who leads the rebellion against Captain Bligh in Charles Nordhoff and James Norman Hall's *Mutiny on the Bounty;* leads a group of mutineers and Tahitians to an isolated island where he attempts to establish a democracy, only to see it fail when the tension between the Tahitians and the whites erupts into violence, to which he falls victim, in *Pitcairn's Island.*

Christian, Jack Identical twin of Sidney Christian, husband of Livia Christian, and uncle of Candy Christian, whom he seduces on the floor of her father's hospital room, in Terry Southern and Mason Hoffenberg's *Candy.*

Christian, Livia Vulgar, sex-starved wife of Jack Christian and aunt of Candy Christian in Terry Southern and Mason Hoffenberg's *Candy.*

Christian, Lucille (Sukie) Daughter of Bill Christian and lover of Percy Munn in Robert Penn Warren's *Night Rider.*

Christian, Sidney Father of Candy Christian; suffers a partial lobotomy at the hands of his gardener but reappears as a dung-covered holy man in Terry Southern and Mason Hoffenberg's *Candy.*

Christian, Uncle Willy Drugstore operator in William Faulkner's *The Town, The Mansion,* and *The Reivers.*

Christian, William Leader of the Roundheads whose execution had been ordered by Charlotte de la Tremouille, Countess of Derby in Sir Walter Scott's *Peveril of the Peak.*

Christiana Wife of Christian; she remains behind in the City of Destruction with her children, but after Christian's death decides to follow in his path; joined by her four sons and Mercy, she is guided by Great-heart through the same perils and trials as her husband, ultimately reaching the Celestial City in Part 2 of John Bunyan's *The Pilgrim's Progress from This World to That Which Is to Come.*

Christiane Franck's wife; narrator's comments about her arguments with Franck suggest marital difficulties, which, however, are never substantiated; unable to accompany Franck and A... on their trip to the port because of her weak physical condition, presumably as a consequence of childbirth; never actually present in the narrative proper of Alain Robbe-Grillet's *Jealousy.*

Christianson, Miss Friend of Lady Macfarren; she plots to make Eleanor (Raymond) Penrhyn look guilty of adultery when David Stuart, thought to be dead, returns; she marries and rules over Lord Peebles in Caroline Norton's *Stuart of Dunleath.*

Christie Lady's maid to Alison (Graeme); she accompanies Henry Dune's family to New York in Robert Louis Stevenson's *The Master of Ballantrae: A Winter's Tale.*

Christie, John London ship chandler who rents rooms to Nigel Olifaunt and Richie Moniplies, believes Nigel has seduced his wife, and pursues Lord Dalgarno to recover his wife in Sir Walter Scott's *The Fortunes of Nigel.*

Christie, Nelly John Christie's wife, who flees with Lord Dalgarno and is reclaimed by John when Dalgarno is killed in Sir Walter Scott's *The Fortunes of Nigel.*

Christie, Rebecca "Jelly" Wife of Thomas Christie; likes to entertain in a grand fashion and is a consummate hostess, circulating among her guests with grace and charm in Frances Sherwood's *Vindication.*

Christie, Thomas Thursday-night dinner guest of Joseph Johnson; one of Joseph's lovers; marries Rebecca "Jelly" Christie; dies of fever in Surinam the same year Mary dies in Frances Sherwood's *Vindication.*

Christie of the Clint Hill Julian Avenel's odious chief retainer; crafty and aggressive, he cowers in the presence of his master, whom he faithfully serves and dies beside in Sir Walter Scott's *The Monastery.*

Christine Granddaughter of Bill Cosey and daughter of May, who has had to endure many hardships in life but does not want people to pity her; works as a prostitute and has acquired valuable jewelry as gifts of her trade; also has been a G.I. bride in Germany and the lover of a black radical by the name of Fruit in the 60s; jailed often for various crimes and is disliked by the townspeople in Toni Morrison's *Love.*

Christine Aunt of Katie, sister of June; recently widowed in Sandra Scofield's *Beyond Deserving.*

Christine Blonde wife of Max; impregnated by Gene Pasternak in John Clellon Holmes's *Go.*

Christine Worker in a laundry across from Sebastian Dangerfield's house; becomes one of Sebastian's girlfriends in J. P. Donleavy's *The Ginger Man.*

Christmas, Joe Possibly a mulatto who is the lover and murderer of Joanna Burden; castrated by Percy Grimm in William Faulkner's *Light in August.*

Christmas, Tom Porter at the local train station; his report leads Larkin to believe erroneously that Rachel Lake went to London with Mark Wylder in J. Sheridan Le Fanu's *Wylder's Hand.*

Christophe, Henri Chief owner of lAuberge de la Couronne, who later becomes the king of Santo Domingo and owns black slaves whom he enlists to build the Citadel La Ferriere; immures his French confessor in cement when the latter tries to leave for France, and is haunted by him; takes ill due to the shock he receives when the confessor rises from the dead; kills himself when he sees that all his slaves have escaped and revolted in the wake of his illness in Alejo Carpentier's *The Kingdom of This World.*

Christopher Fisherman who directs John Buncle to the home of Dorick Watson and is employed by Watson at regular intervals in Thomas Amory's *The Life of John Buncle, Esq.*

Christopher, Annabel The "English Lady-Tiger" of Italian B Films who breaks free of her public image after the suicide of her husband and his carefully crafted attempt to blacken her with responsibility for his death in Muriel Spark's *The Public Image.*

Christopher, Black See Hall, Christopher.

Christopher, Carl Infant son of Annabel and Frederick Christopher; his existence gives purpose to his mother's life after his father's suicide in Muriel Spark's *The Public Image.*

Christopher, Cory Wife of David Christopher, mother of James and Julia Christopher, and daughter of the owners of the farm where the Christophers live in Fred Chappell's *It Is Time, Lord.*

Christopher, David (Davy) Husband of Cory Christopher and father critical of his son, James, but indulgent toward his daughter, Julia; teacher fired for his teaching of science but too proud to ask for reinstatement in Fred Chappell's *It Is Time, Lord.*

Christopher, Frederick Failed actor and screenwriter who tries to destroy his wife through a plot to blame her for his suicide in Muriel Spark's *The Public Image.*

Christopher, James (Jimmy) Son of Cory and David Christopher and husband of Sylvia Christopher; quits his job as production manager of Winton College Press to come to terms with his past and his own identity; eventually starts over by reapplying for his job and returning to his family; narrator of Fred Chappell's *It Is Time, Lord.*

Christopher, Julia Younger sister of James Christopher; model child and responsible adult who claims she always has protected James from the consequences of his actions in Fred Chappell's *It Is Time, Lord.*

Christopher, Sylvia Understanding wife of James Christopher in Fred Chappell's *It Is Time, Lord.*

Christou Storyteller, liar, and good-natured owner of the Cyprus Bar; he was a friend and partner of Ehie Khoury in arms-smuggling to Cypriot rebels, as well as an acquaintance of Townrow; supposedly he tried to kill Townrow in P. H. Newby's *Something To Answer For.*

Christy Laborer who runs errands for Father Oliver Gogarty; he represents the simple and parochial mind of the villagers in George Moore's *The Lake.*

Christy Member of the Northern Irish contingent of the INLA (Irish National Liberation Army) intending to kill Padraic; killed by Padraic in Martin McDonagh's *The Lieutenant of Inishmore.*

Christy, Mrs. Camilla Bellamy's mother, who has wars of words with Edward Bellamy; she does much of the charity sewing work in Ivy Compton-Burnett's *Men and Wives.*

Chromatic, Graziosa Mr. Chromatic's daughter; she weds Sir Patrick O'Prism in Thomas Love Peacock's *Headlong Hall.*

Chromatic, Mr. Squire Headlong's guest for whom all other arts are inferior to music in Thomas Love Peacock's *Headlong Hall.*

Chromatic, Tenorina Mr. Chromatic's daughter; she weds Squire Harry Headlong in Thomas Love Peacock's *Headlong Hall.*

Chronicler/Cronista, The Recorder of courtly events and documenter of official history during the reign of Philip II in Carlos Fuentes's *Terra Nostra.*

Chrono Son of Malachi Constant and Beatrice Rumfoord in Kurt Vonnegut's *The Sirens of Titan.*

Chrysal Spirit of gold trapped in a guinea who narrates the history of his life while in the hands of men, and who promises to communicate the grand secret of nature and spirits to the Adept in Charles Johnstone's *Chrysal; or, The Adventures of a Guinea.*

Chrystal, Charles P. Dean of the Cambridge college who successfully courts Sir Horace Timberlake for a handsome endowment to the college; he joins Arthur Brown to lead in organizing support for Paul Jago as new Master but defects at the last moment to support Crawford instead in C. P. Snow's *The Masters.*

Chrysanthi (Chr'ysomou) Lover of Sotiris Procopirios in Athens in Nicholas Delbanco's *The Martlet's Tale.*

Chrysis The woman of Andros who comes to Brynos, to the dismay of the Greek citizens there whose sons frequent her dinners and discussions, in Thornton Wilder's *The Woman of Andros.*

Chrysostom, Saint Humane fourth owner of Julian the Apostate during his incarnation as a slave; he eventually frees him in Henry Fielding's *A Journey From This World to the Next.*

Chub Irish immigrant and Presbyterian minister; friend of Frank Meriwether, collector of the classical library, and tutor in John Pendleton Kennedy's *Swallow Barn.*

Chubb, Eustace Poet known for his cold war verse in John Updike's *Bech: A Book.*

Chubb, Laurence, Jr. Head of Chubb's safe-making company who shows the South Eastern Railway safes to Miss Miriam in Michael Crichton's *The Great Train Robbery.*

Chubb, Mr. Operator of the Sugar Loaf public house; he has an interest in the electioneering in George Eliot's *Felix Holt, the Radical.*

Chubinov, Vassili Iulievitch Colorless-appearing anarchist descended from monarchs; he is the son of old friends of Nikolai Diakanov, whose heart attack he causes by reporting that Nikolai was betrayed by his secretary, the double agent Monsieur Kamensky, in Rebecca West's *The Birds Fall Down.*

Chubsalid Priest-Supreme of the Church of the Formidable Peace; he insists the Church must be superior to the State and is executed by the Supreme Oligarch in Brian W. Aldiss's *Helliconia Winter.*

Chuchki, Arkikov Eskimo reindeer herder; strikes gold at Seven Above mine in Nome; loses claim due to foreign status; discovers first gold on Nome beaches in James Michener's *Alaska.*

Chu-chu Corrupt judge who accepts a bribe from Mrs. Ma who has killed her husband and blamed the young girl Chang-hi-tang; deprived of his official office by the emperor as punishment in Li Hsing-tao's play *The Circle of Chalk.*

Chucundra Comical muskrat that Rikki meets in the house; afraid of his own shadow, as he cries when Rikki speaks harshly to him, in Rudyard Kipling's "Rikki-tikki-tavi."

Chudleigh, Lord Duke who kills himself on the death of his sickly son because he has no heart to wield the necessary power to run his estates; his property passes to his nephew, Jacob Delafield, in Mrs. Humphry Ward's *Lady Rose's Daughter.*

Chuffey, Mr. Anthony Chuzzlewit's devoted clerk, who is debilitated mentally and physically but remains faithful to Chuzzlewit and his memory, helping to expose Jonas Chuzzlewit's attempt to murder his father in Charles Dickens's *The Life and Adventures of Martin Chuzzlewit.*

Chumfield, Mr. Mayor of Hartlebury and local Tory chairman; he decides to support Aubrey Bohun in the Fanchester election when his own candidate resigns in Benjamin Disraeli's *A Year at Hartlebury; or, The Election.*

Chump, Martha Wealthy, vulgar Irish widow, scorned by the daughters of her business associate and potential husband, Samuel Bolton Pole, in George Meredith's *Emilia in England.*

Chunder, Hurree (the Babu) Although fat and seemingly foolish, an eminent player of the "Great Game" of intrigue for the British army in India; a master of disguise, he joins Kim in tricking the Russian spies in Rudyard Kipling's *Kim.*

Chunga Blind daughter of Anselmo and Antonia; seduced by Anselmo; reopens the brothel The Green House and makes it the most prosperous business in town of Piura in Mario Vargas Llosa's *The Green House.*

Chunsheng Soldier who served in the same battle tunnel with the narrator, Xu Fugui; survived the civil war and the Korean War but died in the political struggle during the Cultural Revolution in China in Yu Hua's *To Live: A Novel.*

Church, Corporal Jonathan (Johnny) Young rebel who is disowned by his father and enlists in Cromwell's army at age sixteen; opposes Cromwell's Irish campaign but is offered a pardon if he will recant his democratic views; chooses to be executed by a firing squad; fathers a child by Nell Lacy; narrator of Mary Lee Settle's *Prisons.*

Church, Roy Agent for the Kansas Bureau of Investigation; works with Harold Nye in breaking the false story of Richard Hickock in Truman Capote's *In Cold Blood.*

Church, Soaphead See Whitcomb, Elihue Micah.

Churchill, Alfred Rambunctious son of the Churchills who grows to manhood in Henry Wadsworth Longfellow's *Kavanagh.*

Churchill, Captain James Twenty-four-year-old romantic who falls in love with Catherine Casement; he is easily affected by the pitfalls of the human condition, especially death, in Kingsley Amis's *The Anti-Death League.*

Churchill, Charles Plump schoolmaster and father of Florence Churchill; he combines a "gross person" with a "fine delicacy of wits"; he astutely recognizes the error Florence has made in marrying Lewis Dodd in Margaret Kennedy's *The Constant Nymph.*

Churchill, Edward Uncle of Jacqueline Churchill, whose marriage to Lewis Rand he opposes; Federalist and veteran of Yorktown in Mary Johnston's *Lewis Rand.*

Churchill, Evelyn Albert Sanger's talented, intelligent, beautiful British second wife, who bears him four children; Evelyn loves Sanger "to distraction" but dies early from a heart condition in Margaret Kennedy's *The Constant Nymph.*

Churchill, Florence Beautiful, good-humored, intelligent cousin to Albert Sanger's children; she falls in love with Lewis Dodd and determines to marry him; achieving her goal, she is devastated when she discovers the love between Lewis and her cousin Teresa Sanger; losing her good humor, she verbally torments Teresa; when Teresa and Lewis run off together, she sets out to find them, determined not to lose Lewis, in Margaret Kennedy's *The Constant Nymph.*

Churchill, Frank Weston Handsome, lively, careless son of Mr. Weston; after his mother's death he was adopted and raised by his wealthy uncle and aunt; secretly engaged to Jane Fairfax, he deflects suspicion by pretending to court Emma Woodhouse; his aunt's opportune death removes the need to keep his engagement secret in Jane Austen's *Emma.*

Churchill, Jacqueline Niece of Edward Churchill; refuses Ludwell Cary's marriage proposal and offends her family by marrying Lewis Rand in Mary Johnston's *Lewis Rand.*

Churchill, Mary Wife of Churchill; encourages her husband to write and scolds him when he does not do so in Henry Wadsworth Longfellow's *Kavanagh.*

Churchill, Mr. Maternal uncle of Frank Churchill; a childless man of wealth, he and his wife have brought Frank up as their adopted son; he is under the direction of his wife and, after her death, is easily manipulated by his nephew in Jane Austen's *Emma.*

Churchill, Mr. Schoolmaster who tries unsuccessfully to write a romance in Henry Wadsworth Longfellow's *Kavanagh.*

Churchill, Mrs. Arrogant, capricious wife of Frank Churchill's uncle; she caused the rupture between the Churchills and Mr. Weston; her sudden death relieves Frank of the necessity for keeping secret his engagement to Jane Fairfax in Jane Austen's *Emma.*

Churchill, Robert Evelyn Churchill's unprepossessing, reserved brother, who is the principal at a university in the British midlands; he accompanies his niece Florence Churchill to the Austrian Tyrol to visit the Sanger household and disapproves of most of the people there in Margaret Kennedy's *The Constant Nymph.*

Church Organist Man who plays the anthem that mesmerizes Soapy and changes him into a repentant soul in O. Henry's "The Cop and the Anthem."

Church-Woodbine, Horace (Woody) Irresponsible banjo player from a family of wealthy horse fanciers; employer of Bad-foot Dixon and Augie in Arna Wendell Bontemps's *God Sends Sunday.*

Churm, Miss Low-class Cockney girl who is very skilled as a painter's model and can assume the bearing and emotion of any class of woman in Henry James's "The Real Thing."

Churnin, Dowell Neighbor of the Warners; retired high school basketball coach whose son was killed in Vietnam; partner with Tom Van Sant in Snell's Greenhouse; dates and later becomes engaged to Barbara Warner in Ann Beattie's *My Life, Starring Dara Falcon.*

Chuzzlewit, Anthony Wealthy and triumphantly stingy brother of old Martin Chuzzlewit; he is proud of the avarice and suspiciousness of his son, Jonas, in Charles Dickens's *The Life and Adventures of Martin Chuzzlewit.*

Chuzzlewit, Diggory Chuzzlewit family forebear who relied heavily for support on an oft-mentioned uncle whose splendid entertainments he called the "Golden Balls" in Charles Dickens's *The Life and Adventures of Martin Chuzzlewit.*

Chuzzlewit, George Bachelor who attends the family gathering at Seth Pecksniff's house; he is so disposed to pimples that the ornaments of his attire seem to have broken out upon him in Charles Dickens's *The Life and Adventures of Martin Chuzzlewit.*

Chuzzlewit, Jonas Vile, crafty, abusive, and murderous son and business partner of Anthony Chuzzlewit; he woos Mercy Pecksniff by pretending to court her sister in Charles Dickens's *The Life and Adventures of Martin Chuzzlewit.*

Chuzzlewit, Martin Extremely wealthy patriarch of the Chuzzlewit family, who suspects everyone he comes in contact with of coveting his money; the selflessness of Mary Graham and Tom Pinch assist his developing benevolence; he is reconciled to his grandson, Martin, and exposes his cousin Seth Pecksniff's hypocrisy in Charles Dickens's *The Life and Adventures of Martin Chuzzlewit.*

Chuzzlewit, Martin (the younger) Grandson to Martin and suitor to his grandfather's paid companion, Mary Graham; having quarreled with old Martin, he ventures abroad to America to make his fortune, taking Mark Tapley as his servant/companion; hardship, illness, and Mark's example of cheerful heroism change him from a selfish man into a more affectionate, appreciative friend and lover in Charles Dickens's *The Life and Adventures of Martin Chuzzlewit.*

Chuzzlewit, Mrs. Ned Strong-minded, disagreeable widow with three red-nosed, unmarried daughters; she is a witness to Charity Pecksniff's triumph-turned-humiliation in Charles Dickens's *The Life and Adventures of Martin Chuzzlewit.*

Chuzzlewit, Toby Chuzzlewit family member, now dead, through whom the Chuzzlewits claim a bend-sinister connection to Lord No Zoo in Charles Dickens's *The Life and Adventures of Martin Chuzzlewit.*

Chzarn, Ghht-Mlark Phagor major of the Borlien guard; she reports secretly to the phagor leader in hiding and sets fire to the Borlien palace in Brian W. Aldiss's *Helliconia Summer.*

Ciccio Dark, passionate Italian, who comes to Woodhouse as a member of the Natcha-Kee-Tawara Troupe; he has mesmeric power upon Alvina Houghton, who goes with him to his remote mountain village in southern Italy in D. H. Lawrence's *The Lost Girl.*

Cicely Wife of Otto and sister of Mrs. Pullbody's sister's husband; she attends Otto during John Lavender's visit to the dentist's office in John Galsworthy's *The Burning Spear: Being the Experiences of Mr. John Lavender in Time of War.*

Cicero Based on a real historical person, Marcus Tullius Cicero; Roman advocate, lawyer, and politician who often hires the private investigator Gordianus in Steven Saylor's *Roman Blood* and many of the other books in the Rome Sub-Rosa series.

Cicero Former slave employed to carry young Martin Chuzzlewit's luggage in New York; his life story, recounted by Mark Tapley, exemplifies American brutality towards Negroes in Charles Dickens's *The Life and Adventures of Martin Chuzzlewit.*

Cicero Roman senator who becomes one of the conspirators against Caesar in Thornton Wilder's *The Ides of March.*

Cienfuegos, Ixca Narrator and mysterious central character; Indian with a double personality as an avatar of the Aztec god of war and a trickster; mythic, handsome, and powerful presence embodying the spirit of indigenous Mexico; responsible for unmasking the decadence of Mexico's upper class; seeks to reclaim the solidity of Mexican nationality and to cleanse Mexico's social classes of inequality in Carlos Fuentes's *Where the Air Is Clear.*

Cifuentes Engineer nearly killed by enemy agents stalking James Wormold because Wormold has taken his identity for an imaginary agent (code identification: 59200/5/2) who allegedly details the mysterious constructions in the Oriente mountains in Graham Greene's *Our Man in Havana.* See also James Wormold.

Cigarette Young, attractive, boyish-looking, cigar-smoking Frenchwoman, a camp follower who leads the troops of the French Foreign Legion to victory at the Battle of Zaraila; she loves Bertie Cecil and sacrifices her life to save him from execution by a firing squad in Ouida's *Under Two Flags*.

Cigny, Isabelle Creole woman of Le Cap, capital city of the French colony Saint Domingue; during the initial days of the slave rebellion of 1791–1802, she shelters Antoine Hébert's mistress, Nanon, who bears Hebert's child in an upstairs room of Isabelle's home; takes his friend Captain Maillart, among other officers, as one of her frequent, casual lovers; escapes Le Cap after the city is subdued in the rebellion in Madison Smartt Bell's *All Souls' Rising*.

Cilissa Orestes' nurse who is greatly devoted to him; when she hears of his (false) death, sadly fetches Aegisthus in Aeschylus's play *The Libation Bearers*.

Cilly Franz Biberkopf's mistress and Reinhold's ex-girlfriend; wants to take revenge on Reinhold for leaving her and plots her payback together with Biberkopf in Alfred Döblin's *Berlin Alexanderplatz*.

Cincia Countess of Cornwall, sister of Queen Eleanor, and member of the royal entourage in Ann Radcliffe's *Gaston de Blondeville*.

Cinder Rival of Mary Pinesett; lover of July, whom she wins by means of a love charm, in Julia Peterkin's *Scarlet Sister Mary*.

Cindy Artist's model who is Philip Weston's customary sexual refuge in Isabel Colegate's *Statues in a Garden*.

Cinnamon Akasaka Made up name by the character; lost his voice because of traumatic memories, but finds a new voice and a more stable relationship to history through writing; person with an ability to form stories, offering an extended lifeline to narratives; enables the protagonist, Toru, computer contact with his missing wife; rescues Toru from drowning in the well in Haruki Murakami's *The Wind-Up Bird Chronicle*.

Cinnamond, Lidy Wife of Stephen Birdwell and lover of Mel Venters in Jessamyn West's *The Friendly Persuasion*.

Cinqbars, Captain Tom (variously George) Member of Rawdon Crawley's regiment and an admirer of Becky (Sharp) Crawley in William Makepeace Thackeray's *Vanity Fair*.

Cinqbars, Lord Charles Ringwood Puny only child of the Earl of Ringwood; his early death signifies the end of Lord Ringwood's title in William Makepeace Thackeray's *The Adventures of Philip on His Way through the World*.

Cinthia Low companion of the bravos and a foil to Rosabella of Corfu in Matthew Lewis's *The Bravo of Venice*.

Cipher X Designer of hula hoops in Ishmael Reed's *The Free-Lance Pallbearers*.

Circe Midwife and housekeeper on the Butler plantation in Danville, Pennsylvania; secretly cares for Pilate Dead and Macon Dead II after their father is killed in Toni Morrison's *Song of Solomon*.

Circumference, Lady Querulous, aggressive noblewoman whose son Lord Tangent dies from an accidental gunshot wound he suffered while attending Llanabba School in Evelyn Waugh's *Decline and Fall*.

Cirillo, Domenico Official physician to the court and personal physician of the Cavaliere and his wife; hanged because he had welcomed the republic's invitation to carry out much-needed reforms in the organization of hospitals and medical care for the poor in Susan Sontag's *The Volcano Lover*.

Cisneros, Damiana One of the women who lives as a spirit or ghost at the Media Luna ranch; helped look after the narrator, Juan Preciado, at birth; serves as a maid and house servant at the ranch in Juan Rulfo's *Pedro Páramo*.

Cissé, Singbin Mara Member of the court of Dankaran Touman; one of the founders of Sundiata in Mema in *Sundiata: An Epic of Old Mali*.

Cissé, Soumaba King of Ghana (Wagadou) and cousin of Moussa Tounkara; grants asylum to Sundiata and his family in *Sundiata: An Epic of Old Mali*.

Cisternas, Antonia de las Beautiful, innocent, impoverished daughter of Elvira de la Cisternas; after Elvira's murder, cut off from her father's family; unaware of Lorenzo de Medina's love, she falls victim to Abbot Ambrosio, who feigns her death and rapes and murders her in a sepulchre, later discovering that she was his sister in Matthew Lewis's *The Monk*.

Cisternas, Beatrice (Bleeding Nun) de las Licentious nun, murdered long ago; as the Bleeding Nun ghost, she haunts Raymond de las Cisternas and foils Agnes de Medina's escape from Lindenberg in Matthew Lewis's *The Monk*.

Cisternas, Elvira (Dalfa) de las Antonia's lowborn but noble-spirited mother; murdered by Abbot Ambrosio (later identified as her son) while preventing Antonia's rape, she reappears as a ghost to predict Antonia's death in Matthew Lewis's *The Monk*.

Cisternas, Raymond de las Marquis who is a virtuous, benevolent relative of Antonia; in love with Agnes; while attempting to elope with his beloved, runs off with the Bleeding Nun instead, in Matthew Gregory Lewis's *The Monk.*

Citizen, The Bigoted leader of the patriotic drinkers in Barney Kiernan's Pub; he throws a biscuit tin at Leopold Bloom in James Joyce's *Ulysses.*

Citizen Barlow African-American young man (late 20s or early 30s); feels guilt since he was responsible for the death of another man; comes to Aunt Ester to have his soul washed by her in August Wilson's *Gem of the Ocean.*

Citizen of Colonus Man who encounters Oedipus near the Furies' grove and orders him to leave the sacred site; asked to tell Theseus, king of nearby Athens, that Oedipus can help him but instead travels to Colonus to confer with its elders in Sophocles' play *Oedipus at Colonus.*

Citrine, Charles (Charlie) Author of the Broadway play *Von Trenck,* which wins a Pulitzer Prize and becomes a successful film; friend of Von Humboldt Fleisher, jilted lover of Renata Koffritz, and seeker of a quiet life through anthroposophy; narrator of Saul Bellow's *Humboldt's Gift.*

Clack, Drusilla Officious, busybody maiden aunt of Rachel Verinder; she tries to save souls by distributing religious tracts and adores the plausible lay preacher Godfrey Ablewhite in Wilkie Collins's *The Moonstone. A Romance.*

Cla-cla Runi's mother; she is killed in W. H. Hudson's *Green Mansions.*

Claggart, Dr. Sympathetic but pessimistic staff psychiatrist who is forced to discharge Bill Plantagenet from City Hospital without having helped him in Malcolm Lowry's *Lunar Caustic.*

Claggart, John (Jemmy Legs) Master-at-arms aboard the *Indomitable* who, upon falsely accusing the young sailor Billy Budd of planning a mutiny, is killed by Budd in Herman Melville's *Billy Budd.*

Claire Daughter of Robert; successful sister of Catherine in David Auburn's *Proof.*

Claire Juliet's cousin who, along with Juliet, is tutored by the young man Saint-Preux, a Swiss commoner; marries a man friendly with Lord Bomston and Saint-Preux, but is later widowed; falls in love with Saint-Preux and marries him after Juliet's death in Jean Jacques Rousseau's *The New Héloïse.*

Claire Sister of Stephen and Rebecca; daughter of Man and Woman; lesbian; and suicidal in Paula Vogel's *The Long Christmas Ride Home.*

Claire Younger sister of Solange; both sisters are maids of the wealthy Madame, for whom they feel both love and resentment; Claire play acts the role of Madame while her sister, Solange, plays the role of Claire while their mistress is absent from the house; her role-reversal shows her hatred of Madame; playing Madame, she insults and abuses Solange (dressed as Claire), as she orders her sister to help her dress; her impersonation shows Madame to be cruel; believes that, in trying to kill Madame, Solange is actually aiming to kill her, Claire; writes an anonymous letter that leads to Monsieur, Madame's paramour, being jailed; fears that Madame will discover their deception, so the maids plan to poison Madame; Claire's plan to give Madame poisoned tea fails; after Madame has departed the house, forces Solange to return to their play and, in the role of Madame, commits suicide by drinking the poisoned tea in Jean Genet's play *The Maids.*

Claire Deceased wife of Konrad Vost and mother of Mirabelle in John Hawkes's *The Passion Artist.*

Claire Discarded mistress of Count Armand de Sacy; courtesan living in forced exile at Bréda in Arna Wendell Bontemps's *Drums at Dusk.*

Claire Syphilitic store owner and wife of Jimmy in Jerry Bumpus's *Anaconda.*

Claire Young, attractive surgeon, who is affianced to Nicholas Marlow; her opened letters to him while he is in Italy serve to confuse the enemy in Eric Ambler's *Cause for Alarm.*

Claire de Bellegarde de Cintré Young widow whose family hopes she will marry a rich man; becomes a nun because her family will not let her marry Christopher Newman in Henry James's *The American.*

Clairval, Madame Wealthy, elderly widow, who is Valancourt's aunt in Ann Radcliffe's *The Mysteries of Udolpho.*

Clamence, Jean-Baptiste Garrulous and narcissistic Parisian lawyer who calls himself a "judge-penitent"; novel's sole controlling voice; fled from the City of Lights and now sits in a squalid bar called Mexico City, a place not unlike Dante's Inferno, located in Amsterdam's wretched sailors' quarter; confesses his past to an acquaintance in the bar, relating that he did nothing when a suicidal woman jumped from a bridge into the Seine and that he has lied to women to gain their affection; seeks to judge himself in Albert Camus's *The Fall.*

Clammidge, Clem (Cousin Clem) Farmhand turned primitive art critic; writes for the *Daily Bugle* in Peter De Vries's *I Hear America Swinging.*

Clammidge, Harry Publisher of the *Picayune Blade* and employer of Chick Swallow in Peter De Vries's *Comfort Me With Apples.*

Clanahan, DeYancey Grandson of Tip Clanahan; defense attorney for Daniel Ponder in Eudora Welty's *The Ponder Heart.*

Clanahan, Tip Friend of Sam Ponder; judge who helps commit Daniel Ponder to an asylum in Jackson, Mississippi, in Eudora Welty's *The Ponder Heart.*

Clancarryl, Lady Camilla Wife of an Irish peer and sister of George Godolphin and Lady Adelina Trelawny, whom she introduces to George Fitz-Edward, her husband's brother, in Charlotte Smith's *Emmeline: The Orphan of the Castle.*

Clancey, William de la Touche Tory sodomite and editor of the anti-American magazine *America* in Gore Vidal's *Burr.*

Clancy Displaced archetypal 1890s police officer in William S. Burroughs's *Exterminator!*

Clancy, Mr. General manager of the Cosmodemonic Telegraph Company; hires Henry Miller to spy on and fire employees in Henry Miller's *Tropic of Capricorn.*

Clancy, Tom Owner of a small inn, the Cat and Bagpipe, near Knaresborough; he tells John Buncle of his cruel landlord, Old Cock, in Thomas Amory's *The Lift of John Buncle, Esq.*

Clandidlem, Lady House guest of the de Courcy family who spreads gossip about Lady Dumbello and Plantagenet Palliser in Anthony Trollope's *The Small House at Allington.*

Clandon-Hartley, Major Herbert Retired, broke British military officer; he avoids his wife's relatives, who are partly responsible for his financial difficulties; he is wrongly suspected by Vadassy of being a spy in Eric Ambler's *Epitaph for a Spy.*

Clandon-Hartley, Maria Dry, austere, Italian-born wife of Major Herbert Clandon-Hartley; having married against her father's wishes, she and her husband have traveled to France in Eric Ambler's *Epitaph for a Spy.*

Clane, John Jester Grandson of Judge Fox Clane and son of Johnny Clane; determined to discover the reason for his father's suicide; loves Sherman Pew in Carson McCullers's *Clock Without Hands.*

Clane, Johnny Son of Judge Fox Clane and father of John Jester Clane; commits suicide after he learns the woman he loves, Joy Little, detests him and loves Nigra Jones in Carson McCullers's *Clock Without Hands.*

Clane, Judge Fox Prejudiced judge and retired statesman whose idea to convince the government to redeem Confederate money leads to Sherman Pew's rebellion and death in Carson McCullers's *Clock Without Hands.*

Clangor, Lady Clara Woman of fashion in William Beckford's *Azemia.*

Clanroyden, Lady See Barbara Dasent.

Clanroyden, Lord See Alexander ("Sandy") Arbuthnot.

Clapp, Mary (Polly) Former servant of the Sedleys who becomes Amelia Sedley's devoted friend in William Makepeace Thackeray's *Vanity Fair.*

Clapp, Mr. Clerk and later landlord to John Sedley in William Makepeace Thackeray's *Vanity Fair.*

Clapp, Mrs. Sedleys' landlady after their loss of fortune requires them to move in William Makepeace Thackeray's *Vanity Fair.*

Clappique, Baron de French merchant, largely a fool, who is also a smuggler and an obsessive gambler at the time of the Communist-Nationalist split in 1927 in Andre Malraux's *Man's Fate.*

Clapsaddle, Captain Daniel Bluff American patriot in Winston Churchill's *Richard Carvel.*

Clapton, Hugh Royalist clergyman and teacher of Johnny Fraser in James Boyd's *Drums.*

Clara Amiable, mature orphaned daughter of Lord Raymond and Perdita; she serves as second mother to the children of Lionel Verney and is one of the three survivors of the plague in Mary Shelley's *The Last Man.*

Clara Clara's daughter and Rosa's clairvoyant sister; foretells her marriage with Esteban Trueb in Isabel Allende's *The House of the Spirits.*

Clara Gentle, high-minded sister of Basil; she disobeys their father by visiting Basil when he is ill; her companionship brings Basil solace and strength in Wilkie Collins's *Basil: A Story of Modern Life.*

Clara Mr. Rochester's third mistress, an honest but uninspiring German girl, whom he sets up in business in Charlotte Brontë's *Jane Eyre.*

Clara Narrator's cousin; bold and determined woman who becomes one of the first female dentists in Cuba; becomes the family's oracle, prescribes painkillers and is the arbiter of fashion; decides to move the mirror—a portal to the world of the dead—from the living room to the dining room, where all could look into it during meals; asks Eulalia from the ghost world to pass a salad bowl to her in the living world; eats the gray lettuce, grows pale, and dies; then is seated at the dinner table in the mirror world of the dead in Maria Elena Llano's "In the Family."

Clara Middle child of the three orphans in the care of Rachel Cooper in Davis Grubb's *The Night of the Hunter.*

Clara Mother of Charles and Susan and wife of Pete; medically and psychologically unstable, demands extra care from those who are close to her in Ann Beattie's *Chilly Scenes of Winter.*

Clara Native American woman who comes to a Montana reservation to care for her bedridden sister Annie George; Clara's relationship with other characters is revealed in the final section of Michael Dorris's *A Yellow Raft in Blue Water.*

Clara Prostitute who befriended Else Crole and appears in the hotel after her death in Graham Greene's *The Confidential Agent.*

Clara, Aunt Thomas Phillips's aunt, a wealthy old woman, who takes care of him financially, sends him to good boarding schools while he is young, lets him visit occasionally when he becomes a sailor, and heaves him all her belongings when she dies in Alan Sillitoe's *Her Victory.*

Clare Black dancing teacher and gigolo whose life is composed of women and drink; he is a confidant of Herbert Gregory and a denizen of the Regina Hotel in Lawrence Durrell's *The Black Book.*

Clare Mother of Ursula; left her husband when Ursula was fifteen in Sandra Scofield's *Beyond Deserving.*

Clare, Ada Beautiful girl, who is John Jarndyce's ward; she falls in love with her cousin, Richard Carstone, whom she eventually marries in Charles Dickens's *Bleak House.*

Clare, Agatha (King) Field's old schoolmate in Isabel Colegate's *Agatha.*

Clare, Angel Clergyman's son and would-be dairyman, who loves and is loved by Tess Durbeyfield; they marry despite her misgivings over her concealed past; when she confesses to him, his intolerance and self-righteousness prevent him from understanding and result in his separation from her; when he realizes his cruelty to Tess, he returns from Brazil to discover that she has been driven by necessity back to her seducer, Alec Stoke-D'Urberville; Clare escapes with Tess for a few days of happiness after she murders Stoke-D'Urberville in Thomas Hardy's *Tess of the D'Urbervilles.*

Clare, Cassius Self-dramatizing father of five; he is married first to Catherine and then to Flavia; he pretends suicide and then suffers a heart attack that resembles his previous drugged state in Ivy Compton-Burnett's *The Present and the Past.*

Clare, Catherine Elton Scrope's sister and Cassius's divorced wife; she returns to get to know her sons, Fabian and Guy, and takes them away with her when Cassius dies in Ivy Compton-Burnett's *The Present and the Past.*

Clare, Cuthbert Angel Clare's conventional clergyman brother who eventually marries Mercy Chant; like Felix Clare, he snobbishly disapproves of Angel's marriage to Tess Durbeyfield in Thomas Hardy's *Tess of the D'Urbervilles.*

Clare, Edward, Lord Tory member of the House of Lords who shows Jenny Rastall about the House, abuses his privilege to claim travel expenses on behalf of charity, and is removed from his board position by Reginald Swaffield in C. P. Snow's *In Their Wisdom.*

Clare, Fabian Cassius's eldest son, whose mother, Catherine, left when he was four years old; he is an angry boy in Ivy Compton-Burnett's *The Present and the Past.*

Clare, Felix Angel Clare's conventional elder brother, a clergyman like his father; he disapproves of Angel's marriage to Tess Durbeyfield in Thomas Hardy's *Tess of the D'Urbervilles.*

Clare, Flavia Present wife of Cassius and the stepmother of Fabian and Guy and the mother of Henry, Megan and Tobias; she treats the children equally, and her friendship with her predecessor, Catherine Clare, makes Cassius jealous in Ivy Compton-Burnett's *The Present and the Past.*

Clare, Francis Eccentric widower neighbor and friend of Andrew Vanstone; he is constantly descanting on the worthlessness of his son, Frank, whom he dispatches to China to earn a living in Wilkie Collins's *No Name.*

Clare, Frank Lazy, selfish lover of Magdalen Vanstone, whom he jilts when he learns that she has lost her inheritance in Wilkie Collins's *No Name.*

Clare, Guy Fabian's full brother, who cannot bear to be parted from him but who loves Flavia Clare as the only mother he has known in Ivy Compton-Burnett's *The Present and the Past.*

Clare, Henry Closest child to Megan in age; he is a son who does not glorify his father even after Cassius's death in Ivy Compton-Burnett's *The Present and the Past.*

Clare, James Angel Clare's father, a clergyman, who hoped his son would follow the same occupation; he represents those in society who are well-meaning but narrow-minded; when Tess (Durbeyfield) walks over fifteen miles to visit him for financial help, thoughts of his stern goodness intimidate her and she returns home in Thomas Hardy's *Tess of the D'Urbervilles.*

Clare, Megan Cassius's seven-year-old daughter; she is thoughtful like Fabian and insightful in Ivy Compton-Burnett's *The Present and the Past.*

Clare, Mother Member of the Anglican Benedictine convent; she appears surprisingly to assist Dora Greenfield in rescuing Catherine Fawley from drowning in Iris Murdoch's *The Bell.*

Clare, Mr. Cassius's father, who says he loved Cassius best in Ivy Compton-Burnett's *The Present and the Past.*

Clare, Mr. Clergyman uncle of Alick Keith; he brings about Rachel Curtis's reconciliation with the Church in Charlotte Yonge's *The Clever Woman of the Family.*

Clare, Mr. Renowned and adored poet, who retires to Ferdinando Falkland's part of England; he takes a liking to Falkland, upsetting Barnabas Tyrrel; he warns Falkland against his too great love of honor and urges him to reconcile with Tyrrel; he makes Falkland the executor of his will, upsetting Tyrrel even more in William Godwin's *Caleb Williams.*

Clare, Mrs. Angel Clare's mother, a good woman, complacent in her ignorance of danger to her son's wife, Tess (Durbeyfield), in Thomas Hardy's *Tess of the D'Urbervilles.*

Clare, Tobias (Toby) Three-year-old boy who pretends to be a minister at the mole's funeral; he is said to have the sense of humor of a savage in Ivy Compton-Burnett's *The Present and the Past.*

Clarence European who disembarks in an unnamed African country as an adventurer or escapee from past troubles; seen as financially destitute from his gambling; already evicted from a colonists' hotel and now faces being turned out by an African innkeeper; descends into a sexual world in which he finds that he has been sold as a sexual slave, a breeding stud service in a harem controlled by a sterile African chief in Camara Laye's *The Radiance of the King.*

Clarence (Amyas le Poulet) Sixth-century associate of Hank Morgan; with Morgan's help, publishes a newspaper in Samuel Langhorne Clemens's *A Connecticut Yankee in King Arthur's Court.*

Clarence (the ghost) Sombre, thin man; he is one of Ida Arnold's lovers in Graham Greene's *Brighton Rock.*

Clarence, George, Duke of Brother of Richard III; condemned to the Tower based on a prophecy created by Richard, whom Clarence trusts; troubled by dreams of those he has killed; murdered by Richard's assassins despite his appeals to their humanity in William Shakespeare's play *Richard III.*

Clarence, Thomas, Duke of Son of Henry IV; gathers with Henry IV, the Earl of Warwick, and his brother Humphrey of Gloucester because of the king's ill health; reveals to Henry that Prince Hal is in London with his tavern friends; when Henry has a fit of apoplexy, fears that Henry will soon succumb to his illness; additionally fears the death of Henry because of bad omens and the superstition of the people; gathers with his brothers to mourn for his father and finds the Lord Chief Justice and Warwick worrying about the future under King Henry V; says the Lord Chief Justice will have to speak kindly of Falstaff now that Prince Hal has become the king; reassured by Henry V that his rule will be just and free from prodigality in William Shakespeare's play *Henry IV, Part Two;* sent with the counsel of English nobles to negotiate the terms of the Treaty of Troyes in William Shakespeare's play *Henry V.*

Clarendon See Hyde, Edward, Earl of Clarendon.

Clarendon, Isabel Wealthy young widow, whose husband has cruelly provided in his will that she must bring up his illegitimate daughter and then turn over the estate to her when she comes of age; she and Bernard Kingcote become lovers but later disagree; ultimately she retains her estate and marries her old lover, Robert Asquith, in George Gissing's *Isabel Clarendon.*

Clarendon, Mr. Husband of Isabel and father of the illegitimate Ada Warren; he mistreats Isabel and injures her after his death by a will which requires her to bring up Ada and which limits her interest in his property to Ada's minority in George Gissing's *Isabel Clarendon.*

Clarenthia Daughter of Turpius and an heiress; she is the best friend of Scipiana and suffers like her, being abducted and seduced by her father; she is loved by Hannibal but loves Lysander in Jane Barker's *Exilius; or, The Banish'd Roman.*

Claret Captain of the *Neversink* in Herman Melville's *White-Jacket.*

Clarice Friend of the narrator, Seline Davis; works at the same dress alteration shop in Jean Rhys's "Let Them Call It Jazz."

Clarice Woman with whom Steven Leadbitter, the hireling, lived for three years and from whom he disengages himself before beginning to chauffeur Lady Franklin and embarking on the tales of family life which entrap him in L. P. Hartley's *The Hireling.*

Clarice Helpful and unintimidating young maid who is assigned to Mrs. de Winter in Dapne Du Maurier's *Rebecca.*

Clarice Illegitimate daughter of Arthur Wiatte, niece of Euphemia Lorimer, and fiancée of Clithero Edny in Charles Brockden Brown's *Edgar Huntly.*

Clarice, Lady Clarice Silly and condescending woman, who marries a man she dislikes and is unhappy in Caroline Norton's *The Wife and Woman's Reward.*

Claridge, Stormy Girlfriend of Ezra Lyttle; uses sex to further her career in Peter Gent's *Texas Celebrity Turkey Trot.*

Clarie See Henderson, Clarence.

Clarimundo, Professor Earns his living in the regular school system and also teaches private classes to well-to-do youngsters; represents the class of society between the haves and have-nots in Erico Verissimo's *Crossroads.*

Clarinau, Calista, Countess of Clarinau Octavio's sister and the unwilling wife of an old Spanish count; she falls in love with Philander, becomes pregnant, and attempts to elope, wounding Clarinau; she flees to a convent, where she takes holy orders when she learns of Philander's infidelity in Aphra Behn's *Love Letters Between a Nobleman and His Sister.*

Clarinau, Count of Calista's jealous, elderly husband, who has killed his first wife; after Calista and Philander elope, he is killed by Octavio, whom he mistakes for Philander in his attempt at revenge in Aphra Behn's *Love Letters Between a Nobleman and His Sister.*

Clarinda, Lady One of Major Fitz-David's many woman friends; the later employer of Sara Macallan's maid, Phoebe, she relays important information to Valeria Macallan in Wilkie Collins's *The Law and the Lady.*

Clarissa Mira's friend in graduate school; abandons her traditional marriage for a lesbian relationship in Marilyn French's *The Women's Room.*

Clarissa Susie's best friend on earth before Susie Salmon's rape and murder at the age of 14; admired by Susie because Clarissa is allowed to do things Susie is not, like wearing platform shoes and smoking; has a boyfriend named Brian in Alice Sebold's *The Lovely Bones.*

Clarisse Young Creole woman who is the love interest of her godmother's son Alcée Laballière; initially spurns Alcée's advances because of his unconventional behavior; goes to the Acadian ball, which Alcée is attending, to profess her love and to bring him home in Kate Chopin's "At the 'Cadian Ball."

Clarisse Young Creole woman, wife of Alcée Laballière; goes on a trip with her children and leaves Alcée at home; unaware that Alcée has a sexual encounter with his former romantic interest, Calixta, while she is away in Kate Chopin's "The Storm."

Clark, Clara Rice University graduate student and lover of Jim Carpenter in Larry McMurtry's *Moving On.*

Clark, G. S. Modern Languages scholar and Cambridge college fellow; a fierce conservative and anti-communist, he gives hostile testimony against Donald Howard in C. P. Snow's *The Affair.* The new Master of the Cambridge college, he pesters Charles Eliot with talk about college matters at the party given by Charles's parents in *The Sleep of Reason.* He wants to deliver the eulogy for Sir Francis Getliffe but yields the honor to Arthur Brown in *Last Things.*

Clark, Howard Farmer in Zebulon County, Iowa; father of sons Loren and Jess Clark; best friend, cohort, and neighbor of Laurence Cook; pretends to arrange reconciliation between Rose, Ginny, and their father, but instead orchestrates a public charge of disloyalty against the two older daughters in Jane Smiley's *A Thousand Acres.*

Clark, Jess Prodigal son of Harold and Verna Clark, who returns to Cabot, Iowa, after spending thirteen years in Vancouver, British Columbia, to escape the draft; sometime Buddhist; imaginative dreamer of alternative farming techniques and products; lover of both Ginny Cook Smith and Rose Cook Lewis; lives with Rose Lewis after her husband, Pete, dies in Jane Smiley's *A Thousand Acres.*

Clark, John CIA field officer who assists in planning and execution of joint CIA and military operations against drug cartels in Colombia; meets Jack Ryan after the passing of their common mentor, James Greer; returns to Colombia to kill or capture intelligence officer turned drug kingpin Felix Cortez; talks James Cutter into committing suicide; and recruits Domingo Chavez for CIA in Tom Clancy's *Clear and Present Danger.* Also appears in *Without Remorse* and *Rainbow Six.*

Clark, Loren Less glamorous son of Harold and Verna Clark, who stays home to help his father farm after Jess moves to Vancouver, British Columbia, during the Vietnam War; imitates his father in mannerisms and habits but not in attitude; friend and neighbor of Ginny Cook Smith and Rose Cook Lewis in Jane Smiley's *A Thousand Acres.*

Clark, Major Jimmy British officer who pays attention to Sarah Layton while she is visiting her uncle and aunt, Arthur and Fenny Grace, in Calcutta; Sarah becomes pregnant from their single sexual encounter in Paul Scott's *The Towers of Silence.*

Clark, Mr. Stout man who works at the wharves; he sends Joe to find Walter Gay for the lost Florence Dombey in Charles Dickens's *Dombey and Son.*

Clark, Nobby Impudent and charming Cockney private who teams up with Roger Henderson when they are stranded in France in W. Somerset Maugham's *The Hour Before the Dawn.*

Clark, Paul Suave rival of Homer Zigler for the affections of Frances Harbach in Clyde Brion Davis's *The Great American Novel.*

Clark, Reverend Young minister from Westbury who presides over Reverend Hooper's deathbed to pray for him; encourages Hooper to shed the black veil before his death, but Hooper shocks him (and everyone else present) with his strength as he refuses to remove the veil in Nathaniel Hawthorne's "The Minister's Black Veil."

Clark, Richard Lame young London clerk, who is rescued from his work by M'Kay and Mark Rutherford to become a shorthand newspaper reporter in Mark Rutherford's *Mark Rutherford's Deliverance.*

Clark, Robert (Bob, David Hawke) Writer and teacher whom Vridar Hunter meets in New York in Vardis Fisher's *No Villain Need Be;* also appears as David Hawke in *Orphans in Gethsemane.*

Clark, Salvatore (Friday, Sal) Bugler for G Company; shares Andy Anderson's and Robert E. Lee Prewitt's love of the blues in James Jones's *From Here to Eternity.*

Clark, Sam Owner of a hardware store and friend of Will Kennicott in Sinclair Lewis's *Main Street.*

Clark, Seward Trewlove Unitarian minister from California who predicts a murder aboard ship in Conrad Aiken's *Blue Voyage.*

Clarke Overseer in Kirby and John's mill in Rebecca Harding Davis's *Life in the Iron Mills.*

Clarke, Betty Poor friend of John Brown's wife; she is assisted as a result of Bryan Perdue's concern in Thomas Holcroft's *The Memoirs of Bryan Perdue.*

Clarke, Daniel See Lester, Geoffrey.

Clarke, Dolly Trevor's complicit secretary who threw Angelica out the window to her death in Carlos Fuentes's *The Hydra Head.*

Clarke, Dorothy Senile neighbor of the Martins; wife of Edward; actual murderer of Robert's daughter Amber and wife, Gwen, in Minette Walters's *The Sculptress.*

Clarke, Edward Neighbor of the Martins; has affair with both Robert Martin and his daughter, accused murderer Olive Martin; husband of senile wife, Dorothy, the actual murderer of both Olive's mother, Gwen, and sister, Amber, in Minette Walters's *The Sculptress.*

Clarke, Franklin Sir Carmichael's brother and prospective heir in Agatha Christie's *The A.B.C. Murders.*

Clarke, Helen Only friend of Mary Katherine, Constance, and Julian Blackwood and only regular visitor to the family home in Shirley Jackson's *We Have Always Lived in the Castle.*

Clarke, Henry Capable certified public accountant with Glymmer, Read who is relatively unaffected by the firm's bankruptcy in Nathan Asch's *The Office.*

Clarke, Jim Husband of Helen Clarke in Shirley Jackson's *We Have Always Lived in the Castle.*

Clarke, Lady Charlotte Wife of Sir Carmichael; she hires Hercule Poirot to investigate her husband's death in Agatha Christie's *The A.B.C. Murders.*

Clarke, Maxwell E. Principal of Calvin Coolidge High School; manages to stay in his office all day, except for a rare public appearance to give a speech on lofty ideals in Bel Kaufman's *Up the Down Staircase.*

Clarke, Mr. Honest carpenter, who is mistakenly accused of theft by Hugh Trevor, later restores Hugh to health, and finally is a recipient of Hugh's patronage in Thomas Holcroft's *The Adventures of Hugh Trevor.*

Clarke, Mrs. Beloved housekeeper for Anna St. Ives's mother during her life and aunt to Peggy and Mr. Webb in Thomas Holcroft's *Anna St. Ives.*

Clarke, Sir Carmichael Third murder victim in Agatha Christie's *The A.B.C. Murders.*

Clarke, St. John Immensely popular novelist of waning prestige who employs Mark Members as secretary in Anthony Powell's *A Buyer's Market.* He fires Members, replacing him with Quiggin, who converts him to Marxism, and later with Guggenbühl, who converts him to Trotskyism, in *The Acceptance World.* He is abandoned by Guggenbühl in *At Lady Molly's.* He backslides politically; at his death he leaves his money to Lord Erridge in *Casanova's Chinese Restaurant.* His books have resisted revival, but he is the subject of a TV documentary in *Hearing Secret Harmonies.*

Clarke, Thomas Attorney, the nephew of Captain Crowe and the godson of Sir Launcelot Greaves; he fears his uncle is losing his mind imitating Sir Launcelot; he flirts with Dolly Cowslip and eventually marries her in Tobias Smollett's *The Adventures of Sir Launcelot Greaves.*

Clark-Matthew, Archie Boisterous nephew of Lady Spencer; well groomed and superior-acting, he gets somewhat drunk and makes crude remarks at the ball in Rosamond Lehmann's *Invitation to the Waltz.*

Clarkson, Mr. Importunate, offensively familiar moneylender, who hounds Phineas Finn to pay up punctually on a bill he had signed as a favor to Lawrence Fitzgibbon in Anthony Trollope's *Phineas Finn.*

Claro, António Supporting actor in forgettable films who seeks revenge and the destruction of his exact double after being pursued and threatened by Senhor Afonso in José Saramago's *The Double.*

Claro, Helena Wife of António Claro who accepts Tertuliano Máximo Afonso as her husband after the men's mutual deceit brings the death of António Claro in José Saramago's *The Double.*

Claros, Colonel Juan Lean and considerate yet stubborn and proud header of the Cape Creux forces who are to aid in the attack on Rosas Bay in C. S. Forester's *Ship of the Line.*

Clarriker, Mr. Manager of a financial house where Herbert Pocket is given a job in Charles Dickens's *Great Expectations.*

Clasby, Jud Hunter, trapper, and instigator of the Indian massacre in Jessamyn West's *The Massacre at Fall Creek.*

Claude, Mlle. Prostitute with whom Henry Miller briefly thinks he is in love in Henry Miller's *Tropic of Cancer.*

Claude, Sir Refined but indecisive aristocrat who marries Ida Farange and later has an affair with Miss Overmore; becomes a surrogate father and object of adolescent affection to Ida's daughter, Maisie; plans to form a family with Miss Overmore and Maisie but is repudiated by the latter in Henry James's "What Maisie Knew."

Claudette, Madame Elderly casino chips beggar and former prostitute in Jorge Amado's *Doña Flor and Her Two Husbands.*

Claudia Child vampire whom Louis treats as a daughter; destroyed by Lestat in Anne Rice's *Interview with the Vampire.*

Claudine Fifteen-year-old who lives in a small village on the northern edge of Burgundy, France; seen as witty and intelligent; attends an all-girls school, where she forms lesbian relationships in Colette's *Claudine at School.*

Claudio Governor (tutor) to Hippolito on his travels; after Hippolito returns from the masked ball, Claudio ventures out in Don Lorenzo's costume and is rescued from attack by

Aurelian; his injuries allow Hippolito to postpone traveling in William Congreve's *Incognita.*

Claudio Hired assassin who kills his master by mistake in Charlotte Dacre's *The Libertine.*

Claudio Isabella's brother; young man who is sentenced to death for bringing pregnancy upon an unwed woman, even though he is engaged to her, in William Shakespeare's play *Measure for Measure.*

Claudio Young soldier in Don Pedro's company and Benedick's companion; falls in love with Hero, young daughter of Leonato; falsely accuses Hero of promiscuity; believes Hero to be dead; vows to marry her cousin in recompense but eventually marries the 'revived' Hero in William Shakespeare's play *Much Ado About Nothing.*

Claudius King of Denmark and, unbeknownst to his subjects, a villain; brother of King Hamlet, whom he poisoned; prizes both the Crown and Queen Gertrude; initially wins over almost everyone in court with his charm and cunning; later is exposed to a watchful few by *The Mousetrap,* a play that recreates his crimes; recognizes his sins in the eyes of heaven yet shows no scruples when it comes to dealing with threats to the throne, notably Hamlet; plots along with Laertes to kill the prince with treachery; accidentally kills Gertrude with a poisoned drink before finally being struck down by the avenging Prince Hamlet in William Shakespeare's play *Hamlet.*

Claudius Murderer of his brother King Hamlet and usurper of his throne; now husband to Gertrude and stepfather to Prince Hamlet in Tom Stoppard's play *Rosencrantz and Guildenstern Are Dead.*

Claudius Lame, stuttering historian and stepgrandson of Augustus; he is virtually ignored by all until he is chosen to succeed Caligula as emperor in Robert Graves's *I, Claudius.* He is a trepid Roman emperor who intends, following initial reforms, to restore the Republic but is prevented by successive crises from doing so; he eventually surrenders power to his wife and niece, Agrippinilla, dies at her hands, and is subsequently deified in *Claudius, the God and His Wife Messalina.*

Claudius, Lucius Wealthy Roman patrician and close friend of Gordianus, a Roman private investigator; a source of much gossip about the Roman ruling class; on his death leaves Gordianus his farm north of Rome in Steven Saylor's *Catalina's Riddle.*

Clausen Sexually frustrated murderer and suicide in Henry Miller's *Tropic of Capricorn.*

Clausen, Anna Sister-in-law of Orin Clausen and neighbor of Chris Van Eenanain and Ellen Strohe in Larry Woiwode's *What I'm Going to Do, I Think.*

Clausen, Orin Brother-in-law of Anna Clausen and Michigan-woods neighbor of Chris Van Eenanam and Ellen Strohe in Larry Woiwode's *What I'm Going to Do, I Think.*

Claverhouse, Janet Sigismund's aged mother, who is devoted to him and his writing in Ivy Compton-Burnett's *Dolores.*

Claverhouse, Sigismund Dramatist of genius who lectures at the women's college that Dolores Hutton attends; he is the love of Dolores's life whom she gives up for her friend Perdita Kingsford and for the sake of Dolores's father in Ivy Compton-Burnett's *Dolores.*

Clavering Cultivated, well-known statesman; he loves Mary, influences her education, and marries her when his wife dies; he ignores public gossip and continues his political career in Caroline Norton's *The Wife and Woman's Reward.*

Clavering, Captain Archibald Lazy brother of Sir Hugh and cousin of Harry; he devotes his energies to horse racing and the pursuit of Lady Ongar, whom he wants to marry for her money; he drowns off Heligoland in a stormy sea in Anthony Trollope's *The Claverings.*

Clavering, Fanny Younger daughter of the Reverend Henry Clavering; she falls in love with the curate, Samuel Saul, and despite initial disapproval from her father she marries him in Anthony Trollope's *The Claverings.*

Clavering, Francis Young son of Sir Francis and Lady Clavering, who is devoted to him in William Makepeace Thackeray's *The History of Pendennis.*

Clavering, Harry Impulsive, pliable son of the rector of Clavering parish; having been jilted by Julia Brabazon (now Lady Ongar), he falls in love with Florence Burton, but when Lady Ongar returns a wealthy widow he succumbs to her attractions; repentant at last, he admits his folly, and Florence forgives him; he becomes heir to the Clavering property after the accidental deaths of Sir Hugh and Archibald Clavering in Anthony Trollope's *The Claverings.*

Clavering, Henry Uncle of Sir Hugh and Archibald Clavering; the benign rector of Clavering parish, he is amiable in all things except when his curate, Mr. Saul, dares to fall in love with Henry's beloved daughter Fanny; after opposing the match, he at last relents; he becomes the twelfth baronet and resigns the living to Mr. Saul after the deaths of his nephews in Anthony Trollope's *The Claverings.*

Clavering, Henry Ritchie (Le Roy Robbins) Englishman who secretly marries Mary Leavenworth in Anna Katharine Green's *The Leavenworth Case.*

Clavering, Hughy Sickly young son and heir and only living child of Sir Hugh Clavering; his death destroys any vestige of satisfaction left in his parents' marriage in Anthony Trollope's *The Claverings.*

Clavering, Lady Good-natured and long-suffering wife to Sir Francis; the reappearance as Colonel Altamont of her presumed-dead first husband threatens her happiness, as does Sir Francis's gambling in William Makepeace Thackeray's *The History of Pendennis.*

Clavering, Lady Hermione Brabazon Elder sister of Julia Brabazon (Lady Ongar); she is abused and neglected by her husband, Sir Hugh Clavering, but is desperate when he is drowned in Anthony Trollope's *The Claverings.*

Clavering, Lee (Clavey) New York journalist and playwright who offers his lover Countess Marie Zattiany a return to youthful passion in Gertrude Atherton's *Black Oxen.*

Clavering, Lucretia Heiress of Miles St. John; her tutoring in evil by Olivier Dalibard leads to the loss of her inheritance and then to a career of crime in the company of his son, Gabriel Varney, in Edward Bulwer-Lytton's *Lucretia.*

Clavering, Mary Elder daughter of the Reverend Henry Clavering; she falls in love with the Reverend Edward Fielding and marries him in Anthony Trollope's *The Claverings.*

Clavering, Mrs. Henry Sweet-natured mother of Mary, Fanny, and Harry and wife of the rector; when Fanny confides Mr. Saul's declaration of love, her mother mediates between her and her father's wrath; she is also instrumental in bringing Harry Clavering and Florence Burton back together in Anthony Trollope's *The Claverings.*

Clavering, Sir Francis Impecunious baronet and Member of Parliament, whose marriage to the rich Lady Clavering is threatened by the reappearance of her first husband in William Makepeace Thackeray's *The History of Pendennis.*

Clavering, Sir Hugh Eleventh baronet, totally selfish and tyrannical in his household; he bullies his frightened wife until he drowns off Heligoland during a fishing trip in Anthony Trollope's *The Claverings.*

Clavis, Christophers Chief astronomer of the Papal College in Rome; sides with Galileo regarding the positions of the Sun and Earth in the solar system in Bertolt Brecht's play *Galileo.*

Clawson, Clif Medical school roommate of Martin Arrowsmith; drops out of school and becomes an automobile salesman in Sinclair Lewis's *Arrowsmith.*

Clay First-person protagonist who narrates the story in the present tense; young student at Camden College in New Hampshire (based on Bennington College, where the author attended as an undergraduate and wrote the first draft of this novel); returns home to Los Angeles for the holiday break, where he crosses paths with many of his old friends while going to parties, concerts, and trendy L.A. spots; bisexual and has sex with an unnamed man, yet still hopes to have a more serious relationship with Blair, a high school girlfriend; finds that his friend Julian is working as a gay prostitute for a drug dealer he owes money to in Bret Easton Ellis's *Less Than Zero;* also appears in and narrates a chapter in Ellis's second novel *The Rules of Attraction;* makes an appearance as a metacharacter in Ellis's *Luna Park.*

Clay First lieutenant aboard the *Justinian* in C. S. Forester's *Mr. Midshipman Hornblower.*

Clay, Ambrose Valentine Uncle of Violet Clay; dabbles at writing, is briefly married to Carol Gruber, and shoots himself in Gail Godwin's *Violet Clay.*

Clay, Catherine South Carolinian and former lover of Chester Hunnicutt Pomeroy; produces a Panamanian marriage certificate showing her marriage to Pomeroy in Thomas McGuane's *Panama.*

Clay, Christine (Gotobed) Film actress found murdered at a seashore retreat in Josephine Tey's *A Shilling for Candles.*

Clay, Collis Unsuccessful suitor of Rosemary Hoyt in F. Scott Fitzgerald's *Tender Is the Night.*

Clay, Dr. Somewhat unctuous rector of the parish at Knowl in J. Sheridan Le Fanu's *Uncle Silas.*

Clay, Father Lonely, homesick Catholic priest in Bamba with whom Henry Scobie stays during his investigation of Dicky Pemberton's suicide in Graham Greene's *The Heart of the Matter.*

Clay, Henry Judge; the mayor of the town 30 years before; dies in Mary McGarry Morris's *Songs in Ordinary Time.*

Clay, John Murderer, thief, and elusive conman long sought by Scotland Yard; grandson of a royal duke; intent on robbing the bank of Mr. Merryweather with the use of the Red-headed League in Sir Arthur Conan Doyle's "The Red-headed League."

Clay, Penelope Ingratiating widowed daughter of Sir Walter Elliot's agent; she establishes herself as a necessary member of the Elliot household, accompanying them to Bath; Elizabeth Elliot ridicules the warning that she might become Lady Elliot, pointing out her freckles and projecting tooth; William Elliot neutralizes the threat by setting her up as his mistress, but her cajoling him into making her his wife is not improbable at the end of Jane Austen's *Persuasion.*

Clay, Robert Adventurer and self-taught engineer in charge of an iron-mining operation in Olancho; enamored of socialite Alice Langham in Richard Harding Davis's *Soldiers of Fortune.*

Clay, Violet Isabel Aspiring artist who leaves her unsatisfactory work in New York as an illustrator of gothic novels to work seriously on her painting in an isolated cabin; narrator of Gail Godwin's *Violet Clay.*

Claybody, Charles Johnson Son of Lord Claybody; his capture of Lord Lamancha reveals the scheme and elicits a laugh and admiration for Lamancha's success in John Buchan's *John Macnab.*

Claybody, Lady Romantic with social ambitions; she enjoys Haripol for its ancient traditions but also exhibits warmth and the ability to laugh at herself during the recovery of her dog, Wee Roguie, in John Buchan's *John Macnab.*

Claybody, Lord Johnson Wealthy, shrewd Scot, owner of Haripol; he exhibits humor and generosity at the unmasking of "John Macnab" in John Buchan's *John Macnab.*

Clayhanger, Clara Pert, vivacious, youngest sister of Edwin Clayhanger; she declines into the fecund, assenting wife of Albert Benbow in Arnold Bennett's *Clayhanger.* A loyal wife, she becomes a prying, embittered sister; her youthful potential has been erased in her submissive wifehood in *These Twain.*

Clayhanger, Darius Successful Bursley printer but an inarticulate, dictatorial father, haunted by his childhood trauma of being driven into the workhouse; his hidden love for and incomprehension of his son, Edwin, and his lingering death form the context of Edwin's conflicts and development in Arnold Bennett's *Clayhanger.*

Clayhanger, Edwin (Teddy) Intelligent, introspective, compassionate, diffident son; his daily conflicts with his tyrannical father, Darius, and his awkwardness with his sisters, aunt, and neighbors provoke his ingenuous astonishment at human behaviour and his constant efforts to adjust his perspective during his coming of age and first love in Arnold Bennett's *Clayhanger.* He attracts Hilda Lessways by his spontaneously stated insights and makes her realize her true love after the disaster of her bigamous marriage to George Cannon in *Hilda Lessways.* His capacity to view daily life with wonder allows him to adjust and to weather the frictions within his marriage and with his relatives in *These Twain.*

Clayhanger, Maggie Older, placid sister of Edwin Clayhanger; she spends her early years as housekeeper for her widowed father and, following his death, keeps house for her brother, Edwin, until his marriage in Arnold Bennett's *Clayhanger.* Maggie's long years of quiet servitude to her relatives are sporadically interrupted with flashes of independent thinking which finally win her brother's respect in *These Twain.*

Claymore, Imogen Grantley Well-placed, vain, and musically unaccomplished young woman whom Oliver unsuccessfully pursues in William Golding's *The Pyramid.*

Claymore, Norman Socially pretentious and arrogant owner of Stilbourne's newspaper; he gets one of the leads opposite his wife in the town opera in William Golding's *The Pyramid.*

Claypole, Noah (Morris Bolter) Big, large-headed charity boy, who works for Mr. Sowerberry; he is knocked down by Oliver Twist when he insults Oliver's mother and later runs off with Charlotte to London, where he spies on Nancy for Fagin in Charles Dickens's *Oliver Twist.*

Claypole, Tom Gossipy, stupid son of a baronet; he marries Flora Warrington in William Makepeace Thackeray's *The Virginians.*

Claythorne, Vera Governess who once deliberately allowed a child to drown; she hangs herself in Agatha Christie's *And Then There Were None.*

Clayton, Anne Owner, with her brother Edward Clayton, of Magnolia Grove plantation; institutes educational and disciplinary reforms on the plantation, which arouse the ire of her neighbors, in Harriet Beecher Stowe's *Dred.*

Clayton, Captain Yorke Zealous joint resident magistrate for several Irish counties who hunts down the law breakers; he marries Edith Jones after she nurses him when he has been shot in Anthony Trollope's *The Landleaguers.*

Clayton, Edward Son of Judge Clayton and fiancé of Nina Gordon; sides increasingly with the abolitionists until he is forced to give up the plantation system and move to Canada with his emancipated slaves in Harriet Beecher Stowe's *Dred.*

Clayton, Gabriel Dipsomaniac sculptor friend of Wilfred Barclay and Johnny St. John John in William Golding's *The Paper Men.*

Clayton, Judge Father of Edward and Anne Clayton; as a North Carolina superior court judge, he is forced to overturn a ruling that Edward won ensuring humane treatment of slaves in Harriet Beecher Stowe's *Dred.*

Clayton, Miss Headmistress of the school Agatha King attends; she writes progress reports to Agatha's father, Orlando King, in Isabel Colegate's *Orlando at the Brazen Threshold.*

Clayton, Mr. Former lover of Mrs. Booby, prior to her marriage; his suit having been thwarted by her mother, he is now married to someone else in Richard Graves's *The Spiritual Quixote.*

Clayton, Mrs. Ambitious mother of Sir George Clayton; upon his receiving an additional large inheritance which expands his prospects, she precipitates Emily Montague's decision to break the arrangement for the proposed marriage to him in Frances Brooke's *The History of Emily Montague.*

Clayton, Sir George Moneyed, "civil, attentive and dull" English baronet in Quebec to honor the arrangements made for his marriage to Emily Montague by his mother and Emily's now-deceased guardian uncle in Frances Brooke's *The History of Emily Montague.*

Clayton, Sir Robert Roxana's financial adviser, who assists her in investing her money in Daniel Defoe's *The Fortunate Mistress.*

Clayton, Tom Union worker who tells the taxi drivers about his experience in an unsuccessful strike in Philadelphia; real name is Clancy, a spy for the owners and a union breaker in Clifford Odets's play *Waiting for Lefty.*

Cléante Orgon's wise brother-in-law; easily sees through Tartuffe's hypocrisy and helps Orgon's family members turn the conman out of the house in Molière's play *Tartuffe.*

Cleanthe Lady of about 50 who behaves like a 15-year-old and who has a discussion with Cleora in which she abuses (in polite terms) Hillario in Francis Coventry's *The History of Pompey the Little.*

Cleary, Sean Unprincipled, self-serving director of guidance for the public schools of Pequot; aids Wissey Jones's attempt to purchase a child genius for experimental research in John Hersey's *The Child Buyer.*

Cleave, Richard (Dick, Philip Deaderick) Captain of the 65th Virginia Infantry under General Jackson; temporarily disgraced and forced to fight under an assumed name, but restored to command; marries Judith Cary after heroic action and revelation of a rival's plotting; appears in Mary Johnston's *The Long Roll* and *Cease Firing.*

Cleaver, Fanny (Jenny Wren) Crippled, shrewish girl, who is a dolls' dressmaker and looks after her drunken father; she rents a room to Lizzie Hexam, is a friend of Riah's, and is instrumental in divining that the dying Eugene Wrayburn wishes to marry Lizzie Hexam in Charles Dickens's *Our Mutual Friend.*

Clegg, Arthur Property owner whose house is the ob-ject of a disputed real-estate transaction, through which Michael Cullen obtains funds to go to London in Alan Sillitoe's *A Start in Life.*

Clegg, Ferdinand Young working-class man who wins a fortune in a football pool, kidnaps Miranda Grey, and holds her prisoner in a cottage basement; his narration reveals the narrowness and deadness of his inner life, epitomized by his butterfly collection and his pathetic attempts to make Miranda fail in love with him in John Fowles's *The Collector.*

Clegg, Harry Barbara Vaughan's lover, an archaeologist working at the Dead Sea excavation sites; his hoped-for marriage to the Roman Catholic Barbara awaits the annulment of his previous marriage to his long-divorced wife in Muriel Spark's *The Mandlebaum Gate.*

Clegg, Harry C. Newspaper reporter in Thomas Berger's *Killing Time.*

Clegg, Hattie Old-maid neighbor of the Ganchions who moves to Houston in William Goyen's *The House of Breath.*

Clegg, Hiram Brunist and eventually bishop of Randolph Junction in Robett Coover's *The Origin of the Brunists.*

Clegg, Humphrey Forty-five-year-old divorced civil servant with the British Foreign and Commonwealth Office; he invites Anthony Keating to go to Wallacia to escort Jane Murray home and also to take and receive some secret papers in Margaret Drabble's *The Ice Age.*

Clegg, Sylvia Ex-wife of Humphrey Clegg, whom she divorced after discovering he was a solitary transvestite in Margaret Drabble's *The Ice Age.*

Clegthorpe, Sam Agnostic who is absurdly named archbishop of Canterbury; also a radical liberal spokesman for agriculture; shot as one of the acrobatic Jumpers at the end of the action in Tom Stoppard's *Jumpers.*

Clelia Extremely beautiful niece of Publius Scipio and one of the heroines of Jane Barker's *Exilius; or, The Banish'd Roman.*

Clellon, Donald First fiancé of Sarah Grimes Wilson; lies about his age and background, causing the engagement to be broken in Richard Yates's *Easter Parade.*

Clem One of the seven dwarfs who wash windows, make Chinese baby food, and live with Snow White in Donald Barthelme's *Snow White.*

Clematis (Clem) Mongrel dog of Genesis; his antics embarrass William Baxter in Booth Tarkington's *Seventeen.*

Clemence Black street woman who assists Palmyre la Philosophe in seeking revenge on Agricola Fusilier in George Washington Cable's *The Grandissimes.*

Clemence, Sam Boyfriend of Mary Kettlesmith in Bernard Malamud's *The Tenants.*

Clemens Monk who announces the ringing of bells throughout Rome for Gregory's arrival and coronation as pope; introduces the reader to the events that led up to Gregory's achievement as the new pontiff in Thomas Mann's *The Holy Sinner.*

Clement Chapman of Wulstead whom Ralph accompanies from Whitwall to Goldburg and who participates in the battle at Upmeads in William Morris's *The Well at the World's End.*

Clement, Arabella Graves Exquisite wife of Hammel Clement; she kills Lord Stivers while defending herself against rape; she is placed on trial, but the justice system proves effective in protecting the innocent and punishing the guilty in Henry Brooke's *The Fool of Quality.*

Clement, Bartholomew Wealthy tradesman who disowns his son Hammel at the urgings of Hammel's stepmother; father and son eventually reconcile in Henry Brooke's *The Fool of Quality.*

Clement, Dennis Sixteen-year-old would-be detective and nephew of Leonard Clement in Agatha Christie's *The Murder at the Vicarage.*

Clement, Father (Clement Blair) Heretic priest, who teaches Catherine Glover a religion of love and peace, and who flees for safety to the Scottish Highlands in Sir Walter Scott's *The Fair Maid of Perth.*

Clement, Griselda Leonard Clement's pretty, much younger wife in Agatha Christie's *The Murder at the Vicarage.* She becomes Miss Jane Marple's great friend and appears in two subsequent mysteries.

Clement, (Stapleton) Hammel (Hammy) Reduced gentleman whose education as a scholar of the classics has rendered him unable to do useful work; he commits crimes to feed his wife and child, who have nearly reached starvation; they are befriended by Henry Clinton, who hires Hammel as a tutor to give Master Harry Clinton moral instruction; Hammel and his father, Bartholomew Clement, are reconciled, and he eventually assumes his father's estate in Henry Brooke's *The Fool of Quality.*

Clement, Karen Hansen Surrogate daughter of Kitty Fremont, lover of Dov Landau, and Jewish refugee in Cyprus; killed during the Israeli War of Independence in Leon Uris's *Exodus.*

Clement, Leonard (Len) Vicar and neighbor of Miss Jane Marple; he is bemused by the antics of his much younger wife, Griselda, in Agatha Christie's *The Murder at the Vicarage.* He appears in *The Body in the Library.*

Clement, Madame Frenchwoman who offers her church pew to an exhausted Monimia (Serafina de Zelos) in London; she sends the crucial letter written by Monimia for Renaldo de Melvil; she agrees to marry Don Diego de Zelos in Tobias Smollett's *The Adventures of Ferdinand Count Fathom.*

Clement, Mrs. Hammel Clement's unsympathetic stepmother, who is responsible for his father's disowning him in Henry Brooke's *The Fool of Quality.*

Clement, Mrs. Prostitute whom Bert Albany trades for another prostitute in E. L. Doctorow's *Welcome to Hard Times.*

Clement, Richard (Dicky) Son of Hammel and Arabella Clement and the occasional companion of Master Harry Clinton in Henry Brooke's *The Fool of Quality.*

Clement, Sir James Baronet who is a Liberal candidate for Parliament in George Eliot's *Felix Holt, the Radical.*

Clemente, Esperanza Nurse and midwife; was raped when she was seventeen; falls in love with and marries Rafael Beltrán in Sandra Benítez's *A Place Where the Sea Remembers.*

Clements, Laurence G. Scholar at Waindell College; his wife rents a room to Timofey Pnin until their daughter returns and forces Pnin to move out in Vladimir Nabokov's *Pnin.*

Clements, Mrs. Kindhearted friend of Anne Catherick as a child; she takes Anne to her London lodging and to Cumberland in quest of Laura (Fairlie), Lady Glyde; she trusts Count Fosco, who dupes her and spirits Anne away from her in Wilkie Collins's *The Woman in White.*

Clemenza, Peter Gangster who remains loyal to the Corleone family in Mario Puzo's *The Godfather.*

Clemmie Ambitious prostitute who tells Arkie McClellan a lie about her new pimp and so causes him to shoot Zebulon Johns Mackie in Fred Chappell's *The Gaudy Place.*

Clennam, Arthur Middle-aged, lonely gentleman, who returns to London after working in China for twenty years; he breaks with his stern stepmother, unhappily loves Pet Meagles, becomes Daniel Doyce's business partner, is imprisoned in the Marshalsea after losing the partnership's money, and befriends and later marries Amy Dorrit in Charles Dickens's *Little Dorrit.*

Clennam, Mrs. Arthur Clennam's old, crippled, hardhearted stepmother; she is bound to a wheel chair, runs the family business, employs Amy Dorrit for needlework, withholds information from Arthur about his birth, negotiates with Rigaud for the iron box containing that information, and suffers a stroke in Charles Dickens's *Little Dorrit.*

Cleo Divorced, consumptive, pot-smoking member of the Hippodrome's cast in Cyrus Colter's *The Hippodrome.*

Cleo Piano player with Walden Blue in John Clellon Holmes's *The Horn.*

Cleófilas Mexican immigrant bride cut off from home and family after moving to Seguin, Texas, with her husband, Juan Pedro; only daughter, previously pampered at home; becomes disabused of romantic notions of life based on the *telenovelas* she watches when she suffers verbal and physical abuse at Juan Pedro's hands; lives by the creek called La Gritona; does not understand the meaning of La Gritona until she meets Felice; finds the courage to finally leave her abusive husband during her second pregnancy and return to her father in Mexico, along with her son, Juan Pedrito, in Sandra Cisneros's "Woman Hollering Creek."

Cleomenes Correspondent of Pharamond on the subject of vanity; he ironically prides himself on his lack of vanity in Sarah Fielding's *Familiar Letters between the Principal Characters of David Simple and Some Others.*

Cleomenes Sicilian lord sent to the Oracle of Delphi along with Dion by King Leontes to inquire about Hermione's fidelity in William Shakespeare's play *The Winter's Tale.*

Cleon Governor of Tarsus and Dionyza's husband; happily receives Pericles, who arrives with corn to aid the famine-stricken city; promises to take care of Marina when Pericles returns to give his daughter over to him; although not involved in his wife's plan to kill Marina, becomes implicated by association, and is burned to death by the citizens once news of the attempted murder spreads in William Shakespeare's play *Pericles.*

Cléonte Respectable young man of middle-class origin who wishes to marry Lucile, the daughter of Monsieur Jourdain, a former tradesman who desires to rise to nobility status; Cléonte is found to be unworthy of Lucile by her father in Molière's play *The Bourgeois Gentleman.*

Cleopatra Narrative exemplar of the female vices of ambition, avarice, and pride; she regards Anthony's suicide with satisfaction since it reveals her power, and ends her own life because of her horror at the prospect of the imprisonment that will follow her failure to seduce Caesar in Sarah Fielding's *The Lives of Cleopatra and Octavia.*

Cleopatra Queen of Egypt and Antony's volatile lover; proud of Antony's love for her; reacts angrily to a messenger's announcement of Antony's marriage to Octavia; appeased only when the messenger returns to inform her that Octavia cannot compare to her; joins forces with Antony upon his return to combat Octavius Caesar; proves a devastating distraction to Antony, who consequently loses the crucial sea battle at Actium; goaded by her servants, makes the catastrophic error of sending the furious Antony a false report of her suicide, which leads Antony to kill himself; thus left alone and at Caesar's mercy, decides to commit suicide rather than be paraded by him in Rome in William Shakespeare's play *Antony and Cleopatra.*

Cleopatra Queen of Egypt and lover of Caesar, by whom she has borne a son; visits Rome on a state visit in Thornton Wilder's *The Ides of March.*

Cleora Celebrated toast (belle) in the meridian of her charms who has a discussion with Cleanthe in which she supports Hillario in Francis Coventry's *The History of Pompey the Little.*

Cleora Subject of a letter from Aurelia to Silvia; she entraps a wealthy man into marrying her and then dies of sorrow as her passion for him is matched by the waning of his for her in Sarah Fielding's *Familiar Letters between the Principal Characters of David Simple and Some Others.*

Clerac, Prince of— (Count de Clerac) Roxana's lover who gives her a sizeable pension after the death of the landlord; Roxana has three sons by him and calls him by the pseudonym of Count de Clerac; after his wife dies, he repents of his affair with Roxana in Daniel Defoe's *The Fortunate Mistress.*

Clergyman Man with no money who borrows from everyone to keep up an appearance and to support his style of life in Charles Johnstone's *Chrysal: or, The Adventures of a Guinea.*

Clergyman Scholar who lodged with the Chandler's-Shopkeeper's mother and who first edited the manuscript in Charles Johnstone's *Chrysal: or, The Adventures of a Guinea.*

Cleric, Gaston Classical scholar and teacher who inspires Jim Burden in Willa Cather's *My Antonia.*

Clerimont, Ned Gentleman and Sir Dauphine Eugenie's friend; along with Dauphine, mocks and plays pranks on Amorous La Foole and John Daw; like Truewit and the other characters, is shocked to discover that Epicoene is a disguised man in Dauphine's service at the end of Ben Jonson's play *Epicoene, or The Silent Woman.*

Clerk, The Poor student of logic at the university who has accompanied the pilgrims on their journey to Canterbury; despite his scholarly background, adheres to Harry Bailey's request to eschew a high and lofty tale and presents a romance similar to that of Cinderella in Geoffrey Chaucer's *The Canterbury Tales.*

Clerk of the Custom-house Colonel Jack's confidant, who holds his money for safe keeping, allowing it to draw interest in Daniel Defoe's *The History and the Remarkable Life of the Truly Honourable Colonel Jacques, Commonly Call'd Col. Jack.*

Clermont, Lord Man who seduces Lady Dellwyn by manipulating her vanity in Sarah Fielding's *The History of the Countess of Dellwyn.*

Clerval, Henry Son of a small-minded merchant, who at first thwarts his university education at Ingolstadt; poetic and loyal, he is the dearly loved friend of Victor Frankenstein; he is strangled by Frankenstein's demon in Mary Shelley's *Frankenstein; or, The Modern Prometheus.*

Cleuch, Jock O'Dawson Dandie Dinmont's neighbor, with whom Dinmont quarrels over boundaries in Sir Walter Scott's *Guy Mannering.*

Cleveland Crewman of the *Justinian* who acts as Simpson's second in C. S. Forester's *Mr. Midshipman Hornblower.*

Cleveland, Angus Powerful, corrupt seventy-year-old political leader, former mayor of Gainesboro, and benefactor of Douglas Taylor, his successor in Julian Mayfield's *The Grand Parade.*

Cleveland, Captain Clement (Clement Vaughan) Pirate; the handsome son of Basil Vaughan and Norna Troil, he adopts the name of Cleveland; when shipwrecked, he is taken into Magnus Troil's household and falls in love with Magnus's daughter Minna; arrested for piracy, he is pardoned because of his past noble deeds in Sir Walter Scott's *The Pirate.*

Cleveland, Flora Competent only child of her absent-minded clergyman father and domestically disorganized mother; she toys with romantic possibilities in the village before she goes up to Oxford in Barbara Pym's *Jane and Prudence.*

Cleveland, Frederick Embittered member of Lord Carabas's party, whose failure to win the party's support of his candidacy for Parliament leads to a duel in which he is unintentionally killed by Vivian Grey in Benjamin Disraeli's *Vivian Grey.*

Cleveland, Jane Forty-one-year-old intellectual eccentric, wife of a country clergyman she met at Oxford; she is a disorganized housewife and mother of a grown daughter; she occupies herself with trying to arrange the life of her protégée Prudence Bates in Barbara Pym's *Jane and Prudence.*

Cleveland, Mr. Tutor and loyal friend to Ernest Maltravers in Edward Bulwer-Lytton's *Ernest Maltravers* and in *Alice.*

Cleveland, Mr. Chauffeur of Miss Ann and her accomplice in crime in Richard Brautigan's *Dreaming of Babylon.*

Cleveland, Nicholas Handsome, bespectacled, vague, middle-aged newcomer clergyman to a village parish; he is bemused by parish disputes and by his wife's unpredictable tangents of thought in Barbara Pym's *Jane and Prudence.*

Cleveland, Sir Harry Ingenuous youth corrupted by exposure to society and then reclaimed to virtue by Miss Bilson, whom he marries, in Sarah Fielding's *The History of the Countess of Dellwyn.*

Clevemore, Sir Henry (nickname "D-G") Director-General of British Secret Intelligence who approves Dr. von Munte's defection in Len Deighton's Berlin Game. He assists in the search for a mole and Bret Rensselaer's downfall in *London Match.*

Clevenger Car test-track owner who takes the hitchhiking David Bell to Texas at the end of Don DeLillo's *Americana.*

Clevering-Haight, Tony Anglican priest who is a friend of Constantine Ormeau in Elizabeth Bowen's *Eva Trout, or Changing Scenes.*

Cleves, Helena (Hellen) Friend and employer of Constantia Dudley; her reputation is ruined by Ormond's refusal to marry her; dies of yellow fever in Charles Brockden Brown's *Ormond.*

Clevinger Friend and fellow squadron member of Yossarian; Harvard undergraduate with much intelligence and no brains; hounded as a troublemaker by Lieutenant Scheisskopf in Joseph Heller's *Catch-22.*

Clewes, Leland Former state department friend whom Walter F. Starbuck betrays; husband of Sarah Wyatt in Kurt Vonnegut's *Jailbird.*

Clewline, Captain Prisoner for indebtedness who seconds Tapley in a prison fight; an alcoholic and a brute since the death of his child, he is a great quarreller with his wife in Tobias Smollett's *The Adventures of Sir Launcelot Greaves.*

Clewline, Mrs. Once a beautiful woman and now an ugly drunkard; in debtors' prison with her husband, she seconds Crabclaw in a prison fight in Tobias Smollett's *The Adventures of Sir Launcelot Greaves.*

Clews, Hasper Tall, taciturn, hypochondriacal Chancellor of the Exchequor and member of the War Cabinet; he has risen to his post from being the son of a nonconformist professor of theology in a minor college in Arnold Bennett's *Lord Raingo.*

Clickett (The Orfling) Micawbers' maid from the workhouse in Charles Dickens's *The Personal History of David Copperfield.*

Cliff Welsh lodger in the small apartment rented by Jimmy and Alison Porter; attempts but fails to keep the married pair from bickering in John Osborne's play *Look Back in Anger.*

Cliff, Miss Grey-haired lecturer in English literature at the women's college that Dolores Hutton attends in Ivy Compton-Burnett's *Dolores.*

Cliffe, Geoffrey Upper-class poet and journalist; he is a ladies' man who finally induces Lady Kitty Ashe to run away with him; he is murdered by a notorious actress in Mrs. Humphry Ward's *The Marriage of William Ashe.*

Clifford One of the circle of Hunt's people whom Kate Fletcher (Armstrong) found interesting when she was sixteen; he is "butch, thick, hairy, squat", and "travels in Oriental fabrics" in Margaret Drabble's *The Middle Ground.*

Clifford, Jane Teacher of English at a midwestern university and lover of Gabriel Weeks in Gail Godwin's *The Odd Woman.*

Clifford, Jerome Lawyer of Barry Muldanno; fears he will be killed by his Mafia-connected client so decides to kill himself before he is killed; tells Mark Sway where the body of a dead senator is buried, then kills himself in John Grisham's *The Client.*

Clifford, Lady Anne Widowed mother of two boys in Dr. Wortle's school; as gossip circulates about the marital status of two of his staff, she is induced by relatives to remove her children in Anthony Trollope's *Dr. Wortle's School.*

Clifford, Lionel Charles Mandeville's fair-haired, good-natured friend and rival at Winchester, whose father is killed fighting for the Royalist cause at Edgehill; he is in every way the archetypal opposite of Mallison; during the Civil War he vies with Charles to become secretary to Sir Joseph Wagstaff and succeeds; later, he marries Charles's sister, Henrietta, in William Godwin's *Mandeville.*

Clifford, Lord Sir Philip Harclay's aristocratic friend, who arranges the joust between Sir Philip and Sir Walter Lovel in Clara Reeve's *The Old English Baron.*

Clifford, Martha Woman who writes a suggestive letter in response to a classified advertisement placed by Leopold Bloom; he decides not to respond in James Joyce's *Ulysses.*

Clifford, Paul (Captain Lovett) Foundling who leads a double life as a man about town and a highwayman; he loves Lucy Brandon and is condemned to death by William Brandon in Edward Bulwer-Lytton's *Paul Clifford.*

Clifford, Sir Coniers Military commander defeated by the Irish in Sophia Lee's *The Recess.*

Clifton, Brother Tod Member of the Brotherhood who is killed by the police and becomes a Brotherhood martyr in Ralph Ellison's *Invisible Man.*

Clifton, Coke Reckless but extraordinary youth, who vies with Frank Henley for the affection of Anna St. Ives; he later attempts to ruin Anna and Frank in a vengeful kidnapping scheme; he finally learns, under Anna's and Frank's instruction, to subdue his passion and pursue virtue in Thomas Holcroft's *Anna St. Ives.*

Clifton, Geoffrey Husband of Katherine; his wife has an affair with Almásy (later the English patient); after discovering the love affair, he crashes his airplane in an attempt to kill all three of them, although he is the only one killed in Michael Ondaatje's *The English Patient.*

Clifton, Katherine Geoffrey Clifton's wife who has an affair with Almásy (later the English patient); is badly injured when Clifton, enraged with jealousy, crashes his airplane to kill all three of them; later dies alone in a desert cave; Almásy puts her body in a plane, but the craft disintegrates by strong winds in Michael Ondaatje's *The English Patient.*

Clifton, Lord Elderly major-domo to Lady Casterley; he takes great interest in the future of Lord Miltoun in John Galsworthy's *The Patrician.*

Clifton, Louisa Anna St. Ives's intimate friend and correspondent, who encourages Anna in her admiration of the noble Frank Henley in Thomas Holcroft's *Anna St. Ives.*

Clifton, Mrs. Virtuous mother of Coke and Louisa; she initially encourages the engagement of Anna St. Ives and Coke and later encourages Coke to forsake his uncontrolled passions in Thomas Holcroft's *Anna St. Ives.*

Climbup, Mr. Promising young man in the Treasury; he argues it is impossible to separate the poor from their poverty in William Beckford's *Azemia.*

Climpson, Alexandra Good-humored, observant middle-aged woman, who works as Lord Peter Wimsey's "inquiry agent" in Dorothy L. Sayers's *Unnatural Death.* She is Katharine Climpson when, as a juror in Harriet Vane's first murder trial, she holds out for a verdict of not guilty in *Strong Poison.*

Clinker, Humphry (Matthew Loyd) Twenty-year-old man, who is employed as Matthew Bramble's footman when John Thomas quits; he embarrasses Tabitha Bramble with his bare posterior, becomes a Methodist preacher, is mistakenly jailed as a highwayman, flirts with Winifrid Jenkins, saves Matthew from drowning, is discovered to be Matthew's natural son, and is allowed to marry Winifrid in Tobias Smollett's *The Expedition of Humphry Clinker.*

Clint Attorney of James Latter; he advises Jim not to go public in a suit against Chester Nimmo because of the damage it may do to Jim's own name in Joyce Cary's *Not Honour More.*

Clinton, Eloisa Daughter of Louisa and Henry Clinton; presumed dead in a boating accident, she is discovered to be the wife of the Sultan of Morocco; the mother of Abenaide, she becomes young Harry Clinton's mother-in-law in Henry Brooke's *The Fool of Quality.*

Clinton, General Governor of New York; he stands by Henry Durie upon the arrival of the Master (James Durie) in Robert Louis Stevenson's *The Master of Ballantrae: A Winter's Tale.*

Clinton, Harriet Child of Matilda (Golding) and Henry Clinton; she dies young from smallpox in Henry Brooke's *The Fool of Quality.*

Clinton, Harry (Henry) Son of Lord Richard Clinton, second Earl of Moreland; because he is reared by peasant foster parents and subsequently by a fugitive uncle who trains him to be the ideal Christian aristocrat, his natural goodness and compassion are not distorted by fashionable society; his lack of affectation and manners cause the fashionable to consider him a fool; he returns home on the deaths of his mother and brother; he marries Abenaide in Henry Brooke's *The Fool of Quality.*

Clinton, Henry (Harry, Dada) Idealized Christian aristocrat, the second son of Richard Clinton, first Earl of Moreland; apprenticed to a London merchant, he becomes wealthy at trade; disgusted at his brother's arrogance, he abducts his nephew Harry Clinton to teach him to be a generous and compassionate steward of God's earthly wealth; he uses the alias Mr. Fenton; he is a generous financial supporter of King William; he is eventually reconciled with his profoundly apologetic brother in Henry Brooke's *The Fool of Quality.*

Clinton, Jacky Child of Matilda (Golding) and Henry Clinton; he dies young from smallpox in Henry Brooke's *The Fool of Quality.*

Clinton, Louisa D'Aubigny Beautiful sister of the Marquis D'Aubigny; unprotected by law, she flees a forced marriage to a favorite of the French king; Henry Clinton rescues her; though her father objects to Clinton's background in trade, she elopes with him and becomes the mother of Eloisa Clinton in Henry Brooke's *The Fool of Quality.*

Clinton, Mr. Dishonest speculator, whom John Meadows uses to get Mr. Merton deep in debt in Charles Reade's *It Is Never Too Late to Mend.*

Clinton, Mrs. Housekeeper for Arthur Villars; she identifies Evelina as the real daughter of Sir John Belmont in Frances Burney's *Evelina.*

Clinton, Schuyler New York senator and chairman of the Foreign Relations Committee; admirer of Madeleine Lee in Henry Adams's *Democracy.*

Clippurse, Mr. Waverly family lawyer who draws up documents necessary to clear Edward Waverly in Sir Walter Scott's *Waverly.*

Clipsby Man in a russet smock who followed the Walsinghams and insults Sir Daniel Brackley to his face in Robert Louis Stevenson's *The Black Arrow: A Tale of Two Roses.*

Clitandre Wealthy young marquis who pursues Célimène and has great influence at the king's court in Molière's play *The Misanthrope.*

Clitheroe, Jack Upset that he has lost his rank of captain in the Irish Citizen Army to Ned Brennan, but regains his composure when Ned informs him that he has been named commandant; dies in the Easter Rebellion of 1916, leaving behind his wife, Nora, who gives birth to a stillborn infant in Sean O'Casey's play *The Plough and the Stars.*

Clitheroe, Nora One of many Irish who live in a common tenement building; learns that her husband has been killed in the Easter Rebellion of 1916; has a stillborn baby a few days later in Sean O'Casey's play *The Plough and the Stars.*

Clive Protagonist and exemplar British aristocrat married to Betty; puts his duty to country highest; controls the other characters on stage; sees sex roles as firmly defined as male and female; expects his son Edward to be a chip off the old block; subscribes to colonialism and the master-slave hierarchy; ironically, falls into an affair with Mrs. Saunders; appears only in the first part of the play in Caryl Churchill's *Cloud 9.*

Clive American millionaire who befriends Sally Bowles and Christopher Isherwood and offers to fly them off to "nowhere" in Christopher Isherwood's *Goodbye to Berlin.*

Clive Surgeon who is very cautious in assessing Captain Sawyer's sanity in C. S. Forester's *Lieutenant Hornblower.*

Clive Young, sharp-suited British espiocrat; he cynically questions Niki Landau and Barley Blair, surreptitiously degrades his American counterparts, and helps run the Russia House's compromising Operation Bluebird in John le Carré's *The Russia House.*

Clive An inside member of the British Communist Party and an acquaintance of Anna Wulf; he is a communist pamphleteer and journalist in Doris Lessing's *The Golden Notebook.*

Clive, Maurice Handsome ex-fiancé of Dulcie Mainwaring in Barbara Pym's *No Fond Return of Love.*

Clocklan, Percy Dublin friend of Sebastian Dangerfield; fakes suicide in the Irish Sea and later re-emerges in London as a mysteriously wealthy man in J. P. Donleavy's *The Ginger Man.*

Clod, Mrs. Shrewish wife of Thomas; she urges him to make extra money by selling trees cut on Lucius Manly's estate in Mary Collyer's *Felicia to Charlotte.*

Clod, Thomas Dull, henpecked tenant on Lucius Manly's estate; he confesses the theft of trees to a stranger who he does not realize is his landlord; Lucius handles the theft in a generous way in Mary Collyer's *Felicia to Charlotte.*

Clodius Lewd wretch who attacks Fabius in Jane Barker's *Exilius; or, The Banish'd Roman.*

Clodius, Marcus Young Roman fop and parasite, who proves a fickle friend to Glaucus in Edward Bulwer-Lytton's *The Last Days of Pompeii.*

Clonbrony, Lady English-born but Irish-reared aristocrat, who denounces her Irish heritage to be allowed to mingle with snobbish English society in Maria Edgeworth's *The Absentee.*

Clonbrony, Lord Irish absentee uprooted from his Irish home by his wife, Lady Clonbrony, and forced to live in England in Maria Edgeworth's *The Absentee.*

Cloten Queen's son; pompous fool repeatedly rejected by Imogen in favor of Posthumus; travels to the forest in search of Imogen and Posthumus, where he meets and immediately challenges Guiderius, Arviragus, and Belarius; duels with Guiderius and is beheaded by him in William Shakespeare's play *Cymbeline.*

Clothier, Mary Widowed mother of Pierce Clothier; she falls in love with Willy Kost but eventually is happily married to John Ducane in Iris Murdoch's *The Nice and the Good.*

Clothier, Pierce Teenaged schoolboy who has a summer-vacation love affair with Barbara Gray in Iris Murdoch's *The Nice and the Good.*

Clotilde French actress who entertains Lord Mon-mouth after his separation from his wife, Lucretia (Colonna), in Benjamin Disraeli's *Coningsby; or, The New Generation.*

Cloudesdale Sir Harry Hotspur's loyal old butler, who is well aware that George Hotspur does no credit to the house of Humblethwaite in Anthony Trollope's *Sir Harry Hotspur of Humblethwaite.*

Cloudesley Son of a peasant on the Danvers estate at Milwood Park; he enters the service of Arthur Danvers, Lord Alton after the latter saves him from prison; his chameleon-like change of character-from a grateful and utterly faithful servant to a greedy, vengeful egotist-occurs after he agrees to become the infant Julian Danvers's foster father; he dies while searching for Julian when he stumbles into an ambush of mountain bandits led by Francesco Perfetti in William Godwin's *Cloudesley.*

Cloudy, Lady Loquacious, empty-headed wife of Sir Christopher Cloudy in Henry Brooke's *The Fool of Quality.*

Cloudy, Sir Christopher Stereotypical member of the gentry who says nothing in Henry Brooke's *The Fool of Quality.*

Clough Crewman aboard the *Indefatigable* in C. S. Forester's *Mr. Midshipman Hornblower.*

Clouston, Jennet Dark and sour-looking Scottish peasant woman, who calls down a curse upon the house of Shaws, the residence of miser Ebenezer Balfour and the future estate of Ebenezer's nephew, David Balfour, in Robert Louis Stevenson's *Kidnapped.*

Clout Gunner's mate aboard the *Atropos* in C. S. Forester's *Hornblower and the Atropos.*

Clov Considered a knight in a game of chess against Hamm's role of the king; the pieces move on the theatrical chess board in a stalemate; feels permanent allegiance to his surrogate father figure Hamm, although constantly threatens to leave the imprisoned domicile; meets Hamm's constant demand; although he constantly questions his life confined with Hamm and wishes to leave the tyrant, cannot for fear of isolation and desolation; shares Hamm's view of the cyclical nature of life with its fused beginnings and endings, and believes that finality to anything is impossible to be reached, which leads him to his chronic inaction about his much-contemplated concern of leaving Hamm in Samuel Beckett's play *Endgame.*

Clover Hutch doe rabbit liberated by Hazel's pioneers; she is the first to bear a litter in the new warren in Richard Adams's *Watership Down.*

Clover, Charles Young man who secures help from Perry Pickle to marry Julia Pickle in Tobias Smollett's *The Adventures of Peregrine Pickle.*

Clover, Louisa Proprietor of a china shop whose missing husband is the object of a search in George Gissing's *The Town Traveller.*

Clover, Minnie Young girl in whom Mr. Gammon shows an interest but whose mother firmly rejects him in George Gissing's *The Town Traveller.*

Clovis, Cletus James (C. J.) Entrepreneur who builds bat towers for insect control in Thomas McGuane's *The Bushwhacked Piano.*

Clovis, Esther Fiercely loyal resident organizing force and research associate of the Learned Society for anthropologists in Barbara Pym's *Excellent Women*. She performs the same functions for the new Research Centre in *Less Than Angels*. Her memorial service occurs in *A Few Green Leaves*.

Clown Agrees to become Wagner's servant, wavers, and is scared into service by Wagner's conjuration of two devils; requests of Wagner to be taught to conjure as well in Christopher Marlowe's play *Dr. Faustus*.

Clown Old shepherd's son who falls victim to Autolycus's tricks; made a gentleman at the end of William Shakespeare's play *The Winter's Tale*.

Clown Sycophantic art teacher at the middle school in Shikoku, the smallest of the four main Japanese islands; ally of the mean-spirited Redshirt; in league with Redshirt to break the loyalty between Botchan and Porcupine; wants to drive Botchan away from the school so he can take over his nice apartment; succeeds in expelling the two teachers, but not before he and Redshirt receive a sound thrashing in Natsume Sôseki's *Bochan*.

Cloyse, Goody One of the characters in Young Goodman Brown's village; he assumes that she is pure of heart and soul, all the while her life is tainted with sin in Nathaniel Hawthorne's "Young Goodman Brown."

Clubber, Lady Wife of Sir Thomas Clubber in Charles Dickens's *The Posthumous Papers of the Pickwick Club*.

Clubber, Sir Thomas Commissioner of the dockyard and a distinguished personage at a ball at the Bull Inn in Rochester in Charles Dickens's *The Posthumous Papers of the Pickwick Club*.

Clubber, The Misses Daughters of Sir Thomas and Lady Clubber in Charles Dickens's *The Posthumous Papers of the Pickwick Club*.

Clubfoot Prisoner who gets himself classified as an invalid, although he is healthy, so he can work in the gulag prison kitchen in Alexander Solzhenitsyn's *One Day in the Life of Ivan Denisovitch*.

Cluffe, Captain Stout, dandyish member of the Royal Irish Artillery and frequent companion of Lieutenant Puddock; he has designs on Rebecca Chattesworth, but when she becomes engaged to Lieutenant Puddock he claims he brought them together; after Paul Dangerfield's identity is revealed, he realizes he saw him hide the murder weapon the night of the attack on Dr. Barney Sturk in J. Sheridan Le Fanu's *The House by the Churchyard*.

Clumly, Esther Blind wife of Fred Clumly; helps temper his zeal for obedience to laws in John Gardner's *The Sunlight Dialogues*.

Clumly, Fred Police chief of Batavia, New York, who finally understands what makes the Sunlight Man behave like a criminal; husband of Esther Clumly in John Gardner's *The Sunlight Dialogues*.

Clump, John Country lad who delivers a letter from Ralph Mattocks; he is disappointed to learn that Dolly Cowslip loves Thomas Clarke in Tobias Smollett's *The Adventures of Sir Launcelot Greaves*.

Clun, Arthur Professor of history who opposes the appointment of Gerald Middleton to the editorship of a new journal; he admires John Middleton's social-welfare activities; he finally supports Gerald after disclosure of the Melpham fraud in Angus Wilson's *Anglo-Saxon Attitudes*.

Cluppins, Elizabeth Brisk, busy-looking friend of Martha Bardell in Charles Dickens's *The Posthumous Papers of the Pickwick Club*.

Clutter, Bonnie Fox Wife of Herbert Clutter and mother of their four children; ill with emotional and physical ailments, she is the last member of the family to be murdered in Truman Capote's *In Cold Blood*.

Clutter, Herbert William Prominent and wealthy owner of River Valley Farm in Holcomb, Kansas; victim of the first and most brutal murder by Perry Smith in Truman Capote's *In Cold Blood*.

Clutter, Kenyon Youngest child and only son of Bonnie and Herbert Clutter; shot to death in Truman Capote's *In Cold Blood*.

Clutter, Nancy Talented and much admired 16-year-old daughter of Bonnie and Herbert Clutter; third murder victim in Truman Capote's *In Cold Blood*.

Clutterbuck. Captain Cuthbert of Kennaquhair Antiquarian and the editor of Benedictine manuscripts containing the stories told in Sir Walter Scott's *The Monastery* and in *The Abbot*.

Clutterbuck, Major Head of a family of eight; his repudiation of the Alpine hotel at which Denry Machin was honeymooning provokes Denry to attempt to draw customers to his hotel from the hotel of their choice in Arnold Bennett's *The Card: A Story of Adventure in the Five Towns.*

Clutton Sardonic, talented artist who studies at Amitrano's Studio in Paris with Philip Carey in W. Somerset Maugham's *Of Human Bondage.*

Cluveau, Albert Cajun who is the occasional fishing companion of Miss Jane Pittman and the hired killer of Ned Douglass in Ernest J. Gaines's *The Autobiography of Miss Jane Pittman.*

Cly, Roger Partner of Solomon Pross and former servant of Charles Darnay, against whom he testifies falsely; he is a spy for the Old Bailey, London criminal court; supposedly dead and buried, he is actually smuggled out of England into revolutionary France; the hoax is uncovered by Jerry Cruncher in Charles Dickens's *A Tale of Two Cities.*

Clyne, Frances Lover of Robert Cohn in Ernest Hemingway's *The Sun Also Rises.*

Clynes Crewman of the *Indefatigable* in C. S. Forester's *Mr. Midshipman Hornblower.*

Clytemnestra Orestes' and Electra's mother; dreams about giving birth to a snake, which now draws blood and milk from her breast; unknowingly receives her son, Orestes, who has disguised himself as a stranger and who falsely reports news of Orestes' death; when finally confronted by her son, holds out her maternal breasts as her defense; upon Apollo's command, however, Orestes kills her in Aeschylus's play *The Libation Bearers.*

Clytemnestra Queen of Argos and wife of King Agamemnon; mother to Orestes and Electra; kills Agamemnon, with the aid of her lover, Aegisthus, upon his triumphant return from Troy; marries Aegisthus and makes him king; aids in imposing a mandatory remorsefulness by all citizens for the crime, and is finally killed by her son Orestes and daughter Electra in Jean-Paul Sartre's play *The Flies.*

Clytemnestra Sister of Agamemnon's wife, Helen, and ruler of Argos during her husband's long absence at Troy; has taken a lover, Aegisthus, with whom she plots to avenge her daughter's death; treacherously butchers Agamemnon in a bathtub, which is but another step in the curse that afflicts the House of Atreus in Aeschylus's play *Agamemnon.*

Clytemnestra Sister of Helen and wife of Agamemnon; conspires with her lover Aegisthus to murder Agamemnon; killed in turn by her son Orestes in John Erskine's *The Private Life of Helen of Troy.*

Clytemnestra's Ghost Appears at the beginning of the play to summon the Furies; dishonored in the underworld for killing her husband, advocates revenge in Aeschylus's play *The Eumenides.*

Clyth, Andrew Powerful Prime Minister; he is influenced by his adored mother to appoint his old Eccles schoolmate Sam Raingo to be Minister of Records and impresses Sam with his comradely demeanor but unique genius for chicanery in Arnold Bennett's *Lord Raingo.*

Coade, Bill Resettlement officer when Timberwork shuts down in Isabel Colegate's *Orlando King.*

Coal, Fletcher Sinister, ambitious, presidential chief of staff; works to suppress Darby Shaw's damaging brief; is politically ruined when the brief is made public in John Grisham's *The Pelican Brief.*

Coates, Bernice Young woman from Massachusetts; joins the WASP to become a pilot during World War II; sister of Jeffrey Coates; occasional lover of Zachary Taylor who assists her in obtaining the legal documents to assume a man's identity; after the war, moves with her partner Florence to Alaska in Marge Piercy's *Gone to Soldiers.*

Coates, Codicil Attorney to the Rookwood family in William Harrison Ainsworth's *Rookwood.*

Coates, Jeff Painter who joins the Office of Strategic Services (OSS) during World War II; brother of Bernice Coates; in his work with an active cell of L'Armee Juive, falls in love with Jacqueline Levy-Monot; they are captured; Jeff commits suicide with a cyanide capsule in Marge Piercy's *Gone to Soldiers.*

Coats, Sarah Ruth Pregnant wife of O. E. Parker; described by him as very plain and ugly; daughter of a gospel preacher; strict Christian who does not smoke, drink, use cosmetics, or speak profanity; dislikes her husband's fetish to cover his body in tattoos; finally throws Parker out of the house after he has the image of Christ tattooed across his back, as she abhors idolatry, in Flannery O'Connor's "Parker's Back."

Cobb, Billy Sportsman and a houseguest at Marlowe in J. Sheridan Le Fanu's *Guy Deverell.*

Cobb, Charles (Cobby) Greedy and crafty bookie who helps finance a jewelry robbery in William Riley Burnett's *The Asphalt Jungle.*

Cobb, Georgiana Fiancée of her neighbor Adam Moss in James Lane Allen's *A Kentucky Cardinal;* dies after giving birth to their son, Adam Cobb Moss, in *Aftermath.*

Cobb, Jeremiah Judge who sentences Nat Turner and Hark to be hanged; Job figure and lonely widower in William Styron's *The Confessions of Nat Turner.*

Cobb, Joe R. Air exec with the 918th Bomb Group in Beirne Lay, Jr., and Sy Bartlett's *Twelve O'Clock High!*

Cobb, Joseph Brother of Georgiana Cobb; West Point cadet in James Lane Allen's *A Kentucky Cardinal;* also appears in *Aftermath.*

Cobb, Margaret Mother of Georgiana Cobb in James Lane Allen's *A Kentucky Cardinal* and *Aftermath.*

Cobb, Maybelline (Mae) Defiant, bedridden wife of Winston Cobb; killed in a fire set by her husband; appears in Hal Bennett's *A Wilderness of Vines, The Black Wine, Wait Until the Evening,* and *Seventh Heaven.*

Cobb, Reverend Winston Preacher in Burnside, Virginia; sex-show performer, blackmailer, and perfume salesman; father of David Hunter, mentor of Kevin Brittain, alter ego of Bill Kelsey, and slayer of his wife, Mae Cobb; apprehended in New Jersey for murdering Dolly Anderson and visited in jail by Joe Market; appears in Hal Bennett's *A Wilderness of Vines, The Black Wine, Lord of Dark Places, Wait Until the Evening,* and *Seventh Heaven.*

Cobb, Sylvia Sister of Georgiana and Joseph Cobb; flirts with Adam Moss in James Lane Allen's *A Kentucky Cardinal;* also appears in *Aftermath.*

Cobb, Thomas Serious young man of quasi-plebeian demeanor whose quarrel with his betrothed, Louise Derrick, starts a fire in the house where she is lodging in George Gissing's *The Paying Guest.*

Cobb, Tom Keeper of the post office at Chigwell and frequenter of the Maypole Inn in Charles Dickens's *Barnaby Rudge.*

Cobble, Father Uncomprehending priest with whom Mick Shaughnessy discusses the De Selby problem in Flann O'Brien's *The Dalkey Archive.*

Cobbley, Eric Struggling artist who is the object of June Forsyte's attempts to help bring him before the public in John Galsworthy's *In Chancery.*

Cobham, Kitty Actress who assumes the identity of the recently dead Duchess of Wharfedale in order to help smuggle orders entrusted to Horatio Hornblower before his capture in C. S. Forester's *Mr. Midshipman Hornblower.*

Coble, Amanda Younger sister of Donny and target of sibling rivalry by her brother in Anne Tyler's "Teenage Wasteland."

Coble, Daisy Mother of Donny and Amanda; once a fourth grade teacher; faces a troubled teenage son who is rebellious, antiauthoritarian, and lacking interest in school in Anne Tyler's "Teenage Wasteland."

Coble, Donny Young teenage boy who has lost interest in his parents and home life and becomes disruptive in school; engages in underage drinking and smoking and skips classes; finds that his hippie-style tutor only enables his problems; finally expelled from school for having beer and cigarettes in his locker; goes from private to public high school, then one day vanishes entirely in Anne Tyler's "Teenage Wasteland."

Cobleigh, James Handsome and charming son of financially ruined parents; puts himself through Harvard Law School and marries socialite Winifred Tuttle; has five children, oldest is Nicholas; philanderer and alcoholic in Susan Isaacs's *Almost Paradise.*

Cobleigh, Jane (Heissenhuber) Tall, outgoing daughter of Richard Heissenhuber and Sarah Taubman; abused by father and stepmother; studies acting in college but abandons career to support husband, Nicholas Cobleigh, in his acting career; mother of two daughters; develops agoraphobia, which threatens her marriage in Susan Isaacs's *Almost Paradise.*

Cobleigh, Nicholas Photogenic scion of New York society mother, Winifred Tuttle, and father, James Cobleigh; excels at sports and studies law; bucks family expectations to become actor; marries Jane Heissenhuber; becomes estranged from family and values by fame in Susan Isaacs's *Almost Paradise.*

Cobleigh, Winifred (Tuttle) Awkward and tomboyish daughter of wealthy New York family; marries James Cobleigh; has five children; battles depression and insecurity throughout her life in Susan Isaacs's *Almost Paradise.*

Cobling, Ben Clara Whittaker's old groom, who supplies information about Whittaker/Dawson family affairs in Dorothy L. Sayers's *Unnatural Death.*

Coburn, Mr. Protestant minister; even though falsely accused of proselytism, he charitably helps the poor Catholic farmers during the blight in Liam O'Flaherty's *Famine.*

Cochrane, Lord Englishman ruined by court martial after years of service; Hornblower continually imagines himself victim of the same fate in C. S. Forester's *Ship of the Line.*

Cock, John Barber who brings his whole family back to London at the first sign of the plague's abating; everyone in his household except his maid dies in Daniel Defoe's *A Journal of the Plague Year.*

Cock, Old Old lawyer who cruelly controls the inheritances and futures of Martha Tilston and Alithea Llansoy; John Buncle with the help of his servant, Soto O'Fin, effects their escape from the villainous guardian and hides the women at Orton Lodge until Old Cock's death in Thomas Amory's *The Life of John Buncle, Esq.*

Cockburn Keeper of the George Inn near Bristo-port in Sir Walter Scott's *Guy Mannering.*

Cockburn, Ensign Peregrine English cousin of Johnny Lacey; sent to Virginia as part of Braddock's force against Fort Duquesne; killed by Indians and stripped of his possessions by Squire Raglan in Mary Lee Settle's *O Beulah Land.*

Cocker, Mrs. Housekeeper who discovers Helen Halliday's skeleton and recovers from a dose of poisoned brandy in Agatha Christie's *Sleeping Murder.*

Cockerell, Jack Head of the English department at Waindell College; does near-perfect but mean impersonations of Timofey Pnin in Vladimir Nabokov's *Pnin.*

Cockeyne, Annette Spoilt young girl at finishing school who attempts suicide when disappointed in love but takes the wrong tablets and survives in Iris Murdoch's *The Flight from the Enchanter.*

Cockney See Shorty.

Cockney Girl Leaves after the party at the house of the famous poet and proceeds to the safety of an underground shelter when the sirens go off announcing the German air raids over London in Muriel Spark's "The House of the Famous Poet."

Cocoanut Called so because of the peculiar shape of his head; young dark-skinned man met by the young white British officer Captain Lionel March aboard the S.S. *Normannia* sailing to Bombay; finagles it so that he and the captain share the same cabin; instigates a homosexual relationship with the captain; carries two passports, thus confusing the protagonist, Lionel March, as to his real name and age; rejected and then killed in a scuffle with Lionel in E. M. Forster's "The Other Boat."

Códac Photographer and one of the three main characters who are all trapped in a socially changing Havana in Guillermo Cabrera Infante's *Three Trapped Tigers.*

Codd, Wayne Cowboy and ranch foreman who hits Nicholas Payne, possibly causing Payne brain damage in Thomas McGuane's *The Bushwhacked Piano.*

Codero, Esperanza Thirteen-year-old Mexican-American girl; attends Catholic school; has three brothers and sisters; hopes for a "real house" someday; narrates Sandra Cisneros's *The House on Mango Street.*

Codger, Miss American literary lady, who wears on her brow a cameo the size and shape of a raspberry tart in Charles Dickens's *The Life and Adventures of Martin Chuzzlewit.*

Codlin, Tom Partner with Harris Short in a traveling Punch and Judy show; he meets with Nell Trent and her grandfather, takes care of the money, is cautious and surly, and states that he is the "open-hearted one" but would turn Nell and her grandfather in for a reward in Charles Dickens's *The Old Curiosity Shop.*

Codlyne, Mrs. Stout widow of a chemist; the increase in taxes on her rented cottages angers her against Mr. Duncalf, her collector, so that Duncalf tells her to place her cottages in other hands; she does so after Duncalf fires Denry Machin, who offers to be her rent collector in Arnold Bennett's *The Card: A Story of Adventure in the Five Towns.*

Cody, Dan Millionaire miner who employs the young James Gatz for five years; leaves money to Gatz, which he does not receive, in F. Scott Fitzgerald's *The Great Gatsby.*

Cody, James M. (Jimmy) Doctor who concludes that Danny Glick was killed by vampires in Stephen King's *'Salem's Lot.*

Coeur, Cindi Lucy Spenser's nom de plume for *Country Daze* magazine in Ann Beattie's *Love Always.*

Coffee, Edward R. (Instant) Impulsive presiding judge; character in Osgood Wallop's *The Duchess of Obloquy* in Peter De Vries's *Mrs. Wallop.*

Coffee, Mr. Ragman and vagrant in Carlene Hatcher Polite's *The Flagellants.*

Coffee-house Orator Domestic tyrant but a true-born Englishman, who uses his rights to abuse the government for the exertion of its power in Francis Coventry's *The History of Pompey the Little.*

Coffey, Father Taciturn priest at Paddy Dignam's funeral in James Joyce's *Ulysses.*

Coffin, China Doff Older sister of Sukie Maceo and neighborhood prostitute in 1930s Harlem; stabs and kills her pimp in Louise Meriwether's *Daddy Was a Number Runner.*

Coffin, Francie Twelve-year-old only daughter and youngest child of Henrietta and Adam Coffin; comes of age in mid-1930s Harlem; narrator of Louise Meriwether's *Daddy Was a Number Runner.*

Coffin, Henrietta Wife of Adam Coffin and mother of James Junior, Sterling, and Francie Coffin; becomes the primary support of the family after her husband abandons them in a Harlem tenement in Louise Meriwether's *Daddy Was a Number Runner.*

Coffin, James Adam Husband of Henrietta Coffin and father of James Junior, Sterling, and Francie Coffin; becomes a number runner and eventually abandons his family after legal fees for Junior absorb his income in Louise Meriwether's *Daddy Was a Number Runner.*

Coffin, James Adam, Jr. (James Junior, Junior) Fifteen-year-old brother of Sterling and Francie Coffin; arrested for the robbery and murder of a white shoe salesman, but released in Louise Meriwether's *Daddy Was a Number Runner.*

Coffin, Sterling Fourteen-year-old brother of Francie and James Junior Coffin; quits high school to take a job because he sees no future as a black person with a diploma in Louise Meriwether's *Daddy Was a Number Runner.*

Coffin, Tom Protestant justice of the peace and member of the Brotherhood of the Rose in Charles Kingsley's *Westward Ho!.*

Cogan, Jack (Jackie) Mafia enforcer who restores order to mob-run enterprises; kills Frankie, Mark Trattman, and Squirrel Amato in George V. Higgins's *Cogan's Trade.*

Cogburn, Reuben (Rooster) Rough talking and riding United States marshal and bounty hunter, often referred to as "Rooster," who is hired by the young woman Mattie Ross to capture Tom Chaney, the killer of her father, in Charles Portis's *True Grit.*

Coggan, Jan Gabriel Oak's good friend, a worker on Bathsheba Everdene's farm in Thomas Hardy's *Far from the Madding Crowd.*

Cogglesby, Andrew Brewer who marries Harriet Harrington, the snobbish daughter of a tailor; she conceals her origins in George Meredith's *Evan Harrington.*

Cogglesby, Harriet Harrington Evan Harrington's snobbish sister, who conceals her father's occupation as a tailor to rise socially by marrying Andrew Cogglesby, a brewer, in George Meredith's *Evan Harrington.*

Cogglesby, Tom Owner of a brewery with his brother Andrew; he engineers numerous odd schemes, including one designed to humble Andrew's snobbish wife in George Meredith's *Evan Harrington.*

Cogshill New captain of the *Renown,* formerly of the *Buckler,* he sits as a member of the court of inquiry regarding the *Renown's* voyage in C. S. Forester's *Lieutenant Hornblower.*

Cohen Elderly furrier who kept the prostitute Melissa Artemis; he dies painfully from uraemia in Lawrence Durrell's *Justine.* Nessim Hosnani's co-conspirator in procuring arms for Palestinian Jews, he has indiscretely confided in Melissa in *Mountolive.*

Cohen, Addy Wife of Ezra Cohen in George Eliot's *Daniel Deronda.*

Cohen, Adelaide Rebekah Daughter of Ezra Cohen in George Eliot's *Daniel Deronda.*

Cohen, Anna Worker burned to death in a fire at Mine. Soubrine's, a fashionable millinery shop in John Dos Passos's *Manhattan Transfer.*

Cohen, Archie Young American volunteer in the Spanish civil war; eventually denounces the Communist party in William Herrick's *Hermanos!*

Cohen, Baruch Mathematical-instrument maker and forty-year-old widower and Jewish brother-in-law of Mr. Marshall; he falls in love with Clara Hopgood and marries Madge Hopgood after Clara decides not to encourage him in Mark Rutherford's *Clara Hopgood.*

Cohen, Bella (Bello) Mistress of a brothel who, in the hallucination of the "Circe" episode, transforms Leopold Bloom into a prostitute; she also calls the police on Stephen Dedalus in James Joyce's *Ulysses.*

Cohen, Benjamin Apprentice for optical-instrument makers in York; he convinces his father, Baruch Cohen, that he is an independent man in Mark Rutherford's *Clara Hopgood.*

Cohen, Bernie Jewish-American citizen who works at the Higate winery for Jake and Claire Levy; volunteer soldier with the Lincoln Brigade; rescuer of Marcel Duboise; meets Barbara Lavette in Paris and falls in love with her in Howard Fast's *Second Generation.*

Cohen, Dr. Medical man discussed by the nurses at St. Andrews, where Rosamund Stacey goes to have her baby in Margaret Drabble's *The Millstone.*

Cohen, Edie Harry's wife who provides the Jewbird with food and shelter; tries to mediate between the bird and her husband; after her husband kills the bird and her son finds the carcass, tells her son the bird was killed by "Anti-Semeets" in Bernard Malamud's "The Jewbird."

Cohen, Ezra Poor Jewish man who owns a pawn shop and is at first mistaken by Daniel Deronda for Mirah Lapidoth's lost brother in George Eliot's *Daniel Deronda.*

Cohen, Gabriel C. (Dutch) Friend of Samuel Paul Berman since grade school in Jay Neugeboren's *Sam's Legacy.*

Cohen, Genghis Eminent philatelist hired to appraise Pierce Inverarity's stamp collection in Thomas Pynchon's *The Crying of Lot 49.*

Cohen, Harry Frozen-foods salesman who resents the Jewbird that takes up residence and requests food; tolerates the bird's presence for his wife and son's sake (because the bird endears himself to Cohen's wife and helps his son with his homework); when he is unsuccessful in persuading the bird to leave, gives him a beating that leads to his death in Bernard Malamud's "The Jewbird."

Cohen, Jacob Alexander Precocious son of Ezra Cohen; Ezra Mordecai Lapidoth tutors him in George Eliot's *Daniel Deronda.*

Cohen, Jasmine Solly and Joss's cousin and Martha Quest's close friend in Doris Lessing's *Martha Quest.* She works with Martha in the Communist Party in *A Proper Marriage,* in *A Ripple from the Storm,* and in *Landlocked.* She is tried for treason in *The Four-Gated City.*

Cohen, Jasper Senior partner in the town law firm who offers Martha Quest a secretarial job, thus giving her the chance to leave behind her parents' farm in Doris Lessing's *Martha Quest.* He later leaves to help run an army in North Africa in *A Ripple from the Storm.*

Cohen, Joey Russian-born childhood friend of Michael Gold in Michael Gold's *Jews without Money.*

Cohen, Joss Jewish intellectual friend of Martha Quest; he experiments with socialism and other political philosophies in Doris Lessing's *Martha Quest,* in *A Proper Marriage,* in *A Ripple from the Storm,* and in *Landlocked.* His expulsion from North Africa by the Colonialist government has brought him to London, England, in *The Four-Gated City.*

Cohen, Maurie Harry and Edie's young son; sweet but not very bright; accepts the Jewbird as a sort of pet and tutor, and studies more diligently under his supervision; finds the dead bird after spring thaw in Bernard Malamud's "The Jewbird."

Cohen, Max Jasper Cohen's brother, also a lawyer, whom Martha Quest dislikes because of his disagreeable and overformal nature in Doris Lessing's *Martha Quest.*

Cohen, Morris (Mike Palgrave) Architect who designs a temple for David Dehn; adopts Dehn's daughter, Rachel Dehn, in Jerome Weidman's *The Temple.*

Cohen, Mr. Orthodox Jewish storekeeper in the station neighboring the Quests' farm, with whose boys Martha Quest develops a friendship in Doris Lessing's *Martha Quest.*

Cohen, Mrs. Mother of Ezra Cohen and assistant in his shop in George Eliot's *Daniel Deronda.*

Cohen, Mrs. An orthodox, rather sad Jewish woman, wife of the storekeeper; she is friendly to Martha Quest and worries incessantly about her two sons in Doris Lessing's *Martha Quest.*

Cohen, Rachel Daughter of David Dehn and Bella Biaggi Dehn, and adopted daughter of Morris Cohen; friend of the reporter who discovers the source of David Dehn's wealth in Jerome Weidman's *The Temple.*

Cohen, Solly Rebellious Jewish intellectual who leaves his home to study at the university in Cape Town in Doris

Lessing's *Martha Quest.* He returns to the city of his province and attempts to bring reforms for the Africans in Doris Lessing's *A Proper Marriage,* in *A Ripple from the Storm,* and in *Landlocked.*

Cohenlupe, Samuel Tricky politician and business associate of Augustus Melmotte; just as Melmotte's trading empire is about to collapse, he decamps with a large sum of money to Europe in Anthony Trollope's *The Way We Live Now.*

Cohenson, Miss Musical-comedy actress; her fabrication of a connection with the famous painter Priam Farll for her reporter friend Charlie Docksay is overheard by Farll, whose reported death is making headlines in Arnold Bennett's *Buried Alive: A Tale of These Days.*

Cohn, Robert Jewish-American novelist in Paris; in love with and violently jealous of Lady Brett Ashley in Ernest Hemingway's *The Sun Also Rises.*

Coigney, M. de Vile unsuccessful pursuer of Charlotta de Palfoy in Eliza Haywood's *The Fortunate Foundlings.*

Coigney, Mademoiselle de Vicious, jealous, and devious pursuer of Horatio; she wants to destroy the Charlotta de Palfoy and Horatio connection in Eliza Haywood's *The Fortunate Foundlings.*

Coil Rustic servant and bagpipe player for the evening dances of the Laird Douglas family at Glenfern Castle in Susan Ferrier's *Marriage.*

Coiler, Mrs. Toady neighbor of the Pockets in Charles Dickens's *Great Expectations.*

Coker Homely barmaid to whom Gulley Jimson owes money; she tries to get Gulley's paintings from Sara Monday and Mr. Hickson, but her plan fails; having become pregnant, she loses her job and is forced to live with her mother in Gulley's old apartment in Joyce Cary's *The Horse's Mouth.*

Cola, Master Vine grower in Sicily in the mid-19th century for whom the protagonist Turiddu Macca is employed; father of the unmarried young girl Santa who Turiddu pretends to court to make Lola, his previous sweetheart, jealous in Giovanni Verga's "Cavalleria Rusticana."

Colamartini, Cristina Schoolmate of Bianchina Girasole; visited in her family's home in Pietrasecca by Bianchina; later joins the underground revolutionaries and seeks to help Paolo Spina escape government forces; dies at the mouths of hungry wolves as she climbs a snowy mountain to help Paolo in Ignazio Silone's *Bread and Wine.*

Colambre, Lord Irish-born but English-reared son of Lord and Lady Clonbrony; he is in love with Grace Nugent; he embarks on a journey to discover his Irish heritage and investigate the condition of his father's estate in Maria Edgeworth's *The Absentee.*

Colbert, Henry Miller and husband of Sapphira Dodderidge Colbert; gives their daughter, Rachel Colbert, money to smuggle Nancy to Canada in Willa Cather's *Sapphira and the Slave Girl.*

Colbert, Martin Rakish nephew of Henry Colbert; his repeated advances toward Nancy cause her to escape to Canada in Willa Cather's *Sapphira and the Slave Girl.*

Colbert, Rachel See Colbert Blake, Rachel.

Colbert, Sapphira Dodderidge (Sapphy, The Mistress) Wealthy Virginia slave owner, wife of Henry Colbert, and mother of Rachel Colbert in Willa Cather's *Sapphira and the Slave Girl.*

Colbrand, Monsieur Swiss attendant of Mr. B—; his appearance and demeanor are frightening in Samuel Richardson's *Pamela, or Virtue Rewarded.*

Colbrook Marine corporal aboard the *Neversink* who saves White-Jacket from a flogging in Herman Melville's *White-Jacket.*

Colburne, Edward (Cap) New England lawyer who relinquishes Lillie Ravenel to John Carter and serves as a captain under Carter in the Civil War; marries Lillie after Carter's death in John William DeForest's *Miss Ravenel's Conversion from Secession to Loyalty.*

Colburne, Lillie Ravenel Carter See Carter, Lillie Ravenel.

Colchnaben, Lady Mother of Lorimer Boyd; hypocritical and jealous of Gertrude Ross, she plots with Alice Ross and Kenneth Carmichael Ross's mother, Margaret Carmichael Ross, against Gertrude; she wants her son to be Sir Douglas Ross's heir in Caroline Norton's *Old Sir Douglas.*

Cold Cuts Alcoholic nightclub singer who works in a morgue and speaks sixteen languages; friend of Jay in Anaïs Nin's *A Spy in the House of Love.*

Colder, Gene Police investigator who is Felicity's lover and vows to find her killer; suspected by Ben Dill as her murderer in Ross Thomas's *Briarpatch.*

Coldfield, Ellen See Sutpen, Ellen Coldfield.

Coldfield, Goodhue Father of Ellen and Rosa Coldfield in William Faulkner's *Absalom, Absalom!*

Coldfield, Rosa Daughter of Goodhue Coldfield in and one of the narrators of William Faulkner's *Absalom, Absalom!*

Coldmoon Scientist and former student of the high school teacher Mr. Sneaze; occasionally entertained at the Sneaze household and closely observed by the narrator, an alley cat adopted by the Sneaze family; seeks to marry Opula Goldfield, the daughter of a prosperous businessman who lives near the Sneaze household, but is turned away; later marries a girl from his hometown in Natsume Soseki's *I Am a Cat.*

Coldridge, Amanda Jill's daughter and Francis Coldridge's stepdaughter, to whom Francis leaves his memoirs of life as it was before the Catastrophe in Doris Lessing's *The Four-Gated City.*

Coldridge, Arthur Phoebe Coldridge's ex-husband, who is a member of the Labour left Party and a Member of Parliament; Phoebe maintains a good relationship with him in Doris Lessing's *The Four-Gated City.*

Coldridge, Colin Mark Coldridge's brother, who is a physicist working at Cambridge on a bomb during the Cold War; accused of spying for the Soviet Union, he decides to flee his country for the Soviet Union in Doris Lessing's *The Four-Gated City.*

Coldridge, Elizabeth Daughter of Mark Coldridge's deceased brother; she visits him because she knows it will create havoc among her stepfamily all of whom see Mark as a traitor; she later becomes involved with Graham Patten and leaves with him in Doris Lessing's *The Four-Gated City.*

Coldridge, Francis Mark Coldridge's son, who suffers from a traumatic relationship with his mentally ill mother; he eventually marries Phoebe Coldridge's daughter, Jill, before establishing a farm commune in Doris Lessing's *The Four-Gated City.*

Coldridge, Galina Colin Coldridge's Russian wife, whom he marries after fleeing England in Doris Lessing's *The Four-Gated City.*

Coldridge, Gwen Phoebe Coldridge's daughter, who rebels against her mother by joining political activities completely at odds with hers; she later moves to the farm commune in Wiltshire in Doris Lessing's *The Four-Gated City.*

Coldridge, Jill Phoebe Coldridge's daughter, who rebels against her mother by joining political activities completely at odds with hers; she later marries Francis Coldridge, moving with him to the farm commune in Wiltshire, and ultimately getting a divorce in Doris Lessing's *The Four-Gated City.*

Coldridge, Lynda Mark Coldridge's mentally ill wife (later ex-wife), who very slowly gains her independence from the hospital and drugs; she is able to predict the imminent disaster that will eventually strike Great Britain in Doris Lessing's *The Four-Gated City.* Her therapist instructs her to write down her thoughts and to assist other mental patients in *Re: Colonised Planet 5, Shikasta.*

Coldridge, Mark Writer for whom Martha Quest works as a secretary and confidante; through Martha's visions, he is able to develop characters and plots for his novels; ultimately he initiates a plan for a rescue mission and rescue points to save people from the destructive environment they have created in Doris Lessing's *The Four-Gated City.*

Coldridge, Paul Sally and Colin's son, who suffers miserably because of his mother's suicide and his father's fleeing; he later becomes rich and helps fund Mark Coldridge's rescue enterprise in Doris Lessing's *The Four-Gated City.*

Coldridge, Phoebe Martha Quest's connection in London; she offers Martha a job working for her ex-brother-in-law, Mark Coldridge, as a secretary; she is herself highly devoted to the Labour party, in which she eventually holds a minor office in Doris Lessing's *The Four-Gated City.*

Coldridge, Sally (Sarah Koenig) Colin's wife, a Jewish refugee from Germany, who commits suicide after her husband flees England for the Soviet Union in Doris Lessing's *The Four-Gated City.*

Coldstream, Giles Rich, anxious, and decidedly alcoholic innocuous weekend guest of Celia and Quentin Villiers; he is obsessed with hosing his teeth; he wants most to do nothing, but he can be aroused to cautious movement by the promise of gin in Martin Amis's *Dead Babies.*

Cole Heads up the advertising agency for which Sam Evans works; first sees Sam as a rising star but then views the young man with misgivings in Eugene O'Neill's play *Strange Interlude.*

Cole, Berkeley A close friend of the narrator who lives on a nearby African farm; has a good spirit and is full of adventure; stays with the narrator when he becomes ill; is encouraged by the doctor to remain in bed until he is well, but travels to Europe anyway; the narrator is sad to learn later that he has died in Isak Dinesen's *Out of Africa.*

Cole, Brian Son of Alderman Cole; he is a fat boy at Seaforth House who out of fear of injury hides equipment to prevent a school boxing tournament which would have pitted him against talented boxers in his weight class in Roy Fuller's *The Ruined Boys.*

Cole, Corporal Richard General Curzon's cousin, son of Stanley and Kate Cole; he is killed in military action after Curzon ignores Kate's written plea for her son's withdrawal and civilian reestablishment in C. S. Forester's *The General.*

Cole, Elizabeth (Litchfield) Deeply troubled woman whose sister killed their tyrannical father in Agatha Christie's *Curtain: Poirot's Last Case.*

Cole, George (Stuffy) Big boy with an overindulgent mother in Louisa May Alcott's *Little Men.*

Cole, John Grady Idealistic 16-year-old from west Texas; accomplished horseman, and confident in his abilities to run the family ranch, despite his mother's objections; runs away to Mexico to live out his dreams of being a mythic cowboy; finds love, adventure, and eventual disillusionment in Cormac McCarthy's *All the Pretty Horses.*

Cole, Harry Blue-collar worker in Chive Ward for ulcer surgery who is bitter towards the bosses of the world; he stays busy helping patients, seeks to keep peace when Ken Adamson and Dai Evans fight, and looks forward to returning home to his wife and son in John Berger's *The Foot of Clive.*

Cole, Kate Wife of Stanley Cole and aunt of General Curzon, for whom she is a source of embarrassment in C. S. Forester's *The General.*

Cole, King Marine whose guitar playing entertains his platoon mates; wounded in France during World War I in Thomas Boyd's *Through the Wheat.*

Cole, Marion Ruth Cole's mother; suffering from grief over the tragic accident that killed her two sons, is drawn into an affair with a much younger man named Eddie O'Hare; affair prompts Marion to leave her husband, Ted, and four-year-old Ruth in John Irving's *A Widow for One Year.*

Cole, Miranda High school teacher and girlfriend of Thomas Skelton in Thomas McGuane's *Ninety-Two in the Shade.*

Cole, Mr. Well-to-do Highbury tradesman, whose social aspirations Emma Woodhouse deplores; she allows herself to be persuaded to attend his and Mrs. Cole's dinner party in Jane Austen's *Emma.*

Cole, Mrs. Kindly madam of a high-class bordello; almost a surrogate mother to Fanny Hill, she oversees most of Fanny's career and helps her mature and gain financial success in John Cleland's *Memoirs of a Woman of Pleasure.*

Cole, Mrs. Unpretentious, ungenteel wife of a prosperous Highbury tradesman; her dinner party is a success in Jane Austen's *Emma.*

Cole, Nat King Hamilton Ashinow's landlord; he joins Hamilton and his friends in drinking and smoking marijuana in Colin MacInnes's *City of Spades.*

Cole, Pauline (M. C. Number Two, Moe) High school cheerleader and girlfriend abandoned by Jack Duluoz in favor of Maggie Cassidy in Jack Kerouac's *Maggie Cassidy;* mentioned in *Book of Dreams* and *Desolation Angels.*

Cole, Peter Young son of Harry Cole; he "lacks confidence" and "has too much imagination" in John Berger's *The Foot of Clive.*

Cole, Phyl Small, dark, energetic wife of Harry Cole; a schoolteacher, she is lovingly called a "great agitator" by her husband in John Berger's *The Foot of Clive.*

Cole, Raymond Fighter and heavy drinker; combat veteran who freezes to death in a cornfield in James Jones's *Some Came Running.*

Cole, Ruth Protagonist; daughter of Marion Cole; an acclaimed novelist who still bears the emotional scars resulting from Marion's abrupt departure from the family in John Irving's *A Widow for One Year.*

Cole, Stanley Radical, who is father of Corporal Richard Cole and husband to Kate; he stands in political opposition to the Victorian conservatism of his celebrated nephew, General Curzon, in C. S. Forester's *The General.*

Cole, Ted Ruth Cole's father; a children's book author and illustrator with a lustful eye who is left to raise his young daughter when his wife, Marion, leaves them in John Irving's *A Widow for One Year.*

Cole, Walter Called Teach, a friend of Don Dubrow, owner of Don's Resale Shop; small-time thug who hangs out at the junk store; plans with Don to steal a coin collection, including American buffalo nickels, from a collector staying in a nearby hotel room in David Mamet's play *American Buffalo.*

Cole, William Boatswain on HMS *Bounty* whose loyalty to Captain Bligh and his regard for Admiralty law cause him to be set adrift with Bligh after the mutiny in Charles Nordhoff and James Norman Hall's *Mutiny on the Bounty;* his faith in God and Bligh, as well as his great strength, help him survive being cast adrift at sea in *Men Against the Sea.*

Coleby, Mr. Prisoner for indebtedness who receives a gift of money from Sir Launcelot Greaves in Tobias Smollett's *The Adventures of Sir Launcelot Greaves.*

Coleman Exploitative cynic and prophet of despair; stabbed by one mistress, he immediately goes to work on and seduces Rosie Shearwater in Aldous Huxley's *Antic Hay.*

Coleman Surgeon's mate who assists in the repair of Captain Sawyer after his tumble in C. S. Forester's *Lieutenant Hornblower.*

Coleman, Alice E. Wife of a northerner who, after being ambushed, dies in her arms in Albion W. Tourgee's *A Fool's Errand.*

Coleman, Claris Daughter of Colonel Coleman and first lover of Clay-Boy Spencer in Earl Hamner, Jr.'s *Spencer's Mountain.*

Coleman, Colonel General manager of the New Dominion Stone Company; buys Clay Spencer's mountain property so Spencer can send his oldest son of college in Earl Hamner, Jr.'s *Spencer's Mountain.*

Coleman, Daisy Meissner Broadway chorus girl and wife of Ray Coleman in Edmund Wilson's *I Thought of Daisy.*

Coleman, Father Good-hearted Jesuit priest, who discusses the church with Lothair but does not bring enough pressure on him to convert and thus incurs the dissatisfaction of Cardinal Grandison in Benjamin Disraeli's *Lothair.*

Coleman, Jane Zachariah's wife, who dislikes his political activity and French friends, and who dies in 1819 while he is in Manchester prison in Mark Rutherford's *The Revolution in Tanner's Lane.*

Coleman, Jewell Glen Davis's longtime girlfriend and the mother of his son David; a hardworking waitress who remains faithful to Glen during the three years he spends in prison in Larry Brown's *Father and Son.*

Coleman, Marie Pauline Daughter of Zachariah and Pauline (Caillaud) Coleman; she lives alone with her widowed father in London; she loathes Thomas Broad and successfully resists his forceful attentions in Mark Rutherford's *The Revolution in Tanner's Lane.*

Coleman, Miss Woman in poor health because of weak lungs, culpable idleness, and a gentleman who disappointed her; she is reunited with her gentleman, Mr. Evans, after her father loses his wealth in George MacDonald's *At the Back of the North Wind.*

Coleman, Miss ("Collie") One of three aging spinsters who live in the May of Teck Chub in Muriel Spark's *The Girls of Slender Means.*

Coleman, Mr. Diamond's father's first employer; he dissipates his wealth in shady speculations urged by his daughter's "gentleman," Mr. Evans; he is finally ruined when North Wind sinks the ship with Mr. Evans aboard in George MacDonald's *At the Back of the North Wind.*

Coleman, Ray Husband of Daisy Meissner Coleman; reporter for the *Telegram-Dispatch* and then for the tabloid *Daily Sketch* in Edmund Wilson's *I Thought of Daisy.*

Coleman, Vance R. (Professor, Slim) Book salesman and would-be entrepreneur; friend of Sidney Wyeth in Oscar Micheaux's *The Forged Note.*

Coleman, Walter ("Bill") Master of Ceremonies at St. Luke's Church, who jealously protects his position and his tailor-made cassock in Barbara Pym's *A Glass of Blessings.*

Coleman, Zachariah Radical Calvinist printer, 30 years old in 1814, who is imprisoned for his connections with the Manchester Blanketeers in 1817; he marries Pauline Caillaud after his release and fathers Marie Pauline Coleman in 1822 in Mark Rutherford's *The Revolution in Tanner's Lane.*

Colepepper, Captain (Peppercull) Cowardly soldier who courts Martha Trapbois for her father's wealth, conspires with Andrew Skurliewhitter to kill and rob old

Trapbois, and is killed by Richie Moniplies after Colepepper murders Lord Dalgarno in Sir Walter Scott's *The Fortunes of Nigel.*

Coles, Anne-Marion College roommate and later correspondent of Meridian Hill in Alice Walker's *Meridian.*

Coles, Arthur Friend and research partner of Colin Pasmore; he tries to help Colin and his wife, Kay, while they are estranged in David Storey's *Pasmore.*

Coles, Irene Boyish and unconventional artist; Elizabeth Mapp dreads her powers of mimicry in E. F. Benson's *Miss Mapp.* She is one of Lucia Lucas's allies in *Mapp and Lucia* and in *The Worshipful Lucia.* Her satire of Botticelli's Venus in Victorian attire caricatures Elizabeth Mapp and is named "Picture of the Year" at the Royal Academy in *Trouble for Lucia.*

Coles, Joel Twenty-eight-year-old handsome, aspiring writer in Hollywood whose career has already jumped off to a promising start, as he has been introduced to the right people; attends a cocktail party given by his employer, the famous director Miles Calman, where he falls in love with Miles's wife Stella in F. Scott Fitzgerald's "Crazy Sunday."

Coleville (or Colevile), Sir John Knight loyal to the archbishop of York; taken prisoner by Falstaff; executed in William Shakespeare's play *Henry IV, Part Two.*

Coley, Captain Kevin Adjutant and frequently the official representative of the prestigious Pankot Rifles in Paul Scott's *The Day of the Scorpion.* He inevitably spends much time with Mildred Layton, wife of the regiment's commander, who is a prisoner of war in Germany, and is revealed to be Mildred's hover in *The Towers of Silence.*

Colfax, Clarence Hotheaded but noble Confederate soldier; suitor of Virginia Carvel in Winston Churchill's *The Crisis.*

Colgate, Father Catholic priest and optimist who says Roger Micheldene's soul is at variance with God; Micheldene, under the influence of alcohol, goes to Colgate's residence and immerses the priest's head in a fishtank in Kingsley Amis's *One Fat Englishman.*

Coligny, Gaspar de Virtuous, honorable French nobleman, who was acquainted with Reginald de St. Leon in his youth, and who, when they meet many years later at the court of Dresden, demands that St. Leon, as a man of honour, account for the astounding change in his fortunes in William Godwin's *St. Leon.*

Colin Young, homosexual server in a Kensington snack bar; he is the object of the hopeless devotion of Leonora Eyre's friend and contemporary Meg in Barbara Pym's *The Sweet Dove Died.*

Colin, Dr. Hard-working, dedicated, early-middle-aged physician employed by the Order in charge of the leper colony; a professed atheist motivated by anger and a strong sense of duty, he finds his salvation in helping others; through his example and uncritical acceptance he helps Querry cure himself of spiritual aridity in Graham Greene's *A Burnt-Out Case.*

Colindale, Ann Gracie Tisbourne's friend, who succeeds in marrying Richard Pargeter in Iris Murdoch's *An Accidental Man.*

Colkitto See M'Donnell, Alister.

Collander, Tom Very successful architect in prison for corruption, keeping almost entirely to himself until Len Wincobank speaks to him; he then proceeds to share with Wincobank ideas which Wincobank finds maddening in Margaret Drabble's *The Ice Age.*

Collatine Virtuous Roman nobleman whose soldier's boasting of his wife's purity and beauty leads directly to her rape and suicide in William Shakespeare's poem *The Rape of Lucrece.*

Colleoni, Mr. Wealthy, powerful, elegant-appearing Jewish leader of a rival extortion mob; he engineers a takeover of Pinkie Brown's (formerly Kite's) mob after Kite's death in Graham Greene's *Brighton Rock.*

Collett, Selina Schoolgirl friend of Aminta Farrell (Lady Ormont); she passes letters to Aminta from Matey Weyburn when they are in school, and when they are adults she-unknowingly-helps bring them together again in George Meredith's *Lord Ormont and his Aminta.*

Colley Red-haired student at Brookfield who has the distinction of being the first boy Mr. Chips punished; he eventually becomes an alderman of the City of London and a baronet whose son and grandson attend Brookfield in James Hilton's *Good-frye, Mr. Chips.*

Colley (the younger) Grandson of the first boy Mr. Chips punished at Brookfield and son of another Brookfield boy; he is the butt of Mr. Chips's joke about the stupidity of the Colleys in James Hilton's *Good-bye, Mr. Chips.*

Collier, Andrew Journalist and half brother of Daniel Compton Wills; discovers his supposed benefactor, Daniel

Cable Wills, is his father and a former member of the OSS and CIA in George V. Higgins's *Dreamland.*

Collier, John Bearer of a marriage proposal from James Hopkins to Sally Oldham; she encourages Collier to advance his own suit and becomes his wife in Lydia Maria Child's *Hobomok.*

Collier, Sally Oldham Friend of Mary Conant; rejects the written marriage proposal of James Hopkins in favor of its bearer, John Collier, in Lydia Maria Child's *Hobomok.*

Colligan, Dr. Physician who treats Anty Lynch for fever; he knocks down her brother, Barry, who has invited the doctor to murder her in Anthony Trollope's *The Kellys and the O'Kellys.*

Collingwood, Lord Cuthbert Vice Admiral of the Mediterranean; he was promoted after battle victories as Captain of the *Trafalgar* in C. S. Forester's *Hornblower and the Atropos.*

Collingwood, Reginald Cabinet minister who is an ally of Roger Quaife in C. P. Snow's *Corridors of Power.*

Collins American sailor who often pays for drinks and entertainment for Henry Miller, Kruger, and Fillmore in Henry Miller's *Tropic of Cancer.*

Collins, Alfred Alcoholic who stopped drinking for a period but who lost all remission, according to the prison officer Jim in Margaret Drabble's *The Ice Age.*

Collins, Audrey Oldest child of Theresa and Dan Collins; sister of Lizzy Collins; friend of Emma and Claire Goodwin in Jane Hamilton's *A Map of the World.*

Collins, Clara Widow of Ely Collins and leader of the Circle in Robert Coover's *The Origin of the Brunists.*

Collins, Dan Husband of Theresa; father of Lizzy and Audrey; friend of Howard; curator for the Dairy Shrine and organist at the Presbyterian Church in Prairie Center in Jane Hamilton's *A Map of the World.*

Collins, Elaine Repressed daughter of Ely Collins; falls in love with Carl Dean Palmers in Robert Coover's *The Origin of the Brunists.*

Collins, Ely Preacher and coal miner; deceased husband of Clara Collins in Robert Coover's *The Origin of the Brunists.*

Collins, Hannah Ann Old and blind Alabama poetess in John Updike's *Bech: A Book.*

Collins, Henry Rich, cranky Englishman who marries Marian Forrester and makes her final years secure in Willa Cather's *A Lost Lady.*

Collins, Jasper Companion of Larry Donovan and Nat Moore in the search for jobs and a meaningful life in Jack Conroy's *The Disinherited.*

Collins, Josh Sardonic computer expert at Darlington University who introduces Robin Dempsey to Eliza, the psychiatric program, in David Lodge's *Small World.*

Collins, Kitty (Mrs. Benjamin Watson, Mrs. Catherine) Maid at the Hutter house; married to Benjamin Watson, who returns to her after an absence of ten years, in Thomas Bailey Aldrich's *The Story of a Bad Boy.*

Collins, Lieutenant Leader of an expedition with Dick Gibson in search of the last living dodo bird on the island of Mauritius during World War II in Stanley Elkin's *The Dick Gibson Show.*

Collins, Lizzy Youngest daughter of Dan and Theresa Collins; victim of drowning in Alice Goodwin's pond; child about whom Alice continues to think in Jane Hamilton's *A Map of the World.*

Collins, Mr. Ferdinando Falkland's steward, considered by Caleb Williams to be one of his closest friends; Caleb learns Falkland's history from Collins; when Caleb asks for Collins's help, Collins replies he will do what he can, but not at the risk of his position in William Godwin's *Caleb Williams.*

Collins, Mrs. Older woman who divides her time between religion and gossip; she goes to Mrs. Thorpe to suggest that Lucy Bentham is the subject of scandal in George Moore's *A Modern Lover.*

Collins, Rupe (Rupie) Bully who encourages Penrod Schofield's antics to take a more aggressive form in Booth Tarkington's *Penrod.*

Collins, Sam (covername: Mellon) Bill Haydon's recruit who becomes Operational Director for British Intelligence; he is dismissed when Operation Testify goes sour in John le Carré's *Tinker, Tailor, Soldier, Spy.* Reinstated by George Smiley for Operation Dolphin, he forces Lizzie Worthington to betray her hover Drake Ko in *The Honourable Schoolboy.* He conspires with Saul Enderby for Smiley's dismissal in *Smiley's People.*

Collins, Theresa Psychologist/therapist; wife of Dan and mother of Audrey and Lizzy Collins; best friend of Alice and witness at her trial; with her family, leaves for Montana following her youngest daughter's death; cares for Alice's children and husband, Howard, during Alice's jail stay in Jane Hamilton's *A Map of the World.*

Collins, William Prosy, self-important clergyman whose practice of studied flattery is not offensive to his patroness, Lady Catherine de Bourgh; heir to Mr. Bennet's entailed estate, he intends to find a wife among the Bennet sisters; after Elizabeth's rejection he proposes successfully to Charlotte Lucas in Jane Austen's *Pride and Prejudice.*

Collins, William David Name given to the baby Leslie Collins adopts in Harriette Simpson Arnow's *The Kentucky Trace.*

Collins II, William David Leslie Son of Virginia gentry and patriot covertly involved in the American Revolution; shoots his own brother at the battle of Camden; cares for and ultimately adopts a child in Harriette Simpson Arnow's *The Kentucky Trace.*

Colliphant, Mr. Dark-haired, dark-faced, heavy-set master of the Works Department; he fails to deal appropriately with the crises created by a visiting Rajah's demand for a special bed in Arnold Bennett's *Imperial Palace.*

Collop, Christopher Fun-loving Anglican clergyman revealed in a spurious editor's note to be the author in Richard Graves's *The Spiritual Quixote.*

Collopy, Mr. Campaigner for public lavatories for women; while in Rome to seek the Pope's assistance for his project, he crashes through a floor because of his enormous weight in Flann O'Brien's *The Hard Life.*

Collwar Deity worshipped by residents of Normnbdsgrsutt in Robert Paltock's *The Life and Adventures of Peter Wilkins.*

Collyer British adjutant in William Faulkner's *A Fable.*

Colmar, Nonie Sexual tease who is part of a company of foreign acrobats; she is murdered by Barney, a dwarf, after she insults his manhood in J. B. Priestley's *Lost Empires.*

Colmar, Sir George Early admirer of Clarissa Harlowe's friend Anna Howe in Samuel Richardson's *Clarissa: or, The History of a Young Lady.*

Colmore, Dorothy Wife of Harold Colmore in Roy Fuller's *The Father's Comedy.*

Colmore, Giles Harold Colmore's son; he is completing his compulsory military service in an African colony when he is arrested for striking an officer who he thinks has brutally interrogated some political prisoners; the charge of assault turns to one of murder on the death of the officer in Roy Fuller's *The Father's Comedy.*

Colmore, Harold Chartered accountant who has risen from humble social origins to become the complacent assistant secretary of a major London industrial company; poised to replace the company's secretary in a post which will ultimately give him a knighthood, he leaves England for an African colony to help organize the legal defense of his son, Giles, who is charged with assault; he is also involved in a relationship with Giles's young woman friend in Roy Fuller's *The Father's Comedy.*

Colocotroni Greek warlord betrayed and later murdered by Bozzari in William Godwin's *Cloudesley.*

Colocotroni, Irene Young Greek woman whom Arthur Danvers, Lord Alton rescues from Bozzari, the murderer of her father; she marries Arthur, but dies in childbirth; her son, Julian, survives but is bilked out of his rightful inheritance by Arthur's younger brother, Richard (Lord Alton), and his accomplice, Cloudesley, in William Godwin's *Cloudesley.*

Colocynth, Comfit Physician who certifies for Mrs. Grizzle that Mrs. Pickle is wrong to douse her infant in cold water in Tobias Smollett's *The Adventures of Peregrine Pickle.*

Colonel Embodiment of the concept of the glory of war and army; dressed up with a patchwork of historical uniforms decorated with bits and pieces of military equipment reminiscent of earlier American wars; represents the American ideal of expansionism through wars; father whose son was badly mutilated in war in Sam Shepard's *States of Shock.*

Colonel Husband of an old woman referred to as the Mummy, and father of the young Adèle, who is actually the biological daughter of fiendish Jacob Hummel; unmasked by Hummel, who shows that the colonel is not in reality a colonel, of noble birth, or Adèle's real father in August Strindberg's play *The Ghost Sonata.*

Colonel Veteran who calls the Doctor to task for his opinions and impudence in Charles Johnstone's *Chrysal: or, The Adventures of a Guinea.*

Colonel Well-born man whose confidence in his own understanding allows him to be defrauded by the Servant's Servant in Charles Johnstone's *Chrysal: or, The Adventures of a Guinea.*

Colonel, The Ranking enemy officer who holds the Cartographer captive in a greenhouse to spite the prison-camp Commandant; he becomes the subject of an inquiry at which the Cartographer is the principal witness in Nigel Dennis's *A House in Order.*

Colonel Pickering Noted phonetician who bets Prof. Higgins to transform Eliza from a flower girl with a Cockney dialect into a refined duchess; unlike the aloof Higgins, Pickering is caring and treats Eliza as a lady even before her transformation in George Bernard Shaw's *Pygmalion.*

Colonna, Fra Wealthy, aristocratic Dominican friar; a sceptic in religion but a zealot in the arts, he makes Gerard's fortune as a copyist of Greek and Latin in Charles Reade's *The Cloister and the Hearth.*

Colonna, Prince Paul Dissolute Roman friend of Lord Monmouth; he is killed in a riding accident in Benjamin Disraeli's *Coningsby; or, The New Generation.*

Colonna, Princess Malicious and greedy second wife, later the widow, of Prince Colonna and friend of Lord Monmouth; she unsuccessfully plots her stepdaughter's marriage to Harry Coningsby and her own marriage to Lord Monmouth in Benjamin Disraeli's *Coningsby; or, The New Generation.*

Colonna, Princess Lucretia Sullen and manipulative daughter of Prince Colonna; she initially intends to marry Harry Coningsby but falls in love with Sidonia, whose rejection of her causes her to marry Lord Monmouth in Benjamin Disraeli's *Coningsby; or, The New Generation.*

Colper, Joe Sales manager of Harris Towers, a condominium complex in *The Condominium,* a novella in Stanley Elkin's *Searches and Seizures.*

Colston, Charlie Mrs. Colston's silly son, who is twenty-eight and eligible for marriage, but whom Catharine Furze rejects when her mother introduces them in Mark Rutherford's *Catharine Furze.*

Colston, Dame Lettie Sister of Godfrey Colston and friendless social reformer; her selfishness, isolation, and fear cause her to misinterpret death's telephone warning and head to her violent death in Muriel Spark's *Memento Mori.*

Colston, Eric Middle-aged failure, who preys on his aged relatives for money in Muriel Spark's *Memento Mori.*

Colston, Godfrey Retired businessman, husband of Charmian Piper; his sexual voyeurism makes him susceptible to Mabel Pettigrew's control, and his long-past indiscretions make him her blackmail victim; his selfishness makes him obtuse to death's call in Muriel Spark's *Memento Mori.*

Colston, Leo Impressionable narrator who at age thirteen visits his classmate's rented estate in Norfolk during Summer 1900 and finds himself messenger and inadvertent panderer for a love relationship; fifty years later he returns to the scene of early trauma to deliver a final message between survivors and a new generation in L. P. Hartley's *The Go-Between.*

Colston, Mrs. Snobbish wife of the brewer in Eastthorp; she condescends to visit Mrs. Furze to collect for a church memorial in Mark Rutherford's *Catharine Furze.*

Colston, Mrs. Widowed mother of Leo Colston; she discourages him from departing Brandham Hall when his own instincts suggest disaster if he remains as go-between in L. P. Hartley's *The Go-Between.*

Colt, Ann Wife of Timothy Colt; shy, awkward former English major who remains devoted to her husband despite his affair with Eileen Shallcross; returns to him after his trial in Louis Auchincloss's *The Great World and Timothy Colt.*

Colt, Ronald Director of the British Institute in Zagazig; he invites Edgar Perry to Zagazig to give a lecture in P. H. Newby's *The Picnic at Sakkara.*

Colt, Timothy (Timmy) Idealistic but angry young lawyer who becomes a partner in a large Manhattan law firm and almost destroys his career and marriage through unethical conduct; husband of Ann Colt in Louis Auchincloss's *The Great World and Timothy Colt.*

Coltham, Geoffrey Critic whose review publicizes Wilfred Desert's religious conversion as an act of cowardice in John Galsworthy's *Flowering Wilderness.*

Coltherd, Little Benjie Boy who teaches Darsie Latimer (Arthur Redgauntlet) the art of fishing and is used as a messenger by Cristal Nixon in Sir Walter Scott's *Redgauntlet.*

Colton Unknown outsider who becomes the first elected sheriff of Tooms County, Alabama, and vows to destroy blacks any way possible to prevent them from advancing in W. E. B. DuBois's *The Quest of the Silver Fleece.*

Colton, Anabel Friend of Isabel Otis, wife of Tom Colton, and a mother submerged in domesticity in Gertrude Atherton's *Ancestors.*

Colton, Thomas (Tom) Practical California businessman, husband of Anabel Colton, politician eager to become a United States senator, and rival of John Gwynne in Gertrude Atherton's *Ancestors.*

Coltsworth, Ralph Suitor preferred by Hagar Ashendyne's family; opposes Hagar's beliefs, but is determined to marry her until she resists his physical advances in Mary Johnston's *Hagar.*

Columbato, Alfonso (Al) Birdy's boyhood friend in real life; the male canary in Birdy's fantasy bird life in William Wharton's *Birdy.*

Columbine, Bess Mistress and partner in crime of Blackjack Mallard; jealous of Mallard's friendship with Amber St. Clare in Kathleen Winsor's *Forever Amber.*

Columbus, Christopher Great mariner portrayed as both valorous and altruistic (the "Harp") and egotistical and duplicitous (the "Shadow") at the time of his canonization by Pope Pius XI; saint whose fame is unlimited and incontrovertible, reaching a planetary wingspan "even larger than the Colossus of Rhodes"; also confesses to profound greed, sexual conquests, unbridled lust for glory, and "deceptions and intrigues trying to gain the favor of the princes of the earth" in Alejo Carpentier's *The Harp and the Shadow.*

Columbus, Christopher Ocean explorer and representative of the new renaissance man in Johannes V. Jensen's *The Long Journey.*

Colville, Anthony Illegitimate son of Lord Scroope (1); he unknowingly marries his sister Gertrude Marlowe; subsequently, as Father Anthony, he devotes himself to study and is an exacting mentor for Matilda and Ellinor before being murdered by Williams in Sophia Lee's *The Recess.*

Colville, Mr. Gentleman with an estate in Jamaica; he knowingly marries the pregnant lover of Lord Scroope (1) and with her raises Anthony Colville in Sophia Lee's *The Recess.*

Colville, Mr. John Falkner's solicitor in his murder trial who obtains his acquittal in Mary Shelley's *Falkner.*

Colville, Theodore Newspaper editor living in Florence; briefly engaged to Imogene Graham, but marries the more suitable Evalina Bowen in William Dean Howells's *Indian Summer.*

Colvin English officer in the pay of Charles, Duke of Burgundy; he is loyal to his employer to the end in Sir Walter Scott's *Anne of Geierstein.*

Colwan, George (the father) Free-living Laird of Dalcastle, who dotes on his son George but rejects his wife's second son, Robert, and dies of grief at George's murder in James Hogg's *The Private Memoirs and Confessions of a Justified Sinner.*

Colwan, George (the son) Elder son of George Colwan the Laird of Dalcastle; he is shadowed, persecuted, and finally murdered by his brother, Robert, in James Hogg's *The Private Memoirs and Confessions of a Justified Sinner.*

Colwan, Rabina ("Lady Dalcastle") Daughter of Baillie Orde; she is the pleasure-renouncing, pious, disapproving wife of the jovial elder George Colwan; hating the name of her husband, she is called Lady Dalcastle as a courtesy; she is mother of the younger George Colwan and of Robert Colwan in James Hogg's *The Private Memoirs and Confessions of a Justified Sinner.*

Colwan, Robert Wringhim Son of Lady Dalcastle (Rabina Colwan) and ward of the Reverend Wringhim; under the influence of Gil-martin and belief in the infallibility of the elect, he murders his brother, George, and several others, commits crimes as Laird of Dalcastle, and finally commits suicide after writing his memoirs in James Hogg's *The Private Memoirs and Confessions of a Justified Sinner.*

Colza, Miss Determinedly youthful maiden lady much given to curls and pink bows, who spies on Margaret Mackenzie and passes information to Mr. Maguire for gossip articles in a Christian journal attacking John Ball; she ends up marrying Maguire in Anthony Trollope's *Miss Mackenzie.*

Comeaux, Bob Physician who works at Fedville medical facility; with the help of John Van Dorn, secretly taints water supply of Ruhr Valley, Louisiana; contamination decreases violent crime, drug addiction, pregnancy, and the spread of AIDS virus in Walker Percy's *The Thanatos Syndrome.*

Comendador Orsini Jacob's boxing manager who is tired of exploiting the aging Jacob; convinced Jacob cannot win another fight; tries to convince Jacob to run away with the purse money before a fight in Santa María, but the proud old boxer refuses to play the cheat in Juan Carlos Onetti's "Jacob and the Other."

Comfort, Aycock Friend of Jack Renfro sentenced with him to Parchman State Penitentiary; maintains the balance of Maud Eva Moody's car while it hangs on the edge of Banner Top in Eudora Welty's *Losing Battles.*

Comfort, Charles Low Church rector of Cawston, neighboring parish to Baslehurst, in Devon; a long-time friend of Mrs. Ray, he pours cold water on her daughter's attachment to Luke Rowan in Anthony Trollope's *Rachel Ray.*

Comfort, James Village blacksmith and volunteer soldier in Thomas Hardy's *The Trumpet-Major.*

Comines, Philip des Shrewd politician and historian of the Duke of Burgundy's court, who is persuaded to join Louis XI in France in Sir Walter Scott's *Quentin Durward.*

Cominius General against the Volscians; a former consul and friend to Coriolanus; when Martius leads the Volscian armies under the walls of Rome, is the first who goes to the camp, trying to speak to him, but Coriolanus refuses to hear his friend in William Shakespeare's play *Coriolanus.*

Comisky, Dan Gambler who promotes free-hanging as a sport and urges Clyde Stout to compete in it in Jack Matthews's *Hanger Stout, Awake!*

Commandant of German Prisoner-of-war Camp An unnamed German officer who disagrees with the sadistic Dr. Halde; he says that the psychologist "does not know about peoples" in William Golding's *Free Fall.*

Commander Jesuit whom Candide meets in Paraguay; turns out to be Cunégonde's brother; attacks the lower-class Candide with his sword when Candide tells him his intention to marry Cunégonde; then killed by Candide, but survives miraculously and is sent first to the galleys, then back to Rome in Voltaire's *Candide.*

Commander of British Forces in America Young, active, and brave Commander with good judgment, who leaves his mother and his beloved to do his duty and fight for his country in Charles Johnstone's *Chrysal: or, The Adventures of a Guinea.*

Commissary Medina Appears as many characters, including frustrated surgeon and painter maintained by Frieda, a lesbian prostitute; also plays a police officer in a love relationship with young Olga, as well as an affair with Seoane, who bears his son, in Juan Carlos Onetti's *Let the Wind Speak;* police officer in Juan Carlos Onetti's *The Body Snatcher* and *Past Caring.*

Commissioner Government Treasury official who bribes Mr. Secretary to spy on London political radicals in Mark Rutherford's *The Revolution in Tanner's Lane.*

Commissioner of Public Safety Magistrate who is officially the head of law and order but fails to establish security; troubled in following Lysistrata's grand ideas of peace through common sense instead of weapons; only a reference to a real historical disaster, the failed expedition to Sicily in 415 B.C.E., makes him uncomfortable in Aristophanes' play *Lysistrata.*

Common, Doll Prostitute and third member of the three-part con operation that includes Face and Subtle; serves as an intermediary between Subtle and Face during their arguments over their roles in the group; desired by Sir Epicure Mammon, and assumes the role of a great lady in her conversation with him; pretends to a madness activated by Mammon's mention of Broughton, under whom she claims to have studied; escapes, along with Subtle, from the house without any reward for her work at the end of Ben Jonson's play *The Alchemist.*

Comnena, Anna Emperor's beautiful and intelligent daughter, who wrote his history, the *Alexiad;* she jealously guards her dignity as a princess and author; though admired by the court for her wisdom and generous nature, she is often neglected by her beloved husband, Nicephorus Briennius, in Sir Walter Scott's *Count Robert of Paris.*

Comnenus, Alexius Emperor of Greece; essentially powerless and ineffectual, he maintains his throne through the wealth and importance of his predecessors; though deeply religious and a defender of the Church, he is nevertheless extremely superstitious in Sir Walter Scott's *Count Robert of Paris.*

Comorin, Mrs. Mistress of Casimir Fleetwood; she is distinguished by her pride of heart, ease of manners, and inexhaustible vitality in William Godwin's *Fleetwood.*

Compeyson Swindler who jilted Miss Havisham on her wedding day; later he is Abel Magwitch's fellow convict and mortal enemy; he betrays Magwitch to the police and finally drowns fighting in the river with Magwitch in Charles Dickens's *Great Expectations.*

Compeyson, Sally Wife of the swindler Compeyson in Charles Dickens's *Great Expectations.*

Compiler Notes and quotations from the "compiler" help to form the history and story of the Paraguayan dictator José Gaspar Rodríguez de Francia; uses library resources such as books, journals, governmental files, and personal documents to explain the personal life of the dictator and his ambitions to save Paraguay; possesses an independent space from which he can launch criticism toward the dictator, with confrontation erupting between the dictator's discourse and the documents collected by the "compiler" in Augusto Roa Bastos's *I, the Supreme.*

Compor, Munn Li Councilman of Terminus who aids Mayor Harla Branno in exiling Golan Trevize, then is himself exiled by Branno and assigned to follow Trevize through space and report on his movements; secretly an agent of the Second Foundation who reports to Stor Gendibal in Isaac Asimov's *Foundation's Edge.*

Composite beings Beings on various planets where the "individual" is a flock of birds or a swarm of insects in Olaf Stapledon's *Star Maker.*

Compson, Benjamin (Benjy, Maury) Idiot son of Caroline Bascomb and Jason Lycurgus Compson III; brother of Caddy Compson, Quentin Compson I, and Jason Compson IV; castrated and committed to an asylum; appears in William Faulkner's *The Sound and the Fury* and *The Mansion.*

Compson, Candace (Caddy) Daughter of Caroline Bascomb and Jason Lycurgus Compson III; sister of Benjy Compson, Quentin Compson I, and Jason Compson IV; mother of Quentin Compson II; appears in William Faulkner's *The Sound and the Fury* and *The Mansion.*

Compson, Caroline Bascomb Wife of Jason Lycurgus Compson III; mother of Benjy and Caddy Compson, Quentin Compson I, and Jason Compson IV in William Faulkner's *The Sound and the Fury.*

Compson, General Neighbor of Colonel Sartoris in William Faulkner's "An Odor of Verbena."

Compson (I), Jason Lycurgus Indian agent who trades a racing mare to Ikkemotubbe for a square mile of land that becomes the center of Jefferson, Mississippi; appears in William Faulkner's *The Sound and the Fury* and *Requiem for a Nun.*

Compson (I), Quentin Son of Caroline Bascomb and Jason Lycurgus Compson III; brother of Benjy and Caddy Compson and Jason Compson IV; following a year at Harvard, he commits suicide; appears in William Faulkner's *The Sound and the Fury; Absalom, Absalom!*

Compson (II), Jason Lycurgus Hunter and Civil War general; only real friend of Thomas Sutpen; appears in William Faulkner's *The Sound and the Fury; Absalom, Absalom!; The Unvanquished; Go Down, Moses; Intruder in the Dust; Requiem for a Nun; The Town;* and *The Reivers.*

Compson (II), Quentin Illegitimate daughter of Caddy Compson and Dalton Ames; appears in William Faulkner's *The Sound and the Fury* and *The Mansion.*

Compson (III), Jason Lycurgus Husband of Caroline Bascomb; father of Benjy and Caddy Compson, Quentin Compson I, and Jason Compson IV; appears in William Faulkner's *The Sound and the Fury* and *Absalom, Absalom!*

Compson (IV), Jason Lycurgus Son of Caroline Bascomb and Jason Lycurgus Compson III; brother of Benjy and Caddy Compson and Quentin Compson I; appears in William Faulkner's *The Sound and the Fury, The Town,* and *The Mansion.*

Compton Airplane pilot who is supposed to fly the injured protagonist, Henry, to the hospital; fails to arrive in time to save Henry's life in Ernest Hemingway's "The Snows of Kilimanjaro."

Compton, Ben Radical intellectual devoted to proletarian issues who is jailed for subversive activities in John Dos Passos's *U.S.A.* trilogy.

Compton, Father Graceless, overworked Roman Catholic priest to whom Sarah Miles goes for counseling and announces her intention to convert to Roman Catholicism; while having dinner with Henry Miles and Maurice Bendrix, he reveals his understanding that Maurice's feelings about Sarah are reflected in his anger in Graham Greene's *The End of the Affair.*

Compton, Gladys Secretary whom J. Ward Morehouse asks to watch over Janey Williams and whose family, as a result, boards her temporarily; sister of Ben Compton in John Dos Passos's *U.S.A.* trilogy.

Comstock, Gordon Middle-class working man who tries to resist the lure of an easy, unthinking life by writing poetry and working at a bookstore instead of at a "good job"; he spends the money he receives for the sale of a poem to an American magazine on a convivial binge that ends in his being arrested and fired; after he gets Rosemary pregnant, he finally marries her and takes the good job and all that comes with it in George Orwell's *Keep the Aspidistra Flying.*

Compton, Molly Lawyer from Washington, D.C.; dates Roger Gaston in Elizabeth Benedict's *Slow Dancing.*

Compton, Mr. Suitor of Alicia Malcolm in contest with her cousin, Sir Edmund Audley, before her marriage to Archibald Douglas in Susan Ferrier's *Marriage.*

Compton, Mrs. Neighbor whom Mr. Blake dislikes, for she is a shoulder to cry on for Louise and too intrusive and compassionate toward Louise for Blake's tastes in John Cheever's "The Five-Forty-Five."

Compton, Private Cockney soldier and companion of Private Carr; he strikes Stephen Dedalus in the brothel district in James Joyce's *Ulysses.*

Comroe, Edgar Night officer at Vandenberg Air Force Base in Michael Crichton's *The Andromeda Strain.*

Comstock, Charlie Reformed alcoholic, pious parishioner of Andrew Mackerel, and copublisher of the Globe in Peter De Vries's *The Mackerel Plaza.*

Comstock, Julia Gordon Comstock's unmarried sister; though she works seventeen hours a day to make her bills, she lends Comstock money when he is low in George Orwell's *Keep the Aspidistra Flying.*

Comtesse de Mirbel Dissolute mother of Jean, a boy and troublemaker whose problems stem from his mother's indifference and cruelty; becomes friends with the narrator, Louis, and Michelle Pian in François Charles Mauriac's *A Woman of the Pharisees.*

Comyn, Lord (Jack) Generous nobleman secretly sympathetic to the American cause; friend of Richard Carvel in Winston Churchill's *Richard Carvel.*

Comyns, Ralph Physical therapist at Emma Lazarus Retirement Home and lover of Mandy Dattner in Alan Isler's *The Prince of West End Avenue.*

Conachar (Eachin M'lan, Hector M'lan) Simon Glover's young apprentice, who rejoins his clan in the Highlands to become its chief; he courts Catherine Glover; he shames himself as a coward when he runs from a fight with Henry Smith; he leaps to his death in a raging torrent in Sir Walter Scott's *The Fair Maid of Perth.*

Conant, Charles Hobomok Son of Mary Conant and Hobomok in Lydia Maria Child's *Hobomok.*

Conant, Jerry Designer and animator of television commercials; husband of Ruth Conant and lover of Sally Mathias in John Updike's *Marry Me.*

Conant, Mary Bride of Hobomok and later of Charles Brown; mother of Charles Hobomok Conant and heroine of Lydia Maria Child's *Hobomok.*

Conant, Mrs. Mary Daughter of an English earl, wife of Roger Conant, and mother of Mary Conant; dies in the Puritan settlement at Salem in Lydia Maria Child's *Hobomok.*

Conant, Roger Stern Puritan father of Mary Conant and husband of Mrs. Mary Conant; forbids his daughter to marry the Episcopalian Charles Brown in Lydia Maria Child's *Hobomok.*

Conant, Ruth Conant Wife of Jerry Conant and lover of Richard Mathias in John Updike's *Marry Me.*

Conari Procurator of Venice whose murder is feigned in Count Rosalvo's plan to ensnare the political conspirators in Matthew Lewis's *The Bravo of Venice.*

Conboy, Catherine M. (Cate) Daughter of Lincoln and Elizabeth Conboy; loves Christian Fraser but marries Ferris Thompson in Jessamyn West's *The Witch Diggers.*

Conboy, Elizabeth (Lib) Wife of Lincoln Conboy and mother of Catherine, James, and Emma Conboy in Jessamyn West's *The Witch Diggers.*

Conboy, Emma Jane (Em) Younger daughter of Lincoln and Elizabeth Conboy in Jessamyn West's *The Witch Diggers.*

Conboy, James (Dandie, Jim) Son of Lincoln and Elizabeth Conboy; marries Poor Farm inmate Norah Tate in Jessamyn West's *The Witch Diggers.*

Conboy, Lincoln (Link) Superintendent of Poor Farm, husband of Elizabeth Conboy, and father of Catherine, James, and Emma Conboy in Jessamyn West's *The Witch Diggers.*

Concasseur, Captain Officer in the Tontons Macoutes, the Haitian secret police; he briefly befriends Major Jones, discovers Jones is trying to trick him, and pursues Jones and Brown; he is killed by Henri Philipot in Graham Greene's *The Comedians.*

Concepta Housekeeper who serves Geoffrey Firmin both his drinks and his "strychnine" (cure for alcoholism) in Malcolm Lowry's *Under the Volcano.*

Concetta Daughter of Don Fabrizio Corbera, prince of Salina in southern Italy and whose family herald is the leopard; loves Tancredi, her father's nephew, but is heartbroken when he elects to marry Angelica, the beautiful but unrefined daughter of a rich peasant in Giuseppe Tomasi di Lampedusa's *The Leopard.*

Concha Young woman and lover of the narrator and protagonist Pablo Ibbieta; her memory is dismissed from Pablo's mind in the hours before he is to be executed as an anarchist by Spain's Republican army during that country's civil war (1936–39) in Jean-Paul Sartre's "The Wall."

Conchis, Maurice Wealthy Greek owner of Bourani, a villa on the island of Phraxos; he lures Nicholas Urfe into his elaborate "god-game", in which he exposes Urfe to a variety of carefully staged experiences using actors and people from Urfe's life in order to teach him his philosophy of life; he half-fabricates long stories about his own past, including one about the Nazi occupation of Phraxos in John Fowles's *The Magus.*

Conchita Older sister of Marela; daughter of Santiago and Cheche; married to Palomo who has taken a mistress; demands that she, too, should enjoy the same equal opportunity and sexual pleasure; takes as her lover the lector Juan Julian in Nilo Cruz's *Anna in the Tropics.*

Conchubar Old King of Ulad who reigns over all other kings, including Cuchulain, in Ireland; arrives to demand that the younger king Cuchulain bow to his demands in order to unify the country; compels Cuchulain, in the name of honor, to carry out a sword fight with the young foreign champion in William Butler Yeats's play *On Baile's Strand.*

Conchubor Aging High King of Ulster who intends to wed the unwilling young maiden Deirdre to make her queen of Ulster; demands her compliance in two days, as she has repeatedly delayed his proposals; his men kill Naisi, her lover, and his two brothers in John Millington Synge's play *Deirdre of the Sorrows.*

Concord, Sophie Negro nurse and friend of Neil Kingsblood in Sinclair Lewis's *Kingsblood Royal.*

Concordance, Mr. Schoolmaster who is a friend of Hugh Strap and who recommends Roderick Random to Mr. Lavement in London in Tobias Smollett's *The Adventures of Roderick Random.*

Condall of Shoreby Old, feverish man, from whom Sir Daniel Brackley extorts a promissory note in Robert Louis Stevenson's *The Black Arrow: A Tale of Two Roses.*

Conder Short, balding newspaperman, who tells elaborate lies about his life; Milly Drover attempts to persuade him to publish a story about Rose Coney's signing of the petition to save Jim Drover from execution in Graham Greene's *It's a Battlefield.*

Condesa, La Insane, drug-addicted Spanish noblewoman deported from Cuba for her political activities; loved by the ship's doctor, Schumann, in Katherine Anne Porter's *Ship of Fools.*

Condor Benevolent autocratic ruler of Eumeswil, a posthistorical state in the Maghreb; overthrew the Tribunes with help of the navy and has since cultivated philosophical and historical interests in Ernst Jünger's *Eumeswil.*

Condorex, Arnold (Lord Mondh) Ambitious and hypocritical politician, who achieves some economic and social power and gains a title; he spars ably with Harriet Hume in an unstable relationship over several years; he sometimes tells her that he thinks of marrying Ginevra, a richer woman from a powerful family; both conceited and insecure, he is interested in politics because he enjoys "the struggle for eminence"; he believes Harriet Hume cannot understand him because he is a man and "a man must rise" in Rebecca West's *Harriet Hume, a London Fantasy.*

Condotti-Pignata, Signor (Cee-Pee) Painter who imagines Cynthia Pomeroy as Primavera in Wright Morris's *What a Way to Go.*

Condu, Count Hungarian vampire imagined by Jack Duluoz in Jack Kerouac's *Doctor Sax.*

Coneg Undunory Myrdem Inggala Queen of Borlien; although greatly loved by the people, she is divorced by her husband for political reasons in Brian W. Aldiss's *Helliconia Summer.*

Coney, Rose Wife of the constable killed by Jim Drover; Milly Drover persuades her to sign the petition for the reprieve of Drover in Graham Greene's *It's a Battlefield.*

Confrey, Mame and Max Restaurateurs in William Faulkner's *Light in August.*

Congo Sailor without attachments or responsibilities; he is an intellectual anarchist against whom free-spirited but otherwise encumbered characters are measured in John Dos Passos's *Manhattan Transfer.*

Congo Witch-Doctor Wizened and old man who wears antelope horns on his head and chants spells; appears as an apparition to the emperor Brutus Jones at a sacrificial altar in the night jungle forest; signs that the fraudulent Jones must be sacrificed to the Crocodile God in Eugene O'Neill's play *The Emperor Jones.*

Coniffe, Katherine Elegant wife of Theodore Coniffe and mother of fifteen-year-old Theresa and thirteen-year-old Sara; at age thirty-eight she discovers to her dismay that she is once again pregnant; she dies delivering a third daughter, Lily, in Mary Lavin's *The House in Clewe Street.*

Coniffe, Lily Youngest of the three daughters of prosperous Theodore Coniffe; her brief marriage to Cornelius Galloway at the age of seventeen is a source of great bitterness to Theresa, her thirty-two-year-old elder sister, in May Lavin's *The House in Clewe Street.*

Coniffe, Sara Second daughter of Theodore Coniffe; the gentle and warm but unassertive aunt of Gabriel Galloway, she timidly tries to shield her orphaned nephew from the harsh Puritanism of her elder sister, Theresa, in Mary Lavin's *The House in Clewe Street.*

Coniffe, Theodore Prosperous and conservative widower; he is the owner of properties in Castlerampart, many of them on fashionable Clewe Street; he is the father of Theresa, Sara, and Lily and the grandfather of Gabriel Galloway in Mary Lavin's *The House in Clewe Street.*

Coniffe, Theresa Eldest and most assertive of the three daughters of Theodore Coniffe; having regarded Cornelius Galloway as her suitor, she was embittered by his marriage to her sister Lily; she is Gabriel Galloway's rigid, Puritanical, class-conscious aunt in Mary Lavin's *The House in Clewe Street.*

Coningsby, Henry (Harry) Orphan grandson of Lord Monmouth; he rejects his grandfather's epicurean materialism for the honest enterprise of the Millbank family; he matures into the principled political leader of the "New Generation" of idealistic young aristocrats in Benjamin Disraeli's *Coningsby; or, The New Generation.*

Coningsby, Lord John Polly Hampton's rich and handsome "official young man" during her debutante season; that she has no interest in encouraging him outrages her mother, Lady Montdore, in Nancy Mitford's *Love in a Cold Climate.*

Coningsby, Mrs. Harry Coningsby's deceased mother, whose portrait Harry discovers in the house of his grandfather's archenemy, Mr. Millbank, in Benjamin Disraeli's *Coningsby; or, The New Generation.*

Conjuror Trendle Conjuror whom Gertrude visits to find a cure for her disfigured arm in Thomas Hardy's "The Withered Arm."

Conklin, Jim Tall soldier fatally wounded in battle; Henry Fleming witnesses his grotesque death throes in Stephen Crane's *The Red Badge of Courage.*

Conklin, Will (Willie) Chief of the Emerald Isle Engine Company; he and his men destroy the Model T of Coalhouse Walker, Jr., and cause the death of many innocent people in E. L. Doctorow's *Ragtime.*

Conmal (Duke of Aros) Renowned translator of Shakespeare into Zemblan; uncle who influences Charles Xavier, the last king of Zembla, to be passionately addicted to literature in Vladimir Nabokov's *Pale Fire.*

Conmee, Father John Jesuit rector of Clongowes School who offers to prevent Father Dolan from pandying Stephen Dedalus in James Joyce's *A Portrait of the Artist as a Young Man.* His perambulations transect the nineteen narratives of "The Wandering Rocks" episode in *Ulysses.*

Connage, Alec Princeton classmate of Amory Blaine and brother of Rosalind Connage in F. Scott Fitzgerald's *This Side of Paradise.*

Connage, Rosalind Great love of Amory Blaine; marries a rich man in F. Scott Fitzgerald's *This Side of Paradise.*

Connal, Black (Captain Connal, Monsieur de Connal) French-educated brother of White Connal; he marries Dora O'Shane when his brother, betrothed to her since her birth, dies in an accident; a coxcomb, gambler, and fortune hunter, Black alienates Harry Ormond at their first meeting but later treats Ormond with genuine regard for both Ormond's character and the money he wants to win from him in Maria Edgeworth's *Ormond.*

Connal, White Shallow "gentleman" betrothed to Dora O'Shane since her birth; he is hard and niggardly with others but extravagant with personal purchases; luckily for Dora, he dies in an accident before he has a chance to wed her in Maria Edgeworth's *Ormond.*

Connell, George Kingham Youngish, ambitious social scientist and criminologist; he is the witness chosen by Frits Krom to substantiate his evidence against Paul Firman in Eric Ambler's *Send No More Roses.*

Connell, John Lover of Louise Bennett Halifax and a friend of Louise's husband, Stephen Halifax; because he is an actor, Louise doubts his sincerity, although her sister, Sarah Bennett, suspects he truly loves Louise in Margaret Drabble's *A Summer Bird-Cage.*

Connemara, Maggie Kind-hearted Dublin prostitute who befriends Gypo Nolan in Liam O'Flaherty's *The Informer.*

Conner, Charlie Hired hand on George Whitney's place; a slave to superstition and an ardent "homeruler", he helps Arthur Green locate Uncle George, missing in Ireland, in C. Day Lewis's *Child of Misfortune.*

Conner, Matt Childhood playmate of Arthur Green; he is now an I.R.A. militant, who leads Arthur into the camp where Uncle George Whitney is captive in C. Day Lewis's *Child of Misfortune.*

Conner, Stephen Current superintendent of the Diamond County Home for the Aged; holds certain ideals about serving humanity and the need for impartiality in dealing with the residents; stoned by some of the old people in John Updike's *The Poorhouse Fair.*

Connie Editorial colleague of Nancy Hawkins at Mackintosh & Tooley in Muriel Spark's *A Far Cry from Kensington.*

Connie Red-haired machinist at Jordan's surgical appliances factory in Nottingham in D. H. Lawrence's *Sons and Lovers.*

Connin, Mr. Hardworking man; the description of his picture paints him as handsome, although he is now very sick and weak; he seems to be a very patient, loving, and sincere husband, father, and family man; he does not have the same religious ritualistic beliefs as his wife; he is perceived as very level-headed in Flannery O'Connor's "The River."

Connin, Mrs. Caring, loving wife and mother who is very confirmed in her faith; she believes that preachers possess healing powers; she is hired by Mr. Ashfield as a sitter; she is not timid and speaks her mind quite often in Flannery O'Connor's "The River."

Connin children, J.C., Spivey, Sinclair, and Sarah seem to be very poor; they are jealous about any other children that their mom brings home in Flannery O'Connor's "The River."

Connoisseur Collector of paintings who is told that he must shoot himself in order to get a good price for his paintings in Charles Johnstone's *Chrysal: or, The Adventures of a Guinea.*

Connolly, Betsy Jekyll See Jekyll, Betsy.

Connolly, Doris The leering teenaged eldest of a trio collectively known as "the Connollies"; presumed war evacuees of unknown origin, they wreak havoc wherever they are sent; Basil Seal billets them on various rural families and accepts payment from the families to place them elsewhere in Evelyn Waugh's *Put Out More Flags.*

Connolly, Father Priest who visits Granny Weatherall at her deathbed in Katherine Anne Porter's "The Jilting of Granny Weatherall."

Connolly, General Capable head of Emperor Seth's army who defeats a rebellion against the Azanian government; he and Basil Seal later disagree, however, and Connolly and the Earl of Ngumo join and succeed in overthrowing Seth's government in Evelyn Waugh's *Black Mischief.*

Connolly, Hector Irish-Catholic newspaperman and author; marries Betsy Jekyll in Nancy Hale's *The Prodigal Women.*

Connolly, Lizzie Occasional girlfriend of Martin Eden in Jack London's *Martin Eden.*

Connolly, Marlene Doris's sister, the drooling youngest of "the Connollies" in Evelyn Waugh's *Put Out More Flags.*

Connolly, Micky The lowering brother of Doris and Marlene in Evelyn Waugh's *Put Out More Flags.*

Connolly, Professor Fawning head of the drama department at Webster, an Ivy League school, whom Victor Milgrim courts in hopes of obtaining an honorary degree in Budd Schulberg's *The Disenchanted.*

Connor, Phil Boss of Ona Rudkus; coerces her into having sex with him in Upton Sinclair's *The Jungle.*

Connor, Walt Night-shift worker at the Past Bay Manufacturing Company factory who is promoted by Carl Belcher and sides with management during the strike; briefly kidnaps Marie Turner and has a relationship with Rose MacMahon in Robert Cantwell's *The Land of Plenty.*

Connors, Andrew Man involved with the IRA who poses as an American and whom Alice Mellings suspects of being a Russian; he inadvertently makes Alice and her comrades conspicuous to the authorities in Doris Lessing's *The Good Terrorist.*

Connors, Ruth Classmate of Susie Salmon; touched by Susie's dead spirit as Susie leaves the earth; becomes fascinated with Susie, despite barely having known her in her life; becomes a friend of Ray Singh; devotes herself to writing about the visions of the dead she sees in Alice Sebold's *The Lovely Bones.*

Connybeare, Wilfred Wealthy brewer and cousin to Nina Woodville; he helps Chester Nimmo make a lot of money in stocks, and his advice helps Chester avoid an insider-information scandal in the Contract Case in Joyce Cary's *Prisoner of Grace.*

Connynge, Mary Deceitful mistress of John Law and, later, of Philippe of Orleans in Emerson Hough's *The Mississippi Bubble.*

Conover, Andrea Biddle Washington mistress of Bruce Gold and daughter of Pugh Biddle Conover in Joseph Heller's *Good as Gold.*

Conover, Pugh Biddle Member of well-connected Virginia gentry and father of Andrea Biddle Conover in Joseph Heller's *Good as Gold.*

Conover, Sarah (Sally) Lover of Ian Sherbrooke in Nicholas Delbanco's *Sherbrookes.*

Conquest, Mrs. Woman to whom George Edwards transfers his affections from Miss Oddly; he is arranging the terms of his marriage when July Wentworth, believed to be dead, appears; Mrs. Conquest nobly yields her claim in John Hill's *The Adventures of Mr. George Edwards, a Creole.*

Conrad Homely, favored son and heir of Manfred; he dies horribly on the eve of his wedding when a monstrous helmet of supernatural origin falls on him in Horace Walpole's *The Castle of Otranto.*

Conradin Ten-year-old sickly boy who detests his guardian and cousin, Mrs. De Ropp, for her suffocating dominance; calls her disdainfully "the Woman"; finds an alternative to the stifling home when he visits the outdoor toolshed, where he secretly keeps a Houdan hen and polecat ferret; sees the toolshed as a refuge and sanctuary; believes the ferret, named Sredni Vashtar, to be a god capable of avenging him against his harsh guardian; elated when the ferret kills the aunt in Saki's "Sredni Vashtar."

Conran, Cathleen Wife of Jack and mother of Rose; she is a fussy, querulous woman in C. Day Lewis's *Child of Misfortune.*

Conran, Jack Irish uncle visited by Arthur and Oliver Green in C. Day Lewis's *Child of Misfortune.*

Conran, Rose Cathleen's provocative and deceitful ten-year old daughter, who cries to her mother in order to escape the consequences of her behavior in C. Day Lewis's *Child of Misfortune.*

Conroy Man involved in a brief relationship with Kate Fletcher Armstrong in Margaret Drabble's *The Middle Ground.*

Conroy, Bill Husband of Stella Conroy; he works at the Polytechnic in Margaret Drabble's *A Summer Bird-Cage.*

Conroy, Gabriel Favorite nephew of his aunts Julia and Kate Morkan; son of their dead sister Ellen; married to Gretta; highly educated and sometimes aloof to the other party gatherers; after the party in a hotel room with his wife, when his desire builds to make love to Gretta, discovers that she harbors memories of a young man named Michael Furey who had died tragically because of his love for Gretta in James Joyce's "The Dead."

Conroy, Gabriel (John Doe, Johnny Dumbledee, Gabe) Gentle giant of a man; good but somewhat clumsy protagonist of Bret Harte's *Gabriel Conroy.*

Conroy, Grace See Salvatierra, Doña Dolores.

Conroy, Gretta Wife of Gabriel, who attends an evening celebration at her husband's aunts' home; recalls aloud painfully to her husband in a hotel room after the party that she had in her youth loved a young man named Michael Furey who had died because of his passion for her in James Joyce's "The Dead."

Conroy, Olympia (Olly) Dutiful wife of Gabriel Conroy in Bret Harte's *Gabriel Conroy.*

Conroy, Stella Cambridge graduate and wife of Bill Conroy; she spends her day in a domestic chaos of crying babies, spilt food, and a cluttered terrace house; she complains that she has no one intelligent to talk to in Margaret Drabble's *A Summer Bird-Cage.*

Conscientious Objector Young Christian Socialist who is recently out of prison; he is defended by John Lavender from attacks by four commercial travellers in John Galsworthy's *The Burning Spear: Being the Experiences of Mr. John Lavender in Time of War.*

Conseil Servant to Professor Pierre Aronnax; traveling with his employer aboard the American frigate *Abraham Lincoln,* a ship on course to rid the ocean of a reportedly mysterious but treacherous giant sea creature; survives an attack on the *Abraham Lincoln* when he is rescued from the sea by Captain Nemo of the futuristic submarine Natilus; observes many wonders while riding in the underwater craft with Captain Nemo in Jules Verne's *Twenty Thousand Leagues Under the Sea.*

Consett, Donald Kay's sociologist husband, who cannot find an academic appointment; he gives lectures to the workers in Robin Middleton's plant and is fired when he discloses a family confidence during one of his lectures in Angus Wilson's *Anglo-Saxon Attitudes.*

Consett, Father Perpetually laughing, untidy, dark-haired, clear-sighted Irish priest, who is Mrs. Satterthwaite's friend; he is hanged by British military authorities in Ulster in Ford Madox Ford's *Some Do Not. . . .* The Roman Catholic Sylvia Tietjens sees him as a saint and martyr who directs her life in *No More Parades* and in *The Last Post.*

Consett, Kay Daughter of Gerald and Ingeborg Middleton; her hand was burned in a fire from an accident caused by her mother when she was a child; she hates her father for reminding her of it in Angus Wilson's *Anglo-Saxon Attitudes.*

Considine, Count William Old family friend and adviser to the O'Malleys in Charles Lever's *Charles O'Malley.*

Constable Officer who arrests Colonel Jack, mistakenly thinking that he is Captain Jack in Daniel Defoe's *The History and the Remarkable Life of the Truly Honourable Colonel Jacques, Commonly Call'd Col. Jack.*

Constable Spokesman for the townspeople of Walthamstow who refuse to allow the poor men from Wapping and the band of thirteen others to pass through their town; he agrees to give the group food if they pass around the town in Daniel Defoe's *A Journal of the Plague Year.*

Constable, Captain Yvonne Firmin's late father in Malcolm Lowry's *Under the Volcano.*

Constable of France Tells the Dauphin that he is wrong to underestimate the English and is mistaken in his opinion of Henry V; compares the French and English soldiers' spirits and finds the French lacking; wishes to rally the troops by pointing out the presumed superiority of the French and shaming them into being better soldiers than the English; predicts that Henry will beg to be ransomed; killed in the Battle of Agincourt in William Shakespeare's play *Henry V.*

Constance Primitive woman inhabiting the forest where Charles Watkins finds himself after his shipwreck; she is perhaps a hallucinatory version of his former mistress, Constance Maine, in Doris Lessing's *Briefing for a Descent into Hell.*

Constance (Cousin) Clare Aubrey's cousin, Jock's wife, and Rosamund's mother; she nurtures her unusual child and is patient about Jock's failures and mean spiritedness in Rebecca West's *The Fountain Overflows.*

Constance, Lady Woman falsely rumored to be engaged to Lord Chelford in J. Sheridan Le Fanu's *Wylder's Hand.*

Constance, Sister (formerly Lady Herbert Somerville) Aristocratic widow and member of an Anglican sisterhood; she helps the Underwood family in Charlotte Yonge's *The Pillars of the House* and in *The Long Vacation.*

Constant, Malachi (Space Wanderer, Unk) Millionaire, messiah, and space traveler in Kurt Vonnegut's *The Sirens of Titan.*

Constantin United Nations simultaneous interpreter and blind date of Esther Greenwood in Sylvia Plath's *The Bell Jar.*

Constantine Young lord who falls in love with Arminda and pursues her in spite of her protests; he dies from a wound she inflicts when he breaks into her room in Penelope Aubin's *The Life and Adventures of the Lady Lucy.*

Constantine Brilliant young physicist who meets Arthur Miles at Cambridge; he is elected to the Royal Society at very young age; he tries to get Miles the directorship of the National Institute in C. P. Snow's *The Search.*

Constantine Son of Helena and Constantius Chlorus; he rises in military and political influence until he becomes the ruler of the Roman Empire in Evelyn Waugh's *Helena.*

Constantine, Carol Painter and wife of Eddie Constantine; they participate in couple swapping, with homosexual overtones, with Irene and Ben Saltz in John Updike's *Couples.*

Constantine, Dr. Physician who examines Samuel Edward Ratchett's body in Agatha Christie's *Murder on the Orient Express.*

Constantine, Eddie Airline pilot married to Carol Constantine in John Updike's *Couples.*

Constantine, Lady Viviette Melancholy young wife, who lives isolated from society because of a promise to her jealous husband, Sir Blount, now off exploring in Africa; she gradually falls clandestinely in love with Swithin St. Cleeve, a handsome young astronomer, and marries him secretly on learning of her husband's death; discovering the marriage invalid because of news of a later date of Sir Blount's death, she gives up St. Cleeve rather than lose him an inheritance; finding that she is pregnant, she desperately marries Bishop Helmsdale; after the bishop's death St. Cleeve returns to claim her, and she dies of heart failure in his arms in Thomas Hardy's *Two on a Tower.*

Constantine, Sir Blount Viviette's jealous husband, off exploring in Africa; instead of dying of fever as reported, he takes to drink and a native wife and eventually his own life, but on a date subsequent to Lady Constantine's clandestine remarriage; Sir Blount has left her an income too small to compensate for the loss of Swithin St. Cleeve's inheritance, should they now repeat their vows in Thomas Hardy's *Two on a Tower.*

Constantinescu, Maria Geoffrey's friend who disrupts life at Ambrose's in Christopher Isherwood's *Down There on a Visit.*

Constantius Chlorus Constantine's father, who is an ambitious Roman military officer; he marries Helena and achieves constant governmental promotions; he ultimately divorces Helena in order to become a Caesar under the Emperor Diocletian; he serves as governor of Dalmatia and eventually is put in charge of Gaul in Evelyn Waugh's *Helena.*

Constanza, Matilda Guest at a ball held at the castle of the Marquis de Mazzini in Ann Radcliffe's *A Sicilian Romance.*

Consuelo Eva Luna's mother, whose life has been both harsh and difficult; bequeaths her daughter the ability to tell stories and with words to create wondrous narratives in Isabel Allende's *Eva Luna.*

Cónsul Introductory narrator who fled into the Colombian wilderness, in José Eustacio Rivera's *The Vortex.*

Contarini, Signora Alcesté Last of Contarini Fleming's mother's family; she marries Contarini and, after a year of traveling with him, dies in childbirth in Benjamin Disraeli's *Contarini Fleming.*

Contarino Boastful, profligate youth and conspirator, who kills himself after realizing he has been trapped by Abellino/Flodoardo (Count Rosalvo) in Matthew Lewis's *The Bravo of Venice.*

Contessa Elderly woman who arranges meetings between handsome Italian gigolos she calls *marchettas* and rich men and women; introduces Mrs. Karen Stone to Paolo in Tennesee Williams's *The Roman Spring of Mrs. Stone.*

Conti Painter; shows Prince Hettore Gonzaga a drawing of Emilia; establishes the connection between the evil Prince and Emilia in Gotthold Ephraim Lessing's *Emilia Galotti.*

Continental Op, The Nameless detective for the Continental Detective Agency who heads the investigation into corruption in Personville in Dashiell Hammett's *Red Harvest.*

Contrite One of the good people of Vanity Fair introduced to Christiana and her party by Mnason in John Bunyan's *The Pilgrim's Progress from This World to That Which Is to Come.*

Control Otherwise unnamed head of British Intelligence London Station; he and George Smiley instigate a complex double-doublecross to protect Hans-Dieter Mundt in John le Carré's *The Spy Who Came In from the Cold.* On the trail of a double agent within his inner circle, he is lured into launching an espionage operation that is in fact a set-up; utterly discredited, he dies not long after losing his position in *Tinker, Tailor, Soldier, Spy.*

"Conversation with My Father, A" Narrator Middle-aged female fiction writer who lives in Manhattan; at her father's request, develops a story about a woman who becomes a junkie in order to bond with her son, who subsequently disowns her; resists the finality of endings that her father wants of her stories in Grace Paley's "A Conversation with My Father."

"Conversation with My Father, A" Narrator's Father Eighty-six years old and disabled by a heart condition; asks his daughter to write a simple, straightforward story about recognizable people; retired doctor and artist who wants his daughter to acknowledge finality and tragedy—in her stories and in her life—to little avail in Grace Paley's "A Conversation with My Father."

Converse, John American journalist in Vietnam who tries to get rich by smuggling heroin into the United States but is captured by Antheil and forced to locate his wife, Marge Converse, who has the heroin in Robert Stone's *Dog Soldiers.*

Converse, Marge Bender Wife of John Converse; pursued by Antheil's men in Robert Stone's *Dog Soldiers.*

Conway Fierce and dissipated-looking Australian from Oxford; possessing a strong, unsatisfied sense of community, he is a header desiring to capture the will of the group, any group, although he is himself without basic belief in C. Day Lewis's *Starting Point.*

Conway, Amanda Young, beautiful fashion model on the rise in New York City who leaves her husband, Jamie Conway, for a more exciting career and life in Paris in Jay McInerney's *Bright Lights, Big City.*

Conway, Bill Boyhood foe of Tom Bailey, until Tom beats him in a fight; tells Ezra Wingate that Tom and others stole Ezra's stagecoach; becomes a grocer with Seth Rodgers in Thomas Bailey Aldrich's *The Story of a Bad Boy.*

Conway, Dodo Often-pregnant Catholic housewife and neighbor of Esther Greenwood in Sylvia Plath's *The Bell Jar.*

Conway, Durfee (Duff) Jazz cornet player executed for murder in Shelby Foote's *Jordan County.*

Conway, Hugh ("Glory") Member of H.M. Consul who is abducted with Miss Roberta Brinklow, Henry D. Barnard, and Captain Charles Mallison when their pilot, Fenner, is mysteriously replaced by Talu, a Tibetan, and flown to Shangri-la, a monastery in Tibet whose monks are hundreds of years old in James Hilton's *Lost Horizon.*

Conway, Isabel Dreamy, aristocratic wife of James Frost; she adapts to a life of relative poverty and publishes a historical romance in Charlotte Yonge's *Dynevor Terrace.*

Conway, Jamie Young writer working in the Department of Factual Verification at a prominent New York magazine; throughout the course of a few days he tries to outstrip mortality with nothing but good will, controlled substances, and wit; ex-husband of Amanda Conway in Jay McInerney's *Bright Lights, Big City.*

Conway, Nora Mother of Duff Conway in Shelby Foote's *Jordan County.*

Conway, Widow Dressmaker and mother of Bill Conway in Thomas Bailey Aldrich's *The Story of a Bad Boy.*

Conyers, Bertha General Conyers's wife, who is twenty years younger than he and twenty years older than her sister, Mildred Haycock, in Anthony Powell's *At Lady Molly's.* She dies in *The Kindly Ones.*

Conyers, General Aylmer Capable soldier and family friend of Nicholas Jenkins's grandparents; an amateur psychologist, he comments on Widmerpool's broken engagement to his sister-in-law, Mildred Haycock, in Anthony Powell's *At Lady Molly's.* After his wife's death Conyers marries Geraldine Weedon in *The Kindly Ones.* His marriage is successful in *The Valley of Bones.* He dies in *The Military Philosophers.*

Conyers, John Poor tenant farmer, for whom Vivian Grey intercedes by flattering Mr. Stapylton Toad to the point that he agrees to stop foreclosure on Conyers's farm in Benjamin Disraeli's *Vivian Grey.*

Coode, John Antithesis of Lord Baltimore; possible hero, possible villain, or possible figment of the imagination in John Barth's *The Sot-Weed Factor.*

Coogan, Signora Rich woman who pays for the companionship of Paolo and takes him to Capri; ridiculed by Paolo and the Contessa in Tennessee Williams's *The Roman Spring of Mrs. Stone.*

Cooger, J. C. Co-owner of Cooger and Dark's combined Shadow Shows and Cross-continental Pandemonium Theater Company; goes backward on the carousel to reverse his age from 40 to 12 years in order to masquerade as "Robert," Miss Foley's nephew; frames Will and Jim for robbery; goes forward on the carousel to become the aged Mr. Electrico in Ray Bradbury's *Something Wicked This Way Comes.*

Cook Blond Dutchman employed by the Swedish Army whose actual name is Peter Lamb; perfidious lover who once broke Yvette Pottier's heart; smokes a special pipe; expresses his bitter cynicism over war in "The Song of the Great Souls of This Earth"; invites Mother Courage to join him in running an inn he has inherited, but stipulates that Kattrin

Haupt, Mother Courage's daughter, cannot come; leaves when Mother Courage refuses to leave her daughter in Bertolt Brecht's play *Mother Courage and Her Children.*

Cook Dr. Benjulia's employee, whose food preparation suffers from her passion for reading novels, especially Samuel Richardson's *Pamela;* until the end of the interview in which Benjulia fires her, she confidently expects his proposal of marriage in Wilkie Collins's *Heart and Science.*

Cook Servant of the charity who saves the best food for his fellow servants and starts a brawl with the Apothecary in Charles Johnstone's *Chrysal: or, The Adventures of a Guinea.*

Cook South Sea native cook who fixes delicacies out of affection for Robert Herrick aboard the pirated schooner *Farallone* in Robert Louis Stevenson's *The Ebb-Tide: A Trio and a Quartette.*

Cook Violent-tempered servant of the Duchess; the chemical assault of her use of pepper is preliminary to her throwing various objects, including fire irons and dishes, at the Duchess and the baby; later, when she is questioned at the trial of the Knave of Hearts, her temper has not improved in Lewis Carroll's *Alice's Adventures in Wonderland.*

Cook Cooks for Mrs. Dawson; sings sad Sicilian songs in a feeble soprano in Frances Sherwood's *Vindication.*

Cook Short, thin woman, employed by the Donnes; she finds the stairs steep and the house eerie in Ivy Compton-Burnett's *Elders and Betters.*

Cook Provincial Lady's servant, who takes revenge against an underequipped kitchen and larder with culinary accidents in E. M. Delafield's *The Diary of a Provincial Lady.*

Cook, Al See Kukolnikov, Alexandr Petrovich.

Cook, Caroline Youngest daughter of Laurence Cook; wife of Frank Rasmussen; sister of Ginny Cook Smith and Rose Cook Lewis; lawyer in Des Moines, Iowa; loses her father's allegiance when she voices concern regarding Larry Cook's plans to bequeath property to his daughters, which Larry perceives as a lack of gratitude and loyalty; recovers her father's affections as she helps her father sue his two older daughters in Jane Smiley's *A Thousand Acres.*

Cook, Ginny See Smith, Ginny Cook.

Cook, John Douglas Under the assumed name Mr. Dundas, the editor of the newspaper that Christopher Kirkland worked on in his first job in London; in his own name, the editor of the *Morning Chronicle* in Mrs. Lynn Linton's *The Autobiography of Christopher Kirkland.*

Cook, Kiddo One of the few Jago "rats" who escape a life of crime; he becomes a respectable vendor and marries Pigeony Poll in Arthur Morrison's *A Child of the Jago.*

Cook, Laurence (Larry and Daddy) Alcoholic, tyrannical, and abusive father of Ginny Cook Smith, Rose Cook Lewis, Caroline Cook; friend and arch-competitor of Harold Clark; grandfather of Pammy and Linda; inheritor of land in Iowa; impulsive Lear-like retiree who at Jess Clark's homecoming party announces his plan to transfer his farm to his daughters; accuses Ginny and Rose of casting him off; temporarily disowns and subsequently collaborates with daughter Caroline regarding the transfer of his land in Jane Smiley's *A Thousand Acres.*

Cook, Lois Unkempt author of *The Gallant Gallstone* who exalts decadence in order to spite beauty in Ayn Rand's *The Fountainhead.*

Cook, Margery London cook who is smitten by Captain Samuel Crowe; she advises him to visit the astrologist in Tobias Smollett's *The Adventures of Sir Launcelot Greaves.*

Cook, Moll Kitchen wench, who discovers Shamela Andrews in the coal-hole after Mrs. Jewkes has dragged the pond, believing her drowned, in Henry Fielding's *An Apology for the Life of Mrs. Shamela Andrews.*

Cook, Mr. Vanessa's father; his trusteeship of Orlo Porter's inheritance gives teeth to his opposition to Vanessa and Orb's engagement; he owns the racehorse Potato Chip in P. G. Wodehouse's *Aunts Aren't Gentlemen.*

Cook, Mrs. Beatrice Latchett (Bea) Mistress of Henry Bech following her sister, Norma Latchett; bland and gentle thirty-four-year-old mother of three in the process of divorcing her husband in John Updike's *Bech: A Book.*

Cook, Rose See Lewis, Rose Cook.

Cook, The Provides the pilgrims who have stopped at a tavern during their travel to Canterbury with a brief tale about a thief who moves in with another man and his prostitute wife; this tale serves as the most churlish fabliau of the three presented in the beginning of Geoffrey Chaucer's *The Canterbury Tales.*

Cook, The Stout, cheerful cook of a capsized ship in charge of bailing out the lifeboat that he and three other survivors try to keep afloat in the Atlantic; rebuked for his unfounded optimism and failure to keep his mind on the problem of survival; becomes preoccupied with the idea of pie and ham sandwiches; later, in the water, lying on his back encircled by a cork life preserver, is able to paddle himself to shore—"as if he were a canoe"—when the lifeboat is swamped in Stephen Crane's "The Open Boat."

Cook, Thomas (Tommy) Law clerk who takes over Mr. Talbot's practice during the Civil War but relinquishes it to Talbot when he returns to New Orleans after the war in Grace King's *The Pleasant Ways of St. Médard.*

Cook, Vanessa Beautiful art student and an old flame of Bertie Wooster; the radical politics she shares with her fiancé, Orlo Porter, arouse her father's opposition to the engagement in P. G. Wodehouse's *Aunts Aren't Gentlemen.*

Cook, Wilmer Boyish thug who works for Casper Gutman and whom Sam Spade calls a gunsel in Dashiell Hammett's *The Maltese Falcon.*

Cooke, Anna Twin sister of Ebenezer Cooke who, Henry Burlingame suggests, might be in reality the woman Cooke really loves in John Barth's *The Sot-Weed Factor.*

Cooke, Ebenezer (Eben) American-born Londoner forced to cross the Atlantic to claim his father's Maryland estates in John Barth's *The Sot-Weed Factor.*

Cooke, Gilbert Bureaucrat in government civil service who works under the direction of Lewis Eliot; his gossip about the suicide of Sheila (Knight) Eliot causes Eliot to have him transferred in C. P. Snow's *Homecomings.*

Cookson, Elsie Previously beautiful and now fat and ugly woman; she was George Bowling's lover when he was young in Lower Binfield; she does not recognize him when he sees her on his outing in George Orwell's *Coming Up for Air.*

Cool, Joe Prison inmate who entrusts Erwin Riemenschneider with Cool's big robbery plan, provided that Riemenschneider will try to get Cool paroled, in William Riley Burnett's *The Asphalt Jungle.*

Cool, Judge Charlie Defender and protector of Dolly Talbo; proposes to her shortly before her death in Truman Capote's *The Grass Harp.*

Cool, Mr. Black teenager living in Napoli; he is attacked by racists and defended by his half brother, Wilf, in Colin MacInnes's *Absolute Beginners.*

Cooler, Colonel Corrupt American officer and Harry Lime's friend who is present at Lime's supposed demise in Graham Greene's *The Third Man and the Fallen Idol.*

Cooley, Benjamin ("Kangaroo") Jewish lawyer and former army officer; he is the charismatic, powerful leader of the Australian paramilitary "Diggers" group; he preaches the "love-ideal" of "mateship" as a new social principle that will save Australia, but he is shot during a political rally and dies at the end of D. H. Lawrence's *Kangaroo.*

Cooley, Gertrude Long-suffering wife of Hubert Cooley and mother of James Lee Cooley in Julian Mayfield's *The Hit.*

Cooley, Hubert Fifty-year-old husband of Gertrude Cooley and father of James Lee Cooley in Julian Mayfield's *The Hit.*

Cooley, James Lee Twenty-six-year-old son of Hubert and Gertrude Cooley, lover of Essie Turner in Julian Mayfield's *The Hit.*

Cooley, Seabright B. (Seab) Senior senator from South Carolina and president pro tempore of the Senate who helps defeat two of his enemies, the president and the president's nominee for secretary of state, in Allen Drury's *Advise and Consent.*

Coon, Jasper Free Soiler who questions why he fights for the Confederacy in Jesse Hill Ford's *The Raider.*

Coonskins See Pitch.

Coop Hollis and Belinda's child, who died of leukemia; the single trait shared by father and son was their dislike of horses in Alice Hoffman's *Here on Earth.*

Coop, Nate Quiet Alaskan native; marries Flossie Flatch; scouts Japanese bases in Aleutian Islands during World War II; works with Flossie to achieve Alaskan statehood in James Michener's *Alaska.*

Cooper, Annabeth Belinda Cooper's mother in Alice Hoffman's *Here on Earth.*

Cooper, April Louise and Nat's daughter and oldest child by nine years; sister of Danny Cooper; gay; well-known singer whose stage name is April Gold; self-centered instigator; is pregnant by artificial insemination in David Leavitt's *Equal Affections.*

Cooper, Belinda Daughter of Annabeth Cooper and sister of Richard Cooper, a pale, red-haired next-door neighbor of March; keeps injured wild animals and nurses them back to health; inherits Guardian Farm; marries Hollis and dies from his abuse and neglect in Alice Hoffman's *Here on Earth.*

Cooper, Charlie Main translator coordinator for Global Foods, who not only introduces Kate Brown to her job, but also fulfills the role as nanny to the many delegates, in the same way that Kate does for her family in Doris Lessing's *The Summer Before the Dark.*

Cooper, Cynthia Albermarle County deputy in Rita Mae Brown's *Cat on the Scent.*

Cooper, Danny Louise and Nat's son and youngest child; brother of April Cooper; gay; life partner of Walter Bayles; lawyer; feels both close to and resentful of his sister, April; moves from California to Connecticut in David Leavitt's *Equal Affections.*

Cooper, Effingham (Effie) Former student of Max Lejour, to whom he makes an annual visit; he has developed a romantic fixation on Hannah Crean-Smith; he conspires unsuccessfully with Marion Taylor to rescue Hannah from Gaze Castle in Iris Murdoch's *The Unicorn.*

Cooper, Emily New member of the Pocahontas Drill Team in the town of Los Robles; at 36, regrets moving into middle age, as she has been married half her life; like the other women on the drill team, secretly marvels at the free life lived by Iomela Ramos, who has left one husband and is living openly with another man, sun bathes with him in the nude, and eats breakfast in the afternoon in restaurants in Jessamyn West's "Love, Death, and the Ladies' Drill Team."

Cooper, Fanny Widow of Henry Cooper, who dies from a snake bite; mother of Carrie, to whom she gives birth after Henry's death, and Sarah; is engaged to and later marries Thomas Keene in Hugh Nissenson's *The Tree of Life.*

Cooper, Ivy The other new girl on the swim team besides Carlin Leander in Alice Hoffman's *The River King.*

Cooper, Louise Wife of Danny Cooper and mother of April and Nat Cooper; older sister of Eleanor Friedman; atheist; has a temper, but loses her "fighting spirit" after she is diagnosed with cancer; lives with cancer for twenty years and dies of it in David Leavitt's *Equal Affections.*

Cooper, Marlene Rich widow and patron of "The Wider Infinity", a setting for séances in Muriel Spark's *The Bachelors.*

Cooper, Master One of the men talking in a tavern in Engsng when the funeral procession of the poor young clerk Hans Schönschreiber passes by in August Strindberg's "A Funeral."

Cooper, Michael Lover of Nell; a reporter for a trade magazine in Elizabeth Benedict's *Slow Dancing.*

Cooper, Minnie Fortyish unmarried spinster who lives in a small house with her invalid mother and aunt; ordinary looking woman who fell behind the other women who married; drinks at times, and has enjoyed men's intimate company in the past; known for her false stories about men; now accuses Will Mayes, a young black man, of molesting her in William Faulkner's "Dry September."

Cooper, Mr. Imprisoned Methodist who praises sin because it may provide grace while he removes William Booth's valuables from his pockets in Henry Fielding's *Amelia.*

Cooper, Mr. Father of Richard and Belinda Cooper; disinherited his son and is killed with his wife in a car wreck before he can reverse his rash decision in Alice Hoffman's *Here on Earth.*

Cooper, Nat Husband of Louise Cooper and father of April and Nat Cooper; computer scientist; has an affair with and loves Lillian Rubenstein-Kraft in David Leavitt's *Equal Affections.*

Cooper, Rachel Elderly woman who takes in Pearl and John Harper after their flight down the river; protects the children from Preacher in Davis Grubb's *The Night of the Hunter.*

Cooper, Reverend Minister in Danville, Pennsylvania, who helps Milkman find his family farm in Toni Morrison's *Song of Solomon.*

Cooper, Richard Husband of March Murray, father of Gwen Cooper, son of Annabeth Cooper, and brother of Belinda Cooper; estranged from his father; a biologist; rejoices in the odd and unprecedented; married to March Murray for eighteen years until she leaves him for Hollis in Alice Hoffman's *Here on Earth.*

Cooper, Sir Anthony Ashley The kinsman of an Oxford friend of Charles Mandeville; to show his appreciation to Charles he provides him with an introduction to Colonel Penruddock in William Godwin's *Mandeville.*

Coot See Harcoot, Asa Bruce.

Coote, Belinda Newly wedded wife of Orlando Eustace, who stabs her to death after an argument over the merits of her sister Maria's painted fan in Thomas Amory's *The Life of John Buncle, Esq.*

Coote, Chester Coote Pallid, class-conscious friend of Helen Walshinghham; he becomes Art Kipps's mentor, advising him how to live like a gentleman but ultimately spurning him when Kipps breaks off with Helen in H. G. Wells's *Kipps: The Story of a Simple Soul.*

Coote, Maria Sister of Belinda Coote; she overpraises a painted fan she owns but which Belinda disparages; the disagreement leads to violent domestic tragedy in Thomas Amory's *The Life of John Buncle, Esq.*

Cope Crewman aboard the *Renown* in C. S. Forester's *Lieutenant Hornblower.*

Cope, Carmen Sylva (Sylvy) Cousin and fiancée of Christian Fraser; loses him first to Catherine Conboy and then to death in Jessamyn West's *The Witch Diggers.*

Copeland, Benedict Mady Ascetic black physician committed to racial progress; his children ignore his teachings in Carson McCullers's *The Heart Is a Lonely Hunter.*

Copeland, Brownfield (Brown) Crazed son of Margaret and Grange Copeland; kills his wife, Mem Copeland, and is later murdered by his father in Alice Walker's *The Third Life of Grange Copeland.*

Copeland, Daphne (Daffy) Eldest daughter of Mem and Brownfield Copeland; committed to an insane asylum in Alice Walker's *The Third Life of Grange Copeland.*

Copeland, Grandpapa Elderly preacher; father and final refuge of Benedict Mady Copeland in Carson McCullers's *The Heart Is a Lonely Hunter.*

Copeland, Grange Georgia black redeemed by love for his granddaughter, Ruth Copeland; his life is chronicled from Prohibition to the Civil Rights movement in Alice Walker's *The Third Life of Grange Copeland.*

Copeland, Josie One-time prostitute and owner of the Dew Drop Inn; vacillates in her allegiance to Grange Copeland, whom she marries, and his son, Brownfield Copeland, in Alice Walker's *The Third Life of Grange Copeland.*

Copeland, Margaret First wife of Grange Copeland; commits suicide after poisoning her illegitimate son Star in Alice Walker's *The Third Life of Grange Copeland.*

Copeland, Mem R. Teacher demoralized by her husband, Brownfield Copeland, who shoots her to death in front of their children in Alice Walker's *The Third Life of Grange Copeland.*

Copeland, Ornette Middle daughter of Mem and Brownfield Copeland; becomes a prostitute in Alice Walker's *The Third Life of Grange Copeland.*

Copeland, Ruth Youngest daughter of Mem and Brownfield Copeland; reared by her grandfather, Grange, who is slain by police after attempting to save her from her father's custody in Alice Walker's *The Third Life of Grange Copeland.*

Copeland, Ted (Teddy) First fiancé of Aline Grey, dies of the flu during World War I in Sherwood Anderson's *Dark Laughter.*

Copeland, William (Willie) Son of Benedict Mady Copeland and brother of Portia; negligent prison guards cause the amputation of his feet from frostbite in Carson McCullers's *The Heart Is a Lonely Hunter.*

Copfee, Beverly Prostitute employed by Maurice Cassard in Ludwig Bemelmans's *Dirty Eddie.*

Coppard, George Nottingham engineer; he is Gertrude Morel's high-minded, stern father in D. H. Lawrence's *Sons and Lovers.*

Coppelius Detestable and satanic old German lawyer who makes mysterious visits to Nathanel's father late at night; Nathanel associates him with the horrible and frightful Sandman; kills Nathanel's father; reappears years later when Nathanel discovers that Coppelius is working with the physics professor Spalanzani to create a human robot in the form of a beautiful woman named Olympia in E. T. A. Hoffmann's "The Sandman."

Copper, Lord English newspaper magnate who sends William Boot as a war correspondent to Ishmaelia; he is confused by Theodore Boot's later substitution at the banquet honoring Boot's journalistic achievement in Evelyn Waugh's *Scoop.*

Copperfield, Clara See Copperfield Murdstone, Clara.

Copperfield, David (Daisy, Trotwood, Doady) Hero and narrator, who relates the story of his life from birth, including his mother's death, his pain and poverty before he lived with his aunt Betsey Trotwood, his school-days, his courtship of and marriage to Dora Spenlow, his career as a writer, and his marriage to Agnes Wickfield in Charles Dickens's *The Personal History of David Copperfield.*

Copperfield, Dora See Spenlow, Dora.

Copperfield, Frieda Wife of J. C. Copperfield, friend of Christina Goering, and intimate companion of Pacifica in Jane Bowles's *Two Serious Ladies.*

Copperfield, J. C. Husband of Frieda Copperfield; enthusiastic man who loves to travel; Frieda finally leaves him in Jane Bowles's *Two Serious Ladies.*

Copperwheat, Stephen British government official who notifies Bernard Sands of the government's subsidy for Vardon Hall in Angus Wilson's *Hemlock and After.*

Coppola, Giuseppe Peddler of optical instruments: eyeglasses, telescopes, and spyglasses; thought by Nathanel to be a double of the sinister and satanic Coppelius; sells a spyglass to Nathanel, which the latter uses to observe the beautiful Olympia in E. T. A. Hoffmann's "The Sandman."

Copthorne, Constance Mistress of Hughie Cantrip; following the crash that killed Hughie and Steven Leadbitter, she delivers the latter's truncated final message to Lady Franklin that he loved her in L. P. Hartley's *The Hireling.*

Cora Prostitute who hangs out at Harry Hope's seedy saloon; her pimp is Chuck Morello, the daytime bartender at the bar; Cora and Chuck fantasize about their future marriage and life on a New Jersey farm, pipe dreams that never materialize in Eugene O'Neill's play *The Iceman Cometh.*

Cora Young, impoverished black student of Eric Eisner's literacy program; suffers from depression and suicidal tendencies in Phillip Lopate's *Confessions of Summer.*

Cora, Aunt Ex-slaveowner who cares for Antoinette Cosway after her brother Pierre's death until Antoinette goes to the Mt. Calvary Convent; she leaves for England for her health and returns for the same reason; she tries to tell Antoinette not to marry Mr. Rochester in Jean Rhys's *Wide Sargasso Sea.*

Coral, Mrs. Diana Delacroix's helpful neighbor in Elizabeth Bowen's *The Little Girls.*

Coralie Pupil attending Mme. Beck's school in Charlotte Brontë's *Villette.*

Coram, Farder Gyptian elder who teaches Lyra to read the alethiometer in Philip Pullman's *His Dark Materials.*

Coramantien, King of Oroonoko's grandfather, who desires Imoinda for his own when he discovers Oroonoko's love for her; he finds the lovers together, but believes Imoinda's false claim of rape and sells her into slavery instead of killing her in Aphra Behn's *Oroonoko.*

Coransee Brother of Teray and son of Rayal and Jansee; challenges his brother for the Pattern, a vast network of mental links in Octavia E. Butler's *Patternmaster.*

Corbaccio Old gentleman and one of Volpone's would-be heirs; gives Mosca a drug for Volpone, which Mosca refuses out of fear that it might be poison; gives Volpone a bag of coins after being informed of Voltore's gold plate gift; disinherits his son Bonario and makes Volpone his heir; readily believes Volpone's lie that Bonario attempted to kill him, Volpone; stripped of all his property by the Venetian court in Ben Jonson's play *Volpone.*

Corbera, Don Fabrizio Aristocratic protagonist who is prince of Salina and whose family herald is the leopard; sharp observer of the events that are precipitating his own demise as well as changing dramatically the destiny of southern Italy; disillusioned with the political state of Italy in Giuseppe Tomasi di Lampedusa's *The Leopard.*

Corbett, Charles Father of the heroine, Emma; he urges her betrothed, Henry Hammond, to renounce either Emma or his commission in the British army; he survives to mourn the deaths of Emma and his son Edward in S. J. Pratt's *Emma Corbett.*

Corbett, Earlie Young black man murdered by Omar Duvall in Mary McGarry Morris's *Songs in Ordinary Time.*

Corbett, Edward Ill-fated brother of the ill-fated heroine, Emma Corbett, in S. J. Pratt's *Emma Corbett.*

Corbett, Emma Heroine who travels to America to join her lover, Henry Hammond, whose regiment is fighting there; she dies in England months after sucking poison from her betrothed's arrow wound in S. J. Pratt's *Emma Corbett.*

Corbett, Luther Grandfather of Earlie in Mary McGarry Morris's *Songs in Ordinary Time.*

Corbett, Mr. Engineer who came to the mines of the Gran Seco from Rhodesia; he is now in charge of the coast garrison held by the rebels in John Buchan's *The Courts of the Morning.*

Corbett, Myna Overweight health food advocate and occasional companion of Gary Harkness at Logos College in Don DeLillo's *End Zone.*

Corbitant Enemy of Hobomok and the Puritan settlers in Lydia Maria Child's *Hobomok.*

Corby, George Young biologist who visits the Anson house years after Paulina's book about her grandfather and his literary work is rejected by publishers; wishes to write an article about an obscure anatomy pamphlet published by Orestes Anson before he had turned his focus from medicine to literature; Corby's interest in her grandfather revives the disillusioned Paulina in Edith Wharton's *The Angel at the Grave.*

Corcoran, Cork Headmaster of Rawcliff School where Colin Saville gets a teaching job; Corcoran extinguishes the small spark of enthusiasm with which Colin is pursuing his vocation and fires him in David Storey's *Saville.*

Corcoran, Fidsey Young hoodlum whom George Kelcey helps win a fistfight in Stephen Crane's *George's Mother.*

Corcoran, Jerome (Corky) Corcoran Son of Timothy and Theresa Corcoran; successful businessman, active in local politics; sexually attractive, flirtatious, and unstable in Joyce Carol Oates's *What I Lived For.*

Corcoran, Jesus Maria Alcoholic, dissipated acquaintance of Pilon, who invites Corcoran to live with him because Corcoran has three dollars, in John Steinbeck's *Tortilla Flat.*

Corcoran, Sean Heavy drinker, brother of Timothy, and uncle of Corky in Joyce Carol Oates's *What I Lived For.*

Corcoran, Theresa Widow of the murdered Timothy; neurotic alcoholic mother of Corky in Joyce Carol Oates's *What I Lived For.*

Corcoran, Timothy Patrick Irish-American man in favor of black workers; murdered on Christmas Eve in front of his own house in Joyce Carol Oates's *What I Lived For.*

Corcos, Ludovic (Ludo) Son of a wealthy Jewish financier; his friend Augustine Penry-Herbert travels with him in Morocco and in Germany in Richard Hughes's *The Wooden Shepherdess.*

Cord, Jonas, Jr. Magnate who takes control of Cord Explosives upon the death of his father; develops an aircraft company, an electronics firm, and a movie company; sacrifices personal happiness for power in Harold Robbins's *The Carpetbaggers.*

Cord, Jonas, Sr. Father of Jonas Cord, Jr., and founder of Cord Explosives and the Cord fortune; dies of an encephalic embolism in Harold Robbins's *The Carpetbaggers.*

Cord, Rina Marlowe See Marlowe, Rina.

Corday, Charlotte Prominent figure in the French Revolution; a young and attractive aristocrat; inveigles her way into Jean-Paul Marat's bath to murder him; idealist who believes that the assassination of revolutionary leader Marat would prevent the slaughter of thousands of innocents, but her actions do not stem the future Reign of Terror that explodes in France after the revolution; is guillotined by the revolutionary courts for treason in Peter Weiss's play *The Persecution and Assassination of Jean-Paul Marat as Performed by the Inmates of the Asylum of Charenton Under the Direction of the Marquis de Sade.*

Corde, Albert Dean of a Chicago university and husband of one of the university's astrophysicists, Minna Raresh; a journalist by trade, nationally known for his columns on the ravages of the inner city and American prisons; spends his Christmas vacation in Romania attending to the dying mother of his wife, while escaping the scandal of the murder of a university student in Saul Bellow's *The Dean's December.*

Corde, Minna Raresh Romanian-born astrophysicist who is married to her university's dean, Albert Corde; is thin and pensive, with a fierce work ethic; suffers greatly at the sudden illness and subsequent death of her mother, Valeria, in Saul Bellow's *The Dean's December.*

Cordelia Daughter of Lear, sister of Regan and Goneril; disowned by her father after she refuses to flatter him by overstating her filial love; marries the king of France, who admires her virtue; returns to England with the army of France to rescue Lear and reclaim his throne from her sisters; captured by Regan and Goneril and murdered in prison on Edmund's orders in Shakespeare's play *King Lear.*

Cordelia Daughter of Nicanor, sister of Oliver, and twin of Ferdinand; she fails to meet a man whom she could marry and remains happily single in Sarah Fielding's *The Cry.*

Cordes, Ramón (Cortés) Itinerant professional revolutionary with a fatal attraction to lost causes; leader of a band of revolutionaries who is taken prisoner and awaits execution in William Herrick's *The Last to Die.*

Cordiala Orphan disguised as a male, Almon; having no one to protect her, she masks herself and runs away to avoid marriage to Clodius; she becomes servant to Clarenthia in Jane Barker's *Exilius; or, The Banish'd Roman.*

Cordiner, Cordelia Swain Psychologist who separates the Swain twins, Wilbur and Eliza, in Kurt Vonnegut's *Slapstick.*

Cordwain, Jenny Rich packer's daughter, who thinks herself more genteel than the impoverished nobility and hires Henrietta Courteney for the fun of having a gentlewoman as her maid; she is betrothed to Lord B—, who loves Henrietta in Charlotte Lennox's *Henrietta.*

Cordwain, Mr. Rich packer, who wishes to marry his daughter into the nobility in Charlotte Lennox's *Henrietta.*

Cordwainer, Peter College friend of Ethan Llewelyn, who believes he should have prevented Peter's suicide two decades ago; Ethan thinks of Peter each time he sees a billboard advertisement for Mother Gettle's Kettle Simmered Soups, made by the Cordwainer family, in Malcolm Lowry's *October Ferry to Gabriola.*

Coredero, Carlos One of Esperanza's brothers who lives largely in a male world in Sandra Cisneros's *The House on Mango Street.*

Coredero, Esperanza Narrator and young girl in a poor and primarily Hispanic section of Chicago; sees how some of the people around her fail to assimilate into American life; embarrassed by her family's impoverished status, the actual poorhouse on Mango Street, for example; although her father says that the house is "temporary" and that the family will get a better one, recognizes that this is not likely to happen in Sandra Cisneros's *The House on Mango Street.*

Coredero, Kiki One of Esperanza's brothers in Sandra Cisneros's *The House on Mango Street.*

Corey Leader of the Indians, a youth movement revolting against an authoritarian United States; his followers disperse and survive in ragtag groups in Marge Piercy's *Dance the Eagle to Sleep.*

Corey, Anna Bellingham Wife of Bromfield Corey; opposes the attachment of her son, Tom Corey, to Penelope Lapham in William Dean Howells's *The Rise of Silas Lapham.*

Corey, Bromfield Boston aristocrat who tries to accept the relationship of his son, Tom Corey, with the Laphams in William Dean Howells's *The Rise of Silas Lapham.*

Corey, Giles Feisty 80-year-old individualist famous for instigating many lawsuits in Salem; does not care what others think; accuses Thomas Putnam of land grabbing and lying to the court; makes the mistake of questioning his own wife to Reverend Hale, which leads to her being accused of witchcraft; held in contempt of court and, refusing to plead guilty to an indictment, is pressed to death by great stones in Arthur Miller's play *The Crucible.*

Corey, Judge Leonidas Member of the educational committee in Morganville, Oklahoma; tries to interest George Brush in Corey's daughter in Thornton Wilder's *Heaven's My Destination.*

Corey, Mississippi Daughter of Judge Leonidas Corey; dines with George Brush and shocks him with her references to drinking and smoking in Thornton Wilder's *Heaven's My Destination.*

Corey, Mister Minister imported by Sally Lacey for Sara Lacey's marriage to Ezekiel Catlett in Mary Lee Settle's *O Beulah Land.*

Corey, Tom Son of Bromfield and Anna Corey; employee in Silas Lapham's paint factory who marries Penelope Lapham in William Dean Howells's *The Rise of Silas Lapham.*

Corfield, Aspasia Aristocrat at whose country house Letty Sewell and Sir George Tressady become engaged in Mrs. Humphry Ward's *Sir George Tressady.*

Corin Old shepherd who attempts, unsuccessfully, to reason with Silvius over his unrequited love for Phoebe; informs Rosalind and Celia of the availability of his master's cottage, which they immediately buy; engages in an exchange with the court jester Touchstone in which he, Corin, argues for country life over courtly life in William Shakespeare's play *As You Like It.*

Corina, Donna Maid of honor to the Queen of Spain; she is loved by Don Fernando de Cardiole but spurns him for Don Pedro de Mendoza in Penelope Aubin's *The Strange Adventures of the Count de Vinevil and His Family.*

Cork, Mrs. London landlady who forces Mrs. Hopgood to move out when she discovers Madge Hopgood is pregnant and unmarried in Mark Rutherford's *Clara Hopgood.*

Cork, Mrs. (Nanny) Silvia Fox Tebrick's old nurse, who discovers her mistress as a fox dressed in her jacket lying in a chair in the Tebricks' bedroom; she recognizes her instantly but hurries away and leaves the house for a cottage near Tangley because she hears Richard Tebrick shooting the family dogs to protect his wife's safety in their home; she later returns to the house to care for the couple and tries to be a civilizing influence on Silvia Fox Tebrick in David Garnett's *Lady Into Fox.*

Cork, Polly Mrs. Cork's granddaughter, who lives at Cork's cottage in Tangley with her father, Simon, Mrs. Cork's son; she befriends Silvia Fox Tebrick when Richard Tebrick decides to relocate to the secluded cottage as a means of protecting his wife's secret in David Garnett's *Lady Into Fox.*

Cork, Simon Son of Mrs. Cork and father of Polly; the Cork cottage becomes a place of refuge for the Tebricks in David Garnett's *Lady Into Fox.*

Corkan, Salko Illegitimate child who is raised by the villagers in Visegrad in Ivo Andrić's *The Bridge on the Drina.*

Corker, Irene Spiteful invalid sister of William Corker, with whom she has lived for twelve years; she "talks like a wife but isn't"; bitterly resentful of her brother's leaving her, she leaves all of her money and property at her death to the Radley Rheumatism Clinic in John Berger's *Corker's Freedom.*

Corker, William Tracey Nondescript, gullible, sixty-three-year-old bachelor, who owns and manages an employment agency in Clapham, England; giving slide shows and lectures of his travels in his spare time, he lives with and is henpecked by an invalid sister for twelve intolerable years until one day, determined to be happy, he declares his freedom from her and leaves her in John Berger's *Corker's Freedom.*

Corkery, Phil Quiet, spare man; an occasional lover of Ida Arnold, he assists her in her quest to find Charles Hale's killers by acting as confidant and by accompanying her to the police station in Graham Greene's *Brighton Rock.*

Corleone, Constanzia (Connie) Daughter of Vito Corleone and wife of the abusive Carlo Rizzi in Mario Puzo's *The Godfather.*

Corleone, Kay See Adams, Kay.

Corleone, Michael Youngest son of Don Corleone; originally determined to stay out of the family business, he takes the place of his father after the old man's death and proceeds to murder all of his family's enemies in Mario Puzo's *The Godfather.*

Corleone, Santino (Sonny) Acting head of the family during the convalescence of his father, Don Corleone, until he himself is killed by rival gangsters in Mario Puzo's *The Godfather.*

Corleone, Vito (Don Corleone, The Godfather) Head of a powerful family of Sicilian gangsters in Mario Puzo's *The Godfather.*

Corley Sexy boyfriend of Celia in Joan Chase's *During the Reign of the Queen of Persia.*

Cornaro Spanish gentleman who sends men out to retrieve his daughter after she marries without his consent; his men mistakenly seize Cornelia and carry her off to Madrid in Sarah Scott's *The History of Cornelia.*

Cornblow Young, amiable interior decorator who believes the work he performs has a "civilizing or priestly function"; he is rejected by Sergeant Jebb because his superior taste makes Jebb recognize that all he himself wants in life is an attic or hotel with no possessions but his books in Storm Jameson's *There Will Be a Short Interval.*

Cornbury, Butler Eldest son of a Devonshire squire; his campaign to represent Baslehurst in Parliament is endorsed by Mrs. Tappitt's social gathering; he kowtows to local gentry, but the Tappitts switch allegiance to his opponent, Mr. Hart, from London; it is a close race, but Cornbury wins the election in Anthony Trollope's *Rachel Ray.*

Cornbury, Patty Comfort Onetime beauty of Devon, now wife of Butler Cornbury and mother of five; she works hard among the country gentry to ensure that her husband is elected Member of Parliament for Baslehurst; she remains loyal to Rachel Ray in the face of local jealousy over the girl's attachment to Luke Rowan in Anthony Trollope's *Rachel Ray.*

Cornbury, Walter Cousin of Patty Cornbury, who encourages him to dance with Rachel Ray at Mrs. Tappitt's ball in Anthony Trollope's *Rachel Ray.*

Cornelia Faithful daughter of Ellen "Granny" Weatherall; one of four children, dutifully brings Granny into her home; calls for a priest, the doctor, and the other children to come to Granny's deathbed; exasperated with her mother but humors her and tries to soothe her last moment in Katherine Anne Porter's "The Jilting of Granny Weatherall."

Cornelia Miranda's friend who tells the story of Prince Henrik's past and of his taking holy orders in Aphra Behn's *The Fair Jilt.*

Cornelia Seven-year-old daughter of Catharina and Johannes Vermeer; challenges Griet's authority and makes trouble for Griet whenever possible in Tracy Chevalier's *Girl with a Pearl Earring.*

Cornelia Virtuous orphan from a well-bred family; she hopes to help the poor, but her great beauty and charm expose her to the jealousy of other women and the lechery of various men in Sarah Scott's *The History of Cornelia.*

Cornelis Brother of Gerard and Sybrandt; expecting to inherit the family business, he dies disappointed at age sixty-five with his mother and father still alive in Charles Reade's *The Cloister and the Hearth.*

Cornelius Roman solider in the Twelfth Legion and companion to Marius; he is known for his purity and his paradoxical severity and hopefulness in Walter Pater's *Marius the Epicurean.*

Cornelius Aristo's friend, a civil servant who negotiates release for Callista on condition she will sign to having sacrificed to the gods in John Henry Newman's *Callista.*

Cornelius Faustus's friend and a famous magician; along with Valdes, is called upon to teach Faustus about magic; stresses the value of incantations as part of Faustus's education in Christopher Marlowe's play *Dr. Faustus.*

Cornelius Physician at Cymbeline's court; ordered by the queen to produce a deadly poison; deeply suspicious of her intentions; instead, produces a sleeping potion that is drunk unknowingly by Imogen in William Shakespeare's play *Cymbeline.*

Cornelius, Frank (Frankie, Mark) Dying tubercular who is the object of Cress Delahanty's infatuation in Jessamyn West's *Cress Delahanty.*

Cornelius, Joyce School bus driver and wife of Frank Cornelius in Jessamyn West's *Cress Delahanty.*

Cornelius, Oswald Hendryks Referred to as Uncle Oswald and born in 1895; womanizer whose motto is never to lie down with the same woman twice; connoisseur of wine, lover of opera, expert on Chinese porcelain, and collector of spiders, scorpions, and walking sticks; describes himself as the greatest Don Juan of all time; an aesthete and dandy who lives life for self-indulgence; wealthy as a result of either immoral or illegal schemes in Roald Dahl's "Bitch."

Cornell, Georgie Twenty-first-century man living in a society dominated by women; escapes enslavement by females in a fantasy of role reversals; protagonist of Thomas Berger's *Regiment of Women.*

Corner, Cecily Sister-in-law of Mr. Brithing's secretary; she reads extensively, is interested in utopias, and longs for a formal education; she is suspicious of marriage and is pursued by the American Mr. Dierck in H. G. Wells's *Mr. Britling Sees It Through.*

Corney, Molly Childhood friend of Sylvia Robson; her coarser nature contrasts with Sylvia's sensitivity and depth of feeling in love and marriage in Elizabeth Gaskell's *Sylvia's Lovers.*

Corney, Mrs. Matron of the workhouse where Oliver Twist was born; she is sweet and sympathetic to Mr. Bumble until she marries him; afterwards, she is shrewish and nags him in Charles Dickens's *Oliver Twist.*

Cornford, Adam Psychiatrist who gives expert testimony for the defense in the trial of Cora Ross and Kitty Pateman in C. P. Snow's *The Sleep of Reason.*

Cornick, Jim Sailor from the ship *Victory* who brings Anne Garland news of Bob Loveday's survival after the Battle of Trafalgar and gossip of Bob's fickle affections in Thomas Hardy's *The Trumpet-Major.*

Cornish, Neil Piano teacher and would-be law student who marries Lulu Bett in Zona Gale's *Miss Lulu Bett.*

Cornwall Husband of Regan, arrogant and greedy; puts Kent in the stocks for confronting Oswald; turns Lear out into the storm; with Regan, blinds Gloucester and is killed by one of Gloucester's servants in Shakespeare's play *King Lear.*

Cornwall-Cope, Denise New wife of Mr. Daintry in Isabel Colegate's *Agatha.*

Cornwallis Head of the British forces in the South; graciously receives Mildred and Henry Lindsay in John Pendleton Kennedy's *Horse-Shoe Robinson.*

Cornwallis, Isabel Director of a traveling ballet company; she practices voodoo and kills chickens when her performances are not sold out; she is strict with her dancers in Colin MacInnes's *City of Spades.*

Cornwallis, William Admiral of the English naval fleet; he commands Hornblower, offering advice, gratitude, and praise; he finally helps Hornblower get promoted to Captain in C. S. Forester's *Hornblower and the Hotspur.*

Coronett, Brother Handsome charismatic preacher; Christianna Wheeler has a sexual dream about Brother Coronett and believes it is partially responsible for the difficult and mysterious pregnancy that results in her quintuplets in Bobbie Ann Mason's *Feather Crowns.*

Corporal See Stefan.

Corpse, The Mummified and later plastered body of Jesus Christ stolen from the Vatican by Plucky Purcell; incinerated along with John Paul Ziller and Mon Cul on the Icarus XC solar balloon in Tom Robbins's *Another Roadside Attraction.*

Corrado Italian brigand who leads Cloudesley to the hideout of St. Elmo and his band and who, on reaching their destination, is killed along with Cloudesley in William Godwin's *Cloudesley.*

Corregidora Portuguese sea captain who in Brazil is a slave breeder and whoremonger; in fathering two females by his own daughters, he ultimately influences the life of Ursa Corregidora in Gayl Jones's *Corregidora.*

Corregidora, Correy (Mama) Daughter of Gram Corregidora and Corregidora; mother by Martin of Ursa Corregidora in Gayl Jones's *Corregidora.*

Corregidora, Dorita (Great Gram) Slave of Corregidora, by whom she has Gram Corregidora; great-grandmother of Ursa Corregidora in Gayl Jones's *Corregidora.*

Corregidora, Gram (Grandmama) Daughter of Dorita and Corregidora; mother, by Corregidora, of Correy Corregidora; grandmother of Ursa Corregidora in Gayl Jones's *Corregidora.*

Corregidora, Ursa (U. C., Ursa Corre, Urs, Ursie) Blues singer descended from the whoremonger Corregidora and instructed by her female forebears to make generations; after her husband, Mutt Thomas, throws her, pregnant, down a flight of stairs, she undergoes a hysterectomy; narrator of Gayl Jones's *Corregidora.*

Corregio, Alfredo Portuguese fisherman who lives for a time with his family in the Meserve's servant house before returning to the shrimping business to handle Jim Meserve's boats in Zora Neale Hurston's *Seraph on the Suwanee.*

Correspondent, The Newspaper reporter stranded with three others on a small lifeboat in the Atlantic after their ship capsizes; diligently shares the duty of rowing with the oiler, despite exhaustion and severe back pain; begins to contemplate, first with terror and later with awe, what he perceives as a universe indifferent to his plight; undergoes a profound transition in his perception of everyday reality; boarded the ship earlier a cynic but gains a sense of comradeship and a keen appreciation for the suffering of others through his struggle and somewhat fortuitous survival in Stephen Crane's "The Open Boat."

Corrie, Felix, Q.C. Wealthy and sophisticated barrister and owner of the country house Newlands; Miriam Henderson's employer, he comes to represent for her narrow and limited masculine logic in Dorothy Richardson's *Honeycomb.*

Corrie, Julia Indulgent mother and bored woman of leisure, whose life-style both attracts and repels Miriam Henderson; she follows the sensational trial of Oscar Wilde with rapt and shocked attention in Dorothy Richardson's *Honeycomb.*

Corrie, Miss See Hogganbeck, Everbe Corinthia.

Corrie, Sybil Twelve-year-old privileged daughter of Felix Cone in Dorothy Richardson's *Honeycomb.*

Corrigan, Fay Very wealthy aunt of Margaret Spencer; she takes Bryan Morley into the Corrigan household in order to send him to Petersons School; her relationship with Bryan becomes questionable as he matures, being more that of lover to lover than guardian to child in David Storey's *A Prodigal Child.*

Corrigan, Harold Wealthy furniture retailer and husband to Fay Corrigan; he finances Bryan Morley's education at Petersons School in David Storey's *A Prodigal Child.*

Corrigan, Miss Red-haired principal of the secretarial school Meg Eliot attends; she helps Meg succeed in her study to find a position in Angus Wilson's *The Middle Age of Mrs. Eliot.*

Corrigan, Mrs. Resident on the street purchased by Hilary Charwell for his clearance project in John Galsworthy's *Swan Song.*

Corrine Wife of Reverend Samuel; unable to have children; fears Olivia and Adam are the children of Nettie and Samuel but is wrong; dies during a mission in Africa in Alice Walker's *The Color Purple.*

Corruthers Political crony of Sammy Scott; known for his underground dirty work in W. E. B. DuBois's *Dark Princess.*

Corson, Lieutenant Veteran army lieutenant who is disillusioned by the Vietnam War and years for the old army; falls in love with Hamijolli Chand in Delhi in Tim O'Brien's *Going After Cacciato.*

Corte, Colonel Ugo Italian revolutionist from Bergamo, operating in groups with Carlo Ammiani; he objects to Milan's initiating a revolt and to Vittoria Campa, a woman, signaling it in George Meredith's *Vittoria.*

Cortese, Dorothea English wife of composer Signor Cortese in E. F. Benson's *Trouble for Lucia.*

Cortese, Signor Acclaimed Italian composer of the opera *Lucretia;* his presence at Olga Bracely's dinner party exposes Lucia Lucas's ignorance of Italian in E. F. Benson's *"Queen Lucia".* He appears in *Lucia in London* and in *Trouble for Lucia.*

Cortez, Felix Cuban emigrant who becomes chief adviser to Colombian drug kingpin Escobedo; seduces FBI director Jacobs's secretary in order to uncover American actions against the Colombian cartels; leads assaults against American light-infantry teams in Colombia; is captured by John Clark and returned to Cuba in Tom Clancy's *Clear and Present Danger.*

Corthell, Sheldon Esthete who courts Laura Dearborn and then attempts to win her once more after her marriage to Curtis Jadwin in Frank Norris's *The Pit.*

Cortleigh, Cardinal Elderly prelate who, in reparation for pains suffered at the Church's hands, offers George Arthur Rose Holy Orders in Frederick William Rolfe's *Hadrian the Seventh.*

Cortright, Edith American-born widow of a British diplomat; lover and traveling companion of Sam Dodsworth in Sinclair Lewis's *Dodsworth.*

Corven, Clare Cherrell, Lady Twenty-year-old daughter of General Sir Conway and Elizabeth Frensham Cherrell; she discusses the background of the Tasburghs with Dinny Cherrell in John Gahsworthy's *Maid In Waiting.* She marries Sir Gerald (Jerry) Corven, seventeen years older than she, in *Flowering Wilderness.* In 1931, at twenty-four, she flees her sadistic husband in Ceylon, meets Tony Croom returning to England, and is divorced with Croom as co-respondent in *Over the River.*

Corven, Sir Gerald (Jerry) Government official in British Colonial service; at forty he marries Chare Cherrell before taking a post in Ceylon in John Galsworthy's *Flowering Wilderness.* He treats his wife sadistically in Ceylon and divorces her in *Over the River.*

Corvino Merchant and one of Volpone's would-be heirs; gives Volpone a pearl as a gift; jealous of his wife Celia, whom he keeps as a prisoner; furious at the scene caused by Volpone (in a mountebank disguise) and chases him and the others away; chastises his wife following the incident; decides to make her sleep with the supposedly ill Volpone in order to help him recover; dismisses her repeated calls for him to reconsider; after Volpone and Mosca's ruse is revealed, he is condemned by the court to wear donkey ears while being paraded through Venice's canals in Ben Jonson's *Volpone.*

Corydon Cobbler of Constantinople in Sir Walter Scott's *Count Robert of Paris.*

Cosette Illegitimate daughter of the beautiful Fantine; entrusted to a foster home by her mother, where she endured harsh treatment; rescued by the protagonist, Jean Valjean, who has promised the dying Fantine that he will raise the child with love; falls in love with the young aristocrat Marius; spared losing both men in her life, as Marius is saved from death at the revolutionary fighting at the barricades and her father is not sent to prison by Inspector Javert in Victor Hugo's *Les Misérables.*

Cosey, Bill Owner of the Hotel and Resort, around whom the story of the women, all of whom were previously in different relationships with him, revolves; hosted the best jazz musicians and drew the finest crowd from the East Coast at his resort until the Civil Rights movement in the 1960s proved fatal to this all-black establishment; known as a ladies' man; although dead for 25 years, is still remembered for his generosity and as a benefactor to the town; connected through marriage to Heed, the grandfather of Christine, and the former husband of May in Toni Morrison's *Love.*

Cosey, Christine Bill Cosey's granddaughter; she and Heed were friends until Heed's marriage; Christine and Heed both vie for Bill Cosey's love and affection; sent to boarding school at the age of 17; maintains her animosity toward Heed throughout her adult life in Toni Morrison's *Love.*

Cosey, Heed Second wife of Bill Cosey, owner of the town's Hotel and Resort, who was married off by her parents at the age of 11; fails to bear Bill children, as he expects; learns to behave more ladylike and deal with her rivalries among the hotel's female employees; illiterate; Heed fights her way to gain respect in the hotel; later inherits the hotel from Bill based on a will written on a napkin, and continues her ferocious love relationship with Christine; lives with Christine in Bill Cosey's house, where the heiress employs Christine as her servant, and the latter continually tries to annoy, even sue, her in Toni Morrison's *Love.*

Cosey, May Bill Cosey's daughter-in-law and the widow of Bill's only son, Billy Boy; successfully bars the friendship between Heed and her daughter Christine and encourages their enmity in Toni Morrison's *Love.*

Cosgrave, Samuel Merchant whose letter reveals to Harriet Fitzpatrick her husband's mercenary motives in marrying her in Henry Fielding's *The History of Tom Jones.*

Cosgrove, Billy Wealthy acquaintance of Father Urban and patron of the Order of St. Clement; offended by Father Urban's attempt to correct his behavior, he abandons both priest and order in J. F. Powers's *Morte D'Urban.*

Cosgrove, Mrs. Hostess who brings young marriageable people together, opposing the aims of the feminists in George Gissing's *The Odd Women.*

Cosimo (Piovasco di Rondo) Baron of the book's title and brother of the narrator; as a young boy has a trivial dispute with his parents and decides to live the rest of his life in the boughs of tall trees; engages in many adventures; grows old living in the trees and is seen as mad by the community; as he nears death, grabs on to a balloon that passes by his tree and floats away, never to be seen again, in Italo Calvino's *The Baron in the Trees.*

Cosimo, Piero di Artist who sees Tito Melema's true nature and shows it in his prophetic paintings in George Eliot's *Romola.*

Cosini, Zeno Protagonist, narrator, and failure in life; recounts the traumatic death of his father, his courtship of four daughters whose names all begin with the letter A, his marriage to the ugly but level-headed Augusta, his affair with the off-key singer Carla Gerco, and the suicide of his acquaintance Guido; finds that his mental health is deteriorating despite his therapy with the psychoanalyst Doctor S in Italo Svevo's *Zeno's Conscience.*

Cosman, Michael General practitioner; best friend and almost lover of Isadora Wing; tells Isadora of her husband's affair in Erica Jong's *How to Save Your Own Life.*

Cosmic Spirit Composite mind, made up of the minds of innumerable beings from throughout the cosmos, which makes contact with its own past (the nebulae) and develops a vision of its creator, the Star Maker, in Olaf Stapledon's *Star Maker.*

Cossar Ferociously determined and single-minded civil engineer and friend of Bensington and Redwood; along with Redwood, Cossar acts as mentor and mediator for the Giants, encouraging their creativity and independence, and, ultimately, their rebellion in H. G. Wells's *The Food of the Gods, and How It Came to Earth.*

Cossar's Sons Three unnamed Giants who become frustrated with the Little People's laws, limits, and fearful narrow-mindedness; Cossar's sons lead the other Giants in rebellion and conquest, refusing to compromise their belief that they are following natural law in claiming the earth for their own in H. G. Wells's *The Food of the Gods, and How It Came to Earth.*

Cosset, Edgar Seventy-year-old uncle of Charles Henri Persaud; former soldier, politician, and statesman; married; has an affair with nephew's sister-in-law Isabel Walker; leaves her on the excuse of a mission to Eastern Europe in Diane Johnson's *Le Divorce.*

Cost, Mr. Agent for the spy ring "The Free Mothers"; with Willi Hilfe, he schemes to frame Arthur Rowe for the apparent murder of Cost at a seance, sending Rowe into hiding; Cost first appears as Travers, a businessman to whom Rowe delivers a suitcase supposedly filled with books but actually containing a bomb which seriously injures Rowe; he later appears as Ford, a tailor's assistant; he commits suicide in Graham Greene's *The Ministry of Fear.*

Costa, Ma Gyptian woman who lived at Jordan College and secretly watched over Lyra during her childhood; protected young Lyra when Lord Asriel killed Mr. Coulter; takes Lyra in to the Gyptian clan in Philip Pullman's *His Dark Materials.*

Costam, Dr. Young, satiric hotel medical man; his treatments of various women's illnesses and emergencies are based upon his belief that the women must be deceived for their own good in Arnold Bennett's *Imperial Palace.*

Costello Kind-hearted policeman, who tends to Alton Locke when he collapses with exhaustion after having been thrown out of his mother's house in Charles Kingsley's *Alton Locke.*

Costello, Bill Sponsor of John Wilder in Alcoholics Anonymous; well-intentioned but platitudinous in Richard Yates's *Disturbing the Peace.*

Costello, Ivan First boyfriend of Maria Wyeth in New York in Joan Didion's *Play It As It Lays.*

Costello, Jim Student at Muskegon Commercial Academy who gets stock tips by telegraph from his father in New York; he is imitated by Loudon Dodd in Robert Louis Stevenson's *The Wrecker.*

Costello, Mrs. Aunt of Frederick Winterbourne; a rich American lady spending time in the best resorts of Europe; met by Winterbourne in Vevey; very exclusive about the people with whom she allows an acquaintance; has a strong sense of decorum and thus refuses to meet commoners such as the Millers in Henry James's *Daisy Miller.*

Coster, Arnold Eighteen-year-old son of Frances and Stephen Coster in 1939; he admires David Renn, comforts a neglected child, Lise Brett, and very briefly loves Georgina Swan in London in Storm Jameson's *Before the Crossing.* In 1945 he is a twenty-four-year-old discharged Airforce Flight-Lieutenant, the private pilot of William Gary, a close companion of Edward West, and the hesitant but successful hover of Lise Brett in Storm Jameson's *The Black Laurel.*

Coster, Frances Dominating wife of Stephen Coster; she seeks to direct and even to smother their son, Arnold, with her anxious solicitude and desire for his safety; against her husband's wishes, she approaches his financial sponsors, Evelyn Lamb and Sir Thomas and Lady Harben, and arranges for Arnold to avoid military service, but he secretly enlists in the air force in Storm Jameson's *Before the Crossing.*

Coster, Stephen Editor of a conservative paper, *The Order;* he is the husband of Frances Coster in an incompatible marriage and the father of Arnold Coster; he seeks financial support from Evelyn Lamb and Nancy, Lady Harben in Storm Jameson's *Before the Crossing.*

Costigan, Captain Jack Pathetically drunken Irishman, the father of Miss Fotheringay (Emily Costigan), in William Makepeace Thackeray's *The History of Pendennis* He reappears, behaving indecorously in *The Newcomes.*

Costigan, Emily (Miss Fotheringay) Beautiful actress encouraged by her father to accept the proposal of the smitten young Arthur Pendennis; persuaded that he is not rich, she breaks the engagement and subsequently, as Miss Fotheringay, goes on the London stage; she marries Sir Charles Mirabel in William Makepeace Thackeray's *The History of Pendennis.*

Costuopolis, Johnny Greek head waiter at the sports club where all of the young people gather nightly for dinner and dancing in Doris Lessing's *Martha Quest.*

Cosway, Antoinette Beautiful West Indian Creole of English descent with long, sad, dark, alien eyes, a pleading expression, and a family history of madness; she marries Mr. Rochester, who renames her Bertha; increasingly unhappy and irrational, she is incarcerated in the attic of her husband's English house in Jean Rhys's *Wide Sargasso Sea.* See Bertha Antoinetta Mason Rochester in *Dictionary of British Literary Characters 18th- and 19th-Century Novels.*

Cosway, Daniel (Boyd) Antoinette Cosway's kinsman, who writes letters to Mr. Rochester telling him of Antoinette's true background and inherited tendency toward madness in Jean Rhys's *Wide Sargasso Sea.*

Cosway, Mrs. (Mrs. Mason) Antoinette's unloving, irrational, and helpless mother; a beautiful West Indian Creole, she is the widowed second wife of an impoverished landowner; she marries the wealthy Mr. Mason but becomes slowly, irrevocably insane and dies when Antoinette is sixteen years old in Jean Rhys's *Wide Sargasso Sea.* See Antoinetta Mason in *Dictionary of British Literary Characters 18th- and 19th-Century Novels.*

Cosway, Pierre Antoinette's younger brother, who "staggered when he walked and couldn't speak distinctly"; he dies as result of fire at Coulibri, their estate, in Jean Rhys's *Wide Sargasso Sea.*

Côte de Grace, Comte Edouard de la Poor French count who refuses to marry Billy Winthrop when he discovers that she has no money in Judith Krantz's *Scruples.*

Cotery, Jack Schoolchum of Lewis Eliot; he urges Eliot not to be hurt by Mr. Peck's insults and warns Eliot in 1925 to stay away from Sheila Knight; he is implicated in the lawsuit for fraud against George Passant in C. P. Snow's *Time of Hope.* He is a businessman and entrepreneur who drops out of the technical school when he loses his subsidy from Calvert to learn printing; he goes into business with financial help from George Passant and seduces Olive Calvert away from Arthur

Morcom; he is tried and acquitted of fraud in *Strangers and Brothers.* He is divorced from his second wife; he is religious and tries to convert Eliot in *The Sleep of Reason.*

Cothope Engineer who assists George Ponderevo in his aeronautical work in H. G. Wells's *Tono-Bungay.*

Cottard, M. Neighbor of Joseph Grand in the French Algerian city of Oran who attempts to commit suicide but is saved by Grand in Albert Camus's *The Plague.*

Cotterill, Councillor Portly, apparently affluent builder; his patronizing responses annoy Denry Machin, and his bankruptcy precipitates Denry's proposal to his daughter, Nellie, in Arnold Bennett's *The Card: A Story of Adventure in the Five Towns.*

Cotterill, Nellie Councillor Cotterill's shy daughter and Ruth Earp's friend; Nellie admires Denry Machin but thinks he will marry Ruth Earp until the day of Nellie's departure as bankrupt for America, when Denry sweeps her off the boat and into an unconventional marriage with him in Arnold Bennett's *The Card: A Story of Adventure in the Five Towns.*

Cotton, Euphrasia (Phrasie) Spinster housekeeper of Hilary Vane; friend of Austen Vane in Winston Churchill's *Mr. Crewe's Career.*

Cotton, Mr. Associate of Mr. Daintry in Isabel Colegate's *Orlando at the Brazen Threshold.*

Cotton, Ralph (Ralphie) Rich and snobbish black student, one of only two, at a private academy; his family discourages his association with George Cain in George Cain's *Blueschild Baby.*

Cotton, Sister Joe Provincially minded woman who works with Mr. Palmiller, chairman of the vice committee in Reedyville, to distribute leaflets against publicly displaying the nude statue of Breckenridge Boutwell as a war memorial in the town in William March's "A Memorial to the Slain."

Coulmier Director of the Clinic of Charenton, a mental asylum; oversees the action as historical figures such as the Marquis de Sade and Jean-Paul Marat and mental patients play roles in the drama in Peter Weiss's play *The Persecution and Assassination of Jean-Paul Marat as Performed by the Inmates of the Asylum of Charenton Under the Direction of the Marquis de Sade.*

Coulson, William Fellow shopman and subsequent partner of Philip Hepburn; his lack of Philip's intensity of feeling provides a contrast in love and daily life in Elizabeth Gaskell's *Sylvia's Lovers.*

Coulter, Burley (Uncle Burley) Wayward bachelor brother of Jarrat Coulter; his wild antics provide down-home Kentucky humor in Wendell Berry's *Nathan Coulter, A Place on Earth,* and *The Memory of Old Jack.*

Coulter, David (Dave) Father of Jarrat and Burley Coulter and Grandpa to Nathan Coulter in Wendell Berry's *Nathan Coulter;* also appears in *The Memory of Old Jack.*

Coulter, Hannah Wife of Nathan Coulter and mother of Mattie Coulter; widow of Virgil Feltner and mother by him of Little Margaret Feltner in Wendell Berry's *A Place on Earth* and *The Memory of Old Jack.*

Coulter, Jarrat Widowed subsistence tobacco farmer in Port William, Kentucky; father of Tom Coulter and Daddy to Nathan Coulter in Wendell Berry's *Nathan Coulter, A Place on Earth,* and *The Memory of Old Jack.*

Coulter, Marisa Mother of Lyra and former lover of Lord Asriel; female scholar and head of the General Oblation Board; kidnaps street urchins for use in intercision experiments to protect them from Dust; kills Lord Boreal and the witch Lena Feldt to discover Lyra's destiny; drugs Lyra and holds her captive; sacrifices herself and Lord Asriel to destroy the Metatron (the voice of the Authority) in Philip Pullman's *His Dark Materials.*

Coulter, Mathew Burley (Mattie) Son of Nathan and Hannah Coulter in Wendell Berry's *The Memory of Old Jack.*

Coulter, Mr. Agricultural "improver" who inspires others with his new, productive farming methods in John Galt's *Annals of the Parish.*

Coulter, Nathan Kentucky tobacco farmer and second husband of widowed Hannah Feltner; narrator of Wendell Berry's *Nathan Coulter;* also appears in *A Place on Earth* and *The Memory of Old Jack.*

Coulter, Tom Oldest son of Jarrat Coulter; leaves home after a fight with his father; killed during World War II in Wendell Berry's *A Place on Earth;* also appears in *Nathan Coulter.*

Counihan, Miss Woman who loves Murphy as long as he is off seeking his fortune in London in Samuel Beckett's *Murphy.*

Counselor, The Lawyer, fellow drinker, and close friend of Frederick Exley; his apartment is a place of retreat after Exley is released from one of his stints in a mental hospital; suffers the ignominy of disbarment, but remains optimistic even as Exley sinks into bitter despair in Frederick Exley's *A Fan's Notes.*

Count Aristocratic father of Miss Julie; his boots, polished by the valet Jean, represent him in the play; is absent from the estate when Miss Julie, after a sudden and brief affair with the hired man Jean, commits suicide out of a loss of honor in August Strindberg's play *Miss Julie.*

Count, The Wealthy aristocrat and head of a family living in a chateau near the Ambricourt Parish in France; sought after by the country priest to help finance needed projects for poor parishioners; engages in numerous affairs, most recently with the hired governess in Georges Bernanos's *The Diary of a Country Priest.*

Count, "The Maid of the Dauber" Wealthy Parisian aristocrat who establishes an unusually beautiful young—but peasant—woman in a luxurious apartment for his pleasure; disturbingly discovers after a few months that the immaculate beauty cannot long be displaced from her humble roots, as he finds her hidden in a closet where she is polishing his black boots in Émile Zola's "The Maid of the Dauber."

Countess Epicene tycoon of feminine hygiene products and owner of the Rubber Rose Ranch; makes Sissy Hankshaw his star model as the Yoni Yum/ Dew Girl in Tom Robbins's *Even Cowgirls Get the Blues.*

Countess Physically ugly but wealthy American lover of Beale Farange while he is married in Henry James's *What Maisie Knew.*

Countess, Dowager of Aristocratic widow whose costume as a nun at a masquerade attracts Mr. B—'s interest; she almost commits bigamy with him in Samuel Richardson's *Pamela, or Virtue Rewarded.*

Countess, The Wife of the count in the chateau near the Ambricourt Parish in France; talks to the country priest about her hysteria over her husband's many infidelities, the latest being an affair with their governess; continues to mourn for her young son who died years earlier; released from her anguish, only to die that very night in Georges Bernanos's *The Diary of a Country Priest.*

Countess of — Model noblewoman, romance-reader, unfashionably intelligent; she begins Arabella's cure by explaining that real, good women have no adventures; she leaves Bath before accomplishing her purpose in Charlotte Lennox's *The Female Quixote.*

Countess of Chell (Interfering Iris) Pretty, young, philanthropic wife; of poor parentage but successfully groomed for a rich marriage, she involves herself in the social progress of the Five Towns; she appreciates the amusing exploits of Denry Machin to the extent of dancing with him at her annual ball, which starts Denry on his career as a "card" in Arnold Bennett's *The Card: A Story of Adventure in the Five Towns.*

Count of Monte Beni See Donatello.

Count of Monte-Cristo See Dantès, Edmond.

Country Girl Traveler on the wagon who is very beautiful and attracts the attention of the Disguised Gentleman in Charles Johnstone's *Chrysal: or, The Adventures of a Guinea.*

Country Girl's Mother Traveler on the wagon who is an unpolished, good-looking woman whose false modesty allows her to drink too freely in Charles Johnstone's *Chrysal: or, The Adventures of a Guinea.*

County Attorney Young man in charge of prosecuting Minnie Wright; referred to as George; believes in her guilt but cannot find a motive for her murdering her husband; acts condescendingly toward the women in the farmhouse and disparages Mrs. Wright's housekeeping abilities in Susan Glaspell's play *Trifles.*

County Clerk, The (Arch Anker) Obscene civil servant working out of the Old Court House in Pigeon Hole; person to whom civil cases are referred so they will not be resolved in William S. Burroughs's *Naked Lunch* and *The Soft Machine.*

County Paris Young noble related to Prince Escalus; seeks the hand of Juliet and secures an arranged marriage to her before the two have even been introduced; visits her tomb after her staged death to grieve; killed in a duel with Romeo, becoming another victim of needless violence in William Shakespeare's play *Romeo and Juliet.*

Coupeau Industrious but cocky zinc worker; marries Gervaise; falls and breaks his leg; turns to drink and dies of alcoholism in the asylum of Sainte-Anne in Émile Zola's *L'Assommoir.*

Coupeau, Nana Young, beautiful, and sexually free woman in Paris in 1867; rises from a poor streetwalker to a high-class stage performer at the Théâtre des Variétés; performs nearly nude in the lead role of *The Blonde Venus;* femme fatale whose beauty and talent to seduce men bring ruin to many desiring paramours; finally dies a horrible death from smallpox in Émile Zola's *Nana.*

Courcy, Olive de Red Cross volunteer in France who passes out stocks of American supplies to the villagers in Willa Cather's *One of Ours.*

Courland, Duke of, John Ernest Biren Consort of the Czarina Anne of Russia and de facto head of state, who jealously guards his power; displeased with William Meadows's growing intimacy with his niece, Isabella Scherbatoff, he orders him arrested in William Godwin's *Cloudesley.*

Court, Alexander Companion of John Bates and Michael Williams on the night before the Battle of Agincourt; meets Henry V in disguise in William Shakespeare's play *Henry V.*

Court, Julius Young, rich, hedonistic owner of a cottage on the grounds of Toynton Grange in P. D. James's *The Black Tower.*

Court, Landry Boyish suitor of Laura Dearborn and worshipful colleague of Curtis Jadwin at the Chicago Board of Trade; marries Laura's sister Page Dearborn and remains determined to become like Jadwin, despite Jadwin's failure as a speculator, in Frank Norris's *The Pit.*

Court, Mont Parole officer of Gary Gilmore in Norman Mailer's *The Executioner's Song.*

Court Clerk Official who accepts the Matron's bribe in order to facilitate her case in Charles Johnstone's *Chrysal: or, The Adventures of a Guinea.*

Courtenay, Hubert Elderly, dignified gentlemanly performer; once a Shakespearean actor, he is now a supporting member of Tommy Beamish's act in J. B. Priestley's *Lost Empires.*

Courtenay, Mr. Oxford tutor responsible for the shaping of the strong moral sense of Jacob Delafield in Mrs. Humphry Ward's *Lady Rose's Daughter.*

Courteney, Charles (Mr. Freeman) Marquis of —'s tutor-companion; he tries to procure Henrietta Courteney as mistress to his charge, then recognizes her as his long-lost sister; he opposes her marriage to the marquis because of parental opposition; he gives up a large portion of his inheritance to arrange an acceptable dowry for her in Charlotte Lennox's *Henrietta.*

Courteney, Henrietta ("Clelia," Miss or Mrs. Benson) Heroine, an orphan cast off by her relatives because of her father's elopement with her mother; she resists forced marriage and conversion to Catholicism and stands up for old aristocratic values in a mercenary world; she shames her family into accepting her by becoming a lady's maid in Charlotte Lennox's *Henrietta.*

Courteney, Mr. Henrietta Courteney's father; the youngest son of the Earl of —, he is disinherited for marrying the daughter of a poor army widow; he dies leaving his family desolate in Charlotte Lennox's *Henrietta.*

Courteney, Mrs. (Miss Carlton) Henrietta Courteney's mother, the daughter of a former army officer; she inspires Mr. Courteney's pity and love when his father rejects her mother's request to reinstate her father's pension in Charlotte Lennox's *Henrietta.*

Courteney, Prudence Frivolous daughter of the Brit-ish ambassador to Azania; one of her love affairs is with Basil Seal; hater a plane in which she is riding crashes in the jungle, and she is captured and eaten by cannibals and inadvertently by Basil in Evelyn Waugh's *Black Mischief*

Courteney, Samson Imperturbable British minister to Azania who seems to regard his job as a perpetual vacation in Evelyn Waugh's *Black Mischief*

Court Envoy Informs Irma and the chief of the rebel conflict taking place outside the The Grand Balcony, a brothel, and of the effective demise of the queen; designates Irma as the new queen in Jean Genet's play *The Balcony.*

Courter, Mary Librarian of River Cover; always calls Geneva first when a book comes in that she thinks Geneva would like in Sandra Scofield's *Beyond Deserving.*

Courtesan of Bologna Owner of Phyllis and Pompey; she gives Pompey to the English fop Hillario in exchange for a gold watch in Francis Coventry's *The History of Pompey the Little.*

Courtier, Charles Forty-year-old radical author of books against war; a longtime friend of Audrey Noel, he courts Lady Barbara Carádoc though discouraged by her family; he gives her up to Lord Harbinger when he goes off to Persia in John Galsworthy's *The Patrician.*

Courtland, Adele Neighbor of the McKelvas and sister of Nate Courtland in Eudora Welty's *The Optimist's Daughter.*

Courtland, Earl of Wealthy English father of Frederick, Lord Lindore and Lady Juliana (Douglas); he opposes her marriage to Henry Douglas on the grounds that it is for love, not for money, in Susan Ferrier's *Marriage.*

Courtland, Nate New Orleans eye specialist and family friend of the McKelvas; treats both Clinton and Becky McKelva's vision problems in Eudora Welty's *The Optimist's Daughter.*

Courtney Lover of Patrick Bateman and best friend of his girlfriend Evelyn; has a boyfriend who is unaware that she is having an affair; comes from money and makes a lot of it herself; street smart, but not smart enough to know that Patrick Bateman is a serial killer in Bret Easton Ellis's *American Psycho.*

Courtney, Duke Father of Iris and husband of Persia; respected middle-class Irish-American businessman in Hammond; loving and mild-tempered until he gambles away his fortune and his family in Joyce Carol Oates's *Because It Is Bitter, and Because It Is My Heart.*

Courtney, Emma Independent-minded but impractical young woman, who repeatedly proposes to Augustus Harley, the last time offering to live common-law; she supports herself by tutoring, loses her money in a bank crash, reluctantly marries Mr. Montague, and becomes his medical assistant in Mary Hays's *Memoirs of Emma Courtney.*

Courtney, Iris Daughter of Duke and Persia Courtney; sensitive and strong-willed; the only witness of the killing of "Little Red"; secret admirer of Jinx; later fiancée of Alan Savage in Joyce Carol Oates's *Because It Is Bitter, and Because It Is My Heart.*

Courtney, Jim Police captain killed by Rico Bandello in the New Year's Eve holdup of the Casa Alvarado nightclub in William Riley Burnett's *Little Caesar.*

Courtney, Leslie Iris's uncle, Duke Courtney's older, bachelor brother; photographer who supports minorities' civil right against a racist community; admirer of Persia in Joyce Carol Oates's *Because It Is Bitter, and Because It Is My Heart.*

Courtney, Mr. Selfish libertine, father of Emma; he spends his money on pleasure, leaving Emma poor, but does teach her to appreciate Roman history and to long for heroic virtue in Mary Hays's *Memoirs of Emma Courtney.*

Courtney, Persia Mother of Iris and wife of Duke Courtney; elegant hostess at Lambert's Tea Room; later divorced from Duke and dies an alcoholic, "loose" woman in Joyce Carol Oates's *Because It Is Bitter, and Because It Is My Heart.*

Courtney, Tom *New York Times* reporter who conducts the first interview with Chance in Jerzy Kosinski's *Being There.*

Courtown, Lord Influential member of the Carabas party, who withdraws his support of Frederick Cleveland's nomination to Parliament, thereby destroying Vivian Grey's political career in Benjamin Disraeli's *Vivian Grey.*

Cousin, Emile Sedate, reserved, cigar-smoking hotel manager upon whom Evelyn Orcham relies in Arnold Bennett's *Imperial Palace.*

Cousin, Henriet Local executioner in Victor Hugo's *Hunchback of Notre Dame.*

Cousin Michael Cousin of Sarah Bennett and Louise Bennett Halifax and the brother of Daphne; a close friend of Sarah, often provided Sarah with a means of temporary independence from Louise while they were all growing up in Margaret Drabble's *A Summer Bird-Cage.*

Couthon Chairman of the French Revolutionary Committee of Public Safety during the Terror in 1793; he yields to Victorine's pleas to release Dupin from prison in Mark Rutherford's *The Revolution in Tanner's Lane.*

Coutras, Dr. French physician who diagnoses Charles Strickland's leprosy and narrates both Strickland's death and the fate of Ata and their young son in W. Somerset Maugham's *The Moon and Sixpence.*

Coventry, Bella Pupil of Jean Muir and almost of age to come out to society in Louisa May Alcott's novella *Behind a Mask.*

Coventry, Gerald Eldest brother in the Coventry family; betrothed to his cousin Lucia, but falls in love with the family governess, Jean Muir; described as aristocratic, handsome, and lazy in Louisa May Alcott's novella *Behind a Mask.*

Coventry, Mrs. Mother of Bella, Ned, and Gerald Coventry; rarely present in the story, except, ironically, to further Jean Muir's deception of the family; often ill and comforted by Jean Muir in Louisa May Alcott's novella *Behind a Mask.*

Coventry, Ned Youngest brother of the Coventry family; the first family member to fall in love with Jean Muir's charms; sent away on commission, during which time he discovers Jean's secret about her identity and returns home to unmask her deception in Louisa May Alcott's novella *Behind a Mask.*

Coventry, Sir John Owner of a large parcel of land and grand estate; falls in love with Jean Muir, who reads to him each night; marries her and allows her, by fraud, to gain his estate in Louisa May Alcott's novella *Behind a Mask.*

Coverdale, Merle Head of the typing pool at Meadows, Meade & Grindley; her affair with the married Vincent Druce ends with her murder in Muriel Spark's *The Ballad of Peckham Rye.*

Coverdale, Miles Narrator who observes the people and events at Blithedale and who claims to have loved Priscilla in Nathaniel Hawthorne's *The Blithedale Romance.*

Coverley, Jack Bristol fop and horseman who flirts with Evelina Anville Belmont without success in Frances Burney's *Evelina.*

Coverley, Major de Magisterially photogenic officer responsible for renting apartments for the use of officers and enlisted men on rest leave in Europe in Joseph Heller's *Catch-22.*

Coverly, Chloe Character in the 20th-century story line of the play, which is divided into two distinct time periods; eager to act as an adult, even though she is 18; considerate of her younger brother Gus; flirtatious with Bernard Nightingale in Tom Stoppard's play *Arcadia.*

Coverly, Thomasina Young girl genius and the daughter of Lord and Lady Coom in an old manor, Sidley Park, in Derbyshire, England; typical young teenager except that she intuitively knows the second law of thermodynamics and other esoteric mathematical concepts; driven by the desire for both academic and sexual knowledge; asks her male tutor Septimas Hodge to explain "carnal knowledge"; develops a mathematical theory on heat, a theme related to both mechanics and sex; sees that sex, because it is a random act, brings chaos to the orderly Newtonian universe; dies tragically, leaving Septimus to try to solve the girl's mathematical hypothesis in Tom Stoppard's play *Arcadia.*

Coverly, Valentine Older brother of Chloe and Gus Coverly; seen as highly intelligent but lacking in sentiment; often explains mathematical concepts to other characters in the play and to the audience in Tom Stoppard's play Arcadia.

Covert, Florence ("Florrie") (Mrs. "Jos" Utlaw) Utlaw's fiancée, daughter of a country clergyman, deeply in love and ambitious for both Utlaw and herself in John Buchan's *A Prince of the Captivity.*

Covey, The Nora Clitheroe's cousin who bemoans that he has been laid off because of the mobilization for Irish independence; claims that fighting will do the poor little good; arrested by British soldiers in a roundup of all Irish men during the Easter Rebellion of 1916 in Sean O'Casey's play *The Plough and the Stars.*

Covielle Cléonte's shrewd servant, who easily manipulates others for moral outcomes in Molière's play *The Bourgeois Gentleman.*

Covill, Mr. Justice Judge who hears the suit of divorce brought by Sir Gerald Corven against his wife, Clare, in John Galsworthy's *Over the River.*

Cowan, Daisy Patricia Sister of Jim Cowan and fiancée of Phillip Laurie in Nathan Asch's *Pay Day.*

Cowan, Eugene Brother of Jim and Daisy Cowan; killed at Verdun in Nathan Asch's *Pay Day.*

Cowan, James (Jim) Dissatisfied bookkeeper who wants to be a traveling salesman and who wanders around New York on the night of the Sacco-Vanzetti executions in Nathan Asch's *Pay Day.*

Cowan, Martha Mother of Jim and Daisy Cowan; tries to keep the family together in Nathan Asch's *Pay Day.*

Cowboy Tall, bronzed cowboy who was on his way to a ranch near the Dakota line and also stays at the Palace Hotel; believes the Swede to be a Dutchman after he has left; tends to the injured Johnnie Scully; later debates with the Easterner about who has fault in the Swede's death and did not prevent the subsequent events in Stephen Crane's "The Blue Hotel."

Cowey, Mrs. Friend of Mrs. Allaby and wife of the celebrated Professor Cowey; a marriage arranger, she suggests Theobald Pontifex for Christina Allaby in Samuel Butler's *The Way of All Flesh.*

Cowlard, Linda "A vast dazzling blonde" and the resident lover of Albert Sanger; Linda is "splendidly stupid" and indolent, but her great beauty attracts Kiril Trigorin when he comes to visit Sanger, and she has an affair with him in Margaret Kennedy's *The Constant Nymph.*

Cowles, T. Trainer of horses who helps Michael Banks to steal a horse but who betrays Banks to Larry, the leader of a group of killers and thieves who want to benefit from Banks's theft in John Hawkes's *The Lime Twig.*

Cowley, Cecil Man who seeks to be with "the right people" in London, Paris, and New York; he is fat, flaccid, coquettish, has a "big snout", and is described as a "cultural insect" with merely superficial interest in the arts; he takes Mary Brett as mistress after she rejects Edward West in Storm Jameson's *The Black Laurel.*

Cowley, Ebenezer Owner of Cowley & Son's store whose reputation as queer torments his son Elmer Cowley in Sherwood Anderson's *Winesburg, Ohio.*

Cowley, Elmer Junior partner of Cowley & Son's store; beats George Willard and leaves Winesburg in a frustrated attempt to deal with his family's reputation as queer in Sherwood Anderson's *Winesburg, Ohio.*

Cowley, Father Bob Debt-ridden priest who owes money to Reuben J. Dodd and accompanies Simon Dedalus in James Joyce's *Ulysses.*

Cowley, Sergeant-Major Army professional with a walrus moustache and scarlet cheeks who serves under Captain Christopher Tietjens on the Western Front; he watches over his men and over Tietjens with motherly tenderness in Ford Madox Ford's *No More Parades.*

Cowperwood, Aileen Butler (Ai, Mrs. Montague) Mistress of Frank Cowperwood in Theodore Dreiser's *The Financier;* unhappily married wife of Cowperwood in *The Stoic* and *The Titan.*

Cowperwood, Frank Algernon (Dickson, Montague) Stockbroker and friend of Philadelphia politicians; husband of Lillian Semple Cowperwood and lover of Aileen Butler; convicted and jailed for unscrupulous business deals in Theodore Dreiser's *The Financier;* released from jail, he is active in the natural gas business; marries Aileen Butler in *The Titan;* attempts to monopolize the London streetcar and subway system; dies in *The Stoic.*

Cowperwood, Henry Worthington Father of Frank Cowperwood; resigns his bank presidency following Frank's involvement in a scandal in Theodore Dreiser's *The Financier.*

Cowperwood, Lillian Semple (Anna Wheeler) Widow of Alfred Semple and first wife of Frank Cowperwood in Theodore Dreiser's *The Financier;* also appears in *The Stoic,* where she is called Anna Wheeler, and *The Titan.*

Cowslip Rabbit who guides conduct in the Warren of the Snares in Richard Adams's *Watership Down.*

Cowslip, Dorothy (Dolly) Supposed daughter of the landlady at Black Lion Inn; she becomes Aurelia Darnel's servant and traveling companion to London, is courted by Tom Clarke, and marries him after she is discovered to be Sir Launcelot Greaves's niece in Tobias Smollett's *The Adventures of Sir Launcelot Greaves.*

Cowslip, Mrs. Landlady of Black Lion Inn who believes her foster child Dolly Cowslip is Tom Clarke's sister in Tobias Smollett's *The Adventures of Sir Launcelot Greaves.*

Cox, Alcmena Guest at a Harrogate dance, where she meets Mr. Dunkley, whom she later marries in Thomas Amory's *The Life of John Buncle, Esq.*

Cox, George Friend of Nelson Dewey; involves Dewey in mining investments that lead to the wealth of both men in August Derleth's *The Shadow in the Glass.*

Cox, Hillary Innocent disfigured by an anarchist's bomb in Robert Herrick's *The Memoirs of an American Citizen.*

Cox, Lieutenant Idle horse-riding crony of Ralph Newton, heir of Newton Priory; he joins in the general dissipation of the Moonbeam pub in Anthony Trollope's *Ralph the Heir.*

Cox, Mr. Astrologer who meets Malcolm on a hotel bench and helps introduce him to life by sending him to the homes of acquaintances in James Purdy's *Malcolm.*

Cox, Mr. London proprietor of Dick Lennox's acting company; he promises to listen to Montgomery's opera but doesn't in George Moore's *A Mummer's Wife.*

Cox, Mr. Publisher of the Hadleyburg newspaper; one of the principal towers of "virtue" in the town, who easily falls prey to the temptation of greed introduced by a mysterious visitor, a revengeful man who intends to corrupt the entire community in Samuel Langhorne Clemens's "The Man That Corrupted Hadleyburg."

Cox, Trina Ruthless investment banker who specializes in hostile takeovers; helps an old college friend, Russell Calloway, to initiate a bid to buy the publishing firm where he is an editor; her relentless and eventually successful seduction of Russell leads to the end of his marriage in Jay McInerney's *Brightness Falls.*

Coyle, Eddie (Eddie Fingers, Paulie) Convicted small-time criminal who sells out other criminals in order to make a deal with federal authorities in George V. Higgins's *The Friends of Eddie Coyle.*

Coyne, Duddy Neighbor of the Bray family; sailor torpedoed and killed in the North Atlantic in Maureen Howard's *Natural History.*

Coyotito Only son of Kino and Coyotito; stung by a scorpion in his bed, is the catalyst for Kino's desire to find a great pearl to pay the doctor; murdered by a thief as the family tries to escape the trackers in John Steinbeck's *The Pearl.*

Coyte, Fred Underachieving son of the wealthy landowner Mrs. Coyte; he becomes engaged to Georgina Nimmo but is later rejected and dies a poor man in Joyce Cary's *Except the Lord.*

Coyte, Mrs. Wealthy landowner who gives the elder Tom Nimmo a job as foreman on her farm in Joyce Cary's *Except the Lord.*

Cozens, Norma The lecturing and intrusive but essentially good-natured wife of an Oxford colleague of Alfred Wincham; she constantly drops in on the recently married Fanny (Logan) Wincham in Nancy Mitford's *Love in a Cold Climate.*

Crab Young man with dyed red hair; a former member of Pinkie Brown's mob, he joins Colleoni's mob; he serves to point out the instability of Pinkie's position as new leader of Kite's mob and thus to further frighten Spicer in Graham Greene's *Brighton Rock.*

Crab Teacher at Swallow Barn; preceptor of Ned Hazard in John Pendleton Kennedy's *Swallow Barn.*

Crab, Dr. Referred to as the mizuage specialist; wins Sayuri's mizuage, and also won Mameha's previously; does little else with his free money than pursue new geisha's mizuage in Arthur Golden's *Memoirs of a Geisha.*

Crab, Launcelot Short, fat surgeon, who is an enemy of Roger Potion; he accepts Roderick Random as an apprentice but sends Roderick off to London when his servant becomes pregnant in Tobias Smollett's *The Adventures of Roderick Random.*

Crabb, Alf Scotland Yard inspector who investigates the death of Nonie Colmar; he is finally no match for the shrewder Nick Ollanton, who enables Barney to escape in J. B. Priestley's *Lost Empires.*

Crabb, Caroline (Calamity Jane) Sister of Jack Crabb in Thomas Berger's *Little Big Man.*

Crabb, Jack (Little Big Man) One-hundred-eleven-year-old survivor of the Battle of Little Bighorn; picaresque hero and narrator of Thomas Berger's *Little Big Man.*

Crabb, Olga Wife of Jack Crabb and mother of their son in Thomas Berger's *Little Big Man.*

Crabbe Recently deceased old don; he was a friend of Nicholas Herrick, William Masson, and Richard Bumpus in Ivy Compton-Burnett's *Pastors and Masters.*

Crabbe, Cissie Provincial Lady's old friend, whose postcards with pictures of exotically distant landmarks have Norwich postmarks in E. M. Delafield's *The Diary of a Provincial Lady.* She also appears in *The Provincial Lady Goes Further.*

Crabbe, Lieutenant Aggressive, patriotic fellow army officer who heads a group to dunk Dan Graveson's head in grease for his Marxist discourses in the mess hall in Alan Burns's *Buster.*

Crabbe, Mickey Politically and sexually impotent Bonn Embassy official; he relates Leo Harting's bar fight in Cologne to Alan Turner in John le Carré's *A Small Town in Germany.*

Crabbe, Timothy Warwick schoolmaster who deciphers part of the manuscript relating Gaston de Blondeville's story in Ann Radcliffe's *Gaston de Blondeville.*

Crabbe, Vincent Slytherin student in Harry Potter's year at school; son of a Death Eater; a bully and enforcer with Gregory Goyle and Draco Malfoy; Slytherin Quidditch team Beater and member of the Inquisitorial Squad in J. K. Rowling's Harry Potter series.

Crabbie, Reverend Dr. Head of the seminary where Woody was enrolled until expelled for theft of a silver dish in Saul Bellow's "The Silver Dish."

Crabbin Confused British Council representative who, believing Rollo Martins, whose pseudonym is Buck Dexter, to be the novelist Benjamin Dexter, a stylist in the Henry James tradition, arranges a lecture for the hack writer of westerns in Graham Greene's *The Third Man.*

Crabclaw, Dr. Physician in London debtors' prison; he fights Mr. Tapley in Tobias Smollett's *The Adventures of Sir Launcelot Greaves.*

Crabshaw, Timothy Cowardly squire to Sir Launcelot Greaves; he loves his horse, Gilbert, and consults an astrologer about the horse's fate in Tobias Smollett's *The Adventures of Sir Launcelot Greaves.*

Crabstick, Patience Lady Eustace's personal maid, implicated in the theft of the Eustace necklace; she later marries Mr. Gager, the detective who proved her guilt in Anthony Trollope's *The Eustace Diamonds.*

Crabtree, Arthur Billy Fisher's fellow worker and friend; he is finally put off by Billy's constant lying in Keith Waterhouse's *Billy Liar.*

Crabtree, Cadwallader Misanthropic old man, who becomes Perry Pickle's companion in London and influences him toward misanthropy; he pretends to be a magician and soothsayer in a scheme with Perry in London and begrudgingly agrees to give away the bride in Perry's marriage to Emilia Gauntlet in Tobias Smollett's *The Adventures of Peregrine Pickle.*

Crabwitz, Mr. Unscrupulous clerk to Thomas Furnival; under an assumed name he tries to buy off Samuel Dockwrath with £1000 in the case of the forged will in Anthony Trollope's *Orley Farm.*

Crackamup, Mr. News editor for a journal; he is assigned the task of running John Lavender's article on a plan to starve German prisoners in John Galsworthy's *The Burning Spear: Being the Experiences of Mr. John Lavender in Time of War.*

Crackenthorp, Father Joe Innkeeper who meets Antony Ewart's ship with horses for Darsie Latimer (Arthur Redgauntlet) and serves the Jacobite conspirators as host for their last meeting in Sir Walter Scott's *Redgauntlet.*

Crackit, Toby Accomplice of Bill Sikes in the attempted housebreaking at Mrs. Maylie's mansion in Charles Dickens's *Oliver Twist.*

Craddock Driver for Eustace Cherrington; his mentioning to the youngster that "we shall be losing you before long", on the assumption, unspoken to the boy, that he will be going to boarding school following receipt of his legacy, inspires the boy to think he is facing imminent death in L. P. Hartley's *The Shrimp and the Anemone.*

Craddock, Alan Eric's older brother, who is a rising Inspector of Education; he tries to dissuade Eric from his life of homosexuality in Angus Wilson's *Hemlock and After.*

Craddock, Alice Name that Mary Reed comes to be known by after she is adopted by Dr. Craddock and his wife (see Mary Alice Reed) in Thomas H. Cook's *The Chatham School Affair.*

Craddock, Celia (Mimi) Eric's American mother, who loses her battle to keep Eric with her in Angus Wilson's *Hemlock and After.*

Craddock, Charles Suspicious husband who dies of anthrax while intending to present a complaint against Dr. Roberts in Agatha Christie's *Cards on the Table.*

Craddock, Edward Joseph Oxford University rowing-man whose last will and testament heaves everything to Zuleika Dobson in Max Beerbohm's *Zuleika Dobson; or An Oxford Love Story.*

Craddock, Eric Twenty-eight-year-old lover of Bernard Sands; he works in a London bookstore and is thought to be a poet; he finally succeeds in breaking from the influence of his mother in Angus Wilson's *Hemlock and After.*

Craddock, Father Brendan Cato Forbes's friend, whose wise advice Cato is too infatuated to take in Iris Murdoch's *Henry and Cato.*

Craddock, Jack Fifty-nine-year-old, short, stout, shrewd meat buyer for the hotel; he marvels at Evelyn Orcham's knowledge of foods yet hack of pretense, but he is shocked at Orcham's taking Gracie Savotte to the Smithfield market in Arnold Bennett's *Imperial Palace.*

Craddock, Mrs. Landlady of Samuel Pickwick's lodgings in Bath in Charles Dickens's *The Posthumous Papers of the Pickwick Club.*

Craddock, Mrs. Philandering wife of Charles Craddock; she dies in Egypt of an infection in Agatha Christie's *Cards on the Table.*

Cradell, Joseph Fellow boarder at Mrs. Roper's with Johnny Eames; he marries Amelia Roper, his landlady's daughter, after she fails to secure Eames in Anthony Trollope's *The Small House at Allington.* He appears briefly in *The Last Chronicle of Barset.*

Crader, Benn Maternal uncle of Kenneth Tractenberg in Saul Bellow's *More Die of Heartbreak;* famous botanist and great reader who believes society can be understood by reading Balzac; abruptly weds socialite Matilda Layamon whom he abandons before their honeymoon in order to study lichens in Antarctica and avoid being used by her family in a scheme to manipulate money from Benn's gangster uncle Harold Vilitzer.

Craft, Mr. Partner in Aaron Burr's law firm in Gore Vidal's *Burr.*

Crafton, Mrs. Lady renowned for the shell collection in her grotto at Fingal, less impressive only than the variety of shells in Harriet Noel's grotto in Thomas Amory's *The Life of John Buncle, Esq.*

Craggs, Howard Left-wing publisher; he employs Gypsy Jones, whose duties presumably include sleeping with him in Anthony Powell's *A Buyer's Market.* His publishing career progresses, and he is knighted in *The Military Philosophers.* He becomes J. G. Quiggin's partner; he marries Gypsy and tolerates her infidelity in *Books Do Furnish a Room.* He dies in *Temporary Kings.*

Craggs, Mrs. Thomas Craggs's wife, who is suspicious of Jonathan Snitchey on principle in Charles Dickens's *The Battle of Life.*

Craggs, Thomas Conservative lawyer and family friend of the Jeddlers and best friend of his partner, Jonathan Snitchey; his death leaves Snitchey bereft in Charles Dickens's *The Battle of Life.*

Craig, Mr. Gardener at Donnithorne Chase; he tries to woo the beautiful Hetty Sorrel even though he is near forty, knock-kneed, and has an odd voice in George Eliot's *Adam Bede.*

Craig, Sam Emily Webb's cousin who has departed Grover's Corners to travel out west; later returns to the New Hampshire town to attend Emily's funeral in Thornton Wilder's play *Our Town.*

Craig, Thomas Employee of Stephen Dudley; his embezzlement causes Dudley's financial ruin; kills Dudley, at Ormond's bidding, and is himself killed by Ormond in Charles Brockden Brown's *Ormond.*

Craigan, Phil Best moulder in the Dupret foundry; he shares his house with and controls the lives of Joe and Lily Gates until his forced retirement saps his strength and his dominance in Henry Green's *Living.*

Craige, Constant Factory owner in debt to Sir Horace Stimms; he houses his underpaid workers in two "infamous" blocks of cottages in Richard Aldington's *The Colonel's Daughter.*

Craigengelt, Captain Shrewd and sinister-looking swindler pretending to support the Jacobite interest; he attaches himself to Bucklaw (Frank Hayston), becoming his constant companion in Sir Walter Scott's *The Bride of Lammermoor.*

Craik (Belfast) Sailor on the *Narcissus* in Joseph Conrad's *The Nigger of the "Narcissus."*

Crail, Captain Captain of smugglers on whose ship the Master (James Durie) arrives at Durrisdeer from France and departs after being stabbed by Henry Durie in Robert Louis Stevenson's *The Master of Ballantrae: A Winter's Tale.*

Crail, Miss Supervisory librarian at the Bayswater Library for Psychic Research whose verbal abuse of Alec Leamas helps Liz Gold fall in love with him in John le Carré's *The Spy Who Came In from the Cold.*

Crainpool Dickensian secretary to Alexander Main; forced to flee for his life for jumping bail in *The Bailbondsman,* a novella in Stanley Elkin's *Searches and Seizures.*

Crake Geneticist and childhood friend of Jimmy; genetically engineers a race of perfect humanlike beings known as the Children of Crake; kills his lover, Oryx, and then himself after releasing a deadly virus in Margaret Atwood's *Oryx and Crake.*

Crale, Amyas Licentious painter, whose wife was convicted of his murder; their daughter, Carla Lemarchant, asks Hercule Poirot to investigate the sixteen-year-old case in Agatha Christie's *Five Little Pigs.*

Crale, Caroline Wife of Amyas Crale, of whose poisoning she was accused and convicted in Agatha Christie's *Five Little Pigs.*

Cramchild, Cousin Dogmatic Bostonian writer of Conversations, in which it is claimed that fairies do not exist; he is berated for his beliefs by the narrator in Charles Kingsley's *The Water-Babies.*

Cramer, Keg Head Neighbor of Nunn Ballew; crass, self-righteous father-in-law of Lureenie Cramer in Harriette Arnow's *Hunter's Horn.*

Cramer, Lureenie Mother of three at age twenty; dreamer deserted by her husband, Rans Cramer; nearly starves to death with her family; dies in childbirth in Harriette Arnow's *Hunter's Horn.*

Cramer, Mark Son of Keg Head Cramer; works in Detroit and fathers a child by Suse Ballew out of wedlock in Harriette Arnow's *Hunter's Horn.*

Cramer, Nurse Freckled army nurse and friend of Sue Ann Duckett in Joseph Heller's *Catch-22.*

Cramer, Rans Husband who deserts Lureenie Cramer; flees the community to avoid arrest and returns after he gets religion in Harriette Arnow's *Hunter's Horn.*

Cramier, Olive Four-years-married wife of Robert Cramier; at age twenty-six she begins an affair with Mark Lennon at Monte Carlo and dies of drowning when she and Mark are attacked in a boat while she is leaving her husband in John Galsworthy's *The Dark Flower.*

Cramier, Robert Forty-two-year-old Member of Parliament who pursues his wife, Olive, when she flees with Mark Lennon and causes her to drown when he attacks them in a boat in John Galsworthy's *The Dark Flower.*

Cramner, Emile Grocery delivery boy with whom Melissa Wapshot has an affair in John Cheever's *The Wapshot Scandal.*

Cramp, Agatha Wealthy white woman dedicated to social service to blacks but opposed to an integrated neighborhood in Rudolph Fisher's *The Walls of Jericho.*

Cramp, Corporal Captain Thornton's subordinate whose duty it is to play Provost-Marshal and hang Dougal in Sir Walter Scott's *Rob Roy.*

Crampley Midshipman on the *Thunder* who hates Roderick Random and loses a fight with him; he is assigned as a lieutenant on board the *Lizzard;* he abuses his surgeon, Tomlins, after assuming command of the ship returning to England; he attempts to leave Roderick to drown with the ship in Tobias Smollett's *The Adventures of Roderick Random.*

Cranage, Ben (Wiry Ben) Worker in Burge's carpentry shop; he teases Seth Bede about his belief in the Methodist religion and, thus, nearly has to fight Adam Bede in George Eliot's *Adam Bede.*

Cranage, Bessy (Chad's Bess) Blacksmith's daughter, who wears large, fake garnet earrings to hear Dinah Morris preach and is persuaded to remove her jewelry as a part of her Methodist conversion in George Eliot's *Adam Bede.*

Cranage, Chad Ben Cranage's cousin, an anti-Methodist blacksmith, in George Eliot's *Adam Bede.*

Cranch, Martha Poor sister of Peter Featherstone; her hopes of inheritance are disappointed in George Eliot's *Middlemarch.*

Cranch, Tom Useless son of Mardia Cranch in George Eliot's *Middlemarch.*

Crandall, Judson "Jud" Kind-hearted and nostalgic eighty-three-year-old neighbor of the Creed family and husband of Norma Crandall; shows Louis the Micmac burying grounds and helps him to bury Winston Churchill; seemingly omniscient regarding Louis's plans for Gage's body after Gage's death; later killed by Gage after Gage's return from the dead in Stephen King's *Pet Sematary.*

Crandall, Norma Arthritic wife of Judson "Jud" Crandall; puts up a healthy facade despite the intense pain of her arthritis; refuses to go to the doctor about her heart condition, and later dies as a result in Stephen King's *Pet Sematary.*

Crane Henry Wilcox's chauffeur in E. M. Forster's *Howards End.*

Crane, Arabella Jasper Losely's rejected mistress, who baffles his schemes and provides proof of Sophy's parentage in Edward Bulwer-Lytton's *What Will He Do With It? by Pisistratus Caxton.*

Crane, Clarissa Popular novelist who is a neighbor of Dollie Stokesay; she is researching medieval history for a new novel but changes her subject after disclosures of truth about the Melpham artifacts in Angus Wilson's *Anglo-Saxon Attitudes.*

Crane, Edwina Superintendent of the Protestant mission schools in the Mayapore District; she and Mr. D. R. Chaudhuri, an Indian teacher from Dibrapur, are attacked by a mob of locals, and Chaudhuri is killed; though Edwina is not severely injured, she never recovers emotionally from the incident and eventually commits suicide in Paul Scott's *The Jewel in the Crown.*

Crane, Esther Daughter of a prosperous black grocer; fascinated by King Barlo in Jean Toomer's *Cane.*

Crane, Evelyn Richard's vivacious, irresponsible, irrevocably attached sister; desirous of their "bolshi" friend, Steve Hallem, she intends her brother for an innocent local, Anna Charteris, who is herself taken with Steve; Evelyn manages an affair with Steve in C. Day Lewis's *The Friendly Tree.*

Crane, Helga Biracial product of a Danish mother and a West-Indian father; educated and restless; spends her young adulthood searching for her identity and proper setting; turning down several eligible suitors, inexplicably chooses a semiliterate preacher and follows him to the backwoods, where she becomes trapped in an endless cycle of pregnancy and illness in Nella Larsen's *Quicksand.*

Crane, Ichabod Schoolteacher from Connecticut who comes to Sleepy Hollow to instruct the children, and does so not as a cruel potentate, but as a discriminating judge who is on good terms with his pupils; renders himself agreeable and useful to the students' parents; also has other duties in the village and carries gossip; woos Katrina Van Tassel and competes with Brom Van Brunt for her hand in marriage; wants to settle down comfortably; appears less physically strong than his handsome rival; after his interview with the heiress goes wrong, leaves and is haunted or hunted into a brook; his body is never found, but also never returns to the village in Washington Irving's "The Legend of Sleepy Hollow."

Crane, Jasper Black Virginian who claims to live with his brother in Harlem; meets Emma Lou Morgan in a movie theater, borrows five dollars from her, and vanishes in Wallace Thurman's *The Blacker the Berry.*

Crane, Kelcey Young trumpeter in John Clellon Holmes's *The Horn.*

Crane, Lewis Army electronics technician who looks for the downed Scoop VII satellite in Michael Crichton's *The Andromeda Strain.*

Crane, Nebraska (Bras) Part-Cherokee Indian boyhood friend of George Webber in Thomas Wolfe's *You Can't Go Home Again* and *The Web and the Rock.*

Crane, Richard Well-born, cynical writer of detective fiction; he is inordinately attached to his sister, Evelyn, with whom he lives in an "agreeable ambiance of privilege"; he is somewhat in love with Anna Charteris in C. Day Lewis's *The Friendly Tree.*

Cranium, Cephalis Daughter of Mr. Cranium; she is sought in marriage by both Mr. Escott and Mr. Panscope in Thomas Love Peacock's *Headlong Hall.*

Cranium, Mr. Phrenologist, who uses skull structure as an index to human personality; he so covets the skull of Cadwallader that he accepts Mr. Escott as his daughter's suitor in exchange for it in Thomas Love Peacock's *Headlong Hall.*

Crankshaw, Jimmy Man who marries Barbara Cherrington; he is "a representative of the Better Sort rather than the Finer Grain", but Eustace Cherrington warms to his friendliness and directness in L. P. Hartley's *The Sixth Heaven.* He and Barbara have a young son whom they name Eustace in *Eustace and Hilda.*

Crankshaw, Mrs. Mother of Barbara Cherrington's husband, Jimmy; she tries a bit of futile match-making for Eustace Cherrington at the wedding of her son in L. P. Hartley's *The Sixth Heaven.*

Cranly Stephen Dedalus's university friend who circulates a petition for universal peace in James Joyce's *A Portrait of the Artist as a Young Man.*

Cranmer, Antonia Wealthy, beautiful, nineteen-year-old woman of Bishoprick; John Buncle's third wife, she dies of smallpox at Orton Lodge after the third year of marriage and is buried at Orton Lodge with Buncle's two earlier wives, Charlotte Melmoth and Statia Henley, in Thomas Amory's *The Life of John Buncle, Esq.*

Cranmer, Faith Hope Cranmer's stepdaughter, who opposes fox hunting and other cruelty to animals in Ivy Compton-Burnett's *Parents and Children.*

Cranmer, Gabriel Cornelia Lucy Perceval Mistress of Overy Hall and wife of Squire Justin Cranmer of Hungrygrain; she has been the victim of Cranmer's fiendish plot to use her as a decoy in his nightmarish schemes to destroy England and to assassinate her cousin, Spencer Perceval, the Prime Minister; after the death of Cranmer she is restored to health and to hope in a happy future with Lord Belses in John Buchan's *The Free Fishers.*

Cranmer, Hope Ridley Cranmer's stepmother and a neighbor of Eleanor Sullivan; there is something second-rate about her in Ivy Compton-Burnett's *Parents and Children.*

Cranmer, Justin Squire of Hungrygrain, a justice of the peace, and deputy-lieutenant for the county of Northumberland; his attempt to kill Anthony Lammas and to assassinate

Spencer Perceval, the Prime Minister, fails when Sir Turnour Wyse shoots Cranmer in John Buchan's *The Free Fishers.*

Cranmer, Paul Ridley's and Faith's quiet father, who is often in the background in Ivy Compton-Burnett's Parents and Children.

Cranmer, Ridley Lawyer who conceals knowledge of Fulbert Sullivan's return in order to try to marry Eleanor Sullivan in Ivy Compton-Burnett's *Parents and Children.*

Cranston, Mrs. Amelia Operator of a boardinghouse for Newport servants in Thornton Wilder's *Theophilus North.*

Cranton, Nobby London jewel thief, a conspirator in the theft of Mrs. Wilbraham's necklace; the body unearthed in the Fenchurch St. Paul churchyard is thought to be his in Dorothy L. Sayers's *The Nine Tailors: Changes Rung on an Old Theme in Two Short Touches and Two Full Peals.*

Crapo, Thomas (Tom) Lowell Friend of Andrew Cather and lover of Cather's wife Bertha Cather in Conrad Aiken's *Great Circle.*

Crash Naval officer convicted of having an illicit affair with a fourteen-year-old Polynesian female in Herman Melville's *Omoo.*

Crashaw One of two cronies on the staff of Lord Raingo's Ministry of Records; Raingo hopes to see them to ease his awkward entry for the first time to the St. James's Club frequented by government members in Arnold Bennett's *Lord Raingo.*

Crasweller, Eva Linguist, musician, and model young citizen of Britannula; she is far from enthusiastic about the euthanasia law condemning her father to be disposed of at sixty-eight years of age; she falls in love with Jack Neverbend in Anthony Trollope's *The Fixed Period.*

Crasweller, Gabriel Best friend of President John Neverbend of Britannula, an ex-British colony off New Zealand; he supports the law demanding that citizens prepare for euthanasia at sixty-eight years of age, but when his own time comes his enthusiasm for the law wanes in Anthony Trollope's *The Fixed Period.*

Cratander Correspondent with Lysimachus on the subject of personal criticism in Sarah Fielding's *Familiar Letters between the Principal Characters of David Simple and Some Others.*

Cratchit, Belinda Bob Cratchit's second daughter in Charles Dickens's *A Christmas Carol.*

Cratchit, Bob Ebenezer Scrooge's clerk and father of Tiny Tim, who acts as a foil to the penny-pinching Scrooge; keeps tardy work habits and is in financial difficulties, yet in spite of these obstacles has a good heart; offsets his boss's stern punctuality and miserly ways by remaining cheerfully unaffected by Scrooge's dour attitude in Charles Dickens's *A Christmas Carol.*

Cratchit, Martha Bob Cratchit's eldest daughter, a milliner's apprentice, in Charles Dickens's *A Christmas Carol.*

Cratchit, Mrs. Wife of clerk Bob Cratchit and mother of six children; she keeps a happy home despite poverty in Charles Dickens's *A Christmas Carol.*

Cratchit, Peter Bob Cratchit's son about whose future his father is hopeful in Charles Dickens's *A Christmas Carol.*

Cratchit, Tim (Tiny Tim) Crippled young son of clerk Bob Cratchit; he exemplifies the piety, charity, and optimism of which Ebenezer Scrooge must learn the importance in Charles Dickens's *A Christmas Carol.*

Cravat, Cimarron (Cim) Son of Sabra and Yancey Cravat and husband of Ruby Big Elk; field geologist in Edna Ferber's *Cimarron.*

Cravat, Donna Daughter of Sabra and Yancey Cravat and wife of the multimillionaire Tracy Wyatt in Edna Ferber's *Cimarron.*

Cravat, Sabra Venable Daughter of Felice and Lewis Venable, wife of Yancey Cravat, and mother of Cimarron and Donna Cravat; strong pioneer who becomes an important newspaper editor and an Oklahoma congresswoman in Edna Ferber's *Cimarron.*

Cravat, Yancey (Cimarron) Husband of Sabra Venable Cravat and father of Cimarron and Donna Cravat; lawyer and newspaperman who becomes governor of the Oklahoma Territory and then Joins Teddy Roosevelt's Rough Riders in Edna Ferber's *Cimarron.*

Craven, Anthony Socialist and Venturist friend of Marcella Boyce in Mrs. Humphry Ward's *Marcella.*

Craven, Louis Friend of Marcella Boyce and editor of Harry Wharton's paper, the *Labour Clarion,* in Mrs. Humphry Ward's *Marcella.*

Craven, Marcella L. (Queenie) Owner of Queenie's Boarding House in Kansas City, where George Brush stays; devout Catholic in Thornton Wilder's *Heaven's My Destination.*

Craven, Nurse Opportunistic manhunter who knows that her patient, Barbara Franklin, is not in bad health in Agatha Christie's *Curtain: Hercule Poirot's Last Case.*

Craven, Stella Villem Craven's wife, who wants her husband to become thoroughly British and therefore forbids George Smihey any contact, forcing Smiley to interrogate Villem secretly in John le Carré's *Smiley's People.*

Craven, Villem (William) Estonian exile and occasional courier for General Vladimir and his freedom movement who risks his British passport and residency to carry Otto Leipzig's clues to Karla's secret to General Vladimir in John le Carré's *Smiley's People.*

Cravens, Wanda Dimwitted widow who is readily seduced by both Justin Miller and Vince Bonali in Robert Coover's *The Origin of the Brunists.*

Craw, Bill Legendary Australian journalist and British Intelligence agent who feeds information on Jerry Westerby's activities to George Smiley and who visibly represents Smiley's disillusion at his betrayal and Westerby's and Luke's death in John le Carré's *The Honourable Schoolboy.*

Craw, Sergeant Legal advisor whose advice to Walter Warmhouse occasions a lawsuit that remains in British courts for thirteen years in an anecdote told by Mr. Fielding in Henry Brooke's *The Fool of Quality.*

Craw, Thomas Carlyle Scots newspaper magnate who leases Castle Gay; sought by Evallonian conspirators who seek to use Craw and his influence to insure British support, he moves under John Galt's tutelage on their walking tour from childish sulkiness and despair to become a "new man", as he recognizes the inadequacy of his former values in John Buchan's *Castle Gay.*

Crawford, Admiral Uncle and, formerly, guardian of the orphaned Henry and Mary Crawford; his contempt for women has helped form Henry's character; his bringing his mistress to his house after his wife's death has driven Mary to seek a home with Mrs. Grant; the admiral effects William Price's promotion to lieutenant at Henry's instigation in Jane Austen's *Mansfield Park.*

Crawford, Andrew Husband for one summer of Emily Grimes; impotent, he hates Emily's sexuality in Richard Yates's *Easter Parade.*

Crawford, Brandon Brother-in-law of Sally Lacey, helps Johnny Lacey with his land claims and is elected with him to the House of Burgesses in Mary Lee Settle's *O Beulah Land.*

Crawford, Elise Sister of Maija von Einzeedle, wife of Reuben Crawford, and lover of Anthony Hope Harding in Nicholas Delbanco's *Small Rain.*

Crawford, Frank Father of Sonny Crawford, former high school principal, and proprietor of a domino parlor in Larry McMurtry's *The Last Picture Show.*

Crawford, Haim Cousin of Bannie Upshire Dudley; member of the Paddy Rollers of Mantipico County in Sarah E. Wright's *This Child's Gonna Live.*

Crawford, Henry Charming, clever, selfish, and unprincipled half brother of Mrs. Grant; he simultaneously gains the affections of Maria and Julia Bertram; after Maria's marriage to Rushworth, he, with his sister Mary's complicity, begins a campaign on Fanny Price; her dislike of him stimulates his admiration of her beauty and sweetness, and he falls in love; though her rejection is unequivocal, he persists, but his chances of success are doomed by the lapse of constancy which results in his adulterous elopement with Maria in Jane Austen's *Mansfield Park.*

Crawford, Jack Chief of the Behavioral Science section of the Federal Bureau of Investigation; supervisor of FBI trainee Clarice Starling, whom he selects to interview serial killer Hannibal Lecter, in Thomas Harris's *The Silence of the Lambs.* Crawford also appears in Harris's *Red Dragon* (1981) and *Hannibal* (1999).

Crawford, Janie Woman whose life story provides the plot of the novel; comes back from a funeral at the beginning and tells the story to her friend Pheoby Watson of her upbringing and three marriages; nicknamed Alphabet as a black child; kisses a boy at her grandmother's house and is married off; escapes from that home with another man, with whom she stays for 20 years; when he dies, marries Tea Cake, her last love, who dies before the story commences; never knew her father or mother; women in town are jealous of her in Zora Neale Hurston's *Their Eyes Were Watching God.*

Crawford, Lord Loyal captain of the archers of the Scottish Guard, well trusted by Louis XI; tall and spare, he is a blunt Scottish nobleman who distinguished himself under Jeanne D'Arc's banner in Sir Walter Scott's *Quentin Durward.*

Crawford, Mary Pretty, witty, accomplished, financially secure, cynical, and unprincipled half sister of Mrs. Grant; she falls in love with Edmund Bertram before she knows he is to be a clergyman; she is her brother Henry's willing confidante and assistant in his games of lovemaking; her cool acceptance of his adulterous liaison with Maria (Bertram) Rushworth opens Edmund's eyes to her character in Jane Austen's *Mansfield Park.*

Crawford, Melancthon American sailor imprisoned by Tripoli pirates; Indian trader and pioneer who is a cofounder of a town in Oklahoma in H. L. Davis's *Harp of a Thousand Strings.*

Crawford, Miss Stephanie Gossipy neighbor of Atticus Finch and one of the family who constantly spread rumors about Boo Radley in Harper Lee's *To Kill a Mockingbird.*

Crawford, Myles Editor of the *Weekly Freeman and National Press* who refuses to give a commission to Leopold Bloom in James Joyce's *Ulysses.*

Crawford, Redvers T. A. Scientist and fellow of the Cambridge college who has a strong reputation for the quality of his research in physiology; he is elected as Master in a close vote over Paul Jago in C. P. Snow's *The Masters.* He is nearing the end of his mastership and conducts the deliberations of the Court of Seniors into the affair of Donald Howard's fellowship; he fi-nally votes for restoration of the fellowship in *The Affair.*

Crawford, Reuben Husband of Elise Crawford in Nicholas Delbanco's *Small Rain.*

Crawford, Sonny Athlete at Thalia High School, roommate of Duane Moore, and lover of Ruth Popper; initiated into adulthood in Larry McMurtry's *The Last Picture Show.*

Crawfurd, David Young, courageous Scots boy-hero; he joins in the effort to combat John Laputa's evil enterprise; later he uses the treasure of Prester John to create a college for black Africans in John Buchan's *Prester John.*

Crawley, Bob Only son of Josiah Crawley; his godfather is Dean Arabin in Anthony Trollope's *Framley Parsonage.* He is a schoolboy in *The Last Chronicle of Barset.*

Crawley, Bute Jovial and impecunious fox-hunting clergyman brother to Sir Pitt Crawley in William Makepeace Thackeray's *Vanity Fair.*

Crawley, Captain Rawdon Handsome, dashing, somewhat stupid second son of Sir Pitt Crawley; he marries Becky Sharp and lives with her in style, largely by her wits, until he suspects her of having an affair with Lord Steyne; he places his son in the custody of his brother and becomes governor of Coventry Island, where he dies in William Makepeace Thackeray's *Vanity Fair.*

Crawley, Emma Accomplished and well-educated but poor and plain and therefore unmarriageable daughter of the Reverend and Mrs. Bute Crawley in William Makepeace Thackeray's *Vanity Fair.*

Crawley, Fanny Emma Crawley's sister and like her in being accomplished, well educated, poor, and plain in William Makepeace Thackeray's *Vanity Fair.*

Crawley, Frank Maxim de Winter's agent and loyal friend, who also befriends the second Mrs. de Winter in Daphne Du Maurier's *Rebecca.*

Crawley, Frank Younger son of the Reverend and Mrs. Bute Crawley in William Makepeace Thackeray's *Vanity Fair.*

Crawley, Grace Josiah Crawley's eldest daughter, a child in Anthony Trollope's *Framley Parsonage.* Lovely, gentle, and remarkably well educated by her father, she is a schoolteacher; her love for Major Henry Grantly is rewarded in their union in Anthony Trollope's *The Last Chronicle of Barset.*

Crawley, James Oafish son of Bute Crawley; his attempts to impress his aunt, Matilda Crawley, are thwarted in William Makepeace Thackeray's *Vanity Fair.*

Crawley, Jane Beloved younger daughter of Josiah Crawley; she comforts her father when he is accused of stealing a cheque in Anthony Trollope's *The Last Chronicle of Barset.*

Crawley, Josiah High-minded clergyman, once a scholar of promise but unlucky in preferment; he has long been the irascible, melancholy perpetual curate of Hogglestock, whose flock are predominately brickmakers; he is charged with the theft of a cheque; driven almost to madness by his own doubts and believed undoubtedly guilty by almost all, he nevertheless holds his own against Mrs. Proudie before he is exonerated and becomes Vicar of St. Ewold's in Anthony Trollope's *The Last Chronicle of Barset.* His friendship with Francis Arabin is mentioned in *Barchester Towers.* He also appears in *Framley Parsonage.*

Crawley, Kate Daughter of the Reverend and Mrs. Bute Crawley in William Makepeace Thackeray's *Vanity Fair.*

Crawley, Lady Grizzel Deceased well-born first wife of Sir Pitt Crawley and mother of Pitt and Rawdon Crawley in William Makepeace Thackeray's *Vanity Fair.*

Crawley, Lady Jane (Sheepshanks) Gentle and virtuous wife of the younger Pitt Crawley in William Makepeace Thackeray's *Vanity Fair.*

Crawley, Lady Rose Ironmonger's daughter and the sickly second wife of Sir Pitt Crawley; only her stepson Pitt treats her with respect; she is the mother of Rose and Violet Crawley; her death enables Sir Pitt to make his unsuccessful proposal of marriage to Becky Sharp in William Makepeace Thackeray's *Vanity Fair.*

Crawley, Louisa Daughter of the Reverend and Mrs. Bute Crawley in William Makepeace Thackeray's *Vanity Fair.*

Crawley, Martha Daughter of the Reverend and Mrs. Bute Crawley in William Makepeace Thackeray's *Vanity Fair.*

Crawley, Mary Josiah Crawley's stouthearted wife, much tried by poverty; stricken with typhus, she is nursed by Lucy Robarts in Anthony Trollope's *Framley Parsonage.* Her greatest trials occur when her husband is accused of theft in *The Last Chronicle of Barset.*

Crawley, Matilda Rich sister of Sir Pitt Crawley; dashing in her youth, she is in old age pathetically flattered by members of her family; she prefers her rakish nephew, Captain Rawdon Crawley, and takes to the governess Becky Sharp, but casts them off after their secret marriage; her favor and money are eventually won by the younger Pitt Crawleys in William Makepeace Thackeray's *Vanity Fair.*

Crawley (2), Matilda Daughter of the Reverend and Mrs. Bute Crawley in William Makepeace Thackeray's *Vanity Fair.*

Crawley (3), Matilda Daughter of the younger Sir Pitt Crawley; she grows up to marry her cousin, young Rawdon Crawley, though she is also courted by Georgy Osborne in William Makepeace Thackeray's *Vanity Fair.*

Crawley, Mr. Impoverished suitor of Jane Wugsby in Bath in Charles Dickens's *The Posthumous Papers of the Pickwick Club.*

Crawley, Mrs. Bute Rector's managing wife, who tries unsuccessfully to secure Matilda Crawley's fortune for her numerous family in William Makepeace Thackeray's *Vanity Fair.*

Crawley, Peter Cowardly, alcoholic attorney-at-law, who is John Meadows's secret agent of "dirty work," going to Australia to attempt to keep George Fielding from returning to claim Susan Merton as his wife in Charles Reade's *It Is Never Too Late to Mend.*

Crawley, (Sir) Pitt Shy and virtuous elder son and heir of Sir Pitt Crawley; he marries Lady Jane Sheepshanks but has vague hankerings after Becky Sharp in William Makepeace Thackeray's *Vanity Fair.*

Crawley, Rawdon Son of Becky (Sharp) and Captain Rawdon Crawley; he is loved by his father but neglected by his mother; eventually inheriting the Crawley property, he supports but will not see his mother in William Makepeace Thackeray's *Vanity Fair.*

Crawley, Rose Elder of Sir Pitt Crawley's young daughters, whom Becky Sharp is hired to teach in William Makepeace Thackeray's *Vanity Fair.*

Crawley, Sir Marmaduke English baronet who hires Juliet Granville to teach the harp to his two sisters in Frances Burney's *The Wanderer.*

Crawley, Sir Pitt Rough and coarse baronet, who employs Becky Sharp as a governess and proposes marriage to her before taking up with Miss Horrocks and succumbing to a stroke in William Makepeace Thackeray's *Vanity Fair.*

Crawley, Violet Younger of Sir Pitt Crawley's daughters, whom Becky Sharp is hired to teach in William Makepeace Thackeray's *Vanity Fair.*

Cray Landing-party member who is in charge of swabbing the cannons for precaution against hot shot in C. S. Forester's *Lieutenant Hornblower.*

Crayton, Colonel Father of Mrs. Beauchamp and husband of Mademoiselle La Rue in Susanna Rowson's *Charlotte.*

Crayton, Mrs. See Mademoiselle La Rue.

Crazy Carl Retarded adult in the town of Maxwell, Georgia, on whose word Henry McIntosh is mistakenly identified as the murderer of Tracy Deen in Lillian Smith's *Strange Fruit.*

Creakle, Miss Daughter of Mr. Creakle; she is rumored to be in love with James Steerforth in Charles Dickens's *The Personal History of David Copperfield.*

Creakle, Mr. Bald, fiery, sadistic head of Salem House school; he always speaks in a whisper but is cruel to the students, except for James Steerforth, whom he treats with favor; he eventually becomes a Middlesex magistrate in Charles Dickens's *The Personal History of David Copperfield.*

Creakle, Mrs. Wife of Mr. Creakle; she breaks the news to David Copperfield of his mother's death and treats him kindly in Charles Dickens's *The Personal History of David Copperfield.*

Cream, William Barber who offers no trust to his customers in Herman Melville's *The Confidence-Man.*

Creamer, Mr. Miss Matilda Crawley's physician at Brighton in William Makepeace Thackeray's *Vanity Fair.*

Creamhair, Lady See Hector, Virginia R.

Crean-Smith, Hannah Heiress who made an unhappy marriage to her bisexual, abusive cousin; guilt and religion have made her an accomplice in her imprisonment at Gaze Castle since, seven years ago, she almost killed her husband during a row over her affair with Pip Lejour; believing her husband about to return, she shoots her keeper, Gerald Scottow, and commits suicide in Iris Murdoch's *The Unicorn.*

Crean-Smith, Peter Hannah's abusive absent husband, who keeps her imprisoned in their isolated house under the watchful eyes of servants, especially his homosexual lover Gerald Scottow; returning after a seven years' absence, he is deliberately killed in a car crash by Denis Nolan in Iris Murdoch's *The Unicorn.*

Crease, Oscar Stepbrother of Christina Lutz and community college teacher and playwright who relies increasingly upon litigation as a means of gaining recognition and capital in William Gaddis's *A Frolic of His Own.*

Creb Powerful Neanderthal shaman, or Mog-ur, whose childhood crippling by a bear is regarded as the source of his mystical potency; teacher and adoptive father of Ayla, who discovers that her mixed-heritage son has a natural Cro-Magnon resilience that is the key to preventing Neanderthal extinction; brother of Brun and Iza in Jean M. Auel's *The Clan of the Cave Bear.*

Crecy, Peter Wealthy friend of Lennie; later, Jill's lover who feels that he has to develop her mentally; marries Donna, but abuses her in Marge Piercy's *Braided Lives.*

Credenza, Louis Senior member of a large property-owning family in northwest Iowa that controls the radio station that employs Dick Gibson in Stanley Elkin's *The Dick Gibson Show.*

Cree, Captain Joe First husband of Julia Cropleigh Cree and pillar of the community; his suicide sets in motion the events of Andrew Lytle's *The Velvet Horn.*

Cree, Foxy (Kennedy) Native American cousin of Rayona Taylor who harasses Rayona when she moves onto his Montana reservation in Michael Dorris's *A Yellow Raft in Blue Water.*

Cree, Julia Cropleigh Youngest of the orphaned Cropleigh children and mother of Lucius Cree; object of the long-suffering love of Pete Legrand, the crazed passion of her brother, Duncan Cropleigh, and the formal devotion of her husband, Joe Cree, in Andrew Lytle's *The Velvet Horn.*

Cree, Lucius Son of Joe and Julia Cropleigh Cree; forced to face the mystery of his family's past when his father commits suicide in Andrew Lytle's *The Velvet Horn.*

Cree, Pauline George Native American woman living on a Montana reservation; younger sister of Ida George and mother of Foxy Cree in Michael Dorris's *A Yellow Raft in Blue Water.*

Creech, Albert Jenkins family's weary, egotistical, self-taught cook, who is loved by Bilison, the emotionally unstable maid; he marries another and leaves the Jenkinses, eventually managing the Bellevue Hotel in Anthony Powell's *The Kindly Ones.* His death is mentioned in *The Military Philosophers.*

Creed, Dr. Louis Middle-aged methodical and organized physician, employed at the University of Maine; has something of a quick temper; saved Norma Crandal's life when she suffered a heart attack; father of Gage and Ellie and husband of Rachel in Stephen King's *Pet Sematary.*

Creed, Eileen "Ellie" Adventurous yet emotionally reserved daughter of Louis and Rachel Creed; has visions of future disasters regarding Louis and Gage in Stephen King's *Pet Sematary.*

Creed, Emmett Head football coach in his first year at Logos College; has a no-nonsense attitude and reputation for winning in Don DeLillo's *End Zone.*

Creed, Joshua (Westminster) Aged newspaper vender, once a butler, who gives evidence to police after Hughes stabs his wife in John Galsworthy's *Fraternity.*

Creed, Mrs. The Costigans' landlady in William Makepeace Thackeray's *The History of Pendennis.*

Creed, Rachel City-born wife of Louis Creed and mother of Gage and Eileen; sister Zelda died of spinal meningitis as a child, and Rachel blames herself; is later killed by Gage after Fage's return from the dead and then buried in the Micmac burying grounds in Stephen King's *Pet Sematary.*

Creed, Winston Churchill Creed family cat that is killed by a passing truck on the highway near the Creed house; is buried in the Micmac burying grounds behind the Pet Sematary, and returns as a changed cat, serving as foreshadowing for future events in Stephen King's *Pet Sematary.*

Creedle, Robert Giles Winterborne's loyal old servant in Thomas Hardy's *The Woodlanders.*

Creek, Catherine Black woman who insists she is an Indian; from childhood on, lives with the Talbo sisters, adoring Dolly and despising Verena, in Truman Capote's *The Grass Harp.*

Creevey, Warren Man of misdirected genius and brilliant intellect whose powers are devoted to goals of self-glorification and who is changed by the self-sacrifice of Adam Melfort in John Buchan's *A Prince of the Captivity.*

Creevy, Mrs. Disagreeable, selfish old woman who runs the Ringwood House Academy for Girls where Dorothy Hare teaches and who forces Dorothy to stay hungry most of the time and will not let her teach the students anything but basic math and penmanship because that is what parents want to see from their daughters in George Orwell's *A Clergyman's Daughter.*

Crefeldt, Countess von Longtime lover of Sigismund Alvan; she has become his staunchest friend by the time he meets Clotilde von Rüdiger, but the Countess feels that marriage to the younger woman would ruin Alvan, and she does not help his suit; she nurses Alvan after he is mortally wounded in George Meredith's *The Tragic Comedians.*

Creighton Officer on the *Narcissus* wounded during a storm in Joseph Conrad's *The Nigger of the "Narcissus".*

Creighton, Colonel Director of the British Secret Service; impressed with Kirn's craftiness and cunning, he recruits him into the "Great Game" of intrigue to collect intelligence for the British army in India in Rudyard Kipling's *Kim.*

Creighton, Fannie Jump Friend and contemporary of Celeste's; plays bridge with Celeste, Fairy, and Ramelle; drinker whose husband leaves her with no money; opens a speakeasy and becomes independent in Rita Mae Brown's *Six of One.*

Crenshaw Shrewd, alcoholic poet; Philip Carey, studying art in Paris, becomes fascinated with Crenshaw, realizing that mediocrity ends in cynical disillusionment in W. Somerset Maugham's *Of Human Bondage.*

Creon Brother-in-law of Oedipus; comes to Colonus ostensibly to invite Oedipus to return to Thebes; instead plans to bury him on the border of Thebes to prevent other cities from benefiting from the grave's power; uses force to compel Oedipus to return by capturing Ismene and Antigone in Sophocles' play *Oedipus at Colonus.*

Creon Jocasta's brother; sent to Delphi to learn how to avert the plague in Thebes; accused of conspiracy and sentenced to death by Oedipus, then reprieved; initially claims to have no interest in ruling but does not hesitate to claim power when given the opportunity; banishes Oedipus in Sophocles' play *Oedipus the King.*

Creon King of Corinth and father of Glauce; makes the tragic mistake of allowing the sorceress Medea to remain one more day in his kingdom, thus giving the raging woman time to plot his murder, along with that of his daughter, in Euripides' *Medea.*

Creon Proud, principled, and stubborn king of Thebes, Antigone's uncle, and Haemon's father; orders that Polynices' corpse remain unburied because he was a traitor; vows to punish anyone defying his order; values adherence to political law over divine law and family; grudgingly agrees to spare Antigone and bury Polynices to save Thebes from divine retribution; recognizes too late that his inflexibility and pride have destroyed his family in Sophocles' play *Antigone.*

Crequy, Clement de Young aristocrat and friend of Lady Ludlow's son; Lady Ludlow tells his story of betrayal and death during the Revolution as an example of the dangers of educating the lower classes in Elizabeth Gaskell's *My Lady Ludlow.*

Crequy, Virginie de Clement de Crequy's cousin, for whom he returns to France; she goes to the guillotine with him in Elizabeth Gaskell's *My Lady Ludlow.*

Crespi, Pietro Handsome Italian who introduces the pianola to the Buendía house; teaches Rebeca and Amaranta to dance; both girls compete for his affection; engaged to Rebeca, who marries José Arcadio; then rejected by Amaranta and commits suicide in Gabriel García Márquez's *One Hundred Years of Solitude.*

Cresseron, Charles de Narrator of the story, a lawyer helping to sort out the tangled wills of the Brandon and Wylder families; he is infatuated with Dorcas Brandon in J. Sheridan Le Fanu's *Wylder's Hand.*

Cressett, Alice Daughter of Barker and bullying wife of Harold Cressett; she cares for her crippled father in his last years; she helps her father blackmail Canon Portway over the Melpham affair and is convicted of killing her husband in Angus Wilson's *Anglo-Saxon Attitudes.*

Cressett, Harold Husband of Alice; he is a victim of British bureaucracy and is made a public cause by John Middleton; he is murdered by his wife in Angus Wilson's *Anglo-Saxon Attitudes.*

Cresset, Earl of Nobleman who dies shortly after his wife, Fanny, runs away in George Meredith's *The Amazing Marriage.*

Cresset, Fanny, Countess of The Earl of Cresset's wife, who runs away from her husband; after his death she marries hardy old Captain Kirby; they have two children, Chillon and Carinthia, in George Meredith's *The Amazing Marriage.*

Cressler, Carrie Confidante of Laura Dearborn; encourages Laura to marry Curtis Jadwin in Frank Norris's *The Pit.*

Cressler, Charles (Charlie) Dealer in grain at the Chicago Board of Trade who is ruined by speculation and commits suicide in Frank Norris's *The Pit.*

Cresswell, Colonel Brother of Adele, Lady Brixton; when Adele purchases Lucia Lucas's Riseholme property, he conveniently makes an offer for Georgie Pillson's in E. F. Benson's *Mapp and Lucia.*

Cresswell, Colonel St. John Southern aristocrat who owns almost everything in Tooms County, Alabama; father of Helen and Harry Cresswell in W. E. B. DuBois's *The Quest of the Silver Fleece.*

Cresswell, Harry Congressman who opposes the education of his black tenants; son of Colonel St. John Cresswell, husband of Mary Taylor, and father of Bertie's mulatto child Emma in W. E. B. DuBois's *The Quest of the Silver Fleece.*

Cresswell, Helen Self-centered daughter of Colonel St. John Cresswell and wife of John Taylor in W. E. B. DuBois's *The Quest of the Silver Fleece.*

Cresswell, Mary Taylor See Taylor, Mary.

Cresswell, Oscar Uncle of the child Paul; comes to know of Paul's secret to horse race betting; though initially surprised, later becomes a partner of the boy and wins a lot of money because of Paul's astoundingly correct guesses for the races; it is to him that Paul divulges the secret of his trying to be lucky because his house is filled with the whispers of the scarcity of money; according to Paul's wishes, secretly arranges a financial agreement with lawyers so that Paul's mother may receive a huge sum of money as a "gift from a relative" in D. H. Lawrence's "The Rocking-Horse Winner."

Cresswell, Penrose Trustee of Maud Ruthyn's estate in J. Sheridan Le Fanu's *Uncle Silas.*

Cressy, Hugh Paulin (Serenus de Cressy) Chaplain and fellow at Merton College, Oxford, who joins a Benedictine monastery in Paris and becomes spiritual advisor to John Inglesant inj. Henry Shorthouse's *John Inglesant, A Romance.*

Creston, Kate Wife of Paul Creston, who has been deceased for a number of years; her memory of a genial and charming woman is carried on by George Stranson's macabre desire to nourish the memory of the dead as though flowers in a garden in Henry James's "The Altar of the Dead."

Creston, Paul Longtime friend of George Stranson; unlike George, who lives wrapped in a cocoon of past memories of his dead fiancée, Paul has remarried after the untimely death of his wife, Kate, in Henry James's "The Altar of the Dead."

Cretan Villagers Ultraconservative, orthodox, and reactionary group; the men hound after and the women shun the attractive but elusive widow, who, after a failed suitor's suicide, is stoned and beheaded by the mob in Nikos Kazantzakis's *Zorba the Greek.*

Cretha Si's wife and the mother of Orfik and Iyfilka in Brian W. Aldiss's *Helliconia Spring.*

Creutzer, Monsieur (Sir) Charles Grandison's governor on his European tour; because of Creutzer's licentiousness, Charles petitions for a replacement to Sir Thomas Grandison, who thereupon decides no governor is necessary in Samuel Richardson's *Sir Charles Grandison.*

Creuzot Tall, fair-skinned Frenchman who operates his own print shop; afflicted with a lung disease in Arna Wendell Bontemps's *Black Thunder.*

Crèvecoeur, Count Philip de Haughty and observant Burgundian knight, marshal of the Duke of Burgundy's household, and Isabelle de Croye's friend; a calming influence on the duke, he serves as his courier in delivering a message of war to Louis XI, who admires him in Sir Walter Scott's *Quentin Durward.*

Crèvecoeur, Countess de Philip de Crèvecoeur's beautiful and spirited wife; she befriends Isabelle de Croye in Sir Walter Scott's *Quentin Durward.*

Crevy, Angela Young woman who joins an older, more advanced social set; she has a dominating power over her jealous and love-sick fiancé Robin Adams, in Henry Green's *Party Going.*

Crew, Peter Unethical solicitor who represents confessed murderer Olive Martin and is later arrested for embezzling Olive's father's legacy in Minette Walters's *The Sculptress.*

Crew, The Thirty African natives and five European pilgrims, including the general manager and Marlow, who sail the company's steamer on the Congo River; attacked by Africans and later find the mysterious Kurtz in Joseph Conrad's *Heart of Darkness.*

Crewe, Alice Pomfret See Pomfret, Alice.

Crewe, Arthur Stepfather of Dixie Morse in Muriel Spark's *The Ballad of Peckham Rye.*

Crewe, Dr. Gruff but kind Gylingden rector when the narrator was a child in J. Sheridan Le Fanu's *Wylder's Hard.*

Crewe, Humphrey Unskilled amateur politician who becomes increasingly shrewd and reforming; unsuccessful suitor of Victoria Flint and husband of Alice Pomfret in Winston Churchill's *Mr. Crewe's Career.*

Crewe, Leslie Half brother of Dixie Morse and member of Trevor Lomas's loutish gang in Muriel Spark's *The Ballad of Peckham Rye.*

Crewe, Luckworth Ambitious advertising agent and entrepreneur with crassly materialistic values; he courts Nancy Lord and participates in Beatrice French's ladies' dress business in George Gissing's *In the Year of Jubilee.*

Crewe, Mavis First G.I. bride from Peckham and mother of Leslie Crewe and Dixie Morse in Muriel Spark's *The Ballad of Peckham Rye.*

Crewkherne, Mrs. Fundamentalist Christian and George Delmont's aunt, whose prejudice against radical political and social notions has disastrous consequences for the Glenmorris family when it informs rumors she spreads about their licentious behavior in Charlotte Smith's *The Young Philosopher.*

Crewler, Caroline Eldest sister of Sophy Crewler and the beauty of the family; she lives with Tommy Traddles and Sophy after they are married in Charles Dickens's *The Personal History of David Copperfield.*

Crewler, Horace Vicar in Devonshire and father of Sophy; he opposes her engagement to Tommy Traddles in Charles Dickens's *The Personal History of David Copperfield.*

Crewler, Louisa Sister of Sophy Crewler; she lives with Tommy Traddles and Sophy after they are married in Charles Dickens's *The Personal History of David Copperfield.*

Crewler, Lucy Sister of Sophy Crewler; she lives with Tommy Traddles and Sophy after they are married in Charles Dickens's *The Personal History of David Copperfield.*

Crewler, Margaret Sister of Sophy Crewler; she lives with Tommy Traddles and Sophy after they are married in Charles Dickens's *The Personal History of David Copperfield.*

Crewler, Mrs. Horace Wife of the Reverend Horace Crewler; like her husband, she opposes her daughter Sophy's engagement to Tommy Traddles in Charles Dickens's *The Personal History of David Copperfield.*

Crewler, Sarah Second eldest sister of Sophy Crewler; she has an ailment of the spine and lives with Tommy Traddles and Sophy after they are married in Charles Dickens's *The Personal History of David Copperfield.*

Crewler, Sophy Fourth daughter of a vicar in Devonshire and "the dearest girl in the world," according to her betrothed, Tommy Traddles; the marriage is opposed by her family because she is so useful in the household in Charles Dickens's *The Personal History of David Copperfield.*

Crews, Tony Black poet; Emma Lou Morgan meets him at a rent party in Wallace Thurman's *The Blacker the Berry.*

Crewsy, Yod Celebrated, loutish pop musician who plagiarizes F. X. Enderby's poetry with the connivance of Vesta

Bainbridge in Anthony Burgess's *Inside Mr. Enderby* and in *Enderby Outside.*

Cribbens (Crib) Prospector with whom McTeague discovers gold in the Panamint Range in Frank Norris's *McTeague.*

Cribiche Young orphan reared by Père Philéas in Grace King's *The Pleasant Ways of St. Médard.*

Crich, Christiana Eccentric, resentful wife of colliery owner Thomas Crich in D. H. Lawrence's *Women in Love.*

Crich, Diana Gerald Crich's young sister who drowns in the lake at Shortlands during the water party in D. H. Lawrence's *Women in Love.*

Crich, Gerald Thomas Crich's son and Gudrun Brangwen's lover; he becomes a wealthy and modern industrialist who is driven by an inner emptiness and his destructive relationship with Gudrun to commit suicide; he dies by freezing in the snow in D. H. Lawrence's *Women in Love.*

Crich, Laura Thomas Crich's daughter who is the bride in the wedding scene that opens D. H. Lawrence's *Women in Love.*

Crich, Thomas Paternalistic old colliery owner in D. H. Lawrence's *Women in Love.*

Crich, Winifred Gerald Crich's precocious youngest sister, who has artistic talent in D. H. Lawrence's *Women in Love.*

Crichton Aide to the British ambassador to Argentina who relieves Charley Fortnum of his position as Honorary Consul in the final pages of Graham Greene's *The Honorary Consul.*

Crick, Alicia Lover of the Reverend Thomas Marshfield in the first of his many adulterous affairs; later lover of Ned Bork; church organist and divorced mother of three in John Updike's *A Month of Sundays.*

Crick, Richard Owner and operator of the dairy farm where Tess Durbeyfield and Angel Clare work and meet in Thomas Hardy's *Tess of the D'Urbervilles.*

Cricket, Mrs. Snooping countrywoman whose discovery of a woman's hair on Aeneas Manston's pillow prepares for the disclosure that he has a wife in Thomas Hardy's *Desperate Remedies.*

Cricklade One of a group of Brookfield boys patrolling the railway lines who asks Mr. Chips what he should do should he meet any strikers in James Hilton's *Good-bye, Mr. Chips.*

Crikey One of a gang of boys in Benditch who blow up an explosives shed with D.'s gun, thus helping D. win a small victory in Graham Greene's *The Confidential Agent.*

Criley, Avis See Elderman, Avis Criley.

Criley, Bradd Grand Republic attorney, friend of Cass Timberlane, and lover of Jinny Timberlane in Sinclair Lewis's *Cass Timberlane.*

Crimp, David Pawnbroker to whom young Martin Chuzzlewit pawns his gold watch; later, as David Crimple, Secretary of the Anglo-Bengalee Disinterested Loan and Life Assurance Company, he lapses into fits of hilarity in Charles Dickens's *The Life and Adventures of Martin Chuzzlewit.*

Crimplesham, Thomas Solicitor who answers Lord Peter Wimsey's advertisement offering the return of the eyeglasses found on the body in Alfred Thipp's bathtub in Dorothy L Sayers's *Whose Body?.*

Crimson Rambler See Rambo, Clarence.

Crimsworth, Edward Tyrannical older brother of William; he runs a successful mill and warehouse, where he employs William for a time; he later goes bankrupt in Charlotte Brontë's *The Professor.*

Crimsworth, Mr. Edward and William Crimsworth's uncle, who is responsible for William until he is nine and then passes on the job of William's education to the Seacombes, the maternal relations, in Charlotte Brontë's *The Professor.*

Crimsworth, Mrs. Edward's attractive wife from a wealthy family, who is later mistreated by her husband in Charlotte Brontë's *The Professor.*

Crimsworth, Victor Son of William and Frances (Henri) Crimsworth; he is attached to his mother and fears his father in Charlotte Brontë's *The Professor.*

Crimsworth, William Reserved "professor" who, orphaned as a boy, receives his education at Eton, tries and dislikes trade with his brother, becomes a teacher in Belgium in several different schools, meets and finally marries Frances Henri, who has his son, and then returns to England, where he retires in Charlotte Brontë's *The Professor.*

Cringer, Mr. Member of Parliament to whom Launcelot Crab sends Roderick Random in London for help to become a surgeon's mate and who refers Roderick to Staytape in Tobias Smollett's *The Adventures of Roderick Random.*

Cringle, Peter First mate and quartermaster of the *Republic,* son of an immigrant who earned a fortune and despised the privileged, of which his son is considered part; watches his father dote on an orphan who had a hard beginning similar to that of Cringle's father; comforts Tommy O'Toole after the boy receives abuse from Captain Falcon; asks to be killed and eaten by his starving shipmates; has this wish carried out in Charles Johnson's *Middle Passage.*

Crinkett, Timothy Mine owner in New South Wales and a partner of John Caldigate in the Polyeuka mine; he follows him to England and tries to blackmail him concerning his association with Euphemia Smith prior to his marriage to Hester Bolton in Anthony Trollope's *John Caldigate.*

Cripple Loyalist soldier who disguises himself as a cripple in order to flee after the defeat at Marston Moor; he goes with the Cavalier and another soldier, who are also in disguise, in Daniel Defoe's *Memoirs of a Cavalier.*

Cripple Billy Orphaned teenager with a crippled arm and leg; raised by Kate and Eileen; loves Helen; goes to Hollywood to do a screen test for a role in Robert Flaherty's film *Man of Aran;* comes down with tuberculosis in Martin McDonagh's *The Cripple of Inishmaan.*

Cripplestraw, Anthony Farm worker for Benjamin Derriman and a volunteer soldier in Thomas Hardy's *The Trumpet-Major.*

Cripps, John Illiterate and cruel husband of Sue Seymour Cripps; following her death, turns their children's home into a low tavern in Harriet Beecher Stowe's *Dred.*

Cripps, Mr. Gossip and deadbeat who hangs around Captain Nat Kemp's tavern and tries to use information he gathers to his own advantage in Arthur Morrison's *The Hole in the Wall.*

Cripps, Sue Seymour (Suse) Daughter of formerly aristocratic Virginian parents and wife of the illiterate John Cripps; owner of Tiff Peyton; dies in poverty after the birth of her third child in Harriet Beecher Stowe's *Dred.*

Crisp, Mr. Chiswick curate who falls in love with Becky Sharp in William Makepeace Thackeray's *Vanity Fair.*

Crisparkle, Mrs. The Reverend Septimus Crisparkle's mother, dainty as a china shepherdess; she is fond of Edwin Drood and Rosa Bud but critical of Neville Landless's character in Charles Dickens's *The Mystery of Edwin Drood.*

Crisparkle, Septimus Minor canon in the Cloisterham Cathedral; he befriends Neville and Helena Landless and prevents John Jasper from assaulting Neville after the disappearance of Edwin Drood in Charles Dickens's *The Mystery of Edwin Drood.*

Critchlow, Mr. Harsh realist and Methuselah of St. Luke's Square; his wry criticisms chart the years; he, late in life, marries the desiccated Miss Insull, clerk of Baines's store, in Arnold Bennett's *The Old Wives Tale.*

Crittenden, Amy Mother of John Buddy Pearson and wife of Ned Crittenden in Zora Neale Hurston's *Jonah's Gourd Vine.*

Crittenden, Ned Stepfather of John Buddy Pearson and husband of Amy Crittenden in Zora Neale Hurston's *Jonah's Gourd Vine.*

Crittendon, Elizabeth Southern lady who has an affair with Nathaniel Franklin after he burns her house in Hervey Allen's *Action at Aquila.*

Crittendon, Margaret Daughter of Elizabeth Crittendon; has an affair with a doomed Confederate soldier in Hervey Allen's *Action at Aquila.*

Croaker Savage, uneducated sexual brute who rapes Anastasia Stoker in John Barth's *Giles Goat-Boy.*

Crocker, Joseph Handsome carpenter whom Isabella Archbald elects to marry in Ellen Glasgow's *The Sheltered Life.*

Crocker, Samuel Post Office clerk who gets into hot water with his superiors for tearing up official papers; he pursues Clara Demijohn but loses her to his rival, Daniel Tribbledale, in Anthony Trollope's *Marion Fay.*

Crockett, Priss Hartshorn Introverted New York socialite and member of the group in Mary McCarthy's *The Group.*

Crocodile God Menacing apparition in the shape of an immense crocodile that emerges from the jungle river to attempt to devour the emperor Brutus Jones as the petty dictator flees for his life from an uprising of his native subjects in Eugene O'Neill's play *The Emperor Jones.*

Croft, Admiral Warm-hearted retired rear admiral, who rents the Elliot estate; his devotion to and touchingly comic dependence on his wife make them a model of marital happiness in Jane Austen's *Persuasion.*

Croft, Art Narrator of Walter Van Tilburg Clark's *The Ox-Bow Incident.*

Croft, Mrs. Proud American centenarian who makes the narrator, her Indian tenant, say "splendid" every time she mentions the American flag; maintains her distance with her tenants; listens to classical music and news on the radio; belongs to the traditional school of thought, as she does not like girls wearing short dresses; sits on her favorite bench all day, but dies succumbing to an injury caused by her fall from the same bench in Jhumpa Lahiri's "The Third and Final Continent."

Croft, Sophia Wife of the admiral and sister to Captain Wentworth; her good-heartedness, candor, and affection for her husband are admired by Anne Elliot in Jane Austen's *Persuasion.*

Croft, Staff Sergeant Samuel (Sam) Fascistic commander of a reconnaissance unit who arranges the death of Robert Hearn in Norman Mailer's *The Naked and the Dead.*

Croftangery, Chrystal First-time author, who asks editing advice of his friend Mr. Fairscribe and winds up narrating Menie Gray's history in Sir Walter Scott's *The Surgeon's Daughter.*

Crofts, Dr. James Physician in Guestwick who marries Bell Dale in Anthony Trollope's *The Small House at Allington.* He appears briefly in *The Last Chronicle of Barset.*

Crofts, Lady Frances Delamere Shameless and unprincipled elder daughter of Lord and Lady Montreville; her affair with Bellozane causes her to separate from her husband; Bellozane kills her brother, Frederic Delamere, in a duel in Charlotte Smith's *Emmeline: The Orphan of the Castle.*

Crofts, Mr. Elder son of Sir Richard Crofts; he ingratiates himself with Lord Montreville's daughter, Lady Frances, and secretly marries her; he agrees to maintain separate residences when she begins an affair with the urbane Chevalier de Bellozane in Charlotte Smith's *Emmeline: The Orphan of the Castle.*

Crofts, Mr. Perverse old man, ugly but rich, who pays fifty guineas for first rights to Fanny Hill's virginity, tries to rape her, and fails grotesquely in John Cleland's *Memoirs of a Woman of Pleasure.*

Crofts, Mr. Solicitor for the defense who thinks his client, Harriet Vane, is guilty in Dorothy L. Sayers's *Strong Poison.*

Crofts, Professor Condescending Emersonian scholar and Shep Stearns's former teacher in Budd Schulberg's *The Disenchanted.*

Crofts, Sir George Man about town in his 50s; shrewd in business and manipulating people; old friend of Mrs. Warren in many ways; wonders if he, like other men in the play, could be the father of Vivie Warren; desires to marry Vivie, but the young woman refuses him in George Bernard Shaw's play *Mrs. Warren's Profession.*

Crofts, Sir Richard Attorney and Member of Parliament; he manages Lord Montreville's affairs and promotes ruthless schemes to prevent a marriage between Frederic Delamere and Emmeline Mobray, whose legitimate claim to the Mowbray estate he suppressed soon after the death of her father in Charlotte Smith's *Emmeline: The Orphan of the Castle.*

Crofut, Mrs. Woman who George Brush believes has many daughters, when in fact she operates a house of prostitution, in Thornton Wilder's *Heaven's My Destination.*

Croisenois, Monsieur de Appealing young man, rich and set to inherit a dukedom; becomes engaged to Mademoiselle de la Mole, who spurns him for Julien Sorel; later killed in a duel over a slur on the young woman's honor in Stendhal's *Red and Black.*

Croisnel, Roland de Nevil Beauchamp's close friend, after Beauchamp saves his life; he disapproves of Beauchamp's plan to elope with his sister Renée (Rouaillout) in George Meredith's *Beauchamp's Career.*

Croke, Captain Unton Officer of the insurgent forces; relentless in pursuit of Sir Joseph Wagstaff and other Royalist fugitives defeated at the battle of Salisbury, he is hoodwinked by Charles Mandeville, who finds an unlikely hiding place for Sir Joseph in William Godwin's *Mandeville.*

Croke, Dr. Acton Eminent London medical specialist who diagnoses the unusual weariness of Sir Edward Leithen and Mr. Palliser-Yeates as boredom with life in John Buchan's

John Macnab. He tells Leithen that he has less than a year to live in John Buchan's *Sick Heart River.*

Croker, Charles Wealthy real estate developer with overextended credit; agrees to endorse innocence of Fareek Fanon, college football star who is an alleged rapist, in return for settlement of his debts; reneges on the deal; loses wife, money, and property; becomes a televangelist for The Stoic's Hour in Tom Wolfe's *A Man in Full.*

Croker, Martha First wife of Charles Croker; mother of three children; educated, intelligent; from an old Virginia family, marries Raymond Peepgas in Tom Wolfe's *A Man In Full.*

Croker, Serena Second wife of Charles Croker; mother of one daughter; beautiful; 36 years younger than Charles in Tom Wolfe's *A Man In Full.*

Crole, Else Fourteen-year-old girl, a servant at D.'s London hotel; she devotedly helps D. until she is murdered by the manageress and K. in Graham Greene's *The Confidential Agent.*

Croll, Herr Augustus Melmotte's confidential secretary, whose refusal to sign as witness papers forged by his employer immediately precedes Melmotte's suicide; he and Madame Melmotte marry in Anthony Trollope's *The Way We Live Now.*

Croly, Miss Grade-school teacher of Felix Fay; encourages Fay to use his imagination in Floyd Dell's *Moon-Calf.*

Cromarty, Sir Francis Retired English general who accompanies the protagonist, Phileas Fogg, during part of his challenging circumnavigation of the globe in Jules Verne's *Around the World in Eighty Days.*

Crombie, Dougal Chieftain and canny header of the Gorbals Die-Hards; he aids Dickson McCunn in rescuing Sakskia, the Russian princess, and preserving her jewels in John Buchan's *Huntingtower.* He again joins forces with McCunn, his benefactor, and Jaikie (John Galt), another former Die-hard, in teaching self-control and objectivity to his boss, Thomas Carlyle Craw, and the quarreling Evallonian political factions in *Castle Gay.* In the confidence of Craw and gradually taking over the position of general manager of the Craw Press, he realizes that a Royalist rebellion would be upset by the new third party, Juventus, and seeks Dickson McCunn's advice and aid again in *The House of the Four Winds.*

Crombie, Hugh and Sarah Hutchins (Widow Hutchins) Operators of the Hand and Bottle Inn in Nathaniel Hawthorne's *Fanshawe.*

Crome, George Captain of the frigate *Syrtis* who allows Hornblower and the Spaniards to return to Ferrol in accordance with the rules of law in C. S. Forester's *Mr. Midshipman Hornblower.*

Crompton, Jack English consulting engineer who tries to help organize the work-relief effort in Crom during the blight in Liam O'Flaherty's *Famine.*

Cromwell (Earl of Essex) Nobleman engaged in the suppression of monasteries in England during the reign of Henry VIII in J. Henry Shorthouse's *John Inglesant, A Romance.*

Cromwell, Clarence (Sinbad) Veteran black Los Angeles police detective; friend of A. M. Valnikov in Joseph Wambaugh's *The Black Marble.*

Cromwell, Oliver Referred to as a "firebrand of war"; he and his Roundhead forces rout the overeager Prince Rupert and his army at Marston Moor in Daniel Defoe's *Memoirs of a Cavalier.* He is a soldier and Protector of the Commonwealth, who pursues King Charles II after the triumph of Parliamentary armies over Stuart forces; he narrowly misses capturing the king at Woodstock Lodge in Sir Walter Scott's *Woodstock.* He explains his presence in Elysium as a reward for sufferings in a second incarnation that made reparation for his disloyalty to Charles I in his first incarnation in Henry Fielding's *A Journey From This World to the Next.*

Cromwell, Oliver (Ironsides) Commander of the Parliamentary army; originally appears to consider his soldiers equals but is corrupted by power and property, betraying his promises to the soldiers opposed to his Irish campaign in Mary Lee Settle's *Prisons.*

Cronstadt, Jabberwhorl (Jab) Friend of Henry Miller; provides one free meal per week for Miller in Henry Miller's *Tropic of Cancer;* poet, musician, weatherman, herbologist, and linguist in *Black Spring.*

Cronstadt, Katya Daughter of Jabberwhorl Cronstadt in Henry Miller's *Black Spring.*

Crook, Eugene (Gene) Crooked banker who swindles Jean Baptiste in Oscar Micheaux's *The Homesteader.*

Crook, Mr. Legal representative of Staffordshire iron merchants; he insists upon payment for his creditors from Mr. Furze in Mark Rutherford's *Catharine Furze.*

Crook, Sir William Friend of Harry Annesley; he offers Harry a post as private secretary when it appears that Peter Prosper has withdrawn his support and favor in Anthony Trollope's *Mr. Scarborough's Family.*

Crookman, Dr. Junius (Doc) Black biologist and physician who develops the Black-No-More process to make blacks white in George S. Schuyler's *Black No More.*

Crooks Black ranch hand who hesitatingly befriends Lennie Small in John Steinbeck's *Of Mice and Men.*

Crookshanks Half cat half kneazle belonging to Hermione Granger in J. K. Rowling's Harry Potter series.

Croom, Arthur Friend of John Laskell; arranges for Laskell's care during his illness in Lionel Trilling's *The Middle of the Journey.*

Croom, James Bernard (Tony) Unemployed young man who meets Clare Corven on a ship from Ceylon; he finds employment caring for Jack Muskham's horses; he becomes co-respondent in Clare's divorce from Sir Gerald Corven in John Galsworthy's *Over the River.*

Croom, Lady Mother of Thomasina, the sister of Captain Brice, and the bossy, wealthy lady of Sidley Park where the young girl Thomasina Covely studies under the tutoring of Septimus Hodge; recognizes Thomasina's intellectual superiority but argues that the girl should look to a suitable marriage rather than academic ends; falls in love with Byron and is upset with his affair with Mrs. Chater; realizes that Septimus is in love with her in Tom Stoppard's play *Arcadia.*

Croom, Nancy (Nan) Wife of Arthur Croom; refuses to accept the reality of death in Lionel Trilling's *The Middle of the Journey.*

Crooper, George Cousin of Johnnie Watson; his prodigious appetite causes him trouble, to the delight of William Baxter, Johnnie Watson, and Joe Bullitt, in Booth Tarkington's *Seventeen.*

Crop, Annie Young daughter of Gideon and Ida Crop; swept off a country bridge to her death during a flood in Wendell Berry's *A Place on Earth.*

Crop, Gideon Tenant farmer of Roger Merchant, husband of Ida Crop, and father of Annie Crop in Wendell Berry's *A Place on Earth.*

Crop, Ida Wife of Gideon Crop, mother of Annie Crop, and object of Ernest Finley's unrequited love in Wendell Berry's *A Place on Earth.*

Cropdale, Tim London author who tricks Birkin out of a pair of boots in Tobias Smollett's *The Expedition of Humphry Clinker.*

Cropleigh, Beverly Woodsman and eldest of the Cropleigh siblings; retreats to Parcher's Cove after his parents are killed in a steamboat disaster in Andrew Lytle's *The Velvet Horn.*

Cropleigh, Dickie Physician and brother of Julia Cropleigh Cree in Andrew Lytle's *The Velvet Horn.*

Cropleigh, Duncan Jealous brother of Julia Cropleigh Cree and probable biological father of her son, Lucius Cree; blown up with his brother Beverly in a dynamite explosion during the Civil War in Andrew Lytle's *The Velvet Horn.*

Cropleigh, Jack (Uncle Jack) Brother of Julia Cropleigh Cree and garrulous uncle of Lucius Cree; tries to instruct and protect his nephew, in the lunging in front of the bullet intended for Lucius; principal narrator of Andrew Lytle's *The Velvet Horn.*

Cropleigh, Julia See Cree, Julia Cropleigh.

Cropper Boarder at Seaforth House school who is in charge of the library in Roy Fuller's *The Ruined Boys.*

Cropper, Evelyn Gotobed Bertha Gotobed's sister and former fellow housemaid in Agatha Dawson's service; she married and emigrated but returns to England for Bertha's funeral in Dorothy L. Sayers's *Unnatural Death.*

Crosbie, Adolphus Unprincipled and selfish minor civil servant, whose social ambition causes him to jilt Lily Dale and marry Lady Alexandrina de Courcy in Anthony Trollope's *The Small House at Allington.* After Lady Alexandria's death his renewed suit is firmly rejected by Lily in *The Last Chronicle of Barset.*

Crosbie, William Provost of Dumfries, who is a friend of Alexander Fairford, and whose letter reporting the disappearance of Darsie Latimer (Arthur Redgauntlet) causes

Alan Fairford's abrupt departure from the court in Sir Walter Scott's *Redgauntlet.*

Crosby Servant and housekeeper to the original Pargiter family; Crosby assists Eleanor in her duties as "angel of the house" in Virginia Woolf's *The Years.*

Crosby Head servant at Anchorstone Hall during the Staveleys' houseparty in L. P. Hartley's *The Sixth Heaven.*

Crosby, Hazel (Mom) Hoosier wife of H. Lowe Crosby; sews the U.S. flag in Kurt Vonnegut's *Cat's Cradle.*

Crosby, H. Lowe Midwestern entrepreneur and patriot; husband of Hazel Crosby in Kurt Vonnegut's *Cat's Cradle.*

Cross, Abel Guard on the Rover Mail; Sir Turnour Wyse appropriates his coach for the last desperate run to Fenny Horton and the defeat of Squire Cranmer's plan in John Buchan's *The Free Fishers.*

Cross, Anthony (Anthony Cruz) Poor, light-skinned love and eventual mate of Angela Murray in Jessie Redmon Fauset's *Plum Bun.*

Cross, Bertha Girl of a poor but genteel background with a troublesome mother; a friend of Rosamund Elvan, she earns money as an artist and eventually marries Will Warburton in George Gissing's *Will Warburton.*

Cross, Lieutenant Jimmy Lieutenant of Alpha Company during the Vietnam War; escapes the fear and the stress of war by occupying his mind with memories of his old sweetheart, Martha; carries a heavy sense of guilt caused by his belief that his preoccupation with Martha prevented him from saving the lives of two of his men in Tim O'Brien's *The Things They Carried.*

Cross, Lucas Drunken shack-dweller whose abuse of his stepdaughter, Selena Cross, drives her to murder him and causes the suicide of his wife, Nellie Cross, in Grace Metalious's *Peyton Place.*

Cross, Mrs. Bertha Cross's ill-tempered mother, who abuses her servants in George Gissing's *Will Warburton.*

Cross, Mrs. Kindly shopkeeper who allows Ernest Pontifex and other schoolboys to run up small debts; Theobald Pontifex's anger results in her shop's being ruled off bounds by the Roughborough school in Samuel Butler's *The Way of All Flesh.*

Cross, Nadine Woman chosen to bear Randall Flagg's child in Stephen King's *The Stand.*

Cross, Nellie Wife of Lucas Cross and mother of Selena Cross; hangs herself in the MacKenzie home as a result of her husband's raping and impregnating her daughter in Grace Metalious's *Peyton Place.*

Cross, Selena Daughter of Nellie Cross, stepdaughter of Lucas Cross, and best friend of Allison MacKenzie; kills her abusive stepfather during an attempted rape and is acquitted of the murder but henceforth shunned by the respectable townspeople in Grace Metalious's *Peyton Place.*

Cross, Sir Henry A supposedly intimidating figure who proves scarcely a threat to General Curzon or anyone else in C. S. Forester's *The General.*

Crossby, Mr. High-spirited journalist and long-distance runner; seeking a story about the archaeological discovery of the Viking barrow of "Harold Blacktooth", he agrees to act as a decoy for Sir Edward Leithen in his attempt to kill a salmon in the waters at Strathlarrig in John Buchan's *John Macnab.*

Crosse, Superintendent Policeman who takes the Assistant Commissioner along to make the arrest of a murderer in Graham Greene's *It's a Battlefield.*

Crossley, Mrs. Neighbor of Jim Hawkins and his mother in Robert Louis Stevenson's *Treasure Island.*

Crossthwaite, John Idealistic, intelligent Chartist tailor, to whom Alton Locke is apprenticed; an advocate of self-sacrifice for the common good, he encourages Alton to become involved in the Chartist movement, finally becoming, like Alton, a Christian socialist and sailing with him for Texas in Charles Kingsley's *Alton Locke.*

Crossthwaite, Katie Supportive wife of the Chartist tailor John Crossthwaite; she helps Lady Ellerton nurse Alton Locke through his fever in Charles Kingsley's *Alton Locke.*

Crosstrees, Lieutenant First officer of a British gunboat sent to end the jurisdiction of John Neverbend as president of the South Seas island of Britannula; he has charge of a 250-ton cannon trained on the capital city to enforce British law in Anthony Trollope's *The Fixed Period.*

Crotchet, Lemma Daughter of Ebenezer Crotchet in Thomas Love Peacock's *Crotchet Castle.*

Crotchet, Young Son of Ebenezer Crotchet; his greed and speculations blight the lives of all around him in Thomas Love Peacock's *Crotchet Castle.*

Croton Giant who helps Vinicius and Petronius locate Lycia, who has gone into hiding with other Christians; killed by Ursus, another giant and devoted servant to Lycia, in Henryk Sienkiewicz's *Quo Vadis.*

Crotti Cocaine merchant involved in a struggle for control of Los Angeles in Paul Cain's *Fast One.*

Crotty, Frank Los Angeles policeman and partner of Thomas Spellacy in John Gregory Dunne's *True Confessions.*

Crouch, Henry Old stooped man who works as a superintendant in the apartment building where George and Dorothy Moore live and where Dorothy shoots Professor Duncan McFee; arm chair philosopher who follows Professor McFee's pragmatism and logic; absurdly named the chairman of the philosophy symposium on the existence of God in Tom Stoppard's play *Jumpers.*

Crouch, Martha Wife of Samuel Crouch; landlady and secret lover of N'Gana Frimbo in Rudolph Fisher's *The Conjure-Man Dies.*

Crouch, Samuel (Easley Jones) Harlem mortician, husband of Martha Crouch, and landlord of N'Gana Frimbo, whom Crouch kills in Rudolph Fisher's *The Conjure-Man Dies.*

Crow (Shaft-speeder) Warrior who leads scouting parties and bears messages in war and peace in William Morris's *The Roots of the Mountains.*

Crow, Canon John Crow's grandfather, whose death at ninety has brought John back to Glastonbury in John Cowper Powys's *A Glastonbury Romance.*

Crow, John Cynical adventurer who returns upon his grandfather's death to Glastonbury after fifteen years in France; he re-encounters and marries his cousin Mary, inveigles a position as Johnny Geard's secretary, and, disdainful of Glastonbury, leaves with Mary for Norfolk in John Cowper Powys's *A Glastonbury Romance.*

Crow, Jonah (J., Jayber, Jaybird) Barber of Port William, Kentucky, and self-taught philosopher in Wendell Berry's *A Place on Earth* and *The Memory of Old Jack.*

Crow, Mary Cousin of John Crow employed as the companion of the spinster Euphemia Drew; she and John become lovers, marry, and, contemptuous of Glastonbury's overawing spiritual character, heave for Norfolk in John Cowper Powys's *A Glastonbury Romance.*

Crow, Philip John Crow's third cousin, an ambitious Glastonbury industrialist who battles Johnny Geard's efforts to revive the town's religious past and the communists' attempts to collectivize its business and industry; he fails on both counts and goes bankrupt, vowing to "begin again" in John Cowper Powys's *A Glastonbury Romance.*

Crowan, Lady Guest at Manderly who asks Maxim de Winter about continuing the tradition of the Manderly costume ball; Maxim's decision to have the ball is the occasion for a public humiliation of his second wife, engineered by Mrs. Danvers in Daphne Du Maurier's *Rebecca.*

Crowd Burmese people in the town of Moulmein, in Lower Burma; the mob's growing size and expectations compel the narrator, a British subdivisional police officer, to shoot a rampaging elephant in George Orwell's "Shooting an Elephant."

Crowd, "Chicamauga" Retreating troops from an unidentified battle or riot on the plantation; throng of blacks is on the way back to the plantation; described as exhausted and defeated; the successive battalions had previously passed the young boy in the opposite direction but have gone unnoticed; the child is attracted by the gleaming blood on their clothing but also frightened by one particular man in the crowd; their course is not disturbed or aided by the boy's presence in Ambrose Bierce's "Chicamauga."

Crowder, Anne Detective-Sergeant Mather's romantically misled fiancée and James Raven's "moll"; after being terrorized by Raven, she joins him in his search for Davis but betrays him to Mather and his death in Graham Greene's *A Gun for Sale.*

Crowder, Ben Tough-minded manager of the Washington baseball team in Mark Harris's *It Looked Like For Ever.*

Crowdey, Jogglebury Chairman of the Stir-it-stiff union; he believes Soapey Sponge is wealthy and invites him to be his houseguest but tries to get rid of him when he finds out otherwise in Robert Surtees's *Mr. Sponge's Sporting Tour.*

Crowdy, Blanche Robarts Buxom sister of Mark Robarts; she marries Squire Crowdy and becomes mistress of Creamclotted Hall in Anthony Trollope's *Framley Parsonage.*

Crowdy, Squire Hearty landowner and husband of Blanche Robarts in Anthony Trollope's *Framley Parsonage.*

Crowe, Captain Samuel Retired merchant marine captain, who travels with his nephew, Thomas Clarke; he admires and imitates Sir Launcelot Greaves, but gives up his mad ambition when he learns from Ferret he has an inheritance; he marries Dorothy Oakley in Tobias Smollett's *The Adventures of Sir Launcelot Greaves.*

Crowe, Mrs. Young woman who travels to interview with the Committee for Aid to the Elderly; she sullenly agrees to accept her aged mother into her home in Angus Wilson's *The Middle Age of Mrs. Eliot.*

Crowe, Letty Spinster in her mid-sixties; she is a clerk in an undefined office who lives alone in a bedsitting room, her retirement plans overthrown by her friend's impending marriage, until her landlady sells the building to an African evangelical pastor in Barbara Pym's *Quartet in Autumn.*

Crowe, Mrs. Obsessive widow whose desire to be near Hadrian VII impells him to join Jerry Sant's blackmailing scheme in Frederick William Rolfe's *Hadrian the Seventh.*

Crowe, Old Old man who lives in the same boarding house as Ida Arnold and partners her as they consult the Ouija Board in Graham Greene's *Brighton Rock.*

Crowe, Thaddeus Honest, successful lawyer, who handles the arrangements on behalf of Fred Neville by which Captain O'Hara is to be paid an annuity of 200 so long as he stays out of Ireland in Anthony Trollope's *An Eye for an Eye.*

Crowell, Joe, Jr. Paperboy who delivers the daily paper to each household in Grover's Corners in Thornton Wilder's play *Our Town.*

Crowell, Si Joe's younger brother who takes over his older brother's newspaper route in Thornton Wilder's play *Our Town.*

Crowhurst, Mrs. Poor woman who is mother of Phoebe and who nurses her during her mortal illness in Mark Rutherford's *Catharine Furze.*

Crowhurst, Phoebe Mrs. Furze's servant, who quits in disgust when she realizes the plot being prepared against Tom Catchpole; she confesses to Catharine Furze her love for Tom before she dies in Mark Rutherford's *Catharine Furze.*

Crowl, Mr. Newman Noggs's fellow lodger, who rails at him when he will not put enough coals on the fire or get him invited to dinner with the Kenwigs in Charles Dickens's *The Life and Adventures of Nicholas Nickleby.*

Crowle, Old Mean-hearted, rough gatekeeper at Bartram-Haugh; at Silas Ruthyn's order he helps keep Silas's ward, Maud Ruthyn, confined to the estate in J. Sheridan Le Fanu's *Uncle Silas.*

Crowling, Mrs. Procuress for Sir Harry Richmond in Charlotte Smith's *The Young Philosopher.*

Crown Catfish Row cotton stevedore and lover of Bess; murders Robbins and is fatally stabbed by Porgy in DuBose Heyward's *Porgy.*

Crowne, Emily William's "elusively radiant" twin, who possesses a "divine purity of outline"; the daughter of Norman Crowne, she inherits his dreaminess and childlike attitude but unlike hem father and brother consciously defies her fate and marries Philip Luttrell, conceives a child, and becomes blissfully happy in Margaret Kennedy's *Red Sky at Morning.*

Crowne, Lenina Attractive genetic worker who after disaffection with Bernard Marx develops an emotional interest in the uncivilized John Savage; conditioned to express affection sexually, she is rebuffed by the naïve youth and eventually brutally murdered by him in Aldous Huxley's *Brave New World.*

Crowne, Norman Handsome, well-born, rich, unstable poet who marries and produces two beautiful children, William and Emily; possessing a "dazzling if fitful genius", he lives in a world of fantasy and is eventually implicated in the death of one of his friends; found innocent, he flees England and dies abroad in Margaret Kennedy's *Red Sky at Morning.*

Crowne, William Handsome, "elusively radiant" twin of Emily Crowne and son of Norman Crowne; like his father, William has poetical genius and is brilliant and unbalanced; he makes an unfortunate marriage to Tilli Van Tuyl and, like his father, is implicated in the death of a man, his cousin Trevor Frobisher, in Margaret Kennedy's *Red Sky at Morning.*

Crowninshield, Alberta Sydna See Vaiden, Alberta Sydna Crowninshield.

Crowninshield, Drusilla Lacefield (Dru) Daughter of Caruthers Lacefield; elopes with Emory Crowninshield the day before she is to marry Miltiades Vaiden; mother of Sydna Crowninshield; appears in T. S. Stribling's *The Forge, The Store,* and *Unfinished Cathedral.*

Crowninshield, Emory Southern genteel aristocrat and husband of Drusilla Lacefield; Confederate major and ardent defender of chattel slavery; appears in T. S. Stribling's *The Forge.*

Crowther, Irene One of Evelyn Morton Stennett's "clients"; on one visit to Irene's, Evelyn is injured during a domestic quarrel between Irene and Joseph Leroy in Margaret Drabble's *The Middle Ground.*

Croy, Kate Secret fiancée of Merton Densher and friend of the dying Mildred Theale; plots to have Densher marry Theale and inherit her money in Henry James's *The Wings of the Dove.*

Croyden, Sarah Actress, confidante of Olivia Lattimore, and abandoned lover and later the wife of Leon Lawrence in Mary Austin's *A Woman of Genius.*

Croye, Lady Hameline de Isabelle de Croye's aunt and guardian; fond of gaiety and absurdly romantic, she imagines Quentin Durward to be infatuated with her and is humiliated to discover his interest lies with Isabelle; eventually she marries William de La Marck in Sir Walter Scott's *Quentin Durward.*

Croye, Lady Isabelle de (Jacqueline) Beautiful Burgundian heiress whom the Duke of Burgundy endeavors to bestow on an odious favorite; fleeing to France, where she uses the name Jacqueline, she is betrayed by Louis XI to William de La Marck; she is rescued by Quentin Durward in Sir Walter Scott's *Quentin Durward.*

Cruchi, Jacopo Innkeeper who incites Angelo Guidascarpi's distrust during his escape from Milan; he regains his trust only to betray him in George Meredith's *Vittoria.*

Cruddock Sir Edward Leithen's manservant in John Buchan's *Sick Heart River.*

Cruickshank, Leola Beautiful but dimwitted schoolmate of Dunstan Ramsay and Boy Staunton; romantically involved with Dunstan briefly following his enlistment, but weds Boy after the war; has two children by her husband, but proves incapable of adapting to the sociocultural demands of Boy's meteoric rise in politics and finance; facing years of Boy's numerous infidelities, neglect, and verbal abuse, commits suicide in Robertson Davies's *Fifth Business.*

Crum Twenty-year-old spendthrift chum of Val Dartie; he is out with Val on an evening when Montague Dartie embarrasses his son in John Galsworthy's *In Chancery.*

Crumb, John Honest, simple, flour-dusted miller, who is devoted to Ruby Ruggles and jealous of her would-be seducer, Sir Felix Carbury; he thrashes his rival and wins Ruby as his bride in Anthony Trollope's *The Way We Live Now.*

Crummins, Ned Laborer who is delivering to Martin Tinman a large mirror broken by Van Dieman Smith (Ribstone); Crummins runs, starting the quarrel between Smith (Ribstone) and Tinman in George Meredith's *The House on the Beach.*

Crummles, Charles Son of Vincent Crummles and an actor in the company since childhood; he later emigrates to Australia in Charles Dickens's *The Life and Adventures of Nicholas Nickleby.*

Crummles, Mrs. Vincent Crummles's wife, who plays tragic roles and dances the hornpipe in her husband's theatrical company in Charles Dickens's *The Life and Adventures of Nicholas Nickleby.*

Crummles, Ninetta (The Infant Phenomenon) Precocious "child" actress, who is kept small in stature by her father, Vincent Crummles, with applications of gin and few hours of sleep; her top billing is resented by other performers in Charles Dickens's *The Life and Adventures of Nicholas Nickleby.*

Crummles, Percy Second son of Vincent Crummles and an actor in his father's theatrical company since childhood; he leaves with his brother for Australia in Charles Dickens's *The Life and Adventures of Nicholas Nickleby.*

Crummles, Vincent Manager of a traveling theatrical company; he hires Nicholas Nickelby and Smike as actors immediately upon seeing them when they need work and asks Nicholas to translate a French play in Charles Dickens's *The Life and Adventures of Nicholas Nickleby.*

Crump, John Secretary of the Imperial Palace Hotel Company; his nervousness at the annual meeting makes him read the notice of meeting in a loud, defiant voice in Arnold Bennett's *Imperial Palace.*

Crump, Lottie Eccentric owner of a London hotel where many of the aristocrats gather in Evelyn Waugh's *Vile Bodies.*

Crump, Mr. Baker in the town of Gylingden who, with John Thomas, brings news of Sir Harry Bracton's entry into the town to try to win the election from Stanley Lake, precipitating

Lake's fateful ride past the uncovered hand of Mark Wylder's corpse in J. Sheridan Le Fanu's *Wylder's Hand.*

Cruncher, Jerry Tellson's Bank employee, who moonlights as a resurrection-man, retrieving bodies from graves to sell to interested parties; he is devoted to Dr. Manette and Lucie Manette and aids Charles Darnay in his escape from France in Charles Dickens's *A Tale of Two Cities.*

Cruncher, (Young) Jerry Son of the resurrectionist; he accompanies his father on burial excavations much to his mother's displeasure in Charles Dickens's *A Tale of Two Cities.*

Cruncher, Mrs. Wife of Jerry Cruncher; she fights with him over his stealing bodies from graves and fears for the safety of her son in Charles Dickens's *A Tale of Two Cities.*

Crupp, Mrs. David Copperfield's landlady while he is lodging in the Adelphi when he first lives in London; she is afflicted with 'spazzums,' which require the administration of brandy in Charles Dickens's *The Personal History of David Copperfield.*

Cruse, Mr. Clergyman and tutor of a student making the Grand Tour; he vies with Mr. M'Gabbery in trying to attract ladies of the party in Anthony Trollope's *The Bertrams.*

Crushton, Mr. The Honourable Crushton, a bosom friend of Lord Mutanhed in Bath in Charles Dickens's *The Posthumous Papers of the Pickwick Club.*

Crusoe, Billie Rebel scientist on a dying planet; sent on an exploratory mission to colonize Planet Blue; falls in love with Spike, a robotic human being; also a scientist on Earth who invents the first robot in Jeanette Winterson's *The Stone Gods.*

Crusoe, Billy Member of Captain Cook's crew; left behind on Easter Island; forms a bond with Spikkers, a shipwrecked Dutchman, in Jeanette Winterson's *The Stone Gods.*

Crusoe (Kreutznaer), Robinson (Bob, Robin) Son of a middle-class merchant; having gone to sea against his father's wishes, he is captured by pirates off the coast of Africa and made a slave for two years before escaping and being brought to Brazil by a Portuguese vessel; later, shipwrecked on the "Island of Despair," he becomes a devout Christian and eventually establishes a home and farm while on the island; after fifteen years of solitude, he discovers another inhabitant, a native whom he names Friday; with Friday, Crusoe saves a Spaniard, the English Captain, and Friday's father, and eventually both Crusoe and Friday are able to leave the island and come to England in Daniel Defoe's *The Life and Strange Surprizing Adventures of Robinson Crusoe of York, Mariner.*

Crutchleigh, Corfe Guest at Brandon Hall's Hunt Ball in J. Sheridan Le Fanu's *Wylder's Hand.*

Crutchleigh, Mr. One of the guests at Brandon Hall's Hunt Ball in J. Sheridan Le Fanu's *Wylder's Hand.*

Crutchleigh, Mrs. Guest at the Hunt Ball at Brandon Hall who disapproves of having a singer performing in J. Sheridan Le Fanu's *Wylder's Hand.*

Cruyer, Richard (Dicky) German Stations Controller and Bernard Samson's boss, who sends Bernard to Berlin for "Brahms Four" in Len Deighton's *Berlin Game.* He conspires for Bret Rensselaer's position in *Mexico Set* and in *London Match.*

Cruz Indian woman, addict, and companion of Tristessa in Jack Kerouac's *Tristessa.*

Cruz, Anthony See Cross, Anthony.

Cruz, Artemio Protagonist in Carlos Fuentes's *The Death of Artemio Cruz.*

Cruz, Catalina Wife of Artemio in Carlos Fuentes's *The Death of Artemio Cruz.*

Cruz, Isabel Mulatta mother of Artemio and sister of Lunero, mistress to the master Atanasio,who drove her off the estate, in Carlos Fuentes's *The Death of Artemio Cruz.*

Crystal Utopian teenager who befriends the isolated William Bamnstaple; Crystal's intelligence makes Barnstaple realize how inferior he is to the Utopians in H. G. Wells's *Men Like Gods.*

Crystal Merchant Employer for whom the protagonist, Santiago, works for a year during his quest; prefers to dream of going on a pilgrimage instead of embarking on a journey to Mecca in real life; fear of failure shakes Santiago into resolving to follow his dream in Paulo Coelho's *The Alchemist.*

Csycsyry, Attila Publican in Fort St. Sebastian; an oft-wounded, now philosophical Transylvanian Protestant; since public houses are not permitted, he calls his business a water room in Bharati Mukherjee's *The Holder of the World.*

Cubitt Slow, large, redheaded man; a member of Pinkie Brown's extortion mob, he witnesses Charles Hale's killing, deserts Pinkie, and tries unsuccessfully to join Colleoni's mob in Graham Greene's *Brighton Rock.*

Cuchulain King of Muirthemne of Ireland; quarrels with the older king Conchubar about why he must be obedient to his elder's higher royal status; meets a foreigner, a young champion, on his land and soon kills the youth in a sword fight; learns from the Blind Man and Fool that the lad was his own son—the son of the foreign queen warrior Aoife; despondent and raging, goes into the sea and drowns in William Butler Yeats's play *On Baile's Strand.;* also appears as legendary figure in Yeats's play *At the Hawk's Well.*

Cuckold Wife murderer and convict who runs a private commissary and tells of a homosexual relationship that parallels that of Zeke Farragut in John Cheever's *Falconer.*

Cuckoo Mistress of Old Lord in the House of Hwang; procuress who moves to Wang Lung's home as Lotus's meddling servant in Pearl Buck's *The Good Earth.*

Cuckow, Tom Man scolded by Ellis Duckworth for not doing a better job of robbing a pardoner; he is one of the few aboard the *Good Hope* who keep their heads during a storm in Robert Louis Stevenson's *The Black Arrow: A Tale of Two Roses.*

Cudjoe Deformed slave fiercely faithful to Lafitte in Joseph Holt Ingraham's *Lafitte.*

Cudlip, Moll Cutpurse sentenced for life to Australia; escapes and lives with her aborigine lover in Charles Nordhoff and James Norman Hall's *Botany Bay.*

Cué, Arsenio Actor and one of the three main characters who are all trapped in a socially changing Havana in Guillermo Cabrera Infante's *Three Trapped Tigers.*

Cuestas, Goyo Old farmhand who, along with his son, steals a phonograph and escapes on horseback through the jungle and across the mountains to Honduras in the hope of selling the artifact for money; get stuck in the mud, sleep under a tree, and are brutally chopped to pieces by four bandits who throw their bodies down into a ravine in Salarrué's "We're Bad."

Cuff, Alastair Director of a family publishing house where George Garner works in Roy Fuller's *The Second Curtain.*

Cuff, Nigel Published critic and cynical friend of Trevor Frobisher; invited by Trevor to join his communal "settlement," Nigel goes with his girlfriend Sally Green to live at the settlement in Margaret Kennedy's *Red Sky at Morning.*

Cuff, Sergeant Richard Grizzled, fatherly detective with a penetrating gaze and a passion for growing roses; he is called in by Lady Verinder to investigate the theft of a valuable diamond, but when his suspicions light on her daughter, Rachel, Lady Verinder discharges him; he helps solve the mystery at last in Wilkie Collins's *The Moonstone. A Romance.*

Cuffee Slave and miller at Beulah; sold as punishment for trying to run away in Mary Lee Settle's *Know Nothing.*

Cuffee Ned Hero of the poor blacks on Bourne Island; led the largest and most successful slave revolt in the island's history in Paule Marshall's *The Chosen Place, the Timeless People.*

Cuitzeo Indian Cousin One of the two husbands of Señora Laurita Aldama; native rebel hunted by landowners in Elena Garro's "Blame the Tlaxcaltecs."

Cujo Friendly Saint Bernard who becomes rabid after being bitten on the muzzle by an infected bat; after killing his owner, Cujo terrorizes Donna and Tad Trenton as he is left to slowly die in Stephen King's *Cujo.*

Culavrov, Louis One of three main characters who are described as thieves, homosexuals, and murderers; arrives in Paris from the country at the age of 20; changes his name to Divine and becomes a thief and male prostitute; ruthless criminal who is unafraid of prison and death; engages in love relationships with Daintyfoot and Our Lady in Jean Genet's *Our Lady of the Flowers.*

Cul de Jatte Fraudulent cripple, who befriends Gerard in Burgundy but is last seen as an inmate of the jail in Hamburgh in Charles Reade's *The Cloister and the Hearth.*

Cullen, Alice Working-class mother of Michael Cullen, whose birth resulted from her liaison with a serviceman during World War II in Alan Sillitoe's *A Start in Life.*

Cullen, Father Outspoken curate of Drumsna and an ally of Father John McGrath in Anthony Trollope's *The Macdermots of Ballycloran.*

Cullen, Lady Cecilia Delicate, shy, tided girl, a hunchback, who is fiercely devoted to Alice Barton and becomes a nun in George Moore's *A Drama in Muslin.*

Cullen, Michael Illegitimate youth who seeks love and fortune through illegal real estate deals and smuggling; he is narrator of Alan Sillitoe's *A Start in Life.*

Cullen, Tom Slightly retarded man who, under the influence of Nick Andros's spirit, saves Stuart Redman's life in Stephen King's *The Stand.*

Culligan, Norah (Norry) Landlady and lover of Charles Fort in Jessamyn West's *The Massacre at Fall Creek.*

Cullen, Rose Embittered, reckless daughter of Lord Benditch; though at first distrustful of D., she finds new purpose for hem life by helping him, falling in love with him, and finally leaving England with him in Graham Greene's *The Confidential Agent.*

Cullen, Tad American pilot and friend of Bill Kendrick; he identifies the dead man on the train as Kendrick in Josephine Tey's *The Singing Sands.*

Culling, Rosamund Everard Romfrey's housekeeper and eventually his wife, a motherlike figure to Nevil Beauchamp; despite her affection for Beauchamp, she inadvertently estranges him from his uncle and from an inheritance in George Meredith's *Beauchamp's Career.*

Culloden, Lord Presbyterian Scottish peer and brother-in-law of Lothair's father; he is one of Lothair's two guardians in Benjamin Disraeli's *Lothair.*

Cullpepper, Alderman Wealthy High Churchman, who allows his young wife to attend Methodist services for diversion, and who good-naturedly opposes Geoffry Wildgoose's assertion that the theater is evil in Richard Graves's *The Spiritual Quixote.*

Cullpepper, Mrs. Young wife of a wealthy alderman; she attends Methodist assemblies and flirts discreetly with Geoffry Wildgoose in Richard Graves's *The Spiritual Quixote.*

Cully, Captain Would-be minstrel and leader of a band of ineffective outlaws in Peter S. Beagle's *The Last Unicorn.*

Culpepper, Catherine Daughter of Spence and Lila Culpepper, who lives nearby and provides emotional support to her mother and father when Lila faces a mastectomy in Bobbie Ann Mason's *Spence and Lila.*

Culpepper, Lee Son of Spence and Lila Culpepper; has abandoned the family farm for factory work but provides some emotional support to his mother and father when Lila faces a mastectomy in Bobbie Ann Mason's *Spence and Lila.*

Culpepper, Lieutenant Third-generation army officer; serves as defense counsel for Robert E. Lee Prewitt's trial in James Jones's *From Here to Eternity.*

Culpepper, Lila Mother of Nancy, Catherine, and Lee Culpepper and wife of Spence Culpepper; endures a mastectomy and, as a result of the operation, must rediscover herself as a mother and a wife in Bobbie Ann Mason's *Spence and Lila.*

Culpepper, Martin (Mart) Town developer and partner of John Barclay; saved from disgrace and financial ruin when his daughter, Molly Culpepper, marries Adrian Brownwell in William Allen White's *A Certain Rich Man.*

Culpepper, Molly See Brownwell, Molly Culpepper.

Culpepper, Nancy Daughter of Spence and Lila Culpepper; moved away from her hometown but returns to provide emotional support to her mother and father when Lila faces a mastectomy in Bobbie Ann Mason's *Spence and Lila.*

Culpepper, Spence Father of Catherine, Nancy, and Lee Culpepper and husband of Lila Culpepper, who undergoes a mastectomy; is challenged to accept the ways his wife and his marriage might change because of the operation in Bobbie Ann Mason's *Spence and Lila.*

Culver, Lieutenant Jack Lawyer on Marine reserve duty and closest friend of Captain Mannix; one of the men ordered on a useless thirty-six-mile hike in William Styron's *The Long March.*

Culwin, Andrew Cold, detached, and hyperrational bachelor who inadvertently exposes a natural terror as horrifying as any supernatural one; enjoys mentoring young men; hosts a dinner party with several friends, including one such young man; as each shares a ghost story, reaches into his own past and reports having encountered ghosts twice in his youth; after putting off a smitten cousin, Alice Nowell, had a haunting vision of evil eyes; three years later, after falsely building up the hopes of a protégé, Gilbert Noyes, again encountered evil eyes; only escaped them once Noyes gave up art and left Culwin's company; after telling his story, finds current protégé Phil Frenham taken aback; finally glimpses himself in a mirror, recognizing the eyes he described as his own in Edith Wharton's "The Eyes."

Cumberland, Richard Asinine young man who wishes to attend society parties to which he is not invited; Max Adey finally invites him to join his holiday party to occupy Amabel, so that Max will be free to romance Julia Wray in Henry Green's *Party Going.*

Cumberland, Sheriff of Kind and courteous sheriff, who escorts Queen Mary of Scotland to England in Sir Walter Scott's *The Abbot.*

Cumberly, Thwaite Philadelphian hired by MacDougal to work with Marietta McGee-Chavéz to populate her Spain in William Goyen's *In a Farther Country.*

Cummings, Harry "Shy youth" who helps his friend Bachir fill orders at the Countess of Varna's flower shop and who complains to an American companion that his position as "Salad-Dresser to the King" affords him no opportunities to rise socially in Ronald Firbank's *The Flower Beneath the Foot.*

Cummings, Major General Edward Commander of troops on the island of Anopopei; predicts a totalitarian future for America in Norman Mailer's *The Naked and the Dead.*

Cummins, Derek Assistant manager in a large corporation; nicknamed the Duck by the women employees during their lunchroom conversation about rape fantasies in Margaret Atwood's "Rape Fantasies."

Cummins, Tom Card player in an anecdote related by Mr. Wicks to Dodson and Fogg in Charles Dickens's *The Posthumous Papers of the Pickwick Club.*

Cummyns, Miss Virtuous friend of Lady Dellwyn; she is spurned when she will not toady, and then is falsely embraced by society when Lady Dellwyn is cast out after her divorce in Sarah Fielding's *The History of the Countess of Dellwyn.*

Cumnor, Lady Local benevolent autocrat and matriarch of the Whig aristocratic influence on the Hollingford community in Elizabeth Gaskell's *Wives and Daughters.*

Cumnor, Lord Friendly and unpretentious landowner; relations between his "great house" (the Towers) and the Gibsons mirror some of the social changes of the period in Elizabeth Gaskell's *Wives and Daughters.*

Cunegonda Governess to Agnes de Medina; she is manipulated by Rodolpha, Baroness Lindenberg to oblige Agnes to enter the convent in Matthew Lewis's *The Monk.*

Cunégonde Daughter of a German baron; grows up in the same household as Candide; object of Candide's love, but her father expels him from this earthly paradise; they are separated throughout the novel and reunite at the end when, alas, Cunégonde has become remarkably ugly; ends up as an excellent pastry chef on a farm with Candide in Voltaire's *Candide.*

Cunningham, Archie One of Louis XI's Scottish Guard archers who save Quentin Durward from hanging in Sir Walter Scott's *Quentin Durward.*

Cunningham, Candace (Candy, The One Who Is Always Wrapped, The Muffled One) Blond American second wife of Colonel Ellellov; fellow student with him at McCarthy College in Wisconsin; wears full purdah to survive the coup Ellellov leads against foreigners; leaves him after his own government falls in John Updike's *The Coup.*

Cunningham, Captain Harold Grumpy and unresponsive but curious-minded husband of Ellie; he watches the beach area through binoculars or sits on the veranda keeping a look-out in Rosamond Lehmann's *A Sea-Grape Tree.*

Cunningham, Ellie Wife of Harold; she has wisdom and insight and believes in miracles; enamoured of Johnny, she feels shy around him in Rosamond Lehmann's *A Sea-Grape Tree.*

Cunningham, John Father of Avis Cunningham Everhard; physics professor who is fired for publishing a prolabor book; disappears during the rise of the Iron Heel in Jack London's *The Iron Heel.*

Cunningham, Martin Friend of the protagonist, Tom Kernan, and elder colleague of Jack Powers; endures an unhappy domestic life because his wife is an incurable alcoholic; plots a scheme to cure Tom Kernan of his drinking problem in James Joyce's "Grace." Sympathetic, failing barrister who seeks assistance for Paddy Dignam's widow with Leopold Bloom in James Joyce's *Ulysses.*

Cunningham, Miz Woman who looks after John and Pearl Harper while Willa Harper is at work; attempts to coerce John into revealing the whereabouts of hidden money in Davis Grubb's *The Night of the Hunter.*

Cunningham, Mr. Old man cared for until his death by Elizabeth Abbott in Anne Tyler's *The Clock Winder.*

Cunshi Wife of the Ecuadorian Indian workman Andres Chiliquinga; forced to sleep with the Spanish master Alfonso Pereira when she is working as a wet nurse for Blanca, Alfonso's wife; later dies from eating rancid meat, the only nourishment left for her family to eat by the greedy Alfonso in Jorge Icaza's *Huasipungo.*

Cupcake, Billy Television evangelist who delivers a eulogy for Trick E. Dixon in Philip Roth's *Our Gang.*

Cupid Arrogant, perverted policeman in Wright Morris's *My Uncle Dudley.*

Cupid, Dan Mischievous grandson of Bombie of the Frizzled Head in James Kirke Paulding's *Koningsmarke.*

Cupp, Ed Leslie's father-in-law; six-foot-eleven Californian whose conversation concerns his troubles with his Mercedes in Walker Percy's *The Second Coming.*

Cupp, Jason Leslie's fiancé (later husband); a Californian, he too is a born-again Christian in Walker Percy's *The Second Coming.*

Cupp, Leslie Barrett Unsmiling daughter of Will and Marion who becomes a born-again Christian and plans to use her mother's money to found a "love-and-faith community" in Walker Percy's *The Second Coming.*

Cupp, Marge Leslie's mother-in-law; an athletic woman whose hobby has become her religion; teaches infants to swim in Walker Percy's *The Second Coming.*

Curate Deranged clergyman whose reckless behavior while hiding from the Martians drives the anonymous narrator, his unwilling companion, to kill him in H. G. Wells's *The War of the Worlds.*

Curate Heartless clergyman, who uses the manuscript of Harley's biography for shotgun wadding in Henry Mackenzie's *The Man of Feeling.*

Curate Jacobite frequenter of the Black Bear in Sir Walter Scott's *Rob Roy.*

Curator Official of the museum and an English informant; shows the Lama a picture of the Lama's monastery, a map of Buddhist holy places; gives the Lama English paper, pencils, and crystal glasses and receives the Lama's iron pen case as a gift; wishes to learn the secret of brush-pen Buddhist pictures in Rudyard Kipling's *Kim.*

Curco, Ernest Las Vegas cab driver whom James Bond employs in Ian Fleming's *Diamonds Are Forever.*

Curdy, Miss Lavinia Friend of Gin-head Susy; searches successfully for a lover in Claude McKay's *Home to Harlem.*

Curé de Torcy Superior and mentor of the young parish priest, the protagonist, in charge of the Ambricourt Parish; thwarts the hopes of the young man, who wants to improve the lives of the poor; believes in the goodness and necessity of poverty for the parishioners in Georges Bernanos's *The Diary of a Country Priest.*

Curfew, Bertie Young man who directs Marjorie Ferrar in a Restoration play; she had a liaison with him in Paris in John Galsworthy's *The Silver Spoon.*

Curfew, Nora Sister of Bertie; she wins the admiration of Michael Mont for her social service in John Galsworthy's *The Silver Spoon.* She helps Fleur Mont run the railway canteen during the General Strike in *Swan Song.*

Curl, Jack Episcopal priest who believes manual labor contributes to his stature as a priest; has so little faith that he cannot even admit a belief in God in Walker Percy's *The Second Coming.*

Curlew, William Richard Pulling's partner, who wanted to get rid of his "perfect" wife; with the help of Pulling, Curlew writes a letter to his wife claiming to be unfaithful, but to his distress she forgives him and he is forced to remain with her in Graham Greene's *Travels with My Aunt.*

Curley Friend admired by Henry Miller because he has no morals or sense of shame; has affairs with three women at the same time in Henry Miller's *Tropic of Capricorn.*

Curley Part-owner of a ranch who vows to kill Lennie Small for having raped Curley's wife in John Steinbeck's *Of Mice and Men.*

Curll, Edmund Bookseller in London made notorious by Pope's *Dunciad* for his frauds and thefts; he shows John Buncle London life, including brothels, and is instrumental in uniting Buncle with his sixth wife, Agnes Dunk, by helping free her from her cruel father, Old Dunk, in Thomas Amory's *The Life of John Buncle, Esq.*

Curlydown, Jemima Irrepressible daughter of a Post Office clerk called to give evidence in the bigamy trial of John Caldigate; she marries another postal official, Samuel Bagwax, in Anthony Trollope's *John Caldigate.*

Curlydown, Mr. Post Office clerk who gives evidence at the bigamy trial of John Caldigate in Anthony Trollope's *John Caldigate.*

Curnow, Dr. Disliked but trusted general practitioner; finding no physical reason for Jake Richardson's declining sex drive, he recommends psychological treatment in Kingsley Amis's *Jake's Thing.*

Curpet, Mr. Small, round-faced man with a neatly trimmed beard; the senior partner in a law firm, he recognizes Richard Larch's dependability and talent for bookkeeping; he surprises Richard with a promotion enabling him to consider marriage in Arnold Bennett's *A Man From the North.*

Curran Past lover of Aunt Augusta Bertram; after working in a circus he established a church for dogs and was often in trouble with the law in Graham Greene's *Travels with My Aunt.*

Curran, Jack Son of Kathleen and Johnny Curran; football star of Boniface College, beer truck driver, and wrestler; falls in love with and marries Mary Odell, who later leaves him; dies fighting a fire in Mark Steadman's *A Lion's Share.*

Curran, Johnny (Old Johnny) Father of Jack Curran and ex-husband of Kathleen Reilley in Mark Steadman's *A Lion's Share.*

Curran, Kathleen See Reilley, Kathleen Lynch.

Curran, Mark Rich art collector, American expatriate, and former lover of Robert Leaver, whose blackmail scheme he foils in Muriel Spark's *Territorial Rights.*

Curran, Mary Cheney Odell First real love of Jack Curran; marries Curran against her parents' wishes and later divorces him in Mark Steadman's *A Lion's Share.*

Currie, Captain Bigoted restaurant manager whom D. encounters at crucial moments; alternately hostile and friendly, he ultimately tries to turn D. over to the police in Graham Greene's *The Confidential Agent.*

Currie, Ned Reporter for the *Winesburg Eagle* who leaves his lover Alice Hindman for greater opportunities in Chicago in Sherwood Anderson's *Winesburg, Ohio.*

Curry, Honey Small-time Irish hoodlum who is involved in Charlie Boy McCall's kidnapping; killed in Newark in a gun battle with the police in William Kennedy's *Billy Phelan's Greatest Game.*

Curry, James (Peppercorn) British dragoon who bribes Wat Adair to betray Arthur Butler; killed at King's Mountain in John Pendleton Kennedy's *Horse-Shoe Robinson.*

Curry, Vera Old woman who is a neighbor of Bernard Sands; she is convicted of blackmail, procuring, and other crimes, largely because of Sands's initiative in Angus Wilson's *Hemlock and After.*

Curryfin, Lord Handsome young nobleman, whose beauty and money attract women to his lectures on fish; he loses himself in constantly changing interests and experiments but finally marries Miss Niphet in Thomas Love Peacock's *Gryll Grange.*

Curtin (Curtis, Curty) American drifter who meets Dobbs in a Mexican oil camp and joins him on a search for gold in B. Traven's *The Treasure of the Sierra Madre.*

Curtin, Marie Asthmatic young socialite and part-time model and writer; lover of Jack Bogardes, Teddy Forster, and Eric Eisner in Phillip Lopate's *Confessions of Summer.*

Curtis Psychologist who marries Gretchen; reads Tarot cards and owns a house in the Berkshires in Elizabeth Benedict's *Slow Dancing.*

Curtis Servant in Petruchio's country home in William Shakespeare's *The Taming of the Shrew.*

Curtis, Charles Father of Kate and Olivia in Rosamond Lehmann's *Invitation to the Waltz* and in *The Weather in the Streets.*

Curtis, Ephraim Captain who rescues Thomas from the Nipmuc ambush; crawled and ran thirty miles to get troops and supplies from Marlborough in Bharati Mukherjee's *The Holder of the World.*

Curtis, George Lost younger brother of Sir Henry Curtis; excluded from his father's inheritance, he assumes the name Neville and journeys into Africa to find King Solomon's mines; he remains stranded in a desert oasis with his servant, Jim, until Sir Henry rescues him in H. Rider Haggard's *King Solomon's Mines.*

Curtis, Grace Quietly satiric elder sister of Rachel Curtis; she attempts unsuccessfully to curb Rachel's excesses in Charlotte Yonge's *The Clever Woman of the Family.*

Curtis, John Richard Curtis's son who has Down's Syndrome in Doris Lessing's *The Diaries of Jane Somers.*

Curtis, Kate Independent, sensible older daughter of Mr. and Mrs. Charles Curtis; she plans to go to Paris to further her education in Rosamond Lehmann's *Invitation to the*

Waltz. She is a capable, experienced wife with four children in *The Weather in the Streets*.

Curtis, Kathleen Richard Curtis's daughter, a student at the University of London, whose time is spent "secretly" trailing Jane Somers and Richard on their dates in Doris Lessing's *The Diaries of Jane Somers*.

Curtis, Kelly Brainy thirteen-year-old seventh grader; best friend of R. B. "Arby" Benton; student assistant of Richard Levine; stowaway onboard RV trailer destined for dinosaur-infested Costa Rican jungle in Michael Crichton's *The Lost World*.

Curtis, Mathew Richard Curtis's bright and ambi-tious son, who looks like his father; he admits to Jane Somers that he is in love with her in Doris Lessing's *The Diaries of Jane Somers*.

Curtis, Mrs. Stubborn landlady to Edgar and Mary Perry; she has owned a beauty parlor in Cairo for twenty years yet is prejudiced against the natives and refuses to learn Arabic in P. H. Newby's *The Picnic at Sakkara*.

Curtis, Mrs. Charles Mother of Kate and Olivia; she expects conventional actions of her daughters in Rosamond Lehmann's *Invitation to the Waltz*. Her superficial, domestic perspective makes it impossible for her to understand Olivia's independent nature in *The Weather in the Streets*.

Curtis, Olivia Naïve, sheltered, seventeen-year-old daughter of Mr. and Mrs. Charles Curtis; she is curious about others and feels that she has had an introduction to life after a party where she meets different characters in Rosamond Lehmann's *Invitation to the Waltz*. At twenty-six she is estranged from her husband, lives an impoverished existence with a cousin, and has an eight-month love affair with Rollo Spencer in *The Weather in the Streets*.

Curtis, Rachel Socially conscious young woman, whose attempts to transcend the restricted life of the seaside resort in which she lives fail until she submits to the guidance of a superior male; she marries Alick Keith in Charlotte Yonge's *The Clever Woman of the Family*.

Curtis, Richard Middle-aged doctor whom Jane Somers meets at a railroad station, and with whom she falls in love; he must eventually move to Canada for his wife's career in Doris Lessing's *The Diaries of Jane Somers*.

Curtis, Sir Henry (Incubu) Powerful, handsome, yellow-bearded Englishman, who accompanies Allan Quatermain on two expeditions into Africa; the first is in search of King Solomon's Mines and Sir Henry's lost brother in H. Rider Haggard's *King Solomon's Mines*. The second expedition is to find a rumored white race, the Zu-Vendi, in *Allan Quatermain*.

Curtis, Sir Walter Man sent by the Earl of Essex (2) to Rouen in search of Lord Leicester and Matilda in Sophia Lee's *The Recess*.

Curtis, Sylvia Richard Curtis's hard-working, brilliant wife, a surgeon, who has always allotted only a certain amount of time to her husband in Doris Lessing's *The Diaries of Jane Somers*.

Curtiss Hercule Poirot's manservant in the necessary absence of George in Agatha Christie's *Curtain: Hercule Poirot's Last Case*.

Curzon, Lieutenant-General Sir Herbert ("Bertie") Central figure whose ascent from an acclaimed commander of the 22nd Lancers in the Boer War to his final post as a general in charge of 100,000 soldiers in World War I is counterpointed by his increasing blindness to a drastically changing world, particularly with regard to wartime tactics and practices; the social status solidified by his marriage to Lady Emily Winter-Willoughby, daughter of the Duke and Duchess of Bude, is accompanied by internal punishments; Curzon grows to understand the anachronism he and his peers have become only in his final symbolic, and somewhat pathetic, attempt to resuscitate the past in C. S. Forester's *The General*.

Cusins, Adolphus Young idealist who is determined to marry Barbara Undershaft, a major in the Salvation Army and daughter of an arms industrialist; a devoted student of Euripides and the Dionysian spirit; becomes swayed from his academic pursuits and ideals by Barbara's father's offer that the young man succeed him at the Armory, and by doing so wins Barbara's hand in George Bernard Shaw's play *Major Barbara*.

Cuss Iping doctor who witnesses Griffin's open invisibility while soliciting his charity at the Coach and Horses, and whose trousers are later stolen by Griffin in H. G. Wells's *The Invisible Man: A Grotesque Romance*.

Cust, Alexander Bonaparte Frustrated possessor of a grandiose name; his travels connect with the murder scenes to a degree beyond coincidence in Agatha Christie's *The A.B.C. Murders*.

Custer, Alex British Council Cultural Affairs officer in Turkey; he takes Philip Swallow to a party in Ankara, where

Philip re-discovers Joy Simpson in David Lodge's *Small World.*

Custer, George Armstrong Famed army cavalry general defeated at Little Bighorn in Thomas Berger's *Little Big Man.*

Cutbeard Morose's supposedly silent barber; following Morose's request, arranges a meeting between Morose and Epicoene; finds Morose a parson who coughs violently; disguised as a lawyer, engages in a long-winded argument regarding divorce with Captain Otter, disguised as a parson, during which both spout off Latin phrases much to Morose's annoyance in Ben Jonson's play *Epicoene, or The Silent Woman.*

Cutbush, Primrose Third-year anthropology student who competes for the Foresight Fellowship in Barbara Pym's *Less Than Angels.*

Cute, Alderman Local justice, red-faced and complacent, determined to "put down" the poor and the distressed in his district in Charles Dickens's *The Chimes.*

Cut-Glass, Lord Eccentric recluse who enjoys his kitchen filled with clocks; member of the colorful and fanciful community of Llaregyb, a mythical seaside village in Wales in Dylan Thomas's play *Under Milk Wood.*

Cuticle, Cadwallader Surgeon aboard the *Neversink* who is interested in morbid anatomy; saves the life of Baldy and kills another sailor by operating on him unnecessarily in Herman Melville's *White Jacket.*

Cutler Gunner aboard the *Indefatigable* in C. S. Forester's *Mr. Midshipman Hornblower.*

Cutler, Rav Yosef Mashpia of Asher Lev; treats Lev compassionately until Lev exhibits his masterpieces in Chaim Potok's *My Name Is Asher Lev.*

Cutler, Sophy Girl who made a play for Jos Sedley in India and whom he likes to speak of in William Makepeace Thackeray's *Vanity Fair.*

Cutrer, Emily Bolling Stoical and aristocratic great aunt and patron of Binx Bolling in Walker Percy's *The Moviegoer.*

Cutrer, Jules Worldly and wealthy husband of Emily Bolling Cutrer and father of Kate Cutrer in Walker Percy's *The Moviegoer.*

Cutrer, Kate Despairing daughter of Jules Cutrer and stepdaughter of Emily Bolling Cutrer; marries Binx Bolling in Walker Percy's *The Moviegoer.*

Cutter, James Vice admiral and national security adviser who urges the president to treat drug smuggling as a terrorist threat and use military force against Colombian cartels; sets up several missions, violates chains of command, and fails to ensure operational security; commits suicide after John Clark shows him the evidence against him in Tom Clancy's *Clear and Present Danger.*

Cutter, Joseph CIA agent who was trained by Miles Kendig but leads the team that pursues Kendig in Brian Garfield's *Hopscotch.*

Cutter, Leo Anna Dunlap's lover; a passionate, unconventional artist who falls deeply in love with Anna and awakens her sexuality, then becomes a scapegoat accused of child abuse in Sue Miller's *The Good Mother.*

Cutter, Wycliffe (Wick) Merciless moneylender who tries to seduce Antonia Shimerda; murders his wife and commits suicide in Willa Cather's *My Antonia.*

Cuttle, Captain Edward (Ned) Loyal friend of Solomon Gills and Walter Gay; he has a hook for a right hand; he supports Gills in his big dreams for Walter, watches the shop while Gills is searching for Walter, and gives Florence Dombey shelter there when she flees her home in Charles Dickens's *Dombey and Son.*

Cutts, Captain Criminal associate of Jasper Losely in Edward Bulwer-Lytton's *What Will He Do With It? by Pisistratus Caxton.*

Cutts, Fiona Daughter of Susan Tolland Cutts; a difficult girl, she has run away from various schools before she becomes a disciple of Scorpio Murtlock and a member of his cult; she marries Russell Gwinnett in Anthony Powell's *Hearing Secret Harmonies.*

Cutts, Mr. Fifty-year-old saddler of Cowfold accused and acquitted of arson; Miriam Tacchi is willing to lie to protect him in Mark Rutherford's *Miriam's Schooling.*

Cutts, Roddy Smiling, assiduously polite Tory member of Parliament who becomes engaged to Lady Susan Tolland in Anthony Powell's *At Lady Molly's.* They are married in *Casanova's Chinese Restaurant* and in *The Kindly Ones.* He has a wartime romance with a cypher decoder and wants a divorce in *The Military Philosophers.* Chastened, he submits to his wife's domination in *Books Do Furnish a Room.* He talks about his daughter, Fiona, in *Hearing Secret Harmonies.*

Cuttwater, Captain Bartholomew (Uncle Bat) Gin-drinking uncle of Bessie Woodward; he lodges with her and her three daughters in Anthony Trollope's *The Three Clerks.*

Cutwright, Doggo Braggart, provincial soldier, and lazy settler at Beulah; moves west beyond Beulah because he hates all symbols of refinement, but leaves his children behind so they can be educated; eventually sides with Johnny Lacey's political opponents in Mary Lee Settle's *O Beulah Land.*

Cutwright, Jacob Drunkard and brother of Doggo Cutwright; tears up and fouls Jarcey Pentacost's books before leaving Beulah with a band of white outlaws who raid the settlement during Johnny Lacey's absence in Mary Lee Settle's *O Beulah Land.*

Cutwright, Leah See Catlett, Leah Cutwright.

Cutwright, Maggie Half-Indian wife of Doggo Cutwright; insulted by the women of Beulah, she steals Sally Lacey's china cup before leaving the settlement in Mary Lee Settle's *O Beulah Land.*

Cuzak, Anton Husband of Antonia Shimerda at the conclusion of Willa Cather's *My Ántonia.*

Cyclops Dimwitted and savage son of the sea god Poseidon; one among the many one-eyed, cannibalistic, giant Cyclopes inhabiting Sicily; herds sheep and is ignorant of agriculture, wine, permanent settlement, and the rule of human and divine law; antithesis of the Greek ideal of moderation, as embodied in Odysseus; captures the Ithacans, devouring two; rendered drunk, and then blinded by Odysseus; as the Ithacans leave, appeals to his divine father for vengeance in Euripides' play *The Cyclops.*

Cylinda Wealthy young woman who exemplifies the dangers of educating females; her "wild imagination" leads her to reject marriage and become the mistress of Nicanor and Eustace; following her repentance she lives a blameless existence with Ferdinand, Portia, and Cordelia in Sarah Fielding's *The Cry.*

Cymbeline King of Britain; father of Imogen, Guiderius, and Arviragus; angered by Imogen's decision to secretly marry the low-born Posthumus instead of Cloten, the son of the queen, under whose negative influence the king has fallen; banishes Posthumus to Italy and imprisons Imogen; supported by the queen and Cloten, refuses to pay Rome the annual tribute demanded to prevent Romet from attacking Britain, thus initiating a war between the two countries; finally comes to his senses following the queen's death; reunited with his children, and agrees to resume paying tribute to Rome at the end of William Shakespeare's play *Cymbeline.*

"Cynecia" Phony heroine sent by Sir George Bellmour to convince Arabella that Charles Glanville is her perjured lover, Ariamenes, in Charlotte Lennox's *The Female Quixote.*

Cynthia Fickle secretary in Section 6A, Overseas Intelligence, and the unresponsive object of Arthur Davis's infatuation in Graham Greene's *The Human Factor.*

Cynthia Tall, busty Swedish girl at the convent who befriends Caithleen Brady and teaches her many things about the real world in Edna O'Brien's *The Country Girls.*

Cynthia Name Mr. Grant gives the marble statue of an angel that stands on the porch outside his monument and statuary business; also the name of Mr. Grant's first wife; the statue is purchased by Queen Elizabeth to adorn the grave of a young female prostitute in her employ in Thomas Wolfe's "The Angel on the Porch."

Cynthia Virtuous wife of Valentine in the happy ending of Sarah Fielding's *The Adventures of David Simple in Search of a Faithful Friend.* She corresponds with Camilla (Simple) in *Familiar Letters between the Principal Characters of David Simple and Some Others.* She suffers greatly after Valentine's death in Jamaica; she returns to England to care for her niece after the death of the latter's parents, David and Camilla Simple, in *David Simple. Volume the Last.*

Cynthia Girlfriend, briefly, of Jesse; leaves him just before he joins Lee Mellon at Big Sur in Richard Brautigan's *A Confederate General from Big Sur.*

Cyon, Lily Shane de See Shane, Lily.

Cyon, René de French diplomat who marries Lily Shane in Louis Bromfield's *The Green Bay Tree.*

Cypher, Humphrey Sergeant-at-arms who advises Hammel Clement after his first arrest in Henry Brooke's *The Fool of Quality.*

Cypress, Hugo Young aristocratic friend and protégé of Guy de Travest; he attends a tension-filled swimming party at Guy's house the night before Iris Storm's death in Michael Arlen's *The Green Hat.*

Cypress, Shirley Well-bred but spirited aristocrat who feels jealous of Iris Storm for saving her girlhood friend Venice Pollen from drowning during their swimming party in Michael Arlen's *The Green Hat.*

Cyprian, Father Parish priest; in 1932 organized a retreat for working women at which some characters in novel met and became friends; in later years they visit him for three weeks each summer in Mary Gordon's *The Company of Women.*

Cyprus, Mr. Visitor at Nightmare Abbey who takes his ideas from Lord Byron's Childe Harold and delivers the Byronic parody "There is a Fever of the Spirit" in Thomas Love Peacock's *Nightmare Abbey.*

Cyril Cancer-stricken, scripture-quoting elderly patient in Clive Ward who is wracked with guilt because of the memory of his rape of his now-deceased wife; he hopes that his daughter, Dorothy, can still be "saved" and prays for "judgement" in John Berger's *The Foot of Clive.*

Cyril Proud, autocratic patriarch and leader of the Christians in Alexandria; he plots and counterplots for the elimination of the Jews, the philosopher Hypatia, and all remaining polytheistic tendencies; his plans succeed but sow seeds of future violence among the Christians in Charles Kingsley's *Hypatia.*

Cyril Husband of Fiona, lover of Catherine, and employer of Rosella; narrator of John Hawkes's *The Blood Oranges.*

Cyril Small boy who is in a railway carriage with his sisters and aunt; he is very curious and naughty and keeps pestering others with questions; he thinks that the bachelor's story is the only beautiful one he has ever heard in Saki's "The Story-Teller."

Cyrus Ancient conqueror; unable to trust himself in the presence of the beautiful captive Panthea, he entrusts her to the care of the virtuous Araspes in a parable told by Henry Clinton in Henry Brooke's *The Fool of Quality.*

Cytheris Famous actress who instructs Pompeia for a part in the Mysteries; visits Turrinus in his self-imposed exile in Thornton Wilder's *The Ides of March.*

Czap, Sybil Mother who sells the story of her son's death to Waldo in Paul Theroux's *Waldo.*

Czienwicz, Casimir (Polack) Polish-American soldier who believes he can beat the system in Norman Mailer's *The Naked and the Dead.*

Czinner, Dr. Richard (covername: Richard John) Doomed political leader and weary refugee; he is captured and condemned by Subotican military authorities while attempting a return to Belgrade to lead a futile uprising and, after breaking away, is shot by the militia and dies in Coral Musker's arms in Graham Greene's *Stamboul Train.*